THE WORLD ECONOMY
TRADE AND FINANCE

SIXTH EDITION

Beth V. Yarbrough
Amherst College

Robert M. Yarbrough
Amherst College

THOMSON
™
SOUTH-WESTERN

Australia · Canada · Mexico · Singapore · Spain · United Kingdom · United States

THOMSON

SOUTH-WESTERN

The World Economy: Trade and Finance, 6e
Beth V. Yarbrough
Robert M. Yarbrough

Editor-in-Chief:
Jack W. Calhoun

Vice President/Team Director:
Michael P. Roche

Senior Acquisitions Editor:
Peter Adams

Senior Developmental Editor:
Jeff Gilbreath

Senior Marketing Manager:
Janet Hennies

Senior Production Editor:
Kara ZumBahlen

Media Production Editor:
Pam Wallace

Media Developmental Editor:
Peggy Buskey

Senior Media Technology Editor:
Vicky True

Manufacturing Coordinator:
Sandee Milewski

Compositor:
Lachina Publishing Services

Printer:
QuebecorWorld, Versailles, KY

Design Project Manager:
Rik Moore

Internal Design:
Rik Moore

Cover Design:
Lou Ann Thesing

Cover Photo Resource:
PhotoDisc, Inc.

Library of Congress Cataloging-in-Publication Data
Yarbrough, Beth V.
 The world economy : trade and finance / Beth V. Yarbrough, Robert M. Yarbrough.—6th ed.
 p. cm.
 Includes bibliographical references and indexes.
 ISBN 0-324-18329-1
 1. Commercial policy. 2. International finance. 3. International economic relations. 4. Economic policy. I. Yarbrough, Robert M. II. Title.
HF1411 .Y34 2002
337—dc21   2002030328

To our student and friend,
Maurita Tam
Amherst College '01
February 18, 1979–September 11, 2001

PREFACE

The success of earlier editions of *The World Economy: Trade and Finance* owes much to developments outside the classroom. Specific episodes come and go, but the pace of world events continues to remind us all of the increasing role international issues play in our economic lives. Turkey and Argentina slip into financial crisis as Asia attempts to crawl out. The European Union and the United States make peace over bananas but test the World Trade Organization's ability to settle disputes by fighting over U.S. tax policy. U.S. policy makers debate whether to reward Pakistan for its support of the war on terrorism by allowing more Pakistani textiles into the United States. The U.S. steel industry, suffering from foreign competition, pressures policy makers to support a world steel cartel. Membership in the European Union moves within sight for several formerly centrally planned economies, such as Poland and Hungary, but others, such as Belarus and Turkmenistan, remain mired in isolation, erratic reform, and recurrent crisis. The euro finally arrives as a "real" currency, one that average citizens use for their day-to-day transactions. The entire Afghan economy needs rebuilding.

What Are We Trying to Do in *The World Economy?*

The pace, scale, and scope of such events underscore the widespread perception of the increased importance of international economics for understanding world events. Luckily, just a few simple tools of economic analysis can provide a great deal of insight into the ever-changing world economy. The goals of this sixth edition of *The World Economy* remain unchanged from those of the first five:

- Present the *basic tools* of international economic analysis clearly, consistently, and comprehensively;
- Provide lots of applications to actual events so students can learn to *use* the tools soundly and confidently to analyze the world economy; and
- Give a sense of the broad range of *challenging and exciting issues* (as well as some humorous ones) that arise in the international economic arena.

Integrated Theory and Applications

By combining up-to-date theory with current events and policy debates, we emphasize learning how to use international economics as a tool for understanding. By the end of the course, students can analyze problems independently, not just those that happen to dominate the headlines at the time of the book's writing. *The World Economy* hasn't ever glorified theory for its own sake. The rule we endeavor to follow remains: *Any theory worth presenting is worth teaching students to use.*

The World Economy is self-contained; it defines all necessary concepts and doesn't rely on students' memories from other economics courses. Frequent data tables tie abstract concepts to their empirical counterparts. *We believe that an international economics course should familiarize students with the empirical reality of the world economy as well as with abstract models of it,* so we present data more frequently than is typical in other texts. We refer often to common errors or misinterpretations in the popular press, because learning how to read the newspaper or listen to the evening news with a keen eye and ear is at least as important as learning how to read the scholarly literature.

The integration of clear, concise theory with up-to-date examples and cases has always set *The World Economy* apart from its competitors. One example of this integration is our focus throughout both the international trade and open-economy macroeconomics sections of the book on policy's distributional consequences. These consequences represent the crux of international economic policy controversies, but many texts shortchange them with a flurry of tangency conditions. We make extensive use of examples from diverse areas of the world economy—Tajikistan, Mexico, India, Egypt, Iceland, and North Korea, not just the United States and a handful of other large industrialized economies. We highlight the relevance of international economic theory for understanding front-page microeconomic issues such as trends in trade and wages, intellectual property protection and piracy in pharmaceuticals, war and trade, the role of science in trade policy, the "resource curse," and the effect of aid on growth. And, we maintain the lively, up-to-date focus throughout Part Two by examining macroeconomic issues such as the development of online currency trading, the United States' external debt, creation of a central bank and currency for the new state of Bosnia, the role of capital flows in financial crises, Japan's long economic slump, the European Union's euro, and countries' adoption of the dollar in lieu of their own national currencies.

Careful, Clear Pedagogy

We number major sections within each chapter of *The World Economy* for easy reference. At crucial points in an argument, we ask students, "Why?" These queries encourage *active* reading, stopping the reader from moving passively through the argument without confronting its underlying logic. Comments from our students indicate that the queries achieve their goal.[1] *The World Economy*'s generous use of graphs, as well as their lively two-color format, make the arguments easy to follow. All graphs are fully integrated into the text and accompanied by self-contained legends. We encourage students to practice active translation between graphs and legends *(Can you cover the graph and draw your own, given the legend? Can you cover the legend and write your own explanation of the graph?)*. Again, the emphasis is on learning to *use* the graphs as tools for understanding, not on memorization or rote manipulation.

Each chapter contains several cases, a summary, a "Looking Ahead" section that links the chapter to the next one, a list of key terms (boldfaced in the text), review questions and problems (including new ones in every chapter of the sixth edition), and a list of supplementary readings. The cases provide examples of the economic concepts and models developed in the chapter as well as extensive empirical information about the countries that make up the world economy. The end-of-chapter "Problems and Questions for Review" highlight major concepts from the chapter and relate those concepts to current policy debates. Many of the end-of-chapter questions from earlier editions now appear in the *Study Guide* (a new version of which accompanies this new edition). Unlike the bibliographies in many textbooks, the readings suggested in *The World Economy* include short, up-to-date articles as well as classic treatises and survey articles, and we note readings as appropriate for introductory, intermediate, or advanced students.

What's New to the Sixth Edition?

Our basic goals, philosophy, and pedagogy remain unchanged, but this sixth edition incorporates many improvements. We've thoroughly updated and revised the book, including the text of each chapter as well as figures, tables, and cases. We've also made the language, headings, figure titles, and case titles more student friendly.

New Cases

We've added many new cases to reflect current events and issues. The new cases are:

- Turning Back Trade Turns Back the Clock
- From Fish to Information Technology
- Socks: Made in USA
- The State of Exports
- Internal Economies of Scale and the Sperm Trade
- Making Cheap Medicine Expensive
- Retaliatory Tariffs
- Designer Grayjeans
- Export Quotas
- Science, or Politics?
- I.D. Cards for Avocados

---

1 Several students have reported making a game of the queries by trying to read each chapter without being "caught" unprepared to answer a query.

- Evading Tax Evasion
- Send Money
- Does Aid Aid Growth?
- Oil Junkies?
- Picking Stocks Means Picking Currencies
- Currency Online
- Rest of Galaxy Enjoys Current-Account Surplus
- GDP: What's in There?
- Best of Both Worlds
- Birth of a Currency
- Pegged, But to What?
- Policy Squeezes: To Do, or Not to Do?
- Dry Cleaning in Tokyo and Mumbai
- Greasing the World Economy
- Do Floating Rates Really Float?
- Standing Ireland in the Corner
- Su Currency Es Mi Currency
- The HIPC Initiative

We've also updated and expanded the cases carried over from the fifth edition.

Intended Audience

By presenting the fundamentals of international economics clearly but rigorously, *The World Economy* becomes adaptable for a variety of courses. Our correspondence with adopters of earlier editions indicates that they use the book successfully in many different ways. Students with only a one-semester introductory economics course as background have no trouble mastering the material; in fact, we use the text extensively in classes at that level. Simply omit the appendixes and choose supplementary reading from the articles denoted as appropriate for beginning students. For students who've completed courses in intermediate micro and/or macro, add the appendixes along with a wider range of supplementary reading. The flexibility of the book also serves beginning graduate students with no specific background in international economics and provides a stepping stone to more advanced texts and the professional literature. The book appeals to students of political science, international relations, and international business by providing economics' unique perspective on international issues.

Alternate Course Outlines

Full-year international economics courses can cover the entire book along with a sizable sample of readings. The micro-macro ordering reflects our own teaching preferences but is easily reversible. In a one-semester course emphasizing microeconomic issues in the world economy, we use Chapters One through Eleven, but users can omit any combination of Chapters Five, Nine, Ten, and Eleven to permit more extensive use of supplementary readings. In a one-semester course emphasizing macroeconomics, we cover Chapters Twelve through Twenty-One, but it's possible to omit any combination of Sixteen, Seventeen, Eighteen, Twenty, and Twenty-One. By limiting outside readings, a one-semester course can cover the essentials of both the micro and macro perspectives. We've taught such a course by concentrating on Chapters Two through Four, Six through Eight, Twelve through Fifteen, and Nineteen. No doubt many other permutations are possible.

Ancillaries by the Text Authors
Study Guide

The sixth edition of *The World Economy* has its own *Study Guide*, available from South-Western through your local or college bookstore or from your South-Western representative. We wrote the *Study Guide* ourselves, carefully coordinating it with the text and using the same careful pedagogy. The *Study Guide* contains:

- A "Quick Quiz" of multiple-choice questions for each chapter, designed to test whether students understood the chapter's main points
- Additional "Problems and Questions for Review" with answers
- Answers to chapter italicized queries
- Matching exercises for key terms in each chapter
- List of key points for each chapter
- Hints for writing a successful term paper on the world economy
- List of source materials for international information and data
- List of Web resources

Instructor's Manual

The *Instructor's Manual,* which we also wrote ourselves, contains:

- Answers to the italicized queries in the text
- Suggested test questions for each chapter
- Answers to the end-of-chapter "Problems and Questions for Review," including those new to the sixth edition
- Chapter-by-chapter key points
- Information on alternate course structures

Acknowledgments

As always, we're grateful to the entire staff of our publisher, now South-Western, for transforming an unruly manuscript into a beautiful book. Peter Adams and Jeff Gilbreath helped make the corporate transition from Harcourt to South-Western painless. Amy Schneider's attentive copyediting helped us keep our economics out of the way of our English and vice versa. Kara ZumBahlen at South-Western and Lorne Franklin and the staff at Lachina Publishing Services managed production beautifully.

Thanks go also to our reviewers. We're grateful to all, and we appreciate the comments we didn't use as much as those we did. Compliments, suggestions, and criticisms from *The World Economy* users continue to play a vital important role in the book's edition-to-edition improvement, so do contact us if you have any comments.

Suggestions and questions—and, yes, even occasional blank stares—from students in the International Trade and Open-Economy Macroeconomics courses at Amherst College constantly help us improve. One of those students, Rajashree Datta, helped compile the original list of Web resources now included in the *Study Guide.*

Our long-time friend and administrative assistant, Jeanne Reinle, keeps us on schedule and in good humor, as well as getting us out of occasional jams. Our boss, Dean Lisa Raskin, generously supports and encourages our work on *The World Economy* and many other projects. If exceptions prove the rule, Lisa must prove all those nasty jokes about deans!

Beth V. Yarbrough
Robert M. Yarbrough
Amherst, Massachusetts
January 2002

CONTENTS

CHAPTER SEVEN

Nontariff Barriers and the New Protectionism   165

CHAPTER EIGHT

Arguments for Restricting Trade   193

CHAPTER NINE

The Political Economy of Trade Policy and Borders   225

CHAPTER TEN

Growth, Immigration, and Multinationals   256

PART TWO: INTERNATIONAL MACROECONOMICS

CHAPTER FIFTEEN
Money, the Banking System, and Foreign Exchange   422

CHAPTER SIXTEEN
Short-Run Macroeconomic Policy under Fixed Exchange Rates   465

CHAPTER SEVENTEEN
Short-Run Macroeconomic Policy under Flexible Exchange Rates   501

CHAPTER EIGHTEEN
The Exchange Rate in Long-Run Equilibrium   529

CHAPTER NINETEEN

Prices and Output in an Open Economy   560

CHAPTER TWENTY

International Monetary Regimes   597

CHAPTER TWENTY-ONE

Macroeconomics of Development and Transition   636

CHAPTER 1

CHAPTER ONE

Introduction to the World Economy

1.1 Why Study International Economics?

The world economy has been a lively place since 1998, when we wrote to introduce the fifth edition of *The World Economy: Trade and Finance*. Discussions of international interdependence fill the news, and the fact that no nation is an economic island has never been more obvious. Citizens of many countries feel increasingly affected by external events over which they, and sometimes their national policy makers, exert less-than-total control. Most of the major economic stories that occupy newspaper headlines are stories about international interdependence, its ramifications, and policy makers' and citizens' attempts to come to terms with it.

Sometimes the stories have a long-run focus: How has Japan's decade-long economic slump affected that country's trading partners? How long will it take for the countries in transition from central planning to develop well-functioning market economies? And sometimes the stories emerge in an instant: How will the September 11, 2001, terrorist attacks in New York and Washington affect the economies of the United States and its trading partners, and for how long?

All of this makes studying international economics more important than ever before, whether you are (or hope to be) a national policy maker, a business owner planning corporate strategy, or simply an informed citizen and voter. *The World Economy: Trade and Finance* provides a basic tool kit. It presents simple models to explain how the world economy works, empirical evidence to evaluate the models' predictions, dozens of case studies and applications from both history and current events around the globe, and lots of useful information about the world economy and the diverse countries that constitute it. When you finish the book, you should feel confident weighing politicians' statements about international economic policy, evaluating the key international influences on a firm or industry, and analyzing the linkages between the economic policies followed by your home country and those followed by the rest of the world.

It's also worth remembering that many of the individuals who formulate the policies we'll analyze in this book have at least some training in economics. Table 1.1 reports the undergraduate training of recent finance ministers (typically in charge of fiscal policy, or government spending and taxation) and central-bank governors (typically in charge of monetary policy, or controlling the money stock) for a sample of developed- and developing-country governments.

1.2 What Do We Mean by International Interdependence?

It's hard to pick up a newspaper or listen to the news these days without hearing about *globalization*. But the term itself usually goes undefined. Does it refer to the fact that consumers in dozens of countries can buy McDonald's Big Macs—although the burgers differ according to local tastes and culinary customs? Or that consumers in

Table 1.1 **Degree Subjects of Top Macroeconomic Policy Makers, 1993**

Country	Finance Minister (Fiscal Policy)	Central-Bank Governor (Monetary Policy)
Britain	Law	Economics
Canada	None	Philosophy, Politics, and Economics
France	Economics	Law/Literature
Germany	Law and Politics	Economics
Italy	Economics	Economics
Japan	Law	Law
United States	Law	Economics
Argentina	Economics	Economics
Brazil	Sociology	Economics
Chile	Economics	Economics
Mexico	Economics	Economics
China	None	Mechanical Engineering
Indonesia	Economics	Economics
South Korea	Public Administration	Economics
Taiwan	Economics	Economics
Thailand	Economics	Economics
Czech Republic	Economics	Economics
Poland	Economics	Economics
Russia	Economics	Economics

Source: *The Economist,* August 14, 1993, p. 63; data from country embassies and central banks.

Mongolia can buy goods from abroad without having to pay any taxes (called *tariffs*) to import them? Or that a British firm can issue bonds denominated in euros and sell the bonds throughout the world? Or that the World Trade Organization can tell the European Union that it can't discriminate against U.S.-based exporters of bananas produced in Central America and exported to Europe? Or that many citizens in remote corners of the globe admire and strive for "Western" values of individual freedom, democracy, and economic growth? The diversity of these issues suggests that the term *globalization* may be so broad and subject to varying interpretations that it loses its ability to communicate effectively. So, marketing considerations aside, most economists prefer to speak instead in terms of **international interdependence** and **international economic integration.** These terms refer to the degree to which economic events in one country affect others and the extent to which markets for goods, services, labor, and capital can operate freely across national boundaries. In other words, to what extent do national boundaries matter; do they block the flow of economic transactions or the effects of economic events and policies?

The term *international interdependence* entered the newspaper-headline vocabulary during the 1970s when the industrialized countries, along with oil-importing developing ones, helplessly endured two rounds of sudden and dramatic oil-price increases by the Organization of Petroleum Exporting Countries (OPEC). By the early 1980s, countries' roles reversed. OPEC watched the price of oil tumble as demand fell because of a policy-induced recession in the industrialized countries. Most industrial and oil-importing developing countries welcomed the fall in oil prices (although not the recession that triggered it), but the decline also heightened the debt problem of several developing-country oil exporters, most notably Mexico. The resulting debt crisis among developing countries, in turn, generated financial uncertainty and a loss of export markets for the developed world and threatened the solvency of several major U.S. commercial banks.

By the 1980s, key industries such as steel and automobiles, once dominated by a handful of U.S. firms, spanned the globe. Many U.S. industries struggled against increasingly potent foreign competition, and one by one those industries sought protection in the form of policy barriers against imports. But industries are themselves interdependent, so one industry's import barriers, which raise the price of that industry's output, can make it more difficult for related industries to remain competitive. For example, when the U.S. steel industry won protection from its foreign rivals, U.S. automobile manufacturers had to pay higher prices for steel and became more vulnerable to competition from foreign car producers. As U.S. auto producers lost their dominance in their home market, they pressured policy makers for their own protection from foreign competition.

Policy makers responded to the auto industry's demands by placing a voluntary export restraint on Japanese automobiles. The restraint, which limited Japanese firms' ability to export cars produced in Japan to the United States, prompted an international relocation of much of the world's auto production. Japanese firms such as Honda and Toyota now produce cars in the United States and export them to Europe, to Asia, and even back to Japan. In fact, it no longer makes much sense to talk about "American" cars or "Japanese" cars. Auto-industry analysts speak instead of "captive imports" (vehicles such as the Geo, made by a foreign-based company but sold through domestic dealerships) and "transplants" (for example, the Ford-Mazda Probe, built domestically by a foreign-based company).

Even though consumers can no longer easily define cars' nationality, firms recognize that as long as domestic interests dominate the policy-making process, it's to the firms' advantage to appear "domestic." So advertising now often emphasizes firms' links to the domestic economy. Figure 1.1 provides a good example; a *Newsweek* advertisement by Toyota highlights the firm's "homegrown success" at its U.S. plants, such as the original one in Georgetown, Kentucky, and implicitly links the firm to a quintessentially American event, the Kentucky Derby.

A product's "nationality" becomes even more difficult to determine once we recognize that firms assemble their products from components manufactured around the world. Ford, for example, assembles its Escort in Germany from parts produced in 15 countries, from Austria to Canada to Japan. Such production linkages represent one type of economic interdependence, a type increasingly prevalent in the world economy. Occasionally, the result is embarrassment—for policy makers intent on giving preference to domestic products to win favor with domestic special-interest groups. For example, a small town in New York, determined to "buy American," bought a $55,000 John Deere excavator in preference over a comparable $40,000 Komatsu model. Town decision makers soon discovered that Komatsu built its machine in Illinois and that Deere built its in Japan.[1]

The debates over international interdependence that heated up in the 1970s and 1980s haven't cooled, but some of the details have changed. For example, one of the most important trends of recent years is developing countries' expanding involvement with the world economy. After decades of attempting to isolate themselves from world markets, many developing countries now open their borders and pursue policies designed to integrate themselves into international economic activity. This trend produces new patterns of international interdependence that bring new debates to the fore. What are the implications for developed countries of trade with developing ones? Is the "commonsense" conclusion—that trade with low-wage countries must lower wages for American workers—correct? In other words, as the title of one article put it, "Are Your Wages Set in Beijing?"[2] As we'll see in Chapter Four, most international economists agree, based on mounting empirical evidence, that trade with low-wage countries has *not* lowered U.S. wages significantly. But the debate continues, and many of the loudest "antiglobalization" critics simply ignore the empirical evidence.

International interdependence and the debates it engenders aren't limited to trade in goods and services. In fact, interdependence in financial markets, where firms and governments borrow, lend, and finance investment projects, has grown even more dramatically than that in markets for goods such as oil, steel, and automobiles. Until the mid-1960s, government regulation of financial flows across national borders, combined with the limitations of transportation and communication technologies, kept national financial markets largely separate. Now, with decreased government regulation and improved technologies, financial activity clusters in international centers such as London, New York, Tokyo, Singapore, Hong Kong, Zurich, Frankfurt, and Paris. The result is a 24-hour market in which the push of a computer button shifts funds from one country or currency to another. Growing numbers of firms based in one country list themselves on foreign stock exchanges to facilitate global finance of their investment projects. Estimates indicate that approximately one in every seven stock (or equity) transactions involves a foreign party.[3] U.S.-based firms now raise funds for investment by issuing bonds denominated not just in dollars but also in euros, yen, Swiss francs, British pounds, and other currencies and sell those bonds around the world.

---

1 *The Economist,* February 1, 1992, p. 26.

2 Richard B. Freeman, "Are Your Wages Set in Beijing?" *Journal of Economic Perspectives,* 1995, pp. 15–32.

3 International Monetary Fund, *World Economic Outlook,* May 1995, p. 80.

Figure 1.1 **Firms Advertise Their Domestic Economic Linkages**

PEOPLE IN

KENTUCKY

BREED HORSES

that sell for

MILLIONS

OF DOLLARS

Luckily they also

PRODUCE SOME MORE

AFFORDABLE

FORMS OF TRANSPORT

In Georgetown, Kentucky, people will proudly tell you stories about their legendary thoroughbred horses. Champion racers, with familiar names like Citation, Whirlaway and Man o' War.

They might also brag a little about some other homegrown success

Toyota Motor Manufacturing

Kentucky, USA

stories. And rightfully so. Because the 400,000 Camrys and Avalons built every year by the people of Toyota Motor Manufacturing in Georgetown are winning hearts around America - and the world.

In every place where Toyotas are built - from Australia, to Thailand, to Kenya - the cars and trucks that are produced there reflect the pride of the people who build them. Because, not coincidentally, they are also the people who drive them.

Here in the U.S., Toyotas are being designed by Californians, tested in Arizona and Michigan, built in Kentucky, California, and soon in Indiana as well. In fact, more than half the Toyotas sold in America are built by Americans.

Toyota understands that growth in the global marketplace only comes when there is a deep understanding and respect of the unique qualities and needs of local operations and people. That's why, around the world, we invest in local design, local manufacturing, parts and jobs.

Sure it makes good business sense for Toyota. But it also makes for increased competitiveness and growth in the economies where we do business.

It's a win/win situation. And if there's one thing the people of Kentucky know - it's how to produce a winner.

TOYOTA People Drive Us

International firms find it advantageous to emphasize their ties to the domestic economy.

Source: *Newsweek Extra*, Winter 1997/98.

Despite rapid growth in virtually all international financial markets, the most dramatic growth of all has occurred in the markets for currencies themselves. In 2001, global turnover in world foreign exchange markets, where national currencies are traded, measured well over $1.2 trillion *per day,* up from around $20 billion per day in 1986, as illustrated in Figure 1.2. This compares with total world merchandise trade of about $6 trillion *per year.* Note, however, the decline in foreign exchange trading registered between 1998 and 2001. Why the drop? Two primary reasons: (1) As 11 members of the European Union switched from their national currencies to the euro during 1999–2002, firms no longer needed to use the foreign exchange market to exchange, say, German marks for French francs. (2) Financial crises in East Asia, Brazil, and Russia put many banks out of business, which consolidated foreign exchange trading among a smaller group of players.

All these international financial markets provide opportunities for **international investment,** which plays a vital role in the world economy. From a lender's perspective, these markets allow individuals, firms, and governments with funds to lend to find the most productive investment projects to fund, regardless of the projects' location. From a borrower's perspective, international financial markets allow individuals, firms, and governments with promising investment projects to seek lenders willing to fund the projects on attractive terms, regardless of the lenders' nationality or place of residence. Still, citizens and policy makers in economies hit by economic crises, such as Mexico in 1994, East Asia in 1997, Brazil and Russia in 1998, and Argentina and Turkey in 2001, ask whether their new financial openness and integration into the world economy caused or contributed to the ensuing crises, in which investment *in*flows suddenly turned into investment *out*flows, with painful consequences.

The growth of international flows of goods and services; financial assets such as stocks, bonds, and currencies; and information reflects, in part, declines in international transportation and communication costs. Sea cargo, air transport, and telephone calls all have become dramatically cheaper (see Figure 1.3), and these trends encourage international economic activity. However, government policies also exert an important influence. Since World War II, more and more governments have recognized the importance of open international markets for goods, services, and investment and reduced their restrictions on international transactions.

Figure 1.2 **Daily Turnover in Foreign Exchange Markets, 1986–2001 (Trillions $)**

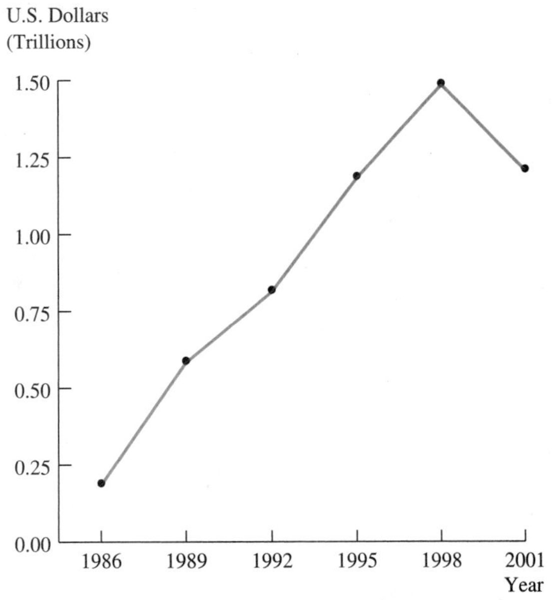

Daily turnover in foreign exchange markets is about a fifth of *annual* trade in goods and services.

Source: Data from Bank for International Settlements (updates available at www.bis.org).

Figure 1.3 **Transport and Communication Costs, 1930–1990 (Index: 1930 = 100)**

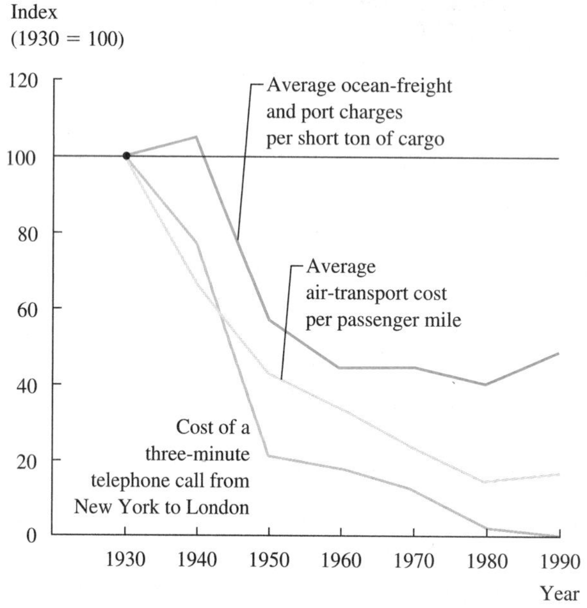

Index
(1930 = 100)

Average ocean-freight and port charges per short ton of cargo

Average air-transport cost per passenger mile

Cost of a three-minute telephone call from New York to London

Year

Declines in transport and communication costs during the twentieth century encouraged increased international economic activity.

Source: Data from Institute for International Economics.

1.2.1 Policy Implications of International Interdependence

The increase in international economic activity, in turn, has far-flung implications for the world political economy. Policy makers in issue areas once considered domestic—such as antitrust policy, regulation, and taxation—now must reckon with those policies' international ramifications. U.S. antitrust policy makers, who approved a merger between General Electric and Honeywell, fumed when the merger failed because European Union antitrust policy makers blocked it. In the North American Free Trade Agreement (NAFTA), U.S. and Canadian environmental interests still fear that firms will exploit Mexico's allegedly lower environmental standards and enforcement by moving to Mexico and exporting goods produced under the laxer standards to U.S. and Canadian markets, although existing empirical evidence doesn't support those fears. With increased international mobility, countries that try to tax their citizens or firms at rates above those in other nations risk losing some of their most productive citizens and enterprises. In all these cases, policies that at first glance appear to have primarily domestic effects turn out to be linked to important international questions as well. Effective economic policy making requires that these international linkages be taken into account.

The implications of interdependence for macroeconomic policy making—that is, for fiscal, monetary, and exchange rate policy—are at least as dramatic as those for microeconomic policy. In Europe, Germany's tight monetary policy to prevent inflation after the country's unification angered other members of the European Union and threatened the group's plans to introduce a common currency for Europe. In Asia, despite the Japanese economy's decade-long slump, Japanese policy makers still resist lobbying by their foreign counterparts to increase the rate of growth of the money supply. Brazil and Argentina suffered "hangovers" or "tequila effects" after Mexico experienced serious macroeconomic instability in late 1994 and early 1995; the same countries experienced shock waves when the Asian and Russian financial crises made international investors more wary of the risks of developing-country markets.

1.2.2 Symptoms of International Interdependence

It's not easy to measure international economic interdependence, but we can examine two symptoms. The first is simply the trend in the extent of trade, or the volume of goods exchanged across national boundaries, illustrated in Figure 1.4. Merchandise trade has expanded rapidly over the past half-century; in fact, since 1950, world merchandise *trade* has grown more than twice as fast as world merchandise *production.* Panel (b) focuses on the past decade, during which trade volume continued to grow much faster than production. These trends indicate an increasingly vital role of international trade in allocating the world's resources. Economics is the study of the allocation of scarce resources among alternative uses, so the importance of international issues in the study of economics also has increased.

As we'll see in Chapters Two and Three, international trade improves individuals' potential well-being by raising incomes and increasing the quantity of goods and services available to consume. Nevertheless, interdependence, of which trade is a symptom, often is viewed as a mixed blessing. For U.S. consumers, trade makes available sugar from Brazil, apparel from China, steel from South Korea, and wine from France. However, U.S. sugar producers, clothing manufacturers, steel producers, and wine growers demand protection from competition by foreign rivals, even though we'll see that the costs of such protection rest squarely on domestic consumers.

Despite dramatic increases in trade worldwide, countries continue to differ significantly in the extent to which they engage in trade. Figure 1.5 presents some examples; it measures a country's involvement in trade by merchandise exports (horizontal axis) and imports (vertical axis) as shares of total output or gross national

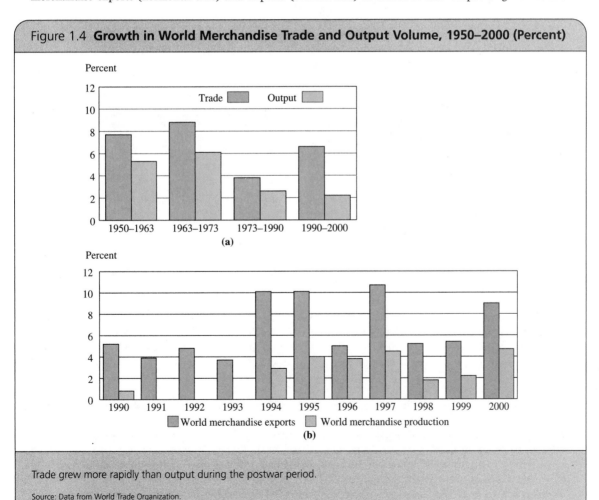

Figure 1.4 **Growth in World Merchandise Trade and Output Volume, 1950–2000 (Percent)**

Trade grew more rapidly than output during the postwar period.

Source: Data from World Trade Organization.

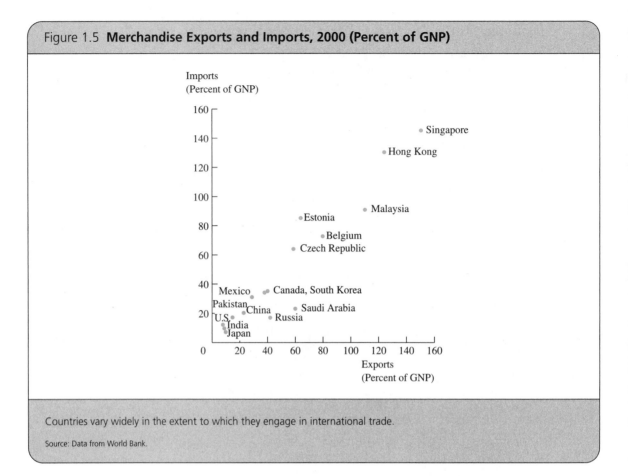

Figure 1.5 **Merchandise Exports and Imports, 2000 (Percent of GNP)**

Countries vary widely in the extent to which they engage in international trade.

Source: Data from World Bank.

product (GNP). The 2000 export shares range from a low of 8 percent for the United States to a high of 150 percent for Singapore, a tiny country that specializes in trade. Import percentages range from Japan's 8 percent to Singapore's 146 percent, again reflecting that country's specialization in assembly and re-export tasks.

Other things being equal, large countries such as the United States tend to engage in less trade, as a share of their production, than do smaller ones. The main reason is easy to see: The size and diversity of the United States mean that domestic markets can efficiently satisfy many needs. On the import side, residents of Rhode Island get corn from Iowa, oil from Texas, and lettuce from California; they go beachcombing in Florida, mountain climbing in Colorado, and whale watching in Alaska. They execute financial deals in New York and watch Hollywood movies. On the export side, U.S. firms enjoy access to a huge domestic market; historically, many small and medium-sized U.S. firms haven't exported, but this is changing. Although still modest by world standards, as indicated in Figure 1.5, U.S. involvement in international trade has increased rapidly in recent years. Figure 1.6, which reports the dollar value of U.S. merchandise imports and exports throughout the postwar era, documents this trend. Note, however, that Figure 1.5 indicates that U.S. imports and exports remain quite small relative to the country's GNP.

Not only do countries engage in trade to differing extents, but their trade tends to cluster with different sets of trading partners. This isn't surprising because transportation costs, while now low by historical standards, still play a role in determining trade patterns. Figure 1.7 highlights this clustering by dividing trade flows into seven major groups or blocs of countries: North America, Asia, Western Europe, Latin America, the Middle East, Africa, and the areas of Central and Eastern Europe along with the Baltic states and the Commonwealth of Independent States (most of the former Soviet Union). Recently, policy makers have expressed concern over the risk that trade patterns will evolve more in the direction of trade blocs—with open intrabloc trade but high

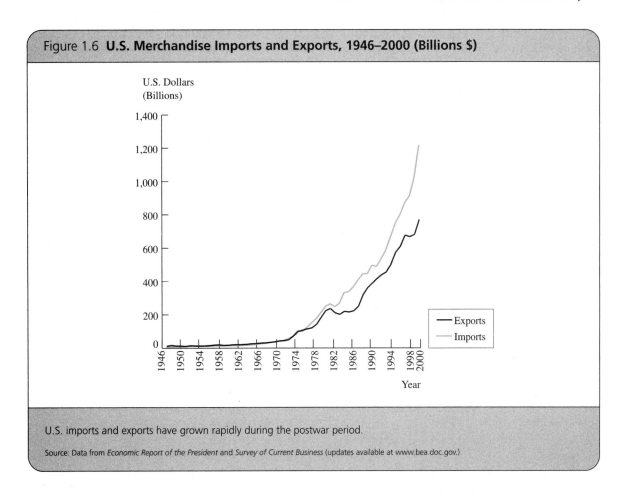

Figure 1.6 **U.S. Merchandise Imports and Exports, 1946–2000 (Billions $)**

U.S. imports and exports have grown rapidly during the postwar period.

Source: Data from *Economic Report of the President* and *Survey of Current Business* (updates available at www.bea.doc.gov.)

barriers to trade between blocs. This concern underlies some economists' criticisms of the European Union and NAFTA, which offer special, favorable terms for intragroup trade. However, Figure 1.7 clarifies that large trade flows continue between North America and Asia and between Western Europe and Asia, despite the EU and NAFTA preferences.

As a symptom of international interdependence, the magnitude and pattern of trade primarily reflect interdependence among producers and consumers in specific markets. International trade in automobiles makes auto consumers and producers worldwide interdependent, and the same is true in thousands of other markets. But economic interdependence goes much deeper. Synchronized changes in macroeconomic activity across countries represent a second important symptom of interdependence. Figure 1.8 illustrates the recent paths of industrial production in a set of major industrialized economies. Notice that the countries exhibit a striking tendency toward simultaneous booms and recessions. This historical evidence suggests that it may be difficult for one economy to expand when its trading partners' economies are growing slowly or shrinking. Note also, however, that the correlation of countries' activity is far from perfect. The 1990s provides a clear example of divergent patterns among the major industrial economies: For most of the decade, the United States and Canada boomed, while Western Europe grew very slowly and activity in Japan stagnated.

Like interdependence within specific markets, macroeconomic interdependence often is viewed as a mixed blessing. In general, macroeconomic spillover effects create the potential for conflict whenever one country perceives a need to pursue contractionary policies (for example, to fight inflation) while its trading partners want to expand (perhaps to counter unacceptably high unemployment). The 1990s provide plenty of examples. Britain withdrew in 1992 from European Union plans for a common currency, at least in part because of its unwillingness to endure the contractionary spillover effects of German macroeconomic policy on the British

Figure 1.7 **Regional Flows of Merchandise Trade, 2000 (Billions $)**

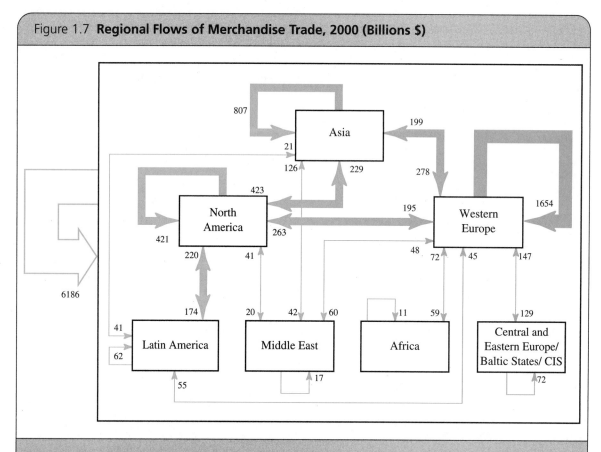

Countries of North America, Western Europe, and Asia engage in large flows of intraregional trade, but also continue to trade actively with countries outside their region. Two-way flows smaller than $50 billion are omitted from the figure.

Source: Data from World Trade Organization.

economy. Germany hoped to keep Italy out of the new EU common-currency area to insulate the group from a possible replay of Italy's historically inflationary policies. American and European policy makers complained to their Japanese counterparts about the latter's reluctance to address Japan's economic problems, a prerequisite to a Japanese role in helping to resolve the Asian financial crisis. And later, already slow-growing Western Europe and Japan despaired over the implications of the 2001 slowdown in U.S. growth.

Despite the clarity of the pattern observable in Figure 1.8, an important cautionary note is in order. Data such as those reported in Figure 1.8 require careful interpretation. After all, each country's experience may have been totally independent of all others'. In other words, it's possible either that mere coincidence produced the pattern apparent in Figure 1.8 or that all the economies responded similarly but independently to outside events. We must take this general caution seriously. Historical evidence can suggest patterns in economic behavior, but can't explain the reasons behind them. Because of the inability of empirical evidence alone to explain observed patterns, we need *theories* of economic behavior to answer questions such as: What are the nature and consequences of the economic ties among the countries of the world economy? How should policy makers respond to particular cases of international economic interdependence?

This book addresses these fundamental questions from the perspective of economics. Within the sphere of countries' international relationships, political and economic elements are difficult, if not impossible, to separate. However, the basic concepts of economic theory can be surprisingly helpful in untangling the maze of

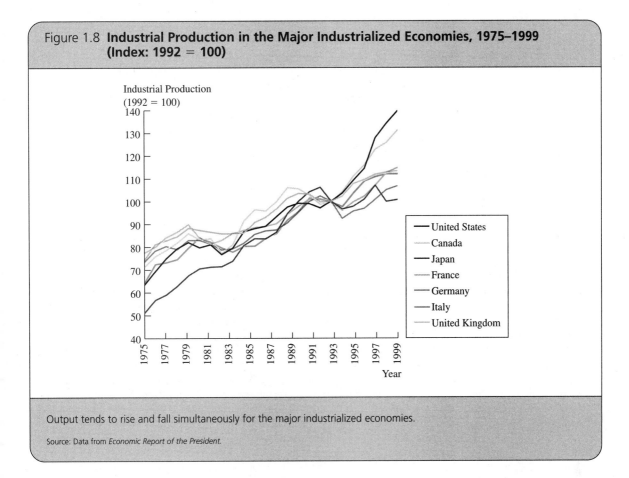

Figure 1.8 **Industrial Production in the Major Industrialized Economies, 1975–1999 (Index: 1992 = 100)**

Output tends to rise and fall simultaneously for the major industrialized economies.

Source: Data from *Economic Report of the President.*

issues that constitutes the world economy. Millions of firms produce hundreds of thousands of commodities in approximately 200 countries, so we need a systematic framework for analysis—and this is what economic theory can provide. Thus, it is this book's perspective more than its subject matter that marks it as a text in international *economics*. The subjects covered—such as international trade, protectionism, growth, the transition from central planning, multinational enterprises, relations between developed and developing countries, inflation, debt, financial crises, and unemployment—are also of direct interest to political scientists, as well as to specialists in international relations, international business, and public policy.

1.3 The Economic Significance of Political Boundaries

International economics traditionally has been the subject of special books and courses, separate from the rest of economics. At the same time, the interaction between international economics and the remainder of economic theory has been rich and, like international trade itself, beneficial to both parties. Economists working specifically on international problems developed many of the analytical techniques now used in all areas of the discipline. Similarly, many recent advances in international economics have built on developments in other areas of economics.

Why does the separate study of international questions persist? The main reason is that the **economic significance of political boundaries** persists. Most people would agree that life in a small New England college town differs radically from life in Los Angeles. From an economist's point of view, however, residents of the two places share a great deal. All use U.S. dollars as a currency or means of payment. All live under a common set of federal laws and a common political and economic system, and many share a common language. All share in the fortunes of the U.S. economy, benefiting from the country's resource endowment and feeling the effects of U.S. policy decisions. Because of all these shared features, most economic transactions between the New Englander and the Californian face a smaller set of barriers than do economic transactions between a U.S. resident and a resident of a foreign country. The Californian can relocate in New England if he or she chooses, and the New Englander is free to migrate to California. If the pattern of interest rates makes deposits in California banks or bonds issued by California firms or government agencies attractive, the New Englander can choose to buy those assets; and vice versa for the Californian buying assets in New England.

National boundaries are economically relevant not only in determining the extent of legal, language, and currency barriers to transactions but in determining economic policy. In other words, the nature of the policy-making process also tends to make international economics a separate field of study. Despite the growing internationalization of many markets, economic policy making remains largely a matter of national sovereignty. In fact, many national governments respond to the perception of increased international interdependence by guarding their sovereign policy-making powers even more jealously. As a result, the policy process typically favors the interests of domestic residents over the interests of the world as a whole. This tendency is easy to understand given the realities of policy making. Decisions on policies that are either universally beneficial or universally harmful are easy—but, unfortunately for policy makers, such easy decisions are rare. The more typical policy decision involves evaluating a policy that benefits some individuals and harms others. In such a situation, we shouldn't be surprised that consideration given to the policy's effect on domestic residents usually outweighs that given to the effect on individuals abroad.

At the same time, it's important to realize that the major popular misconception about international trade policy is that policy choices pit the interests of one country against those of the other. In fact, trade-policy choices rarely take this form. Instead, trade policy primarily affects the distribution of income *within* each country. If the United States blocks imports of Chinese apparel, the main result isn't to help the United States at China's expense; rather, the main effect is to help *American* apparel *producers* at the expense of *American* apparel *consumers*. Similarly, if the U.S. steel industry wins protection from its South Korean competitors, the main losers are American steel consumers, such as the U.S. automobile industry and American car buyers. Economists think that individuals act in their own self-interest, so evaluating the effects of various international trade policies on different interest groups will be one of our major tasks. By understanding a policy's effects on different groups within the economy, we can better understand the observed pattern of political support for and opposition to the policy.

1.4 Studying International Economics

Economists traditionally divide the subject matter of international economics into two parts. The first, called the **theory of international trade,** extends *micro*economic analysis to international questions. Here we consider decisions concerning the quantities of various goods produced, consumed, and traded by different countries. We'll see that the goods and services available for consumers to enjoy are at a maximum when each country specializes in producing those goods that it can produce relatively efficiently. Trade then allows each country's residents to import a variety of other goods to consume. These production and consumption decisions collectively determine the relative prices of both goods and factors of production such as labor, capital, and land. These prices, in turn, determine the distribution of income among individuals in the economy.

Like microeconomics, trade theory traditionally ignores monetary issues by expressing all costs and prices in terms of other goods rather than a monetary unit such as dollars. In other words, goods exchange directly for other goods (one bushel of corn for two bushels of wheat, or four computers for one car). By examining trade's effect on the relative prices of different goods and factors of production, trade theory highlights the distributional impact of trade. Unrestricted international trade can change relative prices, so it also can alter the distribution of income among various groups within each country. An understanding of this interrelationship between trade and income distribution is essential to making sense of the political pressures for **protectionist policies,** which restrict international trade to "protect" domestic producers from foreign competition.

The second major branch of international economics, called *international finance, balance-of-payments theory,* or **open-economy macroeconomics,** applies *macro*economic analysis to aggregate international problems. Major concerns here include the level of employment and output in each economy as well as changes in the price level, balance of payments, and **exchange rates** or relative prices of different national currencies. The most basic issue addressed by open-economy macroeconomics is the interaction of international goals and influences with domestic ones in determining a country's macroeconomic performance and policy. Can a country that engages in international transactions (called an **open economy**) pursue the same macroeconomic policies as a country that engages in no international transactions (a **closed economy**) and achieve the same results? The answer is no; so, understanding the implications of openness turns out to be essential to effective macroeconomic policy making.

As in microeconomic analysis of international trade policy, we'll discover that macroeconomic policies have distributional consequences. Policy choices typically stated in terms of domestic interests versus foreign ones actually involve differences in the interests of various groups *within* each economy. For example, journalists, commentators, and politicians often speak of any currency depreciation (that is, a rise in the exchange rate or the domestic currency price of a unit of foreign currency) as an economic problem in need of a remedy. Indeed, sound economic policy making does require that any country experiencing a chronic currency depreciation consider adjusting its macroeconomic policies. We also must recognize, however, that depreciations *help* some groups within the domestic economy, especially import-competing and export industries. Those same currency depreciations also *hurt* other domestic groups, particularly importers and consumers of imported goods.

International trade and open-economy macroeconomics are the subjects of Parts One and Two of this book, respectively. In each part, we begin by building a simple model and then elaborate on it and apply it to many historical and current events in the world economy. The models are just road maps to describe the way the world economy works. They may seem overly simple and "unrealistic." However, that's the whole point of building models. After all, a road map would be of little practical use if it faithfully illustrated every bump, ant hill, grain of sand, pothole, and roadside sign. We need models like good road maps: as *simple* as possible while still capturing the *key features* necessary to understand the world economy. Once you master the basic models in Parts One and Two, you can use them to analyze not only the applications considered in the text but the constantly changing international economic news.

Economists call models that describe in a simplified way how the world economy works *positive models*. For the most part, we'll employ **positive analysis** in this book, using models to understand how the world economy is structured and how it functions. This approach focuses primarily on explanation and prediction. The goal is to understand the world economy well enough to be able to say, "If event X happens, event Y will follow." For example, after reading Chapter Four we might predict that, given the opportunity to choose between unrestricted trade and protectionism, farmers in Japan would tend to choose protectionism. This prediction *doesn't* depend on whether we, as economists or citizens, believe protectionism is desirable; the prediction follows directly from our model of how the world economy works. We can then look at Japanese farmers' political behavior and see if they do in fact support protectionist policies. (To jump ahead a bit, the answer is yes.)

Another type of analysis, **normative analysis,** *does* depend on our judgments about what is and isn't desirable. For example, if we think trade is desirable because it maximizes the quantity of goods and services available to consumers, we might conclude that Japanese policy makers should pursue open trade policies in the agricultural sector even though Japanese farmers oppose them. Normative analyses rely on our values to determine what types of international economic goals and policies we think policy makers should pursue.

From our discussion of the differences between positive and normative economic analysis, we can see that disagreements over international policy issues can come from at least two sources. First, there may be disagreement about the way the world works. One individual may think that if event X happens, event Y will follow, while another may think that if event X happens, event Z will follow. For example, one person might argue that opening international trade (X) will reduce economic growth (Y) because imported goods will replace domestic production, while someone else claims that opening trade (X) will increase economic growth (Z) by moving resources into their most productive uses. Analysts usually can resolve such disagreements by conducting further empirical research to determine whether Y or Z will follow X.[4]

Disagreements based on normative judgments typically prove more difficult to resolve. Two policy makers may agree that "If we pursue policy X, result Y will follow." But if the two disagree about whether Y is desirable, they will disagree about whether they should pursue policy X. For example, most economists acknowledge that policies of unrestricted international trade would result in the decline of several U.S. industries, including

---

4 On the trade-growth connection, the empirical evidence suggests that countries with open markets experience faster growth. Sebastian Edwards, "Openness, Productivity and Growth: What Do We Really Know?" *Economic Journal,* March 1998, pp. 383–398, summarizes the evidence. See also Jeffrey A. Frankel and David Romer, "Does Trade Cause Growth?" *American Economic Review,* June 1999, pp. 379–399.

nonspecialty steel, some types of automobiles, footwear, and many types of textiles and apparel, because those U.S. industries are relatively inefficient compared with their foreign counterparts. Whether one supports policies of unrestricted trade thus depends in part on one's evaluation of the trade-offs among trade's efficiency benefits, the short-run costs of resource reallocation associated with the decline of certain industries, the costs to consumers of protecting inefficient industries, and the increased interdependence that comes from relying on foreign suppliers.

Throughout this book, both positive and normative issues arise. Although the distinction isn't always sharp, we must keep in mind the conceptual difference between the two. Debates over the desirability of various international economic policies can be useful only when it's clear where the disagreement originates—in our views of the way the world works or in our views of how we would like the world to be.

Throughout the book, we present data on many aspects of the world economy, ranging from the breakdown of trade in Sudan, China's World Trade Organization (WTO) entry, international patterns in labor productivity and wages, the international shipping industry, recent events in the world semiconductor industry, the effect of trade policy on the incidence of malaria in Africa, international food-safety policy, the effect of foreign aid on recipients' growth, online currency trading, the birth of the Bosnian central bank, the economic effects of German unification, the 1997 Thai baht crisis, Japan's policy dilemmas, dollarization, and privatization programs in the formerly centrally planned economies.

A rich variety of sources of additional information about the world economy exists. We've included many in the references at the end of each chapter. In addition, the *Study Guide* written to accompany this book suggests useful leads, including many Web resources, if you want to pursue a particular topic in more detail. If you don't yet have a copy of the *Study Guide,* check with your instructor or your bookstore to order one. Along with data sources on the world economy, the *Study Guide* contains study aids and questions with answers for each chapter in the text, helpful hints for writing economics papers, and much more.

Key Terms

international interdependence	**open-economy macroeconomics**
international economic integration	**exchange rates**
international investment	**open economy**
economic significance of political boundaries	**closed economy**
theory of international trade	**positive analysis**
protectionist policies	**normative analysis**

Problems and Questions for Review

1. For each of the types of cost illustrated in Figure 1.3 (air transport, sea transport, telephone costs), explain why a decline in the cost might lead to an increase in international trade.
2. Look at the data in Figure 1.5. Why might some countries choose to engage more in international trade than other countries?
3. Name some examples of the economic significance of political boundaries.
4. Firms often buy advertising to lobby support for their positions on international trade issues. Suppose that you represent Acme Thingamajigs, a major producer of thingamajigs. What kinds of trade policies for the thingamajig market might you support, and why? What would you consider in deciding whether buying an advertisement to lobby for your position would be worthwhile?
5. Name three recent events in international microeconomics that you hope to understand better after mastering Chapters Two through Eleven. Name three recent events in international macroeconomics that you hope to understand better after mastering Chapters Twelve through Twenty-One.
6. Some economists have argued that increased liberalization of international trade is allowing geographically smaller countries to be economically viable. The number of recognized independent nation-states rose from 74 in 1946 to 192 in 1995.[5] Why might small countries be especially reliant on the availability of open international trade?

---

5 See Alberto Alesina et al., "Economic Integration and Political Disintegration," *American Economic Review* 90 (December 2000), p. 1276.

7. Suppose you had been a German tourist in Moscow on August 26, 1998, when the ruble price of a German mark suddenly rose by 69 percent. How might the ruble depreciation have affected you? Suppose, instead, you had been a Russian firm that used inputs imported from Germany. How might the ruble depreciation have affected you?

8. Look at the data in Figure 1.7, especially the volume of North American exports to North America and Western European exports to Western Europe. How do the sizes of the two trade flows compare? The size of Western Europe's economy is approximately the same size as the U.S. economy. How might you explain the observation that intra–Western Europe international trade is four times the size of intra–North American international trade? *(Hint: Think about what is required for a transaction to be recorded as* international *trade.)*

References and Selected Readings

Bhagwati, Jagdish. *Protectionism.* Cambridge, Mass.: MIT Press, 1988.
A lively treatment of the history and status of protectionism; for all students.

Destler, I. M. *American Trade Politics.* Washington, D.C.: Institute for International Economics, 1995.
Excellent treatment of the historical evolution of U.S. trade policy-making institutions; for all students.

Fieleke, Norman S. "Popular Myths about the World Economy." *New England Economic Review* (July–August 1997): 17–26.
Introductory overview of popular misconceptions about trade.

King, Philip. *International Economics and International Economic Policy: A Reader.* New York: McGraw-Hill, 1995.
An excellent reader for all students. Well organized to follow along with The World Economy.

Krugman, Paul. "Growing World Trade: Causes and Consequences." *Brookings Papers on Economic Activity* 1 (1995): 327–377.
Survey of recent trends in world trade; for intermediate students.

Symposium on "Globalization in Perspective." *Journal of Economic Perspectives* 12 (Fall 1998): 3–72.
Collection of accessible papers on the meaning and effects of globalization.

Yarbrough, Beth V., and Robert M. Yarbrough. "The 'Globalization' of Trade: What's Changed and Why?" In *Studies in Globalization and Development,* edited by S. Gupta and N. K. Choudry. Norwell, Mass.: Kluwer Academic Publishers, 1997.
Recent trends in international trade; for all students.

INTERNATIONAL
MICROECONOMICS

PART ONE

CHAPTER TWO

Comparative Advantage I: Labor Productivity and the Ricardian Model

2.1 Introduction

Countries engage in international trade because they benefit from doing so.[1] The gains from trade arise because trade allows countries to specialize their production in a way that allocates all resources to their most productive uses. Trade plays an essential role in achieving this allocation because it frees each country's residents from having to consume goods in the same combination in which the domestic economy can produce them. If the United States specialized its production but didn't engage in international trade, U.S. residents would have large quantities of wheat and soybeans, airplanes, computers and other high-technology equipment, but no coffee or bananas and few shoes or textiles. Japanese residents, on the other hand, would find themselves well stocked with automobiles and consumer electronics but without gasoline to run the automobiles and confined to a diet consisting largely of fish.

We can easily see the benefits from productive specialization and trade at the individual level. Most individuals choose to specialize in producing one good (for example, the teaching of economics) and then exchange some of that good for other goods to consume (such as food, clothing, and housing). Any individual who attempted to achieve self-sufficiency by producing everything he or she consumed would face a very difficult task and be constrained to a much lower standard of living. Suppose you tried to generate your own electricity and build your own automobile along with growing your own food and building your own house. Providing yourself with these "necessities" would require so much time and effort that there would be little left to produce the "luxuries," such as skis and handheld computers, to which you are accustomed. The same holds true for countries that choose to forgo the opportunities provided by productive specialization and trade. The fact that political boundaries divide the world into nation-states doesn't alter trade's potential for expanding output by efficiently allocating the world's scarce resources to their most productive uses. But policy makers and political economists didn't completely understand this simple point until around 1817, and many still forget or ignore it today.

This chapter demonstrates the existence of gains from trade within the simplest possible context; later chapters extend the analysis to fit reality more closely. The fundamental ideas presented in this chapter—simple though they are—represent not only the heart of international trade theory but also perhaps economics' most enduring contribution to the goal of improving the welfare of the world economy's citizens.

---

1 For convenience, we speak of "countries" engaging in international trade and making production and consumption decisions. In reality—at least in market-oriented economies—individual firms and consumers, not countries or their governments, make most production and consumption decisions and engage in most international trade. In nonmarket economies, government enterprises conduct a large percentage of international trade as well as control production patterns. Chapter Eight examines government involvement in trade for market economies; Chapter Eleven does the same for nonmarket economies.

2.2 Early Thinking about Trade: The Mercantilists

During the seventeenth and eighteenth centuries, the doctrine of **mercantilism** represented the dominant attitude toward international trade. The period was one of nation-building and consolidation of power by newly formed states. Gold and silver circulated as money, so the quantity of these precious metals any country held symbolized that nation's wealth and power. National leaders wanted to accumulate as much gold and silver as possible. Their efforts to accomplish this involved producing and exporting (selling abroad) as many goods as possible while keeping imports (purchases from abroad) to a minimum. When a nation's exports proved more than sufficient to pay for its imports, flows of precious metals settled the account balance; any country that exported more than it imported could enjoy an inflow of gold and silver. The policy prescription based on this mercantilist view was to encourage exports and restrict imports, since mercantilists viewed trade primarily as a way to accumulate gold.

Further, mercantilists assumed trade was a **zero-sum game**—that it couldn't mutually benefit all parties. (Poker is an example of a zero-sum game: Whatever one player wins, the other players lose.) Mercantilists assumed that fixed amounts of goods and gold existed in the world and that trade merely determined their distribution among the various nations.[2]

2.3 The Decline of Mercantilism (and the Birth of Economics)

Late in the eighteenth century, the doctrine of mercantilism came under attack by leaders of the emerging science of political economy. In 1752, David Hume pointed out two weaknesses in the mercantilists' logic.

First, it isn't the quantity of gold and silver a nation holds that matters; rather, it's the quantity of goods and services that the gold and silver can buy. Individuals get satisfaction not by accumulating precious metals for their own sake, but by consuming the goods those metals can buy. Mercantilists wanted to export as many goods and import as few as possible. This implied that other nations would accumulate goods while the mercantilist nation accumulated gold. *(Would you want to live in a country that successfully pursued mercantilist policies?)*

The second problem raised by Hume concerns the long-run viability of mercantilist policies. Suppose a country ran a trade surplus (that is, the value of the country's exports exceeded the value of its imports) and obtained the implied inflow of gold. Gold formed the basis for nations' money supplies during the mercantilist period, so the gold inflow would raise both the money supply and prices.[3] As the prices of the nation's goods rose relative to the prices of other nations' goods, the change in relative prices would make the nation's exports less attractive to foreign buyers and imports more attractive to domestic residents. Exports would fall, and imports would rise. Thus, the price effects of the gold inflow would automatically eliminate the nation's initial surplus. We'll see more about David Hume and his **specie-flow mechanism,** as this automatic-adjustment scenario is called, in Part Two.

A second political economist to question mercantilist policies was Adam Smith, writing in 1776. Smith focused on mercantilists' assumption that trade constituted a zero-sum game. By assuming each country could produce some commodities using less labor than its trading partners, Smith showed that *all* parties to international trade could benefit. How could this be possible? According to Smith, trade improved the allocation of labor, ensuring that each good would be produced in the country where the good's production required the least labor. The result would be a larger total quantity of goods produced in the world. With more goods available for distribution among the nations, each could be made better off. Trade would be a positive-sum game, like a hypothetical poker game in which every player could win simultaneously.

In 1817, David Ricardo showed that even Smith's optimistic view failed to capture all of trade's potential benefits. Ricardo's work provided the basis for our modern understanding of the importance of unrestricted

2 Chapters Nine and Twenty discuss additional aspects of mercantilism. The debate over the causes and consequences of mercantilism can be found in references by Smith, Heckscher, Viner, Ekelund and Tollison, and Irwin in the references at the end of the chapter.

3 The relationship between changes in a nation's money stock and changes in its price level will be a central issue in international macroeconomics in Part Two of the book. For now it suffices to recall that, other things being equal, a change in the money stock causes the price level to move in the same direction.

international trade. We are now ready to examine a modern version of Adam Smith's and David Ricardo's revolutionary views of trade. First we discuss some simplifying assumptions of our analysis. We could relax most of these, at the expense of additional complexity, without altering the fundamental results.[4]

2.4 Keeping Things Simple: Some Assumptions

First, we assume **perfect competition** prevails in both output and factor markets. Each buyer and seller is small enough relative to the market to take the market-determined price as given. Each commodity is homogeneous (that is, all units of each good are identical), and buyers and sellers have good information about market conditions. Entry and exit are easy in each market. The assumption of perfect competition is important, because it implies that the price of each good will equal its **marginal cost** of production, or the change in total cost due to production of one additional unit of output.

Second, we assume each country has a fixed endowment of resources available, and these resources are fully employed and homogeneous. The problem each country faces involves allocating this fixed quantity of resources among production of the various goods residents want to consume.

Third, we assume firms' technologies don't vary. Different countries may use different technologies, but all firms within each country employ a common production method for each good.

Fourth, we assume transportation costs are zero. This implies that consumers will be indifferent between the domestically produced and imported versions of a good when their prices are the same. We also ignore, for now, other barriers to trade.

Fifth, we assume factors of production (or inputs) such as labor and capital are completely mobile among industries within each country and completely immobile among countries. This assumption obviously is too strong to represent an accurate description of the world, and we'll relax the assumption in Chapter Ten. However, resources that are much more mobile within than among countries capture an essential element of the economic significance of political boundaries. Perfect mobility of resources among industries implies that the price of each factor must be equal in all industries within each country. Otherwise, resources would move from low-paying to high-paying industries. Because factors are immobile among countries, the price of each factor generally will differ across countries without trade.

Finally, we assume a world consisting of two countries, each using a single input to produce two goods. For simplicity, we'll refer to the countries as A and B, the single input as L (for *labor*), and the two goods as X and Y.

2.5 The Ricardian World without Trade

The answer to the question "Does international trade benefit its participants?" requires that we compare a world without international trade to one with trade and show that a larger quantity of goods is available in the latter. Economists call the case of self-sufficiency, or no trade, **autarky.** In autarky each nation must produce whatever its residents want to consume, for there's no other way to obtain goods for consumption. In other words, the resource-allocation decision made by a country in autarky is simultaneously a production decision *and* a consumption decision. To make this decision, the country uses two pieces of information. First, it must consider the *production* trade-offs between goods X and Y that are possible given the available resources and technology. Second, it must consider its citizens' preferences, that is, their subjective trade-offs between *consumption* of goods X and Y.

2.5.1 Production in Autarky

We can characterize the various combinations of goods X and Y that countries A and B can produce by developing a production possibilities frontier (or transformation curve) for each country. The **production possibilities frontier** represents all the alternate combinations of goods X and Y a country could produce. To sketch

---

4 Chapters Five and Eight relax the perfect-competition assumption. For the implications of factor growth or mobility, see Chapter Ten. Theories of trade that focus on technology can be found in Chapters Five, Eight, and Ten. Chapter Five contains a discussion of transportation costs. Chapters Six and Seven concentrate on trade restrictions and their effects. The specific-factors model in Chapter Four captures the effects of an input that can't move across industries.

country A's production possibilities frontier, we must know A's resource endowment—the quantity of labor available in A—and the technology available to transform those labor inputs into outputs. We denote country A's *labor* endowment as L^A. Two **input coefficients,** a_{LX} and a_{LY}, summarize the production technology. The input coefficients tell us how many units of *labor* are required to produce one unit of each of the two outputs. In country A, production of one unit of good X requires a_{LX} units of *labor*, and production of one unit of good Y requires a_{LY} units of *labor*.

It helps to have a memory aid for the meaning of the input coefficients. The first letter always refers to the *country,* the first subscript to the *input,* and the second subscript to the *output* produced. For example, a_{LX} might be the number of units of *labor* required to produce a Xerox machine in America, while b_{LY} could denote the number of units of *labor* needed to produce a *yo*-yo in Britain. The best way to become comfortable with the input coefficients is to practice reading them in terms of what they mean rather than the letters themselves. The statement $a_{LX} = 2$ reads "the number of units of *labor* required to produce 1 unit of good X in country A is 2." With a little patience and practice, the input coefficients will become familiar and convenient ways to represent the productive technology available in different countries.

Note the relationship between country A's input coefficients, or technology, and the country's labor productivity. The *more* productive country A's labor is in producing good X, the *fewer* units of labor will be required to produce 1 unit of X, so the *lower* a_{LX} will be. Similarly, *high* labor productivity in the Y industry translates into a *low* value of a_{LY}. Ricardo's model contains only one input (labor), so a country's technology simply reflects the country's labor productivity in the two industries.

If country A chooses to use all its labor in production of good X, it can produce L^A/a_{LX} units of X and zero units of Y. Consider country A with 100 units of labor ($L^A = 100$) where 2 units of labor are required to produce 1 unit of good X ($a_{LX} = 2$) and 5 units of labor are required to produce 1 unit of good Y ($a_{LY} = 5$). If country A chooses to use all the available labor producing good X, it can produce 50 units ($L^A/a_{LX} = 100/2 = 50$). If it chooses instead to use all its labor producing Y, it can produce 20 units of Y and zero units of X. *(Why?)*

Country A also can produce one of a variety of alternate combinations containing some of *both* goods. For every unit of X forgone, A can produce a_{LX}/a_{LY} (or 2/5 in our numerical example) additional units of good Y. By producing 1 fewer unit of X, 2 units of labor ($a_{LX} = 2$) are released—enough labor to produce 2/5 units of Y, since 5 units of labor ($a_{LY} = 5$) are required to produce 1 unit of Y. All the possible production choices can be represented graphically as country A's production possibilities frontier, illustrated in Figure 2.1, where ΔY denotes "change in Y" and similarly for ΔX.

The negative slope of the production possibilities frontier reflects the fact that labor is scarce. Only L^A is available, and it is fully employed. This means the only way to produce more of one good is to produce less of the other. The rate at which one good can be transformed into the other is a_{LX}/a_{LY}, which defines the (absolute value of the) slope of the production possibilities frontier.[5] In economic terminology, the slope gives the **opportunity cost** of good X, or the number of units of good Y forgone to produce an additional unit of good X. This is called the **marginal rate of transformation (MRT),** because it is the rate at which good X can be "transformed" into good Y—by transferring labor out of the X industry and into the Y industry.

In autarky, residents of country A can choose to produce any one of the combinations of goods X and Y on the production possibilities frontier. It also is possible to produce at points inside the frontier, such as point I in Figure 2.1. In the numerical example, country A could produce 10 units of X and 12 units of Y using a total of $2 \cdot 10 + 5 \cdot 12 = 80$ units of labor. However, the country wouldn't choose to locate at an interior point such as I, because it could produce more by moving to a point such as II on the frontier. At each interior point, either some resources are not being used at all or some are not being used to their full productive potential. Points that lie outside the production possibilities frontier, such as III, are desirable but unattainable due to the constraint imposed by the fixed quantity of labor available. For example, country A couldn't produce 20 units of good X along with 20 units of good Y, because such a combination would require 140 units of labor ($2 \cdot 20 + 5 \cdot 20 = 140$) but only 100 units are available.

---

5 The production possibilities frontier is defined by the requirement that all labor be employed. This can be expressed as $L^A = a_{LX} \cdot X + a_{LY} \cdot Y$; in words, the total quantity of labor must equal the quantity employed in producing good X plus the quantity employed in producing good Y. Along a given production possibilities frontier, the total quantity of labor available, L^A, is held constant. For the full-employment condition to continue to hold when output levels of goods X and Y are varied, it must be true that $\Delta L^A = a_{LX} \cdot \Delta X + a_{LY} \cdot \Delta Y = 0$, where Δ, the uppercase Greek letter delta, is a shorthand notation for "change in." Rearranging this expression, it must be true that $\Delta Y/\Delta X = -(a_{LX}/a_{LY})$ gives the slope of the production possibilities frontier.

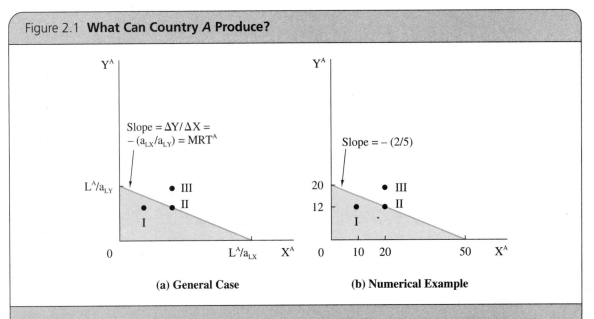

Figure 2.1 **What Can Country *A* Produce?**

(a) General Case

(b) Numerical Example

Country A's production possibilities frontier illustrates the different combinations of good X and Y the country can produce, given its labor endowment and technology. Country A can use its labor endowment (L^A, or 100) to produce L^A/a_{LX} (100/2 = 50) units of good X, L^A/a_{LY} (100/5 = 20) units of good Y, or any intermediate combination. The slope of the frontier ($-[a_{LX}/a_{LY}]$, or $-2/5$) gives the opportunity cost of good X, or the rate at which good X can be "transformed" into good Y.

The **Ricardian model** implies that the production possibilities frontier is a straight line. The slope of the production possibilities frontier represents the opportunity cost of good X, given by a_{LX}/a_{LY}, which is independent of the particular output combination being produced. For this reason, the Ricardian model sometimes is referred to as a **constant-cost model.** In autarky, the shaded triangle formed in Figure 2.1 by the two axes and the production possibilities frontier represents both the **production opportunity set** (the set of all possible combinations of X and Y the country could produce) and the **consumption opportunity set** (the set of all possible combinations of X and Y its residents could consume). The two sets must coincide in autarky, because domestic production is the only source of goods for consumption.

2.5.2 Consumption in Autarky

The production possibilities frontier tells only half the autarky story by revealing all the combinations of goods X and Y it's possible to produce given the available labor and technology. To determine which of the many possible points will be chosen, we must introduce the tastes, or preferences, of the country's residents. We assume that the level of satisfaction or **utility** enjoyed by residents depends on the quantities of goods X and Y available for consumption and that the production/consumption decision is made in such a way as to maximize utility. A graphical technique called an **indifference curve** shows all the different combinations of goods X and Y that result in a given level of utility.

Indifference curves have four basic properties. First, indifference curves are downward sloping. Panel (a) of Figure 2.2 shows why. Initially, the country is located at point 1, consuming X_1 units of good X and Y_1 units of good Y. Which other points would produce the same level of satisfaction as point 1? Surely not the points in area III, because they contain less of each good. Points in area II also must be ruled out, because they contain more of each good and therefore would be preferred to point 1. We are left with areas I and IV. Area I points contain less good X than point 1 but also contain more good Y. Area IV points contain less good Y than point 1 but also contain more good X. Therefore, areas I and IV represent the possibility of *substituting* more of one good for less of the other with no change in overall utility. The fact that residents must be compensated for the

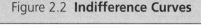

Figure 2.2 **Indifference Curves**

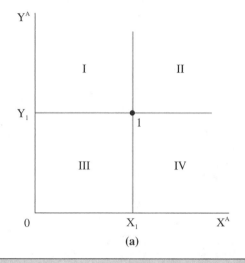
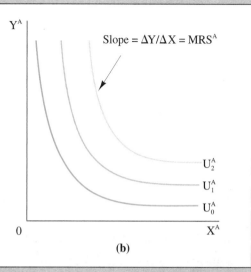

An indifference curve shows all combinations of goods X and Y that give consumers a given level of utility. Panel (a) demonstrates why indifference curves are downward sloping. Residents wouldn't be indifferent between point 1 and any point in areas II or III. Points in area II are preferred to point 1 because they contain more of each good. Points in area III are inferior to point 1 because they contain less of each good. All points that result in a level of utility equal to that attained at point 1 must lie in area I or IV. The indifference curves in panel (b) exhibit four necessary characteristics: each indifference curve is downward sloping and convex, the curves do not intersect, and higher curves are preferred to lower ones.

loss of one good by more of the other good to maintain the same level of utility implies that indifference curves slope downward.

A second requirement is that indifference curves be convex, or bowed in toward the origin of the graph. The slope of an indifference curve represents the rate at which residents are willing to trade off consumption of the two goods; this rate is called the **marginal rate of substitution (MRS).** Convexity of the indifference curve implies that this rate of trade-off changes with movements along the curve. As more X and less Y is consumed (moving down an indifference curve), good Y becomes more highly valued relative to good X; in other words, the amount of additional X required to compensate for further reducing consumption of Y increases.

Suppose, for example, that good X represents food and good Y represents clothing. At a point high and to the left on an indifference curve, a large amount of clothing and very little food would be available. In such a situation, individuals probably would willingly trade a substantial amount of clothing to obtain a small amount of additional food. The marginal rate of substitution between food and clothing would be high, and the indifference curve steep. At a point low and to the right on the same indifference curve, a large amount of food and very little clothing would be available. Individuals then would willingly give up very little clothing to obtain additional food. The marginal rate of substitution between food and clothing would be low, and the indifference curve relatively flat. Therefore, as we move down and to the right along an indifference curve, it becomes flatter as good X becomes less highly valued relative to good Y. The result is a convex indifference curve.

A third characteristic of indifference curves is that they never intersect. Each point, representing a single combination of goods X and Y, lies on one—and only one—indifference curve. Any consumption bundle consisting of given quantities of the two goods produces a unique level of utility, although we'll discuss some potential problems surrounding this requirement shortly.

Finally, higher indifference curves represent higher levels of utility and therefore are preferred to lower indifference curves. This simply reflects the preference for more goods over fewer goods. The indifference curves in panel (b) of Figure 2.2 satisfy the four requirements discussed.

Economists originally developed indifference curves to represent an individual's tastes. Here we are using **community indifference curves** to represent the tastes of residents of a country as a group. This obviously is a much more complicated problem than dealing with the tastes of one individual. We'll use community indifference curves exactly as if they were individual indifference curves. However, we should be aware that this sidesteps some potential problems that arise from the issue of **income distribution.** For example, suppose a country has X_1 units of good X and Y_1 units of good Y. How does the country's utility compare if (1) one individual owns all the X_1 and Y_1 and all other residents have nothing or (2) the X_1 and Y_1 are divided evenly among all individuals? Without making interpersonal comparisons of utility, it's impossible to say. We cannot assume that case 2 implies higher utility just because more people gained than lost in moving there from case 1. There's no "objective" way to compare a loss of utility by one individual with a gain in utility by another. We'll ignore these issues temporarily and return to them in Chapter Four, where we discuss the effects of trade and trade restrictions on a country's distribution of income. For now we should point out that increased availability of goods always raises **potential utility;** whether actual utility increases depends on the distribution of income. Whenever a larger quantity of goods becomes available, it's possible to make every individual better off. Of course, this outcome rarely occurs automatically, so other policies designed to alter the distribution of income often accompany trade policies.

2.5.3 **Equilibrium in Autarky**

In autarky, a country makes its production and consumption decision by maximizing utility subject to the constraint imposed by the production possibilities frontier. Figure 2.3 illustrates this by combining Figure 2.1's production possibilities frontier with the indifference curves from panel (b) of Figure 2.2. Point A* puts residents on indifference curve U_1^A representing the highest level of satisfaction attainable given the country's resource endowment (L^A) and available technology (a_{LX} and a_{LY}). Point A* is the country's **autarky equilibrium.** Given that the country doesn't trade with other countries, point A* represents the allocation of resources between industries X and Y that produces the highest level of utility for domestic residents. Points

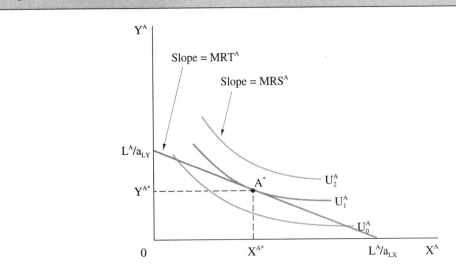

Figure 2.3 **What Would Country *A* Do in Autarky?**

Country A makes its production and consumption decision to maximize utility subject to the constraint imposed by the availability of resources and technology. This decision is represented graphically by the point of tangency between the (highest attainable) indifference curve and the production possibilities frontier at point A*. At that point—and only at that point—the rate at which it is possible to transform good X into good Y (MRT^A) equals the rate at which residents of A are willing to trade off goods X and Y in consumption (MRS^A).

along lower indifference curves (illustrated by U_0^A) are less preferred than A*. Points along higher indifference curves (such as U_2^A) are unattainable because of the resource and technology constraint.

At the autarky equilibrium, the marginal rate of transformation (the rate at which the country is *able* to transform good X into good Y along the production possibilities frontier) equals the marginal rate of substitution (the rate at which residents *willingly* give up some of one good to get more of the other good along an indifference curve). The common slope of the production possibilities frontier and the indifference curve also represents the opportunity cost of good X expressed in terms of good Y. Because all markets are perfectly competitive, the relative price of each good equals its opportunity cost. Therefore, the (absolute value of the) slope of the production possibilities frontier also can be identified with the relative price of good X in country A, or $(P_X/P_Y)^A$, denoting the rate at which units of good X and good Y exchange in the domestic market. This relative price is called the **autarky relative price** of good X in country A. In the numerical example (with $L^A =$ 100, $a_{LX} = 2$, and $a_{LY} = 5$), the relative price of good X in country A equals 2/5 units of good Y because production of an additional unit of good X requires that Y production be reduced by 2/5 units.

We can also calculate the wage rate that will prevail in country A in autarky. We'll use three pieces of information. First, labor comprises the only input, so the marginal costs of producing goods X and Y must equal $a_{LX} \cdot w^A$ and $a_{LY} \cdot w^A$, respectively, where w^A denotes the *wage* rate per unit of labor. Second, because all markets exhibit perfect competition, the price of each good must equal its marginal cost. Therefore, $P_X^A = a_{LX} \cdot w^A$ and $P_Y^A = a_{LY} \cdot w^A$. Third, the wage rate must be equal in the two industries. Otherwise, workers would all want to work in the high-wage industry and production of the other good would fall to zero. Consumers will want to consume *both* goods, so wages must be equal to induce some workers to employment in each industry. Combining these three facts, we arrive at the conclusion that all workers in autarky in country A must earn a wage equal to $w^A = P_X^A/a_{LX} = P_Y^A/a_{LY}$.

2.6 The Ricardian World with Trade

We've seen that in autarky the production opportunity set and consumption opportunity set a country faces are identical. International trade relaxes this restriction on consumption opportunities; residents can consume combinations of the two goods that couldn't possibly be produced domestically. To understand the source of this result, we need to introduce country B, a potential trading partner for country A.

Country B's autarky situation resembles country A's. The consumption possibilities of country B are limited to B's production possibilities, defined by the resource endowment (L^B) and the available technology (b_{LX} and b_{LY}). The two input coefficients again define the number of units of *labor* required to produce a unit of good X in country B (b_{LX}) and the number of units of *labor* required to produce a unit of good Y in country B (b_{LY}). Of course, there's no reason to believe that countries A and B will have identical quantities of labor available or use the same technology. If the technologies differ, the production possibilities frontiers of the two countries generally will have different slopes. In fact, these differences form the basis for mutually beneficial trade. We'll see later that if two countries' production possibilities frontiers have the same slope, trade between the two would be pointless. *(Explain why different relative labor productivity in the two industries across countries generates different slopes of the two countries' production possibilities frontiers.)*

Country B's preferences for goods X and Y can be represented by a set of indifference curves. These must satisfy the four restrictions discussed earlier (see section 2.5.2), but there's no reason to expect the preferences of country B's residents to be identical to those of country A's.

Combining the production possibilities frontier and the set of indifference curves for country B, Figure 2.4 shows B's autarky equilibrium at B*. The slope of B's production possibilities frontier gives the marginal rate of transformation between goods X and Y (MRT^B), or the opportunity cost of good X; the slope of B's indifference curve represents the marginal rate of substitution (MRS^B), or the rate at which residents of B willingly trade off consumption of the two goods. In autarky equilibrium, when country B makes its production/consumption decision to maximize utility subject to the production constraint, these two slopes are equal. The (absolute value of the) slope of country B's production possibilities frontier also gives the autarky relative price of good X in B, or $(P_X/P_Y)^B$. Workers in country B in autarky earn a wage rate of $w^B = P_X^B/b_{LX} = P_Y^B/b_{LY}$ per unit of labor, regardless of whether they work in the X or the Y industry. *(Why?)*

To demonstrate international trade's potential for improving the welfare of residents of countries A and B, it's first necessary to show that the allocation of resources implied by the two autarky equilibria, A* and B*, does *not* maximize total world output. More precisely, by moving away from A* and B*, more of one of the two

Figure 2.4 **What Would Country *B* Do in Autarky?**

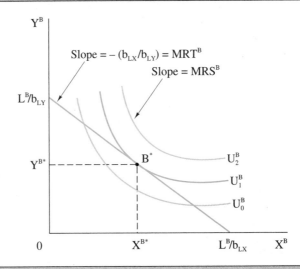

In autarky, country B produces and consumes at B*, the point of tangency between its production possibilities frontier and the (highest attainable) indifference curve, U_1^B.

goods can be produced *without* decreasing production of the other. In other words, we must show that it's possible to produce more output by having countries A and B produce combinations of X and Y different from those represented by A* and B*. Adam Smith first demonstrated this fundamental result using the concept of absolute advantage.

2.6.1 Adam Smith and Absolute Advantage

Country A has an **absolute advantage** in production of good X if $a_{LX} < b_{LX}$, that is, if it takes fewer units of labor to produce a unit of good X in country A than in B. Adam Smith asserted that international trade between two countries would be *mutually* beneficial whenever one country had an absolute advantage in production of one good and the other country had an absolute advantage in production of the other good. For example, if $a_{LX} < b_{LX}$ and $a_{LY} > b_{LY}$, country A has an absolute advantage in production of good X and country B has an absolute advantage in production of good Y; fewer units of labor are required to produce a unit of good X in country A than in B, and fewer units of labor are required to produce a unit of good Y in B than in A. According to the principle of absolute advantage, it would benefit each country to specialize in producing the good in which it has an absolute advantage and to import the good in which it has an **absolute disadvantage.**

To illustrate how specialization and trade between two countries, one of which has an absolute advantage in each of the two goods, can increase world output and utility, we summarize the countries' input coefficients in Table 2.1 in both general terms and a specific numerical example. Starting from the autarky positions, A* and B*, let country A produce one fewer unit of good Y (the good in which A has an absolute *dis*advantage); this frees up a_{LY} (or 5) units of labor. Let country B replace the lost output by producing one more unit of Y; this requires b_{LY} (or 4) units of labor. Total world production of good Y is unchanged. But a_{LY} units of labor have been freed up in A, while only b_{LY} additional units of labor are required in B. Since $a_{LY} > b_{LY}$, this implies $5 - 4 = 1$ unit of labor available for production of *additional* X or Y. The greater the extent of B's absolute advantage in production of Y, the more labor available for additional production. *(Why?)* The reader can use a similar exercise to show that switching a unit of X production from country B to country A produces a similar gain. These gains from specializing according to absolute advantage are possible because such specialization

Table 2.1 **Countries' Productive Technologies**

	General Case		Numerical Example	
	Country A	Country B	Country A	Country B
Labor units needed to produce one X	a_{LX}	b_{LX}	2	3
Labor units needed to produce one Y	a_{LY}	b_{LY}	5	4

The technologies, summarized by the input coefficients for each country, relate the number of units of labor required to produce one unit of each of the outputs.

involves producing each good in the country where it can be produced with less labor. By producing each unit of output using the minimum quantity of labor, the *world's* scarce labor ($L^W = L^A + L^B$) can produce a larger total of goods X and Y.[6]

Adam Smith's discussion represented a giant step forward in understanding the nature and potential of international trade. His main contribution was the idea that trade is *not* a zero-sum game. International trade policy between the United States and China or the European Union isn't like a giant poker game in which one party wins at the other's expense. However, according to Smith, mutually beneficial trade requires each country to have an absolute advantage in one of the goods. This requirement rules out many potential trading relationships in which one of the two countries has an absolute advantage in *both* goods (for example, if $a_{LX} = 2$, $a_{LY} = 5$, $b_{LX} = 8$, $b_{LY} = 10$). But David Ricardo soon demonstrated that even Smith's optimistic view of trade was not optimistic enough.[7]

2.6.2 David Ricardo and Comparative Advantage

Perhaps the greatest of David Ricardo's many contributions to economics was the demonstration that mutually beneficial trade is possible even if one of the potential trading partners has an absolute advantage in production of *both* goods. Failure to understand this simple but important point leads to one of the most common fallacies in modern discussions of international trade and trade policy: the claim that developing economies with low labor productivity relative to the rest of the world should isolate themselves from international trade.

Ricardo articulated the concept of **comparative advantage,** a simple extension of the concept of opportunity cost. Country A has a comparative advantage in production of good X if $(a_{LX}/a_{LY}) < (b_{LX}/b_{LY})$. This simply says that country A has a comparative advantage in production of good X if, to produce an additional unit of good X in A, it is necessary to forgo fewer units *of good Y* than would be necessary to produce the additional unit of good X in country B.[8] This is equivalent to saying that the opportunity cost of good X in country A (measured in units of good Y) is lower than in B.

Table 2.2 reports the opportunity cost of each good in each country in both general form and a numerical example. In country A, $a_{LX} = 2$ units of labor are required to produce 1 unit of good X, and $a_{LY} = 5$ units of labor are required to produce 1 unit of good Y. Therefore, production of 1 additional unit of X means forgoing 2/5 units of Y; in other words, the opportunity cost of producing good X in country A is 2/5 units of Y. Similarly, production of an additional unit of Y in country A is possible only if X production is reduced by 5/2.

---

6 With two goods, the phrase "a larger total of goods X and Y" is defined inadequately, because it's possible to produce more of one good *by producing less of the other.* We use the phrase to convey the notion that it is not possible to produce more of one good *without* reducing production of the other. Moving from a position of autarky to one of productive specialization does allow more of one good to be produced without reducing production of the other good. Once countries are completely specialized, further such gains become impossible.

7 Historians of economic thought disagree whether Adam Smith intended his discussion to also cover cases of comparative advantage. Regardless of one's view on this debate, Smith's achievement in explaining to others the potential benefits of international trade was monumental.

8 To see that (a_{LX}/a_{LY}) is measured in units of good Y per unit of good X, note that a_{LX} is measured in units of labor per unit of X (or labor/X) while a_{LY} is measured in units of labor per unit of Y (or labor/Y). Therefore, a_{LX}/a_{LY} is in units of Y per unit of X (or Y/X).

Table 2.2 **Opportunity Costs of Producing Goods X and Y**

	General Case		Numerical Example	
	Country A	Country B	Country A	Country B
Good X	a_{LX}/a_{LY}	b_{LX}/b_{LY}	(2/5)Y	(8/10)Y
Good Y	a_{LY}/a_{LX}	b_{LY}/b_{LX}	(5/2)X	(10/8)X

The opportunity cost of producing each good in each country equals the number of units of labor required to produce a unit of the good divided by the number of units of labor required to produce a unit of the other good. For example, to produce 1 additional unit of good X in country B requires b_{LX} = 8 units of labor. To obtain those 8 units of labor, Y production in B would have to be cut by 8/10 units, because each unit of Y produced uses b_{LY} = 10 units of labor. Therefore, the opportunity cost of 1 additional unit of X is 8/10 units of Y.

(Why?) In country B, b_{LX} = 8 units of labor are required to produce 1 unit of good X and b_{LY} = 10 to produce 1 unit of Y. This implies that the opportunity cost of producing X in country B is 8/10 units of Y, and the opportunity cost of producing Y in B is 10/8 units of X. In the numerical example, country A has an absolute advantage in *both* goods. *(Why?)* Nonetheless, we'll demonstrate that trade according to comparative advantage can be mutually beneficial.

Note that one country *cannot* have a comparative advantage in production of both goods. *(Why?)*[9] Note too that tastes are irrelevant in determining comparative advantage under constant costs because the slopes of the production possibilities frontiers are constants. Tastes do affect the particular point at which a country will choose to produce in autarky, but the comparison of opportunity costs in the two countries (the determinant of comparative advantage) is the same regardless of tastes.

The principle of comparative advantage states that it will be beneficial for a country to specialize in production of the good in which it has a comparative advantage and to trade for the good in which it has a comparative disadvantage. Such specialization and trade make both countries potentially better off by expanding their consumption opportunity sets. In other words, specialization and trade allow a country's *consumption* opportunity set to expand beyond its *production* opportunity set. Residents can choose to consume combinations of goods that would be impossible to produce domestically.

In autarky, the domestic production possibilities frontier defines both the production and consumption opportunity sets, and its slope defines both the opportunity costs and the relative prices for goods X and Y. We can now demonstrate that specialization and trade along the lines of comparative advantage can increase the total world quantities of the two goods available for consumption and therefore expand the consumption opportunity sets beyond the production opportunity sets.[10]

In Table 2.2, country A has a comparative advantage in good X and country B has a comparative advantage in good Y. *(Why?)* Suppose that beginning at its autarky equilibrium, A*, country A produces 1 additional unit of good X. Its production of good Y must fall by a_{LX}/a_{LY} (or 2/5 in the numerical example), the opportunity cost of good X in A. Now suppose that from its autarky equilibrium, B*, country B produces 1 fewer unit of good X. Its production of good Y rises by b_{LX}/b_{LY} (or 8/10), the opportunity cost of good X in B. Because $(a_{LX}/a_{LY}) < (b_{LX}/b_{LY})$ by the definition of comparative advantage in our example, the same fixed quantity of total labor is now producing the same quantity of good X and a *larger* quantity of good Y than were being produced in autarky. In fact, the increased production of good Y is equal to the difference in opportunity costs $[(b_{LX}/b_{LY}) - (a_{LX}/a_{LY})]$, or (8/10 − 2/5 = 4/10); therefore, the stronger the pattern of comparative advantage, the greater the gains from specialization.

---

9 By definition, country A has a comparative advantage in production of good X if $(a_{LX}/a_{LY}) < (b_{LX}/b_{LY})$ or in good Y if $(a_{LY}/a_{LX}) < (b_{LY}/b_{LX})$. These two statements can't both be true. *(Use the numerical example from Table 2.1 to see why. If one example isn't convincing, make up others by using different numerical values for the input coefficients.)*

10 The appendix to this chapter presents an alternate way to demonstrate this effect of trade, based on the world production possibilities frontier.

The same switching technique (that is, switching production of each good from its comparative-disadvantage country to its comparative-advantage country) can be repeated until each country is completely specialized in the good in which it has a comparative advantage.[11] This is true in the constant-cost model because as countries specialize according to comparative advantage, changes in production don't alter the pattern of costs or comparative advantage, represented by the constant slopes of the production possibilities frontiers.

At points A_p and B_p in Figure 2.5, the total quantity of goods X and Y produced in the world is maximized given the available resources and technology; additional units of either good can be produced *only* by decreasing production of the other.

If the countries can produce more by specializing, why did they not choose to specialize in autarky? The reason is that in autarky, residents of each country must consume goods in the same proportion in which they are produced domestically. If country A specialized completely in production of good X in autarky, its residents would be forced to consume L^A/a_{LX} units of X and none of good Y. However, consumers generally want to diversify their consumption, consuming some of many different goods. This characteristic of tastes effectively rules out production specialization without trade. With trade, a country can specialize its production and then trade some of its domestically produced good (produced at relatively low opportunity cost) for some of the goods produced in other countries (which could be produced domestically only at a relatively high opportunity cost).

2.6.3 International Equilibrium with Trade

Once both countries have opened trade and specialized production according to comparative advantage, at what relative price ratio will trade occur? How many units of its export good (X) will country A have to give up to obtain a unit of its import good (Y)? And how many units of its export good (Y) will country B have to give

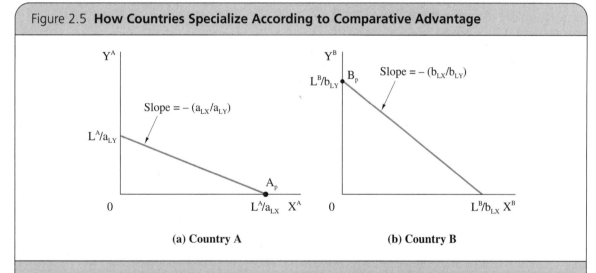

Figure 2.5 How Countries Specialize According to Comparative Advantage

(a) Country A

(b) Country B

Because the opportunity cost of producing good X is lower in country A than in country B, total output of X can be increased without reducing production of good Y by switching X production from B to A. Once A is completely specialized in producing X (at point A_p), further increases in X production require reductions in Y production. Because country B has a comparative advantage in production of good Y, total output of Y can be increased without reducing production of X when B specializes completely in Y (at point B_p).

---

11 Each country will specialize completely as long as tastes for the two goods and the countries' sizes don't differ too much. If tastes are strongly biased toward one good (say, everyone likes to consume lots of X but only a little Y), both countries may continue to produce some X, but the country with a comparative advantage in X will specialize completely. If the countries are very different in size, the small country may not be able to satisfy the large country's demand for the good in which the small country has a comparative advantage. In this case, the small country will specialize completely while the large country will produce some of both goods.

up to get a unit of its import good (X)? First, we can see that the price ratio at which trade occurs (written as $[P_X/P_Y]^{tt}$ and called the **terms of trade**) must lie between the two countries' autarky price ratios, or $(P_X/P_Y)^A < (P_X/P_Y)^{tt} < (P_X/P_Y)^B$. To see why, consider that each country now has two possible methods for turning good X into good Y or vice versa. The first is through domestic production (at a rate defined by the domestic opportunity cost, which equals the autarky price ratio). The second is through international trade (at a rate defined by the international price ratio or terms of trade). Having this choice, a country would never trade voluntarily at international terms of trade less favorable than its own autarky price ratio.

For example, from the point of productive specialization, A_p in panel (a) of Figure 2.5, country A can transform good X into good Y through domestic production at a rate of $a_{LX}/a_{LY} = (P_X/P_Y)^A$ units of Y obtained per unit of X forgone. In order for country A to choose instead to continue to specialize in production of good X and trade some of it to country B in exchange for some good Y, the trade with B must give A at least $a_{LX}/a_{LY} = (P_X/P_Y)^A$ units of Y imports for each unit of X exported. Graphically, beginning at point A_p country A will find it beneficial to trade with country B only if trade occurs at a relative price represented by the slope of a line from point A_p that is *steeper* than A's production possibilities frontier. Residents of A will purchase Y from B if they can do so at a price below the autarky price of Y, or $(P_Y/P_X)^A$. (Note that a low autarky relative price of X is equivalent to a high autarky relative price of Y.) Panel (a) of Figure 2.6 illustrates this restriction imposed by country A on the international terms of trade.

Country B faces a similar choice of technique for obtaining good X. From the point of productive specialization, B_p in panel (b) of Figure 2.5, country B can obtain good X through domestic production by forgoing good Y at a rate of $b_{LX}/b_{LY} = (P_X/P_Y)^B$ per unit of X produced. If country B can obtain X at a more favorable rate through international trade, it will choose to specialize in production of Y and trade with A to get X for consumption. Residents of B will be willing to purchase X from country A at any price below country B's autarky price, $(P_X/P_Y)^B$. Examples of international terms of trade at which B would choose to trade are illustrated in panel (b) of Figure 2.6 by lines from point B_p that are *flatter* than B's production possibilities frontier.

For trade to occur, the terms of trade must satisfy both partners. Therefore, the terms of trade must be equal to the slope of a line that is both steeper than country A's production possibilities frontier and flatter than country B's (that is, $[P_X/P_Y]^A < [P_X/P_Y]^{tt} < [P_X/P_Y]^B$).

Figure 2.6 **At What Terms Will Countries Be Willing to Trade?**

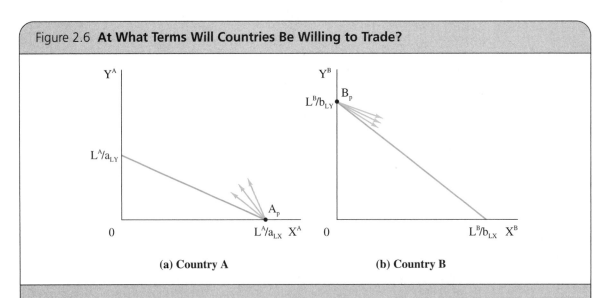

(a) Country A   (b) Country B

For country A to trade voluntarily with country B, the international terms of trade must be more favorable to A than are its own production possibilities or domestic opportunity costs. For any international terms of trade represented as a line from point A_p that is *steeper* than the production possibilities frontier, country A can obtain more units of good Y for each unit of good X forgone through international trade than through domestic production. Because B can get 1 unit of X through domestic production by forgoing b_{LX}/b_{LY} units of Y, B will trade voluntarily only if it can obtain 1 unit of X for fewer than b_{LX}/b_{LY} units of Y. Therefore, all the terms of trade at which country B would willingly trade can be represented by lines from point B_p that are *flatter* than B's production possibilities frontier.

The international terms of trade must satisfy one additional condition beyond those in Figure 2.6: The equilibrium terms of trade also must be the **market-clearing price** for the two goods. In other words, the quantity of good X that country A wants to *export* at the terms of trade must equal the quantity of good X that country B wants to *import* at the same terms of trade. Simultaneously, the quantity of good Y that country B wants to export at the terms of trade must equal the quantity of good Y that country A wants to import. To incorporate this requirement into our graphical framework, we must go beyond Figure 2.6 to see how each country decides how much of goods X and Y to consume under unrestricted trade.

Each country chooses its consumption point in such a way as to maximize utility. We saw the consumption decision under autarky in Figures 2.3 and 2.4. With trade, however, the consumption opportunity set no longer is constrained to equal the production opportunity set. Once country A specializes in producing good X and opens up trade with country B, residents of A can consume any combination of X and Y that lies on the terms-of-trade line through the production point, A_p. From panel (a) of Figure 2.6, we see that this is clearly an improvement over autarky for country A residents. As a result of specialization and trade, they are able to consume larger quantities of both X and Y than they could under autarky; the consumption opportunity set has expanded. From panel (b) of Figure 2.6, we see that residents of country B enjoy a similar expansion of their consumption opportunity set due to specialization and trade. Each country takes advantage of the new opportunities by locating at the point of tangency of the highest possible indifference curve and the terms-of-trade line.

Figures 2.7 and 2.8 show the results for the two countries. Country A *produces* at point A_p and *consumes* at point A_c. Country B *produces* at point B_p and *consumes* at point B_c. The shaded triangles in the figures, known as **trade triangles,** summarize each country's imports and exports as well as the terms of trade. For country A, the base of triangle AA_cA_p, line AA_p, represents exports of good X; the height, line AA_c, gives the imports of Y. The slope of line A_cA_p measures the equilibrium terms of trade. Triangle BB_pB_c in Figure 2.8 summarizes the analogous information for country B. *(What relationship must hold between the lengths of AA_p and BB_c? AA_c and BB_p? The slopes of A_cA_p and B_pB_c? Why?)*

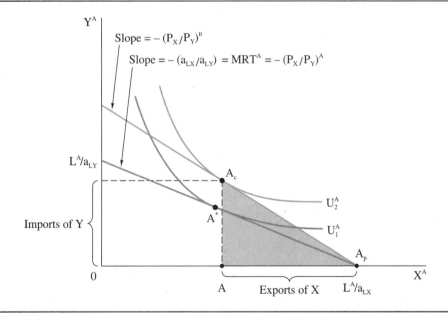

Figure 2.7 **What Would Country *A* Do Under Free Trade?**

Country A *produces* at A_p and *consumes* at A_c, the point of tangency of the indifference curve with the equilibrium terms-of-trade line. At the equilibrium terms of trade, country A's exports of good X equal country B's imports, and A's imports of good Y equal B's exports. Country A's trade triangle is AA_cA_p.

Figure 2.8 **What Would Country *B* Do Under Free Trade?**

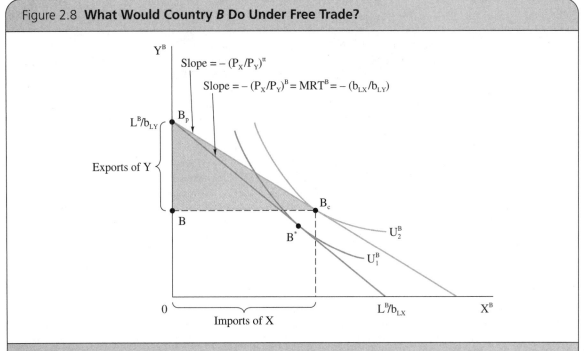

Country B produces at point B_p and consumes at point B_c, exporting good Y and importing good X. This free-trade equilibrium produces a higher level of utility (U_2^B) than was attainable under autarky (U_1^B). Country B's trade triangle is BB_pB_c.

Notice that country B partakes of the gains from trade by specializing according to comparative advantage *even though* B suffers an absolute disadvantage in both goods or, equivalently, even though country B's labor is less productive than country A's in producing both goods. Often-heard claims that countries with low labor productivity need to isolate themselves from trade with more productive economies represent a serious and fundamental fallacy based on a failure to understand comparative advantage. Unfortunately, choosing policies based on this fallacy has proven costly to many developing economies over the last half century.

We can also conclude that wages rise in both countries with the opening of trade. Simply put, this happens because trade allows each country's labor to specialize in producing the good in which it is relatively more productive. Recall that in autarky, $w^A = P_X^A/a_{LX} = P_Y^A/a_{LY}$ and $w^B = P_X^B/b_{LX} = P_Y^B/b_{LY}$, because workers in each country must produce some of both goods. With trade, country A no longer needs to produce any good Y, in which country A labor is *relatively* unproductive; country B no longer has to produce any good X, in which country B labor is relatively unproductive. Therefore, with trade, the conditions defining equilibrium wages in the two countries simplify to $w^{A*} = P_X^{tt}/a_{LX}$ and $w^{B*} = P_Y^{tt}/b_{LY}$. Figures 2.7 and 2.8 show that $P_X^{tt} > P_X^A$ and $P_Y^{tt} > P_Y^B$, as the price of each country's export good has risen with the opening of trade. Each country no longer produces its import good, so the declines in those prices ($P_Y^{tt} < P_Y^A$ and $P_X^{tt} < P_X^B$) that accompany the opening of trade exert no negative effect on wages.

Table 2.3 summarizes trade's effects on production, consumption, prices, and wages in each country. Each produces more of its comparative-advantage good and less of its comparative-disadvantage good. Consumption of both goods can rise in both countries, because productive specialization according to comparative advantage increases the total quantities that can be produced using the two countries' limited resources. In each country, the price of the export good rises, and the price of the import good falls as imports from the lower-cost country become available. Wages rise in both countries as labor shifts to the industry in which it is relatively more productive.

Table 2.3 **What Are the Effects of Trade?**

	Autarky	Free Trade	Effect of Trade
Country A:			
Production	Point A* in Figure 2.7	Point A_p in Figure 2.7	$X\Uparrow$, $Y\Downarrow$
Consumption	Point A* in Figure 2.7	Point A_c in Figure 2.7	$X\Uparrow$, $Y\Uparrow$
Prices	$(P_X/P_Y)^A = (a_{LX}/a_{LY})$	$(P_X/P_Y)^{tt} > (a_{LX}/a_{LY})$	$P_X\Uparrow$, $P_Y\Downarrow$
Wages	$w_A = P_X^A/a_{LX} = P_Y^A/a_{LY}$	$w^{A*} = P_X^{tt}/a_{LX}$	$w^A\Uparrow$
Country B:			
Production	Point B* in Figure 2.8	Point B_p in Figure 2.8	$X\Downarrow$, $Y\Uparrow$
Consumption	Point B* in Figure 2.8	Point B_c in Figure 2.8	$X\Uparrow$, $Y\Uparrow$
Prices	$(P_X/P_Y)^B = (b_{LX}/b_{LY})$	$(P_X/P_Y)^{tt} < (b_{LX}/b_{LY})$	$P_X\Downarrow$, $P_Y\Uparrow$
Wages	$w^B = P_X^B/b_{LX} = P_Y^B/b_{LY}$	$w^{B*} = P_Y^{tt}/b_{LY}$	$w^B\Uparrow$

2.6.4 Who Gains, and by How Much?

We've demonstrated that trade can be mutually beneficial as long as the countries possess a comparative advantage. This does *not* mean that the gains from trade necessarily will be shared equally by the trading partners. Specifying the precise division of the gains from trade between the two countries requires additional information. Figure 2.6 clearly shows that trade expands each country's consumption opportunity set by allowing the country to trade at terms that differ from the autarky price ratio. The implication is that a country will capture a larger share of the gains from trade when the equilibrium terms of trade differ significantly from the country's autarky price ratio (or are very close to the trading partner's autarky price ratio). The importance of this statement lies in its implications for the relationship between country size and the division of the gains from trade.

Economists define a small country as one whose participation in a market is small relative to the overall size of that market, so that the country's decisions don't affect the market price. A large country, in contrast, does affect the market price through its production and consumption decisions, because its activity constitutes a larger share of the market. In trade between a large country and a small country, the *small* country captures the gains because the international terms of trade will be the same as the large country's autarky price.

2.7 The Gains from Trade: Exchange and Specialization

Thus far, we've discussed the gains from trade rather abstractly, implying that all the gains come from specialization according to comparative advantage. In this section, we focus more explicitly on the gains from trade and distinguish two sources.

2.7.1 Gains from Exchange

One portion of the gains from trade, called the **gains from exchange,** comes from allowing unrestricted exchange of goods between countries *without* altering the autarky production patterns. In autarky, the relative prices of the two goods differ between countries, as shown in Figures 2.7 and 2.8. Because the relative price in each country equals the marginal rate of substitution there, the rates at which consumers in the two countries are willing to trade off consumption of the two goods also differ in autarky. In country B, consumers are willing to give up as many as $(P_X/P_Y)^B$ units of good Y for an additional unit of good X; in country A, consumers are willing to give up a unit of good X for as few as $(P_X/P_Y)^A$ units of good Y. By the definition of comparative advantage in our example, $(P_X/P_Y)^A < (P_X/P_Y)^B$. Therefore, an exchange of good X for good Y between countries

A and B could be mutually beneficial: Country A values the Y it can get from B more highly than the X it must give up; likewise, country B values the X it can get from A more highly than the Y it must forgo. Panel (a) of Figure 2.9 illustrates these gains from exchange for country A.

Each country continues to *produce* at its autarky point, but rather than consuming the goods produced domestically, residents of A then exchange with residents of B. Firms in country A will be willing to export good X at any relative price higher than the autarky price in A, $(P_X/P_Y)^A$; consumers in country B will be willing to import good X at any relative price lower than the autarky price in B, $(P_X/P_Y)^B$. *(Why?)* As we've seen, for both countries to trade voluntarily, the international terms of trade must fall between these limits— $(P_X/P_Y)^A < (P_X/P_Y)^{tt} < (P_X/P_Y)^B$. At any terms of trade within this range, the two countries will find exchange mutually beneficial. The precise equilibrium terms of trade at which exchange will occur also require that markets for the two goods clear. The quantity of good X that country A is willing to export in exchange for a quantity of good Y from country B must match the quantity of X that B is willing to import in exchange for its exports of Y. Through this exchange, each country attains a higher level of utility than in autarky.

In panel (a) of Figure 2.9, the move from U_0^A to U_1^A represents the gains from exchange for country A. *(Test your understanding by drawing the corresponding diagram for country B.)* These gains come from simply reallocating the same quantities of goods X and Y produced in autarky between the two countries based on their residents' tastes for each good.

2.7.2 Gains from Specialization

The gains from exchange illustrated in panel (a) of Figure 2.9 obviously don't constitute all of country A's gains from trade. The remainder come from specializing production according to comparative advantage and are called the **gains from specialization.** With open trade, countries no longer choose to produce the same combination of goods they did in autarky. Each country adjusts its production along the production possibilities frontier, producing more of the good in which it has a comparative advantage and less of the good in which it has a comparative disadvantage.

Panel (b) of Figure 2.9 reproduces country A's unrestricted-trade equilibrium from Figure 2.7, but also illustrates how the total gains from trade (the move from U_0^A to U_2^A) can be broken down into the gains from exchange (U_0^A to U_1^A) and the gains from specialization (U_1^A to U_2^A).

2.8 Using Demand and Supply to Analyze Trade

The autarky and trade results developed within the production possibilities frontier/indifference curve framework in this chapter also can be presented using demand and supply curves. The demand/supply framework is useful because it allows us to see more directly the determination of the equilibrium terms of trade; it also will prove convenient for analyzing the effects of trade restrictions in Chapters Six and Seven.

2.8.1 Demand and Supply in Autarky

In autarky, the market for each good in each country is isolated from the market for the same good in the other country; therefore, there are four markets (one for each of the two goods in each of the two countries) represented by the four panels of Figure 2.10. In each market, the interaction of domestic demand and domestic supply determines the good's autarky relative price.

A downward-sloping demand curve for each good represents the tastes of each country's residents. The quantity demanded of each good depends negatively on the good's autarky price, other things being equal.

The opportunity costs of producing the goods determine the shape of the supply curves. The opportunity cost of producing each good in each country is constant out to the maximum amount of the good the country can produce. This gives the supply curves a 90-degree angle: horizontal, then suddenly vertical. The level of output at which the supply curve of good X becomes vertical in panel (a) corresponds to the point at which country A's production possibilities frontier intersects the X axis (that is, L^A/a_{LX}); a similar relationship holds for A's production of good Y in panel (b).

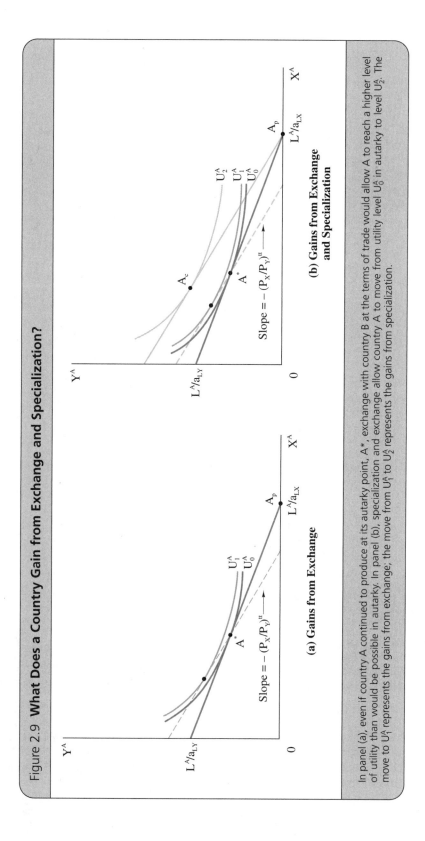

Figure 2.9 **What Does a Country Gain from Exchange and Specialization?**

(a) Gains from Exchange

(b) Gains from Exchange and Specialization

In panel (a), even if country A continued to produce at its autarky point, A*, exchange with country B at the terms of trade would allow A to reach a higher level of utility than would be possible in autarky. In panel (b), specialization and exchange allow country A to move from utility level U_0^A in autarky to level U_2^A. The move to U_1^A represents the gains from exchange; the move from U_1^A to U_2^A represents the gains from specialization.

Figure 2.10 Domestic Markets for Goods X and Y in Autarky under Constant Costs

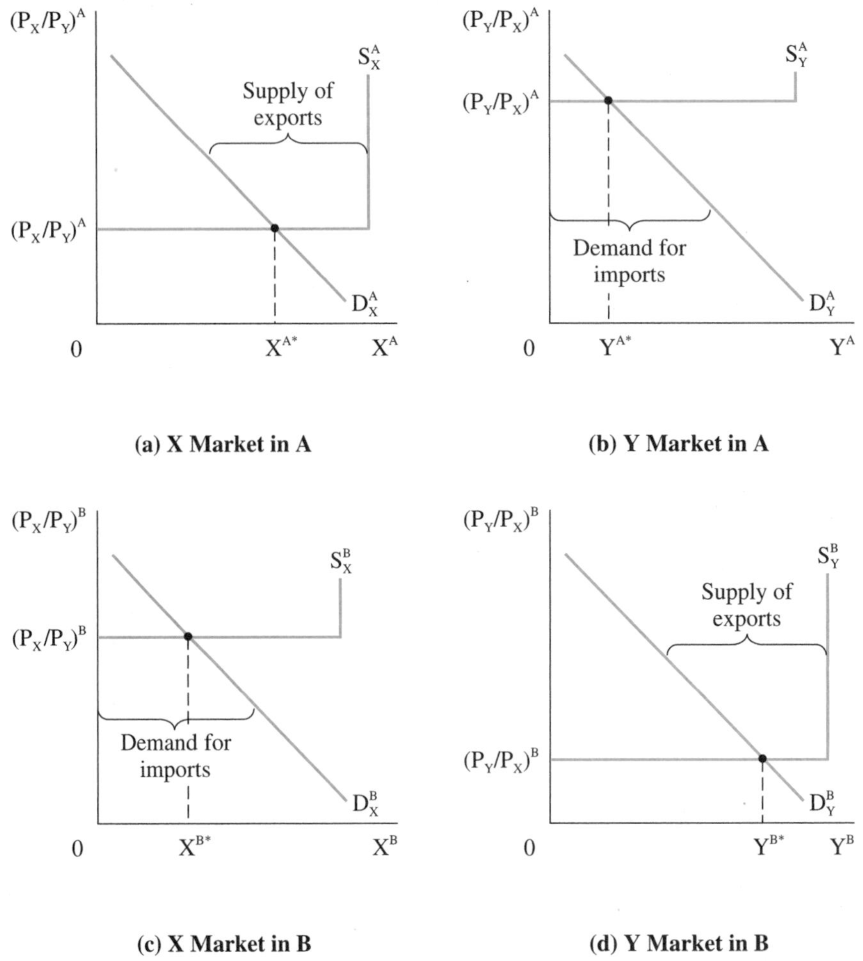

(a) X Market in A

(b) Y Market in A

(c) X Market in B

(d) Y Market in B

In autarky, goods' relative prices are determined by equality of quantity demanded domestically and quantity supplied domestically. Domestic demand for each good depends negatively on the good's relative price. A country can produce each good at a constant opportunity cost to the point where the country's entire labor endowment is employed producing the one good; at that point, it becomes impossible to produce any more of the good, so the domestic supply curve becomes vertical. At relative prices at which domestic quantity demanded exceeds quantity supplied of a good, the domestic short-age results in a demand for imports, as noted in panels (b) and (c). At relative prices at which domestic quantity supplied exceeds quantity demanded of a good, the domestic surplus results in a supply of exports, as noted in panels (a) and (d).

In competitive markets, the price of each good just equals its opportunity cost. The equilibria in the four separate markets represent the same situation as autarky points A* and B* in Figures 2.3 and 2.4. Country A, where the autarky relative price is $(P_X/P_Y)^A$, produces X^{A*} units of X and Y^{A*} units of Y. Country B, with an autarky relative price of $(P_X/P_Y)^B$, produces X^{B*} units of X and Y^{B*} units of Y.

Comparison of the two countries' markets for good X in panels (a) and (c) of Figure 2.10 reveals that country A has a comparative advantage in production of good X. Similarly, country B has a comparative advantage in production of good Y, as shown by comparing panels (b) and (d). *(Why?)*

Figure 2.11 **International Markets for Goods X and Y under Constant Costs**

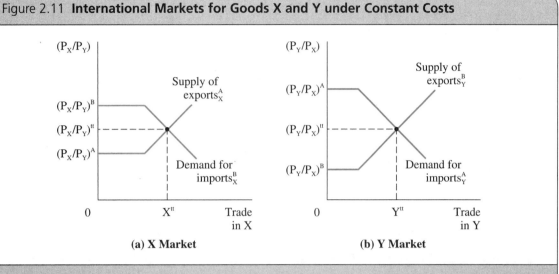

Each country is willing to import its good of comparative disadvantage at prices below its autarky price. At each price, the quantity demanded of imports equals the difference between quantity demanded and quantity produced domestically. Each country also is willing to export its good of comparative advantage at prices above its autarky price. At each price, the quantity supplied of exports equals the difference between quantity supplied and quantity demanded domestically. The equilibrium international terms of trade lie between the two countries' autarky prices. At the equilibrium terms of trade, the quantity one country wants to import matches the quantity the other country wants to export.

2.8.2 Demand and Supply with Trade

Opening trade allows countries A and B to participate in a common international market for each good. The two separate markets for good X in panels (a) and (c) of Figure 2.10 combine to become the international market for good X in panel (a) of Figure 2.11. Similarly, panels (b) and (d) from Figure 2.10 form the basis for panel (b) of Figure 2.11.

Panel (a) of Figure 2.10 demonstrates that country A is willing to export good X at any price greater than $(P_X/P_Y)^A$. The horizontal distance between the domestic demand and supply curves measures the supply of exports offered at each price. The "Supply of exports$_X^A$" line in panel (a) of Figure 2.11 depicts this supply of exports of good X by country A. Note that Figure 2.11's horizontal axis measures the quantity of good X *traded*, not the quantity produced or consumed as in earlier diagrams. Panel (c) of Figure 2.10 shows that country B's residents demand to import good X from A at any price below $(P_X/P_Y)^B$ in quantities given by the horizontal distance between the domestic demand and supply curves. This demand for imports of good X by country B becomes the "Demand for imports$_X^B$" line in panel (a) of Figure 2.11.

Combining the export-supply and import-demand curves yields the unrestricted trade equilibrium in the international market for good X. The international market is in equilibrium when the quantity of the good that one country (A in the case of good X) wants to export at the international terms of trade equals the quantity that the other country (here, B) wants to import on those same terms. The equilibrium price of good X is $(P_X/P_Y)^{tt}$, and country A exports X^{tt} to country B. *(We argued in the production possibilities frontier/indifference curve framework that the international terms of trade would lie between the two countries' autarky price ratios. How does the demand and supply framework in Figure 2.11 reflect this restriction?)*

The same procedure is used to derive the international market for good Y (panel (b) of Figure 2.11) from panels (b) and (d) of Figure 2.10. The demand for imports of good Y by country A comes from panel (b) of Figure 2.10, and the supply of exports of good Y by country B comes from panel (d). *(What determines the vertical intercepts of "Demand for imports$_Y^A$" and "Supply of exports$_Y^B$"?)* The international equilibrium price of good Y is $(P_Y/P_X)^{tt}$, and country B exports Y^{tt} to country A. These results correspond to the information summarized in the trade triangles in Figures 2.7 and 2.8.

In the remainder of the book, we'll use both the demand/supply and production possibilities/indifference curve frameworks. Although the two methods of analysis convey the same basic information, each is more convenient for answering certain questions. As each issue arises, we'll address it with the more appropriate method. Translating back and forth between the two methods also provides practice in working with the basic ideas of international trade theory.[12]

This completes our development of the basic Ricardian model and the demonstration of the gains from productive specialization and trade. We now turn to two cases that report the results of several attempts to test empirically the major implications of the Ricardian theory of trade. Can differences in technology or labor productivity among countries actually explain trade patterns observed in the world economy? Cases One and Two suggest that the answer is yes: Countries *do* tend to export goods in which their labor is relatively productive and to import those in which their labor is relatively unproductive. Case Three examines what happens when civil war shuts down trade between regions of a single country.

U.S./U.K.

CASE ONE:
Can the Ricardian Model *Really* Explain Trade?

The first and best-known effort to test empirically the major implication of the Ricardian model was made by G. D. A. MacDougall in 1951.[13] MacDougall used 1937 data on U.S. and U.K. exports in 25 industries. Recall that the Ricardian model implies that each country tends to export those goods in which it has a comparative advantage. Its comparative advantage lies in those goods in which its labor is highly productive compared to the trading partner's labor.[14] MacDougall combined these two aspects of the Ricardian model to formulate the following testable proposition: Other things being equal, the higher the output per worker in the United States relative to the United Kingdom in a given industry, the higher the exports by the United States relative to those by the United Kingdom in that industry. Figure 2.12 reports this relationship, and its data clearly support the major implication of the Ricardian model: High relative labor productivity in a given industry accompanies a high market share. Later studies confirmed MacDougall's findings using data for different time periods.

Notice how Figure 2.12 confirms the importance of *comparative* as opposed to absolute advantage. U.S. labor productivity exceeded that of the United Kingdom in all 25 industries MacDougall examined. On average, U.S. productivity was approximately twice U.K. productivity, as illustrated by the pale horizontal line in Figure 2.12. If absolute

advantage determined trade patterns, the United Kingdom would not have exported in any of the industries. But because comparative advantage determines trade patterns, the United Kingdom did export—in those industries in which U.K. labor productivity was closer to that of the United States (for example, woolens, beer, and clothing). The United States exported more in those industries where U.S. labor productivity most significantly exceeded that of the United Kingdom (for example, pig iron and tin cans).

Simply reporting MacDougall's results, however, doesn't do justice to the power of the findings or to the Ricardian model. Ricardo originally intended the model as a simple framework for highlighting the principle of comparative advantage rather than as a full explanation for observed trade patterns in the world economy. Both the theoretical model and the empirical tests ignore many relevant issues, such as the presence of nonlabor inputs, tariffs, transportation costs, economies of scale, and product differentiation, each of which will be a focus in later chapters. The theoretical version of the model implies that relative labor productivity (represented by the pattern of input coefficients) determines opportunity costs, which in turn determine autarky price ratios, which in turn determine trade patterns. However, autarky prices typically are unobservable because trade is occurring; thus, empirical tests must seek a direct

---

12 Appendix B to Chapter Three covers a third graphical technique, called the *offer curve* or *reciprocal demand curve*. We can obtain all the information conveyed by offer-curve analysis using either the production possibilities frontier/indifference curve or the demand/supply technique.

13 G. D. A. MacDougall, "British and American Exports: A Study Suggested by the Theory of Comparative Costs," *Economic Journal* 61 (December 1951), pp. 697–724.

14 Highly productive labor in an industry is equivalent to a low input coefficient. The input coefficient (for example, a_{LX}) measures how many units of labor are needed to produce 1 unit of output, while labor productivity (or, $1/a_{LX}$) asks how many units of output 1 unit of labor can produce.

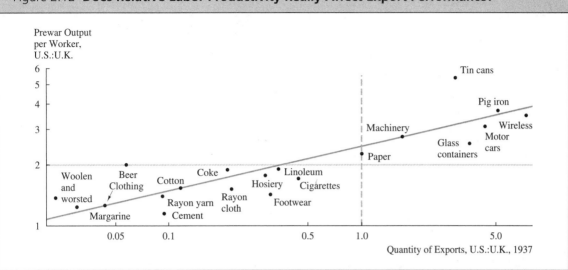

Figure 2.12 Does Relative Labor Productivity Really Affect Export Performance?

The empirical results clearly support the Ricardian hypothesis: A country tends to export goods in which its labor is relatively productive.

Source: G. D. A. MacDougall, "British and American Exports: A Study Suggested by the Theory of Comparative Costs," *Economic Journal* 61 (December 1951), pp. 697–724.

relationship between labor productivity and trade patterns, bypassing the unobservable autarky prices.[15] That this problem in implementing the model empirically cannot disguise the comparative advantage/export relationship is a tribute to the power of Ricardo's insight.

In the two centuries since Ricardo wrote, economists have come to appreciate many explanations for existing trade patterns. However, in recent years, Ricardo's insights, particularly the importance of cross-country differences in technology and labor productivity, once again have come to the forefront. Two major issues in the world economy in the late twentieth century—the need to integrate developing countries and the formerly centrally planned countries into the world economy—help explain this new appreciation of Ricardo's insights. When a country isolates its economy from the rest of the world—as many developing and centrally planned nations did for decades—and then reemerges and tries to integrate itself into the world economy, the years of isolation leave a legacy of backward technology and low labor productivity. Policy makers must evaluate the implications of this legacy and design policies for confronting it. Two centuries after his original contribution, David Ricardo continues to lend a powerful helping hand in this task.

U.S./Germany/Japan

CASE TWO:
Does Labor Productivity *Really* Vary?

We'll see in Chapters Three and Five that differences in relative labor productivity form only one of several possible bases of comparative advantage and that, in turn, comparative advantage is only one of several possible foundations for mutually beneficial international trade. Nonetheless, we can explore at this point whether significant cross-country

15 Occasionally, rare historical circumstances do reveal autarky prices—for example, the case of the opening of Japan to trade during the nineteenth century.

Table 2.4 **Value-Added per Hour Worked in Manufacturing, 1950–1990 (U.S. = 100)**

	1950	1965	1973	1979	1990
Germany/United States: $(1/g_{LX})/(1/a_{LX}) = (a_{LX}/g_{LX})$					
Food, beverages, tobacco	53.1	76.9	68.4	74.1	75.8
Textiles, apparel, leather	44.0	78.1	81.0	85.9	88.2
Chemicals, allied products	32.4	64.3	90.5	106.0	76.7
Basic, fabricated metals	30.9	53.6	67.2	90.1	98.8
Machinery, equipment	43.7	77.1	90.0	110.7	87.6
Other manufacturing	34.2	56.6	68.8	80.1	79.3
Japan/United States: $(1/j_{LX})/(1/a_{LX}) = (a_{LX}/j_{LX})$					
Food, beverages, tobacco	26.7	25.8	39.5	39.8	37.0
Textiles, apparel, leather	24.7	37.5	53.2	54.9	48.0
Chemicals, allied products	13.0	32.1	60.4	78.0	83.8
Basic, fabricated metals	12.5	23.1	61.4	84.3	95.6
Machinery, equipment	8.0	23.5	50.6	79.6	114.4
Other manufacturing	9.7	20.0	34.0	39.8	54.9

Source: Bart Van Ark and Dirk Pilat, "Productivity Levels in Germany, Japan, and the United States: Differences and Causes," *Brookings Papers on Economic Activity: Microeconomics* 2 (1993), p. 17.

differences in relative labor productivity exist. Table 2.4 reports recent estimates of value-added per hour worked for several major manufacturing sectors in Germany and Japan relative to the United States. Value-added is a measure of output, so value-added per hour worked corresponds to the inverse of our input coefficients; a_{LX} reports the number of units of labor required to produce 1 unit of X, so its inverse, $1/a_{LX}$, measures output per unit of labor.

The top half of Table 2.4 compares labor productivity in Germany and the United States in each of six manufacturing sectors. Each number in the table reports value-added per hour of labor in Germany ($1/g_{LX}$ in terms of our input coefficients) divided by value-added per hour worked in the United States ($1/a_{LX}$), or (a_{LX}/g_{LX}). To determine the countries' comparative advantages across two sectors, X and Y, we need to compare (a_{LX}/a_{LY}) and (g_{LX}/g_{LY}). When the former exceeds the latter, Germany has a comparative advantage in good X and the United States in good Y; when the latter exceeds the former, the United States has a comparative advantage in good X and Germany in good Y. The condition (a_{LX}/a_{LY}) > (g_{LX}/g_{LY}) is algebraically equivalent to (a_{LX}/g_{LX}) > (a_{LY}/g_{LY}).[16] So, within each column in the top half of Table 2.4, industries with the highest numbers (that is, sectors with the highest values of [a_{LX}/g_{LX}]) correspond to industries of German comparative advantage relative to the United

States, and industries with the lowest numbers (that is, sectors with the lowest values of [a_{LX}/g_{LX}]) correspond to industries of U.S. comparative advantage relative to Germany.

The data suggest that German labor productivity overall has improved relative to that of the United States, but still lags behind. After solid gains during most of the postwar period, German productivity lost ground relative to that of the United States in several sectors between 1979 and 1990. Note also that the pattern of comparative advantage has shifted. During the early postwar years, German comparative advantage relative to the United States was in food, beverages, and tobacco, along with textiles, apparel, and leather, while the United States exhibited an advantage in chemicals and metals. By 1990, metals showed the strongest German comparative advantage. *(Based on the data in the table, what patterns of imports and exports would you expect between Germany and the United States based on comparative advantage? If trade were based on absolute advantage, what would you predict about U.S.-German trade based on the table? Which fits better with what you know about trade?)*

The bottom half of Table 2.4 performs the same exercise for Japan and the United States. Japan's productivity catch-up during the postwar years is even more impressive than Germany's. In 1950, Japan showed a comparative advantage

---

16 To obtain the second inequality from the first, multiply through by (a_{LY}/g_{LX}).

relative to the United States in food and textiles, and a comparative disadvantage in machinery and other manufacturing. By 1990, Japanese comparative advantage had shifted to metals and to machinery, where Japanese productivity surpassed that of the United States. *(Based on the data in the table,* *what patterns of imports and exports would you expect between Japan and the United States based on comparative advantage? If trade were based on absolute advantage, what would you predict about U.S.-Japan trade based on the table? Which fits better with what you know about trade?)*

Sudan

CASE THREE:
Turning Back Trade Turns Back the Clock

A visitor to the mountains of central Sudan might assume that water has always been gathered by hand from puddles that form when women scoop sand from a riverbed. And perhaps grain has always been milled by hand here, and sesame pressed by hand into oil. But the visitor would be wrong. Twenty years ago, water came from a well equipped with a pump, a motor drove the oil press, and diesel fueled the grinding mill.[17]

What happened? Residents of the area sided with rebels in the country's 19-year-old civil war, prompting the government to blockade trade between the central mountains and the rest of the country. Goods such as salt, sugar, and clothing, produced in or imported into the government-controlled north, rarely reach the south. Metals, machines, and fuel are also rare. A bit of food aid trickles in from international aid agencies. But the civil war has pushed the area back to autarky. Not only has *international* trade been shut down, but the government-enforced embargo has slammed the door on trade even with the rest of Sudan. Since November 1997, U.S. law has prohibited trade, either direct or through third countries, with Sudan, except for U.S. sales of agricultural products, medicines, and medical equipment.[18] The United Nations also forbids trade with Sudan, as punishment for the Islamic regime's alleged involvement in an attempted assassination of Egypt's president. Given the country's isolation, not a lot of current information is available about the details of the economy. The World Bank estimated 2000 per capita income at $320 per year.

Summary

Early trade policies reflected the doctrine of mercantilism, which set a goal of accumulation of gold and silver. At least in the short run, encouraging exports and restricting imports facilitated such accumulation. Mercantilists viewed trade as a zero-sum game that distributed the available gold among countries; whatever one country gained came at the expense of another.

Adam Smith and David Ricardo challenged the zero-sum view of trade. Following the insights of Smith and Ricardo, this chapter demonstrated how the possibility of trading internationally allows a country to separate its production decision from its consumption decision. Gains from trade arise when a country specializes its production according to comparative advantage—based on differences in technology or labor productivity—and then trades with other countries to obtain its preferred set of goods for consumption. The gains in efficiency allow trade to be *mutually* beneficial.

Looking Ahead

The complete specialization of production predicted by the Ricardian model almost never occurs. The two-country, two-good model drastically simplifies the many-country, many-good world economy. In a more realistic setting, most countries produce more than one good, and most goods are produced in more than one country.

---

17 *The Economist,* March 24, 2001, p. 55.

18 For up-to-date information on Sudan and other countries subject to U.S. trade sanctions, go to the Web site of the U.S. Treasury Department's Office of Foreign Assets Control at www.treas.gov/ofac.

There are at least three reasons. First, even in a two-country, two-good world, complete specialization would occur only if there were no restrictions on trade, no transportation costs, and no product differentiation, and if each country were large enough to satisfy world demand for its good of comparative advantage. Second, there are many more goods to be produced than there are countries in the world economy. If all the goods that consumers want are to be produced, most countries must produce multiple goods. This chapter's model can easily be expanded to include many goods. We would simply rank goods according to the extent of a country's comparative advantage, and the country would produce goods high on the list and import goods low on the list. Third, and probably most important, the complete-specialization result follows directly from the assumption of constant costs; we've assumed that comparative advantage never shifts from one country to another— regardless of the degree of productive specialization. Economists believe that constant opportunity cost is the exception rather than the rule. For most production technologies, we expect the opportunity cost of producing a good to rise with the level of production. In Chapter Three, we expand our model of trade to include increasing costs. We'll also see a second major source of comparative advantage: variations in countries' factor endowments. In the process, we'll discover why trade policy has proven so enduringly controversial.

Key Terms

mercantilism	indifference curve
zero-sum game	marginal rate of substitution (MRS)
specie-flow mechanism	community indifference curves
perfect competition	income distribution
marginal cost	potential utility
autarky	autarky equilibrium
production possibilities frontier	autarky relative price
input coefficient	absolute advantage
opportunity cost	absolute disadvantage
marginal rate of transformation (MRT)	comparative advantage
Ricardian model	terms of trade
constant-cost model	market-clearing price
production opportunity set	trade triangles
consumption opportunity set	gains from exchange
utility	gains from specialization

Problems and Questions for Review

1. Let country A's endowment of labor equal 200 and country B's endowment of labor equal 200. The number of units of labor required to produce 1 unit of good X in country A equals 5, and the number of units of labor required to produce 1 unit of good Y in country A equals 4. The number of units of labor required to produce 1 unit of good X in B equals 4, and the number of units of labor required to produce 1 unit of good Y in B equals 8.
   a. Draw the production possibilities frontier for each country. Be sure to label carefully.
   b. Which country has an absolute advantage in which good(s)? Why? What would a theory of absolute advantage imply about the direction of trade? Why?
   c. If free trade according to absolute advantage were allowed, what degree of productive specialization would occur? Why? How much of each good would be produced?
   d. Answer the questions in parts (b) and (c) for the principle of comparative advantage rather than absolute advantage.
   e. How do your answers in (b) and (c) differ from those in (d)? Why?
2. Consider a world consisting of two countries, Continentia and Islandia. Each country has 500 units of labor, the only input. In Continentia, it takes 5 units of labor to produce a computer and 10 units of labor to produce a unit of textiles. In Islandia, it takes 10 units of labor to produce a computer and 5 units of labor to produce a unit of textiles.

a.   Sketch each country's production possibilities frontier. Label the vertical and horizontal intercepts and the slopes.

b.   What is the opportunity cost of producing a computer in Continentia? Why? What is the opportunity cost of producing a unit of textiles in Continentia? Why? What is the opportunity cost of producing a computer in Islandia? Why? What is the opportunity cost of producing a unit of textiles in Islandia? Why?

c.   In autarky, what would be the relative price of computers in Continentia? In Islandia? Why?

d.   Which country has a comparative advantage in producing which good? Why?

e.   If Continentia and Islandia specialize according to comparative advantage, how many computers and how many units of textiles will Continentia produce? Islandia? Why?

f.   After several years of trade, Continentia and Islandia pass new laws stating that half of each country's labor force must be used in each industry. In other words, half of Continentia's labor must produce computers and half must produce textiles. The same is true in Islandia. Under the new laws, how many computers and how many units of textiles will Continentia produce? Islandia? Why?

g.   How big is the economic cost of the laws that restrict specialization and trade between Continentia and Islandia?

3.   Dismalia is a country with an unproductive labor force. It requires more units of labor to produce a unit of any good in Dismalia than in other countries. Dismalia's leaders have decided that the country cannot gain from international trade because the country's labor is so unproductive. Are they correct or incorrect? Explain.

4.   Assume that $L^A = 1,000$; $a_{LX} = 10$; $a_{LY} = 20$; $L^B = 1,000$; $b_{LX} = 20$; and $b_{LY} = 10$.

a.   Sketch and label each country's production possibilities frontier.

b.   Which country has a comparative advantage in which good, and why? Would trade between country A and country B be mutually beneficial? Why or why not?

c.   Now suppose that researchers in country A discover a way to produce both good X and good Y using only half as much labor as before, so now $a_{LX} = 5$ and $a_{LY} = 10$. Sketch and label the new production possibilities frontier. Which country has a comparative advantage in which good, and why? Would trade between country A and country B be mutually beneficial? Why or why not?

5.   Assume that initially $L^A = 1,000$; $a_{LX} = 10$; $a_{LY} = 20$; $L^B = 1,000$; $b_{LX} = 20$; and $b_{LY} = 10$ as in question 4.

a.   Suppose that researchers in country A discover a way to produce good X using only half as much labor as before, so now $a_{LX} = 5$ and $a_{LY} = 20$. Sketch and label the new production possibilities frontier. Which country has a comparative advantage in which good, and why? Would trade between country A and country B be mutually beneficial? Why or why not? Compare your answer with that in question 4, part (c).

b.   Now suppose, instead, that researchers in country A discover a way to produce good Y using only one-quarter as much labor as before, so now $a_{LX} = 10$ and $a_{LY} = 5$. Sketch and label the new production possibilities frontier. Which country has a comparative advantage in which good, and why? Would trade between country A and country B be mutually beneficial? Why or why not? Compare your answer with those in question 4, part (c) and in part (a) of this question.

6.   Suppose labor can't move between industries in either country in the short run. Therefore, each country must continue to produce at its autarky production point. Might it still be worthwhile to allow international trade? Why? How is your answer related to the gains from exchange and the gains from specialization?

7.   Country A can produce 1,000 bushels of corn if it uses all its resources in the corn industry, or 2,000 bushels of wheat if it uses all its resources in the wheat industry; costs are constant. Currently, country A doesn't trade and consumes 500 bushels of corn and 1,000 bushels of wheat.

a.   Draw country A's production possibilities frontier, placing corn on the horizontal axis and wheat on the vertical axis.

b.   Illustrate country A's autarky equilibrium.

c.   A trading partner offers to trade corn and wheat with country A at a price ratio of 1. Show that, even if country A continues to *produce* 500 bushels of corn and 1,000 bushels of wheat, residents of country A would be better off if they exchanged with the trading partner. Would country A export wheat or corn? Would country A import wheat or corn?

   d.   Compared with part (b), how would the amount of trade change if country A specialized its production according to comparative advantage? Would country A specialize in wheat or corn? Would the country specialize partially or completely?
8.   Comment on the following statement. "The Ricardian model of trade assumes each country's fixed endowment of labor is fully employed both in autarky and under unrestricted trade. The model also assumes that technology (labor productivity) does not change. Therefore, the world economy cannot produce more output with trade than in autarky."

References and Selected Readings

Dornbusch, Rudiger, Stanley Fischer, and Paul Samuelson. "Comparative Advantage, Trade, and Payments in a Ricardian Model with a Continuum of Goods." *American Economic Review* 67 (December 1977): 823–839.
A modern version of the Ricardian model, with many goods. For intermediate and advanced students.

Ekelund, Robert B., Jr., and Robert D. Tollison. *Mercantilism as a Rent-Seeking Society: Economic Regulation in Historical Perspective.* College Station, Tex.: Texas A&M Press, 1981.
A modern reinterpretation of mercantilism emphasizing rent seeking. For all students.

Grossman, Gene M., and Elhanan Helpman. "Technology and Trade." In *Handbook of International Economics,* Vol. 3, edited by G. M. Grossman and K. Rogoff, 1279–1337. Amsterdam: North-Holland, 1995.
Advanced survey of the role of technology in international trade theories, including the Ricardian model.

Heckscher, Eli F. *Mercantilism.* London: Allen and Unwin, 1934.
Along with Viner (see below), one of the two classic treatises on mercantilism. For all students.

Hume, David. "Of the Balance of Trade." In *Essays, Moral, Political, and Literary.* London, 1752.
Hume's classic critique of mercantilism.

Irwin, Douglas A. *Against the Tide.* Princeton: Princeton University Press, 1996.
The history of economic thought on the free-trade versus protection issue. For all students.

Krugman, Paul. "What Do Undergrads Need to Know about Trade?" *American Economic Review Papers and Proceedings* 83 (May 1993): 23–26.
An entertaining tour of the many fallacies in supposedly enlightened discussions of international trade policy. Essential reading for all students.

Leamer, Edward E., and John Levinsohn. "International Trade Theory: The Evidence." In *Handbook of International Economics,* Vol. 3, edited by G. M. Grossman and K. Rogoff, 1339–1394. Amsterdam: North-Holland, 1995.
Advanced survey of empirical evidence on international trade theories.

Ricardo, David. *The Principles of Political Economy and Taxation.* Baltimore: Penguin, 1971 (Originally published 1817).
Chapter 7 contains the original, classic version of comparative advantage. For all students.

Smith, Adam. *An Inquiry into the Nature and Causes of the Wealth of Nations.* New York: Random House, 1937 (Originally published 1776).
The book often credited with founding economics as a discipline. The whole book is accessible to students at all levels; Books I and IV contain the specialization argument.

Sykes, Alan O. "Comparative Advantage and the Normative Economics of International Trade Policy." *Journal of International Economic Law* 1 (March 1998): 49–82.
Readable overview of the economist's insights into international trade and trade policy.

Viner, Jacob. *Studies in the Theory of International Trade.* Clifton, N.J.: Kelley, 1965 (Originally published 1937).
Along with Heckscher, one of the two classic treatises on mercantilism. For all students.

CHAPTER TWO APPENDIX

What Can the World Produce?
The World Production Possibilities Frontier

We can see the gains from trade by constructing a world production possibilities frontier illustrating all the combinations of goods X and Y that can be produced using the world's labor according to the pattern of comparative advantage. The technique for constructing the frontier is similar to that used in section 2.5.1. If all the *world's* labor ($L^W = L^A + L^B$) were devoted to producing good X, $[(L^A/a_{LX}) + (L^B/b_{LX})]$ units could be produced; this marks the intersection of the world production possibilities frontier and the horizontal axis at point 1 in Figure 2A.1. Similarly, devoting all labor to producing good Y would permit $[(L^A/a_{LY}) + (L^B/b_{LY})]$ units to be pro-

duced, representing the intersection of the world production possibilities frontier with the vertical axis at point 3 in the figure.

Even though costs of production are constant within each country, giving each *country's* production possibilities frontier its straight-line shape, the *world* production possibilities frontier is *not* a straight line. This is true because the opportunity cost of each good differs between the two countries. We assume for the remainder of this appendix that country A has a comparative advantage in good X, and country B has one in good Y. Any X produced should be produced first in country A, and any Y produced should come first

(continued)

Figure 2A.1 **What Can the World Produce?**

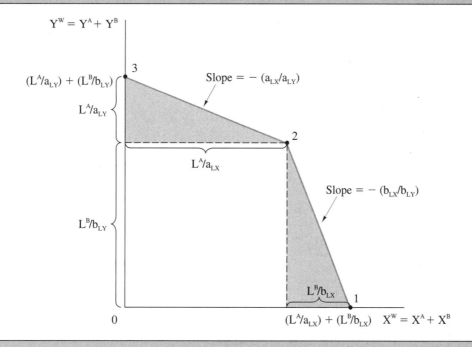

The world production possibilities frontier illustrates the combinations of goods X and Y that can be produced if countries specialize according to comparative advantage. The slopes of the two segments of the world production possibilities frontier represent opportunity costs in the two countries. Moving from point 1 toward point 3, good Y is produced first by country B (from 1 to 2) and then by country A (from 2 to 3). Moving from point 3 toward point 1, good X is produced first by country A (at opportunity cost a_{LX}/a_{LY}) and then by country B (at opportunity cost b_{LX}/b_{LY}).

from country B. *(Why?)* In Figure 2A.1, moving upward and to the left from point 1, where only good X is produced, country B begins to produce good Y; the opportunity cost is b_{IY}/b_{LX}. At point 2, country B can produce no more good Y *(why?)*, so if we continue to move further upward and to the left, the additional good Y must be produced in country A, where the opportunity cost is $(a_{IY}/a_{LX}) > (b_{IY}/b_{LX})$. Similarly, moving downward to the right from point 3, where only good Y is being produced, country A begins to produce good X at an opportunity cost of a_{LX}/a_{IY} per unit. At point 2, country A is completely specialized and can produce no more X. Therefore, any additional X must be produced in country B at an opportunity cost of (b_{LX}/b_{IY}). Note that the two shaded triangles in the figure correspond to the production possibilities frontiers of the two countries, A on the upper left and B on the lower right. *(Suppose the two countries specialize according to their comparative disadvantage rather than their comparative advantage. Construct the world production possibilities frontier under this assumption. How does it compare with the frontier in Figure 2A.1? Why?)*

CHAPTER THREE

Comparative Advantage II: Factor Endowments and the Neoclassical Model

3.1 Introduction

Chapter Two's Ricardian model of production, consumption, and trade is very useful in showing how and why international trade based on cross-country differences in technology or labor productivity can be mutually beneficial. Case One in that chapter showed that repeated empirical tests have supported the major implication of the Ricardian model—the positive relationship between countries' relative labor productivities and relative market shares in various industries. However, another implication of the constant-cost model—complete productive specialization—fails to match what we typically observe in the world economy.[1]

Detailed studies of many industries indicate that the opportunity costs of production increase with output rather than remain constant for most goods. This phenomenon of increasing costs forms the focus of this chapter. We'll see that incorporating increasing costs into the basic trade model can explain the observed partial rather than complete specialization. In addition, the possibility of increasing costs will allow us to explore sources of comparative advantage beyond the differences in relative labor productivity emphasized by Ricardo. Comparative advantage merely reflects differences in opportunity costs between two countries. But why should opportunity costs differ? Within the context of the Ricardian model, the only possible explanation is differences in the productive technologies, captured by the input coefficients that reflect labor productivity. If relative labor productivity were the same in the two countries, the opportunity costs and autarky relative prices would also be the same, and there would be no potential gains from trade. Thus, although the Ricardian model powerfully demonstrates the gains from trade, we want to look for possible additional explanations of *why* opportunity costs differ.

The increasing-cost model also has a second advantage: its ability to explain why international trade policy is so persistently controversial. Strong feelings on both sides of the issue always accompany trade-policy decisions; in each country, some groups advocate unrestricted trade, while others support a variety of restrictions.

3.2 The Neoclassical World without Trade

In this chapter, we continue to use the simplifying assumptions introduced in Chapter Two (see section 2.4). Again our goal is to compare the availability of goods in autarky with that under unrestricted trade. In autarky, each country must make a decision concerning the allocation of its available resources between production of two goods. This decision decides not only the country's production but also its consumption.

---

1 As mentioned in Chapter Two, differences in country size can result in partial specialization by one of the two countries (the large one) even with constant costs. We'll see later that two other circumstances can produce complete specialization in the increasing-cost model: highly dissimilar factor endowments across countries and highly similar factor intensities across industries.

3.2.1 **Production in Autarky**

To incorporate the idea of increasing costs, we need a new element in the model, that is, a second factor of production. Chapter Two's constant-cost model contained only one factor of production, which we called labor; and each unit of labor was a perfect substitute for any other unit of labor. Here, in the **Neoclassical** or **increasing-cost model,** there are two factors of production—we'll call them labor (L) and capital (K)—and they aren't equally effective in producing the two outputs, X and Y. The word *capital,* when used in trade theory, refers to durable inputs such as machines, buildings, iron mines, and tools.

How can we represent the production technology when there are two inputs? A few products may require the two inputs in **fixed proportions.** In such cases, the technology resembles a recipe that calls for ingredients in certain predetermined proportions. A cake recipe that specifies two cups of flour and one cup of milk won't produce a cake if you reverse the proportions of flour and milk. However, most production processes offer a fairly wide range of opportunities for substituting one input for another. For example, automobiles can be built using a large amount of capital equipment, such as mechanized assembly lines and robots, and very little labor. Automobiles also can be built almost entirely by hand, using a large quantity of labor and very little capital in the form of simple tools. The textile industry provides another example. Japan produces textiles using sophisticated, computerized equipment and relatively little labor. At the same time, many developing countries continue to use large quantities of labor along with simple hand looms to make textiles. Economists capture these possibilities for substitution with tools called production functions and isoquants.

Production Functions and Isoquants

For each industry, the recipe specifying the maximum output firms can produce with given quantities of inputs is called the **production function.** We denote the production functions for the X and Y industries in country A by $X^A = f_X^A(L_X^A, K_X^A)$ and $Y^A = f_Y^A(L_Y^A, K_Y^A)$. Plugging the quantities of resources used in each industry into the right-hand side of the production functions, we can determine the output of each industry. For example, if f_X^A is defined as $X^A = 2L_X^A K_X^A$, employment of 3 units of labor and 2 units of capital will produce $X^A = 2 \cdot 3 \cdot 2 = 12$ units of output. Producers can generate a given quantity of output using a variety of combinations of labor and capital, because the two inputs are substitutes for each other. The 12 units of good X produced using 3 units of labor and 2 of capital could also be produced using, for example, 6 units of labor and 1 of capital (because $X^A = 2 \cdot 6 \cdot 1 = 12$) or 2 units of labor and 3 of capital (because $X^A = 2 \cdot 2 \cdot 3 = 12$). The graphical technique for representing these substitution possibilities is called an **isoquant** (or *same-quantity*) map. Each isoquant shows all the different combinations of labor and capital with which it's possible to produce a given amount of output. Figure 3.1 presents an isoquant map for production of good X in country A.

Each isoquant is downward sloping and convex, and higher isoquants correspond to higher levels of output. Isoquants are downward sloping because using less of one input implies that the firm must use more of the other input to maintain the same level of output (that is, to stay on the same isoquant). In other words, the negative slope of an isoquant represents the fact that the two inputs are substitutes—using less of one requires using more of the other. The slope of an isoquant represents the rate at which producers can substitute one input for the other; this rate is called the **marginal rate of technical substitution (MRTS).** The convexity of the isoquant implies that this rate changes along the curve. As more labor and less capital are used (moving down and to the right along an isoquant), it becomes more difficult to substitute additional labor for capital. The amount of additional labor required to compensate for a given reduction in capital increases.

Given all the possible combinations of labor and capital for producing a given level of good X in country A, we must specify how X-producing firms choose a particular production process. Firms' profits equal total revenue minus total cost, so a firm wants to produce its output at minimum cost. Assuming there are only two inputs, an X-producing firm's total costs equal the *w*age rate paid to labor in A (w^A) times the quantity of labor employed (L_X^A) plus the rental rate for capital (r^A) times the quantity of capital employed (K_X^A). The wage rate and the rental rate for capital are called **factor prices** or **factor rewards.**[2] Total costs can be represented as

---

2 Inputs referred to as "capital" are durable in the sense that they provide productive services for more than one period. For example, a machine may last many years even though a firm must purchase it only once. The cost of using such a machine for one period isn't its purchase price but only a portion of that price. Economists refer to the cost of using the machine for one period as the *rental rate,* because it corresponds to the cost of renting the machine for one period rather than purchasing it. In our notation, *r* refers to this rental rate. Of course, the same holds true for labor, since the wage rate represents the cost of "renting" a unit of labor for a specified period, not the price of buying a worker!

Figure 3.1 **Isoquant Map for an X-Producing Firm in Country _A_**

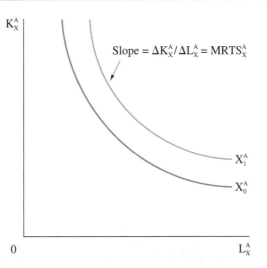

$$\text{Slope} = \Delta K_X^A / \Delta L_X^A = MRTS_X^A$$

Each isoquant depicts all the combinations of labor and capital that can produce a given level of output of good X in country A. Each isoquant is downward sloping, reflecting substitutability of inputs, and convex. Higher isoquants represent higher levels of output (for example, $X_1^A > X_0^A$).

$C = w^A L_X^A + r^A K_X^A$. For example, if the wage rate in country A equals \$10 per unit of labor and the rental rate for capital is \$15 per unit, the total cost for a firm employing 3 units of labor and 2 units of capital would be $C = \$10 \cdot 3 + \$15 \cdot 2 = \$60$.

By using the expression for total cost, we can draw a line representing all the different combinations of L and K a firm could hire for a given level of costs, as in Figure 3.2. If the firm hired only capital, how many units could it hire? The answer is given by the amount of total cost (C) divided by the rental rate (for example, $C/r^A = \$60/\$15 = 4$); this forms the vertical intercept of an isocost line (or _same-cost_ line). Similarly, if the firm hired only labor, the maximum number of units it could hire for a total cost of C would be C/w^A, or $\$60/\$10 = 6$. _(Why?)_ Connecting these two points yields the **isocost line,** which illustrates all the possible combinations of labor and capital the firm could hire for a total cost of C given factor prices of w^A and r^A. The slope of the isocost line is $-(w^A/r^A)$, or $-(2/3)$. _(Why?)_[3] The isocost line for a lower level of total cost (such as \$45) would lie parallel to the one drawn for C = \$60 in Figure 3.2, but shifted in toward the origin.

Combining Figures 3.1 and 3.2 illustrates the firm's choice of production process. For any specified level of output, the firm produces it at minimum cost by choosing the point on the isoquant that lies on the lowest possible isocost line. This occurs at the point of tangency between the isoquant and the isocost line, as illustrated in Figure 3.3. The firm produces output level X_0^A using L_X^{A*} units of labor and K_X^{A*} units of capital at a total cost of $C^* = w^A L_X^{A*} + r^A K_X^{A*}$. At the chosen point, the relative factor prices (given by the absolute slope of the isocost line) just equal the rate at which the firm can substitute the two inputs while maintaining a constant level of output (given by the absolute slope of the isoquant, or the marginal rate of technical substitution). In other words, at this point the rate at which the two inputs can be substituted while keeping total _cost_ constant exactly equals the rate at which they can be substituted while keeping _output_ constant.

---

3 The slope of a line is defined as the rise, or vertical change over the length of the line, divided by the run, or horizontal change over the length of the line. Between the vertical and horizontal intercepts of the isocost line, the vertical change, or change in capital purchased, is $-(C/r^A)$; and the horizontal change, or change in labor purchased, is (C/w^A). Therefore, the slope is $-(C/r^A)/(C/w^A) = -(w^A/r^A)$. With a wage rate of \$10 and a rental rate of \$15, the slope of the isocost would be $-(2/3)$. Hiring an additional unit of labor would require the firm to hire 2/3 units less capital to keep total cost unchanged.

Figure 3.2 **Costs of Different Input Combinations for an X-Producing Firm in Country *A***

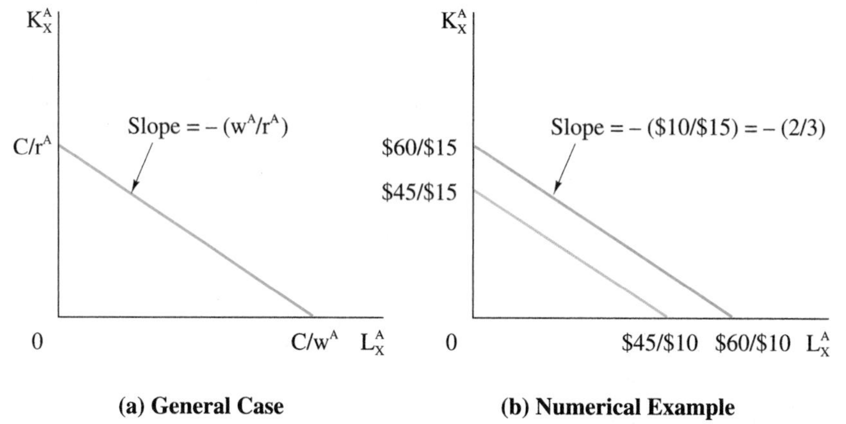

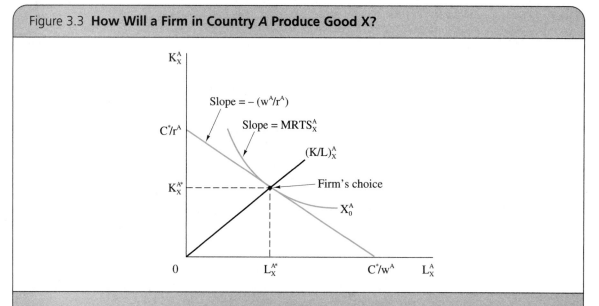

| (a) General Case | (b) Numerical Example |

An isocost line depicts all combinations of labor and capital a firm could hire with a given total cost of C. The (absolute) slope of each isocost equals the ratio of the input prices. Higher isocost lines correspond to higher levels of total costs.

Figure 3.3 **How Will a Firm in Country *A* Produce Good X?**

The firm produces its output at the minimum possible total cost. The point of tangency of an isoquant with an isocost line represents this decision. The firm uses L_X^{A*} units of labor and K_X^{A*} units of capital to produce X_0^A units of output. The slope of the straight line from the origin through the production point indicates the capital-labor ratio.

The Capital-Labor Ratio

The ratio of capital to labor the firm chooses is K_X^{A*}/L_X^{A*} and is called the **capital-labor ratio.** The slope of a ray through the origin and the chosen production point gives the capital-labor ratio, as shown in Figure 3.3.[4] We can relate the capital-labor ratio quite easily to the input coefficients used in Chapter Two.[5] Dividing both K_X^{A*} and L_X^{A*} by the number of units of X being produced gives the number of units of capital and labor used to produce each unit of good X. This corresponds to the definition of the input coefficients from Chapter Two, except that now there are *two* coefficients for the X industry in country A: $a_{KX} = K_X^A/X_0^A$ and $a_{LX} = L_X^A/X_0^A$. The first coefficient represents the number of units of capital used in producing a unit of good X in country A, and the second the number of units of labor used in producing a unit of X in A. Note that $K_X^{A*}/L_X^{A*} = a_{KX}/a_{LX}$.

The major difference between these coefficients and the ones in Chapter Two is that these aren't constants but depend on the relative prices of the two factors of production. The input coefficients have become economic choices. In the constant-cost model, a firm in country A had only one way to produce a unit of good X: Use a_{LX} units of labor. Now the firm can choose from among all the combinations of labor and capital along an isoquant, and the particular combination chosen depends on the relative prices of the two inputs. For example, a fall in the wage rate relative to the rental rate would cause the firm to use more labor and less capital to produce any given output—that is, the capital-labor ratio would fall. *(How can this be demonstrated graphically in Figure 3.3?)*

New General Motors plants around the world provide an example of how a firm's capital-labor ratio responds to different factor prices. Ninety-five percent of the tasks performed at GM's state-of-the-art facility in Eisenach, Germany, are automated (that is, performed using large quantities of capital and little labor) because of Germany's very high labor costs, the highest in the world by most measures. But at GM's even newer facility in Rosario, Argentina, where labor costs are low, only 45 percent of tasks are automated.[6]

Firms that produce good Y in country A go through the same type of decision process as X-producing firms. Each firm chooses its production process to minimize costs, and the choice can be summarized by the ratio of the input coefficients, a_{KY}/a_{LY}. The important point is that the ratios of input coefficients generally will *differ* for the two industries even if the two industries face the *same* relative factor prices, as they will due to mobility of factors within the country. For example, in Figure 3.4 steel-producing firms choose a production technique that uses a large quantity of capital relative to labor, and textile firms choose one using more labor relative to capital, even though both industries face the same prices for labor and capital.

If $(a_{KX}/a_{LX}) > (a_{KY}/a_{LY})$, good X is said to be the **capital-intensive good.** Note that what matters is the amount of capital used *relative* to the amount of labor, not just the amount of capital. Perhaps good Y requires more of both labor and capital than does good X (for example, $a_{LX} = 2$, $a_{KX} = 4$, $a_{LY} = 3$, and $a_{KY} = 5$). Nevertheless, if good X requires *relatively* more capital ($4/2 > 5/3$), good X is capital intensive. As long as there are only two goods and two factors of production, the statement that good X is capital intensive is equivalent to the statement that good Y is **labor intensive.** *(Why?)*[7] In Figure 3.4, steel is the capital-intensive industry and textiles the labor-intensive one.

The production technologies summarized by the four input coefficients provide one of the two pieces of information necessary to sketch country A's production possibilities frontier. The other required information is A's endowment of labor and capital. We assume that country A has L^A units of labor and K^A units of capital. The fact that firms will produce the two outputs using the two factors in different proportions (or different *intensities*) implies that the production possibilities frontier is no longer a straight line as in Chapter Two's constant-cost model; rather, it's concave, or bowed out from the origin. Suppose good X is capital intensive, good Y

---

4 At any point along the ray, the vertical distance from the origin measures the amount of capital used, while the horizontal distance from the origin measures the quantity of labor. Using the rise/run formula for the slope of a line, the slope of a ray from the origin is K_X^A/L_X^A.

5 We'll restrict our attention to production processes in which the firm would choose the same capital-labor ratio regardless of the level of output, as long as factor prices remained the same. Production functions that satisfy this condition are called *homothetic*. In economic terms, the marginal rate of technical substitution depends only on the capital-labor ratio, not on the total quantities of the two inputs used or on the level of output. Graphically, this implies that the tangencies of all isoquants with the corresponding isocost lines lie along a straight line from the origin as long as factor prices do not change. We also assume that constant returns to scale characterize production. This means that changing the usage of both inputs by a certain proportion changes output by that same proportion; we'll relax this assumption in Chapter Five.

6 "GM Is Building Plants in Developing Nations to Woo New Markets," *The Wall Street Journal*, August 4, 1997.

7 The inequality that defines good X as capital intensive directly implies that $(a_{LY}/a_{KY}) > (a_{LX}/a_{KX})$, the definition of labor intensity of good Y.

Figure 3.4 Industries Differ in Their Capital-Labor Ratios

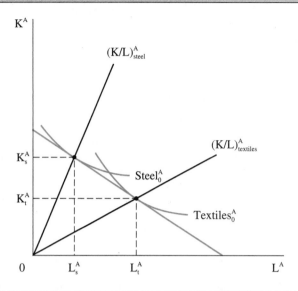

Although both industries in an economy face the same relative factor prices, because factors are mobile between industries, the industries generally choose different capital-labor ratios. This tendency for various industries to utilize factors in different proportions carries important implications for the theory of international trade.

---

is labor intensive, and country A is currently at point 1 in Figure 3.5, producing a large amount of Y and a small amount of X. As the country changes its production along the frontier from point 1 toward point 2, the reduced production of good Y (the labor-intensive good) releases relatively large amounts of labor and small amounts of capital. These released resources are in the "wrong" proportion for the X industry, which is capital intensive. The further the country moves toward point 2, the greater the adjustment that industry X must make in its production process to absorb the resources released by the shrinking Y industry. This increasingly difficult adjustment implies that successive reductions in Y production lead to smaller and smaller increases in the output of good X. This phenomenon is represented graphically by the concavity of the production possibilities frontier.

The (absolute value of the) slope of the production possibilities frontier at each point along the curve represents the opportunity cost of good X in terms of forgone good Y. *(Why?)* As country A produces more and more X along with less and less Y, the opportunity cost of X rises. Similarly, the opportunity cost of producing Y (= 1/absolute slope of the production possibilities frontier) increases as A produces more and more Y along with less and less X. The marginal rate of transformation (MRT^A) no longer is constant as in the constant-cost model of Chapter Two; it now depends on the particular combination of X and Y that country A produces. Opportunity costs rise with production because the two factors of production aren't perfect substitutes for each other; they aren't equally well suited to producing both goods. Efficient production of goods X and Y requires that the two inputs be used with differing intensities in the two industries.

3.2.2 Equilibrium in Autarky

The indifference-curve technique used in Chapter Two to represent tastes for the two goods also applies under conditions of increasing costs. The production possibilities frontier defines the production opportunity set. In autarky, the country's consumption possibilities are limited to these same combinations of X and Y. Residents will choose the point within the opportunity set that lies on the highest attainable indifference curve, thereby

---

Figure 3.5 **What Can a Country Produce under Increasing Costs?**

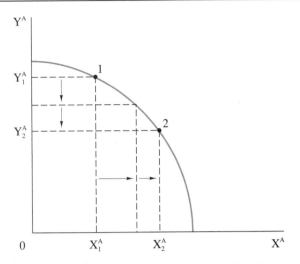

With two factors of production unequally suited for production of the two outputs, the production possibilities frontier bows out from the origin. Reduced production of good Y releases resources in the "wrong" proportion for the X industry. Adjustment becomes increasingly difficult as more and more X is produced, causing X's opportunity cost to rise.

---

maximizing utility subject to the constraint imposed by resource availability and technology. Figure 3.6 illustrates this result.

Country A reaches the highest attainable level of utility at A*, the tangency of indifference curve U_0^A with the production possibilities frontier. The autarky equilibrium involves production and consumption of X^{A*} units of good X and Y^{A*} units of good Y. At the equilibrium, the opportunity cost of X in terms of Y is given by the (absolute) slope of the production possibilities frontier at point A*. All markets are perfectly competitive, so the relative price of good X must equal its opportunity cost; thus, the relative price of X in autarky is given by the (absolute) slope of a line tangent to the production possibilities frontier at A*. Therefore, *in autarky equilibrium, $MRT^A = MRS^A = -(P_X/P_Y)^A$.* These conditions ensure that country A produces so as to achieve the highest possible level of satisfaction given its available resources and technology. The rate at which it's possible to transform good X into good Y in country A (along the production possibilities frontier) equals the rate at which residents of A willingly trade off consumption of the two goods (along the indifference curve). However, by introducing country B as a potential trading partner for country A, we can demonstrate that trade will allow A to achieve an outcome superior to A*, the best possible in autarky.

Country B possesses L^B units of labor and K^B units of capital to allocate between production of goods X and Y. Firms in each industry in country B choose among all the possible production techniques and select the combination of labor and capital that minimizes the cost of production. The chosen production processes can be summarized by the input coefficients (b_{LX} and b_{KX} for the X industry and b_{LY} and b_{KY} for the Y industry), which, like the coefficients in country A, are not constants but choices that depend on the relative prices of the two factors of production in country B. The factor endowment and the production technology in B combine to determine the production possibilities frontier. In Figure 3.6, country B's autarky equilibrium lies at B*, where the production possibilities frontier is tangent to the highest attainable indifference curve. The (absolute) slope of the production possibilities frontier at B* gives the opportunity cost of producing good X in country B. The (absolute) slope of the indifference curve at B* gives the MRS^B, or the rate at which residents of country B willingly trade off consumption of the two goods. All markets are perfectly competitive, so the relative price of each good must equal its opportunity cost; thus, the (absolute) slope of a line tangent to the production possibilities frontier at B* measures the relative price of good X in autarky in country B.

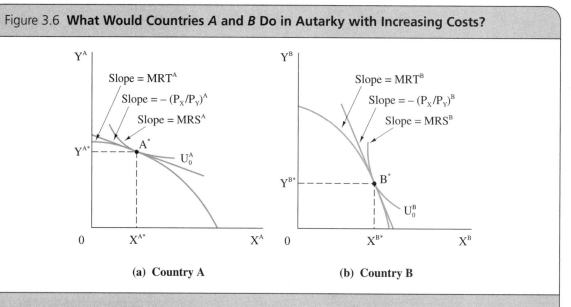

Figure 3.6 **What Would Countries *A* and *B* Do in Autarky with Increasing Costs?**

Country A chooses to locate at the tangency of the highest attainable indifference curve and the production possibilities frontier. The absolute slope of the production possibilities frontier at A* gives the opportunity cost and the relative price of good X. In autarky, country B produces and consumes at B*, thereby achieving the highest level of utility attainable given the constraint imposed by the availability of resources and technology.

3.3 **The Neoclassical World with Trade**

In autarky, the production opportunity set for each country coincides with its consumption opportunity set. Opening up the possibility of trade between countries A and B creates an opportunity for residents of each country to consume combinations of the two goods that lie *outside* the respective production possibilities frontiers. Once again, the key to increased consumption with trade is found in the difference between the autarky relative prices in the two countries.

3.3.1 **Productive Specialization**

In the Neoclassical model, country A is defined as having a **comparative advantage** in production of good X if the relative price of X in A, $(P_X/P_Y)^A$, is lower than that in B, $(P_X/P_Y)^B$. Because all markets are perfectly competitive, this condition also implies that the opportunity cost of good X is lower in A than in B. Graphically, country A has a comparative advantage in good X if the slope of the relative price line in Figure 3.6 representing A's autarky equilibrium is flatter than that representing B's.

Just as in the constant-cost model of Chapter Two, comparative advantage is a natural extension of the concept of opportunity cost. However, in the increasing-cost model, comparative advantage is defined by comparing autarky relative *prices* (which reflect opportunity costs) rather than by directly comparing opportunity *costs*. The reason for this is that, under increasing costs, opportunity costs vary along the production possibilities frontier. By using autarky relative prices, we specify at what points along the two production possibilities frontiers to compare the opportunity costs. This observation points out an important difference between the constant- and increasing-cost models. In both models, determining the direction of comparative advantage involves comparing the slopes of the production possibilities frontiers. Under constant costs, the slope of each frontier is a constant; thus, the determination of comparative advantage doesn't depend on the country's particular location along the frontier. This implies that tastes play no role in the constant-cost model in determining comparative advantage *(why?)*; advantage is determined on the "supply" side of the model by technology rather than on the "demand" side by tastes. Under increasing costs, the determination of comparative advantage requires that we specify the exact points on the production possibilities frontiers at which to compare the

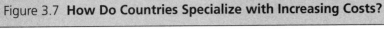

Figure 3.7 **How Do Countries Specialize with Increasing Costs?**

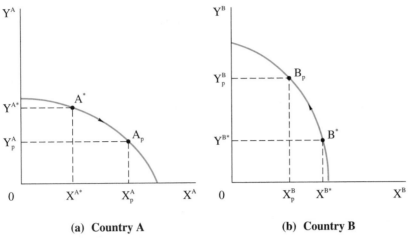

(a) Country A   **(b) Country B**

From the autarky equilibrium, A*, country A specializes in its good of comparative advantage, X. As country A produces more X and less Y, the opportunity cost or relative price of good X rises while that of good Y falls. From the autarky equilibrium at B*, country B increases production of good Y until the opportunity cost of each of the two goods equalizes with that in country A. Specialization continues to point A_p, where the slope of A's production possibilities frontier equals the slope of country B's at B_p.

opportunity costs, because costs change along the frontiers. As we'll see later in section 3.4.2, this fact allows tastes a role in determining comparative advantage.

In Figure 3.6, country A has a comparative advantage in production of good X. *(Why?)* This implies that country B has a comparative advantage in production of good Y. *(Why?)* Suppose each country begins to produce more of the good in which it has a comparative advantage and less of the good in which it has a comparative disadvantage. Each additional unit of good X produced in country A requires forgoing fewer units of good Y than when that unit of X was produced in country B. Similarly, each additional unit of good Y produced in country B requires forgoing fewer units of good X than when that unit of Y was produced in country A. Therefore, specialization according to comparative advantage allows total output to expand; more of one good can be produced *without* producing less of the other good.

In the constant-cost model of Chapter Two, this process of specialization continued until each country produced *only* its good of comparative advantage. Will the complete-specialization result continue to hold under increasing costs? The answer is "probably not." Figure 3.7 illustrates why. As each country begins to specialize by moving along its production possibilities frontier in the direction of the good of its comparative advantage, the opportunity cost of producing that good rises and the cost of producing the good of comparative disadvantage falls. As the cost of producing good X rises in country A and falls in country B, eventually costs in the two countries equalize. Similarly, as the cost of producing good Y rises in country B and falls in country A, costs in the two countries eventually converge. When the cost of producing each good becomes equal in the two countries, the advantage to *further* productive specialization disappears. The optimal degree of productive specialization occurs at points A_p and B_p (the p subscripts denote *production*), where the slopes of the two production possibilities frontiers are equal.[8] Country A produces X_p^A and Y_p^A, and country B produces X_p^B and Y_p^B. Notice

8 It is theoretically possible for two countries to have factor endowments *so* different that no pair of points exists at which the two countries' production possibilities frontiers have the same slope. In this case, each country will specialize completely in its good of comparative advantage (as in the Ricardian model). Countries may also specialize completely if the two industries have very similar factor intensities. In this case, opportunity costs are increasing only slightly, so the production possibilities frontier will be only slightly convex (that is, almost a straight line); and the outcome is like that of the Ricardian model.

that if the two countries' autarky prices (and therefore opportunity costs) were equal, there would be no comparative advantage and no reason to specialize.

The condition illustrated in Figure 3.7 ensures that production is allocated efficiently between the two countries or according to comparative advantage. However, this condition alone isn't sufficient to determine exactly which combinations of goods X and Y the two countries will produce. After all, there are many potential pairs of points at which the slopes of the two production possibilities frontiers are equal; points A_p and B_p in the figure constitute only one possible pair that satisfies the equal-slope requirement. At which of these pairs will production actually occur? To answer this question, we must bring tastes back in.

3.3.2 **International Equilibrium with Trade**

Once productive specialization has occurred so that the two goods' opportunity costs are equalized between the two countries, the goods' relative prices also will be equal in A and B. *(Why?)* Of all the possible sets of relative prices, at which one will trade actually occur? The market-clearing or equilibrium terms of trade will be the one at which the quantity of good X that country A wants to export equals the quantity of X that country B wants to import, and the quantity of Y that B wants to export equals the quantity that A wants to import. This is the international version of the definition of the **equilibrium price** of any good: the price at which quantity demanded equals quantity supplied. In panel (a) of Figure 3.8, country A can trade along the common relative price line representing the international terms of trade to the point of tangency with the highest attainable indifference curve. This occurs at point A_c, which is A's optimal consumption point under unrestricted trade (the c subscript denotes *c*onsumption). Country A produces at A_p, exports $(X_p^A - X_c^A)$ units of good X to country B, and imports $(Y_c^A - Y_p^A)$ units of Y from country B.

Panel (b) of Figure 3.8 represents country B's equilibrium. Residents of B can trade with those of A along the terms-of-trade line. The utility-maximizing consumption choice is B_c. Country B imports $(X_c^B - X_p^B)$ from country A in exchange for exporting $(Y_p^B - Y_c^B)$ to A.

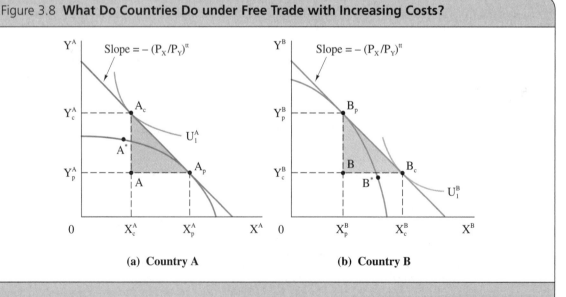

Figure 3.8 What Do Countries Do under Free Trade with Increasing Costs?

(a) Country A

(b) Country B

Country A specializes production in its comparative-advantage good, X, until the opportunity cost of X equalizes in the two countries. Trade occurs along the terms-of-trade line until country A reaches its highest attainable indifference curve at point A_c. The trade triangle is AA_cA_p. Country B specializes in producing good Y until the cost of Y equalizes in the two countries at B_p. Trade occurs along the international terms-of-trade line until country B reaches its highest attainable indifference curve at B_c. The trade triangle for B is BB_pB_c.

Table 3.1 **Effects of Trade**

	Autarky	Free Trade	Effect of Trade
Labor-Abundant Country A:			
Production	Point A* in Figure 3.8(a)	Point A_p in Figure 3.8(a)	$X\Uparrow$, $Y\Downarrow$
Consumption	Point A* in Figure 3.8(a)	Point A_c in Figure 3.8(a)	$X\Uparrow$, $Y\Uparrow$
Prices	$(P_X/P_Y)^A$ =slope of ppf at A*	$(P_X/P_Y)^{tt}$ = slope of ppf at A_p	$P_X\Uparrow$, $P_Y\Downarrow$
Exports	None	$(X_p^A - X_c^A)$	Exports good X
Imports	None	$(Y_c^A - Y_p^A)$	Imports good Y
Capital-Abundant Country B:			
Production	Point B* in Figure 3.8(b)	Point B_p in Figure 3.8(b)	$X\Downarrow$, $Y\Uparrow$
Consumption	Point B* in Figure 3.8(b)	Point B_c in Figure 3.8(b)	$X\Uparrow$, $Y\Uparrow$
Prices	$(P_X/P_Y)^B$ = slope of ppf at B*	$(P_X/P_Y)^{tt}$ = slope of ppf at B_p	$P_X\Downarrow$, $P_Y\Uparrow$
Exports	None	$(Y_p^B - Y_c^B)$	Exports good Y
Imports	None	$(X_c^B - X_p^B)$	Imports good X

Unrestricted trade expands each country's consumption opportunity set by allowing residents to trade at the international terms of trade, obtaining consumption combinations that lie outside the production possibilities frontiers and therefore couldn't be produced domestically. It would be impossible for country A to produce X_c^A units of good X and Y_c^A units of good Y, and country B couldn't produce X_c^B and Y_c^B. Trade also equalizes the opportunity cost of each good across countries by increasing production of each good in the low-cost country and decreasing production in the high-cost one. Table 3.1 summarizes trade's effects on production, consumption, prices, exports, and imports for each good in each country.

3.4 Sources of Comparative Advantage

Under increasing costs, a country has comparative advantage in production of goods whose relative prices are lower there than in the other country. To locate the sources of comparative advantage, it's necessary to examine the determinants of relative prices. As illustrated in Figure 3.6, the interaction of supply (resource availability and technology as summarized in the production possibilities frontier) and demand (tastes as summarized by the indifference curves) determines relative prices in each country. So differences in relative prices can originate from differences in resource availability, technology, tastes, or some combination thereof. We examined the role of technology or labor productivity differences in Chapter Two. Here we restrict our attention to the possible effects of differences in resource endowments and tastes in determining comparative advantage by assuming that the two countries have access to the same technology.

3.4.1 The Role of Factor Endowments

The importance of differences between countries' endowments of various factors of production in determining patterns of opportunity costs was asserted by two Swedish economists, Eli Heckscher and Bertil Ohlin, in the early twentieth century. To demonstrate the role of factor endowments, Heckscher and Ohlin used several simplifying assumptions. In addition to the basic assumptions we've used throughout the first two chapters (see section 2.4), they assumed that tastes and technology did not differ between countries, that countries differed in factor abundance, and that goods differed in factor intensity.

Factor Abundance

First, we must define what Heckscher and Ohlin meant by the assumption that countries differ in **factor abundance.** Abundance can be defined in either of two ways. The first definition is based on relative factor quantities. By this definition, country A is **capital abundant** if $(K^A/L^A) > (K^B/L^B)$—that is, if A has more capital per unit of labor than does country B. Note that A could actually have *less* capital than B yet still be the capital-abundant country (for example, if $K^A = 50$, $L^A = 50$, $K^B = 100$, and $L^B = 150$, so that $K^A/L^A = 1$ and $K^B/L^B = 2/3$). What matters is a comparison of capital *per unit of labor,* or the *ratio* of capital to labor, in the two countries. Given two factors and two countries, if country A is capital abundant, country B must be **labor abundant.** *(Why?)* The quantity-based definition of factor abundance obviously depends only on the supply of factors in each country; the demand for factors plays no role. Table 3.2 highlights the significant differences among countries' factor endowments.[9] *(Which country is the most capital abundant? The least capital abundant?)*

A second possible definition of factor abundance is based on factor *prices* rather than *quantities.* According to the price-based definition, country A is capital abundant if in autarky $(r^A/w^A) < (r^B/w^B)$ or $(w^A/r^A) > (w^B/r^B)$, that is, if the relative rental rate for capital in country A is lower than in B. The price-based definition considers the role of demand for the two factors as well as their supplies, because the price of each factor represents the interaction of both demand and supply. For our purposes, either definition of factor abundance will suffice; however, because the Heckscher-Ohlin model traditionally is associated with the quantity-based definition, we'll use that one.

The Heckscher-Ohlin Theorem

Heckscher and Ohlin combined the notion of factor *abundance* with the idea that different goods involve different factor *intensities* to infer that a country will have a comparative advantage in the good whose production

Table 3.2 **Factor Endowments**

Country	Capital (Billions 1966 $)	Labor (1,000 Persons)	Capital/Labor (Millions 1966 $/Person)	Country	Capital (Billions 1966 $)	Labor (1,000 Persons)	Capital/Labor (Millions 1966 $/Person)
Argentina	24,018	8,496	2.83	Japan	165,976	49,419	3.36
Australia	35,053	4,727	7.42	Korea	3,025	9,440	0.32
Austria	15,653	3,363	4.65	Mexico	21,639	12,844	1.68
Brazil	30,476	26,463	1.15	Netherlands	29,941	4,699	6.37
Canada	76,537	7,232	10.58	Norway	12,883	1,464	8.80
Denmark	13,018	2,230	5.84	Philippines	6,597	12,470	0.53
Finland	13,929	2,176	6.40	Portugal	3,757	3,381	1.11
France	146,052	21,233	6.88	Spain	34,792	11,849	2.94
Germany	181,079	26,576	6.81	Sweden	31,555	3,450	9.15
Greece	7,223	4,314	1.67	Switzerland	23,315	2,843	8.20
Hong Kong	2,087	1,525	1.37	United Kingdom	110,717	25,396	4.36
Ireland	3,370	1,109	3.04	United States	785,933	76,595	10.26
Italy	90,436	19,998	4.52	Yugoslavia	14,023	8,837	1.59

Source: Harry P. Bowen et al., "Multicountry, Multifactor Tests of the Factor Abundance Theory," *American Economic Review* (December 1987), pp. 806–807.

---

9 The tables from which the data in Table 3.2 come list land separately from capital; if land were included in the capital measure, the capital/labor rankings would be different. Chapter Five explores the implications of a more detailed classification of inputs.

involves intensive use of the factor that the country possesses in abundance.[10] Further, under unrestricted trade, the country will export the good in which it has a comparative advantage and import the good whose production involves intensive use of the factor that the country possesses in relative scarcity. We assume that if good X is the capital-intensive good in country A (that is, if $[a_{KX}/a_{LX}] > [a_{KY}/a_{IY}]$), it also will be capital intensive in country B ($[b_{KX}/b_{LX}] > [b_{KY}/b_{IY}]$).[11]

As an example, assume country A is labor abundant ($[L^A/K^A] > [L^B/K^B]$) and good X is labor intensive ($[a_{KX}/a_{LX}] < [a_{KY}/a_{IY}]$ and $[b_{KX}/b_{LX}] < [b_{KY}/b_{IY}]$). These two conditions imply that A has a resource endowment relatively well suited to production of good X, and B has a resource endowment relatively well suited to production of Y. For example, the United States has a resource endowment well suited to the production of wheat; it is farmland abundant, and wheat is a farmland-intensive good. China has a resource endowment well suited to the production of apparel; China is labor abundant, and apparel production is a labor-intensive industry. The production possibilities frontier of each country reflects a **production bias** toward the good of comparative advantage, as shown in the two panels of Figure 3.9.

If tastes were identical in the two countries, as Heckscher and Ohlin assumed, the autarky price of wheat would be lower in the United States and that of apparel lower in China.[12] Each country then would be the low-cost producer of the good that used its abundant factor intensively. Under unrestricted trade, each country would specialize in and export the good that used the abundant factor intensively because of the

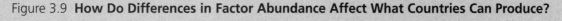

Figure 3.9 **How Do Differences in Factor Abundance Affect What Countries Can Produce?**

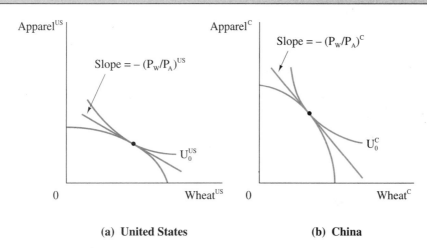

(a) **United States**   (b) **China**

Each country's production possibilities frontier exhibits a bias toward the axis representing the good whose production involves *intensive* use of that country's *abundant* factor of production. This production bias creates a tendency for each country to have a comparative advantage in the good that uses the abundant factor intensively.

---

10 Don't make the mistake of confusing factor abundance and factor intensity. Abundance refers to *countries' endowments* of factors of production. Intensity refers to *industries' usage* of factors of production. For example, the Philippines is (compared with the United States) labor abundant, and the textile industry is (compared with the aircraft industry) labor intensive.

11 The case in which a good is capital intensive in one country but labor intensive in the other is known as a *factor-intensity reversal.*

12 The assumption of identical tastes in the two countries does *not* imply that residents of each will consume the two goods in equal quantities or in equal proportions. Identical tastes are defined as identical sets of indifference curves. Imagine a set of indifference curves drawn on a piece of transparent plastic and placed over two graphs, one containing each country's production possibilities frontier. Even though the indifference curves are identical, the actual consumption point chosen in each graph might differ because of the differences between production possibilities. Only when consumers in both countries face the same output prices, as they would under free trade, would identical indifference-curve maps imply identical or proportional consumption choices.

good's low autarky price. This result is known as the **Heckscher-Ohlin theorem.** *(Using Table 3.1 and the Heckscher-Ohlin theorem, name a country you would expect to export capital-intensive goods. Name a country you would expect to export labor-intensive goods. What do you know about the trade of the countries you named? Does it fit your predictions?)*

A theory of trade based *solely* on production bias due to factor endowments is somewhat artificial. Under conditions of increasing costs, tastes and productive possibilities interact to determine comparative advantage. What ultimately matters is the comparison of autarky price ratios in the two countries. This is distinct from the constant-cost case, in which comparative advantage is determined on the supply side (by the production possibilities frontier) with demand conditions (tastes) determining the volume of trade.

3.4.2 The Role of Tastes

Although the simplest Heckscher-Ohlin model assumes that the production bias resulting from differences in factor endowments forms the basis for trade, there are other possibilities.[13] For example, two countries could have identical production possibilities frontiers (that is, identical factor endowments and technology) but very different tastes. The taste differences would produce different autarky price ratios, as shown in Figure 3.10, and a basis for mutually beneficial trade.

In Figure 3.10, residents of country A have tastes biased toward consumption of good Y, and residents of country B have tastes biased toward consumption of good X. With identical production possibilities, the strong demand for Y in A and for X in B result in different relative prices in each country. This **taste bias** gives country A a comparative advantage in production of good X. Under unrestricted trade, A would specialize in X and B in Y even though the production possibilities are identical. When the identical-taste assumption of Heckscher-Ohlin is relaxed and both factor endowments and tastes are allowed to differ simultaneously, the taste bias can reinforce, partially offset, or totally offset the production bias. Unlike in the constant-cost case,

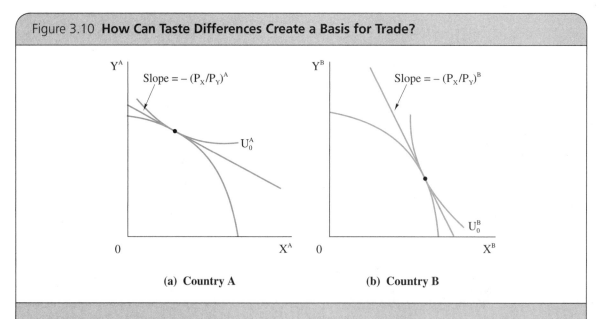

Figure 3.10 **How Can Taste Differences Create a Basis for Trade?**

(a) **Country A**

(b) **Country B**

If tastes differ between countries A and B, the autarky price ratios will differ even if the production possibilities are identical, and a basis for mutually beneficial trade will exist.

---

13 Chapter Two covered technology as a source of comparative advantage. In Chapter Five, we'll add economies of scale as a basis for mutually beneficial trade not based on comparative advantage.

tastes can play a significant role in determining the direction of comparative advantage. Most empirical studies indicate that tastes exhibit a **home bias;** that is, residents of a country tend to consume relatively large quantities of goods produced there and relatively small quantities of goods produced only abroad.

North/South Korea

CASE ONE:
Do Autarky and Trade Matter?
The Two Koreas

No country in the modern world exists in complete autarky. Some, however, come much closer than others.[14] Since Korea split into the Republic of (South) Korea and the Democratic People's Republic of (North) Korea during the Korean War of the early 1950s, the North's philosophy has been one of *juche,* or self-sufficient industrialization. The government of the North, one of the world's last centrally planned Communist regimes, strictly controls foreign trade, along with other contact with the outside world. In fact, experts have called North Korea the "world's most autarchic economy."[15] The South, on the other hand, has pursued outward- or trade-oriented policies despite frequent disputes with the United States over an alleged lack of openness of South Korean markets for U.S. goods. The difference in results is remarkable, as summarized in Table 3.3. The South's per capita gross domestic product exceeds that of the North by a factor of 13; despite the setbacks caused by the Asian financial crisis of 1997, the South's economic growth dwarfs the North's. In fact, North Korea's output shrunk by an average of about 5 percent per year during the 1990s; exports fell by two-thirds during the decade.[16] Estimates indicate that 1999 was the only year during the 1990s during which North Korean GDP grew rather than shrunk. Reasons for the improvement included good weather; increased international aid, especially from South Korea; and

Table 3.3 **Comparison of North and South Korea, 1999**

Indicator	North Korea	South Korea
Territory (1,000 square kilometers)	120	98
Population (million persons)	21.7	46.6
GDP (billions $)[a]	22.6	625.7
Per-capita GDP ($)[a]	1,000	13,300
Economic growth (percent)	1.0	10.0
Exports (millions $)	680	144,000
Imports (millions $)	954	116,000
Telephones (millions)		
Main lines	1.1	23.1
Cellular	0.0	8.6
Televisions (millions)	1.2	15.9
Paved highways (kilometers)	1,997	86,990
Military expenditure (percent of GDP)	25–33	3.2

[a]Converted to U.S. dollars at purchasing-power-parity exchange rates.

Source: Central Intelligence Agency, *The World Factbook* (available at www.cia.gov).

---

14 Similarly, no country practices perfectly free trade. In May 1997, Mongolia became the only country in the world to levy no taxes on trade; see "Those Free-Trading Mongolians," *The Economist,* April 26, 1997.

15 Marcus Noland et al., "Modeling North Korean Economic Reform," *Journal of Asian Economics* 8 (1997), pp. 115–138.

16 "Is North Korea's Free Fall Finally Ending?" *The Wall Street Journal,* May 28, 1999.

a slight weakening of some aspects of the government's stranglehold on the economy.

Of course, North Korea's attempts at self-sufficiency aren't the only cause of its economic problems. Estimates place North Korea's army at 1.2 million people, and military expenditures absorb up to a third of the economy's output. Until 1990, the small amount of trade in which the country engaged took the form of oil imports from the Soviet Union to fuel huge state-owned industrial plants and exports of low-quality goods to Eastern Europe.[17] Since the demise of the Soviet Union, North Korea's factories now run far below capacity because the country lacks the foreign currency to buy oil at world prices on the open market. The decline of central planning in Eastern Europe also eliminated the markets for North Korea's few exports, whose low quality makes them noncompetitive in world markets. This combination of events reduced North Korea's trade by more than 50 percent between 1990 and 1996.[18] These problems led to idle fuelless factories, power outages, famine, and rumors of fatalities from hunger. Kim Il Sung, North Korea's ruler since 1948, died in 1994 and was replaced by his son, Kim Jong Il. Floods and a failed rice crop in 1995 and 1996 forced the country to seek food aid from other countries.

North Korea has responded to its growing economic problems by opening a tiny crack in the door to the outside world. The government now encourages foreign firms to take advantage of North Korea's low wages by investing in a special economic zone, the Rajin-Sonbong Free Economic and Trade Zone, modeled on China's coastal economic zones.[19] But the government keeps that area (strategically placed to handle South Korea–China trade) isolated from the rest of the country to prevent the spread of political ideas; investors have been wary, despite generous tax incentives and relaxed rules that permit 100 percent foreign ownership of new enterprises in the zone.

Talks have been underway for years on several major projects involving North Korea. The first is the reunification of the two Koreas, with the obvious hope that the South could revitalize the North. The costs, however, could be enormous; one estimate placed the cost to bring the North's per capita income up to 60 percent of the South's (the minimum level thought to keep the level of North-South migration manageable) at $1.7 trillion.[20] A second project is the Tumen River Economic Development Area, a free-trade zone among North Korea, China, and Russia, along with Mongolia and South Korea, at the mouth of the Tumen River. The zone could allow North Korea to capture at least a portion of the potential gains from trade. The original idea was to process Russian and Mongolian raw materials with Chinese labor and then export the products through the North Korean port of Rajin. However, despite the area's strategic and commercial importance, strong support from the United Nations Development Program, and over $900 million already having been invested over 10 years, the project seems to have stalled as its participants bicker.[21]

In May 1995, a South Korean firm won government approval for the first joint venture with a firm from the North since the Korean War. North Korea allows Hyundai, in exchange for $1 billion over six years, to operate a tourist service that allows South Koreans to visit—under carefully restricted conditions—the Diamond Mountains in the north. South Korea's state-owned Tobacco and Ginseng Corporation now sends tobacco leaves north, where they are used in One Mind cigarettes, sold in both North and South Korea. Several other South Korean firms have plans for textile and apparel factories, tourist resorts, railroads, telecommunications and electronics factories, and steel mills in North Korea. Chinese and Hong Kong firms also are interested. A handful of international merchant banks have established joint ventures with local North Korean partners. Visitors even report increased government tolerance of black markets, which had been vigorously suppressed for years.

Experts estimate that liberalization of international trade could raise North Korean GDP by 25 to 35 percent. Given the country's resource endowment, especially abundant unskilled and semi-skilled labor, its potential areas of comparative advantage include fish, minerals, textiles, apparel, and a broad range of light manufacturing. Freed from the dictates of central planners, the agricultural and capital-goods sectors—areas of comparative disadvantage—would shrink.

In late 1999, in exchange for North Korean promises to limit its nuclear-weapons and missile-testing programs, the United States eased trade restrictions in place since 1950 that had prohibited trade between the United States and North Korea.[22] After shrinking between 25 and 40 percent during the 1990s, North Korea enjoyed a year of positive economic growth in 1999. Unfortunately for the citizens of North Korea, the government seemed to withdraw once

---

17 This trade pattern also characterized most economies in transition, that is, those in the process of changing from central planning to a market-oriented economy; see section 11.6.

18 "Growing Business Ties Help to Bridge Chasm between North and South Korea," *The Wall Street Journal,* May 9, 1996.

19 Section 9.5.2 examines the role of special economic zones in China's transition.

20 Marcus Noland et al., "The Economics of Korean Unification," Institute for International Economics, Working Paper 97–5, p. 3.

21 "U.N. Extends Strained Asia Trade Project," *The Wall Street Journal,* April 2, 2001.

22 For official up-to-date information on U.S. trade restrictions, go to www.treas.gov/ofac.

again from its engagement with the rest of the world in response to South Korea's support of the antiterrorism campaign launched after the September 11, 2001, terrorist attacks on New York and Washington, D.C. Regardless of the timetables or fates of particular projects, one thing is certain. If North Korea hopes to experience economic growth, open international trade based on comparative advantage will constitute a vital component of the necessary policy changes.

Iceland

CASE TWO:
From Fish to Information Technology

What would the Heckscher-Ohlin model predict about the comparative advantage of Iceland, a small (population 283,000), geographically isolated island in the rugged North Atlantic, just south of the Arctic Circle? For decades, the economy depended heavily on a predictable industry: fishing. The island sits near some of the world's richest fishing grounds. Overfishing reduced fish stocks, but perhaps due to its small size, Iceland has had better success than most other countries in using government restrictions both to reduce the fish catch sufficiently for stocks to recover and to support sustainable fishing and fish-processing industries.

What other industries might the country's factor abundance promote? Abundant cheap energy from hydroelectric and geothermal sources not only provides heat in the cold climate, but also supports a large aluminum industry. Aluminum producers, among the most energy-intensive firms of any industry in the world, routinely locate in low-cost energy areas; for example, most U.S. producers are found in Washington state, home of the lowest U.S. electricity prices.

New technologies have opened up new possibilities for Iceland, reducing the impact of its geographical remoteness. New biotech firms hope to find bases for new medicines among the island's unique ecosystems.[23] The country boasts the highest per-capita Internet and cellular-phone usage in the world, at 70 percent and 73 percent, respectively. The number of software firms doubled between 1995 and 2000. Even the most remote areas, such as tiny Hrisey Island off Iceland's north coast, now enjoy technology links to the rest of the world; residents there operate a call center, placing public-opinion-poll calls.[24]

Iceland's three largest trading partners are the United Kingdom, Germany, and the United States. Despite its heavy trade with members of the European Union, Iceland has resisted joining the EU, because membership would require adherence to the group's Common Fisheries Policy and limit Iceland's ability to manage what Heckscher and Ohlin would have predicted to be its most important industry.

United States

CASE THREE:
Socks: Made in USA

The Heckscher-Ohlin theorem provides the key insight into why the United States imports about two-thirds of its apparel. Most apparel production relies heavily on unskilled labor, a factor relatively scarce in the United States. Major exporters of apparel to the United States include Mexico, countries of the Caribbean, and China, all of which possess abundant unskilled labor (see Case Four for more on China's factor

endowment and trade). We'll see later that the U.S. textile and apparel markets are subject to complex restrictions on trade, so the trade pattern observed doesn't necessarily strictly reflect comparative advantage. In particular, Mexico, a member of the North American Free Trade Agreement, and the countries of the Caribbean Basin Economic Recovery Act group enjoy less restricted access to U.S. markets than do

23 "A Country Which Defies the Elements," *Financial Times,* September 19, 2000; and "Iceland Transforms Itself into a Hotbed of New Industries," *The Wall Street Journal,* March 13, 2001. Visit the Web site of the Trade Council of Iceland at www.icetrade.is/english.

24 "Who Needs Fish? Villagers in Iceland Cast Bets on the Net," *The Wall Street Journal,* August 1, 2000.

other countries. But even though trade restrictions no doubt distort the pattern of exports and imports away from what we would observe under free trade, the Heckscher-Ohlin model explains why we observe large-scale apparel exports to the United States from countries such as Mexico, China, and the Dominican Republic.

So why does the United States manufacture 90 percent of its own socks?[25] Americans buy 3.5 billion pairs of socks each year; most are made in North Carolina and Alabama. Again, the complex set of trade restrictions that limit textile and apparel imports play a role, but the Heckscher-Ohlin framework can help us understand why the U.S. sock industry has outlasted other sectors of U.S. apparel production. Sock production, compared with other apparel manufacturing, uses more capital and skilled labor and less unskilled labor. So sock production better matches the U.S. factor endowment.

The knitting of yarn into socks occurs on computer-controlled knitting machines that run with little human intervention. Unskilled labor tasks involve seaming the toes, stretching and ironing the sock, and packaging, but these labor costs constitute only a small share of the total cost of production. The more important and more costly labor involves the small number of skilled "fixers" who work with the computer-controlled knitting machines and whose job is to spot machine malfunctions or production imperfections and stop the machines for adjustment—before they waste yarn and turn out thousands of unusable socks. Producers sometimes ship unfinished socks to Mexico or Honduras for the unskilled finishing work, but so far, there aren't enough skilled "fixers" abroad. So for now, the capital- and skilled-labor-intensive parts of the production process keep socks "Made in USA."

China

CASE FOUR:
Can Heckscher-Ohlin Explain China's Trade?

The Heckscher-Ohlin theorem predicts that a country will specialize in and export goods that use the country's abundant factors intensively, while importing goods intensive in the country's scarce factors. The United States possesses human capital and arable farmland in abundance, and unskilled labor is the United States' scarce factor. China, on the other hand, possesses unskilled labor in great abundance, but has little arable farmland in comparison with its large population. Therefore, the Heckscher-Ohlin theorem predicts that the United States would export to China products whose production involves intensive use of skilled labor (embodying the country's human capital) and land and that China would export to the United States products intensive in unskilled labor.

From the late 1950s until the mid-1970s, under revolutionary leader Chairman Mao, China's economic policies largely ignored the country's comparative advantage. Beginning at the time of Mao's death in 1976, China began to move, slowly and sometimes erratically, in the direction of larger roles for markets and for international trade in its economy. Have the changes observed over the last 25 years in China's pattern of trade been consistent with the predictions of Heckscher-Ohlin? Several pieces of information suggest that the answer is yes. First, since 1975, the role of food and agricultural products in China's exports has declined dramatically, as reported in Figure 3.11. This is exactly what

we should expect, given the country's relative scarcity of arable farmland. Second, the role of manufactured exports, especially labor-intensive ones such as clothing, has grown dramatically over the same period. Again, this fits the predictions of Heckscher-Ohlin, given China's abundant labor endowment.

The data in Figure 3.11 indicate that, consistent with Heckscher-Ohlin, China has begun to specialize in and export labor- instead of land-intensive products. We can use a second piece of information about China's factor endowment—that its abundance lies in unskilled rather than skilled labor—to examine further the fit between China's experience and the predictions of the Heckscher-Ohlin model. Table 3.4 reports data from a recent study. That study's authors divided a sample of 131 industries into 10 groups (or deciles) according to their skill intensity. Group 1 includes the most skill-intensive industries, and group 10 the least skill intensive. Table 3.4 lists sample industries for each group, along with the group's share of Chinese exports to the United States and of U.S. exports to China.

The pattern of U.S.–China trade in 1990 fits closely with Heckscher-Ohlin-based predictions. U.S. exports to China are concentrated in the high-skill sectors; deciles 1–3 (highlighted in the table) account for 78 percent of U.S. exports. Chinese exports to the United States fall into the lower skill categories; the highlighted groups 9 and 10, the

---

25 See "Socks Are Odd: Made in America," *The Wall Street Journal,* May 3, 2001.

Figure 3.11 **How Have China's Exports Changed, 1975–1990?**

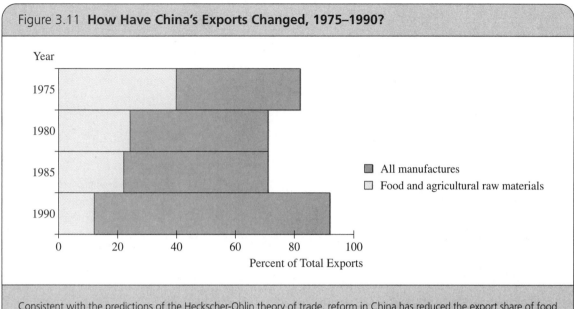

Consistent with the predictions of the Heckscher-Ohlin theory of trade, reform in China has reduced the export share of food and agricultural products (intensive in the country's scarce factor, arable farmland) and increased the export share of manufactures (intensive in the country's abundant factor, labor).

Source: World Bank, *China: Foreign Trade Reform* (Washington, D.C.: World Bank, 1994), p. 5.

Table 3.4 **Skill Composition of U.S.–China Trade, 1990**

Skill Group (Industry Examples)	Percent of Chinese Exports to U.S.	Percent of U.S. Exports to China
Most Skilled		
1 (Periodicals, office and computing machines)	4.8%	**7.7%**
2 (Aircraft and parts, industrial inorganic chemicals)	2.6	**48.8**
3 (Engines and turbines, fats and oils)	3.9	**21.3**
4 (Concrete, nonelectric plumbing and heating)	11.5	4.3
5 (Watches, clocks, toys, sporting goods)	18.9	6.3
6 (Wood buildings, blast furnaces, basic steel)	8.2	1.3
7 (Ship building and repair, furniture and fixtures)	4.1	2.8
8 (Cigarettes, motor vehicles, iron and steel foundries)	5.2	1.8
9 (Weaving, wool, leather tanning and finishing)	**17.2**	0.4
10 (Children's outerwear, nonrubber footwear)	**23.5**	5.2
Least skilled		

Source: Data from Jeffrey D. Sachs and Howard J. Shatz, "Trade and Jobs in U.S. Manufacturing," *Brookings Papers on Economic Activity* 1 (1994), pp. 18, 53.

least skilled, constitute more than 40 percent of the total. Chinese exports in groups 4 and 5 include mostly labor-intensive assembly tasks in the radio, television, and toy industries.

Finally, Figure 3.12 summarizes how the factor intensity of Chinese exports has changed during the reform period since 1975. The figure clearly demonstrates the rapid growth of labor-intensive exports, especially unskilled ones, and the corresponding decline of physical-capital-intensive manufactures along with natural-resource-based products. Overall, the Heckscher-Ohlin model clearly *can* explain the broad patterns of Chinese trade.

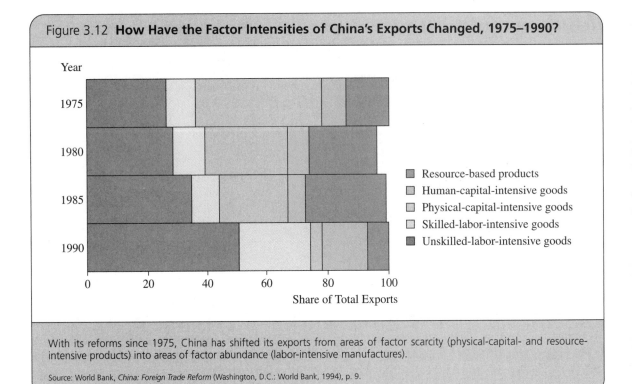

Figure 3.12 **How Have the Factor Intensities of China's Exports Changed, 1975–1990?**

With its reforms since 1975, China has shifted its exports from areas of factor scarcity (physical-capital- and resource-intensive products) into areas of factor abundance (labor-intensive manufactures).

Source: World Bank, *China: Foreign Trade Reform* (Washington, D.C.: World Bank, 1994), p. 9.

Summary

When goods are produced using two inputs that aren't perfect substitutes for each other, the opportunity cost of producing each good rises as more of the good is produced. A country has a comparative advantage in production of a good when the opportunity cost of that good is lower there than in the trading partner. When trade is possible, each country will specialize in and export the good in which it has a comparative advantage. We've now encountered three bases for comparative advantage and mutually beneficial trade: (1) differences in technology or labor productivity, as in Chapter Two's Ricardian model, (2) differences in factor endowments, emphasized in this chapter's Heckscher-Ohlin theorem, and (3) differences in tastes under increasing costs.

Looking Ahead

Chapters Two and Three demonstrated the potential of international trade based on comparative advantage for increasing the welfare of the residents of participating countries. Nevertheless, decisions on trade policy always generate controversy, leading us to suspect that the case for trade must be more complicated than we've seen so far. In Chapter Four, we introduce an effect of trade we've ignored up to now: its effect on the distribution of income *within* each country.

Key Terms

Neoclassical (increasing-cost) model
fixed proportions
production function
isoquant
marginal rate of technical
    substitution (MRTS)

factor prices (factor rewards)
isocost line
capital-labor ratio
capital-intensive good
labor-intensive good
comparative advantage

equilibrium price
factor abundance
capital abundance
labor abundance

production bias
Heckscher-Ohlin theorem
taste bias
home bias (in consumption)

Problems and Questions for Review

1. Assume tastes and technology are identical in Hong Kong and Japan. Assume Hong Kong is labor abundant and Japan is capital abundant. Assume production of clothing is labor intensive and production of automobiles is capital intensive.
   a. Sketch the production possibilities frontiers for Hong Kong and Japan. Explain briefly why you drew them as you did.
   b. In autarky, which country has a comparative advantage in production of which good? Show how you know, or why you don't know.
   c. What does the Heckscher-Ohlin theorem predict would happen if trade were opened between Hong Kong and Japan?
   d. Show and label the autarky and unrestricted-trade equilibria, production and consumption points, imports and exports, autarky price ratios, and terms of trade.
2. Under increasing costs, will two countries find it beneficial to trade if they have:
   a. identical production possibilities and different tastes?
   b. identical tastes and different production possibilities?
   c. identical tastes and identical production possibilities?
   Explain and illustrate.
3. How does a concave, or bowed-out, production possibilities frontier reflect increasing costs?
4. In terms of the production possibilities frontier/indifference curve diagram, explain the effects on North Korea's economy of:
   a. the country's isolation from new technologies.
   b. residents' inability to exchange goods with residents of other countries.
   c. firms' inability to specialize according to comparative advantage.
5. A firm's production function is X = 5LK. Name three input combinations that would allow the firm to produce 100 units of output. In each case, what is the firm's capital-labor ratio? If the wage rate is $10 per unit and the rental rate on capital is $20 per unit, what are the firm's costs for each of the three input combinations?
6. What determines the capital-labor ratio for each good in each country? Why might both industries use a higher capital-labor ratio in one country than in another? Can you think of circumstances in which each industry would exhibit the same capital-labor ratio in both countries? Explain.
7. Why do the autarky relative prices in the two countries form limits or bounds on the international terms of trade? Explain.
8. Suppose that tastes exhibit a home bias in the sense that each country's residents consume relatively large quantities of goods produced domestically and relatively small quantities of goods that must be imported. Would the home bias strengthen or weaken the pattern of production bias based on differing factor endowments? Why? Would the result be more trade or less trade than in the identical-taste case?

References and Selected Readings

Coughlin, Cletus C., and Patricia S. Pollard. "Comparing Manufacturing Export Growth across States: What Accounts for the Differences?" *Federal Reserve Bank of St. Louis Review* 83 (January/February 2001): 25–40.
Introduction to the roles of trade in different U.S. states' economies.

Heckscher, Eli. "The Effect of Foreign Trade on the Distribution of Income." *Ekonomisk Tidskrift* 21 (1919). Reprinted in American Economic Association, *Readings in the Theory of International Trade.* Philadelphia: Blakiston, 1949, Chap. 13.
The original statement of the Heckscher-Ohlin results.

Humphrey, Thomas M. "The Trade Theorist's Sacred Diagram: Its Origin and Early Development." Federal Reserve Bank of Richmond, *Economic Quarterly* 74 (January–February 1988): 3–15.
The history of development of the production possibilities frontier/indifference curve diagram; intermediate.

Jones, Ronald W. "The Structure of Simple General Equilibrium Models." *Journal of Political Economy* 73 (December 1965): 557–572.
For advanced students, the classic mathematical presentation of the basic trade model.

Leamer, Edward, and John Levinsohn. "International Trade Theory: The Evidence." In *Handbook of International Economics,* Vol. 3, edited by G. M. Grossman and K. Rogoff, 1339–1394. Amsterdam: North-Holland, 1995.
Advanced survey of empirical evidence on international trade theories.

Noland, Marcus, et al. "The Economics of Korean Unification." *Journal of Policy Reform* 3 (1999): 255–299.
Empirical estimates of the benefits and costs of unification of North and South Korea.

Noussair, Charles N., et al. "An Experimental Investigation of the Patterns of International Trade." *American Economic Review* 85 (June 1995): 462–491.
Experimental results that suggest trade according to comparative advantage arises in laboratory experiments; advanced.

Ohlin, Bertil. *Interregional and International Trade.* Cambridge, Mass.: Harvard University Press, 1933.
Ohlin's elaboration of Heckscher's earlier work on the factor-proportions model.

Reed, Michael R. *International Trade in Agricultural Products.* Upper Saddle River, N.J.: Prentice-Hall, 2001.
Excellent source of references and applications of introductory trade models to agricultural markets.

Samuelson, Paul A. "The Gains from International Trade." *Canadian Journal of Economics and Political Science* 9 (1939): 195–205.
Early, readable demonstration of how international trade improves potential welfare.

Samuelson, Paul A. "The Gains from International Trade Once Again." *Economic Journal* 72 (1962): 820–829.
Update of the preceding paper.

Saxonhouse, Gary R. "What Does Japanese Trade Structure Tell Us about Trade Policy?" *Journal of Economic Perspectives* 7 (Summer 1993): 21–43.
Surveys empirical tests of how Japan's factor endowment affects the country's trade patterns; accessible to all students.

Trefler, Daniel. "The Case of the Missing Trade and Other Mysteries." *American Economic Review* (December 1995): 1029–1046.
Tests of the Heckscher-Ohlin model find that home bias in consumption and technological differences, along with factor endowments, affect trade patterns; advanced.

CHAPTER THREE APPENDIX A

The Edgeworth Box

One of the inconveniences of attempting to understand the world economy as opposed to a single domestic economy is the need to keep track of so many things at once. Even with our simplifying assumption of only two countries and two industries, the analysis usually requires using at least two graphs simultaneously, such as those in Figure 3.6, representing the situations in country A and country B. Some tasks would be easier if we could combine information about the two countries in a single graph. One convenient tool for accomplishing this is called an *Edgeworth box* (named after, but apparently not invented by, economist and mathematician Francis Edgeworth). Simply put, an Edgeworth box combines two two-axis diagrams (such as those for our two countries or for two industries within a single country) into a single, box-shaped diagram.

We begin by developing an Edgeworth box that combines information about two industries within a single country (the X and Y industries in country A), where each industry uses two inputs: labor (L) and

capital (K). Each industry is characterized by a set of isoquants, as illustrated in Figure 3A.1. The lengths of the axes in Figure 3A.1 are defined by the quantities of labor and capital available in A; it's impossible to use more than L^A units of labor or more than K^A units of capital.

To form an Edgeworth box, we take the Y-industry diagram and rotate it 180 degrees so that the origin lies in its upper right-hand rather than its lower left-hand corner. Next, we move the X-industry and Y-industry diagrams toward each other until the two just touch to form a box, as in Figure 3A.2.

The horizontal dimension of the box measures the total quantity of labor available in A to be allocated between the X and Y industries. The vertical dimension captures the same information about the capital input. Each point in the box, then, represents an allocation of labor and capital between X production and Y production. For example, point I implies that L_{X0}^A units of labor are being used in the X industry and L_{Y0}^A units (read from right to left from the Y origin) in the

(continued)

Figure 3A.1 Isoquant Maps for X and Y in Country *A*

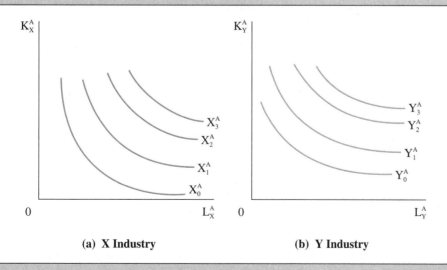

(a) X Industry   **(b) Y Industry**

The country's resource endowment defines the length of each axis. L^A determines the lengths of the horizontal axes, and K^A the lengths of the vertical axes.

Figure 3A.2 **Edgeworth Box for X and Y Production in Country *A***

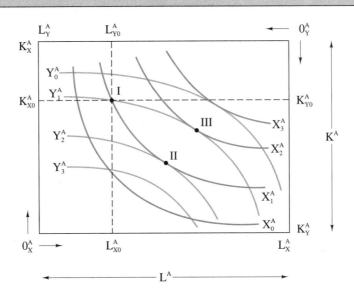

Each point in the box describes an allocation of the total available labor and capital between the X and Y industries. Industry X values are read from left to right and from bottom to top from the 0_X^A origin. Industry Y values are read from right to left and from top to bottom from the 0_Y^A origin.

Y industry. Similarly, point I involves allocating K_{X0}^A units of capital to the X industry and K_{Y0}^A to the Y industry.

Each point in or on the Edgeworth box represents a point inside or on country A's production possibilities frontier. The points lying *on* the production possibilities frontier can be distinguished by the fact that they are tangencies between the X-industry and Y-industry isoquants. This must be true because at any point in Figure 3A.2 that isn't such a tangency, it's possible for country A to produce more of one good without producing less of the other. For example, from point I (a nontangency point), A can produce more good Y without reducing production of X by moving to point II (a tangency point) *or* produce more X without reducing production of Y by moving to point III (another tangency point). Points II and III, therefore, lie on country A's production possibilities frontier, while point I is an interior point, as illustrated in Figure 3A.3.

We can also use the Edgeworth-box technique to consider the gains from specialization and exchange. Let $X^W = X^A + X^B$ represent the total *w*orld quantity of good X produced and $Y^W = Y^A + Y^B$ represent the total world quantity of good Y produced. These two quantities form the dimensions of a second type of Edgeworth box. By allowing more of one good to be produced without producing less of the other, productive specialization according to comparative advantage can increase the size of the box. Using the production possibilities frontiers from Chapter Three, Figure 3A.4 illustrates the increase in the size of the box due to productive specialization. Under autarky, $X^W = X^{A*} + X^{B*}$ and $Y^W = Y^{A*} + Y^{B*}$ from Figure 3.6, while with specialization according to comparative advantage, $X^W = X_p^A + X_p^B > X^{A*} + X^{B*}$ and $Y^W = Y_p^A + Y_p^B > Y^{A*} + Y^{B*}$ from Figure 3.8.

Once productive specialization has increased the quantity of goods available, residents of A exchange with residents of B according to their tastes for the two goods. In Figure 3A.5, tastes are represented by a set of community indifference curves for each country. Beginning at point p (for *p*roduction), trade occurs along a line (whose slope measures the international terms of trade) to a point of tangency between two indifference curves, one for each country. From such a point (denoted c for *c*onsumption), it's impossible to move residents of one country onto a higher indifference curve without moving residents of the other onto a lower curve.

Figure 3A.3 **Country *A*'s Production Possibilities Frontier**

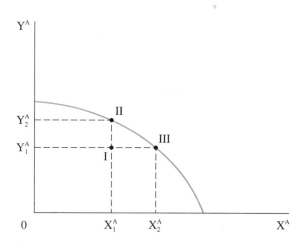

Points I, II, and III correspond to the matching points from Figure 3A.2. All points *on* the production possibilities frontier correspond to points of tangency between an X isoquant and a Y isoquant in the Edgeworth box. All points *inside* the production possibilities frontier correspond to nontangency points in the Edgeworth box, that is, to points from which it is possible to increase production of one good without decreasing production of the other.

Figure 3A.4 **Edgeworth Box for Total World Production of Goods X and Y**

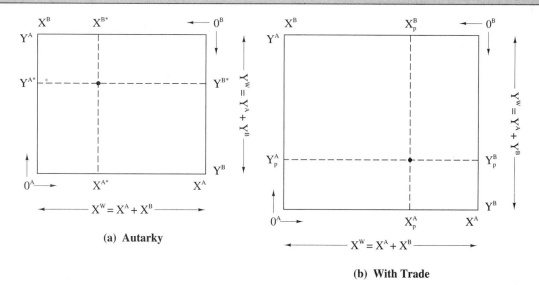

(a) Autarky

(b) With Trade

Production at the autarky production points (A* and B* from Figure 3.6) defines the dimensions of the box in panel (a). The larger dimensions of the box in panel (b) reflect increased production brought about by productive specialization according to comparative advantage (as illustrated in Figure 3.8).

Figure 3A.5 **Edgeworth Box Depiction of Trade between Countries *A* and *B***

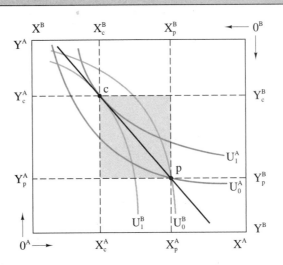

Beginning from the point of productive specialization (p), residents of both countries can make themselves better off through trade, which occurs at the international terms of trade to consumption point c. There it becomes impossible to improve the welfare of residents of one country without reducing the welfare of residents of the other. The two countries' trade triangles compose the shaded rectangle. Its length represents A's exports (and B's imports) of good X, its height represents B's exports (and A's imports) of good Y, and the (absolute) slope of the line that bisects it indicates the equilibrium terms of trade. Points p and c are equivalent to, respectively, points A_p and B_p and points A_c and B_c in Figure 3.8.

CHAPTER THREE APPENDIX B

Offer Curves

Recall from section 3.3.2 that the equilibrium terms of trade between countries A and B must satisfy two conditions: (1) The terms of trade must lie between the two autarky price ratios, or $(P_X/P_Y)^A < (P_X/P_Y)^{tt} < (P_X/P_Y)^B$ if country A has a comparative advantage in production of X, and (2) the amount of a good one country wants to export at the terms of trade must equal the amount of the good the other country wants to import (that is, markets must clear). Finding the equilibrium terms of trade in a production possibilities frontier/indifference curve graph like the one in Figure 3.8 is a matter of artistic trial and error. An alternate graphical technique, known as *offer curves* or *reciprocal demand curves,* has two advantages: Offer curves clearly show the equilibrium terms of trade, while also presenting information about countries A and B in a single graph.

The term *offer curve* refers to the curve's illustration of the "offer" one country would make for trade with another at any given terms of trade—that is, country A's offer curve answers the question, "At each relative price of goods X and Y, what quantities would A want to export and import?" Country B's offer curve presents the same information about the trade offers B would make. The other designation, *reciprocal demand curve,* refers to the curve's emphasis on the relationship between exports and imports; a country exports to receive imports in return, or reciprocally. For each relative price or terms of trade, an offer curve shows how much of its export good a country is willing to give up in exchange for a given amount of its import good. Therefore, an offer curve combines the information in an import demand curve *and* an export supply curve, or in an indifference curve map *and* a production possibilities frontier.

We draw offer curves in a two-dimensional space with the amount of good X traded measured on the horizontal axis and the amount of good Y traded measured on the vertical axis. Note that this differs slightly from most of the graphs we've used so far, which measure the quantities of the two goods produced or consumed on the axes rather than the internationally *traded* quantities.

Figure 3B.1 illustrates the offer curves for countries A and B. The slope of any ray from the origin measures one possible relative price of good X or one possible value for the terms of trade. This is true because the slope of the ray is given by the line's rise (ΔY) divided by the run (ΔX), or how much good Y must be given up to obtain an additional unit of good X through exchange. Steeper rays represent relatively high prices for good X (and relatively low prices for good Y), while flatter rays represent relatively low prices for X (or relatively high prices for Y).

In panel (a) of Figure 3B.1, A's offer curve reflects A's willingness to export larger quantities of good X as the relative price of X rises. The rising relative price of X means that A can obtain more imported Y for each unit of exported X, making exporting more attractive. The curve also reveals A's willingness to import larger quantities of good Y as the relative price of Y falls. The falling price of Y (rising price of X) means Y is less costly in terms of the amount of X that must be exported in exchange. Each point on the curve represents A's desired exports and imports for the terms of trade given by a ray from the origin through that point.

Panel (b) of Figure 3B.1 depicts country B's offer curve. Given the assumption that B has a comparative advantage in good Y, B exports Y and imports X. A steep terms-of-trade line, then, implies that country B's imports of X are expensive in terms of exported Y. As a result, the volume of trade in which B wants to engage is relatively small. Along a flatter terms-of-trade line, the price of B's export good is higher relative to the price of its import good, and B chooses to engage in a larger volume of trade.

Now we can see the convenience of the offer-curve technique for finding the equilibrium terms of trade. Equilibrium occurs at the terms of trade for which A's desired exports of X equal B's desired imports of X, and B's desired exports of Y equal A's desired imports of Y. Obviously, the intersection of the two offer curves meets this condition; thus, $(P_X/P_Y)^{tt*}$ represents the equilibrium at which the markets for goods X and Y clear.

(continued)

Figure 3B.1   **Offer Curves for Countries _A_ and _B_**

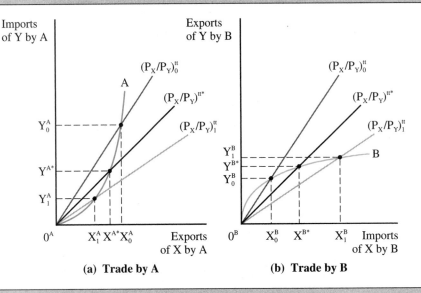

Each country's offer curve illustrates the quantities of the two goods it would want to export and import at different terms of trade, represented by the slopes of rays from the origin.

Figure 3B.2 illustrates the adjustment that brings the terms of trade to equilibrium. If the relative price of good X is too high for market clearing, such as $(P_X/P_Y)_0^{tt}$, A will want to export more X than B will want to import, while B will be willing to export less Y than A will want to import. The excess supply of good X and the excess demand for good Y will cause P_X/P_Y to fall toward equilibrium. On the other hand, if the relative price of good X is too low, such as $(P_X/P_Y)_1^{tt}$, B will want to import more X than A wants to export, and A will want to import less Y than B wants to export. The excess demand for good X and the excess supply of good Y will cause P_X/P_Y to rise.

Finally, note the graphical relationship between the offer-curve diagram and the production possibilities frontier/indifference curve diagram in Figure 3.8. Each point on an offer curve can be thought of as

defining a trade triangle. Recall that the base and height of a trade triangle represent imports and exports of the two goods and that the slope of the third side (hypotenuse) of the triangle measures the terms of trade. In Figure 3B.2, the shaded rectangle depicts the same two trade triangles as in Figure 3.8. The origin in Figure 3B.2 corresponds to the production points, A_p and B_p. The intersection of the two countries' offer curves corresponds to the consumption points, A_c and B_c. The point on the horizontal axis directly below the offer-curve intersection corresponds to point A from Figure 3.8(a), and the point on the vertical axis directly to the left of the offer-curve intersection corresponds to point B from Figure 3.8(b). The slope of the terms-of-trade line, $(P_X/P_Y)^{tt*}$, which bisects the rectangle into the two countries' trade triangles, measures, of course, the equilibrium terms of trade.

Figure 3B.2 **Equilibrium Terms of Trade**

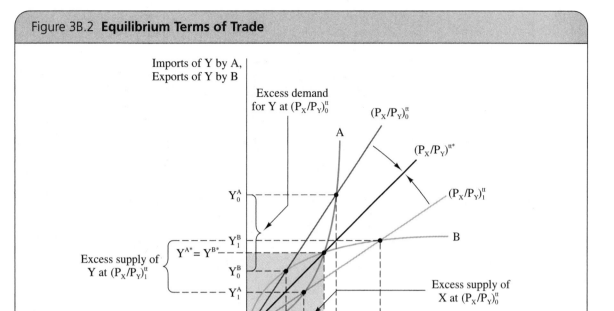

At the equilibrium terms of trade, $(P_X/P_Y)^{tt*}$, the quantity of good X country A wants to export equals the quantity country B wants to import, and the quantity of good Y country B wants to export equals the quantity A wants to import. At any other terms of trade, there is excess supply of one good and excess demand for the other. The shaded rectangle combines the two countries' trade triangles from Figure 3.8.

CHAPTER FOUR

Trade, Distribution, and Welfare

4.1 Introduction

We now come to the heart of the theory of international trade. From the viewpoint of economic *theory*, we'll examine one of the areas in which international trade theory has made major contributions to other aspects of economics: general-equilibrium analysis. From the viewpoint of economic *policy*, we'll explore the primary reason for the controversy that still surrounds the issue of free trade versus protection more than two hundred years after Hume, Smith, and Ricardo.

4.2 Partial- and General-Equilibrium Analysis

General-equilibrium analysis takes into account the interrelationships among various markets in the economy. **Partial-equilibrium analysis,** on the other hand, focuses on events in one or two markets and assumes that other markets remain unaffected. International economists pioneered the use of general-equilibrium analysis, because the issues that arise in an international context often require looking at several markets at once—for example, both foreign and domestic markets or both input and output markets. A typical problem might involve analyzing the effect of unrestricted steel trade on U.S. employment in the automobile industry. Answering such a question requires general-equilibrium techniques.

The general- or partial-equilibrium character of any analysis is a matter of degree, since the two techniques lie on a continuum. At the extreme partial-equilibrium end of the spectrum would be an analysis of the effect of a Florida freeze on U.S. orange prices that ignored the impact on all other markets. At the extreme general-equilibrium end of the spectrum would be a model of the world economy that included every good, every input, and every country and in which "everything depends on everything else." Of course, no such model exists, because it would prove intractable and, therefore, useless. Choosing a point between the extremes of partial- and general-equilibrium analysis is an art—and learning this art is part of becoming an economist. One of the most important skills for any economist to develop is the ability to pick tools and techniques appropriate for the problem at hand. Although partial-equilibrium techniques are important in all areas of economics, including international trade, a true understanding of many international issues requires mastery of some simple techniques of general-equilibrium analysis. In fact, we've already used such techniques to analyze simultaneously events in the X and Y industries in countries A and B.

In Chapters Two and Three, we saw that the mechanism by which unrestricted trade produces a more efficient outcome than does autarky involves the reallocation of production such that relative output prices (which reflect opportunity costs) equalize across countries. This ensures production of each good in the country where its production requires forgoing less in terms of other goods; this is the essence of efficient production. So far, we've treated this change in relative output prices as the end of the story. However, if we move our analysis along the spectrum of techniques toward a more general-equilibrium theory, we must consider that changes in relative output prices will generate changes in other variables, particularly in the rewards or wages paid to factors of production. In other words, *the relative price changes that occur when trade opens alter the distribution of income within each country.* Any policy that alters the distribution of income will generate controversy, because individuals whose positions improve will support the policy, and those who are harmed will oppose it.

4.3 How Do Output Prices Affect Factor Prices? The Stolper-Samuelson Theorem

The changes in relative output prices that accompany the opening of trade follow from changes in the two goods' production levels in each country. Capturing the gains from trade requires productive specialization according to comparative advantage. Production of each good involves using the two inputs in different proportions, so changing the *output* combination alters relative demands for the two *inputs*.[1] This change in relative input demands causes changes in relative input prices and, therefore, in the distribution of income. If production shifts from steel (a capital-intensive good) to textiles (a labor-intensive good), the demand for capital will decrease and the demand for labor will increase. The pattern of factor rewards within the economy will reflect these shifts in demand; the price of capital will fall, and the wage rate will rise.

Under the assumptions of the Heckscher-Ohlin model, opening trade increases production of the good that uses the country's abundant factor intensively, which increases demand for that factor. Similarly, production of the good that uses the scarce factor intensively falls with the opening of trade, decreasing demand for that factor. Remember that each country's endowment of each factor is fixed, so a vertical line represents the supply of each factor. Increased demand for the abundant factor bids up its price, and decreased demand for the scarce factor bids down its price.

As an example, assume country A is labor abundant and good X is the labor-intensive good. According to the Heckscher-Ohlin theorem, under unrestricted trade country A will specialize in producing good X. Production of good X involves intensive use of labor, so the demand for labor in A will increase. Of course, country A will, at the same time, decrease its production of good Y. *(Why?)* The falling production of Y will release some labor previously used in the Y industry; but production of Y is capital intensive, so the amount of labor released will be relatively small.

Panel (a) of Figure 4.1 illustrates these effects of trade on labor demand in country A. In autarky, D_{L0}^A gives the demand for labor. Once trade begins, increased production of good X increases demand to D_{L1}^A, and decreased production of good Y decreases demand to D_{L2}^A. The vertical supply curve, L^A, represents the country's fixed endowment of labor; so trade raises the equilibrium wage from w_0^A to w_2^A.

The effects that occur simultaneously in country A's capital market appear in panel (b) of Figure 4.1. In autarky, the production pattern results in a demand for capital given by D_{K0}^A and an equilibrium rental rate of r_0^A. When trade opens, country A reduces production of good Y, the capital-intensive good, causing demand to shift down to D_{K1}^A. Production of good X increases; but X is labor intensive, so this involves only a small increase in the demand for capital, to D_{K2}^A. The new equilibrium rental rate is r_2^A. Because the wage rate has risen and the rental rate has fallen, the new equilibrium wage-rental ratio, w_2^A/r_2^A, exceeds the ratio that prevailed in autarky, w_0^A/r_0^A. The output price changes that occur when trade opens have redistributed income toward owners of the abundant factor, labor in our example, and away from owners of the scarce factor, capital. These changes in relative factor prices must accompany any change in relative output prices.[2]

In fact, we can make an even stronger statement about the relationship between output prices and factor prices: Each factor price changes in the same direction but *more than proportionally* with the price of the output that uses that factor intensively. For example, if the price of the labor-intensive good rises by 10 percent, the

---

1 For a review, see section 3.2.1, especially Figure 3.4.

2 We'll see in Chapter Ten that, while changes in output prices lead to changes in factor prices, changes in factor quantities (that is, in countries' endowments) do *not* lead to changes in factor prices in the basic trade model. The reason that endowment changes *do not* affect factor prices is the mirror image of the reason that output prices *do*: both lead to changes in the composition of output.

Figure 4.1 How Does Trade Affect the Demand for Inputs in a Labor-Abundant Country?

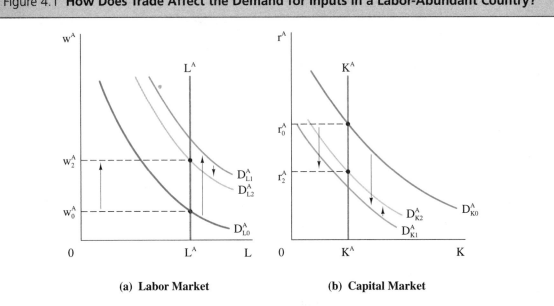

(a) Labor Market   **(b) Capital Market**

As production of the labor-intensive good increases, opening trade generates a net increase in demand for labor. The net effect on demand for capital is negative, because production of the capital-intensive good falls. With fixed factor endowments, the reward paid to the abundant factor (here, labor) rises and that paid to the scarce factor (capital) falls. The wage-rental ratio under unrestricted trade exceeds the ratio under autarky.

wage rate rises by more than 10 percent.[3] If the price of the capital-intensive good remains unchanged when the price of the labor-intensive good rises by 10 percent, the price of capital must fall. To see why, recall that under perfect competition the price of a good must equal its marginal cost, or the change in total cost from producing an additional unit. With two inputs, this requirement can be expressed as $P_X = a_{LX} \cdot w + a_{KX} \cdot r = MC_X$ for good X and $P_Y = a_{LY} \cdot w + a_{KY} \cdot r = MC_Y$ for good Y, because the marginal cost of one unit of output equals the number of additional units of labor used times the wage rate plus the number of additional units of capital used times the rental rate. In other words, the price of a good can be written as a weighted sum of the input prices, where the weights are the input coefficients. The expression for P_Y reveals that if P_Y doesn't change when w rises (due to a rise in P_X), r must fall.[4]

This **magnification effect**—the fact that changes in output prices have a magnified or more-than-proportional effect on factor prices—carries important implications for evaluating the effects of international trade policy. Suppose labor-abundant country A opens trade. The price of labor-intensive good X rises while the price of good Y falls, and the wage rate rises while the rental rate falls. *(Why?)* Now suppose you're a worker in country A. You now earn a higher wage, but you also must pay a higher price for any good X you consume. Are you better off? That is, has your purchasing power or your *real* wage risen? The magnification-effect analysis allows you to answer yes (even if you spend all your income on the now more-expensive good X), because wages have risen proportionally more than the price of good X (that is, $\hat{w}^A > \hat{P}^A_X$, so w^A/P^A_X has risen).

---

3 Similarly, if the price of the labor-intensive good falls by 10 percent, the wage rate falls by more than 10 percent.

4 The result is easy to see if we assume that the input coefficients don't change. Then we can take percentage rates of change of both sides of the price-equals-marginal-cost expressions, which gives $(a_{LX}/MC_X) \cdot \hat{w} + (a_{KX}/MC_X) \cdot \hat{r} = \hat{P}_X$ and $(a_{LY}/MC_Y) \cdot \hat{w} + (a_{KY}/MC_Y) \cdot \hat{r} = \hat{P}_Y$, where "hats" denote percentage rates of change of a variable. If $\hat{w} > \hat{P}_X > \hat{P}_Y = 0$, then $\hat{r}$ must be negative; the marginal cost of Y, which must equal P_Y, can remain unchanged when the wage rate rises only if the price of capital falls. This result continues to hold without the assumption of unchanging input coefficients; for demonstrations using more sophisticated techniques, see the Jones reference at the end of this chapter.

On the other hand, suppose you're a capital owner in country A. The rental rate earned on your capital has fallen, but so has the price you must pay for any good Y you consume. Are you better off or worse off in terms of your purchasing power or *real* return? The magnification effect implies that you are worse off (even if you spend all your income on the now-cheaper good Y), because the rental rate earned on your capital has fallen proportionally more than the price of good Y (that is, $\hat{r}^A < \hat{P}_Y^A$, so r^A/P_Y^A has fallen).

In discussing this link between changes in output prices and changes in factor prices, we've loosely stated one of the basic theorems of international trade theory. This is called the **Stolper-Samuelson theorem** after Wolfgang Stolper and Paul Samuelson, who co-authored the 1941 paper that first demonstrated it. In its most general form the theorem states that, under the assumptions of our model, a change in the price of a *good* changes, in the same direction and more than proportionally, the price of the *factor* used intensively in the good's production.[5] When we add the assumptions of the Heckscher-Ohlin model (which imply that a country has a comparative advantage in the good that uses the abundant factor intensively), the Stolper-Samuelson theorem means that opening trade raises the real reward to the abundant factor and lowers the real reward to the scarce factor. This follows because trade boosts production of the good of comparative advantage, increasing that good's opportunity cost and relative price. The Heckscher-Ohlin model defines comparative advantage in terms of intensive use of the abundant factor, so trade raises the price of the good that uses the abundant factor intensively, thereby raising the abundant factor's real price. Table 4.1 summarizes trade's effects on production, output prices, and factor prices, assuming country A is labor abundant and good X is labor intensive.

The Stolper-Samuelson theorem clarifies one reason for the controversial nature of trade policy. Opening trade leads to output price changes that alter real factor rewards, creating incentives for owners of the abundant input to support opening trade and for owners of the scarce input to resist it. It is important to remember that the country *as a whole* is made potentially better off by trade; that is, the winners from trade (owners of the abundant factor) gain enough from trade to allow them to compensate the losers (owners of the scarce factor) and still be better off. However, such compensation, although theoretically possible, rarely occurs. Therefore, the Stolper-Samuelson theorem clearly pinpoints the existence of at least one constituency for protectionist policies or restrictions on trade: owners of the country's scarce factor. Later, when we discuss various types of protectionist measures and their effects, we'll also examine some policies that aim to eliminate this natural constituency for protection by redistributing the gains from trade to compensate the losers.

The Stolper-Samuelson theorem highlights the relationship between *output prices* and *factor prices* within a single country. The next result to emerge from the basic trade model deals with the relationship between relative factor prices across countries.

Table 4.1 **The Stolper-Samuelson Theorem Says That Opening Trade Changes Output Prices *and* Real Factor Prices**

	Effect of Opening Trade
Labor-Abundant Country A:	
Production	X⇑, Y⇓
Output prices	P_X⇑, P_Y⇓
Factor prices	w⇑⇑, r⇓⇓[a]
Capital-Abundant Country B:	
Production	X⇓, Y⇑
Output prices	P_X⇓, P_Y⇑
Factor prices	w⇓⇓, r⇑⇑

[a]Double arrows denote the magnification effect, or changes in *real* factor prices.

---

5 A slightly different statement of the same result: An increase in the relative price of a good increases the *real* return to the factor used intensively in that good's production and decreases the *real* return to the other factor. Statement of the result in real terms captures the magnification effect, or the fact that factor prices change proportionally more than output prices.

4.4 How Do Factor Prices Vary across Countries? The Factor Price Equalization Theorem

It's easy to see that trade tends to equalize across countries the price of each good traded. Countries' different autarky output prices converge to the international terms of trade. But what about *factor* prices in various countries? If factors of production moved freely across national borders, we'd expect the price of each factor to equalize across countries. Labor would flow from countries with low wages to those with high wages, thereby raising wages in the low-wage countries and lowering wages in the high-wage ones until $w^A = w^B$. Similarly, capital would flow from countries where it received a low reward to those where it received a high reward until $r^A = r^B$. But recall that we're assuming factors of production are *not* mobile among countries.[6] In Chapter One, we argued that restricted mobility of factors among countries constitutes one aspect of the economic significance of political boundaries.[7] While factors aren't actually completely immobile, it is true that factors are much less mobile among countries than within them. Some barriers, such as language or cultural ones, are "natural"; and policy makers impose other artificial barriers, including immigration restrictions and capital controls. Factor immobility implies that there's no obvious mechanism by which unrestricted trade in *outputs* can equalize *factor* prices across countries; but one important role for models is to allow us to see things that aren't obvious.

When trade begins, a country increases its output of the good in which it possesses a comparative advantage. According to Heckscher and Ohlin, production of this good involves intensive use of the country's abundant factor. Thus, according to the Stolper-Samuelson theorem, moving from autarky to unrestricted trade raises the real reward of the abundant factor (which was relatively low in autarky because of the factor's abundance); similarly, such a move lowers the real reward of the scarce factor (which was high without trade because of scarcity). The same adjustment process occurs in the second country, but with the roles of the two factors reversed. *(Could the same factor be abundant in both countries? Why or why not?)* So trade raises the real reward of a factor in the country where that factor is abundant and lowers its real reward in the country where it's scarce. Therefore, *even when factors are immobile between countries, unrestricted trade in goods equalizes the price of each factor across countries.* With free trade in goods and no international factor mobility, $w^A = w^B$ and $r^A = r^B$.[8] This is the logic behind the **factor price equalization theorem,** which Paul Samuelson first demonstrated in 1948. Table 4.2 summarizes the theorem's implications, assuming that country A is labor-abundant and good X is labor-intensive.

The preceding discussion focused on the economy-wide adjustment that results in equalization across countries of each factor's price. We also can view the process of factor price equalization from the viewpoint of how a firm adjusts to trade.

As the world economy moves from autarky to unrestricted trade in outputs, each country increases production of the good that uses the country's abundant factor intensively. Suppose for a moment that firms in each country tried to continue to use capital and labor in the same proportions as they'd been used in autarky (that is, that the input coefficients didn't change). The different output combination produced under trade then would imply more total use of the abundant factor and less total use of the scarce factor in each country. But total usage of each factor in each country (adding the usages by the two industries, X and Y) must equal the fixed endowment of the input. In other words, it must be true, both in autarky and with trade, that

$$L^A = L_X^A + L_Y^A = a_{LX} \cdot X^A + a_{LY} \cdot Y^A,$$
$$K^A = K_X^A + K_Y^A = a_{KX} \cdot X^A + a_{KY} \cdot Y^A,$$
$$L^B = L_X^B + L_Y^B = b_{LX} \cdot X^B + b_{LY} \cdot Y^B,$$
$$K^B = K_X^B + K_Y^B = b_{KX} \cdot X^B + b_{KY} \cdot Y^B.$$

[4.1]

Therefore, a country can't produce a *different* combination of the two outputs while continuing to use the *same* production techniques (that is, capital-labor ratios or input coefficients) as before.[9]

---

6 We'll relax this assumption in Chapter Ten.

7 The degree of factor mobility is an important distinction between interregional and international trade, as discussed in section 9.5.1.

8 Avoid making the common mistake of thinking that factor price equalization implies w = r; it does not.

9 This result can be demonstrated more rigorously by algebraic manipulation of Equation 4.1; see the Jones reference.

Table 4.2 **The Factor Price Equalization Theorem Says That Free Trade in Outputs Equalizes Each *Factor's* Price across Countries**

	Autarky	Effect of Trade	Free Trade
Labor-Abundant Country A:			
Output prices	$(P_X/P_Y)^A < (P_X/P_Y)^B$	$(P_X/P_Y)^A \Uparrow$	$(P_X/P_Y)^{tt}$
Wage	$w^A < w^B$	$w^A \Uparrow \Uparrow$[a]	$w^A = w^B$
Rental rate	$r^A > r^B$	$r^A \Downarrow \Downarrow$	$r^A = r^B$
Capital-Abundant Country B:			
Output prices	$(P_X/P_Y)^B > (P_X/P_Y)^A$	$(P_X/P_Y)^B \Downarrow$	$(P_X/P_Y)^{tt}$
Wage	$w^B > w^A$	$w^B \Downarrow \Downarrow$	$w^B = w^A$
Rental rate	$r^B < r^A$	$r^B \Uparrow \Uparrow$	$r^B = r^A$

[a]Double arrows denote the magnification effect, or changes in *real* factor prices.

Consider the case in which labor-abundant country A opens trade and wants to specialize in producing labor-intensive good X. To increase production of X, country A must decrease production of good Y. This releases a package of inputs composed of capital and labor in the proportion currently used in the Y industry. This package of inputs includes a relatively large amount of capital and a small amount of labor, because Y is the capital-intensive good. The package of resources needed to produce an additional unit of good X using current production techniques includes a relatively large quantity of labor and a small amount of capital. This scenario implies that opening trade causes an excess supply of capital—as firms in the Y industry release more capital than X firms want to hire. There also is an excess demand for labor—as shrinking Y firms release less labor than growing X firms want to hire.

Something must happen to cause the firms to adjust their production techniques. What occurs is a change in the relative prices of the two factors. Capital becomes relatively cheaper, causing Y firms to release less of it and X firms to hire more of it. Labor becomes relatively more expensive, causing Y firms to release more of it and X firms to hire less.

The isoquant diagram of Figure 4.2 illustrates how firms' cost-minimizing production techniques change. Recall that firms in each industry choose their capital-labor ratios by equating the marginal rate of technical substitution (the absolute value of the slope of the isoquant) to the ratio of the factor prices (the absolute value of the slope of the isocost line).[10] We can represent a rise in w/r from $(w/r)_0$ to $(w/r)_1$ as a clockwise rotation of the isocost line, or an increase in (the absolute value of) its slope. Firms respond by using a *higher* capital-labor ratio, $(K/L)_{X1}$ rather than $(K/L)_{X0}$. This adjustment occurs in both industries.

Why would the labor-abundant country need to use a higher capital-labor ratio in production of both goods? When the country engages in trade, it specializes its production according to comparative advantage. This means specializing in production of the good that uses the abundant factor intensively—but the country has available only a fixed quantity of that factor. To produce more of the good that uses the abundant factor intensively, production of each unit of both goods must use less of that factor than before so there will be enough of it to go around. The factor price changes predicted by the factor price equalization theorem provide firms an incentive to undertake the necessary changes in production techniques. Profit-maximizing firms will choose to use more of the scarce factor as it becomes relatively cheaper and less of the abundant factor as it becomes relatively more expensive. This "economizing" on use of the abundant factor allows the country to specialize in producing the comparative-advantage good, which uses the abundant factor intensively.

4.4.1 **An Alternate View of Factor Price Equalization**

Economists initially found the factor price equalization theorem—that is, that trade in outputs could equalize each factor's price across countries even when factors were completely immobile internationally—a very

---

10 For a review, see section 3.2.1.

Figure 4.2 **Changes in Factor Prices Cause Firms to Change Their Capital-Labor Ratios**

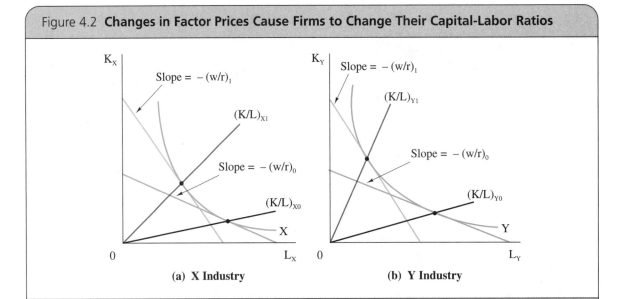

(a) X Industry   **(b) Y Industry**

For the country to increase production of the labor-intensive good (X), firms in both industries must increase their capital-labor ratios. The rise in the wage-rental ratio from $(w/r)_0$ to $(w/r)_1$ brings about this adjustment. Firms choose to use less labor and more capital as labor becomes more expensive relative to capital.

surprising result. Robert Mundell provided an intuitive and insightful explanation. According to Mundell, trade in outputs serves as a "substitute" for trade in factors of production.

For example, when a labor-abundant country exports a unit of a labor-intensive good, it indirectly exports labor to a labor-scarce country. Similarly, when a labor-abundant country imports a capital-intensive good, it indirectly imports capital services from a capital-abundant country. Mundell went even further by "turning the model on its head" and showing that if factors of production were freely traded and outputs immobile among countries, rather than vice versa, trade in inputs would equalize output prices. Unrestricted trade in either output or input markets can serve as a substitute for trade in the other markets. It's easy to find examples of policy makers responding to this linkage between trade policy and immigration policy. NAFTA's improved access for Mexican goods to the U.S. market, for example, reduced pressure for Mexican workers to immigrate illegally to the United States; instead, they can work in Mexico and benefit from U.S. sales of the goods they produce.[11] Similarly, supporters of enlargement of the European Union to include the countries of Central and Eastern Europe hope that better access for those countries' goods in Western European markets will reduce incentives for workers to migrate west.

4.4.2 Why Don't We Observe Full Factor Price Equalization?

We never observe full factor price equalization; it's important to understand why.[12] Figure 4.3 reports one measure of hourly compensation for production workers in manufacturing for 25 countries. Compensation differs by a factor of more than 12; that is, those in the highest-wage country (Germany) are more than 12 times as high as those in the lowest-wage country (Mexico), where wages are still far above those in the lowest-wage countries in the world. Given these data, a reasonable question about the factor price equalization theorem would be: Why are factor prices not equalized? There are several reasons why full factor price equalization isn't observed.

11 "A New Future for Mexico's Work Force," *The Wall Street Journal,* April 14, 2000.

12 The Leamer and Levinsohn and the Rassekh and Thompson articles in the chapter references survey the empirical literature on factor price equalization.

Figure 4.3 **Hourly Compensation Costs for Manufacturing Production Workers, 1999 (U.S. = 100)**

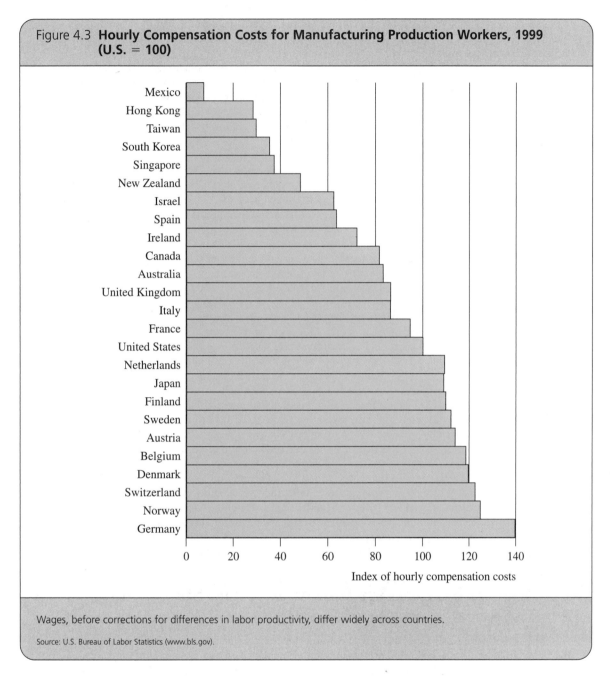

Index of hourly compensation costs

Wages, before corrections for differences in labor productivity, differ widely across countries.

Source: U.S. Bureau of Labor Statistics (www.bls.gov).

First, much of the apparent inequality of income and wealth across countries comes from uneven ownership of human and nonhuman capital. Our basic trade model assumes all labor is homogeneous. However, labor actually differs substantially across countries in terms of human capital—skill, training, education, nutrition, and a variety of other attributes. Wage differences reflect these variations; we wouldn't expect a nuclear physicist with 20 years' experience in Germany to earn the same wage as an unskilled laborer entering the workforce for the first time in Mexico. Also, most individuals in developed countries earn part of their incomes from ownership of capital in addition to what they earn by selling their labor services.

Second, we've assumed that each good is produced using the same production technology in all countries. When someone develops a new and better technology, it tends to spread and replace older, less effective technologies; but the process can be slow, particularly between developed and developing countries. When two countries produce a good using different technologies, the rewards paid to the factors of production won't equalize across countries, even in the presence of trade, although the rewards will tend to move closer together than without trade.

Both differences in ownership of human capital and differences in technology cause factor productivity to vary across countries. Under such circumstances, we wouldn't expect actual factor prices to equalize, but rather factor prices *corrected for productivity differences* to equalize. For example, we would expect countries with labor productivity higher than that of the United States to exhibit wages higher than those in the United States and vice versa. Figure 4.4 presents some evidence on this relationship. The horizontal axis in panel (a) measures each country's labor productivity relative to that in the United States, and the vertical axis measures the country's wage rate compared to that in the United States. The data points for 30 countries, a diverse sample of developed and developing countries, cluster around a 45-degree line, just as we would expect. Panel (b) presents the corresponding information for capital. These data indicate that factor prices, once corrected for productivity differences, do tend toward equality across countries.

Recall that we've argued that countries generally will specialize their production only partially under conditions of increasing costs; in other words, both countries will continue to produce some of both goods. It turns out that factor prices equalize in the basic trade model only when this is true, not when countries specialize completely. So, if countries' factor endowments are so very different that countries specialize completely in their good of comparative advantage, factor price equalization won't occur.

Also, remember that factor price equalization follows from output price equalization. But complete output price equalization doesn't always occur, for reasons including transportation costs, policy barriers to trade, and the existence of goods (for example, haircuts or health care) not easily traded.

Despite these problems, the factor price equalization theorem is useful in understanding trade liberalization's effects. From a theoretical point of view, the theorem highlights the general-equilibrium character of our basic trade model and the importance of a rigorous formulation to derive all its implications. From a policy point of view, the theorem points out that trade in outputs and trade in inputs can be substitutes in terms of their effects on the world economy. Consider the case of an extremely labor-abundant country. In autarky, wages would tend to be very low. Policy makers might be tempted to prescribe policies such as forced emigration to reduce the quantity of labor and raise wages; but the costs of mobility for some factors of production, especially labor, can be very high in both economic and psychological terms. The factor price equalization theorem suggests an important policy alternative: Allow free trade in outputs, specialize in labor-intensive production, and export labor indirectly in the form of labor-intensive goods.[13]

Countries including Ireland, the Philippines, India, Jamaica, and Singapore have begun using new technologies to do just that. With new international computer and telecommunication networks, labor-abundant countries such as those mentioned can perform labor-intensive data-processing tasks for foreign firms. Entering data into computers for new databases, creating telephone directories, maintaining computer files for magazine subscriptions, processing computer records for health insurance companies, and large-scale telephone operations are just a few of the jobs, not all of which are low-skill occupations.

4.5 What If Factors Are Immobile in the Short Run? The Specific-Factors Model[14]

The Stolper-Samuelson and factor price equalization theorems summarize the effects of opening trade on real factor prices under the assumption that factors are completely mobile among industries within a country and completely immobile among countries. In the short run, however, the mobility of factors among

---

13 For our purposes, understanding the mechanism that pushes toward factor price equalization—changes in output mix—is, in fact, much more important than the empirical question of whether factor prices fully equalize. Some elements of recent disagreements between labor economists and trade economists over measuring trade's effect on wages of skilled and unskilled workers hinge on this issue. Work by labor economists tends to ignore changes in the product mix, while work by trade economists recognizes those changes as the channel by which trade affects factor prices. See Case Two.

14 Paul Samuelson, "Ohlin Was Right," *Swedish Journal of Economics* 73 (1971), pp. 365–384, and Ronald W. Jones, "A Three-Factor Model in Theory, Trade, and History," in *Trade, Balance of Payments, and Growth,* eds., Jagdish Bhagwati et al. (Amsterdam: North-Holland, 1971), pp. 3–21, developed the specific-factors model.

Figure 4.4 **Factor Prices Reflect Productivity**

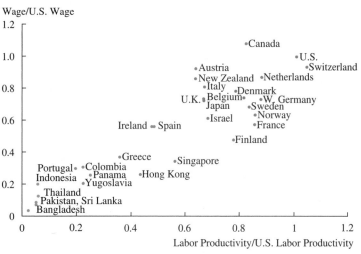

(a) Labor Productivity and Wages

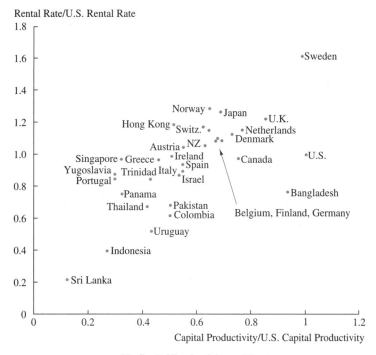

(b) Capital Productivity and Rents

Relative factor price differences across countries match relative productivity differences. Countries with high (low) labor productivity relative to that of the United States tend to have high (low) wages relative to the United States. Countries with high (low) capital productivity relative to that of the United States tend to have high (low) rental rates relative to the United States.

Source: Data from Daniel Trefler, "International Factor Price Differences: Leontief Was Right!" *Journal of Political Economy* 101 (1993), p. 972.

industries may be imperfect. When factors can't move easily and quickly among industries, the short-run effects of opening trade differ from the long-run effects captured by the Stolper-Samuelson and factor price equalization theorems.

4.5.1 Reasons for Short-Run Factor Immobility

Mobility of factors among industries may be less than perfect for several reasons. In the case of physical capital, such as machines and factories, the causes of limited mobility are clear. A machine designed to manufacture shoes can't suddenly manufacture computers. At any moment, a significant share of a country's capital stock takes the form of specialized equipment—equipment suited only for the specific purpose for which it was designed.

How, then, does a country's capital stock change over time to reflect the rising and falling fortunes of various industries? As machines, buildings, and other types of physical capital wear out from use and age, firms set aside funds to replace the equipment when the time comes. These funds are called **depreciation allowances** and comprise a form of saving by firms. Just as an individual might save to have funds to buy a new car when the old one wears out, a firm saves to accumulate funds for replacement of worn-out capital equipment. Although a particular piece of capital equipment often can't be switched to use in a different production process, depreciation funds can be used to buy a different type of capital. In other words, as the economy's capital equipment wears out and is replaced, firms can change the character of the capital stock in response to changes in relative demands for and supplies of various goods. If firms want to produce fewer shoes, some of the machines used in shoe production won't be replaced when they wear out. On the other hand, if firms want to produce more computers, they will not only replace machines worn out in computer production but will invest in additional computer-producing equipment as well.

The preceding arguments for the capital stock also apply, with appropriate modifications, to the country's workforce. Individuals learn certain skills suited for use in specific occupations. Some general skills, of course, apply in a wide range of industries; oral and written communication skills, good interpersonal skills, and desirable work habits such as punctuality prove useful in almost any job. Other skills are more specific. A welder can't become a mathematics professor overnight in response to a decline in the construction industry and a boom in education. Similarly, a mathematics professor can't suddenly become a welder in response to the opposite trend. Individuals can learn new skills, but the process takes time. As older workers retire and new ones enter the labor force, the skill distribution across the labor force slowly changes in favor of growing industries and away from shrinking ones. This captures the labor-force version of the depreciation of the capital stock.

In the long run, the process of depreciation, retraining, and replacement allows both capital and labor to flow from declining industries to rising ones; but such mobility may be limited in the short run. The more specialized the capital equipment and skills and the slower the rate of depreciation in a given industry, the more slowly that industry will adjust to change—including change generated by international trade.

4.5.2 Effects of Short-Run Factor Immobility

Suppose country A uses labor and capital to produce *s*hoes (s) and *c*omputers (c). Labor is perfectly mobile between the shoe and computer industries, but capital is industry specific. Shoe capital (SK) can't produce computers, and computer capital (CK) can't produce shoes. As a result, the wage paid to labor will be equal in the two industries, but the rental rates paid to the two types of capital may differ. *(Why?)*

Figure 4.5 illustrates equilibrium in country A's factor markets. In panel (a), the length of the horizontal axis $(0_s 0_c)$ measures the total quantity of labor available in country A, or L^A. The two vertical axes measure the wage paid to labor in the two industries (w_s on the left axis and w_c on the right). We measure labor used in the shoe industry from left to right from the shoe origin (0_s), and labor used in the computer industry from right to left from the computer origin (0_c). Any point along the horizontal axis represents an allocation of the available labor between the two industries.

The curves VMP_{s0}^L and VMP_{c0}^L represent the *v*alue *m*arginal *p*roduct of *l*abor in the two industries, respectively. The value marginal product of labor equals the increase in revenue to a firm that hires an additional unit of labor, or the marginal product of labor (the number of units of additional output produced when one additional unit of labor is employed) multiplied by the price of the good produced, $VMP^L \equiv MP^L \cdot P$. As the quantity of labor employed in an industry rises, the marginal productivity of labor falls, and with it the value

Figure 4.5 **Effect on Factor Markets of an Increase in an Output Price with a Specific Factor**

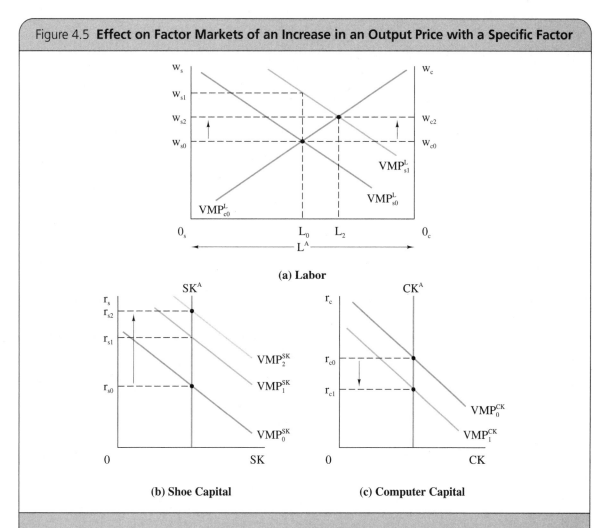

(a) Labor

(b) Shoe Capital

(c) Computer Capital

An increase in the price of shoes raises the wage rate in both industries, but by proportionally less than the rise in the price of shoes. The return to capital specific to the shoe industry rises more than proportionally with the price of shoes, and the return to capital specific to the computer industry falls.

marginal product of labor; therefore, the VMP curves slope downward when viewed from their respective axes.[15] Because we assume the labor market to be perfectly competitive, labor earns a wage in each industry equal to the value of the productivity of the marginal unit of labor in that industry.[16] In the figure, $0_s L_0$ workers work in the shoe industry and $0_c L_0$ workers in the computer industry, equalizing wages at $w_{s0} = w_{c0}$. *(Explain why mobility of labor between industries ensures this division of labor between the industries. What would happen if $w_s > w_c$ or vice versa?)*

---

15 The marginal product of labor eventually falls as the firm uses more labor, because the marginal product of a factor is defined as the change in output resulting from a one-unit change in use of that factor *with the quantities of all other factors held constant.* As more labor is combined with a fixed amount of capital, additional workers eventually become less productive *(think of a simple example);* hence, the marginal product of labor declines.

16 Competitive profit-maximizing firms will hire labor until the additional revenue from hiring an additional worker (VMP^L) is equal to the additional cost incurred by hiring an additional worker (w).

Panels (b) and (c) of Figure 4.5 illustrate equilibrium in the markets for shoe capital and for computer capital. Country A's endowments of these two inputs are fixed at SK^A and CK^A, respectively, so the supply curve of each is just a vertical line. The demand for each type of capital reflects the value of its marginal product, or the additional revenue to a firm hiring an additional unit of the capital. Because the marginal product of each type of capital falls as more is used, the VMP curves slope downward. Each type of capital earns the rental rate at which the quantity available equals the quantity firms want to hire; so the equilibrium rental rates are r_{s0} and r_{c0}.

What happens if the price of shoes (P_s) rises? The value marginal product of labor in the shoe industry rises proportionally with P_s, since $VMP_s^L \equiv MP_s^L \cdot P_s$. The VMP_s^L curve in panel (a) shifts upward. At the initial allocation of labor between the two industries (the vertical line, L_0), $w_{s1} > w_{c0}$. Workers move from the computer industry to the shoe industry until wages again equalize at $w_{s2} = w_{c2}$, with L_2 representing the new allocation of labor between industries.

Notice that wages rise *less* than proportionally with the price of shoes (reflected in Figure 4.5 by the fact that $w_{s2} < w_{s1}$); the magnification effect does *not* apply to the mobile factor when one of the factors is immobile between industries. The rise in the price of shoes exerts an ambiguous effect on workers' real wages or purchasing power. Wages rise, but by less than the rise in the price of shoes. If a worker spent most of his or her income on shoes, the worker's purchasing power would fall because w/P^s falls; but a worker who spent most of his or her income on computers (whose price hasn't changed) would enjoy an increase in purchasing power because w/P_c rises.

Even though capital can't move between industries, the change in the price of shoes still affects capital markets. The marginal product of any factor of production depends positively on the quantity of other factors with which the factor works. As labor moves into the shoe industry, shoe capital has more labor to work with and the marginal product of shoe capital rises, shifting the $VMP^{SK} \equiv MP^{SK} \cdot P_s$ line up to VMP_1^{SK}. The exodus of labor from the computer industry, on the other hand, reduces the marginal product of computer capital and shifts $VMP^{CK} \equiv MP^{CK} \cdot P_c$ down to VMP_1^{CK}. The rise in the price of shoes also causes a proportional shift up in $VMP^{SK} \equiv MP^{SK} \cdot P_s$ to VMP_2^{SK}. The net result is that the rental rate earned by shoe capital *rises more than proportionally* with the price of shoes, while the rental rate earned by computer capital *falls*. The rise in the price of shoes improves the purchasing power of owners of shoe capital, even if they spend most of their incomes on now more-expensive shoes (because r_s/P_s rises), and reduces the purchasing power of owners of computer capital, even if they spend most of their incomes on computers, whose price has not changed. Therefore, the magnification effect *does* hold for the immobile factor. Table 4.3 summarizes these results.

Table 4.3 **Effect of a Rise in the Price of Shoes on Factor Prices When Capital Is Immobile**	
Effect on	
w	$\Uparrow$
Purchasing power of w	?[a] ($w/P_s\Downarrow$, $w/P_c\Uparrow$)
r_s	$\Uparrow$
Purchasing power of r_s	$\Uparrow$[b] ($r_s/P_s\Uparrow$, $r_s/P_c\Uparrow$)
r_c	$\Downarrow$
Purchasing power of r_c	$\Downarrow$[b] ($r_c/P_s\Downarrow$, $r_c/P_c\Downarrow$)

The wage rate rises in both industries, but by less than the increase in the price of shoes. The effect on workers' purchasing power (that is, the *real* wage) depends on the shares of shoes and computers in workers' consumption. The return to shoe capital rises more than the price of shoes, so owners of shoe capital enjoy an increase in buying power regardless of their pattern of consumption. The return to computer capital falls, so owners of computer capital suffer a loss of purchasing power regardless of their pattern of consumption.

[a] No magnification effect.
[b] Magnification effect.

4.5.3 Trade with an Industry-Specific Factor

Short-run immobility of factors among industries implies that the short-run effects of opening trade on the distribution of income differ from the predictions of the Stolper-Samuelson theorem, which applies only when both factors can move between industries. To highlight the importance of the degree of factor mobility in determining the effects on income, we'll continue to consider the case in which labor is highly mobile among industries but capital is immobile in the short run. Suppose a country with a comparative advantage in labor-intensive shoe production and a comparative disadvantage in capital-intensive computer production opens trade. Shoe production rises and computer production falls as the country specializes its production according to comparative advantage.

If both labor and capital were mobile between the two industries, newly unemployed workers from the computer industry would flow into the shoe industry, and the shoe industry would buy unused capital from the computer industry. Given our assumption of mobile labor and immobile capital, workers do flow from the computer to the shoe industry; but the machines formerly used in producing computers are useless in making shoes.

What happens to wages and to the rates of return earned by capital? First, note that the price of shoes rises and the price of computers falls as the production pattern shifts. The price of computers falls because more efficiently produced imports replace relatively inefficient and costly domestic production. The price of shoes rises with the level of production, a reflection of increasing costs. The net effect on wages depends on the magnitudes of the fall in P_c and the rise in P_s. *(How could you illustrate this in Figure 4.5(a)? What would happen to VMP^L_s and VMP^L_c?)* Regardless of whether wages rise or fall, the effect on workers' purchasing power depends on the combination of goods they consume, because w/P_s falls and w/P_c rises. If a worker spends a large share of income on computers (whose price has fallen) and a small share on shoes (whose price has risen), that individual definitely will enjoy an increase in purchasing power, or ability to buy goods. Another worker will be worse off if he or she buys no computers but does buy new shoes, because the price of shoes rises by a greater proportion than do wages. *(Why?)*[17]

The effect on the return to capital is clearer. Owners of capital designed to produce computers are definitely worse off, since the rate of return to computer-specific capital falls and does so by more than the price of computers. Owners of capital designed to produce shoes definitely are better off, because the return to shoe-specific capital rises and by more the price of shoes. In the short run, therefore, the mobile factor's *consumption pattern* and the *industry* that employs the immobile factor determine trade's effect on each factor's real reward. Only in the long run, when all factors can move between industries, does a factor's *relative scarcity or abundance* determine the impact of opening trade.

Table 4.4 illustrates the distinction between trade's short-run and long-run effects on factor prices in terms of our shoe-computer example. In the short run, the returns to capital employed in the expanding shoe industry rise. This creates an incentive for investment in capital designed for shoe production. The other side of the adjustment process is a fall in the returns to capital specifically employed in the computer industry, creating incentives not to replace that capital as it wears out. Again, wages may rise or fall, but the effect on workers' purchasing power will depend on whether workers buy primarily (now cheaper) computers or (now more-expensive) shoes.

In the long run, both workers and capital can move between industries. Wages rise throughout the economy, because the expanding shoe industry is more labor intensive than the contracting computer industry. The return to all capital falls as the economy cuts production of the capital-intensive good, computers. These long-run results coincide with the predictions of the Stolper-Samuelson theorem.

The existence of factors specific to single industries creates a short-run rigidity, or limitation on the economy's ability to reallocate production among industries quickly and at low cost. The more industry-specific the factors of production, the more costly will be any adjustment to relative price changes in terms of temporary unemployment or underutilization of capital. These short-term costs of adjustment can cause policy problems as individuals attempt to insulate themselves from the effects of unfavorable price changes.

---

17 When capital is immobile, an increase in the price of a good causes wages to rise less-than-proportionally with the good's price, as demonstrated for shoes in section 4.5.2. Here the addition of a decline in the price of the second good (computers) causes wages to rise even less. If the decline in the price of computers more than offsets the rise in the price of shoes, wages may fall; but the effect on labor's purchasing power will remain ambiguous, because wages can neither rise proportionally more than P_s nor fall proportionally more than P_c.

	Effect of Trade in	
	Short Run	**Long Run**
w_s	?	⇑
Purchasing power of w_s	?[a]	⇑[b]
w_c	?	⇑
Purchasing power of w_c	?[a]	⇑[b]
r_s	⇑	⇓
Purchasing power of r_s	⇑[b]	⇓[b]
r_c	⇓	⇓
Purchasing power of r_c	⇓[b]	⇓[b]

Table 4.4 **Short- and Long-Run Effects of Trade on Factor Prices and Purchasing Power**

The country has a comparative advantage in production of shoes. In the short run, owners of capital employed in the shoe industry and workers who buy more computers than shoes gain from the opening of trade. And, owners of capital employed in the computer industry and workers who buy more shoes than computers lose. In the long run, workers, the factor used intensively in shoe production, gain from the opening of trade; owners of capital, the factor used intensively in computer production, lose.

[a]No magnification effect.
[b]Magnification effect.

Whenever relative prices change and some industries decline, political pressure for protection builds from resources tied to those industries. However, interference with relative price changes and the resulting factor price changes can be dangerous to the health of the economy as a whole. As we noted in the shoe-computer example, the temporary fall in the rewards to capital in the computer industry and rise in the rewards to capital in the shoe industry create the incentives needed for the economy to adjust to trade by specializing according to comparative advantage. Trade, in turn, improves potential welfare by increasing the total quantity of goods and services available for consumption.

4.6 Trade and Welfare: Gainers, Losers, and Compensation

The Stolper-Samuelson theorem and the specific-factors model explain why various groups in the economy may feel quite differently about trade. Under the assumptions of the Heckscher-Ohlin theorem, a country indirectly "exports" its abundant factor through trade, thereby increasing demand for that factor and raising its real reward. Likewise, the country indirectly "imports" its scarce factor, decreasing demand and lowering the factor's real reward. In the short run, when some factors are industry specific, (1) the real rewards of factors specific to the comparative-advantage industry rise, (2) the real rewards to factors specific to the comparative-disadvantage industry fall, and (3) the real reward to the mobile factor rises (falls) if its owner purchases mainly the comparative-disadvantage (advantage) good. In the long run, the real reward of the abundant factor rises and that of the scarce factor falls. But in Chapter Three we demonstrated that opening trade increases the *total* quantity of goods available and makes it possible for *everyone* to gain. In order for everyone to gain—despite the changes in factor rewards implied by the Stolper-Samuelson theorem and the specific-factors model—a portion of the gains enjoyed by some would have to be used to compensate others for their losses. If this were done, every person, and therefore society as a whole, could be made better off by trade. In general, however, no automatic mechanism exists to make this compensatory redistribution.

These questions of income distribution and the differential impacts of trade on various groups within a country didn't arise in the Ricardian or constant-cost model of Chapter Two. The reason is that the Ricardian model contained only one input, which we called *labor*. In each country, opening trade raised the relative price of the output that the country's labor produced relatively efficiently. Wages rose, and everyone was made better off (see Table 2.3). In reality, however, things aren't so simple.[18] Policy makers usually must deal with questions involving policies that help some groups and harm others.

4.6.1 Potential versus Actual Utility

In Chapters Two and Three, we demonstrated that unrestricted international trade increases the quantity of goods that the world's endowment of scarce resources can produce. With more goods available for consumption, we can see a potential increase in world welfare or utility. Figure 4.6 illustrates this potential increase.[19]

Why must we speak of an increase in *potential* world welfare or utility? We can't say that a move from point 1 (representing autarky) to point 2 (representing unrestricted trade) in Figure 4.6 necessarily increases *actual* utility. After all, we know nothing about the distribution of goods at either point. At point 1, society produces X_1 units of good X and Y_1 units of good Y. One individual may have all the X and all the Y while everyone else has nothing, or the X and Y may be evenly distributed among all individuals. The same holds true at point 2: There are X_2 units of X and Y_2 units of Y available, but we don't know how these goods are distributed. That point 2 lies on a higher indifference curve than point 1 merely implies that moving from 1 to 2 has the *potential* to make every individual better off (for example, if the additional goods were distributed among all individuals).

Figure 4.6 **Trade Increases Potential Welfare**

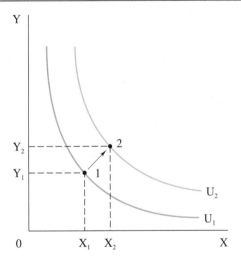

Trade allows production of larger quantities of goods, making a higher indifference curve attainable.

---

18 The result from the Ricardian model carries over to the case of two inputs only if both industries use those inputs in the same proportions. *(Why would the adjustment of production techniques illustrated in Figure 4.2 be unnecessary in this special case?)*

19 For a review of the basics of indifference curves and some hints at the distributional problems involved in using community indifference curves, see section 2.5.2. The distributional issues central to the analysis of community indifference curves don't arise in the case of individual indifference curves because all goods belong to the same individual.

4.6.2 **Comparing Utility: The Pareto Criterion**

Suppose that in moving from point 1 to point 2 in Figure 4.6, the additional goods ($[X_2 - X_1]$ units of X and $[Y_2 - Y_1]$ units of Y) were distributed such that every person ended up with more of each good. In such a case, we could say that the move from point 1 to 2 increased actual welfare or utility according to one possible criterion for judging the effects of a change on welfare. The **Pareto criterion** (named after economist Vilfredo Pareto) says that any change that makes at least one person better off *without* making any individual worse off increases welfare. The example in which increased production was distributed among all residents clearly satisfies this requirement.

The Pareto criterion is a useful benchmark for assessing the welfare effects of various economic policies. Unfortunately, it sidesteps the really tough policy questions. In Chapter One, we suggested that policy makers rarely are lucky enough to evaluate policies that either benefit everyone or harm everyone. Decisions on such policies are relatively easy; both common sense and the Pareto criterion recommend pursuing the former class of policies and avoiding the latter. Far more common are policy questions that involve benefits to some individuals and costs to others. In these cases, neither common sense nor the Pareto criterion provides much assistance.

4.6.3 **Comparing Utility: The Compensation Criterion**

Clearly the Pareto criterion can't answer some questions that arise in evaluating the effect on world welfare of opening international trade. The changes in factor prices predicted by the Stolper-Samuelson and factor price equalization theorems and by the specific-factors model imply that opening trade will harm some groups. In the short run, these groups include owners of any specific factors employed in the country's comparative-disadvantage industry. In the long run, the losers include owners of the factor used intensively in the country's comparative-disadvantage industry.

Several economists have suggested ways to evaluate the welfare effects of policies that benefit some individuals and harm others, thereby circumventing the boundaries of the issues the Pareto criterion can address. The specific proposals vary; however, a simple idea underlies each. The key question is whether the gainers from a policy gain enough to allow them to compensate the losers for their losses and still enjoy a net gain.

Opening international trade satisfies this **compensation criterion** for a welfare improvement. Because the world economy can produce more goods with trade, gainers can, in principle, compensate losers and still be better off. The remaining problems arise because such compensation, though possible, may not occur.

4.6.4 **Adjustment Costs and Compensation in Practice: Trade Adjustment Assistance**

Specialization and trade according to comparative advantage are dynamic processes. Countries gain and lose comparative advantage as demand and supply conditions in various output and factor markets change. Efficiency requires that industries relocate and adapt to these changes, but such adjustment imposes costs. Resources employed in a shrinking industry may suffer losses due to temporary unemployment, relocation, or retraining. The more specifically resources are designed for certain industries, the larger the dislocation costs are likely to be, because specialized resources, by definition, are ill suited for movement among industries. There can be little doubt that these costs and the associated redistributions of income are an important cause of protectionist policies, which rob countries of potential gains from trade. Industries have every incentive to lobby for protection to avoid the adjustment costs associated with changing patterns of comparative advantage.

Adjustment costs create three distinct but related policy problems. The first concerns equity in dealing with individuals adversely affected by trade. We've seen that unrestricted international trade maximizes world welfare. We've also seen that certain groups within the economy are harmed by trade. The extent to which society should compensate those groups represents an important policy question. The second issue concerns how to prevent individuals harmed by trade from successfully lobbying for protectionist policies that reduce total world welfare. The third question is how government can promote the adjustments necessary to realize the full potential gains from international trade.

Many countries have government-administered programs to aid individuals who have lost jobs because of changing patterns of comparative advantage. These programs have the triple purpose of more equitably distributing the adjustment costs incurred to capture the gains from trade, placating the most potent constituency for protectionism, and encouraging and facilitating the necessary adjustments.

The U.S. government administers the **Trade Adjustment Assistance (TAA)** program. The Trade Expansion Act of 1962 contained the first provision for a program aimed specifically at workers displaced for trade-related reasons (in particular, by increased imports resulting from tariff reductions negotiated through the General Agreement on Tariffs and Trade—predecessor to today's World Trade Organization). The act provided extended unemployment benefits plus retraining and relocation funds for workers in industries that could prove liberalization of international trade as the cause of their displacement. Requirements for such proof were quite stringent, and no workers qualified for assistance until 1969. Gradually, Congress eased the requirements, and more workers became eligible for benefits.

The Trade Act of 1974 mandated that imports need only "contribute importantly" to displacement rather than be the direct cause. More important, the 1974 act changed the nature of the link between trade and displacement. Congress had designed the 1962 act with the idea that workers injured *by a government policy* (that is, internationally negotiated reductions in tariffs) should receive compensation. The 1974 act altered the purpose of the program to include compensation of workers injured by increases in imports *regardless of the cause* of those increases. The number of workers receiving assistance grew slowly through the 1970s before exploding in 1980, when automobile workers qualified. Table 4.5 reports cash payments to workers under the TAA program.

Controversy surrounds the TAA program because its three goals, to some extent, inevitably conflict. The goal of compensating workers displaced by international trade can interfere with the goal of facilitating the adjustments required by trade according to comparative advantage. Many economists feel that the TAA program's heavy emphasis on extended unemployment benefits and weak focus on retraining and relocation assistance may actually hinder adjustment. The unemployment benefits may encourage workers to remain unemployed and await recall to their old jobs rather than seek employment in growing industries. Between 1975 and 1987, about $4,400 million went to Trade Readjustment Allowances, or extended unemployment benefits, while only $228 million was spent on retraining, job search, and relocation.

Table 4.5 Trade-Readjustment-Allowance Expenditures

Year	Total Outlays (Millions $)	Year	Total Outlays (Millions $)
1976	$ 79	1988	$186
1977	148	1989	125
1978	257	1990	92
1979	256	1991	116
1980	1,622	1992	43
1981	1,440	1993	50
1982	103	1994	120
1983	37	1995	153
1984	35	1996	166
1985	43	1997	188
1986	116	1998	152
1987	198	1999	196

Source: U.S. Department of Labor.

In response to these criticisms, the Omnibus Trade and Competitiveness Act of 1988 added the requirement that workers must participate in job-training programs to be eligible for TAA payments. About one-third of total program expenditures in 1999 went to training, job-search, and relocation allowances, while two-thirds went to extended unemployment benefits. However, skepticism persists about the effectiveness of the job-training provisions. Proposals currently under consideration include a "wage insurance" component of trade-adjustment assistance. If a displaced worker found a new job, but at a lower wage than the one earned in the original job, government funds would pay the worker a portion of the wage shortfall for a specified period. Such a policy could both encourage workers to find new jobs quickly and increase support for trade liberalization by limiting the risk faced by individuals who might be displaced into lower-wage jobs.

In 1994, the United States added a special transitional-assistance program for workers harmed either by increased imports from Canada or Mexico or by shifts of U.S. production to Canada or Mexico under the North American Free Trade Agreement; Case Four examines that program.

Countries of Asia

CASE ONE:
Trade and Wages I: Asia

Our basic trade model, although a simplified view of the world economy, highlights some common fallacies in discussions of international trade policy. One of the model's most important lessons is the fact that factor prices and the pattern of trade are determined *jointly*. Each affects and is affected by the other. Failure to recognize this two-way interaction can result in nonsensical arguments and poor predictions.

For example, many so-called experts on trade argue that an economy's openness to imports from lower-wage countries will result in massive employment shifts to those countries. You may recall Ross Perot's famous 1992 prediction of a "giant sucking sound" that would move thousands of jobs from the United States to Mexico under NAFTA. Such an argument has many problems (not the least of which is that the prediction didn't come true!), but a pivotal one is its failure to recognize that wages *rise* in low-wage countries as production of labor-intensive goods starts to move there in response to the initially low wages. Thailand, South Korea, Singapore, and Taiwan, for example, all have experienced such wage increases as they removed trade barriers and integrated themselves into the world economy, specializing at first in relatively low-skill labor-intensive goods. Between 1975 and 1999, wages in the newly industrializing Asian economies rose by an average of 11.2 percent each year, despite the effects of the Asian crisis that struck in 1997.[20]

As wages begin to rise, several adjustments occur. First, firms have less incentive, other things being equal, to move their labor-intensive production to the country; so the increase in demand for labor moderates. For example, fewer textile producers moved to Thailand and fewer sports-shoe producers to South Korea in the 1990s than in the 1980s. Instead, production relocated to countries where wages remained low, especially Indonesia, China, and Vietnam. Second, firms in the countries where wages have risen shift into new, less unskilled-labor-intensive lines of production. For example, in the early 1990s, South Korean shoe producers moved from producing sneakers to producing hiking boots and in-line skates, products that lower-wage countries such as China still lacked the skill to produce reliably. More recently, rising wages in China, especially along the export-oriented southern coast, are pushing firms to look elsewhere for unskilled workers.[21] At the same time, improved telecommunications infrastructure in China is allowing Hong Kong banks to shift "back office" service jobs such as data processing to nearby Guangdong, China.[22]

20 Data from the U.S. Bureau of Labor Statistics Web site at www.bls.gov.

21 "China's Increasing Costs of Labor Start to Deter Japanese Businesses," *The Wall Street Journal*, December 14, 1999.

22 "China Proves Its Worth as Companies Look to Cut Costs," *Financial Times*, May 15, 2001.

CASE TWO:
Trade and Wages II: The United States

Recently, policy makers and economists have turned their attention to the possible relationship among three trends in the U.S. economy during the 1980s and 1990s. First, the U.S. merchandise trade deficit (that is, the excess of the total value of imported goods over the total value of exported goods) grew. Second, the upward trend in average U.S. real wages, exhibited through the earlier postwar period, stalled. And third, the wage differential between skilled, well-educated U.S. workers and unskilled, poorly educated U.S. workers expanded. Two obvious questions arise: Did international trade, reflected in the trade deficit, slow the growth in U.S. real wages? And did international trade, especially with low-wage developing countries such as China, cause the real incomes of low-skilled and poorly educated U.S. workers to fall?

Attempts at empirical tests to answer these questions face many obstacles. One is the fact that so many things change simultaneously in the world economy that attempts to identify causality always run the risk of misattributing the cause.[23] A second hurdle follows from the discussion in Case One. Changes in trade patterns may affect wages, but changes in wages also affect trade patterns, and most empirical tests fail to use statistical techniques that can handle the two-way relationship.[24]

Most economists tentatively agree that the trends in wages in the United States during the 1980s and 1990s stem primarily from changes in technology rather than from international trade. The increased importance of knowledge-intensive skills has increased demand for workers who possess those skills and decreased demand for less-educated workers who lack them. Today, even entry-level factory jobs require advanced math and computer skills.[25] The result has been rapidly rising real wages for skilled, educated workers and stagnant or falling real wages for unskilled, poorly educated ones, a trend captured in Figure 4.7.

Why do most economists who have studied this trend carefully attribute it primarily to technological change instead of trade? First, the basic trade model implies that the mechanism through which trade might cause a decline

in wages for unskilled labor would be a fall in the price of unskilled labor-intensive goods (remember the Stolper-Samuelson theorem!). Data on this point are somewhat mixed, but most analysts agree that little evidence of such a price trend exists. Second, if trade reduced the relative wages of unskilled workers in skill-abundant countries such as the United States, that same trade should *increase* the relative earnings of unskilled workers in unskilled-labor-abundant developing countries. *(Why?)* But evidence suggests the opposite: Many unskilled-labor-abundant developing countries (for example, Chile, Colombia, Costa Rica, Mexico, and Uruguay) have experienced the same pattern as in the United States—an increase in the relative wages of skilled workers.[26] Third, if trade depressed the wages of unskilled workers, we should be observing all industries substituting toward using more of those now-cheaper workers. *(Use a diagram similar to Figure 4.2, but with skilled labor on one axis and unskilled labor on the other, to explain why.)* That substitution hasn't happened; instead, most industries now use more skilled labor relative to unskilled labor. Finally, U.S. trade with low-wage developing countries, although it has grown significantly, remains small. U.S. imports from Taiwan, Hong Kong, China, Malaysia, the Philippines, Singapore, and Thailand *combined* equaled only 1.95 percent of U.S. GDP in 1996, up from 0.82 percent in 1982.[27] It's difficult to see how such a small trade share could comprise the primary cause of the trend illustrated in Figure 4.7.

Despite the evidence that technological change rather than trade provides the main explanation for recent wage trends, technological change need not be totally independent of developments on the trade front. Firms that face or anticipate increased competition from imports from low-wage economies may choose either to invest in technology that reduces their use of labor or to outsource low-skill aspects of their production abroad.

Regardless of the final outcome of the debate on the causes of recent wage trends, virtually all economists agree that protection does *not* represent a fruitful approach for

23 The Bhagwati and Kosters reference discusses this problem.

24 This is one reason for the different conclusions about the trade–wage relationship often drawn by labor economists and by trade economists. See the discussion by Leamer and Levinsohn, especially pp. 1349 and 1360–1362.

25 "Manufacturers Decry a Shortage of Workers While Rejecting Many," *The Wall Street Journal,* September 8, 1995, p. A1.

26 Donald Robbins, "Evidence on Trade and Wages in the Developing World," *OECD Development Center Technical Paper* No. 119, December 1996.

27 OECD, *Economic Outlook,* December 1997, p. A70.

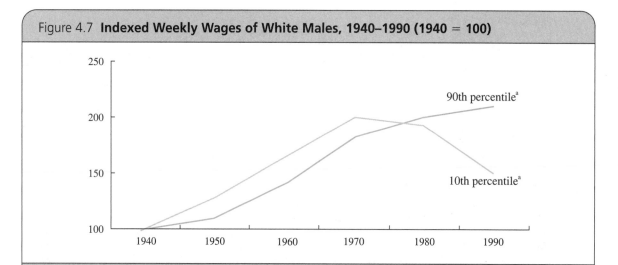

Figure 4.7 **Indexed Weekly Wages of White Males, 1940–1990 (1940 = 100)**

From the mid-1970s through the mid-1990s, wages of high-income workers rose relative to those of low-income workers.

[a]Percentiles refer to percentiles of the wage distribution, where workers in the 99th percentile have the highest earnings.
Source: Elaine Buckberg and Alun Thomas, "Wage Dispersion and Job Growth in the United States," *Finance and Development* (June 1995), p. 17; data from C. Huhn, "Wage Inequality and Industrial Change," National Bureau of Economic Research Working Paper No. 4684, March 1994.

combating the decline in real wages of low-skill workers.[28] Even if increased openness to international trade were the cause of that decline, despite current evidence that suggests otherwise, protection would impose costs on the economy that would far exceed any benefits to low-skill workers. This doesn't mean that low-wage workers must bear all the costs of opening trade. We know that unrestricted international trade allows the economy to produce a larger total quantity of goods and services. We also know that some groups gain and others lose when a country opens trade. But the gains from trade guarantee that winners from trade can compensate losers, allowing all to share in the gains.

Since 1994, there is some early evidence that the gap between wages of educated and uneducated U.S. workers has stopped growing. Workers have responded to the gap by attending college and getting more training.

CASE THREE:
Déjà Vu: Learning from Economic History

Most studies of trade and wages, like those summarized in Cases One and Two, focus on recent events. However, economic history offers richer opportunities to observe this important relationship. During the second half of the nineteenth century, declining transportation costs encouraged international trade. What happened to wages?

Economists Kevin O'Rourke and Jeffrey Williamson indicate that the real wage rates of unskilled urban workers in the United States, Sweden, Britain, Germany, Ireland, and Australia converged.[29] This is exactly what our basic trade model predicts. As the United States and Australia expanded trade, they specialized in goods intensive in their abundant factor, land, while European countries specialized in goods intensive in their abundant factor, labor. The ratio of wages to land rents fell in the United States and Australia, where they had been high in the absence of trade; the wage-rent ratio rose in Europe, where it had been low. The factor price changes were most dramatic in countries that were most open to trade. Around 1895, the move toward free trade stalled, and so did the international convergence of wages; the trend wouldn't resume until the 1950s.

---

28 See, in particular, the Deardorff article in the chapter references.

29 This case draws on the O'Rourke and Williamson book in the chapter references.

N. American Countries

CASE FOUR:
Adjusting to NAFTA

We saw in section 4.6.4 that Trade Adjustment Assistance compensates workers injured by imports. In 1993, the United States faced the politically difficult task of winning congressional approval for the North American Free Trade Agreement, which would eliminate most trade barriers among the United States, Canada, and Mexico. In the United States, most of the political opposition to NAFTA came from workers who feared they would lose their jobs because of increased imports. The U.S. government responded by adding a special provision to the Trade Adjustment Assistance program that would provide transitional assistance to workers. The program provides training, job-search, and relocation assistance to workers in firms affected by imports from Canada or Mexico or by shifts of U.S. production to those countries. Table 4.6 reports the NAFTA Transitional Adjustment Assistance program's experience in 1997.

The NAFTA transitional assistance program, which had cost about $200 million as of 1999, has not been free of controversy. Critics assert that the U.S. Department of Labor, in charge of administering the program, has certified for benefits workers whose job losses have nothing to do with NAFTA. For example, workers at sawmills in Washington state that closed because forest closures to save the spotted owl cut off their supply of logs received certification for benefits under the NAFTA-TAA program. The Labor Department claims the law requires no link of job loss to NAFTA, just a link to imports from Canada or Mexico; log imports rose when some U.S. forests were closed to logging to save the owls' habitat. Critics also express concern that the percentage of petitioners who receive certification has been rising (47,000 workers of 78,000 covered by petitions filed in 2000 received certification). This raises concerns beyond the program's cost. The number of workers certified for benefits under the program provide the statistics for widely circulated reports on NAFTA's economic impact. Therefore, certifying workers whose job loss has nothing to do with NAFTA risks leading to inaccurate estimates of the agreement's effects.[30]

Table 4.6 **NAFTA Transitional Adjustment Assistance, 1997**

Item	Estimated Number of Participants	Costs ($)
Direct Benefits (extra year of unemployment benefits)	n.a.	$14,000,000
Service Benefits	n.a.	$36,800,000
Training	4,400	n.a.
Job search	60	n.a.
Relocation assistance	370	n.a.

Source: U.S. International Trade Commission, *The Year in Trade 1999* (Washington, D.C.: USITC), p. 82.

---

30 You can find other examples of questionable certifications in "Layoffs Not Related to NAFTA Can Trigger Special Help Anyway," *The Wall Street Journal,* June 30, 1997, p. A1.

United States

CASE FIVE:
The State of Exports

Most models of international trade focus on countries as the basic unit of analysis. We've seen, however, that opening trade can create important redistributional effects *within* a country. When various industries and types of inputs aren't spread evenly throughout a country, opening trade can have different effects on regions within a country as well. Figure 4.8 reports U.S. states' export performance between 1988 and 1998 compared with the export performance of the United States as a whole. States shaded in gray, such as

Texas, experienced more rapid export growth than the country as a whole. States shaded in color, such as Massachusetts, experienced export growth less rapid than that of the country as a whole.

The most obvious pattern in the data is the slow export growth of almost all of the Middle Atlantic and New England states. In contrast, all the states bordering Mexico experienced more rapid export growth than the national average.

Summary

This chapter explicitly introduced the concept of general-equilibrium analysis to emphasize some of the many interrelated changes within an economy that result from opening international trade. Figure 4.9 illustrates the key relationships among the various markets.

The basic information the trade model takes as exogenous includes tastes, technology, and factor endowments. These three ingredients form the basis for the demand for outputs and the demand for and supply of factors of production. Factor prices, determined by supply and demand, in turn influence incomes, which feed back through the demand for outputs. Factor prices are linked to output prices (which depend on factor

Figure 4.8 **Net Relative Change in Exports, by State, 1988–1998**

Exports grew more than 30 percent faster than had they grown at the national rate

Exports grew 0–30 percent faster than had they grown at the national rate

Exports grew 0–30 percent slower than had they grown at the national rate

Exports grew more than 30 percent slower than had they grown at the national rate

Twenty-nine states' exports grew more rapidly than U.S. national exports. Twenty-one states' exports grew more slowly than U.S. national exports. Slow export-growth states were concentrated in the Middle Atlantic and New England regions.

Source: Data from Cletus C. Coughlin and Patricia S. Pollard. "Comparing Manufacturing Export Growth across States: What Accounts for the Differences?" Federal Reserve Bank of St. Louis *Review* 83 (January/February 2001), p. 36.

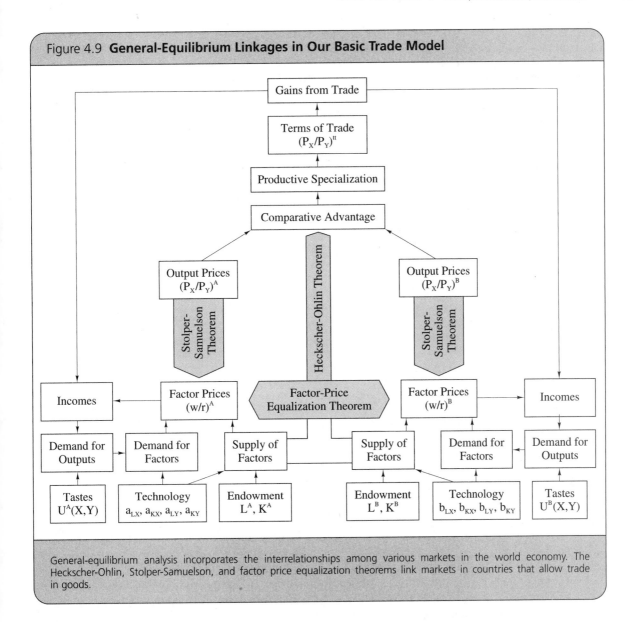

Figure 4.9 General-Equilibrium Linkages in Our Basic Trade Model

General-equilibrium analysis incorporates the interrelationships among various markets in the world economy. The Heckscher-Ohlin, Stolper-Samuelson, and factor price equalization theorems link markets in countries that allow trade in goods.

endowments according to the Heckscher-Ohlin theorem) through the Stolper-Samuelson theorem and to factor prices in the other country through the factor price equalization theorem. Finally, relative output prices in the two countries determine the pattern of comparative advantage and productive specialization. The equilibrium terms of trade resulting from this process determine the size and allocation of the gains from trade.

Looking Ahead

In this chapter, we explored the wide-ranging effects of opening international trade, particularly those on factor prices and the distribution of income. In Chapter Five, we'll examine attempts to test the Heckscher-Ohlin explanation of trade patterns and outline some of the resulting refinements and modifications of the theory. Then we'll turn to trade based on economies of scale rather than on comparative advantage.

Key Terms

general-equilibrium analysis
partial-equilibrium analysis
magnification effect
Stolper-Samuelson theorem
factor price equalization theorem

depreciation allowances
Pareto criterion
compensation criterion
Trade Adjustment Assistance (TAA)

Problems and Questions for Review

1. Suppose that $P_X = a_{LX} \cdot w + a_{KX} \cdot r = 60 \cdot w + 40 \cdot r$ and that $P_Y = a_{LY} \cdot w + a_{KY} \cdot r = 75 \cdot w + 25 \cdot r$.
   a. If $P_X = P_Y = 100$, what are the equilibrium values for the wage rate and the rental rate?
   b. If P_Y rose to 120 and the input coefficients didn't change, what would be the new equilibrium values of w and r?[31]
   c. After the change in part (b), would workers' wages buy more or less good X? More or less good Y? Would capital-owners' rent buy more or less good X? More or less good Y? Have *real* wages risen or fallen? The real rental rate?
   d. Of what trade theorem is your answer to part (c) an example?
2. Farmia is a labor-abundant country that grows coffee and wheat. Assume that labor and land are the only two inputs. Coffee production is labor intensive, and wheat production is land intensive. Labor can work in either the coffee or the wheat industry and can move easily back and forth between the two. But land is specialized; land on the plains is suited to produce wheat and land in the mountains to produce coffee. "Wheat land" is useless in producing coffee, and "coffee land" is useless in producing wheat. If Farmia opens trade with a country with identical tastes, what will happen in the short run to
   a. Farmia's production of wheat and coffee? What information or theorem did you use as the basis for your answer?
   b. Prices of wheat and coffee in Farmia? How do you know?
   c. Wages in Farmia? How do you know?
   d. The price of wheat land in Farmia? How do you know?
   e. The price of coffee land in Farmia? How do you know?
   f. The welfare or purchasing power of workers, owners of wheat land, and owners of coffee land in Farmia? How do you know?
3. This question continues question 1 from Chapter Three.
   a. If both factors of production are mobile between industries, how would the following groups feel about opening trade: capital owners in Hong Kong, labor in Hong Kong, capital owners in Japan, and labor in Japan?
   b. Now assume that labor is perfectly mobile between industries, but that capital is immobile between industries. That is, some capital is suitable for producing automobiles, but not suitable for producing clothing and vice versa. How would the following groups feel about opening trade: owners of auto capital in Hong Kong, owners of clothing capital in Hong Kong, owners of auto capital in Japan, owners of clothing capital in Japan, labor in Hong Kong, and labor in Japan?
4. Suppose two countries allow both free trade in goods and free flows of factors (such an arrangement is called a *common market*). Why would it be difficult to predict the extent and pattern of trade in goods between them?
5. In debates over international trade policy, workers and capital owners in a given industry often take the same side (for example, U.S. auto producers and the United Auto Workers union, or U.S. steel producers and the United Steelworkers union). However, the Stolper-Samuelson theorem predicts that owners of capital and labor would be affected differently by trade. How can international trade theory explain the observation?

---

31 In fact, as we argued in this chapter, the input coefficients *would* change. Using techniques beyond the scope of this book, it's possible to show that the qualitative results derived in this question still hold if the input coefficients change; see, for example, the Jones article in the chapter references.

6. "The Ricardian and Neoclassical models carry different implications about support for and opposition to unrestricted international trade." Explain.
7. Briefly explain why the magnification effect plays an important role in predicting whether various groups in the economy will support or oppose international trade.
8. The labor-abundant countries of Asia have experienced rapidly rising wages since those economies liberalized their international trade policies. Does this observation match the predictions of international trade theory? Explain.

References and Selected Readings

Aghion, Philippe, and Jeffrey G. Williamson. *Growth, Inequality, and Globalization: Theory, History, and Policy.* Cambridge: Cambridge University Press, 1998.
Advanced treatment of the historical relationship between inequality and support for open international markets.

Bhagwati, Jagdish, and Marvin H. Kosters, eds. *Trade and Wages.* Washington, D.C.: American Enterprise Institute, 1994.
Accessible overview of theory and empirical evidence on the relationship between changes in international trade and wages.

"Colloquium on U.S. Wage Trends in the 1980s." Federal Reserve Bank of New York *Economic Policy Review* 1 (January 1995).
Excellent collection of short articles summarizing the latest research on wage trends; for all students.

Deardorff, Alan V. "Technology, Trade, and Increasing Equality: Does the Cause Matter for the Cure?" *Journal of International Economic Law* 1 (September 1998): 353–376.
Argues that the right policies to address income inequality don't hinge on its causes.

Deardorff, Alan V., and Robert M. Stern, eds. *The Stolper-Samuelson Theorem: A Golden Jubilee.* Ann Arbor, Mich.: University of Michigan Press, 1994.
Collection of papers celebrating the 50th anniversary of the Stolper-Samuelson theorem. The papers vary in level of difficulty.

Edwards, Sebastian. "Trade Policy, Growth, and Income Distribution." *American Economic Review Papers and Proceedings* 87 (May 1997): 205–210.
Cross-country empirical study finds no evidence that trade liberalization increases income inequality; for all students.

Feenstra, Robert C. "Estimating the Effects of Trade Policy." In *Handbook of International Economics,* Vol. 3, edited by G. M. Grossman and K. Rogoff, 1553–1596. Amsterdam: North-Holland, 1995.
Advanced survey of the empirical literature on the economic effects of various trade policies.

Feenstra, Robert C. "Integration of Trade and Disintegration of Production in the Global Economy." *Journal of Economic Perspectives* 12 (Fall 1998): 31–50.
Introduction to the globalization of production.

Fieleke, Norman S. "Is Global Competition Making the Poor Even Poorer?" Federal Reserve Bank of Boston *New England Economic Review* (November/December 1994): 3–16.
Introductory overview of the literature on the effect of trade on wages.

Fishow, Albert, and Karen Parker, eds. *Growing Apart.* New York: Council on Foreign Relations, 1999.
Collection of readable papers on nontrade sources of inequality trends.

Grossman, Gene M. "Partially Mobile Capital: A General Approach to Two-Sector Trade Theory." *Journal of International Economics* 15 (1983): 1–17.
For intermediate and advanced students; a model that includes the standard and specific-factor models as special cases.

James, Harold. "Is Liberalization Reversible?" *Finance and Development* 36 (December 1999): 11–14.
Investigates whether antiglobalization forces can reverse progress toward open trade.

Jones, Ronald W. "The Structure of Simple General Equilibrium Models." *Journal of Political Economy* 73 (December 1965): 557–572.
The classic algebraic demonstration of the magnification effect and related ideas.

Leamer, Edward, and James Levinsohn. "International Trade Theory: The Evidence." In *Handbook of International Economics,* Vol. 3, edited by G. M. Grossman and K. Rogoff, 1339–1394. Amsterdam: North-Holland, 1995.
Advanced survey of empirical evidence on international trade theories.

Lerman, Robert I. "U.S. Wage Inequality Trends and Recent Immigration." *American Economic Review Papers and Proceedings* 89 (May 1999): 23–28.
A reevaluation of immigration's effects on wages.

Mundell, Robert A. "International Trade and Factor Mobility." *American Economic Review* 47 (June 1957): 321–335.
Presents the argument that trade in goods and mobility of factors are substitutes. Although the basic argument is highly readable, the graphical proofs may be difficult to follow.

Noussair, Charles N., et al. "An Experimental Investigation of the Patterns of International Trade." *American Economic Review* (June 1995): 462–491.
Experimental results that suggest that factor price equalization arises in laboratory experiments; advanced.

Organization for Economic Cooperation and Development. *Open Markets Matter: The Benefits of Trade and Investment Liberalization.* Paris: OECD, 1998.
Accessible overview of the benefits of economic liberalization.

O'Rourke, Kevin H. "Globalization and Inequality: Historical Trends." National Bureau of Economic Research Working Paper W8339 (available at www.nber.org).
Finds that superior technological progress in richer countries and insufficient globalization, not globalization itself, have caused increased inequality between countries.

O'Rourke, Kevin H., and Jeffrey G. Williamson. *Globalization and History.* Cambridge, Mass.: MIT Press, 1999.
Fascinating applications of the basic trade models to the nineteenth-century Atlantic economy.

Rassekh, F., and H. Thompson. "Factor Price Equalization: Theory and Evidence." *Journal of International Economic Integration* 8 (1993): 1–32.
Useful survey of the literature on factor price equalization.

Rodrik, Dani. "Political Economy of Trade Policy." In *Handbook of International Economics,* Vol. 3, edited by G. M. Grossman and K. Rogoff, 1457–1494. Amsterdam: North-Holland, 1995.
Advanced survey of the literature on distributional aspects of trade policy and their implications for the policy process.

Samuelson, Paul A. "International Factor-Price Equalization Once Again." *Economic Journal* (June 1949): 181–197.
Clarified version of the original demonstration of the factor price equalization theorem. With the exception of a brief mathematical section, the paper is appropriate for students of all levels.

Stolper, Wolfgang, and Paul A. Samuelson. "Protection and Real Wages." *Review of Economic Studies* 9 (November 1941): 58–73.
Original presentation of the Stolper-Samuelson theorem; accessible to intermediate students.

Symposium on "Income Inequality: Issues and Policy Options." Federal Reserve Bank of Kansas City, 1998.
Trends in income inequality and related policies.

Williamson, Jeffrey G. "Globalization, Labor Markets and Policy Backlash in the Past." *Journal of Economic Perspectives* 12 (Fall 1998): 51–72.
Earlier episodes of the trade-and-wages debate; for all students.

CHAPTER FIVE

Beyond Comparative Advantage: Empirical Evidence and New Trade Theories

5.1 Introduction

Chapters Two through Four explored a range of questions, including why nations trade, the direction and volume of trade, and its impact on output prices and factor prices. Economists have suggested several theories to explain international trade patterns, including the Ricardian, Neoclassical, and Heckscher-Ohlin models. It's now time to confront the question of which (if any) of these theories is *the* model that explains observed trade patterns. First, we'll review just what we're trying to explain. Must we adopt a single theory of trade, or might different theories best explain various aspects of trade? Next, after a brief discussion of the role of empirical testing, we'll review the empirical evidence concerning the various models. Finally, we'll discuss some suggested modifications and important recent extensions of international trade theories.

5.2 Questions to Be Answered

The models presented in Chapters Two through Four focus on the determinants of trade patterns. Why does Colombia export coffee, Taiwan computer components, the United States airplanes, Japan automobiles, or Brazil steel? Is one explanation sufficient for all these observations? This chapter argues that the answer to the second question probably is no: Different types of international trade likely require different explanations. For example, unique political and strategic considerations may dictate government imports and exports of military equipment. Trade in manufactured goods may respond to influences different from those that affect trade in primary products. The importance of relative factor endowments in determining trade patterns in oil or diamonds seems much more obvious than in the case of bicycles or shoes. Differences in relative labor productivity probably play a larger role in U.S. exports of computer software than in Saudi Arabian exports of oil.

A large and growing share of trade in many manufactured goods is **intra-industry trade**—trade in which each country *both* imports and exports products from the same industry. Explaining this component of trade requires modifying our basic trade model. Countries tend to trade largely with countries of similar income levels, particularly in manufactured goods; this provides the basis for an alternate theory of trade. The United States and a few other industrialized countries typically produce and export new or high-technology products; this observation gives rise to yet another theory of trade. All these considerations are important to a full explanation of international trade patterns. Simple extensions of the model already introduced can incorporate some of these; others require complementary models.

A second question concerns not the pattern of trade at a given time but how that pattern *changes* over time. In the case of the preceding export examples, Colombia has exported large amounts of coffee for a long time, but all the other exports are recent. Steel, computer components, and automobiles now produced in Brazil, Taiwan, and Japan were, not long ago, produced primarily in the United States. The huge international market in aircraft is relatively new, and computer software didn't even exist until a few years ago. As Case One highlights, using the semiconductor industry as an example, trade patterns can change significantly over time. This carries important implications for trade policy because, as we saw in Chapter Four, such changes can result in significant policy controversy and in pressures for protection.

5.3 How Do We Know If a Theory about Trade Is Correct?

In the previous section, we argued intuitively that some considerations are likely more important than others in explaining various aspects of world trade patterns. In some cases these intuitive arguments seem very persuasive—for example, the importance of relative factor endowments in explaining trade patterns in primary products such as oil or diamonds. In other cases, the arguments seem less immediately compelling. To strengthen our arguments about the important influences on various types of trade, we must turn to empirical tests of the various possible explanations.

Empirical work in international trade theory, both formal and informal, has a long and distinguished history. Adam Smith used his observation that income levels tended to be higher in coastal cities (which engaged actively in trade) than in inland areas (which engaged in little trade) to support his argument that trade can increase income. David Ricardo used his observations of differing opportunity costs in the production of wine and cloth in Portugal and England to argue that unrestricted trade between the two countries could increase the output of both wine and cloth. Certainly these early examples fail the rigorous standards by which economists judge empirical work today. With the development of the science of statistics, the speed of today's computers, and the vast amount of available (albeit imperfect) data on production, consumption, and world trade, the empirical testing of trade theories has grown into a highly technical and exacting field. Nonetheless, the Smith and Ricardo examples remind us that the vital interaction between trade theory and empirical observation has been going on for centuries.

Empirical testing helps economists separate theories with real explanatory power from those that, though plausible, can't really explain observed phenomena. However, we must keep in mind the difficulties inherent in such testing. That the available empirical evidence appears to support a theory can't prove the theory true. A second and yet undiscovered explanation may be the true one despite apparent empirical support for the existing theory. Empirical testing can never prove a theory true, but repeated testing can increase our confidence in the theory. Similarly, empirical results that contradict a theory's implications can't prove the theory false. Such contradictions may weaken our confidence in the theory and lead us to consider alternatives, but there always is a chance that the test itself was faulty in either design or execution. Compromises are necessary in translating a theory's implications into a form suitable for empirical implementation, and these compromises may introduce logical flaws that invalidate the test. Often the most useful outcome of an empirical test is neither validation nor invalidation of the theory in question but refinement of both the theory and the test.

Case One in Chapter Two presented the results of early tests of the Ricardian model. The model's assertion—that differences in relative labor productivity across countries help explain the pattern of trade—appeared strongly supported in tests for several countries and time periods. In the next section, we discuss attempts to test the Heckscher-Ohlin or factor-endowment theory of trade.

5.4 Testing the Heckscher-Ohlin Model

5.4.1 Hurdles to Empirical Testing

The key testable implication of the Heckscher-Ohlin model is that a country will export those goods whose production involves intensive use of its relatively abundant factor and import those goods whose production involves intensive use of its scarce factor. This implies that exports as a group should be more intensive in use of the abundant factor than imports as a group. For several decades after the development of the Heckscher-Ohlin model, it wasn't possible to test the theory empirically using anything more than the simplest observations. England doesn't specialize in growing wheat, or the United States in growing bananas, or France in mining diamonds. All these observations are, of course, consistent with Heckscher and Ohlin's proposal of relative factor endowments as the basis of comparative advantage; but the observations hardly constitute definitive evidence in the theory's favor.

5.4.2 The Leontief Tests

Wassily Leontief laid the groundwork for the first real test of Heckscher and Ohlin's key proposition, using 1947 data for the United States. With no data available on the factor intensity of actual imports (because they were produced outside the United States), Leontief had to use data on **import substitutes** (the U.S.-produced versions of the import goods) as a proxy.

During the period immediately following the Second World War, when Leontief performed these tests, no one seriously questioned the relative capital abundance of the United States. The United States had possessed a highly developed, capital-intensive manufacturing sector before the war, and the war's destruction of much of the rest of the world's capital stock made the United States even more relatively capital abundant. This implied that the goods exported by the United States should be capital intensive relative to goods it imported (as measured by the factor intensity of import substitutes).

Much to everyone's surprise, Leontief found the opposite result: The United States exported labor-intensive goods and imported capital-intensive ones! In fact, Leontief's calculations showed U.S. exports to be about 30 percent more labor intensive than U.S. import substitutes, as Table 5.1 reports. This result was so puzzling that it became known as the **Leontief paradox.** A flurry of research activity emerged to explain the paradox, and the work continues today. Economists performed tests for different countries and for different time periods. Several economists suggested that the use of 1947 data was potentially misleading because the post–World War II world economy was still in a highly disrupted state. Later tests using data for the early 1950s did reduce the magnitude of the paradox; U.S. exports still were labor intensive but by a much smaller margin than 1947's 30 percent. Data for Canada, Japan, East Germany, and India also were examined, with mixed results. For some countries and time periods, the implications of the Heckscher-Ohlin model seemed consistent with observed patterns of trade. In other cases, the Leontief paradox recurred.

In general, it seems fair to say that the simplest version of the Heckscher-Ohlin model does a poor job of explaining trade patterns, particularly in manufactured goods. These results have prompted some analysts to abandon the basic notions of factor abundance and factor intensity as explanations for trade. Others have retained the basic Heckscher-Ohlin framework, incorporated extensions, and relaxed assumptions to produce a more general model of trade still in the spirit of Heckscher-Ohlin. The continuing empirical work on these questions indicates that slightly modified versions of the Heckscher-Ohlin model can explain many aspects of trade quite well. Other aspects, however, seem to require more radical changes and the introduction of considerations outside the Heckscher-Ohlin framework and, in fact, beyond comparative advantage.

In the next section, we present several modifications of the Heckscher-Ohlin model and evaluate their ability to explain trade patterns. Later we consider alternate and complementary theories that explain aspects of trade poorly explained by the Heckscher-Ohlin model.

Table 5.1 **The Leontief Paradox**

	Exports	Import Substitutes
Capital (1947 $)	$2,550,780	$3,091,339
Labor (person-years)	182	170
Capital-labor ratio ($ per person-year)	$ 14,015	$ 18,184

Given the country's apparent capital abundance, everyone expected the United States to export capital-intensive goods. Instead, Leontief found U.S. exports to be about 30 percent more labor intensive than U.S. imports. The numbers reported are inputs per $1 million of exports and import substitutes.

Source: W. W. Leontief, "Domestic Production and Foreign Trade," *Proceedings of the American Philosophical Society,* 1953.

5.4.3 Fine-Tuning the Heckscher-Ohlin Model

The primary modifications of the Heckscher-Ohlin model suggested as possible explanations of the Leontief paradox include the role of tastes, the categorization of inputs, and technology and productivity differences (à la Ricardo).[1]

The Role of Tastes

Recall from Chapter Three that Heckscher and Ohlin assumed tastes were identical across countries to focus on relative factor endowments' role in determining comparative advantage. When tastes are identical, the production bias from different factor endowments implies that a country will have a comparative advantage in the good that uses its abundant factor intensively. Section 3.4.2 showed that large differences in tastes among countries can introduce a taste bias that, in principle, can dominate the production bias. Should this occur, a country will have a comparative advantage in production of the good that uses its scarce factor intensively.

Logically, taste bias might explain the Leontief paradox. If residents of the United States had tastes very strongly biased toward consumption of capital-intensive goods relative to tastes in the rest of the world, the price of capital-intensive goods would be high in the United States; so the country would import capital-intensive goods and export labor-intensive ones. Such a finding wouldn't violate the spirit of the Heckscher-Ohlin model, which merely states that different factor endowments create a production bias toward the good intensive in the abundant factor.

Given that taste bias can logically explain the Leontief paradox, how likely is it to be the paradox's true source? Evidence does exist for a "home bias" in consumption; that is, consumers in a given country tend to consume more domestically produced goods and fewer imports than we might expect. But, for most countries, the observed home bias in consumption probably is unlikely to overwhelm factor-endowment-based differences in production possibilities. Home bias in consumption does seem to play some role in explaining trade patterns; but it can't single-handedly explain the Leontief result.[2]

Classification of Inputs

Attempts to test the Heckscher-Ohlin model of trade have revealed the shortcomings of the traditional two-way classification of inputs as capital or labor.[3] Most modern production processes involve many inputs, some not easily grouped into the capital or labor category. A five-way categorization of inputs can capture the major differences among the factor endowments of various countries much more successfully than can the capital-labor breakdown. Authors have classified inputs in several ways, but the most common includes arable farmland, raw materials or natural resources, human capital, man-made or nonhuman capital, and unskilled labor. Given this more precise categorical breakdown, the United States' factor abundance lies in human capital and arable farmland. This explains U.S. export success in high-technology and research-and-development-intensive industries, such as large-scale computers, and in agricultural products, a seemingly peculiar combination. Once we incorporate this more realistic breakdown of inputs, Heckscher and Ohlin's fundamental notion of comparative advantage based on differing factor endowments and factor intensities does a much better job of explaining trade patterns for many goods.

Technology, Productivity, and Specialization

Recall that Heckscher and Ohlin assumed not only identical tastes, but also identical technologies across countries when they predicted countries would export those goods that used their abundant factors intensively. The identical-technology assumption implies that, with completely unrestricted trade, equalized output and factor prices would lead firms in all countries to adopt identical production processes. *(Why?)*

---

1 A fifth possible explanation—factor-intensity reversals—occurs when a good is labor intensive in one country but capital intensive in the other. Evidence indicates that such reversals are not an empirically important phenomenon.

2 See Trefler (1995).

3 Table 3.2 reports estimates of countries' factor endowments using the capital/labor breakdown.

But we clearly observe technology differences across countries. Some are easy to understand. Warm, sunny countries have access to a technology for producing tropical fruits that colder, less sunny countries can't match. Firms that undertake the research-and-development expenditures necessary to discover an innovative production process typically apply for patents that restrict other firms' abilities to use that process.

Other sources of technological differences across countries, while just as important, are harder to explain. The former Soviet Union trained many talented scientists and engineers. Yet those highly skilled individuals failed to attain the levels of productivity in the Soviet Union that they have since emigrating to the West. One likely reason is that the incentive system in the Soviet Union and other centrally planned economies failed to encourage individual productivity. When considerations such as these result in different countries using different technologies of production, the simple predictions of Heckscher and Ohlin, based on identical technologies, may not follow directly, but must be amended to take account of the cross-country differences in production processes.

The preceding modifications to the Heckscher-Ohlin model appear to produce a framework capable of explaining a significant portion of world trade. Some aspects of trade, however, require alternate, complementary models—including some not based on comparative advantage—to which we now turn.

5.5 Intra-Industry Trade

5.5.1 What Is It, and How Big Is It?

Intra-industry trade—trade in which a single country both imports and exports products in the same industry—comprises a significant share of world trade, particularly in manufactures. How can we estimate the extent of intra-industry trade in a given industry? The most commonly used technique is an *intra-industry trade* (IIT) index,

$$\text{IIT}_X = 1 - \frac{\left|\text{Exports}_X - \text{Imports}_X\right|}{\text{Exports}_X + \text{Imports}_X}, \qquad \textbf{[5.1]}$$

where the vertical bars in the numerator denote absolute value.[4] The IIT index varies from 0 to 1 as intra-industry trade in industry X increases. If a country *only* imports or *only* exports the good in question (no intra-industry trade), the index equals 0. *(Why?)* If a country's X-industry imports and exports are *equal* (maximum intra-industry trade), the IIT index takes a value of 1.

One warning is appropriate concerning the interpretation of intra-industry trade measures: They are very sensitive to the definitions of products or industries used. For example, early estimates suggested that two-thirds of trade in chemicals was intra-industry. The chemical industry is large and diverse; thus, it isn't surprising that most industrialized countries import some types of chemicals and export others, since we would expect different countries to have comparative advantages in different specific chemicals. In general, the more narrowly defined the industry classifications used, the lower the resulting estimates of intra-industry trade.

In addition to the intra-industry trade index for a particular industry, we can define an analogous index for a country's trade as a whole. This involves calculating the ratio on the right side of Equation 5.1 for each industry, summing those ratios across industries, and using the summation in place of the industry ratios as indicated in Equation 5.2, where the symbol Σ represents summation across industries:

$$\text{IIT} = 1 - \frac{\Sigma \left|\text{Exports} - \text{Imports}\right|}{\Sigma \left(\text{Exports} + \text{Imports}\right)}. \qquad \textbf{[5.2]}$$

Calculating the IIT index for a country's overall trade allows comparison across countries of the degree of intra-industry trade. Table 5.2 reports intra-industry trade indexes for a large sample of countries. The table reveals that IIT indexes tend to be substantially higher for industrial countries than for developing ones, reflecting the formers' more extensive manufacturing sectors.

---

4 Strictly speaking, if the country's trade is not balanced (in other words, if total imports do not equal total exports), each export and import term in Equation 5.1 should be replaced by industry exports or imports as a share of total exports or imports.

Table 5.2 **Intra-Industry Trade Indexes**

Developing Countries	IIT Index	Newly Industrializing Countries	IIT Index	Industrial Countries	IIT Index
Algeria	.01	Argentina	.42	Australia	.25
Cameroon	.06	Brazil	.38	Austria	.74
Central African Republic	.01	Greece	.21	Belgium-Luxembourg	.79
Chile	.10	Hong Kong	.41	Canada	.67
Colombia	.20	India	.37	Denmark	.67
Costa Rica	.32	Israel	.62	Finland	.45
Dominican Republic	.07	South Korea	.35	France	.80
Egypt	.07	Mexico	.32	West Germany	.63
El Salvador	.33	Portugal	.33	Ireland	.61
Ghana	.04	Singapore	.67	Italy	.59
Guatemala	.33	Spain	.52	Japan	.26
Guyana	.20	Taiwan	.35	Netherlands	.74
Haiti	.46	Yugoslavia	.51	New Zealand	.26
Ivory Coast	.13	Average	.42	Norway	.44
Jamaica	.14			Sweden	.68
Jordan	.15			Switzerland	.60
Kenya	.14			United Kingdom	.81
Malawi	.06			United States	.59
Malaysia	.32			Average	.59
Morocco	.11				
Nigeria	.00				
Pakistan	.15				
Peru	.10				
Philippines	.15				
Senegal	.19				
Sri Lanka	.05				
Sudan	.01				
Thailand	.17				
Trinidad	.14				
Tunisia	.17				
Turkey	.08				
Average	.15				

Source: Nigel Grimwade, *International Trade: New Patterns of Trade, Production and Investment* (London: Routledge, 1989), p. 127.

Intra-industry trade represents a growing share of total trade, especially among the high-income industrial economies. But why would a country choose to export and import similar goods?

5.5.2 Intra-Industry Trade in Homogeneous Goods

Transportation costs and seasonal trade patterns can explain intra-industry trade in nondifferentiated or **homogeneous goods.** Figure 5.1 illustrates the transportation-cost case. Homogeneous goods most likely to be involved in intra-industry trade include items that are heavy or for some other reason expensive to transport. In Figure 5.1, firm F^A in country A and firm F^B in country B, spatially located as shown, produce such a product. Consumers C^A and C^B buy the product. Because of the firms' and consumers' locations, it may be the case

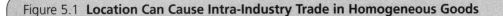

Figure 5.1 **Location Can Cause Intra-Industry Trade in Homogeneous Goods**

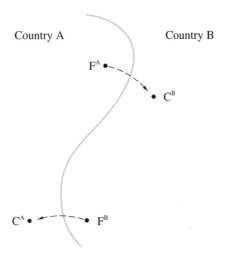

Each country both imports and exports the product because of the greater proximity of consumers to the foreign than to the domestic producer.

that consumer C^A buys from firm F^B and consumer C^B from firm F^A to minimize transportation costs. As a result, countries A and B both import and export the good. Later in this chapter, we'll look in more detail at the issues of transportation costs and the location of industry as possible explanations for the pattern of trade.

Seasonal considerations also can cause intra-industry trade in homogeneous goods. Agricultural growing seasons provide a clear example. A country in the Northern Hemisphere might export agricultural products during the summer and import those same goods from a Southern Hemisphere trading partner during the winter. Governments report most trade statistics on an annual basis, so summer exports and winter imports appear in the statistics as simultaneous exports and imports of the same goods.

5.5.3 Intra-Industry Trade in Differentiated Goods

The basic trade model assumes goods are homogeneous; this is one of the assumptions required for perfectly competitive markets. Homogeneity implies (at least in the presence of transportation costs) that a single good typically wouldn't be both imported and exported by the same country. Rather than import units of the good from abroad, a country would simply choose to consume more of its domestic production and reduce its exports. However, many manufactured goods don't satisfy the homogeneity assumption very well.[5] The example most often cited is automobiles. Around the world, firms produce a variety of types and models of automobiles. All the major industrialized economies both import and export cars.[6] American consumers buy

---

5 Markets with differentiated products but that otherwise satisfy the requirements for perfect competition are called *monopolistically competitive markets.*

6 The automobile industry, as well as other industries, actually engages in two types of intra-industry trade. The first—the focus here—is bidirectional trade in differentiated but similar finished goods such as automobiles. The second, explored later, is trade in component parts; for example, a car may be assembled in the United States from parts produced in 15 different countries. Since the components typically are classified within the automotive-industry category for purposes of governments' trade statistics, such trade in components shows up, along with bidirectional trade in finished automobiles, as intra-industry trade. Some intra-industry trade also is due to an aspect of transportation costs called *cross-hauling*—the fact that once a loaded ship carries goods from country A to country B, the cost of shipping goods back from B to A rather than sending an empty ship is low.

Mercedes-Benzes and Hyundais, while German consumers buy Chevrolets and Saabs. The English drive Fords, and Japanese drive Jaguars. Obviously firms incur substantial costs to ship all these automobiles among countries. This is worthwhile only because consumers don't view the various types of cars as perfect substitutes. An American who buys a BMW or Toyota isn't indifferent between that car and a Ford or Chevrolet. A satisfactory explanation of trade in many manufactured goods requires taking into account such **product differentiation** and the intra-industry trade it generates.

Product differentiation takes us one step toward understanding intra-industry trade, but a true explanation of the phenomenon requires an additional step. Suppose that most Japanese are content to drive Toyotas and Hondas, while most Germans are happy with their Volkswagens and BMWs. Nonetheless a few Japanese want BMWs, and a few Germans want Hondas. Why don't the Japanese produce a few close BMW substitutes and the Germans a few good Honda substitutes? To explain why this adjustment to minority tastes sometimes doesn't occur and intra-industry trade occurs instead, we will need to incorporate the idea of increasing returns to scale, the subject of section 5.6. But first, we need to understand why the difference between inter-industry and intra-industry trade matters for trade policy.

5.5.4 **Why Does It Matter?**

Unlike trade based on comparative advantage, intra-industry trade occurs in greatest volume between developed industrial economies with similar factor endowments, skill levels, and stages of development. The industries most likely to report high intra-industry trade include sophisticated manufactured goods that exhibit product differentiation and whose production processes are characterized by economies of scale.

Intra-industry trade based on transportation costs, seasonal trade, or product differentiation often presents fewer pressures for protection and less political controversy than does inter-industry trade based on comparative advantage. Recall that the redistribution of income caused by inter-industry trade occurs because the *different* factor intensities of industries imply that opening trade alters relative demands for different factors and thereby changes their relative prices. Intra-industry trade, on the other hand, involves trade in goods in the same industry and produced using *similar* factor intensities. Therefore, the changes in factor demands and relative factor prices from such trade tend to be smaller. This may provide one explanation for the pattern of observed trade liberalization since the Second World War. The greatest success in lowering trade barriers has occurred in manufactured-goods industries in which the developed industrial countries engage in large amounts of *intra*-industry trade. In contrast, barriers to trade have been slower to come down in agriculture, primary products, and other sectors in which we would expect resource-based comparative advantage to result in *inter*-industry trade between developed and developing countries.

5.6 **Trade with Economies of Scale**

For some goods, the average cost of production depends on the scale of output, or the number of units of the good produced. If the average cost per unit of a good falls as the scale of production rises, production exhibits **decreasing costs, increasing returns to scale,** or **economies of scale.** Some types of economies of scale can make it difficult for small firms to compete with large ones. Whether economies of scale give an advantage to large firms depends on whether the scale economies are internal or external to the firm.

Internal scale economies occur when the firm's average costs fall as the *firm's* output rises, as in panel (a) of Figure 5.2. The primary sources of internal economies of scale are large fixed costs that can be spread over all the firm's output; examples include research-and-development expenditures and advanced assembly-line production techniques such as robotics. In an industry characterized by such economies, a firm that produces a small output, X^S in Figure 5.2, faces relatively high average costs of AC^S. A *large* firm in the same industry produces more output, X^L, can spread its fixed costs over more units, and therefore achieves lower per unit costs, AC^L. These lower costs allow the large firm to sell its product at a lower price, so we wouldn't expect the small firm to survive in the long run.[7] The automobile industry provides a classic example of an industry characterized by internal economies of scale. Most studies suggest that a small automobile plant that produced only a few cars per year would have much higher average costs per car than would a giant firm such as General

---

7 In the long run, with entry and exit, a firm's price must equal its average costs, implying that the firm earns zero economic profits.

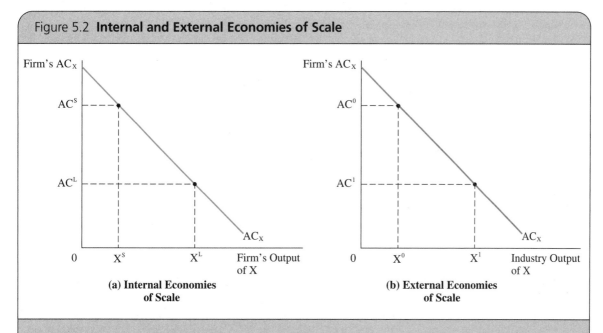

Figure 5.2 **Internal and External Economies of Scale**

(a) Internal Economies of Scale

(b) External Economies of Scale

In an industry characterized by *internal* economies of scale, the firm's average costs fall with increases in the *firm's* level of output. In an industry characterized by *external* economies of scale, firms' average costs fall with increases in *industry* output.

Motors or Toyota.[8] If economies of scale in a particular industry are internal to the firm, large firms have a cost advantage over small ones. The perfectly competitive market structure, in which many small firms take the market price as given, tends to give way to an imperfectly competitive one, in which each firm is large and acts as if it has some control over the price of its product.

External scale economies, on the other hand, occur when the firm's average costs fall as the *industry's* output rises, as in Figure 5.2, panel (b). When the output of the computer industry rises, for example, computer firms' costs fall because the industry becomes large enough to support a pool of skilled labor, along with input suppliers such as semiconductor-chip manufacturers. Therefore, AC^0 represents the average costs of a typical computer firm when the industry is small (industry output X^0), while AC^1 denotes the typical firm's average costs when the industry reaches output level X^1. *(How might this phenomenon explain why so many computer-related firms concentrate in regional centers such as California's "Silicon Valley"?)*

Economies of scale, both internal and external, have important implications for international trade. Such economies create an additional incentive for production specialization. Rather than producing a few units of each good domestic consumers want to buy, a country can specialize in producing large quantities of a small number of goods (in which the industries achieve scale economies) and trade for the remaining goods. Therefore, economies of scale provide a basis for trade *even between countries with identical production possibilities and tastes.* (Recall from Chapters Two and Three that under constant or increasing costs, mutually beneficial trade requires that two countries *differ* in production possibilities, tastes, or both, to generate a pattern of comparative advantage and a motive for trade.)

Figure 5.3, which assumes that countries A and B are identical in both tastes and production possibilities, shows the potential of mutually beneficial trade based solely on economies of scale rather than comparative advantage. Gains from trade occur because the presence of scale economies places a special premium (in the form of cost reductions) on specialization. Just as increasing opportunity costs produced a concave production possibilities frontier in Chapter Three, decreasing opportunity costs result in a *convex* or bowed-in production

8 Internal economies of scale can include plant economies (declining average costs as production in a given *plant* rises) or firm economies (declining average costs as the production of a given *firm* rises, perhaps in multiple plants). The auto industry exhibits both types.

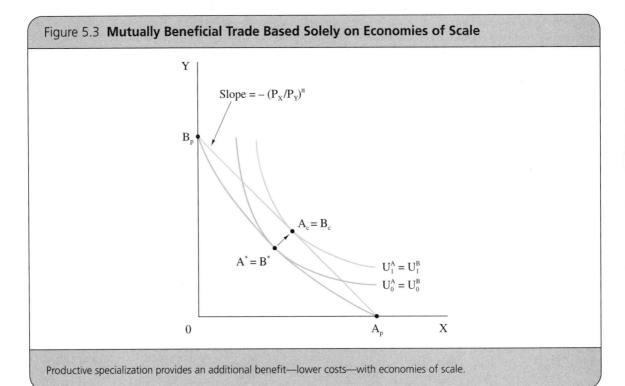

Figure 5.3 **Mutually Beneficial Trade Based Solely on Economies of Scale**

Productive specialization provides an additional benefit—lower costs—with economies of scale.

possibilities frontier. At each point, the (absolute) slope of the frontier reflects the opportunity cost of good X; along a convex frontier such as that in Figure 5.3, this cost *decreases* as a country produces more of good X. Without trade, the two identical countries would produce and consume at their autarky equilibria, A* and B*, placing them on indifference curves U_0^A and U_0^B. Each industry in each country fails to achieve economies of scale because domestic consumers demand some of *both* goods. Alternatively, each country can take advantage of economies of scale by specializing in production of one of the goods. Note an important difference from trade based on comparative advantage: The two countries are identical, so *it doesn't matter which country produces which good.* Suppose A specializes in good X (at point A_p) and B in good Y (at point B_p). The two countries can then trade along the terms-of-trade line to points A_c and B_c, reaching indifference curves U_1^A and U_1^B—a clear improvement for both over the autarky equilibria. Consumers in each economy can have a variety of goods to consume while still enjoying the cost savings from specialized large-scale production.

We'll see that whether trade in the presence of economies of scale will be unambiguously beneficial depends on whether the economies are internal or external to the firm and on the presence or absence of comparative advantage.

5.6.1 Internal Economies of Scale

With internal economies of scale, trade allows consumers to consume a larger variety of goods at lower prices.[9] Generally, we associate more varieties with higher levels of consumer welfare or satisfaction for one of two reasons. For some goods, individual consumers may want to consume several varieties; clothing provides one obvious example. If trade increases the number of styles and fabrics available, most consumers enjoy the expanded choices for variety in their wardrobes. For other goods, each individual may consume a single vari-

---

9 We'll demonstrate that opening trade reduces average costs. As long as entry and exit remain unrestricted, price will equal average costs in the long run because any differential between the two would reflect either positive economic profits (causing entry) or negative economic profits (causing exit).

ety, but different individuals may prefer different varieties. Although an individual may own only one car at a time, some individuals prefer BMW sports cars while others prefer Honda minivans, so the availability of many different varieties improves welfare.

But why should trade increase variety? Without trade, firms produce only for the domestic population. That population may value variety, but because of the population's limited size, firms may produce a limited number of variations to achieve economies of scale. For example, if the domestic population buys a million cars per year, domestic firms may choose to produce, say, a half million each of two varieties, not a hundred thousand each of ten varieties. To produce ten varieties for such a small population would result in high per-unit cost—because of the failure to achieve economies of scale. Trade can help by expanding the consuming population for any firm's product. Firms in one country specialize in one set of varieties, and firms in the other in another set. Consumers then have access to all the varieties through trade, while each firm achieves economies of scale by specializing.

Figure 5.4 illustrates. The four panels represent the markets for goods X and Y in countries A and B. We assume that the costs of producing each good don't vary across countries, so the average-cost curves for good X in panels (a) and (c) match, as do those for good Y in panels (b) and (d). In other words, we assume that the two countries do *not* exhibit a pattern of comparative advantage. To focus on the effect of economies of scale, we also assume that demands for the two goods in the two countries are identical. Curve D_X^A shows country A's demand for good X in panel (a), and D_X^{A+B} shows the total demand for good X, including both countries A and B.[10]

With no international trade, firms in each country would produce for domestic consumers only. Outputs would be X_0^A, Y_0^A, X_0^B, and Y_0^B in the four markets, respectively, where domestic demand intersects the average-cost curve in each case, because long-run equilibrium requires that price equal average cost. The relatively small levels of output would cause firms to forgo economies of scale, so average costs would be relatively high (with superscript zeroes in Figure 5.4); consumers would pay correspondingly high prices. If the two countries opened trade, each could specialize in producing just one of the two goods. The countries are identical, so which country produces which good doesn't matter. Assume country A specializes in good X and country B in Y. Country A would produce X_1^A in panel (a) and serve the entire market for X; its average costs and price would fall to AC_X^1. Country B would produce Y_1^B in panel (d), serve the entire world market for Y, and achieve economies of scale that lower average cost and price to AC_Y^1. *(Explain why, if country A specialized in Y and B in X rather than vice versa, average costs would be AC_X^2 and AC_Y^2.)* Note that the smaller the home market relative to the world market, the bigger the gain from opening trade in goods whose production exhibits internal economies of scale.

Economies of scale contribute a key element to our understanding of intra-industry trade in differentiated products. In industries that exhibit such economies, domestic firms have an incentive to produce for the majority or mass domestic market and to ignore small domestic consumer groups with tastes for different types of products. The costs of small-scale production to satisfy minority tastes would result in very high-priced products. However, if minority tastes in country A match majority tastes in country B, then imports from country B, produced with economies of scale, can satisfy those tastes. At the same time, a few consumers in country B probably will have "type A" tastes that imports from country A can satisfy at low cost.

5.6.2 External Economies of Scale

External economies of scale can help explain the widely observed phenomenon of industrial agglomeration, or the tendency of firms in an industry to cluster geographically. Examples include the watch industry in Switzerland, the high-fashion apparel industry in Italy, the movie industry in Hollywood, and the financial industry in New York and London. Recall that external economies arise when firms' average costs fall as the *industry's* output rises. Such a scenario typically happens when the clustered industry reaches a size adequate to support specialized services such as skilled labor markets and makers of specialized inputs. *(Suppose you own a computer software firm, and your star programmer just quit to start her own firm. Do you think you could find a suitable replacement more quickly if you were located in Palo Alto, California, or in Peoria, Illinois? Why? How would this affect your costs?)* Small firms can remain viable in industries characterized by external economies, unlike the

---

10 The horizontal distance between these two demand curves at any price measures country B's quantity demanded.

Figure 5.4 **Internal Economies of Scale as a Basis for Trade between Identical Countries**

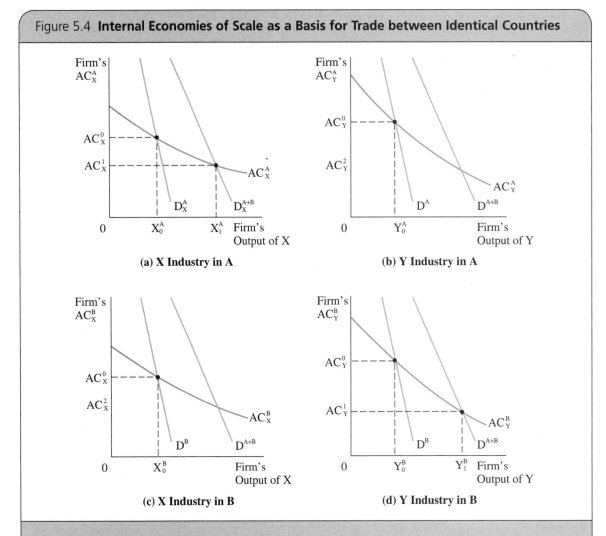

(a) X Industry in A

(b) Y Industry in A

(c) X Industry in B

(d) Y Industry in B

With internal economies of scale and no comparative advantage, international trade permits production of higher levels of output (X_1^A and Y_1^B) at lower costs (AC_X^1 and AC_Y^1) than does autarky (X_0^A, Y_0^A, X_0^B, and Y_0^B at costs AC_X^0 and AC_Y^0). Consumers enjoy both a variety of goods and the cost savings that accompany production specialization.

---

internal-economies case, because industry rather than firm output generates the cost reductions. Even the tiniest computer firm in Silicon Valley can benefit from the rich pool of specialized workers and components available nearby as a result of the industry's agglomeration.

The agglomeration effects generated by external economies of scale can give "historical accident" an important role in determining production and trade patterns. It's easy to see why. Suppose that a few high-fashion firms just happen to locate in northern Italy. Then the next few firms will have lower average costs if they also locate in northern Italy—where they can take advantage of the specialized input markets supported by the earlier firms. This location pattern becomes self-perpetuating and reinforcing. Eventually, no one may even remember the details of how or why the cluster got started in a particular place.

The interaction between external economies of scale and international trade can be either beneficial or harmful, depending on the presence or absence of comparative advantage. Consider first the pure case in which an industry's costs exhibit external economies but are identical in two countries (that is, there is no comparative advantage). Then Figure 5.4's analysis of the benefits from opening trade carries over; we just need to relabel the horizontal axes to measure industry rather than firm output. In this case, external economies provide the *only* basis for trade because no comparative advantage exists, and trade benefits both countries by providing more output at lower costs.

However, things aren't always so simple. Consider Figure 5.5. Now external economies of scale characterize industry X, *and* country A has a comparative advantage in X—in the sense that the average costs of producing good X, *at any given level of industry output,* are lower in country A than in country B. To keep things simple, we continue to assume that the two countries' demands for good X are identical. If the two countries begin in autarky, they will produce X_0^A and X_0^B at average costs of AC^A and AC^B, respectively. *(Why?)* From this autarky starting point, opening trade would benefit each country. Country A, with its cost advantage, would produce X_1 units at cost AC_1, at the point where the total demand curve (D^{A+B}) intersects A's average-cost curve. Consumers in both countries benefit from lower prices and more good X to consume. *(Would consumers in A or B gain more? Why?)*

What if the two countries start out, not in autarky, but trading with each other? If, for some historical reason, country A got started in the X industry first, the outcome would be the same as in the case where the countries move from autarky to trade. Country A will produce X_1 units at cost AC_1, and country B will produce other goods. Here, external economies of scale reinforce country A's comparative advantage, and both countries benefit from trade.

However, if the industry's history is such that country B happened to get an early start, firms from B would end up servicing the entire market, producing X_2 at cost AC_2, under unrestricted trade. In this case, firms from country A might have a hard time breaking into the market *despite their lower average-cost curve* because B's head start gives it the advantage of large scale. A firm in A, wanting to enter the industry, would incur initial average costs of AC_3 and couldn't compete with established firms from country B who can sell at AC_2. This presents a case in which trade may be harmful—in the sense that it allowed country B firms to achieve economies of scale and foreclose entry to country A firms, which have a comparative advantage. Consumers in both countries pay a higher price (AC_2 versus AC_1) for a smaller quantity of good X (X_2 versus X_1) as a result. Historical accident, in the form of country B's head start in the X industry, has combined with external economies of scale to dominate comparative advantage in determining the pattern of trade.

Figure 5.5 **External Economies of Scale and Comparative Advantage**

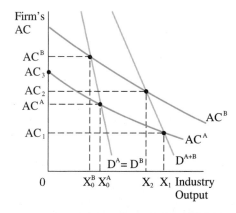

In autarky, country A produces X_0^A at cost AC^A and country B produces X_0^B at cost AC^B. International trade will be mutually beneficial if the country with comparative advantage (here, A) gets a head start in the industry; firms in country A would produce X_1 at cost AC_1. However, if the comparative-disadvantage country (B) gets a head start, firms in the comparative-advantage country may not be able to enter because of their high initial costs (AC_3), and country B firms will produce X_2 at cost AC_2.

Might protection help in cases such as the one in Figure 5.5, where economies of scale result in trade that runs counter to comparative advantage? Maybe, and maybe not. Figure 5.6 illustrates the two cases. In panel (a), if country A's government prohibited imports of X and kept A's market for domestic firms, those firms could achieve partial economies of scale and produce X_4 at AC_4. This would allow them to undersell the country B firms (who under free trade sell at a price equal to AC_2) and capture the rest of the market from the initially advantaged country B firms. Consumers in both countries eventually might benefit from lower prices and increased availability of good X (at AC_5 and X_5) as country A served both markets.[11] But in some cases such a strategy may not work. Panel (b) shows why. There, even a completely protected home market in good X may not allow country A firms to move far enough down their average-cost curve to undersell country B firms; the best A firms can do is output X_6 at a price equal to AC_6, which may not be good enough to displace the B firms, whose initial price equals AC_2. Eventually, if country A did impose protection, the loss of A's market would push B firms upward and to the left along their average-cost curves as industry output fell. The extent to which this occurs and the time horizon over which it happens depend on the exact source of the industry's external economies. In general, existing skilled-labor pools or specialized input markets probably wouldn't disappear very quickly in B, so any increase in B firms' costs due to A's protection of its home market could be slow in materializing. The smaller and slower the increase in B firms' costs, the less likely A's protection would be to allow A firms to capture the market and realize their comparative advantage.

Which case occurs, (a) or (b), depends on a combination of the strength of external economies in the industry (that is, how *steep* are the AC curves?) and the extent of comparative advantage (that is, how large is the *vertical distance* between the two countries' average-cost curves?). With small economies of scale and a strong pattern of comparative advantage, as in Figure 5.6, panel (a), protection of A's home market can permit country A firms to displace the already established country B firms. But with large economies of scale and a weak pattern of comparative advantage, as in panel (b), even protection of their home market may not allow country A firms to catch up with their country B rivals.

Figure 5.6 **Interaction of External Scale Economies and Comparative Advantage**

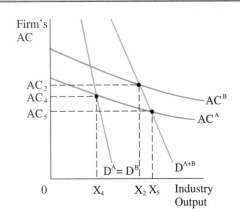

(a) Small Scale Economies, Large Comparative Advantage

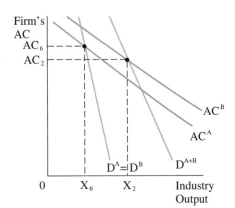

(b) Large Scale Economies, Small Comparative Advantage

Panel (a) combines weak scale economies and strong comparative advantage. Temporary protection of A's market could allow country A firms to capture the market even if country B firms enjoyed a head start. Panel (b) combines strong scale economies and weak comparative advantage. Temporary protection of A's market would not necessarily allow country A firms to capture the market from already established B firms, despite A's comparative advantage.

---

11 In Chapter Eight, we'll discuss some potential problems with these protectionist policies.

5.6.3 Dynamic External Economies

In some cases, firms' average costs depend not on the industry's *current* output but on its *cumulative* output—that is, the total of all past industry production. This occurs when the learning process plays a large role in achieving cost reductions. The downward-sloping curve that captures the negative relationship between cumulative industry output and firms' average costs, illustrated as LC in Figure 5.7, is called the **learning curve**, and the associated economies are called **dynamic external economies.** When these dynamic effects are present, they can reinforce or work against comparative advantage, just like other external economies of scale. In Figure 5.7, where country A has a comparative advantage, learning and comparative advantage could work together under free trade to give consumers the most output at the best price (X_0 and AC_0), but only if the industry got underway first in country A. If a quirk of history gave the B industry a head start, free trade would generate X_1 at price AC_1, definitely an inferior outcome. Despite their comparative advantage, country A firms, with no history of production to let them generate dynamic external economies, might not be able to break into the B-dominated market because of their high initial costs (AC_2), even though they could eventually produce more at lower cost that country B firms. *(Show that trade must be beneficial with a learning curve and no comparative advantage.)*

5.6.4 The Scope of Economies and Learning

Note that all our discussion of external economies of scale has assumed that the industry output of relevance is the *domestic* industry. The other possibility is the case in which firms' costs depend on the output of the *worldwide* industry, either current or cumulative. If this were the case, arguments for protection based on external economies of scale, like the one in Figure 5.6, panel (a), would disappear. To see why, look again at Figure 5.7, and assume that country B has captured the market through historical accident. If country A firms can learn from country B firms' production experience as well as they could learn from domestic firms' experience, then A firms can start producing at cost AC_3, not AC_2. *(Why?)* This allows A firms to undersell their B rivals and capture the market, building on their comparative advantage. They then produce X_0 at a price equal to AC_0.

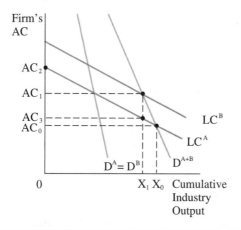

Figure 5.7 **Dynamic External Economies and the Learning Curve**

With a learning curve based on the output of the domestic industry, country A firms can be shut out of the market if country B firms get a head start, despite A firms' comparative advantage. The outcome would be output X_1 produced at cost AC_1. However, if domestic firms can learn from foreign firms' experience, the learning curve won't block entry by firms from country A, whose initial average cost will equal AC_3. The outcome then will be output X_0 at cost AC_0.

Because policy recommendations can hinge on whether dynamic economies of scale depend on output of the domestic or the worldwide industry, answering this question is a high priority. Unfortunately, external economies have proven very difficult to identify and measure. However, in one industry thought to be characterized by strong external economies—the semiconductor industry—recent evidence suggests that effective learning may take place based on foreign as well as domestic production experience.[12] If so, any case for protection disappears.

In summary, economies of scale can provide a basis for trade, even in the absence of comparative advantage. In markets characterized by *internal* economies of scale, international trade allows consumers to enjoy a greater variety of goods while still achieving the cost savings that comes with large-scale production. The resulting trade is intra-industry and may generate fewer political pressures for protection than inter-industry trade because of its smaller impact on relative factor demands, factor prices, and the distribution of income. Trade based on *external* economies of scale can be beneficial or harmful depending on (1) the importance of scale economies relative to comparative advantage, (2) whether historical production patterns follow or run counter to comparative advantage, and (3) whether domestic or worldwide industry output provides the basis for the external scale economies.

Economies of scale as basis for trade is just one of several ways in which the characteristics of available production technologies affect international trade. The next section introduces the idea that changes in technology over time can change the pattern of imports and exports.

5.7 Technology-Based Theories of Trade: The Product Cycle

The Heckscher-Ohlin trade model assumes that all countries have access to and use the same productive technologies. Remember that this implies that the isoquant map for each industry is the same across countries. Even though the isoquant maps are identical, firms in different countries may use different capital-labor ratios in their production processes because of different factor prices that reflect differences in factor endowments. However, with unrestricted trade, factor prices equalize across countries, and all firms use identical production techniques. (The reader may want to review Chapter Three, section 3.2.1, and Chapter Four, section 4.4.)

Some industries probably satisfy the assumption of identical technologies across countries reasonably well. For others, the assumption seems less viable. Consider, for example, the electric-power industry. Countries endowed with large, swiftly flowing rivers have access to a technology for production of electric power not feasible for desert countries. The natural endowment of resources such as rivers is just one possible source of differences in technologies available in various countries. Other sources include technologies kept secret for security reasons (such as nuclear power and some computer capabilities) and legal restrictions such as patents that limit imitation of proprietary technologies. History provides many examples of technological innovations that allowed firms in one country to make significant advances over others at least in the short run, most notably England's industrial revolution of the late eighteenth century, the "second industrial revolution" in late nineteenth- and early twentieth-century America, and the late twentieth-century "computer revolution."

Economists have suggested a number of ways that cross-country differences in technology affect international trade. Here we'll concentrate on one particular technology-based explanation for temporal changes in the observed pattern of trade: the **product-cycle hypothesis,** first articulated by Raymond Vernon in the mid-1960s.[13] The basic idea underlying the product cycle is that certain countries tend to specialize in producing new products based on technological innovation, and other countries specialize in producing already well-established goods. The primary implication of the theory is that as each product moves through its life cycle, the geographic location of its production changes.

Vernon argued that technological innovation and new-product development tend to occur in a few major industrialized economies, particularly the United States. This reflects the countries' highly educated and skilled workforce and the relatively high level of expenditure on research and development. Early production of a new product typically occurs on a small scale as the innovating firm debugs and refines both the product and

---

12 See the Irwin book and the Irwin and Klenow paper in the chapter references.

13 Raymond Vernon, "International Investment and International Trade in the Product Cycle," *Quarterly Journal of Economics* (May 1966), pp. 190–207.

the production process. Firms usually aim this early, small-scale production at the domestic rather than the export market. At first, actual production needs to be located close to consumers so they can provide feedback. Only the technologically innovative firm owns the new technology, so production occurs only in that firm's home country.

Eventually, the firm perfects the product and production accelerates, first for the domestic market and then for export. Domestic consumption and domestic production rise, but production rises more rapidly to accommodate growing export demand. The innovating firm still controls the new technology.

As the production technology becomes standardized (no longer a matter of trial and error and experimentation), the innovating firm may find it profitable to license the technology to other firms both domestically and abroad. It then becomes feasible to relocate production to other countries in which the cost of standardized production is lower. The cost of such production in the innovating country remains relatively high because of its highly skilled labor force. Once production no longer requires the research-and-development and engineering skills of that labor force, relocation of production becomes economical. Some domestic production of the good continues in the innovating country, but exports level off as new, low-cost producers licensed by the innovating firm capture export markets.

Next, imports rather than domestic production begin to serve the domestic market of the innovating country. The technology has diffused completely, and any patents or other proprietary restrictions that once limited its use have expired. Domestic production falls rapidly as the domestic industry loses both its domestic and export markets.

Finally, the product completes its cycle. Although domestic consumption of the good may continue, imports satisfy that consumption. Attention in the innovating country concentrates on new technological innovations, leading to new products in the early stage of their product cycles. Examples of products that appear to have experienced a typical product cycle include radios, black-and-white and then color televisions, and semiconductor chips (see Case One at the end of the chapter).[14]

The textile industry provides a long-term example of the product-cycle scenario at work. The industrial revolution gave England a huge technological advantage in textile production. As the new technologies spread, the textile industry moved to the United States (first to New England, then to the South) and then on to other countries where abundant low-skilled labor permitted production of low-cost textiles using a standardized technology. Today the major centers of textile production are in the labor-abundant countries of Asia. The industry's migration continues; as wages rose in established textile centers such as Hong Kong and Singapore, production shifted to new Asian centers including Malaysia, the Philippines, and China.

The product-cycle hypothesis and other related explanations of trade focus on characteristics of the production process. An alternate theory focuses on the importance of demand characteristics in various countries.

5.8 Overlapping Demands as a Basis for Trade

The Ricardian and Heckscher-Ohlin theories of trade imply that a country will find it most beneficial to trade with countries very *different* from itself. Differences in production possibilities, tastes, or both can form a basis for trade, as demonstrated in Chapter Three. This would lead us to expect large volumes of trade between dissimilar countries, particularly between the capital- and human-capital-abundant developed countries and the mineral- and unskilled-labor-abundant developing countries. World trade figures, however, don't bear out this expectation. The largest share of world trade, particularly in manufactured goods, occurs among the group of developed countries, which have high incomes and similar factor endowments. One explanation of this phenomenon focuses on economies of scale (section 5.6) rather than comparative advantage as the source of trade.

Alternatively, economist Staffan Linder suggested that similarities in *demand* between two countries also can form a basis for trade, especially for manufactured goods.[15] This argument rests on the idea that firms typically don't produce goods solely for export; most produce goods for which domestic demand exists. If a country develops only those industries for which a viable domestic market exists, trade will occur in those products for which domestic consumers and foreign consumers share similar tastes.

---

14 For evidence that the product cycle doesn't characterize most industries, see Joseph Gagnon and Andrew Rose, "Dynamic Persistence of Industry Trade Balances: How Pervasive Is the Product Cycle?" *Oxford Economic Papers*, 1995.

15 Staffan B. Linder, *An Essay on Trade and Transformation* (New York: Wiley, 1961).

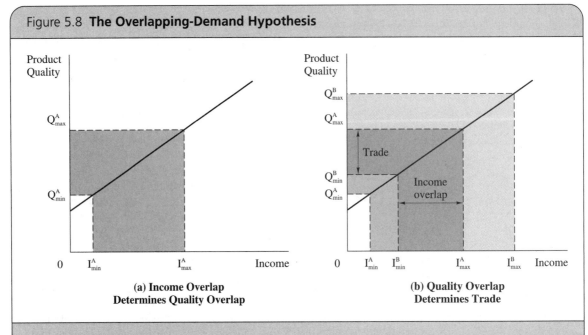

Figure 5.8 **The Overlapping-Demand Hypothesis**

(a) Income Overlap Determines Quality Overlap

(b) Quality Overlap Determines Trade

Linder hypothesized a positive relationship between a country's level of income and the quality of manufactured goods its residents demand. Countries A and B exchange goods in quality range Q_{min}^B to Q_{max}^A, determined by the overlap in their ranges of income.

To formulate empirically testable implications, we must state the hypothesis more precisely. Linder argues that for many manufactured goods, the *quality* of the good that consumers in a particular country demand depends primarily on their income. Consumers with higher incomes tend to demand manufactured goods of higher quality. Panel (a) in Figure 5.8, with income measured on the horizontal axis and quality measured on the vertical one, represents this hypothesized relationship as an upward-sloping line. Of course, the income levels of consumers in any given country vary. In Figure 5.8, panel (a), *i*ncomes for country A range from a low of I_{min}^A to a high of I_{max}^A. Given these income levels, consumers in country A demand goods of *q*uality range Q_{min}^A to Q_{max}^A. If, as Linder suggests, a domestic market is necessary for an industry to develop, country A will produce manufactured goods in the Q_{min}^A to Q_{max}^A quality range.

Figure 5.8, panel (b), introduces a second country with income range I_{min}^B to I_{max}^B and demand for goods in quality range Q_{min}^B to Q_{max}^B. Industries in country B will develop to provide goods in the quality range demanded by B consumers. The overlap in the quality ranges demanded by consumers in countries A and B (Q_{min}^B to Q_{max}^A in panel (b)) represents the goods in which trade between the two countries might occur. The more similar the ranges of income, the larger the overlap in the demanded qualities and the greater the potential for trade.

Empirical evidence on the validity of the overlapping-demands hypothesis is mixed. As mentioned earlier, the large share of trade that occurs among the high-income developed countries provides informal evidence in support. In 1998, 57 percent of all world merchandise exports went from one high-income economy to another, as illustrated in Figure 5.9. Only 36 percent of exports went either from a high-income economy to a developing one or *vice versa*.

More precise tests of the overlapping-demands hypothesis have been less encouraging. However, in evaluating tests of the model, we must remember the problems introduced by differences in the distribution of income across countries. Consider an extreme example. Let all but one consumer in country A have income level I_{min}^A, and let the remaining individual have income level I_{max}^A; let all country B individuals but one have income level I_{max}^B, and let the remaining individual have income level I_{min}^B. The potential for trade is much lower than the illustrated range of overlap in qualities suggests. Because of this problem, tests of the overlapping-demands

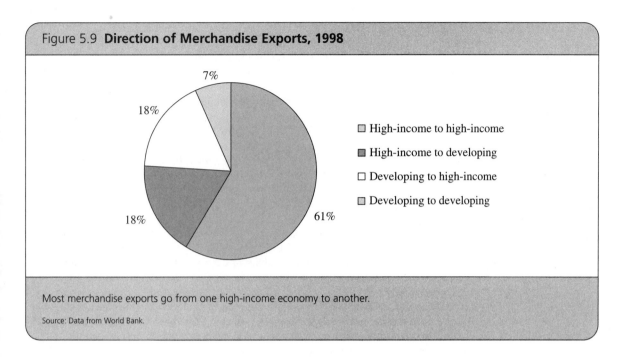

Figure 5.9 **Direction of Merchandise Exports, 1998**

- High-income to high-income
- High-income to developing
- Developing to high-income
- Developing to developing

7%
18%
18%
61%

Most merchandise exports go from one high-income economy to another.

Source: Data from World Bank.

hypothesis require careful corrections for the distribution of income; reliable, internationally comparable data on the distribution of income are difficult to obtain. An additional problem in testing the hypothesis arises because the model's predictions closely match that of a model of intra-industry trade based on economies of scale—both predict high levels of trade in manufactured goods between similar trading partners. The similarity of the models' predictions presents a problem for empirical researchers trying to sort out the relative merits of the two for explaining the pattern of trade observed in the world economy.

Besides theories of trade based on the characteristics of production or of demand, several rely heavily on characteristics of the trade process itself. One consideration we've ignored so far is the role of transportation costs.

5.9 Transportation Costs as a Determinant of Trade

Some goods typically aren't traded internationally. Called **nontraded goods,** the reason for their special status usually involves a prohibitive cost of transporting them from one country to another. The classic example is haircuts (actually a service rather than a good). Although substantial differences exist in the prices of haircuts across countries, trade doesn't develop by shipping haircuts from low-price to high-price countries. The cost of transporting either the barber or the customer to take advantage of the low price in another country would far outweigh the price differential.

For other classes of goods, **transportation costs** may not be prohibitive (that is, high enough to prevent any trade) but still may be high enough to have a significant impact on the pattern of trade. Very heavy goods tend to be more costly to transport. For these, the relationship between the item's weight and value is important. Automobiles, which are relatively heavy but of comparatively high value, are traded; gravel, on the other hand, typically isn't traded internationally because its low value doesn't warrant the high transportation costs implied by its weight. We saw in section 5.5.2 that transportation costs could generate intra-industry trade in heavy homogeneous goods, but only if the placement of national boundaries puts consumers in one country near producers in the other. Also, perishable items must be moved quickly, and rapid means of transportation usually are more expensive than slower means.

Traditionally, economists devoted little attention to the effects of transportation costs on trade. The volume of trade in the world economy certainly is smaller than would be the case if goods could be transported costlessly and instantaneously from country to country. However, as long as transportation costs remain fairly constant over time, their incorporation adds little explanatory power to the models already developed.

When sudden *changes* occur in transportation costs, things become more interesting. Often such changes result from an advance in technology. One example is the development of refrigerated truck and ship transportation. These innovations reduced spoilage by enough to make international trade in many food products feasible for the first time. In the northeastern United States, many of the fresh fruits and vegetables available in stores during the winter come from Latin America. Before invention of refrigerated transport, the spoilage cost of such trade would have been prohibitive. Containerized intermodal cargo shipping provides another example. By prepacking goods in very large, uniformly sized containers that giant cranes can load quickly and efficiently onto ships, trucks, and railroad cars, the cost of hauling many large items long distances has been substantially reduced.

Transportation costs also play an important role in trade with external economies of scale. High transportation costs can contribute to the agglomeration effects common in industries characterized by external economies. Also, past transportation costs may have caused an industry to spring up in a particular location, and external economies of scale may perpetuate that pattern long after the initial transportation-cost reason for it disappears.

Another interesting issue concerning transportation costs is the question of who pays them—the importer or the exporter. In general, the two share the costs. Other things being equal, the less price responsive the demand for the good by the importing country, the larger the share of transportation costs the importer will bear; and the less price responsive the supply of the good by the exporting country, the greater the share of transportation costs the exporter will bear.

Panel (a) in Figure 5.10 illustrates the international market for good X. Country A is assumed to have a comparative advantage in production of X and is willing to export X at any price above its autarky price, P_X^A.[16] The supply curve for exports, $Exports_X^A$, shows how many units of good X country A is willing to export at various prices. Country B has a comparative disadvantage in good X and is willing to import X at any price below

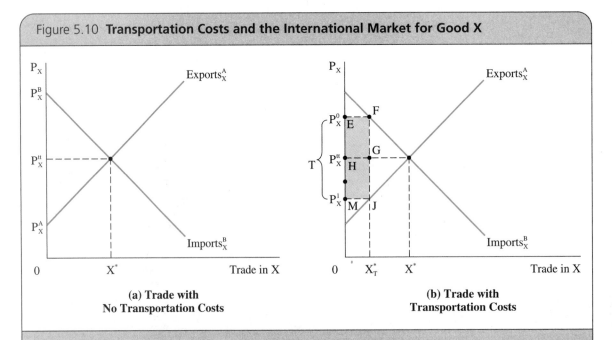

Figure 5.10 **Transportation Costs and the International Market for Good X**

(a) Trade with No Transportation Costs

(b) Trade with Transportation Costs

Transportation costs of T per unit cause the quantity of good X traded to fall from X* to X_T^*. The price consumers pay rises from P_X^{tt} to P_X^0, and the price producers receive falls from P_X^{tt} to P_X^1.

16 To simplify notation, we show the price of good X simply as P_X rather than as the relative price, P_X/P_Y, as in Chapters Two and Three.

its autarky price, P_X^B. The demand curve for imports, Imports$_X^B$, shows how many units of good X country B is willing to import at various prices. The equilibrium outcome with no transportation costs involves X^* units of good X traded at international terms of trade P_X^{tt}.

Next, consider the effect of transportation costs of T per unit of good X transported between countries A and B, as shown in panel (b) of Figure 5.10. T includes the cost of packing and transporting the good as well as insurance premiums for the trip and related expenses. The price paid for good X by consumers in country B must cover *both* the price paid to producers in A and the transportation costs. If $T = P_X^0 - P_X^1$, the new equilibrium volume of good X traded is X_T^*. Consumers in country B pay price P_X^0, and producers in country A get price P_X^1. The difference of T per unit, or $T \cdot X_T^*$ in total, goes to pay the costs of transportation. Transportation costs reduce the volume of trade in good X, just as we would expect.

Producers in country A pay a share of the transportation costs by accepting the lower price P_X^1 rather than the price P_X^{tt} that prevailed without these costs; the area of rectangle HGJM in Figure 5.10, panel (b) shows producers' contribution toward the costs. Consumers in country B share in the burden of the transportation costs by paying the higher price P_X^0; the area of rectangle EFGH represents their contribution. The graphical demonstration that the division of the total transportation costs, area EFJM, between the share borne by producers and that borne by consumers depends on the particular shapes of the demand and supply curves is left to the reader. *(Hint: Draw two graphs with identical demand curves, one with a very steep supply curve and the other with a very flat supply curve.)*

If transportation costs are an important determinant of the pattern of international trade, the choices of firms and industries concerning where to locate also must be significant, because distance from consumers affects transportation costs. In fact, one of the most robust empirical findings in trade is that, other things being equal, the extent to which two countries trade is negatively related to the distance between them.[17] Here we suggest a few basic industry characteristics that play a role in the choice of location.

5.10 Location of Industry

A firm's decision about where to locate depends on, among other things, the characteristics of the production process in the industry. Industries can be classified as resource oriented, market oriented, or footloose.

Resource-oriented industries tend to locate near sources of their inputs or raw materials. One obvious example is mining operations. Once the mineral is out of the ground, the location of each stage of the refining process must be decided. Should the mineral be refined into its final form next to the mine, or should the raw material be shipped to another location for refining? The answer largely depends on how the ore's weight changes as it moves through the stages of refining. Because transportation costs tend to increase with weight, firms have an incentive to avoid moving the good long distances until it is refined to a lighter form. Industries in which the good becomes lighter as it moves through the production stages tend to locate near the source of raw materials to avoid having to move the good until it is in its lighter form.

An example of a **market-oriented industry** is retail sales operations. It wouldn't make sense to locate all bakeries in Iowa just to be near the wheat fields. Bakeries locate near their customers to sell fresh goods made in small batches. Other industries may be market oriented because they involve goods that become heavier or otherwise more difficult to move during the production process. It generally is less costly to gather the inputs to construct a building on the site and then assemble the parts than to build the building and then move it to its site (some small modular buildings provide an exception to the rule); hence, the construction industry locates near its markets. The soft-drink industry provides another example. Most soft-drink companies manufacture a highly concentrated syrup in a centralized location and ship it to local bottling companies, which add carbonated water and distribute the soft drinks to retailers. Shipping the small volume of concentrated syrup is less costly than shipping the much larger volume of soft drink.

A third category of industry has no need to locate near either raw material sources or markets; these industries are characterized as **footloose** or **light industries.** Their products typically neither gain nor lose a significant amount of weight or volume as they move through the stages of production. Goods such as semiconductor chips and electronic components fall into this category because of their high value-to-weight ratios. Such light industries are free to move around the world in response to changes in the prices of inputs and

---

17 Models that incorporate distance between countries as a determinant of the extent of trade are called *gravity models.*

assembly. The product-cycle idea may be important in determining the location of footloose industries. As a product matures, the type of labor and other resources required to produce it may change, causing the industry to relocate. Both the semiconductor and consumer-electronics industries followed this pattern.

Economies of scale also play a role in determining firms' and industries' locations. A firm with substantial internal economies needs a large market to achieve those economies. If transportation costs are low, the firm can serve a large dispersed market and be flexible in its location. But if transportation costs are high, a geographically dispersed market becomes prohibitively expensive, and the firm needs to locate near a large concentration of its customers. We've already seen how external economies of scale can dictate that firms concentrate geographically; but high transportation costs for a firm's final product may counteract the tendency toward agglomeration if the good's consumers are spread over a large area.

U.S./Japan

CASE ONE:
Conducting Semiconductor Trade

Engineers at Texas Instruments and Fairchild invented integrated circuits, or semiconductor chips, in 1958. Since then, the industry has maintained a rapid rate of change. U.S. firms dominated the industry in the early years, but during the late 1970s and 1980s, foreign producers, especially Japanese firms, made rapid gains in manufacturing technology. Worldwide semiconductor sales in 2000 topped $222 billion. Of the top three semiconductor companies in the world in 2000, ranked by worldwide revenue, one was American and two Japanese, as documented in Table 5.3.

Viewing the semiconductor industry as a single entity can be misleading. Relatively early in its life cycle, the industry split into two branches, each with distinct production and trade characteristics. The first branch, highly research-and-development intensive, emphasizes technological innovation and continual introduction of more powerful and self-contained chip designs. This technologically innovative branch of the industry has moved beyond ever-bigger memory chips into so-called designer chips, including microprocessors, microcontrollers, custom-logic chips, and chips for the routers and switches that control Internet traffic. The industry's second branch focuses on standardizing and lowering the cost of large-scale production for existing memory-chip

designs. Memory chips of a given design are a largely homogeneous product (although quality control is crucial), and the primary consideration in capturing market share is lowering manufacturing cost.

Figure 5.11 illustrates the 2000 memory-chip market shares of the Americas (overwhelmingly the United States), Japan, Europe, and non-Japan Asia (primarily Taiwan and South Korea). The United States and Japan together produce about 60 percent of all memory chips. If we include designer chips as well as memory ones, the U.S.-plus-Japan market share rises to about 80 percent, because those countries maintain stronger dominance in the designer-chip sector of the industry.

During the 1990s, several new types of firms appeared in the industry. Some, called foundries or fabs, simply sell their manufacturing services to other firms, which design the chips. Most foundries are based in countries relatively new to the chip industry, such as Taiwan, Malaysia, and China; the largest foundries are Taiwan Semiconductor Manufacturing and United Microelectronics. The counterparts to foundries are "fabless" firms, ones that design chips but leave the *fabrica-tion*, or manufacturing, to foundries (important fabless firms include Broadcom, PMC-Sierra, Vitesse Semiconductor, and

Table 5.3 **Top Three Chip Makers, 2000**

Company	Chip Sales (Billions $)
Intel (U.S.)	$29.8
Toshiba (Japan)	11.2
NEC (Japan)	11.1

Source: Data from Dataquest.

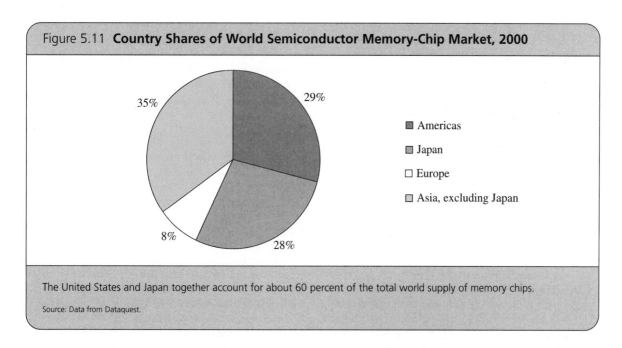

Figure 5.11 **Country Shares of World Semiconductor Memory-Chip Market, 2000**

- Americas
- Japan
- Europe
- Asia, excluding Japan

The United States and Japan together account for about 60 percent of the total world supply of memory chips.

Source: Data from Dataquest.

Xilinx). At first, foundries produced just memory chips; but now they also produce the more sophisticated chips used in communication and consumer-electronics devices.

The design branch of the semiconductor industry remains active in the United States, while the memory branch has moved increasingly to other areas—first Japan, then South Korea and Taiwan, and now China. This reflects U.S. comparative advantage in the research-intensive branch, as opposed to more physical-capital-intensive memory-chip production, where low-cost manufacturing techniques give Asian countries the edge.

In addition to distinct patterns of comparative advantage, the two sectors of the chip industry exhibit different business-cycle patterns. The memory-chip sector is more subject to boom-and-bust cycles. In 1995, memory-chip makers could hardly add production capacity fast enough; 30 new billion-dollar factories were planned or under construction. Many industry analysts proclaimed that the boom-bust days of the 1980s had ended. A *Wall Street Journal* headline in August 1995 declared, "Bad Times Are Just a Memory for DRAM Chip Makers." In February 1996, just six months after bad times had been just a memory, another *Wall Street Journal* headline read, "Dependence on Memory Chips Could Hurt Japan's Firms: Semiconductor Makers Have Failed to Diversify, and Now Prices Are Falling." DRAM (dynamic random access memory) prices fell by one-third to 80 percent in a year, depending on chip type. Firms scrambled to delay or cancel planned construction of new fabrication plants. Worldwide memory-chip sales for 1996, predicted to be $45

billion, turned out to be closer to $25 billion. Soon excess capacity and a collapse of memory-chip prices received blame for triggering a 1997 economic crisis in Asia. Prices recovered in 1999, and by June 2000, the *Wall Street Journal* headline read, "It's Happy Times Again for Memory-Chip Firms." A year later, several new large-scale plants had entered operation, and demand for chips had plummeted with the economic slowdown. DRAM prices fell by 90 percent as the *Financial Times* declared a "Chip Overload." South Korean Hynix, the world's third-largest memory-chip producer, neared default on its debt and received a controversial bailout by its banks, including some funded by the government.

Throughout the semiconductor industry's volatile history, international developments and trade policy have played important roles. In 1986, the United States responded to increasing Japanese dominance of chip production as well as to Japan's entry into the more technologically innovative branch of the industry by pressuring Japan to join a five-year trade pact in chips. The agreement sought to raise the price of Japanese chips in both U.S. and foreign markets and to improve U.S. chip producers' access to the Japanese market.[18] The agreement succeeded in raising chip prices, much to the dismay of the U.S. computer industry (the major buyer of chips), but U.S. chip makers expressed frustration over their lack of increased sales in Japan. Under pressure from domestic chip makers, the United States imposed retaliatory 100 percent tariffs on imports of Japanese televisions, power tools, and laptop computers in 1987.

---

18 On the chip pacts' effects, see the Flamm and Irwin books in the chapter references and section 7.7 on voluntary import expansions.

In 1991, the United States removed the retaliatory tariffs when the two countries extended the chip trade pact for five years. The renewed agreement reduced its earlier emphasis on keeping the U.S. price of Japanese chips high (a concession to the U.S. computer industry) and increased its emphasis on raising the share of foreign chips sold in Japan, including a controversial 20 percent foreign market-share target.

By the time the 1991 semiconductor pact expired in 1996, foreign chip sales in Japan were fluctuating between 20 and 30 percent, and trade tensions fluctuated with the sales figures. The countries negotiated a new agreement, but a much weaker one. The two industries agreed to monitor foreign chips' share of Japan's market, a task assigned to governments under the 1985 and 1991 pacts, while disagreeing about exactly which chips should count as "foreign."

Besides trade in chips themselves, controversy surrounds trade in the machinery used to manufacture chips, such as chemical-vapor deposition and photolithography tools. Japan's share of the world market in this equipment rose during the 1980s, and the U.S. share fell (from 73 percent in 1981 to 43 percent in 1990). U.S. chip makers argued that if Japan came to dominate production of chip-making machinery, they could delay shipment of new technology to the United States, thereby giving Japanese chip makers a jump on their U.S. competitors in new technology chips.

In 1987, U.S. firms joined in a government-supported consortium called Sematech to improve semiconductor manufacturing techniques and bolster U.S. firms that manufacture chip-making equipment. Half of Sematech's $200 million initial budget came from the U.S. government. Many analysts expressed disappointment with Sematech's results, but Congress extended the group's funding in September 1992 for five more years. Japanese firms expressed interest in joining Sematech, but the group restricted membership to U.S.-based firms. Sematech announced in 1994 that when its then-promised government funding expired in 1997, it would stop taking government funds and become a strictly industry-funded research group. It has also diversified internationally; in 1996, seven foreign firms joined one of Sematech's research projects. In 1998, Korean Hyundai, Dutch Philips, Franco-Italian SGS-Thomson, German Siemens, and Taiwan Semiconductor announced a foreign subsidiary, International Sematech. The United States and Japan still dominate production of semiconductor manufacturing equipment; the world's largest producer is Applied Materials, Inc.

Increasingly, the enormous research-and-development expenditures required to produce a new generation of chips have forced firms to join together in these efforts, often across national boundaries. For example, in 2000, American Intel and Micron Technology, Japanese NEC, South Korean Samsung and Hyundai, and German Siemens Infineon Technologies announced a joint project to develop new memory-chip technologies. The semiconductor manufacturing equipment industry's recent challenge has been to develop a new generation of equipment for manufacturing chips from 300-millimeter silicon wafers, up from the current standard of 200-millimeter wafers. Experts have estimated the cost of retooling for the bigger wafers at $35 billion.

Philippines

CASE TWO:
"Getting the Joke" as a Source of Comparative Advantage

Computers have made inroads into cartoon production, especially for blockbuster movies, but much of the industry remains highly labor intensive. Each small movement of a cartoon character requires thousands of panels of patient drawings and paint by artists and animators. Approximately 90 percent of the animation for television cartoons happens in labor-abundant Asia, especially the Philippines, where costs run about half those in the United States.[19]

As wages of Filipino artists and animators rise, cartoon studios are lured toward lower-wage countries such as China and Vietnam. But the Philippines claim a nonwage advantage: The workers there speak English and live in a former U.S. colony. They argue that the result is better cartoons because the workers understand cartoon dialog and "get the joke"—an unlikely but important source of comparative advantage.

---

19 "Asia's Toonsville," *The Economist,* February 22, 1997, p. 75.

CASE THREE:
Around the World in 22 Days

Transportation costs add from 5 to 10 percent to the prices of most internationally traded consumer goods. Until the mid-1970s, most U.S. imports from Asia came across the Pacific Ocean, through the Panama Canal, and up to East Coast ports such as New York. Then the arrival of "intermodal transport," which coordinates containerized shipments by water, rail, and truck, shifted Asia–U.S. trade toward the West Coast ports of Long Beach, Los Angeles, and Seattle. Goods arrived there by ship, where the bus-sized containers were moved onto railroads and trucks for the trip east, along the route illustrated in Figure 5.12, panel (a); the total trip was five or six days faster than the old Panama Canal route. Since 1990, routes appear to be shifting again—this time 9,000 miles across the Indian Ocean, through the Suez Canal, and across the Atlantic to East Coast harbors, along the route shown in panel (b).

The times involved in the Pacific and Suez routes are similar: about 25 days by ship and rail and about 22 days by ship, respectively, made possible by recent improvement in ship speeds relative to rail. Container ships typically travel at between 17 and 23 knots, depending on weather conditions. The new Suez route is somewhat more convenient for Southeast Asian exporters such as Malaysia, Singapore, Thailand, and China. The direct Pacific route, on the other hand, suits Northern Asian exporters Japan and South Korea. Moving an average cargo container from Asia to the United States in 1999 cost around $3,500. The Suez Canal Authority, which sets rates for using the canal, is charged with raising maximum revenues for the Egyptian government (which nationalized the canal in 1952), so the canal authority sets rates to make the Suez trip just cheaper than alternate routes. But as of 2001, the canal carried only about half of its 80-ship-per-day capacity.[20]

Two other economic factors affect exporters' choices of shipping routes. First, the shipping lines that cover each route belong to a cartel that controls rates and other shipping terms. Shipping is one of the few industries in which such cartels are legal in the United States; Congress exempted them from antitrust action in the Shipping Act of 1916. But in 1999 Congress weakened the cartels' power to keep rates high by changing the law to permit shipping firms to reach confidential deals with their customers rather than requiring that all rates be posted publicly. Under the old rules, once rates were posted, cargo had to be carried at that price on a first-come, first-served basis; shipping firms "overbooked," and the resulting waits could be long and costly for customers. Under the new rules, a firm with fresh shrimp to transport can simply pay a higher price for immediate service. The shipping cartels were also weakened during the 1990s by entry of new Asian firms' fleets that didn't join the cartels. About 85 percent of U.S.–Asia shipping capacity belongs to cartel members. As the relative strengths of the cartels on different routes (the Trans-Atlantic Conference Agreement and the Transpacific Stabilization Agreement) fluctuate, relative shipping rates change; exporters respond by moving to the cheaper route. For example, between 1995 and 1997, Atlantic shipping prices remained steady while Pacific prices fell by 12 percent; then, with the onset of the Asian financial crisis, in late 1997, Pacific prices plummeted.

Second, East and West Coast U.S. ports are worked by union stevedores—the International Longshoremen's Association in the east and the International Longshoremen's and Warehousemen's Union in the west. Fluctuations in the two unions' strength, like that of the shipping cartels, alters the cost of having goods unloaded on the two coasts. For example, in 1999, West Coast longshore workers' entry wage was almost double that of East Coast workers;[21] handling a single container cost about $300 at the port of Los Angeles. Port cities watch shifts in these costs closely, because building and modernizing a port requires billions of dollars of investment.

The increased transportation costs caused by the shipping cartels and harbor-service restrictions have a significant impact on world trade. A recent World Bank study found that breaking up shipping cartels could cut transport costs for U.S. trade by up to 25 percent, and that deregulating port services could lower costs by 9 percent.[22]

Hong Kong, a local cargo port for containers coming from and going to China by truck, and Singapore, a transshipment hub where most containers both arrive and leave by boat, are the largest ports in the world. Technology is changing traditional port practices. In the newest facilities, loading, unloading, and container tracking are automated and computerized, requiring little labor. Singapore's PSA Corporation handled 17 million containers in 2000, using its proprietary computer software to track each container and

20 "Too Big for World Trade Demands," *Financial Times,* May 9, 2001.

21 "West Coast Cargo Firms Plan Stingy Labor Talks," *The Wall Street Journal,* May 12, 1999.

22 Carsten Fink et al., "Trade in International Maritime Services: How Much Does Policy Matter?" World Bank Development Research Group.

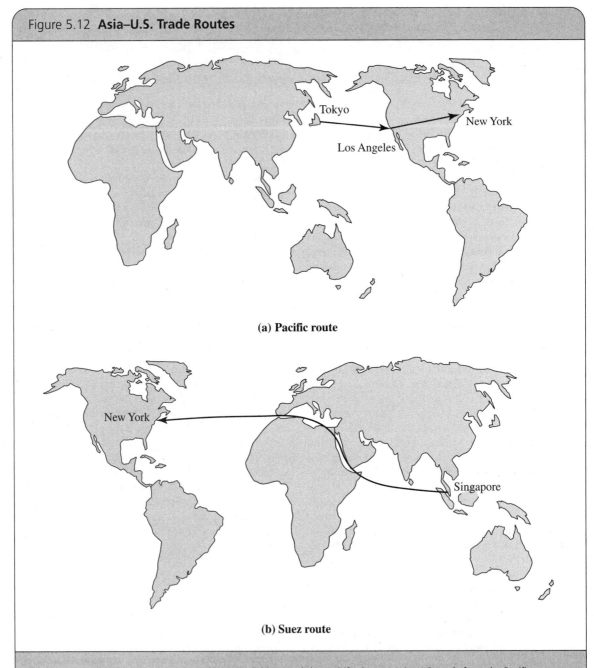

Figure 5.12 **Asia–U.S. Trade Routes**

(a) Pacific route

(b) Suez route

Growth of Southeast Asian exporters and increased ship speeds have shifted some Asia–U.S. trade from the Pacific route to the Suez route.

to ensure that ships remain stable despite loading with thousands of containers each of a different weight; only 1 container in every million shipped through the Singapore port was damaged or misplaced.[23] Such high-tech ports can unload and reload a container ship in about half the time required at older-style U.S. ports (40 versus 76 hours). The Hong Kong port facility can handle 20,000 TEUs (twenty-foot equivalent units, the standard unit of container measurement) per acre per year, compared with only 4,500 TEUs per acre per year at Los Angeles and 2,300 at New York.[24]

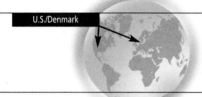

U.S./Denmark

CASE FOUR:
Internal Economies of Scale and the Sperm Trade[25]

Experts estimate that between $50 million and $100 million worth of human sperm are exported each year. Obviously, each country has its own supply, so why international trade in sperm? One answer is internal economies of scale. Sperm sales now require sophisticated tests for genetic defects and infectious diseases. These tests involve high fixed costs for firms to acquire the necessary equipment and expertise. Storage and transportation requirements also are complex, including liquid-nitrogen transportation tanks that maintain freshness for a week; these requirements also add to firms' fixed costs.

As we saw earlier in the chapter, markets characterized by internal economies of scale tend to have only a few firms.

So a small number of firms handle most sperm transactions, and most countries are too small to support a commercial sperm bank. The result: international trade in sperm. Six firms in the United States, such as Xytex Corporation, and Cryos International Sperm bank in Denmark, handle most international transactions. U.S. firms specialize in offering donors from a variety of ethnic backgrounds and in providing buyers lots of information about donors, including photos and, in some cases, videos. Cryos, on the other hand, offers much-in-demand blue-eyed donors and maintains stricter anonymity for its donors.

United States

CASE FIVE:
Multinationals and Intra-Firm Trade

This chapter distinguished between two types of trade: inter-industry trade based on comparative advantage, in which countries import and export goods in different industries, and intra-industry trade based on economies of scale, in which each country both imports and exports differentiated goods in the same industry. Another way of distinguishing "who trades with whom" is to focus on *intra-firm trade*—that is, trade within multinational firms, either between parent and affiliate firms or between affiliates of the same parent. Intra-firm trade accounts for approximately 40 percent of U.S. exports and imports (see panels (a)

and (b) of Figure 5.13). This number has remained relatively constant since the 1980s, reflecting a combination of growth in intra-firm trade as a share of parent company trade and shrinkage in U.S. parent companies' share of total U.S. trade.

Intra-firm trade doesn't occur evenly across countries or industries. Industrial countries have the highest rates of participation in intra-firm trade. Figure 5.14 reports the share of intra-firm trade in total trade for the six top U.S. export markets in 1992. Across 62 export markets, intra-firm transactions account for more than half of all exports with three partners, Russia, Switzerland, and Japan. Across 62 import

---

23 "Singapore Port Positions Itself for IPO This Year," *Financial Times,* February 19, 2001.

24 "U.S. Ports Are Losing the Battle to Keep Up with Overseas Trade," *The Wall Street Journal,* July 9, 2001.

25 "A Most Unlikely Industry Finds It Can't Resist Globalization's Call," *The Wall Street Journal,* January 6, 2000.

Figure 5.13 **Share of U.S. Trade Accounted For by Intra-Firm Trade, 1982–1994**

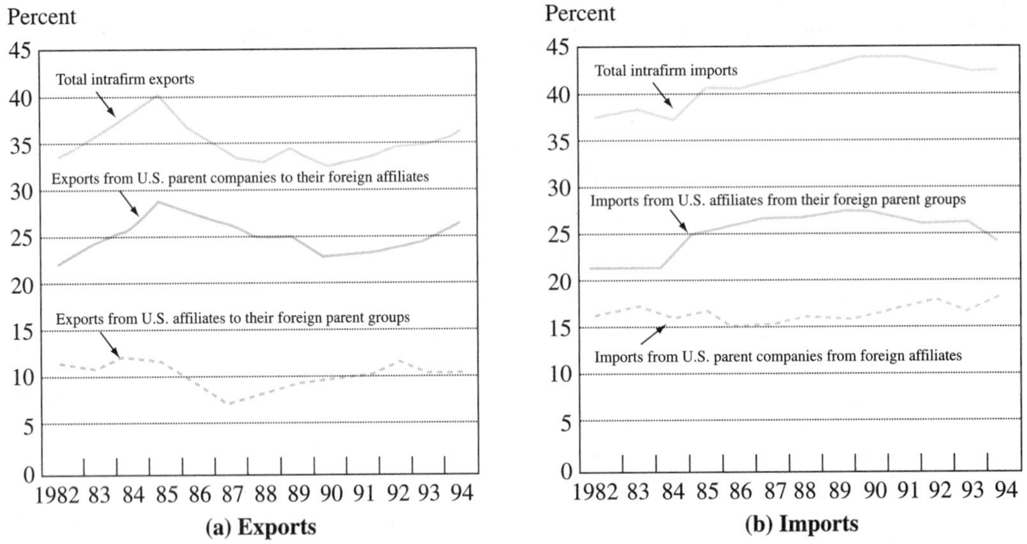

(a) Exports

(b) Imports

Between 35 and 45 percent of U.S. trade occurs within firms, including both affiliate-parent and affiliate-affiliate shipments.

Source: U.S. Department of Commerce.

Figure 5.14 **Intra-Firm Trade Shares of U.S. Trade with Selected Partners, 1992**

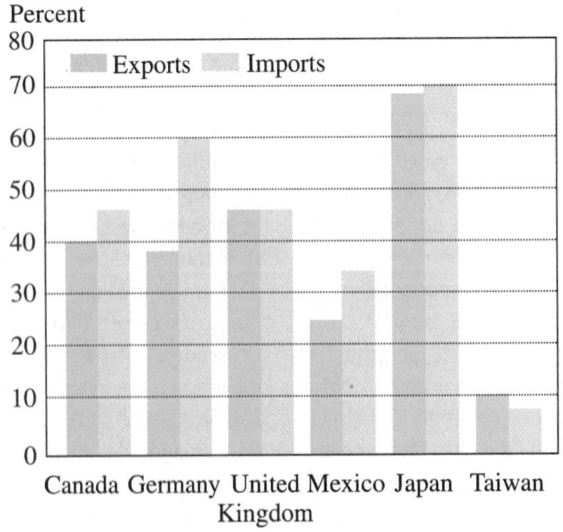

Intra-firm trade accounts for large shares of U.S. imports and exports, especially with developed-country trading partners.

Source: U.S. Department of Commerce.

markets, intra-firm trade makes up more than half of imports from Germany, Ireland, the Netherlands, Sweden, Switzerland, Japan, Singapore, and Trinidad and Tobago.

We'll see in Chapter Ten that economic analysis of multinational firms predicts that such firms would be most likely to arise in industries characterized by high levels of research and development, specialized information, and economies of scale. Figures on U.S. intra-firm trade support this prediction. The U.S. industries with high levels of intra-firm exports relative to total exports include office and computing machines, motor vehicles, electronic components, and pharmaceuticals.

U.S. intra-firm exports consist largely of transactions by U.S. multinational firms, especially shipments from U.S. parents to their foreign affiliates. These exports tend to be materials and components for assembly by foreign manufacturing affiliates. U.S. intra-firm imports consist largely of transactions by foreign multinationals. The U.S. intra-firm trade by foreign multinationals contains more marketing and distribution activities and consists mainly of goods for resale by affiliates without further manufacture.

Summary

International trade is too complex a phenomenon to be explained fully by one simple theory. This chapter explored the ability of the Heckscher-Ohlin model to explain observed trade patterns, along with several alternate theories useful for understanding particular aspects of trade. The Heckscher-Ohlin model does a good job of explaining a large share of trade, with refined definitions of inputs to account for modern production processes. However, growing intra-industry trade in manufactures requires that we move beyond comparative advantage and add economies of scale to our list of bases for mutually beneficial trade. Alternate, complementary explanations include the product cycle, overlapping demands, transportation costs, and location of industry.

Looking Ahead

Chapter Six examines the simplest form of trade restriction: the tariff. By altering relative prices, tariffs change consumption and production decisions as well as redistribute income. The overall welfare effect of a tariff in a small country is negative, but a large country may be able to gain at the expense of its trading partners by imposing a tariff on imports. International negotiations since World War II have significantly lowered overall tariff levels, but high tariffs still distort trade in several important industries.

Key Terms

intra-industry trade
import substitutes
Leontief paradox
homogeneous good
product differentiation
decreasing costs (increasing returns to
    scale, economies of scale)
internal scale economies
external scale economies

learning curve
dynamic external economies
product-cycle hypothesis
nontraded goods
transportation costs
resource-oriented industries
market-oriented industries
footloose (light) industries

Problems and Questions for Review

1. Explain why the data in Table 5.1 present a paradox.
2. a. Write the formula for the intra-industry trade index. Explain why the index takes a value of 0 in industries with no intra-industry trade and a value of 1 in industries with maximal intra-industry trade.
   b. If country A exports $10 million worth of semiconductor chips per year and imports $20 million worth of semiconductor chips per year, what is country A's intra-industry trade index for semiconductor chips? Suppose you had data to calculate the IIT index for 256K DRAMs. How would you expect the two IIT indices to compare? Explain.

3. Use a figure similar to Figure 5.4 to show that international trade is particularly important for small countries in the presence of economies of scale. *(Hint: Alter Figure 5.4 so that country A's demand for each good is half the size of country B's demand.)* Explain.

4. How can international trade theory explain intra-industry trade?

5. The product-cycle theory of trade argues that the economically efficient geographic location of production changes as a good moves through its life cycle. In what sense is this consistent with the Heckscher-Ohlin theory of trade? Why might the kinds of locational shifts suggested by the product-cycle theory result in pressures for protectionist policies?

6. Assume that (1) the computer software industry exhibits external economies of scale, (2) India has a comparative advantage over the United States in producing computer software, (3) the Indian market for software is one-tenth the size of the U.S. market, and (4) the United States has a head start in the industry and currently produces for both the U.S. and Indian markets. Illustrate in a diagram similar to Figure 5.5. What would happen if India protected its software market? On what does your answer depend?

7. Before the Soviet Union collapsed in 1991, Soviet economic planners were famous for keeping transportation costs within the Union artificially low. The Soviet Union was also known for its massive industrial plants, often designed to serve the entire Soviet Union plus its satellite states in Eastern and Central Europe. Explain the relationship between the two policies, and how you would expect the policies to affect the level of trade among the Soviet republics.

8. Why might we expect intra-industry trade based on economies of scale to be less politically controversial than inter-industry trade based on comparative advantage?

References and Selected Readings

Baldwin, Robert E. "Are Economists' Traditional Trade Policy Views Still Valid?" *Journal of Economic Literature* 30 (June 1992): 804–829.
Survey of the literature incorporating imperfect competition and economies of scale and their implications for international trade policy.

Brander, James A. "Strategic Trade Policy." In *Handbook of International Economics,* Vol. 3, edited by G. M. Grossman and K. Rogoff, 1395–1456. Amsterdam: North-Holland, 1995.
Advanced survey of the literature on strategic aspects of trade policy.

Feenstra, Robert C. "Estimating the Effects of Trade Policy." In *Handbook of International Economics,* Vol. 3, edited by G. M. Grossman and K. Rogoff, 1553–1596. Amsterdam: North-Holland, 1995.
Advanced survey of the empirical literature on the economic effects of various trade policies.

Feenstra, Robert C. "Integration of Trade and Disintegration of Production in the Global Economy." *Journal of Economic Perspectives* 12 (Fall 1998): 31–50.
Relationship between trade patterns and production patterns; for all students.

Flamm, Kenneth. *Mismanaged Trade?* Washington, D.C.: Brookings, 1996.
History and economic analysis of the semiconductor industry, including the U.S.–Japan trade pacts.

Grossman, Gene M., ed. *Imperfect Competition and International Trade.* Cambridge, Mass.: MIT Press, 1992.
Collection of important papers on international trade under imperfect competition. Level of papers varies from intermediate to advanced.

Grossman, Gene M., and Elhanan Helpman. "Technology and Trade." In *Handbook of International Economics,* Vol. 3, edited by G. M. Grossman and K. Rogoff, 1279–1338. Amsterdam: North-Holland, 1995.
Advanced survey of technology-related aspects of international trade and trade theory.

Helpman, Elhanan. "The Structure of Foreign Trade." *Journal of Economic Perspectives* 13 (Spring 1999): 121–144.
Interaction between traditional trade models and more modern developments; intermediate.

Hummels, David, et al. "Vertical Specialization and the Changing Nature of World Trade." Federal Reserve Bank of New York *Economic Policy Review* (June 1998): 79–99.
How firms' location of the different stages of their production processes affects trade patterns; intermediate.

Irwin, Douglas A. *Managed Trade: The Case against Import Targets.* Washington, D.C.: The Brookings Institution, 1994.
Excellent, readable analysis of trade agreements such as the U.S.–Japan chip pact.

Irwin, Douglas A., and Peter J. Klenow. "Learning-by-Doing Spillovers in the Semiconductor Industry." *Journal of Political Economy* 102 (December 1994): 1200–1227.
Empirical estimation of learning curves in the semiconductor industry. Advanced.

Komiya, Ryutaro, and Motoshige Itoh. "Japan's International Trade and Trade Policy, 1955–1984." In *The Political Economy of Japan, Vol. 2: The Changing International Context,* edited by Takashi Inoguchi and Daniel I. Okimoto, 173–224. Stanford: Stanford University Press, 1988.
Accessible survey of Japanese postwar trade policy.

Krugman, Paul R. *Development, Geography, and Trade.* Cambridge, Mass.: MIT Press, 1995.
How increasing returns affect locational choice, development, and trade; for all students.

Krugman, Paul. "Increasing Returns, Imperfect Competition, and the Positive Theory of Trade." In *Handbook of International Economics,* Vol. 3, edited by G. M. Grossman and K. Rogoff, 1243–1278. Amsterdam: North-Holland, 1995.
Advanced survey of recent developments in trade theory.

Krugman, Paul R. "Industrial Organization and International Trade." In *Rethinking International Trade,* 226–268. Cambridge, Mass.: MIT Press, 1994.
Advanced survey of the growing overlap in industrial organization and international trade theory.

Leamer, Edward, and James Levinsohn. "International Trade Theory: The Evidence." In *Handbook of International Economics,* Vol. 3, edited by G. M. Grossman and K. Rogoff, 1339–1394. Amsterdam: North-Holland, 1995.
Advanced survey of empirical evidence on international trade theories.

Leontief, Wassily. "Domestic Production and Foreign Trade: The American Capital Position Reexamined." *Economia Internazionale* 7 (February 1954): 3–32.
Presents the empirical evidence that became known as the Leontief paradox. For introductory or intermediate students.

Lewis, Karen K. "Trying to Explain Home Bias in Equities and Consumption." *Journal of Economic Literature* 37 (June 1999): 571–608.
Why are home-country stocks overrepresented in stockholders' portfolios and home-country goods overrepresented in consumers' consumption baskets? Intermediate and advanced.

Murphy, K. M., and A. Schleifer. "Quality and Trade." *Journal of Development Economics* (June 1997): 1–15.
More on the overlapping-demands story.

Session on "Empirical Testing of Trade Theories." *American Economic Review Papers and Proceedings* 90 (May 2000): 145–160.
Advanced treatment of testing trade theories; emphasis on the role of technology.

Trefler, Daniel. "International Price Differences." *Journal of Political Economy* 101 (December 1993): 961–987.
Empirical test of the factor price equalization theorem emphasizing productivity differences. Advanced.

Trefler, Daniel. "The Case of the Missing Trade and Other Mysteries." *American Economic Review* (December 1995): 1029–1046.
Tests of Heckscher-Ohlin; advanced.

Vernon, Raymond. "The Product Cycle Hypothesis in a New International Environment." *Oxford Bulletin of Economics and Statistics* 41 (November 1979): 255–267.
Updated perspective on the product cycle from its original proponent; for introductory or intermediate students.

Westhoff, Frank H., Beth V. Yarbrough, and Robert M. Yarbrough. "Complexity, Organization, and Stuart Kauffman's *The Origins of Order.*" *Journal of Economic Behavior and Organization* 29 (January 1996): 1–25.
Application of complexity theory to the role of "historical accident" in economic history; advanced.

Yarbrough, Beth V., and Robert M. Yarbrough. "International Contracting and Territorial Control: The Boundary Question." *Journal of Institutional and Theoretical Economics* 150 (March 1994): 239–264.
Application of the new economics of organization to the problem of why national boundaries change. For all students.

CHAPTER 6

CHAPTER SIX

Tariffs

6.1 Introduction

Up to this point, we've explored the benefits of unrestricted international trade. Although the methods we've used come from the modern economist's tool kit, the benefits of trade have been known for several centuries, at least since the work of David Hume, Adam Smith, and David Ricardo. Nonetheless, no period of history has been free of a complicated array of trade restrictions. Chapter Four presented several reasons for the controversial nature of trade, particularly its effect of redistributing income within each participating country. The policies countries use to restrict trade are called **barriers to trade,** one of which is the tariff. In this chapter, we explore tariffs' effects on production, consumption, prices, trade volume, and welfare.

A **tariff** is a tax imposed on a good as it crosses a national boundary. Historically, tariffs were the most commonly used type of trade restriction; in recent years, however, use of tariffs in the world economy has declined and use of a variety of other trade restrictions has increased. Average tariff levels have fallen both in the United States and abroad, largely as a result of international negotiations conducted under the General Agreement on Tariffs and Trade (GATT), now called the World Trade Organization (WTO), a forum created after World War II for international negotiation of trade issues.

6.2 Why Would a Country Impose a Tariff?

A country might choose to impose a tariff for any of four reasons. First, a tariff, like any other tax, can discourage consumption of a particular good. Placing a tariff on an imported good makes it relatively more costly to consumers. For example, during the OPEC oil price increases of the 1970s, many policy makers proposed a tariff on oil imports; proponents argued that the United States needed to reduce its consumption of oil, particularly foreign oil, and that a tariff presented one possible incentive.

A second reason for imposing a tariff, like any other type of tax, is to generate revenue for the government. Developed countries rarely impose tariffs specifically to raise revenue, because those countries have the infrastructure necessary to administer other taxes, such as personal and corporate income taxes. Figure 6.1 traces the dramatic historical decline in tariffs' share of U.S. government revenue. However, many developing countries still use tariffs to raise a significant share of the revenue required to finance their governments' activities. Successful administration of an income tax requires a well-developed bureaucracy as well as a literate and settled population; countries lacking these prerequisites find it easier to administer tariffs by patrolling ports and national borders.

A third reason for imposing import tariffs is to discourage imports to decrease a deficit in the balance of trade (that is, a situation in which payments to foreigners for imports exceed receipts from foreigners for exports). A country designing a tariff to reduce a trade deficit would apply the tariff to all imports, or at least to

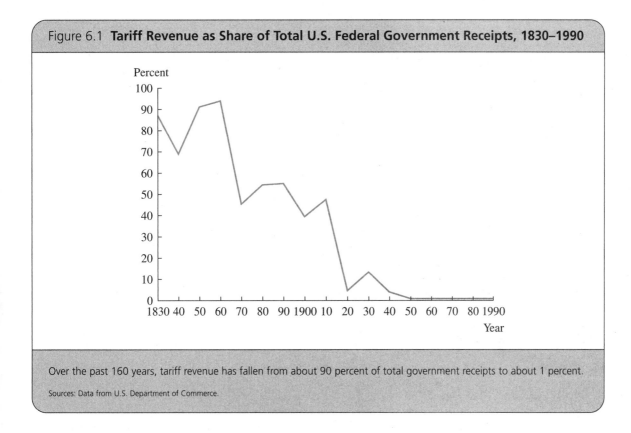

Figure 6.1 **Tariff Revenue as Share of Total U.S. Federal Government Receipts, 1830–1990**

Over the past 160 years, tariff revenue has fallen from about 90 percent of total government receipts to about 1 percent.

Sources: Data from U.S. Department of Commerce.

a wide range of goods, rather than to a single good or a narrow range of goods. We haven't yet developed a framework for analyzing this motive because it involves tariffs as a tool of *macro*economic rather than *micro*-economic policy. In Part Two, we'll see both that tariffs aren't likely to be effective in reducing a balance-of-trade deficit and that proper use of other policy tools makes tariffs for balance-of-trade purposes unnecessary.

The fourth—and most common—purpose of tariffs, and the one on which we'll focus, is as a **protectionist policy**—a way to "protect" or insulate a domestic industry from competition by foreign producers of the same good. A tariff on imports allows domestic producers both to capture a larger share of the domestic market and to charge a higher price than would be possible in the tariff's absence.

Countries impose many more tariffs on imports than on exports, especially developed countries that don't use tariffs as a major source of government revenue. In fact, the U.S. Constitution makes export taxes illegal in the United States, as we'll see in Case Four. So, we'll focus our discussion on import tariffs and, at the end of the chapter, briefly examine the effects of export taxes and the history behind the U.S. prohibition on them.

6.3 Types of Tariffs and Ways to Measure Them

Like any tax, tariffs can be classified as specific or ad valorem.[1] **Specific tariffs** charge a specified amount for *each unit* of the tariffed good imported. For example, the United States charges a tariff of $0.68 per live goat. **Ad valorem tariffs** charge a specified percentage of the *value* of the tariffed good, such as the U.S. tariff of 2.4 percent of a dog leash's value. The fundamental economic effects of tariffs apply to both specific and ad valorem ones. For most of our analysis, specific tariffs will be more convenient because they are easier to depict graphically.

---

1 Compound tariffs combine a specific and an ad valorem tariff on the same good. You can find examples in the U.S. *Harmonized Tariff Schedule*, at www.usitc.gov/taffairs.htm.

Most countries apply tariffs on a detailed product-by-product basis; for example, the U.S. tariff code contains more than eight thousand categories, on which tariffs range from 0 percent to 458 percent.[2] However, economists and policy makers often want a measure of a country's *overall* tariff level. That is, we often want to know about the general level of trade restriction a country imposes in the form of tariffs rather than the amount of the tariff on a narrow product category such as "grapefruit, imported during October" (*yes*, grapefruit imported during October are tariffed at a rate [$0.015 per kilogram] different from grapefruit imported during either August or September [$0.019 per kilogram] or November through July [$0.025 per kilogram]!). This idea may appear simple enough, but measuring a country's overall tariff level turns out to be less simple than it seems.

Tariff rates differ across goods (for example, over 200 separate U.S. tariff rates apply to different types of watches and clocks), so characterizing the overall level of a country's tariff protection requires combining these separate rates into some type of average. There are two basic approaches, each of which has advantages and disadvantages.

The first technique involves a simple unweighted average of industry tariff rates. Consider country A, which imports two goods, X and Y, with imports of X subject to a 25 percent tariff and imports of good Y to a 50 percent tariff. The unweighted average tariff for the country equals $(0.25 + 0.50)/2 = 0.375$ or 37.5 percent. This unweighted-average technique works reasonably well for countries that import approximately equal amounts of different goods—for example, if country A imported $50 worth of X and $50 worth of Y.

But what if country A imported $80 worth of X and $20 of Y? In this case, simply averaging the two tariff rates without taking into account the goods' relative importances in overall imports seems less desirable. This is why the more common measure of tariffs is a weighted-average measure. It involves weighting the tariff rate for each industry by that industry's share of total imports. If country A imported $50 worth of X and $50 worth of Y, then the weighted-average tariff rate would equal $(\$50/\$100) \cdot 0.25 + (\$50/\$100) \cdot 0.50 = 0.375 = 37.5$ percent. Note that with equal imports in both industries, the unweighted and weighted tariff measures give the same result. However, if A imports $80 worth of X and $20 worth of Y, the weighted-average measure equals $(\$80/\$100) \cdot 0.25 + (\$20/\$100) \cdot 0.50 = 0.30$, considerably below the unweighted figure of 0.375. This occurs because the more prevalent import, X, has the low tariff rate. In this case, the weighted-average tariff gives a more accurate picture of country A's overall tariff situation.

For the purpose of measuring a country's overall level of protection, the main problem with both types of average tariffs is that they ignore trade foreclosed by the tariff. In other words, the measures don't take into account that the country might have imported $100 *million* (rather than $100) worth of the two goods with no tariff. The easiest way to see this problem is to consider the extreme case of a **prohibitive tariff,** that is, one high enough to halt trade in the product. Consider again the case where country A imports $50 worth each of goods X and Y. Now suppose country A raises its tariff on good Y from 50 percent to 100 percent, high enough to cause imports of Y to fall to zero. Total imports fall to $50, all good X. The average tariff (whether weighted or not) now equals 25 percent because the tariff on good Y disappears from the calculation. Ironically, the *increase* in the tariff on good Y caused a *decrease* in country A's average tariff. But we wouldn't want to conclude that country A's trade has become more open!

Despite impressive liberalization since World War II, many products remain subject to much higher-than-average tariff rates. In the markets for these products, tariffs (and, in some cases, nontariff barriers as well) continue to distort trade. Even after the Uruguay Round results, approximately 5 percent of developed-country imports remain subject to "peak" tariffs in excess of 15 percent. For example, the United States cut its average tariffs on apparel imports as part of the Uruguay Round, but only from 19.3 to 17.5 percent.[3] In addition, the United States doesn't grant the negotiated tariff reductions, either from the Uruguay Round or from earlier rounds, to some countries, usually for political or security reasons. Regions that in 2001 didn't receive most-favored-nation status, which grants access to the lower tariffs, include Afghanistan, Cuba, Laos, North Korea, and Vietnam.

Because most of the tariff reductions since World War II have taken place in the context of GATT/WTO rounds, nonmember countries often retain high tariffs relative to the members. However, membership has grown rapidly. As of the end of 2000, 140 countries were members and 31 countries had requested accession to the trade group; the newest WTO members include Jordan, Georgia, Albania, Oman, and Croatia, who joined in 2000; and China and Taiwan, who joined in November 2001. Even among WTO members, tariff rates vary

---

2 See the U.S. Harmonized Tariff Code at www.usitc.gov/taffairs.htm.

3 Jeffrey J. Schott, *The Uruguay Round: An Assessment* (Washington, D.C.: Institute for International Economics, 1994), p. 62.

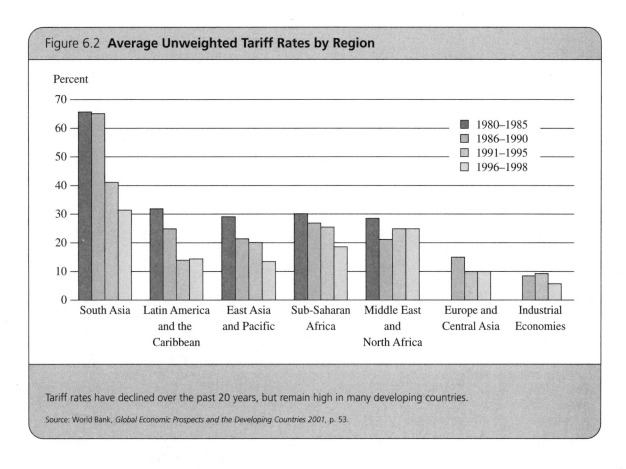

Figure 6.2 **Average Unweighted Tariff Rates by Region**

Percent

Legend:
- 1980–1985
- 1986–1990
- 1991–1995
- 1996–1998

Tariff rates have declined over the past 20 years, but remain high in many developing countries.

Source: World Bank, *Global Economic Prospects and the Developing Countries 2001*, p. 53.

widely by country, by source of imports, and by product. Figure 6.2 indicates regional variations in tariff levels. The industrial economies of North America and Western Europe have the lowest tariffs, and the developing economies of South Asia have the highest; but tariffs in all regions have come down since the early 1980s.

Variation in tariffs across products is as important as variation across regions. Table 6.1 reports average tariffs in effect at the end of the Uruguay Round on industrial products.

Notice two patterns in Table 6.1: developing-country tariffs are higher than industrial-country ones, and the textile and clothing industries have unusually high rates of protection. We'll see more about both issues later.

6.4 What Happens When a Small Country Imposes an Import Tariff?

In analyzing a tariff's effects, the size of the country imposing it matters. We begin with the case of a small country. Remember that *small* refers not to geographic size but to economic size in world markets. A small country is a price taker in world markets; that is, its activity comprises such a small share of total purchases and sales of a good that its actions have no perceptible effect on the world price. In other words, a small country's terms of trade are determined exogenously (outside the country), and the country makes its production and consumption decisions based on those terms of trade.

6.4.1 Effects on Production, Consumption, and Price

We begin by analyzing the partial-equilibrium effects of a small country's imposition of an import tariff. The analysis is a partial-equilibrium one because it focuses on the tariff's effects in the market for the tariffed good and in the country imposing the tariff. Let D^d and S^d in Figure 6.3 represent *d*omestic *d*emand and *d*omestic

Table 6.1 **Post–Uruguay Round Tariff Rates on Industrial Products**

Industrial Product	Average Trade-Weighted Tariff Rate (Percent)		
	Industrial-Economy Imports from Developing Economies	Developing-Economy Imports from Industrial Economies	Developing-Economy Imports from Developing Economies
Fish and fish products	5.0	8.7	15.9
Wood, pulp, paper and furniture	1.5	9.6	7.3
Textiles and clothing	11.1	20.7	21.1
Leather, rubber, footwear, and travel goods	6.1	18.5	8.2
Metals	0.8	13.5	8.5
Chemicals and photographic supplies	2.7	13.0	9.2
Transport equipment	3.9	21.8	10.6
Nonelectric machinery	1.2	14.4	10.2
Electric machinery	2.4	16.0	14.0
Mineral products	1.0	9.4	8.1
Other manufactured articles	2.0	13.9	8.8
All industrial products (excluding petroleum)	3.9	14.7	10.3

Source: Data from Marcelo de Paiva Abreu, "Trade in Manufactures: The Outcome of the Uruguay Round and Developing Country Interests," in Will Martin and L. Alan Winters, eds., *The Uruguay Round and the Developing Countries* (Cambridge: The World Bank, 1996), pp. 66, 75, 79.

supply, respectively, of good Y in the small country. (We omit country superscripts because the analysis refers to a single country.) In autarky, point E represents equilibrium in the market for Y, with Y^0 units produced and sold at price P_Y^0. With unrestricted trade, the equilibrium world price of good Y equals P_Y^1, which is less than P_Y^0. This relationship between the autarky and world prices implies that the country has a comparative disadvantage in good Y, consistent with good Y being the country's imported good.

Because the country is small, it can buy as much good Y as it chooses on the world market at price P_Y^1. The perfectly elastic (horizontal) world supply curve, S^w, represents graphically the country's smallness. Under unrestricted trade, the economy would locate at point F, consuming Y^1 units of good Y, producing Y^2 units domestically, and importing $Y^1 - Y^2$ units, all at price P_Y^1. Even though residents consume more good Y at a lower price under unrestricted trade than in autarky, domestic producers can sell fewer units and only at the lower price. This effect of trade on domestic producers creates pressure for protection from foreign competition. Unrestricted trade doesn't eliminate the domestic Y industry, but lowers both the industry output and the price domestic firms can charge for their product. The cost of domestic production is such that domestic firms can produce units of good Y up to Y^2 more cheaply than they could be imported. Figure 6.3 reflects this, because the domestic supply curve (which represents the domestic cost of production) lies below the world supply curve (which represents the foreign cost of production or the cost of importing) out to Y^2. For all units of good Y beyond Y^2, however, foreign production is less costly than domestic production; thus, the country imports those units under unrestricted trade.

Suppose the country imposes a specific tariff of t per unit on imported Y to improve the position of domestic Y producers. A horizontal line at $P_Y^1 + t$ illustrates the new world supply curve the country faces. The small country can't affect its terms of trade, so the tariff is simply an addition to the domestic price of imports. To import a unit of Y, domestic consumers now must pay P_Y^1 to the foreign producer plus t to the domestic government. Point G represents the new equilibrium. Consumers demand Y^3 units of Y at price $P_Y^1 + t$; domestic producers supply Y^4 units; and $Y^3 - Y^4$ units are imported. By raising the good's effective domestic price, the tariff reduces consumption of good Y, increases domestic production, and cuts imports. Domestic producers of good Y now produce more and can sell at a higher price, but domestic consumers consume less and must pay a higher price.

Figure 6.3 **What Happens When a Small Country Imposes an Import Tariff?**

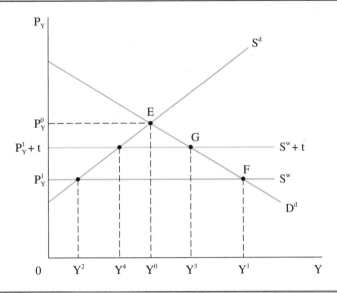

The tariff increases the domestic price of the good by the amount of the tariff, reduces domestic consumption, increases domestic production, and decreases imports.

6.4.2 Effects on Welfare

A tariff's impact on production, prices, and consumption translates into an effect on the small country's welfare. To analyze the change in welfare caused by the tariff, it's useful to separate the effects on consumers from those on producers. For each group we need a measure of welfare, called *consumer surplus* and *producer surplus,* respectively.

Consumer Surplus

Consumer surplus measures the satisfaction consumers receive from a good beyond the amount they must pay to obtain it. In panel (a) of Figure 6.4, the shaded triangle under the demand curve and above the price of the good illustrates the concept of consumer surplus. Recall that the height of a demand curve measures the maximum amount consumers are willing and able to pay for each successive unit of the good. Because no one would pay more for a good than the satisfaction gained from its consumption, the height of the demand curve represents the satisfaction derived from consumption of each unit. If consumers demand Y^0 units, the total satisfaction must equal the area under the demand curve for good Y out to Y_0, or the sum of the satisfactions generated by each unit. But consumers must pay P_Y^0 for each unit; in other words, total expenditures on Y equal the area of rectangle $0P_Y^0CY^0$. This implies that the net satisfaction from consumption of Y^0 units over their cost is the area under the demand curve out to Y^0 and above P_Y^0, or triangle P_Y^0EC.

Producer Surplus

Producer surplus measures the revenue producers receive beyond the minimum required to induce them to supply the good.[4] In panel (b) of Figure 6.4, the area above the supply curve and below the good's price represents producer surplus. The height of the supply curve represents the minimum price at which producers

---

4 The minimum revenue required to induce production is a short-run concept; that is, it includes variable but not fixed costs.

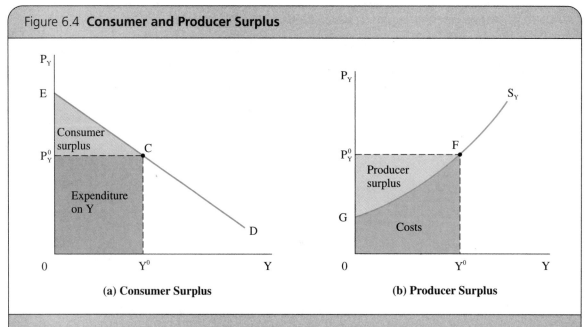

Figure 6.4 **Consumer and Producer Surplus**

(a) Consumer Surplus

(b) Producer Surplus

The consumer surplus generated by consumption of a good equals the value of the satisfaction from that consumption over and above the expenditures necessary to obtain the good. Graphically, consumer surplus can be represented in panel (a) as the area under the demand curve out to the level of consumption and above the good's price. Producer surplus equals the revenue producers receive over and above the minimum necessary to cover production costs. Graphically, producer surplus is reflected in panel (b) by the area above the supply curve and below the good's price.

would willingly supply each unit of the good. The minimum price rises with the level of production because of increasing opportunity costs. If the market price equals P_Y^0 and firms supply Y^0 units, producer surplus is given by the area above the supply curve out to Y^0 and below P_Y^0. Producers receive total revenue equal to area $0P_Y^0FY^0$. The minimum revenue they must receive to produce Y^0 is area $0GFY^0$, which would just cover their production costs. The difference, GP_Y^0F, captures producer surplus.

A Tariff's Effect on Consumer and Producer Surplus

Figure 6.5 shows the welfare effects of an import tariff by a small country in terms of changes in consumer and producer surplus. In autarky, area P_Y^0HE represents consumer surplus. Under unrestricted trade, consumer surplus rises to P_Y^1HF. When the country imposes a tariff, consumer surplus falls to $(P_Y^1 + t)HG$. Therefore, imposition of the tariff reduces consumer surplus by the area bounded by $P_Y^1(P_Y^1 + t)GF$. We can divide this loss of consumer surplus into revenue, redistribution, production, and consumption effects.

In Figure 6.5, rectangle n is the tariff's **revenue effect,** a transfer from consumer surplus to the government that collects the tariff revenue. The total amount of revenue equals the quantity of imports with the tariff, $Y^3 - Y^4$, times the tariff rate per unit, t. Although the tariff transfers this revenue from consumers to the government, most analyses assume the government uses the revenue to finance spending it otherwise would finance with some type of domestic tax. Therefore, the revenue effect of the tariff represents not a net welfare loss to the country but merely a transfer.[5] Consumers of good Y suffer a loss of consumer surplus, but residents of the country also enjoy a reduction in their tax bills made possible by the tariff revenue.

5 One branch of international trade theory suggests that this assumption may not be realistic. Rent-seeking or directly unproductive profit-seeking (DUP) analysis argues that individuals and groups in society lobby to capture the available revenue. Resources will be spent in lobbying up to an amount equal to the reward from lobbying (the tariff revenue), making the revenue a loss to society rather than a transfer. See the Magee, Brock, and Young reference at the end of the chapter.

Figure 6.5 How Does an Import Tariff by a Small Country Affect the Country's Welfare?

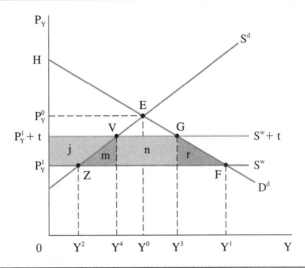

Areas j and n represent transfers of consumer surplus to domestic producers and the domestic government, respectively. Areas m and r represent deadweight losses due to production and consumption inefficiencies generated by the tariff.

Area j in Figure 6.5 is the tariff's **redistribution effect**—the consumer surplus transferred to domestic producers. *(What area in Figure 6.5 represents domestic producer surplus in autarky? With unrestricted trade? With the tariff?)* Like the revenue effect, the tariff's redistribution effect isn't lost to society, but merely transferred from consumers to domestic producers. The transfer takes place through the higher prices consumers pay and domestic producers receive with the tariff. Under unrestricted trade, the revenue domestic Y producers receive is $0P_Y^1ZY^2$. With the tariff, domestic producers receive $0(P_Y^1 + t)VY^4$ in revenue. Increased costs offset a portion of the increased revenue as production rises from Y^2 to Y^4; these increased costs are measured by the area under the domestic supply curve between Y^2 and Y^4. The excess of increased revenue over increased cost is area j, the increase in producer surplus.

Triangle m in Figure 6.5 is the tariff's **production effect**. Units Y^2 through Y^4 are now (with the tariff) produced domestically rather than imported. Each unit is produced domestically at a cost (represented by the height of the domestic supply curve) that exceeds the cost of importing it (represented by the height of the world supply curve, S^w). Area m is a **deadweight loss** to the small country; that is, a loss of consumer surplus *not* transferred to another group in the country but lost through inefficient domestic production. Domestic production of units Y^2 through Y^4 is inefficient because the small country is the high-opportunity-cost producer; foreign firms can produce the good at a lower opportunity cost. Efficiency requires each unit of a good to be produced by the low-opportunity-cost supplier. This condition was satisfied under unrestricted trade (at point F) but isn't satisfied under the tariff. By causing inefficiently high domestic production of good Y, the tariff reduces welfare in the small country by an amount equal to the area of triangle m. The high opportunity cost of domestic production of units Y^2 through Y^4 signals that those resources could be used more productively elsewhere in the economy.

Triangle r in Figure 6.5 represents another deadweight loss to the small country. This **consumption effect** is the loss of consumer surplus that occurs because consumers no longer can obtain units Y^3 through Y^1 at price P_Y^1 with the tariff. For each unit of Y between Y^3 and Y^1, consumers value the good by an amount (measured by the height of the demand curve, D^d) greater than the cost of importing (measured by the height of the world supply curve, S^w). Efficiency requires that each good be consumed to the point at which the marginal benefit from consuming an additional unit just equals the marginal cost of producing it. The unrestricted trade equilibrium (point F) satisfied this condition. The tariff causes consumption to be inefficiently low, thereby lowering welfare.

A Tariff's Net Welfare Effects

The net welfare loss to the small country as a whole from the import tariff equals the sum of areas m and r in Figure 6.5. The remainder of the loss of consumer surplus (areas j and n) is a transfer from domestic consumers to domestic producers (j) and to the government (n). The small country enjoys no gain in welfare to offset the loss of areas m and r. The tariff clearly benefits domestic producers of good Y—but at the direct expense of domestic consumers.

The tariff taxes trade, encourages domestic production, and discourages domestic consumption and imports. The volume of trade falls under the tariff. Imposition of a tariff wipes out a portion of the potential gains from trade by artificially limiting the extent to which a country can specialize production according to its comparative advantage and import goods in which it has a comparative disadvantage. In fact, a tariff set at a high enough rate can stop trade completely, returning countries to autarky and eliminating all the gains from trade. Such a prohibitive tariff would equal $P_Y^0 - P_Y^1$ in Figure 6.5.

Notice that in our analysis of a tariff's welfare effects, we've implicitly used the compensation criterion from section 4.6.3. Domestic producers gain area j from a tariff, and the government gains area n. Domestic consumers lose area $j + m + n + r$. Can the gainers compensate the losers and still be better off? Clearly the answer is no: The gainers from a tariff gain less than the losers lose, making compensation impossible. This is just another way of saying that the tariff imposes a *net* welfare loss on the country equal to area $m + r$.

Under some circumstances, residents of a country may want to create a transfer from consumers to producers and the government. Chapter Eight discusses this possibility as a potential justification for tariffs. In general, however, if a society wants to make such a transfer, there are more efficient ways to do so than through a tariff. This is because a tariff not only creates the transfer but causes deadweight losses $(m + r)$. We'll see in Chapter Eight that other means of accomplishing the transfer can avoid the inefficient production and consumption that create the deadweight losses and, therefore, can effect the desired transfer at a lower opportunity cost to society.

6.4.3 Estimating the Effects of High U.S. Tariffs

We've seen that, while overall tariff levels have fallen dramatically during the postwar period, tariffs remain high in some industries. As of 1990, there were 13 major U.S. industries for which tariffs exceeded 9 percent.[6] The protection of 12 of those 13 industries dates from 1930 or before; the exception is canned tuna, whose protection dates from 1951. Table 6.2 reports estimates of the welfare effects of each industry's tariffs. Areas j, m, n, and r in the table refer to the areas highlighted in Figure 6.5. Consumers in each case lose consumer surplus equal to the total of columns 3, 4, and 5 (or areas $j + m + n + r$). Producers gain the amount in column 3 (area j); and the U.S. government collects tariff revenue equal to the amount in column 4 (area n). Column 5 reports the deadweight efficiency losses (areas $m + r$), which equal the net welfare effect in column 6.[7]

6.5 What Happens When a Large Country Imposes an Import Tariff?

A *large* country constitutes a share of the world market sufficient to enable it to affect its terms of trade. When this condition is satisfied, the country may be able to use an import tariff to improve its terms of trade. Therefore, a large country can in some cases improve its welfare by imposing a tariff, an outcome impossible for a small country. The United States plays a large enough role in many markets to affect world prices through its trade policy. However, many other countries are also large in a few markets. Some developing countries, for example, produce a large share of the world total of some products and therefore possess some market power.

---

6 The Hufbauer and Elliott study restricts attention to industries with U.S. consumption of at least $1 billion per year and potential imports (if tariffs were eliminated) of $100 million or more.

7 The exception is canned tuna, where a tariff-rate quota imposes additional welfare losses, so the amount in column 6 exceeds that in column 5.

Table 6.2 **Welfare Effects of U.S. Tariffs, 1990 (Millions $ per Year)**

Product Category	Tariff Rate (% of P_Y^1)	Redistribution Effect (Area j)	Revenue Effect (Area n)	Production and Consumption Effects (Areas m + r)	Net Welfare Effect on U.S. (−[Area m + r])
Ball bearings	11.0	13	50	1	−1
Benzenoid chemicals	9.0	127	172	10	−10
Canned tuna	12.5	31	31	4	−10
Ceramic articles	11.0	18	81	2	−2
Ceramic tiles	19.0	45	92	2	−2
Costume jewelry	9.0	46	51	5	−5
Frozen concentrated orange juice	30.0	101	145	35	−35
Glassware	11.0	162	95	9	−9
Luggage	16.5	16	169	26	−26
Polyethylene resins	12.0	95	60	20	−20
Rubber footwear	20.0	55	141	12	−12
Women's footwear, except athletic	10.0	70	295	11	−11
Women's handbags	13.5	16	119	13	−13

Source: Data from Gary Clyde Hufbauer and Kimberly Ann Elliott, *Measuring the Costs of Protection in the United States* (Washington, D.C.: Institute for International Economics, 1994), p. 8.

6.5.1 **Effects on Production, Consumption, and Price**

The supply curve of good Y facing the large country is the summation of domestic supply and supply from the rest of the world. In Figure 6.6, S^d represents the *domestic supply*, S^w the *supply from the rest of the world*, and S^{d+w} the total supply. At each price for good Y, we find the total quantity supplied by adding the quantity supplied domestically (read off the domestic supply curve) to the quantity supplied in the rest of the world (read off the rest-of-world supply curve). The total supply curve slopes upward because the large country, as it buys more Y in world markets, pushes up the world price.

Figure 6.7 combines the total supply curve, S^{d+w}, with the domestic demand curve, D^d, to determine the unrestricted trade equilibrium at point C. Domestic residents consume Y^0 units of good Y, of which Y^1 units are produced domestically and $Y^0 - Y^1$ units imported, at the equilibrium price of P_Y^0. For the first Y^1 units of output, domestic production involves a lower cost than importing; beyond Y^1, the domestic country becomes the high-cost producer. Consumer and producer surplus under unrestricted trade equal the areas $P_Y^0 EC$ and $GP_Y^0 F$, respectively.

Now the country imposes an import tariff of t per unit on good Y. The total supply curve shifts upward by t to $S^{d+w} + t$. For each unit imported, domestic consumers must pay the price charged by foreign producers *plus* the tariff. Point H represents the new equilibrium. The domestic price of good Y rises to P_Y^1; Y^2 units are consumed, Y^3 produced domestically, and $Y^2 - Y^3$ imported. Consumer surplus now is $P_Y^1 EH$, and domestic producer surplus is $GP_Y^1 I$. Areas j, m, n, and r represent, respectively, the transfer from consumer to producer surplus (redistribution effect), the deadweight loss from inefficiently high domestic production (production effect), the tariff revenue transferred from domestic consumers to the government (revenue effect), and the deadweight loss due to inefficiently low domestic consumption (consumption effect). Thus far, the analysis exactly parallels that of the small-country case from section 6.4.2.

Notice, however, that area n can't represent the full amount of tariff revenue. Total tariff revenue must equal the quantity of imports ($Y^2 - Y^3$) times the amount of the tariff (the vertical distance between the S^{d+w} and $S^{d+w} + t$ supply curves). The revenue effect, area n, is only a portion of the total revenue—the share paid by domestic consumers in higher prices for good Y (that is, P_Y^1 rather than P_Y^0). Area s represents the remainder

Figure 6.6 **Total Supply Equals Domestic Supply Plus Supply by the Rest of the World**

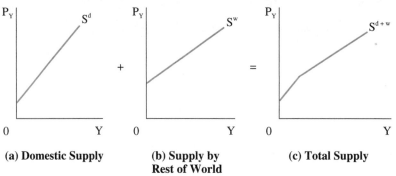

(a) Domestic Supply   **(b) Supply by Rest of World**   **(c) Total Supply**

A large country faces an upward-sloping total supply curve.

Figure 6.7 **How Does an Import Tariff by a Large Country Affect the Country's Welfare?**

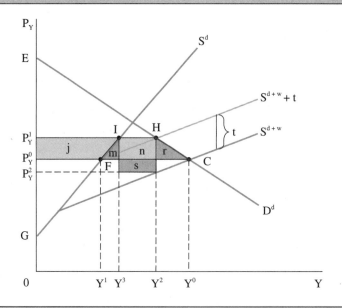

The tariff reduces consumption from Y^0 to Y^2, increases domestic production from Y^1 to Y^3, and decreases imports. The price domestic consumers pay rises from P_Y^0 to P_Y^1, and the price foreign producers receive falls from P_Y^0 to P_Y^2. Area j is a transfer from domestic consumers to domestic producers. Areas m and r are deadweight losses reflecting inefficient production and consumption, respectively. Area n is a transfer from domestic consumers to the government. Area s is a transfer from foreign producers to the domestic government.

of the revenue, the portion of the tariff borne by foreign producers of good Y who must accept lower prices for their product. Before the tariff, foreign producers received P_Y^0 for each unit of good Y exported. With the tariff, they receive only P_Y^2, or the price paid by domestic consumers (P_Y^1) *minus* the tariff, because the tariff goes to the domestic government, not to foreign producers.

Table 6.3 **Possible Net Welfare Effects of a Tariff by a Large Country**	
If:	Then:
$m + r = s$	No net effect on domestic welfare Negative net effect on world welfare
$m + r < s$	Positive net effect on domestic welfare Negative net effect on world welfare
$m + r > s$	Negative net effect on domestic welfare Negative net effect on world welfare

Why does the tariff force foreign producers to accept a lower price for good Y? The tariff raises the price paid by domestic consumers, lowering the quantity of good Y demanded. The tariff-imposing country is large enough, by assumption, for this decline in quantity demanded to have a significant impact on the market. When foreign producers face a substantially lower quantity demanded for their product, their opportunity costs of production fall, and so does price. This effect of the tariff is called the **terms-of-trade effect.**

The analyses of the welfare effects of areas j, m, n, and r are precisely the same as in the small-country case. Areas j and n represent transfers within the country, and m and r are deadweight welfare losses caused by inefficient domestic production and consumption. The large-country case introduces a gain to the tariff-imposing country in the form of tariff revenue paid by foreign producers, area s. If the deadweight losses (the production and consumption effects) exceed this revenue gain (the terms-of-trade effect), imposing the tariff harms the large country. If the revenue gain from foreign producers exceeds the deadweight losses, the large country may improve its welfare by imposing the import tariff. Table 6.3 summarizes these results.

Of course, the tariff still affects the domestic distribution of income. Domestic producers of good Y gain at consumers' expense. In the long run, when resources are free to move among industries, the Stolper-Samuelson theorem implies that owners of resources used intensively in production of good Y gain, while owners of resources used intensively in production of other goods lose (see section 4.3).

The tariff also exerts a redistributive effect among countries. Even if conditions are such that the large tariff-imposing country gains, all its gains come at the expense of its trading partners, which must accept lower prices for their exports. In other words, *a tariff has a negative impact on world welfare regardless of the size of the countries involved.* Tariffs cause inefficient production and consumption patterns and a loss of part of the gains from trade. If the industries involved exhibit economies of scale, tariffs can impose additional costs on the economy by limiting firms' abilities to specialize and capture those scale economies.

6.5.2 Optimal Tariffs and the Threat of Retaliation

We've seen that imposition of an import tariff by a large country has two effects on the country's welfare. The first, called the **volume-of-trade effect,** occurs when the tariff lowers welfare by discouraging trade. Second, by lowering the price foreign producers receive, the tariff causes a terms-of-trade effect that enhances welfare in the tariff-imposing country. The tariff's net effect on the large country's welfare depends on the relative magnitudes of the volume-of-trade and terms-of-trade effects, as noted in Table 6.3. The tariff rate that maximizes the net benefits to the country $(s - [m + r])$ is called the **optimal tariff.** Note that the optimal tariff for a small country always equals zero because of the absence of any terms-of-trade effect $(s = 0)$. For a large country beginning from unrestricted trade, increasing the tariff raises welfare up to a point beyond which welfare begins to decline.

The concept of an optimal tariff deserves some skepticism. Imposition of a tariff reduces total *world* welfare regardless of the size of the countries involved. The source of a large country's ability to affect its terms of trade is simply its ability to force its trading partners to accept lower prices for their exports. Any improvement in its terms of trade that a large country generates by imposing an import tariff also causes a deterioration in the terms of trade of the country's trading partners. The trading partners' losses exceed the tariff-imposing country's gains, because the tariff causes an inefficient pattern of production and consumption. Policies such as optimal tariffs that try to improve the welfare of the domestic country at the expense of others are called **beggar-thy-neighbor policies.**

The beggar-thy-neighbor characteristic of tariffs implies that they risk retaliation by trading partners. The so-called optimal tariff is the one that maximizes the imposing country's welfare, *assuming* that trading partners do nothing in response to having their exports tariffed and their terms of trade harmed. This seems like a rather unrealistic assumption, since the tariff definitely reduces exporting countries' welfare. A tariff by one country invites retaliation, which invites counter-retaliation, and so on. A tariff war that progressively lowers the volume of trade and welfare for all combatants may result.

6.6 How Does a Tariff Affect Factor Prices? Specific Factors and Stolper-Samuelson

Imposition of an import tariff by a small country raises the domestic price of the imported good by the tariff amount. If one or more factors can't move among industries in the short run, the factor specific to the import-competing industry will gain from the tariff, while the factor specific to the export industry will lose, as suggested by the specific-factors model of section 4.5.3. The effect on any factor able to move among industries will depend on the factor owner's consumption pattern. The tariff's welfare effect will be positive if he or she consumes mainly the now-cheaper export good and negative if he or she consumes mainly the now-more-expensive import good.

In the long run, when all factors can move between industries, the tariff has the effects predicted by the Stolper-Samuelson theorem (see section 4.3). That theorem states that a rise in the price of a good will cause a more-than-proportional rise in the price of the input used intensively in that good's production and a fall in the price of the other input. Under the assumptions of the Heckscher-Ohlin theorem, production of the import good will involve intensive use of the scarce factor. Therefore, a tariff, by raising the domestic price of the import good, raises the real reward to the scarce factor and lowers the real reward to the abundant factor.

6.7 Tariffs and Economies of Scale

Thus far, our analysis of tariffs' effects has assumed that comparative advantage—differences in production possibilities or in tastes—forms the basis for trade. In this case, tariffs interfere with the allocation of production to low-cost locations, causing a loss of gains from trade. Recall from section 5.6 that economies of scale provide another potential basis for mutually beneficial trade, one applicable even if two countries have identical production possibilities and tastes. Tariffs also can interfere with this type of trade. With widespread tariffs, each country must produce small quantities of all the goods domestic consumers want to consume, instead of specializing in the export good and producing a large quantity of it, thereby achieving economies of scale. This implies that the costs of tariffs can be even higher in industries characterized by economies of scale. Recent empirical work suggests that a large share of the actual gains from international trade come from exploiting economies of scale, a point of great importance to countries with domestic markets too small to allow their industries to achieve those economies without access to foreign markets.[8]

6.8 The Effective Rate of Protection

It's tempting to assume that domestic producers in all industries with high import tariffs receive high degrees of protection. However, such a simple relationship between tariff rates and degrees of protection doesn't necessarily hold. To determine the actual degree of protection for any domestic industry, we must consider not only tariffs within the industry itself but also any tariffs on inputs the industry uses. The relationship among tariffs in related markets and industries is called **tariff structure.**

Although tariff structure differs across sectors of the economy, tariff rates generally rise as products move through various stages of production, as illustrated in Figure 6.8. Raw materials tend to have lower tariff rates than the finished products ultimately produced with them, a phenomenon known as **cascading tariffs.** The Uruguay Round tariff cuts reduced the difference in tariffs applied to raw materials and finished products by

---

8 See section 5.6 and Chapter Eight's discussion of strategic trade policy in section 8.4.3.

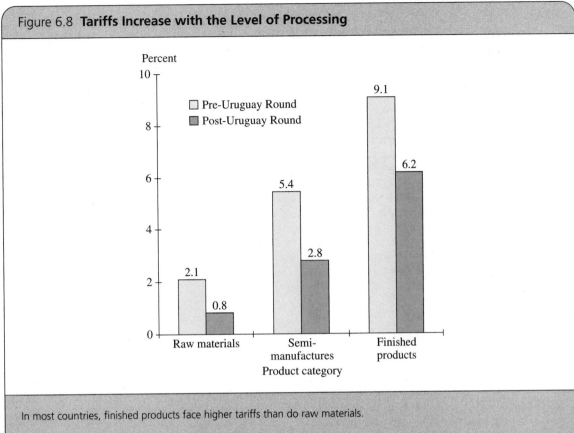

Figure 6.8 **Tariffs Increase with the Level of Processing**

Percent

Pre-Uruguay Round
Post-Uruguay Round

Raw materials: 2.1, 0.8
Semi-manufactures: 5.4, 2.8
Finished products: 9.1, 6.2

Product category

In most countries, finished products face higher tariffs than do raw materials.

Source: Data from General Agreement on Tariffs and Trade.

industrial countries. Figure 6.8 reports that the differential between finished-product and raw-materials tariffs fell from 7.0 percent to 5.4 percent as a result of the Uruguay Round, eliminating cascading tariffs in paper, jute, and tobacco products and reducing them substantially in wood and metal products.[9]

By ignoring the effect of tariff structure, the tariff rate on a final good may provide an inaccurate measure of the effective protection provided to domestic producers. An alternative measure that accounts for the role of tariff structure is the **effective rate of protection (ERP).** To illustrate, suppose a domestically produced television set sells at the world price of $500 under unrestricted trade. The domestic producer uses $300 worth of imported inputs (picture tube, chassis, tuner, and various electronic components). The $200 difference between the world price of the finished television set and the cost of the imported components represents **domestic value-added (V).** Domestic value-added includes the payments made to domestic labor and capital inputs for assembling the imported components into a finished television set. Under unrestricted trade, domestic value-added can't exceed $200, or the price of domestically produced television sets will exceed that of imported ones and the domestic sets won't sell.

An ad valorem tariff of 10 percent on imported television sets would raise the domestic price of an imported TV to $550 (= $500[1 + 0.10]). The price of the domestically produced set then could rise as high as $550 and still compete against imported sets in the domestic market. The nominal tariff rate is 10 percent—but what is the effective rate of protection? The ERP answers the question, "What percentage increase in domestic value-added does the tariff make possible?" Domestic value-added under unrestricted trade (V_0) was $200; a higher level of value-added would have rendered domestically produced television sets noncompetitive by raising their price above the $500 world price. Domestic value-added with a 10 percent tariff on imported television sets (V_1) can rise to $250 (or $550 – $300 worth of imported inputs) and still allow domestic TVs to compete. The effective rate of protection provided for domestic television producers by the 10 percent tariff on imports of finished television sets is ERP = $(V_1 - V_0)/V_0$ = ($250 – $200)/$200 = 25 percent. The 10 percent nominal tariff allows domestic value-added to rise by 25 percent, and this measures the degree of protection for domestic producers.

A 10 percent nominal tariff doesn't always imply an effective rate of protection of 25 percent. The relationship between the nominal tariff rate and the effective rate of protection depends on (1) the share of imported inputs in the production process and (2) the presence or absence of tariffs on imported inputs. To examine the impact on the effective rate of protection of a tariff on imported inputs, consider once again the 10 percent tariff on finished television sets—now accompanied by a 5 percent tariff on imported components used in domestic production of TVs. The 5 percent tariff on inputs implies that domestic producers now must pay $300(1 + 0.05) = $315 for their inputs. Domestic value-added with the tariff package can be as high as V_1 = $500(1 + 0.10) - $300(1 + 0.05) = $550 – $315 = $235 before domestic sets become noncompetitive. This new value-added is the difference between the tariffed price of imported television sets and the tariffed price of imported inputs used in domestic production. The effective rate of protection is ERP = $(V_1 - V_0)/V_0$ = ($235 – $200)/$200 = 17.5 percent. Imposition of the 5 percent tariff on imported inputs lowers the ERP of a 10 percent nominal tariff on finished television sets from 25 to 17.5 percent. The tariff on finished TVs taxes imports of both foreign inputs and foreign assembly costs (foreign value-added). If imported inputs used domestically don't face a tariff, domestic value-added can absorb all the differential.

The general formula for calculating the effective rate of protection is

$$ERP = \frac{t_f - at_i}{1 - a},$$

where t_f is the nominal tariff rate on the imported *finished* good (imported television sets), a is the value of imported inputs as a share of the value of the final good under free trade ($300/$500 = 0.6), and t_i is the tariff on imported *inputs* used by domestic producers.[10] From the general expression for ERP, we can see that whenever the tariff rate on finished goods exceeds the rate on imported inputs ($t_f > t_i$), the ERP is greater than the tariff on finished goods (ERP > t_f). When imported finished goods and imported inputs are tariffed at the same rate ($t_f = t_i$), that rate accurately measures the extent of protection provided for the domestic industry (ERP = $t_f = t_i$). When a country tariffs imported inputs at a rate exceeding that on finished goods ($t_f < t_i$), the effective rate of protection is lower than the tariff rate on finished goods (ERP < t_f). In fact, the ERP can be negative even though t_f is positive! A negative ERP implies that the tariff structure actually makes it harder for domestically produced goods to compete against foreign ones. Other things being equal, the effective rate of protection is higher (1) the higher the nominal tariff rate on finished goods, (2) the lower the tariff rate on imported inputs, and (3) the larger the share of imported inputs in the value of the good (if $t_f > t_i$).[11]

Effective rates of protection differ greatly from actual or nominal tariff rates for many industries. Actual tariff rates significantly underestimate the effective protection received by many industries in the United States as well in other countries. The effective-rate-of-protection idea carries over to nontariff barriers as well; trade barriers on inputs always lower the effective protection given to finished-goods producers.

6.9 Offshore Assembly Provisions

We've already seen that tariff rates typically differ by industry and by country. However, many countries, including the United States, have special tariff provisions that make things even more complicated.[12] Some of the most common are **offshore assembly provisions (OAPs),** which allow reduced tariffs on goods assem-

---

10 With more than one input, the sum of the shares and tariff rates for all inputs replaces the at_i term. It is easy to show that $(V_1 - V_0)/V_0$ = $(t_f - at_i)/(1 - a)$. Letting P denote the price of the finished product, $(V_1 - V_0)/V_0$ = $[P(1 + t_f) - Pa(1 + t_i) - P(1 - a)]/P(1 - a)$ = $(t_f - at_i)/(1 - a)$.

11 Results (1) through (3) can be verified by taking the partial derivatives of the ERP equation with respect to t_f, t_i, and a, respectively.

12 Look at the general statistics chapter of the U.S. Harmonized Tariff Schedule at www.usitc.gov/taffairs.htm.

bled abroad from domestically produced components. Suppose, for example, that the United States imposes a 50 percent tariff on imported cigars and that the Dominican Republic develops an industry that assembles cigars from U.S.-made tobacco.[13] With no offshore assembly provision, a Dominican cigar with a free-trade price of $2 would sell for $3 in the United States, since $3 = $2(1 + 0.50)$; in other words, the tariff would equal $1. The simplest form of offshore assembly provision would state that cigars imported into the United States from the Dominican Republic must pay the 50 percent tariff *only* on Dominican value-added, not on the item's full value. If we assume that each $2 cigar uses $1.50 worth of U.S. tobacco, making Dominican value-added $0.50, then the cigars would sell in the United States for $2 + ($0.50)(0.50) = 2.25. The OAP reduces the tariff from $1 to $0.25 per cigar, although the nominal tariff rate remains 50 percent, by restricting the tariff to foreign value-added and allowing U.S.-made components (in this case, tobacco) to re-enter the United States tariff free. Many countries export to the United States under OAP arrangements, among them the 24 members of the Caribbean Basin Economic Recovery Act, which includes the Dominican Republic. OAP provisions aren't limited to developing countries, but most OAP imports into the United States do come from developing economies, because they tend to have comparative advantages in the labor-intensive assembly tasks that make OAP provisions attractive.

6.10 Taxing Exports

In some cases, countries place trade restrictions such as taxes on exports as well as on imports. Export taxes violate the Constitution in the United States, although other export restrictions are legal. During the framing of the Constitution, southern states, fearful that protectionist-minded northern interests would tax the South's exports of cotton and tobacco, successfully pressured for the export-tax ban.

The goal of an export tax obviously wouldn't be to protect domestic producers from foreign competition. Why might a country tax its own exports? There are two basic reasons.[14] The first is in response to pressure by domestic consumer groups to keep the domestic price of a good low; goods such as food and oil are particularly susceptible to these political pressures. The second possible reason for an export tax applies only to large countries. They may endeavor to exploit their market power by using export taxes to raise the prices foreign buyers must pay. Such a mechanism allowed the Organization of Petroleum Exporting Countries (OPEC) to engineer the infamous oil price increases of the 1970s.

6.10.1 An Export Tax Imposed by a Small Country

Consider the effect of an export tax imposed by a small country—that is, a country that can export all it wants without lowering the world price. In Figure 6.9, point E represents equilibrium under unrestricted trade in the market for good X. The small country produces X^1 units, consumes X^2 units, and exports $X^1 - X^2$ at the world price P_X^1. Note that the world price of good X lies *above* the country's autarky price (P_X^0) because X is the export good in which the country has a comparative advantage.

The country levies a specific tax of t per unit on exports of good X. For each unit exported, domestic producers still receive the world price (P_X^1) from consumers; but the producers must pay t to the domestic government, leaving a *net* price to the producer of $P_X^1 - t$. Domestic production falls from X^1 to X^3, and domestic consumption rises from X^2 to X^4. Exports fall to $X^3 - X^4$.

Domestic producers of good X lose producer surplus equal to f + g + h + j because of the export tax. Area f is a transfer to domestic consumers, who now can buy good X at price $P_X^1 - t$ rather than P_X^1. Area g is a deadweight loss from the inefficient increase in domestic consumption caused by the tax. Too much X is consumed domestically because the marginal benefit of domestic consumption at X^4 (given by the height of D^d) is less than the marginal benefit of foreign consumption of X (measured by the world price foreign consumers are willing to pay for the country's exports). Foreign consumers value the units of good X between X^2 and X^4 more highly than do domestic consumers, but the export tax causes those units to go to domestic consumers. Area h

---

13 The cigar industry is the biggest user of the U.S. offshore assembly provision with the Caribbean countries.

14 A third set of reasons, which underlie the bulk of U.S. export restrictions, include national security, weapons nonproliferation, and foreign policies. For an excellent summary of U.S. export restrictions, including economically and politically motivated ones, see the Richardson book in the chapter references.

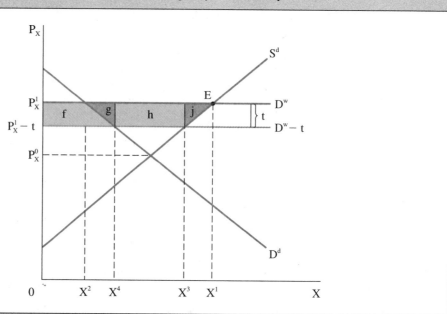

Figure 6.9 **What Happens When a Small Country Imposes an Export Tax?**

The export tax encourages domestic consumption and discourages domestic production and exports. Consumers gain at the expense of domestic producers.

is a transfer from producer surplus to the domestic government in the form of tax revenue. Area j is the dead-weight loss from curtailment of domestic production to X^3. For all units of good X between X^1 and X^3, the cost of producing domestically is less than the cost of producing elsewhere. So long as consumers somewhere in the world are willing to pay P_X^1 for good X, efficiency requires that domestic production be X^1, not X^3.

Some small, very open economies use export taxes primarily as a revenue-generating mechanism, but the most common reason for export taxes is to "protect" domestic consumers from competition by foreign consumers. An export tax by a small country transfers welfare from domestic producers to domestic consumers. The tax causes inefficient production and consumption decisions, so the country suffers a net welfare loss. Domestic producers lose more than domestic consumers gain; therefore, small-country export taxes fail the test of whether gainers can compensate losers.

6.10.2 An Export Tax Imposed by a Large Country

The second reason for export taxes applies only to countries large in the market for the export good under consideration. An export tax may allow such countries to exploit their market position by charging higher prices for their exports than otherwise would be possible. Consider the case of a country that produces a large share of total world output of a particular product, good X. In Figure 6.10, S^d represents the country's domestic supply curve, D^d its domestic demand curve, and D^{d+w} the total world demand curve for good X. The distance between D^d and D^{d+w} at each price measures the rest of the world's demand for good X. Under unrestricted trade, the country would produce X^0 units, of which X^1 would be sold domestically and $X^0 - X^1$ exported; price P_X^0 would apply to both domestic sales and exports.

Now suppose the country imposes a tax of t per unit on X exports; units sold domestically are exempt from the tax. The new world demand curve shifts down by the amount of the tax to $D^{d+w} - t$. Production falls to X^2, with X^3 sold in the domestic market and $X^2 - X^3$ exported. Producers receive price P_X^1 for each unit sold, and

Figure 6.10 **What Happens When a Large Country Imposes an Export Tax?**

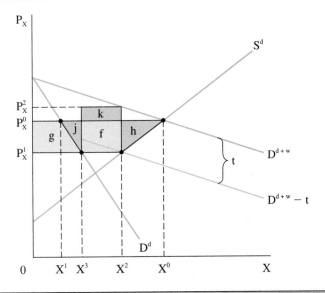

The tax-imposing country suffers deadweight losses equal to area h + j and enjoys a gain in revenue from foreign consumers equal to area k. If (h + j) > k, the country suffers a net welfare loss from the tax. If (h + j) < k, the country enjoys a net welfare gain. The export tax reduces world welfare regardless of the relative sizes of h, j, and k.

the government receives t for each unit exported. Domestic consumers pay P_X^1, but foreign consumers pay P_X^2, with P_X^1 going to producers and t to the exporting-country government.

Domestic consumer surplus rises by area g, as domestic consumers can now buy the good at P_X^1 rather than P_X^0. Domestic producer surplus falls by area f + g + h + j, of which f is a transfer to the government (revenue effect), g is a transfer to domestic consumers (redistribution effect), h is a deadweight loss from the inefficient cut in production (production effect), and j is a deadweight loss caused by the inefficient expansion of domestic consumption (consumption effect). However, area f, the transfer from domestic producers to the domestic government, can't represent all the revenue from the tax. Total tax revenue must equal area f + k, whose length is the quantity exported and whose height is the per-unit export tax. Area k is paid to the domestic government by *foreign* consumers, who now must pay P_X^2 for each unit of good X. Thus, k is a gain to the country imposing the export tax that comes at the expense of trading partners. If this transfer from abroad exceeds the deadweight losses (h + j) from the tax, the tax-imposing country will enjoy a net welfare gain, as Table 6.4 summarizes. The magnitude of the tax that maximizes the net gain (k − [h + j]) is the optimal export tariff.

Because any net gain comes from foreign consumers, the export tax's effect on world welfare is always negative. Attempts to use beggar-thy-neighbor export taxes can backfire. Such policies create an incentive for foreign consumers to find new suppliers, and those suppliers have an enhanced incentive (the higher world price) to enter the market. Ghana and Nigeria suffered such a fate in the cocoa market, and Nigeria and Zaire in palm oil.[15] OPEC's use of export taxes during the 1970s spurred a dramatic decrease in the growth of petroleum use as well as increased production by non-OPEC suppliers such as Britain (from its North Sea reserves) and the United States (from Alaska's north slope). OPEC produced almost half of the world's oil in 1975 but only about 36 percent in 2001.

---

15 World Bank, *World Development Report 1988* (New York: Oxford University Press), p. 91.

Table 6.4 **Possible Net Welfare Effects of an Export Tax by a Large Country**	
If:	Then:
$h + j = k$	No net effect on domestic welfare Negative net effect on world welfare
$h + j < k$	Positive net effect on domestic welfare Negative net effect on world welfare
$h + j > k$	Negative net effect on domestic welfare Negative net effect on world welfare

Countries of Africa

CASE ONE:
Making Cheap Medicine Expensive

The *Anopheles* mosquito carries the protozoan parasite that causes malaria. Experts estimate that between one and two million Africans die of malaria each year. In fact, 90 percent of worldwide deaths from malaria occur in sub-Saharan Africa. No effective malaria vaccine exists; most treatments work only in the short run and have serious side effects. Insecticide-treated bednets provide one of the few effective precautions against contracting malaria. Studies conducted in Africa conclude that bednet use can reduce childhood malaria deaths by almost one-third. Since bednets sell in world markets for about $2.50, surely everyone in malaria-prone areas uses nets. Right?

Wrong. Governments tariffed imported bednets, raising their price out of reach of many residents of Africa's poorest countries. Fourteen sub-Saharan governments tariffed bednets at rates of 30 percent or higher, up to Senegal's 65 percent tariff—even though there were no domestic bednet producers to "protect." The World Trade Organization has pressured governments to lower their tariffs on bednets in an effort to control the spread of malaria.[16]

CASE TWO:
Retaliatory Tariffs

Many of the highest tariffs currently imposed, especially by industrial economies, involve retaliation in ongoing trade disputes. World Trade Organization rules permit tariffs to be imposed as retaliation when members fail to abide by their WTO trade-policy obligations. In July 1999, frustrated by the European Union's long-standing failure to comply with WTO-ordered changes to its trade policy on bananas and hormone-treated beef, the United States imposed retaliatory 100 percent tariffs on $308.2 million worth of EU exports ($191.4 million for the banana dispute and $116.8 million for the beef-hormone fight). Table 6.5 reports the original list of targeted goods; the list changed annually to "spread the pain" among European industries in the hope that they would pressure the Union to comply with the WTO rulings.

Politics on both sides of the Atlantic affected the retaliation list. Motorcycles, for example, appeared on the initial draft list, but disappeared after U.S. motorcycle dealers protested the tariff's potential impact on their business. Note Britain's absence from the list in Table 6.5. Britain opposed the EU ban on imports of U.S. hormone-treated beef, and this opposition spared British exporters their share of the retaliatory U.S. tariffs. Denmark, France, Germany, and Italy, on the other hand, bore large shares of the retaliatory tariffs, because they were the key supporters of the EU's hormone-treated-beef ban. An uneasy 2001 truce in the banana war ended the banana tariffs.

---

16 "Jamming the Net Work," *The Economist,* August 1, 1998, p. 69.

Table 6.5 U.S. Retaliatory Tariffs on EU Exports, 2000

Products from Austria, Belgium, Denmark, Finland, France, Germany, Greece, Ireland, Italy, Luxembourg, the Netherlands, Portugal, Spain, and Sweden:

    Meat of bovine animals, fresh or frozen

    Meat of swine (pork)

    Edible offal of bovine animals

    Roquefort cheese

    Onions, other than onion sets or pearls not over 16 mm in diameter, and shallots

    Truffles

    Dried carrots

    Prepared or preserved liver of goose

    Prepared or preserved liver of any animal other than goose

    Rusks, toasted bread, and other similar toasted products

    Juices of any other single fruit

    Roasted chicory and other roasted coffee substitutes and extracts, essences, and concentrates

    Prepared mustard

Products from France, Germany, and Italy:

    Tomatoes, prepared or preserved otherwise than by vinegar or acetic acid

Products from Germany:

    Guts, bladders, and stomachs of animals (other than fish)

    Soups and broths

    Yarn (other than sewing thread) containing 85 percent or more by weight of artificial staple fibers, singles, not put up for retail sale

Products from France:

    Fatty substances derived from wool grease (including lanolin)

    Chocolate and other cocoa preparations in blocks, slabs, or bars, filled, not in bulk

    Lingonberry and raspberry jams

    Hams, shoulders and cuts thereof with bone in, salted, in brine, dried or smoked

    Products suitable for use as glue or adhesives not exceeding 1 kg, put up for retail sale

Source: U.S. International Trade Commission, *The Year in Trade 1999* (Washington, D.C.: USITC, 2000), p. 59.

China

CASE THREE:
China, Tariffs, and the WTO

China, one of the fastest-growing parties to international trade, badly wanted to join the World Trade Organization and had tried since 1986. China helped found the GATT (predecessor to the WTO) in 1947, but the Taiwan-based government withdrew in 1950 after the Communists took power on the mainland. In 1986, China applied to "resume" its membership. GATT members ruled that membership couldn't be resumed, but that China could negotiate for accession as a new member. The negotiations proved long and acrimonious because of the nonmarket-based nature of China's economy. China wanted to complete an accession agreement before January 1, 1995, so it could be a founding member of the new WTO, which took effect on that date; but negotiators failed to make the deadline. The results of the Uruguay Round enhanced China's incentive to achieve WTO membership. Member countries will phase out the restrictive Agreement on Textiles and Clothing, which severely restricts China's textile and apparel exports, by 2005; but the change applies only to trade with WTO member countries.[17]

The United States made five demands on China to gain WTO membership: (1) implement a single national trade policy for all regions,[18] (2) make the trading system transparent, (3) continue to remove nontariff barriers, (4) commit to move to a full market economy, and (5) agree to special procedures to protect industries in other WTO member countries from surges in Chinese exports. Predictably, the fourth demand proved a major sticking point. China had committed itself to become a "socialist market economy," but policy makers seemed unsure quite what that term might mean.

WTO members claimed that the Chinese tariff system had three problems that hinder China's accession to the group: tariffs were too high, they were too variable across products, and the system was too opaque. Chinese tariffs rose between 1987 and 1992. The Chinese government cut tariffs on more than 3,000 products in 1992, but only to an average tariff rate of about 36 percent. Then Beijing raised tariffs in early 1995 on a list of goods bought primarily by foreigners. Chinese tariff reforms in 1996, shortly after formal WTO accession talks began, lowered average tariff rates from 36 percent to 23 percent; but the new rates remained well above those of most WTO members (see Table 6.1) and even of most developing countries. Some sectors, such as cars, still carried tariffs of 100 percent or more. And the tariff schedule's opacity remained. The new system required wheat importers, up to "a certain level" of imports, to pay tariffs of 1 percent to 35 percent, while imports above "a certain level" had to pay tariffs of up to 180 percent. But the law failed to disclose the "certain level"![19]

Late in 1997, China made additional concessions to try to win WTO membership. The government reduced its weighted-average tariff from 23 percent to 17 percent by cutting rates on more than five thousand items, and it promised to lower tariffs on all industrial goods to an average of no more than 10 percent by 2005.

WTO accession negotiations between China and the United States continued erratically through 1999. In November, the two countries announced successful completion of negotiations. China would reduce its tariffs to an average of 9.4 percent overall and to 7.1 percent on U.S. priority products. Auto tariffs, currently 80 to 100 percent, would fall to 25 percent by 2006; tariffs on telecom equipment would end; and agricultural tariffs would be cut from 31.5 percent to 14.5 percent.

But in mid-2001, China's accession still faced barriers. The Chinese government was hampered in its offers to liberalize trade because government ministries wanted to keep protection for their key constituencies—such as the perennially money-losing auto industry. U.S. demands for strict limits on Chinese agricultural subsidies met political resistance. Members of the European Union wanted better access to China's heavily restricted insurance market. Another protectionist constituency within China included the country's state-trading monopolies and intermediaries. WTO members wanted the right to export to China and sell their products directly to Chinese firms and consumers; the state-trading monopolies and intermediaries, on the other hand, wanted to maintain their exclusive right to sell in China. Some observers feared that tariffs, reduced to gain WTO membership, might be replaced by harder-to-measure nontariff barriers.

In 2001, negotiations finally entered their last stages. China announced it would remove price controls on 128 categories of goods, leaving only 13 categories controlled (for example, natural gas and train tickets). This brought approximately 90 percent of the economy into the market-oriented sector, which China hoped would leave it to be treated as a market economy rather than a nonmarket one in the WTO. When the accession talks ended successfully in late 2001, China had promised to cut its tariffs on many products by 2004 and to cut those on cars to 25 percent by 2006. By 2010, Chinese WTO-promised tariff rates will be 8.9 percent for industrial goods and 15 percent for farm products.

Figure 6.11 illustrates the regional sources of China's imports for 2000. Imports from Asia were dominated by those from Hong Kong, which officially became part of China in mid-1997 but continues to collect and report separate economic and trade statistics.

---

17 A World Bank study predicted a 375 percent increase in Chinese textile and apparel exports in the first 10 years after WTO entry (see "China Textiles Braced for WTO Pain as Well as Gain," *Financial Times,* August 16, 2001).

18 Section 9.5.2 reports on China's special economic zones, which allow more liberal international trade than the rest of the country.

19 See "Under New Laws," *The Economist,* April 13, 1996, p. 62.

Figure 6.11 Regional Sources of Chinese Imports, 2000 (Billions $)

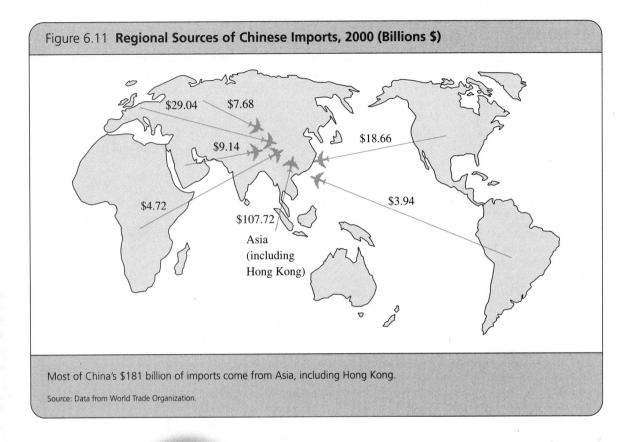

$29.04 $7.68

$9.14 $18.66

$4.72

$107.72
Asia
(including
Hong Kong)

$3.94

Most of China's $181 billion of imports come from Asia, including Hong Kong.

Source: Data from World Trade Organization.

United States

CASE FOUR:
Is It a "Tax" or a "Fee"?

In 1986, as part of the Water Resources Development Act, the U.S. Congress imposed a 0.04 percent tax on the value of imports and exports shipped through U.S. ports, the proceeds of which were earmarked to maintain waterways and port facilities. In 1990, the fee was raised to 0.123 percent. Approximately 3,500 export firms, led by U.S. Shoe Corporation, sued, claiming that the fee taxed exports and was, therefore, unconstitutional. The company argued that the levy constituted a tax on exports, not a fee for harbor use, because it was calculated on the value of goods shipped (*ad valorem*) rather than on a per-ship basis regardless of cargo value.

In 1995, the U.S. Court of International Trade ruled in favor of exporters, but the government appealed. The Supreme Court again ruled against the government in 1998, finding that the tax did indeed violate the U.S. constitutional ban on taxes or duties on exports. The government had to refund the duties already paid by U.S. Shoe and other exporters since 1993, estimated at $750 million. The import charge of 0.123 percent remained in place after the export ruling because Congress has the legal right to tax imports. Not satisfied with rebates for post-1993 taxes, the 3,500 exporters filed suit for rebates of all taxes collected since 1987, when the harbor-use tax went into effect. The U.S. Court of Appeals for the Federal Circuit agreed with exporters. It ruled in February 2000 that all tax revenues must be returned, a total of approximately $1.1 billion.[20]

20 "U.S. Must Refund Harbor-Use Taxes, Appeals Court Says," *The Wall Street Journal*, February 29, 2000.

Summary

This chapter analyzed tariffs' effects on the allocation of resources and distribution of income. Tariffs have a negative effect on welfare in a small country, although a large country may be able to improve its terms of trade and produce an increase in welfare through an import tariff. Even when imposed by a large country, however, a tariff reduces total world welfare and invites retaliation by trading partners.

When imported inputs as well as imports of finished products are considered, nominal tariff rates fail to measure accurately the degree of protection a particular tariff structure provides. The effective rate of protection corrects this problem by taking into account the relationship between tariffs on inputs and those on finished products.

Looking Ahead

The international negotiations sponsored by the GATT/WTO since World War II have produced significant reductions in tariff rates, although trade in certain industries remains subject to high tariffs. Recently, other types of trade barriers—so-called nontariff barriers—have received increasing attention. These barriers have effects at least as harmful as those of tariffs and have proven much less amenable to international liberalization efforts. The "new protectionism" and its increasing use of nontariff restrictions are the subjects of Chapter Seven.

Key Terms

barriers to trade   deadweight loss
tariff   consumption effect
protectionist policy   terms-of-trade effect
specific tariff   volume-of-trade effect
ad valorem tariff   optimal tariff
prohibitive tariff   beggar-thy-neighbor policy
consumer surplus   tariff structure
producer surplus   cascading tariff
revenue effect   effective rate of protection (ERP)
redistribution effect   domestic value-added (V)
production effect   offshore assembly provision (OAP)

Problems and Questions for Review

1. If the world price of automobiles is $10,000 under free trade and if domestic producers of automobiles use $5,000 worth of imported inputs, what is domestic value-added under free trade?
   a. What rate of effective protection would be provided to the domestic auto industry by a 25 percent tariff on imported autos with no tariff on inputs?
   b. What rate of effective protection would be provided to the domestic auto industry by a 25 percent tariff on imported autos with a 25 percent tariff on inputs?
   c. What rate of effective protection would be provided to the domestic auto industry by a 25 percent tariff on imported autos with a 50 percent tariff on inputs?
   d. What rate of effective protection would be provided to the domestic auto industry by a 25 percent tariff on imported autos with a 100 percent tariff on inputs?
2. a. What position would you expect U.S. apparel manufacturers to take on U.S. import tariffs on textiles (that is, fabrics)?
   b. What position would you expect U.S. computer manufacturers to take on U.S. import tariffs on semiconductor chips?

3. This question asks you to analyze the effects of *removal* of a tariff on imported oranges. The following table summarizes situations in the orange market with and without the tariff. The first column describes the situation with a $4.00-per-bushel tariff on oranges. The second column represents the situation after the tariff is removed. You may assume that transportation costs are zero and that the supply and demand curves are straight lines.

	With $4.00 Tariff	With Free Trade
World price of oranges ($/bushel)	$12.00	$12.00
Tariff per bushel ($/bushel)	$4.00	$0.00
Domestic price of oranges ($/bushel)	$16.00	$12.00
Oranges consumed domestically (million bushels/year)	24	28
Oranges produced domestically (million bushels/year)	8	6

   a. Illustrate the effects of *removal* of the tariff. (You may find graph paper useful.) Label the free-trade and tariff equilibria in terms of consumption, domestic production, imports, and domestic and world prices.
   b. Estimate the amount domestic consumers gain from removal of the tariff. Show and explain your work.
   c. Estimate the amount of the *net* effect on the country's welfare from removal of the tariff. Show and explain your work.
   d. In this case, would the optimal import tariff on oranges be negative, zero, or positive? Why? Under what assumptions is the "optimal" tariff really optimal?

4. Country A is labor abundant and practices unrestricted trade with the rest of the world. The country's new minister for trade proposes an import tariff, claiming that such a policy would raise wages relative to the return to capital. Do you agree? Why or why not?

5. Explain why the commonly used empirical measures of average tariff levels tend to *underestimate* actual tariffs.

6. The domestic demand for good X is $D^d = 100 - 20P$. The domestic supply of good X is $S^d = 20 + 20P$.
   a. Draw the domestic demand and supply curves for good X. (Remember that price appears on the vertical axis in the graph.)
   b. If the country allows no trade in good X, what are the equilibrium price, quantity produced, and quantity consumed?
   c. Imports of good X are available in the world market at $P_X = 1$. Draw the total supply curve. If the country allows free trade in good X, what are the equilibrium price, quantity produced domestically, quantity consumed domestically, and quantity imported?
   d. If the country imposes a specific tariff of $t = 0.5$ per unit of imported X, what are the equilibrium price, quantity produced domestically, quantity consumed domestically, and quantity imported?
   e. Who gains and who loses from the tariff? Does national welfare rise or fall?

7. Assume that small country Usia, because of its abundant endowment of forests, has a comparative advantage in producing both logs and lumber (that is, processed logs).
   a. Usia imposes a *prohibitive* export tax on logs. Illustrate the effects of such a tax. Label the effects on consumption, production, exports, world and domestic prices, consumer and producer surplus, and economic efficiency. Explain.
   b. Usia's lumber industry uses logs as its major input. Illustrate the effect of the prohibitive export tax on *logs* on Usia's *lumber* industry. What will happen to consumption, production, price, and exports of lumber because of the tax on log exports? Explain.

8. U.S. presidential candidate and ardent protectionist Patrick Buchanan argues that "Tariffs are taxes, but . . . you don't have to pay them . . . if you Buy American" ("Letters to the Editor," *The Wall Street Journal*, June 2, 1998). Do you agree? Why or why not? Support your argument with an appropriate graph.

References and Selected Readings

Bovard, James. *The Fair Trade Fraud.* New York: St. Martin's Press, 1991.
A treasure trove of examples of protectionist policies written by an outspoken advocate of free trade.

Corbo, Vittori. "Trade Reform and Uniform Import Tariffs: The Chilean Evidence." *American Economic Review Papers and Proceedings* (May 1997): 73–77.
Chile's tariff reform since the 1970s has included not just a reduction in average tariffs, but a shift from highly variable ones across industries to a uniform rate; for all students.

Feenstra, Robert C. "Estimating the Effects of Trade Policy." In *Handbook of International Economics,* Vol. 3, edited by G. M. Grossman and K. Rogoff, 1553–1596. Amsterdam: North-Holland, 1995.
Advanced survey of the empirical literature on the economic effects of various trade policies.

Hufbauer, Gary Clyde, and Kimberly Ann Elliott. *Measuring the Costs of Protection in the United States.* Washington, D.C.: Institute for International Economics, 1994.
Attempt to quantify the cost to U.S. consumers and the U.S. economy as a whole of the structure of protection.

Jackson, John H. *The World Trading System.* Cambridge, Mass.: MIT Press, 1997.
Excellent overview of barriers to trade, including tariffs, by an expert on international trade law; for all students.

Magee, Stephen P., William A. Brock, and Leslie Young. *Black Hole Tariffs and Endogenous Policy Theory.* Cambridge: Cambridge University Press, 1989.
Path-breaking contribution to analysis of tariffs as the outcome of special-interest-group politics; for intermediate and advanced students.

Organization for Economic Cooperation and Development. *Indicators of Tariff and Non-Tariff Barriers.* Paris: OECD, 1997.
Good source of data on trade barriers.

Richardson, J. David. *Sizing Up U.S. Export Disincentives.* Washington, D.C.: Institute for International Economics, 1993.
Readable survey of policies that discourage U.S. exports, along with empirical estimates of the policies' importance.

Rodrik, Dani. "Political Economy of Trade Policy." In *Handbook of International Economics,* Vol. 3, edited by G. M. Grossman and K. Rogoff, 1457–1494. Amsterdam: North-Holland, 1995.
Advanced survey of the literature on distributional aspects of trade policy and their implications for the policy process.

Sazanami, Yoko, Shujiro Urata, and Kiroki Kawai. *Measuring the Costs of Protection in Japan.* Washington, D.C.: Institute for International Economics, 1995.
Attempt to quantify the cost to Japanese consumers and the Japanese economy as a whole of the structure of protection. Intermediate.

Schott, Jeffrey J. *The Uruguay Round: An Assessment.* Washington, D.C.: Institute for International Economics, 1994.
Excellent accessible survey of the issues and results of the Uruguay Round, including tariff reductions.

Trebilcock, Michael J., and Robert Howse. *The Regulation of International Trade.* London: Routledge, 1995.
Comprehensive overview of the world trading system, including tariffs; for all students.

CHAPTER SIX APPENDIX A

Offer Curves and Tariffs

An import tariff's effect on the terms of trade (or lack of effect, in the case of a small country) is easily seen using offer curves. Recall from Appendix B to Chapter Three that an offer curve represents how many units of the export good a country is willing to give up to obtain a unit of the import good. The slope of a straight line through the origin and the intersection of two countries' offer curves captures the equilibrium, or market-clearing, terms of trade.

Figure 6A.1, panel (a), illustrates an offer curve (denoted A) for country A, assuming unrestricted trade. Country A has a comparative advantage in production of good X and exports X to country B in exchange for good Y. Point C, for example, illustrates A's willingness to export X_0 units of X in exchange for Y_0 units of Y. Now suppose country A imposes a tariff on imports of good Y. The effect on A's offer curve is shown by the shift from curve A to curve A_t, where the t subscript denotes *tariff*. The offer curve drawn for a tariff-imposing country is called a *tariff-ridden offer curve*.

Why does A's offer curve shift inward toward the origin as a result of the tariff? One way to answer this is to recall from the analysis of tariffs in Chapter Six that a tariff *reduces* the volume of trade in which the tariff-imposing country wants to engage. This implies that country A will be willing to export a smaller quantity of X in exchange for any given quantity of Y (for example, only X_1 rather than X_0 units in exchange for Y_0).

A second way to consider the shift in A's offer curve caused by the tariff is to note that consumers of Y in country A now must pay *both* the producers of Y in country B and the domestic government for each unit of Y imported. To consume Y_0 units of Y, consumers must pay X_1 units of X to country B and $X_0 - X_1$ to the domestic government. Thus, in total, the price consumers in A are willing to pay for Y_0 units of Y is still X_0 units of X, but now that price is divided between foreign producers and the government. The tariff reduces the amount of good X that country A is willing to offer to country B by the amount of the tariff; the new offer curve reflects this new lower quantity of goods traded. Therefore, country A's offer curve shifts inward, or to the left, by a proportion equal to the tariff rate.

Now that we know the tariff's effect on the offer curve, we can use it to examine the tariff's effect on the equilibrium terms of trade and the importance of country size in determining that effect. First, we assume that country A is small in the markets for goods X and Y; it possesses no market power. In an offer-curve diagram, A's smallness is represented by drawing the trading partner's (country B's) offer curve as a straight line, as in Figure 6A.1, panel (b). The slope of B's offer curve measures the equilibrium terms of trade that, by assumption, A cannot affect. If A imposes an import tariff, shifting its offer curve to A_t, the volume of trade declines (from X_2 and Y_2 to X_3 and Y_3) but the terms of trade aren't affected. Since the decline in the volume of trade has a negative welfare effect on country A (and on B), the overall welfare effect of a tariff by a small country is negative.

Next, we assume that country A is large enough to possess some degree of market power in the markets for goods X and Y. In this case, the trading partner's (B's) offer curve no longer is a straight line but curved, as in panel (a) of Figure 6A.2. Imposition of an import tariff by A improves A's terms of trade, as shown by the increase in the slope of the relative price line. Since the slope of the price line measures the relative price of good X, country A's export good, an increase in the line's slope represents an improvement in A's terms of trade and a deterioration in B's. The imposition of a tariff reduces the volume of trade, just as in the small-country case, but now the terms of trade are affected as well. The net effect of the tariff on country A's welfare depends on the two effects' relative magnitudes.

It's important to note that the improvement in country A's terms of trade through the tariff is synonymous with a deterioration in country B's. Country B is unambiguously harmed by A's tariff and may retaliate by imposing an import tariff of its own on country A's exports.

Figure 6A.2, panel (b), illustrates the possibility of retaliation by B. Should this occur, B's offer curve

(continued)

Figure 6A.1 **Effects of an Import Tariff by Country A**

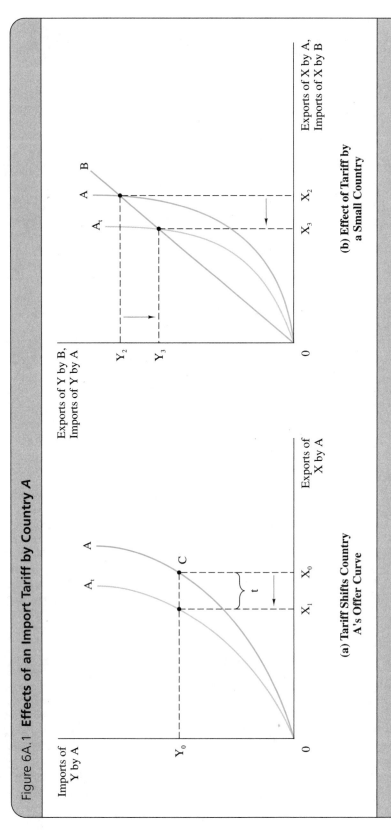

An import tariff of t imposed by country A reduces the volume of trade in which A wants to engage and shifts A's offer curve inward to A_t in panel (a). In exchange for Y_0 units of imports, country A reduces the amount of good X it is willing to export from X_0 to X_1. The difference, $X_0 - X_1$, goes to the government as tariff revenue. In panel (b), country A's smallness is represented by the straight-line shape of trading partner B's offer curve. The slope of B's offer curve determines the equilibrium terms of trade regardless of A's action. The tariff imposed by A reduces the volume of trade from X_2 and Y_2 to X_3 and Y_3, but has no effect on the equilibrium terms of trade.

Figure 6A.2 **Effects of an Import Tariff by a Large Country**

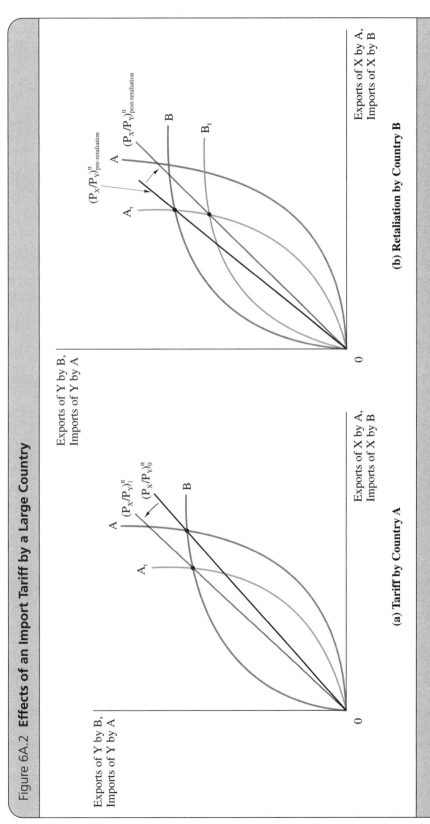

(a) Tariff by Country A

(b) Retaliation by Country B

Country A's large size is represented by the curved shape of trading partner B's offer curve. In panel (a), the imposition of a tariff by A raises the relative price of good X, A's export good, as shown by the increased slope of the straight line from the origin through the new intersection of the two countries' offer curves. Country A's tariff worsens country B's terms of trade and reduces the volume of trade. In response to the damage caused by A's tariff, B may choose to impose an import tariff, shifting its offer curve to B$_t$ in panel (b). The retaliation further reduces the volume of trade. The net effect on the terms of trade depends on the relative sizes of the two countries' tariffs and on the shapes of their offer curves. As drawn, B's retaliatory tariff is too low to restore the terms of trade to their original, pre-tariff level.

shifts inward to B_t, further reducing the volume of trade and shifting the terms of trade in B's favor. Whether the *net* effect on the terms of trade favors A or B depends, of course, on the magnitudes of the original and retaliatory tariffs and on the precise shapes of the countries' offer curves. As drawn, the terms of trade following B's retaliation remain more favorable to A than the pre-tariff terms of trade (omit-ted from the figure). Country B could restore the orig-inal terms of trade by imposing a higher retaliatory tariff. However, the stronger retaliation would reduce further the volume of trade. If a trade war of retalia-tion and counter retaliation erupted, the countries could be driven back to autarky, represented by the origin in Figure 6A.2.

CHAPTER SIX APPENDIX B

General-Equilibrium Tariff Effects in a Small Country

General-equilibrium analysis allows a tariff's effects on consumption and production of both goods to be investigated. In addition, it illustrates more directly the tariff's negative impact on the imposing country's welfare. We continue to assume the country is small, has a comparative advantage in production of good X, and uses the tariff revenue to lower domestic taxes.

In Figure 6B.1, the *production* and *consumption* points under free trade are p^0 and c^0, respectively. We omit the autarky equilibrium and the country superscripts for simplicity. The equilibrium terms of trade are given by the *world* price ratio, $(P_X/P_Y)^w$, and the country's utility level is U_0. Now suppose the country imposes a tariff of t on each unit of good Y imported. The world price of good Y, P_Y^w, isn't affected because of the country's small size. The domestic price of Y in

the small country rises to $P_Y^w + t$. The new relative price ratio relevant for individual domestic producers is $[P_X^w/(P_Y^w + t)]$, which is less than $(P_X/P_Y)^w$. We know that production occurs at the point where the production possibilities frontier is tangent to the price line relevant for domestic producers; this production point with the tariff is p^1 in Figure 6B.1.

As always, the country can trade on world markets to obtain the combination of goods its residents want to consume. At which price ratio does this trade occur? It must occur at $(P_X/P_Y)^w$, because that's the only price ratio at which trade occurs in world markets; the small country's tariff can't affect world prices. Another way to see that $(P_X/P_Y)^w$ is the relevant price ratio for international trade is to note that out of the new domestic price of good Y, only P_Y^w goes

(continued)

Figure 6B.1 **General-Equilibrium Effects of an Import Tariff by a Small Country**

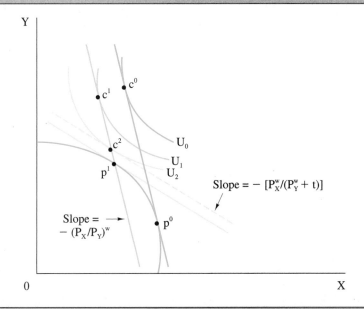

The tariff shifts production from p^0 to p^1, causing a loss of efficiency and a decrease in welfare represented by the move from indifference curve U_0 to U_1. Consumption is based on the domestic price ratio ($P_X^w/[P_Y^w + t]$) and also is inefficient, causing a further reduction in welfare from U_1 to U_2.

to the foreign country while t goes to the domestic government as tariff revenue. Thus, for the importing country as a whole, the price of the import still is only P_Y^w.

At first glance, we'd expect the country to trade along the price line going through the tariff production point p^1 to the point tangent to the highest attainable indifference curve (U_1). If consumption point c^1 were the final equilibrium, there would be only one source of welfare loss from the tariff: the loss caused by inefficient production (p^1 rather than p^0) and represented by the move from utility level U_0 to U_1. However, the actual outcome involves a second welfare loss due to inefficient consumption. The price ratio relevant for individual domestic consumers is $P_X/(P_Y^w + t)$ because for each imported unit of good Y, a consumer must pay P_Y^w to the producer *and* t to the domestic government. The final equilibrium involves trading along the world price line to a point where an indifference curve is tangent to the domestic price line. The final consumption point with the tariff is c^2 on indifference curve U_2. The move from U_1 to U_2 represents the welfare loss due to inefficient consumption.

CHAPTER SEVEN

Nontariff Barriers and the New Protectionism

7.1 Introduction

Nontariff barriers (NTBs) include quotas, voluntary export restraints, export subsidies, and a variety of other regulations and restrictions covering international trade. International economists and policy makers have become increasingly concerned about such barriers in the past few years, for three reasons. First, postwar success in reducing tariffs through international negotiations has made NTBs all the more visible. Nontariff barriers have proven much less amenable to reduction through international negotiations; until recently, agreements to lower trade barriers more or less explicitly excluded the two major industry groups most affected by NTBs, agriculture and textiles. Second, many countries increasingly use these barriers precisely because the main body of rules in international trade, the World Trade Organization, does not discipline many NTBs as effectively as it does tariffs. The tendency to circumvent WTO rules by using loopholes in the agreements and imposing types of barriers over which negotiations have failed has been called the **new protectionism.** The fears aroused by the new protectionism reflect not only the negative welfare effects of specific restrictions already imposed, but also the potential damage to the framework of international agreements when countries intentionally circumvent the specified rules of conduct. Third, countries often apply NTBs in a discriminatory way; that is, the barriers often apply to trade with some countries but not others. In particular, exports from developing countries appear especially vulnerable to restriction through nontariff barriers. NTBs by the European Union, the United States, and Japan apply to a higher percentage of exports from developing countries than from industrial countries. Such barriers can only make the development process more difficult.

7.2 Quotas

The simplest and most direct form of nontariff trade barrier is the import **quota,** a direct restriction on the quantity of a good imported during a specified period. Countries impose quotas for the same reasons as those for imposing import tariffs (see section 6.2). As in the case of tariffs, we'll focus on the protection issue: quotas to protect a domestic industry from foreign competition. Developed countries (for example, Japan, the United States, and the members of the European Union) have used import quotas primarily to protect agricultural producers. Developing countries, on the other hand, have used quotas to try to stimulate growth of manufacturing industries; but we'll see in Chapter Eleven that protection's repeated failure to stimulate manufacturing has persuaded many developing countries to move toward more open trade policies.

The Uruguay Round agreement contained two major developments concerning quotas. First, the accord required countries to convert their quotas to equivalent tariffs, which then fall subject to the agreement's phased-in tariff reductions. Second, countries agreed to establish minimum market access for products, mostly agricultural, previously subject to prohibitive trade barriers. The most notable products subject to the minimum-access rule include Japanese and South Korean rice imports.

Figure 7.1 **What Are the Effects of an Import Quota on Good Y?**

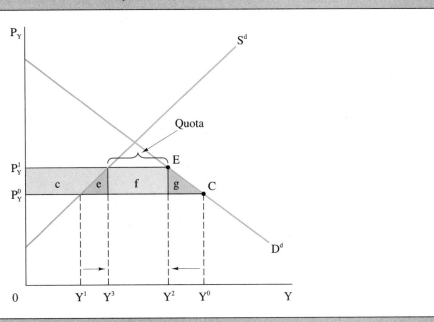

By restricting imports, a quota increases domestic production from Y^1 to Y^3 and decreases domestic consumption from Y^0 to Y^2. The net welfare loss from the quota is shown as the sum of the areas of triangles e and g. Area c represents a transfer from domestic consumers to producers; area f represents the quota rents.

Analysis of an import quota's effects closely resembles that for a tariff. In Figure 7.1, D^d and S^d represent, respectively, the *d*omestic *d*emand and *s*upply for good Y, the import good of the country imposing the quota. For simplicity, the figure omits the total world supply curve of good Y. Assume that the unrestricted trade equilibrium is at point C. Residents consume Y^0 units of good Y, of which Y^1 units are produced domestically and $Y^0 - Y^1$ imported. The price of the good, both domestically and in world markets, is P_Y^0.

Now suppose the country decides that availability of low-cost imports is limiting sales by domestic producers to Y^1. One method to protect the domestic industry from foreign competition is to impose a quota on imports. To find the quota's effect, we define a horizontal line whose length represents the quota (for example, 1 million tons of sugar per year). Then we "slide" the line representing the quota up until it fits horizontally between the domestic demand and supply curves. Point E in Figure 7.1 denotes equilibrium with the quota. The new domestic price of good Y is P_Y^1; at this price, the quantity produced domestically (Y^3) plus the imports allowed under the quota ($Y^2 - Y^3$) equals the quantity demanded by domestic consumers (Y^2).

Area c + e + f + g represents the loss of consumer surplus due to the quota, much as in the case of an import tariff. (The reader can review the concepts of consumer and producer surplus in section 6.4.2.) The basic interpretations of areas c, e, f, and g are the same as the analogous areas in the tariff analysis. Area c is a transfer from domestic consumers to domestic producers able to sell more of their product at a higher price with the quota. Consumers pay the amount represented by c in a higher price (P_Y^1 rather than P_Y^0). Triangle e is a deadweight welfare loss. The quota causes the country to produce units between Y^1 and Y^3 domestically rather than importing them; however, each unit costs more to produce domestically (represented by the height of the domestic supply curve) than to import (represented by P_Y^0). Triangle g is the other deadweight loss, this one caused by inefficient consumption. The quota reduces domestic consumption of good Y from Y^0 to Y^2. For each unit of consumption forgone, the value to consumers (represented by the height of the demand curve) exceeds the cost of importing the good (represented by P_Y^0). Therefore, the reduction in consumption caused by the quota is inefficient.

Area f symbolizes a type of "revenue" generated by the quota, called the **quota rents.** For each unit of good Y imported under the quota ($Y^2 - Y^3$), consumers now pay a higher price. But to whom do the rents go? Under a tariff, the answer is clear: The tariff revenue goes to the tariff-imposing government.[1] Under a quota, the answer is less certain; rents generated by the quota may go to any of several groups, depending on their relative bargaining strengths and the institutional arrangements the government uses to administer the quota. Importers or exporters, foreign producers, or the quota-imposing government may capture the rents; or they may become an additional deadweight loss.

The rents will go to importers if they have the bargaining power to buy $Y^2 - Y^3$ units on world markets at price P_Y^0 and sell them domestically at P_Y^1. This will occur only if importers have some degree of monopoly power; if importing is a competitive industry, importers will bid against one another to buy good Y, and the price producers or exporters charge will rise above P_Y^0. In that case, the sellers of good Y, either producers or exporters, will capture the quota rents represented by area f in Figure 7.1.

Administration of an import quota is less simple than it first appears. The government issues a statement that no more than $Y^2 - Y^3$ units of good Y may be imported. To enforce the restriction, the government must devise a scheme to both keep track of how many units of Y enter the country and allocate the quota among importers. The government may choose to auction import licenses. Under such a system, the rents from the quota would go to the government. An importer able to buy Y on the world market for P_Y^0 would willingly pay approximately $P_Y^1 - P_Y^0$ for a license to import 1 unit of Y. *(Why?)* The total amount for which the government could sell the import licenses would equal the area of rectangle f. Quotas administered under such a scheme are called *auction quotas.*[2]

A third possibility is that area f may end up as an additional deadweight loss; that is, the rents may go to no one. Suppose, for example, that the government doesn't sell import licenses but gives them away on a first-come, first-served basis. Importers then have an incentive to lobby to obtain licenses and otherwise spend resources to obtain them; for example, importers might be willing to wait in line for hours, an allocation method economists refer to as *queuing.* Because the value of a license to import 1 unit of Y is approximately $(P_Y^1 - P_Y^0)$, importers would willingly expend resources equal to that amount to obtain a license. The total resources spent on lobbying or waiting in line equal area f. The process of competition for licenses "uses up" the quota rents, which, in this case, represent an additional deadweight loss from society's viewpoint.

The final possibility is that foreign producers or exporters will capture the rents from the quota. A quota in the form of a voluntary export restraint makes this outcome more likely.

7.3 **Voluntary Export Restraints**

Major world industries—automobiles, steel, and textiles/apparel—are among those subject to trade restrictions known as **voluntary export restraints (VERs).** As the term suggests, importing and exporting countries negotiate agreements for the exporter to "voluntarily" restrict exports. The voluntarism is more apparent than real, because the exporting country often faces the choice of agreeing to the VER, facing a tariff, or, most likely, facing a quota on its exports. U.S. imports of many steel products have been subject to VERs off and on since 1968. The United States negotiated a VER on Japanese automobile imports in 1981 and extended it annually until 1985, after which Japan unilaterally kept the VER in place. The Uruguay Round succeeded in restricting use of VERs, one of the fastest-growing types of protection. Under the new rules, countries can't impose new VERs in response to escape-clause claims of injury by domestic industries, and their existing VERs had to be phased out by 1999. However, we'll see that countries often resolve a dumping or export-subsidy case by signing a suspension agreement, which amounts to a VER by another name.

---

1 Most economic analyses assume that governments use tariff revenue in place of domestic taxes. However, rent-seeking behavior by producers may use up the revenue, adding an additional deadweight loss due to trade restrictions (see footnote 5 in Chapter Six).

2 See C. Fred Bergsten et al., *Auction Quotas and United States Trade Policy* (Washington, D.C.: Institute for International Economics, 1987). Kala Krishna, "The Case of the Vanishing Revenues: Auction Quotas with Monopoly," *American Economic Review* 80 (September 1990), pp. 828–836, demonstrates that auction quotas do not raise revenue under monopoly.

A VER has effects similar to those of a quota. The primary difference lies in the method of administration. In the case of a quota, the importing or quota-imposing country typically handles the administration; under a VER, the exporting country enforces the agreement.[3] This distinction carries important implications for the allocation of the quota rents (area f in Figure 7.1). Administration by the exporting country increases the likelihood that foreign producers or exporters will capture a large share of the rents. Usually the exporting-country government administers the VER by assigning an export limit to each firm. This prohibits competition among the firms and facilitates their charging a higher price (P_Y^1 rather than P_Y^0). As a result, exporters much prefer VERs to tariffs or quotas. Because VERs require negotiations between exporting and importing countries, they typically restrain exports from some but not all suppliers. Exporters not included in a VER agreement can expand exports to fill the gap left by restrained exporters; often, this results in further expansion of the VER as additional exporters become restrained.[4]

The effects of both quotas and voluntary export restraints include a tendency for exporters to raise the average quality of their exported goods. In 1981, Japan agreed under U.S. pressure to restrict its passenger-car exports to the United States to 1.68 million per year. Japanese automobile firms responded by stopping shipments of plain, low-priced models in favor of higher priced ones with more add-on features. This implies that quotas and VERs impose especially high welfare costs on low-income individuals, because the imports such policies eliminate often include the low-cost items bought primarily by low-income families.

As with tariffs, administering quotas or VERs requires defining the categories of goods to be restricted. Product categories tend to be very specific, and exporters can use definitional loopholes to circumvent the restrictions. For example, one clothing exporter got around a quota on two-piece suits by sewing the tops and bottoms together and importing them as jumpsuits. Another circumvented a quota on ski jackets by cutting off the sleeves, importing the sleeveless jackets as vests, then reattaching the sleeves with zippers once the items reached the United States.[5] In 1994, the European Union placed a $81.7 million import quota on "nonhuman dolls" from China, while leaving "human dolls" with no quota. EU officials ruled teddy bears and two popular European dolls, Noddy and Big Ears, subject to the quota. Batman, Robin, and *Star Trek*'s Captain Kirk escaped the quota by an affirmative ruling on their humanity. The biggest controversy surrounded *Star Trek* hero Mr. Spock. Spock's mother was human, which some aficionados claimed should win him exemption, but customs officials used the size of his ears to rule him nonhuman and subject to the quota.[6]

Thus far, with the exception of the rents issue, the effects of quotas and VERs appear identical to those of tariffs. Nonetheless, economists generally think quotas and VERs cause larger losses of welfare than do equivalent tariffs. Section 7.4 examines the reasoning behind this belief.

7.4 Comparison of Tariffs and Quotas

We've seen one major difference between the effects of an import tariff and those of an import quota: The revenue from a tariff goes to the tariff-imposing government, but the quota rent can go to different groups depending on how the government administers the quota. Several other, more subtle differences matter in evaluating the overall effects of the two policies.

Domestic firms in an industry seeking protection typically prefer a quota to other types of import restrictions. One explanation for this preference is the greater certainty associated with a quota's protective effects. A quota assures the domestic industry a ceiling on imports *regardless of changing market conditions*. Even if the domestic industry's comparative disadvantage grows more severe, the quota prohibits consumers from switching to the imported good. Note, however, that the quota does cause a decline in the total quantity demanded by raising the good's domestic price. Therefore, a quota can't keep the domestic industry from facing a shrinking market.

---

3 In this sense, most U.S. quotas operate like VERs, because most are administered by the exporting country. The major exception is the dairy-product program.

4 The Multifiber Agreement (MFA) represents the classic case. In the early 1960s, it began restricting Japanese exports of cotton shirts to the United States. Today, the MFA (now called the Uruguay Round Agreement on Textiles and Clothing) restricts exports of textiles and apparel from virtually all developing countries and to many developed countries. Some aspects of this web of protection will be phased out over the next few years, but only for WTO members.

5 "The Warp and Weft of Anti-Dumping," *The Economist*, November 23, 1991, p. 72.

6 Dana Milbank, "British Customs Officials Consider Mr. Spock Dolls to Be Illegal Aliens," *The Wall Street Journal*, August 2, 1994.

Beyond increasing their market share, domestic firms also seek protection from foreign competition to gain and exploit monopoly power in the domestic market. Suppose an industry following this strategy gains protection in the form of an import tariff. Firms in the industry can raise their prices. However, if they raise prices too much, consumers will switch to the imported good even though they have to pay the tariff. In particular, if domestic firms try to charge a price that exceeds the world price plus the tariff, consumers won't buy from domestic firms. If the industry's protection takes the form of a quota, however, the attempt to monopolize by restricting foreign competition will more likely succeed. Under a quota, domestic consumers *don't* have the option of switching to the imported good. If domestic firms try to exploit a monopoly position by raising prices, the only choice consumers face is to pay the higher prices or consume less of the good. Because successful monopolization of an industry reduces efficiency, economists think the tendency of quotas to facilitate monopolization makes quotas more damaging than tariffs.[7]

Setting aside the issue of who gets the associated rents, it's possible, given any tariff, to define a quota with precisely the same effects on prices, production, consumption, and trade. Similarly, given any quota, it's possible to set a tariff with exactly the same effects. Economists call this result the **equivalence of tariffs and quotas.**[8] We've hinted, however, that as market conditions change, tariffs and quotas cease to have identical effects. Figure 7.2 illustrates this for a large country. Panel (a) analyzes an increase in demand for good Y under a tariff; panel (b) examines the effect of the same increase in demand under a quota. We define the tariff and quota so that at the initial level of demand (D^d), Y^0 units are consumed under both systems, Y^1 units are produced domestically, and $Y^0 - Y^1$ units are imported at price P_Y^0.

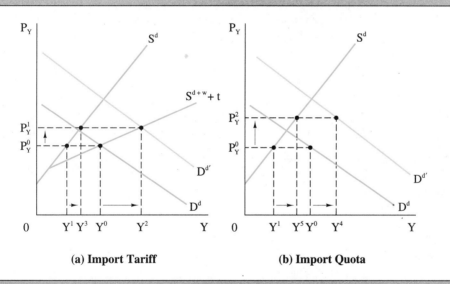

Figure 7.2 **What Happens in Response to Increased Demand under a Tariff and under a Quota?**

(a) Import Tariff

(b) Import Quota

An import quota is more restrictive than an equivalent tariff when demand increases. Under a tariff, imports cover a portion of the increased demand; in panel (a), increased demand causes a larger increase in consumption than in domestic production. A quota forces all increased demand to be matched by increases in (inefficient) domestic production, as panel (b) illustrates. An equal increase in demand causes a larger price increase under a quota than under a tariff.

---

7 Monopolization reduces efficiency by allowing firms to restrict output and charge prices that exceed marginal costs.

8 This result provides the basis for the process of *tariffication,* through which countries replace their quotas with equivalent tariffs, as required by the Uruguay Round. Equivalence also underlies one technique for measuring or quantifying NTBs; see section 7.9.

In panel (a), with an increase in demand to $D^{d'}$, the quantity of good Y consumed rises to Y^2, of which domestic firms produce Y^3 units under a tariff. Note that domestic production rises by *less* than domestic consumption; part of the increased consumption comes from increased imports. The tariff allows increased imports by permitting consumers to either buy domestically or import at a price equal to the world price plus the tariff.

In panel (b), the same increase in demand raises consumption of Y to Y^4 and domestic production to Y^5 under the quota. Increased domestic production exactly *matches* increased consumption, because the quota prohibits any increase in imports. The increased domestic production is inefficient (that is, more costly than increased imports); therefore, the domestic price of good Y rises more under the quota (to P_Y^2) than under the tariff (to P_Y^1). The quota forbids additional imports no matter what price domestic consumers are willing to pay for them. *(Compare the effects of a reduction in domestic supply under a tariff and under a quota.)*

Table 7.1 presents empirical estimates of the effects of several of the most important U.S. quotas and VERs in 1990. Areas c, e, f, and g in the table correspond to the redistribution, production, quota rent, and consumption effects from Figure 7.1. All U.S. quotas except the dairy-products program were administered by exporting countries; so the estimates in Table 7.1 assume that foreign exporters captured the quota rents, making area f part of the U.S.'s net welfare loss from the quotas. By far the biggest welfare loss came from the Multifiber Agreement, which restricted U.S. apparel imports from 47 developing countries. These restrictions cost the United States almost $8 billion a year, and they hindered the growth of developing-country exporters as diverse as Bangladesh, China, Kenya, and Ukraine. The 1995 Uruguay Round Agreement on Textiles and Clothing requires that apparel quotas against WTO members end by 2005, but quotas can continue against non-WTO members. This development created an important additional incentive for China and Taiwan, the second- and fifth-largest apparel exporters to the United States in 2000, to succeed in gaining WTO membership, which they did late in 2001.

Until recently, most attention devoted to trade barriers focused on tariffs and quotas. In the last few years, subtler, more complex restrictions have proliferated. In the following sections, we briefly examine several of these barriers, including export subsidies and countervailing duties, dumping, voluntary import expansions, domestic-content rules and rules of origin, government procurement, and technical standards.

Table 7.1 Costs of U.S. Quotas and VERs, 1990 (Millions $)

Product Category (Tariff Equivalent)	Redistribution Effect (Area c)	Quota Rent Effect (Area f)[a]	Production and Consumption Effects (Areas e + g)	Net Welfare Effect on U.S. ($-$[Area e + f + g])[a]
Protected by import quotas:				
Dairy products (50%)	835	244	104	-104
Peanuts (50%)	32	0	22	-22
Sugar (66%)	776	396	185	-581
Maritime (85%)	1,275	0	556	-556
Protected by VERs:				
Apparel (48%)	9,901	5,411	2,301	$-7,712$
Textiles (23.4%)	1,749	713	181	-894
Machine tools (46.6%)	157	350	35	-385

[a]In all cases except dairy products, quota rents are assumed captured by foreign exporters (and, therefore, a net U.S. welfare loss), because all other quotas are administered by the exporting country. In dairy products, the rents are assumed captured by licensed U.S. importers (and, therefore, not a net U.S. welfare loss).

Source: Data from Gary Clyde Hufbauer and Kimberly Ann Elliott, *Measuring the Costs of Protection in the United States* (Washington, D.C.: Institute for International Economics, 1994), pp. 8–9.

7.5 Export Subsidies and Countervailing Duties

An **export subsidy** is a financial contribution from a government to a firm for export of a commodity; the firm receives the government subsidy along with the price paid by foreign consumers. Note that this definition restricts subsidies to *exports* rather than the country's *export good*. For example, if American Steel Company produces 5 million tons of steel of which it exports 2 million tons, a subsidy of $10 per ton on *exports* implies a total subsidy of $20 million, while a $10-per-ton subsidy on *production* implies a total subsidy of $50 million. Both types of subsidies are important in international trade, but more controversy surrounds export subsidies because they involve differential or discriminatory treatment of domestic sales versus exports. Such subsidies create incentives for firms to export larger shares of their production and sell smaller shares domestically, since the latter don't receive the subsidy payment.

7.5.1 The Importing-Country View

Given the jealousy with which industries guard their domestic markets from foreign competition, it isn't surprising that government subsidization of exports is one of the most controversial issues in international trade policy. Domestic industries often argue that they face unfair competition from rivals subsidized by foreign governments.

Our initial examination of export subsidies' effects takes the perspective of the importing country, which we assume to be small in the market for good Y. (Note that desirability of subsidies from the exporting country's standpoint also is an issue, the subject of section 7.5.2.) The importing country's trading partners subsidize exports of good Y by s per unit.[9] A subsidy is just a negative tax, so it lowers the price at which importing-country consumers can buy the good.

In Figure 7.3, the subsidy shifts the total supply curve for good Y, the country's import good, down by the amount of the subsidy from S^{d+w} to $S^{d+w} - s$. The overall effect is to increase consumption of good Y from Y^0 to Y^2, decrease importing-country production from Y^1 to Y^3, and increase imports from $Y^0 - Y^1$ to $Y^2 - Y^3$. The domestic price of good Y falls from the free-trade price, P_Y^0, to P_Y^1; exporting-country producers willingly sell at a lower price because they now receive the subsidy from their government in addition to the price received directly from consumers. Importing-country consumers gain an amount represented by area e + f + g + h in consumer surplus. *(Why?)* The subsidy harms importing-country producers, as lower-priced imports reduce sales by domestic firms and dictate a lower price. Area e captures this loss of producer surplus, which is transferred to domestic consumers. The remainder of domestic consumers' gains (area f + g + h) come at the expense of exporting countries' taxpayers, who must pay taxes to finance the subsidy.

Importing-country producers of good Y are likely to lobby for protection from subsidized exports to prevent the loss of area e. WTO rules allow for **countervailing duties (CVDs),** or import tariffs designed specifically to offset the competitive advantage provided by trading partners' export subsidies. A countervailing duty of c (= s) per unit in Figure 7.3 eliminates the subsidy's effect on trade by shifting the world supply curve back up to $S^{d+w} - s + c$. Importing-country consumption returns to Y^0 and production to Y^1. Note, however, that one important effect of the subsidy remains, even with the countervailing duty: The importing country continues to gain area g at the expense of exporting-country taxpayers, who still pay a subsidy of s per unit on units Y^1 through Y^0. With the countervailing duty, importing-country consumers don't reap the subsidy directly through lower prices, but the importing-country government collects the countervailing duty and can lower domestic taxes accordingly. Therefore, area g represents a transfer from exporting-country taxpayers (who finance the subsidy) to importing-country taxpayers (who enjoy lower domestic taxes).

Figure 7.3 makes clear that the importing country as a whole loses from a countervailing duty. The duty imposes costs on importing-country consumers (area e + f + g + h) that outweigh the gains to producers (area e) and the government (area g). From the importing-country perspective, countervailing duties represent a victory of protectionist pressures by domestic producers. But from a worldwide view, imposition of a countervailing duty improves total welfare because the cost of the subsidy to exporting countries outweighs the benefits to

---

9 We assume that all exporting countries subsidize, so the importing country can purchase all the good Y it wants at the subsidized price. If a single small country subsidized, buyers would compete for that country's exports, driving the price back up to the initial world price and allowing the subsidizing country's exporters to earn the world price *plus* the subsidy for each unit exported.

Figure 7.3 **What Are the Effects of an Export Subsidy? Importing-Country Perspective**

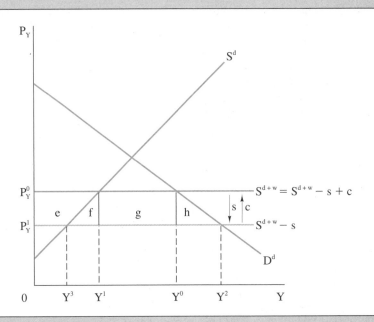

An export subsidy of s per unit increases domestic consumption from Y^0 to Y^2 and reduces domestic production from Y^1 to Y^3. The difference is made up by increased imports now available at a lower price (P_Y^1 rather than P_Y^0). Importing-country producers are harmed (area e), but by less than the gains to importing-country consumers (area e + f + g + h) in the form of lower prices and increased availability of imports. A countervailing duty (c) can offset the subsidy's effects on trade and consumption but will not eliminate a transfer (area g) from exporting-country to importing-country taxpayers.

the importing country. The countervailing duty cancels the production and consumption inefficiencies introduced by the subsidy; only the transfer from taxpayers in the exporting countries to those in the importing country remains.

U.S. law requires firms that allege foreign subsidies to file complaints with the Department of Commerce and the International Trade Commission. Commerce investigates to determine whether a subsidy in fact exists, and the Commission determines whether the subsidy, if any, harms or threatens to harm domestic firms. If both findings are affirmative, the United States imposes a countervailing duty. Table 7.2 summarizes recent investigations. The cases resolved in 2000 with affirmative findings of foreign subsidies and injury covered carbon-steel plate from France, India, Indonesia, Italy, and Korea plus structural steel beams from Korea. As of the end of 2000, the United States had 44 countervailing duties in effect, some of which dated from the late 1970s, that covered goods ranging from steel to pistachio nuts to cotton shop towels and countries from Belgium to Pakistan.

Sometimes, a subsidy investigation leads to a protectionist outcome other than a countervailing duty. A "suspension agreement" occurs if the accused exporter agrees to stop exporting to the United States or to charge higher prices to eliminate the harm to the U.S. industry. In effect, suspension agreements work like VERs: They limit U.S. imports and facilitate noncompetitive pricing among domestic and foreign firms.

The Uruguay Round Agreement requires countries to conduct "sunset" reviews of outstanding countervailing-duty orders when those orders have been in effect for five years. These reviews resulted in revocation of seven U.S. countervailing duties in 2000, including the duties on Venezuelan cement and Israeli phosphoric acid.

Figure 7.4 illustrates the geographic pattern of new countervailing-duty cases reported by WTO member countries in 2000; for each country, the first number in parentheses gives the number of countervailing-duty cases that country *initiated* in 2000 and the second number reports the number of new countervailing-duty investigations to which that country was *subject* in 2000. The European Union initiated the largest number of cases (8); India was the subject of the largest number of investigations (4).

Table 7.2 **U.S. Countervailing-Duty Investigations**

Status	1995	1996	1997	1998	1999	2000
Petitions filed	2	1	6	12	16	12
Final Commerce determinations:						
Negative	0	0	0	0	4	0
Affirmative	5	2	4	1	12	7
Final Commission determinations:						
Negative	2	0	4	0	1	1
Affirmative	3	2	0	1	7	6

Source: Data from U.S. International Trade Commission, *The Year in Trade.*

Figure 7.4 **Countervailing-Duty Actions Reported to the WTO, July 1999–June 2000**

For each country, the two numbers in parentheses report the number of cases as initiator and the number of cases as subject, respectively.

Source: World Trade Organization, *Annual Report 2001.*

7.5.2 The Exporting-Country View

From the importing country's perspective, foreign export subsidies produce a net welfare gain but impose losses on domestic producers who must compete with the subsidized foreign products. The situation in the exporting country is quite different. There, subsidized producers gain at the expense of consumers and/or taxpayers, depending on how many countries in the market subsidize exports.

Figure 7.5 represents the market for good Y in the exporting country. We continue to assume that the country is small in the world market. Point C represents the unrestricted-trade equilibrium. The country produces Y^0 units, consumes Y^1, and exports $Y^0 - Y^1$. Domestic consumer surplus is $P_Y^0 MZ$, and domestic producer surplus is $NP_Y^0 C$.

Scenario 1: What If a Single Exporting Country Subsidizes?

Assume first that the country under consideration is the *only* one providing export subsidies in the market for good Y. The small country's subsidy won't affect the world price of the good, P_Y^0.[10] Exporting firms receive P_Y^0 from foreign consumers *plus* the subsidy, s_1, from the government. Point G in Figure 7.5 represents the new equilibrium. Exporting-country production rises to Y^2 because of the higher total price received for exports. The higher price also creates an incentive for producers to sell more abroad ($Y^2 - Y^3$) and less domestically (Y^3). Domestic consumer surplus falls to $(P_Y^0 + s_1)MH$. Domestic producer surplus rises to $N(P_Y^0 + s_1)G$. In addition, taxpayers pay RHGF to finance the subsidy. Note that import barriers must accompany export subsidies; otherwise foreign producers will bring in the good and re-export it to take advantage of the subsidy. *(Why?)*

The sum of triangles j and k measures the net deadweight loss to the exporting country. Area j is "lost twice"—once in the form of lost consumer surplus and again in the form of subsidy payments by taxpayers—and only "gained once"—in increased producer surplus. Taxpayers pay area k as part of the subsidy, but it doesn't go to producer surplus because of the high cost of producing units Y^0 through Y^2. Overall, exporting-country producers gain at the expense of exporting-country consumers and taxpayers. The welfare losses exceed the gains; thus, the export subsidy fails the compensation test from the exporting country's perspective.

Figure 7.5 **What Are the Effects of an Export Subsidy? Exporting-Country Perspective**

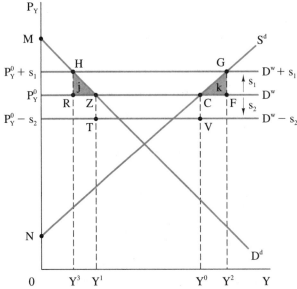

If the small country is the only exporter subsidizing (Scenario 1), export firms receive the world price *plus* the subsidy ($P_Y^0 + s_1$), and the net welfare effect on the exporting country is a loss equal to areas j and k. If all exporters subsidize (Scenario 2), the world price is bid down by the amount of the subsidy (s_2). Exporting firms receive only P_Y^0, and the net welfare loss to the exporting country is area TZCV.

10 See footnote 9.

Scenario 2: What If All Exporting Countries Subsidize?

Now we assume that the country under consideration isn't the only one providing an export subsidy on good Y; *all* exporting countries subsidize. In this case, a subsidy of s_2 $(= s_1)$ dollars per unit on exports of Y shifts down the price exporting-country producers require for sales in the export market.[11] The downward shift represents the amount of the subsidy. Producers are willing to sell abroad at $P_Y^0 - s_2$ in Figure 7.5 because they also receive s_2 from their government for each unit sold abroad; therefore, the total price producers receive, including both the price paid by foreign consumers *and* the subsidy, continues to equal P_Y^0. Exporting-country production doesn't change, nor do domestic producer and consumer surplus. However, taxpayers pay TZCV to finance the subsidy. *(Why?)* The net loss to the country is simply area TZCV, transferred to importing-country consumers in the form of a lower price.

7.5.3 The Controversy over Export Subsidies

Export subsidies raise an obvious question: Why would any country choose to subsidize its exports, thereby providing artificially low-priced imports to foreign consumers? One possible answer lies in the redistribution of income that subsidies generate in the exporting country. If the country is alone in subsidizing (Scenario 1), export-country producers gain and therefore have an incentive to lobby for export subsidies. But if many countries subsidize in the same market (Scenario 2), the subsidies drive down the world price. Producers then cease to gain from the subsidy, but they still won't ask their governments to stop the subsidy. A producer whose government stopped subsidizing while other governments continued to do so couldn't sell any output in the world market. *(Why?)* This explains the importance of WTO negotiations for all member countries to lower export subsidies in agricultural products simultaneously; no single country wanted to lower its subsidies while other countries continued theirs, because that country would lose its export markets.

The clustering of export subsidies in markets for agricultural products provides a clue to a second motivation for the subsidies. Most industrial economies (including the United States, the European Union, and Japan) administer complex agricultural price-support systems that keep prices for those products and farmers' incomes artificially high. When a country imposes a price floor above the equilibrium price of a good—say, wheat—the good's quantity supplied exceeds the quantity demanded. Under a price-support program, the government must prevent the natural fall in price by buying the surplus wheat. Were the government to turn around and sell that wheat domestically, the sales would undermine the domestic price-support system. However, export sales don't undermine the artificially high domestic price. The difference between the high price paid to domestic farmers and the lower world price obtained by the government for export sales represents the subsidy.

The United States and the European Union have bickered for decades over one another's agricultural subsidies. The Uruguay Round Agreement required member countries to cut their agricultural export subsidies, reduce the volume of agricultural exports receiving subsidies, and refrain from granting new subsidies to additional agricultural products. Reaching this compromise between demands for agricultural trade reform and farmers' demands for protection almost derailed the Uruguay Round talks and delayed the agreement for almost four years. Almost a decade later, in 2001, this same old issue almost proved fatal for attempts in Doha, Qatar, to start a new round of WTO talks.

Each year, as part of its report on foreign trade barriers that hinder U.S. trade, the U.S. Trade Representative compiles a list of countries' export subsidies. Table 7.3 lists the export subsidies on specific products included in the 2000 report; many countries in addition to those in the table implement broad export-subsidy programs that favor all or most exports rather than exports of a specific product. Although some manufactured items appear on the list, the prevalence of agricultural products among subsidized exports is striking.

A more complex reason for export subsidies involves the possibility that temporary export subsidies in markets with certain characteristics may allow a country to capture a larger share of the world market that it can then exploit by charging monopoly prices for the good. A full examination of this argument, part of a branch of international trade called *strategic trade policy,* must wait until Chapter Eight.

---

11 When many countries subsidize exports, they drive down the world price by the amount of the subsidy (see footnote 9).

Table 7.3 **Export Subsidies, 2000**	
Country	Subsidized Products
Australia	Automobiles and components, textiles, clothing, footwear, automotive leather
Brazil	Steel, regional aircraft
China	Corn, cotton
European Union	Aircraft, aircraft supplies, shipbuilding
Thailand	Rice
Ukraine	Steel
Venezuela	Coffee, cocoa, fruit, seafood

Source: Data from U.S. Trade Representative, *2000 National Trade Estimate Report on Foreign Trade Barriers* (Washington, D.C., 2000). Available at www.ustr.gov.

Export subsidies rarely take the form of explicit and direct payments from a government to exporting firms. WTO guidelines, even before the Uruguay Round, ruled out such payments on industrial products. Actual subsidies take less direct and visible forms. Defining precisely which actions do and don't constitute subsidies was one of the most difficult issues facing negotiators in the Uruguay Round of WTO talks. One of the most common types of subsidy involves provision of low-cost government loans to firms in certain industries. A second type of subsidy is provision of favorable tax treatment for firms involved in exporting. The Uruguay Round Agreement clarifies that forgone or uncollected government tax revenue, that is, tax credits, does constitute a subsidy under WTO rules.

7.6 Dumping

Perhaps no phenomenon in international trade generates as much controversy and as many calls for protection as does dumping. **Dumping** can be defined in one of two ways.[12] According to the "price-based" definition, dumping occurs whenever a firm sells a good in a foreign market at a price below that for which the firm sells the same good in the domestic market. Under the "cost-based" definition, sale of a good in a foreign market at a price below its production cost constitutes dumping. The definitional distinction is important, because dumping under one definition isn't necessarily dumping under the other. In particular, whenever the domestic price of a good differs from its cost of production, the requirements for dumping differ under the two definitions.

7.6.1 Sporadic Dumping

Economists divide dumping into three categories. The first is **sporadic dumping,** which involves sale of a good in a foreign market for a short time at a price below either the domestic price or the cost of production. This short-lived variety of dumping resembles an international "sale." Stores sometimes sell goods for short periods at prices below their regular prices, often to eliminate undesired inventories. Sporadic dumping is the international equivalent of such sales.

Sporadic dumping may disrupt the domestic market because of the uncertainty generated when foreign supply changes suddenly. However, it's unlikely to cause permanent and serious injury to a domestic industry, just as a store's market position isn't likely to be damaged irrevocably by a competitor's occasional sales. During the brief period of dumping, domestic consumers benefit from availability of the imported good at an unusually low price.

---

12 Many economists agree that rules against dumping should be restricted to predatory dumping (defined in section 7.6.3); the original 1916 U.S. law was so restricted.

7.6.2 **Persistent Dumping**

Persistent dumping, as the term suggests, is continued sale of a good in a foreign market at a price below either the domestic price or production cost, a practice that provides the basis for many calls for protection. The distinction between the price-based and cost-based definitions is crucial in analyzing persistent dumping.

The major cause of persistent dumping according to the price-based definition is international price discrimination. Any firm able to separate its customers into two or more groups with different elasticities of demand for its product and to prevent resale of the good among them can increase profit by charging the groups different prices.[13] This practice is called **price discrimination.** Often a firm serving both a domestic and an export market can charge a higher price to domestic consumers, who typically exhibit a lower elasticity of demand than foreign consumers. Other things being equal, the more and better the substitutes for a good, the higher the elasticity of demand; good substitutes allow consumers to be very responsive to changes in the good's price. In most industries, a firm has more competitors in export markets than in the home-country market; this implies that the elasticity of demand facing the firm in the export market typically exceeds that in the home market and creates an incentive for price discrimination.[14]

Figure 7.6 illustrates the relationship between international price discrimination and persistent dumping. A firm producing good Y faces the situation in panel (a) in the home market and the situation in panel (b) in the export market. The demand curves reflect a higher elasticity of demand for good Y in the export market at any given price; in other words, the firm possesses more market power in the home market than in the export market—an intuitively plausible assumption.

Figure 7.6 **Persistent Dumping as International Price Discrimination**

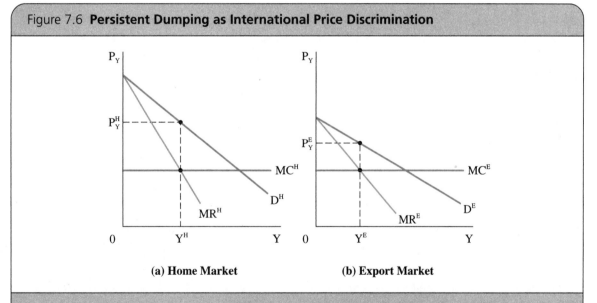

(a) Home Market   **(b) Export Market**

If a firm can prevent resale of its product between domestic and foreign customers, price discrimination based on different elasticities of demand by the two groups will increase the firm's profits. Because of the greater number of competitors in export markets, the firm generally will charge a higher price in the *home* market than in the export market (that is, $P_Y^H > P_Y^E$), generating dumping by the price-based definition.

---

13 A good's elasticity of demand is the percentage change in quantity demanded resulting from a 1 percent change in price (elasticity of demand = % change in quantity demanded/% change in price).

14 In Chapter Eight (section 8.4.2), we discuss the case of two monopolists charging high prices in their respective home markets and dumping (under the price definition) to capture part of the rival's market, a practice known as *reciprocal dumping*.

The firm maximizes profit in each market by producing the level of output at which *marginal cost* (denoted by MC and assumed for simplicity to be constant at all levels of output and equal across markets) equals *marginal revenue* (MR).[15] The height of the corresponding demand curve at the profit-maximizing level of output gives the profit-maximizing price. The price in the *home* market (P_Y^H) exceeds that in the *export* market (P_Y^E) because of the relative inelasticity of home-country demand. The firm dumps by the price-based definition, with a **dumping margin** of $P_Y^H - P_Y^E$. However, such price discrimination produces ambiguous welfare effects. The market power reflected in the firm's ability to charge prices above marginal cost (especially in the home market) reduces economic efficiency and harms consumers, as with any case of monopoly. However, the effect of restricting the firm to charge equal prices in the two markets cannot be ascertained without further information about the market in question. Hence, international trade theory provides no clear rationale for policies that prohibit international price discrimination.

What about persistent dumping under the cost-based definition? Would we expect to observe continual sales of a good below cost? The answer depends on what one means by *cost*. If *cost* is defined as the firm's marginal cost of production, economists think the general answer to the question is no: Firms will not sell a good persistently at a price below its marginal cost of production. Although many industries in many countries ask for protection from foreign competition by pointing to alleged persistent dumping, there are few cases in which such behavior has been observed.

Charges of dumping under the cost-based definition often use a concept of cost other than the exporting firm's *marginal* cost. For example, firms may sell in the short run at prices below their *average total* cost. In fact, we expect firms with significant fixed costs to do so in periods of low demand, such as during recessions. As long as sales bring in revenue sufficient to cover variable cost, the profit-maximizing firm will choose to produce rather than shut down in the short run—even if price falls below average total cost. This holds regardless of whether the firm sells domestically or internationally.[16]

Another problem arises because foreign production costs often are difficult to determine, presenting a temptation to use indirect measures of those costs. Careless use of the cost-based definition of dumping can allow domestic producers to accuse any foreign rival who undersells them of dumping. Assume that American Steel Company loses business to Brazilian Steel Company, which sells steel products at lower prices. American Steel accuses Brazilian Steel of dumping. Since neither American Steel nor U.S. trade-policy makers know Brazilian Steel's cost of production, American Steel argues that Brazilian Steel's prices are below *American Steel's* production cost. Acceptance of such an argument as evidence of dumping sets a dangerous precedent. Domestic producers in *any* comparative-disadvantage industry could accuse foreign rivals of dumping. Recall that a country with a comparative advantage always can sell the industry's product for less than a country with a comparative disadvantage. Disallowing trade based on dumping charges that involve careless use of the cost-based definition of dumping could eliminate all trade based on comparative advantage!

In practice, use of the cost-based definition in dumping cases isn't yet quite as disastrous as the previous example might suggest. When a domestic firm files dumping charges, trade law requires an effort to determine their validity using the price-based definition. If domestic-country prices of the good in question aren't available (for example, if the foreign firm produces only for export), investigators must make an effort to determine the price of the good in a third market. When this fails, investigators seek production costs in the country of origin, followed by production costs in third markets.

The most famous example of this situation involved a 1974 U.S. charge that Poland dumped golf carts in the U.S. market. Poland sold no golf carts domestically, so the price-based definition of dumping proved useless. No one knew the true cost of production by Polish firms because Poland, then a centrally planned economy, didn't use market-determined prices for its inputs. To resolve the case, investigators evaluated the inputs the Polish firm used to make a golf cart at input prices from Spain. The estimated cost turned out to be very close to the price Poland charged for golf carts sold in the United States.

---

15 Marginal revenue is defined as the change in total revenue when the firm changes its level of output by one unit. Under the assumption that the firm has some market power and must charge the same price for all units sold in a given market, marginal revenue at any level of output is less than price. To sell an additional unit of output in any market, the firm must lower its price in that market, and the lower price must apply to all units sold in that market. Therefore, the marginal revenue from sale of the additional unit is less than the price for which the additional unit itself is sold.

16 If sales at high prices in a protected domestic market cover the firm's fixed cost, sales in export markets can occur at any price that covers only the variable cost of production.

Rapid changes in formerly centrally planned economies raise interesting issues for the calculations in dumping investigations. In dumping charges against China, for example, the United States historically used prices from third countries including Germany, Japan, France, Canada, Switzerland, the Netherlands, India, Pakistan, and Thailand to substitute for missing Chinese prices. However, as China has increased the role of market prices in its economy, U.S. dumping-investigation procedures have adjusted and used Chinese prices in some cases.

7.6.3 **Predatory Dumping**

Domestic firms often claim that foreign firms sell in the domestic market at prices below production cost to drive domestic firms from the industry. The alleged purpose behind this strategy of **predatory dumping** is to eliminate domestic competitors and then exploit the newly created monopoly power by raising prices. Although intuitively appealing, several aspects of this story stand up poorly to scrutiny.

First, foreign firms—if indeed they sell at prices below their production cost—suffer losses while dumping. The prospective monopoly power they hope to gain must promise future rewards high enough to compensate for current losses. Second, domestic firms (the "victims") would know that predatory dumping could be only temporary because of the losses it would create for its instigators. If the "unfair competition" is temporary, domestic firms should be able to borrow funds with which to hold out until the foreign firms give up on the attempt to drive rivals out of business. Third, even if predatory dumping drove domestic firms from the industry, the strategy would prove worthwhile only if foreign firms could then exploit their monopoly power by charging higher prices. However, once this occurred, what would prevent domestic firms (either old or new ones) from re-entering the industry and underselling the foreign monopolist? If domestic firms did this, foreign firms would have suffered losses during the dumping episode for little or no future reward. Finally, the predatory-dumping story requires a firm to perceive an opportunity to *monopolize* the industry. But large groups of firms often file dumping charges against dozens of competitors in several countries; the large number of firms involved on both sides of the typical dumping case implies a low probability of monopolization.

The United States' first antidumping law, passed in 1916, applied only to predatory dumping. In the almost 80 years since, no firm has been convicted under that statute. Current dumping cases use statutes that embody much broader definitions of dumping to include that with no predatory intent or effect.

7.6.4 **Policy Responses to Dumping**

Under U.S. trade law, when a domestic firm charges a foreign counterpart with dumping, the U.S. Department of Commerce and the U.S. International Trade Commission conduct investigations. Those investigations must determine (1) whether dumping occurred, and (2) if so, whether it materially injured or threatens to materially injure the domestic industry. If both questions are answered affirmatively, the government imposes an **antidumping duty,** an import tariff equal to the dumping margin (represented by $P_Y^H - P_Y^E$ in Figure 7.6).

Despite rules written into antidumping laws, many analysts argue that U.S. procedures in dumping investigations almost guarantee guilty findings for foreign firms charged with dumping. The computation of dumping margins involves many complex issues, and trading partners complain with some justification that U.S. procedures bias findings toward high dumping margins and, therefore, high antidumping duties. For example, when dumping investigations use the cost-based definition of dumping, cost calculations provide many opportunities for investigators to build in high cost estimates, which lead to finding high dumping margins.

Trading partners also complain about the U.S. practice of demanding extraordinary amounts of detailed information on short notice from firms accused of dumping. If a firm cannot or chooses not to provide any piece of the requested information, the U.S. investigators can use their own "best information available" to substitute for the missing data. In practice, the "best information available" can consist of data provided by the domestic firms seeking protection and, as a result, might be expected to contain a bias toward a large dumping margin.

There is evidence that these procedural issues do appear to bias findings toward high dumping margins and, therefore, high antidumping duties. In U.S. dumping cases between 1995 and 1998, those using the price-based definition found average dumping margins of 3.2 percent, those using constructed values under the cost-based definition found average dumping margins of 25.1 percent, those using surrogate constructed values for nonmarket economies found dumping margins of 40 percent, and those using "best information available" found dumping margins of a whopping 95.6 percent (indicating that foreign firms supposedly were selling products for about half of what it cost to produce them!). A similar differential of findings under the different dumping definitions and investigative procedures also exists in European Union dumping cases over the same period.[17]

Historically, the United States has used antidumping policies much more extensively than other countries. However, in recent years, trading partners have been catching up. Twenty-three member countries reported to the WTO that they had taken antidumping actions in 2000. Figure 7.7 indicates the cases' geographic distribution. For each country in the map, the first number reports the number of antidumping actions *initiated* during the year and the second number reports the number of new antidumping investigations to which the country was *subject*. The European Union (49), the United States (29), India (27), and Argentina (23) reported filing the largest number of cases in 2000. The European Union (32), China (30), and Korea (23) were targets of the largest numbers of dumping accusations by their trading partners.

At the end of 2000, the United States had 200 antidumping orders in effect, covering goods from pineapple to salmon to nails and involving trading partners as varied as Canada and Uzbekistan. Table 7.4 reports the number of U.S. dumping cases in recent years, along with the number of negative and affirmative findings by both the Department of Commerce and the International Trade Commission. Affirmative dumping and injury findings in 2000 covered goods such as aspirin, apple-juice concentrate, and several steel products.

Like subsidy investigations, dumping investigations can lead to a protectionist outcome other than an antidumping duty. Accused exporters can negotiate suspension agreements in which they agree to stop export-

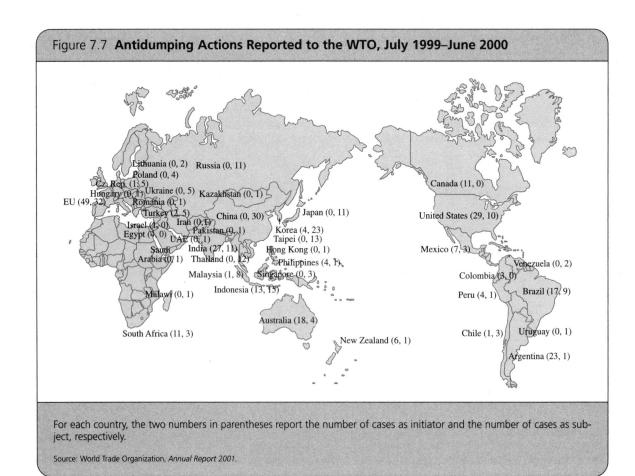

Figure 7.7 Antidumping Actions Reported to the WTO, July 1999–June 2000

For each country, the two numbers in parentheses report the number of cases as initiator and the number of cases as subject, respectively.

Source: World Trade Organization, *Annual Report 2001*.

---

17 Patrick A. Messerlin, "Antidumping and Safeguards," in *The WTO after Seattle*, edited by Jeffrey J. Schott (Washington, D.C.: Institute for International Economics, 2000), p. 169.

Table 7.4 **U.S. Antidumping Investigations**

	1995	1996	1997	1998	1999	2000
Petitions filed	14	20	15	36	61	51
Final Commerce determinations:						
Negative	2	0	1	0	0	1
Affirmative	40	12	17	18	38	39
Suspended	1	1	1	0	0	0
Final Commission determinations:						
Negative	16	3	2	6	18	15
Affirmative	24	8	15	9	21	21
Terminated	3	1	1	0	0	

Source: U.S. International Trade Commission, *The Year in Trade 2001.*

ing to the United States or to raise their prices until the U.S. industry no longer claims injury. Suspension agreements work like VERs; they reduce competition, lead to higher prices, and make it easier for domestic and foreign firms to engage in cartel-like behavior. For example, China agreed to its first suspension agreement in 1995. China agreed to cut its honey exports to the United States to 43.9 million pounds a year for five years (a cut of about 40 percent), to charge a price no lower than 92 percent of the price of non-Chinese imported honey, and to enforce the agreement by issuing quota certificates to Chinese producers. *(How does the pricing rule risk ignoring comparative advantage? Do you think Chinese honey sales were predatory? Why or why not?)* The alternative to the suspension agreement would have been to accept antidumping duties ranging from 127 to 157 percent.

The Uruguay Round elaborated on antidumping rules negotiated as a code during the Tokyo Round. However, progress in dealing with dumping fell far short of that in many other areas. The new agreement does require countries to remove antidumping duties that have been in place for five years unless they can demonstrate that doing so would reinstitute the damage to the domestic industry that led to the initial finding. This provision should help curtail the current practice of more-or-less permanent protection in the form of antidumping duties, a nontrivial accomplishment since many U.S. antidumping duties had been in effect since the 1970s. The U.S. revoked 46 antidumping orders during 2000. But eight duties put in place during the 1970s remained in effect.

7.7 **Voluntary Import Expansions**

A **voluntary import expansion (VIE)** requires a country to import a specified quantity of foreign goods in a given industry. The mandated imports typically are stated as a minimum market share. Failure to achieve the target usually leads to retaliation with tariffs.[18] The exporting country pushing a trading partner to accept a VIE often alleges that foreign trade barriers block exports and necessitate the agreement. On the surface, VIEs appear different from other protectionist policies. After all, VIEs aim to increase, not decrease, trade and claim to offset or break through foreign trade barriers.

VIEs form a key part of "results-oriented" trade policies—that is, policies that focus on generating specific trade *outcomes* rather than on establishing a framework of *rules* under which market forces determine trade patterns. Japan has been a particular target of results-oriented policies, because of the widespread perception that the structure of the Japanese economy embodies many "informal" or "invisible" trade barriers, such as a preference on the part of Japanese firms for long-term business relationships that favor domestic partners. These informal barriers present problems for the international trading system for three reasons. First, their

---

18 See Case One in Chapter Five on the U.S.–Japan semiconductor pact. Chapter Eight (section 8.10) treats more generally the use of protectionist policies to force trade liberalization on trading partners.

very informality makes substantiating their existence, as well as measuring their magnitude or impact, difficult. Second, the complexity of the barriers, if indeed they exist, makes multilateral or even bilateral negotiations for their reduction difficult. Finally, the barriers are embedded in the structure of the economy and culture in such a way that international pressures for change encounter resistance. Proponents of VIEs claim that these factors, taken together, render traditional rules-oriented trade policy ineffective in reducing Japan's informal barriers.

Despite benign first appearances, VIEs can act as powerful tools of protection. They ignore the possibility that the observed outcome in a particular industry simply reflects comparative advantage rather than foreign trade barriers.[19] The agreements allocate specific market shares to foreign and domestic firms, allowing the firms to act as an informal cartel and charge higher prices than would be feasible under market competition. VIEs often allocate the required foreign market share to the country powerful enough to force the import country to negotiate the VIE; again, competition is restricted rather than encouraged, as the VIE itself shuts potential exporters from other countries out of the market. Finally, any industry that potentially could export has an incentive to push for VIEs—even if the industry has a comparative disadvantage. Policy makers tend to measure the "success" of a VIE in increased export sales, regardless of whether those sales coincide with the international pattern of comparative advantage. *More trade, however, is not necessarily better than less trade. Trade produces gains when it's based on either comparative advantage or economies of scale.* VIE-induced exports that run counter to these economic considerations damage foreign producers, may damage consumers, and reduce the efficiency of the world economy, even though they may help some exporting firms.

7.8 Administrative and Technical Standards

Most countries subject international trade to a variety of regulatory standards, some protectionist by design and others unintentionally so. A few of the more common classes of restrictions include domestic-content requirements and rules of origin, government-procurement policies, technical product standards, and regulatory standards. Such policies constitute a continuing source of controversy in the international trading system because of the inherent difficulty in sorting intentionally protectionist policies from those pursued for legitimate domestic reasons but that have unintended negative effects on international trade.

7.8.1 Domestic-Content Requirements and Rules of Origin

Domestic-content requirements mandate that a specified percentage of a product's inputs and/or assembly have domestic origins in order for the good to be sold domestically. Such requirements have three main constituencies. One consists of domestic input producers. For example, most U.S. auto-parts producers support rules to require all cars sold in the United States, especially those produced by Japanese-based firms, to include high percentages of U.S.-made parts. A second constituency includes workers in the domestic industry. A U.S. domestic-content rule on cars, for example, could require Japanese auto producers to perform a high percentage of assembly tasks in the United States, increasing demand for the services of U.S. auto workers. Finally, domestic producers of the good typically support domestic-content requirements because such rules can raise foreign firms' costs and make them less competitive. If U.S.-made labor and auto parts cost more than their Japanese counterparts, then forcing Japanese producers to use more U.S. parts and perform more assembly tasks in the United States could raise Toyota's, Nissan's, and Honda's costs and shift sales toward U.S.-based auto producers.

Worldwide, domestic-content requirements have received most attention in the automobile industry, which in recent years has sponsored almost every type of trade restriction imaginable.[20] The United Auto Workers union has pressured U.S. policy makers to pass domestic-content legislation. The original UAW-supported legislation would have required 90 percent U.S. or Canadian value-added for all manufacturers selling 500,000 or more cars in the United States. The reasons for this pressure are twofold. First, domestic-content requirements would limit imports of foreign-produced automobiles. Second, the requirements would limit

---

19 The quotation in question 4 in the "Problems and Questions for Review" provides one vivid example.

20 Find information on domestic-content requirements for automobiles at www.ita.doc.gov/td/auto/impreq.

outsourcing, in which U.S.-based automobile manufacturers buy inputs and perform assembly functions abroad. Many "American" cars—that is, cars sold by U.S.-based automobile companies—now are built abroad, much to the dismay of American auto workers. Auto makers have adopted Japan's high-technology assembly methods and use them in factories around the world. Also, many car parts, including engines and transmissions, now are built in Canada, Mexico, and Brazil, imported into the United States, and placed in "American" cars. U.S. companies aren't the only ones taking advantage of low-cost production in developing countries; Volkswagen and Nissan, for example, maintain assembly operations in Mexico. Foreign-based auto producers, including Honda, Toyota, and BMW, also build cars in the United States. For cars sold in the United States, the vehicle-identification number (VIN) provides information about the country where the car was assembled. Cars assembled in the United States have VINs beginning with 1 or 4, while cars assembled in Japan begin with J and in Sweden with Y, for example. *(Where was your car assembled?)*

Modern worldwide production makes it difficult or impossible to determine the "nationality" of a product. A car may be assembled in England from parts produced in Brazil and sold by a firm owned primarily by Germans. One U.S. pro-protection interest group wants to require all goods to carry labels listing how much of the goods' value-added comes from each country. The South Dakota legislature carried the idea further by proposing that all goods be labeled with three flags: to denote the countries of the producing firm's ownership, the product's manufacture, and the parts used in the product. Since 1994, cars sold in the United States have required stickers stating the percentage of parts from U.S. and Canadian sources.

Direct political pressure from protectionist-oriented special-interest groups isn't the only reason for increased domestic-content requirements. When groups of countries negotiate reductions in their barriers to trade, those reductions sometimes apply *only* to members of the group. These agreements require a version of domestic-content rules, often called **rules of origin;** otherwise, nonmember countries could use the agreements to circumvent tariffs. For example, if Canada's import tariffs exceed those of the United States, countries exporting to Canada would like to ship their goods to the United States, pay the low U.S. tariff, and then ship to Canada duty-free from the United States under the North American Free Trade Agreement. To prevent this, agreements such as NAFTA contain provisions that limit duty-free access to goods "originating" in the member countries.[21] In practice, this involves complicated and politically sensitive issues, as members of the European Union and NAFTA have discovered.

Under NAFTA, most goods qualify for duty-free treatment if they *either* contain a specified percentage of North American content *or* are sufficiently "transformed" in North America to change tariff classification.[22] For goods in sensitive sectors (autos, computers, and textiles and apparel), *both* conditions must be satisfied. Autos, in particular, must contain 62.5 percent North American content.

The Uruguay Round agreement set in motion a three-year process to develop harmonized rules of origin for WTO member countries. Suggested disciplines include requiring rules to be consistent and impartial, prohibiting retroactive application of rule changes, and restricting the frequency of rule changes to every three years, since frequent changes in rules disadvantage exporters.

Domestic-content rules and rules of origin discourage production of goods in the countries where opportunity costs are lowest. Thus, such rules reduce the gains from trade. The potential losses may be particularly large in industries, such as the automobile industry, that involve many diverse manufacturing and assembly tasks. A single country isn't likely to have a comparative advantage in every aspect of the automobile production process, from research-and-development-intensive design to labor-intensive assembly. Arrangements such as outsourcing reflect firms' attempts to perform each manufacturing and assembly stage in the country of comparative advantage. As a result, outsourcing not only contributes to efficient production of automobiles but also supports developing countries' attempts to build manufacturing sectors. A developing or newly industrializing country finds it difficult to build a complete automobile industry that can compete with the established industries in the developed economies. An alternative is to specialize in particular stages of the production process appropriate for the country's factor endowment; but domestic-content rules and rules of origin by developed countries restrict such specialization and harm developing countries.

---

21 The alternative is to form a customs union with a common external tariff on trade with nonmembers; we'll discuss this option in section 9.4.1.

22 On tariff classification, see section 6.3.

7.8.2 Government-Procurement Policies

Our analyses of international trade have relied on profit-maximizing motives of firms and utility maximization by consumers. We assume that consumers and firms try to buy at the lowest and sell at the highest available prices. The interaction of buyers' and sellers' decisions in each market determines the prices of goods and, in turn, the prices of factors of production. A large amount of trade, however, is undertaken by entities that may not respond to these motives of profit and utility maximization, at least in the simple terms in which we have defined them. Governments are foremost among the trading entities with unique goals.

We've seen several effects of government involvement in international trade: agricultural price supports and the role of government subsidization of exports. Two other areas involve even more direct government roles in international trade. First, governments actually buy and sell many goods and services in international markets. Second, government-owned industries and government-run monopolies make purchases and sales. These phenomena are called **government-procurement policies.**

Most countries have **buy-domestic requirements,** which either legally or informally require governments to purchase domestically made goods on a preferential basis. The strength of the requirements varies considerably. Some prohibit government purchases of certain imports outright; for example, laws require many governments to use the domestic airline exclusively and to patronize only domestic insurance firms. Other laws mandate strict guidelines for giving preference to domestic over foreign producers. The Buy American Act of 1933 required a 6 percent margin of preference for domestic producers of goods bought by the government. In other words, a foreign firm would have to sell at a price more than 6 percent below the domestic firm's price to win the contract.[23] For military or defense-related goods, the margin of preference expanded to 50 percent.

Many of the most controversial government-procurement practices are much more subtle and informal than the provisions of the Buy American Act and its foreign counterparts. For example, governments may keep their bidding practices secret so foreign firms won't have information about the procedure and timing for submission of bids for government contracts. Government agencies may advertise contracts in media unlikely to be available to foreign firms and may keep bids secret to prevent scrutiny of the award process. The Tokyo Round of trade negotiations addressed some of these problems with a government-procurement code, and the Uruguay Round built on this effort. The code has only 28 signatory countries and applies only to specified government agencies and projects, but it represents a step forward in recommending that government bidding procedures be well specified and open. The Uruguay Round rules apply to procurement of services as well as goods and to some purchases by subfederal governments and public utilities. However, governments still can practice many forms of preference for domestic firms.

Even more controversy arises when the government owns sizable industries, as in the cases of postal, telephone, and telegraph services (PTTs) in Asia, Europe, and most developing economies. The governments involved often claim to maintain these monopolies for purely domestic reasons, including national security and protection of domestic consumers from exploitation by private monopolies. The complex web of restrictions on imports of goods used in these industries suggests that protection of the domestic industry from foreign competition may be another government goal. The scope of the problem varies widely across countries with the extent of public ownership of industry. National policies typically restrict imports of telecommunications equipment, data processing, and computer-oriented technology by PTTs. Most governments recognize the need to privatize or deregulate their utilities, both to improve the industries' efficiency and to avoid trade disputes, but progress in this reform has varied widely across countries.

7.8.3 Technical, Administrative, and Regulatory Standards

Governments regulate various aspects of activity within their economies and carefully guard their rights to do so. Regulations may include health, safety, and product-labeling requirements, as well as controls over entry into certain professions and access to certain types of mass media. Domestic considerations motivate many of these **technical barriers to trade.** Governments require imported foods to meet hygienic standards, toys and autos to meet safety standards, and products to conform to labeling laws to prevent fraud and provide consumer information.

---

23 Many U.S. states have gone even further with "buy in the state" legislation, which gives preference to in-state firms for goods purchased by state and local government agencies. Los Angeles requires a specified percentage of *local* value-added for purchases related to its mass-transportation system.

As in the case of government-owned telecommunications monopolies, some of the observed restrictions clearly have protectionist effects. In some cases, these effects are so strong that one must suspect the proclaimed domestic goals of the restrictions as mere covers for protectionist intent. Because of the difficulties in sorting legitimate domestic policy goals from protectionist ones, efforts at international negotiations to lower technical barriers to trade have met with relatively little success. Taken individually, the rules may seem small and rather insignificant in terms of cost. When taken together, however, the costs become substantial. Eliminating these costs by removing technical barriers to trade provided a major stimulus to the European Union's efforts to develop a completely open market for trade among its members. However, loopholes for safety and environmental regulations allow member countries to continue technical standards that restrict trade even within the European Union.

7.9 How Can We Measure Nontariff Barriers?

Nontariff barriers present major hurdles to analysts interested in measuring the range and magnitude of those barriers. Deciding exactly what should count as a nontariff barrier can be difficult in itself. Once we decide which barriers to include, at least four different measures can be calculated.

The most common empirical measure of NTBs is the **coverage ratio,** or the value of imports subject to NTBs, divided by total imports. Consider a simple example. Country A imports $60 worth of good X and $40 worth of good Y, so A's total imports equal $100. Imports of X are subject to a quota under which a maximum of $60 worth of X can be imported, and imports of Y are free of any NTBs. NTBs affect $60 out of the country's $100 worth of imports, so country A's NTB coverage ratio equals ($60/$100) = 0.6. The major problem with the coverage ratio is that *incipient* trade, shut off by trade restrictions, isn't counted. With no quota on good X, perhaps country A would have imported $5,000 worth of X; but the loss of the additional $4,940 worth of trade doesn't enter the coverage-ratio calculation. Another problem involves measuring changes in NTBs. Suppose, beginning with the situation just outlined, country A tightens the quota on good X until no imports can enter, while good Y remains unrestricted. Now none of country A's imports are covered by NTBs, so the new coverage ratio is ($0/$40) = 0. Counterintuitively, *tightening* the quota, by stopping all trade in the restricted good, *lowered* the NTB coverage ratio![24]

An alternative measure, called the **implicit tariff,** uses the equivalence between tariffs and quotas (see section 7.4). The idea is to calculate the tariff rate that would have the same effect on trade as the existing quota or other nontariff barrier. The Uruguay Round required that countries calculate implicit tariffs in order to accomplish the required *tariffication,* that is, switching their agricultural protection policies from quotas to tariffs, which would then be cut according to the Uruguay Round tariff-reduction timetable. Canadian quotas on agricultural products had been so high that their implicit tariff rates, imposed in 1995, ranged up to 335 percent. Even after the Uruguay Round phased-in tariff reductions, Canadian tariffs would still be prohibitive—285 percent on imported chicken cuts, 187 percent on eggs, and 272 percent on yogurt.[25] The United States filed a complaint under the North American Free Trade Agreement dispute-settlement procedure, arguing that NAFTA required elimination of all tariffs between Canada and the United States by 1998. Canada argued that its WTO tariffication obligation took precedence over the NAFTA tariff-elimination commitment. A NAFTA dispute-settlement panel ruled in favor of Canada.

The most comprehensive measures of nontariff barriers are producer- and consumer-subsidy equivalents. An industry's **producer-subsidy equivalent (PSE)** measures the difference between the income industry producers receive *with* their NTBs and the income producers would receive *with no* such barriers, and expresses that difference as a percentage of the income-without-barriers figure. If producers earn $3 million with a quota but would earn only $2 million under free trade, the producer-subsidy equivalent is ($3 million − $2 million)/$2 million = 0.5 or 50 percent. Economists have calculated producer-subsidy equivalents for many agricultural products because those products are subject to so many NTBs. Table 7.5 reports one set of estimates that compares agricultural PSEs for several major agricultural producers; Switzerland's agricultural producers, for example, received 76 percent more income in 1997 than they would have in the absence of government assistance to the industry, including price supports facilitated by import barriers.

---

24 Average tariff measures exhibit the same weakness; see section 6.3 in Chapter Six.

25 U.S. International Trade Commission, *The Year in Trade 1996* (Washington, D.C.: USITC, 1997), p. 88.

Table 7.5 **Producer-Subsidy Equivalents in Agriculture, 1997**		
	Producer-Subsidy Equivalent (Percent of Value of Production)	Consumer-Subsidy Equivalent (Percent of Value of Consumption)
Switzerland	76	−53
Norway	71	−50
Japan	69	−46
Iceland	68	−35
European Union	42	−25
Turkey	38	−34
Poland	22	−20
Canada	20	−14
United States	16	−8
Hungary	16	−9
Mexico	16	0
Czech Republic	11	−4
Australia	9	−5
New Zealand	3	−6

Source: Data from Organization for Economic Cooperation and Development, *Agricultural Policies in OECD Countries 1998* (OECD: Paris, 1998), pp. 30–33.

Table 7.5 also reports the **consumer-subsidy equivalent (CSE),** which performs the same exercise for an industry's consumers. If, because of an import quota, consumers must pay $5 million for a good they could get for $4 million without the quota, the quota's consumer-subsidy equivalent is ($4 million – $5 million)/$4 million = –0.25 or –25 percent. Note the negative sign; the quota forces consumers to pay higher prices, hence in effect they receive a *negative* subsidy. Generally, protectionist policies including NTBs affect producers and consumers in an industry in opposite ways. Therefore, the producer- and consumer-subsidy equivalents for an industry have opposite signs. *(Name a trade policy with a negative PSE and a positive CSE, and vice versa.)*

CASE ONE:
Has Trade Policy Gone Bananas?

The members of the European Union have a long history of protectionism in the banana market. Before the 1992 completion of Europe's internal market, only Germany, the biggest per capita banana-consuming country in the world, allowed free trade in bananas. Other EU members had *two* banana policies. They imported small, expensive bananas from a group of African, Caribbean, and Pacific (ACP) exporters, mostly former European colonies such as Cameroon and St. Lucia, through a special trade agreement with the European Union; these bananas paid no tariff and faced no quotas. At the same time, all non-German EU members applied a 20 percent tariff on all so-called "dollar bananas"—larger, cheaper bananas grown in Latin America. France, Italy, Portugal, Spain, Greece, and the United Kingdom also applied quotas against dollar bananas. As a result, banana prices varied widely within the EU, from $125 per ton in Portugal to $700 per ton in Spain. *(Which producers do you think have a comparative advantage in bananas— the ACP producers, or the Latin American dollar-banana producers? Why?)*[26]

---

26 Banana production per acre is approximately three times as high in dollar-banana countries as in the Caribbean; and the cost of producing a dollar banana is approximately half that of an ACP banana ("Expelled From Eden," *The Economist,* December 20, 1997, p. 37).

The EU's 1992 program required free movement of goods across the Union, a plan that would destroy the market for expensive ACP bananas, since dollar bananas could enter the EU through Germany and move on to other countries. The Union responded by replacing member countries' national banana restrictions with an EU-wide policy. Germany took its case to the European Court of Justice, insisting on its right to free trade in bananas, but lost.

Under the post-1992 European Union Banana Regime, up to 857,700 metric tons of ACP bananas could enter the EU tariff-free each year; additional ACP bananas had to pay a tariff of ECU750 per ton.[27] The first 2 million metric tons of dollar bananas each year owed a tariff of ECU100 per ton; additional dollar bananas faced an ECU850 tariff. Also shut out of the EU market were countries such as Ghana, which, as a new producer, wasn't entitled to an EU import license. The Banana Regime's cost to European consumers has been estimated at $2 billion per year.[28]

When dollar-banana producers Colombia, Costa Rica, Guatemala, Nicaragua, and Venezuela complained to the GATT, the organization ruled that the EU Banana Regime was illegal, but the EU blocked adoption of the report.[29] The EU offered the five countries a "Framework Agreement on Bananas," which promised to increase their EU quota by 10 percent and lower the tariff against their banana exports by 25 percent—in exchange for the countries' dropping their complaint and promising not to challenge the EU Banana Regime in the future. The agreement also guaranteed the signatories country-specific quotas and allowed the exporting countries to administer the quotas, ensuring that they could capture the valuable quota rents. The five Latin American countries, except for Guatemala, accepted the terms of the Framework Agreement, but only Colombia and Costa Rica actually implemented its terms.

Chiquita and members of the Hawaii Banana Industry Association complained to the U.S. Trade Representative, claiming that the new EU Banana Regime and Framework Agreement shut them out of their traditional role as banana ripeners and distributors of dollar bananas to European markets. In 1995 and 1996, the United States initiated a WTO dispute-settlement procedure, joined by Ecuador, Guatemala, Honduras, and Mexico. Caribbean (ACP) banana exporters claimed that elimination of their preferential access to EU markets would lead to the collapse of their banana-dependent economies and to social unrest. The United States also began an investigation into the implications for U.S. companies of Colombia's and Costa Rica's implementation of the Framework Agreement, which restricted the role of U.S. firms such as Chiquita Brands and Dole Food.

In 1997, the WTO ruled that the EU Banana Regime violated the Union's WTO obligations; the EU appealed, but lost again. A WTO-appointed arbitrator ruled that the Union had until January 1, 1999, to bring its banana policy into line with its WTO obligations. In June 1998, the EU finally made some minor changes to its Banana Regime. It abolished the regime's licensing requirement but maintained the quota on dollar bananas. U.S. trade officials went "bananas" in response, claiming that the EU Banana Regime still violated WTO rules and threatening trade sanctions in retaliation.

In December 1998, the U.S. government announced a list of 15 European exports—from coffee makers to pecorino cheese—on which the U.S. would impose 100 percent retaliatory import tariffs by March 1999 unless the European Union complied with WTO rulings against the Banana Regime. The EU, on the other hand, hoped to stall by demanding a time-consuming WTO investigation of the minor changes made in the Regime after the initial WTO rulings. Most trade experts agreed that the EU's changes weren't sufficient to bring EU banana policy into compliance with WTO obligations; but those same experts also agreed that unilateral retaliation by the United States would be a step down the slippery path to a possible trade war. In April 1999, the WTO ruled, as expected, that the EU's changes to its Banana Regime didn't bring the policy into WTO compliance. The United States imposed the threatened 100 percent retaliatory tariffs on $191.4 million of EU exports.

In late November 1999, the European Union put forward a proposal for further changes in the Banana Regime, which would allow a fixed quota of bananas to enter the EU on a first-come, first-served basis regardless of country of origin; but ACP bananas would pay lower tariffs than dollar bananas. According to the proposal, the changes would remain in effect until 2006, at which time the complex Banana Regime would be replaced with a simple tariff scheme still giving preference (that is, lower tariffs) to ACP producers. Shortly thereafter, Caribbean banana producers—the supposed beneficiaries of the EU Regime—announced that they preferred the policies demanded by the United States. Then six European companies hit by the U.S. retaliatory tariffs, including an Italian battery manufacturer and a German cardboard-box producer, sued the European Union for damages, claiming that their businesses were harmed by the EU's slow response to the WTO rulings. And a banana split appeared between former allies Chiquita and Dole. Chiquita opposed the 1999 and 2000 EU proposals, which allowed bananas in on a first-come, first-served basis. Chiquita's European market share had dropped dramatically in recent years, and the firm wanted licenses allocated based on historical market

27 Such policies are called *tariff-rate quotas*. European Currency Units (ECU) are a currency measure used in the European Union pre-1999.

28 "Expelled from Eden," *The Economist,* December 20, 1997, p. 36.

29 The ability of the "defendant" country to block unfavorable findings weakened the GATT dispute-settlement procedures. Important elements of this deficiency were remedied in the 1994 agreement that changed the GATT into the new WTO.

shares from pre-1993 when it dominated the banana business. Dole, on the other hand, opposed allocation based on historical data, because its market share was growing. Both Dole and Chiquita sued the EU over its failure to propose a WTO-compatible banana policy.

Finally, in April 2001, the United States and the European Union reached an agreement. The European Union would allocate banana import licenses based on 1994–1996 market shares (thereby helping Chiquita at Dole's expense), enlarge the quota for Latin American bananas, and shrink slightly the quota set aside for ACP producers. In return, the United States dropped its retaliatory tariffs as of July 1.

EU Countries

CASE TWO:
Designer Grayjeans

Recall that firms with some market power can earn higher profits by engaging in price discrimination. This involves separating customers into groups with different price elasticities of demand for the product and charging higher prices to the low-elasticity customers. But for this pricing strategy to work, customers must not resell the product between groups. In other words, the firm's price discrimination won't work if a high-elasticity-of-demand customer can buy the good at a low price and then turn around and resell it to a low-elasticity-of-demand customer for a higher price. One way firms try to prevent such resale is by permitting only licensed dealers to sell their product.

Levi Strauss, the famous maker of jeans, uses this technique. When Tesco, a discount supermarket in the United Kingdom, started selling Levi's jeans bought from non-Levi's sources in the United States, Canada, and Mexico, Levi Strauss filed a case with the European Court of Justice demanding an end to the practice. Levi refused to license Tesco to sell jeans, claiming that its staff lacked the necessary training. A Levi spokesman asserted that "Customers need advice on what's on offer and the difference between loose and baggy, straight and slim. . . . Staff have to explain how one blue is different from another blue."[30]

Products such as the Levi's jeans sold by Tesco—bought in countries where Levi's sells its jeans for a lower price—are called *gray-market* or *parallel imports.* They aren't counterfeit goods, because they *are* Levi's jeans, but they travel through unlicensed distribution channels, thereby eroding the original seller's (Levi's) ability to price discriminate between markets.

Under EU trademark law, before the Levi's/Tesco case, goods could be sold legally in the European Union after they had been brought into the Union by a licensed supplier; the legal status of goods that entered the Union through an unlicensed channel wasn't clear. If the Levi case had led the Union to change its law to conform with international trademark rules, this murky restriction no longer would have applied; retailers could have imported from outside the Union without the original manufacturer's consent. The result would have been lower prices for European consumers, and a transfer from manufacturers to retailers. But that's *not* what happened. The European Court of Justice ruled in favor of Levi Strauss, saying that parallel imports were permitted only if consent by the trademark owner could be "unequivocally demonstrated."

Egypt

CASE THREE:
Export Quotas

Occasionally, countries use quotas to limit their own exports. Egypt's market for cotton provides one example.[31] Textile experts around the world recognize the exceptional quality of Egyptian cotton; its long, straight, durable fibers produce

---

30   "Levi Puts Case for Its 'Special' Sales Skills," *Financial Times,* January 16, 2001.

31   This case draws on "Cash Crop Labours under State Controls," *Financial Times,* May 9, 2001.

premium-quality fabrics. The cotton has been traded on international markets since the nineteenth century, making it the country's longest-standing cash crop.

During the 1960s and 1970s, when Egypt adopted a centrally planned economic system, the government nationalized trade in cotton, as well as the downstream spinning, weaving, and textile sectors. The government bought the entire cotton crop at a bureaucratically determined price to supply the state-owned spinners. Only lint, the leftover product from the first stage of the cotton-refining process, was exported. Reforms began in 1994, and cotton growers no longer must sell their entire crop to the state. The government also has allowed private firms to enter the cotton trade, previously a state monopoly.

However, the still-state-owned spinning and weaving industries, big employers in Egypt, couldn't compete if they had to pay world market prices for their main input—cotton. So, to keep the inefficient spinners and weavers in business, the government restricts cotton exports. For the 2000–2001 season, exporters could sell abroad only 50,000 tons each of long-staple and extra-long-staple cotton, or about 25 percent of the total crop. The government reserved the remainder of the cotton crop for the domestic spinning and weaving industries, thereby keeping the prices those industries must pay artificially low.

This export-quota policy generates all the usual inefficiencies associated with restrictions on international trade, plus an additional one. The outdated, heavily indebted Egyptian state-owned spinning and weaving industries don't have the technology or marketing expertise to take full advantage of the special qualities of Egyptian cotton. Most of the products manufactured in Egypt could be made with much cheaper, lower-quality cotton from abroad, saving the premium-quality Egyptian varieties for use in products where quality really matters. And, of course, to create a domestic market for inefficiently produced domestic garments, Egypt restricts apparel imports at the expense of Egyptian consumers' wallets. Under WTO rules, these apparel-import restrictions must go by 2002.

Summary

In this chapter, we examined the effects of import quotas, voluntary export restraints, export subsidies and countervailing duties, dumping, voluntary import expansions, domestic-content rules and rules of origin, government-procurement policies, and technical standards. For a variety of reasons, these restrictions have been much more difficult to deal with in the context of international negotiations than the tariffs discussed in Chapter Six. Economists have dubbed the failure to eliminate these barriers to trade and increased reliance on nontariff forms of trade restriction the *new protectionism*, which restricts trade in goods ranging from steel to honey to jeans.

Looking Ahead

Despite arguments that unrestricted trade maximizes welfare for the world as a whole, pursuit of free trade as a policy clearly is the exception rather than the rule. The effect of trade on the distribution of income and the adjustment costs incurred when resources must move from a comparative-disadvantage industry to one of comparative advantage provide two explanations for the existence of trade restrictions. In Chapter Eight, we examine in more detail arguments presented in favor of tariffs, quotas, and other barriers to trade.

Key Terms

nontariff barrier (NTB)
new protectionism
quota
quota rents
voluntary export restraint (VER)
equivalence of tariffs and quotas
export subsidy
countervailing duty (CVD)
dumping
sporadic dumping
persistent dumping
price discrimination
dumping margin

predatory dumping
antidumping duty
voluntary import expansion (VIE)
domestic-content requirements
outsourcing
rules of origin
government-procurement policies
buy-domestic requirements
technical barriers to trade
coverage ratio
implicit tariff
producer-subsidy equivalent (PSE)
consumer-subsidy equivalent (CSE)

Problems and Questions for Review

1. Imports of peanuts into the United States are subject to a quota, set at about 1.7 million pounds per year.
   a. Illustrate the free-trade equilibrium in the market for peanuts. Then show the quota's effects on domestic consumption, domestic production, imports, and price. Label carefully.
   b. What are the quota's welfare effects, including both the distributional effects and the overall (net) effect on the United States? Relate the effects to your diagram in part (a).
   c. In 1990, a severe drought hit Georgia, where most U.S. peanuts are grown. Illustrate the effects of the drought, assuming that policy makers don't change the quota. What happens to domestic production, domestic consumption, imports, and price as a result of the drought?
   d. Assume that the United States is a small country in the peanut market. Now suppose that the peanut market is subject to an import tariff *instead of* the quota. *The tariff is set at a level that results in the same pre-drought level of production, consumption, and price as under the quota in part (a).* Illustrate the effects of the tariff *before* the drought.
   e. Compare the effects of the drought under the tariff with those under the quota. What are the similarities and differences?

2. This question asks you to address several issues related to dumping, using as an example U.S. accusations that Japanese firms dumped laptop-computer screens in the United States in 1991.
   a. A lawyer for Compaq, a U.S. computer manufacturer, was quoted in *The Wall Street Journal* (February 11, 1991), asserting, "There are no U.S. suppliers for these products [the screens for laptop computers], and therefore there can be no dumping." Is the lawyer correct or incorrect, and why?
   b. According to *The Wall Street Journal,* the U.S. Department of Commerce has "decided that display prices set by Japanese companies in their home market may be artificially low. Rather than comparing U.S. prices with Japanese prices, Commerce is now coming up with its own 'fair' price based on a formula accounting for the costs of materials, research, and return on investment." Do you think this procedure is more or less likely to result in imposition of antidumping duties than one in which prices charged for Japanese displays in the United States are compared with actual prices for the same displays in Japan? Why? As an economist, which procedure would you prefer to see used? Why?

3. Country A is a small country with a comparative advantage in good X. The government of country A provides X producers with a subsidy of $10 for each unit of X exported. The governments of all other X-exporting countries also subsidize exports of X by $10 per unit. Evaluate the following statement: "Producers of good X in country A don't really gain from the subsidy. Nevertheless, they are unwilling to have their government stop the subsidy."

4. Do you agree or disagree with the argument in the following letter to the editor from *The Wall Street Journal* (February 14, 1985)? Support your answer with a brief economic analysis. You may take the numbers reported in the letter as factual for purposes of your argument.

   > [A recent letter to the editor] claims that the [United Auto Workers'] request for continued auto restraints on the part of Japanese auto manufacturers is protectionist and anti-competitive. At present, the UAW wants to limit imports of Japanese autos to 17 percent of the U.S. market. This seems fair enough after one examines auto sales in Japan during 1984. According to *The Japan Times,* 5,471,982 cars were sold in Japan last year, of which only 41,982 were foreign. American auto sales totaled 2,382—or less than one-half of 1 percent! These figures show that a much higher degree of protectionism exists in Japan than in the U.S., a fact that should be remembered by both American policy makers and Japanese who accuse the U.S. of being anti-competitive and protectionist.

5. The domestic demand for good X is $D^d = 100 - 20P$. The domestic supply of good X is $S^d = 20 + 20P$.
   a. Draw the domestic demand and supply curves for good X. [Remember that price appears on the vertical axis in the graph.]
   b. If the country allows no trade in good X, what are the equilibrium price, quantity produced, and quantity consumed?
   c. Imports of good X are available in the world market at $P_X = 1$. Draw the total supply curve. If the country allows free trade in good X, what are the equilibrium price, quantity produced domestically, quantity consumed domestically, and quantity imported?

d. If the country imposes an import quota of 20 units of good X, what are the equilibrium price, quantity produced domestically, quantity consumed domestically, and quantity imported?

e. Who gains and who loses from the quota? Does national welfare rise or fall?

f. Compare your answers with those for question 6 in Chapter Six.

6. This question continues question 7 from Chapter Six. The country of Usia has a prohibitive export tax on logs. Both Usia and Themia export lumber made from logs. Usia files a complaint against Themia alleging that the government of Themia subsidizes lumber exports and that Themia's subsidized exports steal markets from Usia's lumber producers. The government of Themia is angered by Usia's accusation and countercharges that Usia's prohibitive export tax on *logs* amounts to an export subsidy for Usia's *lumber* producers. Briefly evaluate Themia's charge.

7. Protectionist responses in dumping cases include antidumping duties and suspension agreements, which act like VERs. Compare the implications of the two for net domestic welfare. *(Hint: Who is likely to capture the tariff revenue or quota rent in each case?)*

8. In 1996, potato growers in northern Maine suffered their third year of bad harvests. They did, however, expect prices for their potatoes to rise as a result. Instead, imports of Canadian potatoes rose.

a. Illustrate in a demand-and-supply diagram why, in the absence of imports, a bad domestic harvest would have boosted domestic potato prices.

b. Also illustrate why the possibility of Canadian imports prevents the price increase. (You may assume that the United States is a small country in the potato market.)

c. In which case is the sum of U.S. producer and consumer surplus greater, the case with no imports, or the case with imports?

d. How would you expect Maine potato growers to react to the increased imports?[32]

References and Selected Readings

Baldwin, Richard E. "Regulatory Protectionism, Developing Nations, and a Two-Tier World Trade System." *Brookings Trade Forum* (2000): 237–294.
The potential of discriminatory protectionist policies to restrict developing countries' full access to the world trade system.

Berry, Steven, et al. "Voluntary Export Restraints on Automobiles: Evaluating a Trade Policy." *American Economic Review* 89 (June 1999): 400–430.
Careful assessment of the gainers and losers from U.S. auto VER; intermediate.

Bhagwati, Jagdish, and Robert E. Hudec, eds. *Fair Trade and Harmonization, Vols. 1 and 2.* Cambridge, Mass.: MIT Press, 1996.
Collection of papers on NTBs. Level of papers varies.

Deardorff, Alan V., and Robert M. Stern. *Measurement of Nontariff Barriers.* Ann Arbor: University of Michigan Press, 1998.
Comprehensive examination of measurement issues related to NTBs.

Engel, Eduardo M. R. A. "Poisoned Grapes, Mad Cows, and Protectionism." *Journal of Policy Reform* 4 (2000): 91–112.
When do domestic policies cross the line and become protectionism? For all students.

Feenstra, Robert C. "Estimating the Effects of Trade Policy." In *Handbook of International Economics,* Vol. 3, edited by G. M. Grossman and K. Rogoff, 1553–1596. Amsterdam: North-Holland, 1995.
Advanced survey of the empirical literature on the economic effects of various trade policies.

Graham, Edward M., and J. David Richardson, eds. *Global Competition Policy.* Washington, D.C.: Institute for International Economics, 1997.
Excellent, accessible overview of countries' competition policies and their international implications.

Hindley, Brian, and Patrick A. Messerlin. *Antidumping Industrial Policy.* Washington, D.C.: American Enterprise Institute, 1996.
Brief, accessible overview of the current state of antidumping policy and suggested reforms.

Hufbauer, Gary C., and Kimberly A. Elliott. *Measuring the Costs of Protection in the United States.* Washington, D.C.: Institute for International Economics, 1994.
Estimates the costs of protection to the U.S. economy; for all students.

---

32 NAFTA prevented Maine potato growers from getting the quota or tariff protection they wanted. However, they did persuade U.S. officials to begin around-the-clock rigorous inspections of all Canadian potato imports. Inspectors rejected approximately 20 percent of imports based on alleged faulty labeling or grading. See "Big Potatoes," *The Economist,* January 20, 1996.

Irwin, Douglas A. *Managed Trade: The Case against Import Targets.* Washington, D.C.: American Enterprise Institute, 1994.
Accessible analysis of the protectionist effects of voluntary import expansions.

Jackson, John H. *The World Trading System: Law and Policy of International Economic Relations,* 2nd ed. Cambridge, Mass.: MIT Press, 1997.
Excellent and readable treatment of legal aspects of trade, including subsidies and dumping.

Jones, Kent A. *Export Restraint and the New Protectionism.* Ann Arbor: University of Michigan Press, 1994.
Analysis of negotiated export-restraint agreements; intermediate.

Leidy, Michael. "Antidumping: Unfair Trade or Unfair Remedy?" *Finance and Development* 32 (March 1995): 27–29.
Introductory overview of the protectionist effects of antidumping policies.

Organization for Economic Cooperation and Development. *Indicators of Tariff and Non-Tariff Trade Barriers.* Paris: OECD, 1997.
Good source of data on OECD members' trade barriers.

Reed, Michael R. *International Trade in Agricultural Products.* Upper Saddle River, NJ: Prentice-Hall, 2001.
Excellent source of information on protection in agricultural markets.

Rodrik, Dani. "Political Economy of Trade Policy." In *Handbook of International Economics,* Vol. 3, edited by G. M. Grossman and K. Rogoff, 1457–1494. Amsterdam: North-Holland, 1995.
Advanced survey of the literature on distributional aspects of trade policy and their implications for the policy process.

Sazanami, Yoko, Shujiro Urata, and Kiroki Kawai. *Measuring the Costs of Protection in Japan.* Washington, D.C.: Institute for International Economics, 1995.
Attempt to quantify the cost to Japanese consumers and the Japanese economy as a whole of the structure of protection. Intermediate.

Staiger, Robert. "International Rules and Institutions for Cooperative Trade Policy." In *Handbook of International Economics,* Vol. 3, edited by G. M. Grossman and K. Rogoff, 1495–1552. Amsterdam: North-Holland, 1995.
Advanced survey of the literature on how rules and institutions at the international level affect national trade policies.

Stiglitz, Joseph E. "Dumping on Free Trade: The U.S. Import Trade Laws." *Southern Economic Journal* (1997): 402–424.
Argues for a larger role for national welfare in determining policy toward imports; for all students.

Sykes, Alan O. *Product Standards for Internationally Integrated Goods Markets.* Washington, D.C.: The Brookings Institution, 1995.
Excellent treatment of the role for and protectionist potential for product standards.

Trebilcock, Michael J., and Robert Howse. *The Regulation of International Trade.* London: Routledge, 1995.
Accessible survey of the legal aspects of trade restrictions.

Trefler, Daniel. "Trade Liberalization and the Theory of Endogenous Protection." *Journal of Political Economy* 101 (February 1993): 138–160.
Empirical study of the determinants and effects of U.S. import restrictions; advanced.

United States International Trade Commission. *The Year in Trade.* Washington, D.C.: USITC, annual.
Excellent survey of current trade issues for all students. Available on CD-ROM.

United States Trade Representative. *National Trade Estimate Report on Foreign Trade Barriers.* Washington, D.C.: USTR, annual.
Annual summary of foreign countries' trade barriers that restrict U.S. exports.

Wall, Howard J. "Using the Gravity Model to Estimate the Costs of Protection." *Federal Reserve Bank of St. Louis Review* 81 (January/February 1999): 33–40.
Investigation of how much protection distorts trade patterns; intermediate.

Westhoff, Frank H., Beth V. Yarbrough, and Robert M. Yarbrough. "Harassment versus Lobbying for Trade Protection." *International Trade Journal* 9 (Summer 1995): 203–224.
Examines use of protection, especially antidumping and countervailing duty policy, to harass foreign producers; intermediate.

World Trade Forum. *Regulatory Barriers and the Principle of Non-Discrimination in World Trade Law.* Ann Arbor: University of Michigan, 1999.
Collection of accessible papers on discriminatory trade barriers.

World Trade Organization. *Annual Report.* Geneva: WTO, annual.
Excellent source on current international trade and trade-related issues; for all students.

CHAPTER EIGHT

Arguments for Restricting Trade

8.1 Introduction

Chapters Six and Seven showed how international trade restrictions reduce world welfare by distorting the relationship between a good's price and its opportunity cost, causing inefficient production and consumption decisions. Efficiency requires that each good be produced at the level at which the value consumers place on the good (price) just equals the opportunity cost of producing it (marginal cost).

In this chapter, we probe the results of Chapters Six and Seven for weaknesses. Are there circumstances in which unrestricted trade isn't efficient or doesn't maximize world welfare? Can protection ever increase welfare, not just for some groups at the expense of others, but for the country or the world as a whole? Are there major aspects of the world economy that we ignored in the earlier chapters? In particular, might goals other than efficiency justify the use of protection?

8.2 Categories of Arguments for Trade Restrictions

In policy debates over international trade, many arguments for protection emerge. It's useful to categorize the arguments into three major groups.

Arguments that question the *assumptions* we used to develop the basic trade model comprise the first group. Assumptions frequently challenged include those of perfect competition and no externalities in either production or consumption. The situation in which all these assumptions are met is called **optimal market conditions.** The presence of a violation of one of the assumptions—for example, a monopolized industry or an externality—is referred to as a **domestic distortion.** In Chapters Two through Seven, we demonstrated that *under optimal market conditions, unrestricted trade produces an efficient result and trade restrictions reduce world welfare.* Once we relax the assumption of optimal market conditions, the efficiency of unrestricted trade may or may not continue to hold. This chapter examines these issues.

A second category of arguments for trade restrictions focuses on the *distributional effects* of trade. International trade affects the distribution of income both within each country and among countries. Both effects generate constituencies for restricting trade. Proponents of arguments in this category often couch them in somewhat deceptive terms. An explicit argument to tax domestic consumers and give the proceeds to producers in a certain industry would have scant political appeal; but an argument phrased in nationalistic terms that emphasizes preventing "them" (foreign producers) from taking something from "us" (a domestic industry) tends to meet with more success—even if it misrepresents the actual effects of the policy under consideration. Therefore, domestic producers seeking protection rarely claim to seek to improve their own welfare at the expense of other domestic consumers; instead, groups try to identify their own interests with those of the country as a whole to make their calls for protection seem more patriotic and less self-interested.

A third group of justifications for protection includes so-called *noneconomic arguments*. The term doesn't imply that the arguments have nothing to do with economics or that economics has nothing to say about their relative merits. This group of arguments does, however, emphasize elements beyond the narrow scope of economics by pointing out that a society typically values things such as national security and equity along with economic efficiency. Economists still have an important role to play in evaluating these justifications for protection: primarily providing information about the trade-offs between economic efficiency and other societal goals, so an informed policy decision can be made. If a society desires (as all do) to pursue goals in addition to economic efficiency, what kinds of policies will best achieve those goals with a minimum cost in terms of lost efficiency?

8.3 What about "Infant" Industries?

One of the oldest arguments for protection, the **infant-industry argument,** makes a case for short-term protection of a new industry temporarily unable to compete with experienced rivals in other countries. Advocates of infant-industry protection admit that trade restrictions cause welfare losses along the lines discussed in Chapters Six and Seven. But, they argue, those short-term losses will be more than offset when the industry matures and can compete without protection in world markets. Figure 8.1 illustrates the short- and long-run effects of infant-industry protection for the Y industry, where we assume for simplicity that protection takes the form of a prohibitive import tariff imposed by a small country.

Figure 8.1 **How Does Protection Affect an Infant Industry?**

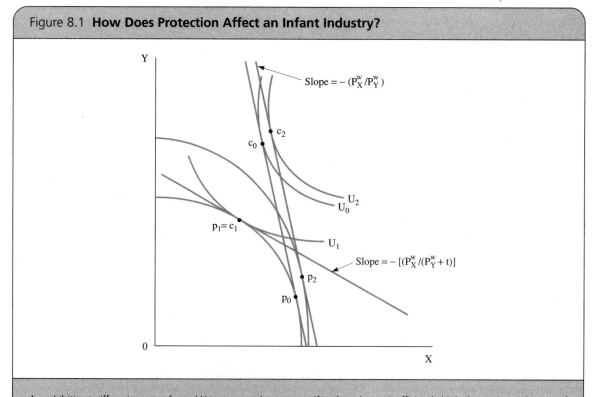

A prohibitive tariff on imports of good Y imposes a short-run welfare loss due to inefficiently high domestic production of Y (p_1 rather than p_0) and inefficiently low domestic consumption (c_1 versus c_0). If the infant industry matures and becomes capable of competing in world markets without protection, the country's production possibilities frontier will expand beyond the frontier that would have existed without the temporary protection afforded the Y industry. The economy then will be able to produce at p_2 and consume at c_2, a previously unattainable outcome.

Without protection, domestic production initially occurs at p_0 and consumption at c_0. *(Why?)* A prohibitive import tariff on good Y shifts production and consumption to p_1 and c_1, reducing welfare from U_0 to U_1.[1] But if temporary protection allows the Y industry to perfect its production techniques, train its workforce, and develop management skills, this improved productivity will shift the production possibilities frontier outward.[2] At this point, policy makers remove the protection (theoretically), and the industry should be able to compete with foreign rivals. The country is assumed to be small, so development of the new industry doesn't affect world prices. The new long-run equilibrium involves production at point p_2 and consumption at c_2. Welfare has increased to utility level U_2 from U_0 before the protection of the infant Y industry.

Economists generally are rather skeptical of arguments for protection of infant industries. The first and perhaps foremost reason is the difficulty in spotting good candidates for protection. Many firms and industries are born each year, and many don't survive. A policy of infant-industry protection requires policy makers to recognize *in advance* industries that have a potential comparative advantage, that is, those that could, on maturing, compete successfully in world markets. A wrong decision could prove very costly, involving years of inefficiency with no reward.[3] The challenge of picking winners becomes even harder once we realize that patterns of comparative advantage change over time.

Suppose a certain industry were recognized widely as an excellent prospect. In this case, why would the industry need even temporary protection? If private investors expected the industry to succeed, they would willingly invest in it and even suffer short-run losses in return for the promise of future profits.[4] The infant-industry argument must assume that government policy makers somehow are better able than private investors to spot winners. But private investors have a sizable economic incentive to search out good prospects, so many economists doubt policy makers' ability to do better. Even if government policy makers somehow became aware of a new industry likely to succeed but overlooked by private investors, an alternative to infant-industry protection would be for the government to provide investors with information about the industry to encourage them to take advantage of the profitable opportunity.

A second problem with evaluating infant-industry protection is that early support of an industry that turns out successful can't prove that the protection itself constituted a wise policy. For the protection to provide *net* benefits, the industry must be successful enough to more than offset the efficiency losses incurred during the protection period. Perhaps the industry would have succeeded without protection, implying that the costs incurred were wasted. Also, the resources spent in developing one infant industry could have been spent on another industry, one that might have been even more successful.

A third problem is based on the politics of the policy-making process. The infant-industry argument justifies only *temporary* protection. Historically, removal of protection has proven very difficult. Even if changing conditions allow a now-mature industry to compete successfully without protection, maintaining that protection still permits the industry to gain at the expense of domestic consumers and foreign producers. This creates an incentive for producers in the industry to lobby for continuing protection even after any infant-industry justification fades.

Perhaps the most important basis for economists' skepticism toward infant-industry protection is the availability of superior policies for dealing with infant industries. Assume that an industry does exist that could develop successfully if it received short-run assistance (that is, ignore the problem of sorting potential winner industries from losers, and assume that future gains will exceed current welfare losses). Assume also that private investors won't invest in the industry despite its promise. The policy that encourages the industry to develop at minimal efficiency cost to the economy is a production subsidy. This represents the first example of

---

1 A prohibitive tariff shifts the country back to its autarky equilibrium. A lower tariff would place the country at some point between the free-trade and prohibitive-tariff outcomes.

2 This process often is called *learning by doing* (see section 5.6.3).

3 Even Japan, whose rapid growth and industrialization during the 1950s and 1960s many attribute to successful use of infant-industry policies, made a number of costly blunders along these lines. See Case Four and Table 8.6 later in the chapter.

4 This can happen only in countries with developed financial markets to channel funds effectively from savers to investors. Some developing countries still lack access to such markets, although many developing countries have integrated themselves into world financial markets over the past decade. For countries that remain isolated, removing barriers to world capital markets probably represents a more promising policy than infant-industry protection justified by presence of those barriers.

Figure 8.2 How Does an Import Tariff or a Production Subsidy Affect an Infant Industry?

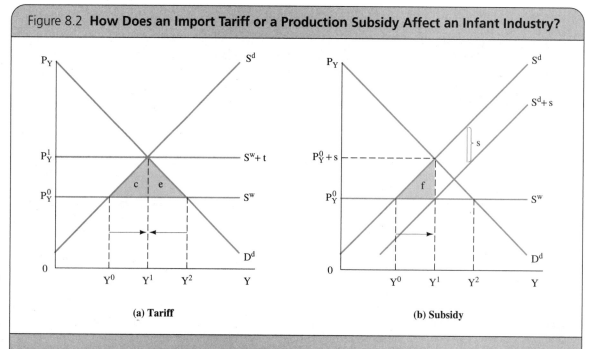

(a) Tariff

(b) Subsidy

The import tariff both increases domestic production of good Y from Y^0 to Y^1 (the desired goal) and decreases domestic consumption of Y from Y^2 to Y^1 (an additional source of inefficiency). The production subsidy increases domestic production but leaves consumption unaffected.

what will emerge in this chapter as a general rule: *The least-cost policy in response to a distortion is the policy that attacks the problem directly rather than indirectly.* In the case of an infant industry, the goal is to encourage production in the industry to facilitate learning and the perfection of productive techniques. If increasing *production* is the goal, the direct policy is to temporarily *subsidize production,* not to restrict trade, even temporarily.

Figure 8.2 illustrates the superiority of a direct policy, a production subsidy, over an indirect policy, an import tariff. Panel (a) repeats the effects of a prohibitive tariff on imports of good Y, and panel (b) shows the effects of a production subsidy to Y producers. Both policies generate equal increases in domestic production. The tariff operates by artificially raising the price of imports from P_Y^0 to P_Y^1 (where $P_Y^1 = P_Y^0 + t$), which allows domestic producers to raise their price to P_Y^1 and encourages domestic production to expand from Y^0 to Y^1. By raising the price of good Y, the tariff also discourages consumption of Y, and consumption falls from Y^2 to Y^1. The sum of the areas of triangles c and e captures the total loss of welfare to the country from the *two* inefficiencies caused by the tariff.[5]

The production subsidy of s (= t) per unit in panel (b) also encourages domestic producers to produce a larger quantity of good Y at each price paid by consumers, because firms receive the subsidy payment along with that price. Domestic production rises from Y^0 to Y^1. The subsidy to producers doesn't affect the price consumers face (P_Y^0) and leaves consumption of good Y unchanged. The area of triangle f measures the net welfare loss caused by the subsidy; for each unit of Y between Y^0 and Y^1, the opportunity cost of domestic production exceeds the cost of imports. Of course, domestic taxpayers must finance the subsidy; but the full amount of the subsidy, with the exception of area f, is transferred to domestic producers. Therefore, only area f represents a deadweight loss to society.

The two policies have identical impacts on domestic production of good Y, so the import tariff and the production subsidy are equally effective in helping the infant industry develop. The production inefficiencies,

---

5 Section 6.4 presents a more detailed treatment of the effects of an import tariff by a small country.

represented by triangle c in the case of the tariff and by triangle f in the case of the subsidy, are identical. The tariff involves a second inefficiency, represented by triangle e, in the form of a distortion of the consumption decision caused by the change in P_Y. The production subsidy, by attacking the problem more directly, can encourage domestic production at a lower cost in lost economic efficiency. The production subsidy also has an additional advantage over the tariff: The visible budget cost of the subsidy makes the policy's cost transparent, allowing an informed debate in society about the desirability of supporting the particular industry in question. The tariff, on the other hand, involves costs "hidden" in higher consumer prices.

Brazil's Informatics Law provides the most infamous example of an infant-industry protection policy that backfired. Since 1975, Brazil had informally prohibited imports of electronics products, including microchips, fax machines, and especially personal computers. In 1984, the extremely restrictive Informatics Law replaced the informal prohibitions. As Brazil's secretary for science and technology put it, "It was enough for a Brazilian company to say that it was planning to develop the same thing eventually and imports were banned." The law was intended to build a domestic electronics industry by creating "market reserves," that is, reserving the domestic market for domestic firms by prohibiting imports and banning foreign companies from building local electronics manufacturing facilities. The law had unintended but predictable results: an uncompetitive and technologically outdated Brazilian electronics industry, and electronics products that cost two and a half times the products' world prices. Even Brazilian electronics firms—the supposed beneficiaries of the law—complained that it made reasonably priced, high-quality parts unavailable, thereby making it impossible for Brazilian firms to produce goods that could compete in world markets. Finally, growing opposition to the law produced change. New policies eliminated the market reserve (but replaced it with high tariffs) and allowed foreign firms to own up to 49 percent stakes in joint ventures with Brazilian partners; but government procurement of informatics and telecommunications equipment still grants strong preferences to domestic firms.

8.4 What If Markets Aren't Competitive?

8.4.1 The Optimal Tariff: Monopoly in a World Market

We've already seen one argument for protection based on monopoly power: the optimal tariff argument in section 6.5.2. When a single country comprises a large enough share of the world market in a good to achieve some market power, that country may be able to gain at the expense of its trading partners by imposing a tariff.

Figure 8.3 presents the graphical analysis of the optimal tariff. The country is large enough that its imposition of a tariff on imports of good Y forces exporting countries to accept a lower price (P_Y^2 instead of P_Y^0). As a result, foreign producers pay a portion of the tariff revenue by accepting lower prices for their product. If the revenue gained from foreign producers (area s in Figure 8.3) exceeds the deadweight efficiency losses caused by the tariff (the sum of triangles m and r), the tariff-imposing country enjoys a net welfare gain *at the expense of the exporting country.* The optimal tariff rate is the one that maximizes this net gain or (area s − area [m + r]).

Note that, unlike some arguments for protection discussed in this chapter, the optimal tariff argument takes a national perspective; that is, the imposing country gains, but total world welfare suffers from the imposition of an optimal tariff. Use of an optimal tariff, like any other exploitation of monopoly power, is a beggar-thy-neighbor policy. Gains come only at the expense of others, and the gains to the monopolist are smaller than the losses imposed on others (in the case of the optimal tariff, domestic consumers and foreign producers). In addition, use of an optimal tariff invites retaliation by trading partners, which would further reduce the gains from trade.

8.4.2 Protection and Monopolized Industries

Another monopoly-based argument for protection focuses not on the monopoly power of a *country* in a world market, as in the case of the optimal tariff, but on the monopoly power of *firms* in a domestic industry. Recall the mechanism by which trade expands world output under perfect competition. In autarky, the opportunity cost of producing a good differs across countries. Under perfect competition, the price of a good equals its opportunity cost; thus, the relative price of a good also varies across countries in autarky. Unrestricted trade equalizes the relative price of a good across countries by allowing productive specialization and exchange. Under unrestricted trade, the relative prices of a good equalize across countries, as do the good's opportunity

Figure 8.3 **What Are the Effects of a Tariff on Imports by a Large Country?**

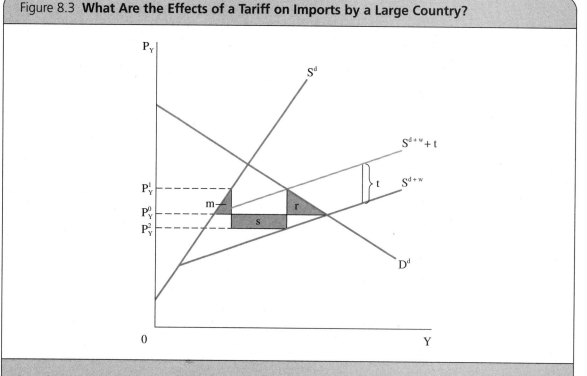

By exploiting its monopoly power, the country can gain the equivalent of area s in revenue from foreign producers. The areas of triangles m and r measure the deadweight welfare losses due to the tariff. The optimum tariff maximizes the net gain to the country from the tariff (area s − area [m + r]).

costs of production. Unrestricted trade satisfies the criteria for efficiency: Each good is produced at the lowest possible opportunity cost and to the point at which price equals marginal cost. The equality of relative prices and opportunity costs that follows from the assumption of perfect competition generates this efficiency result.

Price and Opportunity Cost for a Monopolist

When we relax the perfect-competition assumption and allow a firm to monopolize an industry, the good's price no longer equals its marginal cost. A monopolist will produce the level of output at which marginal revenue equals marginal cost, as in Figure 8.4. Because price exceeds marginal revenue for a monopolist (see footnote 15 in Chapter Seven), marginal cost is less than price in a monopolized industry. The *m*onopolist produces a smaller level of output and charges a higher price (Y^M and P^M in Figure 8.4) than if the industry were organized *c*ompetitively (Y^C and P^C).

More important from the standpoint of international trade, monopoly power in a market causes relative prices to fail to reflect the true opportunity costs of production. If both the X and Y industries are perfectly competitive in country B, then $P_X^B = MC_X^B$ and $P_Y^B = MC_Y^B$, so

$$P_X^B/P_Y^B = MC_X^B/MC_Y^B, \qquad\qquad [8.1]$$

or relative prices reflect opportunity costs.

Graphically, the autarky production and consumption decision in a country in which both industries are perfectly competitive appears as in Figure 8.5. The autarky price ratio just equals the marginal rate of substitution along the indifference curve and the marginal rate of transformation, or relative opportunity costs, of the

Figure 8.4 **How Does a Monopolist Choose Its Output and Price?**

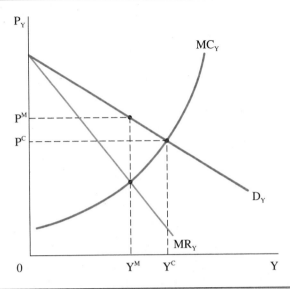

A monopolist maximizes profit by producing where marginal revenue (MR) equals marginal cost (MC). The monopolist's output (Y^M) is lower and price (P^M) higher than the perfectly competitive outcome (Y^C and P^C). Marginal revenue is less than price for the monopolist, so price exceeds marginal cost. Consumers value the marginal unit produced by the monopolist by more than the opportunity cost of producing it; thus, the monopolist's output is inefficiently low.

two goods. (For a review, see section 3.2.2.) Production and consumption occur at point $p_0 = c_0$ on indifference curve U_0. This outcome is efficient in the restricted sense that U_0 represents the highest level of utility attainable *without trade*.

If one industry—say, Y—is monopolized in country A, then $P_X^A = MC_X^A$ but $P_Y^A > MC_Y^A$; so,

$$P_X^A/P_Y^A < MC_X^A/MC_Y^A, \qquad\qquad [8.2]$$

and relative prices don't reflect opportunity costs. Inefficiency results. In Figure 8.5, monopolization of the Y industry causes country A to locate at point $p_1 = c_1$ on indifference curve U_1. The monopoly price charged for good Y restricts both production and consumption of that good. Not only does country A fail to realize the potential gains available through international trade, the monopoly causes utility even in autarky to be lower than if both industries were competitive.

Trade with a Monopolized Industry in Both Countries

Suppose monopolies characterize the Y industry in both countries A and B. In autarky, both countries suffer from the monopoly-induced inefficiency illustrated in Figure 8.5. Allowing international trade can improve the welfare of both countries. Forced to compete with its foreign rival, each firm, formerly a domestic monopolist, lowers its price and increases its output.

Actual international trade may or may not occur. If the two countries are identical and the monopolized industry produces a homogeneous good, there's no need for actual trade. The important point is that just the *possibility* of trade forces the firms to compete by lowering price and expanding output. A firm that failed to respond in this way to the opening of trade would find itself undersold in its domestic market by its foreign

---

Figure 8.5 How Does a Monopoly Affect Production and Consumption in Autarky?

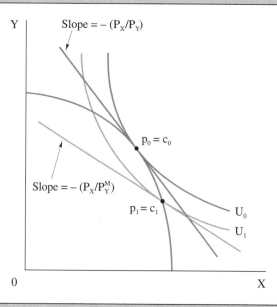

With two perfectly competitive industries, production and consumption occur at $p_0 = c_0$. The relative production costs of the two goods (represented by the slope of the production possibilities frontier) equal both the goods' relative prices (represented by the slope of the price line) and consumers' marginal rate of substitution between the goods (represented by the slope of the indifference curve). The introduction of a monopoly in Y raises the relative price of good Y to P_Y^M, which is greater than its opportunity cost. Production and consumption occur at point $p_1 = c_1$, where the slope of the production possibilities frontier exceeds that of the price line and indifference curve. The monopoly lowers the level of utility attainable in autarky from U_0 to U_1.

---

rival.[6] Lowering barriers to international trade in a monopolized industry can produce gains even greater than those from opening trade in a competitive industry, because gains come from undermining monopoly power in the market as well as from the usual specialization and exchange. Although the welfare of each country improves as trade enhances efficiency, the new rivalry harms the (former) monopolists by restricting their ability to act as monopolists. This is just one of many cases where it is important to remember that *a country's welfare and the welfare of a particular firm or group of firms are not the same.* Restrictions on international trade can help firms, but almost always at the expense of consumers and the rest of the economy.

Trade with a Monopolized Industry in One Country

Now suppose the Y industry is monopolized in country A but competitive in country B. Intra-country competition among the country B firms results in a price of good Y equal to Y's opportunity cost in country B. The monopoly in A, however, charges a price for good Y above the opportunity cost of production. Therefore, if the cost of producing good Y is the same in both countries, B firms will offer the good for sale at a lower price than the A firm. With no restrictions on trade in good Y, the B firms can export to A, breaking the A firm's monopoly. So, *given similar costs of production, countries tend to export goods produced by industries that are structured competitively compared to their foreign rivals.*

The policy process through which governments withdraw the special privileges they've granted to monopoly firms is called *deregulation.* The Organization for Economic Cooperation and Development (OECD), a group of

---

6 A monopolist's efforts to maintain the monopoly price in the domestic market and capture a share of the rival's market by cutting price there can result in dumping charges. Such behavior is called *reciprocal dumping.*

Table 8.1 **Price Reductions after Deregulation**	
Sector	Country (Percent of Price Reduction)
Electricity	Japan (5), Norway (18 to 26), United Kingdom (9 to 15)
Financial services	United Kingdom (70), United States (30 to 62)
Telecommunications	Finland (66), Japan (41), Korea (10 to 30), Mexico (21), United Kingdom (63)
Air transport	Australia (20), Spain (30), United Kingdom (33), United States (33)
Road transport	France (20), Germany (30), Mexico (25), United Kingdom (19)

Source: Data from OECD, *The OECD Report on Regulatory Reform—Synthesis Report* (Paris: OECD, 1997).

29 mostly industrial economies, conducted a study of deregulation to measure the economic gains it provides by reducing firms' abilities to restrict output and charge high monopoly prices. The study found significant price reductions in specific sectors following deregulation. Table 8.1 summarizes some of the price-reduction findings. The report also indicated that continued regulatory reform could increase GDP by as much as 3 to 6 percent in Japan and in the more heavily regulated countries of Europe.

Maintaining a domestic monopoly in an industry structured competitively in other countries requires import barriers to prevent the monopoly, with its artificially high price, from being undersold. This provides a useful explanation for several long-standing trade disputes between the United States and other countries, including members of the European Union, over trade in utility-related goods, such as telecommunications and power-generating equipment. In the late 1970s and 1980s, the United States deregulated many of its utilities industries, such as telephone, airlines, railroads, and trucking, making them more competitive. Prices fell dramatically in the United States following deregulation. Although other countries have engaged in some utility deregulation, the pace of the process has been far slower than in the United States, so prices remain high abroad. The trade disputes involve U.S. firms' complaints about trade barriers that other countries' economies maintain to block access of the now-cheaper U.S. goods.

More generally, unrestricted international trade, along with antitrust policy or regulation, can be a powerful tool in limiting monopoly power. The size of a country's domestic market may support only a small number of firms and, as a result, allow them significant monopoly power. By allowing foreign firms to compete in the domestic market, international trade can limit domestic firms' ability to raise price above marginal cost. In fact, free trade can force a monopolist to act as if its industry were perfectly competitive!

Figure 8.6 illustrates the situation facing a domestic monopolist that produces good Y in a small country. With no trade, the firm would choose to produce the level of output, Y^M, at which marginal revenue equals marginal cost, and to charge the monopoly price, P^M. But if the small country allows international trade in Y, foreign producers will undersell the monopolist. The importing country is small, so consumers can import as much good Y as they want at the world price of P^W, which isn't affected by the small country's monopolized industry. With trade, if the monopolist tries to charge any price above P^W, it can't sell any of its product. Therefore, the monopolist will charge P^W and produce Y_0, the output at which the firm's marginal cost equals the world price. Consumers will import $Y_1 - Y_0$. Unrestricted trade forces the monopolist to behave as if the industry were perfectly competitive. This happens because trade makes the scope of the relevant industry worldwide, and the worldwide industry *is* competitive, despite the small country's monopoly firm.

Tariffs and Quotas with Monopoly

Panel (a) in Figure 8.7 illustrates that a tariff on a good produced by a small country's monopoly firm generates exactly the same effects as if the industry were competitive and subject to a tariff. The tariff raises the price the monopolist can charge by the amount of the tariff, t, to $P^W + t$. The monopolist produces a higher level of output, Y_3, and consumption falls to Y_4. Unless the tariff is prohibitive, the possibility of international trade still limits the monopolist from charging the full monopoly price.

Panel (b) shows the monopolist's price and output choices when protection takes the form of a quota rather than a tariff. The quota shifts the demand curve facing the monopolist to the left by the amount of the quota, from D to D^Q. The marginal revenue curve corresponding to D^Q is MR^Q. The monopolist produces the level of

Figure 8.6 **International Trade Causes a Monopolist to Behave as If the Industry Were Competitive**

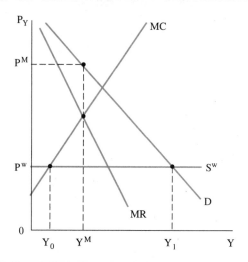

A monopolist in a small country can't ignore the competitive nature of the worldwide industry under free trade. With no trade, the monopolist produces Y^M and charges P^M. With trade, the monopolist produces Y_0 and charges the world price, P^W.

Figure 8.7 **A Monopolist Behaves Differently under a Tariff and a Quota**

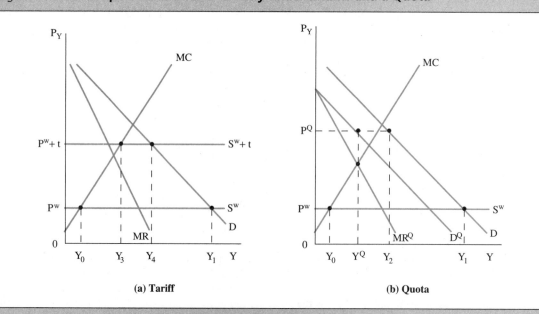

(a) Tariff

(b) Quota

The quota allows the monopolist more market power. The firm produces less output ($Y^Q < Y_3$) and charges a higher price ($P^Q > [P^W + t]$) under a quota (panel (b)) than under a tariff (panel (a)).

output at which marginal cost equals this new marginal revenue, or Y^Q in panel (b), and charges price P^Q, which we read off the quota-adjusted demand curve. Consumers purchase Y_2 units, of which they import $Y_2 - Y^Q$.

Comparing panels (a) and (b) in Figure 8.7, note that the tariff and the quota cause the monopolist to behave differently, even when we define the two policies to allow the same quantity of imports. The tariff does allow the monopolist to produce more and charge a higher price than under unrestricted trade. But the monopolist knows that raising price above $P^W + t$ will cause consumers to buy from foreign suppliers. This constraint on the monopolist's behavior evaporates under the quota. No matter how high the monopolist raises price, consumers can't shift to imports. So quotas allow monopolists to act more like monopolists; they produce less and charge higher prices than under tariffs.

When domestic firms sell in export markets, any monopoly power they have allows them to raise prices at the expense of foreign rather than domestic consumers. This idea of capturing monopoly profits on foreign sales provides the basis for a branch of international-trade theory known as strategic trade policy.

8.4.3 Strategic Trade Policy

Strategic trade policy focuses on trade policy among small interdependent groups of players—firms and governments—in which any action brings a reaction, leading to games of strategy. For example, when can a firm deter a foreign rival from entering a profitable export market; or when can country A, through its choice of trade policy, cause country B to pursue a policy more favorable to A than the policy B otherwise would follow? Here we examine the strategies firms use and whether government policies can or should be used to help domestic firms fare well in international markets. There are two basic types of strategic trade policy models, based on the concepts of *profit shifting* and *the learning curve*. We'll examine each and then address practical problems and dangers related to strategic trade policy.

Profit-Shifting Strategic Trade Policy

Firms behave strategically in international markets when the number of firms is small enough to confer on them some degree of market power. Then, firms treat one another as rivals and respond to one another's actions. If the world market for a good is one in which economic profits exist, individual firms will enact strategies designed to capture the largest possible share of those profits.[7] In designing its strategy, each firm will take account of rivals' reactions.

From a national perspective, each country wants its firms in the international market to capture the largest possible share of available profits.[8] This goal coincides with the goal of the firms themselves. Typically, when the goal of individual firms matches that of policy makers, there's little need for active government policy; individual firms, acting in their own self-interest, accomplish the policy makers' goal as well. In situations involving games of strategy, however, this intuitively plausible result can break down. Even though firms and policy makers have the same goal in mind (maximizing the country's share of the profits available in an international market), there may be a role for an active policy to accomplish the **profit shifting.** In other words, government policy may be able to accomplish something domestic firms, either individually or as a group, can't do.

Assume that a market consists of one firm in country A and one firm in country B.[9] Now suppose the A firm wants to capture a larger share of the international market and its profits. If the A firm expands production with no reduction in output by the B firm, the market price will fall and both firms will be worse off. Obviously, what the A firm wants is for the B firm to cut production and allow the A firm to expand its market share; however, the B firm has no incentive to go along.

One possibility is for the A firm to try to bluff the B firm into reducing output; for example, the A firm might announce, "If you don't cut production by 20 percent, I'll expand production and drive the price of the product so low that you'll suffer losses." From the B firm's perspective, the question is whether that threat is credible;

---

7 Recall that economic profits exist only in markets characterized by some degree of monopoly power, at least in the long run. In perfectly competitive markets, any positive economic profits lead to entry by additional firms, which eventually drives economic profit to zero.

8 Of course, monopoly profits come at consumers' expense. The perspective taken in the strategic trade policy literature is that, assuming an international monopoly exists along with its burden on consumers, each country will want its firms to capture the largest possible share of worldwide profits. The only alternative is to allow foreign firms to capture them.

9 Economists call markets that consist of two firms *duopolies,* a special case of oligopoly.

that is, should the B firm expect the A firm to carry out the threat? The answer is no. The threat isn't credible, because carrying it out obviously would impose losses on the A firm. Thus, the B firm, unimpressed with the threat, carries on business as usual, thwarting the A firm's effort to capture a larger share of the market.

Now enter the country A government. Can it devise a policy that will make the country B firm take the A firm's threat seriously? If so, the A firm can force the B firm to cut production, allowing the A firm to take up the slack and the accompanying profits. Suppose, for example, that the government of country A promises its domestic firm an export subsidy so the firm will find it still profitable to export even if the market price of the good falls to a very low level (as it would if the A firm carried out its threat to increase production). Then the A firm's threat becomes credible; carrying it out no longer will impose losses on the A firm but still will do so on the B firm. Without any retaliatory intervention by the government of country B, the B firm will respond by cutting production, allowing the A firm to expand its market share. The promised export subsidy facilitates the A firm's success by giving it the ability to credibly threaten the B firm.

The country A *firm* clearly gains; it captures a larger share of the world market and is able to charge a higher price thanks to the foreign rival's retreat. Whether country A *as a whole* gains is a more complicated question. Domestic taxpayers must pick up the tab for the subsidy. But, depending on the number of firms in the market and on consumption patterns, the increased monopoly profits earned by the domestic firm in foreign markets may outweigh the cost to domestic taxpayers of the subsidy. If so, the subsidizing country enjoys a net gain from its profit-shifting policy. This is possible *only* if the government can alter the strategic interaction between the two firms, causing them to make different choices than they would in the absence of the government's policy. The subsidy payment itself can only transfer income from taxpayers to the subsidized firm. The country as a whole can gain *only* if the subsidy causes the domestic firm to behave more aggressively, which, in turn, causes the foreign firm to retreat and produce less. This scenario is possible only in markets with a small number of firms, each of which possesses market power. Profit-shifting strategic trade policy can't work in competitive industries.

The Learning Curve and Strategic Trade Policy

Learning-curve models of strategic trade policy are similar to infant-industry models. As we saw in section 5.6.3, the basic idea is that firms in some industries learn by producing, a phenomenon known as *moving down the learning curve* or *learning by doing*. As the firm accumulates production experience, its production costs fall, making it more competitive in world markets. If the industry is one in which the presence of economic profits characterizes the world market, domestic firms' ability to capture a larger share of export markets means an ability to capture a larger share of those profits. The goal of government policy in such a scenario is to provide domestic firms in these industries with large enough markets to allow the firms to move down their learning curves.[10]

One obvious way to provide domestic firms with a large market is to restrict imports to reserve the domestic market for domestic firms. Tariffs, quotas, or a variety of other import restrictions can accomplish this task. If the domestic market is large enough to allow domestic firms to move down their learning curves, protection of the domestic market may, by making the domestic firms *more* competitive, allow those firms to capture larger shares of export markets. Such a policy will have the secondary effect of making foreign rivals *less* competitive by reducing their scale of production and raising their costs. Protection of the domestic market thus becomes a tool for expanding export markets.

Domestic *firms* clearly gain from the export-promotion policies. Domestic *consumers,* however, must pay higher prices in the protected home market. Thus, the country *as a whole* enjoys a net gain only if the domestic firm sells a large share of its output abroad so that foreign rather than domestic consumers bear most of the burden of the high prices. Once again, there's little doubt that protection can help the firms receiving protection; but the overall net welfare effects, even domestically, still are likely to be negative.

Problems and Precautions

What are the practical problems and possible dangers in using strategic trade policies? One of the most basic problems in trying to apply such a policy is defining the nationalities of firms. Given the spread of multinational enterprises, joint ventures, partnerships, and foreign stock ownership, firms' nationalities have become

---

10 The learning-curve argument for protection applies only if firms can learn from domestic but not foreign firms' production. Evidence suggests this isn't the case, at least in some industries; see section 5.6.4.

much less clear in recent years. Determining exactly which firms a government would want to assist with the tools of strategic trade policy becomes problematic. If the U.S. government wanted to shift economic profits toward "American" firms, exactly which firms would it assist? Firms whose stock is owned primarily by U.S. citizens, firms with production plants located in the United States, or firms that use inputs manufactured in the United States?

A second problem centers on the sensitivity of strategic trade policy recommendations to the precise assumptions of the model. For example, in profit-shifting models, if we assume that firms practice their rivalry by setting prices (and allowing quantities to be determined by market conditions) rather than by setting quantities (and allowing prices to be determined by market conditions), the optimal strategic policy recommendation switches from an export subsidy to an export tax.[11] Similarly, changes in assumptions about the number of domestic firms in the industry can shift the policy prescription from an export subsidy to an export tax, similar to the optimal export tax of section 6.10.2. Monopoly profits—the competition for which forms the basis for all strategic trade policies—may disappear if entry occurs in response to the policies; thus, strategic trade policies prove useless or counterproductive in industries without substantial entry barriers. All these considerations contribute to the difficulty of pinpointing industries that satisfy the requirements for successful strategic trade policy. Studies by many researchers suggest that the commercial aircraft industry probably satisfies the criteria as well as any existing industry. Case One in this chapter uses the rivalry between U.S.-based Boeing and Europe-based Airbus to highlight some of the issues involved in strategic trade policies.

Like all beggar-thy-neighbor policies, strategic trade policies rely on the assumption that rival governments don't retaliate. If, in the profit-shifting case, both governments subsidize their respective firms, both countries end up worse off than in the no-subsidy case. Taxpayers in both countries bear the burden of the subsidies, but neither firm can enjoy the increased monopoly profits that come with increased market share, because neither firm will back down in the face of the other firm's government-backed threats.

Another issue concerns the distributional effect of such policies. As noted earlier, the pool of profits over which firms and governments fight the strategic-trade-policy battle comes from higher prices paid by consumers. Therefore, even though some may see it as preferable for "domestic" rather than "foreign" firms to capture those profits, the issue of government-assisted redistribution from consumers to (large, profitable, multinational) firms remains.

Finally, but perhaps most important, when a government chooses to become involved in an active policy of trade intervention, the system is subject to abuse by special-interest groups. In spite of stringent industry-characteristic requirements for successful strategic trade policy, producers in virtually all industries have an incentive to lobby for trade restrictions, in the guise of strategic trade policy, to gain protection from foreign rivals.

8.5 **What If There Are Externalities?**

Among the assumptions we used in deriving the result that unrestricted trade maximizes world welfare was the absence of externalities in either production or consumption. An **externality** exists when production or consumption of a good generates effects on bystanders not taken into account in the production or consumption decision.

Pollution provides the most common example of an externality. Without anti-pollution laws, a chemical firm may dump its waste materials into a river. The resulting pollution imposes costs on individuals outside the firm (such as families who live near the river and want to use it for recreation, or firms downstream that want clean river water to use in their plants). The chemical firm, meanwhile, has no incentive to take these external costs into account in making its decisions. Pollution generates a **negative externality,** one that imposes *costs* on others. When production of a good involves negative externalities, output of that good tends to be inefficiently high from society's point of view. The chemical firm produces too much output because it fails to consider a portion of the cost of producing the chemicals, that is, pollution.

Production also may involve **positive externalities** by generating *benefits* for third parties not considered in the decision-making process. In this case, a firm will tend to produce too little of the good from society's

---

11 In the formal language of strategic trade theory, price-setting behavior characterizes models having Bertrand assumptions and quantity-setting behavior characterizes models having Cournot assumptions.

perspective. Suppose a firm, in the process of producing its output, teaches workers skills also useful in other firms. The other firms get benefits from the original firm's production. The original firm has no incentive to weigh the benefits of its training to other firms in deciding how much to produce or how many workers to train.

Consumption also can involve either negative or positive externalities. Consumption of cigars or cigarettes, for example, imposes costs on nonsmokers. As long as smokers ignore these costs in deciding how much to smoke, too much smoking occurs from society's perspective. Education is a good whose consumption generates positive externalities. An education clearly benefits the individual obtaining it, but by producing a more informed voter and citizen, it also benefits others. If individuals ignore these external benefits, they will choose inefficiently low levels of education.

Efficiency requires that each activity be conducted to the point at which its marginal benefit equals its marginal cost. The relevant benefits and costs include those enjoyed or suffered by individuals *other than* the consumers or producers of the good. Externalities represent costs and benefits ignored in the decision-making process, so they can cause inefficient outcomes. Many types of government policies seek to eliminate or reduce the inefficiencies caused by positive and negative production and consumption externalities. Proponents of protectionism or trade-restricting policies often cite externalities as justifications for the policies they propose. The next two sections examine trade restrictions as ways to deal with externalities.

8.5.1 **Production Externalities**

Increasing (decreasing) production in industries that involve positive (negative) production externalities can raise welfare. We begin by considering the case of a positive production externality where the policy goal is to increase production to capture the external benefits associated with a higher level of output. Chapters Six and Seven explored several restrictions on international trade that have the effect of increasing domestic production.

Suppose production in the Y industry provides valuable worker training that benefits firms outside the industry. The country under consideration has a comparative disadvantage in production of Y and therefore imports a large percentage of the Y consumed. Imposing a restriction on Y imports, such as a tariff or quota, would allow the country to increase domestic production of Y and capture the external benefits of the additional training. Figure 8.8 assumes that the (small) country chooses to impose a tariff on imports.[12] Panel (a) reproduces the effects of an import tariff in a small country. Panel (b) represents the external benefits from the worker training involved in producing good Y. The height of the *marginal external benefit* (MEB) curve in panel (b) measures the extra benefit to third parties (for example, firms able to hire workers trained in the Y industry) for each unit of good Y produced domestically. At each level of Y output, the total area under the MEB curve gives the total external benefits generated by that production level. The tariff increases domestic production of Y from Y_0 to Y_1, which leads to an increase in external benefits equal to the shaded area in panel (b). The tariff also imposes the standard welfare losses represented by the shaded triangles in panel (a).

The net welfare effect of the import tariff depends on the relative sizes of the shaded areas in the two panels. If the standard welfare losses from the tariff exceed the external benefits of expanded production, the tariff reduces welfare. If the external benefits of increased domestic production more than offset the welfare losses in panel (a), the tariff increases net welfare.

Although we can't be certain whether a tariff would improve welfare compared with the case in which policy makers simply ignore the positive production externality, we can be sure that a superior policy for dealing with the externality exists. The tariff confronts the production externality *indirectly*—by restricting imports. A policy that *directly* encouraged increased production of Y would be an improvement. One such policy would be a production subsidy to the Y industry. Just as in the infant-industry case, the direct production subsidy would encourage production without introducing a distortion of prices affecting consumption.

Panel (c) of Figure 8.8 shows the effect of a subsidy to Y producers. The domestic supply curve shifts down by the amount of the subsidy, and domestic production rises from Y_0 to Y_1. We chose the amount of the subsidy (s) to have precisely the same effect on domestic Y production as the tariff (t) in panel (a); therefore, the external benefits (in panel (d)) generated by the increased production in response to the subsidy are identical to those in panel (b) in response to the tariff. However, the welfare losses are smaller under the production subsidy

---

12 Neither the assumption that the country is small nor that the trade restriction takes the form of a tariff affects the general result; the assumptions are for simplicity only.

Figure 8.8 **An Import Tariff and a Production Subsidy by a Small Country in Response to a Positive Production Externality**

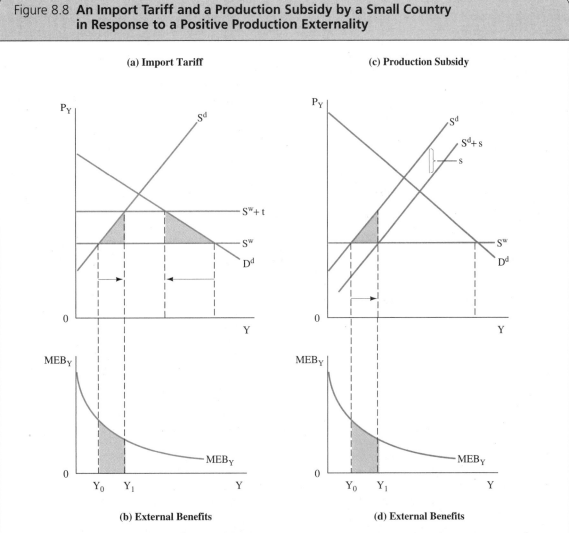

Panel (a) represents the standard analysis of the effects of a tariff. The Y industry generates positive production externalities measured by the height of the marginal external benefit curve in panel (b). By increasing domestic production of good Y from Y_0 to Y_1, the tariff allows the country to capture external benefits equal to the shaded area in panel (b). The shaded triangles in panel (a) represent the standard deadweight welfare losses from the tariff. The difference between the shaded area in panel (b) and the sum of the shaded areas in panel (a) gives the tariff's net welfare effect. The production subsidy in panel (c) increases domestic production without distorting prices and consumption. The country captures the same external benefits as under the import tariff, but avoids the welfare loss caused by inefficient consumption.

(panel (c)) than under the import tariff (panel (a)). The tariff causes domestic consumption of good Y to fall, while the production subsidy leaves the consumption decision unaffected. The efficiency loss from the subsidy consists of the single shaded triangle in panel (c). By creating the same external benefits at lower welfare cost than with the tariff, the subsidy constitutes a superior policy for handling the positive production externality.

In the preceding example, we assumed that the positive production externality takes the form of worker training. If this is the case, an even better and more direct policy involves a subsidy on employment in the Y industry. A subsidy to employment rather than production will have a greater effect on employment. A production subsidy gives firms an incentive to increase output by increasing use of both labor and capital. An employment subsidy creates a more direct incentive for firms to hire and train more workers, thereby producing more external benefits. The superiority of an employment subsidy over a production subsidy for dealing with this particular type of externality is just another application of the general rule that direct policies generate more efficient outcomes than indirect ones. A production subsidy increases employment indirectly by increasing output; an employment subsidy increases employment directly.

What happens if production of a country's import good results in negative rather than positive externalities? In this case, the industry's output will be too high from society's point of view because firms ignore part of the production cost. One policy for discouraging production is a subsidy on imports (that is, a negative tariff), but this is indirect and alters the consumption as well as the production decision. A better policy would be a domestic production tax that would reduce domestic production and the associated external costs without altering consumption. *(Draw diagrams similar to those in Figure 8.8 that compare an import subsidy and a production tax as responses to a negative production externality.)*

The good a country exports also may involve either positive or negative production externalities. Trade-oriented solutions, such as export subsidies (to encourage production in cases of positive externalities) or export taxes (to discourage production in cases of negative externalities), introduce a new source of inefficiency by distorting prices and interfering with consumption decisions. Direct production subsidies or taxes avoid these effects and take account of the externality at a smaller cost in lost efficiency.

8.5.2 **Consumption Externalities**

When consumption of a good generates positive or negative externalities, consumption subsidies or taxes lead to more efficient outcomes than do trade restrictions. The reason is analogous to the production externality case: If the problem concerns the level of consumption, the best policy is one that alters consumption directly without interfering with production decisions. Consumption subsidies or taxes accomplish this; trade restrictions don't.

Consider a case of a negative consumption externality: cigarette smoking. Panel (a) of Figure 8.9 represents conditions in the market for cigarettes. Panel (b) illustrates the external cost imposed on nonsmokers by cigarette consumption. The height of the *marginal external cost* curve (MEC) measures the additional cost imposed on third parties by each unit of cigarettes smoked. We assume cigarettes are the country's import good. The small country can discourage consumption of cigarettes by imposing an import tariff as in panel (a). The society suffers the usual deadweight welfare losses from altered consumption *and* production. In panel (b), the society avoids the external costs represented by the shaded area underneath the MEC curve (in other words, this area illustrates the *benefits* of the tariff policy). Whether the tariff improves welfare depends on the relative magnitudes of these effects.

Again, a superior policy exists in the form of a consumption tax. Such a tax could reduce consumption of cigarettes by the same amount as the tariff in Figure 8.9 does, but without creating the inefficient increase in domestic production the tariff causes. *(Demonstrate this result with a diagram.)*

When a country's import good creates a positive consumption externality, policy makers can choose between an import subsidy and a consumption subsidy. The import subsidy lowers domestic production, while the more direct policy leaves production unaffected.

The same logic applies when a country's export good exhibits externalities in consumption. In the last few years, controversy has surrounded U.S. export policy regarding tobacco and cigarettes. Policy makers, as we'll see later in the chapter (see section 8.10), have taken aggressive steps to open foreign markets to U.S. products in these industries. The markets in question include those in the former Soviet Union, Eastern Europe, and Asia. Anti-smoking activists charge policy makers with hypocrisy for forcing open export markets at the same time that they discourage smoking at home for health-related reasons. Policy makers respond that foreigners already smoke cigarettes, usually those produced by foreign governments' tobacco monopolies, and that aggressive U.S. market-opening efforts merely allow U.S. firms to capture their fair share of those markets.

Externalities on a larger scale lead to one of the hot topics in current international trade policy debates: the environment.

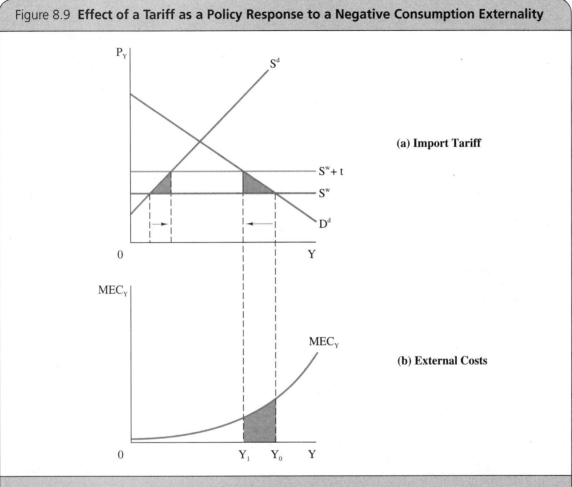

Figure 8.9 **Effect of a Tariff as a Policy Response to a Negative Consumption Externality**

An import tariff reduces consumption, allowing the country to avoid the external costs represented by the shaded area in panel (b). The tariff also imposes the welfare losses associated with the two triangles in panel (a). The tariff's net welfare effect is uncertain. However, a consumption tax would be a superior policy, since it could reduce consumption by the same amount as the tariff does but without leading to inefficiently high domestic production.

8.5.3 **International Trade and the Environment**

Growing concerns about the environment have made environmental issues a source of increasing controversy in international trade policy.[13] There are three basic problems or issues: how to conduct international trade while allowing individual countries to choose their own preferred levels of environmental protection, how to encourage international cooperation in safeguarding and improving the environment, and how to prevent feigned concern over the environment from serving as a cover for protectionism.

The World Trade Organization doesn't provide explicit rules concerning environmental policy. The WTO does require countries' environmental policies to apply equally to domestic and foreign products. For example,

---

13 Jagdish Bhagwati, "The Case for Free Trade," *Scientific American* (November 1993), pp. 42–49; and Herman E. Daly, "The Perils of Free Trade," *Scientific American* (November 1993), pp. 50–57, provide two diverse perspectives. See also the Lomborg book in the chapter references.

the WTO would permit a country to ban automobiles because of the pollution they generate, but wouldn't permit a country to exclude foreign automobiles on pollution grounds while allowing sale of equally polluting domestically produced cars. Countries are free to exclude *products* that fail the import country's environmental standards; for example, the WTO permits countries to ban food products if they fail to meet hygienic standards that apply to both domestic and imported foods. However, the WTO doesn't allow countries to exclude imports based on the environmental consequences of the *process* used to produce them. Thus, a country couldn't exclude food imports by claiming that the foreign factories where the products were packed generated air pollution that exceeded the import-country's standards.

The most famous case revolving around the "product versus process" distinction involved the United States, Mexico, and tuna. The United States banned tuna imports from Mexico, Venezuela, and Vanuatu because those countries used purse-net fishing techniques that killed dolphins in the eastern Pacific Ocean. Mexico protested to the WTO, which ruled the U.S. ban illegal in 1991. Nothing about the tuna product itself violated U.S. environmental standards, and the WTO doesn't allow one country to impose its regulations concerning production processes, such as fishing techniques, on other countries. The ruling outraged many U.S. environmentalists, who were never fans of the WTO or an open international trade regime. In 1994 the European Union filed another WTO complaint against the U.S. tuna ban, and the WTO again ruled the ban illegal. U.S. legislation in 1997 provided for an end to unilateral U.S. bans on imported tuna once a legally binding international dolphin conservation program—the Panama Declaration, signed by 11 countries including the United States and Mexico—was in place.

Another case along the same lines involved shrimp and turtles. The United States banned shrimp imports from countries that catch shrimp with nets that also trap sea turtles. India, Malaysia, Pakistan, and Thailand protested the ban to the WTO. The organization's initial ruling went against the United States, which later appealed. The WTO appeal decision recognized the U.S. right to protect sea turtles, but said the protection must come through negotiation of international agreements rather than unilateral import bans.

Many environmentalists claim that trade liberalization harms the environment by encouraging commercial development and facilitating firms' moves to countries of least stringent regulation. For example, opponents of the North American Free Trade Agreement claimed it would erode U.S. progress on the environment by allowing firms to serve the U.S. market by producing in Mexico, where some regulations are less strict. However, strong counterarguments exist. Evidence indicates that the cost of environmental compliance, even in countries with stringent regulations, comprises too small a share of total costs to provide much incentive to relocate. Evidence also suggests that the main determinant of demand for environmental protection is income; the wealthy can afford it while the poor can't.[14] Hence, supporters claim that free trade, by raising income, increases demand for environmental protection. Trade also spreads newer, cleaner technologies, both directly and by raising income to pay for them. Growing evidence also suggests that the price-support schemes and elaborate protection granted to agriculture by most developed countries have led to overclearing of land, overuse of fertilizers, overuse of water, and other negative environmental consequences. Agricultural trade based on patterns of comparative advantage rather than complicated price-control schemes would generate far less environmental degradation.

The arguments for a positive relationship between trade openness and the environment received new empirical support in the early 1990s when revolutions swept Eastern Europe and revealed the environmental messes the Iron Curtain had concealed. The centrally planned economies of Eastern Europe had isolated themselves from the trading system, denied firms access to new and cleaner technology, and provided firms with artificially cheap energy. The result: massive environmental problems that the countries' poorly performing economies couldn't afford to clean up.

Some types of environmental problems call more strongly for international cooperation than others. Many types of pollution have primarily local effects and, thus, reasonably are subject only to domestic rules. Other types, such as air pollution, release of greenhouse gases with climatic consequences, acid rain, and deforestation, can have international or even global effects and are more reasonably subject to mutually agreed international rules. Often, what is needed is not so much new environmental rules but changes in existing domestic or international policies that have adverse environmental consequences. For example, Borneo has been a prime offender in rapid cutting of its tropical rain forest. Part of the reason is its policy of short-term logging

---

14 For example, urban pollution appears to decline sharply with income after a country attains an income level of approximately $5,000 per capita per year. Chapter Eleven contains more discussion of environmental issues between developed and developing countries.

concessions that give a firm rights to log a piece of land for only 20 to 25 years. With no future rights to the land's productivity, concessionaires have little incentive to manage the forest with environmentally responsible techniques; instead, they cut as much as possible as quickly as possible and move on to the next piece of land.[15] These issues, particularly deforestation, often pit richer industrialized countries (many of whom cut most of their forests decades ago) against poorer developing ones. One proposed solution is for developed countries to pay developing nations for the carbon-absorbing services of their forests, thereby providing a financial incentive for poor countries to maintain rather than cut their forests.

Sound environmental policy requires insulating it from protectionists who disguise their self-interested arguments as concern for the environment. In the guise of environmentalism, Germany passed legislation (the "Töpfer Law") requiring firms that sell in Germany to collect their used packaging and recycle it. While such a policy may provide some environmental benefits, it also discriminates against foreign firms that, because of transportation costs and lack of established local distribution networks, have a much harder time complying with the regulation. To cite another example, South Korea passed a Toxic Substances Control Act that required that any firm selling a chemical product in South Korea provide a list of ingredients, their proportions, and the manufacturing process used to produce the chemical. Foreign chemical companies were suspicious of the law's true intent because South Korea has a growing chemical industry and has been trying to move into specialty chemicals, where technologies the country doesn't yet have are needed. U.S. chemical firms claimed that the new disclosure rules use environmentalism to disguise an attempt by South Korean chemical firms to obtain trade secrets from foreign firms.

8.6 Shouldn't the "Playing Field" Be Level?

Explicit calls for prohibitive tariffs are rare, but policy debates resound with arguments for "scientific" tariffs, which have the same effect as prohibitive ones. A **scientific tariff** is specifically designed to offset the cost advantage enjoyed by foreign producers of the tariffed good. For example, if Japanese auto makers can produce a subcompact car for $1,718 less than the cost of an equivalent American car, the scientific tariff on each imported Japanese subcompact car will be $1,718.[16]

Proponents of scientific tariffs argue that international trade is inherently unfair whenever domestic producers must compete with foreign producers who enjoy lower production costs. They argue that trade can be fair only when all producers begin on an equal footing by having equal costs. Domestic producers seeking protection often cite the need for a "level playing field."

The primary fallacy in the argument for a scientific tariff lies in its failure to recognize across-country cost differentials as a reflection of comparative advantage. Every country will be the low-cost producer of some goods—those in which it has a comparative advantage—and the high-cost producer of other goods—those in which it has a comparative disadvantage. International trade's potential to increase world output and welfare comes from exploiting these very cost differences. Across-the-board scientific tariffs would eliminate all trade based on comparative advantage. The result would be a return to autarky and a significant reduction in world welfare.

8.7 How Can We Compete with Low-Wage Countries?

In high-wage developed countries such as the United States, one of the most commonly heard justifications for protection is labor's supposed inability to compete with low-wage foreign labor. How can it be fair to expect goods produced in the United States to compete with those produced in developing countries using labor that is paid subsistence wages for work in sweatshop conditions? Proponents of this argument assert that American labor can compete under these conditions only by accepting a significantly lower standard of living.[17] The fact is that products in many U.S. industries *do* compete successfully in world markets against goods produced

---

15 *The Economist,* August 8, 1991, 36.

16 Robert B. Cohen, "The Prospects for Trade and Protectionism in the Auto Industry," in *Trade Policy in the 1980s,* edited by William R. Cline (Washington, D.C.: Institute for International Economics, 1983), p. 553.

17 See Case Two in Chapter Four.

using foreign labor that is paid only a small fraction of the wages earned by U.S. labor. High wages don't render an industry uncompetitive *so long as labor's productivity justifies them.*

The United States, with its highly skilled labor force and abundant capital stock relative to the rest of the world, has a comparative advantage in industries that involve intensive use of human capital and research-and-development skills. By world standards, U.S. workers in these industries are highly paid but also highly productive. On the other hand, the United States suffers a comparative disadvantage in goods involving intensive use of unskilled labor, which is relatively scarce in the United States. Trade according to comparative advantage moves these industries to low-wage countries—those with abundant unskilled labor. The result is a higher level of world output and a higher standard of living for residents of *both* the United States and labor-abundant countries.

As productivity rises in a country, so do wages. In a world where production facilities are increasingly mobile, firms are attracted to countries with workers who are highly productive relative to the wages they earn. As firms relocate to take advantage of the high ratio of productivity to wages, they bid up those wages.[18] Taiwan, Hong Kong, South Korea, and Singapore, often referred to as the "Four Tigers" because of their impressive success in industrialization and exporting during the 1970s and 1980s, provide an outstanding example. As recently as 15 years ago, wage rates there were very low by world standards, and firms from all over the world moved labor-intensive tasks there. Then wages in the four countries began to rise rapidly; firms now shift instead to Indonesia, Malaysia, Thailand, China, the Philippines, and other unskilled-labor-abundant countries where wages remain low.

High wages *not* justified by high productivity *do* make industries uncompetitive. The U.S. automobile and steel industries, for example, lost their ability to compete in world markets largely because of increases in union wage rates far in excess of productivity gains.[19] When workers in an industry succeed in raising wages above the value of the productivity of labor, the industry loses its ability to export and also must have protection from foreign competition in the domestic market. Although firms and workers in such industries typically rationalize protection on the grounds of saving domestic jobs, evidence from the steel and auto industries doesn't support this view. The increased profitability based on protectionism in those industries tended to go to even higher wages; hence, layoffs continued. The United Auto Workers union membership, for example, fell by more than half during the 1980s and 1990s, from 1.5 million members in 1979 to fewer than 672,000 in 2000. Stringent union work rules that hindered flexibility and productivity, combined with high wages, continued to hamper the domestic industry even after two decades of protection.

8.8 How Do We Handle National Security and Defense?

Some industries have particular strategic importance, making countries hesitant to depend on imports. Two examples are the food and steel industries. The strategic importance of food is obvious, and the military applications of steel make that industry crucial during periods of conflict. Another industry in which the United States has used a national security argument to limit imports is petroleum.

The national security and defense argument for protectionist policies has several weaknesses. First, in the event of war or other catastrophe, it may be more effective to build new capacity for production of some needed goods than to rely on outdated and inefficient plants. During World War II, for example, the United States built many new plants, including some to produce goods previously supplied by Germany. During the Gulf War, the United States chartered on the world market half the ships used to carry equipment to the Gulf—despite the Jones Act, which has protected the U.S. shipping industry since 1920 by requiring that all domestic maritime trade be conducted on ships that are U.S. owned, built, and staffed.[20]

Even in industries that require continuous maintenance of productive capacity, trade restrictions represent inefficient means for doing so. Production subsidies can encourage domestic production of strategic goods without altering consumption patterns. Why should consumers have to pay higher prices for all goods contain-

---

18 See Case One in Chapter Four.

19 Mordechai E. Kreinin, "Wage Competitiveness in the U.S. Auto and Steel Industries," *Contemporary Policy Issues* 4 (1984), pp. 39–50. The same argument has been made about management compensation in the two industries.

20 "Ruling the Waves," *The Economist,* March 23, 1991, p. 81.

ing steel in order to maintain capacity for steel production in the event of war? A direct production subsidy to the steel industry can avoid the effect of higher prices on consumers. Taxpayers must finance the subsidy, but all taxpayers presumably benefit from the national security provided.

We can illustrate another common fallacy in the national security argument using U.S. policy toward the petroleum industry. When imported oil was cheaply available from the Persian Gulf (before 1974), the United States chose to limit imports. The logic behind the policy was to avoid becoming dependent on imported petroleum, the supply of which could be cut off in war. The import restrictions kept U.S. petroleum prices artificially above world prices with the stated goal of encouraging the search for oil reserves in the United States. The strategy worked, but it had unfortunate consequences. The United States searched for, found, and used a large share of its oil reserves during a period when low-cost imports were freely available. Once the OPEC oil embargo of 1974 ended the availability of low-cost imports, the United States sorely missed its already-used reserves. A better strategy—and one that several countries, including the United States, gradually have adopted—would have been to buy imported oil and stockpile it for emergencies. Not only would the stockpiles have been relatively inexpensive, but also domestic reserves would have been saved for the day when imports ceased to be available.

A wide range of industries, including some surprising ones, use the national security argument for protection. Of course, industries have an incentive to use any politically successful argument to obtain protection. The U.S. footwear industry, for example, argued in 1984 that national security dictated protection for shoes because in time of war, soldiers must have boots for combat. The national security argument's vulnerability to special interests asking for self-interested protection represents a serious problem.

8.9 Aren't Goods *and* Money Better Than Just Goods?

The "goods versus goods *and* money" argument for protection appeals to "common sense." When a consumer buys a domestic good, both the good and the money paid for it remain in the country; but when a consumer buys an import, the good comes into the country and the money leaves. Proponents of this protectionist argument claim that it must be better to keep both the good and the money than just the good, so a country must be better off producing everything domestically than engaging in international trade.

The fallacy in this argument lies in its failure to recognize that the country loses something when a consumer buys a domestically produced good—even though both the good and the money remain in the country. It loses the resources used up in producing the good. Whenever these resources have a higher value than the price that would have been paid for importing the good, the country is better off importing. This is just another way of stating the principle of comparative advantage. *(Why?)* Also, as we'll see in Part Two of the book, income spent on imported goods doesn't disappear forever; it returns in the form of foreign demand for domestically produced goods or foreign capital flows into the domestic economy.

8.10 Can We Threaten Other Countries into Trade Liberalization?[21]

An argument heard often (especially in the United States) supports protectionism, or, more precisely, *the threat of* protectionism, as a means to lower foreign trade barriers. If domestic special-interest groups in a foreign country succeed in winning protection from competition, how can trading partners overcome the influence of those interest groups to achieve liberalization? One possible answer is "with the threat of retaliation."

A case involving the Japanese tobacco and cigarette industry illustrates this idea. For years, import tariffs and marketing restrictions closed the industry to foreign competition. In 1987, Japan Tobacco, a government-owned monopoly since 1898, held 98 percent of the Japanese cigarette market (the second-largest market in the world at 300 billion cigarettes per year, where 60 percent of men and 15 percent of women smoked). The United States threatened to restrict Japanese exports in retaliation under Section 301 of the 1974 Trade Act, which provides for retaliation against "unfair" trade practices by U.S. trading partners. The threat worked: Japan removed its tariffs and other restrictions on imported cigarettes. In the first two years, U.S. cigarette sales

---

21 See section 7.7 on voluntary import expansions, as well as Case One in Chapter Five.

in Japan rose by about 500 percent. Japan Tobacco, forced by continuing Japanese restrictions on imports of raw tobacco to buy domestically grown tobacco at two to three times world prices, found it increasingly difficult to compete. However, a study of the cost to Japanese consumers of protection found that, as of 1989, tobacco products still enjoyed nontariff barriers equivalent to a 241 percent tariff.[22] Although Japan Tobacco has since been privatized, the Japanese government still holds a two-thirds stake in the firm.

Similar stories apply in other Asian cigarette markets, among the world's fastest-growing ones as smoking declines in the United States and Western Europe. For example, Thailand formerly banned imported cigarettes as well as cigarette advertising. The United States filed a case with the World Trade Organization, claiming that the Thai bans violated WTO rules. The WTO panel ruled the import ban illegal because it discriminated between foreign and domestic cigarettes (thereby making Thailand's claimed public-health justification implausible), but upheld Thailand's right to ban cigarette advertising for health reasons so long as the ban applied equally to domestic and foreign products. Four years later, imports still accounted for only about 3 percent of Thai cigarette sales.

Several bilateral agreements between the United States and Asian countries have been renegotiated to allow those countries to restrict tobacco-product advertising for public-health reasons, with the United States retaining the right to monitor the restrictions to ensure that they don't discriminate against imported products. The most recent dispute, in 2001, involved U.S. opposition to a plan by South Korea to impose a 40 percent tariff on imported cigarettes. Again, the United States argued that such protection of Korean producers from foreign competition shouldn't be allowed under the guise of public policy to reduce smoking.

The United States now exports more than 150 billion cigarettes annually. In addition, U.S.-based firms such as Philip Morris produce billions more cigarettes abroad, particularly in Eastern Europe, where the firms have purchased most of the formerly state-owned tobacco monopolies. U.S. cigarette export policies remain controversial for two reasons. First, they represent cases of the United States using its size and power to threaten other countries into changing policies that run counter to U.S. commercial interests. Second, many individuals argue that the U.S. government shouldn't aid U.S. firms' foreign tobacco sales at the same time that public policies in the United States discourage smoking for health reasons. Public pressure has led to some policy changes. In mid-1998, new guidelines to all U.S. embassies ordered that embassy personnel shouldn't promote the sale of tobacco or tobacco products and that diplomats should support rather than oppose local antismoking laws, so long as those laws apply on a nondiscriminatory basis to both domestic and imported tobacco.[23]

Despite apparent "success" stories such as the cigarette cases, many economists remain skeptical of protectionist threats as a tool for trade liberalization. Supporters insist that threats are the only way to eliminate foreign trade barriers supported by deeply entrenched and politically powerful special-interest groups. Detractors insist that the United States should concentrate on reducing its own trade barriers before issuing threats to trading partners about theirs. Skeptics also point out the danger of introducing a world trading system based on who has the power to issue effective threats rather than on the multilateral, nondiscriminatory framework of the World Trade Organization.

The Omnibus Trade and Competitiveness Act of 1988 increased the scope for protectionist threats by the United States, especially in the form of so-called **super-301 cases.** Under this provision, the U.S. Trade Representative must issue an annual report on policies designed to facilitate U.S. exports. Most years the report contains a list of countries that maintain "priority" unfair trade barriers with the most deleterious effects on U.S. exports. Negotiations follow, and if the named country refuses to make policy changes acceptable to the United States, retaliation can follow. The 2001 report named no specific countries.

A related provision of the 1988 trade act, called **special-301,** provides a framework for the United States to threaten retaliation against countries that don't enforce to U.S. satisfaction copyrights, patents, trademarks, and other intellectual property rights. Many countries don't have or enforce laws that limit firms' ability to copy other firms' inventions or products without paying fees to the innovating firm. U.S. firms, especially producers of pharmaceuticals, chemicals, plant varieties, computer software, movies, and books, claim to lose millions of dollars in sales each year because illegal copies produced abroad replace those sales. In 2001, the U.S. Trade Representative placed 32 countries on its Watch List, including 16 on its Priority Watch List. Without

---

22 Yoko Sazanami et al., *Measuring the Costs of Protection in Japan* (Washington, D.C.: Institute for International Economics, 1995), p. 24.

23 Carla Anne Robbins and Tara Parker-Pope, "U.S. Embassies Stop Assisting Tobacco Firms," *The Wall Street Journal*, May 14, 1998.

Table 8.2 **Cost to Consumers per U.S. Job Gained in Protected Sectors**

Sector (Date)	Loss of Consumer Surplus per Job Gained by Protection
Textiles and apparel (1990)	$144,751
U.S.–Japan semiconductor agreement (1989)	$525,619
Steel antidumping and countervailing duties (1993)	$835,351

Source: Data from Gary Clyde Hufbauer and Kimberly Ann Elliott, *Measuring the Costs of Protection in the United States* (Washington, D.C.: Institute for International Economics, 1994), pp. 15, 20.

improvement, countries on the Priority Watch List move to the Priority Country List, which means negotiations with the United States and the risk of retaliation. Ukraine became a Priority Foreign Country in 2001 because of its production and export of pirated "optical media"—primarily CDs.

Supporters of protectionist policies use many variations of the arguments presented in this chapter. Our primary aim has been to look logically at the arguments and evaluate their merits and demerits. The general conclusion: Protectionism isn't the best policy response to most of the problems discussed in the chapter. Regardless of the guise in which the argument appears, it's wise to approach any demand for trade-restricting policies as a request for protection from foreign competition. The most common motive underlying such requests, whether stated or not, is an effort to improve the welfare of the industry seeking protection at the expense of other groups both in the domestic economy and abroad. There's no doubt that protection can bring additional revenues to firms in protected industries, but such benefits rarely match, much less exceed, the losses to domestic consumers. One commonly used indicator of the effect of protection is the loss of consumer surplus for each job added in the protected sector. Table 8.2 reports this indicator for several cases of highly protected U.S. industries. U.S. consumers lost almost $150,000 in consumer surplus for each job created by protection of the U.S. textile and apparel industries, over $500,000 in consumer surplus for each job created by the bilateral agreement with Japan on semiconductor trade (see Case One in Chapter Five), and over $800,000 for each job created by applying antidumping and countervailing duties in the steel industry.

 CASE ONE:
Games at 35,000 Feet

Most analysts agree that if any industry fits the requirements for strategic trade policy as discussed in section 8.4.3, the commercial aircraft industry does.[24] Worldwide, the number of new commercial aircraft demanded in any given year typically amounts to fewer than a thousand. Plane models are designed for specific distance ranges and numbers of passenger seats, as Table 8.3 illustrates; so the number sold of any particular model of aircraft is even smaller, rarely more than a hundred per year. In the table, model names beginning with the letter *A* are Airbus models; three-digit model numbers beginning with *7* are Boeing planes.

The bulk of the cost of a new family of commercial aircraft comes in the early research, development, and design stages. A firm incurs these costs regardless of how many planes actually end up being produced, so cost per plane declines significantly as the firm produces more planes of a given model, spreading the fixed cost over a larger number of units. Analysts estimate the break-even (that is, zero-profit) number of planes of a given model at around 600; selling fewer planes means that revenues fail to cover the large research-and-development costs. The combination of limited demand, high research-and-development costs (about

24 This case draws on Richard Baldwin and Paul Krugman, "Industrial Policy and International Competition in Wide-Bodied Jet Aircraft," in *Trade Policy Issues and Empirical Analysis,* edited by Robert E. Baldwin (Chicago: University of Chicago Press, 1988), pp. 45–78.

Table 8.3 **Commercial Aircraft Market Niches**

Range	Size (Number of Seats)				
	Small (100–150)	Medium (150–200)	Large (200–300)	Jumbo (300–500)	Super-Jumbo (550–800)
Medium (1,500–3,500 miles)	717, 727, 737 A318, A319, A320	737, 757, 767 A321	767 A300		
Long (3,500–7,000 miles)		757, 767 A310	767, 777 A300, A340	747, 777 A330, A340	
Very long (over 7,000 miles)		Boeing "Sonic Cruiser"	Boeing "Sonic Cruiser"	747, 777 A340	A380

$12 billion per model), and economies of scale or learning curve means that the worldwide aircraft industry can support only a few firms, probably only two.

Those firms currently are American Boeing and European Airbus. Boeing and the United States claim that Airbus exists only through government subsidies. The European governments involved deny this, claiming that they fully expect Airbus to repay all its borrowing, making the aid loans rather than subsidies. Under the terms of the European government loans to Airbus, the firm must repay only if it earns a profit—something the firm claimed to do for the first time in 1990. Although Airbus entered the market in 1970, many initial years of losses wouldn't be unusual given the cost structure of the industry, especially the high up-front research-and-development costs.

Recently the possible introduction of "super-jumbo" jets—to carry 550 to 800 passengers over 7,000-mile routes—has generated debate within the aircraft industry. Boeing, in a surprise move in 1993, announced a joint study with the four Airbus member firms (before 2001, Airbus was a consortium of firms rather than a single legal entity) for joint development of a super-jumbo jet, a project expected to cost between $10 billion and $15 billion. Each plane likely would have cost over $230 million, and only major airlines flying long international routes—Japan Airlines, Lufthansa, British Airways, Singapore Airlines, and United Airlines—would buy them. The total market was estimated at 500 planes, so at most one producer could profitably produce

such a plane. In 1995, after two years' study, Boeing and the European firms suspended their joint development plans, citing weak potential demand for a super-jumbo jet. The next year, the super-jumbo idea reemerged; but this time Airbus and Boeing had separate plans. Before plans could take shape, the Asian financial crisis of 1997 placed the super-jumbo game on hold because Asian airlines, with their long and heavily traveled routes, constituted the primary potential market for the super-jumbos.

A hypothetical strategic, or game-theory, model helps highlight the issues. If Airbus decided to produce a super-jumbo (the A380), should Boeing also enter the market (with the 747-500X and 747-600X)? How might government subsidies to Airbus, if indeed they existed, affect Boeing's decision? Table 8.4 represents how the two firms' hypothetical profits depend on their decisions whether to enter the new super-jumbo market. Each row in the table corresponds to a decision by Boeing and each column to a decision by Airbus. Each of the four decision combinations represents a possible outcome of the game (one on the lower right where neither firm enters the new market; one on the upper left where both enter; and two where one enters but the other doesn't). For each outcome, the first numerical entry in the table reports the profit (or loss, if negative) earned by Boeing and the second the profit (or loss) earned by Airbus.

Table 8.4 assumes that either firm can profitably enter the new super-jumbo market if the other firm doesn't; but if both enter, both will incur losses of 100 because each firm's

Table 8.4 **Hypothetical Profits or Losses for Boeing and Airbus**

		Airbus	
		Enter	Don't Enter
Boeing	Enter	−100, −100	500, 0
	Don't Enter	0, 500	0, 0

Table 8.5	**Hypothetical Profits or Losses for Boeing and Airbus with a Subsidy to Airbus**		
		Airbus	
		Enter	Don't Enter
Boeing	Enter	−100, 100	500, 0
	Don't Enter	0, 700	0, 0

sales will be too small to cover its large fixed cost. If Airbus already were committed to entry, Boeing would choose not to enter, thereby earning zero rather than the losses of 100 that would come from joining Airbus in the market.

But what if Airbus weren't already committed to entry? Each firm would want to enter the market and would want to do so alone. Airbus would enter only if it believed that Boeing wouldn't, and similarly for Boeing. *(Why?)* This is where strategic trade policy might play a role. Suppose European governments committed themselves to subsidize Airbus by 200 if Airbus entered the market, regardless of what Boeing did.

Table 8.5 captures the new game. With the subsidy, Airbus is better off entering no matter what Boeing does.[25] Equally important, Boeing now knows that Airbus *will* enter, so Boeing will choose not to, giving Airbus its most favorable outcome of entering the new market alone. The European subsidy, by confirming that Airbus will enter no matter what, deters entry by Boeing and allows Airbus to capture all the profits in the market (here, 500) plus the subsidy.[26]

But the United States could play the subsidy game too, offering Boeing a subsidy of 200 for entry regardless of what Airbus does. *(How would the new table look?)* If this happened, both firms would enter and both would earn profits of 100 (actually a loss of 100 plus the 200 subsidy). Both countries make themselves worse off in this case, because taxpayers bear the burden of the subsidies to induce their respective firms to enter an unprofitable market.

Efforts to restrict such subsidies are difficult to negotiate, as we saw in section 7.5. Each country wants to force its trading partners to stop subsidizing and then continue its own subsidies. *(Why?)* In addition to the problem of retaliation or "competitive subsidies," this type of strategic trade policy poses another problem: The success of the policy depends critically on the precise configuration of the numbers in the table. Most analysts see little evidence that the benefits to

Europe of Airbus have exceeded the costs of the subsidies provided. In other words, governments can end up subsidizing their firms to enter markets that turn out to be not very profitable. Airlines around the world, however, have benefited from the lower plane prices generated by Airbus's rivalry with Boeing.

So what actually happened in the aircraft game? As of 2000, Airbus and Boeing foresaw different patterns of future development in world air travel. Airbus envisioned more and more people wanting to travel between the world's huge hub airports (such as London and Tokyo), while Boeing thought travelers would want to bypass those hubs with more point-to-point service on smaller planes (such as from Portland, Oregon, to Nagoya, Japan). As a result, Airbus forecast demand for 1,500 super-jumbo jets over the next 20 years, while Boeing claimed that airlines wouldn't want more than 500.

Based on these differing visions, Airbus committed itself in 2000 to develop its super-jumbo, the A380. Boeing considered creating a "stretch" 747 that could carry 100 extra passengers while avoiding the huge research-and-development expenditure involved in a whole new aircraft model. But then Boeing had another idea consistent with our game-theory model: Why enter the risky super-jumbo market *with* Airbus, when it could create a new market it could have to itself? So Boeing announced plans to develop a new mid-sized (100–300 passengers), long-range (9,000 nautical miles) plane that could travel at Mach 0.95 to Mach 0.98, just below the speed of sound. The company bet that airlines would buy its "Sonic Cruisers" for point-to-point service that could cruise at 45,000 feet and shave one hour off typical flight times for each 3,000 miles flown.

Boeing and Airbus aren't the only pair to play a version of the aircraft game. Canada's Bombardier and Brazil's Embraer have fought similar battles over the regional, short-range jet market for planes that carry fewer than 100 passengers.

---

25 In the formal language of game theory, Airbus now has a dominant strategy—enter.

26 Of course, the subsidy itself simply transfers income from European taxpayers to Airbus; Europe as a whole can gain from the subsidy only if it deters entry by Boeing and allows Airbus to capture the market.

CASE TWO:
No, The *Other* Type of Dumping

Usually, when the word *dumping* arises in a trade-policy discussion, it refers to sales of a good in an export market at a price below the price charged in the home market. Recent discussions between the United States and China, however, involved *dumping* in the more everyday sense, as in garbage. China buys large quantities of discarded material from industrial countries to reclaim the metal, plastic, and other recyclable materials using the country's abundant, cheap labor force. However, falsified documents sometimes facilitate entry for huge container ships of pure garbage, which can be hidden in China's vast, sparsely populated northwest countryside and go undetected by lax environmental-law enforcement.

Most African and Latin American countries banned garbage trade in 1991. Now China's rapid growth, which results in large quantities of domestically produced waste, is forcing the country to strengthen its own laws and enforcement. New rules require a license from the National Environmental Protection Agency (NEPA) to import trash, and both the NEPA and customs officials must certify that each shipment contains high recyclable content and doesn't contain certain toxic materials. But enforcement is difficult and costly. When unacceptable shipments arrive, false documents often impede a "Return to Sender" solution.

The relevant international rules on exporting garbage constitute the Basel Convention, a 1994 agreement among 100 countries that bans export of hazardous waste from rich countries to poor ones. Administering the Basel Convention has proven less straightforward than anticipated. In fact, some of the developing countries that originally promoted the agreement now believe it harms them. Most signatories are happy with a ban on international shipment of waste for *disposal*. The controversial part of the agreement is its ban on exports of hazardous materials for *recycling*. Many developing countries, including Malaysia, India, and China, rely heavily on imported scrap to produce steel, paper, aluminum, lead, copper, and zinc, among other raw materials. The scrap is cheaper than virgin materials and requires less processing. Firms that perform the recycling as well as those that use the recycled materials worry that the Basel ban will shut off their supplies of scrap, since many of the scrap products, such as old auto batteries, are at least potentially hazardous. The outcome—and whether the agreement helps or hurts the developing countries that wanted it—will depend in part on how strictly the ban is interpreted. If defined broadly, the term *hazardous* could include many products widely used in developing countries' recycling industries. A narrower definition could keep those industries viable while preventing wholesale dumping in poor countries of materials with no economic use but much potential for environmental damage.

U.S./Canada

CASE THREE:
Spawning a Trade Dispute

Canada and the United States share the Pacific salmon fishery, one of the world's most valuable and biologically complex fish resources.[27] The fishery extends through Washington, Idaho, Oregon, and Alaska and through British Columbia and the Yukon, along the Fraser, Skeena, and Thompson rivers. The most important fish include chinook, sockeye, pink, chum, and coho salmon, several subspecies of which are classified as threatened or endangered under the U.S. Endangered Species Act.

Managing a salmon fishery is complicated by the salmon life cycle. The fish migrate for hundreds or thousands of miles, from U.S. and Canadian rivers to the middle of the northern Pacific, and then back to their original river to spawn. The commercial harvest along the U.S.–Canadian border inevitably involves U.S. boats catching "Canadian" fish, and vice versa, because fish from U.S. and Canadian rivers mingle in the ocean and on the return trip to their respective rivers. When fish were plentiful, disputes were

27 Before countries extended their fishery conservation zones to 200 miles offshore during the 1970s, Japan and the former Soviet Union also fished the Pacific salmon fishery.

rare. But now, salmon stocks are in severe decline. High harvest rates, industrial development along rivers and coastlines, and more dams and reservoirs mean the salmon no longer reproduce at the rate of the harvest. The decline in the number of available fish has generated increased tension between U.S. and Canadian fishing boats—and between trade policy makers in the two countries.

The United States and Canada signed the Pacific Salmon Treaty in 1985 after 14 years of negotiations. Under the treaty, the two countries negotiated total allowable salmon catches and allocated the catch between boats from the two countries so that U.S. interceptions of "Canadian fish" and Canadian interceptions of "U.S. fish" balanced. But Canadians perceived U.S. demands that Canada reduce its catch of Snake River chinook as unreasonable and, in 1994, imposed a fee of C$1,500 on U.S. fishing boats passing through Canadian waters. The United States declared Snake River chinook endangered in response. Unable to settle the dispute themselves, the two countries hired an arbitrator who, though agreeing with the Canadian position, resigned in frustration over the split in the parties' positions.

In 1997, Canada continued to claim that U.S. boats were catching many more Canadian salmon than the U.S. salmon caught by Canadian boats. The Canadian government warned the United States and then seized several U.S. fishing boats on their way through Canadian waters from Washington to Alaska, and British Columbian fishing boats temporarily blockaded a U.S. ferry bound for Alaska.

In 1998, while negotiations continued, Canada banned fishing of coho salmon in Canadian waters due to the species' declining numbers, especially in the Skeena River run where Canadians claim Alaskan boats netted 600,000 coho in 1997. Canada also announced a buyback of fishing licenses to reduce the number of Canadian boats fishing both the Pacific and Atlantic coasts. But Canada acknowledged that its cutbacks would do little to improve fish stocks if the United States didn't follow along and stop fishing practices that allegedly included taking 35 million more Canadian-spawned salmon than allowed under the 1985 treaty. The week before the July 1 opening of the 1998 salmon season, Canada and Washington State reached two agreements to cover catches of coho, chinook, and sockeye. Under the new agreements, Washington state boats must cut their catch of coho headed for British Columbia's Upper Thompson River by 22 percent, while Canadians must catch 50 percent fewer Washington-bound chinook. The sockeye agreement limits Washington State boats to 24.9 percent of the year's allowable catch of (Canadian) Fraser River sockeye. Talks between Canada and Alaska failed to lead to an agreement.

A year later, in 1999, the two countries reached a new 10-year agreement. New provisions include abundance-based management (that is, flexible catch limits based on a species' abundance or scarcity in a particular year) and $140 million worth of spending by the United States on habitat restoration and other efforts to rebuild fish stocks.

Japan

CASE FOUR:
MITI Miracles?

For years, in debates over the desirability of strategic trade policies (STP) of the type discussed in section 8.4.3, proponents of STP pointed to the postwar growth of the Japanese economy and attributed that growth to strategic trade policies by Japan's Ministry of Trade and Industry (MITI). Many took MITI's success for granted and focused their attention on how other countries might emulate that success. In particular, how could bureaucrats in charge of STP pick winning industries for support and avoid political pressures to support losers?

A recent study by Beason and Weinstein examines Japanese industrial policy and sectoral growth between 1955 and 1990 to see if MITI in fact succeeded in promoting industrial growth to the extent widely believed. Unlike anecdotal stories that pick out a rapid-growth industry in Japan (say, autos or semiconductors) and then look for any past government support of that sector, the Beason and Weinstein study compares 13 different industries and asks whether those

that got lots of government largesse performed better than those that got less. Beason and Weinstein ranked each of the 13 industries according to the amount of four different types of government support it received: subsidized loans, subsidies, effective rate of trade protection, and tax relief. Table 8.6 reports the rankings for each industry. Mining got the most government support in three of the four categories, and processed food got the most trade protection.

Several patterns stand out in Table 8.6. First, rather than a coherent policy of supporting some sectors and not others, most industries got help on some margins and not on others. Textiles, for example, got lots of subsidies, trade protection, and tax relief, but little access to loans. Processed food got lots of trade protection, but little support in the other areas. Second, and more important, the sectors that received the *most* government help had the *lowest* growth rates. Such a pattern is discernible through casual inspection of the table, but statistical tests by Beason and Weinstein confirm

Table 8.6 **Japanese Government Support of Industry, 1955–1990**

Sector	Annual Growth of Output (%)	Loans	Subsidies	Protection	Tax
			Sector Ranking (1 = Most Support; 13 = Least Support)		
Electrical machinery	12.2	8	9	8	8
General machinery	11.4	12	4	11	8
Transport equipment	10.8	7	11	4	8
Fabricated metal	10.1	10	6	12	7
Oil and coal	9.8	2	13	7	3
Precision instruments	9.3	13	10	6	8
Ceramics, stone, glass	8.7	5	8	9	3
Pulp and paper	7.7	6	5	10	13
Chemicals	7.6	3	7	5	3
Basic metals	7.2	4	2	3	6
Processed food	6.3	9	12	1	12
Mining	3.8	1	1	13	1
Textiles	2.7	11	3	2	2

Source: Richard Beason and David E. Weinstein, "Growth, Economies of Scale, and Targeting in Japan (1955–90)," *Review of Economics and Statistics* (May 1996).

it: Government support went primarily to slow-growth industries, and industries that grew quickly typically did so with relatively little government help. The authors also divided the 1955–1990 interval into two subperiods: 1955–1973, when most analysts conclude that the Japanese government and MITI in particular were most actively involved in the economy, and 1973–1990, when such involve-ment occurred on a lesser scale. In each subperiod, the same result holds; more government support was associated with slower growth. It appears that, despite MITI's public-relations success at convincing many otherwise, Japanese policy mak-ers did exactly what policy makers in most other countries tend to do: They granted support to declining industrial sec-tors in response to political lobbying.

U.S./E.U.

CASE FIVE:
Science, or Politics?

The World Trade Organization allows member countries to ban food products for safety reasons. However, to prevent protectionism in the guise of food-safety concerns, all restrictions must apply equally to domestically produced and imported products and must be based on scientific evidence.

In 1989, the European Union banned imports of U.S. beef based on the common U.S. industry practice of using growth hormones to increase cattle's leanness and growth rates. The United States issued a WTO challenge of the ban and won in 1997. The EU appealed the WTO decision and lost again in 1998. The WTO ruled that the EU ban lacked the necessary scientific evidence and that the EU must remove the ban by mid-1999 in order to comply with the union's WTO obliga-tions. The EU refused, citing European consumers' concerns over growth hormones' health effects, despite the lack of hard scientific evidence. The United States offered to label all its exported beef as "Made in America," so consumers could decide whether they wanted to consume it. European policy makers refused the offer, demanding that beef be labeled as hormone treated. In 1999, faced with the EU's repeated refusal to lift the ban as ordered by the WTO, the United States requested and received WTO permission to retaliate by imposing 100 percent tariffs on $116.8 million worth of European exports.

What constitutes "scientific evidence" in such disputes? Usually the standards set by the Codex Alimentarius, established by the United Nations Food and Agricultural Organization and the World Health Organization in 1962 to recommend, based on scientific assessments, food-safety standards. But European Union trade policy makers aren't satisfied with those rules. In the upcoming round of WTO negotiations, the EU wants to incorporate a "precautionary principle," which would allow the union to restrict access for food products about whose safety consumers have concerns but no scientific evidence. Agricultural exporters, on the other hand, see in the union's new demands only a continuation of EU agricultural protectionism.[28]

Summary

In this chapter we analyzed the merits of many arguments for international trade restrictions, including those based on infant industries, monopolies, strategic trade policy, externalities, scientific tariffs, competition with low-wage foreign suppliers, national security, "goods versus goods and money," and protectionist threats to open markets. Several of the arguments contain valid elements, but more direct policies (such as production or consumption taxes or subsidies) generally produce results superior to those from restricting international trade. Restrictions on trade aren't the most effective policies for dealing with domestic distortions.

Looking Ahead

A tension between the self-interested, nationalistic policies pursued by individual interest groups and countries and the broader perspective of the gains from an open and liberal trading system dominates the history of international trade. In Chapter Nine we explore this tension, focusing on the history of international trade policy and on the development of regional trading groups that extend beyond the boundaries of a single country. We also examine the role of national borders and the differences between interregional and international trade.

Key Terms

optimal market conditions
domestic distortion
infant-industry argument
strategic trade policy
profit shifting
learning-curve models

externality
negative externality
positive externality
scientific tariff
super-301 cases
special-301

Problems and Questions for Review

1. Small country Dismalia "imports" education by sending its students to school abroad. Education generates positive consumption externalities for Dismalia, and the marginal external benefits decline with the quantity of education. As the new Dismalian Minister of Education, you must develop policy proposals for dealing with this issue.
   a. First, present to the Dismalian Minister of Trade a proposal for how trade policy might be applied to the problem. Explain the economic logic of your proposal and illustrate graphically the policy's effects.
   b. For the Dismalian Minister of the Budget, you must present a proposal for how domestic policy might be applied to the problem. Explain the economic logic of your proposal and illustrate graphically its effects.
   c. Given the choice of policies outlined in (a) and (b), what is your recommendation, and why?

---

28 See "Is EU's Environmental Push Protectionism?" *The Wall Street Journal*, August 8, 2001.

2. Evaluate the following comment: "Economists have estimated that protection of the U.S. textile and apparel industry results in 169,000 more jobs in that sector than would be the case with no protection. Clearly, this is a case in which protection is justified because it works; Americans are better off."

3. Analyze the following statement: "If an American buys a car produced in the United States, both the car and the money stay in the United States. If an American buys a car produced in Japan, then the car comes to America, but the money goes to Japan. Clearly, the first case is better for America because Americans get both the car and the money."

4. Good X exhibits a negative production externality, all effects of which are local; that is, production of X imposes costs on third parties, but only those who live near the production site.
   a. Good X is country A's import good, and the country also produces some good X domestically. From a national perspective, would you recommend an import tariff, a production tax, a consumption tax, or none of the above?
   b. Good X is country A's import good, and country A can't produce good X domestically. From a national perspective, would you recommend an import tariff, a production tax, a consumption tax, or none of the above?
   c. Good X is country A's export good, and some domestic production of good X is consumed domestically. From a national perspective, would you recommend an export tax, a production tax, a consumption tax, or none of the above?

5. Briefly explain why a policy other than a trade restriction generally can handle a domestic distortion at lower cost than can a trade restriction.

6. For each of the following justifications for protection, propose an alternate policy:
   a. An infant industry.
   b. National defense reasons for not wanting to rely on imports.
   c. A negative production externality in the country's export good.
   d. A negative consumption externality in the country's import good.

7. Name two channels through which international trade may improve environmental quality.

8. Small country Alpha exports lumber products obtained by cutting Alpha's forests. Cutting the forests creates negative external effects in Alpha (soil erosion, loss of wildlife habitat, and so forth). The marginal external costs rise with the level of production of lumber products. As the new Alphan Minister for the Interior, you are charged with devising policy proposals for dealing with the problem.
   a. First, you must present to the Alphan Minister of Trade a proposal for how trade policy might be applied to the problem. Explain the economic logic of your proposal and use graphs to illustrate.
   b. For the Alphan Minister of Domestic Agriculture, you must present a proposal for how domestic policy might be applied to the problem. Explain your proposal, and use graphs to illustrate.
   c. Given the choice of policies you outlined in (a) and (b), what is your recommendation, and why?
   d. Suppose now that Alpha's cutting of its forests has negative externalities abroad as well as domestically (for example, the worldwide climatic effects of destruction of forests). What are the implications for the economic efficiency of free trade from a worldwide perspective? What policy problems might such a situation present? Why?

References and Selected Readings

Aaronson, Susan Ariel. *Taking Trade to the Streets*. Ann Arbor: University of Michigan Press, 2001.
Fascinating history of public resistance to open international markets.

Acheson, Keith, and Christopher Maule. *Much Ado about Culture: North American Trade Disputes*. Ann Arbor: University of Michigan Press, 1999.
Excellent, readable treatment of trade policy toward cultural or entertainment industries.

Bagwell, Kyle, and Robert W. Staiger. "The WTO as a Mechanism for Securing Market Access Property Rights: Implications for Global Labor and Environmental Issues." *Journal of Economic Perspectives* (Summer 2001): 69–88.
Discusses the WTO as a forum for countries to exchange property rights in market access.

Baldwin, Robert E. "Are Economists' Traditional Trade Policy Views Still Valid?" *Journal of Economic Literature* 30 (June 1992): 804–829.
Assesses free trade considering strategic trade policy arguments; for all students.

Basu, Kaushik. "Child Labor: Cause, Consequences, and Cure, with Remarks on International Labor Standards." *Journal of Economic Literature* 37 (September 1999): 1083–1119.
Accessible overview of a controversial issue.

Bayard, Thomas O., and Kimberly Ann Elliott. *Reciprocity and Retaliation in U.S. Trade Policy.* Washington, D.C.: Institute for International Economics, 1994.
Empirical examination of the efficacy of reciprocity as a basis for trade policy; for all students.

Bhagwati, Jagdish, and Robert E. Hudec, eds. *Fair Trade and Harmonization, Volumes 1 and 2.* Cambridge, Mass.: MIT Press, 1996.
Collection of articles on trade effects of across-country differences in policies; intermediate.

Bhagwati, Jagdish, and V. K. Ramaswami. "Domestic Distortions, Tariffs, and the Theory of Optimum Subsidy." *Journal of Political Economy* 71 (February 1963): 44–50.
A classic paper comparing tariffs with other policies as responses to domestic distortions; for intermediate students.

Brander, James A. "Strategic Trade Policy." In *Handbook of International Economics,* Vol. 3, edited by G. M. Grossman and K. Rogoff, 1395–1456. Amsterdam: North-Holland, 1995.
Advanced survey of the literature on strategic aspects of trade policy.

Brown, Drusilla K. "Labor Standards: Where Do They Belong on the International Trade Agenda?" *Journal of Economic Perspectives* (Summer 2001): 89–112.
Argues against imposition of universal labor rules through the WTO; accessible to all students.

Esty, Daniel. *Greening the GATT.* Washington, D.C.: Institute for International Economics, 1994.
Good overview of issues involved in extending international trade rules to cover the environment; for all students.

Feenstra, Robert C. "Estimating the Effects of Trade Policy." In *Handbook of International Economics,* Vol. 3, edited by G. M. Grossman and K. Rogoff, 1553–1596. Amsterdam: North-Holland, 1995.
Advanced survey of the empirical literature on the economic effects of various trade policies.

Fieleke, Norman S. "Popular Myths about the World Economy." Federal Reserve Bank of Boston, *New England Economic Review* (July–August 1997): 17–26.
Introductory overview of popular misconceptions about trade, including some of the arguments covered in this chapter.

Golub, Stephen S. "Are International Labor Standards Needed to Prevent Social Dumping?" *Finance and Development* (December 1997): 20–23.
Accessible discussion of the relationship between labor standards and trade.

Graham, Edward M., and J. David Richardson, eds. *Global Competition Policy.* Washington, D.C.: Institute for International Economics, 1997.
Excellent, accessible overview of countries' competition policies and their international implications.

Grossman, Gene M., and Elhanan Helpman. "Technology and Trade." In *Handbook of International Economics,* Vol. 3, edited by G. M. Grossman and K. Rogoff, 1279–1338. Amsterdam: North-Holland, 1995.
Advanced survey of technology-related aspects of international trade and trade theory.

Irwin, Douglas. *Against the Tide.* Princeton: Princeton University Press, 1996.
Excellent history of arguments for protection; for all students.

Irwin, Douglas A. *Managed Trade: The Case against Import Targets.* Washington, D.C.: American Enterprise Institute, 1994.
Accessible analysis of the protectionist effects of voluntary import expansions, or threatened protection to force down foreign trade barriers.

Irwin, Douglas A. "Mercantilism as Strategic Trade Policy: The Anglo–Dutch Rivalry for the East India Trade." *Journal of Political Economy* 99 (December 1991): 1296–1314.
Argues that the seventeenth-century Dutch East India Company practiced strategic trade; parts are accessible to all students.

Irwin, Douglas A., and Peter J. Klenow. "Learning-by-Doing Spillovers in the Semiconductor Industry." *Journal of Political Economy* 102 (December 1994): 1200–1227.
Empirical examination of the application of learning-curve models to the semiconductor industry; intermediate and advanced.

Jha, Prabhat, et al. "Death and Taxes: Economics of Tobacco Control." *Finance and Development* 36 (December 1999): 46–50.
Controversies over domestic and international tobacco policies.

Johnson, Harry G. "Optimal Trade Intervention in the Presence of Domestic Distortions." In *Trade, Growth, and the Balance of Payments,* edited by Richard Caves, Harry Johnson, and Peter Kenen. New York: Rand McNally, 1965.
The classic paper on the theory of protection with domestic distortions; for intermediate students.

Krueger, Anne O. *American Trade Policy.* Washington, D.C.: American Enterprise Institute, 1995.
Analysis of recent protectionist trends in U.S. trade policy; for all students.

Krugman, Paul. "What Should Trade Negotiators Negotiate About?" *Journal of Economic Literature* (March 1997): 113–120.
Arguments for and against harmonization; for all students.

Krugman, Paul R. "The Narrow and Broad Arguments for Free Trade." *American Economic Review Papers and Proceedings* 83 (May 1993): 362–366.
Consideration of the merits of free trade in light of many of the issues raised in this chapter; for all students.

Lomborg, Bjorn. *The Skeptical Environmentalist: Measuring the Real State of the World.* Cambridge: Cambridge University Press, 2001.
Professor of statistics and former Greenpeace member refutes many of the doomsday statistics widely cited by environmental activists.

Richardson, J. David. *Sizing Up U.S. Export Disincentives.* Washington, D.C.: Institute for International Economics, 1993.
Readable survey of policies that discourage U.S. exports, along with empirical estimates of the policies' importance.

Rodrik, Dani. "Political Economy of Trade Policy." In *Handbook of International Economics,* Vol. 3, edited by G. M. Grossman and K. Rogoff, 1457–1494. Amsterdam: North-Holland, 1995.
Advanced survey of the literature on distributional aspects of trade policy and their implications for the policy process.

Session on "Ineffectiveness of Economic Sanctions." *American Economic Review Papers and Proceedings* 89 (May 1999): 403–420.
How effective are trade sanctions in changing target countries' behavior? For all students.

Steer, Andrew. "Ten Principles of the New Environmentalism." *Finance and Development* (December 1996): 4–7.
Accessible overview of trade and the environment.

Thomas, Vinod, and Tamara Belt. "Growth and the Environment: Allies or Foes?" *Finance and Development* (June 1997): 22–24.
Introduction to the relationship between growth and environmental issues.

Tyson, Laura D'Andrea. *Who's Bashing Whom?* Washington, D.C.: Institute for International Economics, 1993.
The case for strategic trade policy.

Uimonen, Peter, and John Whalley. *Environmental Issues in the New World Trading System.* New York: St. Martin's Press, 1997.
Interaction between environmental and trade issues.

CHAPTER NINE

The Political Economy of Trade Policy and Borders

9.1 Introduction

The history of international trade and trade policy perhaps is best characterized as a reflection of countries' ambivalent feelings toward trade. Since the decline of mercantilism in the early nineteenth century, many countries have lauded free trade as an ideal. During the same two centuries, however, actual trade policies have been littered with relics of mercantilist thought and with protectionist policies won by inefficient domestic industries in the lobbying battles that typically determine nations' trade policies.

From the viewpoint of world welfare as a whole, the national character of international trade policy has advantages and disadvantages. On the positive side, the constitutional prohibition against tariffs among U.S. states undoubtedly has contributed to the United States' remarkable growth and stability over the last two hundred years. On the negative side, trade policy's national character tends to perpetuate the erroneous mercantilist view of trade as a zero-sum game—that one country's gains must come at its trading partners' expense rather than from improved efficiency.

The fact that most trade policy is nationally determined draws our attention to the existence, definition, and economic significance of national borders, as well as to those cases in which policy making occurs at levels other than a national one. First, we recognize that sometimes countries form themselves into groups and determine jointly a range of economic policies. The European Union and the North American Free Trade Agreement represent the best-known of many examples. By extending beyond the boundaries of a single country, these groups internationalize both economic activity and decision making. Trade among group members takes on some, but not all, the characteristics of a country's internal trade.

Second, regions within a single country may differ in their factor endowments, market sizes, or economic policies. Differences between the northern and southern United States, for example, have played an important role throughout the country's economic history. The same holds true for Italy, Mexico, Brazil, and many other countries. In other cases, policy makers subject subnational regions to different policies, as in the special economic zones along China's southern coast, where economic activity follows a more market-oriented path than in the country's interior. Trade between distinct regions, called *interregional trade,* exhibits both similarities to and differences from international trade. Understanding these similarities and differences helps illuminate the role of international trade and highlights more precisely the economic significance of national borders.

Finally, recent events in the world economy remind us that even the definition of countries can change. At the same time that some groups of countries join to coordinate their economies and trade policies, other nations disintegrate. Examples of the first trend include the former East and West Germanys, the members of the European Union, and the NAFTA trio—Canada, Mexico, and the United States. The demise of the Soviet Union, civil war in the former Yugoslavia, the breakup of Czechoslovakia, and tensions between Quebec and the rest of Canada represent just a few examples of the opposite tendency of nation-states to break into smaller policy-making units. Trade between East Germany and West Germany constituted inter*national* trade, while trade between the Czech and Slovak regions of Czechoslovakia was inter*regional* trade. Now, the situation has reversed; trade in the Czech and Slovak case now crosses a national border while German trade no longer does.

In this chapter, we address the domestic political processes that determine national trade policies, the history of the world trading system, and cases of supranational and subnational trade policies.

9.2 The Political Economy of National Trade Policy

In Chapter Eight, we saw that despite the many guises of arguments for protection, almost all could be met with a superior policy that wouldn't sacrifice the gains from trade. The problems best solved by trade protection are few. Nonetheless, protectionist policies are numerous, diverse, and widespread. Thus far, we've explained protection's overwhelming presence in the world economy based on trade's distributional effects. International trade alters relative prices, thereby helping some groups, hurting others, and creating a natural constituency for protectionist policies. Chapters Two and Three, however, demonstrated that the benefits of unrestricted international trade outweigh the costs—in the sense that the winners can compensate the losers and still enjoy net gains. So why does unrestricted trade remain the exception rather than the rule? The keys to solving this puzzle lie in understanding the *distribution* of trade's costs and benefits and its implications for the political process through which most countries make trade-policy decisions.

The costs of international trade (for example, the decline of comparative-disadvantage industries) tend to be concentrated on a relatively small number of individuals. The benefits of international trade, on the other hand, come primarily in the form of lower prices for consumers and are spread over a large group, with each individual capturing only a small portion. This implies that in a direct referendum in which individuals costlessly voted on the question, "Should the country impose a tariff on imports of good X?" the vote should be a resounding no, because consumers of X typically outnumber producers of X by a wide margin. If it were costly to vote (perhaps because each voter must take time to gather information on the issue and go to the polling place), the referendum's outcome would be less certain. Each producer of good X would have a larger stake in the issue than each consumer, making producers likely to vote. Consumers, although they have a larger stake *as a group,* might find *as individuals* that the cost of voting exceeded the potential benefits of avoiding the tariff.

But countries rarely make trade policy decisions by direct referendum. In such a referendum, each individual votes on a specific issue, not on a list of candidates, one of whom then "represents" the voter on a number of questions. This turns out to be an important distinction. Rarely is a voter lucky enough to find a candidate who perfectly represents that voter's views on all issues; typically, picking a candidate requires trade-offs. Each voter has a priority regarding issues. For producers of good X, the tariff question is likely to decide which candidate gets their vote. For consumers of good X, the small effect the tariff would have on each individual makes the tariff a lower priority issue. As a result, a vote-maximizing candidate will more likely follow the wishes of X producers and support the tariff.

A related phenomenon that also pushes policy in a protectionist direction concerns the costs of organization. The fact that a small number of individuals bear the costs of trade while the benefits are much more widely dispersed implies that pro-protectionist supporters will be more successful in organizing an effective lobbying force than will supporters of unrestricted trade. Suppose Congress holds a hearing in Washington, D.C., that will influence the vote on the tariff. Who will undertake the inconvenience and expense to go to Washington to make their feelings known—workers and producers in the X industry or consumers? Workers and producers will, because failure to get a tariff will impose a cost on each individual high enough to justify the expense of the trip. An individual consumer, on the other hand, has too small a stake in the issue to make the trip even though consumers' stake as a group is very large. Members of Congress see a biased sample of their constituents and become more likely to vote for the tariff.

This systematic pro-protection bias in the policy-making process carries over to the laws that govern the making of international trade policy. One of the clearest examples is **Section 201** of the Trade Act of 1974, the "escape clause" that allows the United States to abandon its tariff-reduction obligations under the WTO whenever imports are a substantial cause of serious injury or threat to a domestic industry. Under the law, the U.S. International Trade Commission investigates an industry's claim of injury. If the ITC finds that imports indeed injure or threaten to injure the domestic industry, the commission must recommend to the president relief in the form of a tariff, quota, or Trade Adjustment Assistance eligibility for the industry.[1] Nowhere does the law require that the ITC take the interests of consumers into account. The president, having instructions to weigh a broader set of considerations, may accept the ITC's recommendation or reject it in the national economic interest.

Of course, opening trade injures a country's industries of comparative disadvantage, as predicted by the specific-factor model and the Stolper-Samuelson theorem derived in Chapter Four. But the benefits of trade in terms of lower prices and improved efficiency more than offset these losses. The wording of Section 201, by limiting ITC consideration to the interest of domestic producers, biases trade policy toward protectionism. This bias has become stronger as successive amendments to the original Section 201 have restricted the freedom of the ITC and the president to refuse to recommend or implement import relief, part of an overall tendency by Congress to acquire more control over the making of international trade policy.

Given the pro-protection bias in the policy-making process, how does trade liberalization ever get accomplished? One way is by informing voters of the often-hidden costs of protection. Even though an individual consumer may lose a relatively small amount from a single protectionist measure, such as the U.S. sugar quota or antidumping duties on foreign steel, such measures taken together impose enormous costs on consumers as a group, particularly low-income ones. Laws that require the hidden costs of protection to be spelled out can help voters make more informed decisions. For example, as we saw in Chapter Eight, most arguments for protection can be met with alternate policies that provide equivalent benefits at lower efficiency costs.

Since World War II, international negotiations through the GATT/WTO have persuaded many countries to lower their trade barriers. One reason negotiations may succeed in cases where countries aren't willing to liberalize unilaterally is that the reciprocity involved in negotiations creates another pro-liberalization constituency: export industries. In the context of reciprocal negotiations, a country lowers its trade barriers in exchange for trading partners lowering theirs. Therefore, the opposition of import-competing producers can be balanced by support from exporters who benefit from increased openness of foreign markets.

9.3 How Did We Get Here? A Brief History of International Trade Policy

9.3.1 Before Smith, Ricardo, and Hume: Mercantilism

The first dominant theory of international trade was **mercantilism,** which prevailed from the Renaissance until the early nineteenth century. This was the era of nation-building and consolidation of power by emerging nation-states. Rulers raised armies, built navies, and went to war to protect their newly formed territorial dominions—an expensive process. These rulers viewed international trade primarily as a way to finance the expenditures involved in building their nations.

The use of paper money (dollar bills, euro notes, and paper yen) hadn't yet spread during the mercantilist era. "Money," or the means of payment, consisted of precious metals, primarily gold and silver, called specie. Policy makers' goal for international trade was to accumulate as much specie as possible, because ownership of gold and silver provided the wherewithal to pay armies and build ships. Policies that encouraged exports and restricted imports contributed to this accumulation. Whenever a nation exported more than it imported vis-à-vis another country, the deficit country (the one for which the value of imports exceeded the value of exports) paid the balance of its account to the surplus country (the one for which the value of exports exceeded the value of imports) in gold or silver.[2]

Mercantilism dominated thought on international trade for a remarkably long period. Eventually the Classical economists in England began to point out critical weaknesses in the mercantilist view.[3] One important point was that all nations couldn't conduct successful mercantilist policies simultaneously. One country's

---

1 Before the Uruguay Round agreement, escape-clause cases often culminated in negotiation of a voluntary export restraint (VER), but the agreement limits this source of VER proliferation.

2 Section 2.2 discusses mercantilism in more detail.

3 Section 2.3 contains more discussion.

exports are by definition another's imports, so one country's "success" necessarily implied the "failure" of another. In fact, mercantilists viewed international trade as a zero-sum game: Whatever specie one nation accumulated necessarily came at the expense of another. As we learned in Chapter Two, Adam Smith's and David Ricardo's work on absolute and comparative advantage transformed the perspective on trade into a positive-sum view.

David Hume continued the critique of mercantilism by arguing that even when one country succeeded from the mercantilist viewpoint, that success couldn't continue in the long run. The accumulation of specie or money had the effect of raising prices in the successful mercantilist country.[4] As prices rose relative to those in other countries, imports became relatively cheaper and more attractive while the desirability of the country's exports waned. The very success in accumulating specie caused imports to rise and exports to fall, eliminating the surplus that had facilitated the accumulation process. So any mercantilist "success" was short-lived at best.

Finally—and perhaps most importantly—specie was useful only insofar as it represented purchasing power, or the ability to buy goods and services that generate consumer satisfaction. If a country exported to the limits of its ability and imported nothing, it would accumulate specie but would have little in the way of goods and services.

9.3.2 Britain and the Rise of the United States

At the close of the eighteenth century, world events combined with the effects of the Classical economists' work moved trade policy away from mercantilism and toward liberalization. The Industrial Revolution created British textile, iron, and steel industries that, because of their technological superiority and scale economies, could serve the entire world. Opening export markets and locating foreign sources of raw materials became Britain's policy priorities. Invention of railroads and steamships provided the inexpensive land and sea transport needed to expand world trade. All these events edged Britain toward a policy of relatively unrestricted international trade throughout the first half of the nineteenth century, although wars and recessions interjected temporary periods of renewed trade restrictions.[5]

Before the American Revolution, the colonies used tariffs to generate government revenue. Protection of domestic industries wasn't a major issue, because British law prevented the colonies from developing manufacturing to compete with British industry. During the Revolution, American manufacturing grew to replace no-longer-available British imports. In what has become a common historical pattern, the end of the war coincided with demands for protection by the new American industries that had enjoyed insulation from foreign competition during the Revolution. The protection of domestic manufacturing joined revenue generation as a major reason for the tariffs instituted by the United States, which passed its first comprehensive trade legislation in 1789.

Strong disagreement over the proper course of international trade policy characterized the first half of the nineteenth century in the United States. The North, with its dominant manufacturing interests, favored protective tariffs. The South, on the other hand, was still an agricultural economy and favored unrestricted trade. The South exported raw materials, primarily cotton and tobacco, in exchange for manufactures from Britain and Europe. The North might have pushed for tariffs on exports as well as imports, but the South had inserted a clause into the Constitution prohibiting such taxation. Disagreement continued up to the Civil War of the 1860s, when the North used tariffs to finance its victorious war effort and then continued to impose tariffs to protect its manufacturing interests after the South's defeat.

During the late 1800s, tariffs rose in both Britain and the United States. Germany and France were growing and industrializing rapidly, eroding Britain's technological advantage from the Industrial Revolution. During the first decade of the twentieth century, tariffs' negative effects on world growth and trade were gaining recognition. Policy makers laid plans for tariff reductions, but World War I intervened before any serious liberalization could take place. As usual, the war and its aftermath created renewed demands for protection in most countries, and tariff levels continued to rise. The U.S. economy enjoyed phenomenal growth relative to the rest of the world during this period, and U.S. trade policy became increasingly important as a worldwide model.

---

4 Part Two discusses the relationship between the supply of money and prices.

5 On Britain's mid-nineteenth-century trade liberalization, see Beth V. Yarbrough and Robert M. Yarbrough, *Cooperation and Governance in International Trade,* in the chapter references.

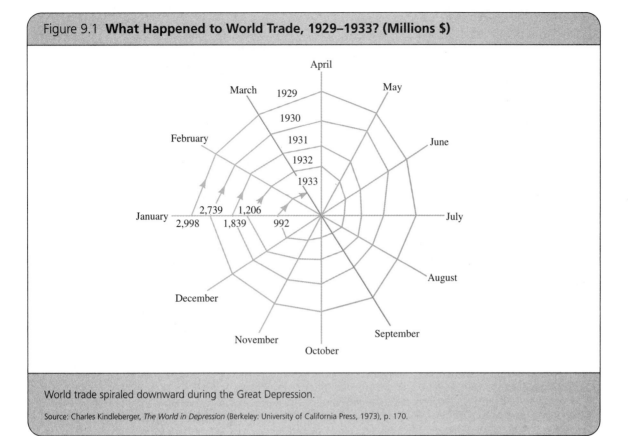

Figure 9.1 **What Happened to World Trade, 1929–1933? (Millions $)**

World trade spiraled downward during the Great Depression.

Source: Charles Kindleberger, *The World in Depression* (Berkeley: University of California Press, 1973), p. 170.

Unfortunately, the model set by the United States rested on the **Smoot-Hawley tariff bill of 1930,** which raised tariffs to an average of 53 percent. Other economies retaliated by raising their own trade barriers, and the volume of world trade plummeted as the world economy entered the Great Depression. Figure 9.1 summarizes the downward spiral of world trade during 1929–1933. Countries attempted to "export" their unemployment problems by blocking imports, a classic example of a beggar-thy-neighbor policy. Analysts disagree over the precise degree of blame for the Great Depression that rests on the Smoot-Hawley bill, but clearly the bill didn't help solve the severe economic problems of the time.

9.3.3 The Reciprocal Trade Agreements Act of 1934

Despite the dubious value of U.S. leadership in the Smoot-Hawley episode, the United States soon recognized the need for trade liberalization as a way to emerge from the Great Depression. In 1934, a radical change in U.S. trade policy produced the **Reciprocal Trade Agreements Act (RTAA),** which set the stage for a half-century of liberalization. Not only did the act reduce the Smoot-Hawley-level tariffs; it also changed the institutional arrangements for making U.S. trade policy.[6] Previously Congress had sole responsibility for tariffs and determined, on a unilateral and product-by-product basis, U.S. tariff levels. The RTAA switched authority over tariffs to the executive branch of government and authorized tariff negotiations with other countries. For the first time, countries could negotiate, coordinate, and cooperate in their (still nationally determined) international trade policies.

---

6 Political scientist I. M. Destler argues in *American Trade Politics* that this institutional change was a key element in the liberalization that followed.

Table 9.1 **Tariff Reductions, 1934–2001**

GATT/WTO Conference	Average Cut in All Duties	Remaining Duties as a Proportion of 1930 Tariffs	Number of Participants
Pre-GATT (1934–1947)	33.2%	66.8%	23
First Round (Geneva, 1947)	21.1	52.7	23
Second Round (Annecy, 1949)	1.9	51.7	13
Third Round (Torquay, 1950–1951)	3.0	50.1	38
Fourth Round (Geneva, 1955–1956)	3.5	48.9	26
Dillon Round (Geneva, 1961–1962)	2.4	47.7	26
Kennedy Round (Geneva, 1964–1967)	36.0	30.5	62
Tokyo Round (Geneva, 1974–1979)	29.6	21.2	99
Uruguay Round (Geneva, 1987–1994)	38.0	13.1	125
Doha Round (Geneva, 2001–)	n.a.	n.a.	144

Source: Data from Real Phillipe Lavergne, "The Political Economy of U.S. Tariffs" (Ph.D. thesis, University of Toronto, 1981); reproduced in Robert E. Baldwin, "U.S. Trade Policy Since World War II," in *The Structure and Evolution of Recent U.S. Trade Policy,* edited by R. E. Baldwin and A. O. Krueger (Chicago: University of Chicago Press, 1984), p. 6; updated to include the Uruguay and Doha Rounds.

The RTAA remained the backbone of U.S. trade policy through 11 revisions and extensions until the Trade Expansion Act of 1962 replaced it 28 years later. Table 9.1 documents the success in tariff reduction under the RTAA and summarizes the reductions achieved in negotiations between 1934 and 1962 as well as more recent events.

Another innovative aspect of the RTAA was its recognition of the interdependence of trade policies by the United States and its trading partners. The argument that U.S. tariff reductions would encourage reciprocal reductions by other countries and thereby stimulate U.S. exports (important to agricultural interests) was critical to passage of the 1934 act.

9.3.4 Post–World War II Trade Policy

Soon war again interrupted world trade. Emerging from World War II as the only major industrial economy with its capital stock intact, the United States took a strong leadership position in pushing for postwar trade liberalization. The policy resulted from a combination of economic and political interests. Clearly the dominant country in technology and industrial strength, the United States had vast export opportunities it could exploit only in a relatively open trading environment. American intellectual and political leaders also believed that building economic linkages through trade could promote world peace. A related concern was the desire to help Europe reunite and rebuild quickly, to limit the spread of Soviet influence through Europe.

The U.S. commitment to open trade was reflected primarily in its support of a strong institutional framework for international economic and political interaction. That framework included the **International Monetary Fund (IMF),** responsible for helping member countries with short-run balance-of-payments problems; the **World Bank** to deal with economic development issues; and the **General Agreement on Tariffs and Trade (GATT),** predecessor of today's **World Trade Organization (WTO).** These institutions still form the basic structure for international economic relations in the monetary, development, and trade spheres, although each has evolved and others have emerged in the intervening decades.

Even in the postwar heyday of trade liberalization, the United States continued to exhibit ambivalence toward trade. The GATT was meant as a preliminary to formation of the more extensive and formal International Trade Organization (ITO), but the U.S. Congress refused to ratify the ITO because of fear of losing control over U.S. trade policy to an international organization. As a result, the GATT became the basis for international trade-policy negotiations.[7] Congress repeatedly authorized the president to seek further reciprocal

---

7 The Jackson book in the chapter references includes an excellent treatment of the history of the GATT.

tariff reductions through negotiations with trading partners, but at the same time imposed increasing restrictions on the liberalization process. Perhaps the clearest example of these restrictions was the insistence in 1947 that a formal escape clause be included in all tariff treaties. The **escape clause** permits cancellation of tariff reductions shown to cause injury to a domestic industry. As earlier chapters of this book show, the gains from international trade come from specialization and exchange according to comparative advantage and exploitation of economies of scale. The process of specialization inherently involves shrinkage or elimination of some industries. The idea of an escape clause, if carried to its logical limit, could eliminate trade, because trade always injures a nation's comparative-disadvantage industries. The escape clause represents just one example of a number of **safeguards** imposed in an effort to avoid the adjustment costs involved in trade's reallocation of resources.

In the United States, Congress has alternately tightened and loosened safeguard provisions with evolving perceptions of international trade. We can see these changing views by briefly examining the main trade acts passed since the 1950s: the Trade Expansion Act of 1962, the Trade Act of 1974, the Trade Agreements Act of 1979, the Trade and Tariff Act of 1984, the Omnibus Trade and Competitiveness Act of 1988, and the Uruguay Round Agreements Act of 1994.[8] Each act attempted to reclaim for Congress a portion of the control over international trade policy delegated to the president during the Depression and World War II.

9.3.5 Trade Policy in the 1960s and 1970s

The Trade Expansion Act and the Kennedy Round

The trade policies of the 1940s and 1950s involved extensions of the Reciprocal Trade Agreements Act. Congress had authorized the president to negotiate tariff reductions with trading partners, but throughout the period it gradually tightened restrictions on the president's actions, particularly through changes in the safeguard provisions. Partly as a result of this increased protectionist sentiment, President Kennedy sought to regain momentum in trade liberalization by designing a comprehensive trade bill to replace, rather than merely revise and extend, the RTAA. The result was the Trade Expansion Act of 1962 (TEA).

In addition to granting the president authority to negotiate reductions of up to 50 percent in tariffs through the GATT, the TEA contained three provisions important for their lasting effect on world trade policy. The first resulted not from the bill itself but from the political process necessary to obtain its passage. To gain the political support of representatives from the southern states (site of the U.S. textile industry), Kennedy agreed to impose quotas on cotton textile imports and to partially exempt textiles from the negotiations to take place under the proposed bill. These quotas and exemptions grew through the years, in the form of the **Multifiber Agreement (MFA),** into one of the world's most far-reaching and restrictive sets of trade barriers (and probably the most damaging to developing economies).

The Trade Expansion Act also introduced two rather sweeping changes into the institutional arrangements for tariff negotiations. The form of negotiations shifted from a *product-by-product format* to an *across-the-board,* or *linear, format.* Before the TEA, countries had negotiated tariffs for each product separately. The process was slow and tedious, and countries often proved unwilling to consider reductions on a large number of goods. Under the TEA, a single negotiated tariff-cutting formula would apply to all products. Each country then could submit a list of exceptions, or products on which it would not cut tariffs. The new approach speeded up the negotiation process somewhat; however, arrival at the tariff-cutting formula was slow as each country tried to fine-tune the formula to its own advantage. In the end, the Kennedy Round of tariff reductions conducted under the GATT by authority granted by the TEA achieved a tariff cut of approximately 36 percent by the major industrial countries (see Table 9.1).

The other institutional innovation introduced in the Trade Expansion Act was the addition of the **Trade Adjustment Assistance** (TAA) program to U.S. safeguard provisions. Before the act, if imports resulting from a tariff reduction injured an industry, the only remedy was reinstitution of the tariff. Trade Adjustment Assistance constituted an alternate way to deal with injury: directly compensate injured firms and workers for their losses. Compensation could take the form of extended unemployment benefits, retraining, and relocation

---

8 Robert E. Baldwin, *The Political Economy of U.S. Import Policy* (Cambridge, Mass.: MIT Press, 1985), provides a useful account of the ebb and flow of support for pro-trade and protectionist policies and the reflections of those sentiments in the postwar trade bills. Most provisions of each bill take the form of amendments of earlier bills; thus, U.S. trade law is cumulative. For example, Section 201 of the Trade Act of 1974, as amended by the later acts, still forms the basis of U.S. escape-clause law.

assistance for workers; low-interest loans and other assistance to help firms move into new product lines; and even restitution to whole communities harmed by an industry's decline. Trade Adjustment Assistance provided a way to capture the benefits from unrestricted trade while assisting those harmed by it; in other words, the program attempted to provide the compensation discussed in earlier chapters on the distributional effect of trade.[9]

Following the success of the TEA and the accompanying Kennedy Round talks, protectionist pressures rose in the United States. U.S. industries claimed that other countries, especially members of the European Community, violated the spirit if not the letter of the GATT agreement by replacing their tariffs with nontariff barriers. The Trade Adjustment Assistance program, expected to reduce pressure by domestic industries for protection, had little actual effect during the 1960s, due to its stringent eligibility requirements. For eligibility, an industry had to prove that a tariff reduction had injured it and had been the primary cause of injury (that is, had caused at least 51 percent of the industry's problems). These requirements were interpreted strictly, and essentially no assistance was paid under the TAA program until 1969. The politically powerful AFL-CIO labor group, dissatisfied with the adjustment assistance program, reversed its historical support of trade liberalization in favor of import restrictions. Not until 1974 was Congress willing to pass another trade bill authorizing a further round of tariff negotiations.

The Trade Act of 1974, the Tokyo Round, and the 1979 Trade Agreements Act

The Trade Act of 1974 resembled the 1962 TEA in several respects. The 1974 bill granted the president an impressive 60 percent tariff-reduction authority, but at the same time placed additional constraints on the president's liberalization efforts and continued Congress's campaign to reclaim its power over trade policy. As in 1962, obtaining adequate support for the trade bill required major concessions to the textile industry. The United States extended the existing set of import quotas from cotton textiles to cover wools and synthetics. Congress specifically excluded several items from the president's tariff-cutting authority, including footwear, an industry of particular interest to developing countries.

The bill strengthened the role of the International Trade Commission, then known as the Tariff Commission, relative to the president in the interpretation and enforcement of safeguards against injury to domestic industries. Rules requiring stronger enforcement against "unfair" foreign trade practices such as subsidies and dumping were included. The president received authority to negotiate reductions in nontariff trade barriers as well as tariffs, but only with the specific approval of Congress.

Finally, the act loosened eligibility requirements for compensation under the Trade Adjustment Assistance program in two important ways. Injury to a domestic industry no longer had to be directly linked to a government policy (the reduction of tariffs) but only to increased imports. And increased competition from imports had to represent an "important" cause of the injury but no longer the "primary" one.

These rules set out in the Trade Act of 1974 laid the groundwork for U.S. participation in the Tokyo Round of GATT talks, which lasted from 1974 to 1979 and reduced the major industrial economies' tariff rates by approximately 30 percent. On other issues, the Tokyo Round, which was more ambitious than earlier talks in addressing problems associated with nontariff barriers, had mixed success. Because of the price-support systems we discussed in the context of export subsidies (see section 7.5), trade barriers on most agricultural products proved immune to progress. Developing countries' concerns received somewhat more attention than in earlier rounds of talks, but lack of progress in the crucial agricultural, textile, apparel, and footwear industries continued.

The Tokyo Round broke controversial ground by reaching several agreements accepted by only a subset of the then more than 90 GATT member countries. Nine such **codes** were negotiated, with additional signatories free to join later. Areas covered by the codes included subsidies and countervailing duties, government procurement, standards or technical trade barriers, import licensing, customs valuation, antidumping, trade in civilian aircraft, trade in dairy products, and trade in bovine meat. Some of the codes proved more successful than others, but the idea of codes or mini-agreements remains controversial, because they represent a move away from the more traditional multilateral approach of the GATT.

The Tokyo Round left the international trading system with a number of unresolved issues, including developed-country barriers against developing-country exports, mutually acceptable interpretations of safe-

---

9 See the discussion of Trade Adjustment Assistance in section 4.6.4 and Case Four in Chapter Four.

guard provisions, and procedures for settling disputes within the GATT. The United States ratified the results of the Tokyo Round negotiations in the Trade Agreements Act of 1979. That act also further limited the executive branch's discretion over trade policy by requiring more extensive monitoring of trade agreements and reporting to Congress.

9.3.6 Trade Policy in the 1980s and 1990s

The Trade and Tariff Act of 1984

The Trade and Tariff Act of 1984 is best known for its approval of an historic shift in U.S. trade policy: It gave the president authority to negotiate *bilateral* trade treaties. Since World War II, the United States had insisted that trade liberalization be accomplished *multilaterally* through the GATT to ensure that all member countries benefited from liberalization on a nondiscriminatory basis. Throughout the early 1980s, the United States promoted a new round of multilateral GATT trade talks and sought support from its trading partners for the venture. The world economy was mired in both a global recession, which increased protectionist pressures, and a developing-country debt crisis; this unfortunate combination of circumstances threatened to stymie progress toward opening trade. Other countries resisted U.S. appeals to support a new round of GATT talks. So U.S. policy makers turned to bilateral agreements for two reasons: as an alternate path to liberalization and as an attempt to pressure trading partners to support a new GATT round or risk being left out of the liberalization process.

The Omnibus Trade and Competitiveness Act and the Uruguay Round Agreements Act

Finally, a 1986 meeting of trade ministers in Uruguay launched a round of GATT talks known as the **Uruguay Round.** Goals included complete elimination of tariffs by the major trading partners; extension of GATT rules to previously neglected areas such as trade in services and agriculture; clarification of GATT's institutional role, especially in dispute settlement; better enforcement of property rights in intellectual property such as computer software and movies; and limiting use of nontariff trade barriers, particularly voluntary export restraints.

Although the Uruguay Round talks began in late 1986, it wasn't until 1988, in the Omnibus Trade and Competitiveness Act, that Congress actually granted the executive branch the formal authority to participate and to negotiate tariff reductions of up to 50 percent. The 1988 act also required domestic industries seeking import relief under the Section 201 escape clause to show that they were prepared to make "positive adjustment" to import competition. Although subject to a range of interpretation, this change at least provided the opportunity to halt the trend toward long-term, permanent protection for the country's comparative-disadvantage industries.

Despite the provision for participation in the GATT talks and the modification of Section 201 to take some account of patterns of comparative advantage, the origin of many of the 1988 act's elements lay in concern over the U.S. trade deficit and in the often-cited decline in the country's "competitiveness." As a result, many parts of the 1,000-page bill represented moves toward protectionism. Under the amended Section 301, domestic industries found it easier to claim (sometimes falsely) that they were injured by imports facilitated by foreign unfair trade practices, thereby justifying relief or retaliation.[10] The 1988 bill transferred responsibility for initiating Section 301 cases from the president to the U.S. trade representative, a move expected to make firms more likely to obtain affirmative findings in unfair trade cases.

The Uruguay Round talks were scheduled for completion by the end of 1990. If submitted to Congress by May 1991, the results of the round could have been approved under a special **fast-track** process that expedites congressional action by prohibiting amendments and limiting the time Congress has to consider the bill.[11] However, a deadlock between the United States and the European Community over always-controversial agricultural export subsidies prevented agreement, and talks broke down in 1990. The United States wanted the agreement to eliminate agricultural subsidies, and the EC wanted to keep intact its subsidy-based Common Agricultural Policy.

---

10 Recall that Section 301 of the Trade Act of 1974 is the foundation of U.S. trade law dealing with "unfair" trade practices of foreign countries. See also section 8.10.

11 The *fast-track* terminology for Congressional authorization of trade negotiations has since been changed to *trade-promotion authority*.

The Uruguay Round continued past its original deadline under a two-year extension of the president's negotiating authority granted by Congress in 1991. Key countries had reached tentative agreement in many areas, including industrial subsidies, antidumping duties, foreign investment, dispute settlement, safeguards, and bringing textile trade into the GATT system. Negotiations, however, follow a format in which no part of an agreement becomes final until the entire agreement becomes final. Continuing disagreement between the EC and the United States over the depth of cuts in farm subsidies threatened the whole negotiation, after five years' work.

Congress extended fast-track authority for the Uruguay Round for the final time in 1993, but only until December 15 of that year. U.S. policy makers took a risk that, by signaling that they would walk away from the entire venture if talks didn't conclude by the end of the year, they could pressure recalcitrant Europeans to compromise on agriculture. The gamble paid off, and GATT members approved the Uruguay Round agreement in 1994.

In the end, the Uruguay Round accomplished many of the tasks on its ambitious agenda. The major results included the following:

1. The agricultural provisions significantly reduced export subsidies and imposed some discipline on domestic subsidies. The agreement also required tariffication of existing nontariff barriers and made the resulting tariffs subject to cuts averaging 36 percent. In agricultural markets completely closed to imports, the agreement required reduction of trade barriers sufficient to allow minimum access for imports.

2. In textiles, the bilateral quotas of the Multifiber Agreement were slated to be removed by the end of a 10-year transition period. Most of the protection would remain in place until the end of that period, and high tariffs would remain in many textile and apparel sectors even after the quotas disappeared.

3. Overall progress on tariffs included cuts averaging almost 40 percent plus complete elimination of tariffs by industrial countries in several important sectors. A much higher percentage of world trade would occur duty free after the Uruguay Round, and many developing economies agreed to bind (that is, promise not to raise) tariffs on a large share of their imports.

4. The agreement clarified the distinction between acceptable and unacceptable subsidies. Developing countries' subsidies were subject to discipline for the first time.

5. The new General Agreement on Trade in Services began the task of developing a framework of rules for trade in services comparable to existing rules for trade in goods.

6. The agreement strengthened international rules for enforcement of intellectual property rights including patents, trademarks, copyrights, and industrial secrets. After specified transition periods, the rules would apply to developing as well as developed countries.

7. Most important, the agreement strengthened the structure of the GATT framework itself by establishing the World Trade Organization (WTO). The new organization brought together the 50-year accumulation of GATT rules and agreements under one umbrella. The WTO would exist as a "single undertaking," so member countries would subscribe to all rules and responsibilities, rather than picking and choosing as in the past. An improved dispute-settlement procedure would handle all disputes and improve members' compliance with their obligations.

The Doha Round

The eight-year Uruguay Round negotiations exhausted participants. But the history of trade policy has caused many observers to suggest the "bicycle" theory: If the liberalization process stops moving forward, it tends to fall over. So, exhausted or not, negotiators agreed at the end of the Uruguay Round to a schedule of future talks on specific issues. New talks on trade in agriculture and services started in early 2000. Many WTO members hoped to launch a new round of comprehensive negotiations; but early talks bogged down. In addition to issue-specific disagreements, WTO members faced the nontrivial task of agreeing on a strategy for approaching the new round. Most members agreed that the Uruguay Round's eight-year length overtaxed everyone's patience, suggesting that the new round should aim for a more reasonable three-to-four year completion schedule. But this raised a problem: a short time horizon required a limited and manageable agenda. But constraining the number of items on the agenda limits countries' ability to negotiate trade-offs among issues (for example, giving up something you want in agriculture in order to get something you want in services).

Finally, in late 2001, WTO members agreed, in Doha, Qatar, on a draft agenda for a new round of trade talks. Items on the agenda include (as always!) difficult and controversial ones. The United States and many developing countries want drastic changes in the European Union's Common Agricultural Policy, which turns Western European countries that would import agricultural goods under free trade into heavily subsidized exporters. Almost everyone wants the United States to stop its aggressive use of import-blocking antidumping policies; and many countries (including the United States) hope to stop the further spread of antidumping laws. Labor and environmental groups in the rich industrialized economies hope to make future trade agreements contingent on developing countries' adherence to high labor and environmental standards; but developing countries view these demands as thinly disguised protectionism on the part of the developed world. And developing economies that face public-health crises, such as the AIDS epidemic, wanted and won more generous provisions for exemptions from patents that protect the property rights of pharmaceutical firms.

The ongoing work of the WTO is just one of the paths by which governments have addressed many of the economic goals expressed at the end of World War II. As mentioned earlier, one of those goals was a quick rebuilding of Western Europe. The United States encouraged not only the rebuilding of individual European economies but also the economic and political unification, or *integration,* of Western Europe as a means of preserving the peace. Policy makers saw the nationalistic character of prewar political and economic policies as a cause of the war that devastated both sides.

The integration of Europe greatly affected postwar trade policy, providing one example of institutions' role in transcending the strictly national character of economic policies. Ironically, some policy makers now cite Europe's integration as a danger sign for the world trading system. European success in moving toward an open market within the European Union, along with the formation of NAFTA and many other integration groups, raise fears that the trading system will break into blocs, or regional areas *within* which trade is relatively free but *between* which protectionism dominates. To understand and evaluate these concerns, we must analyze economic integration's impact on the world trading system.

9.4 Economic Integration and Regional Trading

The combination of countries' variation in economic size and the importance of economic size in determining a country's role in world markets provides a powerful incentive for nations to form themselves into groups. At the same time, the unique situation each country faces forms a barrier to smooth coordination and cooperation within such groups. Each country wants to retain its national economic goals and its power over policies for pursuing them, while capturing the ability to make decisions that transcend national boundaries. One attempt to obtain the benefits of both nationalism and supranationalism involves the creation of groups of countries that explicitly agree to coordinate certain aspects of their policies.

9.4.1 Stages of Integration

Integration, or the formation of countries into groups, can be either political or economic, and the distinction between the two often blurs. Five stages of economic integration represent increasing degrees of unification, as illustrated in Figure 9.2.

The lowest level of integration is formation of a **preferential trading arrangement (PTA).**[12] Under this system, member countries agree to maintain lower barriers to trade within the group than to trade with nonmember countries. Each country continues to determine its own policies, but the trade policy of each includes preferential treatment of group members. One simple example of such an arrangement would be a differential tariff whereby each member placed a tariff on imports from member countries equal to half its tariff on imports from nonmembers. Panel (a) of Figure 9.3 illustrates such an arrangement in a three-country world where countries A and B form a PTA while C remains a nonmember.

The next stage of integration is a **free-trade area,** which involves eliminating barriers to intra-group trade while allowing each country to maintain its own nationally determined barriers to trade with nonmembers; NAFTA is an example. A free-trade area may apply to all goods or to only a specified list.[13] Free-trade areas

---

12 In the literature on economic integration, the terms *preferential trade arrangement* (PTA) and *regional trade arrangement* (RTA) also are used as generic names for all five stages of integration.

13 In order not to violate the WTO nondiscrimination requirement, a free-trade area or customs union (discussed shortly) must remove the barriers to all or almost all trade between members.

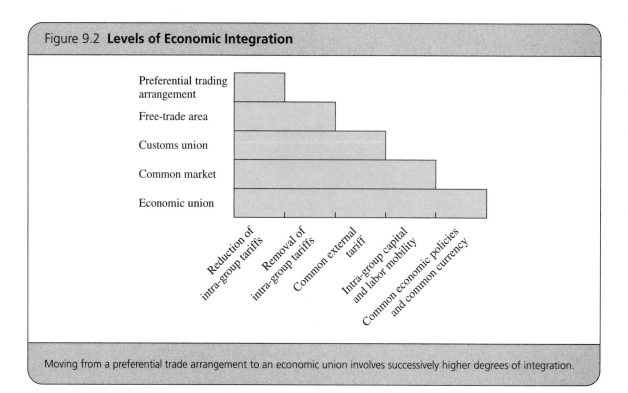

Figure 9.2 **Levels of Economic Integration**

Moving from a preferential trade arrangement to an economic union involves successively higher degrees of integration.

have the advantage of requiring agreement among member countries on only a narrow range of issues. One disadvantage of this limited form of integration lies in the area of enforcement. Panel (b) in Figure 9.3 depicts a free-trade area in which country A maintains a 10 percent tariff on imports from C, and country B imposes a 20 percent tariff on goods from C. This situation produces an incentive for C to ship goods ultimately destined for B through A, paying the 10 percent tariff and then shipping duty-free from A to B, thereby avoiding B's 20 percent tariff. Transshipment problems arise whenever member countries try to maintain different tariff levels on trade with nonmembers.[14]

One way to ameliorate the transshipment problem involves moving to the next level of integration by forming a **customs union.** With this arrangement, intra-group trade faces no barriers and members maintain a **common external tariff (CET)** on trade with nonmembers. If countries A and B from the previous example formed a customs union, a uniform tariff would apply to goods from C; it could be 10 percent, 20 percent, or a compromise, perhaps 15 percent, as in panel (c) of Figure 9.3. In the case of the most successful economic integration, the European Union, CET levels equal the average of the members' pre-integration tariff rates. The CET eliminates the incentive for transshipment that happens under a preferential- or free-trade agreement.

The fourth stage of economic integration is a **common market,** which extends free trade among members to factors of production (labor migration and capital flows) as well as to goods and services. In addition, common-market members typically maintain fixed exchange rates among their national currencies.[15] The European Union refers to the "four freedoms" that make it a common market: free intra-group movement for labor, goods, services, and capital, although several of the freedoms remain less than perfect.

The most extensive form of economic integration, an **economic union,** means common, group-determined economic policies as well as a common currency or money. Economic union proves very difficult to achieve and maintain, because it requires member countries to agree on a very wide range of issues and policies. Even countries that are politically, economically, and culturally similar find differences in their individual situations that make such agreement difficult. While political boundaries have economic significance, economic barriers have

---

14 The U.S.–Israel Free Trade Agreement and NAFTA seek to avoid transshipment by restricting tariff-free treatment to goods produced in the partner country. These restrictions require rules of origin (see section 7.8.1).

15 Chapter Twelve and later chapters examine the implications of fixed exchange rates.

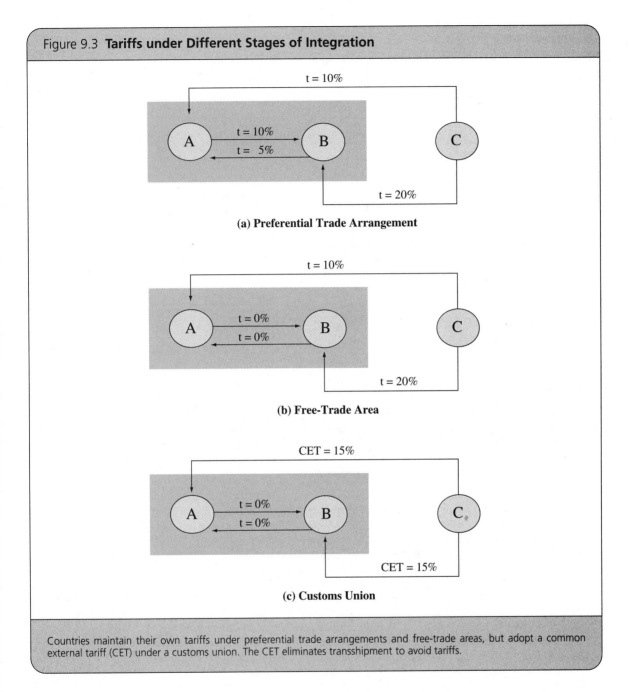

Figure 9.3 **Tariffs under Different Stages of Integration**

(a) Preferential Trade Arrangement

(b) Free-Trade Area

(c) Customs Union

Countries maintain their own tariffs under preferential trade arrangements and free-trade areas, but adopt a common external tariff (CET) under a customs union. The CET eliminates transshipment to avoid tariffs.

political implications as well. Historically, countries have been extremely reluctant to forgo the exercise of their national sovereignty in the interest of an economic union; this is one reason why the European Union's efforts to become a true economic union have been so controversial and have attracted so much attention.

9.4.2 Trade Creation and Trade Diversion: Integration and Welfare

The overall welfare effects of economic integration are ambiguous and require case-by-case judgment. We can see the reason for this ambiguity by recognizing integration as simultaneously a policy of protection (against nonmembers) and a move toward free trade (with members). The protectionist element of integration is called

Figure 9.4 **Welfare Effects of a Free-Trade Area in Good X**

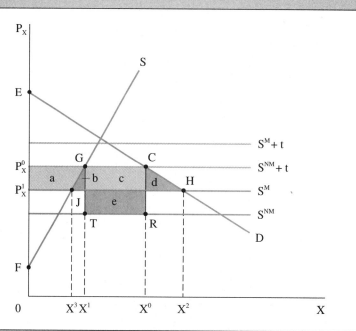

S^M denotes the supply of good X by *member* countries and S^{NM} the supply by *nonmember* countries. Formation of a free-trade area causes a move from point C to point H. Trade increases as imports rise from $X^0 - X^1$ to $X^2 - X^3$. Trade also is diverted from nonmember countries toward member countries, causing an efficiency loss represented by the area of rectangle e.

trade diversion. This refers to the diversion of trade from nonmembers to members caused by the discrimination inherent in integration. The trade-liberalization element of integration is called **trade creation.** Integration reduces or eliminates protection among member countries and allows them to specialize and trade according to comparative advantage and to exploit potential economies of scale. If trade creation exceeds trade diversion, economic integration increases member countries' welfare. If trade diversion dominates trade creation, welfare falls.

Figure 9.4 illustrates integration's trade-creating and trade-diverting effects. We take the point of view of a small country considering elimination of trade barriers on good X with a group of countries (that is, the formation of a free-trade area in good X). D and S, respectively, represent the country's domestic demand for and supply of good X. S^M denotes the supply of good X from other countries that would be *members* of the free-trade area; S^{NM} is the supply of X by countries that would be *non*members.

Before integration, imports of good X from all countries are subject to a tariff of t per unit; thus, $S^M + t$ and $S^{NM} + t$ represent the effective supply curves for imports from the two possible sources. Point C represents the initial equilibrium. Residents of the country consume X^0 units of X at price P_X^0, of which X^1 are produced domestically and $X^0 - X^1$ are imported from countries that, if integration occurred, would be nonmembers. No imported X comes from would-be members, because nonmembers supply the good at a lower price than do members. Graphically, this is reflected by the fact that S^{NM} lies below S^M, or $S^{NM} + t$ lies below $S^M + t$. Consumer surplus is given by the area of triangle $P_X^0 EC$, and the surplus of domestic producers by area $FP_X^0 G$. The government collects the equivalent of the area of rectangle TGCR in tariff revenue.

After formation of a free-trade area, the relevant supply curves are S^M (because imports from member countries no longer are subject to the tariff) and $S^{NM} + t$ (because imports from nonmembers remain subject to the tariff). The new equilibrium is at point H. Residents consume X^2 units of X at price P_X^1, and X^3 units are produced domestically. The remainder ($X^2 - X^3$) are imported, but now from member countries. *(Why?)* Consumer surplus rises by a + b + c + d, and domestic producer surplus declines by area a. The government no longer collects any tariff revenue, because all imports now come from member (tariff-free) countries. Area c, which previously went to the government as tariff revenue, now goes to consumers in the form of reduced prices for good X. Area b is a net gain from increased efficiency; the units of X between X^3 and X^1 previously were produced domestically at relatively high costs (represented by the height of the domestic supply curve) but now are imported at lower costs (represented by the height of S^M). This efficiency gain captures one part of integration's trade-creation effect. Area d denotes the other trade-creation effect. As lower-cost imports become available, consumption increases from X^0 to X^2. For each additional unit of consumption, the value to consumers (represented by the height of the demand curve) exceeds the opportunity costs of production (represented by the height of S^M). The total trade-creating effect of the elimination of the tariff on imports from member countries equals the sum of areas b and d.

Area e in Figure 9.4 illustrates integration's trade-diverting effect. Notice that before integration, all imports came from nonmember countries, the low-cost producers of good X. After integration, all imports come from higher-cost member country producers. This switch from low-cost to high-cost sources of imports represents trade diversion. Before integration, area e was a portion of the tariff revenue going to the domestic government. After formation of the free-trade area, e becomes a deadweight loss. Each unit of imports between X^1 and X^0 now is being produced at an opportunity cost represented by the height of S^M rather than the lower opportunity cost given by the height of S^{NM}.

We can determine the free-trade area's overall effect on the small member country's welfare by comparing the trade-creation and trade-diversion effects. If trade creation dominates, formation of a free-trade area enhances welfare; if trade diversion exceeds trade creation, the group reduces welfare. Note that if member countries include the low-cost producers of good X, there will be no trade-diversion effect and integration will unambiguously increase welfare. *(To see this, switch the labels of S^M and S^{NM} and of $S^M + t$ and $S^{NM} + t$ in Figure 9.4.)* Note also that if the tariff is low enough to make the tariff-inclusive price of nonmember imports still lower than the price of tariff-free member imports, the free-trade area will have no trade-creating or trade-diverting effects—because no trade will occur with member countries even if the group does form.

We can formulate some general rules about when trade creation will be likely to dominate trade diversion or vice versa. First, the higher member countries' initial tariffs, other things equal, the more trade creation induced by integration and, therefore, the more likely integration will improve members' welfare. Second, lower member barriers against trade with nonmembers translate into less trade diversion and make welfare-enhancing integration more likely. Finally, the more members the better, because the group will more likely include low-cost producers. As noted earlier, when the low-cost producers of the good are group members, no trade diversion occurs. Another way of viewing this last rule is to notice that a free-trade area that included *all* countries could not generate any trade diversion, because the good's lowest-cost producers would, by definition, be members.

Economists estimate the overall impact of integration by calculating the effects corresponding to areas a, b, c, d, and e in Figure 9.4 for each good traded. In the case of the European Union, most analysts agree that trade creation outweighs trade diversion for most manufactured goods. However, the opposite holds for the group's highly protected agricultural sector.

9.4.3 **Additional Considerations**

The analysis of economic integration in Figure 9.4 is static, focusing on the reallocation of resources caused by elimination of barriers to intra-group trade over a short time period. Integration may also have dynamic effects—that is, it may cause the member economies to evolve differently over time. A complete analysis of integration's welfare effects must include an examination of the effects of these dynamic changes.

Economic integration increases the size of the "domestic" market. In industries that exhibit economies of scale, the increased market size may allow firms to achieve the economies necessary for them to become competitive in export markets, as we saw in Chapter Five.

Increased market size also may allow a group of countries to exercise some monopoly power in world markets. A group of "small" countries may, by banding together, be able to act as a "large" country and impose an optimal tariff or export tax (see sections 6.5.2 and 6.10.2). This pooling of power also may be important within international organizations and in other bargaining situations. One often-cited reason for the formation of the European Community in 1957 was to present the United States with a more nearly equal partner in terms of bargaining strength.

An additional source of dynamic benefits from economic integration takes the form of increased competitive pressures on industries within the integrated group. Once intra-group trade barriers fall, industries face competition from their counterparts in other member countries. If the group allows market forces to determine success and failure, intra-group specialization will develop along the lines of comparative advantage. Monopolization and the associated inefficiencies will be less likely to develop and persist. Groups forgo these potential benefits if they "assign" industries to the various members or otherwise prohibit competition within the group. The question of distribution of industries across member countries has proven troublesome, especially among groups of developing countries whose members are eager to industrialize.

Besides the static and dynamic welfare effects of any particular integration group, the trend toward the formation of such groups affects the fundamental norms of the international trading system. The postwar GATT/WTO system rests on a foundation of multilateral nondiscriminatory liberalization that treats all trading partners equally, in principle if not in practice. Many policy makers and economists express concern that this system may lose out to one based on bilateral arrangements and discriminatory treatment of trading partners, in which regional trading blocs partition the world trading system into a small number of groups, each practicing discriminatory protection against nonmembers.

Supporters of regional trading groups point out that more progress on difficult issues may be possible when participants are a small group of like-minded countries.[16] As the GATT/WTO membership has grown from 23 members to more than 140 (see Table 9.1) and become more diverse, negotiations there have become more unwieldy. At the same time, changes in the nature of trade policy and of protection have complicated the negotiation process. Tariffs have fallen substantially, and the most important issues in the world trading system now include much more complex policies—subsidies, antidumping policies, informal protectionism, and voluntary import expansions. These developments, taken together, may suggest a role for small-group trade agreements, along with the WTO.

9.4.4 Efforts at Integration: Success and Failure

Since World War II, attempts at economic integration have come in two waves. The first, in the 1960s, included numerous groups of developing economies that attempted to follow the European Community model. The definition and goals of economic integration suggest that we might expect groups of small developing countries to be most likely to choose integration as a policy. However, most early attempts at integration among developing countries met with only mediocre success, and many arrangements throughout Africa and Latin America collapsed within a few years of initiation.

The second wave of economic integration began in the mid-1980s and continues today. The United States has, for the first time, entered bilateral trade arrangements, and the European Community has expanded its membership and its integration agenda. Developing countries also are participating in this second wave of integration. Some groups that formed earlier have been revived, and new groups have formed in Africa, Latin America, the Middle East, and Asia. Outside the European Union and the North American Free Trade Agreement, the groups that have received the most attention, because of their rapidly growing and industrializing economies, are the Southern Common Market (Mercosur), which includes Argentina, Brazil, Paraguay, and Uruguay, and the Association for South East Asian Nations (ASEAN, composed of Brunei, Cambodia, Indonesia, Laos, Malaysia, Myanmar, the Philippines, Singapore, Thailand, and Vietnam).

WTO member countries that form integration groups must report their actions to the WTO, because such groups don't apply the most-favored-nation and nondiscrimination principles that underlie the WTO. Article 24 of the original GATT agreement does permit economic integration so long as (1) trade liberalization applies to "substantially all" intra-group trade and (2) group barriers to trade with nonmembers aren't higher than before the group formed. Since 1948, hundreds of integration groups have notified the GATT/WTO of their existence; but only about a hundred remain in effect (of which almost 30 are bilateral agreements between the European Union and one nonmember country), and only a handful of those have had a substantial and sustained impact on trade.[17] Figure 9.5 reports recent shares of intra-group trade for the EU, NAFTA, ASEAN, and Mercosur.

---

16 See Beth V. Yarbrough, "Preferential Trade Arrangements and the GATT: EC 1992 as Rogue or Role Model?" in the chapter references.

17 For lists, see the World Trade Organization, *Annual Report.*

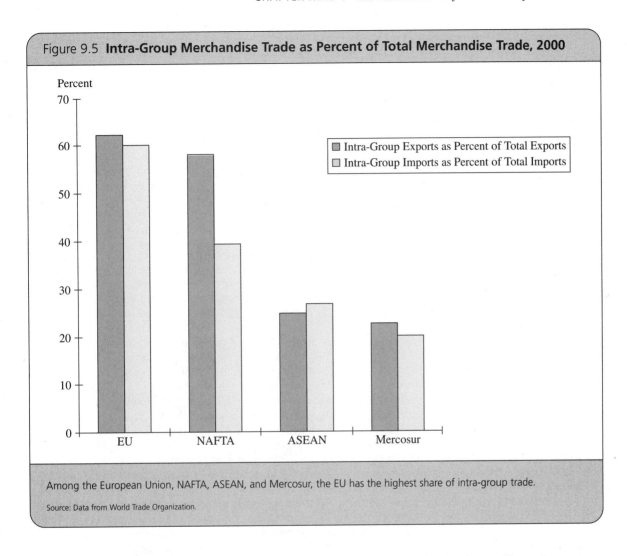

Figure 9.5 **Intra-Group Merchandise Trade as Percent of Total Merchandise Trade, 2000**

Among the European Union, NAFTA, ASEAN, and Mercosur, the EU has the highest share of intra-group trade.

Source: Data from World Trade Organization.

The history of failed and only moderately successful attempts at economic integration testifies to the strong desire for national sovereignty in economic policy making—even though political boundaries are largely arbitrary from the standpoint of the organization of economic activity. Generally speaking, integration efforts among developed economies have enjoyed more success than those among developing ones. Some reasons for this pattern emerge from the simple graphical analysis of a free-trade area in Figure 9.4. Several African integration groups, for example, included economies with highly similar factor endowments and trade stemming almost exclusively from factor-endowment-based comparative advantage. Prior to integration, members imported largely the same goods from the same nonmember countries. Such a pattern provides little scope for trade creation. *(Why?)* In addition, the first wave of integration among developing economies coincided with the height of popularity of import-substitution development strategies based on extensive import restrictions.[18] Therefore, much of the trade liberalization envisioned in the integration treaties never actually occurred.

Among developed economies, especially in the European Union, beneficial effects of integration came largely from intra-industry trade based on economies of scale. So trade creation was possible despite the similarities of members' factor endowments.

The second historical wave of integration differs from the first in its inclusion of groups whose members encompass countries at widely divergent levels of development. NAFTA provides one example, as does the

---

18 Section 11.4 compares import-substitution and outward-oriented development strategies.

expansion of the EU to include countries less developed than the original members. Developing economies can achieve two major benefits from integration with developed ones. The first is market access on a preferential basis. The "Europe Agreements," for example, grant many countries of Eastern and Central Europe extensive access to the markets of the European Union, although sensitive industrial sectors and agriculture remain restricted; most of the countries covered by the agreements hope to qualify eventually for full EU membership. The second benefit is a means of credibly committing the developing-country government to market-oriented reforms and open economic institutions. Mexico, eager to guarantee that it would not reverse its dramatic economic reforms of the late 1980s, saw NAFTA as a way of making a public commitment to that effect.

The developed members of developed-developing integration groups, on the other hand, hope to discourage labor migration and to support the developing economies' commitments to market-oriented reforms. Both these elements play a large role in the relationships between the EU and the transitional economies of Central and Eastern Europe and between Mexico and the United States.

The European Union

The 1957 Treaty of Rome established the six-member European Community—Belgium, Luxembourg, the Netherlands, France, Germany, and Italy. The treaty's goals included formation of a common market with shared agricultural policies and aid programs to facilitate development of the less-developed areas within the community. More fundamentally, the goal was a unified Europe, both to prevent the intra-European rivalries that had resulted in two world wars in 30 years and to present the United States with a more equal economic and political rival.

The group satisfied its customs-union goals within about a decade of the original treaty, but efforts at further integration stalled. In 1971, the EC agreed to a 10-year plan to achieve a full economic union. An incomplete common market evolved; however, many nontariff barriers and impediments to labor and capital flows remained, most of them intimately connected to issues of national sovereignty over economic policy making. Decision-making complexity grew as membership expanded. With the addition of Spain and Portugal in 1986, the EC became the world's largest market in terms of population and the second largest in terms of GDP.

In 1987, the EC passed the Single Europe Act, an amendment to the Treaty of Rome designed to recapture momentum toward integration and to complete the open internal market by 1992. The act facilitated achievement of these goals by limiting the ability of a single member country to veto EC proposals. It also expanded the EC bureaucracy based in Brussels and the scope of EC policy making in areas such as the environment, monetary policy, health and safety standards, and foreign policy.

In 1991, the EC made another major commitment toward moving to an economic union and changed the group's name from the European Community to the European Union. The Maastricht Treaty pledged member countries to coordinate their monetary, foreign and security, and immigration and policing policies. Most important, the treaty outlined a schedule and procedure by which the members would move to a common currency (the euro) and a common European central bank to conduct monetary policy for the group.[19]

In 1994, the EU and the European Free Trade Association (EFTA), minus Switzerland and Liechtenstein, signed an accord to form the European Economic Area (EEA), which grants all members free trade in goods, services, capital flows, and labor flows, except for agriculture. Since, three EFTA members—Austria, Finland, and Sweden—have moved to full EU membership. In Figure 9.6 the 15 current EU members are indicated by light shading. The darker-shaded countries (plus Cyprus) have applied for membership; and the Union has committed itself to enlargement by 2004, although many controversial issues must be hammered out before any new members join.

Many of the most controversial issues that face Europe's integration efforts also face the world trading system: trade in services, agricultural policy, government procurement, technical barriers to trade, and capital mobility. These issues present difficulties because they involve a delicate balance between international cooperation and national sovereignty. Although *EC92* became a buzzword for regional economic integration, analysts and policy makers now realize that integration is a continuing process, not a goal achievable by a set date such as December 31, 1992.

In general, the issues facing the European Union highlight the fundamental dilemma confronting the world economy: how to capture the gains from international cooperation and trade while maintaining politically

---

19 Chapter Twenty contains an examination of the monetary aspects of the EU, including the common currency.

Figure 9.6 **European Union Members and Applicants, 2001**

Many countries want to join the 15-member European Union.

acceptable levels of national control over economic, political, and social policy making. This dilemma becomes even more apparent as EU members move beyond a common market toward the goal of an economic and political union, with a common currency and common macroeconomic policies, and as the union encompasses a larger and more diverse membership.

The North American Free Trade Agreement

The North American Free Trade Agreement (NAFTA), linking the United States, Canada, and Mexico, exhibits several unique characteristics. First, an unusual process led up to the agreement. Mexico approached the United States about a free-trade agreement after launching a series of economic reforms, which included the elimination of its long-standing program of import substitution, in 1987. Shortly thereafter, the United States signed the Canada–United States Free-Trade Agreement. When the United States consented to talks with Mexico, Canada asked to join in a three-way agreement to reach "from the Yukon to Yucatan." Talks began in 1991, and the three countries initialed a 2,000-page agreement in 1992, subject to legislative approval in each country. After a long and controversial approval process, the agreement took effect on January 1, 1994. Figure 9.7 illustrates the pattern of trade among the three NAFTA members.

NAFTA broke ground for free-trade agreements because of its members' very different levels of economic development. Mexico had two primary reasons for desiring such an agreement with the United States. As illustrated in Figure 9.7, over 80 percent of Mexican exports go to the United States, so assured access to the

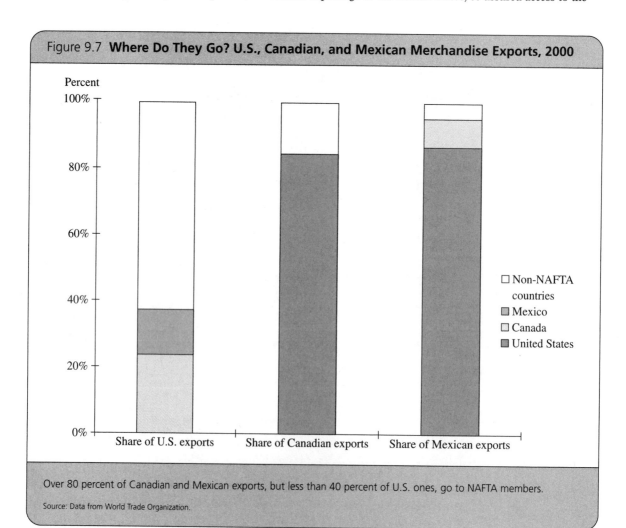

Figure 9.7 **Where Do They Go? U.S., Canadian, and Mexican Merchandise Exports, 2000**

Over 80 percent of Canadian and Mexican exports, but less than 40 percent of U.S. ones, go to NAFTA members.

Source: Data from World Trade Organization.

market of Mexico's large neighbor plays a big role in the long-run viability of Mexican reforms and growth. Economic reforms in Mexico have an erratic history, and many such attempts have failed. The agreement with the United States helped demonstrate the Mexican government's commitments to reform and to open trade; such government credibility improved Mexico's ability to attract foreign investment and reestablish creditworthiness after the country's debt problems of the 1980s. In return for these benefits, Mexico made politically difficult concessions, including opening its markets for financial services, securities, and insurance as well as many parts of its oil industry—a politically sensitive move because the oil industry's nationalization coincided with Mexico's revolution. Mexico also improved the transparency of its trade laws, which, like those in many developing countries, tended to be opaque, *ad hoc,* and arbitrary.

As a large economy, the United States had a substantially smaller stake in an agreement than Mexico, because the bulk of the gains from trade between a large and a small economy go to the smaller economy, as we learned in Chapters Two and Three. Nonetheless, over 80 percent of U.S. exports to Mexico were subject to Mexican tariffs (at an average rate of 10 percent), which the agreement would eliminate. By 1996, Mexican tariffs on U.S. exports had fallen to 2.9 percent.

Under the terms of NAFTA, tariffs on approximately half of members' trade were removed immediately. Remaining tariffs will be phased out by 2010. The most sensitive items, on which some tariffs will remain until 2010, include sneakers, ceramic tile, household glassware, orange juice concentrate, peanuts, broccoli, asparagus, and melons. In agriculture, existing quotas were converted to equivalent tariffs, and those tariffs will be reduced by 2010.

One of the stickier negotiating points in NAFTA involved rules of origin that specify how much North American content a product must contain to qualify for duty-free treatment, especially in the automobile, textile and apparel, and television industries.[20] The U.S. auto industry pressed for very high (70 percent) content rules. Canada and Mexico resisted, fearful that such rules would inhibit Japanese auto producers from investing in plants in Canada and Mexico to serve the U.S. market—because such plants typically import many auto parts from Japan. A last-minute compromise set the rules of origin for autos at 62.5 percent of value. In textiles and apparel, textiles must be woven and processed in North America to qualify for duty-free movement until 2004; apparel made from qualifying textiles also qualifies.

These stringent rules of origin probably represent the biggest threat for substantial trade diversion from NAFTA, because they exclude low-cost Asian suppliers of textiles and auto parts. If the Uruguay Round agreement succeeds in eventually dismantling the Multifiber Agreement, freer worldwide trade in textiles will reduce NAFTA's trade-diversion impact in textiles, but high textile tariffs that will remain still imply a potential for substantial trade diversion. *(Why?)*

In any free-trade agreement, procedures for settling disputes and escape-clause provisions are two of the key elements. NAFTA created the North American Trade Commission, consisting of three cabinet-level officials, to hear disputes. If a member country claims that another member's exports injure one of its industries, the country can stop its tariff reduction or return to the most-favored-nation (pre-NAFTA) tariff rate for that industry. Each country can do this only one time per industry, and for a maximum of three years.

Opposition to NAFTA from pro-protection forces in the United States centered on three issues: the agreement's environmental impact, the effects of differences between labor standards and wages in the United States and Mexico, and the possibility of sudden large import surges from Mexico, particularly in a few agricultural products. To gain the domestic political support necessary for passage through Congress, the United States negotiated three "side agreements" to cover some of these concerns. The environmental and labor-standard side agreements provide mechanisms to monitor members' compliance with their respective national laws and regulations and procedures for disputes. The side agreements encourage transparency and voluntary compliance and allow fines and trade sanctions only as last resorts and only for certain classes of violations. In the case of sudden and large import surges, the side agreement provides a monitoring system to allow governments to anticipate problems in import-competing industries.

NAFTA's success, like that of the European Union, has created a waiting list of would-be members throughout the Western Hemisphere. Talks began in mid-1995 for Chile's accession to the agreement. Mexico already had a free-trade agreement with Chile, and Canada signed one in 1997.

On an even larger scale, the 34 Western Hemisphere countries with democratically elected governments pledged in 1994 to begin work toward a Free Trade Area of the Americas, to be completed no later than the end

---

20 Section 7.8.1 introduces domestic-content rules and rules of origin.

of 2005. The initiative was formally launched in 1998, but the group's large, diverse membership makes concrete progress in reducing trade barriers difficult. Latin American countries emphasize the importance of disciplining U.S. antidumping policies and agricultural subsidies; the United States, to the extent it will address these issues at all, prefers to do so in the context of the WTO.

Mercosur

Brazil, Argentina, Paraguay, and Uruguay agreed in 1991 to form a free-trade area called Mercosur (or the Southern Cone Common Market). In the group's first five years, intra-group trade increased by a factor of four, and in 1996 Chile and Bolivia signed free-trade agreements with Mercosur. Despite early successes, the group hasn't been without problems (including average tariffs against nonmembers of about 20 percent). Its members have histories of high rates of protection, military dictatorships, and erratic trade liberalization. Auto and auto-parts trade between Brazil and Argentina remains restricted and will until 2006. Economic crises, in Brazil in 1999 and Argentina in 2001, strained relations with the group, as the two imposed unilateral restrictions on one another's exports.

Important sectors such as capital goods, informatics, telecommunications, and sugar remain outside Mercosur's liberalization at least for the short term. Perhaps more important, some analysts have questioned how much of Mercosur's increased internal trade represents trade creation and how much represents trade diversion. The fastest growing sectors of intra-group trade include capital-intensive items such as autos, buses, and agricultural machinery, in which none of the Mercosur members may be low-cost producers relative to nonmembers.

9.5 **Interregional Trade**

National boundaries distinguish inter*regional* from inter*national* trade. When boundaries change, formerly interregional trade becomes international, or vice versa. Trade between Russia and Ukraine, interregional during the Soviet Union's existence, now goes in the international ledger. And in 1997, when Hong Kong became part of China, trade between the two switched from international to interregional. Historically, most periods of widespread changes in national boundaries have coincided with major wars; for example, the end of World War II brought dramatic changes to Europe's map. More recently, an unusual number of border adjustments have occurred more peacefully, including the unification of Germany and the breakup of Czechoslovakia.

National boundaries are somewhat arbitrary from the perspective of the organization of economic activity.[21] Economic interaction between Toronto and Detroit dwarfs that between Toronto and Vancouver, or between Detroit and Seattle. Although economic activity across national borders sometimes exceeds the level of activity within borders, political boundaries do have major economic consequences. Economic policies, laws, tastes, currencies, and economic and political systems are just a few of the dimensions on which political borders matter.

Trade barriers, in particular, influence the spatial organization of economic activity. Regions within a country (that is, areas between which relatively free trade prevails) typically exhibit greater specialization than do countries themselves, in part because national trade barriers preclude countries' further specialization.

9.5.1 **The Role of Factor Mobility**

Another dimension of economic policy that distinguishes interregional from international trade patterns is factor mobility.[22] Labor and capital move more easily within than between countries because of both natural and policy-induced barriers to intercountry mobility. The high rate of factor mobility within a national economy carries an important implication: Because factors tend to flow out of the low-productivity regions within an economy, reduced wages or returns to capital can't offset low factor productivity.

---

21 Sometimes, however, economic considerations help explain changes in national boundaries; see, for example, Beth V. Yarbrough and Robert M. Yarbrough, "International Contracting and Territorial Control" and "Unification and Secession" in the chapter references.

22 Jacob Viner, writing in 1937, emphasized the role of factor immobility in distinguishing international trade.

Consider a simple example in which labor is the only input. There are two geographical areas, A and B. First, assume that A and B represent countries, between which labor can't move. Labor in country A is more productive than labor in country B. This results in a situation identical to Chapter Two's Ricardian model. B's relatively unproductive labor still can compete with country A's more productive labor, at least in some goods, by accepting lower wages that reflect the lower productivity.[23] This is just comparative advantage again. Even if B's labor is less productive than A's in every industry, B still can export those goods in which B's labor is *relatively* productive.

Now, introduce one change. Areas A and B now represent regions within a single country, so labor can move easily between the two. But labor in A remains more productive than labor in B. A wage differential no longer will allow area B to produce and export goods to area A, because labor will flow from B to A in response to A's higher wages. Factors migrate from the low-productivity to the high-productivity area, instead of remaining in the low-productivity area and accepting a lower wage. This mobility improves efficiency because the labor moves to the area where it can be more productive, but less productive regions are abandoned.

Of course, factors of production are neither perfectly immobile between countries nor perfectly mobile within countries. Given a pattern of productivity differences across two geographic areas, the higher the factor mobility between the two, the more equal the wages and the more unequally dispersed the population. The lower the degree of factor mobility, the bigger the wage differential and the more equally dispersed the population.

9.5.2 The Role of Economic Policy

The majority of government policies with greatest relevance for trade are defined at the national level. U.S. imports pay the same tariff whether they land at New York or Seattle. Occasionally, however, governments show their ambivalent feelings toward trade by applying different trade rules in different regions of a country. Such policies are used most often by policy makers with histories of relatively closed, inward-looking economic policies who recognize the need to allow more trade to improve economic performance but are hesitant to give up the control that closed borders imply.

The most common forms of subnational trade policy are special economic zones or export-processing zones. **Special economic zones (SEZs)** typically allow more generous rules for trade and for inward foreign direct investment than apply in the rest of the country. The goal is to encourage such investment, which brings access to foreign technology, manufacturing expertise, and knowledge of world export markets. Foreign firms that invest in such zones may receive exemption from certain taxes or minimum wage laws, as well as reduced site-rental charges, help with infrastructure, and other inducements. **Export-processing zones** concentrate on attracting firms that assemble products for export. These zones provide low-cost infrastructure such as port facilities, power supplies, and rail connections. Tariff exemptions, particularly on imported inputs, also play an important role.

Some of the most dramatic examples of special economic zones come from China, where they enjoy considerably more administrative autonomy than other areas and have been encouraged by the central government to serve as laboratories for economic and social policy experiments, including investment not covered by the country's central economic plan.[24] The Chinese SEZs are particularly interesting because they link particular provinces of China with more open nearby economies such as Taiwan. Fujian and Guangdong provinces, on China's south coast, received designation as experimental reform regions in 1978, when China first began opening up to the world economy. Since, the Chinese government has created several additional zones; their economic success, along with their rapidly rising incomes, has created popular pressure to allow the trade reforms to spread to the rest of the economy. Widespread smuggling also constrains the central government's ability to maintain divergent policies in different areas.

The most successful zone is the Greater South China Economic Region, which encompasses Guangdong and Fujian provinces, Hong Kong (now part of China), and Taiwan. Businesses in the zone combine China's cheap labor and land with Hong Kong's marketing links and transportation network, and with Taiwan's capital, manufacturing technology, and management skills. Shoes and toys comprise large shares of production in

---

23 On the role of wage differentials in Ricardian comparative advantage, see sections 2.5.3 and 2.6.3.

24 On China's SEZs, see World Bank, *China: Foreign Trade Reform* (Washington, D.C.: World Bank, 1994), pp. 221–251.

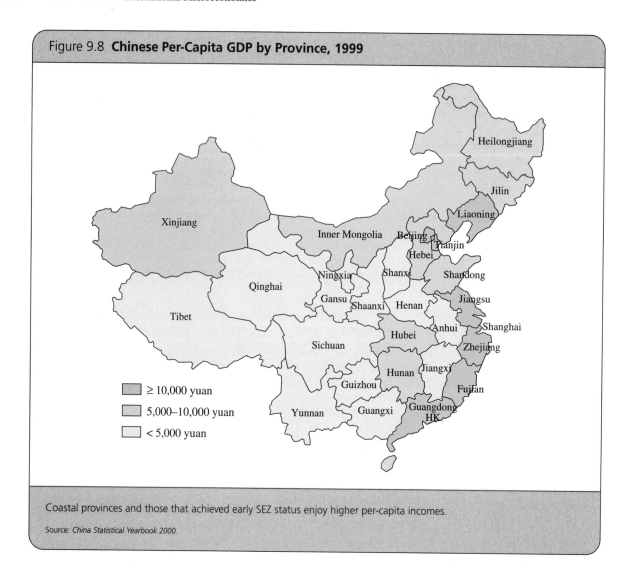

Figure 9.8 **Chinese Per-Capita GDP by Province, 1999**

Coastal provinces and those that achieved early SEZ status enjoy higher per-capita incomes.

Source: *China Statistical Yearbook 2000.*

the region. The income consequences of the zones are apparent in the map in Figure 9.8. In 1999, as part of a package designed to lure investment funds to the economically lagging interior, China announced that every province would be allowed an economic and technological development zone.

Latin American and other Asian economies also created many special economic zones and export-processing zones during the 1980s. The zones played an important role in demonstrating the potential of open international trade to raise incomes and allow developing economies to move into manufacturing. As we mentioned in the case of China, the success of open regions within the economy typically creates political pressure for national policy reform. As many developing and transitional countries open their economies to international trade, the significance of their special zones declines. For example, the liberalization of Mexico's trade policy and the provisions of the NAFTA reduce the special role for the *maquiladora* program. Even some of the world's very closed economies, including North Korea and Iran, use special economic zones to try to capture some of the benefits of openness without allowing foreign political ideas and culture to reach their populations.[25]

---

25 On North Korea, see Case One in Chapter Three. On Iran, see "Iran's Little Welcome Mats," *The Economist,* October 17, 1998, 51.

CASE ONE:
NAFTA Traffic Jams

Before the NAFTA agreement, U.S. trucks could go only 20 miles into Mexico and Mexican trucks only 20 miles into the United States. Products destined for points farther away had to be reloaded onto domestic trucks for the rest of the trip. NAFTA was supposed to change all that. By late 1995, trucks from both countries would have access to all the border states: four in the United States (California, Arizona, New Mexico, and Texas) and six in Mexico. State and federal transportation and law enforcement officials of both countries spent a lot of time preparing for the change, especially ensuring that Mexican trucks could meet U.S. safety and insurance regulations and that those regulations would be enforced. After five years under the border-state system, all limits on access to international traffic would end in 2000.

Just two weeks before the scheduled 1995 implementation, the U.S. Teamsters Union (with 1.5 million members) cited safety concerns and unfair competition from Mexico's lower-paid truckers and pressured the United States to renege, which it did. Mexico claimed that the United States violated the NAFTA agreement. The four U.S. border-state governors reaffirmed their states' ability to conduct the necessary safety inspections and patrols, since they had already hired extra officers and built extra inspection stations. Mexican truckers repeatedly blockaded busy border crossings in Laredo, Brownsville, and McAllen, Texas, in protest. Finally Mexico filed a case under NAFTA's dispute-resolution provisions. In early 2001, a five-member binational panel ruled in Mexico's favor, but not before the Clinton administration had succeeded in stalling the issue past the 2000 U.S. presidential election, in hopes of winning Teamster Union support for candidate Al Gore. The new Bush administration expressed its intention to comply with the NAFTA ruling, allowing in Mexican trucks that passed U.S. safety inspections; but a year later, political pressure from the Teamsters still stymied the plan.

Mexico hasn't been alone in its frustration with trucks and NAFTA. Mexico had promised permission for U.S. firms to drive larger (53-foot) trailers in Mexico than previously permitted. In particular, Mexico promised national treatment (that is, treatment equivalent to that granted Mexican trucks) to U.S. parcel-delivery companies such as United Parcel Service. U.S. firms claimed that they were restricted to smaller mini-bus trucks, which raised their costs and forced them to transfer large shipments to Mexican firms. Mexico claimed that the larger tractor-trailer trucks were permissible only for "freight," not for "small parcels." In 1995, UPS responded to the truck-size restriction and to time-consuming Mexican border inspections (in which inspectors opened *every* box—even if many were identical) by halting its U.S.–Mexico ground service, although it continued air service and ground delivery within Mexico. The United States filed a dispute-settlement case under NAFTA, the first case to claim that Mexico treated a U.S. firm unfairly.

In addition to these "one-sided" issues, both Americans and Mexicans are frustrated with border delays at major U.S.–Mexico border crossings, especially Laredo, Texas. It often takes 12 hours for a truck to cross the Rio Grande on the way from Detroit or Chicago to Mexico City or vice versa. Few rail lines cross the border, so most goods (around 85 percent) must move by truck. And NAFTA's very success in boosting North–South trade in North America has strained the border's ability to cope with so many trucks. The Laredo crossing, built to handle about 750 trucks per day, now sees about 4,000, carrying an average of $65 million worth of goods every day. As Table 9.2 reports, rail and air transport also shows dramatic increases between pre-NAFTA 1990 and post-NAFTA 1996.

Table 9.2 **Monthly Laredo, Texas, Border Traffic, Pre- and Post-NAFTA**

Traffic Type	July 1990	July 1996
Tractor-trailer trucks	28,000	88,000
Rail cars	5,100	11,700
Air cargoes	630	2,800

Source: Data from U.S. Customs Service.

CASE TWO:
I.D. Cards for Avocados

NAFTA implementation hasn't meant an end to trade disputes among the member countries, but post-NAFTA talks did end an 81-year-old trade fight between the United States and Mexico. U.S. officials detected avocado-seed weevils in Mexican-grown avocados in 1914 and banned them (the avocados, along with the weevils) to avoid pest infestation of the U.S. crop. During the 1970s, Mexico repeatedly requested an end to the quarantine, but U.S. officials continued to report finding weevils, both in growing areas of the Mexican state of Michoacan and in illegal fruit confiscated at border crossings.

After investing heavily to improve its production, packing, and shipping processes and pest control, Mexico tried again in the 1990s to end the U.S. avocado quarantine. A tiny victory came in 1993 when the U.S. altered rules to allow imported Hass avocados into Alaska—a state that while geographically very large isn't famous as a major guacamole consumer.

With the advent of NAFTA, U.S. non-avocado agricultural interests began to fear that if the U.S. avocado quarantine stayed in place, Mexico might respond with standards to keep out U.S. wheat or fruit. Finally in 1997, after several scientific studies of the alleged risks and several rounds of public hearings, the U.S. Department of Agriculture approved imports of Mexican avocados from specifically approved groves in Michoacan, but only from November through February each year, only into 19 northeastern U.S. states plus the District of Columbia, only under an elaborate system of multilayered anti-weevil safeguards, and subject to a quota of 12,000 tons. Avocados shipped to the permitted northeastern states must be sent in sealed containers. Each individual avocado must have its own "sticker of origin." States that still quarantine Mexican avocados watch out for the stickers, which would indicate illegal avocado trade.

How does the ban affect avocado prices? Fruit that sell in Mexican supermarkets for $0.30 per pound sell for $4.00 a pound just three miles north, across the Mexico–California border.[26] The quarantine on fresh avocados also generates some other interesting trade effects; for example, if you eat guacamole in a restaurant chain or buy it in a grocery store, chances are it was made in Mexico. "For discount chains like Taco Bell, Simplot [the Mexican producer] prepares a squirtable avocado paste used as a condiment. For Chili's and TGIF, chains targeting more affluent diners, Simplot ships a watery mash, into which kitchen workers add avocado chunks to give the guacamole more of a made-on-site look. Diners shouldn't be fooled, though. Simplot also provides the chunks—which are frozen at the same facility that makes the paste."[27]

CASE THREE:
Life before NAFTA

The North American Free Trade Agreement didn't mark the beginning of special trade relations between the United States and Mexico. For 30 years, firms have located in the Mexican border region to service the U.S. market. The pre-NAFTA arrangements reflected special provisions of both U.S. and Mexican tax and tariff law. Mexican tax law allowed tariff-free entry for any imported inputs that would be assembled and then reexported. And section HTS 9902.00.80 of the U.S. Harmonized Tariff Schedule allowed tariff-free re-imports into the United States of U.S.-manufactured parts and products not "transformed" in Mexico. In other words, U.S.-made components could be assembled in Mexico and the final product exported to the United States, with U.S. tariffs due only on Mexican value-added, not on the value of the original components.[28]

The restrictions to products not "transformed" in Mexico limited the program to assembly-type tasks performed by Mexico's abundant low-skilled and semi-skilled workers

---

26 "Bitter Fruit: Spats Persist Despite NAFTA," *The Wall Street Journal,* June 19, 2000.

27 "That Order of Guacamole Was Probably Mashed Up South of the U.S. Border," *The Wall Street Journal,* January 19, 2000.

28 See section 6.9 on offshore-assembly provisions.

Figure 9.9 *Maquiladora* **Establishments, 1996**

The *maquiladora* region along the southern side of the U.S.–Mexican border is a major center of electronics assembly operations.

rather than imports of raw materials manufactured into their final form in Mexico. The Mexican program, which gave the border region its *maquiladora* name (after the share of flour a miller gets in return for milling grain), allowed components and raw materials from anywhere in the world into Mexico tariff-free, to be held in bonded warehouses until processed by a manufacturer. The finished product could then be reexported, with only the Mexican value-added portion subject to Mexican taxes. Figure 9.9 locates key *maquiladora* centers along with some of the major firms in each. The largest *maquiladora* employers by industry are electronics, transportation equipment, and apparel, which is the fastest-growing as NAFTA liberalizes apparel trade within North America.

The *maquiladora* program's goal was to help Mexico industrialize by encouraging foreign companies to locate there and train manufacturing workers. The original program limited the special provisions to a narrow band along the Mexican border. The program's own success led to over-crowding, strain on the local infrastructure, and environmental problems as so many firms located in the region. The NAFTA program, by eventually extending tariff-free trade to all areas, should alleviate some of these problems by allowing assembly for the U.S. and Canadian markets to occur anywhere in Mexico. By 1996, the share of *maquiladora* plants located in the Mexican border states (Baja California, Coahuila, Chihuahua, Nueva Leon, Sonora, and Tamaulipas) had dropped from 100 percent to 86 percent, even though the NAFTA provisions for tariff-free assembly in southern states were still being phased in (see Table 9.3). One of the fastest-growing nonborder areas is Aguascalientes, north-west of Mexico City and about 500 miles from the U.S. border. By 1998, the area boasted major investments by U.S. and Japanese firms in autos, semiconductors and other electronics, copiers, and auto parts.

NAFTA also will gradually lift previous restrictions on sale of *maquiladoras'* products in Mexico. Since NAFTA reduces the special character of *maquiladoras* by liberalizing trade

Table 9.3 **Location of *Maquiladoras,* 1996**

Mexican State	Number of Maquiladoras	Number of Employees
Aguascalientes	49	11,781
Baja California	793	159,519
Baja California Sur	7	1,936
Coahuila	212	62,984
Chihuahua	371	215,423
Durange	79	20,677
Guanajuato	40	8,868
Jalisco	59	13,725
Edo de Mexico YDF	55	8,851
Nuevo Leon	99	32,032
Puebla	34	12,046
Sonora	192	58,886
Tamaulipas	307	122,500
Yucatan	41	8,031
All others	73	17,599
Total, frontier states	1,974	651,344
Total, all states	2,411	754,858

Source: Data from John E. Cremeans, ed., *Handbook of North American Industry: NAFTA and the Economies of Its Member Nations* (Lanham, MD: Bernan Press, 1998), p. 30.

on a broader basis, we would expect *maquiladoras* to grow more slowly relative to other U.S.–Mexico trade after NAFTA implementation than before. *Maquiladoras'* share of manufactured exports did fall from 42 percent in 1993 to 38 percent in 1996.

Other changes are also affecting the program. Beginning in late 2000, imported inputs' duty-free entry into Mexico became contingent on North American origin. In other words, inputs from the United States and Canada still get in duty-free, but inputs from Asia no longer do. The impact of the new rules should be modest for most firms, however, for three reasons. First, the North American content for most *maquiladora*-assembled products is already very high, so most inputs will maintain their duty-free status. Second, Mexico continues to sign free-trade agreements with other countries and groups of countries, including the European Union, so inputs from those areas also maintain their duty-free access to Mexican assembly plants. Finally, input suppliers always have the option of moving their production to Mexico, to be near their assembly plants.

Summary

Within each economy, a complex political bargaining process determines national trade policy. The history of international trade relations chronicles the interaction of nations' political and economic self-interests. Despite the dominance of nations in the world economy, political boundaries remain somewhat arbitrary from the standpoint of organization of economic activities. This has resulted in the evolution of economic institutions, such as economic integration groups, that extend beyond the boundaries of a single nation.

Looking Ahead

In Chapter Ten, we relax the assumption that each country contains a fixed quantity of capital and labor to be allocated among industries. We examine the implications of economic growth, international labor migration, and capital flows. Free movement of factors of production generates distributional effects similar to those of free movement of goods and services. These distributional consequences create pressures for policies that restrict the international mobility of both capital and labor.

Key Terms

Section 201
mercantilism
Smoot-Hawley tariff bill of 1930
Reciprocal Trade Agreements Act (RTAA)
International Monetary Fund (IMF)
World Bank
General Agreement on Tariffs and
    Trade (GATT)
World Trade Organization (WTO)
escape clause
safeguards
Multifiber Agreement (MFA)
Trade Adjustment Assistance
codes

Uruguay Round
fast track (trade promotion authority)
integration
preferential trading arrangement (PTA)
free-trade area
customs union
common external tariff (CET)
common market
economic union
trade diversion
trade creation
special economic zone (SEZ)
export-processing zone

Problems and Questions for Review

1. We have seen that trade policy has predictable distributional effects. In particular, protection of a domestic industry tends to help domestic producers in that industry at the expense of domestic consumers. In almost any industry, the number of consumers outweighs the number of producers; and we know that the loss in consumer surplus as a result of protection outweighs the gain in producer surplus. How, then, can we explain the success of domestic producers in winning protection through the political process?

2. What is fast-track (or trade-promotion) authority? Using the political economy of trade policy argument, why might such authority be important to the process of trade liberalization?

3. Country A exports $500 worth of components to country B, where workers assemble the components into a finished product, the world price of which is $1,000. Country B exports the finished good to country A.
    a. If country A imposes a 5 percent ad valorem tariff on imports and country B imposes a 10 percent ad valorem tariff on imports, how much tariff will be paid at each stage of the transaction?
    b. If the two countries have special tariff provisions that allow (1) components intended for assembly and re-export and (2) the component-re-export share of finished goods to enter tariff-free, how much tariff will be paid at each stage of the transaction?

4. Country A is a small country considering joining a free-trade area for trade in good X. The cost of importing a unit of good X from countries that would *not* be members of the potential group is $10 per unit. The cost of importing a unit of good X from countries that would be members of the potential group is $20 per unit. Currently, country A applies a $5-per-unit tariff on imports of good X from all sources. If the free-trade group forms, will there be any trade creation? Any trade diversion? Why?

5. Use the illustration of trade creation and trade diversion in Figure 9.4. Under what conditions is trade creation likely to outweigh trade diversion? Under what conditions is trade diversion likely to outweigh trade creation?

6. Country A is a small country considering joining a free-trade area for trade in good X. The cost of importing a unit of good X from countries that would *not* be members of the potential group is $10 per unit. The cost of importing a unit of good X from countries that would be members of the potential group is $20 per unit. Currently, country A applies a $10-per-unit tariff on imports of good X from all sources. If the free-trade group forms, will there be any trade creation? Any trade diversion? Why?

7. Suppose a labor-abundant economy that does *not* engage in international trade creates a special economic zone with free trade with the rest of the world. If labor were immobile geographically within the country, what would you expect to happen? If labor were mobile geographically within the country, what would you expect to happen? Why?

8. Consider two trends in the post–World War II world economy: (a) The number of independent countries rose from 74 in 1946 to 192 in 1995, and (b) barriers to international trade fell dramatically. How does the theory of international trade suggest these two trends might be related?

References and Selected Readings

Alesina, Alberto, and Enrico Spolaore. "On the Number and Size of Nations." *Quarterly Journal of Economics* (November 1997): 1027–1056.
The economics of national boundaries; intermediate.

Alesina, Alberto, et al. "Economic Integration and Political Disintegration." *American Economic Review* (December 2000): 1276–1296.
Argues that open trade policies allow countries to be geographically smaller.

Baldwin, Richard E., and T. Venables. "Regional Economic Integration." In *Handbook of International Economics,* Vol. 3, edited by G. M. Grossman and K. Rogoff, 1597–1644. Amsterdam: North-Holland, 1995.
Advanced survey of the literature on the causes and implications of regional trade groups.

Baldwin, Robert E. "The Political Economy of Trade Policy." *Journal of Economic Perspectives* (Fall 1989): 119–136.
More on political economy explanations for protection; for all students.

Bhagwati, Jagdish, et al., eds. *Trading Blocs.* Cambridge, Mass.: MIT Press, 1999.
Collection of papers on the effects of regionalism.

Destler, I. M. *American Trade Politics.* Washington, D.C.: Institute for International Economics, 1995.
A political scientist's analysis of American institutions that make trade policy and how their evolution has affected policy outcomes; for all students.

Feenstra, Robert C. "Estimating the Effects of Trade Policy." In *Handbook of International Economics,* Vol. 3, edited by G. M. Grossman and K. Rogoff, 1553–1596. Amsterdam: North-Holland, 1995.
Advanced survey of the empirical literature on the economic effects of various trade policies.

Fieleke, Norman S. "The Uruguay Round of Trade Negotiations: An Overview." Federal Reserve Bank of Boston, *New England Economic Review* (May–June 1995): 3–14.
Accessible overview of the main accomplishments of the Uruguay Round.

Folsom, Ralph H., et al. *NAFTA: A Problem-Oriented Coursebook.* St. Paul, Minn.: West Group, 2000.
Everything you could ever want to know about the nitty-gritty of NAFTA rules.

Grossman, Gene M., and Elhanan Helpman. *Special Interest Politics.* Cambridge, Mass.: MIT Press, 2001.
Theoretical models of how special-interest groups affect the political process through voting and financial contributions; intermediate and advanced.

Hufbauer, Gary Clyde, and Jeffrey J. Schott. *NAFTA: An Assessment.* Washington, D.C.: Institute for International Economics, 1993.
Issue-by-issue assessment of NAFTA; for all students.

Hufbauer, Gary Clyde, and Jeffrey J. Schott. *Western Hemisphere Economic Integration.* Washington, D.C.: Institute for International Economics, 1994.
Prospects for extending NAFTA-like agreements to other countries; for all students.

Irwin, Douglas A. "The GATT in Historical Perspective." *American Economic Review Papers and Proceedings* 85 (May 1995): 323–328.
Excellent short article on the role of the GATT in trade liberalization.

Jackson, John H. "The Role and Effectiveness of the WTO Dispute Settlement Mechanism." *Brookings Trade Forum* (2000): 179–236.
Assessment of one of the Uruguay Round's chief accomplishments.

Jackson, John H. *The World Trading System.* Cambridge, Mass.: MIT Press, 1997.
Introduction to the history and structure of the GATT by a leading legal scholar of that institution.

Krueger, Anne O. "Are Preferential Trading Arrangements Trade-Liberalizing or Protectionist?" *Journal of Economic Perspectives* 13 (Fall 1999): 85–104.
Balanced assessment of PTAs' potential effects by one of the strongest proponents of open international trade.

Krugman, Paul. "Growing World Trade: Causes and Consequences." *Brookings Papers on Economic Activity* 1 (1995): 327–377.
Essay on recent trends in world trade; intermediate.

Lawrence, Robert Z. *Regionalism, Multilateralism, and Deeper Integration.* Washington, D.C.: Brookings, 1996.
Relative abilities of regional and multilateral institutions to handle nonborder trade issues; for all students.

Lipsey, Richard. "The Theory of Customs Unions: A General Survey." *Economic Journal* 70 (1960): 496–513.
A survey of the classic papers that developed the theory of customs unions; for intermediate students.

Magee, Stephen P., William A. Brock, and Leslie Young. *Black Hole Tariffs and Endogenous Policy Theory.* Cambridge: Cambridge University Press, 1989.
A recent classic on the political economy of protection; for intermediate and advanced students.

Mansfield, Edward D., and Helen V. Milner. *The Political Economy of Regionalism.* New York: Columbia University Press, 1997.
Collection of papers on various aspects of PTAs; for all students.

Panagariya, Arvind. "Preferential Trade Liberalization: The Traditional Theory and New Developments." *Journal of Economic Literature* 38 (June 2000): 287–331.
Intermediate-level survey of the implications of PTAs.

Rodrik, Dani. "Political Economy of Trade Policy." In *Handbook of International Economics,* Vol. 3, edited by G. M. Grossman and K. Rogoff, 1457–1494. Amsterdam: North-Holland, 1995.
Advanced survey of the literature on distributional aspects of trade policy and their implications for the policy process.

Schott, Jeffrey J. *The Uruguay Round: An Assessment.* Washington, D.C.: Institute for International Economics, 1994.
Issue-by-issue assessment of the round's accomplishments and shortcomings; for all students.

Schott, Jeffrey J., ed. *The WTO after Seattle.* Washington, D.C.: Institute for International Economics, 2000.
Implications of the Seattle protests for trade liberalization.

Special Issue on "Multilateral Trade Negotiations: Issues for the Millennium Round." Federal Reserve Bank of St. Louis *Review* 82 (July/August 2000).
Accessible survey of issues likely to play important roles in the next round of WTO negotiations.

Spruyt, Hendrik. *The Sovereign State and Its Competitors.* Princeton: Princeton University Press, 1994.
Political scientist's analysis of the development of the modern territorial nation-state; for all students.

Staiger, Robert. "International Rules and Institutions for Cooperative Trade Policy." In *Handbook of International Economics,* Vol. 3, edited by G. M. Grossman and K. Rogoff, 1495–1552. Amsterdam: North-Holland, 1995.
Advanced survey of the literature on how rules and institutions at the international level affect international trade policies.

Symposium on "The North American Economy." *Journal of Economic Perspectives* 15 (Winter 2001): 81–144.
NAFTA's effects on its members' economies.

United States International Trade Commission. *The Year in Trade.* Washington, D.C.: USITC, annual.
Accessible source of recent developments in the WTO and PTAs; available on CD-ROM.

Westhoff, Frank H., Beth V. Yarbrough, and Robert M. Yarbrough. "Preferential Trade Agreements and the GATT: Can Bilateralism and Multilateralism Coexist?" *Kyklos* 47 (1994): 179–195.
Interaction of bilateral and multilateral trade-liberalization agreements; intermediate.

Yarbrough, Beth V. "Preferential Trade Arrangements and the GATT: EC 1992 as Rogue or Role Model?" In *The Challenge of European Integration,* edited by Berhanu Abegaz et al., 79–117. Boulder, Colo.: Westview Press, 1994.
Overview of the effects of preferential trade agreements on the world trading system; for all students.

Yarbrough, Beth V., and Robert M. Yarbrough. *Cooperation and Governance in International Trade: The Strategic Organizational Approach.* Princeton: Princeton University Press, 1992.
An analysis of bilateralism, minilateralism, and multilateralism in trade policy; for all students.

Yarbrough, Beth V., and Robert M. Yarbrough. "International Contracting and Territorial Control: The Boundary Question." *Journal of Institutional and Theoretical Economics* 150 (March 1994): 239–264.
Examines the role of economics in disputes over national boundaries; for all students.

Yarbrough, Beth V., and Robert M. Yarbrough. "Unification and Secession: Group Size and 'Escape from Lock-In,'" *Kyklos* (1998): 171–195.
The economics of national unifications and secessions; intermediate.

CHAPTER TEN

Growth, Immigration, and Multinationals

10.1 Introduction

Chapters Two through Nine examined international trade's effects on production, consumption, output and input prices, and the distribution of income under the assumptions of fixed factor endowments and fixed technology. In terms of the schematic diagram in Figure 4.9, factor endowments and technology, along with tastes, form the "fixed" foundation on which our basic trade model rests. These assumptions seem appropriate for many countries and time periods in which endowments and technology, while not really constant, change only slowly. For other periods and countries, however, changes in endowments and technology lie at the very heart of events. Many examples come to mind: the Industrial Revolution in late eighteenth-century Britain, the massive European immigration to America during the nineteenth century, the worldwide spread of multinational corporations since World War II, the increased pace of foreign investment in the United States in the 1980s, and recent immigration waves to the United States and Western Europe.

Trade represents just one type of international interaction in which countries find it beneficial to engage. We've seen, for example, that a labor-abundant country can exploit its comparative advantage by specializing in and exporting labor-intensive goods. However, such a country might also borrow abroad to increase its capital stock or allow workers to emigrate. If the country is too small for domestic firms to achieve economies of scale, policies that permit inward and outward foreign direct investment might allow both domestic and foreign firms to produce at large enough scale to achieve gains from trade based on scale economies. In other words, *factor flows between countries represent another way countries can use economic interaction to benefit from their differences.*

In this chapter, we extend our basic trade model to consider issues related to economic growth and factor mobility. Thus far, we've viewed trade only in static terms—that is, comparing a country's situation under unrestricted trade with its situation at the same time and in the same circumstances but without trade. When we introduce dynamic considerations such as economic growth, the basic characteristics of the world economy, including the pattern of comparative advantage, can change over time.[1] These changes can dramatically alter the pattern of trade and governments' policies toward trade. For example, Britain, which came to dominate the world textile industry through the technological advances of the Industrial Revolution, lost that industry to the United States because of changing patterns of comparative advantage. The United States, in turn, lost the tex-

---

1 Our analysis of economic growth actually provides an example of comparative-static rather than dynamic analysis. Comparative-static analysis compares the pre-growth and post-growth equilibria in the economy. A dynamic analysis also would examine the path along which the economy moves from the old equilibrium to the new one. Dynamic analysis lies beyond the scope of this book.

tile industry to the labor-abundant countries of Asia. In fact, many U.S. industries now asking for protection from the rigors of foreign competition once were industries of U.S. comparative advantage—not just textiles, but steel, automobiles, televisions, and semiconductor chips.

During the past few years the study of economic growth has become, literally, a growth industry within economics. To keep the scope of the discussion manageable, we'll limit our attention to the relationship between economic growth and international trade. Economic growth is a complex phenomenon, particularly when viewed as an objective of economic policy making. The debate among economists and policy makers over what types of policies promote economic growth has been long and lively, going back to Adam Smith and the founding of economics as a field of study. In this chapter, our perspective differs from that of a policy maker interested in promoting economic growth. We are interested primarily in the *effects* of growth rather than how to bring it about. In Chapter Eleven, we'll examine the pursuit of growth from the viewpoint of developing countries.

For our purposes, we can define **economic growth** simply as a shift outward of a country's production possibilities frontier. Any change that allows the economy to produce a larger quantity of goods (that is, more of one good and no less of any other) represents economic growth. Recall from the discussion of production possibilities frontiers in Chapters Two and Three that the position of a country's frontier depends on the endowment of resources and on the technology with which the country can transform those resources into goods. The major sources of economic growth, then, are (1) increases in the quantities of resources available to the country and (2) technical progress, or improvements in available production technology. Empirical evidence suggests that increases in resources have accounted for somewhat less than half of economic growth in the modern period, and technical progress for somewhat more than half.[2]

Early economic growth theories focused on increases in stocks of labor and capital, but more recent work emphasizes the role of knowledge and education in the technical progress that generates ongoing economic growth.[3] Called **endogenous growth theory,** these new approaches to growth recognize knowledge or ideas as an input, along with capital and labor, in an economy's ability to produce goods and services. An economy produces knowledge by investing in education and research, which requires forgoing current consumption, just as investing in physical capital does. Unfortunately, economists' understanding of the growth process, especially the role of knowledge creation, still has a long way to go. Growth rates among countries differ dramatically (see Figure 10.1) for reasons not fully understood, although most economists agree that governments' different policy choices play a major role in explaining countries' differential growth experiences.

As noted in Chapters One and Nine, the assumption that factors of production move much more freely within than among countries seems realistic. Although a significant amount of inter-country factor movement does occur, it remains small relative to intra-country movement for two basic reasons. First, most governments maintain some restrictions on flows of both capital and labor across their national boundaries. The United States, for example, restricts immigration of labor, and Mexico imposes limits on foreign-owned production facilities in some industries. Second, even without such government restrictions, the differences in costs involved in inter-country versus intra-country mobility would produce a differential rate of movement. In the case of labor, some of the additional costs of inter-country mobility include the costs—both financial and psychological—of overcoming language and cultural barriers. In the case of capital, additional costs take the form of risks associated with owning capital in a foreign country, such as the risk of expropriation or of unfavorable changes in the value of the foreign country's currency. The important point is that, as long as political boundaries continue to have economic significance, inter-country mobility will remain less than intra-country mobility.

Factor mobility among countries raises issues similar to those surrounding economic growth. In fact, we can view factor mobility as simultaneous positive growth in one country (the country of immigration, or host) and negative growth in another (the country of emigration, or source). Because factor mobility raises additional distributional issues, we'll separate the discussions of growth (sections 10.2 and 10.3) and factor mobility (section 10.4), despite the close relationship between the two.

---

2 Case One provides more information on this issue.

3 The key citations are Robert M. Solow, "A Contribution to the Theory of Economic Growth," *Quarterly Journal of Economics* 70 (1956), pp. 65–94; and Paul M. Romer, "Endogenous Technological Change," *Journal of Political Economy* 98 (1990), pp. S71–S102, respectively.

Figure 10.1 **Growth Rates for 114 Countries, 1960–1985**

Percentage Growth Rate of Per-Capita GDP
(Annual Rate, Compounded Continuously)

Dollar Level of Per-Capita GNP in 1960
(Measured in 1980 International Prices)

Source: Gene M. Grossman and Elhanan Helpman, *Innovation and Growth in the Global Economy* (Cambridge, Mass.: MIT Press, 1991), p. 3; data from Robert Summers and Alan Heston, "A New Set of International Comparisons of Real Product and Price Levels: Estimates of 130 Countries," *The Review of Income and Wealth* 34 (1988), pp. 1–25.

10.2 **Economic Growth I: More Inputs**

Economists classify economic growth resulting from increased factor endowments according to the relative changes in the endowments of capital and labor. A country's labor endowment can grow in three ways. First, the population can grow because of an increase in the birth rate relative to the death rate. Second, immigration can lead to population changes (see section 10.4.1). Third, available labor can increase due to a rise in *labor-force participation,* or the working portion of the population. A country's capital stock is its accumulation of durable factors of production such as machines and buildings. Capital accumulates whenever residents choose to consume less than the total amount of current production, setting a portion of output aside for increasing future productive capacity.

Figure 10.2 **What Are the Effects of Balanced Growth?**

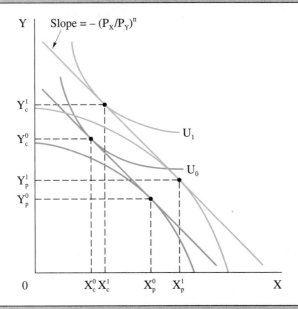

Balanced growth increases production and consumption of each good, imports, exports, and the volume of trade in the same proportion as the factor endowments. The country superscript is omitted for simplicity. Subscript p refers to production, c to consumption, 0 to pre-growth, and 1 to post-growth.

10.2.1 **More Labor *and* Capital**

Economists refer to a proportional increase in a country's endowments of both capital and labor as **balanced growth.** Such growth generates an outward shift of the production possibilities frontier that maintains the frontier's original shape, as Figure 10.2 illustrates. The country in the figure is small in the sense that it can't alter the international terms of trade. When both goods exhibit constant returns to scale, balanced growth shifts the production possibilities frontier outward in the same proportion as the increase in the factor endowments, because constant-returns-to-scale production means that output increases proportionally with a proportional increase in all inputs. For example, after a doubling of the endowments, the new frontier intersects both axes at points twice as far from the origin as the original frontier. Balanced growth increases production of both goods, consumption of both goods, imports, and exports proportionally with the endowments.

How does balanced growth affect welfare, both of the growing country and of its trading partners? First, what about the growing country itself? It's tempting to answer quickly that welfare increases—based on the rise in consumption of both goods. Such a reply, however, would ignore the fact that the country's population also may have increased. *Total* consumption of both goods has risen, but that bigger total may be spread across a larger population. If the increased availability of labor that led to growth was due to an increase in population, then *per-capita* consumption (that is, total consumption divided by population) wouldn't change. *(Why?)* But if the increased availability of labor resulted from increased labor-force participation, then per-capita consumption would rise. Individuals who previously had consumed but not produced (labor-force nonparticipants) now would produce as well as consume, allowing per-capita consumption to rise. Economists call growth's effect on per-capita consumption at unchanged terms of trade the **income effect** of growth. The income effect of balanced growth equals zero if labor growth comes from population growth but is positive if labor growth comes from increased labor-force participation. For a small country, the income effect captures growth's entire impact

Table 10.1 **How Does Balanced Growth Affect Welfare?**		
	Small-Country Case	**Large-Country Case**
Effect on growing economy:		
Income effect	0 (if population ⇑); + (if labor force ⇑)	0 (if population ⇑); + (if labor force ⇑)
Terms-of-trade effect	0	−
Change in export price	0	⇓
Change in import price	0	⇑
Net effect on per-capita consumption	0 (if population ⇑); + (if labor force ⇑)	Depends on magnitudes of income and terms-of-trade effects
Effect on trading partner:		
Income effect	0	0
Terms-of-trade effect	0	+
Change in export price	0	⇑
Change in import price	0	⇓
Net effect on per-capita consumption	0	+

because the country can't, by definition, change its terms of trade. So the overall effect of balanced growth in a small country can be zero (if due to population growth) or positive (if due to increased labor-force participation), as summarized in Table 10.1's first two columns.

What about growth's effects on the growing country's trading partners? They experience no income effect because growth abroad doesn't shift their production possibilities frontiers. They also experience no terms-of-trade effect since the growing country is too small to generate any. Therefore, balanced growth in a small country leaves the country's trading partners unaffected.

For a country large enough to affect the international terms of trade, the income effect is only one of two components of growth's effect on welfare. The second component, the **terms-of-trade effect,** captures the effect of changes in relative output prices. A country's terms of trade just equal the price of its export good(s) relative to the price of its import good(s). If country A exports X and imports Y, its terms of trade are $(P_X/P_Y)^{tt}$. Decreases in this ratio represent deterioration in the terms of trade, while increases represent improvement. If country B exports Y and imports X, its terms of trade are $(P_Y/P_X)^{tt}$, or the reciprocal of A's terms of trade. Deterioration in a country's terms of trade reduces its total consumption, because the country receives fewer units of its import good in exchange for each unit of its export good. Balanced growth causes a country to want to engage in a larger volume of trade at the original terms of trade, so the relative price of the country's import good rises (because of increased demand) and that of its export good falls (because of increased supply). This change in relative prices represents a deterioration in the terms of trade from the growing country's perspective and an improvement from the perspective of the trading partner. Note this implies that balanced growth in a large country improves the trading partner's welfare: The trading partner experiences no income effect and a positive terms-of-trade effect.

Figure 10.3 shows the effects of a deterioration in the growing country's terms of trade. At constant terms of trade, given by $(P_X/P_Y)^{tt}_0$, balanced growth would move the country from U_0 to U_1. Remember that the increase in total consumption doesn't necessarily translate into an increase in per-capita consumption, because U_0 and U_1 may be drawn for different population sizes. For a large country, balanced growth increases the desired volume of trade at the original terms of trade and causes the terms of trade to deteriorate to $(P_X/P_Y)^{tt}_1$. This terms-of-trade effect moves the country to U_2. Thus, the welfare effects of balanced growth are less encouraging for a large country than for a small one. The net effect of balanced growth on per-capita consumption in a large country depends on (1) the source of the growth in the labor endowment (population versus labor-force participation), and (2) the relative magnitudes of the income and terms-of-trade effects, as summarized in Table 10.1's right-hand column.

Figure 10.3 **What Are the Effects of a Deterioration in a Country's Terms of Trade?**

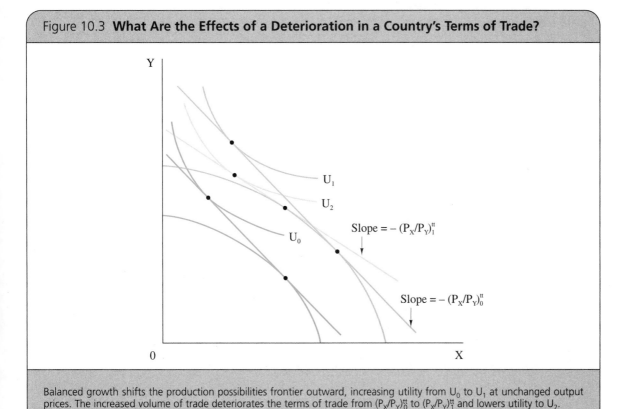

Balanced growth shifts the production possibilities frontier outward, increasing utility from U_0 to U_1 at unchanged output prices. The increased volume of trade deteriorates the terms of trade from $(P_X/P_Y)_0^{tt}$ to $(P_X/P_Y)_1^{tt}$ and lowers utility to U_2.

10.2.2 Just More Labor

An increase in the labor endowment with a constant capital endowment shifts the production possibilities frontier asymmetrically. The shift exhibits a bias toward production of the labor-intensive good, assumed in Figure 10.4 to be good X. The intersection of the new production possibilities frontier with both axes shifts outward, reflecting the fact that the additional labor could be used to produce more of either good, but the shift along the X axis is larger. The economy's overall capital-labor ratio falls. The effect on the economy of a decline in the capital-labor ratio depends on whether the country imports or exports the labor-intensive good and on the terms-of-trade effect.

First, consider the effect on a small country. In Figure 10.4, the increased labor endowment causes such a country to increase production of the labor-intensive good and reduce production of the capital-intensive good, as represented by the move from point I to point II. This somewhat peculiar-sounding result provides an example of the **Rybczynski theorem.** The theorem states that when the terms of trade are constant (as in a small country), an increase in the endowment of one factor with the other factor endowment held constant *increases* production of the good intensive in the increased factor and *decreases* production of the good intensive in the constant factor.[4]

---

4 Using more advanced techniques, we could demonstrate a much more general form of the Rybczynski theorem. For any change in factor endowments at unchanged output prices, the output of the labor-intensive commodity always changes in the same direction and more than proportionally with the endowment of labor. If the endowment of labor increases, output of the labor-intensive good increases by a larger percentage. If the endowment of labor decreases, output of the labor-intensive industry shrinks by a larger percentage. Similarly, output in the capital-intensive industry changes in the same direction and more than proportionally with the capital endowment. If X is the labor-intensive good, $\hat{X} > \hat{L} > \hat{K} = 0 > \hat{Y}$. In Figure 10.4, output of good Y must shrink because the rate of growth of the capital endowment is zero. This phenomenon provides another example of the magnification effect discussed in Chapter Four.

Figure 10.4 **What Are the Effects of Labor Endowment Growth?**

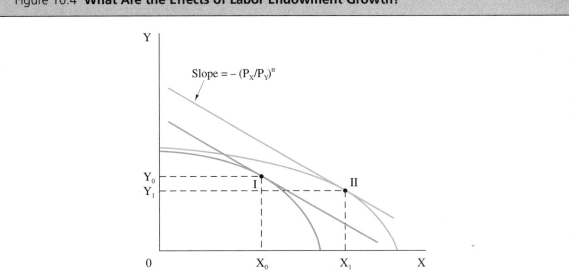

Good X is the labor-intensive good. With a constant capital endowment, output of the labor-intensive good rises more than proportionally with the labor endowment and output of the capital-intensive good falls; this provides an example of the Rybczynski theorem.

Why would economic growth cause a country to reduce production of one of the two goods? To take advantage of the increased availability of labor and increase output of the labor-intensive good, the labor-intensive industry must obtain some additional capital, because even the labor-intensive industry uses some capital along with labor. With the country's capital endowment held constant, the only source of additional capital is that employed in the capital-intensive industry. Therefore, the capital-intensive industry must shrink to facilitate the expansion of the labor-intensive industry made possible by the increased labor endowment.

Often viewed as a theoretical curiosity, the Rybczynski theorem actually carries important implications. For example, suppose a country undergoes a large-scale inflow of labor such as those from the former Soviet Union to Israel or from Mexico to the United States. If the growing country's product mix didn't change, the labor inflow would reduce wages (more on this in section 10.4.1). However, if the country receiving the inflow increases its production of the labor-intensive good and decreases its output of the capital-intensive good, as implied by the Rybczynski theorem, the economy can absorb the new labor without a reduction in the wage.[5]

Growth of a country's labor endowment increases output of the labor-intensive good relative to the capital-intensive good. If the labor-intensive good is the country's export good, this tends to increase the volume of trade and is referred to as *export expanding*. If the labor-intensive good is the country's import good, increased domestic production of it reduces desired imports and is *import replacing*.

The pattern of domestic consumption of the two goods also influences labor growth's net effect on trade. When domestic consumption of the import good rises relative to that of the export good, the effect is export expanding—that is, it represents a force that tends to increase the volume of trade. If consumption of the export good rises relative to that of the import good, the volume of trade falls and the effect is import replacing. The total effect of labor-endowment growth on the volume of trade depends on the combination of the effects on production and consumption; the volume of trade can rise, fall, or remain unchanged.

Economic growth based on increased population coupled with a constant endowment of capital generally creates a negative income effect. The increased population implies that each worker now has less capital with

Table 10.2 **How Does Labor-Endowment Growth Affect Welfare?**		
	Small-Country Case	Large-Country Case
Effect on growing economy:		
Income effect	– (if population ⇑); + (if labor force ⇑)	– (if population ⇑) + (if labor force ⇑)
Terms-of-trade effect	0	– (if export-expanding); + (if import-replacing)
Net effect on per-capita consumption	– (if population ⇑); + (if labor force ⇑)	Depends on signs and magnitudes of income and terms-of-trade effects
Effect on trading partner:		
Income effect	0	0
Terms-of-trade effect	0	+ (if export-expanding); – (if import-replacing)
Net effect on per-capita consumption	0	+ (if export-expanding); – (if import-replacing)

which to work, so labor's marginal product falls. Total consumption rises, but at a lower rate than the population growth; thus, per-capita consumption falls. As in the case of balanced growth, the income effect changes if the increased availability of labor comes from greater labor-force participation rather than increased population. Increased labor-force participation results in positive income effects, or increases in per-capita consumption.

A small country's labor growth doesn't affect its trading partners. They experience no income effect; and growth in the small country doesn't alter the terms of trade, so they experience no terms-of-trade effect either. Table 10.2 summarizes the welfare effects of small-country labor growth.

For a large growing country, the impact of labor-endowment growth on the terms of trade is uncertain. If the growth is export expanding, it tends to worsen the terms of trade by increasing the supply of the export good and demand for the import good. On the other hand, if the growth is import replacing, the terms of trade improve as the supply of the export good falls along with the demand for imports. Therefore, the total effect of labor growth on per-capita consumption in a large country is ambiguous for three reasons: (1) The income effect of growth depends on whether the labor growth comes from a growing population or increased labor-force participation; (2) the effect of labor growth on the volume of trade, and therefore on the terms of trade, is ambiguous; and (3) if the income and terms-of-trade effects work in opposite directions, either effect may dominate. When a large country grows, its trading partners experience a terms-of-trade effect but no income effect. Therefore, export-expanding growth in one country helps its trading partners, while import-replacing growth harms them.

10.2.3 **Just More Capital**

The overall effects of growth due to an increased endowment of capital in a large country are ambiguous, as in the case of labor-based growth. The major change in the analysis is a definitely positive income effect in the case of capital-based growth. Total consumption rises; and because the population doesn't change, a rise in per-capita consumption follows. For a small country, in which growth generates no terms-of-trade effect, capital-based growth must increase per-capita consumption. Again, growth in the small country has no effect on its trading partners.

In a large country, the terms-of-trade effect can be either positive or negative, making the overall effect of growth on both countries uncertain. If the growth is import replacing, the growing country's terms of trade improve and the overall effect on its welfare is positive, while the trading partner suffers from the deterioration in its terms of trade. If the growth is export expanding, the growing country's terms of trade deteriorate and the overall effect of growth on its welfare is ambiguous, while the trading partner gains from the improvement in its terms of trade. Table 10.3 summarizes the results for both the small-country and large-country cases.

Table 10.3 **How Does Capital-Endowment Growth Affect Welfare?**	Small-Country Case	Large-Country Case
Effect on growing economy:		
Income effect	+	+
Terms-of-trade effect	0	− (if export-expanding); + (if import-replacing)
Net effect on per-capita consumption	+	Depends on sign and magnitudes of income and terms-of-trade effects
Effect on trading partner:		
Income effect	0	0
Terms-of-trade effect	0	+ (if export-expanding); − (if import-replacing)
Net effect on per-capita consumption	0	+ (if export-expanding); − (if import-replacing)

10.2.4 **An Extreme Case: Immiserizing Growth**

For many years, economists have recognized the theoretical possibility that, in some cases, increased production could lower welfare through its deteriorating effect on the terms of trade. In 1956, Jagdish Bhagwati rigorously analyzed this situation and named it **immiserizing growth.** Sections 10.2.1, 10.2.2, and 10.2.3 covered several cases in which economic growth lowers per-capita consumption. We might expect such a result when growth takes the form of a growing population. The case of immiserizing growth as developed by Bhagwati is somewhat more surprising in its implication that growth could lower per-capita consumption even if population remains constant. The source of immiserizing growth is a strongly negative terms-of-trade effect. Therefore, the problem can affect only large countries, which have some influence on international terms of trade.

The possibility of immiserizing growth is illustrated in Figure 10.5, drawn under the assumption that growth doesn't result from an increase in population. The move from U_0 to U_1 represents growth's income effect. Because growth is biased toward production of the export good (X), the country's terms of trade deteriorate sharply, from $(P_X/P_Y)_0^{tt}$ to $(P_X/P_Y)_1^{tt}$, reducing welfare from U_1 to U_2 and leaving the country worse off than in its pre-growth situation (U_0).

Many conditions must be satisfied for the immiserizing-growth result to emerge. First, growth itself must be relatively modest; if it is substantial, the positive income effect (represented in Figure 10.5 by the move from U_0 to U_1) will swamp any negative terms-of-trade effect and growth will enhance welfare. Second, growth must significantly increase supply of a country's exports and demand for its imports, to generate a large terms-of-trade effect. Third, the elasticity of trading partners' demand for the country's exports must be sufficiently low for increased exports to lower their price substantially. Finally, the country must depend heavily on foreign trade so that changes in the terms of trade exert a large impact on its welfare. In Chapter Eleven, where we discuss problems facing developing countries, the possibility of chronic deterioration in the terms of trade will play a role. Little evidence, however, suggests that immiserizing growth actually occurs; the phenomenon appears to be more a theoretical possibility than an empirical reality.

Historical periods involving rapid economic growth based solely on increases in factor endowments have been rare. More commonly, periods of rapid growth have followed technological advances or technical progress. Of course, one frequent outcome of technical progress is to turn something not previously viewed as an important resource into a valuable factor of production (for example, development of the internal combustion engine and the resulting importance of petroleum).

10.3 **Economic Growth II: More Productivity**

Economists refer to an increase in productivity as **technical progress.** Defining and measuring it is notoriously difficult. In general, technical progress occurs whenever a larger quantity of goods can be produced from

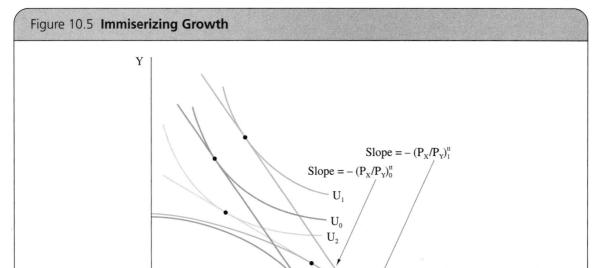

Figure 10.5 **Immiserizing Growth**

With unrestricted trade, growth at unchanged terms of trade shifts out the production possibilities curve, allowing the country to reach U_1 rather than the pre-growth U_0. If the increased volume of trade significantly worsened the terms of trade, the country could end up on U_2, which lies below U_0.

a given quantity of resources or, equivalently, a given quantity of goods can be produced from a smaller quantity of inputs. Technical progress involves an increase in the *productivity* of capital, labor, or both. For small countries, technical progress generates an unambiguously positive welfare effect; per-capita consumption rises. For large countries, the income effect of technical progress is unambiguously positive, but the terms-of-trade effect may be negative.

10.3.1 Types of Technical Progress

Nobel prize winner Sir John Hicks provided the classification system commonly used by economists for the various types of technical progress. Hicks classified technical progress according to its effect on the cost-minimizing capital-labor ratio that firms choose to use at unchanged factor prices.

Neutral technical progress leaves firms' chosen capital-labor ratio unchanged. It increases the productivity of both capital and labor proportionally such that at any given capital-labor ratio (K/L), the marginal rate of technical substitution (MRTS) between the two inputs remains unchanged.[6] Figure 10.6 represents neutral technical progress in production of good X. (The reader may want to review the use of isoquants and the firm's choice of the cost-minimizing capital-labor ratio in section 3.2.1.) After the technical progress, smaller bundles of capital and labor than before can produce output X_0, but the new isoquant representing X_0 retains the same shape as the old one—just shifted in toward the origin. At the same relative factor prices, the firm chooses the same capital-labor ratio as before.

---

6 By definition, the marginal rate of technical substitution equals the ratio of the *marginal products* of the two inputs ($-[MP_L/MP_K]$), where an input's marginal product equals the increase in output made possible by use of one additional unit of the input with the quantity of the other input held constant. Neutral technical progress raises MP_L and MP_K proportionally, leaving MRTS unchanged.

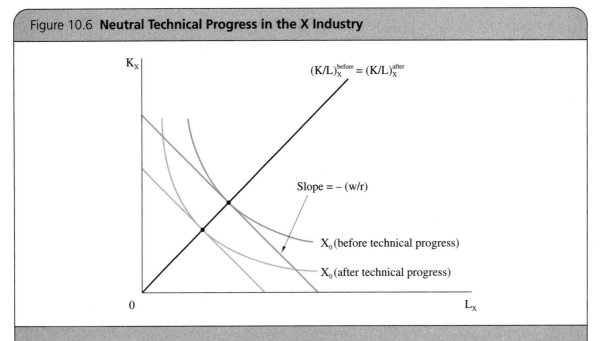

Figure 10.6 **Neutral Technical Progress in the X Industry**

Technical progress shifts the isoquant that represents production level X_0 in toward the origin. The isoquant retains its original shape, and firms' capital-labor ratio is unchanged at the old relative factor prices.

Capital-saving technical progress raises the marginal productivity of labor relative to that of capital. At unchanged factor prices, firms choose a lower capital-labor ratio (hence the term *capital-saving*). Graphically, such progress implies that for any given capital-labor ratio (along any ray from the origin), the new isoquant is steeper than the old one because the slope, given by $-(MP_{LX}/MP_{KX})$, is greater (see Figure 10.7).

Note two sources of potential confusion. First, *capital*-saving technical progress makes an industry more *labor* intensive. Second, capital-saving technical progress doesn't save just capital; it saves *both* capital and labor in the sense that good X now can be produced using less of both resources than before. The term *capital-saving* indicates only that firms will employ less capital per unit of labor.

Similarly, **labor-saving technical progress** involves an increase in the marginal product of capital relative to that of labor. The cost-minimizing capital-labor ratio rises. *(We leave construction of a diagram representing labor-saving technical progress to the reader.)*

10.3.2 How Does Increased Productivity Affect Welfare?

The fundamental effect of any type of technical progress on the production possibilities frontier is clear: The frontier shifts outward. The precise shape of the shift, however, depends on several considerations. The frontier represents two industries, each of which can enjoy technical progress of any type and at any rate. For example, industry X might experience rapid capital-saving progress and industry Y slow neutral progress. Because of the many possible combinations, we'll restrict our attention to the case of neutral progress.

In the event that both industries enjoy neutral technical progress at the same rates, the production possibilities frontier shifts out at the rate of the increased productivity while maintaining its original shape. Figure 10.2, drawn to represent balanced factor growth, also can represent neutral technical progress in both industries.

The welfare analysis of balanced growth also carries over, with one important exception. Recall that balanced growth's income effect equaled zero when population grew at the same rate as output, leaving per-capita

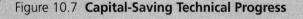

Figure 10.7 **Capital-Saving Technical Progress**

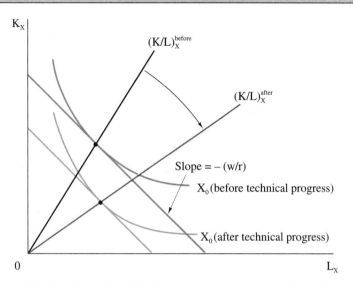

Capital-saving technical progress raises the marginal productivity of labor relative to that of capital. At unchanged factor prices, firms use a lower capital-labor ratio. Along any ray from the origin (for any given K/L), the new isoquant is steeper than the old one.

consumption unchanged.[7] Neutral technical progress involves productivity growth rather than population growth, so the increased output raises per-capita consumption. Therefore, neutral technical progress in both industries exerts a definitely positive income effect. For a small country, the income effect constitutes the only component of the welfare impact, and thus the overall effect is favorable. The welfare impact on a large country depends on the relative strengths of the positive income effect and the negative terms-of-trade effect, identical to that in the case of balanced growth.

What if neutral technical progress occurs in only one industry? The intersection of the production possibilities frontier with the axis representing the static industry remains unaltered, while the intersection with the axis representing the progressive industry shifts outward at the rate of the increased productivity. A small country would reduce output in the static industry and increase output of the progressive one.

Figure 10.8 captures the effect of single-industry neutral progress in a small country. The production point after technical progress must lie southeast of the original production point. How do we know? The production possibilities frontier's slope represents the opportunity cost of good X in terms of forgone good Y. Neutral technical progress in the X industry reduces the amount of resources required to produce a unit of good X and, therefore, the opportunity cost of good X in terms of good Y. At the point on the new frontier directly to the right of the original production point, the new frontier must be flatter than the old one to capture the new lower opportunity cost of good X; and the point on the new frontier with a slope equal to that at the original production point must lie to the southeast.

Again, the welfare effect on the small country is unambiguously positive. Total consumption rises with an unchanged population, implying increased per-capita consumption. For a large country, the total welfare effect is ambiguous because of the possibility of a deterioration in the terms of trade. In theory, technical progress could cause immiserizing growth in a large country. If the progress were strongly biased toward the export

---

7 Balanced growth creates a positive income effect if increased labor availability comes from greater labor-force participation rather than population growth.

Figure 10.8 **What Are the Effects of Neutral Technical Progress in the X Industry?**

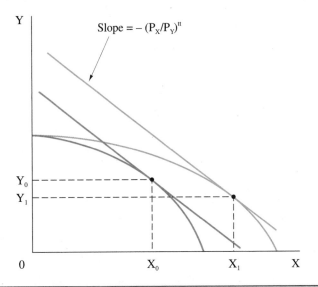

Slope = $- (P_X/P_Y)^{tt}$

With neutral technical progress in industry X, a small country reduces production of good Y and increases production of good X.

good, increased production of that good might lower its price sufficiently to offset the positive income effect on welfare. The conditions discussed in section 10.2.4 as necessary to the immiserizing-growth result apply not only to factor endowment–based growth but to technical progress. Again, little empirical evidence documents actual occurrence of immiserizing growth.

For the trading partners of a large country experiencing technical progress, the welfare effect depends on what happens to the terms of trade. If the terms of trade turn in favor of the country experiencing progress, trading partners suffer. If the progressive country experiences a deterioration in its terms of trade, trading partners benefit from the technical progress.

Thus far, we've analyzed the effects of economic growth in one country, assuming that the fundamental situation in the other country remains unchanged, although we've seen that factor-endowment growth or technical progress in a large country affects its trading partners through the terms-of-trade effect. When factors of production can move between countries, we must extend the analysis to include the direct impacts in both countries.

10.4 **What If Factors Can Move?**

The basic trade model of Chapters Three and Four assumes that factors of production are completely immobile between countries. Nonetheless, with unrestricted trade, factor prices tend to equalize across countries according to the factor price equalization theorem (see section 4.4). Trade in goods substitutes for trade in factors, because exports of a capital-intensive good are equivalent in their effects to exports of capital.

The link between factor mobility and international trade in goods and services lies at the center of several current international policy debates. Consider the North American Free Trade Agreement (NAFTA) implemented by the United States, Canada, and Mexico in 1994. Proponents argued that the agreement would enlarge the U.S. market for Mexican goods, raise incomes in Mexico, and decrease Mexican migration, especially illegal migration, to the United States. This view presents trade in goods and services as a substitute for factor mobility. On the other hand, opponents of the agreement claimed that firms would move from the United States to Mexico to "exploit" its low-wage labor. Along similar lines, the governments of Western Europe debate whether to lower trade barriers and admit the cheaper products from Eastern Europe or to maintain trade barriers in goods and services, especially agriculture, and risk massive migration from East to West.

Achievement of complete factor price equalization would remove the major incentive for inter-country factor movements: obtaining higher factor rewards. We'll see that some reasons for factor movement persist even with complete factor price equalization, but the primary cause of factor movements is differences in factor prices across countries. As long as capital or labor earns a higher reward in one country than in another, the differential provides an incentive for factor movements.

Section 4.4 indicated the relatively stringent requirements for complete factor price equalization. For example, the presence of either trade barriers or nontraded goods (such as haircuts) can prevent complete equalization. Trade barriers play a particularly strong role in generating factor movements. The development of U.S. production facilities by Japanese automobile producers provides one outstanding example. The United States first subjected imports of Japanese automobiles to voluntary export restraints in 1981, and the Japanese feared even stronger trade restrictions. One way to guarantee continued access to the U.S. market was to build production facilities in the United States—and firms, especially Toyota and Honda, chose to do just that. Today "Japanese" auto firms produce hundreds of thousands of cars each year in the United States.

The welfare analysis of factor movements involves four questions. First, how does factor movement affect total world output; can factor mobility increase the efficiency of the world economy in a manner similar to trade in outputs? Second, how does factor movement affect the division of welfare between the two countries? Third, how does factor movement affect the distribution of income within each country? And fourth, how does the movement affect the factors that move? The answer to the fourth question is the easiest to predict: Assuming factor movements take place voluntarily, the owners of the factors that move must expect to be better off, or they wouldn't move.

Inter-country movements of capital and of labor generate similar effects. However, the particular motivations and some of the issues that arise differ between the two classes of factors; so we'll analyze separately the effects of labor mobility (section 10.4.1) and capital mobility (section 10.4.2).

10.4.1 Inter-Country Labor Mobility

Labor generally flows less easily than capital across national boundaries. This reflects the special character of labor as a factor of production: A unit of labor is embodied in a human being. The person has tastes and preferences, a culture, a language, and friends and family. Individuals don't feel indifferent about where they work or the conditions under which they work; many considerations other than the wage rate enter into the work decision. The owner of a machine, on the other hand, probably doesn't care about the machine's location or working conditions so long as the equipment isn't abused in such a way as to reduce its productivity and value.

Despite the financial and personal costs involved, growing numbers of individuals have chosen to immigrate. Immigrants comprise 17 percent of Canada's population. In the first few years after the Berlin Wall opened in 1989, 1 in 16 residents of the eastern German states moved to the western states.[8] North Africans comprise a growing share of the population in Europe; the many Algerians in France provide one example. Singapore employs hundreds of thousands of foreign workers, including many from Malaysia who cross the border daily to work. Malaysia, on the other hand, also hosts foreign workers, of whom most are undocumented and come from Indonesia and Bangladesh. Approximately five and a half million Filipinos work abroad as nurses, nannies, maids, and crew aboard the world's merchant ships. The United States, which takes in more immigrants each year than any other country, apprehends more than 1.5 million individuals illegally crossing the border from Mexico each year, and experts estimate that only 10 to 50 percent of those who cross illegally are caught.

Incentives for Migration

When labor moves between countries, the reasons can be economic or noneconomic, and often the two are interconnected. The periods of mass migration to America during the nineteenth and early twentieth centuries reflected immigrants' desire for religious and political freedom and for the economic freedom to better

---

8 Greg Steinmetz, "West German Riches Are Luring Easterners Desperate for Work," *The Wall Street Journal*, July 7, 1997.

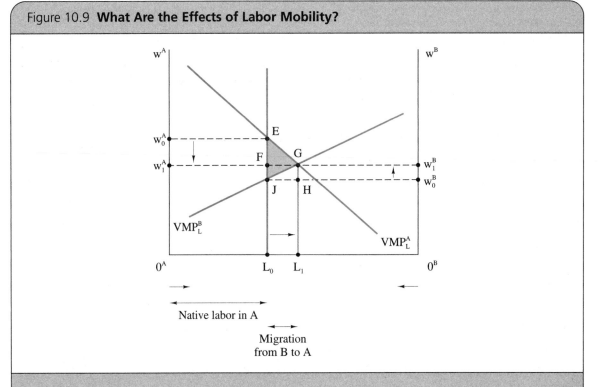

Figure 10.9 **What Are the Effects of Labor Mobility?**

Labor's ability to move from country B to country A in response to a wage differential raises total world output by an amount represented by the area of triangle EGJ. Country A gains, and country B loses. In A, capital owners gain relative to labor; in B, workers gain relative to capital owners.

themselves and improve opportunities for their children. These motives remain important today. Although a complex web of influences determines an individual's decision to move to another country, we'll focus on economic motivations and assume that an individual moves when the reward paid to labor is higher in the destination country.

Figure 10.9 provides a convenient guide for analyzing labor mobility's effects. The world is assumed to be composed of two countries, A and B. The length of the horizontal axis (distance $0^A 0^B$) represents the total quantity of labor in the world. The two vertical axes measure the wage paid to labor in the two countries (w^A on the left axis and w^B on the right). L_0 represents the initial allocation of labor between countries A and B; so $0^A L_0$ units of labor work in A, and $0^B L_0$ in B.

In each country, labor earns a *wage* rate (w) equal to the value of the marginal unit of labor's productivity. The *value* of the *marginal product of labor* (VMP_L) equals the marginal product of labor (the number of units of additional output produced when 1 additional unit of labor is employed) multiplied by the price of the good produced. As the quantity of labor increases in a given country, the marginal productivity of labor declines and, with it, the value of that productivity and the wage rate.[9] The curves VMP_L^A and VMP_L^B represent the values of the marginal product of labor in countries A and B, respectively. With the initial allocation of labor between countries, workers in A earn w_0^A and workers in B earn w_0^B. The higher wage in A reflects labor's higher marginal productivity in A (point E) relative to B (point J).

If they can, workers from country B will migrate to A to obtain higher wages. This incentive will cause the workers represented by the distance between L_0 and L_1 to move. Once sufficient migration has occurred to reach the new labor allocation at L_1, wage rates in the two countries will equalize at $w_1^A = w_1^B$.

---

9 For a review of the law of diminishing returns, see the discussion of Figure 4.5.

Labor Migration's Effects

Our first task is to determine how labor movements in response to wage differentials affect the efficiency of the world economy. Does such mobility increase or decrease total world output? The shaded area (triangle EGJ) in Figure 10.9 represents an increase in total world output from the mobility of labor. Each unit of labor between L_0 and L_1 produces more in country A than in country B; that the VMP_L^A curve is higher than the VMP_L^B curve throughout the L_0 to L_1 range reflects this productivity differential. Higher wages in A signal to workers the greater value of labor's marginal product in A, attracting them to the area where they will be more productive. As labor is used more efficiently, total output increases.

How are the gains represented by area EGJ divided between countries A and B? The controversial nature of emigration and immigration policies leads us to suspect—correctly—that the gains aren't divided equally among all interested parties. Country A as a whole gains from the immigration. The net gain is the sum of gains by capital owners in A, losses by native country A workers, and gains by the immigrants themselves. Country B as a whole loses from its emigration, but workers in B gain relative to owners of capital. As we predicted earlier, the immigrants themselves gain.

The net gain to country A equals the sum of the value of the marginal product of all labor units between L_0 and L_1, or area EGL_1L_0. The original work force from A loses area $w_0^A EFw_1^A$ because of immigration's negative effect on the wage rate. Area FGL_1L_0 represents the income earned by immigrants in country A. Area JHL_1L_0 just replaces the income they could have earned in country B, but FGHJ shows the net increase in their income that provided the incentive for migration. Owners of the fixed quantity of capital in A gain as the marginal product of capital rises because of the availability of more labor for use along with the capital.[10] Country B's output falls by JGL_1L_0 as a result of the emigration. Workers who remain in B gain area $Gw_1^Bw_0^BH$ in increased wages, but B's capital owners lose as the marginal product of capital falls. Table 10.4 summarizes these effects.

Opposition to Immigration Policies

The preceding analysis makes clear why labor groups typically favor strong limits on immigration: Open immigration can lower wages of domestic workers (including earlier immigrants) who compete with new immigrants in labor markets. When immigrant workers are unskilled, the negative impact on wages affects primarily unskilled domestic workers and other recent immigrants. Recent waves of immigrants to the United States, for example, possess skill levels below those of earlier immigrants.[11] Empirical evidence suggests that in developed countries, unskilled migrants sometimes fill jobs not wanted by domestic workers, minimizing immigration's effect on wages. Overall, most empirical studies find only small effects of immigration on wages.[12] Of course, there also can be noneconomic reasons for opposing open immigration, including cultural prejudice or racism, but even these seemingly noneconomic arguments may reflect fear of immigration's economic effects.

Table 10.4 **Effects of Labor Migration from Country B to Country A**	
Effect on:	
Capital owners in A	+
Native labor in A	−
Immigrants	+
Net effect on A	+ (area EGL_1L_0)
Capital owners in B	−
Labor remaining in B	+
Net effect on B	− (area JGL_1L_0)
Net effect on world	+ (area EGJ)

---

10 Recall that an input's marginal product measures the change in total output resulting from use of one more unit of the input, with the quantities of all other inputs held constant. An input's marginal product is increased by availability of a larger quantity of other inputs used together with it; a reduction in the use of other inputs lowers the marginal product.

11 See the Borjas articles in the chapter references.

12 We'll see one reason why later.

Table 10.5 **Immigration to the United States by Top Source Countries, Fiscal Year 1998**	
Country	Immigrants (Thousands)
Mexico	131.6
China	36.9
India	36.5
Philippines	34.5
Dominican Republic	20.4
Vietnam	17.6

Source: Data from U.S. Immigration and Naturalization Service.

Another reason for opposition to open immigration has emerged in recent years as governments have taken on larger roles in assuring residents minimal levels of food, housing, medical care, education, and income—even if they are unable or unwilling to work. Countries that provide generous levels of such social benefits may fear an influx of immigrants who won't work and produce, as did the immigrants in Figure 10.9, but instead live on government-provided benefits at the expense of domestic workers and working immigrants. Immigrants to the United States during the 1950s and 1960s didn't avail themselves of public assistance at rates exceeding those for domestic residents. However, this no longer is the case. Recent arrivals have drawn public assistance at high rates relative to earlier immigrant arrivals, and their use of public assistance appears to be growing over time.[13] The rate of dependence on public assistance varies widely across source countries and with the immigrants' age. Table 10.5 lists the six countries from which the United States accepted the most immigrants in 1998.

Another issue that adds controversy to immigration policies is developing countries' concerns about **brain drain,** the tendency of the most highly skilled, trained, and educated individuals from developing countries to migrate to the industrialized countries. Developing countries argue that they expend scarce resources to educate and train these individuals only to lose the return on their investment to other nations, particularly the United States. Africa, according to a 2001 report by the International Organization for Migration, loses 23,000 college graduates annually, mostly to Europe and the United States. India produces approximately 100,000 engineers each year from the country's technical institutes and colleges; usually between 50,000 and 60,000 go to the United States; and for each 1,000 who leave, only one or two return.[14] One positive result: rising salaries at home for Indian technology workers.

Theory, Evidence, and Politics: An Important Caveat

As noted earlier, empirical evidence suggests that any negative effect of immigration on wages is small. This may seem puzzling, given our analysis of Figure 10.9. However, notice something important about that analysis. It assumes, albeit implicitly, that the country produces only *one* good. What if, instead, we incorporate the idea from earlier chapters that countries produce at least two goods, a labor-intensive one and a capital-intensive one, and that those goods can be traded internationally? Then, an inflow of labor makes a country more labor abundant and causes it to shift toward producing labor-intensive goods and away from producing capital-intensive ones. The result is an increase in the demand for labor to match the increased supply.

In fact, this is what the Rybczynski theorem tells us. *The country's product mix changes with changes in its factor endowment. Therefore, factor prices needn't change in response to factor inflows and outflows.* One way to remember this important caveat is to note that the Rybczynski theorem says that changes in factor *quantities* (that is, changes in a country's endowment) lead to changes in the *quantities* of different goods produced (that is, changes in the product mix), *not* to changes in factor *prices*. This is a cousin to the Stolper-Samuelson theorem from Chapter Four, which states that changes in product *prices* lead to changes in factor *prices*.

---

13 See the Borjas articles in the chapter references.

14 "Soaring Indian Tech Salaries Reflect the Country's Brain Drain," *The Wall Street Journal,* August 21, 2000.

Of course, if the world practiced complete free trade in all goods, factor-price equalization would remove much of the economic incentive for migration. Similarly, complete factor mobility would equalize factor prices and remove the cost differentials that form the foundation for comparative-advantage-based trade in goods. When both trade in goods and factor mobility occur, but imperfectly, it becomes difficult to predict the relative magnitudes of the two. Nonetheless, it's important to keep in mind that the product-mix response to changing factor endowments can mitigate much of the factor-price response we might expect in the simple one-good world analyzed in Figure 10.9.

Immigration Policy

Over the last century, U.S. immigration policy changed dramatically four times, affecting both the overall magnitude and composition of immigration flows. In the late nineteenth century, the United States restricted many classes of immigration, including an almost total ban on people from Asia. Beginning in the 1920s, national-origin quotas severely restricted entry from Southern and Eastern Europe by allocating visas to maintain the ethnic balance of the 1920 U.S. population. By 1965, the national-origin quotas had become politically unacceptable, and immigration policy shifted to a system that provided easy entry for people with family ties to U.S. residents and earlier immigrants.

By the 1980s, U.S. immigration controversies centered squarely on Mexico. The 1986 Immigration Reform and Control Act aimed to eliminate illegal foreign workers, especially those from Mexico, from the U.S. labor market in two ways. First, the bill granted amnesty to foreign workers who had been in the United States illegally since before 1982 and could document their residence or who had worked in U.S. perishable-crop agriculture for at least 90 days during the previous year. By the end of the program, 3.2 million individuals, 90 percent from Mexico, had gained permanent-resident status through the amnesty program. Second, to reduce the demand for illegal labor, the bill imposed penalties known as employer sanctions on firms that hired illegal workers. U.S. agricultural interests incorporated provisions into the bill for temporary admission of foreign workers during the harvest season, since foreign workers, most from Mexico and other parts of Central America, harvest many U.S. crops.

Predictably, based on our graphical analysis in Figure 10.9 and on the results reported in Table 10.4, U.S. labor unions found the 1986 bill too weak, believing that it allowed too much competition from foreign workers for jobs in the United States. U.S. firms, on the other hand, particularly in industries such as the Los Angeles–based garment industry, found their operations threatened by the reduction in the supply of illegal labor. Many leaders of the Hispanic community also opposed the bill's provisions for penalties on firms that hire illegal workers, fearing that firms would choose to avoid the risk of hiring improperly documented workers by refusing to hire Hispanics. The first few years after the 1986 bill saw a decline in the number of illegal entrants apprehended along the U.S.–Mexico border, but the decline was short lived.

Immigration law adjustments made in 1995 cut legal immigration back to 675,000 per year, of which up to 465,000 would go to family members of U.S. residents; up to 140,000 to individuals with special skills needed in U.S. labor markets; up to 10,000 to investors (individuals who invested at least $1 million in a business to employ at least 10 workers or $500,000 in a rural area); and up to 55,000 to "diversity immigrants"—visas to be awarded by lottery to individuals from countries other than the principal sources of current U.S. immigration. Shortages of high-tech workers during the U.S. technology boom of the late 1990s created political pressure to raise the number of skilled-based visas. Congress obliged by raising the number of workers admitted on three-year H1-B visas to 195,000 per year. Unfortunately for the holders of H1-B visas, the increase came shortly before the technology boom slowed; because each visa is sponsored by the worker's employer, H1-B workers who lose their jobs also lose their status to stay in the United States legally.

An International Issue

The United States isn't alone in its ongoing debate over immigration policy. Current controversy in developed countries over immigration policy centers around their desires to both encourage inflows of skilled, especially high-tech, workers and limit inflows of unskilled workers. Norway needs more doctors and seeks immigrants from Germany, France, and Austria. Much of Europe, especially Britain and Germany, joins developing countries such as China, India, and South Africa in worrying about a brain drain of their skilled workers to the United States. German immigration laws make it very difficult for German firms to hire skilled workers from outside the European Union; only 884 permits were granted in 1999.[15] Canada grants well over half of its legal entries to workers with special skills needed in Canada, whereas in the United States most legal entries go to individuals with family ties to people already in the country, regardless of skills or employability. Even Japan, whose resident foreigners constitute barely 1 percent of the population, faces pressure to allow more immigration, both to attract more skilled workers and to offset the demographic effects of the country's rapidly aging population.

Experts estimate that at least 500,000 illegal immigrants enter the European Union annually. At the same time South Africa loses many of its skilled workers to developed countries, it expels each year about 100,000 illegal unskilled immigrants from the rest of Africa, still leaving between 2 million and 8 million undocumented individuals in the country. The U.S. Immigration and Naturalization Service estimates that approximately 5 million illegal aliens live in the United States, almost 3 million of them from Mexico. Even immigration-averse Japan tolerates small amounts of illegal immigration by individuals willing to do hard, dirty, or dangerous jobs. And, anticipating the need to care for rapidly increasing numbers of elderly Japanese, the government has proposed admitting large numbers of low-skilled nursing assistants.[16]

In 1986, when the European Union granted membership to Spain, Portugal, and Greece, residents of the new members had to wait seven years before becoming eligible to work in another member country. As negotiations progress on EU expansion to include countries of Central and Eastern Europe, the existing members want to impose again a seven-year moratorium on free movement of labor from the new members. For the countries seeking EU membership, the proposed delays sound like an offer of second-class standing in the group. Many workers from Eastern and Central Europe already work illegally in the EU—for example, Albanians and Bulgarians who cross the border into Greece.

In parts of the former Soviet Union, the emigration situation is even more striking. Experts estimate that the former Soviet republic of Armenia lost between 800,000 and 1.5 million people (between one-quarter and one-half of the population) between the breakup of the Soviet Union in 1991 and 2001.[17]

Labor Mobility without Immigration?

Recently firms have begun to use several arrangements that amount to labor mobility without migration. The first arrangement is **outsourcing** or offshore assembly, in which a firm performs each step in a manufacturing process in the country with a comparative advantage in that particular stage. Components for a finished product may be produced in many countries, and labor-intensive assembly of the components often occurs in labor-abundant developing countries. Such offshore assembly operations make up a large share of manufactured imports into the United States from developing countries, especially Mexico. In many cases, including Mexico's, special tax and tariff arrangements have encouraged firms to use offshore assembly.[18]

Sometimes technology makes possible even more innovative ways of accomplishing labor mobility without migration. A U.S.–India satellite linkup permits U.S. computer firms such as Texas Instruments to use Indian computer programmers for programming tasks. The U.S. firms send software design specifications to India by satellite link; the Indian software engineers develop and test the software in India and then transmit it back to the United States. Some firms estimate that the arrangement could cut programming costs in half. Indian programmers earn more than they would otherwise in India but less than programmers in the United States. Highly trained programmers remain in India (along with their earnings), instead of migrating to the United States as part of the brain drain; as a result, India now exports billions of dollars worth of computer software each year. Programmers in Novosibirsk, Siberia, have started a similar program.

Another sector moving rapidly to use labor abroad is remote services, which includes call centers and back-office operations. Again, India, along with Ireland and the Philippines, provides many of these services. Mortgage, credit-card, and insurance companies increasingly rely on the staff of foreign call centers to handle customers' e-mail and telephone questions, perform data-entry operations (such as keeping up with airline customers' frequent-flier miles), transcribe medical and legal dictation, and conduct basic research. Countries

---

15 "Germany Faces Storm over Tech Staffing," *The Wall Street Journal,* March 7, 2000.

16 "The Door Opens, a Crack," *The Economist,* September 2, 2000.

17 "At Last a State, Armenia Loses People," *The Wall Street Journal,* July 6, 2001.

18 See section 6.9. Case Three in Chapter Nine examines Mexico's *maquiladora* plants, which have grown along the U.S.–Mexico border and specialize in assembly operations.

in which a large share of the population speaks English well have a big advantage in attracting these jobs. The tasks involved don't require highly skilled workers, so firms resist paying high developed-country wages; but the tasks aren't yet routine enough to be performed by machines. Training often includes understanding American regional accents as well as lessons on American culture, so U.S. callers won't realize that the person answering their question isn't in the United States.

Constraints on the growth of such operations in some countries include the poor quality of utility infrastructures (for example, local power failures are common) and expensive telephone services because of not-yet-deregulated national telephone monopolies. But some developed countries with modern utility infrastructures and strong telecommunications networks are getting in on the trend. The Canadian Maritime provinces, for example, suffer high rates of unemployment after losing their traditional fishing and mining industries but have attracted several call centers, including those of Staples, Xerox, and AT&T.

10.4.2 Inter-Country Capital Mobility

Capital mobility among countries exceeds labor mobility largely because it doesn't require people to move; a capital owner can stay in one place while the capital flows from country to country in response to differences in available returns and other relevant considerations. The term *capital mobility* is somewhat deceptive. In economic discussions of international trade, *capital* typically refers to durable productive inputs such as factories, machines, and tools. But *capital mobility* refers not to actual international movement of such inputs but to international borrowing and lending activity.

There are two main classes of capital mobility. The first is international **portfolio investment,** or the flow across national boundaries of funds to finance investments in which the lender doesn't gain operating control over the borrower. Whenever an individual, firm, or government buys bonds issued by a foreign firm or government, the transaction transfers funds and represents a portfolio investment. This type of transaction involves very low transaction and transportation costs, so portfolio investment represents the most mobile component of capital. Often all that's involved is an electronic transfer of funds, accomplished almost instantaneously at very little cost using modern computer technology.

If a U.S. firm issues bonds (borrows) and sells some of those bonds to a resident of Germany (who thereby makes a loan to the U.S. firm), the transaction represents a **capital outflow** or an **international purchase of assets** from Germany's perspective and a **capital inflow** or **international sale of assets** from the perspective of the United States. The U.S. firm typically uses the borrowed funds to buy a piece of physical capital such as a new factory building; so the U.S. capital stock rises and the German capital stock falls relative to what it would have been had the German resident lent his or her funds domestically to a German firm—even though no one packed up a factory and shipped it from Germany to the United States.

The other component of capital flows is **direct investment,** which gives the lender operating ownership of and control over the borrower. For example, if a U.S. firm buys a German firm or establishes a subsidiary in Germany, the transaction represents an outward foreign direct investment from the U.S. point of view and an inward foreign direct investment from the German perspective. The line between portfolio and direct investment is somewhat fuzzy. If a U.S. firm buys stock in a Japanese corporation, the buyer may or may not gain operating control—depending on the magnitude of the purchase relative to the Japanese firm's outstanding stock. U.S. government statistics assume that ownership of 10 percent or more of a firm's outstanding stock gives the holder operating control and therefore classifies the investment as a direct one.

Recent Patterns in International Capital Mobility

Worldwide, two trends characterize direct investment patterns. The first is rapid, if erratic, growth. In 1980, the value of the stocks of inward and outward foreign-direct-investment assets in the world economy equaled 4.9 percent and 5.4 percent, respectively, of the value of world gross domestic product (output) at the time. By 1998, those percentages had risen to 13.7 and 14.1. Between 1982 and 1999, the total value of annual world exports grew by three-and-a-half times (from $2,041 billion to $6,892 billion) and annual outflows of foreign direct investment grew by more than 20 times (from $37 billion to $800 billion).[19] The late 1980s and late 1990s were characterized by dramatic surges in the rate of foreign direct investment, which had grown much more slowly from 1973 to 1984 and during the recession of the early 1990s.

---

19 United Nations, *World Investment Report 2000*, pp. 317, 4.

Figure 10.10 Top Source and Host Countries for Foreign Direct Investment, 1999

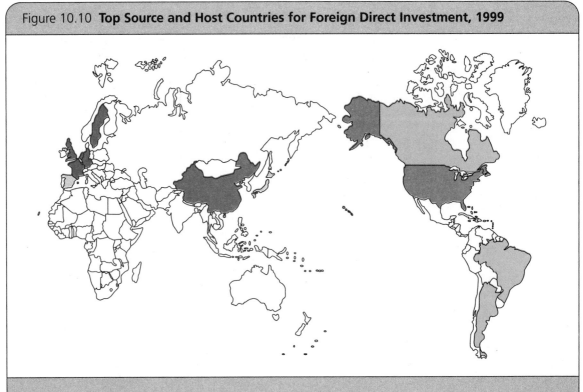

The top 10 source countries are lightly shaded. Medium shading denotes the top 10 host countries. Darkly shaded countries make both the top-hosts and the top-sources lists.

Source: Data from United Nations, *World Investment Report 2000*.

The second notable trend is a diversification of the source and host countries. In 1980, the value of the stocks of inward and outward foreign-direct-investment assets for developing economies as a group equaled 5.4 percent and 0.9 percent, respectively, of the developing countries' output. By 1998, those percentages had risen to 20.0 and 6.7.

While foreign direct investment flows to developing countries have risen, the flows remain relatively concentrated. Of $208 billion of foreign direct investment flows into developing economies in 1999, $85 billion went to Asia, $90 billion to Latin America and the Caribbean, $24 billion to the European economies in transition, and $9 billion to Africa. However, those flows were concentrated toward a few countries. Five countries took almost 70 percent of the $208 billion total; China alone (including Hong Kong) accounted for 31 percent.

Figure 10.10 illustrates the top 10 host and source countries for foreign direct investment in 1999. Countries making the source list but not the host list are shaded lightly in the figure. Countries making the host list but not the source list are denoted by medium shading in the figure. Seven economies make both lists; they are shaded darkly. Note that the most active participants in foreign direct investment, both hosts and sources, continue to be industrial economies.

Table 10.6 shows the relative sizes of the stocks of portfolio and direct foreign investment held by private U.S. residents in recent years. As the table makes evident, direct investment dominated U.S. private international portfolio investment. This pattern contrasts with that of British investment during Britain's economic dominance in the late nineteenth century. Britain's assets consisted largely of portfolio investment, exemplified by British purchases of bonds to finance worldwide railroad construction, particularly in the United States. Note that Table 10.6 reports private investment; it doesn't include holdings of foreign assets by the U.S. government. In evaluating the overall investment position of the United States, government holdings as well as private holdings matter, but government borrowing and lending respond to different motivations than do pri-

Table 10.6 Private U.S. Investment Abroad, Assets at Year End, 1950–1999 (Billions $)

Year	Direct Investment[a]	Bonds	Stocks	Total[b]
1950	$ 11.8	$ 3.2	$ 1.2	$ 17.5
1960	31.9	5.5	4.0	44.4
1970	78.2	13.2	6.4	105.0
1980	396.2	43.5	18.9	701.0
1990	620.0	144.7	197.6	1,923.3
1995	884.3	355.3	699.1	3,014.8
1996	970.8	398.0	875.5	3,477.4
1997	1,023.9	445.0	1,001.3	4,021.0
1998	1,207.1	576.7	1,476.2	4,846.3
1999	1,331.2	556.7	2,026.6	5,668.4

[a]Valued at current cost.
[b]Total includes categories besides direct investment, bonds, and stocks; therefore, components don't sum to total.

Sources: William H. Branson, "Trends in United States International Trade and Investment since World War II," in *The American Economy in Transition,* edited by Martin Feldstein (Chicago: University of Chicago Press, 1980), p. 237; *Economic Report of the President; Survey of Current Business.*

vate borrowing and lending. For now, we'll focus on the voluntary transactions undertaken by the private sector. In Part Two of the book, we'll explore in detail the role of government borrowing and lending and its impact on the world economy.

The rate of foreign investment in the United States during the 1980s exceeded that of U.S. investment abroad. The result was a net capital inflow, implying that the United States borrowed abroad more than it lent abroad, as a comparison of Table 10.6 and Table 10.7 reveals. In the mid-1980s, the stock of U.S. assets held by foreigners surpassed the stock of foreign assets held by private parties in the United States. The United States became, for the first time in 70 years, a debtor nation.[20] As the comparison of Tables 10.6 and 10.7 documents, the rapid change in U.S. status from creditor to debtor resulted not from a decline in U.S. investment abroad but from a rapid increase in foreign investment in the United States. Note that U.S. direct investment assets held abroad still exceed foreign direct investment assets in the United States.

The most politically controversial aspect of foreign investment in the United States involved Japanese direct investment during the 1980s. Japanese firms invested heavily in the United States and made highly visible purchases such as Rockefeller Center in New York, Columbia Pictures, the Beverly Wilshire Hotel, Firestone Tire and Rubber, the Seattle Mariners baseball team, and the Pebble Beach golf course. Many pundits extrapolated that pace of investment into the future and concluded that the United States soon would be owned and controlled by the Japanese. But, as happens with many economic trends, the 1990s brought a sharp reversal; the rate of foreign investment in the United States declined, including that by Japan.

Not only did the Japanese buying trend not last forever, but many of the transactions also turned out to be great deals for the U.S. sellers, because Japanese investors bought just before the early-1990s plummet in U.S. real estate values. For example, a Japanese investor bought the Los Angeles Hotel Bel-Air in 1989 for $110 million and sold it in 1994 for $60 million. Similarly, the Japanese investor who bought the Pebble Beach Golf Links in Pebble Beach, California, paid $841 million in 1990 and sold the course in 1992 for $500 million. Even the Rockefeller Center purchase didn't turn out well for the buyer. A Japanese firm paid $1.4 billion for 80 percent ownership of the complex between 1989 and 1991; the owners later were in bankruptcy.[21]

---

20 This statement isn't without controversy. Because of measurement difficulties and differences in accounting procedures, no single number can claim to represent the net investment position of the United States. In particular, measures are sensitive to how assets are valued—at historical cost, at current cost, or at market value. We'll see more about this controversy in Chapter Thirteen.

21 "Japan's U.S. Property Deals: A Poor Report Card," *The Wall Street Journal,* June 9, 1995.

Table 10.7 **Nonofficial[a] Foreign Investment in the United States, Assets at Year End, 1950–1999 (Billions $)**

Year	Direct Investment[b]	Bonds	Stocks	Total[c]
1950	$ 3.4	$ 0.2	$ 2.9	$ 8.0
1960	6.9	0.6	9.3	18.4
1970	13.3	6.9	18.7	44.8
1980	125.9	25.6	64.6	367.7
1990	467.3	408.1	221.7	2,051.1
1995	654.5	923.5	465.4	3,282.0
1996	729.1	1,184.7	571.3	3,786.1
1997	751.8	1,380.0	859.9	4,627.0
1998	928.6	1,638.9	1,110.3	5,353.2
1999	1,125.2	1,724.5	1,445.6	6,102.2

[a]As reported by the Department of Commerce and reproduced in Tables 10.6 and 10.7, the U.S. and foreign investment positions aren't precisely comparable, because foreign assets in the United States include nonofficial assets held by foreign governments, while U.S. assets abroad exclude all government-held assets, whether official or nonofficial.
[b]Valued at current cost.
[c]Total includes categories besides direct investment, bonds, and stocks; therefore, components don't sum to total.

Sources: William H. Branson, "Trends in United States International Trade and Investment since World War II," in *The American Economy in Transition*, edited by Martin Feldstein (Chicago: University of Chicago Press, 1980), pp. 239, 245; *Economic Report of the President; Survey of Current Business*.

In the past few years, foreign investors have snapped up assets in Asia, particularly in the economies hardest hit by the Asian financial crisis. Japan's decade-long economic slump also attracted buyers. French Renault bought Nissan, Japan's second-largest auto maker. A British company bought J-Phone, Japan's third largest mobile phone firm. And Japanese assets bought by U.S. investors include many of Japan's golf courses, such as Golf Seiyo and Forest Miki.[22]

Figure 10.11 indicates the regional allocation of U.S. outward and inward direct foreign investment for 1999. Although Japanese investment in the United States captured most of the political attention, Japan always ranked behind the United Kingdom as the largest source of foreign direct investment in the United States; by 1999, Japan had fallen to eighth. The United Kingdom, Canada, Switzerland, and Japan were the top four recipients of U.S. 1999 foreign direct investment.

Incentives for International Capital Movements

Several incentives exist for capital owners to move their capital across national boundaries. We focus first on incentives for portfolio investment; section 10.4.4 will consider multinational enterprises as a vehicle of foreign direct investment. The primary incentive for capital movements, of course, is the opportunity to earn a higher rate of return. Different tax laws among countries also affect capital flows, as we'll see in section 10.4.3.

Another major reason for capital mobility is individuals' and firms' desire to diversify their assets to reduce risk. Evidence suggests that most individuals are risk averse. This just means that given a choice between two assets, one with a certain return and the other with a return that is uncertain but expected to equal, on average, the certain return on the other asset, most individuals will choose the certain return.[23] Most investment decisions involve a trade-off between the rate of return and the level of risk; by tolerating more risk, an investor often can earn a higher rate of return.

---

22 "Fair Game for Buyers at Japan's Golf Clubs," *Financial Times,* May 19, 2001.

23 *If you were offered a choice between (1) $5 with certainty and (2) a gamble with a 50 percent chance of winning $10 and a 50 percent chance of winning nothing, which would you choose?* If you chose (1), you exhibited aversion to risk, because the expected value of the two offers is equal (at $5) while offer (1) involves no risk.

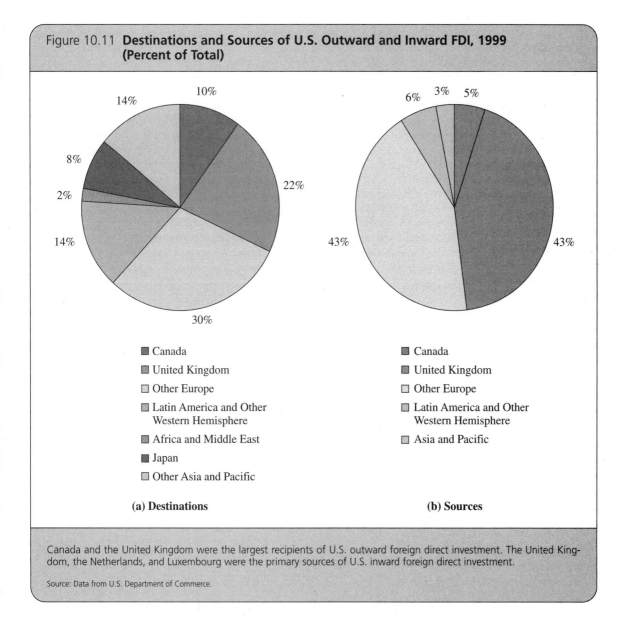

Figure 10.11 **Destinations and Sources of U.S. Outward and Inward FDI, 1999 (Percent of Total)**

(a) Destinations

(b) Sources

Canada and the United Kingdom were the largest recipients of U.S. outward foreign direct investment. The United Kingdom, the Netherlands, and Luxembourg were the primary sources of U.S. inward foreign direct investment.

Source: Data from U.S. Department of Commerce.

To reduce the riskiness of a portfolio or group of assets, an investor need not hold only low-risk, low-return assets. One can do better by diversification. **Diversification** refers to holding a variety of assets, chosen so that when some perform poorly, others are likely to perform well. An owner of an orange grove in Florida and a hotel on a Florida beach wouldn't be very well diversified. A severe freeze, for example, would both kill the orange trees and ruin the hotel business. Owning an orange grove in Florida and a New England ski resort would represent better diversification. A severe winter might kill the orange trees, but it would help the ski business; a warm winter, on the other hand, might mean no skiing but a great orange crop. Diversification generally means owning assets that any given set of circumstances would affect differently.

A role for international capital mobility in diversification is obvious. Holding all one's assets in a single country heightens risk because it subjects all the assets to common events. A political disturbance in the country or an economic slump or recession could cause all the assets to perform poorly. Holding assets in several countries, on the other hand, can diversify these risks. If one country pursues a policy that turns out to be disastrous, the policy would harm only a subset of the assets. Asset holders' risk aversion creates a motivation for capital mobility even under conditions of full factor price equalization.

Yet another motivation for capital mobility focuses on mobility as a way of trading goods across time, called **intertemporal trade.** Without international borrowing and lending, each country must divide its current production between current consumption and investment in tools to improve future output. The sum of consumption and investment must equal output each period for each country. Intertemporal trade, however, relaxes this constraint. A country with a net capital inflow borrows from the rest of the world. Residents of the country can consume and invest more than current production by borrowing, but they will have to consume and invest less than production later when they repay the loans. Such borrowing by a developing country, for example, might allow the country to take advantage of productive investment opportunities that its current low level of production couldn't fund. A country with a net capital outflow, on the other hand, lends to the rest of the world. Residents consume and invest less than current production, lend their savings to foreigners, and can consume and invest more than production in the future when borrowers repay the loans with interest. In the 1970s, for example, oil-exporting countries suddenly found themselves with more current income than they could consume or invest profitably in their home economies; therefore, they used the savings to buy assets abroad.

Such intertemporal exchange in assets can be mutually beneficial in much the same way as ordinary trade in goods and services. In fact, we can even phrase the story in terms of comparative advantage. Countries with an abundance of current production and a scarcity of domestic investment opportunities exhibit a comparative advantage in "current goods" relative to "future goods." Such countries can specialize in producing current goods by lending abroad and import future goods when the borrowers repay. On the other hand, countries with a scarcity of current production and an abundance of domestic investment opportunities hold a comparative advantage in future goods relative to current goods. They can import current goods by borrowing abroad and export future goods when they repay their loans.

Capital Mobility's Effects

Analysis of the effects of capital mobility is very similar to that for labor mobility. Figure 10.12 modifies the labor-mobility diagram from Figure 10.9. From an initial allocation of capital between the two countries represented by K_0, capital flows from country B to country A in response to the higher rate of return in A, $r_0^A > r_0^B$. Area EGJ measures the positive effect on world output from capital's shift from B to A. This gain comes from using the units of capital between K_0 and K_1 in the country with the higher value marginal product of capital (VMP_K).

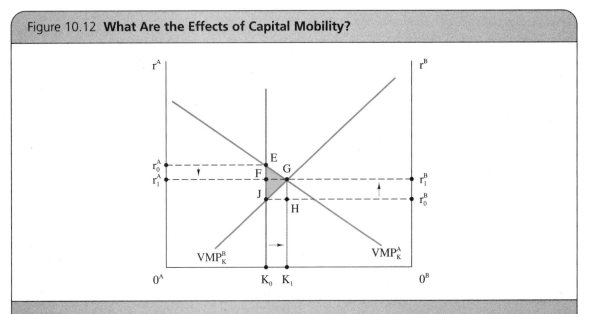

Figure 10.12 **What Are the Effects of Capital Mobility?**

Beginning at point E, capital flows, in response to the higher rate of return in country A, improve efficiency and increase output by EGJ. Both countries gain because ownership of the migrant capital remains with country B. In A, workers gain relative to capital owners; in B, capital owners gain relative to workers.

The allocation of capital mobility's benefits differs from the case of labor mobility. With labor mobility, not only the labor power itself migrated but also the owner of the labor. When capital migrates, its owner typically stays in country B. The migrant capital earns FGK_1K_0 in A, a gain of FGHJ over what it earned in B. This represents a gain to country B, which enjoys the income from the capital because its owner still resides there. Country A gains EGF, the productivity of the migrant capital above the return paid to it. The emigrant country loses in the case of labor mobility but gains from capital mobility, because it retains the ownership of and rights to the income from the migrant capital. Therefore, both countries enjoy a net gain; as usual, however, some groups within each country gain while others lose.

Owners of "native" capital in A suffer a reduction in their rate of return from r_0^A to r_1^A because of the capital inflow. Workers in A gain as the marginal productivity of labor rises from the availability of additional capital with which to work. Owners of capital that remains in country B benefit from the rise in the return to capital that occurs after the capital outflow. Workers in B have less capital to work with, suffer reduced marginal products, and earn lower wages. Therefore, it's not surprising that most labor groups favor restrictions not only on labor immigration but on capital outflows. Table 10.8 summarizes these results.

So far we've considered only factor mobility resulting from inter-country differentials in the rewards paid to factors of production. An additional consideration arises when governments tax the rewards paid to inputs.

10.4.3 Taxation and Factor Mobility

Most governments levy taxes on income earned by both workers and owners of capital. The rates of taxation and the precise rules defining taxable income vary widely from country to country, creating additional incentives for inter-country factor mobility. Ireland, for example, attracted many writers and poets by exempting from taxation all income earned from such activities. Several movie stars, rock stars, and athletes (including David Bowie, Michael Caine, Roger Moore, and Sean Connery) left England to avoid its high tax rates, formerly as high as 83 percent. England responded by lowering its top income tax rate dramatically and lured most of its tax exiles home.

Our analysis so far suggests that factor mobility increases world efficiency by drawing resources to those locations where they can be most productive. This conclusion does *not* apply, however, to mobility motivated solely by countries' differing tax rates and rules. Although such mobility clearly benefits the migrant labor or capital, it doesn't contribute to the efficiency of the world economy.[24] On the other hand, it does raise some interesting policy issues.

Taxation of wages and capital income have similar effects. The following discussion focuses on taxation of wages. The results carry over, with minor modifications, to taxation of capital. Figure 10.13 resembles Figure 10.9, which illustrated the effects of labor mobility. To keep the analysis simple, Figure 10.13 assumes that the initial allocation of labor between countries A and B (represented by L_0) is the efficient one; that is, at L_0 the values of the marginal productivity of labor and wage rates are equal in the two countries. Now

Table 10.8 **Effects of Capital Flow from Country B to Country A**	
Effect on:	
Owners of native capital in A	−
Laborers in A	+
Net effect on A	+ (area EGF)
Owners of capital remaining in B	+
Laborers in B	−
Owners of migrant capital	+
Net effect on B	+ (area FGJ)
Net effect on world welfare	+ (area EGJ)

24 This statement ignores supply-side or incentive arguments that, for example, individuals work more when they face low marginal tax rates because the after-tax return to working is higher.

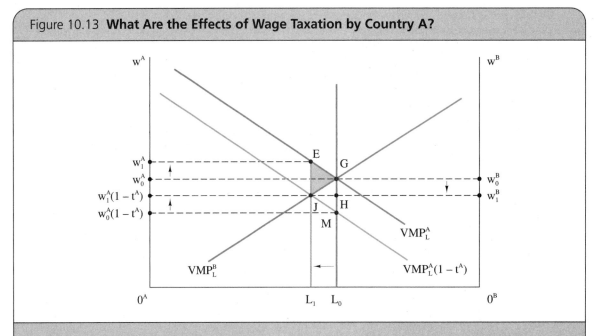

Figure 10.13 **What Are the Effects of Wage Taxation by Country A?**

Beginning with an efficient allocation of labor between A and B, taxation of wages by A reduces total output by EGJ. Workers between L_1 and L_0 migrate to B in response to a differential in wages net of taxes, but gross returns reflect true labor productivity. Immigration harms workers in B. Workers in A are better off than they would be in the presence of the tax and with no labor mobility.

suppose country A imposes a tax on wages at a rate denoted by t^A, where $0 < t^A < 1$.[25] For each dollar of wages earned, a worker must pay t^A in taxes, leaving a net reward or "take-home pay" of $\$1(1 - t^A)$. At any wage rate w^A, labor suppliers get to keep only $w^A(1 - t^A)$. Workers no longer choose between countries A and B by comparing $VMP_L^A = w^A$ with $VMP_L^B = w^B$; now the relevant comparison from the individual worker's point of view is between net or after-tax wages in the two countries, or $VMP_L^A(1 - t^A) = w^A(1 - t^A)$ and $VMP_L^B = w^B$. At L_0, $w_0^A(1 - t^A) < w_0^B$; thus, country A's taxation of wages causes the units of labor between L_1 and L_0 to migrate to country B to avoid the tax. Remember that L_0 represents the efficient, or output-maximizing, allocation of labor between the two countries. The workers who migrate in response to country A's tax are less productive in B than in A (reflected in the fact that VMP_L^A lies above VMP_L^B between L_1 and L_0); but because of the tax in A, workers earn higher *net* wages by working in B. Area EGJ measures the total *loss* of world output from the tax-migration effect.

Total output in A falls by EGL_0L_1. Workers who remain in A earn w_1^A but get to keep only $w_1^A(1 - t^A)$. They're worse off than before the tax (because $w_1^A[1 - t^A] < w_0^A$) but better off than if the tax had occurred with restrictions on labor mobility, in which case net wages would have fallen all the way to $w_0^A(1 - t^A)$. *(Why?)* Capital owners in A earn less because their capital has less labor with which to work than before the imposition of the tax. The country A government collects $w_1^A EJ w_1^A(1 - t^A)$ in tax revenue. Note, however, that labor's ability to move to avoid the tax reduces the government's ability to raise revenue by taxing wages. With completely immobile labor, the same tax rate depicted in Figure 10.13 would have raised $w_0^A GM w_0^A(1 - t^A)$ in revenue.

Total output in country B rises by JGL_0L_1. Native workers in B lose $Gw_0^B w_1^B H$ because of the inflow of workers, and owners of capital gain. The mobility of labor drives the wage rate in B down to equality with the *net* wage in A, even though wages in B remain untaxed.

---

25 For simplicity, we assume a constant tax rate; that is, the tax system is proportional. The tax liability equals a constant proportion (t^A) of the wage. Systems in which the tax rate rises with income are progressive, while those in which it falls with rising income are regressive. In Figure 10.13, we depict the tax, for simplicity, by a parallel shift of the VMP curve. In reality, the new curve would be steeper than the original one.

Country A's taxation of wages distorts the labor market and results in inefficient labor migration from A to B. Workers flow to the country in which they can earn the higher net wage, but gross rather than net wages reflect true productivity.

Figure 10.13 assumes that only country A taxes wages. In reality, most countries do; and the size of the distortion created by those taxes depends on relative tax rates. If countries A and B tax wages at the same rate and use the same definitions for taxable income, the taxes don't create any incentive for labor migration, because workers face the same taxes no matter where they live and work. *(How would you represent this case in Figure 10.13?)*[26] As long as the only choice labor has is whether to live and work in country A or country B, taxation has no net effect through migration when countries impose equal taxes.[27]

Because of the importance of *relative* tax rates, governments worry about other countries' tax policies. During the 1980s, top income tax rates trended downward in the major industrial economies. That the trend was in the same direction for the various countries limited incentives for migration in response to the tax changes. Even with the downward trend, substantial differences in tax rates remain. Simple comparisons can be misleading, however. For example, in some countries much of the relevant taxation occurs at the provincial or state rather than the federal level, and overall tax liability always depends on definitions of taxable income and allowable deductions as well as tax rates.

The pattern in corporate tax rates, or taxes on capital, is similar to that in personal income taxes. Differences in tax rates remain a source of controversy, particularly among the members of the European Union as they try to harmonize their economies. Despite the distorting effects of differences in taxes on capital, rates in 2001 ranged from Ireland's 20 percent to Italy's and Belgium's 40 percent.

So far, our examination of taxation's effects has maintained one subtle but important assumption: Income was subject to taxation by only one country at a time. By moving from A to B, workers could avoid paying the tax levied by A but became subject to any tax levied by B. Luckily for tax attorneys, the real-life situation is much more complex. A citizen working or investing abroad or a firm earning income abroad often faces taxation by both the domestic and foreign governments. This raises several policy issues.

Double taxation, or taxation of the same income by two governments, creates a strong disincentive for factor mobility. Many governments agree, through tax treaties, to reduce if not eliminate double taxation by granting either tax credits or tax deductions for taxes paid to foreign governments. A tax credit reduces the tax liability to country A by the full amount of the tax paid to country B. A tax deduction reduces the income subject to taxation in A by the amount of the tax paid to B. The tax credit eliminates double taxation, leaving a total tax liability equal to the higher of the two countries' tax rates. The tax deduction, on the other hand, reduces but doesn't eliminate double taxation. The negotiation of tax treaties reflects a delicate balancing of costs and benefits in terms of the revenue of the governments involved. Even with tax treaties, international mobility of factors of production reallocates the world's tax base, providing another source of controversy over policies toward factor mobility.

Most industrial countries, including the United States, use a residence-based tax system that taxes U.S. residents' income even if earned outside the country but doesn't tax interest income paid to foreigners. Many developing countries, on the other hand, use a source-based tax system that taxes any income originating in the domestic economy but not domestic citizens' income earned abroad. The combination of the two systems creates an incentive for capital flows from developing countries to industrial countries. *(Why?)*

10.4.4 **Multinational Enterprises and the World Economy**

One of the major economic trends of the postwar period has been the growth of firms across national boundaries, a source of both political and economic controversy. Estimates indicate that intra-firm trade within multinationals accounts for about one-third of all world trade, and that multinationals' exports to non-affiliates

---

26 Add a $VMP_L^B(1 - t^B)$ curve to represent the net return to labor in country B. If $t^B = t^A$, the new curve will intersect $VMP_L^A(1 - t^A)$ at point M. No labor will migrate. Gross wages will be equal at $w_0^A = w_0^B$, and net wages will be equal at $w_0^A(1 - t^A) = w_0^B(1 - t^B)$.

27 Taxation may cause some individuals to choose not to work; in that case, it will lower the total quantity of labor available. Even if taxation has no effect on total world output, distributive effects remain. The tax transfers the revenue raised from workers to the government, and the overall outcome depends on how government chooses to use the revenue.

account for another third, leaving only one-third of all trade to national rather than multinational firms.[28] The world's top 100 non-financial multinational enterprises employ more than 6 million workers and have foreign annual sales of more than $2 trillion.[29]

Definition

We can define **multinational enterprises (MNEs)** simply as firms that manage and control facilities in at least two countries. This simple definition, however, doesn't clearly separate multinational enterprises from other firms; the main source of ambiguity is the meaning of "manage and control." Would a firm based in country A, which owns half the shares of stock of a firm in country B, be an MNE? From the standpoint of economic theory, the primary issue in establishing whether an enterprise qualifies as an MNE is whether decisions made in one country direct and allocate resources located in another. This transcending of national boundaries makes MNEs both economically important and controversial.

Multinational enterprises can be classified into three groups based on the pattern of organization of their production. Some MNEs produce basically the same or similar goods in several countries; these are called *horizontally integrated MNEs*. For example, Toyota produces automobiles in both Japan and the United States. Other enterprises produce inputs in one country that they then use to produce another good in another country; these are referred to as *vertically integrated MNEs*. For example, the General Motors plant in Tonawanda, New York, produces engines to supply GM auto plants worldwide. The third possibility involves production of different or even totally unrelated goods in various countries; such arrangements are called *diversified* or *conglomerate MNEs*. For example, Japanese electronics firms such as Toshiba, Matsushita, and Sony manufacture a wide range of electronics products around the world. Early MNEs clustered in agricultural and mining sectors, where industrial economies invested in developing countries' raw-materials sectors; but the bulk of multinational activity now occurs in manufacturing, especially in the electronics, automobile, chemical, and pharmaceutical industries.

The MNE phenomenon isn't new, but the multinationalization of production has grown rapidly since World War II. Advances in transportation and communications technologies have increased the feasibility of global production. U.S. intra-MNE trade, that between U.S. parent firms and their foreign affiliates, comprises about 40 percent of all U.S. merchandise exports and imports. Case Five in Chapter Five provides more detail on patterns of intra-firm trade by MNEs.

The central questions to be answered concerning multinational enterprises include the reasons for their existence, their welfare implications, and the policy issues they raise for both parent and host governments. We now turn to each of these issues.

Why Go Multinational?

For years, most analysts of multinational enterprises viewed them as vehicles for spreading capital from one country to another, a perspective known as the **capital arbitrage theory of multinationals.** In capital-abundant countries, capital tends to earn a low return compared with that in capital-scarce countries. This difference in returns creates an incentive for capital owners to shift their resources from low-return to high-return countries, as discussed in section 10.4.2. Such activity increases total world income because it moves capital from areas of low productivity to those of higher productivity. However, the capital arbitrage view seems inconsistent with at least three aspects of observed MNE behavior. First, MNE capital doesn't flow primarily from capital-abundant to capital-scarce countries. We've seen that a large share of inward foreign direct investment goes to developed, capital-rich economies, not to developing capital-scarce ones. Second, in many countries inflows and outflows of MNE capital occur simultaneously. Figure 10.10 revealed that seven of the 10 leading FDI *host* countries also number among the top 10 *source* countries. Third, although MNEs often do move capital from one country to another, such movements aren't necessary because MNEs can borrow funds locally for their subsidiaries. Rather than simply moving capital, multinationals change where goods get produced and who maintains control over that production. Overall, the capital-arbitrage hypothesis appears unsatisfactory as an explanation of the MNE phenomenon.

---

28 WTO (1996), 44.

29 United Nations, *World Investment Report 2000*, p. xv.

When seeking to understand the observed location of production facilities around the world, economists think first of the low-cost way to serve markets. The theories of comparative advantage and trade based on scale economies are, after all, theories of the *location* of production: Industries tend to locate where they can produce a product at the lowest possible opportunity cost. However, this rule alone can't explain the existence of multinational enterprises, because all firms in each country could be locally owned and controlled. For example, the fact that Honda sells automobiles in both Japan and the United States doesn't imply that the firm must own and control separate production sites in Japan and Marysville, Ohio. Alternatives include (1) production just in Japan with export to the U.S. market and (2) licensing by Honda of a U.S. company to produce and sell Hondas in the United States in exchange for a license fee. That Honda now also exports automobiles from its U.S. plants to Japan further complicates the picture!

A theory of the MNE phenomenon must explain why an enterprise chooses multinationalism over exporting or licensing. Why does the firm choose to produce abroad *and* to maintain domestic ownership and control of that production? In other words, why does the enterprise choose to have its decision making and control of resources cross national borders? After all, multinationalism clearly involves costs. The firm must move goods, employees, and information around the world and learn the laws and customs of multiple countries. The headquarters in the parent country must spend resources monitoring the activities of its foreign affiliates. Occasionally hosts even expropriate investor assets. For example, when China's First Automobile Works' license to build Audi automobiles expired in 1997, the firm simply expropriated the technology and put its own Red Flag logo on the cars.[30] Given these costs, an MNE must expect significant benefits from centralized control of foreign facilities.

In choosing between exporting and producing abroad as alternate methods to serve a foreign market, the presence or absence of trade barriers is one important determinant of strategy. If the foreign market is protected by tariffs, quotas, or other restrictions on imports, exporting becomes less attractive relative to producing abroad. Statistical studies have confirmed that trade barriers encourage MNE activity. Even during the Great Depression, U.S. firms set up production facilities behind the Smoot–Hawley retaliatory tariffs passed by many countries. More recently, some developing countries have used this response as a strategy for attracting foreign investment. The tactic involves imposing import restrictions high enough to force foreign firms that want to sell in the market to establish local production facilities. Some Japanese investment in the United States, such as that in the auto industry, also fits this pattern, sometimes called *tariff-jumping,* or *market-access, foreign direct investment.* Foreign direct investment can also defuse protectionist political sentiment in the host country; this is called *quid pro quo investment.*

Empirical evidence indicates that deliberate use of high trade barriers to attract inward foreign direct investment can work but has some negative consequences. Most important, the investment attracted tends to be simply production units to serve the domestic market, not technology transfer or export-oriented production. Also, high trade barriers can make the domestic MNE affiliate less competitive by raising the cost of imported inputs it uses.

The non-export alternative to forming an MNE is to license a foreign firm to serve the foreign market. Examination of this alternative takes us closer to the frontiers of MNE research. Empirically, MNEs cluster in industries with large research-and-development or technological-innovation components, such as electronics, chemicals, and pharmaceuticals. The special character of information, technology, and other outputs of the research-and-development process provide a key to understanding the choice between licensing and multinationalism. Suppose that a firm in country A, through a costly research-and-development program, discovers a lower-cost technology to produce good X. The firm adopts the new technology in the domestic market and wants to use it to sell in country B. The firm has no production facilities in B, and B's trade barriers against imports make exporting infeasible. The firm can either acquire or build production facilities in B, thereby becoming an MNE, or sell the right to use the new technology to an existing firm in B. Consider the second alternative, licensing. How much would the A firm charge for the license, and how much would the firm in B be willing to pay for it? The character of new technology makes it difficult to arrive at a mutually acceptable price. The firm in B has no incentive to accept the A firm's word on the new technology's worth—because of the A firm's incentive to exaggerate it. But if the A firm reveals the technological secret to the firm in B to establish the innovation's value, the B firm may steal the design and use it without paying any license fee. The

30 Craig S. Smith and Rebecca Blumenstein, "In China, GM Bets Billions on a Market Strewn with Casualties," *The Wall Street Journal,* February 11, 1998.

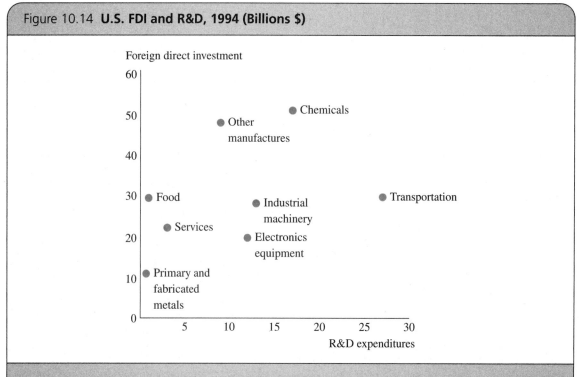

Figure 10.14 **U.S. FDI and R&D, 1994 (Billions $)**

Industries with high levels of research-and-development expenditure tend to generate high levels of foreign direct investment.

Source: Data from U.S. Bureau of Economic Analysis.

combination of the A firm's incentive to overstate the new technology's value and the B firm's motive to steal the underlying information can make a licensing agreement difficult to achieve.

These problems may be particularly acute in developing countries that have weak or nonexistent systems of patent and trademark protection for inventions. For these reasons, firms in technologically innovative or research-and-development-intensive industries tend to choose multinationalism over licensing. By forming an MNE, the firm maintains *control* over its technology while using it to serve foreign markets. Figure 10.14 reveals that U.S. foreign direct investment tends to be higher in industries, such as chemicals, that involve high levels of research and development.

Substitute for or Complement of Trade?

We've seen that both international trade and foreign direct investment by MNEs are growing rapidly—much more rapidly, in fact, than production. But how might the two trends be related? In particular, does more MNE activity tend to be associated with more international trade, or less? Existing empirical evidence suggests that the tentative answer is *both*. Some types of foreign direct investment substitute for trade in goods, while other types encourage more such trade.

If firms go multinational primarily to locate their production according to comparative advantage, then international trade tends to increase. If, for example, U.S.-based auto firms produce cars for the U.S. market in Mexico rather than in the United States because of Mexico's cost advantage, then more international trade in cars occurs. On the other hand, some firms may go multinational to gain better access to local markets. Japanese auto firms use their U.S. production facilities primarily (although no longer exclusively) to serve the U.S. market. To the extent that this production replaces U.S. car imports from Japan, international auto trade falls.

MNEs' Effects

The effect of multinational enterprises, both overall and on parent and host countries separately, is a subject of disagreement. Insofar as MNEs play a role in moving production to its least-cost locations and contribute to the spread of technological improvements, total world output increases. This makes possible an increase in total world welfare and potentially (though not necessarily) improves welfare in parent and host countries alike. MNEs may facilitate achievement of scale economies by handling some functions, such as research and finance, centrally while continuing to adapt to local conditions in other areas of operation (for example, labor relations and marketing). By handling many transactions internally, the MNE may be able to guarantee supplies of raw materials (by owning its own) and to build more reliable distribution networks.

Most of the controversy surrounding multinationals relates to the division of their benefits and costs between parent and host countries. U.S. labor organizations, for example, claim that the multinationalization of production by U.S. firms "exports" jobs. Because of the scarcity and relatively high wages of unskilled labor in the United States, firms tend to move abroad production that involves intensive use of unskilled labor. Assembly tasks, such as those in apparel, consumer electronics, and some high-technology products, often are conducted for U.S. companies by operations in labor-abundant and low-wage countries, from Mexico to China.

Claims by labor groups that this constitutes export of jobs that rightly belong to U.S. workers are subject to several important qualifications. The movement of production processes to areas of low-cost production maximizes total world output and income. In many cases firms face a choice between moving abroad or stopping production completely; that is, solely domestic production may cease to be viable due to comparative disadvantage. If foreign production operations make inputs cheaper for U.S. producers, the competitive positions of those producers improve. Increased foreign production also increases employment in management and research within the parent country. To the extent that foreign production raises foreign incomes, demand for U.S. exports increases, raising employment in export-oriented industries. Multinational enterprises play important roles in spreading training, as well as norms of corporate governance, accounting, and law. And the firms' ability to leave a country may constrain governments' abilities to pursue bad policies without accountability.

The proliferation of multinationals also tends to spread the technology developed in parent countries to the rest of the world. Developing countries have complained that MNEs keep research-and-development operations clustered in the industrialized countries rather than spreading facilities that would allow developing countries to become more self-sufficient in research and development and in technological innovation. Most empirical studies, however, find both that MNEs transfer advanced technology to their hosts and that the presence of MNEs enhances the efficiency of local firms. The trend of increased technology transfer through MNEs reflects the firms' growing globalization, in which the full range of firm activities occurs in locations throughout the world. General Motors, for example, has five state-of-the-art factories in Argentina, Poland, China, Thailand, and Brazil. The five utilize advanced technologies not present in any of the firm's U.S. plants, and local engineers played central roles in the design of all five.

Developing countries also charge that MNEs' sheer size and economic strength allow them to exploit their host countries. This alleged exploitation takes a variety of forms: bargaining with the host government for excessive tax concessions, paying unfairly low prices for raw materials removed from the host country, and issuing deceptive financial statements to repatriate all the benefits from the operation to the parent country. *(Refer back to Figure 10.12. What area represents the amount MNEs would need to extract to leave the host country no better off than before the investment?)* An additional concern is MNEs' general domination of the host's economy and culture, which can cause a loss of indigenous values and damage to local enterprises. Local firms in the host country, of course, have an incentive to block the entry of MNEs that would compete in the local market.

A final source of contention between MNEs and their parent and host governments arises not because of the multinationals themselves but rather because of governments' policies toward them. An MNE exists under the jurisdiction of several governments, and one of the most controversial questions surrounding these arrangements concerns those governments' rights to tax the MNE.[31] By moving production facilities around the world, multinationals reallocate the tax base among countries, as we saw in section 10.4.3, sometimes with significant distributional consequences.

---

31 The discussion of taxes and factor mobility in section 10.4.3 applies to multinational enterprises as well as labor.

Government Policies toward MNEs

Historically, government policies toward multinationals have been erratic. Countries vacillate between explicitly encouraging foreign investment and legally forbidding it. Current policies toward both inward investment (as viewed by the host country) and outward investment (as viewed by the parent country) differ widely across countries, although the last few years have seen a general move toward greater encouragement of foreign investment. Between 1991 and 1999, countries worldwide made 1,035 changes in laws covering foreign direct investment; and the United Nations characterizes 94 percent of those legal changes as having created a more open environment for foreign direct investment.[32]

However, despite the desire, particularly by developing countries, to attract foreign capital, many countries continue to restrict the entry and behavior of MNEs. Common host-country policies include bans from MNE participation in certain industries, limits on dividend payments and repatriation of profits to the parent country, requirements that MNEs buy specified percentages of inputs locally, local ownership requirements, minimum export limits, and ceilings on royalty payments for technology owned by parent-country firms. Industries in which governments often restrict MNE participation include banking, insurance, telecommunications, pharmaceuticals, computers, and advertising.

At the same time such restrictions make foreign investment less attractive, many host-country governments offer tax incentives to multinationals to locate in their countries. Other incentives include government provision of infrastructure such as roads, ports, railroads, and other facilities, as well as exemption from tariffs on imported inputs. Host countries end up using these incentives to compete for investments by firms such as General Electric, Intel, Microsoft, and Toyota. For example, after several episodes of tightening restrictions on foreign firms, China announced in 1999 that it would provide firms that transferred technology to China with exemptions from income and sales taxes.[33] To the extent that the *total* amount of investment remains unaffected by these fiscal incentive packages, such competition merely reallocates investment among host countries and transfers resources from the "winning" hosts to the MNEs that benefit from the incentives.

Parent-country governments generally place far fewer restrictions on MNE behavior than do hosts. As mentioned earlier, labor groups often argue that multinationalization leads to job loss, despite a lack of empirical evidence of any such economy-wide effects. In the United States there have been union-backed efforts to pass domestic-content legislation for the automobile industry, but the attempts have failed so far, except for NAFTA's stringent rules of origin.

CASE ONE:
Growth Myths and Miracles

We've seen in this chapter that a country's output can grow in two basic ways—more inputs or higher productivity. Either shifts the country's production possibilities frontier outward. We can make the growth relationship a bit more precise by stating it as an equation, often referred to as the *growth-accounting equation:*

Rate of growth of output =

Rate of growth of labor inputs + Rate of growth of capital inputs + Rate of growth of productivity

The last term on the right-hand side of the equation is called **total factor productivity** (TFP) and refers to organizational

and technological advances that allow the country to produce more output from the same amount of labor and capital resources. In other words, TFP captures changes in the effectiveness with which labor and capital resources are used.

Much of the recent increase in economic research on the subject of growth has taken the form of empirical studies of the growth-accounting equation to discover how much of observed growth should be attributed to the equation's various right-hand-side terms for different countries and time periods. Table 10.9 presents results from one study. The table reports the percentage of output growth attributable to labor, capital, and productivity for seven industrial countries during 1960–1989. With the notable exceptions of the United

---

32 United Nations, *World Investment Report 2000,* p. xv.

33 "China Takes Steps to Increase Investment," *The Wall Street Journal,* September 10, 1999.

Table 10.9 **Percent of Output Growth Attributable to Labor, Capital, and Productivity, 1960–1989**

	Percentage of output growth						
	U.S.	Canada	Japan	France	U.K.	Italy	Germany
Labor input per capita	32.2%	27.5%	37.5%	−5.9%	−7.1%	−0.6%	−11.3%
Capital input per capita	41.7	50.6	12.7	46.4	49.8	44.8	53.7
Productivity	26.2	21.8	49.8	59.6	57.3	55.8	57.6
Output per capita	100.0	100.0	100.0	100.0	100.0	100.0	100.0

Source: Data from Chrys Dougherty and Dale W. Jorgenson, "International Comparisons of the Source of Economic Growth," *American Economic Review Papers and Proceedings* (May 1996), p. 26.

States and Canada, TPF accounted for very large shares of growth. Unfortunately, the data that underlie such studies are subject to significant measurement error, and the findings of different studies vary significantly.

The division of economic growth into its input and productivity components took central stage in a debate over Asia's (pre-financial-crisis) growth experience. The growth of several Asian economies since the 1960s was widely touted as a "miracle"—often attributed by noneconomists and even by a few economists to a unique combination of Asian cultural values and government industrial policies. Economist Paul Krugman triggered the debate in 1994 by arguing that the Asian "miracle" was in fact a "myth."[34] He suggested that Asian economies had experienced such high growth rates mainly by utilizing more resources—that is, working harder and forgoing consumption to invest more—not by increasing their productivity. In fact, he even compared the Asian experience to that of the Stalinist era in the former Soviet Union. The USSR achieved very high growth rates dur-

ing the 1950s and 1960s by reducing consumption and investing at unprecedented rates. Output grew, but only so long as the unsustainable level of investment continued. Much of the investment went to unproductive projects, as directed by central planners; and growth collapsed (as, eventually, did the Soviet Union itself). No one suggested—even later in light of their severe financial crisis—that the Asian economies would suffer a series of Soviet Union–like collapses. The question was whether they would again reach the dramatic growth rates they experienced during the past couple of decades or whether their growth rates would settle down to a couple of percentage points faster than those in the industrial market economies. Once the region recovers from its late-1990s financial crisis, will the countries' emphasis on education generate rising productivity to sustain rapid growth? Or will the rapid increases in their rates of labor and capital utilization simply come to an inevitable end, leaving growth rates much like those in the rest of the world?

CASE TWO:
Evading Tax Evasion

As technologies for moving capital around the world improve, national governments worry more about their ability to maintain their tax bases. The industrial economies joined in a program, called the Financial Action Task Force, to dissuade other countries from engaging in Harmful Tax Practices, or tailoring a country's tax regime to erode the tax base of other countries. Examples include low rates of taxation on foreign capital that cause saving and investment which otherwise would happen in another country to

migrate (tax competition), as well as facilitating evasion of other countries' taxes. The targets of the campaign are offshore financial centers that offer low or no taxes along with strict bank-secrecy laws conducive to tax evasion and money laundering. The industrialized countries claim that these tax havens siphon saving and investment from abroad and that the bank-secrecy laws block needed cooperation between countries in money-laundering and tax-evasion investigations.

---

34 "The Myth of the Asian Miracle," *Foreign Affairs* (1994).

Table 10.10 **Financial Action Task Force Money Laundering Blacklist, June 2001**			
Removed from Blacklist	Still on Blacklist, but Making Progress	Still on Blacklist, and Facing Increased Countermeasures	Added to Blacklist
Bahamas	Cook Islands	Nauru	Egypt
Cayman Islands	Dominica	Philippines	Guatemala
Liechtenstein	Israel	Russia	Hungary
Panama	Lebanon		Indonesia
	Marshall Islands		Myanmar
	Niue		Nigeria
	St. Kitts and Nevis		
	St. Vincent and the Grenadines		

Source: Data from Financial Action Task Force Report. Updates available at the OECD Web site at http://www.oecd.org.

European governments, with their relatively high tax rates, wanted the task force to focus on both tax competition and tax evasion/money laundering. The United States, on the other hand, feared that listing low tax rates as a Harmful Tax Practice would provide governments an excuse for maintaining high rates. Eventually, pressure from the United States caused the group to reduce its emphasis on tax competition and to focus on cooperation against money laundering.

Bermuda, Cyprus, Mauritius, the Cayman Islands, Malta, San Marino, the Isle of Man, Netherlands Antilles, and Seychelles reached agreements to alter their laws and practices sufficiently to avoid being named on a list of countries engaged in Harmful Tax Practices. But other offshore centers didn't.[35] In late 2000, the Financial Action Task Force produced a report naming 15 financial centers as blacklisted for inadequate laws and enforcement against money laundering. The results of a June 2001 report update are listed in Table 10.10. Nauru, the Philippines, and Russia, having failed to make progress since being blacklisted in the first report, moved a step closer to facing sanctions, which might include restrictions on overseas operations of banks based in the recalcitrant countries and enforcement of more detailed information and reporting requirements for transactions in those countries.

After the terrorist attacks of September 11, 2001, the push to curtail international money laundering and unregulated financial flows took on a new urgency, as evidence accumulated that terrorist organizations used both informal money-shifting networks and commercial banks to move funds around the world.

CASE THREE:
Saving, Investment, and Intertemporal Trade

With no international capital mobility, each country's saving must equal its investment, because the only way to obtain funds to finance an investment project is to forgo current consumption, that is, to save. In such a world, a graph with national investment rates on the horizontal axis and national saving rates on the vertical one would show countries as a series of dots on an upward-sloping 45-degree line. Countries with low saving and investment rates would appear as dots on the lower, left-hand end of the line, and those with high saving and investment rates on the upper, right-hand end of the line.

Of course, capital isn't completely immobile. Most countries have removed many (but not all) of their legal barriers to capital flows, at least in the industrialized world. But a

35 For updates, go to the Tax section of the OECD Web site at www.oecd.org.

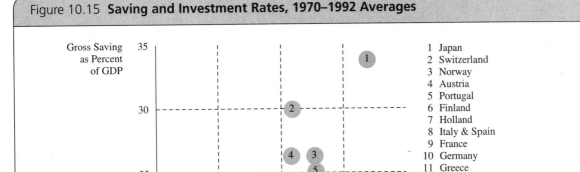

Figure 10.15 **Saving and Investment Rates, 1970–1992 Averages**

1	Japan
2	Switzerland
3	Norway
4	Austria
5	Portugal
6	Finland
7	Holland
8	Italy & Spain
9	France
10	Germany
11	Greece
12	Australia
13	Iceland & New Zealand
14	Canada
15	Belgium
16	Ireland
17	Turkey
18	Sweden
19	Denmark
20	United States
21	Britain

Despite increased capital mobility, countries with low (high) rates of saving tend to also have low (high) rates of investment expenditure.

Source: Martin Feldstein, "Global Capital Flows," *The Economist,* June 24, 1995, p. 73.

graph of countries' actual saving and investment rates, shown in Figure 10.15, looks remarkably similar to the 45-degree line we just described. Of the 23 industrialized countries included, not a single one pairs low saving and high investment or high saving and low investment; the maximum difference between the two rates for any country equals about 4 percent.

Countries' saving rates differ for several reasons. Cultures place different levels of importance on thriftiness. A country's age, demographic, and labor-force participation patterns affect saving because individuals' saving behavior varies considerably over their life cycle. Tax systems can encourage or discourage saving. Countries with generous public and private retirement systems may experience lower levels of nonretirement saving than those in which individuals feel more responsible for their own retirement income.

Figure 10.15 has at least two possible interpretations. The first takes the figure as evidence of a lack of international capital mobility. Countries' saving and investment rates match closely, just as we argued would be the case if mobility

were zero. This suggests that capital may not flow from countries with poor investment opportunities to those with good ones.

The second interpretation argues that perhaps countries with high saving rates happen to be the same countries that offer good investment opportunities, while countries with low saving rates offer few or poor investment opportunities. Countries that experience rapid economic growth, for example, tend to both save and invest at high rates. Countries whose economic policy makers follow policies that lead to stability foster both saving and investment in their economies. Other countries' policy makers cause uncertainty and instability that discourage both saving and investment.

Unfortunately, economists don't have enough information about the potential gains from intertemporal trade to choose confidently between Figure 10.15's two interpretations. We do know, however, that international capital mobility has risen in recent years and that countries' saving and investment rates diverge more now than in earlier years.

CASE FOUR:
Send Money

We saw in section 10.4.1 that labor mobility's effects on the country of emigration depend on whether workers who move send any of their earnings back home. Officially, the 5.5 million Filipinos working abroad in 152 countries (mostly the United States, Saudi Arabia, and Malaysia) sent $6.79 billion in worker remittances to family back in the Philippines in 1999.[36] Experts estimate that another $3 billion was sent outside the banking system, thereby escaping measurement.

The Philippines aren't alone in heavy reliance on worker remittances. Families in Haiti, Jamaica, the Dominican Republic ($1.5 billion), Trinidad, Cuba ($800 million), and Guyana receive hundreds of millions of dollars each year from family members working in the United States, Canada, and the United Kingdom. Total annual remittances to Latin America and the Caribbean have risen from about $7 billion in 1993 to over $20 billion in 1999; the worldwide total stands at about $70 billion per year, according to International Monetary Fund estimates. For the six countries listed in Table 10.11, annual remittances equal 10 percent or more of the country's gross domestic product.

While total remittances amount to huge sums, the individual transactions typically are quite small. Family members abroad send an average of about $250 eight to ten times per year. So the $20 billion in total remittances mean approximately 80 million separate transactions. Most go by Western Union; typical fees take more than 10 percent of the sum remitted. In addition, 5 percent of the sum remitted usually goes to foreign-exchange fees.

After the September 11, 2001, terrorist attacks on the United States, information surfaced that the perpetrators had used an informal and unregulated international money-moving network called *hawala* to handle their financial needs. Several *hawala* operations had their funds frozen as part of the anti-terrorism campaign. Unfortunately, while having the beneficial effect of making it harder to finance terrorism, loss of this network also left many foreign workers with fewer alternatives for sending remittances home to countries with poorly developed banking systems.

Table 10.11 **Remittances as a Percent of Gross Domestic Product, 2000**

Country	Remittance (Percent)
Haiti	17.0%
Nicaragua	14.4
El Salvador	12.6
Jamaica	11.7
Dominican Republic	10.0
Ecuador	10.0

Source: Data from Multilateral Investment Fund, Inter-American Development Bank.

Summary

Economic growth's effect on welfare is more complex than a first glance suggests. The two components are the income effect (which applies to both small and large countries) and the terms-of-trade effect (which applies only to large countries). When growth results from increased factor endowments, the direction of the income effect depends on the relative increases in total consumption and population. If total consumption rises at a faster rate than population, per-capita consumption rises. The terms-of-trade effect can be either positive or negative, depending on growth's impact on the desired volume of trade at the original terms of trade. The overall effect of factor-endowment-based economic growth on welfare is uncertain for both large and small countries.

---

36 "Bolstering the Economy from Afar," *Financial Times,* September 26, 2000.

Economic growth due to technical progress improves the welfare of small countries by raising per-capita consumption. For large countries, the terms-of-trade effect can be either positive or negative. The possibility of a strongly negative terms-of-trade effect outweighing the positive income effect implies that growth can be immiserizing, although little empirical evidence supports this view.

International mobility of factors of production increases the efficiency of the world economy when it is based on differential productivity across countries. Mobility also alters the distribution of income in each country between capital owners and labor, making policies that promote or restrict mobility controversial. When artificial incentives such as differential tax rates cause migration of capital or labor, the migration reduces the efficiency of the world economy.

Looking Ahead

Chapter Eleven focuses on special trade-related problems facing developing countries. It examines the role of international trade in growth and development, as well as the use of trade restrictions for dealing with the special problems of development. We also explore the experience of a new class of developing economies—those in transition from central planning.

Key Terms

economic growth
endogenous growth theory
balanced growth
income effect
terms-of-trade effect
Rybczynski theorem
immiserizing growth
technical progress
neutral technical progress
capital-saving technical progress
labor-saving technical progress
brain drain

outsourcing
portfolio investment
capital outflow
international purchase of assets
capital inflow
international sale of assets
direct investment
diversification
intertemporal trade
multinational enterprise (MNE)
capital arbitrage theory of multinationals
total factor productivity

Problems and Questions for Review

1. Technological advances in computer hookups and satellite communications have allowed U.S.-based computer software development firms to use computer programmers in India for programming tasks. The firms send program specifications to India via satellite; the Indian programmers do the programming (at wages below those of U.S. programmers) and transmit the completed programs back to the United States via satellite.
   a. Explain whether you expect the following groups to support or oppose the new arrangements and why: U.S. computer software development firms, U.S. computer programmers, computer programmers in India.
   b. What effect might such policies have on the brain drain?
2. Which of the following groups would you expect to support the policy of allowing U.S. offshore assembly provisions? For each group, briefly explain why.
   a. Workers in labor-abundant developing countries.
   b. Capital owners in labor-abundant developing countries.
   c. Labor in the United States.
   d. Capital owners in the United States.
3. U.S. automobile manufacturers took a variety of positions on U.S. limits on auto imports from Japan. Ordinarily, we would expect domestic producers to favor such restrictions. What might explain the observation that some domestic producers didn't favor the import restrictions?

4. a. Illustrate an equilibrium situation with an efficient allocation of capital between two developing countries, A and B, and with no taxation of capital income in either country. Be sure to label carefully and explain.

    b. Illustrate the effects if country A imposes a tax (at rate t^A) on capital income. What are the tax's implications for capital mobility, efficiency, and country A's government budget?

    c. Illustrate the effects if country B also imposes a tax at rate $t^B = t^A$ on capital income. What are the tax's implications for capital mobility, efficiency, and for the two countries' government budgets, compared with the situation in part (b)?

    d. Developing countries often grant tax concessions (that is, partial or complete tax exemptions) to multinational firms in an effort to attract capital inflows. What happens if country A grants concessions and country B doesn't? What happens if both countries grant concessions? Why might countries want to negotiate agreements that limit concessions they can grant to multinational firms?

5. Explain the similarities between balanced growth and neutral technical progress. Can the welfare effects of the two differ? Why, or why not?

6. Countries A and B, the only two countries in the world, follow free trade in goods X and Y. Country A has a comparative advantage in good X, which is labor intensive.

    a. Compare the wage rates in the two countries under free trade.

    b. Now country B imposes a tariff on X imports. If labor can move between countries, will the tariff create an incentive to move from A to B, from B to A, or neither? Why?

7. Each year, labor flows from Mexico to the United States. If the United States and Mexico eliminated barriers to trade in goods and services, would you expect the migration to increase or decrease? Why? Might your answer differ for the short run and the long run? Why?

8. Country A and Country B use labor and capital to produce a single good. Each country has the same amount of capital and the same technology. The value marginal product of labor in each country depends on how many workers are employed according to the following schedule:

Number of Workers Employed	Marginal Product of Last Worker	Price of Output	Value Marginal Product of Last Worker
1	10	$10	$100
2	9	$10	$90
3	8	$10	$80
4	7	$10	$70
5	6	$10	$60
6	5	$10	$50
7	4	$10	$40
8	3	$10	$30
9	2	$10	$20
10	1	$10	$10

Initially, there is no labor mobility, and 8 workers are employed in country A and 4 workers in country B. If labor mobility were allowed, what would happen to employment, production, and wages in each country?

References and Selected Readings

Aghion, Philippe, and Peter Howitt. *Endogenous Growth Theory.* Cambridge, Mass.: MIT Press, 1998.
Advanced textbook on the theory of economic growth.

Aghion, Philippe, et al. "Inequality and Economic Growth: The Perspective of the New Growth Theories." *Journal of Economic Literature* 37 (December 1999): 1615–1660.
Advanced; what do new theories about growth imply about inequality's impact on growth?

Barro, Robert J. *Determinants of Economic Growth.* Cambridge, Mass.: MIT Press, 1997.
Accessible overview of the recent empirical literature on economic growth.

Bhagwati, Jagdish N. "Immiserizing Growth: A Geometrical Note." *Review of Economic Studies* (June 1956): 201–205.
The original demonstration of immiserizing growth.

Borjas, George J. "The Economics of Immigration." *Journal of Economic Literature* 32 (December 1994): 1667–1717.
Review of the recent literature and recent events; for all students.

Borjas, George J., et al. "How Much Do Immigration and Trade Affect Labor Market Outcomes?" *Brookings Papers on Economic Activity* (1997): 1–90.
Survey and empirical evidence on immigration, trade, employment, and wages; for all students.

Carrington, William J., and Enrica Detragiache. "How Extensive Is the Brain Drain?" *Finance and Development* 36 (June 1999): 46–49.
How much do developing countries lose as a result of skilled workers emigrating to developed countries?

Easterly, William. *The Elusive Quest for Growth: Economists' Adventures and Misadventures in the Tropics.* Cambridge, Mass.: MIT Press, 2001.
Easy-to-read but highly informative tour of development policies.

Forbes, Kristin J. "A Reassessment of the Relationship between Inequality and Growth." *American Economic Review* 90 (September 2000): 869–887.
Advanced; finds a short-run positive effect of inequality on growth.

Frankel, Jeffrey A., and David Romer. "Does Trade Cause Growth?" *American Economic Review* 89 (June 1999): 379–399.
Strong evidence that open trade contributes to growth, not the other way around.

Graham, Edward M. *Fighting the Wrong Enemy: Antiglobal Activists and Multinational Enterprises.* Washington, D.C.: Institute for International Economics, 2000.
Readable treatment of the benefits of multinational enterprises.

Graham, Edward M., and Paul R. Krugman. *Foreign Direct Investment in the United States.* Washington, D.C.: Institute for International Economics, 1995.
Measurement and implications of foreign direct investment in the United States; for all students.

Gropp, Reint, and Kristina Kostial. "FDI and Corporate Tax Revenue: Tax Harmonization or Competition?" *Finance and Development* 38 (June 2001): 10–13.
Global patterns in tax rates.

Grossman, Gene M., and Elhanan Helpman. "Technology and Trade." In *Handbook of International Economics,* Vol. 3, edited by G. M. Grossman and K. Rogoff, 1279–1338. Amsterdam: North–Holland, 1995.
Advanced survey of technology-related aspects of international trade and trade theory.

Gu, Wulong, and Mun S. Ho. "A Comparison of Industrial Productivity Growth in Canada and the United States." *American Economic Review Papers and Proceedings* 90 (May 2000): 172–175.
Has productivity in the United States and Canada converged or diverged?

Jones, Charles I. *Introduction to Economic Growth.* New York: Norton, 1998.
Textbook on growth theory; intermediate to advanced.

Jones, Charles I. "On the Evolution of the World Income Distribution." *Journal of Economic Perspectives* (Summer 1997): 19–36.
Changes over time in the international distribution of income; intermediate.

Jones, Ronald W. *Globalization and the Theory of Input Trade.* Cambridge, Mass.: MIT Press, 2000.
Advanced treatment integrating trade in factors of production.

Klenow, Peter, and Andrés Rodríguez-Clare. "The Neoclassical Revival in Growth Economics: Has It Gone Too Far?" *NBER Macroeconomics Annual* (1997): 73–114.
The debate over neoclassical versus endogenous growth theory; intermediate.

Lee, Frank C., and Jianmin Tang. "Productivity Levels and International Competitiveness between Canadian and U.S. Industries." *American Economic Review Papers and Proceedings* 90 (May 2000): 176–179.
How productivity affects industries' trade performance.

Lerman, Robert I. "U.S. Wage Inequality Trends and Recent Immigration." *American Economic Review Papers and Proceedings* 89 (May 1999): 23–28.
A reevaluation of immigration's effects on wages.

Little, Jane Sneddon. "U.S. Regional Trade with Canada during the Transition to Free Trade." Federal Reserve Bank of Boston, *New England Economic Review* (January–February 1996): 3–21.
Introduction to the interaction of international trade and foreign direct investment.

Loungani, Prakash, and Assaf Razin. "How Beneficial Is Foreign Direct Investment for Developing Countries?" *Finance and Development* 38 (June 2001): 6–9.
Evaluating the impact of FDI on host countries.

Mankiw, N. Gregory. "The Growth of Nations." *Brookings Papers on Economic Activity* 1 (1995): 275–326.
Overview of economic growth models; intermediate and advanced.

Markusen, James R. "The Boundaries of Multinational Enterprises and the Theory of International Trade." *Journal of Economic Perspectives* 9 (Spring 1995): 169–190.
Relationship between multinational firms and patterns of international trade; intermediate students.

Mataloni, Raymond J., Jr. "A Guide to BEA Statistics on U.S. Multinational Companies." U.S. Department of Commerce, *Survey of Current Business* 75 (March 1995): 38–55.
Detailed guide to U.S. government statistics on multinationals.

Organization for Economic Cooperation and Development. *Migration and Regional Economic Integration in Asia.* Paris: OECD, 1998.
Introduction to recent migration trends in Asia.

O'Rourke, Kevin H., and Jeffrey G. Williamson. *Globalization and History.* Cambridge, Mass.: MIT Press, 1999.
Fascinating exploration of immigration in the nineteenth-century Atlantic economy.

Pritchett, Lant. "Divergence, Big Time." *Journal of Economic Perspectives* (Summer 1997): 3–18.
Argument that incomes of rich and poor countries are diverging; for all students.

Rybczynski, T. M. "Factor Endowment and Relative Commodity Prices." *Economica* 22 (November 1955): 336–341.
The original statement of the Rybczynski theorem; for intermediate students.

Schuknecht, Ludger. "A Trade Policy Perspective on Capital Controls." *Finance and Development* 36 (March 1999): 38–41.
Uses the basic trade model to illustrate the benefits of open international capital flows.

Stiglitz, Joseph E., and Shahid Yusuf. *Rethinking the East Asian Miracle.* Oxford: Oxford University Press, 2001.
Collection of readable essays on various aspects of East Asia's amazing growth, in light of the area's late-1990s financial crisis.

Symposium on "Slow Growth in Africa." *Journal of Economic Perspectives* 13 (Summer 1999): 3–88.
Why have most countries in Africa grown so slowly?

Temple, Jonathan. "The New Growth Evidence." *Journal of Economic Literature* 37 (March 1999): 112–156.
Intermediate/advanced overview of the recent empirical evidence on causes of economic growth.

Webb, Roy H. "National Productivity Statistics." Federal Reserve Bank of Richmond, *Economic Quarterly* 84 (Winter 1998): 45–64.
An introduction to measures of productivity, changes in productivity over time, and explanations for those changes.

Wong, Kar-yiu. *International Trade in Goods and Factor Mobility.* Cambridge, Mass.: MIT Press, 1995.
Advanced international textbook emphasizing factor mobility.

World Bank. *World Development Report.* New York: Oxford University Press, annual.
The 2000/2001 issue focuses on poverty, and the 2001/2002 issue on institutional prerequisites for markets.

World Trade Organization. *Trade and Foreign Direct Investment: Annual Report 1996,* Vol. I. Geneva: WTO, 1996.
Excellent introductory survey of theory and evidence on foreign direct investment and its relation to trade.

Development, Transition, and Trade

11.1 Introduction

The basic theories of international trade developed in Chapters Two through Ten apply to countries regardless of their levels of economic development. The gains from specialization and exchange exist for the United States and Kazakhstan and for Singapore and Ethiopia. Regardless of what country imposes them, tariffs and quotas harm domestic consumers, deny the protected industries scale economies, and risk creating bloated and inefficient monopoly firms with the political clout to maintain their protected status at the expense of the rest of the domestic economy.

Despite the general applicability of what we've learned about international trade, developing countries undeniably face special challenges. The post–World War II development record presents a juxtaposition of dismal failures and sparkling successes. The challenge to economists and policy makers is clear: Understand the development process well enough to explain the successes and learn to apply their lessons to remedy the failures.[1]

Consider some of the failures. Five developing countries experienced drops of more than 2 percent in their per-capita incomes during 1999–2000: Chad, Côte d'Ivoire, Eritrea, Kenya, and Zimbabwe.[2] Of course, many types of disturbances can cause short-run declines in output, but even over the long run, some countries have experienced large declines in per-capita income. During the three decades from 1965 to 1998, the Democratic Republic of the Congo (formerly Zaire), Kuwait, Nicaragua, Niger, United Arab Emirates, and Zambia each experienced an average annual decline of 2 percent or more in per-capita GNP.

Annual per-capita income in Ethiopia in 2000 was $100. A baby born in 1999 in Sierra Leone faced an infant-mortality rate of 283 per thousand live births and a life expectancy of 37 years. Experts estimate that 57 percent of Nepali children under five years old suffered from malnutrition during 1992–1998. Only 6 percent of Nepal's population had access to sanitation in 1990–1996, and only 7 percent of Eritreans had access to safe drinking water. In 1998, 93 percent of adult women in Niger could not read; only 24 percent of primary-school-age children there attended school. Measured by the World Bank's standard—living on less than $1 per day—1.2 billion people in 1998 endured extreme poverty.

Despite these clear indicators of past failures and future challenges, the development record isn't uniformly bleak. Six geographically diverse developing economies—Dominican Republic, South Korea, Moldova, Mozambique, Nicaragua, and Turkmenistan—increased their per-capita incomes by more than 8 percent during 1998–1999. Botswana, China, Hong Kong, South Korea, Oman, Singapore, and Thailand each experienced average annual per-capita income growth of 5 percent or more for the three decades from 1965 through 1998.

---

1 For an up-to-date analysis, see World Bank, *Globalization, Growth, and Poverty.*

2 Data come from the World Bank's *World Development Indicators 2000* and *World Development Report 2000/01.*

Between 1970 and 1998, infant mortality in the low-income economies fell from 113 per thousand live births to 68. For girls, primary school enrollment rose from 67 percent of the relevant age group to 82 percent between 1980 and 1997. Many other indicators of well-being show similar gains. Developing countries as a group, and even the 64 low-income ones, have made dramatic progress. A handful of countries have done so to the point that the term *developing* no longer seems to fit.

In this chapter, we focus on the trade-related issues facing developing countries. First, we define and evaluate the magnitude of the development task. Next, we highlight several distinct subgroups of developing countries that face somewhat different sets of problems and concerns. Finally, we outline the experience and prospects of both traditional developing economies and the economies in transition from central planning.

11.2 Defining Development

The ultimate goal of a country's development process is to improve its residents' well-being, but there's neither an indisputable definition of economic development nor an unambiguous standard by which to measure a country's development status.

Per-capita gross national product or income represents the most widely used single indicator of development. **Gross national product (GNP)** measures the value of a country's yearly output.[3] International organizations divide countries into several development groups based on per-capita income, or GNP divided by population. The World Bank classifies countries into "high-income economies" with annual per-capita incomes above $9,266 in 2000, "upper-middle-income economies" with per-capita incomes between $2,996 and $9,265, "lower-middle-income economies" with per-capita incomes between $756 and $2,995, and "low-income economies" with per-capita incomes below $755. That 2.5 billion people live in low-income economies, while only 903 million live in high-income economies, highlights the magnitude of the development task.

As an indicator of development, per-capita GNP is far from perfect. First, it fails to account for variation in the scope of market transactions in different economies. Economic transactions typically count in GNP only if they occur in an organized market. As a country develops, an increasingly large share of its economic activity typically moves into organized markets; for example, commercially bought food and restaurant meals often replace home-grown and prepared food. Therefore, much of the economic activity in developing countries fails to show up in per-capita GNP figures, causing those figures to overestimate the gap between developing and developed countries.

A second shortcoming of differences in per-capita income as an indicator of development is that such differences, dramatic as they are, fail to capture many issues relevant to development. For example, average infant mortality and life expectancy at birth in low-income countries are 116 per thousand and 59 years, respectively, compared with 6 per thousand and 78 years in the high-income countries. A final weakness of focusing exclusively on per-capita income as a development indicator is that it fails to indicate the distribution of income across the population.

Table 11.1 reports countries' 2000 per-capita incomes, 1999 infant-mortality rates, and Gini indices, a measure of how equally income is distributed across the population. The Gini index varies from zero to one hundred; a value of zero indicates a perfectly equal income distribution (every individual has income equal to per-capita income), and a value of one hundred denotes the extreme of unequal distribution (one individual receives all the income). For the countries reported, the Gini index varies from the Slovak Republic's 19.5, where the highest-income 20 percent of the population earns 31 percent of all income, to Sierra Leone's 62.9, where the highest-income 20 percent of the population earns 63 percent of all income.

Table 11.1 reveals that individual countries often fare quite differently in terms of different indicators of well-being; some enjoy high per-capita income although other indicators of well-being lag, while others exhibit the opposite pattern. Compare, for example, Armenia and Haiti. Per-capita incomes are very similar, yet Haiti's infant-mortality rate remains six times as high as Armenia's. Or, consider Tajikistan and Thailand. Although Thailand's income equals almost 12 times Tajikistan's, the two countries have almost identical infant-mortality rates.

---

3 More precisely, gross national product is the sum of the current market values of all currently produced final goods and services over a specified time period, such as one year.

Table 11.1 **Per-Capita Income, Infant Mortality, and Gini Index of Income Distribution**

Country	Per-Capita Income, 2000 ($)	Under-5 Mortality per 1,000 Live Births, 1999	Gini Index	Country	Per-Capita Income, 2000 ($)	Under-5 Mortality per 1,000 Live Births, 1999	Gini Index
Algeria	$ 1,590	39	35.3	France	$23,670	5	32.7
Angola	240	208	n.a.	Georgia	590	20	37.1
Argentina	7,440	22	n.a.	Germany	25,050	5	30.0
Armenia	520	18	44.4	Ghana	350	109	39.6
Australia	20,530	5	35.2	Greece	11,960	7	32.7
Austria	25,220	5	23.1	Guatemala	1,690	52	55.8
Azerbaijan	610	21	36.0	Guinea	450	167	40.3
Bangladesh	380	89	33.6	Haiti	510	118	n.a.
Belarus	2,990	14	21.7	Honduras	850	46	59.0
Belgium	24,630	6	25.0	Hungary	4,740	10	24.4
Benin	380	145	n.a.	India	460	90	37.8
Bolivia	1,000	83	58.9	Indonesia	570	52	31.7
Botswana	3,300	95	n.a.	Iran, Islamic R.	1,630	33	n.a.
Brazil	3,570	40	59.1	Ireland	22,960	7	35.9
Bulgaria	1,510	17	26.4	Israel	16,310	8	35.5
Burkina Faso	230	210	48.2	Italy	20,010	6	27.3
Burundi	110	176	33.3	Jamaica	2,440	24	36.4
Cambodia	260	143	40.4	Japan	34,210	4	24.9
Cameroon	570	154	n.a.	Jordan	1,680	31	36.4
Canada	21,050	6	31.5	Kazakhstan	1,190	28	35.4
C. African Rep.	290	151	61.3	Kenya	360	118	44.5
Chad	200	189	n.a.	Korea, Rep.	8,910	9	31.6
Chile	4,600	12	57.5	Kuwait	n.a.	13	n.a.
China	840	37	40.3	Kyrgyz Rep.	270	38	40.5
Hong Kong	25,950	5	n.a.	Lao, PDR	290	143	37.0
Colombia	2,080	28	57.1	Latvia	2,860	18	32.4
Congo, D. Rep.	100	161	n.a.	Lebanon	3,750	32	n.a.
Congo, Rep.	630	144	n.a.	Lesotho	540	141	56.0
Costa Rica	3,960	14	45.9	Lithuania	2,900	12	32.4
Côte d'Ivoire	660	180	36.7	Macedonia	1,710	17	n.a.
Croatia	4,510	9	29.0	Madagascar	260	149	46.0
Czech Rep.	4,920	5	25.4	Malawi	170	227	n.a.
Denmark	32,020	6	24.7	Malaysia	3,380	10	49.2
Dominican Rep.	2,100	47	47.4	Mali	240	223	50.5
Ecuador	1,210	35	43.7	Mauritania	370	142	37.3
Egypt	1,490	54	28.9	Mexico	5,080	36	51.9
El Salvador	1,990	36	50.8	Moldova	400	22	40.6
Eritrea	170	105	n.a.	Mongolia	390	73	33.2
Estonia	3,410	12	37.6	Morocco	1,180	62	39.5
Ethiopia	100	166	40.0	Mozambique	210	203	39.6
Finland	24,900	5	25.6	Myanmar	n.a.	120	n.a.

(continues)

Table 11.1 *(continued)*

Country	Per-Capita Income, 2000 ($)	Under-5 Mortality per 1,000 Live Births, 1999	Gini Index	Country	Per-Capita Income, 2000 ($)	Under-5 Mortality per 1,000 Live Births, 1999	Gini Index
Namibia	$ 2,050	108	n.a.	South Africa	$ 3,020	76	59.3
Nepal	220	109	36.7	Spain	14,960	6	32.5
Netherlands	25,140	5	32.6	Sri Lanka	870	19	34.4
New Zealand	13,080	6	n.a.	Sweden	26,780	4	25.0
Nicaragua	420	43	60.3	Switzerland	38,120	5	33.1
Niger	180	252	50.5	Syria	990	30	n.a.
Nigeria	260	151	50.6	Tajikistan	170	34	n.a.
Norway	33,650	4	25.8	Tanzania	280	152	38.2
Pakistan	470	126	31.2	Thailand	2,010	33	41.4
Panama	3,260	25	48.5	Togo	300	143	n.a.
P. New Guinea	760	77	50.9	Tunisia	2,090	30	41.7
Paraguay	1,450	27	57.7	Turkey	3,090	45	41.5
Peru	2,100	48	46.2	Turkmenistan	840	45	40.8
Philippines	1,040	41	46.2	Uganda	310	162	37.4
Poland	4,200	10	31.6	Ukraine	700	17	29.0
Portugal	11,060	6	35.6	United Kingdom	24,500	6	36.1
Romania	1,670	24	28.2	United States	34,260	8	40.8
Russia	1,660	20	48.7	Uruguay	6,090	17	42.3
Rwanda	230	203	28.9	Uzbekistan	610	29	33.3
Saudi Arabia	6,900	25	n.a.	Venezuela	4,310	23	48.8
Senegal	500	124	41.3	Vietnam	390	42	36.1
Sierra Leone	130	283	62.9	Yemen, Rep.	380	97	33.4
Singapore	24,740	4	n.a.	Zambia	300	187	52.6
Slovak Rep.	3,700	10	19.5	Zimbabwe	480	118	56.8
Slovenia	10,070	6	28.4				

Source: Data from World Bank, *World Development Report 2001/02.*

Lumping all low- and middle-income economies together under the rubric "developing countries" conceals important differences, both in the well-being of their residents and in the trade-related issues of primary concern to policy makers in the various countries. Table 11.2 divides the low- and middle-income economies by region and reports their basic development indicators.

Note the differences revealed in Table 11.2. Sub-Saharan Africa suffers low per-capita GNP, negative long-term growth rates, short life expectancy, and high illiteracy. The East Asia region, on the other hand, although per-capita GNP remains low, has enjoyed very rapid long-term economic growth along with life expectancy that approaches that in high-income economies; but illiteracy remains high. Latin America and the Caribbean enjoy the highest incomes among developing countries, as well as long life expectancy and low rates of illiteracy, but their low long-term growth rate reveals continuing economic difficulties.

Increases in per-capita income are essential to the development process. Even small differences in rates of economic growth can substantially alter the length of time required to, say, double a country's per-capita income. Table 11.3 provides a rough rule for the relationship between growth rates and length of time required to double income. Consider the implications. The growth rate of 2.2 percent recorded by low- and middle-income developing countries as a group between 1965 and 1998 (from Table 11.2) produces a doubling of

Table 11.2 Low- and Middle-Income Economies' Development Indicators

Country Group	GNP per Capita 2000 ($)	Annual Growth, 1965–1998 (Percent)	Life Expectancy, 1999	Adult Female Illiteracy, 1999 (Percent)
All low income	$ 420	3.7%	59	49%
All middle income	1,970	1.9	69	20
Lower middle income	1,140	n.a.	69	23
Upper middle income	4,620	2.2	69	11
All low- and middle-income	1,230	2.2	63	33
Sub-Saharan Africa	480	−0.3	47	49
East Asia and Pacific	1,060	5.7	69	22
South Asia	460	2.7	63	59
Europe and Central Asia	2,010	n.a.	69	5
Middle East and North Africa	2,040	0.2	68	48
Latin America and Caribbean	3,680	1.3	70	13

Source: The World Bank, *World Development Indicators 2000* and *World Development Report 2001/02.*

income in approximately 32 years. Growing instead at the 5.7 percent rate experienced by the East Asian and Pacific economies doubles incomes in about 12 years. Achieving even the more modest goal of boosting growth from 2.2 percent to 3.2 percent would cut the doubling period from 32 years to 22.

11.3 Development Issues

Since the 1940s, when developing economies began to achieve political independence in large numbers, policies to foster economic development have been an area of active research, both theoretical and empirical. Individual countries have followed a variety of policies in their efforts to develop; as we've seen, the results have been mixed. Some, such as Taiwan, South Korea, Hong Kong, and Singapore, have achieved economic success that even the high-income economies envy. Others, including many in sub-Saharan Africa, continue to suffer severe economic deprivation.

Nonetheless, developing countries as a group have shared some commonalities. Historically, most followed policies that favored the industrialized sectors of their economies over primary-product production, for reasons we explore later. Most isolated themselves, at least to some degree, from the international trading system. And the state dominated the typical developing-country economy, enforcing elaborate protection and trade-control schemes, managing huge state-owned enterprises, deciding which firms got funds for new investment projects, and administering detailed "plans" for the country's development.

Many economists and policy makers believed during the 1950s and 1960s that the fundamental results of international trade theory didn't apply to developing economies as they did to developed ones, because the basic structure of developing economies was different. Policy makers from most developing countries argued that their undeveloped status warranted special assistance from the developed economies and fundamental changes in the international trading system. These calls for change became known as the **North–South debate,** because most developed economies lie in the Northern Hemisphere temperate zone.[4]

The developing economies' divergent experience during the past 25 years, especially the impressive growth and industrialization of several Asian economies, has made developing countries' policy concerns and interests more diverse, as the more successful economies have come to hold more in common with the high-income

---

4 Bloom and Sachs (1998) argue that a tropical location presents a very high hurdle to economic growth.

Table 11.3 **Growth Rates and Length of Time Required to Double Income**			
Growth Rate (%)	Approximate Years to Double Income	Growth Rate (%)	Approximate Years to Double Income
1%	70	6%	12
2	35	7	10
3	24	8	9
4	18	9	8
5	14	10	7

economies than with the least-developed ones. In addition to these changes, advances in economists' understanding of the development process have produced a new consensus that, despite lively disagreements over details, accepts two basic points: (1) International trade theory *does* apply to developing countries, and (2) the market-based international trade system benefits developing countries that choose to participate and contributes in many complex and subtle ways to successful development.

We can organize our discussion around five basic trade-related issues that have played central roles in policy debates. As the developing countries' experiences have diverged, some of the issues remain more salient for some countries than for others.

1. What is the proper role of agriculture and other primary-product sectors in a developing economy, and what are appropriate policies toward those sectors? Until the 1970s, most developing countries specialized in primary products, including agriculture, metals, and minerals; a large number still do.
2. What is the appropriate role of industrialization in development, and what policies can achieve the desired goals? Historically, most developing-country policy makers viewed economic development as synonymous with industrialization. We'll see that, in their attempts to industrialize, economies have followed two alternate strategies: inward-oriented import substitution and outward-oriented development, which differ dramatically in their focus on industrialization and in their policies toward trade.
3. How can countries with modest resources gain access to new productivity-enhancing technologies? Developing countries' low incomes limit the resources available to spend on research and development. One possible shortcut involves borrowing and adapting technology from more advanced economies, but the international system of patents and the monopoly power held by some technologically innovative firms constrains such borrowing. On the other hand, industries in the industrialized economies—semiconductors, movies, and computer software, for example—claim that they lose millions in revenues as a result of unauthorized copying of their products by counterfeiters based in developing economies.
4. How can developing countries borrow to gain the advantages of intertemporal trade without encountering debt crises of the type that made the 1980s a "lost decade" in terms of growth for many borrowers? Many developing countries continue to exhibit very low saving rates, making them dependent on foreign borrowing to finance investment. They still face the problem of how to maintain policies that create enough confidence in their economies' future performance to allow them to borrow to finance development-related investment.
5. To what extent is there an inevitable trade-off between economic growth and environmental quality? High-income developed economies (not to mention vocal "antiglobalization" activists) press the developing economies to adopt more stringent environmental protections. Developing countries guard their right to exploit their resources as they see fit, despite developed countries' wishes to restrict practices such as cutting of tropical rain forests that may have global climatic consequences.

11.4 Agriculture, Industry, or Both?

There are few areas of economics in which the views held by most economists have changed more than in the field of development.[5] During the 1950s and 1960s, certain stylized facts about developing economies and the

---

5 This section draws on Krueger (1997) and Bruton (1998).

nature of the world economy, now recognized as erroneous and misleading, were widely accepted. Also, many important elements of the relevant international economic theory (for example, the effective rate of protection, the superiority of subsidies over protection for dealing with domestic distortions, and the analysis of trade policy with economies of scale) had not yet been discovered.

11.4.1 Views on Development, Circa 1950–1965

The central stylized fact of development economics during the 1950s and early 1960s was the belief that poor developing economies were fundamentally and structurally different from rich developed ones. The two primary aspects of difference centered on the relationships between agriculture and manufacturing and between capital and labor.

Developing economies were widely seen as prisoners of their dependence on agriculture and other primary products and their corresponding dependence on imported manufactured goods from the developed countries. All agriculture was perceived as labor intensive and all manufacturing as capital intensive, while developing economies typically were labor abundant and developed ones capital abundant. Many economists and policy makers drew the inference that specialization and trade according to comparative advantage would make developing economies permanent agricultural producers. Developing countries also claimed that their terms of trade deteriorated over time as prices of the primary products they exported fell relative to those of the manufactured goods they imported.[6] Given these views, the conclusion was that international trade according to comparative advantage would condemn developing economies to permanently low and erratic export earnings and income because of their specialization in agriculture and other primary products.

Developing countries were also thought to have far too much labor—so much that its marginal product was low or even zero—and far too little capital. Economists believed that the "traditional structure" of labor-abundant, agriculturally oriented economies made them unresponsive to prices, incentives, and other market forces. This implied that development, which was thought to require an escape from dependence on agriculture, could only be brought about by dramatic government policies that forced the economies out of their traditional *status quo.* Most important were policies to encourage capital-good imports that could support domestic manufacturing at the expense of agriculture and thereby change the fundamental structure of developing economies to one more like that of the developed economies—capital abundant and dominated by manufacturing.

11.4.2 Import Substitution

Economic historians often call international trade the "engine of growth." Historically, periods of rapid growth in international trade have corresponded with periods of rapid increases in world output. Nonetheless, until recently most developing countries sought to limit their exposure to the world trading system by following an **import-substitution** development strategy, which involved extensive use of trade barriers to protect domestic industries from import competition. Import substitution focused on eliminating imported manufactures and encouraging the growth of domestic manufacturing. Many developing countries followed import-substitution policies during the 1950s and 1960s, and a few continue to do so.

The policies' logic followed directly from the stylized facts discussed earlier. If industrialization was necessary for development and if free trade would leave developing countries specialized in agriculture, then government policy had to generate investment in new manufacturing industries. The infant-industry argument for protection, outlined in Chapter Eight, also played an important role in import substitution. If mature manufacturing industries already existed in the developed countries, potential entrants from developing economies couldn't compete in the short run with those established competitors. Temporary infant-industry protection, however, might support new developing-country firms; those firms could eventually become competitive, at which time government could remove the protection.

The precise form and extent of import substitution differed from country to country. Brazil's "Law of Similars" declared that firms that imported goods similar to ones produced domestically would lose their access to government credit, tax privileges, and right to bid on government contracts. In India, all imports required a license, and firms petitioning for one had to provide a letter from all potential domestic suppliers explaining

---

6 A country's terms of trade consist of the price of the country's export good(s) relative to the price of its import good(s). A rise in this ratio is an improvement in the terms of trade and a fall is a deterioration.

why the domestic firms couldn't meet the specifications. Turkey maintained a list of goods for which import licenses could be granted; once domestic production of an item began, the good was removed from the list. In other words, imports that competed with domestic goods were effectively banned.

Because the import-substitution policy package emphasized production of manufactured goods for the domestic market (that is, to substitute for imports), the policies typically penalized the agricultural and export sectors of the economy. These sectors were often taxed, denied access to credit, and refused permits for imported inputs they needed. In many cases, for example, import barriers restricted farmers' access to new agricultural technology and to productivity-enhancing improvements such as tractors and new, improved seed varieties. Governments maintained monopolies in farm products and forced farmers to sell to those monopolies at prices far below market levels, discouraging production. Again, the logic could be found in the accepted stylized facts about developing economies, the nature of markets, and the development process. If the structure of agriculture made it a dead end, and if the static nature of traditional societies made them unresponsive to prices and other incentives, then development policy needed to shrink that sector and shift resources into manufacturing. Domestic politics also contributed to these counterproductive agricultural policies in many countries because small-scale rural farmers typically possessed little political influence compared with urban elites who benefited from low food prices and government assistance to manufacturing.

11.4.3 As the World Learns: Changing Views on Development

Since about 1965, the views of most economists and policy makers on the development process have changed dramatically. Many of the stylized facts accepted earlier have now been recognized as incomplete, irrelevant, or just plain wrong.

Developing economies do differ from developed ones—in their capital-labor ratios, their histories and political institutions, and their endowments of expertise and entrepreneurship. However, *developing economies respond to prices and incentives and can benefit from international trade based on comparative advantage or economies of scale just as developed economies do.*

Countries' comparative advantages evolve over time, and developing economies can and do specialize in manufacturing. The agricultural and manufacturing sectors each contain goods whose production is labor intensive (for example, rice and apparel) and products whose production is capital intensive (for example, wheat and steel). The comparative advantage for labor-abundant developing economies lies in labor-intensive agricultural products *and* labor-intensive manufactures; the comparative advantage for capital-abundant developed economies is in capital-intensive agricultural products *and* capital-intensive manufactures. Therefore, labor abundance doesn't imply a comparative advantage in agriculture and a comparative disadvantage in manufacturing, as had been thought earlier. Similarly, investment in education, skills, and human capital allow developing economies to alter their factor endowments and shift their comparative advantage toward more skill- and technology-intensive products.

The presumed long-run deterioration of developing countries' terms of trade also turned out to be wrong. Empirical investigations have demonstrated that developing countries' terms of trade exhibit little or no long-run tendency to decline. Periods of decline, such as the 1980s, certainly do occur and make the development process more difficult. Countries that depend on one or a few export products, such as the oil-exporting developing countries, can experience dramatic shifts in their terms of trade. But the earlier presumption of a permanent downward trend in the terms of trade for all developing countries involved in primary-product markets was simply mistaken.

The Failure of Import Substitution

Evidence suggests that forgoing gains from trade to develop domestic manufacturing industries through import substitution does *not* constitute a promising development strategy; in fact, the results of import substitution disappointed, exactly as our basic trade model would lead us to expect.

Several problems contributed to the apparent failure of many import-substitution programs. Most important, the infant-industry argument, as we saw in Chapter Eight, suffers from serious weaknesses. A period of temporary government support is no substitute for comparative advantage, and an industry without comparative advantage will remain an infant forever. In many developing economies, shortages of skilled labor, experienced management, clear and well-enforced property rights and contract law, and entrepreneurship hampered the emergence of successful industrial enterprises. Under these circumstances, an import-substitution policy based on import barriers simply guaranteed the continued existence of an inefficient domestic industry, often a monopoly—at the expense of domestic consumers and taxpayers. To make matters worse, many of the developing countries that pursued import substitution most aggressively were small, so their attempts to develop manufacturing based solely on the domestic market doomed firms to produce at inefficiently small scale.

Import substitution also failed for reasons having as much to do with politics as with economics. The strategy's emphasis on manufacturing tempted many developing economies to pour vast resources into building highly visible and symbolic national industries, such as steel, autos, chemicals, and national airlines, without regard for comparative advantage or economies of scale. Active involvement by governments in favoring some sectors of the economy over others asked governments to predict which industries would succeed. Such predictions run a high risk of failure as patterns of comparative advantage change. Even in Japan, a success story overall, the industries that proved most successful often weren't the ones favored by the government during the years of import substitution in the 1950s and 1960s, as we saw in Case Four in Chapter Eight. Governments often failed in the task of choosing industries to support because they picked in part based on special-interest groups' political pressure for protection rather than on economic analysis. Political factors also made the switch away from import substitution difficult, even after the strategy's failure became apparent. Capital owners and workers in industries created by import-substitution policies were potent political forces to block a shift toward other development strategies. And, since import-substitution policies placed so much power in the hands of government planners and bureaucrats, they often proved understandably reluctant to move toward more market-oriented policies that reduced their control and prestige.

Somewhat more surprising than its other shortcomings is the fact that import substitution failed to decrease dependence on imports. By artificially encouraging industrialization even in areas of comparative disadvantage, import substitution actually increased dependence on the imported inputs and capital goods required to keep production going in the protected industries. Because of the inefficient nature of many of the manufacturing processes, the value of these imports often exceeded that of the finished manufactured goods imported before institution of an import-substitution policy. The inefficiencies of import-substitution policies multiplied when the chosen industries exhibited economies of scale, because the domestic market typically was too small to support production at a scale sufficient to achieve those economies.

The import-substitution blueprint for development involved an attempt to replicate developed economies with their high capital-labor ratios and dominant manufacturing sectors. When developing countries emphasized *capital*-intensive production despite their *labor* abundance, they suffered high unemployment and chronically low wages and incomes. Low domestic income, in turn, limited the domestic market for the manufactured goods that governments so carefully cultivated. The protected industries couldn't export—because of their comparative disadvantage—but had little domestic market.

Lessons from the Newly Industrializing Countries

Some developing economies switched away from import substitution early (Taiwan was among the first) and opened their economies to trade. Details differed from country to country, but common elements included reducing import protection, removing policy biases against exports and agriculture, and allowing manufacturers to produce for export as well as for the domestic market. Economies that made these policy shifts enjoyed remarkable rates of economic growth and industrialization. Some, including Taiwan, South Korea, Hong Kong, and Singapore, earned the name **newly industrializing countries (NICs)** for their swift move along the development path. They weathered the OPEC-induced oil price increases of the 1970s better than other developing economies, even though they imported most or all of their oil requirements, and they resumed post-oil-shock growth more quickly.

Most indicators suggest that these newly industrializing economies now have more in common with the developed countries than with the low-income developing ones, as Table 11.4 reports. They built major export industries including steel, shipbuilding, chemicals, semiconductors, and computers. They undertook foreign investment projects in Asia, as well as in the United States and Europe. They even started financing foreign-aid projects in less-developed economies. Observing these countries' successes helped to change attitudes about development, since their experience challenged old assumptions—such as the ones about developing countries' alleged permanent condemnation to agriculture and inability to build export industries.

Scholars and policy makers debate the precise reasons for the NICs' successes. In particular, disagreement persists concerning the extent to which the governments directed investment to specific industries (that is, "picked winners"). Most analysts agree, however, that the key was the shift away from import substitution

Table 11.4 **Newly Industrializing Countries' Economic Indicators, 2000–2001**				
Country	Per-Capita GDP ($ at Purchasing Power Parity)	Exports (Billions $)	Imports (Billions $)	Male Life Expectancy at Birth
Hong Kong	$25,400	$204.0	$215.0	77
Singapore	26,500	137.0	127.0	77
South Korea	16,100	172.6	160.5	71
Taiwan	17,400	148.4	140.0	74

Source: Central Intelligence Agency, *World Factbook 2001.*

toward policies that opened the economy to international trade, foreign investment, foreign competition, and new technology and know-how. The new policies respected patterns of comparative advantage, the importance of achieving economies of scale, and the role for exports.

11.4.4 Outward-Oriented Development

As we've seen, industrialization traditionally has been viewed as a crucial step in the process of economic development. The record of success in industrialization varies. The United States and Japan were, not too many years ago, developing countries and now are industrial giants in the world economy. More recent years have seen other success stories, including Taiwan, South Korea, and Brazil. The experiences of other countries, such as India and many in sub-Saharan Africa, have been less encouraging, sometimes for obvious reasons and sometimes for less obvious ones. Overall, the developing countries' shares of production and export of manufactures have increased significantly over the past three decades, but most of the early growth has come in middle-income developing countries rather than low-income ones.

One of the most dramatic events in the world economy during the 1980s was the shift of many developing countries from inward-looking import-substitution policies to more outward-oriented policies that recognized a role for exports. **Outward-oriented growth** is best characterized as open to the world economy. This development strategy involves exploiting comparative advantage and economies of scale and importing goods costly to produce domestically. Industrialization for its own sake receives less emphasis here than under an import-substitution policy. Countries specialize production along the lines dictated by their comparative advantage, which may be resource based, and in sectors where export success can allow them to achieve economies of scale. Industrialization is a natural outcome of the overall development process rather than a goal pursued for its own sake.

Because of the critical importance of the import-substitution/outward-oriented policy choice for world welfare, economists have devoted a great deal of time and effort to examining the implications of each. One of the world's leading authorities on economic development, Anne Krueger of the International Monetary Fund, supervised one study while she served as Chief Economist for the World Bank. The Krueger analysis found that the evidence overwhelmingly favors outward-oriented policies as a strategy for development. Countries that pursue such policies have higher average growth rates than countries that pursue import substitution. In addition, individual countries typically experience spurts in their growth rates when they switch from import substitution to outward-oriented policies. Finally, despite its lesser emphasis on industrialization, an outward-oriented policy appears to promote higher growth rates in manufactured exports than does a policy that targets industrialization through import substitution.

To understand the differential success of import-substitution and outward-oriented development strategies, recall how early chapters of this book emphasized the importance of market-determined prices in guiding resources to their highest-valued use. An inward-oriented strategy, or import substitution, involves circumventing market forces to alter prices and encourage domestic manufacturing regardless of the pattern of comparative advantage and without regard to the prospects for achieving economies of scale. Such a strategy typically involves extensive use of tariffs, quotas, and import-licensing schemes, often justified by appeals to the infant-industry argument for protection (see section 8.3). The second strategy, an outward-oriented one, stresses specialization according to comparative advantage and reliance on sectors where firms can achieve economies of scale rather than an attempt at artificially induced industrialization.

11.4.5 Lessons

Few economists today expect or recommend a return to policies like import substitution. Most now agree than openness plays complex and essential roles in development: It provides access to consumer goods, new technology, and managerial and entrepreneurial resources; and it provides domestic firms with market discipline, incentives to reduce costs, and motivation to innovate as they face competition from foreign firms.

Despite these broad areas of new consensus, areas of disagreement remain. The World Bank study described earlier, for example, has been criticized for its allegedly overly optimistic and simplistic view of the benefits of an outward orientation. Critics of the new enthusiasm for outward-oriented development strategies emphasize the daunting difficulty of the development task and caution that mere openness to international trade, while it may facilitate that task, can hardly transform it into a quick and simple one. Successful development requires sound policies, implemented effectively from a base of good information. Important resources include not just labor and capital, but human skills, policy competence, entrepreneurship, the ability to learn and adapt, credible and trustworthy business and government institutions, and an understanding of each economy's unique history, politics, and culture. Given this demanding recipe, in which openness to international trade is one of many important ingredients, it seems likely that the development record will continue to be a mixed one.

11.5 North–South Issues

Thus far, we've focused on developing countries' own policies and how they affect the prospects for successful development. But, of course, external considerations such as the health of the overall world economy and the policies followed by developed countries and international organizations also affect developing economies. Sometimes developing countries want developed ones to change their policies or want international organizations to allow them special privileges because of the difficult development tasks they face. Three specific areas of ongoing disagreement and negotiation concern agricultural policy, technology-transfer and intellectual-property issues, and the environment.

11.5.1 Agricultural Policy

Recall that the main goal of import substitution involved shifting resources out of the traditional agricultural sector and into manufacturing. Import-substitution policies discriminated against agriculture in many ways. Agricultural prices were kept artificially low, which discouraged production. It also kept incomes low for the majority of the population, which limited domestic demand for new, domestically produced manufactured goods. Workers who lacked the skills to work in industry became unemployed as the agricultural sector stagnated or shrunk. As the severe long-run distortions caused by import-substitution policies came to be recognized, developing economies and their advisors also began to appreciate the important roles for agriculture in a developing economy—even one that hopes to eventually become more involved in manufacturing.

When developing economies switched their policies to ones that respected their comparative advantage in agriculture and began to try to export agricultural products, they found that developed countries' agricultural policies limited the developing countries' abilities to export primary products. In the developed countries, agricultural policies have primarily domestic goals, including raising agricultural prices and supporting domestic farmers' incomes. However, as we saw in Chapters Seven and Eight, these domestic policies often require trade-policy supplements, especially import quotas and export subsidies. Table 11.5 reports the tariff-equivalent rates of import protection for eight agriculture sectors for a sample of 11 developed countries at the beginning of the Uruguay Round negotiations. Recall that the tariff-equivalent rate of protection is the tariff rate that would have the same trade-reducing effect as the existing system of tariffs and quotas; in other words, it provides a single measure of the level of tariff and nontariff protection. Notice that most of the tariff equivalents measured well over 100 percent. Unfortunately, these developed-country agricultural policies seemed to ignore the impact on developing countries.

Table 11.5 **Tariff-Equivalent Rates of Protection, Beginning of Uruguay Round (Percent)**								
Country	Rice	Wheat	Coarse Grains	Sugar	Beef & Veal	Pork	Poultry	Dairy
Australia	0.0%	0.0%	0.4%	52.4%	0.0%	0.0%	0.0%	6.7%
Canada	0.9	57.7	34.7	34.7	38.0	0.0	226.0	288.4
United States	5.0	6.0	8.0	197.0	31.0	0.0	7.0	144.0
European Union	360.5	155.6	134.4	297.0	125.4	51.7	44.5	288.5
Japan	n.a.	239.6	233.1	126.1	38.5	87.3	14.0	489.4
New Zealand	0.0	0.0	7.2	2.9	0.0	20.0	28.5	19.6
Austria	0.0	400.0	241.0	178.0	239.0	178.0	38.0	463.0
Finland	10.0	352.0	204.0	493.0	394.0	320.0	264.0	389.0
Norway	454.0	495.0	394.0	n.a.	405.0	428.0	379.0	435.0
Switzerland	67.0	179.0	242.0	273.0	479.0	227.0	767.0	795.0
Turkey	50.0	200.0	200.0	150.0	250.0	250.0	30.0	200.0

Source: Data from General Agreement on Tariffs and Trade.

A second aspect of developed countries' agricultural policies makes it more difficult for developing-country agricultural producers to move into refining and processing of their agricultural products. We saw in section 6.8 that the **effective rate of protection (ERP)** provided by a given nominal tariff on a finished product depends on the tariffs levied on inputs used in producing it. The lower the tariffs on inputs, other things equal, the higher the rate of protection on the finished good. The developed countries' practice of **cascading tariffs,** or **tariff escalation,** imposes increasing tariff rates as a good moves through the stages of production; tariffs are lowest on raw materials and highest on finished goods. The result is often an effective rate of protection on processed and finished goods several times their nominal tariff rates. In reaching developed-country markets, developing countries face increasingly high barriers as they attempt to move into processing and manufacturing.

These agriculture-related issues ranked high on developing countries' lists of concerns about the world trading system in the 1980s. The beginning of the Uruguay Round of GATT talks in 1986 involved special attempts to encourage active participation by developing countries, and the debates over agricultural policy played a key role. Earlier GATT rounds had ignored agricultural trade, although it was a major concern of developing countries and a major source of trade disputes, because the developed economies didn't want to face the domestic political consequences of changing their highly protectionist agricultural policies. Early in the Uruguay Round, developed countries promised to include agriculture in the talks in exchange for developing countries' active participation and their consent to include trade liberalization in services on the agenda as well.

In the end, the Uruguay Round made progress in agricultural reform. Several of the changes enhance developing countries' access to export markets in the developed countries. WTO members no longer can grant new export subsidies to agricultural goods. Developed countries were given six years to cut their existing export subsidies by 36 percent, and each country's volume of subsidized exports had to fall by 21 percent. Developing countries were required to institute similar changes, but at rates of 24 percent and 14 percent on the amount and volume of subsidies, respectively. Countries also were required to reduce their aggregate domestic subsidies to farmers by 20 percent.

The Uruguay Round agreement also required developed member countries to convert all nontariff barriers into their tariff equivalents, which then became subject to the negotiated schedule of tariff reductions—of 36 percent over six years. However, a look at the tariff-equivalent rates of protection in Table 11.5 makes clear that even after the 36 percent reductions, agricultural tariffs by developed countries will still be very high, much higher than those on manufactured goods. The Uruguay Round agreement also required developing countries to convert their nontariff barriers to tariffs and then cut those tariffs, but with cuts of 24 percent over 10 years. For the least-developed economies, the agreement required binding agricultural tariffs at current levels, but no cuts.

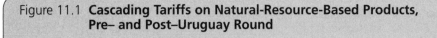

Figure 11.1 **Cascading Tariffs on Natural-Resource-Based Products, Pre– and Post–Uruguay Round**

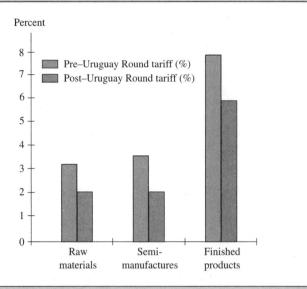

Uruguay Round tariff cuts on resource-based semi-manufactured and finished goods exceeded those on raw materials. This reduced the effective rate of protection for processed and finished goods.

Source: GATT, *The Results of the Uruguay Round of Multilateral Trade Negotiations: Market Access for Goods and Services* (Geneva: GATT, 1994.)

Markets subject to prohibitive quotas in the past, such as the Japanese rice market, had to provide minimum access to imports. In addition, the agreement reduced cascading tariffs. As Figure 11.1 illustrates, absolute tariff cuts on natural-resource-based finished products (2 percent) exceeded those on raw materials (1 percent) and semi-manufactures (1.5 percent), so the effective rates of protection provided to semi-manufactures and finished products in developed countries fell. This should make it easier for developing countries to shift into processing and manufactures related to their primary-product sectors.

Developing countries that are actual or potential agricultural exporters hope to make further progress during the Doha Round of WTO negotiations. The wish list hasn't changed much since the Uruguay Round: reduced developed-country barriers against agricultural imports and cuts in developed countries' export subsidies for agricultural products. The political opposition to theses changes hasn't shifted much either; European Union opposition to changes in its subsidy-based Common Agricultural Policy, in particular, remains strong, especially in France.

11.5.2 Technology, Intellectual Property, and Development

Technology, viewed from the economist's perspective, is simply the set of rules that govern how inputs can be transformed into goods and services. Improvements in technology allow more goods and services to be produced from the same quantity of inputs, or the same quantity of goods and services to be produced from a smaller quantity of inputs. Technological improvement contributes to economic development by increasing the output a country can produce given its resource endowment.[7]

The research and development (R&D) process that leads to technological innovations is long, expensive, risky, and skill intensive. It's also subject to economies of scale, implying that R&D on a very small scale is

---

7 Section 10.3 analyzed the effect of technical progress on economic growth.

inefficient. These characteristics of the R&D process make it difficult for developing countries to create their own indigenous technologies, resulting in dependence on the developed world for technological innovation.

Technology Transfer and Appropriateness

Developing economies point to two aspects of current technology arrangements that they believe work to their disadvantage. The first is the terms on which developing-country firms can gain access to new technologies, often through multinational enterprises. The second issue concerns the nature of the technology itself and its appropriateness for developing countries.

In the industrial market economies, where most technological innovation historically has taken place, private firms typically conduct most research, spurred by the promise of profit from any forthcoming innovations. An international system of patents—legal restrictions on uncompensated use of technology developed by others—protects technology from being freely copied, a protection that allows firms engaged in research to capture the return necessary to justify their efforts. If a newly developed innovation were freely available to all, research might slow as the incentive to innovate evaporated.

The prices firms charge for licenses to use their new technologies do slow the spread of technology from developed to developing countries. In the past, many multinational enterprises maintained their technologically innovative research-and-development divisions in their home countries and restricted the degree of **technology transfer** to their foreign subsidiaries. Critics of multinationals claimed that these policies prevented developing countries from using the technologies to advance the rest of their economies. However, as we saw in Chapter Ten, multinational firms increasingly use their newest techniques in foreign plants and conduct research there. The distinction between typical parent-country activities and typical host-country activities is fading for most multinationals as they move toward true global production.

The more relevant question isn't whether developing economies would benefit if given free access to all technology created by developed-country firms (an unlikely scenario), but whether developing countries that open themselves to trade gain access to useful technologies and grow faster than countries that insulate themselves from the world trading system. Recent experience provides a clear answer to this question.[8] Although the most successful developing economies differ widely in the extent to which they've welcomed foreign direct investment by multinational enterprises, virtually all have imported and exported relatively freely and used their trade to learn about and master technologies created abroad.

Most major technological advances have occurred in physical-capital-abundant and human-capital-abundant countries, where firms' goals for technological improvement include substitution of abundant capital for relatively scarce unskilled labor. Developing countries, however, claim that they need a different type of technology, because they tend to have abundant unskilled labor and little physical or human capital. The appropriate technologies in such situations typically would be more labor intensive. Thus, multinational enterprises often receive blame for introducing inappropriate technology. But firms, whether multinational or domestic, respond to the incentives they face in choosing technologies and production processes. In the past, many developing economies' import-substitution policies encouraged firms to use highly capital-intensive technologies, because capital-intensive industries gave the appearance of successful industrialization. Without such artificial incentives, multinational firms producing in labor-abundant countries have an incentive to use technologies that take advantage of the availability of low-wage labor. Thus, labor-abundant developing countries must recognize that the production techniques that use their labor and, thereby, raise wages, may not correspond to the symbolically important capital-intensive industrialization typical of industries such as steel and chemicals. And within any given industry, production techniques in labor-abundant countries will be more labor intensive than those used in other countries. Recall the example from Chapter Three of General Motors' two state-of-the-art production facilities. The plant in Germany, a capital-abundant, high-wage country, is 95 percent automated, while the plant in Argentina, a labor-abundant, low-wage country, is 45 percent automated.

Intellectual Property

Trade disputes over **intellectual property** involve trade in goods that infringe on foreign copyrights, trademarks, industrial secrets, and patents, including counterfeit goods. Industries in which intellectual-property issues play a large role include pharmaceuticals, computer software, music recordings, computers, books, and

---

8 See, for example, Edwards (1998) and Frankel and Romer (1999).

movies.[9] These issues have only recently earned a prominent role in international trade negotiations. Earlier, developed economies tended to ignore whatever losses their firms sustained due to unauthorized copying, and developing economies openly claimed the right to copy at will in order to diffuse the benefits from technological advances and to avoid the monopoly prices charged by innovating firms for their technologies.

More recently, trade in goods containing important intellectual-property elements has grown much faster than trade overall. This trend has caused firms in developed economies to take their lost revenues more seriously, since the developed economies exhibit strong comparative advantage in most of the relevant industries. In addition, the growth of developing economies' markets has made innovating firms eager to sell there, but the developing countries' weak intellectual-property laws and enforcement have limited the profitability of doing so.

Several developing economies have moved unilaterally to strengthen their intellectual-property protection. Although this trend represents in part a response to pressure from developed countries, especially the United States, other reasons exist as well. Some of the more successful developing economies have begun to innovate and to shift into industries where they themselves desire intellectual-property protection. Other countries hope, by strengthening their rules, to encourage inward foreign direct investment and foreign firms' willingness to share new technologies with their local affiliates.

Several factors complicate international negotiations over intellectual-property rules. One is the difficulty in determining the optimal level of protection. Any system of intellectual-property rules represents a trade-off between the incentives to innovate (which rest on strong protection) and the benefits from rapid diffusion (which come from weak or nonexistent rules). Probably a more important impediment to successful negotiations is the obvious distributional consequence of rule changes. Unlike negotiations to lower most trade barriers, which produce gains for all countries, strengthening intellectual-property protection is likely to generate gains for some (developed and a few advanced developing economies) and losses for others (most developing economies), at least in the short run. Each country knows into which group it falls, so gaining consensus is difficult. Countries that expect to be technology importers for the foreseeable future have little incentive to accept stronger intellectual-property rules, and countries that are or expect to become technology exporters have every incentive to push for strong rules.

The Uruguay Round did produce an agreement on intellectual property. Members now grant *national treatment,* which means that foreign intellectual property receives protection equal to that granted to domestic intellectual property. Countries must grant any protection given to one trading partner to all under the agreement's most-favored-nation provision. Members also agreed to respect copyrights, trademarks, industrial-design secrets, and patents, with rules to be phased in over a 1-year period for developed countries, 5 years for developing countries and economies in transition, and 11 years for the least-developed economies.

During the agenda negotiations to begin the new Doha Round, WTO members clarified that existing WTO intellectual property rules allow countries to engage in compulsory licensing of pharmaceuticals necessary to respond to public health crises. This clarification had been sought by poor countries facing large-scale AIDS infections and by pharmaceutical firms in countries such as India and Brazil, which specialize in copying existing drugs. U.S.-based drug companies claimed that the clarification would do little to alleviate the AIDS crisis in poor countries, since lack of treatment resulted more from poverty, lack of basic medical infrastructure, and poor health policies than from lack of access to state-of-the-art medicines.

11.5.3 **Debts for Development**[10]

In 1982, Mexico announced that it could no longer afford to make the scheduled payments on its debt, and the debt owed by developing economies moved to the front page of newspapers worldwide. A full decade passed before policy makers declared the "end of the debt crisis." During that decade, developing countries' inability to make interest and principal payments on their debt periodically threatened the stability of the world financial system and continually strained relations between developed-country creditors and their developing-country debtors. While the crisis aspect of the developing-country debt has passed, its effects linger.

---

9 One example: China imposed an import quota that allows in only 10 foreign films annually; but less than a week after the film's U.S. release, counterfeit DVDs of *Harry Potter and the Sorcerer's Stone* sold on Beijing streets for 5 yuan ($1.20) complete with Chinese subtitles.

10 Here we'll analyze developing-country debt from a microeconomic perspective; in Chapter Twenty-One, we focus on the macroeconomic aspects of the debt. In Chapter Fifteen, we'll examine the Asian currency and financial crisis.

Defining and Measuring External Debt

Developing economies always have relied heavily on borrowing from abroad to finance the domestic investment that plays a vital role in development. The extent and exact nature of the borrowing have varied through time. Before World War I and again between World War I and World War II, British private investors financed much of the investment in the then-developing world (including the United States) by buying bonds. After World War II, the newly created international institutions, the International Monetary Fund and the World Bank, began making development-oriented loans. At the same time, private investors from developed countries undertook large-scale foreign direct investment in the developing world, at first in mining and mineral industries and later in manufacturing. Newly independent developing economies in the 1960s often viewed these foreign investors as exploiters and sought alternate sources of funding that would maintain more local control. They found such a source in the mid-1970s when members of OPEC lacked adequate domestic investment opportunities for their burgeoning oil revenues. The OPEC countries deposited their funds in banks, mostly in the United States, which then made bank loans to developing economies.

All these sources of borrowing—bonds sold abroad to private investors, official lending, foreign direct investment, and foreign bank loans—together constitute **external debt,** that is, borrowing from abroad.[11] Developing countries' sources of borrowing vary greatly in their importance over time, but all four types continue to be used. Table 11.6 divides developing countries' recent long-term borrowing into its main components. Note that private capital flows have grown rapidly while flows of official assistance, from developed-country governments and international organizations, have shrunk. Private capital flows go primarily to middle-income rather than low-income countries. In middle-income developing economies, private investors now fund even infrastructure projects such as power plants, once a mainstay of official development assistance. Official assistance goes to low-income countries and, increasingly, to humanitarian assistance and aid to countries in crisis.

Developing countries' external debt now totals well over $2 trillion. However, in analyzing debt, knowing the total quantities owed—even when the amounts are measured in trillions—isn't sufficient; different types of debt carry different implications. Figure 11.2 diagrams a useful taxonomy. Total debt can be divided into short-term debt, long-term debt, and use of credit from the International Monetary Fund (IMF). The bulk of developing-country debt (over 80 percent as of 1999) falls into the long-term category; this means the principal needn't be repaid until well in the future, and only interest payments are required in the short term. Long-term debt is classified by the identity of the debtor—the private sector or the public sector. Public-sector debt refers to amounts either owed by or guaranteed by the developing-country government; private-

Table 11.6 **Long-Term Capital Flows to Developing Countries, 1990–1999 (Billions $)**										
Type of Flow	1990	1991	1992	1993	1994	1995	1996	1997	1998	1999
Official flows	$55.9	$62.3	$54.0	$ 53.4	$ 45.9	$ 53.9	$ 31.0	$ 39.9	$ 50.6	$ 52.0
Private flows	42.6	61.6	99.7	165.8	174.5	203.3	282.1	303.9	267.7	238.7
Portfolio flows	18.5	26.4	52.2	99.8	85.7	98.3	151.3	133.6	96.8	46.7
Debt flows	15.7	18.8	38.1	48.8	50.5	62.2	102.1	103.4	81.2	19.1
Bank lending	3.2	5.0	16.4	3.5	8.8	30.4	37.5	51.6	44.6	−11.4
Bond financing	1.2	10.9	11.1	36.6	38.2	30.8	62.4	48.9	39.7	25.0
Other	11.3	2.8	10.7	8.7	3.5	1.0	2.2	3.0	−3.1	5.5
Equity	2.8	7.6	14.1	51.0	35.2	36.1	49.2	30.2	15.6	27.6
Foreign direct investment	24.1	35.3	47.5	66.0	88.8	105.0	130.8	170.3	170.9	192.0
Private flows' share (percent)	43.2	49.7	64.9	75.6	79.2	79.0	90.1	88.4	84.1	82.1

Source: Data from World Bank, *Global Development Finance 2000.*

---

11 With the "end of the debt crisis," stock markets in developing economies have begun to attract investment funds from abroad. This represents a fifth component of external debt, but it was trivial during most of the crisis of the 1980s.

sector debt is owed by individuals and firms and not guaranteed by government. About 75 percent of total long-term developing-country debt is public or publicly guaranteed. For short-term debt (loans with maturities of one year or less), available statistics don't distinguish between public- and private-sector debt. About 10 percent of developing countries' short-term debt consists of past-due unpaid interest (called *interest arrears*) on their long-term debt.

The distinction between public and private debtors is important because of its implications for the remedies available when repayment problems arise. Governments owed or guaranteed almost all the developing-country debt during the 1980s (around 90 percent), so the defaults feared during the debt crisis would have been **government** or **sovereign defaults** rather than defaults by private firms or individuals. This effectively ruled out the legal remedies a bank normally would pursue against a firm or individual who failed to make loan payments. However, even governments have incentives not to default on their loans. The primary reason: Such behavior can result in inability to borrow in the future, at least for several years.[12] Loss of borrowing privileges, in turn, limits access to trade by eliminating a major source of trade financing. An additional incentive rests on the threat of seizure by creditors of any assets that the debtor government owns abroad.[13]

Just as debt can be divided according to type of *debtor,* either public or private, it can be classified by type of *creditor.* The main classification distinguishes between **official debt,** owed to governments and international organizations, and **commercial,** or **unofficial,** or **market debt,** owed to private sources, including commercial banks. During the 1950s and 1960s, the bulk of development loans were of the official type. Throughout the 1970s, commercial banks became more involved in making loans to developing countries. In 1999, about 55 percent of developing-country governments' debt was owed to other governments and international organizations; the remaining 45 percent was owed to private creditors, including U.S., European, and Japanese banks as well as private bondholders.

We also can classify borrowing by the nature of the payments owed by debtors to creditors. The two main types are borrowing using **debt instruments** and borrowing using **equity instruments.** Debt instruments obligate the debtor to make payments of a fixed amount to the creditor at a specified date, regardless of the profitability of the financed project and regardless of economic circumstances. Borrowing by issuing bonds and through bank loans both fall into this category. The alternative is equity finance, in which debtor and creditor agree to share in the fortunes of a project, good or bad, with the shares determined in advance. Historically, equity finance in developing economies occurred primarily through foreign direct investment, which also facilitates technology transfer and provides access to international export markets. Only recently have stock markets in some developing economies evolved to the point that they attract significant flows of portfolio equity finance from investors in developed economies.[14] Borrowing through equity has the advantage that when an investment project turns out badly, the payments owed by the debtor to its creditors automatically fall, eliminating the risk of default. One reason developing countries encountered problems with their accumulation of borrowing in the 1980s was that most of the debt took the form of bank loans and bonds rather than equity. When projects failed and debtors' economic circumstances deteriorated, the same loan payments still came due. In 1999, private capital flows to developing countries included 8 percent debt finance and 92 percent equity finance, including both foreign direct investment (80 percent) and portfolio equity investment (12 percent).

General Rules of Debt

That many developing countries face large external debts doesn't necessarily signal a problem. We've seen that intertemporal trade, in which countries with low current saving but plentiful investment opportunities borrow from countries with high current saving but scarce investment opportunities, generates gains from trade. We'd expect this type of borrowing by developing countries from developed countries to produce gains for both debtors and creditors. However, all borrowing, whether by individuals, firms, or governments, must conform to a few simple rules to avoid repayment and default problems.

---

12 History reveals that punishment for debt repudiation doesn't last forever. Most of the countries of Latin America, for example, defaulted on loans during the 1930s. But by the early postwar years, those countries were borrowing again in international capital markets. Likewise, the defaulters of the 1980s soon were able to borrow again.

13 During the summer of 2001, Russia pulled two of its military jets out of the Paris Air Show early to avoid having them impounded in retaliation for Russia's nonpayment of a multimillion-dollar debt to a Swiss firm. See "Russian Jets Flee Paris and the Repo Man," *Financial Times,* June 23, 2001.

14 Recall that direct investment gives the buyer operating control, while portfolio investment doesn't.

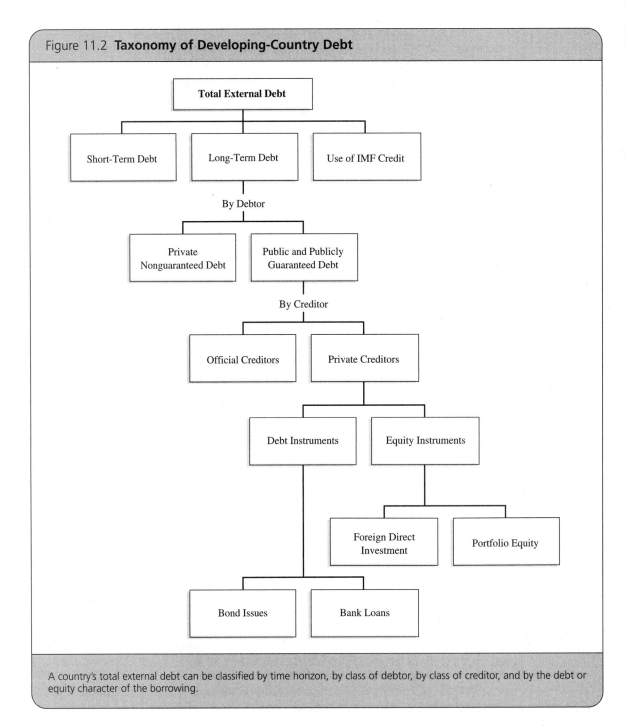

Figure 11.2 **Taxonomy of Developing-Country Debt**

A country's total external debt can be classified by time horizon, by class of debtor, by class of creditor, and by the debt or equity character of the borrowing.

The economic implications of debt depend on the amount of funds borrowed, the use to which the funds are put, the terms of the borrowing, and the borrower's future prospects and general economic circumstances. Only when one considers all these aspects can one appraise a particular country's debt situation. Generally, borrowing presents no problem as long as (1) the funds finance investment projects that produce returns sufficient to pay the interest on the loan (to "service the debt," in banking jargon); (2) the **maturity** of the loan, or the time over which it must be repaid, matches that of the financed investment projects; and (3) the possibility of unforeseen events is evaluated in calculating the total acceptable amount of debt.

In evaluating any debt, the most important question concerns the use of the funds. When a borrower uses debt to finance consumption in excess of income, the borrowed funds don't produce the returns to cover repayment. The debtor can't even make interest payments as they come due, much less repay the loan's principal, or the sum originally borrowed. This inability to repay is called **insolvency.** If, on the other hand, a borrower finances investment projects that produce a return sufficient to cover repayment, then both the debtor and the creditors benefit. Therefore, developing countries need an effective banking system and financial markets to channel funds to *productive* investment projects; this is essential both to avoid debt crises and to maximize the economic growth potential of the borrowing.

A second source of potential debt problems concerns the relationship between the maturity, or time horizon, of the borrowing and the time frame of the funded projects. Many of the potentially productive investments undertaken in developing countries involve long-term projects that can't be expected to pay off for several years. Loans that come due before the investment projects they fund become productive lead to a **liquidity problem;** the borrower can afford to repay eventually—but not on schedule. One common response to inability to service existing debt is to borrow more to cover the interest payments. Often these additional loans are short-term ones. The funds go to pay interest on earlier loans or, in some cases, to finance consumption-oriented expenditures, so they don't generate returns for repayment. The short-term nature of the additional debt can aggravate an already bad situation, and default becomes a serious possibility.

A final potential error by borrowers and lenders is to assume that the economic conditions prevailing at the time loans are made will continue indefinitely. An individual analogy would be to borrow an amount based on current income with no regard for the possibility of unemployment, illness, or other causes of reduction in income. A country deciding the amount it can prudently borrow must forecast not only its own economic prospects, but those of the larger world economy, since external events can exert a big impact on a country's ability to repay.

What Went Wrong in the 1980s?

Unfortunately, much of the borrowing by developing countries during the 1970s broke at least one of these general rules, and some of it violated all three, leading to the 1980s debt crisis. In some countries, such as Mexico (current external debt, $160 billion), the bulk of the investment funded by borrowing was undertaken by the public rather than the private sector, and a large portion went into inefficient state-owned industries. Before their recent reforms, developing-country governments typically sold food, gasoline and other forms of fuel, and basic utility services such as electricity at artificially low prices. Insofar as borrowed funds went into investment to produce goods then sold at prices below their production costs, the funds actually paid for current consumption. Venezuela (current external debt, $37 billion) tried to industrialize "overnight" using borrowed funds and, in the process, invested heavily in inefficient industries that produced no return. Peru (current external debt, $32 billion) also borrowed heavily and used the funds to subsidize highly inefficient state-run enterprises. Argentina (current external debt, $144 billion) spent a large share of its borrowed funds on military hardware. Many of these investments produced zero, or even negative, economic returns; so the debtors suffered crises of insolvency.

Changes in the nature of developing-country debt also led to liquidity problems that contributed to the 1980s crisis. Before the 1970s, most developing countries borrowed almost exclusively from official lenders such as the World Bank and the IMF, whose lending constituted long-term debt at concessional, or below-market, interest rates. As middle-income countries' borrowing moved to private sources of funds such as the recycled OPEC oil revenues during the 1970s, loan terms shortened and banks charged market interest rates. Many countries used these short-term loans to finance long-term investment projects that, even if successful, couldn't possibly produce returns in time to repay the loans. Venezuela, for example, incurred a large amount of short-term debt for long-term industrialization projects and encountered a liquidity crisis.

The 1980s crisis also occurred in part because both debtors and creditors failed to account for the possibility of future changes in the world economy. During the 1970s, when many of the loans that led to the crisis were made, commodity prices were booming, and developing countries guessed wrong concerning the permanence of those price increases. Those lucky enough to have stocks of minerals and other products enjoying rising prices invested heavily in increased capacity designed to take advantage of the high prices. Unfortunately, by the time the investments got under way, the high prices were a thing of the past. Investments that would have been very profitable at 1974 prices turned out to be very unprofitable at the prices prevailing in 1979 and 1980, when the debt came due.

Along with faulty forecasts of future commodity prices, developing countries based their borrowing in the 1970s on the assumption that developed countries' economic policies would remain more or less unchanged. Instead, the 1980s opened with developed countries making determined efforts to reduce their inflation rates. The resulting recession cut deeply into their demand for developing countries' exports, but the debtors had counted on revenue from those exports to cover debt payments. Prices for primary products, the leading exports for many debtor economies, collapsed as demand in the developed economies fell. To make matters worse, the recession in the developed economies increased pressures by their domestic industries for protection from foreign competition, so developed-country markets became less open to developing-country exports. The dramatic changes in developed countries' economic policy also caused real interest rates to rise, and much of the developing-country debt was subject to floating interest rates, so payments on the existing debt rose. The same economic forces that cut demand for their exports and raised interest rates on their outstanding loans also caused the value of many debtors' national currencies to fall (or *depreciate)* against the U.S. dollar. Most of the debt was denominated in dollars, so the amount of debt rose sharply when measured in the debtors' local currencies.

Developing-country debtors hoped that the painful combination of recession, reduced export demand, higher interest rates, and currency depreciations was temporary. In an effort to avoid the painful adjustment to these adverse circumstances, many borrowers simply borrowed more to finance spending at current levels. Such decisions contributed to both the liquidity and solvency problems facing debtors. The burgeoning debt-service burdens faced by several middle-income developing countries (especially Argentina, Brazil, and Mexico) began to dry up the sources of private borrowing. The OPEC oil-revenue surpluses disappeared as OPEC fell victim to internal cheating; and banks, so eager to lend in the 1970s, sharply curtailed their lending to developing-country governments. Additional loans were required to prevent default on existing loans; official lenders, especially the IMF, found themselves acting as lenders of last resort and playing an increasing role as arbitrators between debtor countries and creditor banks.

Legacy of a Crisis: Is It Over, and What Did We Learn?

The day-to-day threat of simultaneous major sovereign defaults by large developing countries no longer hangs over the international financial system as it did throughout the 1980s. Situations in many debtor countries have improved to the point that a new flow of much-needed private capital is under way, eloquent testimony to investors' confidence in the countries' economic stability. Nonetheless, potential debt problems remain in at least two senses: the continuing high levels of debt in the low-income economies and the continuing heavy reliance by most developing countries on external capital flows to fund development-related investment.

The debt crisis of the 1980s centered on middle- rather than low-income developing countries for two reasons. First, low-income developing economies—because of their civil wars, poor governance, weak macroeconomic policies, inadequate infrastructures, and unskilled workforces—never gained access to the large-scale private commercial bank lending that played a key role in the crisis. Figure 11.3 locates the severely indebted low-income countries and summarizes their borrowing by type of creditor; they continue to borrow largely from official development agencies that provide long-term loans at concessional interest rates. In 1998, 65 percent of these countries' borrowing came from official sources. As a result, low-income economies escaped the sudden inability to repay that hit the middle-income countries who borrowed from commercial banks during the years of plentiful OPEC funds. Second, because the low-income economies remain small relative to the world economy as a whole, their financial difficulties don't threaten the stability of the world financial system as simultaneous difficulties in Brazil, Mexico, and Argentina did.

The debt crisis of the 1980s was a crisis of the middle-income economies, so the responses focused on those economies as well. The severely indebted low-income economies continue to face huge external debts with little prospect of repayment; their external debt totaled $362 billion in 1999. Burundi, Democratic Republic of Congo, Ethiopia, Guinea-Bissau, Nicaragua, Rwanda, Sierra Leone, and Sudan each owe debt more than 500 times their respective annual export earnings. Moreover, many of the severely indebted low-income economies lack the basic institutional structures essential for economic growth and development. Some have suffered decades-long government policies that produce income insufficient to feed their populations, much less repay debt. Most long ago stopped making payments on their medium- and long-term debt to private creditors and fell behind in payments to governments and international agencies. Much of these countries' debt has been forgiven already. A 1996 IMF/World Bank HIPC Debt Initiative (*Heavily Indebted Poor Countries*) promises to

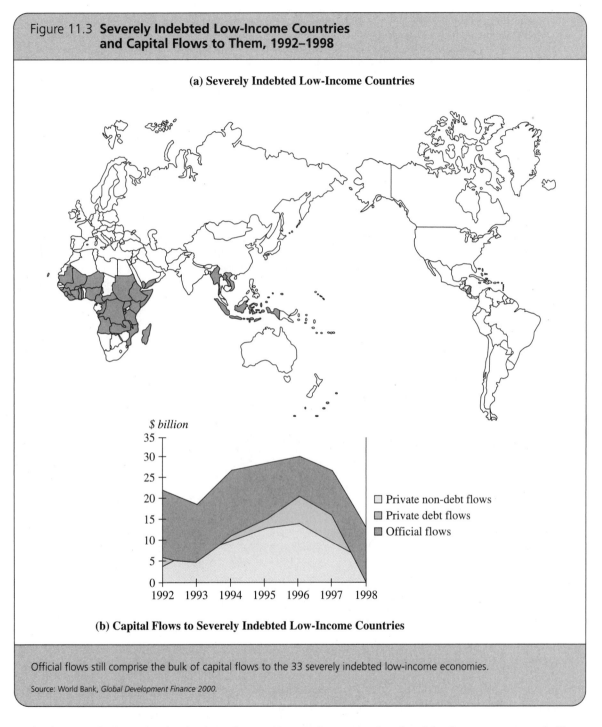

Figure 11.3 **Severely Indebted Low-Income Countries and Capital Flows to Them, 1992–1998**

(a) Severely Indebted Low-Income Countries

(b) Capital Flows to Severely Indebted Low-Income Countries

Official flows still comprise the bulk of capital flows to the 33 severely indebted low-income economies.

Source: World Bank, *Global Development Finance 2000.*

forgive more for countries that institute the macroeconomic, structural, and social reforms necessary to facilitate growth, avoid future debt problems, and alleviate poverty.

Most analysts agree that some debt forgiveness is essential to provide incentives for reform. Countries with huge debt accumulations know that if they reform and grow, most of the benefits will go to their creditors; this weakens the incentives for good policies and growth. But debt forgiveness also carries costs. It can adversely affect the debtors' future ability to borrow and can reduce the pressure on debtor governments to alter the policies that led to debt problems of such magnitudes. In the long run, only fundamental policy reforms to support economic growth, combined with continued support from creditors, will allow these countries to overcome their debt. In this sense, the debt problem continues.

A second, more general legacy of the 1980s debt crisis is developing countries' continued heavy reliance on capital flows from abroad to finance investment. As noted earlier, the post-crisis renewal of capital flows into developing economies represents the most often-cited basis for proclamation of the debt crisis's end. A substantial portion of these inflows probably represents the return of flight capital that flowed out during the crisis; this repatriation is a one-time phenomenon and can't be counted on as a permanent method of external finance. The revival of capital flows to developing economies in the 1990s differs in several ways from earlier flows. Today, *private* capital flows account for a much larger share of the total. On the debtor side, private borrowers play a bigger role; large-scale sovereign borrowing is less prevalent than in the 1970s, in part because developing countries' reforms have assigned governments more limited roles in the economy. Recent flows also include more equity instruments, both foreign direct investment and portfolio equity, than the bank-loan-heavy flows of the 1970s.

As Mexico learned in 1994 and several Asian economies learned in 1997, foreign capital inflows are potentially reversible; so economies dependent on such flows face particular pressures to maintain policies that support investor confidence. Those same policies can encourage domestic saving and provide a domestic source of funds for development-related investment.[15] Private investors watch developing countries' policies closely for signs of trouble. The recent rapid growth of private capital flows to these countries has been uneven, as investors look for sound economic policies and good growth prospects. Table 11.7 reports the regional breakdown of private capital flows and their division between low- and middle-income recipients. The table also lists the top five recipient countries, which together account for almost three-fifths of the total, but for a smaller share now than in 1990.

Some of the debt crisis's legacies take the form of even more general lessons about the world economy. The successful growth of many developing economies over the past three decades has rendered them an important

Table 11.7 Net Private Capital Flows to Developing Countries, 1990–1998 (Billions $)

Country Group or Country	1990	1991	1992	1993	1994	1995	1996	1997	1998
All developing countries:	44.4	56.9	90.6	157.1	161.3	184.2	243.8	256.0	267.7
Sub-Saharan Africa	0.3	0.8	−0.3	−0.5	5.2	9.1	11.8	8.0	3.5
East Asia and the Pacific	19.3	20.8	36.9	62.4	71.0	84.1	108.7	89.0	67.2
South Asia	2.2	1.9	2.9	6.0	8.5	5.2	10.7	9.0	7.6
Europe and Central Asia	9.5	7.9	21.8	25.6	17.2	30.1	31.2	41.0	53.3
Latin America and Caribbean	12.5	22.9	28.7	59.8	53.6	54.3	74.3	95.0	126.9
Middle East and North Africa	0.6	2.2	0.5	3.9	5.8	1.4	6.9	14.0	9.2
Income group:									
Low-income countries	11.4	12.1	25.4	50.0	57.1	53.4	67.1	88.7	52.4
Middle-income countries	32.0	44.0	64.8	107.1	104.2	130.7	176.7	210.0	215.3
Top country destinations (1998):									
Brazil	0.5	3.6	9.8	16.1	12.2	19.1	14.7	43.4	54.4
China	8.1	7.5	21.3	39.6	44.4	44.3	52.0	60.8	42.7
Mexico	8.2	12.0	9.2	21.2	20.7	13.1	28.1	20.5	23.2
Russia	5.6	0.2	10.8	3.1	0.3	1.1	3.6	12.5	19.3
Argentina	−0.2	2.9	4.2	13.8	7.6	7.2	11.3	19.8	18.9

Source: World Bank, *World Development Indicators.*

---

15 Case Three in Chapter Ten examines the continued correlation between domestic saving and investment.

force in the world economy. Trade and capital flows between developed and developing economies are substantial, so problems in either area no longer can be ignored in the other. The debt crisis forced recognition of this increased interdependence. The crisis also forced developing economies to undertake structural reforms and to support institutional structures such as the WTO and NAFTA for codifying those reforms, thereby helping to ensure that they remain in place. The crisis reinforced the importance of the different implications of various types of external borrowing. The large role of bank loans in the 1980s crisis reminded debtors and creditors of the appropriate roles for debt instruments and equity instruments in foreign borrowing. Debtors and creditors alike were reminded of the importance of competent domestic institutions, especially a sound banking system and other financial markets, in assuring that borrowed funds are used effectively to facilitate economic growth and development (not to mention repayment). Finally, the crisis highlighted the futility of debtor–creditor deadlock once a crisis erupts. Only when debtors and creditors worked together, with support from other governments and international organizations, did the worst of the crisis end.

11.5.4 Economic Development and the Environment

Although scholars and policy makers long have recognized links between international trade and environmental policies, recent increased concern with environmental issues has moved the trade–environment link to center stage.[16] This applies especially to developing countries, because environmental quality represents an essential element in the improved quality of life that is development's ultimate goal, and because some forms of environmental degradation hinder productivity and development prospects.

Several characteristics of environmental issues combine to produce controversy and difficulties in international policy making. First, a lack of scientific consensus on the physical effects of some classes of pollution (for example, "greenhouse gases" and the extent and implications of any accompanying global warming) makes agreements difficult to reach because each side of the debate can point to reputable scientific studies that support its position. Second, countries with different income levels demand different levels of environmental quality or protection, just as they demand different qualities of housing, food, or transportation. Again, this greatly complicates international agreements. Low-income developing countries fear having the high-income developed countries' relatively stringent environmental standards imposed on them. Third, environmental restrictions provide an easy disguise for protectionism. For example, a developed country wanting to protect its vegetable producers from competition by developing-country producers might ban imports and claim that those producers use environmentally unacceptable chemicals or pesticides.[17] Finally, different population densities, geography, and past pollution levels imply that countries' *assimilative capacities* (that is, their abilities to absorb new pollution with minimal damage) vary widely. A factory whose air pollution might impose heavy health costs if placed in the Los Angeles basin might pose few costs in North Dakota. The Los Angeles basin has a relatively high population density, a geographical configuration in which sea winds trap pollution against the mountains that ring the basin, and a high existing level of many pollutants; North Dakota's situation, and hence its assimilative capacity, is quite different.

Differences among types of pollution also complicate the link between international trade and the environment. Some types (for example, water pollution) have primarily local effects and can be dealt with through domestically financed local policies. Others have cross-border, or even global, effects and require more international coordination of policies as well as more cooperative financing. For example, habitat destruction that reduces biological diversity and deforestation that leads to global climatic consequences impose costs on the entire world. Solving these problems requires international cooperation. Potential approaches include payments by wealthy countries to developing countries for the "species-diversity services" and "carbon-absorption services" provided by their forests. Such payments would provide incentives for developing countries to conserve their habitat and forests.

The environmental priorities of developed and developing countries differ. If you ask an individual in a high-income, developed country about environmental problems, his or her response probably would deal with issues such as carbon dioxide emissions from automobiles, depletion of the ozone layer by chlorofluorocarbons, global warming, and hazardous waste disposal. The same question posed to a resident of a low-income

---

16 Chapter Eight (section 8.5.3) contains a more general discussion of international trade and the environment. Here, we restrict our attention to issues of particular concern to developing economies.

17 Section 8.5.3 outlines WTO rules on environmental protection through trade policy.

developing country would more likely elicit concern over unsafe drinking water, lack of sanitation facilities, soil depletion, and indoor smoke from burning wood or dung for cooking. These understandable differences in priorities, along with inevitable controversy over who pays for cleanup, go a long way toward explaining the difficulties in international discussions about the environment.

Increasingly, specialists in the environment recognize that the logical first step toward improvement involves curtailing policies that actually encourage environmental damage. Examples of such policies include subsidized use of fossil fuels and water, lack of private-property rights for poor farmers in their land, insulation of state-owned industries (which tend to be heavy polluters) from competitive forces, and rewarding aggressive land clearing by awarding ownership of land to those who clear it.[18] All these policies are prevalent in developing countries, and all take a heavy toll on the environment. Fortunately, elimination of these policies would improve economic efficiency, facilitate international trade liberalization, *and* raise incomes as well as improve the environment. Therefore, the commonly held idea that economic development and international trade necessarily come at an environmental cost clearly is wrong; the truth is much more complex.

11.6 Developing Markets: Economies in Transition

Between 1989 and 1991, the breakup of the Soviet Union and the overthrow of Communist governments in its Central and Eastern European satellite states revealed a new group of developing economies. Forty years of central planning had left a zone of outdated technology, environmental disasters, dilapidated factories, and frustrated citizens. Even areas such as East Germany, industrialized and modern before coming under Soviet domination at the end of World War II, had declined into backwardness compared with the Western market economies. Because the most fundamental task facing the formerly centrally planned countries was the shift to market-oriented economies, they came to be called **economies in transition.**[19] As a group, they have much in common with other developing economies, but face some unique problems and opportunities. To understand the special character of the trade-related aspects of their development prospects, we must briefly turn back the clock and return to central planning.

11.6.1 International Trade and Central Planning

A **market-based economic system** relies on *prices* to allocate resources, signal trends, and provide incentives. If a good's price rises, this signals increased scarcity, and consumers have an incentive to consume less of the good and producers an incentive to make more of it. Similarly, a rise in an input's price informs firms that the input has become scarcer and gives them an incentive to use less of it and more of other relatively cheaper inputs. A **centrally planned economy,** in contrast, relies instead on government *planning* to decide what and how much to produce and how much to pay factors of production. When government bureaucrats rather than market forces set prices, no automatic mechanism exists to equate quantity supplied with quantity demanded, and shortages and surpluses are more the rule than the exception.

Market-determined prices play a central role in international trade theory (for example, as the basis for the definition of comparative advantage), so that theory says little about how centrally planned economies conduct their international trade policies. In practice, autarky, or self-sufficiency, often was an explicit policy goal. Planners viewed trade as a necessary evil whereby export goods were produced to obtain only those imports impossible to produce domestically. Like policy makers in many other developing economies, central planners also placed great weight on industrialization as a policy goal.

The Soviet Union moved to a system of central planning in the 1920s, approximately a decade after the 1917 revolution brought the Communists to power. From the late 1920s until the end of World War II, the Soviet state pursued national self-sufficiency and industrialization, accompanied by a disastrous collectivization of agriculture. Following World War II, the Soviet Union extended its power into Central and Eastern Europe and integrated those economies into its self-sufficient industrial system. The countries formed the **Council for Mutual Economic Assistance (CMEA, or COMECON)** to manage and coordinate their intra-

---

18 See section 8.5.3 for specific examples.

19 Other economies throughout the world, including about 30 in Africa, also abandoned central planning during the 1980s and early 1990s. These countries typically aren't included in "economies in transition," although they face many of the same challenges.

group trade. Original CMEA members were the Soviet Union, Poland, Hungary, Czechoslovakia, Bulgaria, and Romania; later, East Germany, Vietnam, Cuba, and (temporarily) Albania joined.

Trade within the CMEA grew rapidly, expanding from less than one-third of members' total trade to over three-fourths in just the first five years. The Soviet Union exported oil to other members in return for manufactured goods such as tractors, buses, and forklifts. Although the planners didn't believe in international trade according to comparative advantage, they did believe in specialization and economies of scale. Many goods were produced in a single enormous plant that served the entire CMEA market.[20] Even basic goods such as steel and automobiles came from a mere handful of factories. As a result, the CMEA countries traded heavily with one another even though they traded relatively little with the West, especially during periods of heightened Cold War tensions. The Soviet Union linked its own republics even more tightly; only the Russian Republic exported less than 30 percent of it output in 1988, and 10 republics exported more than 50 percent. In 1989, 90 percent of Belarus's trade was with other Soviet republics; 80 percent of all Soviet trade occurred among the Soviet republics themselves.

The CMEA trading system, inefficient as it was (for reasons we'll see in a moment), did allow the centrally planned economies to escape some of the negative effects of their isolation from the rest of the world trading system.[21] Unfortunately, the pattern of trade established under the CMEA made the 1989–1991 revolutions more painful and complicated some countries' transitions to market economies. Bulgaria, for example, conducted approximately 80 percent of its trade with CMEA members, so the sudden collapse of the Soviet Union abruptly halted most of Bulgaria's trade.

The CMEA economies' isolation from the rest of the world wasn't just a matter of ideological refusal to accept the theory of comparative advantage or of political tensions with the West. To be feasible, a centrally planned system *must* insulate itself from contact with market economies; otherwise, trade at market-determined world prices will erode the government's ability to impose its artificial prices and centrally planned resource allocation. For example, the Soviet Union emphasized production of capital and military goods in its planning and left little productive capacity for consumer goods. The results were queues, waiting, rationing, and high black-market prices for consumer goods. If the Soviet government had allowed free trade, Soviet consumers would have purchased Western consumer goods and Western firms would have bought the capital goods on which the Soviet government kept prices artificially low (that is, a fraction of the opportunity cost of producing them). To avoid these deviations from the state's economic plan, a centrally planned economy must prevent a free flow of goods between itself and market economies.

CMEA countries achieved this separation primarily through use of monopoly state bureaucracies to handle all foreign trade.[22] Typically the state planning ministry worked with a ministry of foreign trade to decide which goods the country would need but not be able to produce domestically. To obtain these imports, they made plans to use other goods as exports. The foreign-trade ministry then informed the official state-trading bureaucracy of the necessary imports and exports. This bureaucratic process greatly interfered with the efficiency of trade. Goods often failed to arrive as planned. Firms hoarded inputs so they could continue to produce when input shipments failed to appear. The result was an economy of enormous enterprises, each of which tried to maintain self-sufficiency to the extent possible within the central-planning system.

The nature of the centrally planned economies imposed several other barriers to efficient international trade. First, planners didn't allow their currencies to be traded in foreign-exchange markets; in particular, the currencies weren't *convertible* into other currencies. If a Czechoslovakian firm exported machinery to the Soviet Union and received payment in rubles (the Soviet currency), Czechoslovakia could spend the proceeds only on imports from a country willing to accept rubles in payment, most likely the Soviet Union itself. If the ruble had been freely convertible, Czechoslovakia could, for example, have exchanged the rubles for Japanese yen in the foreign-exchange market and used the yen to import goods from Japan. But the centrally planned economies maintained artificial exchange rates for their currencies just as they maintained other artificial prices, so unrestricted trade in currencies had to be avoided. The result was bilateralism; that is, each country

---

20 In the Soviet Union, of 5,884 product lines, 77 percent were supplied by a single producer ("Remaking the Soviet Union," *The Economist,* July 13, 1991, 23).

21 Ignoring the political barriers to East–West trade, most intra-CMEA trade represented trade diversion (see section 9.4.2). However, during the Cold War and Soviet domination of Eastern Europe, trade with the West was severely limited, so the choice was between no trade and intra-CMEA trade.

22 Lenin imposed a state monopoly on foreign trade shortly after the 1917 revolution in Russia; most other socialist economies followed.

had to import and export approximately equal amounts with each trading partner, because the proceeds from exports took the form of nonconvertible currencies useful only on imports from the issuing country. This bilateralism ignored patterns of comparative advantage and led to inefficient trade flows at prices that bore little resemblance to market-determined world prices.

The planning system presented an additional barrier to trade with market economies by giving producers no incentive to make the types of high-quality goods demanded in world markets. Under central planning, the rewards producers earned were only weakly connected to the quality or desirability of their product. Producers couldn't keep any profits that resulted from a superior product, so quality tended to be low and erratic. Such products couldn't compete with Western-made goods in world markets, but traded in CMEA transactions at prices that ignored the goods' shoddy quality.

The CMEA amounted to a trading system that ignored comparative advantage, overemphasized regional specialization and economies of scale, channeled trade to group members at the expense of potential trade with the West, and ignored market prices and product quality. Needless to say, its historical legacy didn't facilitate transition.

11.6.2 **The Painful Transition from Central Planning**

Even before the massive political and economic change that swept Central and Eastern Europe and the Soviet Union between 1989 and 1991, some of the centrally planned economies liberalized their trade procedures to allow firms that wanted to import or export to deal more directly with foreign firms. Most notably, as part of the Soviet Union's economic restructuring or *perestroika,* new trade laws allowed Soviet firms to trade directly with foreign firms as of 1989. The Soviet Union also expressed interest in joining GATT, forerunner of today's WTO, but Western nations were skeptical about the feasibility of applying GATT's market-oriented rules to an economy so insulated from world markets. In efforts to improve product quality and upgrade their technology, several countries including the Soviet Union started to encourage joint ventures with Western firms.

Between 1989 and 1991, economic and political reforms in Eastern Europe and the Soviet Union grew from a trickle to a torrent. One by one, authoritarian regimes fell, and new governments pledged themselves to the difficult task of transition to market-oriented economies. As this process continues, each country faces unique problems and challenges, but there are elements common to all.

Although analysts agree that the economies of the former Soviet Union and Central and Eastern Europe will perform much better under market systems than under central planning, things got worse before they got better. With the threat of Soviet military intervention gone, so was the incentive to accept the system's poor-quality goods. Demand shifted to better, Western-made goods. The massive government-owned factories lost their only markets. The CMEA disbanded as members shifted their trade to the West. Countries such as Hungary and Czechoslovakia that had relied on exports of manufactured goods saw the (artificial) prices of those goods collapse when confronted with world market prices for higher-quality goods. Some economies tried to shift exports to the West, but their outdated technology and trade barriers in developed-country markets limited this ability in the short run.

Several economies in transition instituted large-scale reforms early, signaling a dramatic shift to a market orientation. For these countries—including Albania, the Baltic republics, the Czech Republic, Mongolia, Poland, the Slovak Republic, and Slovenia—the worst of the short-run shock of transition seems to be over, and growth rates are climbing, albeit erratically. For others, late or overly timid reforms or special difficulties such as massive corruption or armed conflicts have their economies still mired in the downturn phase of transition.

One additional problem in evaluating the early performance and prospects of the transitional economies was the lack of reliable data on key economic variables such as gross national product. Existing data from the central-planning era had two problems. First, GNP calculations in centrally planned economies often included only the state-owned sector of large industries. Typically, this represented the least productive sector, especially as reforms removed the subsidies that had allowed these "dinosaur" industries to survive. As reforms took hold and small, privately owned firms appeared, this dynamic sector of the economy provided a growing share of income and employment but failed to find its way into official accounts. The second data problem reflected the effect of inconvertible currencies. Cross-country comparisons of GNP figures require that data be "translated" from domestic currency units (the Soviet ruble, or the Polish zloty) to a common unit, usually the U.S. dollar. This translation process uses the exchange rate, or the value of one currency expressed in units of the other currency. But, as we've noted, the centrally planned economies maintained highly artificial exchange rates. This implies that economic data calculated using such rates were highly suspect at best. At least a portion of the dramatic declines in reported income levels in the transitional economies after 1989 reflected the use of more realistic exchange rates for the calculations. Table 11.8 reports estimates of GNP per-capita during transition for the former Soviet Republics and the Central and Eastern European economies; however, the World Bank cautions that the early figures, especially those for the former Soviet Union, must be regarded as tentative.

The transitional economies as a whole grew in 1997 for the first time in seven years. On average, an economy suffered 3 years of falling output after introducing sustained reforms. Industry's share of output has fallen in most of the countries, while services have grown and agriculture has grown in some and declined in others. By the end of transition's first decade, the countries' economic and policy performances had become highly differentiated. Some had built impressive track records of reform and had realistic hopes of joining the European Union; others had hardly started down the road to reform and recovery.

Table 11.8 Per-Capita GNP for the Economies in Transition, 1989–2000 ($)

Country	1989	1990	1991	1992	1993	1994	1995	1996	1997	1998	1999	2000
Albania	n.a.	n.a.	n.a.	n.a.	$340	$380	$670	$820	$750	$810	$870	n.a.
Bulgaria	$2,320	$2,250	$1,840	$1,330	1,140	1,250	1,330	1,190	1,140	1,230	1,380	$1,510
Czechoslovakia	3,540	3,140	2,470	n.a.	n.a.	n.a.	n.a.	n.a.	n.a.	n.a.	n.a.	n.a.
Czech Rep.	n.a.	n.a.	n.a.	2,450	2,710	3,200	3,870	4,740	5,200	5,040	5,060	4,920
Slovak Rep.	n.a.	n.a.	n.a.	1,930	1,950	2,250	2,950	3,410	3,700	3,700	3,590	3,700
Hungary	2,590	2,780	2,720	2,970	3,350	3,840	4,120	4,340	4,430	4,510	4,650	4,740
Poland	1,790	1,690	1,790	1,910	2,260	2,410	2,790	3,230	3,590	3,900	3,960	4,200
Romania	n.a.	1,640	1,390	1,130	1,140	1,270	1,480	1,600	1,420	1,390	1,520	1,670
Yugoslavia	2,920	3,060	n.a.	n.a.	n.a.	n.a.	n.a.	n.a.	n.a.	n.a.	n.a.	n.a.
Croatia	n.a.	n.a.	n.a.	n.a.	n.a.	2,560	3,250	3,800	4,610	4,520	4,580	4,510
Macedonia	n.a.	n.a.	n.a.	n.a.	n.a.	820	860	990	1,090	1,290	1,690	1,710
Slovenia	n.a.	n.a.	n.a.	n.a.	n.a.	7,040	8,200	9,240	9,680	9,760	9,890	10,070
Soviet Union	n.a.	n.a.	n.a.	n.a.	n.a.	n.a.	n.a.	n.a.	n.a.	n.a.	n.a.	n.a.
Armenia	n.a.	2,380	2,150	780	660	680	730	630	530	480	490	n.a.
Azerbaijan	n.a.	1,640	1,670	740	730	500	480	480	510	490	550	610
Belarus	n.a.	3,110	3,110	2,930	2,870	2,160	2,070	2,070	2,150	2,200	2,630	2,990
Estonia	n.a.	4,170	3,830	2,760	3,080	2,820	2,860	3,080	3,330	3,390	3,480	3,410
Georgia	n.a.	2,120	1,640	850	580	n.a.	440	850	840	930	620	590
Kazakhstan	n.a.	2,600	2,470	1,680	1,560	1,160	1,330	1,350	1,340	1,310	1,230	1,190
Kirgizstan	n.a.	1,570	1,550	820	850	630	700	550	440	350	300	270
Latvia	n.a.	3,590	3,410	1,930	2,010	2,320	2,270	2,300	2,430	2,430	2,470	2,860
Lithuania	n.a.	3,110	2,710	1,310	1,320	1,350	1,900	2,280	2,230	2,440	2,620	2,900
Moldova	n.a.	2,390	2,170	1,300	1,060	870	920	590	540	410	370	400
Russia	n.a.	3,430	3,220	2,510	2,340	2,650	2,240	2,410	2,740	2,300	2,270	1,660
Tajikistan	n.a.	1,130	1,050	490	470	360	n.a.	340	330	350	290	170
Turkmenistan	n.a.	1,690	1,700	1,230	n.a.	n.a.	n.a.	940	630	n.a.	660	840
Ukraine	n.a.	2,500	2,340	1,820	2,210	1,910	1,630	1,200	1,040	850	750	700
Uzbekistan	n.a.	1,340	1,350	850	970	960	970	1,010	1,010	870	720	610

Source: World Bank, *World Development Report; World Development Indicators;* United Nations, *Human Development Report.*

11.6.3 The Reform Agenda and Prospects

The list of major transition tasks included eliminating price controls and introducing market-determined prices, cutting government subsidies to industry, removing restrictions on private ownership and market activities, cutting military spending and the role of government in the economy, assuring macroeconomic stability, providing incentives for improved productivity and quality, privatization, designing systems for effective corporate governance, and creation of independent central banks to administer monetary and foreign-exchange policies. In the former Soviet Union, even more fundamental reforms such as building a legal system to protect private property, a framework for enforcement of contracts, and a transparent accounting system were (and still are) needed; some of the economies of Central and Eastern Europe, with their shorter histories of central planning, were luckier in these regards.

Most analysts and policy makers agreed on most items on the reform list. However, there were two controversies. The first concerned the proper speed and ordering of reforms. Faced with such a daunting list, should one attempt all the reforms simultaneously and as quickly as possible? Or should one concentrate on a few elements at a time and allow for lengthy adjustment periods? History provides few models of such broad political and economic change; therefore, substantial disagreement remains on this question. Poland followed the sudden or "big bang" approach on January 1, 1990, when it cut tariffs and moved its zloty currency toward convertibility. Many economists argue that opening international trade supports the other needed reforms by providing information about market prices, putting competitive pressure on domestic firms to improve quality, and providing access to new technology, an area in which most of the economies in transition lag seriously behind the West. The former Soviet Republics have, with few exceptions, taken more gradual approaches, but have met with only erratic success. China's gradualism, in which liberalization began in agriculture during the late 1970s and only gradually extended to industry, has been somewhat more successful. Table 11.9 reports the transitional economies' status on the major margins of reform.

The data in Table 11.9 highlight the countries' diverse policies and progress. Some, such as the Czech Republic, Estonia, Hungary, Lithuania, Poland, and Slovenia, show substantial reform on all margins, with all scores of 3 or 4. Others, such as Belarus and Turkmenistan, have hardly begun their reform tasks. Still others, such as Bulgaria and Romania, show substantial progress on some margins of reform and almost none on others. Generally, the countries of Central and Eastern Europe have undertaken the most complete reforms; Central Asian countries, on the other hand, lag behind.

A second debate over reform concerns how (and how much) to cushion the effects of transition on individuals and firms. On the one hand, failure to provide social cushions generates social and political discontent that may threaten the reform process. On the other hand, too much cushioning removes the essential incentives to adjust and prolongs the inevitable pain of transition. As price controls are removed, particularly for key goods such as energy, food, and housing, citizens bring tremendous political pressure to raise wages to maintain their purchasing power. But the low productivity in many sectors doesn't justify those higher wages, so yielding to the political pressure prolongs the transitional period of increased unemployment.[23]

The short-run economic prospects vary substantially across Eastern Europe and the former Soviet Union. In some countries, such as Hungary, central planning was never complete and substantial market expertise exists within the population. In others, such as the former Soviet Union, a longer and more exclusive history of socialism means that few citizens possess significant market experience. The share of the state sector in the economies varied substantially before reforms began. For example, in the mid-1980s, 97 percent of value-added originated in the state sector in Czechoslovakia, East Germany, and the Soviet Union, but only 65 percent in Hungary.[24] So the magnitude of the privatization task—a slow and difficult aspect of reform—differs across countries. In some countries, the population strongly supports reform; other countries face more troubling and unstable domestic political situations or even civil or interstate conflict.

The former Soviet republics faced several additional problems. The breakup of the country severed long-standing supply relations, leaving factories without supplies and component producers without customers. Unlike most Eastern European economies, the Soviet planning system encompassed agriculture as well as industry, so both sectors had to undergo the transition process. Separated from the national framework of the Soviet Union, the republics lacked the institutions of a typical nation-state, including central banks and legal

---

23 See Cases One and Two in Chapter Four and section 8.7 on the relationship among wages, productivity, and competitiveness.

24 *The Wall Street Journal,* July 23, 1991.

Table 11.9 Transitional Economies' Reform, 2001 (4+ = Market Economy, 1 = Little Progress)

Country	Private-Sector Share of GDP (Percent)	Enterprises — Privatization		Governance and Restructuring	Markets and Trade — Price Liberalization	Trade and Foreign-Exchange System	Competition Policy	Financial Institutions — Banking Reform & Interest-Rate Liberalization	Securities Markets & Non-bank Financial Institutions
		Large-Scale	Small-Scale						
Albania	75	2+	4	2	3	4+	2−	2+	2−
Armenia	60	3	4−	2	3	4	2	2+	2
Azerbaijan	60	2	3+	2	3	3+	2	2+	2−
Belarus	20	1	2	1	2	2	2	1	2
Bosnia and Herzegovina	40	2+	3−	2−	3	3	1	2+	1
Bulgaria	70	4−	4−	2+	3	4+	2+	3	2
Croatia	60	3	4+	3−	3	4+	2+	3+	2+
Czech Rep.	80	4	4+	3+	3	4+	3	4−	3
Estonia	75	4	4+	3+	3	4+	3−	4−	3
FR Yugoslavia	40	1	3	1	3	3	1	1	1
FYR Macedonia	60	3	4	2+	3	4	2	3	2−
Georgia	60	3+	4	2	3+	4+	2	2+	2−
Hungary	80	4	4+	3+	3+	4+	3	4	4−
Kazakhstan	60	3	4	2	3	3+	2	3−	2+
Kirgizstan	60	3	4	2	3	4	2	2+	2
Latvia	65	3	4+	3−	3	4+	2+	3+	2+
Lithuania	70	3+	4+	3−	3	4+	3	3	3
Moldova	50	3	3+	2	3+	4+	2	2+	2
Poland	75	3+	4+	3+	3+	4+	3	3+	4−
Romania	65	3+	4−	2	3+	4	2+	3−	2
Russia	70	3+	4	2+	3	3−	2+	2−	2−
Slovak Rep.	80	4	4+	3	3	4+	3	3+	2+
Slovenia	65	3	4+	3−	3+	4+	3−	3+	3−
Tajikistan	45	2+	4−	2−	3	3+	2−	1	1
Turkmenistan	25	1	2	1	2	1	1	1	1
Ukraine	60	3	3+	2	3	3	2+	2	2
Uzbekistan	45	3−	3	2−	2	2−	2	2−	2

Source: Data from European Bank for Reconstruction and Development, *Transition Report 2001.*

frameworks to deal with the bankruptcies that constitute an inevitable part of the transition process. The republics had to decide how closely to cooperate and what functions to share within the Commonwealth of Independent States, a loose confederation joined by most former Soviet republics. Prospects for economic growth and development vary widely among the republics based on different size, resource endowments, international linkages, damage from broken supplier relationships, environmental problems, ethnic tensions, and degrees of political instability.

Like other developing countries, the economies in transition also face the hurdle of developed-country trade barriers. Industries in which the emerging economies have comparative advantage—such as agriculture, textiles, and steel—are precisely those industries in which many developed countries erect the highest trade barriers. The Uruguay Round reforms, once in full effect, will improve market access for the economies in transition. In addition, for transitional economies with WTO membership, the reforms require them to continue to dismantle their own trade barriers, although the agreement permits a slower liberalization schedule for developing and transitional economies than for developed ones. As of 2001, many transitional economies had attained full WTO membership; most of the others, including Russia, had requested membership.

For all but the least reformed transitional economies, divergent performance increasingly reflects policy choices rather than initial conditions. Difficult work remains, especially in the areas of capital- and financial-market reforms, enterprise restructuring and governance, and government reform of tax systems and corruption. There are reasons for optimism. All the economies should be able to attain substantial productivity gains from restructuring their enterprises. And most enjoy highly educated and skilled workforces. However, everyone now recognizes that building market institutions and policies is a long-term job that requires persistence and, sometimes, resourcefulness and stamina in the face of opposition by vested interests.

CASE ONE:
Does Aid Aid Growth?

Developing countries have received billions of dollars in aid over the past several decades. Most studies, however, have found virtually no relationship between the amount of aid a country receives and growth of its per-capita income. Recently, economists Craig Burnside and David Dollar set out to take a more careful look, using better data and statistical techniques than earlier studies. The investigation covered 56 developing countries from 1970 until 1993. What did the investigators find?

First, they confirmed findings of many other studies that a developing country's growth depends heavily on its own economic policies. This led Burnside and Dollar to wonder if aid does affect growth, but only in countries following growth-conducive policies. What if aid acts basically as an income transfer? If the recipient government invests the additional income in productive projects, income will rise. This will be likely to happen in countries where governments choose their own policies with an eye toward growth. But if governments simply consume the additional income, aid won't enhance growth; this is most likely to occur in countries whose governments follow distorting policies that discourage investment and growth.

Policies found in many studies to be conducive to growth include low inflation, an absence of government budget deficits, and openness to trade. For countries meeting these conditions, Burnside and Dollar find that aid does help growth.

Have donors responded by giving more aid to countries whose governments follow good policies? Apparently not. Bilateral aid in particular (that is, aid from a single donor government to a single recipient government) seems unaffected by the wisdom of the recipient's policy choices. Such aid appears to lead to a rise in government consumption, not to a rise in investment or growth. Multilateral aid, on the other hand (that is, aid administered by international organizations and regional development banks), responds more to recipient policy and is less likely to go toward increased government consumption.

With the end of the Cold War, which created political and security reasons for particular aid patterns regardless of growth goals, donors may start to focus development aid where studies suggest it will have the strongest growth-enhancing effect: in countries whose governments follow good economic policies. Such a shift in aid allocation might also nudge bad-policy governments to reconsider their policy choices.

CASE TWO:
Location, Location, Location, and TADAZ

Residential real-estate agents say the key to a property's marketability and value is "location, location, location." The same is true for the economic viability of many industries. During the 1920s, in addition to collectivizing Soviet agriculture, Joseph Stalin created the landlocked republic of Tajikistan in Central Asia. The mountainous republic's chief resource was its rivers. Thirty-five years later, Soviet planners decided to use those rivers to provide hydroelectric power to a giant aluminum smelter at Tursunzadeh. (Recall that an important characteristic of Soviet economic planning was building huge specialized factories designed to serve the entire Soviet Union and its satellite states.) The 865-acre smelter, known as TADAZ, started to produce in 1975; by 1989 it produced 416,000 tons of aluminum, which supplied half of Tajikistan's export revenue.[25] The smelter received plentiful electricity at subsidized prices; other Soviet republics bought the aluminum, while the plant's transportation also was subsidized.

The Soviet breakup brought problems. The smelter is hundreds or thousands of miles from both its raw-material sources and its potential markets. Loss of its Soviet-financed transportation and large electricity subsidies meant that, at world prices, the smelter's inputs were worth more in alternate uses than the value of the aluminum it produced. In other words, every $1 million worth of aluminum produced used up resources worth more than $1 million.

After the Soviet breakup, political instability and civil conflict plagued Tajikistan; but slow economic reform now has begun. The government has committed itself to devise a plan, with assistance from the World Bank, to restructure TADAZ, which employs 12,000 workers. Aluminum prices rose in 2000, and TADAZ raised its output by 15 percent to 270,000 tons, about two-thirds of its 1989 production. Experts view privatization of TADAZ any time soon as unlikely; but some disagreement exists about whether the smelter, if radically restructured, could produce profitably while paying market prices for its electricity usage. For now, the explicit electricity subsidies that prevailed during the Soviet era have disappeared. Instead, TADAZ simply hasn't paid its electric bills (experts call such cases *implicit subsidies*); the smelter has, however, reached an agreement to pay $8.3 million to the state electricity company to cover its arrears.

CASE THREE:
Open to Development

We saw in Chapter Ten that a country can grow in two ways: using more inputs or using inputs more productively. The latter path involves boosting total factor productivity, a measure of how efficiently an economy uses its inputs. Total factor productivity rises because of technological innovations, including organizational ones, that allow a given quantity of inputs to produce more output. Table 11.10 reports estimates of the contributions of the various sources of growth for developing countries as a group and for subsets of developing countries divided by their growth rates. Notice that high rates of total factor productivity distinguish the high-growth economies from the medium-growth ones and, especially, from the low-growth ones, which actually suffered a large decline in productivity between 1982 and 1991.

What contributes to growth in total factor productivity? One source of innovation, especially for poor developing economies, is borrowing technology from abroad through imports or foreign direct investment. This suggests that, in addition to providing a one-time increase in output as traditional trade models suggest, openness may raise a country's rate of growth by encouraging increases in its total factor productivity.

A recent study by Sebastian Edwards empirically examines this proposition. Do countries that make themselves open to trade grow faster? The answer appears to be yes. Edwards used a sample of 93 countries and nine different measures of openness between 1980 and 1990. He found that, for every one of the nine measures, more-open countries exhibited higher rates of total factor productivity growth.[26]

25 "Helter-Smelter: Why Tajikistan Has an Aluminum Plant," *The Wall Street Journal,* July 2, 1998.

26 See Edwards (1998), as well as Frankel and Romer (1999).

Table 11.10 **Contributions to Growth, 1971–1991**

| | Share in Total GDP Growth | | |
	1971–1981	1982–1991	1971–1991
Developing countries:			
Average GDP	100.0	100.0	100.0
Capital contribution	51.7	47.6	48.1
Labor contribution	26.7	31.0	25.0
Total factor productivity	21.7	23.8	25.0
High-growth countries:			
Average GDP	100.0	100.0	100.0
Capital contribution	49.3	47.1	47.2
Labor contribution	21.3	17.6	18.1
Total factor productivity	29.3	33.8	34.7
Medium-growth countries:			
Average GDP	100.0	100.0	100.0
Capital contribution	54.5	41.4	50.0
Labor contribution	32.7	44.8	35.7
Total factor productivity	12.7	10.3	16.7
Low-growth countries:			
Average GDP	100.0	100.0	100.0
Capital contribution	57.6	75.0	57.1
Labor contribution	30.3	137.5	42.9
Total factor productivity	12.1	–112.5	0.0

Source: Data from United Nations Industrial Development Organization, *Industrial Development Global Report 1997*, p. 9.

India

CASE FOUR:
Reproducing Pharmaceuticals

For years, firms in many developing countries have copied products created by developed-country firms. Developing countries' lack of intellectual-property laws or failure to enforce them let this copying continue with no remuneration to the innovative firms. India, for example, built a thriving pharmaceutical industry centered in Mumbai and Hyderabad. Indian law protected patents on the *process* for making a drug but not on the *product* itself, so Indian firms could copy drugs legally—so long as they altered slightly the manufacturing process for the active ingredient's molecule. Analysts estimate that this allowed Indian drug manufacturers to spend less than 2 percent of their sales revenue on research and development, compared with the 16 percent spent by the U.S. firms that develop and test most new drugs.

Intellectual-property provisions of the Uruguay Round agreement promised to change the situation for developing countries that, like India, belong to the WTO. Under the agreement, all new product or process innovations receive 20 years of patent protection from the date of application. However, the WTO gave the least-developed countries such as India up to 11 years (until 2005) to implement the new rules; innovations already in the pipeline received no protection.

The 2005 deadline created a big incentive for Indian pharmaceutical firms to copy as many drugs as possible as quickly as possible. Consider Viagra, Pfizer's popular anti-impotence pill. Within months of the drug's 1998 U.S. debut, several Indian firms were producing Viagra's active ingredient, sildenafil citrate, selling it illegally at home (where it had yet to be approved by the Indian government), and exporting it. The black market price was reported to be $13 per tablet (compared with $10 for a Pfizer tablet in the United States), but experts expected the domestic price of

Indian tablets to fall to between $1 and $2 by the time government approval legalized domestic sales.

Pfizer, Eli Lilly, Warner-Lambert, and other U.S. pharmaceutical firms often don't sell their latest drugs in India (or in other piracy-prone countries such as Argentina) because the local knockoffs undercut the innovators' prices. Once the Uruguay Round agreement takes full effect, unlicensed pharmaceutical firms may find their copying of patented drugs restricted. But countries such as India and Argentina may also enjoy more foreign direct investment and technology sharing by the innovators themselves once their research activities receive some protection. In fact, Eli Lilly, AstraZeneca, and other foreign pharmaceutical firms have plans in place for more research and production in India after January 1, 2005—the date India is scheduled to begin recognition of international drug patents.

Perhaps the most visible issue concerning intellectual property rights in pharmaceuticals centers on the extent of countries' right to override patents in public-health crises by engaging in compulsory licensing, that is, by copying pharmaceuticals without the innovating firm's permission when that firm refuses to license the product. WTO rules do allow such licensing; that permission received clarification during negotiations to begin the new Doha Round. Developing countries such as India and Brazil, with large copy-based pharmaceutical industries, along with some medical and AIDS activist groups, claimed a victory. But many public-health experts pointed out that licensing issues for state-of-the-art drugs were, at most, secondary problems in treating public-health crises such as AIDS in poor developing countries; more substantial barriers to be overcome include poverty, lack of basic medical infrastructure, and poor health policies.

CASE FIVE:
Oil Junkies?

Consider the following unflattering description of oil-endowed economies: "[O]il revenues are to the Middle East what heroin is to the junkie. Day to day, shooting up keeps you from feeling sick; over time, though, it keeps you from being healthy. . . . The oil producers are addicts. They prefer the comfortable squalor of staying hooked to the work it would take to kick the habit."[27]

Economists have noted for decades that economies with abundant endowments of natural resources, such as oil, often perform poorly. Think, for example, about the economies of the Middle East and North Africa. In fact, the tendency earned a seemingly oxymoronic name: the **resource curse**. How can resources be a curse when they are, after all, what makes possible production of the goods and services we want? What's special about natural resources, as opposed to labor or capital, that might make too much a bad rather than a good thing?

First, an increase in natural resources tends to increase that sector's output at the expense of manufacturing. We can think of this as an application of the Rybczynski theorem from Chapter Ten. Recall what that theorem tells us: When a small country experiences an increase in its endowment of one input (here, oil reserves), output of the good that uses that input intensively (here, oil) will rise more than proportionally *and* output of the other good (here, manufacturing) will fall. Shrinkage of the other sector must happen to free

up the labor and capital needed for expansion of the oil sector. So large natural-resource endowments can lead to lack of development of other sectors of the economy.

Second, prices and revenues from natural-resource products can be volatile. For an economy highly dependent on such products, income and government tax revenues reflect this volatility. So it's important for policy makers to manage prudently. When prices and revenues are high, policy makers must have both the foresight and the political will to put some away for the proverbial rainy day (the best-known example is Norway's Norwegian Government Petroleum Fund). Or, to put it differently, using up oil and gas reserves depletes the country's capital stock. So unless part of the revenues earned from the oil and gas go into productive investment projects to increase the other components of the capital stock, the country's ability to produce income over time will decline. But many poor developing and transitional economies lack the policy-making expertise and credibility to handle such management.

Third, the availability of "windfall" wealth from natural resources can destroy incentives to invest in education and technological innovation—key elements for sustained economic growth. For a personal-level analogy, think how you might have behaved differently if you'd won the lottery at age 18; would you have invested in a college education? Living off a windfall is always easier than working to create

---

27 James Surowiecki, "The Real Price of Oil," *The New Yorker,* December 3, 2001, 41.

Table 11.11 **Resource Dependence of Oil- and Gas-Rich Transitional Economies, 2000**					
	Azerbaijan	Kazakhstan	Russia	Turkmenistan	Uzbekistan
Oil and gas exports as percent of total exports	85.2%	46.8%	50.4%	81.0%	12.3%
Oil and gas exports as percent of GDP	30.5	24.7	21.5	68.7	4.3
Oil and gas revenues as percent of total government revenues	36.2	27.5	30.1	42.0	14.8
FDI in oil and gas sector as percent of total FDI	80.5	69.7	n.a.	n.a.	n.a.

Source: Data from European Bank for Reconstruction and Development, *Transition Report 2001*.

something, so the availability of oil or gas resources can reduce the incentives for entrepreneurship. When there's enough oil for the entire population to live off it, at least for a while, the lack of incentives for entrepreneurship and other economic activity erodes the basis for growth.

Fourth, in many developing and transitional economies, the natural-resource sectors are dominated by the government or newly privatized monopolies. Competitive pressures are suppressed through entry or ownership restrictions. Once again, incentives to innovate disappear, even in the resource sector.

Finally, the existence of rents from natural-resource monopolies often leads to corruption and political fights over the division of those rents. Consumers want, and often get, highly subsidized energy prices, which encourage overly rapid depletion of the resource. The politically powerful fight over access to reserves and pipelines. Promising pipeline routes lead to territorial disputes and even armed conflicts, which drain the country's ability to produce.

Among the transitional economies, Russia, Kazakhstan, Azerbaijan, Turkmenistan, and Uzbekistan have rich oil and gas reserves; Table 11.11 summarizes the degree of their dependence on their resource sectors.

How will this affect their transitions and future growth? Will they avoid the resource curse, or will they follow the unfortunate economic paths of Nigeria, Saudi Arabia, Algeria, and Iran? So far, the evidence suggests that the resource-endowed transitional economies performed less well during 1989–2000 on the European Bank for Reconstruction and Development's indicators of progress in transition than did other transitional economies. All of the problems mentioned here have been in evidence, albeit to differing degrees in the various countries.

Summary

The basic economic theory of international trade as developed in Chapters Two through Ten applies to developed and developing countries alike. But developing countries face special concerns regarding specialization in primary products, their desire for industrialization, access to new technologies, external borrowing to finance investment, environmental policies, and integration into the world economy. The process of economic development is long and difficult and offers few easy answers or quick fixes. But active participation in the world economy, based on comparative advantage and economies of scale, appears to offer a brighter future for the developing nations than the price-distorting and inward-looking policies prevalent in the past.

Looking Ahead

Thus far, we've ignored the fact that economic transactions across national borders involve use of more than one currency or unit of money. In Chapter Twelve, we explore the mechanics of dealing in different currencies and the policies open to governments for determining the value of their currencies relative to those of other countries.

Key Terms

gross national product (GNP)
North–South debate
import substitution
newly industrializing countries (NICs)
outward-oriented growth
effective rate of protection (ERP)
cascading tariffs (tariff escalation)
technology
technology transfer
intellectual property
external debt
government (sovereign) defaults
official debt

commercial (unofficial, or market) debt
debt instruments
equity instruments
maturity
insolvency
liquidity problem
economies in transition
market-based economic system
centrally planned economy
Council for Mutual Economic Assistance
  (CMEA, or COMECON)
resource curse

Problems and Questions for Review

1. Developing countries often accuse developed ones of pursuing trade policies that impede the ability of developing countries to export to developed countries. Briefly describe two examples of trade policies that provide some support for the developing countries' position, including why the policies you cite might harm developing countries.

2. Suppose you've been called in as a consultant to a country trying to decide whether to take out a substantial amount in foreign bank loans. What basic questions would you ask the country in order to obtain information to evaluate the desirability of the borrowing? Briefly explain the importance of each of your questions and how the answer to each would affect your recommendation.

3. In India's pharmaceutical and biotechnology industries, most firms simply manufacture drugs and vaccines discovered and developed by foreign firms. However, a few Indian firms engage in research and development to develop new drugs and vaccines. How would you expect these two groups of Indian firms to differ in their views on India's intellectual-property laws? In particular, which group would you expect to support stronger patent protection?

4. Cashew nuts provide the second-largest source of export revenue for Mozambique. The country imposes a 20 percent export tax on unprocessed cashews to support a cashew-processing industry that removes the kernels from their outer shells. A World Bank study found that cashew farmers would be much better off if the government simply removed the export tax on unprocessed cashews, but the government refused. Explain the policy and its expected beneficiaries and losers. Does the export tax represent an example of import-substitution development strategy or an outward-oriented one?

5. Explain why cascading tariffs provide high rates of effective protection for finished products.

6. Briefly describe several reasons why developing and developed countries often have difficulty reaching agreements in negotiations over environmental issues.

7. Explain why, using the theory from earlier chapters of the book, you might expect outward-oriented development strategies to be more successful than strategies based on import substitution.

8. Explain two reasons why the successor states to the former Soviet Union experienced a more painful and prolonged economic downturn from the events of 1989–1991 than did most of the formerly centrally planned states of Eastern Europe.

References and Selected Readings

African Development Bank. *African Development Report.* Oxford: Oxford University Press, annual.
Analysis and data of development-related activities in Africa.

Bannister, Geoffrey J., and Kamau Thugge. "International Trade and Poverty Alleviation." *Finance and Development* 38 (December 2001): 48–51.
Channels through which trade can alleviate poverty.

Bardhan, Pranab. "Corruption and Development: A Review of Issues." *Journal of Economic Literature* (September 1997): 1320–1346.
Accessible overview of the effects of and policies toward corruption.

Behrman, Jere, and T. N. Srinivasan, eds. *Handbook of Development Economics.* Amsterdam: North-Holland, 1995.
Collection of advanced review articles on the major topics in the field.

Bloom, David E., and Jeffrey D. Sachs. "Geography, Demography, and Economic Growth in Africa." *Brookings Papers on Economic Activity* 2 (1998): 207–296.
Argues for an important role of geography in Africa's slow growth.

Broadman, Harry G. "Competition and Business Entry in Russia." *Finance and Development* 38 (June 2001): 22–25.
Introduction to the continuing monopoly problem in Russia.

Bruton, Henry J. "A Reconsideration of Import Substitution." *Journal of Economic Literature* (June 1998): 903–936.
Strengths and weaknesses of import substitution and outward-oriented development; for all students.

Burnside, Craig, and David Dollar. "Aid, Policies, and Growth." *American Economic Review* 90 (September 2000): 847–868.
Does foreign aid contribute to recipients' economic growth?

Calamitsis, Evangelos A. "Adjustment and Growth in Sub-Saharan Africa." *Finance and Development* 36 (March 1999): 6–9.
Progress and continuing problems in Africa.

Clague, Christopher, ed. *Institutions and Economic Development.* Baltimore: Johns Hopkins University Press, 1997.
Collection of accessible applied papers on the roles of governance in development.

Collier, Paul, and Jan Willem Gunning. "Explaining African Economic Performance." *Journal of Economic Literature* 37 (March 1999): 64–111.
Survey of why African economic growth has lagged behind that of other regions.

Eaton, Jonathan, and Raquel Fernandez. "Sovereign Debt." In *Handbook of International Economics,* Vol. 3, edited by G. M. Grossman and K. Rogoff, 2031–2077. Amsterdam: North-Holland, 1995.
Advanced survey of the literature on developing-country debt.

Edwards, Sebastian. "Openness, Productivity, and Growth: What Do We Really Know?" *Economic Journal* (March 1998): 383–398.
More evidence on the complex relationship between trade and growth.

European Bank for Reconstruction and Development. *Transition Report.* London: EBRD, annual.
Excellent source of up-to-date analysis and data on the transitional economies.

Frankel, Jeffrey A., and David Romer. "Does Trade Cause Growth?" *American Economic Review* 89 (June 1999): 379–399.
Strong evidence that open trade contributes to growth, not the other way around.

Hernández-Catá, Ernesto. "Sub-Saharan Africa: Economic Policy and Outlook for Growth." *Finance and Development* 36 (March 1999): 10–13.
How African countries' policies affect their growth.

Klitgaard, Robert. *Tropical Gangsters.* New York: Basic Books, 1990.
A Harvard University economist's entertaining story of his experiences with corruption while working on a World Bank project in Equatorial Guinea.

Krueger, Anne O. "Trade Policy and Economic Development: How We Learn." *American Economic Review* (March 1997): 1–22.
Accessible review of recent changes in views toward development by one of the field's leading authorities.

Krueger, Anne O. "Whither the World Bank and the IMF?" *Journal of Economic Literature* (December 1998): 1983–2020.
Former World Bank Chief Economist on the two institutions' futures; for all students.

Lau, Laurence J., et al. "Reform without Losers: An Interpretation of China's Dual-Track Approach to Transition." *Journal of Political Economy* 108 (February 2000): 120–143.
Advanced treatment of China's gradual shift toward markets.

Leipziger, Danny M. "The Unfinished Poverty Agenda: Why Latin America and the Caribbean Lag Behind." *Finance and Development* 38 (March 2001): 38–41.
Poverty problems and policies in Latin America.

Maskus, Keith E. *Intellectual Property Rights in the Global Economy.* Washington, D.C.: Institute for International Economics, 2000.
Accessible discussion of striking a balance between incentives for innovation and spreading the benefits of new ideas.

Megginson, William L., and Jeffry M. Netter. "From State to Market: A Survey of Empirical Studies on Privatization." *Journal of Economic Literature* 39 (June 2001): 321–389.
Readable survey of what economists have learned from the privatization experience of the last two decades.

Meier, Gerald, and Joseph Stiglitz, eds. *Frontiers of Development.* New York: Oxford University Press, 2001.
The past and future of development economics.

Mshomba, Richard E. *Africa in the Global Economy.* Boulder, Colo.: Lynne Rienner, 2000.
Excellent introduction to the role of international trade and trade policy in Africa.

Murdoch, Jonathan. "The Microfinance Promise." *Journal of Economic Literature* 37 (December 1999): 1569–1614.
The role of small-scale credit in developing countries.

Perkins, Dwight H., et al. *Economics of Development.* New York: Norton, 2001.
Textbook covering a wide range of development issues.

Reed, Michael R. *International Trade in Agricultural Products.* Upper Saddle River, NJ: Prentice-Hall, 2001.
Excellent introductory applications of trade models to agricultural markets.

Rodrik, Dani. "Political Economy of Trade Policy." In *Handbook of International Economics,* Vol. 3, edited by G. M. Grossman and K. Rogoff, 1457–1494. Amsterdam: North-Holland, 1995.
Advanced survey of the literature on distributional aspects of trade policy and their implications for the policy process.

Rodrik, Dani. "Understanding Economic Policy Reform." *Journal of Economic Literature* (March 1996): 9–41.
The politics of policy reform; for all students.

Ryan, Michael P. *Knowledge Diplomacy: Global Competition and the Politics of Intellectual Property.* Washington, D.C.: Brookings, 1998.
Introduction to policies toward intellectual-property rights.

Sachs, Jeffrey D., and Wing Thye Woo. "Understanding China's Economic Performance." *Journal of Policy Reform* 4 (2000): 1–50.
How China's transition experience has differed from those of many other transitional economies.

Session on "Agriculture and Transition: The First Decade." *American Economic Review Papers and Proceedings* 89 (May 1999): 265–275.
Several short papers on one of the aspects of transition that many countries have found difficult.

Sharer, Robert. "Trade: An Engine of Growth for Africa." *Finance and Development* 36 (December 1999): 26–29.
How countries' low involvement in trade has hampered their growth.

Special issue on "Trade-Related Aspects of Intellectual Property Rights." *Journal of International Economic Law* 1 (December 1998).
How international law treats intellectual property rights, and how that treatment affects international trade.

Symposium on "Globalization and Africa." *Finance and Development* 38 (December 2001): 2–36.
Variety of perspectives on how integration into the world economy could improve Africa's growth.

Symposium on "Taking the Offensive against Corruption." *Finance and Development* 37 (June 2000): 2–19.
Series of papers on policies to discourage corruption.

Symposium on "Trade." *Finance and Development* 37 (June 2000): 22–36.
Collection of papers on trade's role in development.

Tybout, James. "Manufacturing Firms in Developing Countries: How Well Do They Do, and Why?" *Journal of Economic Literature* 38 (March 2000): 11–44.
Intermediate/advanced overview of the mixed performance of developing countries' manufacturing sectors.

United Nations Industrial Development Organization. *Industrial Development: Global Report.* Oxford: Oxford University Press, annual.
Excellent source of analysis and data on industrialization.

World Bank. *Globalization, Growth, and Poverty.* Washington, D.C.: The World Bank, 2002.
Up-to-date analysis of economic integration's effects on poverty.

World Bank. *World Development Report.* New York: Oxford University Press, annual.
Devoted to examination of various aspects of development; accessible to all students. The 2000/2001 issue focuses on poverty; the 2001/2002 issue focuses on institutional prerequisites for markets. Also contains large collection of data.

World Trade Forum. *State Trading in the Twenty-First Century.* Ann Arbor: University of Michigan Press, 1998.
The continuing role of government monopolies and trading companies in world trade.

Yarbrough, Beth V., and Robert M. Yarbrough. "Unification and Secession: Group Size and 'Escape from Lock-In.'" *Kyklos* (1998): 171–195.
Changing national borders as a way of overcoming political opposition to reform; intermediate.

Yusuf, Shahid. "The Changing Development Landscape." *Finance and Development* 36 (December 1999): 15–18.
How have development issues and challenges changed in recent years?

INTERNATIONAL
MACROECONOMICS

PART TWO

CHAPTER TWELVE

Currency Markets and Exchange Rates

12.1 Introduction

From a macroeconomic perspective, one fundamental characteristic distinguishes international economic activity from domestic: International transactions typically involve more than one currency or monetary unit. Whether a German buys an Italian sports car, a British airline buys a Boeing airplane, a Korean firm borrows from a Japanese bank, or an American buys stock in a Chinese firm, the transaction requires that one country's currency be exchanged for another's. Thus far, we've avoided the complications multiple currencies introduce by focusing on trade in real rather than monetary terms. In this chapter, we add another layer of realism to our analysis by examining the mechanics of currency markets and their role in international trade and financial activity.

12.2 Exchange Rates and Prices

12.2.1 What Do Prices Tell Us?

In Chapters Two through Eleven, we examined how individuals and firms decide what goods to produce, consume, and trade. We saw that they use relative prices as guides for making these decisions. Relative prices convey information about the opportunity costs of various goods. In day-to-day transactions, however, we rarely see relative prices directly. It would be unusual to walk into a store and find the price of a pound of apples listed as two pounds of bananas or to shop for a car and find a sticker price of 20 personal computers. Instead, we use **money prices;** they tell how many units of money (dollars in the United States, yen in Japan, baht in Thailand, pesos in Mexico, or yuan in China) we must pay to buy apples, bananas, a car, or a personal computer. If individuals and firms are to make everyday economic decisions according to comparative advantage, these money prices must reflect relative prices or opportunity costs.

Suppose that good X sells in the United States for $10 per unit and good Y for $5 per unit. The *ratio* of these two money prices ($P_X/P_Y = \$10/\$5 = 2$ units of Y per unit of X) gives the opportunity cost or relative price of good X; to obtain a unit of good X, we must forgo 2 units of good Y. Similarly, $P_Y/P_X = \$5/\$10 = 0.5$ units of X is the opportunity cost of Y; a consumer must forgo 0.5 units of X to obtain a unit of Y. The **relative price** of a good is sometimes referred to as its real price; this means the price is measured in "real" units (other goods) rather than monetary or "nominal" units such as dollars or yen. The simple relationship between money prices and relative prices allows individuals to enjoy the convenience of using money prices for everyday decisions without losing the information about opportunity costs that relative prices convey.

Notice that money prices can change while relative prices remain unchanged—as long as all money prices change proportionally. If the money prices of goods X and Y doubled from the previous example to $P_X = \$20$ and $P_Y = \$10$, the relative prices of X and Y still would be 2 units of Y and 0.5 units of X, respectively. This will prove important in our analysis of inflation in Chapters Eighteen and Nineteen. After all, inflation is simply a persistent proportional rise in all money prices, so it should leave relative prices unchanged.

12.2.2 How Can We Compare Prices in Different Currencies?

We've solved the puzzle of the relationship between relative and money prices in a single currency. Now, we need an additional step to compare prices stated in different currency units. How can we compare the price of an item selling for 10 dollars in the United States ($P^{US} = \$10$) and 5 pounds sterling in Britain ($P^B = £5$)? We need to know the exchange rate between pounds and dollars. We define the **exchange rate** (e) as the number of units of *domestic* currency required to purchase 1 unit of the *foreign* currency—in our example, the number of U.S. dollars required to buy 1 British pound sterling. In shorthand notation, $e = \$/£$; for example, if the exchange rate (e) is 2, then buying 1 pound requires 2 dollars ($e = \$2/£1$).

The exchange rate can also be expressed as the number of units of *foreign* currency required to buy 1 unit of *domestic* currency, or $e' = £/\$$. Of course, e' just equals $1/e$. Writers use both definitions, and we'll see that the daily *Wall Street Journal* reports both. To avoid confusion, form the habit of checking carefully when reading about exchange rates (as well as while traveling) to see which definition is being quoted. Buying 2 dollars with 1 pound ($e = \$2/£1$) is quite a different matter than buying 2 pounds with 1 dollar ($e' = £2/\$1$). In this book, we'll define the exchange rate as the domestic currency ($\$$) price of foreign currency unless specified otherwise.

Suppose the United States and Britain both produce an identical good. At $P^{US} = \$10$, $P^B = £5$, and $e = \$2/£1$, individuals would be indifferent between buying the U.S. good and buying the British good, ignoring transportation costs. To obtain the £5 to buy the British good, an American would have to give up $10, or $2 for each pound; this makes the dollar price the same for both the British- and U.S.-made goods. Similarly, a British resident would have to give up £5 to buy the $10 necessary to buy the U.S. good; thus, the price of the two goods would also be the same when measured in pounds. If $e > 2$, at $P^{US} = \$10$ and $P^B = £5$, individuals from both countries would have an incentive to buy the U.S.-made good. *(Why?)* If $e < 2$, individuals would have an incentive to buy the British good. *(Why?)*

Now consider goods produced uniquely in one country, say, tickets to the National Football League's Super Bowl, produced only in the United States and priced in dollars, and tickets to the Wimbledon tennis tournament, produced only in Britain and priced in pounds. Assume for simplicity that a Super Bowl ticket costs $125 and a ticket to Wimbledon costs £75. The exchange rate between dollars and pounds allows potential purchasers to compare the relative prices of the two tickets, even though their money prices are denominated in different currencies. In 1992, the exchange rate between dollars and pounds was $e = \$1.77/£$. From an American's perspective, a Super Bowl ticket cost $125, while a ticket to Wimbledon cost an amount equal to the dollar price of a pound multiplied by the pound price of a Wimbledon ticket, or ([$1.77/£] · £75) = $132.75. So the relative price of the two sporting events was equal to $125/$132.75 = 0.94. A resident of Britain would compare the prices in pounds; and the pound price of a Super Bowl ticket equals the dollar price of the ticket divided by the dollar price of a pound; so ($125/[$1.77/£])/£75 = 0.94—the same result. From either nationality's perspective, the exchange rate in 1992 made the Super Bowl less expensive than Wimbledon, because the pounds necessary to buy a Wimbledon ticket were relatively expensive compared with the dollars necessary to buy a Super Bowl ticket. But by 2001, the dollar price of a pound had fallen from $1.77 to $1.41. The change in the exchange rate raised the Super Bowl's relative price from an American's perspective to $125/([$1.41/£] · £75) = $125/$105.75 = 1.18. Similarly, a British resident would find that a Super Bowl ticket now cost $125/($1.41/£) = £88.65, while a Wimbledon ticket cost £75; and £88.65/£75 = 1.18. The fall in the dollar price of pounds between 1992 and 2001 raised the price of Super Bowl tickets relative to Wimbledon tickets, from either an American or a British perspective.

From these examples, we can see that *a change in the exchange rate, other things equal, changes all foreign prices relative to all domestic prices.* When the dollar price of the pound falls (e decreases), American goods become more expensive relative to British goods. If the dollar price of the pound rises (e increases), American goods become cheaper relative to British ones. This simple observation explains why individuals, firms, and governments care about the value of the exchange rate: Changes in the exchange rate can alter the relative prices of domestic and foreign goods, and this shifts demand away from the goods that become more expensive and toward the ones that become cheaper.[1]

---

1 Note that we've held the prices of the goods themselves constant; we'll relax this assumption later.

If exchange rates or the relative prices of various currencies never changed, we wouldn't have much reason to study the effects of using different currencies. Exchange rates would be merely a minor nuisance—like the fact that distances are measured in inches, yards, and miles in the United States and in centimeters, meters, and kilometers in Canada. But what if the "rate of exchange" between miles and kilometers weren't a constant (= 0.62 mile/1 kilometer) but varied over time? Travelers then would need a theory to explain the relationship. Similarly, because exchange rates aren't constant but change over time, we need a theory to explain them. So let's turn to an analysis of foreign exchange markets.

12.3 Foreign Exchange Markets

12.3.1 What Are They?

The **foreign exchange market** is the generic term for the worldwide institutions that exist to exchange or trade different countries' currencies. Most of the approximately 200 countries in the world use a unique currency or monetary unit, from Afghanistan's afghani to Zimbabwe's dollar (*not* the same as the U.S. dollar); international trade requires some mechanism for exchanging them. With so many different currencies, there are literally thousands of exchange rates, because each currency has a relative price in terms of every other.

In practice, many smaller countries' currencies rarely are traded (professional foreign exchange traders call them "exotics"), and some nonmarket and developing economies don't allow their currencies to trade freely in foreign exchange markets. Figure 12.1 reproduces a recent set of daily exchange rate quotations from *The Wall Street Journal.* The daily lists include only about 50 of the most heavily traded currencies. The first two columns in Figure 12.1 report the exchange rate as this book defines it: the number of U.S. dollars required to buy a unit of foreign currency (e). The two columns on the right report the number of units of foreign currency required to purchase a U.S. dollar ($e' = 1/e$). *(Verify the relationship between e and e' for several of the currencies.)* The prices quoted are for the large commercial transactions ($1 million or more) that constitute the bulk of the market activity. For small "retail" transactions, such as those undertaken by individuals or small firms, higher prices prevail to cover banks' costs of handling them.

Each Monday, *The Wall Street Journal* publishes a more complete listing of exchange rates, including more than 200 currencies. This listing quotes rates for the previous two Fridays, so the change in a currency's value over the preceding week can be calculated. Figure 12.2 reproduces a recent listing. *(Are the quotations e or e'? Can you find currencies on the list for which e = e'? Why?)*

The primary participants in foreign exchange markets include banks (who execute about 90 percent of foreign exchange market transactions), firms, foreign exchange brokers, and central banks and other official government agencies. Most transactions are made by electronic transfer and involve the exchange of large bank deposits denominated in different currencies. There are separate, much smaller markets for the exchange of actual cash or bank notes; this form of foreign exchange is more expensive to buy because banks incur the costs of transporting the cash and guarding it from theft. Just as each country's domestic money supply consists primarily of bank deposits rather than cash, activity in the foreign exchange market consists mainly of transactions in bank deposits denominated in the various currencies.[2] This is important to keep in mind in the discussion that follows: "Selling dollars and buying pounds" really means using funds from a bank deposit denominated in dollars to open or add to a bank deposit denominated in pounds.

12.3.2 What Types of Transactions Happen in Foreign Exchange Markets?

We'll see that the decisions by actors in the foreign exchange market to buy and sell bank deposits denominated in different currencies determine the equilibrium exchange rates between various pairs of currencies. But why do those actors buy and sell deposits in different currencies? The basic answer is that each bank, firm, or individual must choose how to allocate its available wealth among various assets. An **asset** is simply something of value, such as a house, a diamond, an acre of land, a bank deposit, a share of Microsoft stock, or a U.S. Treasury bond. An **asset portfolio** is a set of assets owned by a firm or individual. *Portfolio choice* refers to allocating one's wealth among various types of assets, some of which may produce pleasure from consumption (for

---

2 The bank deposits traded in the foreign exchange market consist of large time deposits or certificates of deposit, not part of the issuing country's money stock.

Figure 12.1 Exchange Rate Quotations, December 14, 2001

CURRENCY TRADING

Friday, December 14, 2001
EXCHANGE RATES

The New York foreign exchange mid-range rates below apply to trading among banks in amounts of $1 million and more, as quoted at 4 p.m. Eastern time by Reuters and other sources. Retail transactions provide fewer units of foreign currency per dollar. Rates for the 12 Euro currency countries are derived from the latest dollar-euro rate using the exchange ratios set 1/1/99.

Country	U.S. $ EQUIV. Fri	Thu	CURRENCY PER U.S. $ Fri	Thu
Argentina (Peso)	1.0009	1.0009	.9991	.9991
Australia (Dollar)	.5195	.5186	1.9251	1.9281
Austria (Schilling)	.06561	.06488	15.242	15.413
Bahrain (Dinar)	2.6525	2.6525	.3770	.3770
Belgium (Franc)	.0224	.0221	44.6831	45.1861
Brazil (Real)	.4208	.4216	2.3765	2.3720
Britain (Pound)	1.4534	1.4407	.6880	.6941
1-month forward	1.4509	1.4381	.6892	.6954
3-months forward	1.4460	1.4331	.6916	.6978
6-months forward	1.4388	1.4261	.6950	.7012
Canada (Dollar)	.6405	.6373	1.5614	1.5692
1-month forward	.6403	.6371	1.5618	1.5697
3-months forward	.6400	.6369	1.5624	1.5701
6-months forward	.6401	.6369	1.5623	1.5702
Chile (Peso)	.001490	.001491	670.95	670.65
China (Renminbi)	.1208	.1208	8.2768	8.2770
Colombia (Peso)	.0004323	.0004315	2313.00	2317.30
Czech. Rep. (Koruna)				
Commercial rate	.02772	.02741	36.072	36.483
Denmark (Krone)	.1213	.1199	8.2431	8.3432
Ecuador (US Dollar)-e	1.0000	1.0000	1.0000	1.0000
Finland (Markka)	.1518	.1502	6.5859	6.6600
France (Franc)	.1376	.1361	7.2658	7.3476
1-month forward	.1375	.1359	7.2751	7.3571
3-months forward	.1371	.1356	7.2914	7.3742
6-months forward	.1368	.1352	7.3116	7.3950
Germany (Mark)	.4616	.4565	2.1664	2.1908
1-month forward	.4610	.4559	2.1692	2.1936
3-months forward	.4600	.4548	2.1741	2.1987
6-months forward	.4587	.4535	2.1801	2.2049
Greece (Drachma)	.002649	.002620	377.46	381.69
Hong Kong (Dollar)	.1282	.1282	7.7998	7.7998
Hungary (Forint)	.003666	.003621	272.75	276.17
India (Rupee)	.02092	.02092	47.810	47.790
Indonesia (Rupiah)	.0000981	.0000989	10195	10110
Ireland (Punt)	1.1463	1.1335	.8724	.8822
Israel (Shekel)	.2353	.2360	4.2498	4.2374
Italy (Lira)	.0004663	.0004611	2144.74	2168.88

Country	U.S. $ EQUIV. Fri	Thu	CURRENCY PER U.S. $ Fri	Thu
Japan (Yen)	.007851	.007933	127.38	126.05
1-month forward	.007863	.007946	127.18	125.84
3-months forward	.007886	.007971	126.80	125.46
6-months forward	.007926	.008010	126.17	124.85
Jordan (Dinar)	1.4108	1.4108	.7088	.7088
Kuwait (Dinar)	3.2658	3.2637	.3062	.3064
Lebanon (Pound)	.0006609	.0006606	1513.00	1513.75
Malaysia (Ringgit)-b	.2632	.2632	3.8000	3.8000
Malta (Lira)	2.2416	2.2242	.4461	.4496
Mexico (Peso)				
Floating rate	.1098	.1098	9.1100	9.1110
Netherlands (Guilder)	.4097	.4051	2.4410	2.4685
New Zealand (Dollar)	.4182	.4186	2.3912	2.3889
Norway (Krone)	.1125	.1114	8.8913	8.9779
Pakistan (Rupee)	.01646	.01646	60.750	60.750
Peru (new Sol)	.2914	.2914	3.4318	3.4315
Philippines (Peso)	.01921	.01923	52.055	51.995
Poland (Zloty)-d	.2497	.2493	4.0055	4.0120
Portugal (Escudo)	.004503	.004453	222.07	224.57
Russia (Ruble)-a	.03297	.03297	30.335	30.335
Saudi Arabia (Riyal)	.2666	.2666	3.7509	3.7509
Singapore (Dollar)	.5443	.5466	1.8372	1.8295
Slovak Rep. (Koruna)	.02093	.02068	47.778	48.356
South Africa (Rand)	.0820	.0869	12.2000	11.5050
South Korea (Won)	.0007807	.0007877	1280.90	1269.60
Spain (Peseta)	.005426	.005366	184.30	186.37
Sweden (Krona)	.0948	.0951	10.5523	10.5165
Switzerland (Franc)	.6132	.6052	1.6309	1.6524
1-month forward	.6132	.6051	1.6309	1.6525
3-months forward	.6132	.6052	1.6308	1.6524
6-months forward	.6137	.6056	1.6295	1.6513
Taiwan (Dollar)	.02903	.02906	34.450	34.410
Thailand (Baht)	.02284	.02289	43.775	43.680
Turkey (Lira)-f	.00000069	.00000071	1450000	1410000
United Arab (Dirham)	.2723	.2723	3.6730	3.6728
Uruguay (New Peso)				
Financial	.07220	.07184	13.850	13.920
Venezuela (Bolivar)	.001331	.001331	751.25	751.50
SDR	1.2692	1.2676	.7879	.7889
Euro	.9028	.8928	1.1077	1.1201

Special Drawing Rights (SDR) are based on exchange rates for the U.S., German, British, French , and Japanese currencies. Source: International Monetary Fund.
a-Russian Central Bank rate. b-Government rate. d-Floating rate; trading band suspended on 4/11/00. e-Adopted U.S. dollar as of 9/11/00. f-Floating rate. eff. Feb. 22.

The daily *Wall Street Journal* reports exchange rates (both e and e') for about 50 widely used currencies.

Source: *The Wall Street Journal.*

example, houses, compact-disk players, sports cars), and some of which produce income (for example, interest from bank deposits or capital gains from stock). We'll assume that each firm or individual already has decided how to split the available wealth between pleasure-producing, consumption-oriented assets such as houses and income-generating wealth such as bank deposits; and we'll focus on allocation *within* the second group. In particular, because the demand for bank deposits denominated in various currencies determines exchange rates, we need to examine what determines that demand.

The primary determinant of any particular asset's desirability is its expected rate of return, or the expected future change in its value expressed as a percent of its purchase price. Maximizing wealth requires that individuals and firms try to add to their portfolios those assets whose value will rise in the future and eliminate from their portfolios those assets whose value will fall. Of course, asset owners can't know perfectly today what will happen to the value of different assets in the future, so portfolio choice requires collecting the available information on different assets and forming expectations about their future rates of return. Before we explore in detail the implications for the demand for bank deposits in different currencies, we can see that maximizing the rate of return from an asset portfolio could lead to four basic circumstances in which an individual or firm

Figure 12.2 **Extended Exchange Rate Quotations, December 14, 2001**

WORLD VALUE OF THE DOLLAR

The table below, based on foreign-exchange quotations from Reuters, gives the rates of exchange for the U.S. dollar against various currencies as of Friday, December 14, 2001. Unless otherwise noted, all rates listed are middle rates of interbank bid and asked quotes, and are expressed in foreign-currency units per one U.S. $.

Country (Currency)	Value 12/14/01	Value 12/07/01	Country (Currency)	Value 12/14/01	Value 12/07/01
Afghanistan (Afghani) c	4750	4750	Latvia (Lat)	0.6235	0.6262
Albania (Lek)	137	137.86	Lebanon (Pound)	1513	1513.5
Algeria (Dinar)	76.7297	77.5031	Lesotho (Maloti)	12.151	10.901
Andorra (Franc)	7.2541	7.3658	Liberia (US $)	1	1
Andorra (Peseta)	184.3306	186.77	Libya (Dinar)	0.6416	0.6416
Angola (Readj Kwanza)	18.2458	18.2458	Liechtenstein (Swiss Franc)	1.629	1.6599
Antigua (East Caribbean $)	2.67	2.67	Lithuania (Lita)	3.998	3.998
Argentina (Peso)	0.9991	0.9991	Luxembourg (Franc)	44.614	45.371
Armenia (Dram)	566.28	564.45	Macau (Pataca)	8.033	8.032
Aruba (Florin)	1.79	1.79	Macedonia (Denar)	67.33	67.33
Australia (Dollar)	1.9251	1.9453	Madagascar (Malagasy Franc)	6250	6433
Austria (Schilling)	15.2418	15.4723	Malawi (Kwacha)	67.01	67.05
Azerbaijan (Manat)	4677	4677	Malaysia (Ringgit) e	3.8	3.8
Bahamas (Dollar)	1	1	Maldives (Rufiyaa)	11.77	11.77
Bahrain (Dinar)	0.377	0.377	Mali Rep (CFA Franc)	725	737.2
Bangladesh (Taka)	56.95	56.95	Malta (Lira)	0.4461	0.451
Barbados (Dollar)	1.99	1.99	Martinique (Franc)	7.2546	7.3777
Belarus (Ruble)	1572	1564	Mauritania (Ouguiya)	269.05	268.5
Belgium (Franc)	44.6831	45.3589	Mauritius (Rupee)	30.25	30.25
Belize (Dollar)	1.97	1.97	Mexico (Peso)	9.11	9.2015
Benin (CFA Franc)	725	737.2	Moldova (Leu)	13.09	13.14
Bermuda (Dollar)	0.99	0.99	Monaco (Franc)	7.2546	7.3777
Bhutan (Ngultrum)	47.83	47.81	Mongolia (Tugrik) m	1101	1100
Bolivia (Boliviano) f	6.8285	6.82	Monserrat (East Caribbean $)	2.67	2.67
Bosnia & Herzegovina (Convertible Mark)	2.1632	2.1996	Morocco (Dirham)	11.3756	11.527
Botswana (Pula)	7.1635	6.7341	Mozambique (Metical)	23025	23000
Bouvet Island (Krone)	8.8775	8.9731	Myanmar (Kyat)	6.7042	6.7256
Brazil (Real)	2.3765	2.389	Namibia (Dollar)	12.255	11.09
Brunei Darussalam (Dollar)	1.8342	1.8331	Nauru Island (Australia $)	1.9244	1.9427
Bulgaria (Lev)	2.1533	2.1879	Nepal (Rupee)	75.938	75.938
Burkina Fas (CFA Franc)	725	737.2	Netherlands (Guilder)	2.441	2.4779
Burundi (Franc)	850.8	852.35	Netherlands Antilles (Guilder)	1.78	1.78
Cambodia (Riel)	3835	3835	New Zealand (Dollar)	2.3912	2.4125
Cameroon (CFA Franc)	725	737.2	Nicaragua (Cordoba Oro)	13.76	13.73
Canada (Dollar)	1.5614	1.5752	Nigeria (Naira) m	119.5	120
Cape Verde (Escudo)	119.8	119.8	Norway (Krone)	8.8913	8.9726
Cayman Islands (Dollar)	0.82	0.82	Oman (Sul Rial)	0.38507	0.38507
Central African Rep (CFA Franc)	725	737.2	Pakistan (Rupee)	60.75	60.45
Chad (CFA Franc)	725	737.2	Panama (Balboa)	1	1
Chile (Peso official)	543.99	543.81	Papua New Guinea (Kina)	3.7888	3.8619
Chile (Peso)	670.95	673.15	Paraguay (Guarani) d	4675	4720
China (Yuan)	8.2768	8.2772	Peru (Nuevo Sol) d	3.4318	3.432
Colombia (Peso) o	2313	2310	Philippines (Peso)	52.055	51.95
Comoros (Franc)	545.026	552.0594	Pitcairn Island (NZ $)	2.3932	2.4108
Congo Dem Rep (Congolese Franc)	326.75	325.55	Poland (Zloty) o	4.0055	4.0805
Congo Republic (CFA Franc)	725	737.2	Portugal (Escudo)	222.0669	225.4253
Costa Rica (Colon)	340.7	340.14	Puerto Rico (US $)	1	1
Croatia (Kuna)	8.1624	8.323	Qatar (Rial)	3.6397	3.5405
Cuba (Peso)	1	1	Reunion, Ile de la (Franc)	7.2546	7.3777
Cyprus (Pound)	0.6356	0.647	Romania (Leu)	31605	31730
Czech Republic (Koruna)	36.0715	37.0645	Russia (Ruble) m, b	30.335	30.075
Denmark (Krone)	8.2431	8.3703	Rwanda (Franc)	451.76	450.95
Djibouli (Franc)	170	170	Samoa, American (US $)	1	1
Dominica (East Caribbean $)	2.67	2.67	Samoa, Western (Tala)	3.522	3.522
Dominican Republic (Peso) d	16.4	16.4	San Marino (Lira)	2141.42	2177.79
Ecuador (US $) g	1	1	Sao Tome and Principe (Dobra)	8937.2	8937.2
Egypt (Pound)	4.535	4.26975	Saudi Arabia (Riyal)	3.7509	3.7504
El Salvador (Colon) d	8.752	8.752	Senegal (CFA Franc)	725	737.2
Equatorial Guinea (CFA Franc)	725	737.2	Seychelles (Rupee)	5.618	5.618
Estonia (Kroon)	17.264	17.558	Sierra Leone (Leone)	1975	1975
Ethiopia (Birr) o	8.422	8.422	Singapore (Dollar)	1.8372	1.833
European Union (Euro)	1.1077	1.1244	Slovakia (Koruna)	47.7775	48.513
Faeroe Islands (Danish Krone)	8.2313	8.3731	Slovenia (Tolar)	243.285	247.175
Falkland Islands (Pound)	0.6888	0.6999	Solomon Islands (Dollar)	5.5166	5.4953
Fiji (Dollar)	2.2728	2.2718	Somalia (Shilling) d	2620	2620
Finland (Markka)	6.5859	6.6855	South Africa (Rand) c	12.2	11.065
France (Franc)	7.2658	7.3757	Spain (Peseta)	184.3	187.0872
French Guiana (Franc)	7.2546	7.3777	Sri Lanka (Rupee)	93	93.15
Gabon (CFA Franc)	725	737.2	St Christopher (East Caribbean $)	2.67	2.67
Gambia (Dalasi)	17.525	17.525	St Helena (Pound)	0.6888	0.6999
Germany (Deutsche Mark)	2.1664	2.1992	St Lucia (East Caribbean $)	2.67	2.67
Ghana (Cedi)	7225	7260	St Pierre (Franc)	7.2546	7.3777
Gibraltar (Pound)	0.6888	0.6999	St Vincent (East Caribbean $)	2.67	2.67
Great Britain (Pound Sterling)	0.688	0.6977	Sudan (Dinar) c	258.7	258.7
Greece (Drachma)	377.455	383.145	Sudan Rep (Pound)	2587	2587
Greenland (Danish Krone)	8.2313	8.3731	Suriname (Guilder)	2178.5	2178.5
Grenada (East Caribbean $)	2.67	2.67	Swaziland (Liiangeni)	12.151	10.901
Guadeloupe (Franc)	7.2546	7.3777	Sweden (Krona)	10.5523	10.4807
Guam (US $)	1	1	Switzerland (Franc)	1.6309	1.6592
Guatemala (Quetzal)	8.005	7.975	Syria (Pound)	49	49
Guinea Bissau (CFA Franc)	725	737.2	Taiwan (Dollar) o	34.45	34.41
Guinea Republic (Franc)	1970	1957.5	Tanzania (Shilling)	917	915
Guyana (Dollar)	180.5	180.5	Thailand (Baht)	43.775	43.825
Haiti (Gourde)	25.5	27.25	Togo, Rep (CFA Franc)	725	737.2
Honduras (Lempira) d	15.85	15.87	Tonga (Pa'anga)	2.1887	2.2249
Hong Kong (Dollar)	7.7998	7.7993	Trinidad and Tobago (Dollar)	6.115	6.12
Hungary (Forint)	272.75	280.045	Tunisia (Dinar)	1.443	1.4595
Iceland (Krona)	103.32	108.1	Turkey (Lira) h	1450000	1456000
India (Rupee) m	47.81	47.81	Turkmenistan (Manat)	33.79	33.79
Indonesia (Rupiah)	10195	10365	Turks & Caicos (US $)	1	1
Iran (Rial) o	1750	1750	Uganda (Shilling)	1725	1725
Iraq (Dinar) o	0.311	0.311	Ukraine (Hryvnia)	5.35	5.297
Ireland (Punt)	0.8724	0.8856	United Arab Emirates (Dirham)	3.673	3.673
Israel (Shekel)	4.2498	4.228	Uruguay (Peso) m	13.85	13.97
Italy (Lira)	2144.7386	2177.1743	Vanuatu (Vatu)	145.28	146.1
Ivory Coast (CFA Franc)	725	737.2	Vatican City (Lira)	2141.42	2177.79
Jamaica (Dollar) o	47.05	47.05	Venezuela (Bolivar) d	751.25	750
Japan (Yen)	127.38	125.54	Vietnam (Dong) o	15086	15091
Jordan (Dinar)	0.7088	0.7088	Virgin Islands (US $)	1	1
Kazakstan (Tenge)	150.3	149.99	Yemen (Rial) a	169.2	169.2
Kenya (Shiling)	78.45	78.85	Yugoslavia (New Dinar)	66.4834	66.4834
Kiribati (Australia $)	1.9244	1.9427	Zambia (Kwacha)	3885	3925
Korea, North (Won)	2.2	2.2	Zimbabwe (Dollar)	55.45	55.45
Korea, South (Won)	1280.9	1269			
Kuwait (Dinar)	0.3062	0.3067			
Laos (Kip)	7600	7600			

US $ per national currency unit. a - parallel. b - Russian Central Bank rate. c - commercial. d - freemarket. e -Government rate. f - financial. g - Adopted US $ as of 9/11/00. h- Floating rate as of 2/22/01. m - market. o- official.

Each Monday, *The Wall Street Journal* reports exchange rates (e') from the previous two Fridays for about 200 currencies.

Source: *The Wall Street Journal.*

might make transactions in the foreign exchange market. For now, we restrict our attention to the **spot foreign exchange market,** that is, the market in which participants trade currencies for current delivery, which usually means delivery within two business days.

Clearing

Suppose a U.S. firm decides to buy a bond issued by a British firm.[3] The U.S. firm typically enters the spot foreign exchange market to buy the pounds in which the British firm issuing the bond wants to be paid. This happens when the U.S. firm instructs its bank to debit its dollar account and credit the pound bank account of the British firm. This type of transaction often is referred to as the **clearing** function of the foreign exchange market. The American firm demands foreign exchange (bank deposits denominated in pounds) in exchange for domestic currency (bank deposits denominated in dollars). In fact, it doesn't matter who (buyer or seller) actually conducts the foreign exchange transaction. At some point, if a U.S. firm buys a British bond, a dollar deposit will be exchanged for a pound deposit. The location of the foreign exchange transaction doesn't really matter, because arbitrage links foreign exchange markets all over the world. This means that the rate at which dollar deposits exchange for pound deposits will be approximately the same whether the buyer of the bond makes the foreign exchange transaction in New York or the seller of the bond makes the transaction in London.

Arbitrage

Arbitrage refers to the process by which banks, firms, or individuals (mainly banks in the case of foreign exchange) seek to earn a profit by taking advantage of discrepancies among prices that prevail simultaneously in different markets. For example, suppose $e^{NY} = \$2/£1$ in New York and $e^L = \$2.20/£1$ in London, and you have \$100 to use to arbitrage the foreign exchange market. You could use the \$100 deposit to buy a £50 deposit in New York and then use the £50 deposit to buy a \$110 deposit in London. You'd make a profit of \$10 (or a \$10/\$100 = 10 percent rate of return), ignoring transaction costs—which are close to zero in the foreign exchange market because most trading is done electronically in very large denominations. Of course, you wouldn't be the only person doing this. Not only is the transaction very profitable; it also involves no risk, because the New York and London transactions can be made simultaneously. In the process of making your profitable transaction, you increase the demand for pound-denominated deposits in New York (where you supplied \$100 to demand £50) and increase the demand for dollar-denominated deposits in London (where you demanded \$110 by supplying £50). This causes e^{NY} to rise and e^L to fall. Such arbitrage continues to be profitable until the two exchange rates (e^{NY} and e^L) equalize at some value between \$2.00 and \$2.20 per pound.

Arbitrage ensures not only that dollars and pounds exchange at the same rate in New York and London but also that exchange rates will be consistent across currencies. Suppose exchange rates were such that you could buy 1 euro (€) for 1 dollar, 1 pound for 2 euros, and 3 dollars for 1 pound. Such a situation is referred to as *inconsistent* and wouldn't persist in the presence of arbitrage. What if you again had \$100 to use in arbitrage? You could use your \$100 bank deposit to buy a €100 deposit, use the 100 euros to buy £50, and use the 50 pounds to buy \$150—a 50 percent rate of return for your efforts! Of course, the example exaggerates the inconsistency of the rates, and you wouldn't be fortunate enough to be the only one seeking to take advantage of the situation. Your efforts, along with those of others, would tend to raise the dollar price of euros, the euro price of pounds, and the pound price of dollars, thereby eliminating the opportunity for profitable arbitrage and ending the **inconsistent cross rates.** Because of the possibility of such **triangular** (three-currency) **arbitrage,** we expect that $\$/£ = \$/€ \cdot €/£$. *(Why?)*

Until recently, cross exchange rates rarely were reported. Most foreign exchange transactions took place through a two-step process with the dollar serving as an intermediary, or vehicle, currency. Someone who wanted to exchange Swiss franc deposits for yen deposits would trade the francs for dollars and the dollars for yen. However, with the acceleration of international trade and financial activity in the past few years, more transactions have begun to occur directly between nondollar currencies. *The Wall Street Journal* now prints a daily chart of cross exchange rates for eleven major currencies, shown in Figure 12.3. The chart reports both e and e′ for each currency pair. For example, the first column reports the price of a U.S. dollar in terms of each of the other currencies (e′), and the last row reports the U.S. dollar price of each of the other currencies (e). *(Use the data in the chart to check the consistency of the cross rates for several currencies. Also, check the relationship between e and e′.)*

---

3 A bond is just an IOU. The U.S. firm lends funds to the British firm in return for a promise of future repayment with interest.

Figure 12.3 **Cross Exchange Rates, December 14, 2001**

KEY CURRENCY CROSS RATES

Late New York Trading Friday, December 14, 2001

	Dollar	Euro	Pound	SFranc	Guilder	Peso	Yen	Lira	D-Mark	FFranc	CdnDlr
Canada..........	1.5614	1.4096	2.2693	0.9574	.63966	.17139	.01226	.00073	.72073	.21490	....
France..........	7.2658	6.5596	10.5601	4.4551	2.9766	.79756	.05704	.00339	3.3539	....	4.6534
Germany........	2.1664	1.9558	3.1486	1.3283	.88751	.23780	.01701	.00101	....	.29816	1.3875
Italy..............	2144.7	1936.3	3117.1	1315.1	878.63	235.43	16.837	....	990.00	295.18	1373.6
Japan............	127.38	115.00	185.13	78.104	52.184	13.982	....	.05939	58.798	17.531	81.581
Mexico..........	9.1100	8.2245	13.240	5.5859	3.7321	....	.07152	.00425	4.2051	1.2538	5.8345
Netherlands ...	2.4410	2.2037	3.5477	1.4967	....	.26795	.01916	.00114	1.1268	.33596	1.5633
Switzerland	1.6309	1.4724	2.3704	....	.66813	.17902	.01280	.00076	.75282	.22446	1.0445
U.K...............	.68800	.6212	....	.4219	.28187	.07553	.00540	.00032	.31760	.09470	.44066
Euro	1.10770	....	1.6099	.67917	.45378	.12159	.00870	.00052	.51129	.15245	.70941
U.S...............	....	.9028	1.4534	.61316	.40967	.10977	.00785	.00047	.46160	.13763	.64045

The daily *Wall Street Journal* reports cross exchange rates (both e and e') for 11 widely traded currencies.

Source: *The Wall Street Journal.*

For the many currencies for which cross rates still aren't reported, the best guess is the rate that would be consistent in the sense defined earlier. *(Use Figure 12.2 to predict the cross rates between the Panamanian balboa and the Belizian dollar and between the Angolan readjusted kwanza and the Turkish lira.)* The degree to which consistency holds for a given currency depends on the extent of arbitrage activity allowed. If government policies restrict purchases and sales of a currency, inconsistent cross rates may persist.

Hedging

Another reason for making transactions in the spot foreign exchange market is hedging. **Hedging** is a way to transfer part of the **foreign exchange risk** inherent in all noninstantaneous transactions, such as international trade, that involve two currencies. For example, suppose you're a U.S. importer who just purchased £1,000 of goods from a British exporter; payment is due in pounds in 30 days. You face two alternatives (we'll see a third later): (1) You can enter the spot foreign exchange market now, buy a £1,000 deposit at the current spot exchange rate, and earn interest on it until the payment to the exporter is due in 30 days, or (2) you can hold your dollars in a deposit and earn interest for 30 days until the payment comes due, at which time you enter the spot foreign exchange market and buy a £1,000 deposit at what is *then* the spot exchange rate. In other words, you can choose whether to hold a pound deposit or a dollar deposit as an asset in your portfolio over the next 30 days.

If you choose the first option and buy pounds now, you're hedging to avoid the foreign exchange risk that the dollar price of pounds could rise. If you wait (take option 2), the exchange rate might rise during the 30-day period, meaning you'll have to pay more dollars for the £1,000. During the 30-day period under option 2, you're said to hold a **short position** in pounds—that is, you're short of pounds you'll need at the end of the 30 days. Option 1 (buying now the pounds you'll need in 30 days) allows you to avoid this short position and the associated foreign exchange risk. Once you've purchased the pounds, changes in the exchange rate no longer affect you. You're then said to hold a **balanced, or closed, position** in pounds: You own just as many pounds as you need to cover your upcoming pound payment.

Entering the foreign exchange market to hedge is a way to avoid foreign exchange risk; it insulates your wealth from the effects of adverse changes in the exchange rate. But what if you hedge and buy your pounds now; then, in 30 days, you happen to glance at *The Wall Street Journal* and find that the dollar price of pounds has fallen? You could have bought the pounds now for less than you paid for them 30 days ago. Hedging allowed you to avoid the possibility that pounds would become more expensive, but it didn't allow you to take advantage of the possibility of pounds becoming cheaper.[4]

---

4 For a small set of heavily traded currencies, a recently developed financial instrument known as an option contract provides still another alternative. Case One at the end of the chapter explains these contracts.

Speculation

Speculation is yet another reason to make transactions on the spot foreign exchange market. In one sense, **speculation** is just the opposite of hedging: It means deliberately making your wealth depend on changes in the exchange rate by (1) buying a deposit denominated in a foreign currency (taking a long position) in the expectation that the currency's price will rise, allowing you to sell it later at a profit, or (2) promising to sell a foreign-currency deposit in the future (taking a short position) in the expectation that its price will fall, allowing you to buy the currency cheaply and sell it at a profit. When you speculate, changes in the exchange rate affect your wealth. Exchange rate movements in the direction you expected increase wealth, but those in a direction opposite to that anticipated reduce it. The line between hedging and speculation is a fuzzy one; choosing not to hedge is one kind of speculation. However, the term *speculation* often is reserved for cases in which someone buys (sells) a bank deposit denominated in a currency solely because he or she expects the currency's price to rise (fall), with no link to financing another transaction, as in the case of the hedging decision.

12.3.3 **Buying Currency** *Now* **for Delivery** *Later*

The major markets for foreign exchange other than spot markets are forward markets. Here participants sign contracts for foreign-exchange deliveries to be made at some specified future date (usually in 30, 90, or 180 days). The important thing is that the price of the foreign exchange is agreed on *now* for *future* delivery. The **30-day forward rate** for pounds is simply the dollar price at which you can buy a contract today for a pound deposit to be delivered in 30 days. The percentage difference between the 30-day *forward* rate (e^f) on a currency and the spot rate is called the **forward premium** if positive and the **forward discount** if negative.[5] If pounds sell at a 10 percent forward premium against dollars, the dollar price of a pound deposit to be delivered in 30 days is 10 percent higher than the dollar price of a pound deposit delivered today (that is, the spot rate). If a forward pound to be delivered in 180 days costs 5 percent less than a pound delivered today, the pound sells at a 5 percent 180-day forward discount against the dollar. Active forward markets exist in a relatively small number of currencies. Figure 12.1 reports 30, 90, and 180-day forward rates for the British pound (£), the Canadian dollar (Can$), the French franc (F), the German mark (DM), the Japanese yen (¥), and the Swiss franc (SF). (*In Figure 12.1, which currencies sell at a forward premium against the dollar? Which sell at a forward discount?*)

As we've already seen, every international transaction that doesn't occur instantaneously involves a foreign exchange risk for one of the parties, because the spot exchange rate may change unexpectedly during the transaction's time horizon.[6] The existence of forward markets allows parties to transfer these risks.

Suppose you're a U.S. firm holding $1,000. What if you expect the dollar to lose value against the pound (that is, the dollar price of a pound to rise) over the next 30 days? You can buy a pound deposit now in the spot market, hold it for 30 days, and then sell it in the spot market in exchange for dollars; or you can buy a pound deposit now in the spot market *and* buy a dollar deposit in the 30-day forward market to "freeze" the price at which you can buy dollars in 30 days; or you can simply hold dollars over the entire period. Which alternative will maximize your expected rate of return depends on (1) the forward exchange rate, (2) short-term interest rates available on deposits denominated in the two currencies, (3) the spot rate you expect to prevail in 30 days, and (4) the current spot rate. If you choose to buy pounds now in the spot market and sell them in the future spot market, the current and future spot exchange rates and the interest rate on pound-denominated deposits will determine your rate of return. This is a risky strategy—because the future spot rate can't be known now; so whether you would make this choice depends on your attitude toward risk and on your expectation about the future spot rate. If you buy pounds now in the spot market *and* buy dollars in the forward market, your rate of return will depend on the current spot rate, the forward rate, and the interest on the pound-denominated deposit you will hold for 30 days. If you simply hold a dollar-denominated deposit, your rate of return will depend on the interest rate available on dollar-denominated deposits.

---

5 A forward premium or discount can be defined for any time horizon; 30 days is only one example. Note that, for any two currencies, a forward premium on one is equivalent to a forward discount on the other. If the pound sells at a forward premium against the dollar ($[e^f - e] > 0$), the dollar sells at a forward discount against the pound ($[e'^f - e'] < 0$). Therefore, when using the term *forward premium* or *forward discount*, one must specify the currency.

6 The appropriate definition and measurement of foreign exchange risk is a matter of controversy. Here we mean simply that changes in the value of the exchange rate during a transaction may alter the rate of return anticipated by the parties at the time they agreed to the transaction.

The collective decisions of many individuals weighing the alternatives outlined previously determine the equilibrium relationships among the current spot rate, the forward rate, short-term interest rates on deposits denominated in the two currencies, and individuals' expectations of the future spot rate. The efforts of all individuals in the economy to maximize the expected rates of return on their asset portfolios result in two conditions—called *interest-parity conditions*—that summarize the relationships between spot and forward exchange rates and short-term interest rates on assets denominated in the two currencies.

12.4 **Interest Parity**

Uncovered interest parity applies to transactions in which participants don't use forward markets to transfer foreign exchange risk, and covered interest parity applies to transactions in which they do. We examine each in turn.

12.4.1 **Uncovered Interest Parity**

Suppose the 30-day interest rate on dollar-denominated deposits is 1 percent, the 30-day interest rate on comparable pound-denominated deposits is 2 percent, and the spot exchange rate between dollars and pounds is e = \$2/£1. If you have \$1,000, should you buy a £500 bank deposit or keep the funds in a dollar deposit over the next 30 days?

If you keep your \$1,000 in a dollar-denominated deposit at 1 percent interest, you'll end up with \$1,010, or a rate of return of 1 percent (the interest rate on dollar-denominated deposits). If you use your \$1,000 in the spot foreign exchange market to buy a £500 deposit, it will mature in 30 days and earn 2 percent interest in pounds. Then, you can take your £510 (£500 of principal plus 2 percent interest) and convert them back into dollars at the then-current spot exchange rate. The rate of return on your deposit measured in dollars will depend on the spot exchange rate at the end of the 30-day period.[7] For example, if the spot rate doesn't change over the 30 days, you'll end up with \$1,020. The dollar rate of return on the pound deposit will equal 2 percent, and you'll be glad you chose the pound deposit over the dollar deposit. But what if the spot rate during the 30-day period falls to e = \$1.50/£1? Then, when you convert your £510 back into dollars, you'll get only \$765, a dollar rate of return of *negative* 23 percent, consisting of the 2 percent interest on the pound deposit plus a *loss* of 25 percent from holding pounds, which lost 25 percent of their value against the dollar over the 30 days because [\$1.50/£1 − \$2.00/£1]/(\$2.00/£1) = −25%. In this case, you'd have been much better off taking the 1 percent interest rate and rate of return on the dollar-denominated deposit.

Obviously, whether there's an incentive to buy the pound-denominated deposit depends not only on a comparison of interest rates but also on what the individual expects to happen to the spot exchange rate during the life of the deposit. There's no way of knowing in advance (before making the decision about which deposit to purchase) what the future value of the spot rate will be. The individual must form an expectation about the future spot rate and base the asset decision on that; this expectation is called the **expected future spot rate,** e^e (that is, what people expect *today* about the spot rate that will prevail in the future). If the expectation turns out to be correct, the outcome of the decision will please the individual. If the expectation turns out to be wrong, the individual may regret the decision after the fact, even though it was made on the best information available at the time.

When all individuals in the economy choose between purchasing dollar- and pound-denominated deposits in a way to maximize expected rate of return, the result is a relationship among interest rates, the current spot rate, and individuals' expectations of the future value of the spot rate. The expected dollar rate of return on a dollar-denominated deposit is just the interest rate available on such deposits, $i^\$$. The expected dollar rate of return on a pound-denominated deposit has two components: the interest rate on a pound-denominated deposit, $i^£$, and the expected rate of change in the value of pounds relative to dollars, $([e^e − e]/e)$. Portfolio owners will buy more pound-denominated deposits if the return on dollar-denominated deposits is less than the expected return on pound-denominated ones. Algebraically,

---

7 Note that investors generally care about rates of return in their *domestic* currency and that when comparing assets' rates of return, they must always be expressed in the *same* currency.

General Case:

If $i^\$ < i^\pounds + (e^e - e)/e$, purchase pound-denominated deposits.

[12.1]

Numerical Example:

$1.5\% < 1\% + [(\$2.02/\pounds1 - \$2.00/\pounds1)/(\$2.00/\pounds1)] = 2\%$;

therefore, purchase pound-denominated deposits,

where $i^\$$ is the interest rate on dollar-denominated deposits, $i^\pounds$ is the interest rate on comparable pound-denominated deposits, e^e is the spot rate individuals *expect* to prevail at the end of the deposit's life, and e is the current spot rate. In the preceding numerical example, the rate of return on dollar-denominated deposits is 1.5 percent. The interest rate on the pound-denominated deposit is only 1 percent, but the dollar price of pounds is expected to rise by $(\$2.02 - \$2.00)/\$2.00 = 1\%$. Therefore, the expected dollar rate of return on the pound-denominated deposit $(= 1\% + 1\% = 2\%)$ exceeds that on the dollar-denominated one $(= 1.5\%)$, and portfolio owners will choose to buy pound-denominated deposits to earn the higher expected rate of return. *(What if $i^\$ = 1\%$, $i^\pounds = 2\%$, $e = \$2/\pounds1$, and $e^e = \$2/\pounds1$?)*

On the other hand,

General Case:

If $i^\$ > i^\pounds + (e^e - e)/e$, purchase dollar-denominated deposits.

[12.2]

Numerical Example:

$3\% > 1\% + [(\$2.02/\pounds1 - \$2.00/\pounds1)/(\$2.00/\pounds1)] = 2\%$;

therefore, purchase dollar-denominated deposits.

In this case, the dollar rate of return on dollar-denominated deposits $(= 3\%)$ exceeds that on pound-denominated ones $(1\% + 1\% = 2\%)$. The extra interest on dollar deposits is large enough to compensate for the expected foreign-exchange loss (1%) in holding dollars. Therefore, portfolio owners will switch out of pounds and into dollars. *(What decision would investors make if $i^\$ = 1\%$, $i^\pounds = 2\%$, $e = \$2/\pounds1$, and $e^e = \$1.50/\pounds1$?)*

From the rules in Equations 12.1 and 12.2, we can see that there will be no incentive to shift from one currency to the other when the expected dollar rates of return on the two types of deposits are equal. This equilibrium condition is known as **uncovered interest parity.** It holds when

General Case:

$$i^\$ = i^\pounds + [(e^e - e)/e].$$

[12.3]

Numerical Example:

$2\% = 1\% + (\$2.02/\pounds1 + \$2.00/\pounds1)/(\$2.00/\pounds1) = 2\%$.

The relationship in Equation 12.3 is an *equilibrium condition* because when the condition doesn't hold, expected rates of return on the two deposits differ and we expect portfolio owners to reallocate their portfolios between deposits denominated in the two currencies. When the condition does hold, the two assets carry the same expected rates of return and we expect the allocation of deposits between the two currencies to be in equilibrium, with no tendency to change.[8]

---

8 More precisely, uncovered interest parity requires $i^\$ = i^\pounds + ([e^e - e]/e) \cdot (1 + i^\pounds)$. The second term on the right-hand side appears because the interest earned on a pound-denominated asset, as well as the principal, must be reconverted into dollars and thus is subject to the premium or discount on foreign exchange. Because interest rates typically are less than 10 percent, at least in the major industrialized economies, the extra term is close to 1 and often is dropped, leaving the simplified expression for uncovered interest parity in Equation 12.3.

An alternative way of writing the uncovered interest-parity condition from Equation 12.3 puts the **interest differential** ($i^\$ - i^\pounds$) on the left-hand side. The remaining term on the right-hand side is the expected increase (if positive) or decrease (if negative) in the value of pounds against dollars, expressed in percentage terms. Uncovered interest parity holds when $i^\$ - i^\pounds = [(e^e - e)/e]$, or when the difference in interest rates on deposits denominated in two currencies equals the percentage difference between the expected future spot exchange rate and the current spot rate between those currencies. If the interest differential in favor of dollar-denominated assets is less than the expected increase in value of pounds against dollars ($[i^\$ - i^\pounds] < [(e^e - e)/e]$), portfolio owners have an incentive to sell dollar-denominated deposits and purchase pound-denominated ones; this is equivalent to the situation in Equation 12.1. On the other hand, if the interest differential in favor of dollar-denominated assets exceeds the expected increase in value of pounds against dollars ($[i^\$ - i^\pounds] > [(e^e - e)/e]$), portfolio owners will sell pound-denominated deposits and purchase dollar-denominated ones; this is just another way of stating the situation in Equation 12.2.

How do portfolio adjustments bring about the interest-parity equilibrium? Suppose the condition in Equation 12.1 holds. The interest rate available on dollar-denominated deposits exceeds that on pound-denominated deposits ($i^\$ - i^\pounds > 0$), but by less than the percentage by which the pound is expected to gain value against the dollar ($[e^e - e]/e$). Portfolio owners will buy pound-denominated deposits because the expected gain in the form of increased value of pounds will more than offset the forgone interest; in other words, because the expected rate of return on pound deposits exceeds that on dollar deposits. As many market participants try to buy pound deposits and few want to sell them, the price of pound deposits relative to that of dollar deposits rises. In other words, the current spot price of pounds rises.[9] *(Why?)* The increase in e lowers the right-hand side of Equation 12.1, leading toward interest parity as in Equation 12.3.

The portfolio-choice activities discussed in this section clearly involve a foreign exchange risk. The total expected return on an asset includes the interest earned *and* the expected gain or loss on the value of the currency. Individuals, firms, and banks make decisions based on what they *expect* to happen to the spot exchange rate in the future. If those expectations turn out to be incorrect, enormous losses can result. Many banks hesitate to take large open positions in foreign currencies because of the possibility of large losses; most banks' foreign exchange activities focus on transactions central to their customers' day-to-day international trade and financial dealings. There are exceptions, however; Citibank, Deutsche Bank, and Chase Manhattan, for example, actively trade foreign exchange.

For those who want to speculate in foreign currencies beyond the extent of ordinary international trade and finance activities, the International Monetary Market (part of the Chicago Mercantile Exchange) provides a forum for the sale and purchase of foreign exchange futures contracts. Figure 12.4 presents futures price quotations from *The Wall Street Journal* for eight currencies.

Futures contracts are similar to, but distinct from, forward contracts. Both involve buying or selling currency deposits for future delivery with the price determined today. Futures contracts are for uniform amounts and delivery dates (see Figure 12.4), while forward contracts can be negotiated for amounts and delivery dates tailored to the parties' specific needs. On Friday, December 14, 2001, you could buy a contract for 125,000 euros to be delivered in March 2002 for $0.8902 per euro; a similar contract for euros to be delivered in June 2002 would have cost $0.8969 per euro. *(Does this indicate that most market participants in December 2001 expected the euro to appreciate or to depreciate against the U.S. dollar between March 2002 and June 2002? How do you know?)* Because of their uniform nature, futures contracts are liquid or tradable. Also, because the futures market imposes significant margin requirements (money put "up front" to guarantee that the buyer will honor the contract), speculators are free to use the market. Forward contracts, on the other hand, usually are arranged between a bank and a customer or between two banks. Most banks engage in forward contracts primarily to provide clearing and hedging services for customers, although in the process they can carry large short or long currency positions for brief periods.[10]

---

9 In this simple, partial-equilibrium model of the foreign exchange market, we assume that adjustment takes the form of changes in the exchange rate alone, not in interest rates. Later chapters will incorporate the foreign exchange market into a general-equilibrium model of the macroeconomy, which will allow interest rate adjustment as well.

10 Case Three discusses another type of risk banks face in foreign exchange markets.

Figure 12.4 **Currency Futures Prices, December 14, 2001**

FUTURES PRICES

CURRENCY

	OPEN	HIGH	LOW	SETTLE	CHANGE	LIFETIME HIGH	LIFETIME LOW	OPEN INT.
Japan Yen (CME)-12.5 million yen; $ per yen (.00)								
Dec	.7914	.7934	.7817	.7857	− .0066	.9880	.7817	53,582
Mr02	.7970	.7972	.7851	.7893	− .0066	.8760	.7851	97,372
June	.7920	.7920	.7919	.7931	− .0066	.8776	.7919	20,383
Est vol 13,977; vol Thu 22,722; open int 171,692, −762.								
Deutschemark (CME)-125,000 marks; $ per mark								
Dec	.4678	.4617	.4568	.4623	+ .0056	.4742	.4400	194
Est vol 16; vol Thu 73; open int 194 unch.								
Canadian Dollar (CME)-100,000 dlrs.; $ per Can $								
Dec	.6382	.6410	.6367	.6409	+ .0029	.6825	.6230	31,280
Mr02	.6362	.6407	.6362	.6405	+ .0029	.6725	.6230	42,288
June	.6385	.6403	.6380	.6406	+ .0029	.6700	.6230	2,302
Sept	.6381	.6405	.6381	.6408	+ .0029	.6590	.6234	718
Dec	.6383	.6409	.6383	.6411	+ .0029	.6555	.6236	522
Est vol 14,315; vol Thu 18,042; open int 77,112, +348.								
British Pound (CME)-62,500 pds.; $ per pound								
Dec	1.4402	1.4570	1.4400	1.4544	+ .0124	1.5600	1.3600	23,660
Mr02	1.4338	1.4496	1.4324	1.4468	+ .0124	1.4700	1.3810	18,543
Est vol 5,793; vol Thu 10,112; open int 42,244, +23.								
Swiss Franc (CME)-125,000 francs; $ per franc								
Dec	.6043	.6145	.6043	.6140	+ .0083	.6382	.5506	28,364
Mr02	.6057	.6148	.6048	.6140	+ .0083	.6370	.5540	24,912
Est vol 11,426; vol Thu 17,495; open int 53,310, −5,383.								
Australian Dollar (CME)-100,000 dlrs.; $ per A.$								
Dec	.5183	.5200	.5171	.5192	+ .0005	.5641	.4802	7,483
Mr02	.5154	.5170	.5141	.5163	+ .0005	.5300	.4810	16,268
June	.5135	.5135	.5135	.5134	+ .0005	.5150	.4885	353
Est vol 2,052; vol Thu 5,473; open int 24,119, −11.								
Mexican Peso (CME)-500,000 new Mex. peso, $ per MP								
Dec	.11035	.11050	.10958	.10985	+ 00007	.11100	.09100	13,335
Mr02	.10810	.10870	.10750	.10785	+ 00007	.10870	.09770	24,316
Est vol 6,270; vol Thu 7,263; open int 37,966, −68.								
Euro FX (CME)-Euro 125,000; $ per Euro								
Dec	.8928	.9053	.8925	.9041	+ .0107	.9632	.8337	39,124
Mr02	.8902	.9022	.8891	.9010	+ .0108	.9640	.8336	76,728
June	.8969	.8985	.8964	.8986	+ .0108	.9275	.8365	396
Est vol 31,913; vol Thu 39,664; open int 116,315, −2,189.								

Futures markets permit traders to buy uniform contracts of currency for future delivery with the price and delivery date specified today.

Source: *The Wall Street Journal.*

12.4.2 Covered Interest Parity

Undertaking a transaction in the forward market at the same time the portfolio decision is made can cover foreign exchange risk. A U.S. resident who purchases a pound-denominated deposit in the spot market could buy dollars (by selling pounds) in the forward market at the same time, thereby avoiding the risk that the price of dollars might rise during the deposit's life. For an individual using the forward market to cover foreign-exchange risk, the relevant information for choosing between a dollar-denominated deposit and a pound-denominated one still includes a comparison of the rates of return on the two deposits. The rate of return on the dollar deposit is still just $i^\$$. Pound deposits' return consists of two components: the interest rate ($i^£$) and the forward premium. Letting e^f represent the *f*orward rate,

General Case:

If $i^\$ < i^£ + [(e^f − e)/e]$, purchase pound-denominated deposits.

[12.4]

Numerical Example:

$$1.5\% < 1\% + [(\$2.02/£1 − \$2.00/£1)/(\$2.00/£1)] = 2\%;$$

therefore, purchase pound-denominated deposits.

Here, the rate of return on pound deposits exceeds that on dollar deposits, so portfolio owners shift toward pounds. Dollar deposits pay a higher interest rate than pound ones, but pounds sell at a forward premium (or, equivalently, dollars sell at a forward discount). The foreign-exchange premium earned by holding pounds over the 30 days more than makes up for the forgone interest.

Just as a high dollar interest rate doesn't necessarily imply that portfolio owners would switch toward dollars, a high pound interest rate needn't imply a shift toward pounds. In Equation 12.5, the pound interest rate exceeds that on dollars, but the return on dollar deposits still exceeds that on pound deposits.

General Case:

If $i^\$ > i^£ + [(e^f - e)/e]$, purchase dollar-denominated deposits.

[12.5]

Numerical Example:

$1\% > 2\% + [(\$1.50/£1 - \$2.00/£1)/(\$2.00/£1)] = -23\%$;

therefore, purchase dollar-denominated deposits.

In summary, both the interest differential and the forward premium or discount on foreign exchange must be taken into account in choosing among deposits denominated in different currencies based on their rates of return. When individuals in the economy make their decisions based on the relationships in Equations 12.4 and 12.5, the resulting equilibrium condition is **covered interest parity.** This condition holds whenever the rates of return on dollar- and pound-denominated deposits are equal.

General Case:

$$i^\$ = i^£ + [(e^f - e)/e].$$

[12.6]

Numerical Example:

$$2\% = 1\% + [(\$2.02/£1 - \$2.00/£1)/(\$2.00/£1)] = 2\%.$$

When interest parity holds, the rates of return on dollar- and pound-denominated deposits are the same, so no incentive exists to alter the composition of asset portfolios. Therefore, currency markets are in equilibrium.

We can also express covered interest parity as a comparison of the interest differential and the forward premium or discount on foreign exchange (the percentage difference between the forward and spot exchange rates). When $i^\$ - i^£ = [(e^f - e)/e]$, rates of return on the two types of assets are equal, and foreign exchange markets are in equilibrium. If $i^\$ - i^£ > [(e^f - e)/e]$, portfolio owners will shift toward dollar assets; and if $i^\$ - i^£ < [(e^f - e)/e]$, they'll switch toward pounds.

Table 12.1 summarizes the interest-parity results. The spot exchange rate responds to changes in domestic interest rates, foreign interest rates, the expected future spot rate, and the forward rate. When these changes cause portfolio owners to shift toward domestic-currency deposits, the exchange rate tends to fall. When something happens to cause portfolio owners to shift toward foreign-currency deposits, the spot exchange rate tends to rise.[11]

12.4.3 Does Interest Parity Hold?

Covered interest parity is one of the most frequently tested relationships in international macroeconomics.[12] The empirical support for the relationship is quite strong, but the results are sensitive to the testing technique. In particular, the parity relationship holds more closely when all deposits used in the test are issued in a single

---

11 We'll see in section 12.7 that the government may choose to fix or peg the exchange rate, not allowing the changes implied here.

12 Testing uncovered interest parity is much more difficult, because the relationship involves the unobservable expected future spot exchange rate rather than the observable forward rate.

Table 12.1 **Interest Parity and the Exchange Rate**

Variable	Shift in Expected Return-Maximizing Asset Portfolio	Effect on Spot Exchange Rate
Domestic interest rate (i):		
Increase	Toward domestic-currency-denominated deposits	e falls (domestic currency appreciates)
Decrease	Toward foreign-currency-denominated deposits	e rises (domestic currency depreciates)
Foreign interest rate (i*):		
Increase	Toward foreign-currency-denominated deposits	e rises (domestic currency depreciates)
Decrease	Toward domestic-currency-denominated deposits	e falls (domestic currency appreciates)
Expected future spot rate (e^e):		
Increase	Toward foreign-currency-denominated deposits	e rises (domestic currency depreciates)
Decrease	Toward domestic-currency-denominated deposits	e falls (domestic currency appreciates)
Forward rate (e^f):		
Increase	Toward foreign-currency-denominated deposits	e rises (domestic currency depreciates)
Decrease	Toward domestic-currency-denominated deposits	e falls (domestic currency appreciates)

country. For example, a test using dollar-denominated and pound-denominated certificates of deposit (CDs) both issued by a Zurich bank typically will show a tighter parity relationship than a test using a dollar-denominated CD from a New York bank and a pound-denominated CD from a London bank. This is why, in our discussion of interest parity, we speak of the interest rates on deposits denominated in different *currencies* ($i^\$$ and $i^£$) rather than the interest rates in different *countries* (i^{US} and i^B).

Why the difference? One factor in addition to the expected rate of return that influences individuals' portfolio decisions is the risk that a country might impose restrictions on the movement of funds across national boundaries. A high rate of return on a deposit issued by a London bank would be worth little to an American if Britain imposed controls that prevented the owner from converting the proceeds of the deposit into dollars and moving them back to the United States. In comparing a dollar-denominated CD issued by a New York bank and a pound-denominated CD issued by a London bank, three things differ: (1) the currency, (2) the bank, and (3) the country. The interest-parity relationship addresses factor 1. For major banks in industrialized countries, factor 2 is of little significance, because bank failures are rare and, when they occur, deposits usually are backed by government insurance such as that provided by the U.S. Federal Deposit Insurance Corporation. But factor 3 can interfere with interest parity, especially in times of uncertainty—when market participants might expect changes in government policy.

By testing interest parity using deposits issued in the same country but in different currencies, the risk of government restrictions on movement of funds is equalized across currencies, allowing a purer test of interest parity. Offshore currency markets provide the perfect opportunity for testing interest parity. **Offshore deposits (or Eurocurrencies)** are currencies held in deposit outside their country of issue; in other words, a dollar deposit held anywhere outside the United States is a Eurocurrency (or Eurodollar) deposit, regardless of who owns the deposit.[13] Among offshore deposits held in the same country but denominated in different currencies, interest parity holds so tightly and routinely that dealers use the relationship as a shorthand way to calculate the forward rates they offer.

13 Section 12.9 discusses Eurocurrency markets.

12.5 **Demand and Supply in the Foreign Exchange Market**

Up to now our reliance on the standard demand-and-supply framework in analyzing the market for foreign exchange has been implicit. In this section, we'll develop a simple model of the demand for and supply of foreign exchange based on the interest-parity conditions. We'll see that equilibrium in the foreign exchange market and interest parity are equivalent conditions.

The demand for and supply of foreign exchange are similar in many respects to those for any other asset. The important thing to remember is that the demand for a currency is really the demand for deposits denominated in that currency, not demand for actual paper money. The **demand curve for a foreign currency** shows how many units of the currency individuals would want to hold at various exchange rates. In other words, the demand curve summarizes the relationship between the quantity demanded and the price of a foreign currency, holding constant the other economic variables that affect quantity demanded. Similarly, the **supply curve for a foreign currency** shows how many units of foreign-currency deposits are available for individuals to hold at various exchange rates.

The supply-and-demand model of the foreign exchange market is a partial-equilibrium model and, as such, ignores many interconnections among variables. Despite this limitation, the model is a useful first step in understanding the determination of exchange rates and their role in the international macroeconomy. Fuller elaboration of the relationships between exchange rates and the rest of the macroeconomy forms the basis of later chapters.

The interest-parity relationships developed in section 12.4 suggest that individuals allocate their asset portfolios among deposits denominated in different currencies by comparing expected rates of return, which depend on interest rates, spot exchange rates, expected future spot exchange rates, and forward rates. When the interest-parity conditions are satisfied (as in Equations 12.3 and 12.6), individuals are content to hold their existing portfolios; there's no incentive to shift from deposits denominated in one currency toward those denominated in another. So the foreign exchange market is in equilibrium when, given current interest rates, spot and forward exchange rates, and exchange rate expectations, individuals are content to hold in their portfolios the existing supply of deposits in each currency. In other words, interest parity and equilibrium in the foreign exchange market are two ways of looking at the same relationships.

12.5.1 **The Demand for Foreign Exchange**

The relationship between the quantity demanded of foreign exchange and the spot exchange rate (expressed as the domestic-currency price of a unit of foreign currency) is a *negative* one: As the exchange rate rises, the quantity of foreign exchange demanded falls. It's easy to see why. As the spot exchange rate rises, each unit of foreign currency becomes more expensive in terms of domestic currency. Given existing interest rates, expected future spot rates, and forward rates, foreign-currency deposits become less attractive assets than domestic-currency ones because the expected return on foreign-currency deposits falls. As a result, individuals choose to hold fewer foreign-currency deposits in their portfolios. *(Use the expressions for interest parity in Equations 12.3 and 12.6 to verify that a rise in the value of e, holding the other values constant, changes the situation from interest-parity equilibrium to one in which individuals substitute away from foreign-currency deposits.)* On the other hand, a fall in the exchange rate makes foreign-currency deposits more attractive because their expected rate of return rises, causing individuals to want to hold more in their portfolios. *(Use the expressions for interest parity in Equations 12.3 and 12.6 to verify that a fall in the value of e, holding the other values constant, changes the situation from interest-parity equilibrium to one in which individuals demand a larger quantity of foreign-currency deposits.)*

The negatively sloped line in Figure 12.5 illustrates the negative relationship between the quantity demanded of foreign exchange and the exchange rate. Just as in other goods or asset markets, the exchange rate is only one of several determinants of quantity demanded. Each demand curve is drawn for fixed values of the domestic interest rate ($i^\$$), the foreign interest rate ($i^£$), the expected future spot rate (e^e), and the forward rate (e^f). A change in any of these values causes individuals to demand a different quantity of foreign-currency-denominated deposits at each value of the spot exchange rate; this causes the entire demand curve to shift.

If the domestic interest rate rises, the demand curve for foreign exchange shifts to the left. The higher rate of interest paid on domestic-currency deposits causes individuals to shift their portfolios away from foreign-currency deposits and toward domestic-currency ones whose rate of return has risen. A fall in the domestic interest rate shifts the demand curve for foreign exchange to the right. *(Use Equations 12.1 through 12.6 to ver-*

Figure 12.5 **The Exchange Rate and the Quantity Demanded of Foreign Exchange**

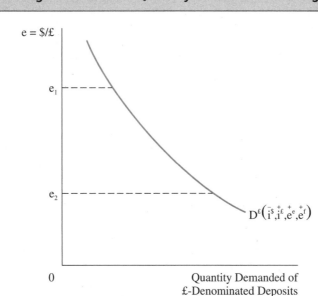

For given values of $i^\$$, $i^£$, e^e, and e^f, a high exchange rate (such as e_1) makes foreign-currency-denominated deposits less attractive relative to domestic-currency ones. The result is a low quantity demanded. A fall in the exchange rate from e_1 to e_2 makes foreign-currency deposits relatively more attractive to portfolio holders, increasing the quantity demanded. Increases in $i^£$, e^e, or e^f shift the demand curve to the right; increases in $i^\$$ shift it to the left.

ify.) In Figure 12.5, the $(-)$ sign over the domestic interest rate $(i^\$)$ term represents this relationship; when the domestic interest rate changes, the demand curve for foreign exchange shifts in the *opposite* direction.

A rise in the interest rate on foreign-currency deposits raises the quantity of those deposits demanded at any given value of the exchange rate; the demand curve shifts to the right. *(Why?)* A fall in the foreign-currency interest rate lowers the rate of return on foreign-currency deposits and shifts the demand curve to the left. The $(+)$ sign over the foreign interest rate $(i^£)$ term represents the positive relationship between the foreign interest rate and the quantity demanded of foreign-currency-denominated deposits; a change in $i^£$ shifts the demand curve in the *same* direction.

Using Equations 12.1 through 12.3, we can see that a rise in the expected future spot exchange rate increases the quantity demanded of foreign exchange. Such a change means that the dollar price of pounds is expected to rise; during the change, individuals want to hold pounds (which are becoming more valuable), not dollars (which are becoming less valuable). So the expected exchange rate term in Figure 12.5 has a $(+)$ sign; the demand for pounds shifts in the same direction as any change in e^e.

Similarly, Equations 12.4 through 12.6 imply that a rise in the forward exchange rate causes an increase in the quantity demanded of foreign exchange. Converting the proceeds of pound-denominated deposits back into dollars brings more dollars when e^f rises, so holding pound-denominated deposits now becomes more attractive. The sign over e^f in Figure 12.5 is $(+)$; when the forward rate changes, the demand for pounds shifts in the same direction.

The model of the demand for foreign exchange just developed is an *asset-oriented model*. It focuses on demand for foreign-currency deposits *as assets*. It may be tempting to ask, "What about international trade? Don't Americans demand yen to buy Toyotas, while Japanese demand dollars to buy Boeing 777s?" The answer, of course, is yes. Holding foreign-currency deposits for making trade transactions rather than as interest-bearing assets is called the *liquidity* or *transactions motive*. But in today's world economy, international financial activity dwarfs such considerations. Experts estimate that fewer than 5 percent of foreign-exchange transactions reflect trade in goods and services. In 2001, foreign exchange transactions total about $1.2 trillion *per day,* representing about one-fifth of the value of all world merchandise trade *for an entire year!* Also, as we've seen in this chapter, an international trade transaction, such as the purchase of an imported good, typically involves an asset decision, since immediate payment usually isn't required; the buyer must decide which currency to hold over the payment interval. Since asset-oriented financial transactions have come to dominate actual foreign exchange markets over the last few years, it's only appropriate that economists' models reflect this important change in the nature of the world economy.

12.5.2 The Supply of Foreign Exchange

Individuals determine the *demand* for foreign exchange through their efforts to earn the highest expected rates of return on their asset portfolios, as reflected in the interest-parity conditions. In contrast, government policies, together with banks' loan decisions, determine the *supply* of deposits denominated in foreign currency. We'll explore this process in some detail later. For now, it suffices to point out that private individuals' transactions can't create or destroy foreign-currency-denominated deposits.[14] An individual can only sell a deposit to another individual, firm, or bank or buy a deposit from another individual, firm, or bank.[15] In either case, the total stock of foreign-currency-denominated deposits remains unchanged; it will simply have been reallocated between portfolio holders.

Because the stock of foreign-currency-denominated deposits available at any time is fixed, we can represent the supply of foreign exchange by a vertical line, $S^£$, in Figure 12.6. The supply curve is vertical because the supply of deposits in existence at any time doesn't depend on the exchange rate. Now we can combine the demand for and supply of foreign exchange to see how they determine exchange rates.

Although we can draw demand and supply curves for foreign exchange, governments choose whether to allow the forces of demand and supply to determine the value of exchange rates for their respective currencies. In each country, the government decides the type of policy to follow regarding the exchange rate. Economists call this policy the **exchange rate regime.** There are four main types of regime: (1) flexible or floating exchange rates, (2) fixed or pegged exchange rates, (3) managed floating (a mixture of flexible and fixed), and (4) exchange controls. In the remaining chapters, we'll discuss all four systems. We begin with the simplest: the flexible or floating exchange rate.

12.6 How Are Exchange Rates Determined under a Flexible-Rate Regime?

Since the early 1970s, most countries have moved toward the use of **flexible,** or **floating, exchange rates.** Under such a regime, the demand for and supply of each currency in the foreign exchange market determine the exchange rate. We can treat the market for foreign exchange as a competitive one, because millions of individuals, firms, and banks participate; foreign exchange is a homogeneous commodity; market information is good; and market entry and exit are unrestricted. The market for foreign exchange under a flexible regime works much like the market for any other good: The price (the exchange rate) moves to the level that equates quantity demanded to quantity supplied. In the case of the foreign exchange market, the good in question is an asset in the form of bank deposits denominated in a foreign currency. The exchange rate adjusts until the quantity of foreign-currency-denominated deposits individuals want to hold equals the quantity available, or equivalently, until the expected rates of return on domestic- and foreign-currency-denominated deposits are equal, or until interest parity holds.

---

14 In the same sense, individual deposit transactions don't create or destroy domestic bank deposits. If an individual writes a $15,000 check for a new car, his or her account balance falls by $15,000, but the car dealer's account rises by the same amount. Total deposits remain unchanged; they've merely been reallocated between individuals. Cash transactions can affect total deposits but represent such a small share of activity that we can ignore them.

15 We ignore for now the possibility that the individual will buy from or sell to a *central* bank (that is, the government monetary authority); we'll cover this case in the forthcoming discussion of foreign exchange market intervention.

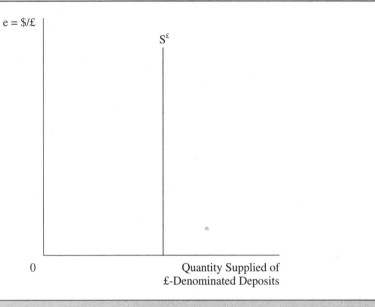

Figure 12.6 **The Supply of Foreign Exchange**

$e = \$/£$

$S^£$

0

Quantity Supplied of
£-Denominated Deposits

The quantity of pound-denominated deposits available is determined by government policies and banks' loan decisions. At each point in time, this quantity is independent of the exchange rate; therefore, a vertical line represents the supply of foreign-currency-denominated deposits.

Figure 12.7 shows the equilibrium exchange rate, e_3, between the dollar and the pound. If the exchange rate were *above* the equilibrium (for example, at e_1), individuals would want to hold *fewer* than the existing quantity of pound-denominated deposits. A surplus of foreign exchange would cause the price to fall as individuals offered to sell pound-denominated deposits in exchange for dollar-denominated ones. If the exchange rate were *below* the equilibrium rate (for example, at e_2), individuals would want to hold *more* than the existing quantity of pound-denominated deposits. A shortage of foreign exchange would cause individuals to bid up its price as they offer to buy pound-denominated deposits in exchange for dollar-denominated ones. Only at e_3, where quantity demanded equals the quantity supplied of foreign exchange, is the market in equilibrium. At that exchange rate (given the values of $i^\$$, $i^£$, e^e, and e^f), individuals are content to hold exactly $S^£$ of pound-denominated deposits in their portfolios, and interest parity is satisfied because the expected rates of return on dollar-denominated and pound-denominated assets are equal.

Under a flexible exchange rate regime, the price mechanism equates the quantity demanded of each currency with the quantity supplied; therefore, the foreign exchange market clears. Later chapters will explore the arguments for using a flexible exchange rate regime as well as the implications of such a regime for various macroeconomic policies.

When the exchange rate is flexible, we call a rise in the market-determined rate a **depreciation** of the currency whose price has fallen and an **appreciation** of the currency whose price has risen. A change in the rate from e_1 to e_3 represents a depreciation of the pound or, equivalently, an appreciation of the dollar. A move from e_2 to e_3 involves a depreciation of the dollar and an appreciation of the pound. Note that in discussing an appreciation or a depreciation we must always refer to a specific currency. A change in any exchange rate always involves an appreciation of one currency *and* a depreciation of another, so saying "the exchange rate between yen and francs appreciated" conveys no information. *Either* the yen appreciated against the franc (implying that the franc depreciated against the yen) *or* the franc appreciated against the yen (implying that the yen depreciated against the franc).

Figure 12.7 **Equilibrium in the Foreign Exchange Market under a Flexible Rate Regime**

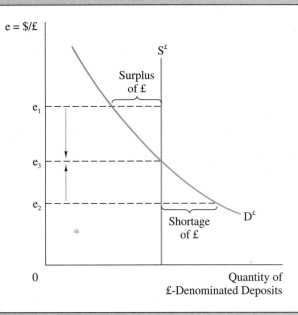

The exchange rate moves to equate the quantity demanded and the quantity supplied of pounds. The equilibrium exchange rate is e_3; at that exchange rate, portfolio owners willingly hold the existing quantity of pound-denominated deposits given the values of $i^\$$, $i^\pounds$, e^e, and e^f.

Any change in economic conditions that increases the demand for pounds causes the pound to appreciate (e to rise). Such changes could include a rise in $i^\pounds$, a fall in $i^\$$, or a rise in e^e or e^f, as in Figure 12.8. A fall in the demand for pounds causes a depreciation of the pound (a fall in e). This might result from a fall in $i^\pounds$, a rise in $i^\$$, or a fall in e^e or e^f.

12.7 **How Are Exchange Rates Determined under a Fixed-Rate Regime?**

Exchange rates haven't been flexible through most of modern economic history; in fact, peacetime flexible rates were rare until the early 1970s. Instead, most governments used **fixed** or **pegged exchange rates** for their respective currencies. Such a practice works much like fixing the price of any good. The demand for and supply of foreign exchange still exist, but they don't determine the exchange rate as they would in a flexible rate system. Central banks (such as the U.S. Federal Reserve, the Bank of England, the European Central Bank, or the Bank of Japan) must stand ready to absorb any excess demand for or supply of a currency to maintain the pegged rate.[16]

Suppose the U.S. government decides to peg the exchange rate between dollars and pounds at e_1^p in Figure 12.9. At that rate, the quantity supplied of pounds exceeds the quantity demanded. The high dollar price of the pound makes dollar-denominated deposits attractive relative to pound-denominated ones, so the quantity demanded of pounds is low. The surplus of pounds in the foreign exchange market at e_1^p creates a tendency for

---

16 In some countries, government agencies other than the central bank can also intervene in foreign exchange markets. The U.S. Treasury, for example, sometimes intervenes using its Exchange Stabilization Fund. However, interventions by these agencies typically do not have the important macroeconomic effects (in particular, increasing or decreasing the money supply) that central banks' interventions do; so we'll focus on central banks' role in foreign exchange markets.

Figure 12.8 **Shifts in the Demand for Foreign Exchange Change the Exchange Rate**

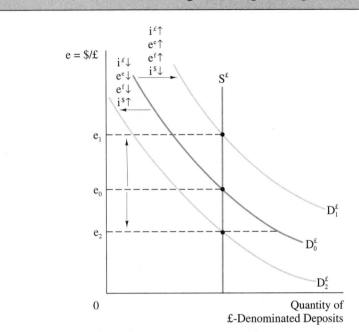

Increases in $i^£$, e^e, or e^f increase the demand for pound-denominated bank deposits and cause the pound to appreciate against the dollar. Increases in $i^\$$ decrease the demand for pound-denominated deposits and cause the pound to depreciate against the dollar.

the exchange rate to fall (that is, for the pound to depreciate against the dollar) as individuals try to sell pound-denominated deposits in exchange for dollar ones.

To keep the exchange rate at e_1^p, the U.S. central bank must step into the market and buy up the surplus pound-denominated deposits. This is called a policy of **intervention** in the foreign exchange market. Individuals sell the pound-denominated deposits they don't want to the U.S. central bank in return for dollar-denominated deposits at a rate of e_1^p per pound. The horizontal distance between $D^£$ and $S^£$ at e_1^p in Figure 12.9 represents the magnitude of the required intervention.

Alternatively, if the central bank chooses to adjust the pegged exchange rate downward from e_1^p, the policy is called a **revaluation** of the dollar. A revaluation under a pegged exchange regime is analogous to an appreciation under a flexible regime; that is, both revaluation and appreciation refer to a rise in the value of the currency (here, the dollar) relative to another currency (the pound).

Suppose, on the other hand, that the U.S. government decided to hold the exchange rate between dollars and pounds at e_2^p, below the equilibrium rate in Figure 12.10. At e_2^p, the quantity demanded of pounds exceeds the quantity supplied. The low value of the exchange rate makes pound-denominated deposits more attractive and dollar-denominated deposits less so. The forces of supply and demand in the foreign exchange market put upward pressure on the dollar price of pounds. If the exchange rate is to stay at e_2^p, the central bank must intervene in the foreign exchange market to supply enough pounds to cover the difference between the quantity individuals demand and the quantity supplied at e_2^p. For intervention purposes, governments hold stocks of deposits denominated in various foreign currencies, called **foreign exchange reserves.** In our example, the U.S. central bank would sell a portion of its pound reserves by buying dollar-denominated deposits with those pound-denominated deposits, thereby satisfying portfolio owners' demand for pounds.

If a central bank tried to hold the exchange rate between its currency and another at a level below equilibrium for a long period, it eventually would deplete its foreign exchange reserves. Then the policy choices would

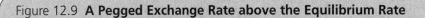

Figure 12.9 **A Pegged Exchange Rate above the Equilibrium Rate**

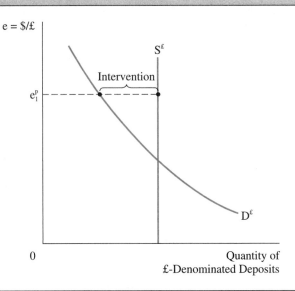

To maintain the exchange rate at e_1^p, the central bank must stand ready to absorb the excess quantity supplied of pounds. The U.S. central bank intervenes by buying pound-denominated deposits at a price of e_1^p; the horizontal distance between $D^£$ and $S^£$ at e_1^p represents the magnitude of the required intervention.

be to borrow reserves from other central banks or from the International Monetary Fund to continue the intervention, reset the pegged exchange rate at a level more consistent with equilibrium in the foreign exchange market, or allow the exchange rate to float to its equilibrium value.[17] If the central bank chooses to reset the exchange rate at a level higher than e_2^p, the policy is called a **devaluation** of the dollar against the pound, analogous to a depreciation under a flexible exchange regime.

Later we'll discuss at length the implications of a fixed exchange rate regime for the conduct of macroeconomic policy. For now, note that the type of foreign exchange risk analyzed in our discussions of hedging arises from the possibility that the spot exchange rate will *change* over time. If it were possible for governments' monetary authorities to peg e such that everyone was certain the exchange rate would never change, there wouldn't be any foreign exchange risk of this type. There would be little need for a forward market, because everyone would know that foreign exchange could be bought in the future at the same price prevailing today. Such fixed exchange rates would eliminate many but not all the roles of private foreign exchange markets—if the exchange rate were fixed within very narrow bands that were permanent and dependable. Unfortunately, history suggests that no fixed rate system can provide that degree of certainty, since there always is a possibility that, due to shifts in the demand for and supply of a currency, the government may become unable or unwilling to maintain the pegged rate. We'll see in later chapters that these issues played a big role in the Asian financial crisis of 1997–1998. Banks and other firms in countries such as Thailand and Indonesia took out loans denominated in foreign currencies under the assumption that their governments would maintain fixed exchange rates at their

17 Central banks enter agreements, called swaps, to lend specified amounts of their currencies to one another for intervention. For example, if the U.S. Federal Reserve ran short of pounds while trying to hold the dollar price of pounds below the equilibrium rate, it could borrow pounds from the Bank of England, to be repaid at a later date after U.S. pound reserves were replenished. The Federal Reserve Bank of New York's quarterly publication, *Treasury and Federal Reserve Foreign Exchange Operations*, reports recent trends in exchange rates and activity in the U.S. swap accounts.

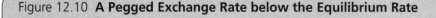

Figure 12.10 **A Pegged Exchange Rate below the Equilibrium Rate**

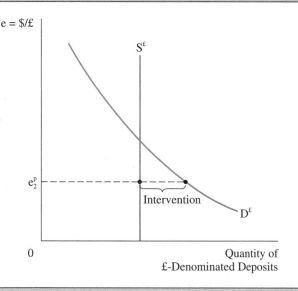

At e_2^p, the quantity demanded of pounds exceeds the quantity supplied. The central bank can maintain the rate at e_2^p if it intervenes by supplying pound-denominated deposits to the market from its foreign exchange reserves.

current values. Faced with mounting economic problems, governments instead devalued the currencies or, in some cases, abandoned the pegs and allowed the currencies to depreciate. Banks and firms, which had assumed they'd be able to buy foreign currency in the future at the long-standing fixed rates, suddenly faced much higher prices for the foreign currency they needed to repay their loans.

12.8 The Effective Exchange Rate

An exchange rate is merely the relative price of two currencies, reflecting the relative demands for and supplies of deposits denominated in those currencies, so a currency may *appreciate* against some currencies at the same time it *depreciates* against others. This means it's not possible, based on a **bilateral exchange rate,** to determine whether a currency generally is appreciating or depreciating in foreign exchange markets. Nonetheless, it often is useful to have an indicator of the trend of a currency's overall movement relative to other currencies "on average." **Effective exchange rates** serve this purpose. The effective exchange rate of the dollar, for example, provides a measure of the dollar's value relative to U.S. trading partners' currencies as a group.

Several government agencies, international organizations, and private financial institutions compute effective exchange rates for the U.S. dollar and other currencies. Table 12.2 reports one of four measures of the effective exchange rate of the dollar calculated by the Federal Reserve Board, for the years since the dollar began to float. This particular measure, called the major currencies index, now includes the euro, Canadian dollar, Japanese yen, Swedish krona, Swiss franc, British pound, and Australian dollar.

Various measures of the effective exchange rate differ primarily in the weights attached to the bilateral exchange rates in the calculation. Over short periods, these differences in weighting procedures can cause substantial variation in measures of the effective exchange rate. For example, during the Asian financial crisis of 1997–1998, measures that weighted Asian currencies heavily showed a larger appreciation of the dollar, because the dollar's value rose particularly sharply against the currencies belonging to those trading partners.

Table 12.2 **Major Currency Index Effective Exchange Rate of the U.S. Dollar, 1973–2000**			
Year	Effective Exchange Rate (Index: March 1973 = 100)	Year	Effective Exchange Rate (Index: March 1973 = 100)
1973	101.0	1987	104.8
1974	98.6	1988	112.6
1975	101.5	1989	108.2
1976	94.6	1990	113.1
1977	95.0	1991	115.1
1978	103.4	1992	117.1
1979	104.7	1993	114.0
1980	104.9	1994	116.0
1981	96.1	1995	122.9
1982	87.2	1996	117.4
1983	84.3	1997	108.8
1984	79.2	1998	104.4
1985	76.3	1999	106.3
1986	92.7	2000	101.6

As reported here, the index reports the trade-weighted value of foreign currencies in terms of the U.S. dollar; therefore, an increase in the index represents a depreciation of the dollar.

Source: Data from Board of Governors of the Federal Reserve System (updates are available at www.federalreserve.gov).

12.9 Offshore Currency Markets

Recall that an offshore deposit is simply a bank deposit denominated in the currency of a country *other than* the one in which the deposit is located. A dollar deposit in a London bank or a pound deposit in a Hong Kong bank both constitute offshore deposits, regardless of their owners' nationalities. What makes a deposit part of the offshore currency market is the combination of the bank's location and the deposit's currency of denomination.

One obvious question about offshore currency markets concerns why they exist at all. Why would anyone want to hold a deposit in a country other than the one issuing the currency? There are three answers to this question, two primarily economic and the other political; they are the reasons most often cited for the emergence and rapid growth of offshore currency markets.

Governments regulate banking within their borders. The United States, for example, imposes reserve, disclosure, and insurance requirements and many other restrictions on U.S. banks. Similar regulatory patterns exist in other countries, although the details vary considerably. There are several reasons for extensive regulation of the industry. Because of the links between banking and the money-creation process (see section 15.2.3), smooth functioning of the banking system constitutes an important element in the successful conduct of monetary policy. Confidence in the banking system is critical; the reserve, insurance, and disclosure requirements that governments impose on banks help ensure stability in banking and promote the public's confidence.

While the various government banking regulations provide benefits, they also raise banks' costs of doing business. Banks—at least those in the United States—are privately owned, profit-maximizing businesses, so the costs of regulation imply that banks must pay lower interest rates to depositors and charge higher ones to borrowers to operate profitably. Any bank that can partially escape the costly national regulations can lower its operation costs and thus afford to pay higher interest rates to depositors and charge lower rates to borrowers. Offshore markets achieve this goal. The U.S. government, for example, has little control over a bank that accepts deposits denominated in dollars in other countries. Even for overseas branches or subsidiaries of a U.S. bank, a foreign location reduces the government's power to regulate it. Countries that choose not to regulate banking heavily attract international banking activity. By escaping regulation, banks operating in these countries can offer more attractive interest rates to both depositors and borrowers. Countries that have deliberately fostered the growth of offshore banking include Britain, Switzerland, Panama, Bahrain, the Cayman Islands, Singapore, and Hong Kong.

Other countries, including the United States, Germany, and Japan, historically have used regulation to discourage borrowing and lending in foreign currencies within their borders. However, with the rapid growth of the offshore segment of the banking industry, the United States has adjusted its regulations to allow U.S. banks to capture a larger share of the growing business. The primary change came in 1981, when the government granted approval for international banking facilities (IBFs) to operate within the United States. IBFs accept deposits and make loans in any currency, including dollars, but only to foreigners. In return for reduced regulation, the IBFs agree not to compete with commercial banks for domestic business.

With the rapid growth of international trade and financial activity, firms' demand for offshore banking services has grown as well. When a firm buys and sells in many countries around the world, the ability to hold bank deposits in different currencies and locales becomes an important part of minimizing the costs of doing business. Firms' increased needs for international financial services help explain the rapid growth of offshore markets.

We can trace the third—and political—reason for offshore deposits to 1950s Cold War tensions between the United States and the Soviet Union. As part of its efforts to modernize and develop its economy, the Soviet Union entered into growing trade relations with Western economies, which meant dealing in dollars. However, the Soviet Union and the other Eastern European nonmarket economies were reluctant to hold dollar deposits in the United States, fearing that if hostilities escalated, the United States would seize or "freeze" their assets. To avoid the possibility of having their assets frozen, the Soviets searched for a bank outside the United States that would accept dollar-denominated deposits and located one in Paris.

Foreign branches and subsidiaries of the largest U.S. banks now dominate the offshore currency market. About half of all offshore deposits are denominated in dollars. In the market's early years, the bulk of activity consisted of dollar deposits held in Europe, which explains why offshore deposits often are called *Eurocurrencies* or *Eurodollars*. As a larger number of currencies have come to be used actively in offshore currency markets, the markets themselves have proliferated throughout the world. Offshore banking activity tends to move to areas of least regulation. Such activity originally centered in Europe, with London still the dominant location (although about 85 percent of the activity there is undertaken by foreign institutions). More recently offshore banking has expanded to a number of Asian centers, such as Tokyo and Singapore, making the term *Eurocurrency* less descriptive of the entire phenomenon.

The primary effect of offshore currency markets has been to increase the mobility of financial capital. Previously it was difficult to buy short-term assets denominated in foreign currencies. Investment abroad took the form of direct investment, purchases of common stock or equity in foreign firms, or purchases of foreign bonds. Now, offshore bank deposits provide a way to hold assets denominated in foreign currencies for very short periods, often only a few days. Most deposits in the offshore market are time deposits with maturities ranging from overnight to a few years.

CASE ONE:
Multinationals and Foreign Exchange

The analysis in this chapter makes clear that any noninstantaneous transaction involving more than one currency involves a foreign exchange risk. If the exchange rate between the relevant currencies changes significantly during the transaction, the terms of the transaction will deviate *ex post* from those originally negotiated. As reductions in transportation and communication costs have encouraged firms to become more international in their production, finance, and marketing operations, firms' exposure to foreign exchange risk has grown. Businesses and the financial institutions that serve them have developed several techniques to manage these risks.[18]

---

18 These techniques can't eliminate foreign exchange risk, but they transfer the risk from one party to another.

For large multinational firms, internal hedging (that is, offsetting one division's long position in a currency against another division's short position) provides the most common way of handling exchange risk. The costs involved in internal hedging often prove less than that of using a bank's forward foreign exchange services. If a firm's chemical division expects to be paid 1 million euros in 30 days for goods exported to Germany while the plastics division owes 1 million euros for imported raw materials, a simple internal transfer of the euros from chemicals to plastics can hedge against foreign exchange risk while avoiding the cost of forward contracts.

For smaller, less internationalized firms, forward markets provide the most widely used method of managing foreign exchange risk. By allowing a firm to contract to buy or sell a currency in the future at a prespecified price, forward markets facilitate planning by eliminating uncertainty about the domestic-currency value of future revenues earned in foreign currencies and future costs owed in foreign currencies. Forward contracts can be expensive, however, especially during times when foreign exchange market participants perceived exchange risk to be high—exactly when firms would most want to hedge. Also, banks typically offer forward contracts in only a few major currencies and only for relatively short durations (typically less than two years). For other currencies and longer-term risks, firms must pursue other strategies to cover their foreign exchange risk.

One possibility for avoiding losses due to currency fluctuations is the design of contracts that allow flexibility in the timing of receipts and payments. A U.S. firm importing ¥1 billion of goods from Japan may request contractual terms that allow payment at any time within a 180-day period following the delivery date. If the U.S. firm expects the dollar to appreciate against the yen, the firm may postpone payment as long as possible to obtain the best expected price on the yen. If, on the other hand, the firm expects the dollar to depreciate, the firm may pay the bill right away to avoid the possibility that the dollar price of yen will rise. The same idea can be used to alter the timing of foreign-currency-denominated export receipts.

Another strategy involves holding domestic bank deposits denominated in foreign exchange. As of 1990, U.S. firms can hold such accounts, insured by the Federal Deposit Insurance Corporation. The accounts, with minimum deposits of $20,000–$25,000, are invested in foreign time deposits (CDs) with maturities of three months to one year. But, again, a relatively small number of currencies are available.

Still another possibility is a financial instrument called an *option contract*. Buying an option contract guarantees the buyer the right to purchase (or sell) a specified quantity of a currency at a future date for a predetermined price called the *strike price*. The contracts are called *options* because the buyer has the option whether to exercise the contract; for-

ward or futures contracts, on the other hand, obligate the buyer to accept delivery at the specified date and price. Option contracts for future purchases of a currency are *calls*, and option contracts for future sales are *puts*. Figure 12.11 reproduces a set of price quotations for currency options.

A call option guarantees that the holder of the contract won't have to pay a price higher than the contract's strike price, because the owner will exercise the call if the spot price exceeds the strike price. *(Why?)* Note in Figure 12.11 that call-option prices rise for contracts with lower strike prices. A put option guarantees that the holder won't have to sell currency for a price below the strike price; the owner will exercise the put if the spot price is below the strike price. *(Why?)* For puts, note that prices rise for contracts with higher strike prices. Option contracts therefore provide the possibility of combining hedging and speculation. The holder of an option contract can still enjoy the benefits of favorable movements in the exchange rate (the speculative element) while limiting the effects of unfavorable movements (the hedging element). The Philadelphia Stock Exchange and Chicago Mercantile Exchange dominate currency options markets in the United States.

Some firms follow the ultimate strategy to avoid foreign exchange risk. They insist on being paid in their own currencies even on foreign sales, forcing customers to bear the risk. Such arrangements occur primarily in markets where the selling firm has substantial market power; otherwise, customers can threaten to go to a competitor with more willingness to take on the risk. In 2000–2001, as the British pound appreciated dramatically against the new euro, manufacturers in Britain, including Unilever and Toyota, demanded billing from their suppliers in euros—in order to avoid the painful combination of euro revenues and pound payments.

The Asian financial crisis caused many firms that historically had left exchange risk unhedged to reconsider, especially after they were surprised by the dramatic July 1997 devaluation of the Thai baht. But many of the Asian currencies most affected by the crisis—the baht, the Korean won, the Indonesian rupiah, and the Malaysian ringgit, for example—are only thinly traded, so forward contracts are unavailable or very costly. Nonetheless, firms such as computer manufacturer Digital Equipment started to hedge.[19] Dell Computer routinely buys currency options in all currencies in which the company operates. Other firms deliberately took out loans in the Asian currencies in which they expected to earn revenues, so if a devaluation lowered the revenues' dollar value, the firm enjoyed the offsetting benefit of repaying the loan with devalued currency. Avon Cosmetics chose to buy most of its raw materials and do most of the manufacturing for its Asian cosmetics sales in its biggest Asian markets (China, Indonesia, the Philippines, and Japan);

---

19 Darren McDermott, "Asian Turmoil in Currencies Creates Risks," *The Wall Street Journal,* August 15, 1997.

Figure 12.11 **Quotations on Foreign Exchange Option Contracts, December 14, 2001**

FUTURES OPTIONS PRICES

CURRENCY

Japanese Yen (CME)
12,500,000 yen; cents per 100 yen

STRIKE	CALLS-SETTLE			PUTS-SETTLE		
PRICE	Jan	Feb	Mar	Jan	Feb	Mar
7800	1.36	....	2.24	0.43	0.99	1.32
7850	....	....	....	0.59	....	....
7900	0.74	1.34	1.68	0.81	1.41	1.75
7950	0.51	1.10	....	1.08	1.67	....
8000	0.35	0.89	1.21	1.42	1.96	2.27
8050	0.23	0.72	....	1.80	2.28	....

Est vol 2,237 Th 566 calls 1,668 puts
Op int Thur 30,866 calls 39,593 puts

Canadian Dollar (CME)
100,000 Can.$, cents per Can.$

STRIKE	CALLS-SETTLE			PUTS-SETTLE		
PRICE	Jan	Feb	Mar	Jan	Feb	Mar
6300	1.10	....	1.35	0.05	....	0.31
6350	0.67	....	1.01	0.12	....	0.46
6400	0.32	0.58	0.73	....	....	0.68
6450	0.13	....	0.52	....	....	0.97
6500	....	0.23	0.35	....	....	1.29
6550	....	....	0.23	....	....	....

Est vol 147 Th 33 calls 158 puts
Op int Thur 19,291 calls 4,043 puts

British Pound (CME)
62,500 pounds; cents per pound

STRIKE	CALLS-SETTLE			PUTS-SETTLE		
PRICE	Jan	Feb	Mar	Jan	Feb	Mar
1430	2.14	....	3.20	0.46	1.10	1.52
1440	1.48	2.20	2.64	0.80	1.52	1.96
1450	0.88	1.70	2.10	1.20	....	....
1460	0.54	1.24	1.68	1.86	....	3.00
1470	0.34	0.94	....	2.66	....	....
1480	0.20	0.76	1.06	....	....	....

Est vol 807 Th 53 calls 131 puts
Op int Thur 3,128 calls 5,695 puts

Swiss Franc (CME)
125,000 francs; cents per franc

STRIKE	CALLS-SETTLE			PUTS-SETTLE		
PRICE	Jan	Feb	Mar	Jan	Feb	Mar
6050	1.14	....	....	0.24	....	....
6100	0.79	1.22	1.49	0.39	....	1.09
6150	0.52	....	....	....	....	....
6200	0.33	....	1.02	0.93	....	1.62
6250	0.21	....	....	....	....	....
6300	0.13	0.46	0.68	....	....	....

Est vol 253 Th 795 calls 753 puts
Op int Thur 3,723 calls 3,361 puts

Euro Fx (CME)
125,000 euros; cents per euro

STRIKE	CALLS-SETTLE			PUTS-SETTLE		
PRICE	Jan	Feb	Mar	Jan	Feb	Mar
8900	1.47	2.06	2.42	0.37	0.96	1.33
8950	1.13	1.76	....	0.53	1.16	....
9000	0.84	1.49	1.92	0.74	1.39	1.82
9050	0.62	1.26	....	1.02	1.65	....
9100	0.44	1.07	1.47	1.34	....	2.36
9150	0.30	0.90	....	....	....	....

Est vol 2,317 Th 1,586 calls 742 puts
Op int Thur 22,491 calls 14,318 puts

Options contracts give buyers the option to buy or sell currency at a future date at the prespecified strike price.

Source: *The Wall Street Journal.*

that strategy assured that any devaluation that lowered revenues would also lower costs.[20] The company also denominated its operational loans in local currency. In addition, Avon ordered its Asian operations to convert their earnings to dollars weekly rather than monthly.

Traditionally, Asian firms hedged currency risks less than U.S. or European firms, in part because so many Asian countries pegged their currencies to the dollar. Even in November 1997, well into the financial crisis, a survey of 110 chief financial officers (CFOs) at a CFO forum in the Philippines

---

20 Fred R. Bleakley, "How U.S. Firm Copes with Asia Crisis," *The Wall Street Journal,* December 26, 1997.

found that only 42 percent hedged their companies' foreign exchange risk. Of those that did, most relied on forward contracts. But as the Asian crisis shook those pegs, more firms began to hedge, again using a variety of techniques. Japanese auto manufacturer Mitsubishi responded to the weakness of the Thai baht by boosting production facilities in Thailand and replacing inputs previously imported from Japan with local ones. Since the Asian financial crisis, firms around the world report placing a higher priority on financial market expertise, especially foreign exchange trading, in recruiting for CFO and chief executive officer positions.

CASE TWO:
Picking Stocks Means Picking Currencies

We saw in this chapter that the expected dollar rate of return on a deposit denominated in foreign currency has two components: the interest rate on the deposit plus the expected appreciation or depreciation of the currency relative to the dollar. A similar rule applies to other assets, including stocks. The dollar rate of return on a share of Mexican stock, for example, equals the change in the stock's peso price plus any change in the dollar value of the peso. Table 12.3 reports rates of return in local currency and in U.S. dollars for 13 countries' stock indexes during 1999.

All the countries experienced high rates of local-currency return; 1999 was, in much of the world, a crisis-recovery year. For most of the countries in the table, the return measured in U.S. dollars differed significantly from the local-currency return. In Turkey, a large depreciation of the lira cut the dollar return on Turkish stocks by a third. Indonesia and Japan, on the other hand, experienced significant currency appreciations against the dollar, so their dollar stock returns exceed the local-currency ones. Hong Kong, with its fixed exchange rate relative to the U.S. dollar, exhibited equal returns in both currencies.

Anyone owning stock in a foreign firm experiences a rate of return that reflects both the firm's performance and changes in the value of the foreign currency. Managers of international mutual funds vary widely in the degree to which they hedge to avoid this foreign exchange risk, but funds' policies toward foreign exchange rarely appear in the fund prospectus.[21]

Table 12.3 **Local-Currency and Dollar Stock Returns, 1999**

Market	Percent		Market	Percent	
	Local Currency	Dollar		Local Currency	Dollar
Turkey	183.8%	126.6%	Hong Kong	52.4%	52.0%
Russia	123.2	96.2	Brazil	95.9	51.2
South Korea	67.9	72.3	Sweden	50.6	45.3
Indonesia	55.5	66.8	South Africa	49.1	44.5
Mexico	54.8	58.4	France	41.3	25.9
Japan	46.0	57.8	U.S.	17.8	17.8
Singapore	55.9	54.9			

Source: Bank for International Settlements.

---

21 For some examples, see "Fund Managers Disagree on Value of Currency Hedging," *The Wall Street Journal*, February 1, 2001.

CASE THREE:
Herstatt Risk

On June 26, 1974, German Bankhaus I. D. Herstatt collapsed after major losses on its foreign currency trading operations. German bank regulators closed Herstatt at 3:30 P.M. Frankfurt time. The bank had already *received* the day's payments on its foreign-exchange contracts; but, because of the hour, it hadn't yet *made* its dollar payments to U.S. banks. The episode eventually cost U.S. banks about $200 million, and the risk when a bank on one side of a foreign exchange contract fails to pay up had earned a name: Herstatt risk. It is also called settlement risk, since the problem stems from settling payments for foreign exchange contracts across markets in different time zones. When a bank is victimized by a partner's failure to honor a contract, the victim may become unable to honor its own contracts, lacking the foreign currency to do so; so the problem can spread quickly through the world financial system. Healthy banks may refuse to trade with those in trouble, afraid of themselves falling victim. The size of the average currency trade has grown to over $10 million, so failure of even a single transaction can have a large impact.

A 1994 study of the problem by the Federal Reserve Bank of New York found banks lulled into complacency in dealing with each other. A bank would often settle several contracts with a single partner on consecutive days without having received any payment in return, thereby accumulating significant exposure to Herstatt risk. Central bankers issued stern warnings to banks in 1996: (1) Do something as an industry about Herstatt risk or face increased regulation of currency trading, and (2) don't expect to be bailed out by taxpayers if you suffer Herstatt-type losses.

Banks responded by joining netting pools, which pool trades in a particular currency, net out offsetting ones, and settle any differences at the end of the day. Trading in net rather than gross terms reduces significantly the volume of currency traded and the associated risk. In late 2000, Hong Kong became the first Asian market to offer "real-time, gross settlement" in both local currencies and U.S. dollars. Each transaction, regardless of time of day, is settled immediately and for the full gross amount; participants no longer have to wait until New York markets open to get their dollars, thereby reducing Herstatt risk.

An even larger-scale solution is also in the works, called CLS Bank for "continuous linked settlement." CLS Bank will handle settlements in seven currencies for about 30 banks. At midnight Central European Time each day, CLS Bank will announce to each member bank how much of each currency it needs to settle its payments with other member banks. Each bank will send its currency to CLS Bank between 7 and 9 A.M. Payments by CLS to members will be made only when both sides of the transaction are ready. If the plan works and member banks play by the rules, CLS Bank members won't face any Herstatt risk, at least when dealing with other member banks.

CASE FOUR:
Currency Online

Foreign exchange trading for major institutional clients is moving online. Thirteen big traders that together account for 31 percent of all foreign exchange market revenues (including Morgan Stanley Dean Witter, Goldman Sachs, JP Morgan, and Bank of America) formed FXall. A rival trading system, Atriax, claims Citigroup, Chase Manhattan, Deutsche Bank, and Reuters as members; together the 50 founding banks in Atriax account for more than half of all foreign exchange trading, and the group plans to offer trades in more than one hundred currencies.[22]

Experts estimate that only about 10 percent of foreign exchange trades happen online now but expect that number to grow to 50 percent within a couple of years. The old system—trading through brokers over the telephone—can lead to costly errors. Competition between FXall and Atriax will make it easier for clients to compare prices and services, squeezing the already-tiny margins between the prices asked and bid on a currency; this will be good news for clients but bad news for the trading banks.

Online trading also promises to make foreign currencies easier to handle for small firms and individuals for whom foreign exchange transactions have historically been either very costly or impossible. Automated online trading seemingly bypasses the big trading banks, so clients can buy currencies

---

22 You can find exchange-rate quotes at either group's Web site (www.fxall.com or www.atriax.com).

in amounts as small as $1 and with bid-ask spreads as low as 0.02 percent of the currency's value. But if quantities supplied and demanded for a currency don't match across the online trading firm's many small clients, the firm must still access the regular interbank foreign exchange market to cover the difference.

Unfortunately, the largely unregulated nature of foreign currency markets combined with the anonymity of online trading creates ample opportunity for fraud. In the United States, the foreign exchange market is exempt from oversight by the Commodity Futures Trading Association, which regulates other futures markets. Why? Because activity in foreign exchange markets historically was limited to large banks, institutional investors, and other so-called sophisticated professional participants. But now advertisements on cable television and the Internet, often promising high rates of return with no mention of risks, encourage online speculative trading by ordinary individuals. The result: one of the fastest-growing categories of fraud.[23]

Summary

This chapter outlined foreign exchange markets' role in the world economy. Transactions involving more than one currency are a hallmark of international trade and finance. Activities in the foreign exchange market include clearing, arbitrage, hedging, and speculation, as portfolio owners choose assets with the highest expected rates of return. These activities create relationships among interest rates, spot and forward exchange rates, and expected exchange rates called *covered* and *uncovered interest parity*. The chapter used a partial-equilibrium demand and supply framework based on interest parity to examine the determination of the spot exchange rate along with the mechanics of the two simplest exchange rate regimes—a flexible rate system and a fixed rate system.

Looking Ahead

Chapter Thirteen introduces the balance of payments as the summary of all transactions of domestic individuals, firms, and governments with their foreign counterparts. It examines the various accounts of the balance of payments and explores some popular but misleading misconceptions.

Key Terms

money price
relative price
exchange rate
foreign exchange market
asset
asset portfolio
spot foreign exchange market
clearing
arbitrage
inconsistent cross rates
triangular arbitrage
hedging
foreign exchange risk
short position
balanced (closed) position
speculation
30-day forward rate
forward premium
forward discount

expected future spot rate
uncovered interest parity
interest differential
covered interest parity
offshore deposits (Eurocurrencies)
demand curve for a foreign currency
supply curve for a foreign currency
exchange rate regime
flexible (floating) exchange rate
depreciation
appreciation
fixed (pegged) exchange rate
intervention
revaluation
foreign exchange reserves
devaluation
bilateral exchange rate
effective exchange rate

---

23 See "Currency Scams Set Off Red Alerts as Investors Lose Millions of Dollars," *The Wall Street Journal,* December 9, 1998, and "Online Currency Trading Vexes Regulators," *The Wall Street Journal,* August 14, 2000.

Problems and Questions for Review

1. Assume that a fixed exchange rate regime is in effect.
   a. Countries A and B have agreed to peg the exchange rate between their currencies (the alpha, α, and the beta, β, respectively) at $\alpha 1/\beta 2$. Initially, this exchange rate corresponds to equilibrium in the foreign exchange market. Illustrate the initial situation in the market for beta-denominated deposits; be sure to label your graph carefully.
   b. Country A undertakes an economic policy that lowers the interest rate on alpha-denominated deposits (i^α). Explain and illustrate the effects of the policy in the market for beta-denominated deposits.
   c. If the two countries want to maintain the original exchange rate of $\alpha 1/\beta 2$, what must Alphabank (country A's central bank) do?
   d. Time passes, and the situation remains as described in part (c). Individuals in the two countries begin to anticipate a change in the pegged exchange rate. What type of change (that is, in which direction) would they be likely to expect? Why?
   e. Illustrate how the change in expectations described in part (d) would affect the market for beta-denominated deposits. Would the expectations make a change in the actual exchange rate more likely or less likely? Would the expectations be likely to make any change in the exchange rate larger or smaller? Why?
   f. Can your answers to parts (d) and (e) help explain the observation that policy makers and central bankers in countries facing likely currency devaluations often publicly deny that any devaluation is forthcoming? Why? Might there be a long-run cost to repeated such denials that turn out to be false? Why?

2. In 1998, India marketed $2 billion worth of Resurgent India bonds to Indians living abroad. The five-year bonds are denominated in foreign currency, not Indian rupees. Explain in what sense this transfers the foreign exchange risk from buyers of the bonds to the Indian government.

3. You have $2,000. The current interest rates on dollar- and pound-denominated deposits for 180-day maturity are $i^\$ = 0.02$ (2 percent) and $i^\pounds = 0.03$ (3 percent), respectively. The current spot exchange rate is e = $2/£1.
   a. What are your three basic choices of strategy over the next 180 days?
   b. If you (and everyone else) were certain that the exchange rate between dollars and pounds would not change over the next 180 days, what would you do? What would you have at the end of 180 days?
   c. Assume that you do not mind bearing foreign exchange risk. You expect the spot rate in 180 days to be $1.90/£1. What strategy would you follow, and why? After 180 days, the actual spot rate turns out to be $1.80/£1. Are you pleased with your decision? Why or why not?
   d. Now assume you are risk averse. The 180-day forward rate is $2.02/£1. What strategy do you follow?

4. Assume for simplicity that Germany and the United States are the only two countries in the world.
   a. Illustrate equilibrium in the foreign exchange market, using Deutsche marks (DM) as the foreign currency. Label your graph carefully.
   b. Suddenly, because of costs associated with unifying (formerly) East and West Germany, everyone expects the Deutsche mark to appreciate against the dollar. Illustrate and explain the effect of the change in expectations on the foreign exchange market, including the equilibrium exchange rate.
   c. What is the relationship between what everyone thought would happen and what actually happens? What might this imply about exchange rate volatility?

5. Suppose wheat sells for $3.00 per bushel in the United States and for 90 rubles per bushel in Russia. Ignoring transportation costs, what exchange rate between the dollar and the ruble would make consumers indifferent between buying U.S. and Russian wheat? Explain.

6. On January 31, 2000, *The Wall Street Journal* reported, "The euro's sharp plunge against the U.S. dollar last week has forced Europe's policy makers to confront the question of what, if anything, they should do about it. They have four options: do nothing, talk it up, intervene, or raise interest rates." Explain each of the four options using the basic supply/demand diagram of the foreign exchange market between the dollar and the euro.

7. As of September 8, 1992, the exchange rate between the Swedish krona and the dollar was $1/k5.5. The interest rate on krona-denominated deposits was 0.12 (or 12 percent), and the interest rate on dollar-denominated deposits was 0.03 (or 3 percent).
   a. Assume that the foreign exchange market is in equilibrium given the situation described. Is the *expected* spot exchange rate between the krona and the dollar closer to $1/k5.0, $1/k5.5, or $1/k6.0?

(Hint: There's no need for complicated numerical calculations.) Explain how you know, and provide the equation for equilibrium in the foreign exchange market that you used to arrive at your answer. Illustrate the equilibrium in a graph of the foreign exchange market between the dollar and the krona. Be sure to label your graph.

b. On September 9, 1992, the expected future spot rate fell. Illustrate the effects of the change in expectations on the graph of the foreign exchange market. If policy makers did nothing, what would happen to the exchange rate? Explain why.

c. Instead of doing nothing, Swedish policy makers raised interest rates on krona-denominated deposits. Use the equation for equilibrium in the foreign exchange market and your graph of the foreign exchange market to explain and illustrate the effect of the Swedish policy.

d. After several days, Swedish policy makers reduced interest rates on krona-denominated deposits back to about 0.12 (or 12 percent), their original level. Yet the exchange rate between the krona and the dollar remained approximately unchanged in the short run. What could account for this scenario? *(Hint: What effect, if any, might the temporary rise in interest rates have on exchange rate expectations? Why?)*

8. Comment on the following statements.

a. "In 1993, short-term Mexican bonds paid an interest rate of over 17 percent, Argentine bonds over 23 percent, Indonesian certificates of deposit over 15 percent, and Philippine Treasury bills over 12 percent. U.S. interest rates on dollar-denominated assets during the same period ranged from 3 to 6 percent, depending on the type of asset. This is proof that portfolio owners don't pursue high rates of return. Otherwise, no one would have held any dollar assets in 1993."

b. "During 1992, Brazil's currency depreciated by 95 percent against the dollar, Turkey's lira by 46 percent, Peru's new sol by 41 percent, Poland's zloty by 34 percent, and Russia's ruble by 100 percent. Surely no one holds deposits denominated in these currencies, because of their volatility."

References and Selected Readings

Coughlin, Cletus C., and Patricia S. Pollard. "A Question of Measurement: Is the Dollar Rising or Falling?" Federal Reserve Bank of St. Louis, *Review* (July–August 1996): 3–18.
Introduction to measures of the effective exchange rate.

Dominguez, Kathryn M., and Jeffrey A. Frankel. *Does Foreign Exchange Intervention Work?* Washington, D.C.: Institute for International Economics, 1993.
Examination of the ability of intervention to affect exchange rates; intermediate.

Frankel, J. A., and A. K. Rose. "Empirical Research on Nominal Exchange Rates." In *Handbook of International Economics,* Vol. 3, edited by G. M. Grossman and K. Rogoff, 1689–1730. Amsterdam: North-Holland, 1995.
Survey of what economists know from empirical work on foreign exchange markets; intermediate to advanced.

Giddy, Ian H. *Global Financial Markets.* Lexington, Mass.: D. C. Heath, 1994.
Textbook covering international financial markets; intermediate.

Isard, Peter. *Exchange Rate Economics.* Cambridge: Cambridge University Press, 1995.
Excellent survey for advanced students.

Lewis, K. "Puzzles in International Financial Markets." In *Handbook of International Economics,* Vol. 3, edited by G. M. Grossman and K. Rogoff, 1913–1972. Amsterdam: North-Holland, 1995.
Survey of unsolved puzzles concerning international financial markets, including foreign exchange markets; intermediate to advanced.

Neely, Christopher J. "Are Changes in Foreign Exchange Reserves Well Correlated with Official Intervention?" Federal Reserve Bank of St. Louis, *Review* 82 (September/October 2000): 17–32.
Empirical investigation of how accurately changes in reserves reflect intervention; intermediate and advanced.

Pollard, Patricia S. "The Creation of the Euro and the Role of the Dollar in International Markets." Federal Reserve Bank of St. Louis, *Review* (September/October 2001): 17–36.
How will the euro affect international use of the dollar? For all students.

Tavlas, George S. "The International Use of Currencies: The U.S. Dollar and the Euro." *Finance and Development* (June 1998): 46–49.
Why a few currencies dominate international transactions; for all students.

CHAPTER THIRTEEN

The Balance-of-Payments Accounts

13.1 Introduction

Countries differ widely in their degree of *openness,* or the extent to which they engage in economic activity across international boundaries. The United States is, by world standards, a relatively closed economy, as measured by its ratio of exports or imports to gross national product (GNP), although its degree of openness has increased in recent years. Between 1965 and 2000, U.S. **merchandise exports** (exports of physical goods) rose from 4 to 8 percent of GNP and merchandise imports from 3 to 13 percent. These trade percentages remain small, but fewer than ten countries have GNPs as large as U.S. merchandise exports!

Table 13.1 provides a perspective on openness by reporting merchandise exports as a share of GNP for a sample of countries. The ratios range from 6 percent of GNP in Mozambique to 125 percent in Malaysia, an economy that specializes in assembly and trade.

Although important, merchandise trade is only one of many types of economic activity that occur internationally. Another significant dimension of openness is trade in **services**—banking, insurance, travel, transportation, consulting, and other economic activities in which the item traded isn't a physical good. Trade in services represents one of the fastest-growing areas in the world economy, although data are difficult to obtain because of measurement problems. As we saw in Chapter Seven, nontariff barriers and regulatory restrictions also plague trade in services. The developed economies traditionally have been net exporters of services; that is, the value of their service exports has exceeded that of their service imports, because of their highly developed

Table 13.1 **Merchandise Exports as a Percentage of GNP, 2000 (Percent)**			
Country	Exports as Percent of GNP	Country	Exports as Percent of GNP
Mozambique	6%	Mexico	33%
Brazil	9	China[a]	36
India	9	Russia	44
Central African Republic	19	Hungary	59
Malawi	22	Malaysia	125

[a]Includes Hong Kong.

Source: World Bank.

Table 13.2 **Commercial Service Exports, 2000 (Millions $)**

Country	Commercial Service Exports	Country	Commercial Service Exports
Mozambique	n.a.	Mexico	$ 9,634
Brazil	$ 8,846	China[a]	72,213
India	17,569	Russia	13,563
Central African Republic	n.a.	Hungary	6,204
Malawi	n.a.	Malaysia	13,579

[a]Includes Hong Kong.

Source: World Trade Organization.

markets in banking and insurance and their populations of skilled consultants. Table 13.2 reports commercial service exports for the same sample of countries covered in Table 13.1.

Financial and investment activities such as purchases and sales of stocks, bonds, and other financial assets and of physical capital such as factories, machines, and land constitute a third major category of international transactions. Reductions in transportation and communication costs have resulted in growing internationalization of both production and financial markets. It's no longer unusual for a U.S.-based firm to buy a plant in Europe financed with bonds sold worldwide and denominated in several currencies. Table 13.3 summarizes the magnitude of net private international investment flows for our sample countries.

A set of accounts called the country's **balance-of-payments (BOP) accounts** summarizes all these transactions by individuals, firms, and governments of one country with their counterparts in the rest of the world. Like any single set of numbers, the BOP accounts can't capture the full extent of the complex economic interactions among countries. In addition, a number of misconceptions that cause both confusion and bad economic policy surround the balance-of-payments accounts. This chapter introduces the fundamental definitions and mechanics of the balance-of-payments accounts, explores the associated misconceptions, and relates the accounts to the currency markets and exchange rates we learned about in Chapter Twelve.

13.2 What's in the Balance-of-Payments Accounts?

The balance-of-payments accounts summarize all the transactions undertaken by residents of one country with the rest of the world, so we can divide them into subaccounts that correspond to the various categories of international transactions in which individuals, firms, and governments participate. The actual balance-of-payments accounts, as reported quarterly for the United States by the Department of Commerce, are quite complex, involving about 70 categories of transactions. Table 13.4 reproduces a recent report.

Table 13.3 **Net Private Investment Flows, 1999 (Millions $)**

Country	Net Private Investment Flows	Country	Net Private Investment Flows
Mozambique	$ 374	Mexico	$ 3,780
Brazil	22,793	China[a]	40,632
India	1,813	Russia	26,780
Central African Republic	13	Hungary	4,961
Malawi	60	Malaysia	3,247

[a]Excludes Hong Kong.

Source: World Bank.

Table 13.4 U.S. International Transactions, 2000 (Millions $)[a]

Line		2000
	Current Account	
1	**Exports of goods and services and income receipts:**	**$1,414,925**
2	Exports of goods and services	1,069,531
3	Goods, balance of payments basis	773,304
4	Services	296,227
5	Transfers under U.S. military agency sales contracts	14,604
6	Travel	85,153
7	Passenger fares	21,313
8	Other transportation	29,847
9	Royalties and license fees	37,955
10	Other private services	106,493
11	U.S. government miscellaneous services	862
12	Income receipts	345,394
13	Income receipts on U.S.-owned assets abroad	343,052
14	Direct investment receipts	149,459
15	Other private receipts	189,765
16	U.S. government receipts	3,828
17	Compensation of employees	2,342
18	**Imports of goods and services and income payments:**	**−1,797,061**
19	Imports of goods and services	−1,438,011
20	Goods, balance of payments basis	−1,222,772
21	Services	−215,239
22	Direct defense expenditures	−13,884
23	Travel	−65,044
24	Passenger fares	−23,902
25	Other transportation	−40,713
26	Royalties and license fees	−16,331
27	Other private services	−52,486
28	U.S. government miscellaneous services	−2,879
29	Income payments	−359,050
30	Income payments on foreign-owned assets in the United States	−351,194
31	Direct investment payments	−65,683
32	Other private payments	−177,839
33	U.S. government payments	−107,672
34	Compensation of employees	−7,856
35	**Unilateral current transfers, net:**	**−53,241**
36	U.S. government grants	−16,448
37	U.S. government pensions and other transfers	−4,711
38	Private remittances and other transfers	−32,082
	Capital and Financial Account **Capital Account**	
39	**Capital account transactions, net**	680

(continues)

Table 13.4 **U.S. International Transactions, 2000 (Millions $)**[a]

Line		2000
	Financial Account	
40	**U.S.-owned assets abroad, net (increase/financial outflow (−)):**	**−553,349**
41	U.S. official reserve assets, net	−290
42	Gold	
43	Special drawing rights	−722
44	Reserve position in the International Monetary Fund	2,308
45	Foreign currencies	−1,876
46	U.S. government assets, other than official reserve assets, net	−715
47	U.S. credits and other long-term assets	−4,887
48	Repayments on U.S. credits and other long-term assets	4,064
49	U.S. foreign currency holdings and U.S. short-term assets, net	108
50	U.S. private assets, net	−552,344
51	Direct investment	−161,577
52	Foreign securities	−123,606
53	U.S. claims on unaffiliated foreigners reported by U.S. nonbanking concerns	−156,988
54	U.S. claims reported by U.S. banks, not included elsewhere	−110,173
55	**Foreign-owned assets in the United States, net (increase/financial inflow (+)):**	**952,430**
56	Foreign official assets in the United States, net	35,909
57	U.S. government securities	29,532
58	U.S. Treasury securities	−11,377
59	Other	40,909
60	Other U.S. government liabilities	−2,540
61	U.S. liabilities reported by U.S. banks, not included elsewhere	5,790
62	Other foreign official assets	3,127
63	Other foreign assets in the United States, net	916,521
64	Direct investment	316,527
65	U.S. Treasury securities	−52,206
66	U.S. securities other than U.S. Treasury securities	465,858
67	U.S. currency	1,129
68	U.S. liabilities to unaffiliated foreigners reported by U.S. nonbanking concerns	105,728
69	U.S. liabilities reported by U.S. banks, not included elsewhere	79,485
70	**Statistical discrepancy (sum of above items with sign reversed):**	**35,616**
70a	Of which seasonal adjustment discrepancy	
	Memoranda:	
71	Balance on goods (lines 3 and 20)	−449,468
72	Balance on services (lines 4 and 21)	80,988
73	Balance on goods and services (lines 2 and 19)	−368,480
74	Balance on income (lines 12 and 29)	−13,656
75	Unilateral current transfers, net (line 35)	−53,241
76	Balance on current account (Lines 1, 18, and 35 or lines 73, 74, and 75)	−435,377

[a]Credits (+), debits (−).

Source: U.S. Department of Commerce (updates are available at the department's Web site, www.bea.doc.gov).

For our purposes, a much simpler classification will suffice. Individuals and firms engage in international transactions when they buy or sell goods or services abroad; borrow or lend abroad (that is, sell or buy financial assets); or buy or sell buildings, equipment, or land located abroad. Government agencies also can engage in any of these transactions plus other "official" transactions outside the province of private individuals and firms. We can use this simple classification to define three basic accounts: the current account, the (nonofficial) capital and financial account, and the official settlements account.

As we'll see, the balance-of-payments accounts consist of a **double-entry bookkeeping system.** This means that each international transaction appears twice, because every transaction has two sides. For example, when the United States exports a Boeing plane to Britain, Britain also makes a payment to the United States. The plane flows in one direction, while the payment flows in the other; *both* enter the double-entry bookkeeping system of the balance-of-payments accounts of *both* the United States and Britain. Or, when a U.S. firm buys a factory in China, the title to the factory flows from China to the United States *and* payment for the factory from the United States to China; two entries appear in each country's balance-of-payments accounts. Often the two entries reflecting the two sides of a single transaction occur in different accounts (for example, one in the current account and one in the capital and financial account). But before we can analyze the dual entries for various types of transactions, we must understand the differences among the current, capital and financial, and official settlements accounts.

13.2.1 **What Goes in the Current Account?**

The major categories of transactions within the **current account** are (1) merchandise exports and imports, (2) imports and exports of military services, travel and transportation, and other services, (3) current income received and paid on international investments, and (4) unilateral transfers, including worker remittances and pension payments. Table 13.5 reports the status of the various current-account components for the United States.

Each category of current-account transactions includes both exports by the United States (entered as **credits** [+] in the bookkeeping sense because they generate *receipts* from foreigners to U.S. residents) and imports by the United States from the rest of the world (entered as **debits** [−] because they generate *payments* from U.S. residents to foreigners). A net value entered with a negative sign means that imports (payments by U.S. residents) exceeded exports (receipts) in that category; a positive value represents exports (receipts) in excess of imports (payments).

The final column in Table 13.5 reports the **current-account balance.** This equals the sum of all the other entries and represents the difference between total exports or receipts (credits) by U.S. residents for current transactions and total imports or payments (debits) by U.S. residents for current transactions. Again, a negative value implies that debits exceed credits. To understand better the various categories in Table 13.5, we can illustrate each with examples of typical entries.

Table 13.5 **U.S. Current Account, 1960–2000 (Millions $)**

Year	Net Merchandise Trade	Net Services Exports	Net Investment Income	Net Unilateral Transfers	Current-Account Balance
1960	$4,892	−$1,382	$3,379	−$4,062	$2,824
1965	4,951	−287	5,350	−4,583	5,431
1970	2,603	−349	6,233	−6,156	2,331
1975	8,903	3,503	12,787	−7,075	18,116
1980	−25,500	6,093	30,073	−8,349	2,317
1985	−122,173	295	20,592	−22,700	−123,987
1990	−109,030	27,901	24,174	−34,669	−91,624
1995	−173,729	73,838	19,275	−34,638	−115,254
2000	−449,468	80,988	−13,656	−53,241	−435,377

Source: U.S. Department of Commerce (updates are available at the department's Web site, www.bea.doc.gov).

Merchandise Trade

The largest source of credits in the U.S. current account is merchandise exports. This category includes shipments abroad of a variety of items: agricultural products, high-technology goods such as the software exported by Microsoft, and the aircraft exported by Boeing. The sum of the value of all the goods exported by American individuals, firms, and government agencies (excluding the military) equals merchandise exports. Imports of goods include the value of all U.S. merchandise purchases: automobiles from Japan, coffee from Brazil, crude oil from Saudi Arabia, VCRs from South Korea, and apparel from China.

Since the mid-1970s, the value of U.S. merchandise imports has exceeded the value of U.S. merchandise exports; this is called a **deficit** on the **merchandise trade balance.** During the 1950s and 1960s, the United States ran a **surplus** on its merchandise trade balance; that is, the value of exports exceeded the value of imports. For the past few years, the large U.S. merchandise trade deficit (reaching well over $400 billion in 2000) has received much attention.[1] Pundits have proposed many policies for reducing the deficit, often claimed to cause "exportation of jobs" and "deindustrialization." Unfortunately, many of the policy proposals amount to protectionism, as they attempt to restrict imports from countries with a comparative advantage in the production of items such as steel, automobiles, apparel, and footwear. We'll explore some misconceptions surrounding the effects of a trade deficit later. For now, note that the merchandise trade balance is only one of several components of the current account, which in turn is only one of several components of the balance-of-payments accounts. A deficit in the merchandise trade balance is *not* the same as a balance-of-payments deficit (a concept we haven't yet defined), although the popular press often confuses the two.

Services

The services category of current-account transactions includes military transactions, travel and transportation, royalties, education, accounting, banking, insurance, and consulting. A U.S. resident vacationing in France or attending Oxford University imports a service; that import enters the U.S. balance-of-payments accounts as a current-account debit because it involves a payment to foreigners. When Mexico hires a U.S. petroleum engineer to work in its oil industry, the United States, in effect, exports the consultant's services to Mexico, a credit in services from the U.S. point of view. The United States typically runs a surplus (credits > debits) in the services account, primarily because U.S. firms provide large shares of the insurance, transportation, and financial services that constitute integral parts of international trade activity.

Net merchandise trade and net services trade often are combined to report the **balance on goods and services,** or the value of U.S. exports of goods and services (credits) minus the value of U.S. imports of goods and services (debits).

Investment Income

The third category of transactions in the current account captures interest, dividends, and other income Americans receive from investments they own abroad (credits) and payments by Americans to foreigners as income earned on foreign-owned investments in the United States (debits). This account does *not* include new investments but merely the current income from those made previously. Included as credits are all interest, dividends, and other income earned by American residents on the $7 trillion of foreign assets they own. To remember that these receipts are credits, it helps to recall that they involve payments *to* U.S. residents *from* foreigners, just as U.S. merchandise exports (which are credits) do. Debit entries include all the interest, dividends, and other income paid to owners of the $8.6 trillion of foreign-owned assets in the United States. Like U.S. merchandise imports, these represent debits on the U.S. current account because they involve payments *from* U.S. residents *to* foreigners. Despite the fact that the value of U.S. assets owned by foreigners has exceeded the value of foreign assets owned by U.S. residents for more than a decade, the United States continued to run a small surplus in the net investment income subaccount until 1998, when for the first time since World War II foreigners earned income on their investments in the United States that exceeded the income Americans received on their investments abroad.

---

1 For example, the U.S. government recently commissioned a 12-member panel to study the issue. You can find their 2000 report (U.S. Trade Deficit Review Commission, *The U.S. Trade Deficit*) at www.ustdrc.gov.

Unilateral Transfers

The final category of current-account transactions, unilateral transfers, includes transactions that aren't purchases or sales of either goods or services. Unilateral debits include U.S. nonmilitary aid to foreign countries (government aid or private charity); worker remittances, or funds sent back to the home country by individuals working in the United States; and pensions paid to former U.S. residents now living abroad. The United States consistently runs a deficit in unilateral transfers.

Current-Account Balance

The sum of the current-account components—merchandise trade, services, investment income, and unilateral transfers—gives the country's current-account balance. As Table 13.5 reports, in most years between World War II and the late 1970s the United States had a current-account surplus, although occasionally current-account debits exceeded current-account credits. Since the late 1970s, however, a deficit has characterized the current account, reaching over $400 billion in 2000.

The Current Account and Individual Transactions: An Analogy

When studying the balance-of-payments accounts for the first time, the greatest danger is missing the forest (the logic and meaning of the accounts) for the trees (the details about the types of transactions in each account). Now that we've examined each tree in the current account, we can use an analogy to think about the forest. The analogy is between the economic transactions undertaken by an individual and those recorded in a country's balance-of-payments accounts. Table 13.6 suggests a correspondence between the entries in the current account and the economic transactions of a typical individual (that is, if each individual kept balance-of-payments accounts, what would they look like?).

Credits in the current account correspond to current receipts or income for the individual. This income could come from production and sale of a good (in which case it would be like a merchandise export in the current account), from the return on a previously purchased stock or bond (like investment income in the current account), from the sale of a service (like service exports in the current account), or from some type of gift or pension (analogous to a unilateral transfer receipt in the current account). Debits in the current account correspond to current expenditures by an individual. The individual may make expenditures on goods (like a merchandise import), make interest payments on a loan (analogous to investment payments in the current account), pay for a service (corresponding to a service import), or give a gift (a unilateral transfer payment).

The sum of a country's current-account credits is analogous to the total of an individual's current income, and the total of current-account debits corresponds to the total of an individual's current expenditures. A current-account surplus (credits > debits) is similar to a situation in which an individual's current income

---

Table 13.6 Analogy between Transactions in the Current Account and Typical Economic Transactions of an Individual

Current-Account Transaction	Analogous Individual Economic Transaction
Merchandise exports	Value of goods produced and sold by the individual
Investment income	Income from assets (stock dividends, bond interest, etc.)
Service exports	Value of services sold (wages, etc.)
Unilateral receipts	Gifts, pension payments, etc. received
Merchandise imports	Value of goods purchased (food, clothing, etc.)
Investment payments	Payments on loans, mortgages, etc.
Service imports	Services purchased (insurance, medical care, etc.)
Unilateral payments	Gifts, etc. given
Sum of current-account receipts or credits	Current individual income
Sum of current-account payments or debits	Current individual expenditures
Current-account surplus	Current income > current expenditures
Current-account deficit	Current expenditures > current income

exceeds current expenditures. A deficit on the current account (debits > credits) matches the situation of an individual whose current expenditures exceed current income.

Just as current income and expenditures fail to capture all the relevant dimensions of an individual's economic situation, the current account gives an incomplete record of a country's transactions with the rest of the world. In both cases, the primary items missing include borrowing and lending activity, purchases and sales of assets, and changes in the stock of cash or money balances. For an individual, if current income exceeds current expenditures, the "excess" income must be used to make new loans, pay off old loans, buy an asset (such as a house or shares of stock), or increase money balances (for example, a checking account). On the other hand, if an individual's current expenditures exceed current income, the difference must be covered by borrowing, selling an asset, or running down money balances. A similar logic applies for a country and carries us beyond the current account to the other balance-of-payments accounts.

13.2.2 What Goes in the Capital Account?

The **capital account** records international borrowing and lending and purchases and sales of assets.[2] When a U.S. resident (individual, firm, or government agency) purchases a foreign asset or makes a foreign loan, the asset or IOU is imported into the United States and enters as a debit in the U.S. capital account, known as a **capital outflow.** The asset could be a bond issued by a British firm, a house in France, or shares of stock in a Japanese company. The way to remember that a capital outflow is a debit (like the *import* of a good) is to think of it as *importation* of the title to the asset or of the IOU. Capital outflows from the United States represent *increases* in U.S. ownership of foreign assets. The figure reported in the capital account of the balance-of-payments accounts is a net value; it reflects the net increase (if negative) or decrease (if positive) in U.S. ownership of foreign assets, because debits (payments to foreigners) enter the balance-of-payments accounts with a negative sign and credits (receipts from foreigners) with a positive sign.

One effect of using the net figure is to make the volumes of capital flows appear much smaller than they actually are. For example, if one U.S. resident purchases $10 million worth of bonds from a British firm and another individual sells $9 million worth of Japanese bonds, the figure in the U.S. capital account will report a net capital outflow of $1 million ($9 million − $10 million), even though $19 million of bonds have changed hands. Also, annual balance-of-payments accounts don't reflect purchases of foreign assets resold within the same year.

Credit transactions in the capital account occur when foreign residents buy assets such as bonds, stocks, or land in the United States. It may help to think of the United States as *exporting* the titles to the assets or IOUs for the loans; thus, these **capital inflows** are credits in the U.S. balance-of-payments accounts, as are *exports* of goods. Capital inflows also are reported in net terms, so the figure reflects the net increase (or decrease, if negative) in foreign ownership of U.S. assets.

The difference between net capital inflows and net capital outflows is the capital-account balance: a surplus if inflows (= credits) > outflows (= debits) and a deficit if inflows < outflows.[3] Until recently, the United States consistently ran a capital-account deficit, buying more assets abroad than the rest of the world bought in the United States. The 1980s, however, brought a change in the pattern: The pace of U.S. investment abroad slowed dramatically (though only temporarily), while the growth of foreign investment in the United States accelerated. Table 13.7 reports the U.S. capital-account balance.[4]

Again, an analogy with an individual helps clarify the role of capital-account transactions in the world economy. Table 13.8 suggests correspondences between typical transactions undertaken by an individual and

---

2 Strictly speaking, what we call the *capital account* is now called the *capital and financial account* in government reports. However, both to keep things simple and for consistency with popular usage, we'll call it just the *capital account*.

3 The account as reported by the Department of Commerce includes all borrowing/lending and purchases/sales of assets by individuals, firms, and governments. For our purposes, we exclude transactions by central banks—changes in official reserve assets—and report them separately as the official settlements account to be discussed in the next section. Other borrowing/lending and purchases/sales of assets by governments are part of the (nonofficial) capital account.

4 Official transactions aren't included but are discussed separately in the next section under the official settlements account; therefore, the figures in Table 13.7 refer to the nonofficial capital account.

Table 13.7 **U.S. Nonofficial Capital Account, 1960–2000 (Millions $)**

Year	Net U.S. Purchases of Assets Abroad (Increase or Capital Outflow [−])	Net Foreign Purchases of U.S. Assets (Increase or Capital Inflow [+])	Capital-Account Balance
1960	−$6,244	$821	−$5,423
1965	−6,941	607	−6,334
1970	−11,818	−550	−12,368
1975	−38,854	10,143	−28,711
1980	−78,813	47,115	−31,698
1985	−36,032	147,501	111,469
1990	−71,853	107,082	35,229
1995	−317,711	355,681	37,970
2000	−553,059	916,521	363, 462

Source: U.S. Department of Commerce (updates are available at the department's Web site, www.bea.doc.gov).

Table 13.8 **Analogy between Transactions in the Capital Account and Typical Economic Transactions of an Individual**

Capital-Account Transaction	Analogous Individual Economic Transaction
Net capital outflows	(New loans made) minus (receipts for loans paid off) plus (purchases of assets) equals (net change in amount of lending outstanding and increase in assets owned)
Net capital inflows	(New loans taken out) minus (old loans paid off) plus (sales of assets) equals (net change in amount of borrowing outstanding and decrease in assets owned)
Capital-account balance	(Net change in amount of borrowing outstanding) minus (net change in amount of lending outstanding) minus (net change in assets owned) equals net decline (if +) or increase (if −) in ownership of assets
Capital-account surplus	Net change in borrowing plus sales of assets > net change in lending plus purchases of assets equals decline in net ownership of assets
Capital-account deficit	Net change in borrowing plus sales of assets < net change in lending plus purchases of assets equals increase in net ownership of assets

capital-account transactions. At the individual level, net capital outflows represent the net change in the individual's lending plus purchases of other assets. Net capital inflows represent the individual's net change in borrowing plus sales of assets. A surplus in the capital account occurs when net capital inflows exceed net capital outflows. The capital account is in deficit when the overall flow of capital out of a country exceeds the flow coming in. Note the somewhat counterintuitive terminology here: A capital-account *surplus* denotes a *decline* in the net domestic ownership of foreign assets, while a capital-account *deficit* corresponds to an *increase* in such ownership.

13.2.3 **What Goes in the Official Settlements Balance?**

Unlike the current and capital accounts, all transactions in the official settlements account are conducted by "official" government authorities, usually central banks, rather than by individuals or firms. The **official settlements balance** reports the net change in a country's stock of foreign exchange reserves (see section 12.7)

Table 13.9 **U.S. Official Settlements Balance, 1960–2000 (Millions $)**			
Year	Net U.S. Official Reserve Assets (Increase [−])	Net Foreign Reserve Assets in U.S. (Increase [+])	Official Settlements Balance
1960	$2,145	$1,473	$3,618
1965	1,225	134	1,359
1970	2,481	6,908	9,389
1975	−849	7,027	6,178
1980	−8,155	15,497	7,342
1985	−3,858	−1,119	−4,977
1990	−2,158	33,910	31,752
1995	−9,742	109,768	100,026
2000	−290	35,909	35,619

Source: U.S. Department of Commerce (updates are available at the department's Web site, www.bea.doc.gov).

and official government borrowing.[5] Increases in the level of U.S. reserves or decreases in the level of reserves held by foreign central banks in the United States enter as debits in the U.S. official settlements account. (It may help to think of increases in U.S. foreign exchange reserves as *imports* of foreign exchange.) Decreases in U.S. central bank reserves or increases in foreign central banks' reserves held in the United States represent credits (think of decreases in U.S. reserves as *exports* of foreign exchange and, therefore, as a credit).[6] Table 13.9 reports the transactions on the U.S. official settlements balance. We'll see later in the chapter that whether governments undertake these transactions depends on whether the exchange rate is fixed or flexible.

The easiest way to see the relationship between the official settlements balance and the rest of the balance-of-payments accounts is through the analogy developed earlier with the transactions of an individual. The balance on the current account represents the relationship between the individual's current income and current expenditures. The capital account represents changes in the individual's borrowing and lending or purchases and sales of assets. Suppose the sum of the individual's current income, borrowing, and revenue from sales of assets exceeds the sum of current expenditures, loans made, and purchases of assets. What happens to the difference? It goes into the individual's cash balances.[7] On the other hand, how does an individual handle a situation in which the sum of current expenditures, loans made, and purchases of assets exceeds the sum of income, borrowing, and revenue from sales of assets? This is possible only if the individual possesses cash balances that can be depleted to cover the shortfall.

---

5 For simplicity, we assume that all transactions in the official settlements account represent changes in the levels of official foreign exchange reserves resulting from intervention in foreign exchange markets. In reality, several other types of transactions show up in the account. For example, if a foreign central bank (say, the Bank of Japan) reduces its reserve holdings of a currency (such as the euro) by selling the currency and buying U.S. Treasury bills, the transaction will appear as an increase in foreign official holdings in the United States (a credit in the U.S. official settlements account) even though the purpose was not to intervene in foreign exchange markets to affect the exchange rate between yen and dollars. In addition, government agencies other than the central bank (for example, the U.S. Treasury Department through its Exchange Stabilization Fund) occasionally intervene in foreign exchange markets; but we can ignore such cases.

6 In recent years, it's become increasingly common for foreign central banks to hold a portion of their dollar reserves outside the United States. When central banks undertake intervention using these reserves, the U.S. official settlements account doesn't capture the activity. Because of this phenomenon, changes in the level of reserve assets as reported in the official settlements account have become somewhat less reliable as measures of the extent of intervention to affect the value of other currencies relative to the dollar.

7 Consider a simple numerical example. Suppose that in a given month an individual earns a salary of $2,000, takes out a new-car loan from the bank for $15,000, and sells a used car for $5,000. During the same month, the individual buys a new car for $15,000 and spends $3,000 on routine expenses (rent, food, clothing, and so on). What must be true about the individual's cash balances? They rise by $4,000, or the difference between $22,000 and $18,000.

Table 13.10 **A Country's Current, Capital, and Official Settlements Balances Must Sum to Zero Just Like an Individual's Total Receipts and Total Payments**

Balance-of-Payments Accounts	Individual Transactions
Current-account balance	Current income − current expenditures
+ Capital-account balance	+ Net new borrowing + net revenue from sales of assets
+ Official settlements balance	+ Change in cash balances
Zero	Zero

Transactions on the official settlements account play the same role as increases or decreases in the individual's cash balances: They cover or compensate for any differences between total payments and total receipts in the other accounts, as summarized in Table 13.10. For the individual, the sum of income minus expenditures, borrowing minus lending, revenue from sales minus purchases of assets, and changes in cash balances *must* sum to zero. *(Why?)* In the balance-of-payments accounts, the sum of the current-account balance, the capital-account balance, and the official settlements balance must sum to zero. If the combined balance on the current and capital accounts is in deficit (debits > credits), there must be an offsetting surplus (credits > debits) in the official settlements account. With a surplus in the current and capital accounts, the official settlements account must be in deficit.

When the U.S. Department of Commerce collects data for the balance-of-payments accounts, many transactions are missed or unreported. This occurs for a variety of reasons. The United States doesn't closely monitor tourism and imports brought into the United States by travelers, so many goods enter and exit the country unreported. Tax avoidance provides an incentive for some types of capital flows to go undisclosed (and therefore untaxed). These imperfections in data collection are reflected in the **statistical discrepancy,** or the amount by which the sum of the current, capital, and official settlements balances as actually calculated fail to sum to zero. The magnitude of the statistical discrepancy has grown over the last few years along with international trade and financial activity. The discrepancy now ranges yearly from several hundred million dollars to around $100 billion, as shown in Table 13.11.

From one perspective, these numbers are quite large; in fact, in several years since 1960, the U.S. statistical discrepancy was larger than the current-account balance! From another perspective, the statistical discrepancy is remarkably small given the task of accounting for all transactions between U.S. residents and the rest of the

Table 13.11 **U.S. Statistical Discrepancy, 1960–2000 (Millions $)**

Year	Current-Account Balance	Capital-Account Balance	Official Settlements Balance	Statistical Discrepancy
1960	$2,824	−$5,423	$3,618	−$1,019
1965	5,431	−6,334	1,359	−457
1970	2,331	−12,368	9,389	−219[a]
1975	18,116	−28,711	6,178	4,417
1980	2,317	−31,698	7,342	20,886[a]
1985	−123,987	111,469	−4,977	17,494
1990	−91,624	35,229	31,752	24,643
1995	−115,254	37,970	100,026	−22,742
2000	−435,377	364,142	35,619	35,616

[a]Small allocations of special drawing rights in 1970 and 1980 are omitted.

Source: U.S. Department of Commerce (updates are available at the department's Web site, www.bea.doc.gov).

world. Once we take the existence of the statistical discrepancy into account, the fundamental relationship that must hold for U.S. transactions with the rest of the world becomes:

$$\text{Current-account balance} + \text{Capital-account balance} \\ + \text{Official settlements balance} + \text{Statistical discrepancy} = 0 \qquad \textbf{[13.1]}$$

Next, we must address a question that probably has occurred already to the careful reader: If the components of the balance-of-payments accounts always sum to zero, what do we mean by a balance-of-payments surplus or deficit? As a first step toward answering this question, we must recall that each international transaction has two sides and, therefore, enters *twice* in the double-entry bookkeeping system that comprises the balance-of-payments accounts. This guarantees that Equation 13.1 holds, because any credit entry automatically generates an equal debit entry somewhere in the accounts. To see the logic of the double-entry system, let's look at a few hypothetical transactions.

13.2.4 How Double-Entry Bookkeeping Works: Some Illustrative Transactions

The simplest international transaction from a balance-of-payments perspective is barter, or the exchange of two goods without use of money. Suppose Coca-Cola exports $1 million worth of Coke to Poland in exchange for $1 million worth of Polish beer.[8] How would the Department of Commerce record the transaction in the U.S. balance-of-payments accounts? The soft-drink export is a $1 million credit in the merchandise category of the current account, and the beer import is a $1 million debit, also in the merchandise category. Note that although trade has increased, both the merchandise trade balance and the current-account balance remain unaffected—because both debits and credits have risen by the same amount. This occurs whenever both the debit and credit entries for a given transaction occur in the same account. *(How would the transaction appear in Poland's balance-of-payments accounts?)*

Now suppose Coca-Cola exports $1 million worth of Coke to Britain and the British importer pays with a check for the pound equivalent of $1 million, which Coca-Cola deposits in its London bank. The Coke export is again a $1 million credit entry in the merchandise category of the U.S. current account. But the payment for the Coke—the check—is a capital outflow, a debit in the U.S. capital account, because a U.S. resident now owns an asset (the pound bank deposit in London) previously owned by the British importer.[9] The U.S. merchandise trade balance (as well as the current account) shows a $1 million credit entry *(Why?)*, while the U.S. capital account shows a $1 million debit entry *(Why?)*. *(How would the transaction appear in Britain's balance-of-payments accounts?)*

Now consider a third possibility. A private charity in the United States ships $1 million worth of Coke to a foreign country as aid following an earthquake that destroyed the sources of pure drinking water. What happens in the U.S. balance-of-payments accounts? The export of Coke is still a $1 million credit in the merchandise subaccount of the U.S. current account, but the United States expects no payment in return for the aid. So what's the second side of the transaction? This is where the unilateral transfer subaccount comes in; the second entry is a $1 million debit under unilateral transfers. The net effect is an increase of $1 million in the merchandise trade balance but no effect on the current-account balance *(Why?)*. *(Show the transaction's effect on the recipient's balance-of-payments accounts.)*

Now consider a transaction that occurs solely in the capital account. Suppose Coca-Cola buys a $1 million building in London to open a production facility there. The firm pays the building's owner with a check for $1 million. The U.S. capital account shows a debit and a credit of $1 million. The debit represents Coca-Cola's "import" of the title to the building, and the credit Coke's "export" of ownership of the funds represented by the check. *(Show the entries in Britain's balance-of-payments accounts.)*

---

8 Such transactions are called *countertrade*.

9 Alternatively, Coca-Cola could exchange the pound deposit for a dollar deposit at a New York bank. In this case, the New York bank would now be holding $1 million worth of pounds. For our purposes, this wouldn't affect the way the transaction is recorded in the balance-of-payments accounts.

As these transactions illustrate, every transaction creates *both* a credit *and* a debit entry in each country's balance-of-payments accounts, and the two entries always are equal in magnitude. Therefore, total credits always equal total debits (as in any double-entry bookkeeping system), although the debit and credit entries from any given transaction don't necessarily occur within the same account. But if total credits equal total debits, what do we mean by a balance-of-payments surplus or deficit?

13.3 What Are Balance-of-Payments Surpluses and Deficits?

The balance-of-payments accounts always "balance" in the sense that total credits equal total debits. Just as for an individual, total receipts must equal total payments once changes in asset holdings and cash balances are taken into account. This type of balance in the balance-of-payments accounts is trivial and arises from accounting and bookkeeping conventions, not from the theory of international trade and finance. The fact that an individual's total receipts must equal total payments tells us very little about that individual's economic circumstances. Likewise, the fact that total receipts from the rest of the world must equal total payments to the rest of the world reveals little about a country's economic situation.

Examination of the balance (or lack thereof) in the balance of payments in the *nontrivial* sense requires distinguishing between two types of transactions: autonomous and accommodating ones. We refer to transactions that individuals, firms, or government agencies undertake for their own purposes (such as utility maximization by individuals, asset portfolio decisions, profit maximization by firms, and foreign-policy goals by government) and whose goals are unrelated to the balance of payments as **autonomous, or independently motivated, transactions.** These transactions represent the routine international trade and finance that constitute world economic activity. A U.S. resident buying a pair of Italian shoes, a U.S. firm selling a bond to a German resident, and the U.S. government sending foreign aid to Afghanistan constitute actions taken for their own interests and independently of their effects on the balance of payments. The transactions may affect the balance of payments, but those effects are unintentional and not the goal of the transaction.

For our purposes, we can identify the sum of the current-account balance, the capital-account balance, and the statistical discrepancy as the balance on autonomous transactions.[10] The current and nonofficial capital accounts include all the trade and finance activities undertaken by individuals, firms, and governments without regard for their balance-of-payments effects. The statistical discrepancy measures omitted or mismeasured current- and capital-account transactions.[11] The sum of autonomous transactions is the country's balance of payments (BOP) with the rest of the world:

$$\text{Current-account balance} + \text{Capital-account balance} + \text{Statistical discrepancy} = \text{Balance of payments (BOP)} \qquad [13.2]$$

If total autonomous credits exceed total autonomous debits, a **balance-of-payments surplus** (BOP > 0) exists. An excess of autonomous debits over credits is a **balance-of-payments deficit** (BOP < 0). The balance of payments shows whether a country's trade and finance activities (that is, its autonomous transactions) involve receipts from foreigners in excess of payments to foreigners (a surplus) or payments to foreigners in excess of receipts from foreigners (a deficit).

In each of the illustrative transactions discussed previously, the net effect on the balance of payments is zero. In the first, the Coke-for-beer barter transaction, both the debit and the credit sides of the current account rise by $1 million, leaving the current-account balance unchanged. The capital account and the statistical discrepancy remain unaffected; therefore, Equation 13.2 implies that the transaction doesn't change the country's balance of payments. In the second transaction, in which exported Coke is paid for by a check deposited in a

---

10 As noted in footnotes 2 through 4, official transactions actually are recorded in a separate subaccount *within* the capital and financial account. We treat official transactions separately; when we speak of the capital account, we mean the nonofficial capital account.

11 We attribute the statistical discrepancy to mismeasurement in the current and capital accounts rather than in the official settlements account because the last includes only official government transactions subject to few measurement errors, omissions, or revisions.

London bank, the current-account balance rises by the $1 million credit while the capital-account balance falls by a $1 million debit; again the two parts of the transaction offset, leaving the overall balance (the left-hand side of Equation 13.2) unaffected. In the third transaction, the charity shipment of Coke is recorded as a $1 million credit in merchandise exports and a $1 million debit in unilateral transfers within the current account, leaving the current account and the balance of payments unaffected. In the fourth transaction, the purchase of a factory abroad appears as a $1 million debit and the payment by check as a $1 million credit, both in the U.S. capital account. For all four transactions, *both* the debit and credit entries occur on the left-hand side of Equation 13.2. All the entries are independent or autonomous, undertaken by private parties for reasons unrelated to the balance of payments.

The second class of transactions is **accommodating, or compensatory, transactions.** These are official government actions taken for balance-of-payments purposes; they correspond to the transactions in the official settlements account—changes in central banks' stocks of foreign exchange reserves. A comparison of Equations 13.1 and 13.2 reveals the relationship between the official settlements balance and the balance of payments. Rearranging Equation 13.1, the sum of the current-account balance, the capital-account balance, and the statistical discrepancy equals the *negative* of the official settlements balance:

$$\text{Current-account balance} + \text{Capital-account balance} + \text{Statistical discrepancy} = \\ -\text{ Official settlements balance} \qquad \textbf{[13.3]}$$

Combining this with Equation 13.2, the balance of payments just equals the negative of the official settlements balance:

$$\text{Balance of payments} = -\text{ Official settlements balance} \qquad \textbf{[13.4]}$$

The balance of payments represents the difference between credits and debits for autonomous transactions undertaken by individuals, firms, and governments. Any deficit or surplus must be "accommodated," or "compensated for," by official transactions on the official settlements account because a country's total receipts from foreigners must equal its total payments to foreigners (that is, the balance-of-payments accounts must balance in the double-entry bookkeeping sense). To highlight this point, we can rewrite Equation 13.4 as the explicit relationship between autonomous and accommodating transactions:

$$\text{Balance on autonomous transactions} + \text{Balance on accommodating transactions} = 0 \quad \textbf{[13.5]}$$

To understand better the significance of the distinction between autonomous and accommodating transactions in defining and interpreting the balance of payments, it's useful to relate the ideas and definitions developed in this chapter back to Chapter Twelve's model of the demand for and supply of foreign exchange.

13.4 What's the Connection? The Balance of Payments and the Foreign Exchange Market

Before more explicitly introducing the demand for and supply of foreign exchange as a way to view the balance of payments, we need to distinguish between the overall, or multilateral, balance-of-payments accounts and the bilateral balance-of-payments accounts. The **overall, or multilateral, balance-of-payments accounts** are the ones discussed so far; they record all the transactions between U.S. residents and the rest of the world as a whole. The **bilateral balance-of-payments accounts** report receipts and payments between the United States and one other country; there's one set of bilateral balance-of-payments accounts for each country with which the United States interacts. The multilateral balance-of-payments accounts simply aggregate the bilateral ones.

In relating the balance-of-payments accounts to demand and supply in foreign exchange markets, it's convenient to assume that there are only two countries (such as the United States and Britain) in the world, so we can give specific names to the currencies involved.

Recall from Chapter Twelve that the foreign exchange market is in equilibrium when the quantity of foreign-currency-denominated deposits individuals want to hold in their asset portfolios just equals the quantity of foreign-currency-denominated deposits available. Figure 13.1 reproduces Figure 12.7, the graphical representation of such an equilibrium, using pounds as the foreign currency.

The supply of foreign-currency deposits, represented by the vertical line $S^{\pounds}$, is determined by government policies and banks' lending decisions, independent of the exchange rate. The demand for foreign-currency deposits reflects the asset-portfolio decisions of individuals and firms based on the interest parity conditions from section 12.4. The higher the value of the spot exchange rate (for given values of $i^{\$}$, $i^{\pounds}$, e^{e}, and e^{f}), the higher the expected rate of return on domestic-currency deposits and the more attractive those become relative to foreign-currency deposits. *(Why? For a review, see section 12.5.1.)* Therefore, we represent the demand curve for foreign-currency deposits as a negatively sloped line. Changes in interest rates, the expected future spot rate, or the forward rate shift the demand curve in the directions indicated by the $(+)$ and $(-)$ signs in Figure 13.1, as portfolio owners respond to changes in the expected rates of return on the two types of deposits.

When quantity demanded and supplied of a good aren't equal, what usually happens to bring a market back into equilibrium? Given no government interference with the forces of supply and demand, price adjusts to equate quantity demanded and quantity supplied. This is the case in foreign exchange markets when the exchange rate (the domestic-currency price of foreign currency) is flexible. If the quantity supplied of foreign

Figure 13.1 **Foreign Exchange Market Equilibrium under a Flexible Exchange Regime**

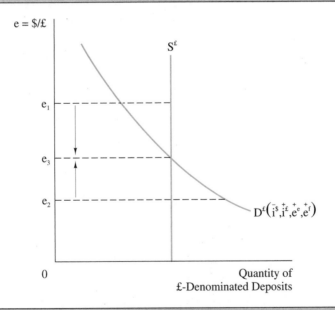

The exchange rate moves to equate the quantity demanded and supplied of pound-denominated deposits. The equilibrium exchange rate is e_3. At e_1, individuals aren't willing to hold the existing supply of pound-denominated deposits. As individuals try to exchange their excess pound-denominated deposits for deposits denominated in dollars, they must accept fewer dollars per pound; and the dollar price of pounds falls toward e_3. At e_2, individuals want to hold more than the existing supply of pound-denominated deposits. Individuals enter the market trying to exchange dollar-denominated for pound-denominated ones, thereby bidding up the dollar price of pounds to e_3.

exchange exceeds the quantity demanded (as at e_1), the domestic currency appreciates (e falls); if the quantity demanded of foreign exchange exceeds the quantity supplied (as at e_2), the domestic currency depreciates. *(Explain why, using the interest parity conditions.)* In contrast, under a fixed exchange rate regime, some other mechanism must equilibrate the foreign exchange market. In the next two sections, we examine the relationship among the balance of payments, demand and supply in foreign exchange markets, and exchange rates, first under a flexible and then under a fixed exchange rate regime.

13.4.1 The Balance of Payments, Foreign Exchange Markets, and a Flexible Exchange Rate

The demand for foreign exchange as developed in Chapter Twelve reflects all the autonomous transactions in the balance-of-payments accounts. In these transactions, individuals and firms exchange goods, services, and financial assets, paid for with deposits denominated in various currencies.[12] Portfolio owners hold foreign-currency-denominated deposits to buy foreign goods and services, to earn interest on the deposits, to purchase other foreign assets (bonds, factories, and so forth), and to speculate by holding foreign exchange in the hope of an appreciation against the dollar. These transaction categories correspond to the various categories of autonomous transactions in the current and capital accounts of the balance-of-payments accounts. The balance of payments is in equilibrium when individuals are willing to hold as assets any foreign-currency-denominated deposits received in payment for international transactions.

Consider a hypothetical transaction. A resident of Britain uses a £1,000 check to purchase a bond issued by a U.S. firm. The foreign exchange market is in equilibrium at e = $2/£1, as in Figure 13.2. If the firm selling

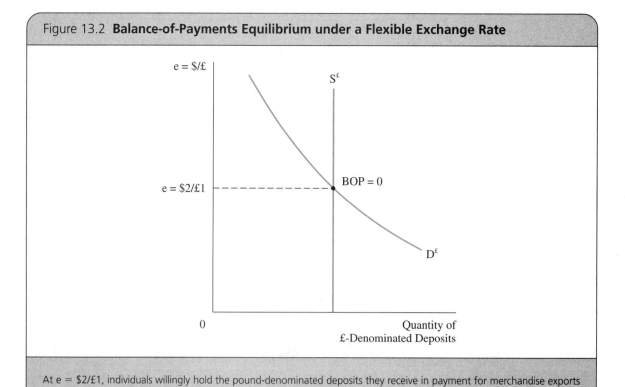

Figure 13.2 **Balance-of-Payments Equilibrium under a Flexible Exchange Rate**

At e = $2/£1, individuals willingly hold the pound-denominated deposits they receive in payment for merchandise exports and other transactions. Autonomous debits match autonomous credits in the balance-of-payments accounts (BOP = 0).

---

12 Of course, some transactions are arranged using barter and others using actual currency rather than payment by check, but the overwhelming majority of international transactions are financed by check or bank deposit.

the bond is content to hold the £1,000 in its asset portfolio and deposits the check in a London bank, the total demand for pound-denominated deposits remains unchanged. The £1,000 deposit simply has been reallocated from the individual who purchased the bond to the firm that sold it.

The transaction appears in the U.S. balance-of-payments accounts as a capital-account credit of $2,000 (= £1,000 · $2/£1) and a capital-account debit of $2,000. *(Why?)*[13] But suppose the bond seller doesn't want to hold the pounds and instead sells the pound-denominated deposit to the firm's New York bank in return for a $2,000 deposit. If e = $2/£1 is the equilibrium exchange rate, by definition someone *will* be content to hold the pound-denominated deposit, perhaps the New York bank or one of its other customers. *(Why?)* Again the total demand for pound-denominated deposits remains unchanged. Portfolio owners are content to hold $S^£$ pound-denominated deposits (including the £1,000 involved in our hypothetical transaction) at e = $2/£1. The autonomous demand for pound-denominated deposits equals the quantity available. The British resident who buys the U.S. firm's bond makes available the £1,000 deposit, and the U.S. firm or its bank is willing to hold that deposit. The current- and capital-account balances sum to zero.

If, given current interest rates and expected and forward exchange rates, *no one* wants to hold the pound-denominated deposit, e = $2/£1 is *not* the equilibrium exchange rate. The firm that received the pound-denominated deposit in payment for the bond will be willing to sell it for *less* than $2,000, receiving less than $2 for each £1. The pound depreciates against the dollar (see Figure 13.3). If the equilibrium value of the exchange rate is, say, $1.80/£1, the U.S. balance of payments reports the transaction as a $1,800 capital-account credit for "export" of the bond (= £1,000 · $1.80/£1) and a capital-account debit of $1,800 for "importing" ownership of the deposit. Again autonomous debits equal autonomous credits; the balance of payments is in equilibrium at e = $1.80/£1.

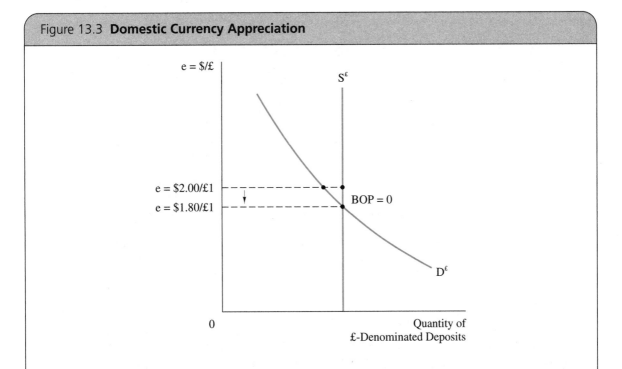

Figure 13.3 Domestic Currency Appreciation

The dollar appreciates from $2/£1 to $1.80/£1 to encourage individuals to hold more pound-denominated deposits in their asset portfolios. The balance of payments is in equilibrium at e = $1.80/£1, where autonomous debits equal autonomous credits.

---

13 The bookkeeping for each country's balance-of-payments accounts is conducted in the domestic currency.

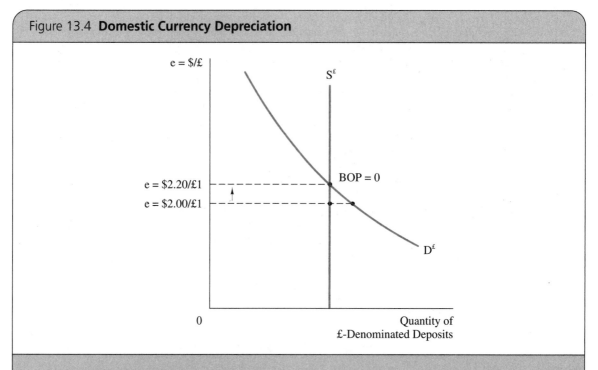

Figure 13.4 **Domestic Currency Depreciation**

The dollar depreciates from $2/£1 to $2.20/£1 to discourage individuals from holding pound-denominated deposits in their asset portfolios. At e = $2.20/£1, autonomous debits equal autonomous credits and the balance of payments is in equilibrium.

On the other hand, if at current interest rates and expected and forward exchange rates, many portfolio owners want to purchase the pound-denominated deposit at a price of e = $2/£1 to add to their portfolios, the price of the deposit will be bid up. Each pound will bring the firm more than $2, and the pound will appreciate against the dollar, as in Figure 13.4. If the equilibrium exchange rate turns out to be $2.20, the transaction appears in the U.S. balance-of-payments accounts as a $2,200 capital-account credit (for export of the bond) and a $2,200 capital-account debit (for import of the deposit). Autonomous debits and credits in the current and capital accounts remain equal, so the balance of payments is in equilibrium at $2.20/£1.

In both cases (Figures 13.3 and 13.4), the exchange rate adjusts until someone becomes willing to hold the pound-denominated deposit at current interest rates, although not necessarily the same firm that originally received it in payment for the bond exported to Britain. This is the essence of a flexible exchange rate regime. Under such a regime, governments allow the market forces of supply and demand to determine the price of foreign exchange, here the exchange rate between dollars and pounds. The exchange rate adjusts until individuals willingly hold the existing supply of pound-denominated deposits in their asset portfolios. As long as individuals and firms are willing to hold the existing supply of deposits at the current exchange rate, autonomous credits equal autonomous debits and the balance of payments balances (BOP = 0). *A flexible exchange rate guarantees that the equality between autonomous debits and credits will hold and, therefore, that the balance of payments will be neither in surplus nor in deficit.* This adjustment process occurs in each foreign exchange market where the dollar exchanges for a trading partner's currency. Often the dollar appreciates against some currencies (to eliminate a bilateral U.S. balance-of-payments surplus) and depreciates against others (to eliminate a bilateral U.S. BOP deficit).

Another perspective on the balance of payments under a flexible exchange regime focuses on the official settlements account. Recall that the balance of payments equals the negative of the official settlements balance (see Equation 13.4). The transactions on the official settlements account represent changes in the central bank's stock of foreign exchange reserves. The cause of changes in the level of these reserves is intervention in foreign exchange markets to maintain the exchange rate at a level away from equilibrium (see section 12.7).[14] Under a flexible rate regime, authorities make no effort to hold the exchange rate away from its equilibrium level and, therefore, engage in no foreign exchange intervention that would lead to changes in foreign exchange reserves. With no changes in the official reserves, the official settlements balance equals zero—another way of saying that the balance of payments is in equilibrium (BOP = 0).

Under a perfectly flexible exchange rate regime, the balance-of-payments concept is not very meaningful, since the exchange rate always will move to keep the balance of payments balanced or in equilibrium. "Balance" in the balance of payments is just another way of looking at equilibrium in the market for foreign exchange. Since a perfectly flexible exchange rate, by definition, guarantees foreign exchange market equilibrium, equilibrium in the balance of payments also follows.

This does *not* imply that either the merchandise trade balance or the current account necessarily will be in balance under a flexible exchange rate regime. A current-account deficit (or surplus) merely requires an offsetting surplus (or deficit) on the capital account. There's a widespread misconception, often repeated in the popular press, that the theory of flexible exchange rates claims that such a system will balance either the merchandise trade account or the current account. Since the move away from a fixed exchange rate regime in the early 1970s, deficits and surpluses have been observed widely in the merchandise trade and current accounts of many countries. This is the basis of frequently heard claims that flexible exchange rates don't work the way economic theory suggests. This argument reveals two misunderstandings. First, as we've noted, the theory of flexible exchange rates does *not* claim that deficits or surpluses in the merchandise trade or current accounts will disappear under flexible exchange rates—only that balance-of-payments deficits or surpluses will. Second, the exchange rate regime in use since the early 1970s, although much more flexible than the earlier system, is *not* a purely flexible exchange rate regime. Monetary authorities still intervene in foreign exchange markets to affect exchange rates, although, as we'll see, the extent and frequency of intervention differ widely over time and across countries.

13.4.2 The Balance of Payments, Foreign Exchange Markets, and a Fixed Exchange Rate

Under a fixed exchange rate regime, the demand for and supply of foreign exchange still reflect the autonomous transactions in the balance of payments. However, governments don't allow the forces of demand and supply to determine the exchange rate; instead, policy makers peg, or fix, the exchange rate at a certain level by intervening in foreign exchange markets to buy and sell assets denominated in various currencies (for a review, see the discussion in section 12.7).

Figure 13.5 reproduces Figure 12.9, which illustrates an exchange rate pegged above the equilibrium rate. Consider again a U.S. firm that sells a £1,000 bond to a resident of Britain and receives payment by a check for £1,000. At the fixed exchange rate, e_1^p, the firm doesn't want to hold the pound-denominated deposit in its portfolio. Overall, at e_1^p, the quantity supplied of pounds in the foreign exchange market exceeds the quantity demanded. Portfolio owners aren't willing to hold the existing supply of pound-denominated deposits because the expected rate of return on dollar deposits is higher than that on pound deposits. With the exchange rate pegged, market forces can't restore equilibrium by bidding down the value of pound-denominated deposits, as happened under a flexible rate regime in section 13.4.1. If the dollar price of pounds is to remain at e_1^p, either the U.S. or British central bank, or both, must intervene to eliminate the excess supply of pounds. The intervention consists of permitting individuals or firms holding unwanted pound-denominated deposits to exchange them for dollar-denominated ones with the central bank at a rate of e_1^p.

Under the rules of the fixed exchange rate system that governed the international monetary system from the end of World War II until 1971—called the **Bretton Woods system**—each central bank was responsible for intervening to maintain the value of its currency relative to the U.S. dollar. In other words, with the situation depicted in Figure 13.5, the Bank of England, the British central bank, intervened. Anyone holding unwanted pound-denominated deposits could take them to the Bank of England and exchange them for deposits denominated in dollars, receiving e_1^p dollars per pound. To purchase the pounds, the Bank of England

---

14 See footnote 5.

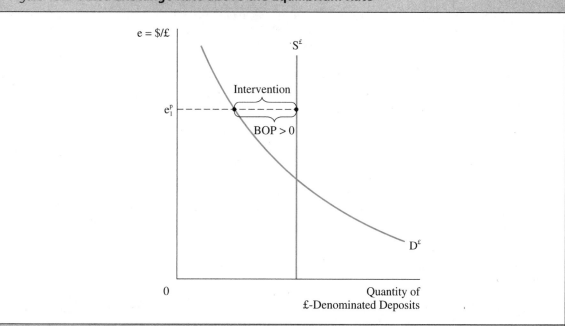

Figure 13.5 **Fixed Exchange Rate above the Equilibrium Rate**

At e_1^p, individuals aren't willing to hold the existing supply of pounds. To maintain the exchange rate at e_1^p, a central bank must absorb the excess supply of pounds. Individuals holding unwanted pound-denominated deposits can exchange them with the central bank for dollar-denominated deposits at a rate of e_1^p. The intervention enters the U.S. balance-of-payments accounts as a debit in the official settlements account, accommodating the surplus (BOP > 0) in the autonomous current and capital accounts.

would use dollar-denominated deposits from its stock of foreign exchange reserves held in the United States. The size of the Bank of England's pound purchase would equal the difference between the quantity demanded and the quantity supplied of pounds at e_1^p. The result would be a decrease in the Bank of England's stock of dollar reserves held in the United States. Recall that such a decrease in British reserves would appear as a debit in the U.S. official settlements balance, because that account records changes in *both* U.S. official reserves and foreign official reserves held in the United States (see section 13.2.3). The debit in the official settlements balance just matches the surplus (BOP > 0) in the U.S. balance of payments, as indicated by Equation 13.4.

Consider our hypothetical transaction in which a U.S. firm receives a £1,000 check in payment for a bond sold in Britain, and assume that $e_1^p = \$2.50/£1$. The firm sells the pound-denominated deposit to the Bank of England in return for a $2,500 dollar-denominated deposit. The net effect on the U.S. balance-of-payments accounts is an autonomous capital-account credit of $2,500 (= £1,000 · $2.50/£1) for "export" of the bond and an official settlements debit of the same amount for the Bank of England's sale of $2,500 of its dollar reserves. *(Why?)* Using Equation 13.4, the result is a U.S. balance-of-payments surplus of $2,500. *(What is the corresponding situation in Britain's balance-of-payments accounts?)*

The analysis of a balance-of-payments deficit under a fixed exchange rate proceeds similarly. Figure 13.6 repeats Figure 12.10's depiction of an exchange rate fixed below the equilibrium level. At the relatively low dollar price of pounds represented by the fixed exchange rate, e_2^p, portfolio owners want to hold more than the existing stock of pound-denominated deposits. Some individuals who want to buy pound-denominated deposits can't do so at the current exchange rate. The U.S. balance of payments with Britain shows a deficit. With no intervention, the dollar will depreciate against the pound. To prevent depreciation of the dollar, one of the central banks must intervene to supply pound-denominated deposits to the foreign exchange market. The Bank of England may sell pound-denominated deposits in exchange for dollar-denominated deposits and add

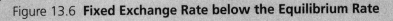

Figure 13.6 **Fixed Exchange Rate below the Equilibrium Rate**

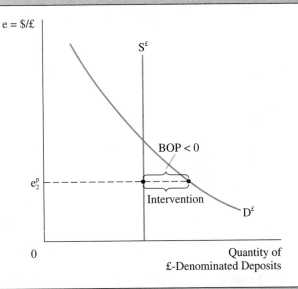

At e_2^p, the quantity demanded of pounds exceeds the quantity supplied. The exchange rate can be maintained at e_2^p only if a central bank supplies pounds to the market through intervention. Individuals who want pound-denominated deposits can purchase them at the central bank at a price of e_2^p. The U.S. balance-of-payments accounts record the intervention as an accommodating official settlements credit, reflecting the BOP deficit (BOP $<$ 0).

the dollars to its foreign exchange reserves in the United States (a credit in the U.S. official settlements account), or the U.S. Federal Reserve may sell pound-denominated deposits from its foreign exchange reserves (also a credit in the U.S. official settlements account). In either case, the balance-of-payments deficit at e_2^p reflected in the excess demand for pounds is just matched by a credit on the official settlements balance of the U.S. balance of payments, as indicated by Equation 13.4.

Suppose a U.S. resident buys £5,000 worth of stock in a British firm. At the pegged exchange rate (say, $1.50/£1), the individual isn't able to buy a pound-denominated deposit with which to pay for the stock because the quantity demanded of such deposits exceeds the quantity available. But the Bank of England can prevent appreciation of the pound by selling a £5,000 deposit to the individual at the pegged exchange rate (at $e = \$1.50/£1$, the £5,000 deposit will exchange for a $7,500 deposit). The transaction's effect on the U.S. balance of payments will consist of a $7,500 autonomous capital-account debit for the "imported" ownership of the stock and an accommodating $7,500 official settlements credit for the increase in dollar reserves held by the Bank of England. From Equation 13.4, the United States has a $7,500 balance-of-payments deficit (BOP $<$ 0) with Britain. *(How would the transaction affect Britain's balance-of-payments accounts?)*

Earlier we noted that under flexible exchange rates a currency may simultaneously appreciate against some currencies and depreciate against others. With a fixed exchange regime, a similar phenomenon occurs when the quantity demanded of some currencies exceeds the quantity supplied while for other currencies the opposite holds true. A central bank may find it necessary to intervene by simultaneously purchasing one currency and selling another from its reserves. Suppose, for example, that the United States wants to maintain fixed exchange rates between the dollar and the pound and between the dollar and the euro. If demand and supply in the two foreign exchange markets create pressure for the dollar to depreciate against the pound (excess demand for pounds) and to appreciate against the euro (excess supply of euros), the Federal Reserve can intervene by selling pound deposits from its reserves and purchasing euro-denominated ones. The balance on the multilateral official settlements account shows the net change in U.S. reserves (assuming the Bank of England and the European Central Bank undertake no intervention).

CASE ONE:
The U.S.–China Trade Deficit: $10 Billion or $40 Billion?

The U.S. merchandise trade deficit with China is a politically sensitive topic. Many U.S. industries would like protection against Chinese imports; those industries with heavy protection, especially the apparel sector, would like even more. U.S. protectionist forces routinely cite figures on the bilateral trade deficit; however, the two countries disagree significantly about the correct figure. U.S. figures for 1996 place the deficit at just under $40 billion, second in size only to the U.S. trade deficit with Japan. China, on the other hand, claims that the right number for 1996 is less than $10 billion. How can the numbers diverge so dramatically?

One answer is Hong Kong. A big share of China's trade flows through Hong Kong and did so even before the former British colony's 1997 reversion to Chinese sovereignty.[15] Official U.S. trade figures count all China's exports through Hong Kong as imports from China. But China counted that trade as exports to Hong Kong until 1993. In other words, a sweater exported from China to the United States through Hong Kong would appear in U.S. trade statistics as an import from China, but in Chinese trade statistics as an export to Hong Kong, not the United States. Since 1993, China has begun to identify exports' final destinations; but many transactions go unrecorded or misrecorded. Also, the United States doesn't count its own exports to China that pass through Hong Kong as going to China.

A second statistical problem that Hong Kong introduces concerns its own value-added. Suppose the sweater mentioned earlier is shipped unfinished from China to Hong Kong, where the final manufacturing steps are taken before the finished product goes to the United States. Accurate trade accounts would show part of the sweater's value coming from China and part from Hong Kong. U.S. statistics, however, typically assign the full value as an import from China.

In 1997, the Chinese government shared previously secret trade data with the U.S. Department of Commerce and a team of U.S. academic economists who specialize in international trade. The purpose was to reconcile the two countries' statistics. The economists found that the correct number fell between U.S. and Chinese estimates, somewhere in the $21 billion to $26 billion range.

Similar problems plague data on foreign direct investment. Numbers reported by source countries rarely match those reported by host countries. And, again, the China–Hong Kong case provides a dramatic example. For 2000, Hong Kong reported receiving $64 billion in foreign direct investment, placing behind just the United States and China in the world ranking of FDI recipients. But how could Hong Kong, with a population of 7 million and annual GDP of $162 billion, absorb $64 billion of foreign direct investment in a single year? The answer, again, seems to be: China. Experts expect that a large share of Hong Kong's inward foreign direct investment is merely making a temporary stop on its way to China.[16]

CASE TWO:
The United States as a Debtor

A country's **net foreign wealth,** or **net international investment position,** equals the difference between the value of foreign assets the country's residents own and the value of the country's domestic assets owned by foreigners. Unlike the purchases and sales of assets recorded in a country's capital account, net foreign wealth or international investment position represents asset ownership accumulated over time; in other words, while transactions in the capital account are flows, net foreign wealth or international investment position is a stock. A country's net foreign wealth is negative when foreigners currently own more assets in the country than the country's residents own abroad. This all seems straightforward. However, controversy surrounds the measurement of U.S. net foreign wealth. What's the value of U.S. assets owned by foreigners, and what's the value of foreign assets owned by Americans? When did the United States

---

15 Even after the 1997 Chinese takeover of Hong Kong, the government continues to report the province's trade statistics separately from those of the rest of China.

16 "FDI Is Hong Kong's $64 Billion Question," *Financial Times,* March 30, 2001.

become a debtor in the sense of having a negative net foreign wealth? And how big is the debt?

There are at least three ways of valuing assets. Until recently, U.S. Department of Commerce statistics valued assets at historical cost, or their original purchase price. In other words, if a U.S. firm bought a factory in Britain in 1950, government statistics still reported the value of that asset in 1990 at the original 1950 purchase price. Most economists agree that this is a poor way to measure asset value. Most U.S. purchases of foreign assets occurred in years prior to the bulk of foreign purchases of U.S. assets, so measuring at historical cost tends to understate the value of U.S.-owned foreign assets relative to foreign-owned U.S. assets.

The two alternate methods of valuing assets attempt to estimate their current values rather than relying on historical values at the time of purchase. One current-valuation method estimates assets' current cost, or the cost of purchasing them now. The other method estimates market value, or the price for which each asset could be sold now. Both measures are difficult to estimate, but conceptually superior to the old historical-cost method. When U.S. net foreign wealth became negative and by how much depend on the measure used, as reported in Table 13.12.

Although the U.S. international investment position has been negative since some point during the 1980s by all three measures reported in Table 13.12, the United States continued to earn positive current net income on its foreign investments until 1998. That is, U.S. owners of foreign assets earned more income from those assets than foreign owners of U.S. assets earned each year until 1998 (see Table 13.5).

The United States' negative net foreign wealth position often is compared with the debt of developing countries. U.S. external debt is equivalent in size to over half of the total external debt of all developing economies (which totals over $2.5 trillion)—making the United States by far the world's largest debtor. If the developing-country debt threatened the stability of those economies and the world financial system during the 1980s, as we saw in Chapter Eleven, mustn't the same be true of the U.S. external debt? Not necessarily. First, the U.S. debt, though large in absolute terms, remains relatively small compared with the size of the U.S. economy, while several developing countries' debts equal many times their respective annual GDPs. Second, the U.S. debt is denominated in dollars, the country's own domestic currency, while the developing countries owe debt denominated largely in foreign currencies, which means

Table 13.12 **U.S. International Investment Position (Billions $)**

	Historical Cost			Current Cost			Market Value		
Year	U.S. Assets Abroad	Foreign Assets in U.S.	U.S. Net Foreign Wealth	U.S. Assets Abroad	Foreign Assets in U.S.	U.S. Net Foreign Wealth	U.S. Assets Abroad	Foreign Assets in U.S.	U.S. Net Foreign Wealth
1982	$ 838.1	$ 688.6	$149.5	$1,100.6	$ 736.6	$ 364.0	$ 954.9	$ 696.4	$ 258.5
1983	887.5	781.5	106.0	1,169.2	1,068.3	337.4	831.8	800.7	267.6
1984	895.9	892.6	3.3	1,177.5	1,081.8	232.9	944.7	905.9	175.9
1985	949.7	1,061.1	−111.4	1,296.4	1,171.1	125.3	1,288.3	1,159.8	128.5
1986	1,073.3	1,341.1	−267.8	1,468.8	1,434.2	34.6	1,566.4	1,441.3	125.1
1987	1,167.8	1,536.0	−368.2	1,625.4	1,648.2	−22.8	1,709.0	1,650.9	58.1
1988	1,253.7	1,786.2	−532.5	1,841.0	2,002.8	−161.8	2,006.6	2,019.2	−12.6
1989				2,076.0	2,319.8	−243.8	2,348.1	2,418.6	−70.5
1990				2,180.0	2,426.4	−246.4	2,291.7	2,498.7	−207.0
1991				2,285.1	2,611.1	−326.0	2,468.4	2,788.3	−319.9
1992				2,325.0	2,798.0	−473.0	2,464.2	2,993.7	−529.5
1993				2,742.5	3,112.6	−370.1	3,055.3	3,330.2	−274.9
1994				2,899.0	3,310.7	−411.7	3,178.0	3,499.5	−321.5
1995				3,272.7	3,960.4	−687.7	3,700.4	4,337.9	−637.5
1996				3,720.7	4,591.3	−870.5	4,284.5	5,115.8	−831.3
1997				4,237.3	5,460.9	−1,223.6	5,007.1	6,329.6	−1,322.5
1998				5,079.1	6,190.9	−1,111.8	6,045.5	7,453.2	−1,407.7
1999				5,889.0	6,971.5	−1,082.5	7,173.4	8,647.1	−1,473.7
2000				6,167.2	8,009.9	−1,842.7	7,189.8	9,377.2	−2,187.4

Source: U.S. Department of Commerce (updates are available at the department's Web site, www.bea.doc.gov).

those economies must run current-account surpluses to earn the foreign exchange to make their debt payments. Finally, we saw in Chapter Eleven that whether debt presents a problem depends on the uses to which borrowed funds are put. For countries with a comparative advantage in future production (that is, low current income but plentiful investment opportunities), borrowing provides a way to use those opportunities. The projects funded by such borrowing earn returns sufficient to repay the loans and make both debtors and creditors better off by creating gains from intertemporal trade. Borrowing to finance consumption beyond a country's income, on the other hand, fails to generate returns to repay the loans and leads to debt problems.

CASE THREE:
Rest of Galaxy Enjoys Current-Account Surplus

Official statistics indicate that the entire world economy runs an annual current-account deficit of almost a quarter trillion dollars. Since Earth doesn't yet conduct interplanetary trade, something must be wrong with the numbers. In principle, the world's current-account balance must equal zero, because every transaction generates equal debit and credit entries in the world balance-of-payments accounts. We've seen that each country's balance-of-payments accounts typically include a statistical-discrepancy term to cover unreported or misreported data. But we might expect countries' statistical discrepancies to more-or-less offset in any given year, leaving the world accounts in rough balance. Instead, the world current account has shown a deficit every year since the mid-1970s, except for 1997; and the deficit is growing.

Experts have offered several explanations. If exports get recorded before imports because of transportation delays, then during periods of growing world trade, the current account could appear to be in deficit. More flexible exchange rates, in place since the early 1970s, may make it more common for the same good to be recorded at different export and import values if the exchange rate changes during the transaction. Trade liberalization may leave countries with less incentive to count their trade carefully, especially imports, since less tariff revenue is at stake. Trade over the Internet may slip through cracks in the data-collection process. Emerging market economies, which may have less data-collection resources and expertise, account for a growing share of trade. And financial crises can create incentives for exporters to understate their exports in order to export the undeclared earnings illegally. No one really knows how much of the observed discrepancy should be attributed to these various possible explanations. But economists and policy makers are actively studying the problem. They realize that good policy making requires good information.

Summary

The balance-of-payments accounts record transactions between residents, firms, and government agencies in one country and those in the rest of the world. Goods, services, loans, and a variety of assets are traded internationally, and a country's balance-of-payments accounts reflect all these transactions.

One of the simplest and most useful schemes for examining the balance-of-payments accounts divides transactions into current, capital, and official settlements accounts. By accounting convention, the accounts must "balance" in the trivial sense, so the sum of the balances on the current and capital accounts (plus the statistical discrepancy) equals the negative of the balance on the official settlements account. The current account, capital account, and statistical discrepancy represent autonomous transactions; when these three entries sum to zero, payments balance in the nontrivial sense. Transactions for which both entries occur in the current or the nonofficial capital account exert no effect on the balance of payments. The official settlements account records changes in the level of official foreign exchange reserves (accommodating transactions) and captures the effects of government intervention in foreign exchange markets when exchange rates aren't completely flexible. Transactions for which one entry occurs in the official settlements balance do alter the balance of payments. Figure 13.7 summarizes the balance-of-payments accounts and the effect of various classes of transactions.

A number of popular misconceptions surround the balance of payments. Two of the most widespread concern the relationship between the merchandise trade balance and the balance of payments. First, a balance-of-payments deficit (or surplus) is *not* the same as a merchandise trade deficit (or surplus). The merchandise trade

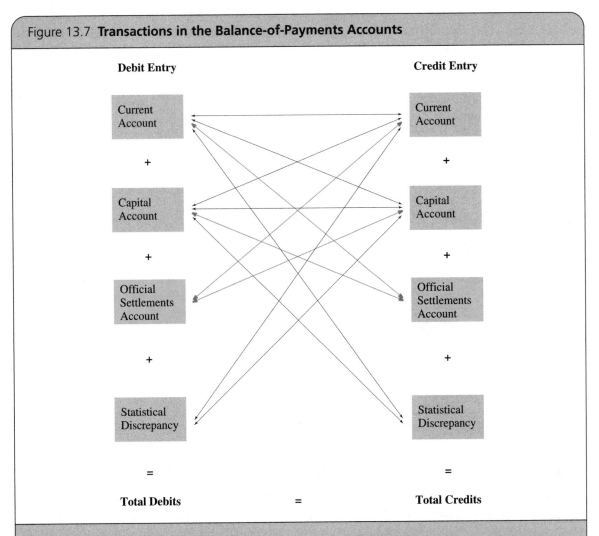

Figure 13.7 **Transactions in the Balance-of-Payments Accounts**

The sum of the current-account balance, the nonofficial capital-account balance, the official settlements balance, and the statistical discrepancy must equal zero. Transactions for which both the debit and the credit entry appear in the (autonomous) current or capital accounts don't affect the balance of payments (BOP = CAB + KAB = − OSB). Such transactions are represented by solid black lines in the figure. Transactions for which either the debit or credit entry occurs in the (accommodating) official settlements balance do affect the balance of payments and are represented by solid color lines in the figure.

balance reflects trade in goods only, while the balance of payments records trade in goods and services as well as borrowing/lending and purchases/sales of assets. Second, a perfectly flexible exchange rate assures balance-of-payments equilibrium, but not balance in either merchandise trade or the current account. A flexible exchange rate moves to equate the quantity demanded and supplied of a currency in the foreign exchange markets. Like the balance-of-payments accounts, the demand for a currency reflects not only trade in goods but trade in services, assets, and loans.

Looking Ahead

A country's international economic relations, including its balance of payments, matter primarily because they affect and are affected by domestic economic performance. The various components of the balance-of-payments accounts can affect domestic output, employment, prices, and interest rates as well as exchange rates. Chapter Fourteen begins the process of integrating international considerations—foreign exchange markets and the balance of payments—into a simple model of the macroeconomy.

Key Terms

merchandise exports
services
balance-of-payments (BOP) accounts
double-entry bookkeeping system
current account
credit
debit
current-account balance
deficit
merchandise trade balance
surplus
balance on goods and services
capital account
capital outflow

capital inflow
official settlements balance
statistical discrepancy
autonomous (independently motivated)
   transactions
balance-of-payments surplus
balance-of-payments deficit
accommodating (compensatory) transactions
overall (multilateral) balance-of-payments
   accounts
bilateral balance-of-payments accounts
Bretton Woods system
net foreign wealth (net international
   investment position)

Problems and Questions for Review

1. For the year 2004, country A has a current-account balance of −1,000 and a (nonofficial) capital-account balance of +1,500 (measured in units of country A's currency).
    a. What's the status of country A's 2004 balance of payments? What happened to country A's net investment position during 2004?
    b. What would happen under a flexible exchange regime? Why?
    c. Now assume that country A operates under a fixed exchange rate regime. If foreign central banks didn't buy or sell any country A deposits during 2004, what happened to the country's central bank's foreign exchange reserves during 2004? How would this be recorded in country A's balance-of-payments accounts?
    d. Continue to assume that country A operates under a fixed exchange rate regime. Foreign central banks sold 500 worth of deposits denominated in country A's currency. How would this be recorded in country A's balance-of-payments accounts?
2. State whether each of the following represents a debit or a credit on the U.S. current account (for now, ignore the "second side" of each transaction).
    a. Purchase of a Boeing aircraft by a Chinese airline
    b. Expenditures by an American on vacation at EuroDisney
    c. Purchase by a U.S. automaker of Brazilian steel
    d. A U.S. telecommunications company hires a French firm to launch a new space satellite
    e. A Hong Kong-based corporation pays its annual dividend to its U.S. stockholders
3. Under the Bretton Woods system of pegged exchange rates in effect from the end of World War II to the early 1970s, suppose that (then West) Germany had a balance-of-payments deficit with the United States. According to the rules of the Bretton Woods system and ignoring other countries, what would have happened, and how would it have been reflected in the U.S. balance-of-payments accounts?
4. Evaluate the following statements:
    a. "The theory of flexible exchange rates doesn't work. Otherwise, the United States couldn't have a $450 billion merchandise trade deficit."
    b. "Look at Tables 13.7 and 13.12. The U.S. capital-account balance and net international investment position never even show the same number for any given year. Obviously, the statistics can't be trusted."

5. Assume that the United States operates under a flexible exchange rate regime. Comment on the following statement: "The U.S. current-account deficit provides a measure of how much the United States must borrow abroad."

6. For each of the following transactions, show the entries in the balance-of-payments accounts for each of the countries involved and the overall effect on each country's balance of payments.

    a. In the 1980s, Pepsico (a U.S.-owned firm) sold $3 billion worth of Pepsi syrup to the Soviet Union in exchange for $3 billion worth of Stolichnaya vodka and ships. The exchange rate between dollars and rubles was $1/ruble0.5.

    b. A U.S. book publisher sells $20,000 of books to China and is paid with a check for 80,000 yuan that the publisher holds in an account in Beijing. The equilibrium exchange rate is $1/yuan4.

    c. A U.S. firm imports SF5,000 worth of goods from Switzerland. In the foreign exchange market, the firm is unable to purchase a Swiss franc deposit (with which to pay for the goods) at the pegged exchange rate of $1/SF2. The firm buys an SF5,000 deposit from the U.S. central bank.

    d. General Motors issues $10 million of new bonds, sells them to residents of Mexico, and uses the proceeds to buy an automobile factory in Mexico. The equilibrium exchange rate is $0.10/P1.

    e. Seagram sells Can$1 million worth of liquor to a U.S. distributor, who pays Seagram with a Can$1 million deposit in a New York bank. Seagram decides to keep the deposit. The equilibrium exchange rate is U.S.$1/Can$1.

    f. A British firm purchases a U.S. supercomputer and pays with a £100,000 deposit in a New York bank. The computer seller doesn't want to hold the pounds and sells them to the U.S. central bank at a pegged rate of $2/£1.

    g. Nissan (a Japanese auto firm) buys a factory in England and pays the British seller for the land and building with a ¥1 billion account in a Tokyo bank. The British seller decides to keep the yen deposit. The exchange rate is £1/¥200.

    h. A German firm hires a British attorney as a consultant. The attorney is paid with a €1,000 deposit in a Frankfurt bank, which she sells to the Bank of England (the British central bank) in exchange for a deposit of £350.

7. Briefly explain why equilibrium in the foreign exchange market and equilibrium in the balance of payments are two ways of looking at the same phenomenon.

8. Can a country have a

    a. current-account deficit, capital-account surplus, and flexible exchange rate? Why or why not?

    b. current-account deficit, capital-account deficit, and flexible exchange rate? Why or why not?

    c. merchandise trade deficit, capital-account deficit, and flexible exchange rate? Why or why not?

    d. current-account surplus, capital-account surplus, and fixed exchange rate? Why or why not?

    e. current-account surplus, capital-account surplus, official settlements balance surplus, and fixed exchange rate? Why or why not?

References and Selected Readings

Carlson, Keith M. "The U.S. Balance Sheet: What Is It and What Does It Tell Us?" Federal Reserve Bank of St. Louis, *Review* 73 (September–October 1991): 3–18.
An introduction to national accounting; for all students.

Cooper, Richard N. "Is the U.S. Current Account Deficit Sustainable? Will It Be Sustained?" *Brookings Papers on Economic Activity* (2001): 217–226.
Emphasizes the role of capital flows into the United States as a source of the U.S. current-account deficit.

Feenstra, Robert C., et al. "Discrepancies in International Data: An Application to China–Hong Kong Entrepôt Trade." *American Economic Review Papers and Proceedings* 89 (May 1999): 338–343.
Difficulties in measuring countries' trade accurately; more on the subject of Case One.

Fieleke, Norman S. "The Soaring Trade in 'Nontradables.'" Federal Reserve Bank of Boston, *New England Economic Review* (November–December 1995): 25–36.
Accessible overview of the rapidly growing trade in previously nontraded goods.

Fieleke, Norman S. "Unilateral International Transfers: Unrequited and Generally Unheeded." Federal Reserve Bank of Boston, *New England Economic Review* (November–December 1996): 27–38.
Introduction to the role of unilateral transfers in the balance-of-payments accounts.

Graboyes, Robert F. "International Trade and Payments Data: An Introduction." Federal Reserve Bank of Richmond, *Review* 77 (September–October 1991): 20–31.
Outline and assessment of data on international trade and finance.

Hervey, Jack L., and Loula S. Merkel. "A Record Current Account Deficit: Causes and Implications." Federal Reserve Bank of Chicago, *Economic Perspectives* (Fourth Quarter 2000): 2–13.
Why does the United States exhibit such a large current-account deficit, and what are its implications?

Hooper, Peter, and J. David Richardson, eds. *International Economic Transactions.* Chicago: University of Chicago Press, 1991.
Collection of papers on the problems of measuring international transactions; level of papers varies.

International Monetary Fund. *Annual Report on Exchange Arrangements and Exchange Restrictions.* Washington, D.C.: International Monetary Fund, annual.
Comprehensive country-by-country report of exchange restrictions.

International Monetary Fund. *International Capital Markets.* Washington, D.C.: International Monetary Fund, annual.
Comprehensive survey of recent events in world capital markets.

McKinnon, Ronald I. "The International Dollar Standard and the Sustainability of the U.S. Current Account Deficit." *Brookings Papers on Economic Activity* (2001): 227–240.
Emphasizes the vehicle-currency role of the dollar as a source of sustainability for the U.S. current-account deficit.

Obstfeld, M., and K. Rogoff. "The Intertemporal Approach to the Current Account." In *Handbook of International Economics,* Vol. 3, edited by G. M. Grossman and K. Rogoff, 1731–1800. Amsterdam: North-Holland, 1995.
Survey of the literature on the current account as intertemporal trade; advanced.

Primo Braga, Carlos A. "The Impact of the Internationalization of Services on Developing Countries." *Finance and Development* (March 1996): 34–37.
Introduction to the growing international trade in services.

"Statistical Discrepancies in the World Current Account." *Finance and Development* (March 1997): 24–25.
More on Case Three, how world current-account balances fail to sum to zero; for all students.

U.S. Department of Commerce Bureau of Economic Analysis. *The Balance of Payments of the United States.* Washington, D.C.: U.S. Government Printing Office, 1990.
Detailed report on the presentation of U.S. government statistics on international transactions.

U.S. Trade Deficit Review Commission. *The U.S. Trade Deficit: Causes, Consequences, and Recommendations for Action.* Washington, D.C: U.S. Trade Deficit Review Commission, 2000.
Report of blue-ribbon panel on the trade deficit; available at www.ustdrc.gov.

Wei, Shang-Jin. "Local Corruption and Global Capital Flows." *Brookings Papers on Economic Activity* 2 (2000): 303–354.
How and to what extent does corruption affect the pattern of capital flows?

World Bank. *Global Development Finance.* Washington, D.C.: World Bank, annual.
Comprehensive report on capital flows to and from developing countries.

CHAPTER FOURTEEN

The Market for Goods and Services in an Open Economy

14.1 Introduction

Thus far, we've examined foreign exchange markets (Chapter Twelve) and the balance-of-payments accounts (Chapter Thirteen) in relative isolation from other elements of the international macroeconomy. The next few chapters integrate exchange-rate and balance-of-payments considerations into a simple model of the macro-economy. Our goal is to understand better the interactions between international and domestic elements in determining macroeconomic performance and the effectiveness of macroeconomic policy.

This is an area in which one hears many claims and counterclaims in the popular press. Critics of international openness claim that merchandise-trade deficits reduce economic growth and "deindustrialize" the U.S. economy. So-called experts disagree whether the U.S. trade deficit reflects unfair trade practices abroad, an attractive investment environment in the United States, or simply the interplay of domestic and foreign macro-economic policies. NAFTA opponents allege that the agreement's opening of the Mexican economy contributed to the country's 1994 peso crisis. Critics of the European Union's macroeconomic integration worry that the lowering of economic barriers between countries lessens national policy makers' control over the macroeconomy. And policy makers the world over worry about catching at least a cold from other countries' economic illnesses.

These complex issues involve the interaction of many economic variables, including output, price levels, rates of inflation, employment, exchange rates, and interest rates. Therefore, the perspective of this and subsequent chapters will alternate between partial-equilibrium analyses, which focus on a small subset of the interactions, and more general-equilibrium analyses, which, although more complicated, permit a broader view. We'll see that many disagreements and contradictory statements concerning international macroeconomics stem from ignoring or misunderstanding the relationship between partial- and general-equilibrium analyses. Statements that hold true when we consider only one market in isolation may be false once we introduce a more complete set of economic interactions.

Our investigation of the international macroeconomy will focus on three key markets: that for domestically produced goods and services (the subject of this chapter) and those for money and for foreign exchange (the subjects of Chapter Fifteen). Along the way, we'll mention several common sources of confusion and disagreement that have important effects on public opinion and on the policy-making process.

14.2 How Do We Measure a Country's Output?

The market for goods and services produced by the domestic economy provides the first building block of our model of an open macroeconomy. The most commonly used measures of an economy's goods and services output are **gross national product (GNP)** and **gross domestic product (GDP).** Both measure the sum of the market values of all final goods and services produced by the economy in a given period (typically a year, although the government reports figures quarterly). Several features of this definition deserve note.

First, GNP and GDP exclude most goods and services not transacted through markets. Thus, both measures fail to reflect items such as homegrown food and housekeeping by family members—even though those goods and services contribute to society's economic welfare. Both measures also ignore the economy's production of "bads," such as pollution and congestion, because these costs aren't transacted in markets. Therefore, GDP and GNP don't necessarily accurately reflect residents' economic well-being.[1]

Second, calculation of GNP or GDP involves adding the *values* of all goods and services produced in the economy, evaluated at market prices. This step facilitates the aggregation of many diverse goods and services into a single measure. We can't simply add in physical units (bushels, dozens, and so forth) the automobiles, bananas, computers, and dynamite produced, because each good is measured in different units. But market prices can translate the quantity of each good and service into a dollar value; and we can add the dollar values because they're measured in a common unit.

Third, GNP and GDP include only production of *final* goods and services, not intermediate ones; this convention avoids double-counting. If we included the values of silicon production, semiconductor-chip production, and computer production in GNP, we would count the value of the silicon three times, because the values of both chips and computers include the value of the silicon used as an input.

Finally, GNP and GDP refer to production within a specified period. For example, consider an economy with a GDP of $9,963 billion. With no time period specified, this figure conveys little information. If the figure were a daily one, the economy would be enormous (approximately 365 times the size of the U.S. economy in 2000). If the figure referred to a decade, the economy would be much smaller (approximately one-tenth the size of the 2000 U.S. economy).

The difference between GNP and GDP lies in their definitions of "the economy." Gross *national* product refers to the output produced by a country's factors of production—regardless of where in the world the production takes place. Gross *domestic* product refers to output produced within a country's geographical boundaries—regardless of the resources' nationality. The output of a U.S. resident temporarily working in Germany, for example, is a part of U.S. GNP but not U.S. GDP, and a part of German GDP but not German GNP. Beginning with a country's GDP, we can arrive at its GNP by adding the country's receipts of factor income from the rest of the world and subtracting the country's payments of factor income to the rest of the world. Table 14.1 performs this exercise for the United States for a sample of years.

Table 14.1 **U.S. GDP and GNP, 1960–2000 (Billions $)**

Year	GDP	Plus: Receipts of Factor Income from the Rest of the World	Less: Payments of Factor Income to the Rest of the World	Equals: GNP
1960	$ 536.6	$ 5.0	$ 1.8	$ 529.8
1965	719.1	8.1	2.7	724.5
1970	1,035.6	13.0	6.6	1,042.0
1975	1,630.6	28.2	14.9	1,643.9
1980	2,784.2	81.8	46.5	2,819.5
1985	4,180.7	108.1	87.7	4,201.0
1990	5,743.8	177.5	156.4	5,764.9
1995	7,265.4	222.8	217.5	7,270.6
2000	9,963.1	370.6	374.9	9,958.7

Source: U.S. Department of Commerce (updates are available at www.doc.gov).

---

1 Despite this disclaimer, empirical evidence suggests that many important measures of well-being (for example, life expectancy and infant-mortality rates) are highly correlated with countries' GNP and GDP.

Until recently, most countries emphasized GDP in their economic reporting, while the United States emphasized GNP. In late 1991, the U.S. Department of Commerce announced that it would begin to focus more on GDP as its primary measure of output, although both figures would continue to be collected and reported. For the United States, differences between the two measures are tiny. For countries with a greater divergence between factor-income receipts from the rest of the world and factor-income payments to the rest of the world, the GNP versus GDP distinction makes a bigger difference. For example, in 1999, GNP was 12 percent greater than GDP for Singapore, but 19 percent less than GDP for Ireland. Countries, such as Singapore, that are net providers of factor services to the rest of the world have GNPs that exceed their respective GDPs. Countries, such as Ireland, that are net importers of factor services have GNPs smaller than their GDPs. International factor payments include not only wages and salaries, but also interest and dividends and firms' profits.

14.3 What Determines Output and Income in an Open Economy?

One useful way to think about the market for goods and services at the macroeconomic level is to imagine the entire economy as composed of one giant firm, Nation Inc. The firm earns revenue by producing output that it sells at market prices. The firm's revenue equals the value of its output (the economy's GDP); this revenue, in turn, goes to pay the firm's inputs. Households in the economy own these inputs (labor services, raw materials, factories, and so on); so the revenue earned by Nation Inc. is paid out as income to households. Therefore, the economy's GDP (represented by Nation Inc.'s revenue) also equals the total income of households in the economy (represented by Nation Inc.'s payments to inputs).[2] This equality between the value of output or GDP and the value of **national income** is important for understanding the determination of the equilibrium level of GDP.

The next step involves analyzing the sources of demand for Nation Inc.'s output. Nation Inc. can sell its output to four basic groups: individuals, the firm Nation Inc. itself, government agencies, and foreigners. When individuals buy goods and services such as food, automobiles, books, and medical care, the spending is referred to as **consumption expenditure (C).** When Nation Inc. retains a portion of the goods and services it produces (for example, machine tools, hammers, and personal computers) to use to produce next year's output, this spending is **investment expenditure (I).**[3] Local, state, and federal government agencies purchase a variety of goods and services (such as file cabinets, missiles, and telephone service); these are called **government purchases (G).** Government purchases refer only to government spending on goods and services and exclude government spending that simply transfers income between groups within the economy, such as Social Security, unemployment-insurance, and public-assistance benefits. Finally, **export expenditures (X)** represent spending by foreigners on the domestic economy's output.

We must make one adjustment before we can add consumption, investment, government purchases, and exports to arrive at total expenditure on Nation Inc.'s output. Consumption expenditure by individuals, investment expenditure by firms, and government purchases each typically include some purchases of foreign-produced goods, or **import expenditures (imp),** which we must subtract to obtain a measure of total expenditure on the output of the *domestic* economy. After this adjustment, we can write total *e*xpenditures (E) on Nation Inc.'s output as:

$$E = C + I + G + X - \text{imp} \qquad \text{[14.1]}$$

Equilibrium in the market for domestically produced goods and services requires that this expenditure just equal GDP, or the value of the economy's output of goods and services (denoted by Y):

$$Y = C + I + G + X - \text{imp} \qquad \text{[14.2]}$$

---

2 In the national-income accounts, two entries preclude exact equality between GDP and national income: the capital consumption allowance, or depreciation, and indirect business taxes. Neither is a part of national income. For simplicity, we assume both to be zero to create exact equality between GDP and national income. This simplification doesn't affect the basic results of the analysis.

3 Without our simplifying assumption of only one firm, investment includes one firm's purchases of other firms' outputs.

Table 14.2 **Components of U.S. GDP, 1960–2000 (Billions $)**

Year	Y	=	C	+	I	+	G	+	X	−	imp
1960	$ 526.2		$ 332.2		$ 78.8		$ 113.2		$ 25.3		$ 22.8
1965	719.1		444.3		118.0		153.0		35.4		31.5
1970	1,035.6		648.1		150.2		236.1		57.0		55.8
1975	1,630.6		1,029.1		225.4		362.6		136.3		122.7
1980	2,784.2		1,760.4		465.9		572.8		278.9		293.8
1985	4,180.7		2,704.8		715.1		875.0		303.0		417.2
1990	5,743.8		3,839.3		799.7		1,176.1		557.3		628.6
1995	7,265.4		4,957.7		1,038.2		1,355.5		818.4		904.5
2000	9,963.1		6,757.3		1,832.7		1,743.7		1,097.3		1,468.0

Source: U.S. Department of Commerce (updates are available at www.doc.gov).

In words, the value of the economy's output (the left-hand side of Equation 14.2) must equal total expenditures made on that output (the right-hand side of Equation 14.2).[4] If we think of the economy as a single firm, the value of Nation Inc.'s output must equal the amount of revenues it takes in from selling that output. Table 14.2 reports GDP, consumption, investment, government purchases, exports, and imports for the United States for a sample of years, illustrating the relationships from Equations 14.1 and 14.2.[5]

Equation 14.2 provides the basic framework for our analysis of the market for goods and services, but it can't reveal much until we understand how its various terms are determined as well as which economic variables are held constant in the analysis. Remember that the Y on the left-hand side of Equation 14.2 represents the value of the economy's output, or GDP; however, Y also represents the total income of the individuals in the economy (also known as *national income*).[6] This must hold true because Nation Inc. pays out the total value of its revenues to the owners of the resources it uses; these payments represent income to the recipients.

The amount of consumption expenditure (C) depends on income. In the case of one individual, the proposition that consumption depends positively on that individual's income seems intuitively appealing. The same relationship holds for the economy as a whole: Higher incomes coincide with higher consumption expenditures, and lower incomes with lower consumption expenditures, other things held constant. We can represent this relationship in shorthand form with $C(\overset{+}{Y})$, where the plus sign represents the positive relationship between income and consumption. When income rises, consumption rises, but by less than the increase in income; the remainder of the additional income goes into saving. Economists call the share of the increase in income consumed the **marginal propensity to consume (mpc),** a fraction between 0 and 1. For example, if a $1,000 increase in national income causes consumption to rise by $800, the marginal propensity to consume equals $\Delta C / \Delta Y = \$800/\$1{,}000 = 0.8$.[7]

Investment includes firms' purchases of new capital equipment (machines, factories, and so on) to produce future output, along with changes in firms' inventories. The level of investment expenditure in the economy depends primarily on the interest rate, i, which measures the opportunity cost of using funds in a particular investment project.[8] If a firm borrows funds to finance an investment project, it's easy to see that the interest

---

4 Equation 14.2 can be either an identity (a relationship that's always true—by definition) or an equation true only in equilibrium. If we define expenditure as including even unplanned changes in inventories (that is, accumulations of unsold output by firms), Equation 14.2 holds as an identity. If we define expenditure as excluding unplanned changes in inventories, Equation 14.2 holds only when no such changes occur. We use the second interpretation here.

5 In Table 14.2, the categories of expenditure include unplanned changes in firms' inventories so that the equality of income and expenditure holds as an identity in each period (see footnote 4).

6 GDP excludes factor income earned abroad, but includes payments to foreign factors employed in the domestic economy.

7 Recall that Δ denotes "change in," so ΔC represents the change in consumption expenditures.

8 If individuals in the economy expect inflation, we must distinguish between real and nominal interest rates, with real rates determining investment behavior. We assume temporarily that expected inflation equals zero so that real and nominal rates of interest are equal.

rate represents the opportunity cost of the borrowed funds. At first, it may seem less obvious that the interest rate also measures the relevant opportunity cost when the firm uses internal (nonborrowed) funds. But remember that opportunity cost always measures forgone opportunity. A firm that undertakes an investment project using $1,000 of its own funds forgoes the opportunity to lend out those funds and earn interest. Therefore, the interest rate measures the opportunity cost of the funds used for investment—regardless of whether the funds are borrowed or not. When the interest rate is low, so is the opportunity cost of funds with which to undertake investment projects; and firms undertake a relatively large number of projects. With a higher interest rate, the higher opportunity cost of funds makes fewer investment projects worthwhile. We can represent this negative relationship between the rate of interest and investment by $I(\bar{i})$.

Explaining the determinants of the level of government purchases is an important but complex and elusive goal. Two subfields within economics, public finance and public-choice theory, address this question directly. For our macroeconomic purposes, it suffices to assume that the level of government purchases of goods and services is determined exogenously, that is, outside our model. We'll take government purchases as a policy variable, one of policy makers' fiscal policy tools; and we can examine the effects of changes in fiscal policy on the economy's performance.

Exports, or purchases of domestically produced goods and services by foreigners, depend primarily on income in trading-partner countries and on the relative prices of domestic and foreign goods. To keep things simple by examining one country at a time, we assume that foreign income is just a constant, Y*. (Whenever possible, we'll let an * denote a magnitude for the foreign country; for example, if Y refers to domestic income, Y* refers to foreign income.) Higher foreign incomes imply higher levels of foreign spending on all goods and services, including imports from the domestic economy. Therefore, foreign income and the domestic economy's exports are positively related. As in the case of government purchases, we can investigate the effects of changes in the level of foreign income even though we won't build an explicit model of its determinants.

Demand for exports also depends on their prices relative to the prices of their foreign-produced counterparts. The price of domestically produced goods is P, the domestic price level, measured in the domestic currency.[9] The domestic-currency price of foreign-produced goods equals their foreign-currency price (P*) multiplied by the exchange rate, or the domestic-currency price of a unit of foreign currency. *(Why?)*[10] Therefore, we can define R, the relative price of domestically produced goods and services, as:

$$R \equiv P/eP^* \qquad\qquad \textbf{[14.3]}$$

The higher the relative price, R, the more expensive are domestic goods relative to foreign ones and the lower the domestic economy's ability to export. The lower the relative price, the less expensive are domestic goods compared with foreign ones and the higher the level of domestic exports. In other words, exports depend positively on foreign income and negatively on the relative price of domestic goods, or $X(\overset{+}{Y}{}^*, \overset{-}{R})$.

The relative price of domestic and foreign goods, R, also is known as the **real exchange rate.** The domestic country's currency undergoes a real appreciation whenever R rises and a real depreciation when R falls. A real appreciation decreases the country's ability to export, and a real depreciation increases that ability. Note that a nominal appreciation of a country's currency (that is, a fall in e) leads to a real appreciation *if* there's no offsetting change in the domestic or foreign price level. Similarly, a nominal depreciation (that is, a rise in e) with no change in either price level implies a real depreciation as well.

The determinants of imports simply mirror the determinants of exports. Imports depend on domestic income and on the relative prices of domestic and foreign goods, or the real exchange rate. Imports rise with domestic income and with the relative price of domestic goods, $imp(\overset{+}{Y}, \overset{+}{R})$. *(Why?)* The share of any rise in income that goes to increased imports is known as the **marginal propensity to import (mpi),** which, like the marginal propensity to consume, is a fraction between 0 and 1. If an increase in income of $1,000 leads to a $100 increase in imports, the marginal propensity to import equals $\Delta imp/\Delta Y = \$100/\$1,000 = 0.1$.

---

9 The price level measure that takes into account prices of all the goods and services included in GDP is the *GDP deflator.* The deflator measures changes in prices over time by comparing the value of a given level of production at two sets of prices, one from a base year and the other from the current year.

10 Whenever we compare two prices, we must express them in a common currency. This is why we compare P with eP*, not P with P*. For a review, see section 12.2.

We now have the tools to depict graphically the relationship between national income and total expenditure on the economy's output of goods and services. The panels of Figure 14.1 combine consumption, investment, government purchases, exports, and imports to construct total expenditure. Panel (a) illustrates the positive relationship between consumption and income; the slope of the consumption line equals the marginal propensity to consume, or $\Delta C/\Delta Y$. The consumption line doesn't go through the origin but has a positive vertical intercept. This intercept captures the fact that if some disaster reduced national income to zero in one period, consumption wouldn't fall to zero but would continue at a positive level financed out of accumulated saving.

Figure 14.1 **Expenditure on Domestically Produced Goods and Services Depends on Income**

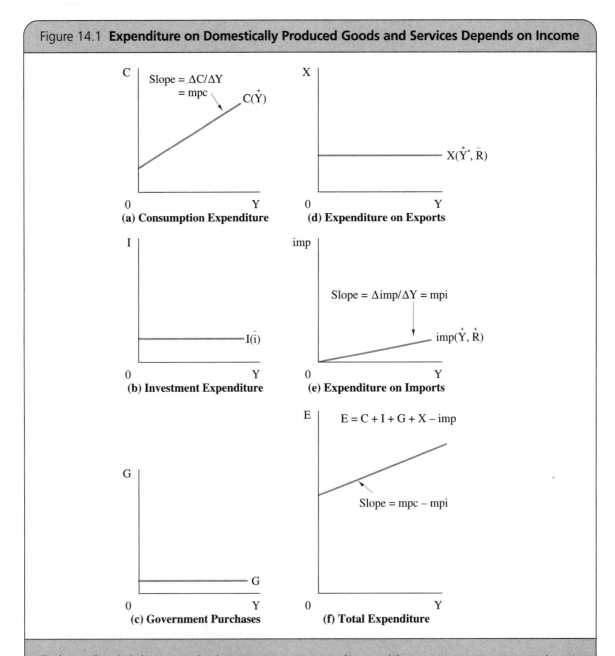

Total expenditure includes consumption, investment, government purchases, and the current account or net exports (exports minus imports). Income affects consumption and imports by the marginal propensities to consume and import, respectively.

Panel (b) shows a horizontal line because we've assumed, for simplicity, that investment doesn't depend on income. The height of the investment line depends on the interest rate. The government purchase and export lines (panels (c) and (d), respectively), also are horizontal, since we assume that both spending categories are independent of income. Panel (e) exhibits a positive slope to capture the positive relationship between domestic income and expenditures on imports; the slope of the line measures the marginal propensity to import.

Total expenditure (panel (f)) is simply the sum of the various expenditure components (note that imports enter with a *negative* sign). The slope of the total expenditure line gives the effect of a change in income on total expenditure ($\Delta E/\Delta Y$). A rise in income causes two of the expenditure components to increase: consumption by the marginal propensity to consume and imports by the marginal propensity to import. The slope of the expenditure line equals the sum of these effects, where the change in imports again enters with a negative sign. Therefore, the slope of the total expenditure line equals (mpc − mpi).

Panel (f) of Figure 14.1 illustrates the relationship between the economy's national income or GDP (measured on the horizontal axis) and total expenditure on domestically produced goods and services (measured on the vertical axis). The market for goods and services will be in equilibrium when national income or GDP equals total expenditure (see Equation 14.2). We can easily find the point that satisfies this condition—by sketching in a 45-degree line, as in Figure 14.2. Recall that along any 45-degree line, the quantity measured on the horizontal axis equals the quantity measured along the vertical axis; here this implies that national income equals total expenditure. The equilibrium level of income or GDP is Y_0.

At income levels below Y_0 (such as Y_1), expenditure exceeds the value of the economy's output of goods and services. When firms sell more goods and services than they produce, they see their inventories decline unexpectedly and respond by producing more. As a result, the value of output rises, moving Y toward Y_0. On the other hand, at levels of income above Y_0 (such as Y_2), income exceeds expenditure. The value of goods and services produced exceeds the expenditures made to buy them. Inventories begin to accumulate, and firms respond by reducing production. Income falls toward Y_0. The equilibrium at Y_0 is based on the assumption that

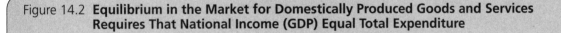

Figure 14.2 Equilibrium in the Market for Domestically Produced Goods and Services Requires That National Income (GDP) Equal Total Expenditure

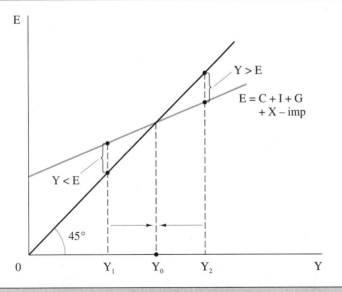

The market for goods and services is in equilibrium at Y_0. At incomes below Y_0 (such as Y_1), expenditure exceeds income, inventories decline, production increases, and income rises. At incomes greater than Y_0 (such as Y_2), income exceeds expenditure, inventories accumulate, production decreases, and income falls.

i, Y*, G, and R are fixed at the levels in Figure 14.1. A change in any of these variables will *shift* the expenditure line, resulting in a different equilibrium income; we'll explore the details of such changes later.

Now that we've seen how to determine the equilibrium level of income or GDP, we turn to investigations of international trade's effects and of events that alter the economy's equilibrium income.

14.4 How Does International Trade Affect the Market for Goods and Services?

The current account is one component of the market for domestically produced goods and services.[11] The other balance-of-payments accounts discussed in Chapter Thirteen don't enter directly into the market for goods and services. Although simple, this point is important to remember to avoid confusion and spot common errors. The model of the market for goods and services presented in section 14.3 often is used to draw sweeping conclusions concerning the relationship between a country's income or output and its balance of payments. This is obviously inappropriate, since the model contains only a small subset of the transactions recorded in the balance-of-payments accounts. The model does, however, produce some useful insights into the interaction between the current account and national income.

The most important lesson to be learned is that the relationship between national income and the current account is an interactive one; that is, income affects the current account *and* the current account affects income. We can see this interaction clearly in Figure 14.3, which combines the export and import panels from Figure 14.1. Recall that exports are independent of the level of domestic income, while imports rise with income.

Holding constant foreign income (Y^*) and the relative prices of domestic and foreign goods or real exchange rate (R), the *c*urrent *a*ccount will be in balance (neither in surplus nor in deficit) at only one income, denoted Y_{ca} in Figure 14.3. When income falls below Y_{ca}, the resulting decline in imports produces a current-account

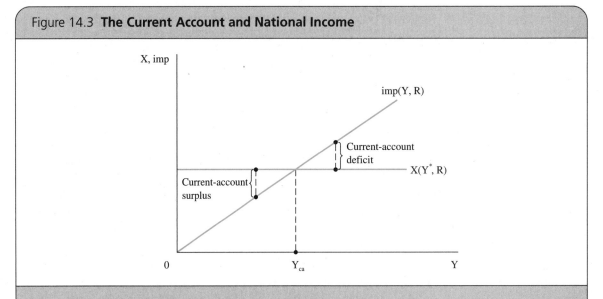

Figure 14.3 The Current Account and National Income

Because imports increase with income, other things equal, increases in income lead to current-account deficits, and decreases in income to surpluses. Income Y_{ca} represents the income at which the current-account balance equals zero. There's no necessary relationship between Y_{ca} and the level of income at which the market for goods and services is in equilibrium.

---

11 In fact, the market for domestically produced goods and services includes only part of the current account—that is, net exports of goods and services.

surplus (X > imp). When income rises above Y_{ca}, imports rise and the current account moves into deficit (imp > X). *The level of income at which the market for goods and services is in equilibrium (Y_0 in Figure 14.2) and the level of income at which the current account balances (Y_{ca} in Figure 14.3) generally aren't the same.* Only an unlikely coincidence would produce a situation in which the two income levels coincided.

So far we've focused on income's effect on the current account: *Other things equal,* higher incomes are associated with current-account deficits and lower incomes with current-account surpluses. But other things aren't always equal. We must also consider the effect of changes in the current account on income. Suppose, for example, that an increase in foreign income from Y_0^* to Y_1^* increases the demand for exports, shifting up the total expenditure line, as in panel (a) of Figure 14.4. (You may want to review the effect of a change in exports on total expenditure in Figure 14.1.) The increased expenditures on domestic output run down inventories and cause firms to increase their production. The equilibrium level of domestic income rises from Y_0 to Y_1. The current account moves toward a surplus, but by *less* than the initial increase in exports would indicate. The increased exports lead to increased domestic income, which in turn raises imports and partially offsets the initial positive effect on the current account.[12] Once adjustment is complete, income is higher than in the initial equilibrium, and the current account will have moved toward a surplus. Similarly, a decrease in exports will move the current account toward a deficit and lead to a decrease in income that partially offsets that deficit. *(Illustrate the effects of a decrease in exports in a graph similar to Figure 14.4.)*

These results are simple but important, because they point out a common error. Earlier we argued that, other things equal, an increase in income leads to a current-account deficit (through an increase in imports) and a decrease in income to a current-account surplus (through a decrease in imports). But Figure 14.4 illustrates a rise in income accompanied by a move toward a surplus in the current account. There's no contradiction between the two lines of reasoning; in Figure 14.4, we can illustrate them by distinguishing between *movements along* the expenditure curves and *shifts* in the curves.

A change in income (represented by a horizontal *movement along* an expenditure curve in Figure 14.4) changes imports in the same direction. As a result, any rise in income causes a move toward a deficit in the current account, while a fall in income causes a move toward a current-account surplus. But a change in exports or imports caused by something *other than* a change in domestic income (such as a change in foreign income) *shifts* the expenditure curve in panel (a) of Figure 14.4 and changes the equilibrium level of income. The new level of income is reflected in panel (b) in a new current-account value read from the intersection of the import line and the *new* export line at the new equilibrium income. The increase in imports causes the current-account surplus to be smaller than it would be otherwise; but the rise in income nonetheless accompanies a move toward a surplus in the current account.

Because of the two-way interaction between income and the current account, we must draw conclusions with care. In some situations, income may rise while the current account moves toward a deficit; in others, income may rise while the current account moves toward a surplus. The relationship depends on what causes the initial change.

14.4.1 A Note on Terminology

A move toward a surplus in the current account commonly is referred to as an *improvement* and a move toward a deficit a *deterioration* or *worsening* of the current account. Although this terminology is convenient in the sense that it is easier to say "the current account improved" than to say either "the current account moved toward a surplus" or "the current-account deficit declined," it also is potentially misleading. Speaking of a move toward a surplus as an improvement implies that such a move is desirable—which isn't necessarily the case.

---

12 You may wonder whether imports might rise by more than exports, leading to a deficit on the current account. The answer is no, and the logic goes like this: Suppose Y^* rises by \$1, causing foreign imports to rise by mpi* · ΔY^* = mpi* · \$1. With only two countries in the world, foreign imports equal domestic exports, so ΔX = mpi* · \$1. Domestic income rises by the increase in domestic exports multiplied by the spending multiplier (defined in section 14.5.1), so ΔY = mpi* · \$1 [1/(1 − mpc + mpi)]. This causes domestic imports to rise by mpi · ΔY = mpi · mpi* · \$1 [1/(1 − mpc + mpi)]. Because the marginal propensity to consume must lie between zero and one, we can show that the increase in domestic exports (ΔX = mpi* · \$1) exceeds the increase in domestic imports (mpi · mpi* · \$1 [1/(1 − mpc + mpi)]). Therefore, the rise in Y^* must move the domestic current account toward a surplus.

Figure 14.4 **Interaction between Changes in the Current Account and Changes in Income**

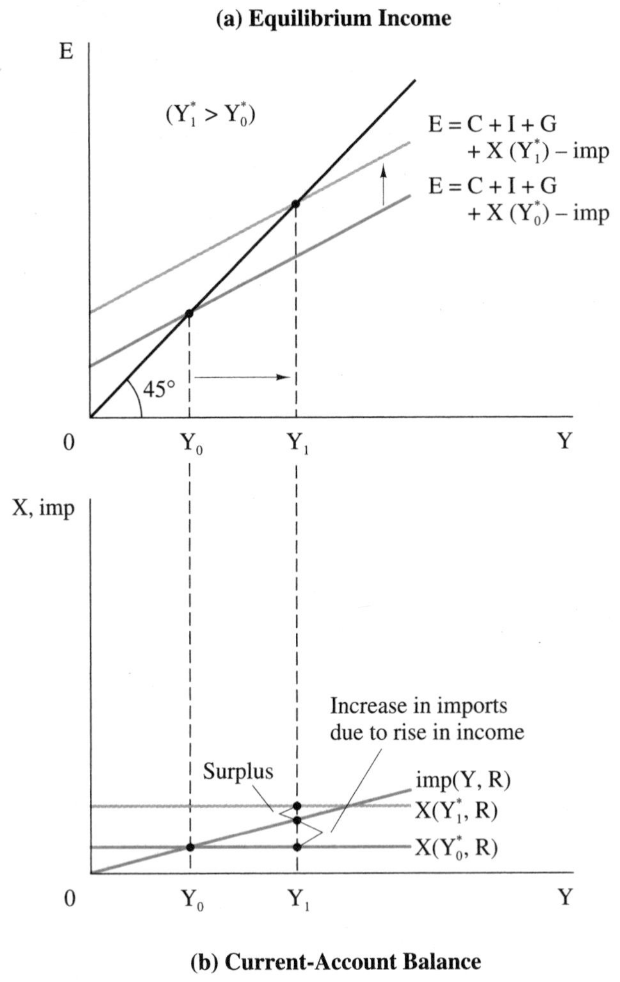

(a) Equilibrium Income

$(Y_1^* > Y_0^*)$

$E = C + I + G + X(Y_1^*) - imp$

$E = C + I + G + X(Y_0^*) - imp$

$45°$

$0 \quad Y_0 \quad Y_1 \quad \quad Y$

X, imp

Increase in imports
due to rise in income

Surplus

$imp(Y, R)$
$X(Y_1^*, R)$
$X(Y_0^*, R)$

$0 \quad Y_0 \quad Y_1 \quad \quad Y$

(b) Current-Account Balance

The net effect of an increase in exports (caused here by an increase in foreign income) on the current account is smaller than the original increase in exports. Domestic income rises, producing a partially offsetting increase in imports.

Surpluses aren't necessarily good, just as deficits aren't necessarily bad. In fact, economies that grow rapidly relative to the rest of the world and provide many profitable investment opportunities tend to run current-account deficits. Those deficits are matched by capital inflows (capital-account surpluses) as foreign investors take advantage of the profitable opportunities provided by the growing economy. Similarly, a surplus may (but doesn't always) reflect a stagnant economy in which imports fall with declining income and foreign investors see few profitable investment opportunities. We can judge the desirability of a surplus or a deficit only in light of the country's overall economic situation.

There's another reason to avoid words with positive or negative connotations when describing economic events or situations: Such phenomena typically affect different individuals or groups in the economy differently. An entertaining editorial in *The Economist* noted this problem:

It is bound to end in tears: some economists are trying to give their dismal science sex appeal. To make dry numbers more alluring, economic and financial commentators add emotive adjectives or nouns: gloom, worsening, cheer, improved. But the next time you spot the word *gloom* in a headline or read that a trade balance has deteriorated, ask this question: gloom for whom? The answer may be surprisingly cheery. . . . Economic commentators take note. Trade surpluses and deficits increase, rise, grow, widen or swell, but they never improve.[13]

Make it a habit to avoid terminology with inappropriate positive or negative connotations.

14.5 What Causes Changes in the Market for Goods and Services?

So far, variables held constant in the analysis include government purchases (G), the relative prices of domestic and foreign goods or the real exchange rate (R), and the interest rate (i). We can determine the effects of each of these variables on income and the current account using the graphical framework developed in the preceding sections.[14] When we refer to "the" equilibrium level of income in the economy, we really mean the particular level of income that represents equilibrium in the market for goods and services *given* the values of other variables, including G, i, Y*, P, P*, and e, as well as the marginal propensities to consume and import. A change in any of these variables changes the income at which the value of goods and services produced (Y) equals expenditure on goods and services (E).

14.5.1 Fiscal Policy and the Spending Multiplier

A change in government purchases of goods and services provides one example of a **fiscal policy,** a policy that uses changes in government spending or taxation to affect the macroeconomy's performance. Government purchases constitute one category of total expenditure on domestically produced goods and services (see Equation 14.2), so the *initial* effect of a change in government purchases is an equal change in total expenditure. Figure 14.5 depicts such a change as an increase from G_0 to G_1. Equilibrium income rises as a result, and the current account moves toward a deficit.

The magnitude of fiscal policy's effect on income depends on the **spending multiplier.** A $1 increase in government purchases generates an income increase of $1 times the spending multiplier. The value of the multiplier is given by $1/(1 - mpc + mpi)$, where mpc denotes the marginal propensity to consume and mpi denotes the marginal propensity to import. A high marginal propensity to consume increases the value of the multiplier by causing a larger share of the additional income to be passed along in the form of increased consumption expenditure. A high marginal propensity to import decreases the value of the multiplier, because income spent on imports "leaks" out of the domestic economy.

Suppose, for example, that the initial increase in government purchases $(G_1 - G_0)$ equals $1,000. Income immediately rises by $1,000. The $1,000 rise in income increases spending on domestic output by $1,000(mpc − mpi). *(Why?)* This second round of increased spending is passed on as additional income out of which the recipients spend $1,000(mpc – mpi)(mpc – mpi) on domestic output. This process—often called the **round-by-round effect,** because additional spending gets passed on in the next "round" as an increase in income—continues until the initial $1,000 in government purchases has increased income by $1,000(1/[1 − mpc + mpi]).[15] Therefore, the total change in the equilibrium level of income caused by a change in government purchases is:

$$Y_1 - Y_0 = [1/(1 - mpc + mpi)] (G_1 - G_0) \qquad \textbf{[14.4]}$$

---

13 *The Economist,* August 31, 1991, 16.

14 Other variables also can be changed, including the marginal propensities to consume and import; we leave these analyses to the reader.

15 This follows from the fact that $1 + $1(mpc − mpi) + $1(mpc − mpi)(mpc − mpi) + $1(mpc − mpi)(mpc − mpi)(mpc − mpi) + . . . = $1/(1 − [mpc − mpi]) = $1/([1 − mpc + mpi]). Each term corresponds to an increase in income of which a share equal to (mpc − mpi) is spent on domestic goods and therefore passed on as an increase in income to another individual in the economy.

Figure 14.5 **A Rise in Government Purchases Raises Equilibrium Income and Moves the Current Account toward a Deficit**

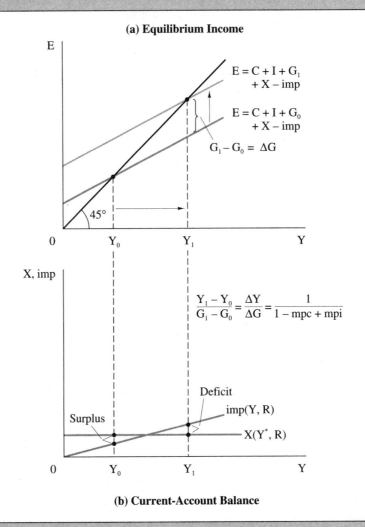

(a) Equilibrium Income

(b) Current-Account Balance

The amount of the increase in income per unit increase in government expenditure is known as the spending multiplier and is equal to $1/(1 - mpc + mpi)$.

Because a rise in government purchases increases income, imports rise and the current account moves toward a deficit, as represented in panel (b) of Figure 14.5.

14.5.2 **Relative Prices of Domestic and Foreign Goods: The Real Exchange Rate**

Changes in the relative price of domestic and foreign goods or real exchange rate, R, also alter equilibrium income and the current account. A real appreciation of the domestic currency, or a rise in R, reflects domestic goods becoming more expensive relative to foreign ones. Exports fall (shown as a downward shift in the export line in

Figure 14.6 **A Domestic Real Appreciation Reduces Income and Moves the Current Account toward a Deficit**

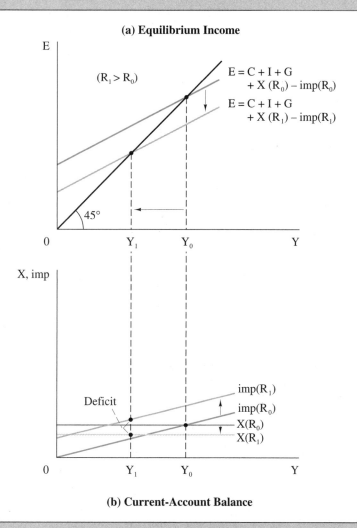

(a) Equilibrium Income

$(R_1 > R_0)$

$E = C + I + G + X(R_0) - imp(R_0)$

$E = C + I + G + X(R_1) - imp(R_1)$

45°

Y_1 Y_0 Y

X, imp

$imp(R_1)$

Deficit

$imp(R_0)$

$X(R_0)$

$X(R_1)$

Y_1 Y_0 Y

(b) Current-Account Balance

If domestic goods become relatively more expensive, demand shifts to imports, income falls, and the current account moves toward a deficit.

Figure 14.6), and imports rise (shown as an upward shift in the import line).[16] These responses result from individuals shifting their purchases from now-more-expensive domestic goods to now-cheaper foreign goods.

Total expenditure on domestically produced goods and services falls, and the total expenditure line shifts down. As expenditure on domestically produced goods declines, inventories accumulate and domestic firms cut their production. Income falls by an amount equal to the magnitude of the shift down in total expenditure multiplied by the spending multiplier, $(1/[1 - mpc + mpi])$. Because of the decline in income, individuals curtail

---

16 For simplicity, we assume the demands for imports and exports are price elastic. A rise in the relative price of domestic goods increases the quantity of imports and decreases the quantity of exports. The effects on the *value* of imports and exports depend on the cause of the change in relative price (P, e, or P*) and on the elasticities of demand. See the section on the J curve and footnote 17.

their spending, including spending on imports. The current account moves toward a deficit, but by somewhat less than the initial impact of the change in R, because of the partially offsetting effect of the decline in income and imports.[17]

Relative price or real exchange rate changes sometimes stem from deliberate economic policies. Economists call these policies, designed to alter the allocation of expenditure between domestic and foreign goods, **expenditure-switching policies.** The nominal exchange rate enters into the relative price of domestic and foreign goods or real exchange rate ($R \equiv P/eP*$), so changes in the nominal exchange rate under either fixed or flexible exchange rate regimes can alter relative prices, at least in the short run. Under a fixed exchange rate regime, a nominal devaluation (a rise in the domestic currency price of foreign currency, e) will lower the relative price of domestic goods (or, equivalently, generate a real devaluation) so long as price levels, P and P*, don't respond to offset completely the effect of the rise in e. A similar statement holds for a depreciation under a flexible exchange rate regime. We'll see in later chapters that there are reasons to doubt that a devaluation or depreciation will leave P and P* unaffected in the long run.

This effect of the exchange rate on relative prices historically has played an important role in international economic policy making. During the Depression of the 1930s, countries desperately tried to increase export markets for their goods as a means of combating unemployment. Country after country devalued its currency in an effort to achieve a real devaluation and a competitive advantage at the expense of its trading partners. Like other policies designed to benefit one country at the expense of others, such **competitive devaluations** are known as **beggar-thy-neighbor policies.** The nominal devaluations often failed to achieve the desired results because as soon as one country devalued its currency against its trading partners', the trading partners retaliated by devaluing their own currencies, leaving the initial exchange rate and relative prices little changed. At the same time, protectionist policies such as the Smoot-Hawley tariff in the United States were on the rise, effectively eliminating the possibility that international trade could help pull the world economy out of its depression.

Movements in nominal exchange rates, unless accompanied by offsetting price-level movements, always have distributive consequences within the domestic economy. Export-oriented and import-competing industries lose and domestically oriented (nontradable) industries gain from currency appreciations. Domestic consumers also gain as the domestic-currency price of imported goods falls, lowering the cost of living. Currency depreciations have the opposite effects, helping industries involved in international trade at the expense of nontrade industries and domestic consumers. These distributive effects help explain why the exchange rate never is perceived by everyone as being at the "right" level. During the 1970s, the dollar depreciated heavily against other major currencies, and the politicians seen as responsible lost public support. The early 1980s provided an example of the opposite phenomenon: The dollar appreciated substantially against other currencies, and support grew for policies designed to depreciate the dollar as well as for protectionism aimed at reducing the U.S. current-account deficit. The late 1980s and early 1990s produced substantial depreciations of the dollar against trading-partner currencies, especially the yen and Deutsche mark, a trend policy makers sought to interrupt through foreign exchange market intervention. By the late 1990s, dollar appreciation again made the headlines, especially against the depreciating Asian currencies during the Asian financial crisis and against the euro during that new currency's debut years.

A Caveat: J-Curve Effects

We just argued that a real depreciation (or real devaluation) of the domestic currency lowers the relative price of domestically produced goods and services, increases exports, reduces imports, and thus moves the current account toward a surplus. This adjustment process, however, may not occur immediately. In fact, in the short run, a depreciation or devaluation of the domestic currency can even push the domestic current account toward a further *deficit.* To see why, it helps to write out the expression for the current-account balance, as in Equation 14.5:

$$\text{Current-account balance} = (\text{Price of exports} \cdot \text{Quantity of exports})$$
$$- (\text{Price of imports} \cdot \text{Quantity of imports}) \qquad \textbf{[14.5]}$$
$$= (P \cdot Q_X) - ([e \cdot P*] \cdot Q_{imp}),$$

---

17 We know that the *net* effect on the current account is a move toward a deficit, because otherwise a net move toward a surplus would *increase* expenditure on domestically produced goods and services and *raise* income. But it is the *fall* in income that causes the secondary move toward a surplus on the current account to begin with. Hence, a net surplus on the current account from a rise in R produces a contradiction. We can show this algebraically using the technique from footnote 12.

where Q_X and Q_{imp} represent the *quantities* of exports and imports, respectively. When e rises, the price of imports rises immediately, but the quantity of imports may take some time to adjust downward in response to the price change, because current imports and exports typically occur based on orders placed months in advance—before the devaluation or depreciation. If so, the *value* of imports will rise in the short run. Similarly, the domestic currency depreciation makes exports more attractive to foreign buyers, but those buyers may not adjust immediately to the price change. The result of quantities' slow adjustment to the relative price changes caused by a domestic currency depreciation or devaluation can be a short-run move toward a further deficit in the current account. *(Use Equation 14.5 to explain why.)*

As time passes, import and export quantities do adjust. The quantity of imports falls, and the quantity of exports rises. This distinction between the short-run and long-run effects of a real depreciation or devaluation is called the **J-curve** phenomenon. Figure 14.7 illustrates the logic behind the name. The horizontal axis measures time; the vertical axis measures the current-account balance. As the story opens, the current account is in deficit. The devaluation or depreciation of the domestic currency occurs at time t_0. Initially the current-account deficit grows because the domestic-currency price of imports rises. *(To test your understanding, explain what would happen to the J-curve analysis if contracts for imports were written in domestic currency, that is, if the prices paid for imports were set in terms of domestic rather than foreign currency.)* As time passes, export and import quantities begin to adjust. Export receipts rise, and expenditures on imports fall. The deficit stops growing, and the current account moves toward a surplus. The time path of the current account following the rise in e traces out a shape similar to the letter *J*.

Is the J curve just a theoretical curiosity, or is there evidence that it accurately describes the actual effects of exchange rate changes? Unfortunately, this question doesn't have a simple or definitive answer. The presence or absence of the J curve hinges on the demand elasticities for imports and exports.[18] These elasticities

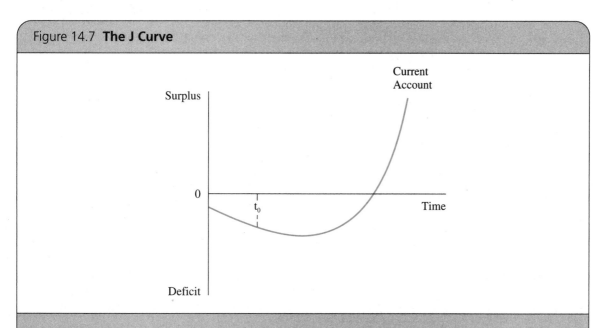

Figure 14.7 **The J Curve**

Policy makers devalue the domestic currency at time t_0. The devaluation immediately raises the domestic-currency price of imports. The quantities of imports and exports don't adjust right away, so the current-account deficit grows in the short run. As time passes, the quantity of imports falls and the quantity of exports rises. Eventually, the current account moves toward a surplus. The time path of the devaluation's effect on the current-account balance traces out a pattern similar to the letter *J*.

---

18 Letting ε_{imp} and ε_X represent the elasticities of demand for *imports* and exports, respectively, the effect of a domestic currency depreciation on the current-account balance equals $\varepsilon_X + \varepsilon_{imp} - 1$. Therefore, the more elastic the demands, the more a depreciation will shift the current account toward a surplus. If $(\varepsilon_X + \varepsilon_{imp}) > 1$, the current account does move toward a surplus; this is known as the *Marshall-Lerner condition*.

differ across historical periods and countries, so we observe the J curve in some cases and not in others. Recent experience suggests that industrial countries often experience J-curve effects for six months to a year following currency devaluations or depreciations. But even in cases with a pronounced J curve caused by low short-run elasticities, evidence shows long-run elasticities high enough for real currency depreciations or devaluations to move the current account toward a surplus.

14.5.3 **Interest Rates**

Changes in interest rates alter equilibrium income by changing investment expenditure. A rise in interest rates discourages investment (see section 14.3). Investment expenditure is one component of total expenditure on the economy's output, so a fall in investment reduces total expenditure and causes a decline in income. This is illustrated in Figure 14.8, in which the interest rate rises from i_0 to i_1. The decline in income equals the change in investment expenditure multiplied by the spending multiplier $(1/[1 - \text{mpc} + \text{mpi}])$. The decline in income reduces imports and moves the current account toward a surplus. We don't yet have a theory of what causes changes in the interest rate but will develop one in Chapter Fifteen, where we add money to our model of the macroeconomy.

14.5.4 **Summary of Effects on Income and the Current Account**

Changes in variables that increase total expenditure on domestically produced goods and services increase the income consistent with equilibrium in the market for goods and services. Such changes include increases in government purchases or foreign income and decreases in the relative price of domestic goods and services or in the domestic interest rate. Table 14.3 summarizes these effects.

Increases in government purchases and decreases in interest rates move the current account toward a deficit. Increases in foreign income or decreases in the relative price of domestic goods and services (whether caused by a fall in P, or a rise in P* or e) move the current account toward a surplus.

14.6 **Interdependence: Protectionism, Income, and the Current Account**

Despite protectionism's popularity as a response to a current-account deficit, economic analysis suggests that such a response is ineffective at best and damaging to the world economy at worst. Problems with protection include repercussions from the adverse effect of protectionism on trading partners' economies, the possibility of retaliation, and the economic inefficiencies introduced by trade barriers.

Just as exports provide a source of demand for domestic products, imports provide a source of demand for trading-partner economies. Protectionism by one country, to the extent it succeeds in reducing that country's demand for foreign goods, reduces foreign incomes. The reduction in foreign incomes then feeds back into the domestic economy through a reduction in foreign demand for exports. Because of these linkages among economies, artificial reductions in imports through protectionism result in reductions in exports.[19]

The history of protectionist legislation makes clear that protectionism by one country in the world trading system leads to similar protectionism by other countries. Beggar-thy-neighbor policies of any type, by their very nature, spread quickly from one country to another. Each country's exports constitute its trading partners' imports, so successful efforts by one country to alter its current account always produce consequences for trading partners' current accounts. Retaliation adds one more reason why the belief that protectionism can reduce imports while leaving exports unchanged is naive. In fact, if protectionism simultaneously switches expenditure from foreign- to domestically produced goods for all countries, current-account balances remain unchanged, other things equal, because exports simply decline by the same amount as imports.

Finally, the most important reasons for avoiding protectionist policies formed the basis of Chapters Two through Eleven. Unrestricted international trade allows the world's scarce resources to produce the maximum quantity of goods and services. By interfering with the efficient allocation of resources, barriers to trade reduce the world economy's ability to produce goods and services. The result: fewer goods available for consumption and higher prices.

---

19 This interdependence generalizes to other changes in spending.

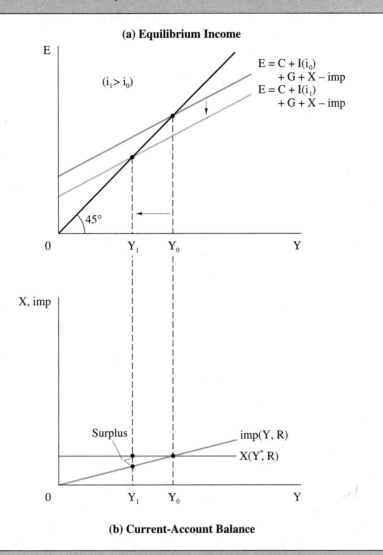

Figure 14.8 **A Rise in the Interest Rate Reduces Income and Moves the Current Account Toward a Surplus**

(a) Equilibrium Income

E

$(i_1 > i_0)$

$E = C + I(i_0)$
$\quad + G + X - imp$
$E = C + I(i_1)$
$\quad + G + X - imp$

$45°$

$0 \qquad Y_1 \quad Y_0 \qquad\qquad Y$

X, imp

Surplus

$imp(Y, R)$
$X(Y^*, R)$

$0 \qquad Y_1 \quad Y_0 \qquad\qquad Y$

(b) Current-Account Balance

A rise in the interest rate increases the opportunity cost of funds for investment. Investment expenditure falls, reducing total expenditure and the equilibrium level of income. The fall in income reduces imports, and the current account moves toward a surplus.

14.7 The "Twin Deficits"

In the popular- or business-press coverage of the U.S. economy during the 1980s and early 1990s, one of the most commonly encountered subjects was the **"twin deficits."** The term refers to the combination of a government budget deficit and a current-account deficit, both of which grew substantially during the 1980s in the United States. In what sense are the two deficits "twins"? After all, the government budget deficit equals the amount by which government purchases of goods and services exceed the net tax revenues government takes in $(G - T)$, while the current-account deficit refers to the amount by which the value of a country's imports

Table 14.3 **Effects on Equilibrium Income and the Current Account**

Variable	Effect on Equilibrium Income	Effect on Current-Account Balance
Increase total expenditure (E):		
Increase in G	+	−
Increase in Y*	+	+
Decrease in R	+	+
Decrease in P	+	+
Increase in P*	+	+
Increase in e	+	+
Decrease in i	+	−
Decrease total expenditure (E):		
Decrease in G	−	+
Decrease in Y*	−	−
Increase in R	−	−
Increase in P	−	−
Decrease in P*	−	−
Decrease in e	−	−
Increase in i	−	+

exceeds the value of its exports.[20] Given these definitions, a direct connection between the two isn't immediately obvious.

Repeating the information from Equation 14.2, we know that national income equals the sum of consumption expenditure, investment expenditure, government purchases, and the current-account balance or net exports of goods and services ($CA = X - imp$):

$$Y = C + I + G + X - imp = C + I + G + CA \qquad \textbf{[14.6]}$$

Rearranging Equation 14.6, we can see that $Y - (C + I + G) = CA$, or that a country's current account reflects the difference between the country's national income (Y) and its residents' spending on goods and services ($C + I + G$). If residents buy more goods and services than the country produces, the country runs a current-account deficit (imports more goods and services than it exports), and the country must borrow from foreigners to cover its excess spending. From a balance-of-payments perspective, this is just another way of saying that a current-account deficit must be covered by a capital-account surplus, or a decline in the country's net foreign wealth. A country that produces more goods and services than its residents buy, on the other hand, runs a current-account surplus, and sells the excess to foreigners. The current-account surplus is matched by a capital-account deficit, or an increase in the country's net foreign wealth.

From the standpoint of the households receiving national income, there are three outlets for that income: It can be spent on consumption (C), paid to the government in taxes (T), or saved (S):[21]

$$Y = C + T + S \qquad \textbf{[14.7]}$$

Combining and rearranging Equations 14.6 and 14.7, we get an expression that highlights the relationship between the government budget and the current account:

$$S - I = (G - T) + (X - imp) = (G - T) + CA \qquad \textbf{[14.8]}$$

---

20 Note the other components of current account discussed in section 13.2.1.

21 By definition, saving equals income minus consumption expenditures and taxes.

The difference between saving and investment in the economy (S – I) must equal the sum of the government budget surplus (G – T < 0) or deficit (G – T > 0) and the current-account surplus (CA > 0) or deficit (CA < 0). The two terms on the right-hand side of Equation 14.8 are "twins" in the sense that, for given values of saving and investment, a change in one necessarily accompanies an offsetting change in the other; the larger the budget deficit (that is, the larger G – T), the larger the current-account deficit. Given private saving and investment in the economy, when government spends more than the revenue it takes in, the country must borrow abroad to finance that spending. (Recall that a current-account deficit implies a capital-account surplus or net borrowing from abroad.)

We can rearrange Equation 14.8 to note that:

$$I = S - (G - T) - CA \qquad \textbf{[14.9]}$$

An open economy has three sources of funds to finance investment: domestic private saving, a government budget surplus, or borrowing from abroad. Saving represents individuals in the economy forgoing current consumption and using the income not consumed to fund investment projects that increase future output. A government budget surplus occurs when government doesn't spend all the tax revenue it takes in (G − T < 0); we can think of this as public saving by the government, and the excess funds can finance investment projects. The sum of private saving (S) and public or government saving $(-[G - T])$ is called national saving. Finally, the country can import more goods and services than it exports (CA < 0), use the net imports for investment purposes, and borrow from foreigners.

To take yet another perspective, we can rearrange Equation 14.8 to focus on private saving in the economy:

$$S = I + (G - T) + CA \qquad \textbf{[14.10]}$$

When individuals in the economy save, that saving can go into any of three channels: domestic investment projects (I), purchases of bonds issued by the domestic government to cover its spending in excess of tax revenues (G − T), or purchases of foreign assets and loans to foreigners (CA).

Equation 14.10 also suggests why many analysts proposed policies to increase domestic saving as a means of reducing the twin deficits. Higher saving raises the left-hand side of Equation 14.10, allowing any given budget deficit to coincide with a smaller current-account deficit (or, equivalently, allowing any given current-account deficit to be associated with a smaller budget deficit). But evaluating policy proposals for dealing with the twin deficits requires more than the information provided in Equation 14.10. In particular, we need to understand how the variables in the equation are related, both to each other and to other important macroeconomic variables—tasks for the next three chapters. Before undertaking those tasks, we can summarize this chapter's results in a form handy for later use.

14.8 A Concise Graphical Summary: The IS Curve

Our goal is to combine the insights from this chapter's examination of the market for goods and services with an understanding of the markets for money and foreign exchange. To help accomplish that goal, a graphical technique called an IS curve will prove useful. An **IS curve** summarizes the relationship between income and the interest rate that must hold for the market for goods and services to be in equilibrium. When we use IS curves, we'll assume that the price level (P) is fixed so that changes in nominal GDP (or Y, in our notation) translate directly into changes in real GDP, which we denote as Q, where $Y \equiv Q \cdot P$.

In section 14.5.3, we argued that a rise in the interest rate would, by discouraging investment, lower the income at which the market for goods and services was in equilibrium. Figure 14.9 repeats panel (a) of Figure 14.8, showing the effect of an increase in the interest rate on the income (now real GDP) at which the market for goods and services is in equilibrium. When the interest rate rises from i_0 to i_1, firms face an increased opportunity cost of funds for investment and investment expenditure falls from $I(i_0)$ to $I(i_1)$. Because investment expenditure is one component of total expenditure on the goods and services produced by the domestic economy, total expenditure falls. Firms find their inventories accumulating and respond by cutting their output, so GDP falls from Q_0 to Q_1. Similarly, a fall in the interest rate would require an increase in income for the market for goods and services to remain in equilibrium.

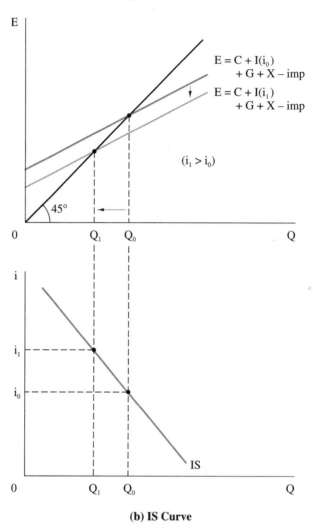

Figure 14.9 **The IS Curve**

(a) Equilibrium Income

$E = C + I(i_0) + G + X - imp$

$E = C + I(i_1) + G + X - imp$

$(i_1 > i_0)$

45°

(b) IS Curve

An increase in the interest rate raises the ópportunity cost of funds for investment, discourages investment, and lowers total expenditure on goods and services. The IS curve in panel (b) represents all combinations of domestic income and interest rate consistent with equilibrium in the market for goods and services. The IS curve is negatively sloped; a rise in the interest rate lowers investment expenditure and the equilibrium level of income.

We can summarize the *negative* relationship between income and interest rate necessary to maintain equilibrium in the market for goods and services by a downward-sloping line as in panel (b) of Figure 14.9. We call this an *IS curve*, so named because in a closed economy the market for goods and services is in equilibrium when *investment* equals *saving*. In an open economy the relationship becomes more complex, making the IS terminology less descriptive. Nevertheless, we'll use the standard term, keeping in mind that the IS curve shows the combinations of income and interest at which the market for goods and services is in equilibrium.

Figure 14.10 **Variables That Shift the Total Expenditure Line Also Shift the IS Curve**

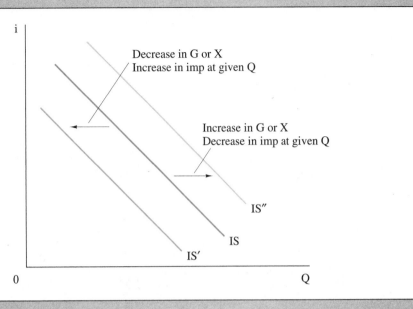

Decrease in G or X
Increase in imp at given Q

Increase in G or X
Decrease in imp at given Q

IS″

IS

IS′

Changes that increase total expenditure (for example, an increase in G) shift the IS curve to the right. Changes that decrease total expenditure (for example, a decrease in G) shift the IS curve to the left.

An IS curve is drawn assuming that government expenditure (G), exports (X), and the marginal propensity to import are fixed. Changes in any of these variables shift the entire IS curve. In fact, a change in any variable, *other than the interest rate,* that shifts the total expenditure line also shifts the IS curve.[22] Any change that shifts the total expenditure line *up* shifts the IS curve to the *right,* and any change that *lowers* the total expenditure line shifts the IS curve to the *left.* For example, a rise in either government expenditure or exports raises total expenditure and therefore raises income at each level of the interest rate (see Equation 14.1). An increase in G or X thus shifts the IS curve to the right. An exogenous increase in imports reduces total expenditure and, given the interest rate, reduces income, shifting the IS curve to the left. Figure 14.10 summarizes these changes. The IS curve summarizes the requirements for equilibrium in the market for goods and services in a single line, a convenient way to carry this chapter's results forward and to integrate them with other elements of the world macroeconomy.

United States

CASE ONE:
GDP: What's in There?

We've seen that we can divide a country's gross domestic product among several different categories of expenditure: consumption, investment, government purchases, and net exports. But what do we know about the types of spending recorded in each of these categories? Government statistics break C, I, G, X, and imp down into more detailed accounts that may be useful in developing a sense of the economic activity underlying the national-income accounts. Figure 14.11

22 Changes in the interest rate cause movements along an IS curve rather than shifts in the curve, because the interest rate is the variable graphed on the diagram's vertical axis.

Figure 14.11 **U.S. Expenditure, 2000**

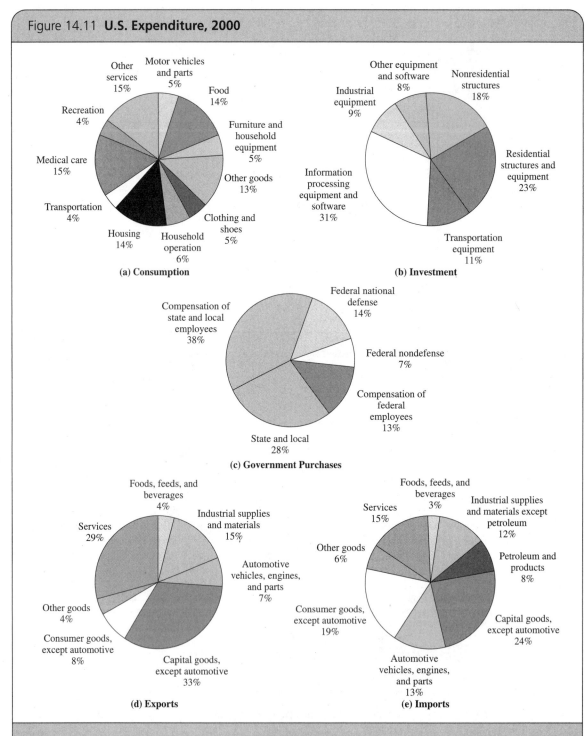

(a) Consumption

(b) Investment

(c) Government Purchases

(d) Exports

(e) Imports

We can divide U.S. 2000 GDP into consumption expenditure, investment expenditure, government purchases, and net exports (exports minus imports). Each category includes many types of spending.

Source: Data from U.S. Department of Commerce (updates are available at www.doc.gov).

reports the major types of spending for the U.S. economy in 2000.

The largest categories of Americans' $6.8 trillion of consumption expenditures in 2000 included medical care (15%), other services (15%), housing (14%), and food (14%). Firms spent 31 percent of their $1.8 trillion of 2000 investment expenditures on information processing equipment and software, a category that had represented only 14 percent of investment spending just a decade earlier in 1990. Government purchases figures reveal two interesting facts. First,

when we think of government spending, we often think of the federal level of government; but state and local governments account for two-thirds of the total $1.7 trillion in government purchases in the United States. Second, compensation of government employees accounts for just over half of all government purchases.

Almost two-thirds of U.S. exports in 2000 fell into just two categories: capital goods (except automotive) and services. U.S. imports were dominated by capital goods (except automotive) and consumer goods (except automotive).

U.S./Mexico

CASE TWO:
The Peso and Mexico–U.S. Trade

Between November 1994 and March 1995, the peso price of a dollar almost doubled (see Figure 14.12, panel (a)), from about three and one-half pesos per dollar to almost seven. Mexican exports to the United States became much cheaper as a result, and Mexican imports from the United States much more expensive. Mexico's bilateral trade balance with the United States moved from a small deficit to a sizable surplus (see Figure 14.12, panel (b)) in response to the sudden change in relative prices. Adding to the shift in trade patterns was a large decline in Mexico's national income brought about by some of the same economic conditions that led to the peso depreciation.

We'll see more about the Mexican episode in later chapters. But we can already understand part of what happened leading up to the 1994 crisis and devaluation. Mexico undertook a broad and successful program of economic liberalization starting in 1987 and culminating with the signing of NAFTA with the United States and Canada. But, despite the impressive liberalization, problem areas remained—a weak and largely unreformed financial and banking system and potential political instability related to alleged government corruption, for example. In 1994, an economic downturn was magnified by two political assassinations and a rebellion in the southern part of the country. Foreign-exchange mar-

ket participants started to expect a peso devaluation; that is, the expected future spot peso price of dollars (e^e) rose. The expected rate of return on peso-denominated assets fell, and both Mexican and foreign investors started to move funds out of pesos in anticipation of a devaluation. The Mexican government pegged the peso–dollar exchange rate; so the Mexican interest rate rose substantially, from about 10 percent in early 1994 to almost 20 percent by the end of the year, to maintain interest parity. This rise in i discouraged investment expenditures and further reduced national income, as this chapter's model predicts. Finally, the Mexican central bank ran short of dollar reserves with which to buy pesos in the foreign exchange market and had to devalue on December 20, 1994.

By the end of 1995, the worst of the crisis had ended. The post-crisis period has, so far, been one of relative stability in Mexico. Even the 2000 election generated few economic jitters, unusual in a country with a dramatic history of election-related economic crises. The peso, now floating in foreign exchange markets, has depreciated against the dollar.[23] Mexico maintains a bilateral trade surplus with the United States as the two economies continue to experience increased trade and economic integration under NAFTA.

---

23 We'll see later, when we relax the assumption of a fixed price level, that currencies of high-inflation countries tend to depreciate against currencies of low-inflation countries. Throughout the period, Mexico's inflation rate exceeded the U.S. inflation rate.

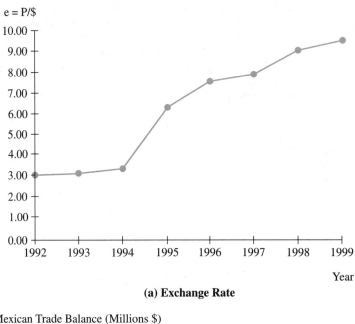

Figure 14.12 **Peso–Dollar Exchange Rate and Mexico–U.S. Trade Balance, 1992–1999**

(a) Exchange Rate

(b) Mexican Bilateral Trade Balance

The large peso depreciation against the dollar in December 1994 lowered the relative price of Mexican goods and services and moved Mexico's bilateral trade balance with the United States from a small deficit to a large surplus.

Source: Data from U.S. Census Bureau and International Monetary Fund.

CASE THREE:
The Macroeconomics of German Unification

In 1990, the Federal Republic of (West) Germany and the (East) German Democratic Republic unified into a single economic and political entity. The act carried dramatic macroeconomic implications, as we'll see at several points over the next few chapters. Table 14.4 highlights a few key macroeconomic variables for Germany and how they were affected by unification and the policies that accompanied it.

Prior to unification, the Federal Republic of Germany ran a surplus on its current account, and the Deutsche mark price of a U.S. dollar stood at e = DM1.88/$1.[24] Fiscal policy exerted little net effect on the macroeconomy as the government budget surplus equaled less than one-half of 1 percent of GDP. With unification in 1990, government spending soared, the Deutsche mark appreciated dramatically against the dollar as well as other currencies, and the interest rate rose.[25] The current-account surplus shrank, and the growth

rate of real GDP accelerated, just as this chapter's model would lead us to expect. The expansionary fiscal policy continued for several years, and the DM price of the dollar remained low. The current account shifted into deficit, reflecting reduced demand for German goods and services. At the same time, the rising interest rate reduced domestic investment in Germany. The combination of these two forces pushed the German economy into recession, and real output actually fell in 1993.

German policy makers' responses included reducing the government budget deficit and lowering the interest rate by pursuing somewhat more expansionary monetary policies (the subject of Chapter Fifteen). By 1994, real GDP was growing again, but the Deutsche mark hadn't reversed its appreciation relative to the dollar, and the German current account remained in deficit.

Table 14.4 **German Macroeconomic Indicators, 1989–1994[a]**

Year	Current-Account Balance (Billions $)	Structural Fiscal Balance (Percent of GDP)[b]	e = DM/$	Percent Change in Real GDP	Interest Rate (Percent)
1989	$57.3	−0.4%	1.88	3.6%	6.6%
1990	46.9	−3.5	1.62	5.7	8.0
1991	−19.2	−5.3	1.66	2.9	8.9
1992	−21.0	−3.6	1.56	2.2	9.4
1993	−14.8	−2.0	1.65	−1.1	7.4
1994	−22.6	−1.0	1.62	2.3	5.3

[a]Figures through 1990 refer to Federal Republic only.
[b]Government budget surplus (+) or deficit (−) evaluated at potential output and expressed as a percent of GDP.

Source: International Monetary Fund, *World Economic Outlook*; *Economic Report of the President*.

Summary

The current account's effect on equilibrium in the market for goods and services is one avenue by which international trade affects the performance of the domestic economy. But the relationship between income and the current account is more complex than is often recognized. Changes in the current account do affect national income, but changes in national income affect both the current account and the incomes of trading-partner

---

24 Since we focus in this case on the German economy, we report the exchange rate, e, as the German (domestic) currency price of U.S. (foreign) currency, or the Deutsche mark price of a dollar.

25 We'll see in later chapters that there are reasons to expect a currency appreciation and a rise in the interest rate to follow expansionary fiscal policy.

countries. Other important considerations determining equilibrium in the market for goods and services include fiscal policy, the relative prices of domestic and foreign goods or real exchange rate, and interest rates.

Looking Ahead

In section 14.5.3, we saw that for every possible interest rate there exists a different equilibrium income. This implies that to determine actual equilibrium income, we need to know the interest rate. This chapter focused solely on the market for goods and services, so we don't yet have a way to determine the interest rate. In Chapter Fifteen, we'll combine the market for goods and services developed here with the markets for money and foreign exchange. Using a general-equilibrium approach with all three markets will allow us to examine income, the interest rate, and the balance of payments (or the exchange rate) simultaneously.

Key Terms

gross national product (GNP)

gross domestic product (GDP)

national income

consumption expenditure (C)

investment expenditure (I)

government purchases (G)

export expenditures (X)

import expenditures (imp)

marginal propensity to consume (mpc)

real exchange rate

marginal propensity to import (mpi)

fiscal policy

spending multiplier

round-by-round effect

expenditure-switching policy

competitive devaluation

beggar-thy-neighbor policy

J curve

"twin deficits"

IS curve

Problems and Questions for Review

1. Beginning from a position of equilibrium in the market for goods and services and in the current account, government expenditure rises by 100. The marginal propensity to consume is 0.6, and the marginal propensity to import is 0.1. *Ignoring the effects on other countries,* by how much will equilibrium GDP change? What happens to exports? To imports? To the current account?

2. Between 1992 and 1998, the U.S. government budget moved from a large deficit to a small surplus, and the current-account deficit grew. What do you think happened to the relationship between saving and investment in the United States over the same period? Explain.

3. Assume that the United States and Japan are the only countries in the world. Beginning from a position of equilibrium in the U.S. and Japanese markets for goods and services, suppose Japan increases government spending by 1,000.
    a. If the Japanese marginal propensity to consume equals 0.7 and the Japanese marginal propensity to import equals 0.2, what will happen to Japanese income (Y^J) as a result of the fiscal expansion?
    b. What will happen to U.S. exports of goods and services because of the Japanese fiscal expansion?
    c. Assume that the U.S. marginal propensity to consume is 0.9 and the U.S. marginal propensity to import is 0.1. What will happen to U.S. income (Y^{US}) as a result of the Japanese fiscal expansion?
    d. What is the net effect of the Japanese fiscal policy on the U.S. current-account balance?
    e. Illustrate the U.S. results of the Japanese policy. (Don't worry about the numerical precision of your graph; just illustrate the qualitative effects.)

4. Suppose the government institutes a tax cut. What would be the effects on equilibrium income and the current-account balance?

5. State how you would expect each of the following groups to feel about a real depreciation of the U.S. dollar. Briefly explain your reasoning.
    a. Boeing (one of the largest U.S. exporters)
    b. The United Auto Workers Union
    c. The owner of a small U.S. shop that sells foreign-made handicrafts
    d. A dedicated consumer of fine French wines

6. Explain: "Other things equal, a high marginal propensity to import reduces the macroeconomic impact of fiscal policy."
7. Explain how the fact that one country's imports constitute its trading partners' exports can lead to international business cycles; that is, to situations in which trading partners experience simultaneous economic booms or simultaneous recessions.
8. Suppose an auto producer obtains all its components in Britain, with their costs denominated in pounds. The firm sells most of its cars in the euro zone of Europe. How would a 20 percent appreciation of the pound against the euro affect the firm?

References and Selected Readings

Baxter, M. "International Trade and Business Cycles." In *Handbook of International Economics,* Vol. 3, edited by G. M. Grossman and K. Rogoff, 1801–1864. Amsterdam: North-Holland, 1995.
Survey of research on the relationship between international trade activity and macroeconomic cycles; intermediate and advanced.

Boskin, Michael J. "Economic Measurement: Progress and Challenges." *American Economic Review Papers and Proceedings* 90 (May 2000): 247–252.
Accessible overview of issues in measuring countries' GDP and trade.

Obstfeld, M., and K. Rogoff. "The Intertemporal Approach to the Current Account." In *Handbook of International Economics,* Vol. 3, edited by G. M. Grossman and K. Rogoff, 1731–1800. Amsterdam: North-Holland, 1995.
Survey of research on the current account from the perspective of intertemporal trade; advanced.

Obstfeld, Maurice, and Kenneth Rogoff. *Foundations of International Macroeconomics.* Cambridge, Mass.: MIT Press, 1996.
Advanced textbook on international macroeconomics.

Pollard, Patricia S., and Cletus C. Coughlin. "Going Down: The Asian Crisis and U.S. Exports." Federal Reserve Bank of St. Louis, *Review* 81 (March/April 1999): 33–46.
Accessible overview of how the early stages of the Asian financial crisis affected U.S. exports.

U.S. Trade Deficit Review Commission. *The U.S. Trade Deficit: Causes, Consequences, and Recommendations for Action.* Washington, D.C: U.S. Trade Deficit Review Commission, 2000.
Report of blue-ribbon panel on the trade deficit; available at www.ustdrc.gov.

CHAPTER FIFTEEN

Money, the Banking System, and Foreign Exchange

15.1 Introduction

This chapter constructs the second and third building blocks of our model of an open macroeconomy: the markets for money and foreign exchange. Chapter Fourteen explored the effect of openness on the market for goods and services. We saw that an economy that engages in international trade has an additional source of demand for its output (exports) and an additional leakage of domestic expenditure out of the domestic economy (imports). The current account, or the difference between the value of goods and services exports and the value of goods and services imports, provides one avenue through which the exchange rate and events in trading-partner economies affect the domestic economy.

An economy's openness also affects its money market, but in a more subtle way than it does the market for goods and services. At first glance the money market in an open economy appears identical to that in a closed one, which you may remember from introductory economics or other courses in macroeconomics. Later in the chapter, we'll see that the effect of openness on the money market, though subtle, is perhaps the most important key to understanding policy options in the world macroeconomy.

Of course, the most obvious effect of openness on the macroeconomy involves the introduction of a foreign exchange market. We examined the essentials of the foreign exchange market in an asset-oriented demand/supply framework in Chapter Twelve and related it to the balance-of-payments accounts in Chapter Thirteen. Later in this chapter, we'll translate our findings from those chapters into a form more convenient for combining with the market for goods and services from Chapter Fourteen.

15.2 Money

15.2.1 What's Money?

As a first important step in studying money's role in the world macroeconomy, we must recall economists' definition of money, which differs somewhat from the popular usage. To an economist, **money** is an asset that its owner can use directly as a means of payment. Currency (coins and paper notes in various denominations) held by the public and checkable deposits, or deposits on which checks can be written, constitute a country's money stock.[1] Either form of money, currency or checks, can be used directly (that is, without an intermediate exchange) to pay for goods and services.

---

1 Traveler's checks also are included. The large time deposits transacted in the foreign exchange market *don't* constitute part of a country's money stock. Be careful not to confuse the foreign exchange market with the money market.

Nonmoney assets, such as stocks, bonds, real estate, certificates of deposit, and diamonds, also represent purchasing power to their owners, but they typically can't be used directly as a means of payment. If an owner of shares of Microsoft stock, a U.S. Treasury bond, or a diamond ring decides to use that asset's purchasing power to buy a new car, the transaction requires two steps, or exchanges. First, the individual must find someone to buy the asset; this involves exchanging the asset for money. Second, the individual uses the money obtained in the first step to buy the car. Only an unlikely coincidence would find two individuals directly exchanging Microsoft stock for a car. Such **barter** exchanges—transactions that don't use money as an intermediate step—are rare, because they require a *double coincidence of wants.* The owner of Microsoft stock may find it difficult to locate an individual who both has the desired type of car for sale and wants to buy Microsoft stock. Money eliminates the need for this coincidence by allowing monetary exchange to separate the car-stock transaction into two pieces.

Note that the economist's definition of money is narrower than the popular one, which identifies money with purchasing power, income, or wealth. A statement such as, "I want to take a vacation, but I don't have enough money," usually means that the individual has chosen not to spend a portion of his or her limited income or purchasing power on a vacation. The individual might have $5,000 in his or her checking account (more than enough money for a vacation, by the economist's definition) but have higher-priority uses for it. The shortage, then, isn't really one of *money* but one of *purchasing power* or *income.* Another way to view the distinction between money and income is to realize that a shortage of money, by the economist's definition, rarely is a problem. As long as an individual owns some nonmoney assets, he or she can obtain more money simply by selling a nonmoney asset. In discussing the market for money, we must keep in mind the distinction between money and purchasing power or income.

Money serves its purpose primarily because individuals believe it will continue to do so. A music store owner doesn't hesitate to accept a $20 bill in payment for a compact disk, because the owner believes that he or she, in turn, can use the $20 to buy some other good or service. It's this faith in money's acceptability as a means of payment—rather than any intrinsic value of the paper itself—that allows it to facilitate transactions effectively. Historically many curious items have functioned as money, including beads, seashells, beer, and cigarettes. The specific physical form of money is relatively unimportant as long as it is commonly accepted as payment.[2]

We denote a country's **nominal money stock,** or the money stock measured in current dollars, as M. The term *stock* denotes the quantity of dollars existing *at a point in time* in the same way the term *housing stock* refers to the number of houses that exist at a given time.[3] Table 15.1 reports the U.S. nominal money stock from 1960 through 2000. The reported measure, called *M1,* includes currency and checkable deposits as well as minor items such as traveler's checks. The government also reports several broader measures of money, but for our purposes M1 will suffice. U.S. M1 has increased by a factor of about 8 since 1960; but the annual rate of change in the money stock has been erratic, ranging from a decline of 4 percent in 1996 to an increase of 17 percent in 1986.

Table 15.1 **U.S. Nominal and Real Money Stocks (M1), 1960–2000**

Year	M1 (Billions $)	M1/P (Billions 1992 $)	Year	M1 (Billions $)	M1/P (Billions 1992 $)
1960	$140.7	$604.7	1985	$ 619.9	$ 789.4
1965	167.8	672.2	1990	825.8	882.3
1970	214.4	703.4	1995	1,129.0	1,047.7
1975	287.5	683.1	2000	1,088.1	n.a.
1980	408.9	677.8			

Source: Data from Board of Governors of the Federal Reserve System (updates are available at www.federalreserve.gov).

---

2 It's helpful if money is durable and easily measured and transported, conditions satisfied by paper currency.

3 Recall that the alternative type of measure is a *flow,* which refers to a quantity (such as GDP) per unit of time.

Before going on to discuss money demand, we'll make one adjustment. Because economists traditionally analyze money demand in real rather than nominal terms, it's convenient to translate the money stock into real terms as well. As always, we can accomplish this translation easily by dividing the nominal money stock by a price index. The **real money stock** at any time equals the nominal money stock, M, divided by a price index, here the GDP deflator, P:

$$\text{Real money stock} = \text{Nominal money stock/Price index} = M/P \qquad \textbf{[15.1]}$$

The real money stock is measured in constant dollars or at the price level in effect during the base year on which the price index is calculated. Over periods of rising prices, the nominal money stock grows faster than the real money stock. During periods of falling prices, the real money stock grows faster than the nominal money stock. Table 15.1 also reports the U.S. real money stock for 1960–2000. Because prices rose each year, the nominal money stock exceeds the real money stock for each year after the base year—here 1992—and the real money stock stated in 1992 dollars exceeds the nominal money stock for each year before 1992. *(Verify these relationships in Table 15.1.)*

15.2.2 The Demand for Money

Money is defined as a group of assets that can be used directly to make purchases, so individuals choose to hold a portion of their total wealth in the form of money primarily for its convenience in making transactions. The demand for money reflects the quantity of currency and checkable deposits the public wants to hold to make purchases.[4] In 2000, money holdings in the United States averaged over $4,000 per person (including children), with almost $1,900 per person in the form of currency.[5]

Studies of individuals' money-demand behavior suggest that they care primarily about how many goods and services they can buy with their money balances. In other words, individuals don't choose the number of *dollars* to hold in the form of money but the amount of *purchasing power* over goods and services to hold in that form. This explains why economists usually formulate their models of money demand in terms of **real money balances,** or nominal money balances divided by the price level. These models recognize that if the price level in the economy suddenly doubled while nothing else changed, individuals would choose to double the number of dollars held in money balances, to maintain the purchasing power of their money balances.[6]

If individuals choose to hold money for its transactional convenience, the quantity of money held should reflect the volume of transactions. We can incorporate this relationship into our model by assuming that the demand for real money balances depends on real income, Q.[7] When real income is high, individuals undertake a large number of transactions and therefore demand a large quantity of real money balances. Low levels of real income, on the other hand, are associated with lower volumes of transactions and correspondingly lower real money balances. Letting L represent the demand for real money balances, we can express the positive relationship between real income and money demand as $L(\overset{+}{Q})$.

If money provides convenience for making transactions, why don't individuals choose to hold all their assets in this form? Because an individual holding money incurs a cost: the forgone interest the individual could have earned on other assets, such as bonds. Generally, money balances earn no interest, although finan-

---

4 This discussion concentrates on the transactions demand for money, that is, the demand for money resulting from its convenience as a means of payment. Other reasons suggested for holding money include precautionary and speculative motives. Standard macroeconomics texts discuss these at length; including them here would add little to the discussion. Empirically it's difficult to separate money held for the various purposes.

5 In fact, no one really knows the location of a large portion of the U.S. currency in circulation. Experts think that much of the currency facilitates illegal transactions (for example, the drug trade) and circulates in foreign countries that lack reliable domestic currencies.

6 If a portion of the goods and services that individuals purchase is imported, real money balances are more appropriately measured as nominal balances divided by a price level that's a weighted average of the domestic and foreign price levels, with the weights reflecting the shares of domestic goods and services and imports in total spending. Nonetheless, the real money stock typically is reported as the nominal money stock divided by the domestic price level.

7 Real income, Q, equals nominal income or GDP divided by the price level: $Q \equiv Y/P$.

cial innovations such as NOW accounts partially relaxed this rule.[8] Even though some forms of money, such as NOW and other interest-bearing checking accounts, do earn interest, the rates paid remain lower than those on nonmoney assets such as bonds. Therefore, the differential between the interest paid on NOW accounts and the interest paid on bonds still represents an **opportunity cost of holding money.**

When the interest rate is high, the opportunity cost of holding money assets also is high, and individuals choose to hold a smaller fraction of their assets in money; in other words, they demand a relatively small quantity of money. At a lower interest rate, the opportunity cost of holding money is smaller and the quantity demanded of money is higher. We can combine the negative relationship between money demand and the interest rate with the earlier result for income and summarize the two as $L(\overset{+}{Q}, \overset{-}{i})$.

Figure 15.1 depicts the relationship among the quantity of real money balances, the interest rate, and income. We measure the interest rate, which represents the opportunity cost of holding money, on the vertical axis and the quantity of real money balances on the horizontal one. The downward-sloping demand curve for money shows the negative relationship between the interest rate and the quantity demanded of money. A single money-demand curve assumes a fixed level of real income, for example, Q_0. Changes in real income shift the money-demand curve, just as a change in income shifts the demand curve for other goods. An increase in real income to $Q_1 > Q_0$ shifts the money-demand curve to the right, because at any given interest rate individuals demand a larger quantity of money than before. The higher real income is associated with a desire to undertake more economic transactions; this makes it worthwhile to forgo interest on more funds in order to have money for convenience in making those additional transactions.

Figure 15.1 The Demand for Real Money Balances Depends Negatively on the Interest Rate and Positively on Real Income

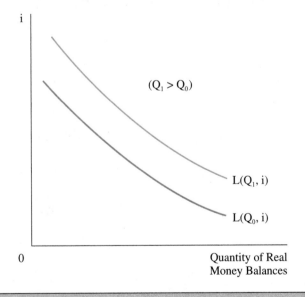

The negative slope of each demand curve (drawn for a fixed level of income) represents the negative relationship between the interest rate and the quantity demanded of real money balances. Changes in income shift the demand curve for real money balances. Here a rise in income from Q_0 to Q_1 shifts the demand curve to the right.

---

8 NOW accounts are *negotiable orders of withdrawal*, basically interest-paying checking accounts. The government's measure of M1 includes such accounts, since they're checkable deposits. The holder of a NOW account does earn interest, but less than that on alternative assets such as bonds.

15.2.3 Where Does Money Come From, and What Determines How Much There Is?

In a modern economy, the nominal money stock is the outcome of a process involving the central bank (often called a country's *monetary authority*), commercial banks, and the public. While this process seems a bit mysterious at first, it will become clearer if you make sure to keep the definition of money in mind: Money is simply a type of asset, one that can be used directly as a means of payment.

The central bank creates the base for a country's money stock by buying nonmoney assets (in particular, government bonds or foreign exchange) from the public, using checks written by the central bank and drawn on itself.[9] These checks are unique because they *create* money rather than merely *transfer* money from one person to another. When a party other than the central bank writes a check, that check just transfers funds from the person writing the check to the person receiving it, leaving no effect on the total quantity of checkable deposits and, therefore, no effect on the money stock. In contrast, when the central bank buys a bond using one of its special checks, the seller exchanges a nonmoney asset (the bond) for money. The check written by the central bank represents money because the recipient can either (1) cash the check and receive currency, or (2) deposit the check in a checkable bank deposit. In either case, the funds represent an addition to the country's money stock because, by definition, the money stock includes both currency and checkable deposits (see section 15.2.1). To see more concretely how this money-creation process works, it helps to look at the balance sheets for the central bank and for the country's commercial banks. These balance sheets are often called "T accounts," for a reason that will become obvious when we examine them.

The Central-Bank Balance Sheet

Any organization's balance sheet records the assets owned by the organization as well as its liabilities, or what the organization owes to others. Balance sheets are governed by the principles of double-entry bookkeeping, which we encountered already in the balance-of-payments accounts. Traditionally, assets appear on the left side of a balance sheet and liabilities on the right, giving the balance sheet a structure reminiscent of the letter *T*. Table 15.2 provides a simplified balance sheet for country A's central bank, Alphabank. We can call it the Stage I balance sheet because it presents the initial situation from which we'll later want to initiate some changes.

On the asset side, Alphabank owns two main types of assets. The first consists of foreign exchange reserves—the stocks of foreign currencies the central bank holds in case it decides to intervene in the foreign exchange market. We assume that Alphabank holds foreign currencies in an amount with a domestic-currency value of $1,000.[10] The second type of assets is domestic ones. This category can include many different items, but for our purposes the most important is domestic government bonds. We assume that Alphabank holds $2,500 in such bonds, the accumulation of the bank's earlier bond purchases. Alphabank's total assets equal $3,500, or the $1,000 of foreign exchange reserves plus the $2,500 of domestic government bonds.

Table 15.2 **Central-Bank Balance Sheet for Alphabank (Stage I)**

Assets		Liabilities	
Foreign exchange reserves (FXR)	$1,000	Commercial banks' deposits in Alphabank	$ 500
Domestic government bonds (GB)	$2,500	Currency held by the public	$2,000

---

9 It's important to distinguish between (1) issuance of a new government bond that may be sold to the public and (2) the central bank's purchase of an outstanding (previously issued) bond from the public. Bonds are just IOUs, so issuance of a new government bond constitutes a loan from the bond purchaser to the government. In the United States, the Department of the Treasury handles this type of transaction. The central bank (the Federal Reserve in the United States) doesn't issue new bonds (that is, borrow from the public); rather, it purchases bonds from the public that the public had purchased earlier from the Treasury. In so doing, the central bank exchanges monetary for nonmonetary assets, thereby "creating money."

10 Just as in the balance-of-payments accounts, the foreign-currency value of foreign exchange reserves is multiplied by the exchange rate to record the reserves' value in domestic-currency units.

Central banks also have two main types of liabilities. First, commercial banks hold deposits at the central bank, much as individuals and firms hold deposits at commercial banks. In fact, a central bank often is referred to as a "bank for banks." The commercial banks' deposits at the central bank belong to their commercial bank owners and can be withdrawn; therefore, from the central bank's perspective, they're liabilities. In our Table 15.2 example, these liabilities equal $500. Currency held by the public, $2,000 in our example, also appears as a central bank liability.[11] In our example, Alphabank's total liabilities equal $2,500, or $500 in commercial bank deposits plus $2,000 in publicly held currency.

The difference between an organization's total assets and its total liabilities equals its net worth. For our purposes, the central bank's net worth isn't important, so we can simply ignore it in our example in Table 15.2. The balance sheet is a double-entry bookkeeping system, so any time assets change, liabilities must change by the same amount. Suppose the central bank buys an asset, either a domestic government bond or some foreign exchange. The bank pays for its purchase either with a check or with currency. If it pays by check, the seller of the asset will deposit the central bank's check in a commercial bank, after which the commercial bank will deposit the check in its own account at the central bank. Therefore, the first category of Alphabank's liabilities—commercial banks' deposits—rise by the amount of the asset purchase. If Alphabank pays instead with currency, then currency held by the public rises by the amount of the purchase. So any increase in Alphabank's assets is matched by an equal increase in its liabilities. Using the same logic, if Alphabank sells an asset, its liabilities also fall by an equal amount. This happens because the buyer of the asset pays for it either with a check (which causes commercial banks' deposits at the central bank to fall when the check "clears") or by cash (which causes currency held by the public to fall).

The process just described captures the key steps in how the central bank increases or decreases the country's money stock. When the central bank expands its assets by buying either domestic government bonds or foreign exchange, its liabilities also expand. Those liabilities consist of commercial banks' deposits at the central bank and currency held by the public. We already know that currency held by the public is one of the two components of the money stock; the other component is checkable deposits. So our next job is to discover the relationship between commercial banks' deposits at the central bank, which appear as a liability in the central bank's balance sheet, and the amount of checkable deposits in the economy. To do this, we need another balance sheet—this time that of commercial banks.

The Commercial-Bank Balance Sheet

Each commercial bank, like any other firm or organization, has its own balance sheet. However, we're interested in the macroeconomy and, in particular, in the banking system's role in determining the size of country's money stock. We aren't interested in the performance of individual banks. Therefore, rather than looking at a single commercial bank's balance sheet, we examine in Table 15.3 the "consolidated" balance sheet of all commercial banks as a group. Again, assets appear on the left side and liabilities on the right side of the T.

Commercial banks hold many types of assets. We can focus on just three. First, consider commercial banks' reserves (not to be confused with the central bank's *foreign exchange* reserves). Modern economies operate under a **fractional reserve banking system.** Under such a system, banks can lend funds from the deposits

Table 15.3 **Consolidated Balance Sheet for Country A's Commercial Banks (Stage I)**

Assets		Liabilities	
Reserves	$ 500	Deposits	$5,000
Loans	$4,500	Borrowing	$1,000
Other assets	$1,500	Net worth	$ 500

11 This seems odd in a modern banking system, but it made sense for the historical period when banks developed their accounting conventions. At the time, currency was "backed" by gold or silver, which meant that if someone took paper currency to the central bank and demanded gold or silver in exchange, the central bank was required to oblige the request. Therefore, currency was a liability from the viewpoint of the central bank.

they accept, because government regulation requires banks to hold only a fraction (say, 10 percent) of their deposits on hand to cover customers' possible withdrawals.[12] When you deposit $5,000 in a commercial bank, the bank must hold $500 (10 percent of $5,000) in reserves in case you want to make a withdrawal.[13] The bank holds these reserves in a deposit at the central bank, and they are an asset from the commercial bank's perspective. Note in Table 15.2 that they're also a liability from the central bank's point of view.

The second category of commercial bank assets is loans. Once the bank satisfies its reserve requirement, it can loan out the remainder of the funds you deposited. These loans ($4,500 in Table 15.3) are also a bank asset, because they represent something that the borrowers owe to the bank. Commercial banks earn most of their revenue from making loans on which they charge interest. The third asset category—other assets—can include many different items. Banks may own office buildings, real estate, government bonds, or (in some countries) corporate stock. We assume in the example that commercial banks own $1,500 worth of such assets.

Commercial bank liabilities come in two main types. Customers' deposits (here, $5,000) are liabilities from the banks' perspective (although assets from the customers') because customers own the deposits and can withdraw them. Commercial banks may also owe other commercial banks or the central bank if they've borrowed funds; our example assumes that banks have borrowed $1,000.

The net worth of country A's commercial banks (here, $500) just equals the value of their total assets ($6,500) minus the value of their total liabilities ($6,000). Net worth must be positive or the banking system is insolvent; that is, if net worth were negative, banks couldn't pay off what they owe to depositors and other creditors. In fact, international banking standards followed by most industrial economies require net worth equal to at least 8 percent of assets. The other requirement that commercial banks' balance sheet must meet is that banks' reserves must satisfy the government's reserve requirement, which we assumed to be 10 percent. Also, banks tend not to hold more reserves than necessary because doing so involves forgoing making loans, which, again, provide the primary source of banks' revenues. In Table 15.3, banks have made as many loans as they can. They hold $500 in reserves, which equals the required 10 percent of their $5,000 in deposits.

Changing the Money Stock by Buying or Selling Government Bonds

Now we can use the central- and commercial-bank Stage I balance sheets to see exactly how and by how much a central bank asset purchase or sale changes the country's money stock. Suppose, beginning from the Stage I situation represented in Tables 15.2 and 15.3, that Alphabank buys a $1,000 government bond from an individual using one of its special checks. The bond seller exchanges a $1,000 nonmoney asset (the bond) for $1,000 of money. The $1,000 Alphabank check represents money because the recipient can either cash the check at his or her commercial bank and receive $1,000 in currency (which is money) or deposit the check in a checkable bank deposit (which is money). To take the empirically more important case, let's assume the latter. The bond seller deposits the $1,000 Alphabank check in his or her commercial bank. That bank, in turn, sends the check to Alphabank, which credits the commercial bank's account for $1,000.

What's happened in our balance sheets? In Table 15.4's Stage II balance sheets, Alphabank's holdings of domestic government bonds have risen by $1,000, as have Alphabank's liabilities in the form of commercial banks' deposits there. In Table 15.4's commercial bank balance sheet, deposits have risen by $1,000. Reserves also have risen by $1,000 because the commercial bank sent Alphabank's check back to the central bank and the check was credited to the commercial bank's account. What's happened to the money stock? The amount of currency held by the public ($2,000) hasn't changed, and checkable deposits have risen by $1,000; so thus far, the central bank's purchase of a government bond has increased the country's money stock by the amount of the bond purchase, or $1,000.

However, Alphabank's purchase of a $1,000 bond from the public actually increases the money stock by considerably more than this initial $1,000. The additional money-stock expansion happens because of the fractional-reserve banking system. When the seller of the government bond deposits the $1,000 Alphabank check in a commercial bank, the bank need hold only $100 (10 percent of $1,000) in reserves in case depositors want

---

12 Banks would choose to hold some reserves even without government regulation, because a bank that lent out all its deposits and couldn't meet its depositors' requests for withdrawals wouldn't stay in business very long.

13 Unfortunately, both the funds banks hold to cover withdrawals and the central bank's stock of foreign currencies are called "reserves." To minimize confusion, we'll refer to the foreign currencies as *foreign exchange,* or *international, reserves.*

Table 15.4 **Balance Sheets for Alphabank and for Commercial Banks (Stage II)**			
Alphabank's Assets		**Alphabank's Liabilities**	
Foreign exchange reserves (FXR)	$1,000	Commercial banks' deposits in Alphabank	$ 500
			+$1,000
Domestic government bonds (GB)	$2,500	Currency held by the public	$2,000
	+$1,000		
Commercial Banks' Assets		**Commercial Banks' Liabilities**	
Reserves	$ 500	Deposits	$5,000
	+$1,000		+$1,000
Loans	$4,500	Borrowing	$1,000
Other assets	$1,500	Net worth	$ 500

to make a withdrawal. The other way of thinking about the situation is to note that in Table 15.4 commercial banks are now holding $1,500 in reserves and $6,000 in deposits. Only $600 (10 percent of $6,000) in reserves is required for this level of deposits, so the banking system can make more loans. But how many more? The key to answering this question lies in seeing that additional loans made by the banking system increase deposits at commercial banks by the amount of the new loans.

To see why, suppose an individual borrows $900 from the bank to buy a computer. The bank credits the borrower's account with the $900. Once the individual buys the computer, the $900 deposit moves into the computer dealer's bank account as a deposit.[14] The computer dealer's bank must then hold 10 percent of the new $900 deposit, or $90, in reserves and can lend the remaining $810, which in turn ends up as an additional deposit. This "round-by-round" process, called **deposit expansion,** ends when the commercial banking system can no longer make any additional loans because it's required to hold all available funds as reserves. At the end of this process, the money stock will have grown by a multiple (called the **money multiplier**) of Alphabank's original $1,000 purchase of the government bond. The money multiplier, or the relationship between the size of the original central bank purchase and the size of the total change in the money stock, depends on the fraction of deposits banks hold as reserves and on how much money the public chooses to hold in currency rather than in checkable deposits.[15] So the answer to the question, "How many more loans can the commercial banking system make?" is that it can expand loans until the corresponding increase in deposits brings total deposits to the maximum level supportable by the existing amount of reserves. In Table 15.4, the reserves of $1,500 could support up to $15,000 in deposits with our assumed required reserves of 10 percent. In the Stage II balance sheet, commercial banks have $6,000 in deposits; so they can make $9,000 (= $15,000 – $6,000) in new loans. Those new loans will find their way into commercial bank deposits, bringing them up to the allowable $15,000. At that point, commercial banks can't expand loans further. Table 15.5 updates the balance sheets to Stage III in order to take account of the deposit-expansion process.

Stage III is the end of the process. What's happened to country A's money stock as a result of Alphabank's purchase of a $1,000 government bond? Currency held by the public hasn't changed, but checkable deposits have risen by a total of $10,000. This increase has two components: (1) the initial $1,000 increase from the bond seller's deposit of Alphabank's check into a commercial bank, and (2) the secondary $9,000 increase from the deposit-expansion process that the initial increase in commercial banks' reserves made possible.

---

14 Recall that we care what happens at the macroeconomic level, not at particular banks. We're working with commercial banks' consolidated balance sheet, so it doesn't matter if the computer buyer and computer seller bank at different commercial banks.

15 We can write the money multiplier as mm = (c + 1)/(c + d), where c denotes the ratio of currency to deposits held by the public and d the reserve-to-deposit ratio of banks. If we make the simplifying assumption that there's no cash in the economy (that is, that c = 0), then the money multiplier simplifies to mm = 1/d. For a more extensive discussion of the money multiplier and the money creation process, see any intermediate macroeconomics or money and banking text.

Table 15.5 Balance Sheets for Alphabank and for Commercial Banks (Stage III)

Alphabank's Assets		Alphabank's Liabilities	
Foreign exchange reserves (FXR)	$1,000	Commercial banks' deposits in Alphabank	$500
			+$1,000
Domestic government bonds (GB)	$2,500	Currency held by the public	$2,000
	+$1,000		
Commercial Banks' Assets		**Commercial Banks' Liabilities**	
Reserves	$500	Deposits	$5,000
	+$1,000		+$1,000
			+$9,000
Loans	$4,500		
	+$9,000	Borrowing	$1,000
Other assets	$1,500	Net worth	$500

Policies by which the central bank changes the nominal money stock by buying or selling government bonds are called **open market operations.** A central bank purchase of bonds increases the money stock. The same type of policy in reverse, in which case the central bank *sells* government bonds to the public rather than buying them, can decrease the money stock. Open market sales cause bank deposits to shrink as individuals exchange their deposits (money) for bonds (nonmoney assets).

Changing the Money Stock by Buying or Selling Foreign Exchange

The central bank can obtain exactly the same effects on the money stock in another way: It can purchase or sell foreign exchange rather than domestic government bonds.[16] Suppose the quantity supplied of foreign-currency-denominated assets exceeds the quantity demanded in the foreign exchange market. Individuals currently hold foreign exchange in excess of the amount they want to hold in their asset portfolios; they want to exchange the excess foreign-currency assets for domestic-currency ones. The central bank can buy the excess foreign-currency-denominated assets from the public just as it did the government bond in the earlier example. It purchases the assets with its special check. The deposit-expansion process operates again, increasing the money stock by a multiple of the central bank's purchase. In fact, a central bank's purchase of $1,000 of foreign-currency-denominated assets from the public has exactly the same effect on the money stock as did the $1,000 open market purchase of a government bond. *(Beginning from the situation in Tables 15.2 and 15.3, explain the effects of central bank intervention to buy $500 of foreign exchange; show your analysis in tables like Tables 15.4 and 15.5.)*

If the quantity demanded of foreign exchange in the economy exceeds the quantity supplied, the central bank can sell foreign exchange from its international reserves. The effect is identical to that of the central bank's open market sale of government bonds; that is, the money stock falls by the amount of foreign exchange reserves sold times the money multiplier.

Summing Up

The size of a country's money stock is the outcome of the processes just outlined. Because the stock rises whenever the central bank purchases either government bonds or foreign exchange and falls whenever it sells either government bonds or foreign exchange, the size of the money stock at any time is determined by the quantity of government bonds and foreign exchange currently held by the central bank. We've seen, however,

---

16 Other policy options through which the central bank can alter the money stock include changes in the required reserve ratio for banks and changes in the discount rate, or the interest rate at which the central bank lends reserves to commercial banks.

Table 15.6 **Money Stock Expansion and Contraction**	
Central Bank Operation	Effect on Money Stock
Open Market Operations:	
Purchases of government bonds from the public	Rises by mm · ΔGB
Sales of government bonds to the public	Falls by mm · ΔGB
Foreign Exchange Market Intervention:	
Purchases of foreign-currency assets	Rises by mm · ΔFXR
Sales of foreign-currency assets	Falls by mm · ΔFXR

that each purchase or sale has a multiplier effect on the money stock, so the current money stock (M) equals the money multiplier (mm) times the government bonds (GB) and foreign exchange reserves (FXR) held by the central bank:[17]

$$M = mm(GB + FXR) \qquad \text{[15.2]}$$

Table 15.6 summarizes the effects of central bank open market operations and foreign exchange intervention on the domestic money stock. In each case, the change in the central bank's asset holdings changes the money stock in the same direction and by more than the asset purchase or sale.

15.2.4 **Money Market Equilibrium**

Equilibrium in the money market requires that the real money stock, the outcome of the central bank operations just described, equal the quantity of real money balances demanded by the public:

$$M/P = L(\overset{+}{Q}, \overset{-}{i}) \qquad \text{[15.3]}$$

The nominal money stock, M, depends on the actions of the central bank, as we just saw. In the remainder of this chapter, we'll assume that the price level, P, is fixed. (Later chapters will explore the importance of price flexibility.) Other variables, in particular the interest rate and income, must adjust to equate the quantity demanded of money (the right side of Equation 15.3) to the stock of money created by the central bank (the left side of Equation 15.3).

Panel (a) of Figure 15.2 combines the money-demand curves from Figure 15.1 with a vertical money-supply curve that represents the size of the money stock (M_0/P) created by the central bank. If the current level of income in the economy is Q_0, the money market will be in equilibrium only if the interest rate equals i_0, the rate at which the quantity of real money balances individuals want to hold equals the quantity of real money balances the central bank has created.

What would happen at other interest rates? Suppose the interest rate were i_1. Panel (a) suggests that, at that relatively high interest rate, individuals choose to hold little of their wealth in money because of its high opportunity cost. The quantity of money individuals want to hold falls short of the quantity the central bank has created. Individuals try to eliminate their unwanted money balances by buying other assets such as interest-bearing

---

17 With minor adjustments, the term in parentheses in Equation 15.2 represents what's known as *high-powered money,* or the *monetary base.* This is the determinant of the money stock that the central bank can affect directly through its policy choices. The money multiplier depends on the willingness of banks to lend, the central bank's regulated minimum reserve requirement imposed on banks, and the public's currency/deposit ratio (see footnote 15). Together, high-powered money and the money multiplier determine the money stock. In Equation 15.2, foreign exchange reserves are measured in units of domestic currency.

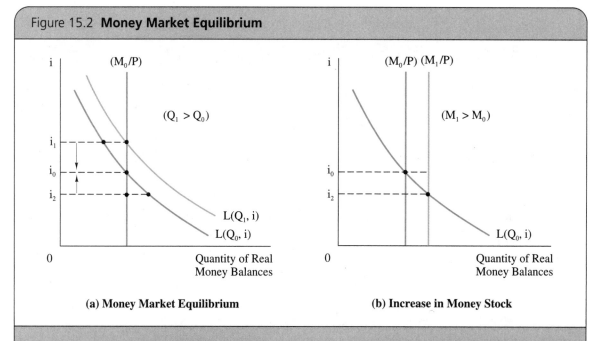

Figure 15.2 **Money Market Equilibrium**

(a) Money Market Equilibrium

(b) Increase in Money Stock

The equilibrium interest rate is the opportunity cost of holding money at which individuals willingly hold the existing stock of real money balances. Increases in income raise the demand for money and increase the interest rate, as in panel (a), where a rise in income from Q_0 to Q_1 raises the interest rate from i_0 to i_1. Increases in the money stock produce a fall in the interest rate, inducing individuals to hold the new higher level of real money balances, as in panel (b), where the nominal money stock rises from M_0 to M_1 and reduces the equilibrium interest rate from i_0 to i_2.

bonds. This process bids up the price of bonds or, equivalently, pushes down the interest rate.[18] Once the rate falls to i_0, individuals in the economy are content to hold (M_0/P) in real money balances, because the opportunity cost of doing so is lower than at i_1.

Suppose the interest rate initially were i_2. At such a low interest rate, individuals want to hold a large portion of their wealth in the form of money—more money than the central bank has created, because money provides convenience for making transactions and at i_2 the opportunity cost of not holding bonds is low. As individuals try to sell bonds to increase their money holdings, the price of bonds falls or (equivalently) the interest rate rises. When the rate reaches i_0, the opportunity cost of holding money has risen sufficiently to make individuals content to hold only (M_0/P) in real money balances.

Changes in income shift the demand for money, as we saw in section 15.2.2. When income rises from Q_0 to Q_1, individuals in the economy undertake more transactions and need more real money balances to do so conveniently. The demand curve shifts to the right, as in Figure 15.2, panel (a). At the old equilibrium interest rate, i_0, individuals now want to hold more than the existing quantity (M_0/P) of real money balances. They try to sell bonds to reach the desired level of money balances and push up the interest rate to i_1 in the process.

18 The simplest form of bond is an IOU promising to pay the owner (lender) the face value (say, $1,000) on a certain future date. Such a bond sells for less than its face value, because the purchaser (lender) must wait until the future date to receive the $1,000, and $1,000 received in the future has a value today of less than $1,000 even if future receipt is certain. The seller of the bond (borrower) willingly pays the difference between the face value and the purchase price to borrow funds over the bond's life. In other words, the seller willingly pays, and the purchaser demands, interest on the loan. When the demand for bonds is high (such as when individuals are holding a larger-than-desired portion of their assets in money), the purchase price of bonds gets bid up. The mirror image of this price increase is the fact that bond sellers need pay only a relatively low rate of interest because individuals are eager to lend (buy bonds). When the demand for bonds falls, so does the purchase price. Sellers must then pay higher rates of interest (that is, accept lower purchase prices for a given face value of a bond).

Table 15.7 **Summary of Money-Market Effects on the Interest Rate**

Variable	Effect on Equilibrium Interest Rate
Income (Q):	
Increase	+
Decrease	−
Nominal Money Stock (M):	
Increase	−
Decrease	+
Price Level (P):	
Increase	+
Decrease	−
Demand for Money (L):	
Exogenous increase	+
Exogenous decrease	−

The demand for money also can shift for other (exogenous) reasons. For example, the widespread availability of automatic teller machines reduces the demand for money by providing easier access to nonmoney assets such as savings accounts. Such an institutional innovation shifts the demand for money to the left and, other things being equal, results in a lower interest rate in the economy.

Panel (b) of Figure 15.2 illustrates the effect of a change in the size of the money stock. If the central bank buys government bonds or foreign-currency assets, the money stock rises from (M_0/P) to (M_1/P). At the old equilibrium interest rate, i_0, the existing money stock now exceeds the quantity of real money balances individuals want to hold given their income, Q_0. To reduce their money holdings, individuals try to purchase bonds, and the interest rate falls to i_2. If the central bank were to cut the money stock by selling government bonds or foreign-currency assets, individuals would respond by trying to sell bonds, and the interest rate would rise. For now, we continue to assume that the price level remains unchanged, but note that a rise in the price level reduces the real money stock, while a decline in the price level raises the real money stock.

Table 15.7 summarizes the key relationships required for money-market equilibrium. An increase in income, a decrease in the nominal money stock, a rise in the price level, or an exogenous increase in money demand raises the equilibrium interest rate. A fall in income, an increase in the nominal money stock, a fall in the price level, or an exogenous decline in money demand lowers the interest rate at which individuals in the economy are content to hold the existing money stock.

To make it easier to combine our insights from the money market with those from the markets for goods and services and foreign exchange, we can summarize the money-market results in an LM curve.

15.2.5 A Concise Graphical Summary: The LM Curve

Panel (a) of Figure 15.3 illustrates one point of equilibrium in the money market, point I. The real money stock equals M_0/P. Real money demand is given by $L(Q_0, i_0)$, because income equals Q_0 and the interest rate equals i_0. Panel (b) marks the combination of income (Q_0, measured on the horizontal axis) and interest rate (i_0, measured on the vertical axis) that corresponds to the equilibrium at point I.

Now suppose income rises to Q_1. Panel (a) shows that at the original interest rate (i_0) and the new, higher level of income (Q_1), the new quantity demanded of money exceeds the unchanged money stock; that is, $M_0/P < L(Q_1, i_0)$. In panel (b), the (Q_1, i_0) point corresponds to a quantity demanded of money that exceeds the money stock. Given this situation, individuals attempt to obtain the additional desired cash balances by selling other assets, particularly bonds. Increased bond sales lower the price of bonds, and a fall in the price of bonds is equivalent to a rise in the interest rate. The interest rate will continue to rise until individuals are content to hold the quantity of money available (M_0/P). Point II represents the new equilibrium, and we mark the corresponding combination of income and interest (Q_1, i_1) in panel (b). The original rise in income required a rise

Figure 15.3 **The LM Curve Represents Equilibrium in the Money Market**

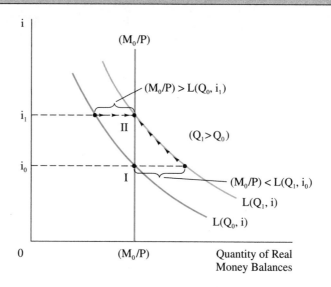

(a) Money Market Equilibrium

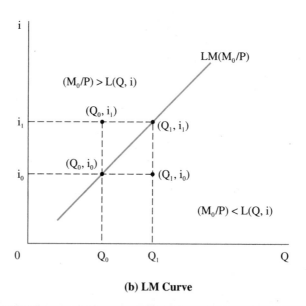

(b) LM Curve

A rise in income from Q_0 to Q_1 increases the demand for money. To reequate quantity demanded with the fixed stock of money, the interest rate must rise. Similarly, a rise in the interest rate lowers the quantity demanded of money. With the stock of money fixed, income must rise to increase the demand for money. Therefore, the interest rate and income combinations consistent with equilibrium in the money market are *positively* related. The curve summarizing this positive relationship between i and Q is called an LM curve, because at each point on it the quantity demanded of money (L) equals the money stock (M/P). To the right of the LM curve, the quantity demanded of money exceeds the money stock; to the left of it, the quantity demanded of money is less than the money stock.

in the interest rate to reequate the quantity demanded of money with the money stock. The rise in income increased the demand for money, and the rise in the interest rate raised the opportunity cost of holding money, causing an offsetting decline in quantity demanded. Note that throughout the process, the stock of money remained at M_0/P.

Beginning again at the original equilibrium, point I, suppose events in the economy cause the interest rate to rise from i_0 to i_1. With income at Q_0, the rise in the interest rate causes the quantity demanded of money to fall below the level of the money stock. In panel (b) of Figure 15.3, the point (Q_0, i_1) corresponds to a situation in which the quantity demanded of money is less than the money stock. The money market can be in equilibrium at an interest rate of i_1 only if income rises to Q_1, raising the demand for money and restoring equilibrium at point II. Again, the money stock doesn't change between points I and II.

The upward-sloping curve in panel (b) of Figure 15.3, called an **LM curve,** shows the various combinations of income and interest at which the money market is in equilibrium. The term *LM curve* refers to the fact that, at every point along the curve, the quantity demanded of money (L) equals the fixed money stock (M/P). At points to the right of the LM curve, the quantity demanded of money exceeds the money stock; at points to the left, the opposite holds. *(Why?)*

When the real money stock changes, the LM curve shifts. Since we assume that the price level is fixed, only a change in the nominal money stock, M, can cause a change in the real money stock. As illustrated in Figure 15.4, increases in the nominal money stock shift the LM curve to the right. In panel (a), the nominal money stock rises to M_1, shifting the money stock line to the right. At income Q_0, equilibrium now requires an interest rate of i_2 at point III. A lower interest rate ($i_2 < i_0$) induces individuals to hold the larger stock of money.

The same argument holds at income Q_1. The interest rate must fall from i_1 to i_3 for the quantity demanded of money to rise. At i_1, the opportunity cost of holding money was too high for the public to willingly hold the new, larger money stock. Panel (b) of Figure 15.4 marks the new combinations of income and interest that result in money market equilibrium given the new money stock. (As a reminder, we label each LM curve according to the real money stock on which it is based.)

15.2.6 **Money in Open versus Closed Economies**

As mentioned in section 15.1, the money market in an open economy at first glance appears identical to that in a closed economy. Money demand depends on domestic income and the interest rate, which must adjust to keep money demand equal to the money stock. The effects of openness enter through the additional mechanism by which the central bank can create or destroy money, that is, purchases or sales of foreign exchange. In fact, we'll see later in the chapter that the nature and extent of a central bank's ability to control the money stock hinge on the nature of the country's international linkages, particularly the exchange rate regime under which it operates. But first we investigate the banking system as a potential source of macroeconomic instability.

15.3 **Banking Crises**

15.3.1 **How Important Are Banking Problems?**

In most countries the banking system gets relatively little attention as long as it works well. However, most countries do, at one time or another, experience banking-sector problems. The aftermath of Asia's severe financial crisis, much of it rooted in the region's banks, has dominated recent headlines; but the International Monetary Fund reports that 130 of its member countries, approximately three-quarters of all IMF members, experienced "significant banking sector problems" between 1980 and 1996. Figure 15.5 locates those countries and reveals that they include all regions of the world economy and developed as well as developing economies.

For reasons we'll examine shortly, banking crises can impose large costs on an economy. To give just one example, when banks fail and become unable to pay back their depositors, governments often step in and either provide the failed banks with resources to continue to function, or directly pay depositors their losses. Several countries' banking crises in recent years have cost the respective governments the equivalent of significant shares of the country's annual GDP. Figure 15.6 provides some examples. Argentina's 1980–1982 crisis ended up costing the Argentine government almost 60 percent of annual GDP. Note the appearance of the U.S. savings and loan crisis at the bottom of Figure 15.6. The cost to the U.S. government came to less than 5 percent of GDP, but the absolute amount was huge—in the neighborhood of $180 billion.

Figure 15.4 Effect of an Increase in the Real Money Stock on the LM Curve

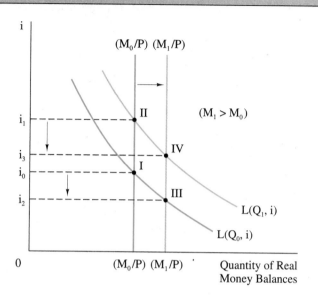

(a) Money Market Equilibrium

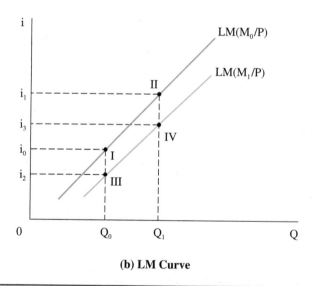

(b) LM Curve

An increase in the real money stock (caused here by an increase in the nominal money stock from M_0 to M_1 with the price level constant) shifts the LM curve to the right. Any given level of income now requires a lower interest rate for money market equilibrium.

Figure 15.5 **Countries Experiencing Banking Sector Problems, 1980–1996**

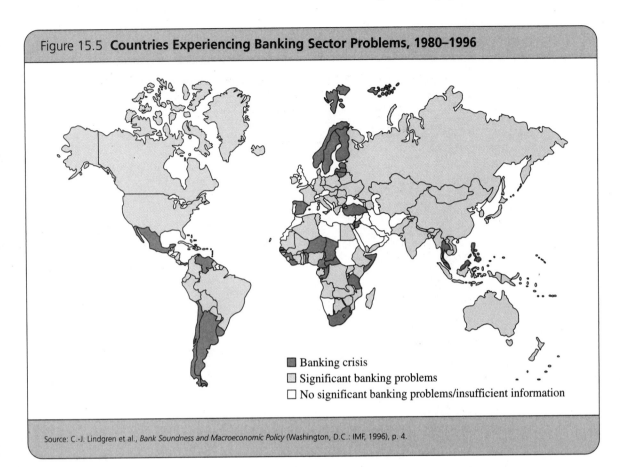

■ Banking crisis
□ Significant banking problems
□ No significant banking problems/insufficient information

Source: C.-J. Lindgren et al., *Bank Soundness and Macroeconomic Policy* (Washington, D.C.: IMF, 1996), p. 4.

15.3.2 **What Does It Mean for a Bank to Be "Unsound"?**

Recall from our discussion of commercial banks' balance sheets that banks' total assets, by definition, equal their total liabilities plus their net worth. A useful way to think about net worth (also called *bank capital*) is as what would be left over for the owners of the bank if its assets were used to pay off all its liabilities. Net worth also represents the funds that the bank's owners or stockholders have at stake.

A bank can be unsound in one of two ways, both serious but one more so than the other. Illiquidity occurs when a bank's assets are sufficient to cover its liabilities, but there is a time-horizon mismatch. Liabilities are due *now;* revenue from the assets isn't available until *later.* For example, in January 1998, South Korean banks announced that they couldn't repay the approximately $20 billion in short-term borrowing that they owed to foreign banks. The creditors postponed repayment (called *rolling over the debt*), hoping to be paid when the economic situation in South Korea improved.

If a situation of short-term illiquidity fails to improve, it can turn into the long-term, often fatal problem of insolvency. This occurs when the value of a bank's assets is insufficient to cover the value of its liabilities. Net worth is negative. The bank must then be "recapitalized" (for example, by merging with a healthy bank), bailed out by the government at taxpayers' expense, or allowed to fail. One of Asia's most famous investment banks—Peregrine Investments Holding, Ltd., of Hong Kong—failed in January 1998. Its assets included large holdings of Indonesian and other Asian "junk" bonds, the values of which had declined sharply along with Asian currencies and stock markets. Peregrine's assets fell below the level of its liabilities, and the bank became insolvent.[19] Several international banks considered a merger with the troubled Peregrine, but a deal never materialized and the bank closed.

---

19 In addition, Peregrine reportedly had about $10 worth of "off balance sheet" exposure to Indonesia for every dollar of "on balance sheet" exposure; the former consisted primarily of foreign-exchange contracts.

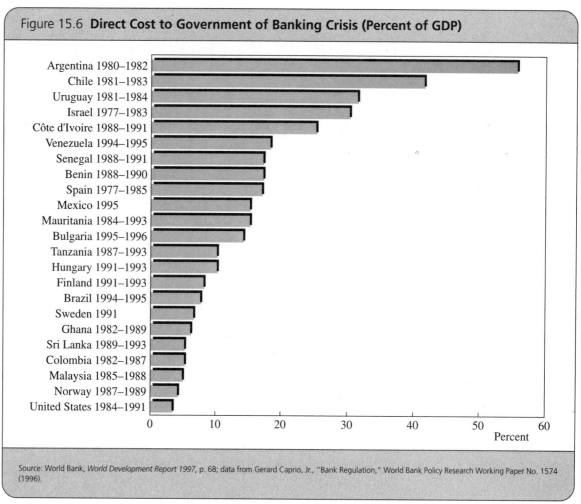

Figure 15.6 **Direct Cost to Government of Banking Crisis (Percent of GDP)**

Source: World Bank, *World Development Report 1997*, p. 68; data from Gerard Caprio, Jr., "Bank Regulation," World Bank Policy Research Working Paper No. 1574 (1996).

15.3.3 What Are Some Recipes for Banking-System Problems?

A Run on an Individual Bank

A bank's health always depends on its depositors' confidence in the value of its assets. After all, the bank uses depositors' funds to buy the assets; depositors' ability to get their funds back hinges on the bank's assets maintaining their value. If a bank's depositors lose confidence in the integrity of its assets, each depositor will want to withdraw his or her funds. But all depositors can't get their funds simultaneously, even from a healthy bank. The reason is that many of the bank's assets can't be sold quickly to pay off depositors. Suppose, for example, that the bank has used its deposits to make a 30-year mortgage loan on a family's new home. If depositors suddenly want to withdraw all their funds, the bank can't simply call the family that bought the new house and tell them that they must repay the entire $250,000 immediately! Moreover, if the bank suddenly tries to sell off large quantities of its assets to meet depositor withdrawals, it may end up having to accept lower prices for those assets, thereby further damaging the bank's health.

In terms of the balance sheet, a sudden run initially causes both the bank's deposits and its reserves to fall by equal amounts. It will have to curtail its loans or sell assets to cover withdrawals and bring reserves back up to the required level. Depending on the severity and duration of the run, the bank may become illiquid or even insolvent. Still, a run on a particular bank shouldn't have a significant effect on the country's money supply, because depositors will move their funds to other banks, so *total* checkable deposits in the consolidated banking system should remain the same.

A bank run does pose dangers, however. It may spread to other banks, with consequences we'll investigate in a minute. One bank's sudden large-scale asset sales may reduce the value of other banks' assets if, for example, all own large quantities of local real estate. Finally, in an economy with only a small number of banks and other financial institutions, a single bank's stoppage of loans may curtail the flow of credit to firms in the economy and slow overall economic activity.

Policy makers can help stop a bank run by promising to lend the bank funds to cover depositors' withdrawals. In the balance sheet, this policy intervention shows up as a rise in the bank's borrowing on the liability side and in reserves on the asset side. These increases offset the decline in deposits on the liability side and in reserves on the asset side caused by the run itself. With prompt intervention to restore depositors' confidence, a basically sound bank is likely to survive the run.

Economy-Wide Bank Runs

When many or all of a country's banks fall victim to a run, the consolidated banking system's total deposits and reserves fall. All banks must curtail their loans or sell other assets to try to cover the withdrawals and bring reserves back up to their required levels. Unlike the case of a run on a single bank, the country's money stock falls unless policy makers act, because the banking system's total deposits fall. If policy makers fail to act and allow the money stock to decline, this can cause a further loss of confidence or trigger a recession.[20] Central bank policy makers can help prevent this by promptly lending banks reserves (often called the central bank's *lender-of-last-resort function*) or conducting open-market purchases to boost reserves.

During 2001, after several years of recession, Argentina's banking system lost about 20 percent of its deposits to slow runs. In early December, the government responded with a ceiling on cash withdrawals of $250 per week per person; but the economy's problems had grown so severe that before Christmas the president resigned amid economic and political chaos.

Bad Loans

Banks are in the business of making loans. This both provides banks themselves a source of income—interest on the loans—and provides firms and consumers in the economy with a source of borrowed funds with which to buy goods and services and to fund investment projects. But a loan's value as an asset to the lending bank depends on the loan's being repaid. When banks make loans that end up "not performing" (banking jargon for not being repaid), the value of the banks' loan assets declines.

If widespread loan nonperformance is a temporary problem, banks become illiquid and unable to make timely payments on their own borrowing. If widespread loan nonperformance is a long-term problem, then banks become insolvent. In November 1997, Hokkaido Takushoku Bank, Japan's tenth largest, failed because of its bad loans. The bank's losses exceeded its net worth, so all of the owners' equity stake in the bank went to pay creditors; Japan's Deposit Insurance Corporation, run by banks themselves rather than the Japanese government, absorbed the rest of the losses.

Estimates of bad loans still on surviving Japanese commercial banks' balance sheets range from $265 billion to $1,900 billion. China's four big state-owned banks hold bad loans estimated at between $240 billion and $600 billion. Most analysts agree that these lingering bad loans, which reduce confidence in the banks, interfere with firms' ability to obtain loans for promising investment projects, and place a huge drain on government budgets, represent the biggest hurdle to full recovery of the Asian economies.

Declines in Value of Nonloan Assets

As we mentioned earlier, banks can hold many types of assets other than loans. The macroeconomic effects of declines in the value of nonloan bank assets are similar to the effect of bad loans discussed earlier. If banks hold corporate stocks in their portfolios, for example, stock market declines reduce the value of the banks' assets.[21] If banks hold long-term bonds in their portfolios, increases in interest rates reduce the market value of those

---

20 We'll see in detail in Chapters Sixteen and Seventeen how and why a contraction of the money supply can reduce a country's GDP.

21 Because of stocks' price volatility, U.S. banking regulators restrict stock ownership by U.S. banks; but most corporate stock in Asia is owned by banks, a fact that contributed to the area's late-1990s banking crisis.

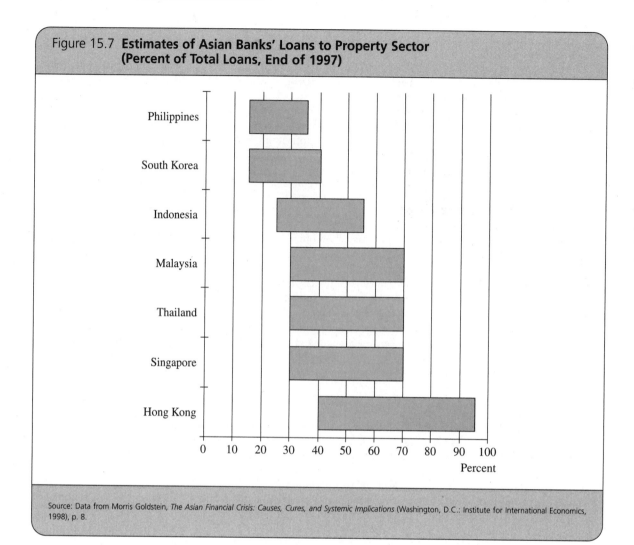

Figure 15.7 **Estimates of Asian Banks' Loans to Property Sector (Percent of Total Loans, End of 1997)**

Source: Data from Morris Goldstein, *The Asian Financial Crisis: Causes, Cures, and Systemic Implications* (Washington, D.C.: Institute for International Economics, 1998), p. 8.

assets by pushing down bond prices. If banks hold inflation-hedge assets such as real estate in their portfolios, reductions in the rate of inflation or increases in interest rates reduce the market value of those assets. All these problems are especially likely if government banking regulators restrict banks' asset purchases to the domestic market, thereby limiting their ability to diversify risk.

Loss of value of banks' nonloan assets contributed heavily to the financial crisis in Asia. It's easy to see why. First, many banks held large shares of their total asset portfolios in a very narrow class of assets, such as local real estate. When banks encountered problems and started to sell assets, their actions caused local real estate prices to drop, further damaging banks' balance sheets. Figure 15.7 reports banks' local real estate holdings as of the end of 1997 for the economies most affected by the Asian financial crisis. Hong Kong property values fell by about 40 percent during 1997–1998. In addition to the countries listed in the figure, the value of commercial real estate in Japan fell by 80 percent between 1991 and 1998, with dramatic consequences for Japanese banks' balance sheets.

As we mentioned earlier, in many Asian economies, banks rather than individuals or other firms own most corporate stock. When stock prices plummeted in 1997 and 1998, so did the value of these bank assets. Figure 15.8 reports the declines in several Asian stock market indices between mid-1997 and mid-1998.

Stock market losses, along with bad loans, caused much of Japan's decade-long banking problems. Accounting rules changed in late 2001 so that banks had to report on their balance sheets their stock-portfolio assets at current market value rather than historical value (that is, the value of the shares at the time they were pur-

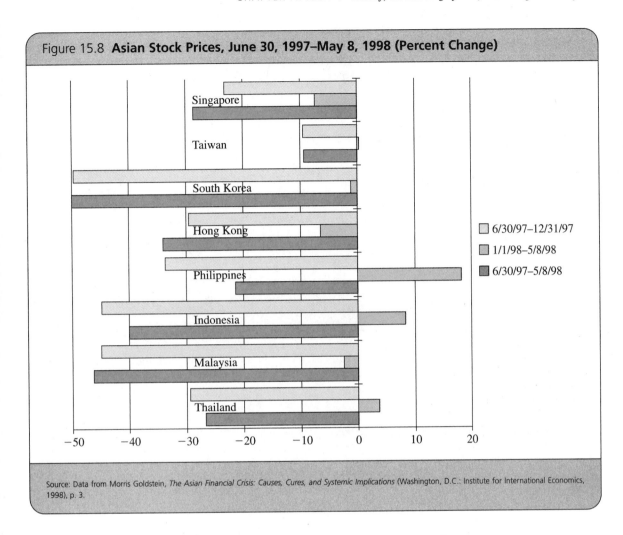

Figure 15.8 **Asian Stock Prices, June 30, 1997–May 8, 1998 (Percent Change)**

Source: Data from Morris Goldstein, *The Asian Financial Crisis: Causes, Cures, and Systemic Implications* (Washington, D.C.: Institute for International Economics, 1998), p. 3.

chased, often before the 1990 stock market collapse). This new "mark-to-market" rule reduced the banks' stock assets, as shown on their balance sheets, by ¥4.7 trillion.

Corruption and Political Favors

Poorly managed and inadequately supervised banks may make loans to insiders or to politicians, spend the banks' income on lavish salaries and perquisites for employees, or undertake overly risky investments. After all, most of the funds that banks spend ultimately belong to someone else—depositors. So bank managers may not be as careful as they would be if all the funds they spent were their own. This is why regulators encourage or require that net worth equal at least 8 percent of a banks' assets. Recall that net worth is what the bank owners have at stake in the operation; it's the maximum amount owners stand to lose if they run the bank unwisely. Regulators want to keep that amount high enough to provide an adequate incentive for bank managers to act prudently with depositors' funds. However, banks in many developing economies, including many in Asia, receive lax supervision and regulation.

When corruption affects a banking system, the economy's most productive firms may have trouble getting loans, which go instead to the politically well connected. This reduces economic output and growth. Taxpayers often bear the cost of bailing out corrupt and politically influential bankers, even in countries without formal deposit insurance programs. Table 15.8 lists countries with formal deposit insurance at the time of the Asian financial crisis; note the absence of the key Asian economies. The Indonesian and South Korean governments did pledge, well into the crisis, to provide deposit insurance. Such moves can avert political instability, since

Table 15.8 Countries with Explicit Deposit Insurance Systems

Africa	Asia	Europe		Middle East	Western Hemisphere
Kenya	Bangladesh	Austria	Italy	Bahrain	Argentina
Nigeria	India	Belgium	Luxembourg	Kuwait	Brazil
Tanzania	Japan	Bulgaria	Netherlands	Lebanon	Canada
Uganda	Marshall Is.	Czech Rep.	Norway	Oman	Chile
	Micronesia	Denmark	Poland		Colombia
	Philippines	Finland	Portugal		Dominican Rep.
	Taiwan	France	Spain		El Salvador
		Germany	Sweden		Mexico
		Greece	Switzerland		Peru
		Hungary	Turkey		Trinidad/Tobago
		Iceland	United Kingdom		United States
		Ireland			Venezuela

Source: Morris Goldstein, *The Asian Financial Crisis: Causes, Cures, and Systemic Implications* (Washington, D.C.: Institute for International Economics, 1998), p. 48.

without such insurance the public can perceive bank bailouts as help for the rich while small savers lose their life savings. Individuals may hesitate to save unless the government guarantees their deposits against loss. But if the government provides such guarantees, they may reduce bankers' incentives to be prudent, since taxpayers will pick up the tab for any losses.

Corruption and banks run on a political rather than an economic basis played important roles in the Asian financial crisis. Bangkok's Bank of Commerce failed in 1996 after making extensive bad loans to politicians, but the government bailed out the bank. Indonesian banks held an estimated $700 million in loans to the former president's son for his "national car" project. No single region, however, has a monopoly on corruption. A Berlin-based organization called Transparency International collects data on the level of government and business corruption in various countries; Figure 15.9 presents some of their findings. Countries near the top of the figure have low levels of corruption, and those near the bottom have high levels.

Foreign-Exchange Problems

Often banks borrow in foreign currency (usually U.S. dollars), sell it for local currency, and then buy assets denominated in the local currency. For example, an Indonesian bank might take out a dollar-denominated loan from a U.S. bank, sell the dollars for rupiah, and use the rupiah to buy a piece of Jakarta real estate. If the domestic currency is devalued or depreciates against the foreign currency (here, the rupiah against the dollar), the bank may not be able to repay the loan because the domestic-currency price of buying the necessary dollars rises. In terms of the banks' balance sheet, the domestic-currency value of liabilities (borrowing) rises.

In 1997, Indonesian banks and other firms had high levels of dollar-denominated liabilities when the Indonesian government suddenly stopped pegging the value of the rupiah to the dollar. Between July 1997 and early 1998 the rupiah's value fell by more than 70 percent relative to the dollar. Indonesia had to appeal to the International Monetary Fund for a bailout to avoid the banks' defaulting on their loans. The Indonesian and South Korean governments both stepped in to guarantee their banks' foreign loans, shifting the foreign exchange risk from banks to the governments. Banks in other Asian countries experienced similar problems as the Thai baht, South Korean won, and Malaysian ringgit all declined dramatically against the dollar beginning in mid-1997, as illustrated in Figure 15.10.

15.3.4 Why Do Banking Problems Spread?

Once one or a few banks encounter problems of the types just discussed, those problems often spread to other banks in the same country and even to those across the region and around the world. This *contagion* happens

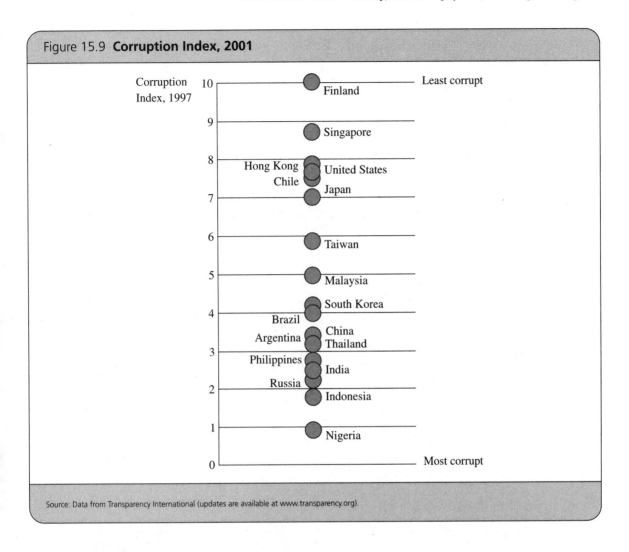

Figure 15.9 **Corruption Index, 2001**

Source: Data from Transparency International (updates are available at www.transparency.org).

in part simply because of the nature of the banking business. All banking systems are based on confidence—depositors' confidence that they can safely place their funds in a bank. Any event that shakes this fundamental confidence can have wide-ranging effects. For example, a run on one weak bank can easily spread to healthy ones, especially if ignored or mishandled by policy makers.

We've seen that one bank's liabilities often comprise another bank's assets. So if Bank A borrows from Bank B and becomes unable to repay its loan, Bank B may be forced into illiquidity or even insolvency.[22] And if Bank B had borrowed from Bank C, then the value of C's assets also decline. In Asia, many banks own stock in other banks; when Hokkaido Takushoku bank failed, for example, its major stockholders included Long-Term Credit Bank of Japan and Nippon Credit Bank.

If one bank suffers a run and has to sell off assets quickly to cover withdrawals and rebuild its reserves, those sales may lower the market value of other banks' similar assets, especially if banks hold regionally or sectorally undiversified portfolios, as is often the case. Asian banks, for example, held large shares of their asset portfolios in local real estate, as we saw in Figure 15.7.

---

22 On the related counterparty or Herstatt risk, see Case Three in Chapter Twelve.

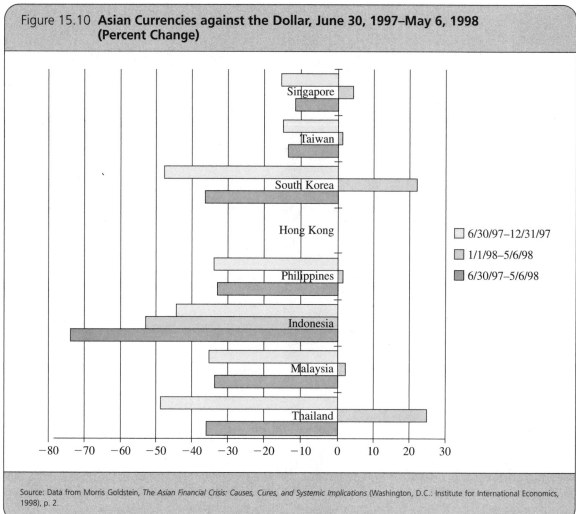

Figure 15.10 **Asian Currencies against the Dollar, June 30, 1997–May 6, 1998 (Percent Change)**

Source: Data from Morris Goldstein, *The Asian Financial Crisis: Causes, Cures, and Systemic Implications* (Washington, D.C.: Institute for International Economics, 1998), p. 2.

Once a banking crisis gets started, fixing the problems become difficult. Foreign banks start to charge banks in the troubled country a premium to borrow because of the increased default risk. Japanese banks, for example, have had to pay a "Japan premium" of up to 1 percent to borrow from foreign banks since the early 1990s. Often, weak banks need to be closed, but doing so during a crisis can further erode the public's confidence. Governments tend to bail out banks, especially big ones judged "too big to fail," and force taxpayers to bear the cost. In the long run, such policies can encourage reckless lending behavior by bankers, who assume that the government will save them if they run into difficulties because of overly risky loans.

15.3.5 **Why Do Banks Matter So Much?**

Why can trouble in a single sector—banking—cause such multifaceted microeconomic and macroeconomic problems? The answer lies in recognizing the many crucial roles that banks play in an economy.

In market-oriented economies, banks allocate capital; that is, they channel savers' funds to firms to finance investment projects. When a banking system works well, the most economically promising firms get funding, and their productive investment projects help the economy grow. When the banking system works poorly, politically connected or bureaucratically targeted firms get funding, and their unproductive projects become a drain on the economy. If the public perceives corruption in the banking system, that perception can discourage saving. To prevent this from happening, the government may have to provide full deposit insurance to reassure potential depositors; but the insurance, in turn, can discourage bankers' prudence by shifting the cost of bank failure from bank owners to taxpayers who typically fund the deposit insurance.

Banks also play a key role in monetary policy. We've seen in this chapter how banks interact with the central bank and the public to determine the size of the money stock. In the next few chapters we'll see how changes in the size of the money stock, in turn, can affect the economy's macroeconomic performance. A banking system with too many bad loans on its books may hesitate to extend additional loans, thereby reducing the central bank's ability to alter the size of the money stock through the deposit-expansion process described in section 15.2.3. Many experts see this problem as the major continuing problem in the Japanese economy. In addition to hampering monetary policy, a weak banking system carries important fiscal implications. Figure 15.6 revealed that government bailouts of failed banks often involve large costs to the government; and this can limit governments' ability to provide needed spending for other sectors of a struggling economy.

Weak banks also constrain policy makers' ability to carry out the macroeconomic policies needed by the rest of the economy. We'll see much more about this in later chapters, but we can already understand the basic reason why. Suppose that macroeconomic conditions were such that a devaluation of the domestic currency seemed the appropriate policy, but the countries' shaky banks hold large amounts of foreign-currency-denominated liabilities and domestic-currency-denominated assets. Policy makers might find themselves unwilling or unable to devalue for fear of pushing the banks into illiquidity or insolvency. Or, suppose a history of high inflation has led to high prices for real estate, an asset whose price tends to rise during expected inflation. Normally, policy makers would pursue policies to reduce inflation. But if banks, already weak, hold large amounts of real estate in their asset portfolios, policy makers may hesitate to reduce inflation, because to do so would likely cause a substantial drop in real estate prices.

Banks play key economic roles in virtually all economies. But their role is more crucial in some than in others because the availability of other, nonbank financial institutions varies widely. In developed industrial economies, for example, there may be a large number of commercial banks, plus investment banks, active government and corporate bond markets, and stock markets in which firms can issue stock to raise funds to finance investment projects. In some developing economies, on the other hand, there may be a mere handful of banks, no bond markets, and no stock markets. The few banks constitute firms' only source of investment funds. Figure 15.11 shows banks' share of financial intermediation for a sample of countries in 1994. *Financial intermediation* refers to channeling saving to investors. In the United States, commercial banks accounted for only 23 percent of this activity. Note that banks dominate financial intermediation in the Asian economies included in the figure, with the exception of South Korea. For Hong Kong, Indonesia, Japan, Malaysia, Singapore, Taiwan, and Thailand, banks' share ranges from 64 to 94 percent. This high level of dependence on the banking system for financial intermediation makes bank soundness even more important than in countries such as the United States. In addition, some of these economies have small numbers of banks, so trouble at even a few can significantly affect firms' ability to obtain investment funds and, therefore, the growth of the overall economy.

Governments in developing economies, including the newly industrializing ones in Asia, sometimes deliberately concentrate financial intermediation in the hands of banks because it allows government policy makers—who supervise, regulate, and sometimes own the banks—to influence the allocation of credit. Favored sectors, including heavy industry such as cars, steel, chemicals, and semiconductors in Asia, get plentiful credit at low interest rates. Firms are discouraged from issuing bonds or raising investment funds through other financial markets that would dilute the government's role. The result can be an economy dependent on large quantities of short-term bank debt, vulnerable to banking crises, with poor information about the true economic prospects of most firms. Open bond and stock markets, on the other hand, facilitate long-term debt, make the economy less dependent on banks, and encourage firms to provide the transparent and reliable disclosure of financial statistics demanded by nonbank lenders.

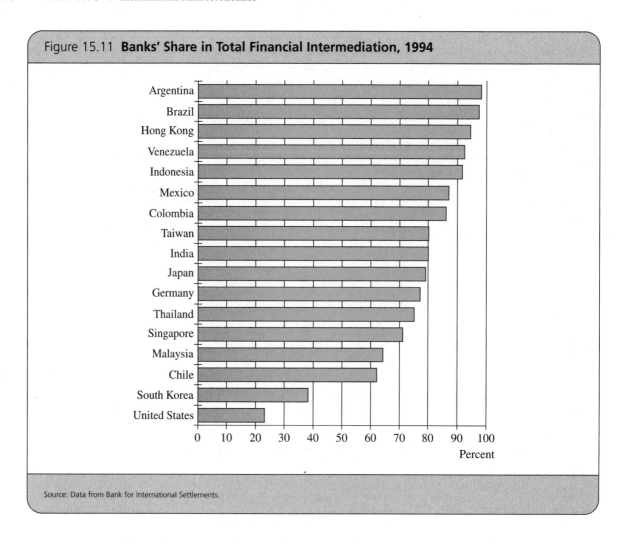

Figure 15.11 **Banks' Share in Total Financial Intermediation, 1994**

Source: Data from Bank for International Settlements.

15.4 **Foreign Exchange**[23]

We've now seen the basic mechanics and roles of the markets for goods and services, money, and foreign exchange. Before we can explore the details of the interaction among these three markets, we need to translate our knowledge of the foreign exchange market and balance of payments into a more convenient form.

Recall from Chapter Thirteen that the balance-of-payments accounts classify autonomous foreign exchange transactions (that is, those arising in the course of day-to-day economic transactions by individuals, firms, and government agencies) into two major subaccounts: the *current account*, composed mainly of purchases and sales of goods and services, and the *capital account*, which reflects international borrowing and lending or purchases and sales of financial assets and direct investment.[24]

When the sum of the current- and capital-account balances equals zero, the quantity demanded of foreign exchange equals the quantity supplied and the balance of payments is in balance. When the sum of the current- and capital-account balances is negative, the quantity demanded of foreign-currency-denominated deposits exceeds the quantity available and the domestic balance of payments is in deficit. A positive sum of the current-

23 The following discussion assumes that the reader is familiar with the material covered in Chapter Twelve; if not, we suggest a review at this point.

24 In the actual government accounts, what we refer to as the *capital account* is the *financial and capital account.*

and capital-account balances corresponds to a quantity of available foreign-currency-denominated deposits that exceeds the quantity demanded and a balance-of-payments surplus.

15.4.1 Equilibrium in the Foreign Exchange Market, Again

Because the current and capital accounts reflect different classes of economic transactions (purchases/sales of goods and services versus borrowing/lending and direct investment), each account responds to different economic variables. The current account depends on domestic and foreign incomes and on the relative prices of domestic and foreign goods and services. A rise in foreign income increases exports and moves the current-account balance toward a surplus. Increased domestic income has the opposite effect by raising imports. A rise in the relative price of domestic goods or real exchange rate $(R \equiv P/eP^*)$ reduces exports and increases imports, moving the current account toward a deficit. (For a review, see sections 14.4 and 14.5.2.) Letting CAB denote the *current-account balance*, a plus sign denote a move toward a surplus, and a minus sign denote a move toward a deficit, we can summarize the effects on the current account:

$$CAB(\overset{+}{Q^*}, \overset{-}{Q}, \overset{-}{R}) \qquad [15.4]$$

The capital account depends on relative interest rates on domestic and foreign assets and on the spot exchange rate, the forward rate, and the expected future spot rate. Other things being equal, a rise in the foreign interest rate, i^*, makes foreign assets more attractive, resulting in a capital outflow and a move toward a deficit in the domestic capital account. A rise in the domestic interest rate, i, has the opposite effect, generating a capital inflow and a capital-account surplus. A rise in the spot exchange rate lowers the expected return on foreign assets and causes a capital inflow, while a rise in the forward rate raises the expected return on foreign assets and produces a capital outflow. Given domestic and foreign interest rates, an expectation that the domestic currency will depreciate in the future makes foreign assets more attractive and produces a capital-account deficit. Letting KAB denote the capital-*account balance* (since K has symbolized capital throughout this book):

$$KAB(\overset{-}{i^*}, \overset{+}{i}, \overset{+}{e}, \overset{-}{e^f}, \overset{-}{e^e}) \qquad [15.5]$$

When the sum of the current- and capital-account balances equals zero, the overall balance of payments is in equilibrium. The market for foreign exchange also is in equilibrium, since the quantity demanded of foreign-currency-denominated assets equals the quantity available:

$$CAB + KAB = 0 \text{ for BOP equilibrium} \qquad [15.6]$$

We can rearrange Equation 15.6 slightly:

$$CAB = -KAB \text{ for BOP equilibrium} \qquad [15.7]$$

Figure 15.12 represents graphically this requirement for equilibrium in the balance of payments or the foreign exchange market by a negatively sloped 45-degree line along which Equation 15.7 holds. At points above and to the right of the line, the balance of payments shows a surplus (BOP > 0) because either (1) the current-account surplus exceeds the capital-account deficit (in area 1), (2) both the current and capital accounts are in surplus (in area 2), or (3) the capital-account surplus exceeds the current-account deficit (in area 3). Below and to the left of the line, the balance of payments is in deficit (BOP < 0). In area 4, the current-account deficit exceeds the capital-account surplus. Area 5 represents combinations at which both the current and capital accounts are in deficit. In area 6, the current-account surplus is too small to offset the deficit in the capital account.

In the remainder of this section, we'll assume that foreign income, relative prices of domestic and foreign goods and services, foreign interest rates, the spot exchange rate, the forward exchange rate, and the expected

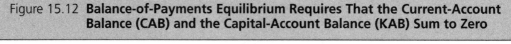

Figure 15.12 Balance-of-Payments Equilibrium Requires That the Current-Account Balance (CAB) and the Capital-Account Balance (KAB) Sum to Zero

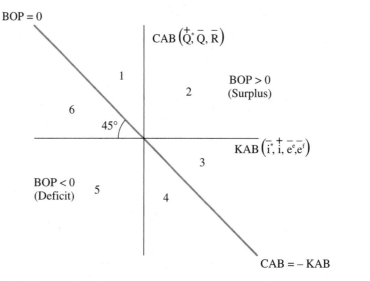

Along the negatively sloped 45-degree line, the balance of payments is in equilibrium. Below and to the left of the line, there is a deficit; above and to the right of the line, the balance of payments is in surplus.

future spot exchange rate are fixed, so we can concentrate on the relationship between domestic income and interest rate that must hold for equilibrium in the foreign exchange market. Figure 15.13, panel (a), repeats Figure 15.12 with these simplifications.

Beginning at any point on the 45-degree line in panel (a) of Figure 15.13 (such as point I), let domestic income rise, say, from Q_0 to Q_1. The fact that point I lies *on* the balance-of-payments line implies that the interest rate equals i_0 such that $CAB(Q_0) = -KAB(i_0)$, as required for balance-of-payments equilibrium. The increase in income moves the current-account balance toward a deficit, because $CAB(Q_1) < CAB(Q_0)$ as Equation 15.4 implies. This is represented graphically as a move downward to point II, at which the balance of payments is in deficit because $CAB(Q_1) < -KAB(i_0) = CAB(Q_0)$. Restoring balance-of-payments equilibrium requires that the interest rate rise by enough to generate an increased capital inflow sufficient to offset the current-account move toward a deficit.[25] We denote the new interest rate as i_1, where $CAB(Q_1) = -KAB(i_1)$. Point III in panel (a) of Figure 15.13 represents this new equilibrium.

Generally, any rise in domestic income moves the CAB toward a deficit; therefore, maintaining foreign exchange market equilibrium requires a rise in the interest rate to generate an offsetting move toward a surplus in the KAB. Similarly, a fall in the interest rate moves the KAB toward a deficit (as individuals want to hold more foreign-currency-denominated assets) and requires a fall in income to reduce imports and move the CAB toward a surplus.

15.4.2 Another Concise Graphical Summary: The BOP Curve

We can summarize the relationship among income, the interest rate, and the balance of payments by stating that the various combinations of domestic income and interest rate that result in foreign exchange market equi-

---

25 We'll see that the magnitude of the rise in interest rates depends on the degree of capital mobility. The more mobile is capital, the smaller the rise in i required to generate a capital inflow sufficient to restore balance-of-payments equilibrium.

Figure 15.13 **Effects of Domestic Income and Interest on the Market for Foreign Exchange**

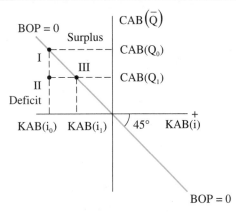

(a) Balance-of-Payments Equilibrium

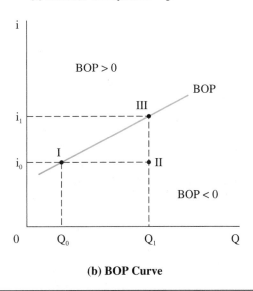

(b) BOP Curve

Starting from a point of balance-of-payments equilibrium, point I, in panel (a), an increase in domestic income from Q_0 to Q_1 moves the current-account balance toward a deficit, resulting in a balance-of-payments deficit at an unchanged interest rate (point II). To cause increased capital inflows with which to offset the decreased current-account surplus, the interest rate must rise from i_0 to i_1 (point III). At point III, the balance of payments is again in equilibrium, but with a smaller current-account surplus and capital-account deficit than at the original equilibrium, point I. The BOP curve in panel (b) represents all the combinations of domestic income and interest rate at which the balance of payments and the foreign exchange market are in equilibrium. Because increases in income move the CAB toward a deficit while increases in interest rates move the KAB toward a surplus, the BOP line is upward sloping. Points I and III in panel (b) refer to those combinations of income and interest resulting in equilibrium points I and III in panel (a).

librium lie along an upward-sloping line as illustrated in panel (b) of Figure 15.13. We label this line a **BOP curve,** because it reflects all combinations of income and interest rates that correspond to *balance-of-p*ayments (and foreign exchange market) equilibrium.

Although the balance of payments is in equilibrium at every point along the BOP curve, each point reflects a different situation for the current and capital accounts. Points on the lower left end of the BOP curve correspond to low levels of income and interest, implying current-account surpluses and capital-account deficits. At the upper right end of the BOP curve, high income results in a current-account deficit and a high interest rate produces an offsetting capital-account surplus. The BOP curve alone can't determine at which point the economy will operate; but once we combine the markets for goods and services, money, and foreign exchange we can determine the point at which all three markets are in equilibrium. First, we need to know what shifts the BOP curve.

The BOP curve is drawn for given values of foreign income (Q^*), relative foreign and domestic prices or real exchange rate (R), foreign interest rate (i^*), forward rate (e^f), and expected exchange rate (e^e). Changes in any of these variables shift the entire BOP curve. At any given level of domestic income, a rise in foreign income or a decline in the relative price of domestic goods moves the CAB toward a surplus. Balance-of-payments equilibrium then requires a lower interest rate to produce an offsetting KAB move toward a deficit. Since BOP equilibrium requires a lower interest rate at any given level of income, the BOP curve shifts to the right. A similar analysis in the other direction implies that a fall in foreign income or a rise in the relative price of domestic goods shifts the BOP curve to the left; each level of domestic income requires a higher interest rate for balance-of-payments equilibrium.

Increases in the foreign interest rate, expected depreciations of the domestic currency, or increases in the forward rate encourage capital outflows, moving the KAB toward a deficit. An offsetting move toward a surplus in the current account requires a fall in domestic income to reduce imports. Because a lower level of domestic income is required at each domestic interest rate, the BOP curve shifts to the left. Figure 15.14 summarizes these results and lists the causes of shifts to the left and to the right of the BOP curve.

Two Special Cases: Capital Mobility and the BOP Curve

We just argued that balance-of-payments equilibrium requires a *positive* relationship between income and the interest rate. A rise in income increases imports and moves the current account toward a deficit, so BOP equilibrium requires a rise in the interest rate to generate an offsetting move toward surplus in the capital account. How big an increase in the interest rate is required depends on how sensitive international capital flows are to changes in interest rates. If asset owners don't respond strongly to changes in international interest rate differ-

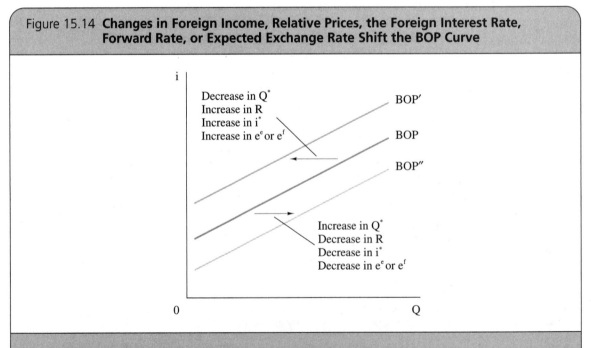

Figure 15.14 **Changes in Foreign Income, Relative Prices, the Foreign Interest Rate, Forward Rate, or Expected Exchange Rate Shift the BOP Curve**

A decrease in Q*, or an increase in R, i*, e^e, or e^f shifts the BOP line to the left. An increase in Q*, or a decrease in R, i*, e^e, or e^f shifts the BOP line to the right.

entials, then a large increase in the interest rate may be necessary to induce a capital inflow sufficient to offset the current-account deficit. In such circumstances, the BOP curve will be steeply upward sloping. *(Why?)* On the other hand, asset owners may be highly sensitive to even small changes in the international pattern of interest rates. If so, only a tiny rise in the domestic interest rate will bring about a capital inflow sufficient to restore balance-of-payments equilibrium. Graphically, this implies that the upward-sloping BOP curve will be relatively flat. *(Why?)* In other words, the slope of the BOP curve indicates the degree of capital mobility, or how sensitive international capital flows are to changes in domestic and foreign interest rates. Low capital mobility implies a steep BOP curve, and high capital mobility a flat one.

We'll see in the next two chapters that the degree of capital mobility exerts an important influence on the macroeconomy and on the effectiveness of macroeconomic policies. To examine the effects of differing degrees of capital mobility, it often proves useful to focus on two extreme cases: that of perfect capital immobility (or zero mobility) and that of perfect mobility.

Under perfect capital *im*mobility, the nonofficial capital account as described in Chapter Thirteen contains no transactions, because both capital inflows and outflows equal zero by definition. No autonomous international borrowing and lending occurs, regardless of the interest rate differentials among countries. With no capital-account transactions, the balance of payments (normally BOP = CAB + KAB) consists solely of the current account (BOP = CAB). If the current account is in deficit, the balance of payments is in deficit; with a current-account surplus, a balance-of-payments surplus exists. The requirement for balance-of-payments equilibrium reduces to the requirement that the current-account balance equal zero.

Recall from section 14.4 that there exists only one level of income at which the current-account balance equals zero. The interest rate becomes irrelevant to balance-of-payments equilibrium with no capital mobility; thus, the BOP line becomes vertical, as in Figure 15.15, panel (a). To the right of the BOP line, the balance of payments lies in deficit; to the left of the line, a BOP surplus exists. A rise in foreign income (Q*) or a fall in the relative price of domestic goods and services (R) increases exports at each level of domestic income and causes the income consistent with balance in the current account to rise, so the BOP curve shifts to the right. A

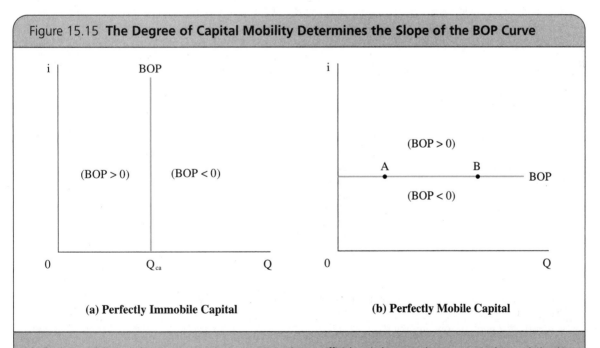

Figure 15.15 The Degree of Capital Mobility Determines the Slope of the BOP Curve

(a) Perfectly Immobile Capital

(b) Perfectly Mobile Capital

Perfectly immobile capital means no transactions occur in the nonofficial capital account in response to changes in i or i*. The balance of payments includes only the current-account balance, which equals zero at a single level of income, Q_{ca}, in panel (a). Perfectly mobile capital means that infinitesimal changes in the interest rate generate large international capital flows, implying a horizontal BOP curve as in panel (b).

decline in foreign income or a rise in the relative price of domestic goods and services decreases exports at each level of income and shifts the BOP curve to the left. *(Why?)*

We now move to the opposite assumption, that of perfect capital mobility. The assumption of perfect capital mobility simply means that investors, in deciding which assets to hold, consider only interest rates and exchange rates (including the forward rate and the expected future spot rate). In other words, investors have no built-in preferences for assets denominated in one currency versus those denominated in another, and government policies don't restrict capital flows. Under perfect capital mobility, the balance-of-payments line becomes horizontal, as illustrated in panel (b) of Figure 15.15. Recall that in the presence of an active capital account we draw each BOP line for given values of the foreign interest rate, the exchange rate, and forward and expected spot exchange rates. This implies that any rise in the domestic interest rate causes a capital inflow and a move toward a surplus on the capital account. (For a review, see the discussion of interest parity in section 12.4.)

How does the assumption of perfect capital mobility produce a horizontal BOP line? In Figure 15.15, panel (b), the balance of payments is in equilibrium at point A; this is true because A lies on the BOP line, which, by definition, represents points of balance-of-payments equilibrium. Beginning at A, suppose a disturbance in the economy raises income. Imports rise with income, and the current account moves toward a deficit. To maintain balance-of-payments equilibrium, the capital account must generate an offsetting move toward surplus. With perfectly mobile capital, how large an increase in the domestic interest rate is required to generate this capital-account surplus? The answer is that an infinitesimal (essentially zero) rise in the interest rate will suffice. The reason is that investors will respond immediately to the slightest rise in domestic rates by moving their funds into the domestic economy.

In terms of the interest parity condition discussed in Chapter Twelve, massive capital flows in response to even minute changes in relative interest rates maintain the equilibrium or parity condition. Therefore, the balance of payments is in equilibrium at B—with a larger current-account deficit and capital-account surplus than at A. All points above the BOP line correspond to situations of balance-of-payments surplus, and those below the line represent balance-of-payments deficits. *(Why?)* An increase in the foreign interest rate, the forward exchange rate, or the expected future spot rate raises the expected return on foreign-currency-denominated assets and shifts the BOP line up, because a higher domestic interest rate is required to induce asset owners to hold domestic-currency assets. A fall in the spot exchange rate has a similar effect. *(Use interest parity to explain why a fall in i^*, e^e, or e^f or a rise in e would shift the BOP curve down.)*

Our models of the goods and services, money, and foreign exchange markets are now complete and summarized in the IS, LM, and BOP curves, respectively, each of which represents the combinations of domestic income and interest rates at which quantity demanded equals quantity supplied in the respective market.

15.5 **Bringing It All Together**

Recall that *general equilibrium* refers to simultaneous equilibrium in several related markets. General-equilibrium analysis of an open macroeconomy examines the interaction of the goods and services, money, and foreign exchange markets in determining the economy's performance. Because we've summarized the requirement for each market's equilibrium with a curve relating domestic income and interest rates, we can combine the three markets easily to facilitate a general-equilibrium analysis.

Figure 15.16 brings together the IS, LM, and BOP curves that represent equilibrium in the markets for goods and services, money, and foreign exchange, respectively. The IS curve is downward sloping and the LM and BOP curves upward sloping, reflecting our assumption of an intermediate degree of capital mobility.

A point at which all three curves intersect represents a general equilibrium in the economy. No such intersection occurs in Figure 15.16. In fact, there appears to be no reason to expect such an intersection to occur; the figure suggests that perhaps only a coincidence would result in a common intersection and general equilibrium. This somewhat pessimistic-sounding situation disappears, however, once we recognize several linkages among the three markets. These linkages guarantee that (in the absence of interference) the IS, LM, and BOP curves will move to a point of common intersection and that the economy will reach a general equilibrium. This is an important and somewhat surprising result, especially since we've assumed throughout this chapter that the price level is fixed, thereby ruling out one of the economy's most powerful self-adjustment mechanisms.

The exact nature of the linkages among the three markets depends on the exchange rate regime under which the economy operates. Flexible exchange rates imply linkages that are somewhat easier to see than those under fixed rates. So, let's begin with a flexible-rate regime and then move on to adjustment under a fixed-rate regime.

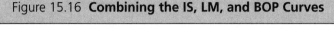

Figure 15.16 **Combining the IS, LM, and BOP Curves**

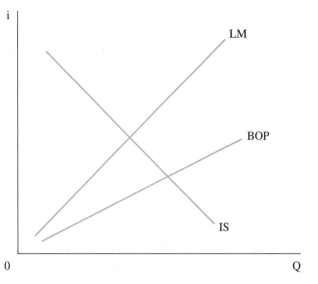

A general equilibrium in the economy requires that the three curves share a common point of intersection. At such a point, the markets for goods and services, money, and foreign exchange are all in equilibrium simultaneously at the given combination of Q, i, and e.

15.6 How a Flexible Exchange Rate Regime Works

Under a perfectly flexible exchange rate regime, the exchange rate continually adjusts to keep the balance of payments in equilibrium and, equivalently, to keep the quantity demanded of foreign exchange equal to the quantity supplied. These changes in the exchange rate shift both the IS and BOP curves until they reach a general equilibrium on the LM curve.

Note that because of the negative slope of the IS curve and the positive slopes of the LM and BOP curves, the IS curve will intersect each of the other two, but not necessarily at the same point. Point I in Figure 15.17 illustrates a case in which the markets for goods and services and for money are in equilibrium, but with a balance-of-payments surplus with the exchange rate at e_0.[26] The surplus in the BOP at point I is evident from I's position above and to the left of the BOP curve drawn with $e = e_0$ (see section 15.4.2). Because the quantity supplied of foreign exchange exceeds the quantity demanded (by the definition of a balance-of-payments surplus), the domestic currency appreciates, or the domestic currency price of foreign currency falls from e_0 to e_1. The appreciation raises the relative price of domestic goods, since $R \equiv P/eP^*$. Exports fall and imports rise, shifting the IS curve to the left from IS to IS'.[27]

An appreciation of the domestic currency also shifts the BOP curve to the left. The currency appreciation affects both balance-of-payments accounts. The current-account balance moves toward a deficit as exports fall and imports rise. *(Why?)* The capital account also moves toward a deficit. (If you've forgotten why the exchange rate has this effect on the capital account, you may want to review section 12.4 on interest parity.) Since the balance of payments originally was in surplus at point I, the changes in both accounts move it toward

---

26 We wouldn't actually observe a point such as I under a perfectly flexible exchange rate, because the exchange rate adjusts instantaneously. Nonetheless, an examination of point I proves useful for understanding the nature of the adjustment process.

27 Recall from section 14.8 that events that lower total expenditure on domestic goods and services also shift the IS curve to the left.

Figure 15.17 Automatic Adjustment from a Position of Balance-of-Payments Surplus under a Flexible Exchange Rate

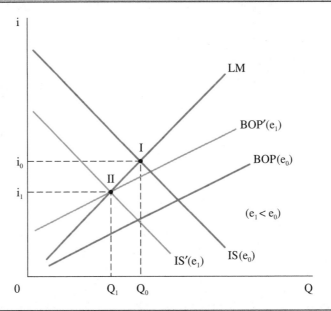

The balance-of-payments surplus at point I causes the domestic currency to appreciate, shifting the BOP and IS curves to the left. Point II represents equilibrium with income equal to Q_1, the interest rate at i_1, and the domestic-currency price of foreign currency at e_1.

---

equilibrium. The new BOP line (BOP′) represents the combinations of income and interest that place the balance of payments in equilibrium given the new, lower value of the exchange rate, e_1. The IS and BOP curves come to a rest once they share a common intersection with the LM curve. At that point (point II in Figure 15.17), all three markets are in equilibrium simultaneously at income Q_1, interest rate i_1, and exchange rate e_1. Table 15.9 reports the automatic adjustments in response to the balance-of-payments surplus.

We can use a similar analysis to show that if the IS and LM curves intersect below and to the right of the BOP curve, indicating a BOP deficit, the domestic currency will depreciate. The IS curve will shift to the right *(Why?)*, as will the BOP line *(Why?)*. Again, general equilibrium will occur when income, the interest rate, and the exchange rate have adjusted such that all three markets are in equilibrium simultaneously, as reported in Table 15.10.

In the process of shifting the IS, LM, and BOP curves, it's important to keep in mind the major results obtained so far. First, a general equilibrium in the economy requires a combination of income, interest rate, and exchange rate such that all three markets are in equilibrium simultaneously.

Second, even with prices held fixed, the economy contains self-adjusting mechanisms for bringing the three major markets into equilibrium. We call these mechanisms *self-adjusting,* or *automatic,* because they require no explicit policy actions. Under a flexible exchange rate regime, the currency appreciates in response to a balance-of-payments surplus and depreciates in response to a deficit as a result of market forces, not government action. Once the exchange rate adjustment begins, individuals respond by altering their relative purchases of foreign and domestic goods, services, and assets. This process brings income, the interest rate, and the exchange rate to levels that clear all three markets, although the adjustment may be gradual.

Third, the model highlights the pitfalls of drawing conclusions from analysis of only one market. If we consider only the market for goods and services or only the market for money, point I in Figure 15.17 appears to be an equilibrium. Imagine a situation in which output Q_0 corresponds to an acceptable level of employment (or unemployment) such that policy makers want the economy to operate at point I. If we ignore the balance of

Table 15.9 **How Does the Economy Adjust from a BOP Surplus under a Flexible Exchange Rate?**[a]

Variable	
Domestic income (Q)	Falls
Domestic interest rate (i)	Falls
Exchange rate (e)	Falls (domestic currency appreciates)
Money stock (M/P)	None

[a]Here we assume an intermediate level of capital mobility. Chapter Seventeen will focus on the implications of different degrees of capital mobility for the adjustment process and for macroeconomic policy.

Table 15.10 **How Does the Economy Adjust from a BOP Deficit under a Flexible Exchange Rate?**[a]

Variable	
Domestic income (Q)	Rises
Domestic interest rate (i)	Rises
Exchange rate (e)	Rises (domestic currency depreciates)
Money stock (M/P)	None

[a]See note in Table 15.9.

payments, the tendency of the economy to move to point II will be difficult to understand. By taking into account the balance of payments, however, it becomes easy to see why the economy ends up at point II. If point II is unacceptable, moving the economy away from it will require some type of active macroeconomic policy. We'll analyze such policies in Chapters Sixteen and Seventeen. There we'll see that a general-equilibrium framework is essential not only for understanding where the economy tends to move independently but also for predicting accurately the effects of the various economic policies available. Just as a model that includes only the market for goods and services can wrongly imply that the economy will be in equilibrium at Q_0 and i_0, so can it produce misleading results concerning economic policies' effects in an open economy.

15.7 How a Fixed Exchange Rate Regime Works

It may seem obvious that the economy can adjust to reach a general equilibrium under a flexible exchange rate regime, since the exchange rate provides an automatic adjustment mechanism. But what about an economy under a completely fixed exchange rate regime in which even policy-induced changes in the pegged rate (that is, devaluations and revaluations) are ruled out? Do we have any reason to expect the economy to self-adjust and reach general equilibrium under such circumstances? The answer is yes, because a direct link exists between the nominal money stock and the balance of payments under a fixed-rate regime.

With a flexible exchange rate, a currency appreciation or depreciation corrects any balance-of-payments surplus or deficit. In terms of the IS-LM-BOP graph, the change in the exchange rate shifts the IS and BOP curves until they intersect on the LM curve (which remains stationary throughout the adjustment process). Under a fixed exchange rate regime, the IS and BOP curves no longer handle the adjustment. Instead, the LM curve moves to the intersection of the stationary IS and BOP curves, because surpluses or deficits in the balance of payments automatically cause changes in the money stock. (It may prove useful to review Figure 15.4's analysis of the effect of a change in the nominal money stock on the LM curve.) To understand this process, we need to examine the link between the balance of payments and the money stock under a fixed exchange rate.

15.7.1 **Fixed Exchange Rates and the Nominal Money Stock**

Recall that within a fixed exchange rate regime, the central bank maintains the pegged exchange rate by intervening to buy any excess supply of foreign exchange or to sell foreign exchange to cover any excess demand. As we'll see, such intervention by the central bank restores foreign exchange market equilibrium at the pegged exchange rate. The mechanics of foreign exchange market intervention are quite simple. When the balance of payments is in surplus, the central bank must purchase from the public the excess of quantity supplied over quantity demanded of foreign exchange. These purchases raise the central bank's stock of foreign exchange reserves (FXR). As Equation 15.2 indicates, the money stock rises by the amount of the FXR purchase multiplied by the money multiplier.

Figure 15.18 ties Chapter Twelve's analysis of the foreign exchange market to intervention's effect on the money stock, using pounds to represent foreign exchange. To maintain the exchange rate at e^p, the central bank must buy the excess supply of foreign exchange at that rate. It makes this purchase with one of its special checks. The central bank's foreign exchange reserves rise by ΔFXR; the money stock rises by $mm \cdot \Delta FXR$ through the money-creation process discussed in section 15.2.3.[28]

Figure 15.19 illustrates how the rise in the money stock restores foreign exchange market equilibrium at the pegged exchange rate, e^p. Panel (a) traces events in the money market. Prior to the central bank's intervention,

---

Figure 15.18 **Effect of Intervention on the Money Stock under a Fixed Exchange Rate**

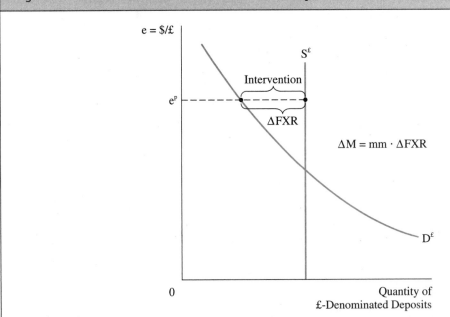

At the pegged rate, e^p, the quantity of foreign exchange supplied exceeds the quantity demanded. To prevent the dollar from appreciating, the U.S. central bank must buy the excess pounds. The central bank adds the purchased pounds to its foreign exchange reserves. The central bank check with which the pounds are bought creates the basis for an expansion of the U.S. money stock. The money stock rises by $mm \cdot \Delta FXR$.

---

28 In Chapter Sixteen, we'll see that this result hinges on an assumption that the central bank doesn't *sterilize* or engage in open market operations designed to offset intervention's effect on the domestic money stock. As Equation 15.2 makes clear, if central bank purchases or sales of government bonds cancel out the effect of purchases or sales of foreign exchange ($\Delta GB = -\Delta FXR$), the money stock will remain unchanged.

the money stock is (M_0/P) and the equilibrium interest rate is i_0. Panel (b), representing the foreign exchange market, shows that the foreign exchange market is *not* in equilibrium at e^p and i_0. Given those values of the exchange rate and the domestic interest rate (along with i^*, e^e, and e^f), portfolio owners want to hold less than the existing stock of pound-denominated assets. The central bank must step in to buy up the excess supply, adding the pounds to its international reserves and expanding the domestic money stock by $mm \cdot \Delta FXR$. The rise in the domestic money stock shifts the money supply line in panel (a) to the right, from (M_0/P) to (M_1/P), where $(M_1/P) = (M_0/P) + (mm \cdot \Delta FXR)$. At the old equilibrium interest rate, i_0, individuals don't want to hold the new, higher level of real money balances. They try to buy bonds to lower real money balances to the desired level and, in the process, push the interest rate down to i_1. At i_1, individuals are content to hold the new, larger domestic money stock. The lower interest rate also affects the foreign exchange market. Because i has fallen, asset owners want to shift their portfolios toward more pound-denominated deposits, since dollar-denominated ones now pay a lower rate of return. This shifts the demand for pound deposits to the right, achieving interest parity and foreign exchange market equilibrium at e^p.

To retrace the argument, the initial excess supply of pound deposits at e^p and i_0 necessitated central bank intervention to buy foreign-currency assets. The intervention increased the domestic money stock and lowered the domestic interest rate, thereby making asset owners content to hold the existing quantity of foreign-currency assets.

If the exchange rate is fixed at a level below the equilibrium rate, the quantity demanded of foreign exchange exceeds the quantity supplied (see, for example, Figure 12.10). The central bank intervenes to sell foreign exchange from its reserves. Because the central bank's foreign exchange reserves fall by the amount of the excess demand at e^p, the domestic money stock falls by $mm \cdot \Delta FXR$. The decline in the domestic money stock pushes up the domestic interest rate and restores equilibrium in the foreign exchange market by decreasing demand for foreign-currency-denominated deposits. Interest parity holds at the pegged exchange rate and the new, higher domestic interest rate.

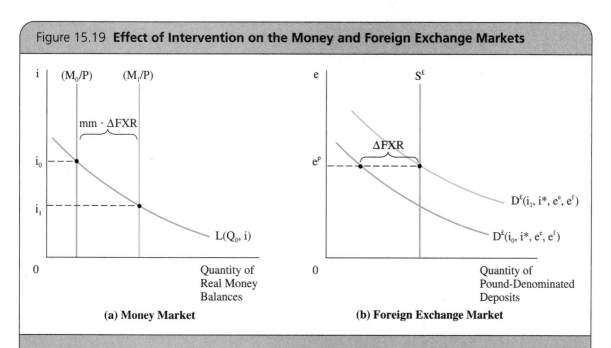

Figure 15.19 **Effect of Intervention on the Money and Foreign Exchange Markets**

(a) Money Market

(b) Foreign Exchange Market

\When the central bank intervenes by buying the excess supply of foreign-currency-denominated deposits in the foreign exchange market (panel (b)), the domestic money stock rises (panel (a)). The larger domestic money stock pushes down the equilibrium interest rate in panel (a), lowers the rate of return on domestic-currency deposits, and raises the demand for foreign-currency deposits in panel (b). The intervention restores interest parity at the original exchange rate (e^p) and a lower domestic interest rate.

15.7.2 **The Money Stock and Automatic Adjustment**

As long as a balance-of-payments surplus exists, the central bank's foreign exchange market intervention will cause the money stock to expand, shifting the LM curve to the right. A balance-of-payments deficit, on the other hand, will shrink the money stock, shifting the LM curve to the left. These adjustments ensure that the LM curve will move to the point of intersection with the IS and BOP curves, resulting in a general equilibrium in the economy.

Figure 15.20 traces the economy's adjustment from a position of surplus in its balance of payments. At the intersection of the IS and LM curves (point I), the balance of payments is in surplus, because the point lies above and to the left of the BOP curve. In the foreign exchange market, there's an excess supply of foreign-currency-denominated deposits. To restore balance-of-payments equilibrium, the central bank must buy the excess foreign exchange, causing the domestic money stock to rise from M_0 to M_1 and shifting the LM curve to the right. The adjustment process is complete when the LM curve reaches a point of intersection with both the IS and BOP curves (point II). There, all three markets are in simultaneous equilibrium at the existing income, interest rate, and exchange rate.

Table 15.11 summarizes the economy's automatic adjustment from a point of balance-of-payments surplus under a fixed exchange rate regime.

Figure 15.21 illustrates adjustment from a position of balance-of-payments deficit. At the intersection of the IS and LM curves (point I), the balance of payments is in deficit. To restore balance-of-payments equilibrium, the central bank must sell foreign exchange, causing the money stock to fall from M_0 to M_1 and shifting the LM curve to the left. The adjustment process is complete when the LM curve has shifted to a point of intersection with both the IS and BOP curves (point II). Table 15.12 lists each variable's contribution to the adjustment process.

We've demonstrated that linkages among the goods and services, money, and foreign exchange markets ensure that the economy can reach a point of general equilibrium even if prices are fixed. The exact mechanism

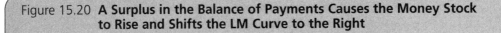

Figure 15.20 A Surplus in the Balance of Payments Causes the Money Stock to Rise and Shifts the LM Curve to the Right

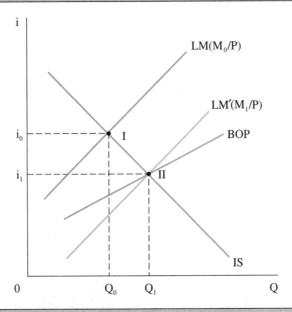

A balance-of-payments surplus corresponds to an excess supply of foreign exchange. To maintain the pegged exchange rate, the central bank must intervene, buying foreign exchange and adding it to the bank's reserves. The increase in reserves raises the domestic money stock from M_0 to M_1.

Table 15.11 How Does the Economy Adjust from a BOP Surplus under a Fixed Exchange Rate?[a]

Variable	
Domestic income (Q)	Rises
Domestic interest rate (i)	Falls
Exchange rate (e)	No Change
Money stock (M/P)	Rises

[a]Here we assume the degree of capital mobility to be intermediate. In Chapter Sixteen, we'll look in detail at the importance of the extent of capital mobility for the automatic adjustment process and for fiscal and monetary policies.

Table 15.12 How Does the Economy Adjust from a BOP Deficit under a Fixed Exchange Rate?[a]

Variable	
Domestic income (Q)	Falls
Domestic interest rate (i)	Rises
Exchange rate (e)	No Change
Money stock (M/P)	Falls

[a]See note in Table 15.11.

Figure 15.21 A Deficit in the Balance of Payments Causes the Money Stock to Fall and Shifts the LM Curve to the Left

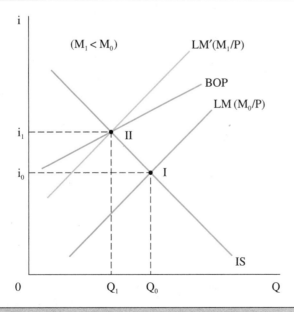

A BOP deficit corresponds to an excess demand for foreign exchange. To maintain the pegged exchange rate, the central bank must intervene, supplying foreign exchange from its reserves. The loss of reserves lowers the domestic money stock from M_0 to M_1.

by which adjustment occurs depends on the exchange rate regime in operation. Under a flexible-rate regime, the *exchange rate* adjusts to equilibrate the balance of payments. Graphically, changes in the exchange rate shift the IS and BOP curves to a common intersection with the LM curve. Under a fixed-rate regime, the *money stock* adjusts through the central bank's foreign exchange intervention policies. Graphically, this is reflected in a shift of the LM curve to a common intersection with the IS and BOP curves. Note that the mechanism by which adjustment occurs carries important implications for the macroeconomy. For example, comparing Tables 15.9 and 15.11, we can see that automatic adjustment from a balance-of-payments surplus reduces income under a flexible exchange rate (because the currency appreciation raises the relative price of domestic goods and services relative to foreign ones) but increases income under a fixed exchange rate (because the money-stock growth lowers the interest rate and encourages investment).

Under either exchange rate system, the adjustment is automatic in the sense that the only policy required is that the central bank follow the "rules" of the exchange regime in effect. The rules of a flexible-rate regime are to allow the forces of demand and supply to determine the exchange rate. The rules of a fixed-rate regime are to intervene to buy and sell foreign exchange from international reserves to maintain the pegged exchange rate.

CASE ONE:
Best of Both Worlds

Deposit insurance systems, under which the government guarantees that bank depositors won't lose their deposits in the event of a bank failure, provide policy makers with a dilemma. On the one hand, such plans deepen confidence in the banking system. This encourages saving and helps get saving into banks, where lenders can channel it to investors to finance investment projects that help the economy grow. But if depositors and lenders believe that the government will cover any losses that happen because of overly risky loans or other bad decisions, banks lose the incentive to behave prudently with depositors' funds. Economists call this problem *moral hazard.* Economists' awareness of this dilemma has grown since the financial crises in Latin America, Mexico, and Asia, all of which involved huge bad-loan problems in the banking system.

So what's a policy maker to do? The answer is to try to tailor a deposit insurance system in such a way to get the maximum confidence-building benefits while minimizing the moral-hazard problem. One approach is to limit the amount of insurance coverage per depositor to a set amount, say $100,000 (a per-account limit is less effective, because large depositors just open multiple accounts to get full coverage). This ensures that small depositors don't lose their life savings; but it leaves large depositors, presumably those most capable of monitoring the prudence of the bank's behavior, with uninsured funds, thereby providing an incentive for them to police bank managers' lending decisions. Almost all of the

explicit deposit insurance systems in effect contain limits on amounts covered; most governments with unlimited systems in effect plan to introduce limits (for example, Mexico). Japan had a deposit insurance ceiling in effect until 1996, when the country's severe financial-sector problems generated political pressure to suspend the ceiling, but only temporarily for five years to increase depositors' confidence in the system. So far, that same political pressure has led to postponement of reinstitution of the insurance ceiling.

A second element of an optimal deposit insurance system involves making participation compulsory for banks. Otherwise, banks who plan to make overly risky loans will participate, while more-prudently-run banks won't. Ideally, the insurance system can be funded by banks, with the premium charged each bank dependent on the level of risk of that bank's asset portfolio. Again, this creates an incentive for banks to be careful; by creating a prudent asset portfolio, the bank can reduce its insurance premiums (just as you can reduce your life insurance premiums by not smoking). Finally, to work effectively, the system should be established—with full and explicit rules—*before* a crisis. Governments must beware of implicit or murky insurance promises that passively encourage depositors and bank owners to count on being bailed out in a crisis. Such a situation encourages risky banking behavior that can bring on a crisis; once a crisis develops, the government will face strong political pressure to deliver on even implicit promises.

CASE TWO:
Where the Foreign Exchange Reserves Are

Central banks hold foreign exchange reserves in case they want to intervene in the foreign exchange market. These reserves are a central bank asset and determine, along with the central bank's domestic assets and the money multiplier, the size of the country's money stock. The quantity of reserves that countries hold varies widely. Of the countries included in the International Monetary Fund's *International Financial Statistics Yearbook 2000*, Equatorial Guinea held the smallest amount of total reserves ($2.75 million) and

Japan the largest ($288 billion). Figure 15.22 reports the six countries with the largest total reserve holdings, including gold, in 1999.

Japan accumulated $170 billion in additional reserves between 1994 and 1999 as it intervened periodically to lower the dollar price of yen in response to a sluggish Japanese economy. Of all foreign exchange held in reserves in 2000, dollars make up about 68 percent of the total.

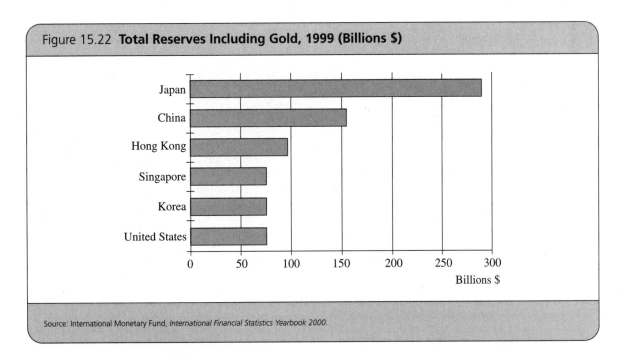

Figure 15.22 **Total Reserves Including Gold, 1999 (Billions $)**

Source: International Monetary Fund, *International Financial Statistics Yearbook 2000*.

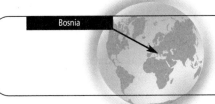

Bosnia

CASE THREE
Birth of a Currency

The 1995 Dayton Peace Accord created a new Bosnian state after three years of war among Serbs, Croats, and Bosnian Muslims in Bosnia and Herzegovina. Terms of the settlement

included creation of a new central bank and currency, the Bosnian marka.[29] Since the breakup of the former state of Yugoslavia, three currencies had been widely used in the

---

29 See "Building Bosnia on Banknotes," *The Economist,* May 1, 1999.

war-ravaged territory: the German mark, the Yugoslavian dinar, and the Croatian kuna. But participants at the Dayton talks thought a new currency could help reunite Bosnia.

The Bosnian constitution created a central bank that works as a currency board. This means that the bank can't buy government bonds, but can only buy and sell foreign exchange reserves to keep the marka's exchange rate pegged, originally to the German Deutsche mark at an exchange rate of M1/DM1 and now to the euro at a rate of M1/€0.51. Such a system is designed to develop confidence in the new currency by maintaining a fixed value relative to a trusted foreign currency. The new constitution also embodies other confidence-building rules. For example, it specifies that until at least 2003 the central bank must be run by someone *not* from Bosnia or any neighboring state. A Frenchman did the early groundwork for the new currency; the current governor of the Central Bank of Bosnia hails from New Zealand.

Not everything went smoothly in introducing the new currency. Serbs, Croats, and Bosnian Muslims argued for months about the design of the new bank notes, especially whether they should feature Roman script or Cyrillic script (they now have both) and which famous writers would adorn them (different denominations now feature writers favored by each group). Once over these initial hurdles, the new currency has fared well. Markas circulate widely in Sarajevo. The population's trust in the new currency is symbolized by the fact that shopkeepers don't even separate Bosnian marka notes from Deutsche mark notes in their cash drawers. Outside Sarajevo, in areas dominated by one of the three dominant factions, the marka remains less widely used. Areas of Bosnia with large Croat populations favor the Croatian kuna; Serb areas still use the dinar, although that currency's dramatic loss of value has discouraged even its Serb users.

Summary

An economy is in general equilibrium when the markets for goods and services, money, and foreign exchange all clear at a common income, interest rate, and exchange rate. The economy contains self-adjusting mechanisms for reaching a general equilibrium under both fixed and flexible exchange rate regimes.

Under a flexible-rate regime, imbalances in the balance of payments cause *exchange rate* changes. These changes alter the relative prices of domestic and foreign goods, affecting both the market for goods and services and the current account. Under a fixed-rate regime, imbalances in the balance of payments cause changes in the *money stock*. The central bank must intervene in foreign exchange markets to maintain the pegged exchange rate in the face of a deficit or a surplus. This intervention causes changes in the stock of foreign exchange reserves and in the money stock. Since 1973, the major currencies have operated under a mixed exchange regime involving some flexibility of rates in response to market forces and some intervention by central banks.

Looking Ahead

This chapter argued that an economy contains self-adjusting mechanisms that bring the markets for goods and services, money, and foreign exchange into equilibrium under either a fixed or flexible exchange rate regime. However, these automatic mechanisms may operate slowly or produce side effects that conflict with other goals. For this reason, policy makers may choose to conduct a variety of policies that attempt to either speed up or hinder the adjustment process. These policies are the subject of Chapter Sixteen.

Key Terms

money
barter
nominal money stock
real money stock
real money balances
opportunity cost of holding money

fractional reserve banking system
deposit expansion
money multiplier
open market operation
LM curve
BOP curve

Problems and Questions for Review

1. Explain the mechanics of the money creation process in an open economy, focusing on differences from the closed economy case. Be sure your answer includes an equation for the money stock in an open economy and a discussion of the relationship between foreign exchange intervention and the domestic money stock.

2. Explain the following statement: "Macroeconomic policy makers can control either the money stock or the exchange rate, but not both."

3. Begin with the situation reported in the consolidated banking system's balance sheet in Table 15.3. A bank run causes the banking system to lose $500 in deposits. If individuals hold the $500 that they withdraw from banks in currency, what is the run's effect on the money stock? Explain.

4. Explain the following statement: "The central bank can have the same effect on the domestic money stock by buying (or selling) either government bonds or foreign exchange."

5. Use a diagram similar to Figure 15.19 to predict the effect of an increase in the domestic money stock on the exchange rate under a flexible exchange rate regime. Explain.

6. Country A keeps its exchange rate fixed. Currently, the markets for goods and services and for money are in equilibrium, but country A's balance of payments is in deficit.
   a. Assume that capital is perfectly immobile. Once automatic adjustment eliminates the balance-of-payments deficit, will country A's income be higher or lower than before? Why?
   b. Assume that capital is perfectly mobile. Once automatic adjustment eliminates the balance-of-payments deficit, will country A's income be higher or lower than before? Why?

7. a. Draw a diagram of the domestic money market in equilibrium.
   b. Draw a diagram of the foreign exchange market in which the quantity demanded of foreign exchange exceeds the quantity supplied at the current fixed exchange rate.
   c. Illustrate the effects of intervention by the central bank to supply foreign exchange.
   d. Explain how the intervention restores interest parity at the original exchange rate.

8. Using the framework from problem 7, explain the following comment: "Central bank intervention is more successful when it affects market participants' expectations."

References and Selected Readings

Adams, Charles, et al., eds. *Managing Financial and Corporate Distress.* Washington, D.C.: Brookings, 2000.
How countries can mitigate the macroeconomic consequences of firm failures.

Burnside, Craig, et al. "Understanding the Korean and Thai Currency Crisis." Federal Reserve Bank of Chicago, *Economic Perspectives* (Third Quarter 2000): 45–60.
Argues that expected future government liabilities (for pensions and financial bailouts) contributed to the financial crises.

DeLong, J. Bradford. "Financial Crises in the 1890s and the 1990s: Must History Repeat?" *Brookings Papers on Economic Activity* 2 (1999): 253–294.
Commonalities and differences between the two end-of-century financial crises.

Dominguez, Kathryn M., and Jeffrey A. Frankel. *Does Foreign Exchange Intervention Work?* Washington, D.C.: Institute for International Economics, 1993.
Examines intervention's ability to affect exchange rates and the money stock; intermediate.

Fischer, Stanley. "On the Need for an International Lender of Last Resort." *Journal of Economic Perspectives* 13 (Fall 1999): 85–104.
The pros and cons of international lending to banks in the midst of financial crises.

Furman, Jason, and Joseph E. Stiglitz. "Economic Crises: Evidence and Insights from East Asia." *Brookings Papers on Economic Activity* 2 (1998): 1–136.
Argues that the crisis was caused by a loss of confidence rather than by weak fundamentals or bad policy making.

Garber, P., and L. Svensson. "The Operation and Collapse of Fixed Exchange Rate Regimes." In *Handbook of International Economics,* Vol. 3, edited by G. M. Grossman and K. Rogoff, 1865–1912. Amsterdam: North-Holland, 1995.
Survey of research on fixed exchange rate regimes, including the money stock–balance of payments link; intermediate and advanced.

Goldstein, Morris. *The Asian Financial Crisis.* Washington, D.C.: Institute for International Economics, 1998.
Accessible overview of the origins and implications of the Asian financial crisis.

Hardy, Daniel C. "Are Banking Crises Predictable?" *Finance and Development* (December 1998): 32–35.
Introduction to the early indicators of banking-sector problems.

Harwood, Alison, et al., eds. *Financial Markets and Development.* Washington, D.C.: Brookings, 1999.
Collection of papers on financial markets' role in development.

Helfer, Ricki Tigert. "What Deposit Insurance Can and Cannot Do." *Finance and Development* 36 (March 1999): 22–25.
The benefits and costs of deposit insurance in financial crises.

Hume, David. "On the Balance of Trade." In *Essays, Moral, Political, and Literary,* Vol. 1. London: Longmans, Green, 1898 [1752].
The classic work on automatic adjustment of the balance of payments, including the original statement of the specie-flow mechanism; for all students.

Kaminsky, Graciela, and Carmen M. Reinhart. "The Twin Crises: The Causes of Banking and Balance-of-Payments Problems."
American Economic Review 89 (June 1999): 473–500.
Advanced discussion of the relationship between banking and payments crises.

Kester, Anne Y. "Improving the Framework for Reporting on International Reserves." *Finance and Development* 37 (June 2000): 49–52.
How reporting standards could improve market participants' information about central banks' reserves.

Lindgren, Carl-Johan, et al. *Bank Soundness and Macroeconomic Policy.* Washington, D.C.: International Monetary Fund, 1996.
Interrelationship between the banking system and macroeconomic policy; for all students.

Moskow, Michael H. "Disruptions in Global Financial Markets: The Role of Public Policy." Federal Reserve Bank of Chicago, *Economic Perspectives* (Third Quarter 2000): 2–8.
What can policy makers do to prevent or respond to problems in international financial markets?

Neely, Christopher J. "The Practice of Central Bank Intervention: Looking under the Hood." Federal Reserve Bank of St. Louis, *Review* 83 (May/June 2001): 1–10.
Accessible overview of the mechanics of foreign exchange market intervention.

Peek, Joe, and Eric Rosengren. "Implications of the Globalization of the Banking Sector: The Latin American Experience." Federal Reserve Bank of Boston, *New England Economic Review* (September/October 2000): 45–62.
How has internationalization affected the performance of Latin American banks?

Pollard, Patricia S. "The Creation of the Euro and the Role of the Dollar in International Markets." Federal Reserve Bank of St. Louis, *Review* (September/October 2001): 17–36.
How will the euro affect international use of the dollar? For all students.

Quirk, Peter J. "Money Laundering: Muddying the Macroeconomy." *Finance and Development* (March 1997): 7–10.
Macroeconomic effects of money laundering; for all students.

Sarno, Lucio, and Mark P. Taylor. "Official Intervention in the Foreign Exchange Market: Is It Effective and, If So, How Does It Work?" *Journal of Economic Literature* (September 2001): 839–868.
Survey of the empirical evidence on sterilized intervention's effectiveness.

Schinasi, Garry J., et al. "Managing Global Finance and Risk." *Finance and Development* 36 (December 1999): 38–41.
The risk of international financial flows.

Special issue on "Lessons from Recent Crises in Asian and Other Emerging Markets." Federal Reserve Bank of New York, *Economic Policy Review* 6 (September 2000).
What can market participants and policy makers learn from the crisis experience?

Summers, Lawrence H. "International Financial Crises: Causes, Prevention, and Cures." *American Economic Review Papers and Proceedings* 90 (May 2000): 1–16.
Accessible discussion by the former U.S. Treasury Secretary, now president of Harvard University.

Symposium on "Global Financial Instability." *Journal of Economic Perspectives* 13 (Fall 1999): 3–84.
Collection of papers on the causes and effects of the financial turmoil of the late 1990s.

Symposium on "Reform and Restructuring in Asia." *Finance and Development* 38 (March 2001): 2–28.
Policy changes instigated by the crisis.

Tavlas, George S. "The International Use of Currencies: The U.S. Dollar and the Euro." *Finance and Development* (June 1998): 46–49.
Introduction to the determinants of which currencies are widely used in international transactions.

CHAPTER SIXTEEN

Short-Run Macroeconomic Policy under Fixed Exchange Rates

16.1 Introduction

Among the many purposes of studying an open macroeconomy is to understand better the implications of openness for macroeconomic policy. The effectiveness of various policies depends, often in crucial ways, on the nature and extent of a country's linkages with the larger world economy. These linkages include the magnitude of trade in goods and services, the integration of financial markets reflected in capital flows, and the type of exchange rate regime used for facilitating currency transactions.

Because these linkages vary across countries as well as over time, the effectiveness of different macroeconomic policies also varies across these dimensions. For example, during the 1950s and 1960s the degree of international capital mobility and the magnitude of capital flows were limited. Most governments regulated international borrowing and lending, limiting the flows of funds into and out of their economies. The absence of highly developed institutions through which to facilitate international capital flows, such as Eurocurrency markets[1] and bonds issued in multiple currencies, also contributed to a relatively low degree of international capital mobility. During the past quarter-century, the growth of a truly international capital market has been one of the major developments on the world scene. Governments of the major industrial economies and of many developing ones have loosened their regulation of capital flows, and elaborate institutions have evolved to handle the resulting transactions.

These developments carry major implications for businesses, which can now conduct production, marketing, and borrowing and lending operations on a worldwide scale. Less recognized but equally important are the implications for formulating macroeconomic policy. For example, changes in capital markets, along with the move to more flexible exchange rates, have made fiscal policy a less effective tool for managing the economy than in the 1950s. In general, changes in either the degree of capital mobility or the exchange rate regime will alter the expected effectiveness of the basic tools of macroeconomic policy.

This chapter examines the goals of macroeconomic policy in an open economy; defines some general principles useful in designing policies to meet those goals; and explores the effectiveness of three major types of macroeconomic policy: fiscal, monetary, and exchange rate policy, under a fixed exchange rate using the IS-LM-BOP model from Chapter Fifteen. Why analyze a fixed exchange rate regime when the United States and most other industrial economies shifted to more flexible-rate regimes in the early 1970s? First, exchange rates for most currencies have been fixed throughout most of modern macroeconomic history. To understand that history, including its lessons for today and the future, we must understand the basic functioning of a fixed exchange

---

1 Eurocurrencies are offshore deposits denominated in the currency of a country other than the one in which the deposits are located. Section 12.9 discusses Eurocurrencies.

Table 16.1 IMF Members Maintaining Less-Flexible Exchange Rates, March 31, 2000

Exchange Rate Regime (Number of Countries)	
Exchange arrangements with no separate legal tender[a] (38)	*Another currency as legal tender:* Ecuador, Kiribati, Marshall Islands, Micronesia, Palau, Panama, San Marino
	East Caribbean Common Market: Antigua & Barbuda, Dominica, Grenada, St. Kitts & Nevis, St. Lucia, St. Vincent & the Grenadines
	CFA Franc Zone: Benin, Burkina Faso, Cameroon, Central African Republic, Chad, Republic of Congo, Côte d'Ivoire, Equatorial Guinea, Guinea-Bissau, Gabon, Mali, Niger, Senegal, Togo
	Euro area: Austria, Belgium, Finland, France, Germany, Ireland, Italy, Luxembourg, Netherlands, Portugal, Spain
Currency board arrangements[b] (8)	Argentina, Bosnia & Herzegovina, Brunei Darussalam, Bulgaria, Hong Kong, Djibouti, Estonia, Lithuania
Other conventional fixed peg arrangements (including de facto peg arrangements under managed floating)[c] (45)	Aruba, The Bahamas, Bahrain, Bangladesh, Barbados, Belize, Bhutan, Botswana, Cape Verde, China (Mainland), Comoros, Egypt, El Salvador, Fiji, Iran, Iraq, Jordan, Kuwait, Latvia, Lebanon, Lesotho, Macedonia FYR, Malaysia, Maldives, Malta, Morocco, Myanmar, Namibia, Nepal, Netherlands Antilles, Oman, Pakistan, Qatar, Samoa, Saudi Arabia, Seychelles, Solomon Islands, Swaziland, Syrian Arab Republic, Tonga, Trinidad & Tobago, Turkmenistan, United Arab Emirates, Vanuatu, Zimbabwe
Pegged exchange rates within horizontal bands[d] (6)	Cyprus, Denmark, Greece, Iceland, Libya, Vietnam
Crawling pegs[e] (5)	Bolivia, Costa Rica, Nicaragua, Tunisia, Turkey
Exchange rates within crawling bands[f] (7)	Israel, Honduras, Hungary, Poland, Sri Lanka, Uruguay, Venezuela
Managed floating with no preannounced path for exchange rate[g] (27)	Algeria, Azerbaijan, Belarus, Burundi, Cambodia, Croatia, Czech Republic, Dominican Republic, Ethiopia, Guatemala, Jamaica, Kenya, Kyrgyz Republic, Lao PDR, Malawi, Mauritania, Nigeria, Norway, Paraguay, Romania, Singapore, Slovak Republic, Slovenia, Suriname, Tajikistan, Ukraine, Uzbekistan

[a]The currency of another country circulates as the sole legal tender or the member belongs to a monetary or currency union in which the same legal tender is shared by the members of the union.
[b]A monetary regime based on an implicit legislative commitment to exchange domestic currency for a specified foreign currency at a fixed exchange rate, combined with restrictions on the issuing authority to ensure the fulfillment of the legal obligation.
[c]The country pegs its currency (formally or de facto) at a fixed rate to a major currency or a basket of currencies where the exchange rate fluctuates within a narrow margin of at most ±1 percent around a central rate.
[d]The value of the currency is maintained within margins of fluctuation around a formal or de facto fixed peg that are wider than ±1 around a central rate.
[e]The currency is adjusted periodically in small amounts at a fixed, preannounced rate or in response to changes in selective quantitative indicators.
[f]The currency is maintained within certain fluctuation margins around a central rate that is adjusted periodically at a fixed preannounced rate or in response to changes in selective quantitative indicators.
[g]The monetary authority influences the movements of the exchange rate through active intervention in the foreign exchange market without specifying, or pre-committing to, a preannounced path for the exchange rate.

Source: International Monetary Fund.

rate system. Second, as reported in Table 16.1, two important groups of countries continue to maintain less-flexible exchange rates. Adoption of a common currency such as the euro, used by most members of the European Union, represents the ultimate fixed exchange rate system (the exchange rate between a "German euro" and a "French euro" equals one, by definition), although the currency floats against nonmember currencies. Also, many developing economies continue either to fix their exchange rates relative to a major currency (for example, Hong Kong) or to actually use a major currency as their domestic money (for example, Ecuador). Thus, policy decisions by EU members and by many developing economies remain bound by the structure and rules of a fixed-rate regime.

Third, even the governments of economies such as the United States, which operate under flexible exchange rates, engage in foreign exchange market intervention on occasion. When they do, knowledge of how a fixed exchange rate system works is an important prerequisite to understanding the intervention's impact on the macroeconomy.

16.2 Macroeconomic Goals in an Open Economy

16.2.1 Internal and External Balance

A complete list of economic goals would constitute a book in itself. The main goals for an economic system include the efficient allocation of resources to produce goods and services wanted by society, an acceptable rate of economic growth, and an acceptable distribution of income. The study of each of these goals and the inter-relationships among them constitutes economics as a discipline. We examined the efficient allocation of resources to produce the goods most desired by society in Part One. We explored international trade's effect on economic growth in Chapter Ten and its impact on the distribution of income in Chapters Four and Ten.

Here we focus on the two primary macroeconomic goals of an open economy—usually referred to as *internal* and *external balance*. **Internal balance** involves the full use of the economy's resources, or full employment, along with a stable price level. We'll examine directly not the level of employment or unemployment but the corresponding level of output or income. At income levels "too low" from the perspective of internal balance, the employment rate is too low or the unemployment rate too high. Unemployed resources indicate that the economy fails to produce as many goods and services as it can, a situation that clearly makes society worse off. However, if the unemployment level falls too low to attain the internal-balance goal, prices begin to rise and inflation may emerge as a problem.[2]

But what exactly does a "too low" or "too high" rate of unemployment mean? We can't define full employment as a given percentage of unemployment measured by governments' official statistics (for example, 2, 4, or 6 percent). The percentage of measured unemployment properly identified with "full employment" depends on factors such as the pattern of wages in the economy, demographics (the age, gender, health, and educational characteristics of the population), and citizens' tastes for income versus leisure. We can, however, rule out a zero rate of unemployment as a reasonable or desirable policy goal. For an economy to function efficiently, workers must sometimes spend time searching for the employment in which they'll be most productive. During that search, workers may be unemployed, but such temporary unemployment ultimately raises productivity through a better match between workers and jobs. In the remainder of this chapter, we'll assume that there exists a desired output for the economy that corresponds to "full" employment, given the society's resources, technology, and tastes for leisure, and that the goal of internal balance consists of maintaining that level of output.

At first glance, the external-balance goal appears more easily definable. We might argue that an economy achieves **external balance** when the quantity demanded of foreign exchange equals the quantity available—that is, when the foreign exchange market is in equilibrium. Under a fixed exchange rate regime, such external balance occurs when the balance of payments balances (BOP = 0). The analogous definition of external balance under a flexible exchange rate regime corresponds to a situation in which the domestic currency neither appreciates nor depreciates against other currencies. However, we'll see that in reality the goal of external balance is subtle and complex.

Policy makers often have preferences for the status of particular subcategories within the balance-of-payments accounts (for example, a balanced merchandise trade account or current account) along with a goal of overall balance. But those preferences may differ across time and across countries. The current account provides no clear value to serve as a policy goal, as does full employment or low inflation on the internal-balance side. A current-account balance of zero, for example, may make sense as a policy goal in some circumstances, but not as a general rule. We've seen at several points that international borrowing and lending (or intertemporal trade) can provide gains from trade to both the borrowing and the lending country by allowing them to be net

---

2 So far, we've ignored inflation, or a sustained rise in the price level, through our assumption of fixed prices. Chapters Eighteen and Nineteen will relax that assumption and raise questions about macroeconomic policies' ability to alter real income, at least in the long run. For now, we merely note that attempts to use macroeconomic policy to increase real output above a level sustainable given the economy's availability of resources will promote inflation. Inflation poses problems for an economy, so avoidance of inflation constitutes a major goal of macroeconomic policy making, as does avoidance of unemployment.

importers and net exporters, respectively, of current goods and services. In such circumstances, policy makers needlessly forgo the gains from intertemporal trade if they pursue a current-account balance of zero. Temporary disasters, such as earthquakes or wars, provide a second reason for tolerating current-account imbalances. A country that suffers a sudden but temporary reduction in its productive capacity can borrow from foreigners to "smooth" or spread the disaster's negative effect on consumption over several years rather than bearing the entire burden in a short period.

Nonetheless, large and persistent current-account deficits or surpluses cause policy makers concern. Large deficits, which imply large-scale foreign borrowing, raise the risk that some of the borrowed funds may go not to fund worthwhile investment projects but to either excessive current consumption or unproductive "white-elephant" investments. If this happens, the funds will fail to earn a rate of return sufficient to repay the loans, and the debtor may be forced to either default or undergo costly adjustment policies to avoid default. Countries that borrow heavily abroad also must worry about foreigners' perceptions of their economic policies and performance. If foreign investors begin to suspect unwise use of borrowed funds, they may become unwilling to lend, forcing the debtor to suffer through a sudden reduction in its ability to borrow to finance its current-account deficit.[3]

Large and persistent current-account surpluses pose more subtle concerns for policy makers. They correspond to large and persistent capital-account deficits, or accumulation of foreign assets, and to lower levels of domestic investment than would occur in the absence of the current-account surplus. Policy makers must wonder why foreign investments appear so much more attractive than domestic ones, when a higher rate of domestic investment might foster domestic economic growth, as well as a larger tax base on which to collect government revenue. In addition, the accumulation of foreign lending runs the risk that some borrowers may be unable to repay their obligations. Countries with large current-account surpluses also often receive intense political pressure from the corresponding deficit countries to reduce exports, accept protectionist policies against exports, or endure accusations of unfair trade practices.

Market forces, combined with governments following the rules of the exchange rate regime in effect, will produce external balance in the sense of balance-of-payments equilibrium, but not necessarily external balance by other definitions governments may have in mind, such as target levels for the current account. Therefore, in our analysis of macroeconomic policies' effects, we'll track not only their impact on the macroeconomy as a whole, but also their effects on the current-account balance.

16.2.2 Targets and Instruments

The overall goal of macroeconomic policy making in an open economy is to help the economy achieve the desired performance. We've defined this objective as simultaneous achievement of internal and external balance. The word *objective* is subtly deceptive here, because there actually are two objectives: internal balance *and* external balance. In the terminology of the theory of economic policy, these objectives are **targets,** that is, the desired consequences of policy.

Instruments, on the other hand, are the policy tools available to pursue the targets. Possible policy instruments include fiscal policy (changes in government expenditure or taxation), monetary policy (changes in the money stock), and exchange rate policy (devaluation or revaluation). However, not all these instruments will always be accessible to the policy maker; for example, according to the discussion of automatic balance-of-payments adjustment under fixed exchange rates in section 15.7, monetary policy vanishes as an instrument under a fixed-rate regime. One of the major tasks of open-economy macroeconomics is to determine under what circumstances each potential instrument will be both available and effective.

The definitions of targets and instruments appear straightforward and may seem to do little more than give labels to common sense. However, further examination reveals that the targets and instruments concepts yield important insights and that the distinction between targets and instruments is less clear than common sense suggests.

The major insight gleaned from the targets and instruments view concerns the important relationship between the number of targets and the number of available instruments. A rule of successful policy making is that at least one instrument must be available for each target. Simple physical analogies prove useful in consid-

---

3 Mexico's situation in 1994, reported in Case Three, provides one example. The Asian crisis, discussed in Cases Two, Four, and Five, provides another.

ering this point. The game of bowling, for example, involves aiming a single instrument (a bowling ball) at multiple targets (10 pins). The object of the game, to hit multiple targets with a single instrument, is feasible only because the prearrangement of the pins makes it possible (but not easy!) to hit them all with a single ball. Only when multiple targets are closely related—so that the requirement for achieving one is similar to that for achieving another—is the multiple-target/single-instrument game possible; the game of bowling wouldn't work if the 10 pins were scattered over an area the size of a football field rather than arrayed in the usual tight pattern. Macroeconomic policy makers rarely are lucky enough to have their multiple targets placed in such a convenient pattern. As a result, reaching N macroeconomic targets typically requires at least N instruments.

Despite its useful insights, the distinction between targets and instruments is less sharp than it first appears. Additional targets tend to appear on closer examination. For example, exchange rate policy is one of the previously mentioned instruments. Under a flexible exchange rate regime, exchange rate changes automatically achieve external balance defined as balance-of-payments equilibrium. In the United States, this process produced a substantial appreciation of the dollar against most other currencies in the early 1980s. The flexibility of the exchange rate facilitated external balance; however, many individuals in the United States and abroad expressed dissatisfaction with the dollar's value relative to other currencies. U.S. farmers blamed the high value of the dollar for their inability to export agricultural products. U.S. automobile producers and firms in other import-competing sectors of the economy blamed the dollar for a "flood of imports" that "exported jobs." Some commentators worried that large-scale capital inflows meant foreign investors, especially those from Japan, were "buying up" the United States. Debt-ridden developing countries blamed the worsening of their already severe debt problems on their currencies' depreciations against the dollar.

Each of these elements of dissatisfaction reflects an additional target. Farmers want a value of the dollar that enhances their ability to export; import-competing industries want a value of the dollar that lessens their import competition; opponents of foreign investment in the United States want a value of the dollar that discourages such investment; and debtor countries want a stable value of their currencies against the dollar because of their dollar-denominated debts. In other words, the exchange rate, because of its distributional effects, can itself become a target rather than an instrument.

In spite of these pitfalls, the terminology of targets and instruments proves useful in examining the prospects for macroeconomic policy in an open economy. Achievement of any number of targets requires at least an equal number of instruments. This means that policy makers must be on the lookout for hidden targets and for instruments that may be unavailable or ineffective in some circumstances.[4] Additional targets and missing instruments present problems for policy makers. The primary determinants of effective instruments for the policy maker are (1) the degree of international capital mobility and (2) the nature of the exchange rate regime. We'll explore the effects of each combination in turn, beginning with macroeconomic policy under a fixed exchange rate and immobile capital.

16.3 **Macroeconomic Policy with Immobile Capital**

Economists developed their early analyses of macroeconomic policy in an open economy using the assumption of capital *im*mobility, that is, the absence of private international capital flows. From a 1990s perspective, this assumption seems quite unrealistic; however, until the 1960s capital immobility was a more reasonable supposition than a glance at today's active capital markets suggests.[5] Most governments regulated private capital flows heavily, because most policy makers viewed such flows as a source of instability and therefore something to avoid. Further, many of the institutions that facilitate private capital flows today had not yet developed. The markets for Eurocurrencies didn't exist, nor did today's extensive international linking of bond and stock markets. Today, the degree of capital mobility varies widely across countries, but most still maintain some restrictions on nonofficial capital-account transactions.

Under perfect capital immobility, no private capital flows occur to enter the nonofficial capital account as described in Chapter Thirteen. Since private capital inflows and outflows equal zero, the capital-account

---

4 For example, for monetary and fiscal policy to constitute two instruments, the central bank must pursue a policy *independent* of the expenditure and taxing patterns of the fiscal authority. This isn't the case in countries whose central banks are expected to expand the money supply to offset any interest rate rise generated by expansionary fiscal policies.

5 Obstfeld and Rogoff, pp. 1734–1735, present a very brief history of international capital flows.

balance simply equals a constant, which we can set arbitrarily at zero for simplicity. No private international borrowing and lending occurs, regardless of the interest rate differentials among countries. With no capital account (KAB = 0), the balance of payments (BOP = CAB + KAB) consists solely of the current account. If the current account is in deficit, the balance of payments is in deficit; with a current-account surplus, a balance-of-payments surplus exists. The requirement for external balance reduces to the requirement that the current-account balance equal zero. The variables that ordinarily affect the capital account—domestic and foreign interest rates and forward and expected future exchange rates (i, i^*, e^f, and e^e)—no longer play a role in determining the country's balance of payments, because private capital flows don't respond to changes in those variables.

Recall from section 14.4 that only one level of income exists at which the current-account balance (and therefore, with no capital mobility, the balance of payments) equals zero. We'll denote that level of income as Q_{EB}, for *external balance*. Capital immobility renders the interest rate irrelevant to balance-of-payments equilibrium, so the BOP line becomes vertical, as in Figure 16.1, rather than upward sloping, as we saw in section 15.4.2. The degree of capital mobility doesn't affect the IS and LM curves, which represent equilibrium in the markets for goods and services and for money, respectively.

In Figure 16.1, Q_{IB} denotes the level of income consistent with *internal balance*, or full employment. All three key markets—goods and services, money, and foreign exchange—are in equilibrium at the intersection of the IS, LM, and BOP curves, and that equilibrium income satisfies the requirements of both internal and external balance (that is, $Q_{IB} = Q_{EB}$). But so far, we have no reason to expect the incomes consistent with internal balance (full employment) and external balance (balance-of-payments equilibrium) to coincide.[6] If the lucky coincidence illustrated in Figure 16.1 held, there would be little need for macroeconomic policy.

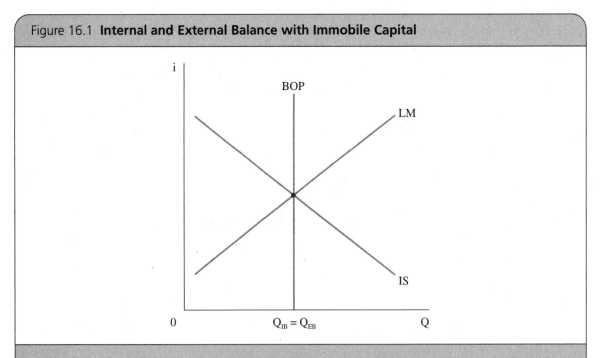

Figure 16.1 **Internal and External Balance with Immobile Capital**

The economy is in equilibrium at the intersection of the IS, LM, and BOP curves, which represent the three major markets: goods and services, money, and foreign exchange. As drawn, the equilibrium income satisfies both internal balance (full employment, represented by Q_{IB}) and external balance (balance-of-payments equilibrium, represented by Q_{EB}).

---

6 Once we introduce price flexibility in Chapters Eighteen and Nineteen, the economy will contain an adjustment mechanism with which to equate the incomes required for internal and external balance, at least in the long run.

We've seen that the economy does contain a self-adjustment mechanism for reaching external balance under a fixed exchange rate regime (see section 15.7). If the balance of payments is in deficit (at a point to the right of the BOP curve), the quantity demanded of foreign exchange exceeds the quantity available. To prevent the domestic currency from depreciating, the central bank intervenes to supply foreign exchange from its international reserves. The resulting loss of reserves causes the money stock to fall and the domestic interest rate to rise. Graphically, the reduction in the money stock shifts the LM curve to the left until it intersects the IS and BOP curves at Q_{EB}. The new equilibrium level of income is lower, because the higher interest rate discourages investment expenditure; the reduction in income curtails imports and eliminates the current-account deficit. The higher interest rate also reduces the quantity of real money balances individuals in the economy choose to hold, making them content with the new lower money stock.

Similarly, a balance-of-payments surplus (at any point to the left of the BOP curve) requires central bank intervention to buy foreign exchange. Reserves rise, and the money stock increases. The LM curve shifts to the right until it intersects IS and BOP at Q_{EB}. The lower rate of interest in the economy induces greater investment and higher income, as well as making portfolio owners content to hold the larger stock of money balances now available in the economy. The increased income encourages imports and eliminates the balance-of-payments surplus.

With the price level fixed (an assumption we've not yet relaxed), no analogous mechanism exists to enable the economy to reach internal balance if the income required for internal balance differs from that for external balance, as is generally the case. The primary role of macroeconomic policy under such circumstances would be to bring the economy into internal balance. The list of possible policy instruments to be considered includes fiscal, monetary, and exchange rate policies. We now consider each in turn. For each analysis, we begin with the economy in external balance at a level of income below that required for internal balance, or full employment. *(In each case, the reader should test his or her understanding by constructing the reasoning that would apply if the economy found itself in external balance at an income level above that required for internal balance, thereby creating a threat of inflation.)*[7]

16.3.1 **Fiscal Policy**

Expansionary fiscal policy can take the form of increased government spending on goods and services or of decreased taxes. The expansionary impact of a tax cut works through the effect on consumption: Lower taxes leave a larger share of income available for consumption.[8] Either form of expansionary fiscal policy shifts the IS curve to the right (for a review, see section 14.8).

In Figure 16.2, we selected the magnitude of the fiscal policy to shift the IS curve from IS^0 to IS^1—just enough to cause it to intersect the LM^0 curve at the income corresponding to internal balance. Initially the economy moves into internal balance. The interest rate rises because the increased income raises the demand for money, requiring a rise in the interest rate to lower money demand to match the constant money stock. The rise in income also causes a current-account deficit as imports rise with income. The deficit requires intervention by the central bank to maintain the fixed value of the exchange rate, and the money supply falls, shifting the LM curve back to LM^1. Income falls back to its original level, eliminating the current-account deficit, but with a higher interest rate at the new equilibrium.

Although income ultimately remains unchanged by the fiscal policy, the pattern of spending in the economy does change. The new equilibrium involves a higher level of government spending. The overall level of spending can't be higher, however, since output both begins and ends at Q_{EB}; therefore, the higher interest rate has curtailed the level of private investment spending, a phenomenon known as **crowding out.** When capital is immobile, increased government spending completely crowds out private investment; that is, private investment spending falls by the full amount of any rise in government purchases. This outcome follows from the rise in the interest rate caused by the combination of the increased government spending and the reduction in the money stock generated by the current-account deficit. Fiscal policy proves unsuccessful in expanding the economy to achieve internal balance; in fact, it leaves income completely unaffected.

---

7 See footnote 2.

8 Tax cuts may also encourage production if they take the form of lower marginal tax rates. These effects are referred to as the *supply-side impact* of tax cuts.

Figure 16.2 **Short-Run Effects of Fiscal Policy with Immobile Capital**

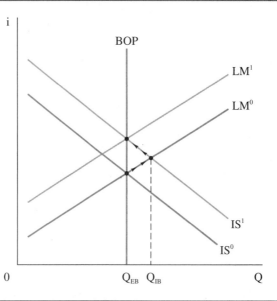

An increase in government purchases raises total expenditure and shifts the IS curve to the right. Income rises as the economy moves to the intersection of the new IS curve with the LM curve. The rise in income increases imports, producing a balance-of-payments deficit. The central bank must intervene to supply foreign exchange, reducing foreign exchange reserves and the money stock. The LM curve shifts to the left and restores equilibrium at the original income, but at a higher interest rate. Complete crowding out renders fiscal policy ineffective for achieving internal balance.

16.3.2 Monetary Policy

Monetary policy also turns out to be incapable of achieving internal balance under fixed exchange rates and immobile capital. The reason for the failure here is even more apparent than in the case of fiscal policy. Under fixed exchange rates, the central bank must intervene in the foreign exchange market to maintain external balance; otherwise, the fixed exchange rate can't be maintained. This intervention alters the domestic money stock. In other words, policy makers must allow the domestic money stock to grow and shrink according to the requirements for external balance.

Figure 16.3 illustrates the basic problem. Beginning from equilibrium at the intersection of IS^0, LM^0, and BOP, expansionary monetary policy shifts the LM curve to LM^1 in an effort to reach internal balance at Q_{IB}. The increase in the money stock lowers the interest rate; investment rises, and the increase in total expenditure raises income. But the rise in income increases imports and causes a balance-of-payments deficit. Intervention in the foreign exchange market to maintain the pegged value of the exchange rate then causes a loss of reserves, shrinking the money stock and shifting the LM curve back to its original position. The interest rate returns to its original level, the temporary increases in investment and income disappear; and imports fall. These adjustments restore external balance but leave the goal of internal balance unachieved.

16.3.3 Sterilization

The monetary authority's primary means for bringing about an expansion of the money stock involves open market operations, or purchases of government bonds from the public (see section 15.2.3). The money stock equals the product of the money multiplier (mm) and the central bank's assets. These assets, in turn, include the central bank's stock of government bonds (GB) accumulated through open market operations plus its foreign exchange reserves (FXR). The central bank accomplishes the move from LM^0 to LM^1 in Figure 16.3 by a

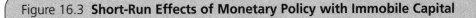

Figure 16.3 **Short-Run Effects of Monetary Policy with Immobile Capital**

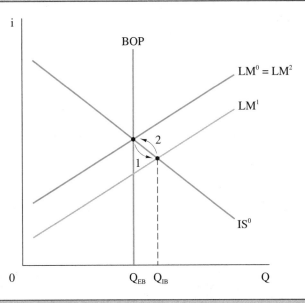

Monetary policy can't achieve internal balance under a fixed exchange rate and perfect capital immobility. Any attempt to increase the money stock (LM⁰ to LM¹) raises income and imports, causing a balance-of-payments deficit. The deficit requires intervention in the foreign exchange market to supply foreign exchange. Reserves fall, offsetting the initial increase in the money stock (LM¹ to LM²).

purchase of government bonds that increases the money stock by $\Delta M = mm \cdot \Delta GB$. The resulting balance-of-payments deficit and intervention then cause the money stock to fall by $\Delta M = mm \cdot \Delta FXR$, where $\Delta FXR < 0$ because the central bank must *sell* reserves.

Since only one income level coincides with external balance with completely immobile capital, the money stock must fall all the way back to its original level—the only one consistent with Q_{EB}. Therefore, the loss of foreign exchange reserves must fully offset the purchase of government bonds so that

$$\text{Total } \Delta M = mm\,(\Delta GB + \Delta FXR) = 0,$$

$$\text{or} \qquad\qquad \textbf{[16.1]}$$

$$-\Delta FXR = \Delta GB$$

The central bank loses foreign exchange reserves equal to the amount of government bonds it purchased. Monetary policy's only lingering effect is a change in the central bank's portfolio of assets. After its intervention, the bank holds a larger quantity of government bonds and a smaller quantity of foreign exchange reserves, but its total assets and the money stock remain unchanged.

Policy makers hardly can expect monetary policy to achieve internal balance if it can't even increase the money stock! A policy that appeals to many central bankers under these circumstances is a **sterilization policy.** The idea is to prevent the loss of foreign exchange reserves from affecting the money stock, thereby maintaining LM^1 and Q_{IB} in Figure 16.3. To sterilize, the central bank simply buys more government bonds to offset any loss of foreign exchange reserves, or:

$$\Delta GB = -\Delta FXR \qquad\qquad \textbf{[16.2]}$$

The incentive to pursue sterilization is obvious. Policy makers typically are much more sensitive to problems of internal imbalance (that is, unemployment) than to those of external imbalance. Sterilization attempts to prevent the realities of external requirements from interfering with domestic economic priorities. But, as we'll see, such attempts aren't likely to succeed.

Equations 16.1 and 16.2 make clear the mechanics of sterilization policy: As the loss of foreign exchange reserves reduces the central bank's assets, the bank offsets the loss with additional open market operations that raise GB. But such a policy isn't viable in the long run.[9] As long as the government pursues sterilization policy, the economy fails to reach external balance—because sterilization blocks the necessary downward adjustment in the size of the money stock. A balance-of-payments deficit persists, requiring continued sales of foreign exchange reserves to maintain the exchange rate. However, the central bank's stock of such reserves is finite, and eventually the reserves will run out. Then policy makers face a choice: cease sterilization and allow the money stock to shrink back to LM^2 or alter the exchange rate with a devaluation, the policy to which we now turn.

16.3.4 **Exchange Rate Policy with Immobile Capital**

Under fixed exchange rates with capital immobility, exchange rate policy has the power to remove the fundamental barrier to simultaneous internal and external balance. This barrier is the fact that each target requires a unique level of income, that is, Q_{IB} for internal balance and Q_{EB} for external balance. If the two income levels differ, as they generally do, the two targets must conflict. Neither fiscal nor monetary policy, alone nor used together, can resolve this conflict. The advantage of exchange rate policy is that it can *change* the level of income required for external balance; in other words, changes in the exchange rate can alter Q_{EB}, making it equal to Q_{IB}.

Recall that a government fixes its exchange rate by announcing the price at which it will buy and sell foreign exchange and then following through on the promise to exchange foreign for domestic currency at that price as demanded by participants in the foreign exchange market. To devalue or revalue its currency, the government simply announces a change in the price at which it will trade foreign exchange.

Figure 16.4 illustrates the use of exchange rate policy—in particular, a devaluation—to effect a solution to the same problem we've been examining: $Q_{EB} < Q_{IB}$. With fixed domestic and foreign price levels, a devaluation of the domestic currency lowers the relative price of domestic goods ($R \equiv P/eP^*$), encourages exports, and discourages imports.[10] The devaluation shifts both the IS and BOP curves to the right. By lowering the relative price of domestic goods, the devaluation raises exports relative to imports at each level of income. Therefore, the income at which exports equal imports (Q_{EB}) rises, which shifts the BOP curve to the right.[11] The increase in net exports due to the devaluation also shifts the IS curve to the right by raising total expenditure on domestic goods and services. To achieve the goal of simultaneous internal and external balance, the devaluation must be just enough to shift the BOP curve such that $Q_{IB} = Q_{EB}$.

The devaluation shifts the BOP curve from BOP^0 to BOP^1 and the IS curve to IS^1. Initially the economy moves to the intersection of the new IS curve with the original LM curve, LM^0. The effect on income is positive, but income remains below the full-employment level. The balance of payments moves into surplus temporarily, causing central bank intervention to buy foreign exchange. The money stock rises with the stock of foreign exchange reserves, which shifts the LM curve to the right. The new equilibrium occurs at the intersection of IS^1, LM^1, and BOP^1, which satisfies both the internal- and external-balance goals. By shifting the income required for external balance from Q_{EB}^0 to Q_{EB}^1, equal to the level consistent with internal balance, the devaluation eliminates the basic policy conflict that prevented both fiscal and monetary policies from achieving the two targets.

---

9 In the case of mobile capital, sterilization may affect the perceived riskiness of foreign and domestic assets, thereby altering portfolio decisions and rendering sterilization somewhat effective, at least in the short run. See section 16.4.2.

10 The assumption of fixed domestic and foreign price levels proves important because, once we relax it, changes in the exchange rate may not affect the relative prices of foreign and domestic goods. Since $R \equiv P/eP^*$, it remains unaffected if P rises proportionally with e or P^* falls proportionally with a rise in e. In other words, changes in the nominal exchange rate (e) imply corresponding changes in the real exchange rate (R) only if price levels are somewhat rigid.

11 Recall that the change in the exchange rate exerts no influence on the capital account when capital is completely immobile.

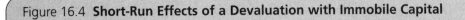

Figure 16.4 Short-Run Effects of a Devaluation with Immobile Capital

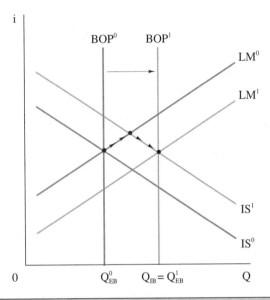

A devaluation of the domestic currency lowers the relative price of domestic goods and services. Exports rise relative to imports, shifting the IS and BOP curves to the right. The initial effect is to create a balance-of-payments surplus. Intervention in the foreign exchange market then increases the money stock. This increase restores equilibrium at a point that satisfies both internal and external balance. The key to this result is the devaluation's ability to alter the income consistent with external balance to match that required for internal balance.

Our analysis makes clear why governments might choose to devalue their currencies. The policy is simple in the sense that it requires merely an announcement of the government's intention to buy or sell foreign exchange at a different price; therefore, the policy change can be accomplished quickly. We've seen that governments with fixed exchange rates and immobile capital can't use fiscal or monetary policy effectively to influence the economy's performance. Exchange rate policy, by generating changes in the size of the money stock indirectly, provides an alternative policy. And, if the central bank is running short of reserves, a devaluation can replenish them.

16.3.5 Summary of Policy Effects with Immobile Capital

Under conditions of perfectly immobile capital and a fixed exchange rate, exchange rate policy is policy makers' only effective tool for altering domestic income in the short run. Neither fiscal nor monetary policy is effective, because attempts to use either generate offsetting changes in the money stock through foreign exchange market intervention. The money stock must adjust to achieve external balance (equivalent to current-account balance). Only exchange rate policy has the power to change the income consistent with external balance to match that consistent with internal balance, thereby permitting policy makers to achieve both targets. Table 16.2 summarizes these results.

16.4 Macroeconomic Policy with Perfectly Mobile Capital

As mentioned earlier, the assumption of international capital immobility has grown increasingly unrealistic in recent years. To see the effect of changing degrees of capital mobility, we now move to the opposite assumption: that of **perfect capital mobility.** This simply means that investors, in deciding which assets to hold, consider

Table 16.2 **Short-Run Policy Effects with Immobile Capital**

Policy	Effect on Equilibrium Q	Effect on Equilibrium Current-Account Balance	Effect on Equilibrium Money Stock
Fiscal Policy:			
Increase in G	0[a]	0[b]	–
Decrease in G	0[a]	0[b]	+
Monetary Policy:			
Increase in M	0	0[b]	0[c]
Decrease in M	0	0[b]	0[c]
Exchange Rate Policy:			
Devaluation	+	0[b]	+
Revaluation	–	0[b]	–

[a]Effect completely crowded out by offsetting impact of interest rate on investment.
[b]With completely immobile capital, only a current-account balance of zero is consistent with balance-of-payments equilibrium.
[c]Effect of initial monetary policy completely offset by foreign exchange market intervention.

only interest rates and exchange rates, including the forward rate and the expected future spot rate. In other words, investors have no built-in preferences for assets denominated in one currency versus those denominated in another, and government policies don't restrict capital flows.

Under perfect capital mobility, the capital account plays the dominant role in foreign exchange markets. Recall that the balance-of-payments or BOP line depicts all the combinations of income and interest rate consistent with foreign exchange market equilibrium, or with interest parity. We draw each BOP line for given values of the foreign interest rate, exchange rate, and forward and expected spot exchange rates.[12] This implies that any rise in the domestic interest rate causes a capital inflow and a move toward a surplus on the capital account.[13]

How does perfect capital mobility produce a horizontal BOP line? In Figure 16.5, the balance of payments is in equilibrium at point A; this is true because A lies on the BOP line, which, by definition, represents points of balance-of-payments equilibrium. Beginning at A, suppose income rises. Imports rise with income, and the current account moves toward a deficit. To maintain balance-of-payments equilibrium, there must be an offsetting move toward surplus on the capital account. With perfectly mobile capital, how large an increase in the domestic interest rate is required to generate this capital-account surplus? An infinitesimal rise will suffice because under perfect capital mobility, investors respond immediately to the slightest rise in domestic rates by moving funds into the domestic economy.[14]

In terms of the interest parity condition discussed in Chapter Twelve, massive capital flows in response to even minute changes in relative interest rates maintain the equilibrium or parity condition. Therefore, the balance of payments is in equilibrium at B, but with a larger current-account deficit and capital-account surplus than at A. All points above the BOP line correspond to situations of balance-of-payments surplus, and those below the line represent balance-of-payments deficits. *(Why?)*

We now turn to the question of the ability of fiscal, monetary, and exchange rate policies to achieve internal and external balance with perfect capital mobility. We'll continue to assume that the problem the economy faces is one of unemployment.

---

12 See section 15.4.2.

13 For a review, see the discussion of interest parity in section 12.4.

14 This assumes that the country can't affect world interest rates. Although called the *small-country assumption,* this condition holds true for most countries.

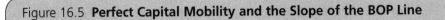

Figure 16.5 Perfect Capital Mobility and the Slope of the BOP Line

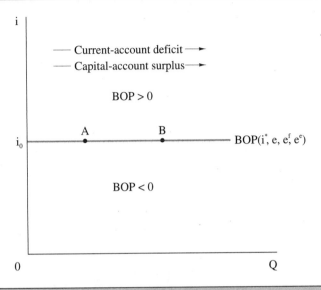

The BOP line is horizontal in the case of perfect capital mobility. A BOP line is drawn for given values of the foreign interest rate and of spot, forward, and expected future spot exchange rates. Given these values, even a tiny increase in the domestic interest rate causes capital inflows. Moving to the right along the BOP line (such as from point A to point B), the current account moves toward a deficit as a result of rising income and imports, and the capital account moves toward a surplus. Above the BOP line, the balance of payments is in surplus; below it, the balance is in deficit.

16.4.1 Fiscal Policy

The change in assumption from perfectly immobile to perfectly mobile capital carries radical implications for fiscal policy's effectiveness under fixed exchange rates. Recall that with no capital mobility, fiscal policy results in complete crowding out and leaves income unaffected. However, with perfect capital mobility in response to international interest differentials, fiscal policy is highly effective in raising income and achieving simultaneous internal and external balance.

Figure 16.6 traces the effects of an expansionary fiscal policy. Beginning in equilibrium at the intersection of IS^0, LM^0, and BOP, an increase in government spending shifts the IS curve to IS^1. Initially the economy moves to the intersection of the new IS curve with LM^0. The rise in income increases the demand for money; because the money stock doesn't change, the interest rate must rise to bring the quantity demanded of money back down to equality with the existing money stock. The rise in the domestic interest rate generates capital inflows and a balance-of-payments surplus. Note that the balance of payments is in surplus even though imports have risen with income; this occurs because, under perfect capital mobility, the capital flows made in response to interest rate changes dominate changes in the current account. To maintain the fixed exchange rate in the face of the BOP surplus, the central bank must purchase foreign exchange; this intervention raises the domestic money stock and shifts the LM curve to LM^1. A new equilibrium occurs at the intersection of IS^1, LM^1, and BOP.

Internal balance has been achieved (assuming that fiscal policy shifts the IS curve to the right by an amount sufficient to ensure that the new IS curve intersects BOP at Q_{IB}). The interest rate remains at its original level; the balance of payments is again in equilibrium, but with a larger current-account deficit and capital-account surplus. *(Why?)* The central bank also holds a larger stock of foreign exchange reserves, acquired through its intervention.

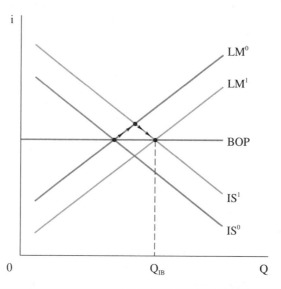

Figure 16.6 **Short-Run Effects of Fiscal Policy with Perfectly Mobile Capital**

An expansionary fiscal policy, by raising income, causes the interest rate to rise. The response is a capital inflow that more than offsets the move toward deficit on the current account. Because the balance of payments is in surplus, foreign exchange market intervention increases the domestic money stock. This increase prevents crowding out; thus, the expansionary fiscal policy raises total expenditure and income. This contrasts with the case under immobile capital, in which expansionary fiscal policy causes a balance-of-payments deficit and a decrease in the domestic money stock.

The key to understanding capital mobility's crucial role in the success of fiscal policy is the policy's effect on the balance of payments. With no capital mobility (see Figure 16.2), expansionary fiscal policy causes a balance-of-payments *deficit*. It (temporarily) raises income and moves the current account into deficit, and there is no possibility of offsetting capital flows. The balance-of-payments deficit, through the automatic adjustment mechanism, *reduces* the money stock. The fall in the money stock counteracts the fiscal policy's expansionary effect (see fiscal policy's impact on the money stock in Table 16.2).

Perfectly mobile capital reverses the effect of fiscal policy on the balance of payments. Although an expansionary policy still moves the current account toward a deficit, this effect is more than offset by the capital inflow in response to the rise in the domestic interest rate. The net effect is a balance-of-payments *surplus,* which, through the automatic adjustment mechanism, results in an *increase* in the money stock. Thus, capital mobility causes expansionary fiscal policy to generate an accompanying increase in the money stock, rather than a decrease as under capital immobility. The expansion of the money stock prevents the interest rate from rising and short-circuits the crowding-out mechanism. The increase in government spending doesn't cause an offsetting decrease in private spending (that is, investment), and total expenditure and income rise.

An alternative way to view fiscal policy's success with mobile capital focuses more directly on the requirements for internal and external balance. With no capital mobility, external balance requires a unique income—the one consistent with a balanced current account. With capital mobility, *any* income can be consistent with external balance (represented graphically by a horizontal BOP line). Since capital mobility guarantees that external balance can occur at any income level, the policy problem reduces to one of reaching internal balance.

16.4.2 **Monetary Policy**

Capital mobility greatly enhances fiscal policy's ability to alter the economy's equilibrium level of income. However, this isn't true for monetary policy. Monetary policy can't affect income under a fixed exchange rate regardless of the degree of capital mobility.

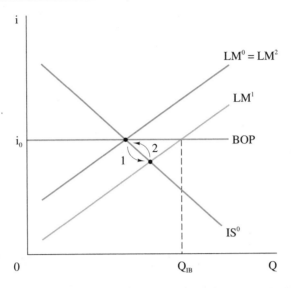

Figure 16.7 **Short-Run Effects of Monetary Policy with Perfectly Mobile Capital**

Beginning from a point of equilibrium, expansionary monetary policy causes a fall in the interest rate and a capital outflow. The resulting balance-of-payments deficit requires intervention to sell foreign exchange from reserves. The loss of reserves reduces the money stock; this process continues until M is back at its original level.

Expansionary monetary policy (represented by Figure 16.7's shift from LM^0 to LM^1) initially lowers the domestic interest rate and raises income, resulting in capital outflows as well as a current-account deficit. The balance-of-payments deficit requires sales of foreign exchange reserves until the money stock falls back to its original level.

Sterilization, Once Again

Recall that to sterilize, the central bank simply buys government bonds to offset any loss of foreign exchange reserves caused by intervention (see section 16.3.3). As the loss of foreign exchange reserves reduces the central bank's assets (GB + FXR), the bank offsets the loss with additional open market operations that raise GB.

Could policy makers permanently prevent the shift of LM back to LM^2 in Figure 16.7 through sterilization? Given the model developed so far, the answer is no. Sterilization isn't viable in the long run, because as long as the central bank pursues such a policy, the interest rate remains below the rate consistent with interest parity and the economy can't reach external balance. The persistent balance-of-payments deficit requires continued sales of foreign exchange reserves to maintain the fixed exchange rate. But each central bank's stock of such reserves is finite and eventually would be depleted, forcing policy makers to choose between a currency devaluation and the reduction in the money stock represented by the leftward shift of the LM curve to LM^2 in Figure 16.7.

An alternate way to recognize sterilization's futility is to recall that a balance-of-payments deficit reflects excess demand for foreign-currency deposits in the foreign exchange market, such as the one depicted in panel (a) of Figure 16.8. A fall in the domestic money stock, through foreign exchange market intervention to supply foreign currency, can eliminate such excess demand because, as the money stock falls, the domestic interest rate rises (shown in panel (b)). The increase in the domestic interest rate increases the expected return on domestic-currency-denominated deposits, reduces the demand for foreign-currency-denominated ones in panel (a), and restores equilibrium in the foreign exchange market at e_0.[15] Sterilization, by preventing the decline in the

---

15 Figure 15.20 illustrates the corresponding case of monetary adjustment to eliminate a balance-of-payments surplus.

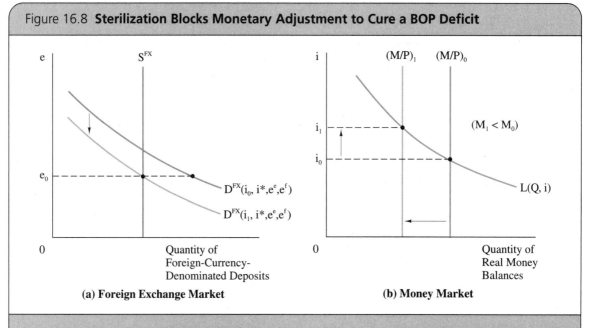

Figure 16.8 **Sterilization Blocks Monetary Adjustment to Cure a BOP Deficit**

(a) Foreign Exchange Market

(b) Money Market

With a balance-of-payments deficit, intervention reduces the money stock and raises the domestic interest rate in panel (b), which reduces demand for foreign-currency-denominated deposits in panel (a). Sterilization uses open market operations to offset intervention's effect on the money stock. The domestic interest rate fails to rise, and the balance-of-payments deficit persists.

money stock and the increase in the interest rate, blocks this adjustment process and keeps the economy out of external balance because the excess demand for foreign-currency deposits at the fixed exchange rate persists.

Empirical evidence, however, suggests that central banks do sterilize. In fact, popular discussions of monetary policy often ignore completely the link between a country's balance of payments and its money stock, because they assume that sterilization automatically accompanies any foreign exchange market intervention. Questions regarding the viability of sterilized intervention have become the subject of active research by both academic economists and policy makers. Two considerations, when integrated into the model developed so far, suggest channels through which sterilized intervention—that is, intervention that doesn't affect the money stock—might alter the demand for foreign-currency-denominated deposits to restore equilibrium in the foreign exchange market at the fixed exchange rate.

Suppose that in allocating their asset portfolios between foreign-currency- and domestic-currency-denominated deposits, investors care about the perceived riskiness of each type of deposit as well as its expected return.[16] To hold an asset perceived as risky, investors will demand a higher expected rate of return in compensation, and they will be willing to hold an asset carrying little risk at a lower expected rate of return. If assets denominated in different currencies vary in their perceived riskiness, the interest parity condition will contain a **risk premium,** σ, that represents the extra return investors require to compensate them for the additional risk in holding a particular currency.[17] In Equation 16.3, σ will be positive if domestic-currency assets require a risk premium, implying that domestic assets must carry a higher interest rate. The domestic interest rate can be lower relative to the foreign interest rate if σ is negative, that is, if foreign-currency assets require a risk premium.

$$i - i^* = [(e^e - e)/e] + \sigma \qquad \textbf{[16.3]}$$

16 This condition is known as *imperfect asset substitutability*, in contrast to *perfect asset substitutability*, in which investors care only about expected rates of return in choosing among assets.

17 In the economics literature, the lowercase Greek letter *sigma* (σ) constitutes the standard notation for variability or risk in a variable.

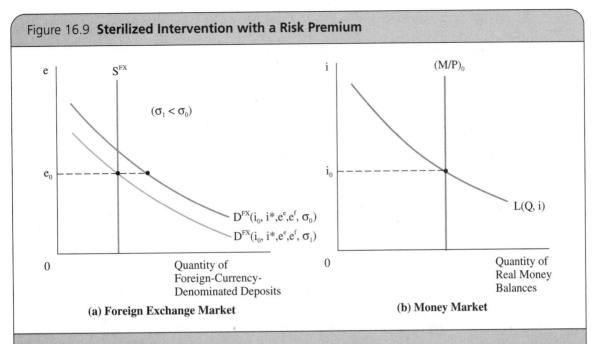

Figure 16.9 **Sterilized Intervention with a Risk Premium**

With a balance-of-payments deficit, sterilized intervention reduces the quantity of government bonds held by the public. If this reduces the risk premium (σ) demanded by market participants, the demand for foreign-currency deposits falls, and the balance-of-payments deficit is eliminated in panel (a), even though sterilized intervention fails to alter the size of the money stock or the interest rate in panel (b).

The existence of a risk premium in the interest parity condition carries several important implications. The most important is that, as the quantity of the domestic government's bonds held by the public rises, the risk premium on domestic assets may rise because a large share of such bonds in investors' portfolios makes the investors' wealth more vulnerable to changes in the exchange rate. Under such conditions, expansionary domestic monetary policy (that is, a central bank purchase of government bonds that expands the domestic money stock) may reduce the risk premium by reducing the number of domestic government bonds held by the public. Similarly, contractionary monetary policy (that is, a central bank sale of government bonds that reduces the domestic money stock) may increase the risk premium.

A risk premium that changes in this way with domestic monetary policy implies that sterilized foreign exchange market intervention might affect the demand for foreign-currency-denominated deposits. Recall that a government sterilizes its intervention by purchasing or selling government bonds to offset the intervention's effect on the domestic money supply, as summarized in Equation 16.2. With no risk premium, sterilized intervention leaves the domestic money stock and interest rate unchanged. However, with a risk premium, if the central bank sterilizes a sale of foreign exchange by buying bonds, the quantity of government bonds that the public must hold falls, and this may cause the risk premium on domestic-currency assets to fall. If so, the domestic interest rate consistent with interest parity falls, as indicated in Equation 16.3.

Figure 16.9 illustrates the implications for a country with a balance-of-payments deficit. To hold the exchange rate fixed, the central bank intervenes to supply foreign exchange but also sterilizes by buying government bonds so that the money stock remains unchanged in panel (b). The central bank's bond purchase leaves fewer bonds to be held by the public, reduces the perceived riskiness associated with holding domestic bonds, and lowers the risk premium, σ. The reduction in risk makes investors more willing to hold domestic-currency-denominated assets and less willing to hold foreign-currency-denominated ones at any given interest rate. The demand for foreign-currency assets in panel (a) shifts to the left and restores balance-of-payments equilibrium at the fixed exchange rate of e_0. Because of the variable risk premium, sterilization doesn't block foreign exchange market equilibrium, as it does in the absence of a risk premium. In other words, a risk premium may allow even sterilized intervention to shift the demand for foreign-currency assets.

The second channel through which sterilized intervention may be able to shift the demand for foreign-currency assets, even in the absence of a risk premium, relies on market participants using intervention as a source of information, or a **signal,** about future macroeconomic policy. When a government intervenes, even on a sterilized basis, market participants may interpret the intervention as a sign that future government policies will push the exchange rate in the direction indicated by the intervention. For example, if a central bank sells foreign exchange and buys domestic bonds, market participants may expect future macroeconomic policies aimed at reducing the domestic-currency price of foreign currency. If so, the expected future exchange rate (e^e) may fall, which would shift the demand for foreign-currency-denominated assets to the left, even though the domestic money stock remained unchanged.

Governments that attempt to use such signaling too often, however, will suffer a loss of credibility. Unlike the risk-premium effect, the signaling effect of sterilized intervention requires that market participants take such intervention as a credible indication of future government policies. Too many episodes of faulty signals lead market participants to ignore future signals.

Several empirical studies have found that sterilized intervention can alter the demand for foreign-currency-denominated assets, but often only insignificantly. Generally, however, studies of sterilized intervention's effectiveness lead to mixed results for several reasons. First, detailed intervention data often are kept secret by central banks, so many studies rely on somewhat unreliable data. Second, statistical studies suffer from observers' lack of knowledge of what would have happened in the absence of intervention. Third, the risk-premium and signaling hypotheses rest on effects that we might expect to vary across time and across countries. Investors may demand risk premiums for some currencies and not others or during some periods and not others; some risk premiums may respond to factors other than the quantity of government bonds held by the public. Similarly, market participants may accept sterilized intervention as a policy signal from some governments and not from others. Therefore, there may be no single correct answer to whether sterilized intervention "works."

Many economists remain skeptical, for several reasons, of sterilized intervention's ability to alter the exchange rate.[18] First, they point out that intervention is most likely when exchange rates reach extreme values; such episodes, however, correspond to times when exchange rate trends are most likely to reverse themselves even without intervention. Therefore, attributing such trend reversals to sterilized intervention runs the risk of interpreting something that would have happened anyway as an effect of intervention. Second, central banks may choose to intervene only when they believe market conditions are such that intervention can alter the path of the exchange rate. Finally, if central banks continue intervention until the exchange rate trend changes, then intervention will, by definition, be followed by trend reversal and will appear to "work."[19] Most economists agree that sterilized intervention, while it may exert some small short-run influence in foreign exchange markets in some circumstances, *cannot* be used to overcome trends in the foreign exchange market or to avoid the fundamental monetary adjustment necessary to achieve external balance under a fixed exchange rate.

16.4.3 Exchange Rate Policy

As with fiscal policy, changes in the exchange rate can achieve internal balance under a fixed-rate regime with perfect capital mobility. The devaluation doesn't affect the BOP curve as long as the forward and expected future spot exchange rates move in tandem with e. This will be the case when foreign exchange market participants expect the devaluation to be permanent, but don't expect it to lead to further devaluations. When these assumptions are met, the forward premium (or discount) on foreign exchange and the expected rate of future depreciation (or appreciation) remain unchanged during the devaluation. Therefore, for any given value of the foreign interest rate, the same domestic interest rate that was consistent with balance-of-payments equilibrium before the devaluation is still consistent with equilibrium after the devaluation.

A devaluation shifts the IS curve in Figure 16.10 to the right by lowering the relative price of domestically produced goods and services. The economy moves to the intersection of the new IS curve with LM^0. The interest rate rises because the rise in income raises money demand, and the rise in the interest rate reequates the quantity demanded of money with the money stock. The balance of payments moves to surplus because of increased capital inflows brought on by the higher interest rate.

---

18 The Obstfeld article in the chapter references contains a useful discussion.

19 This is akin to the old saying that you always find a lost object in the last place you look for it—because when you find it you stop looking in additional places.

Figure 16.10 **Short-Run Effects of a Devaluation with Perfectly Mobile Capital**

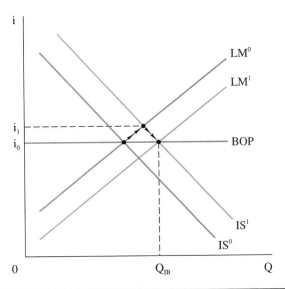

A devaluation of the domestic currency shifts the IS curve to the right. At first, the balance of payments moves to a surplus because of an increased capital inflow. Intervention in the foreign exchange market increases the domestic money stock and shifts the LM curve from LM^0 to LM^1. The interest rate returns to i_0.

The BOP surplus requires central bank intervention to buy foreign exchange, swelling the money stock and moving the LM curve from LM^0 toward LM^1. Equilibrium is restored at the intersection of IS^1, LM^1, and BOP. The devaluation raises income by generating an increase in the money stock through the automatic adjustment mechanism. The devaluation also moves the current account toward a surplus and raises the central bank's stock of foreign exchange reserves. While devaluations can serve as an important tool of macroeconomic policy, they do run certain risks. In particular, a devaluation may lead market participants to anticipate further devaluations. If so, a devaluation can precipitate a balance-of-payments crisis, along the lines suggested in the following section.

16.4.4 **Changes in Exchange Rate Expectations**

Even under a pegged exchange rate, participants in foreign exchange markets may come to believe that the government will be unwilling or unable to maintain the current pegged value. For example, individuals might come to expect a devaluation of the domestic currency because the central bank is running short of foreign exchange reserves, because of prolonged domestic unemployment, or because of a large chronic current-account deficit. Figure 16.11 depicts the effects of such a change in expectations. Initially the economy is in equilibrium at the intersection of IS^0, LM^0, and BOP^0. Suddenly e^e rises from e_0^e to e_1^e, which causes the BOP line to shift up to BOP^1. Because the actual exchange rate hasn't changed, the rise in e^e requires a higher domestic interest rate to make portfolio owners content to hold the existing stock of domestic-currency-denominated deposits in the face of the expected devaluation. *(Explain why, using the interest parity condition from section 12.4.1.)*

At the intersection of IS^0 and LM^0, the balance of payments is in deficit with $e^e = e_1^e$ because of the low domestic interest rate. Intervention by the central bank to hold the exchange rate at its peg lowers the domestic money stock and shifts the LM curve to the left to LM^1. The capital flight in response to the expected devaluation requires a rise in the domestic interest rate, thereby reducing investment and income. Maintaining the exchange rate in the face of the expected devaluation also causes the central bank to expend part of its foreign exchange reserves. This loss of reserves may cause foreign exchange market participants to anticipate a further

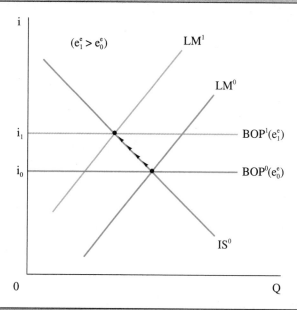

Figure 16.11 Short-Run Effects of an *Expected* Devaluation with Perfectly Mobile Capital

An expected devaluation of the domestic currency (a rise in e^e) shifts the BOP line from BOP^0 to BOP^1. At i_0, the domestic balance of payments is in deficit. As the central bank intervenes to supply foreign exchange, the domestic money stock falls and the LM curve shifts from LM^0 to LM^1. A new equilibrium occurs at the intersection of IS^0, LM^1, and BOP^1.

devaluation, which can set the entire process in motion again. The result can be a vicious circle in which the loss of reserves creates expectations that require further central bank intervention to protect the exchange rate, further reducing its reserves. The possibility of such vicious circles has led many analysts to question the viability of fixed but adjustable exchange rates under perfect capital mobility, especially for governments that lack a reputation for keeping their policy promises.

16.4.5 Summary of Policy Effects with Perfectly Mobile Capital

With perfectly mobile capital, fiscal policy and exchange rate policy can alter the level of income in the domestic economy. Monetary policy, in contrast, remains ineffective, as in the immobile-capital case. Fiscal policy and exchange rate policy work through their abilities to generate changes in the domestic money stock, as reported in Table 16.3.

16.5 Macroeconomic Policy with Imperfectly Mobile Capital

The two assumptions we've used so far concerning the capital market—zero capital mobility and perfect capital mobility—represent extremes. Although such extremes rarely are observed in the world economy, they provide useful benchmarks to understand capital mobility's role in determining the effectiveness of macroeconomic policies. We now turn to the case in which the degree of capital mobility falls between the two extremes: Investors do respond to international changes in interest rates by altering the compositions of their portfolios; however, the responses may not be instantaneous, investors may prefer assets denominated in certain currencies, and government policies may restrict mobility.

Table 16.3 Short-Run Policy Effects with Perfectly Mobile Capital

Policy	Effect on Equilibrium Q	Effect on Equilibrium Current-Account Balance	Effect on Equilibrium Money Stock
Fiscal Policy:			
Increase in G	+	−	+
Decrease in G	−	+	−
Monetary Policy:[a]			
Increase in M	0	0	0[b]
Decrease in M	0	0	0[b]
Exchange Rate Policy:			
Devaluation	+	+	+
Revaluation	−	−	−

[a]Foreign exchange market intervention unsterilized.
[b]Effect of initial monetary policy completely offset by foreign exchange market intervention.

In this section, we examine the effectiveness of fiscal, monetary, and exchange rate policy in achieving internal balance under this intermediate degree of capital mobility. As we might expect, the results lie between those of the two extreme cases. Fiscal policy is effective in raising income (as in the perfect capital mobility case), but some degree of crowding out occurs (as in the perfect capital immobility case). Monetary policy remains ineffective, and a devaluation can still achieve internal balance.

When capital is imperfectly mobile, a question arises concerning the relative slopes of the LM and BOP curves. The more mobile is capital, the flatter the BOP curve. *(Why?)* We'll examine the case in which the BOP curve is flatter than the LM curve: that of high capital mobility. *(For each policy discussed, the reader should test his or her understanding by constructing a similar analysis under the assumption that capital is somewhat less mobile and the BOP curve thus is steeper than the LM curve.)*

16.5.1 Fiscal Policy

Fiscal policy raises income through the following chain of events, illustrated in Figure 16.12. The initial expansionary policy shifts the IS curve from IS^0 to IS^1 and raises income, increasing the demand for money. Because the money stock doesn't change, the interest rate must rise to cause an offsetting decline in the quantity demanded of money. The rise in the interest rate implies increased capital inflows and a balance-of-payments surplus. The surplus raises the money stock through the automatic adjustment mechanism under a fixed exchange rate. The rise in the money stock shifts the LM curve to the right, from LM^0 to LM^1.

The new equilibrium involves a higher income and a higher interest rate. The two must occur together because the higher income moves the current account toward a deficit. External balance, then, requires an increased capital inflow, which occurs with imperfect capital mobility only in response to a higher domestic interest rate.

16.5.2 Monetary Policy

Regardless of the degree of capital mobility, monetary policy can't raise income under a fixed exchange rate regime. This is because the money stock must vary with the requirements of external balance through foreign exchange market intervention.

The more mobile capital is, the more futile are attempts to use expansionary monetary policy to raise income, even in the short run. The more sensitive capital flows are to interest rate changes, the larger and more rapid is the capital outflow in response to the temporary drop in the domestic interest rate that follows an open market purchase (see arrow 1 in Figure 16.13). A larger and more rapid capital outflow implies a larger, more immediate balance-of-payments deficit and greater, more rapid losses of foreign exchange reserves (represented by arrow 2 in Figure 16.13).

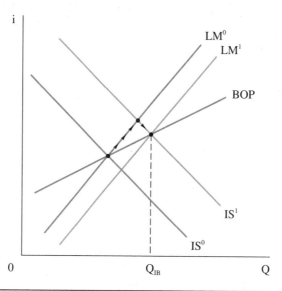

Figure 16.12 **Short-Run Effects of Fiscal Policy with Imperfectly Mobile Capital**

Expansionary fiscal policy shifts the IS curve to the right. The rise in the interest rate generates capital inflows, and foreign exchange market intervention increases the money stock. The new equilibrium occurs at a higher income and interest rate.

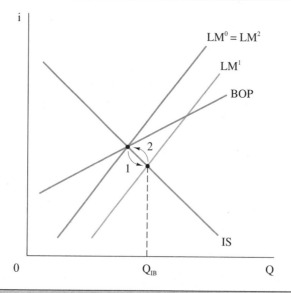

Figure 16.13 **Short-Run Effects of Monetary Policy with Imperfectly Mobile Capital**

Expansionary monetary policy shifts the LM curve to the right and lowers the interest rate. Capital outflows cause a balance-of-payments deficit; the central bank must intervene to sell foreign exchange. The decline in foreign exchange reserves cuts the money stock to its original level. The new equilibrium is at the original income and interest rate.

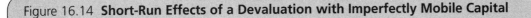

Figure 16.14 Short-Run Effects of a Devaluation with Imperfectly Mobile Capital

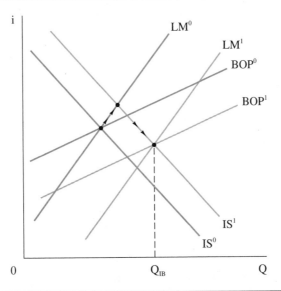

A devaluation of the domestic currency shifts both the IS and BOP curves to the right by lowering the relative price of domestic goods and services. The balance-of-payments surplus results in an increase in the domestic money stock. The new equilibrium occurs at a higher income level and a lower interest rate.

16.5.3 Exchange Rate Policy

A devaluation raises income when capital is imperfectly mobile. The change in the exchange rate lowers the relative price of domestically produced goods and services, which shifts both the IS and BOP curves to the right.[20] The resulting balance-of-payments surplus leads to a rise in the stock of foreign exchange reserves and in the domestic money stock, shifting the LM curve from LM^0 to LM^1 (see Figure 16.14). The devaluation succeeds in raising income to a level consistent with internal balance.

16.6 A Special Case: The Reserve Country

Thus far, we've examined the case of a single country that fixes its currency's value against the currency of a single trading partner by intervening in the foreign exchange market to exchange domestic-currency deposits for foreign-currency ones as demanded by participants in the foreign exchange market. In practice, hundreds of currencies exist in the world economy (see Figure 12.2), but fixed exchange rate regimes typically don't involve each country intervening in hundreds of separate foreign exchange markets to fix their respective currencies against each of the other currencies. Instead, countries agree, either implicitly or explicitly, on a single currency to act as the **reserve currency.** Each central bank announces a fixed exchange rate between its domestic currency and the reserve currency, which the bank holds as its foreign exchange reserves. The system of fixed rates between each nonreserve currency and the reserve currency indirectly produces fixed exchange rates between each pair of nonreserve currencies.

---

20 If the devaluation is expected to be permanent, but doesn't generate expectations of further devaluations, then e and e^e move together, the original interest rate remains consistent with interest parity, and the BOP line shifts solely because of e's impact on the current account through the relative price of domestic goods and services ($R \equiv P/eP^*$). If the devaluation alters market participants' expectations of the future exchange rate, those changes must be taken into account in shifting the BOP line. Devaluation-induced changes in expectations can have dramatic consequences, as in Mexico in 1994 and Asia in 1997; see Cases Two and Three.

Under the **Bretton Woods** system of fixed exchange rates, in effect from the end of World War II until 1973, the U.S. dollar served as the reserve currency. Non-U.S. central banks held most of their international reserves in dollars, and each bank intervened as required to hold the exchange rate between its currency and the U.S. dollar at the agreed rate.[21] Private arbitrage kept cross exchange rates between nondollar currencies fixed, because whenever an exchange rate became inconsistent with the two respective dollar exchange rates, the situation created a profitable arbitrage opportunity.[22] Suppose, for example, that in 1967 the fixed exchange rates between the dollar and the pound and between the dollar and the mark were \$2.75/£1 and \$0.275/DM1, respectively, and that the Bank of England and Bundesbank bought or sold dollars from their reserves to maintain those rates. The consistent exchange rate between pounds and marks would be DM10/£1. Any other exchange rate would allow profitable arbitrage. Consider what would happen if the cross exchange rate fell to DM9/£1. Arbitrageurs could use \$2.75 to buy DM10, use the 10 marks to buy £1.11, and turn those pounds into \$3.05, earning a riskless profit of \$0.30. The impact of the arbitrage would raise the mark price of a pound back toward the consistent rate, DM10/£1.

Existence of a reserve currency creates a special situation for policy makers in the reserve-currency country, the United States in the case of the Bretton Woods system. The reserve-currency country never has to intervene in the foreign exchange market, because each nonreserve central bank handles the task of keeping its exchange rate fixed relative to the reserve currency. Another way of noting the special situation is to realize that a world of N countries and N currencies has $N - 1$ exchange rates against the reserve currency. For example, if Britain, Germany, and the United States composed the entire world economy (N = 3), there would be only two ($N - 1 = 3 - 1 = 2$) exchange rates relative to the dollar (\$2.75/£1 and \$0.275/DM1). Consistency determines the third rate, so that $£/DM = £/\$ \cdot \$/DM$, as we saw in section 12.3.2.

This asymmetry carries an important implication: The reserve-currency country *can* use monetary policy to pursue internal balance even under a fixed exchange rate. Recall that monetary policy fails for nonreserve countries because they must intervene to cover any balance-of-payments surpluses or deficits, and such intervention offsets the effect of the initial monetary policy. The reserve country, in contrast, never has to intervene, so it can use monetary policy. In fact, it can conduct monetary policy not only for itself, but also for the entire set of countries in the fixed exchange rate system. Figure 16.15 shows why. Panel (a) represents the situation in the reserve country. We omit the BOP line from the diagram because, as we just argued, the reserve-country central bank needn't intervene to offset any balance-of-payments surplus or deficit that might arise. In effect, the reserve country is unconstrained by external balance, because other countries adjust to keep the reserve country in balance-of-payments equilibrium. Panel (b), which illustrates events in a representative nonreserve economy, does contain a BOP line, because the nonreserve-country central bank has the responsibility to intervene to keep its currency's exchange rate fixed against the reserve currency.

Suppose the reserve country conducts an expansionary monetary policy that shifts its LM curve to the right. The domestic interest rate falls, and the balance of payments moves into deficit. In the nonreserve country, the BOP line shifts down. This occurs because the lower interest rate in the reserve country generates a capital outflow from the reserve country into the nonreserve country and makes a lower interest rate in the nonreserve country consistent with interest parity. As the nonreserve country's BOP line shifts down, the economy experiences a balance-of-payments surplus from the capital inflow. To prevent its currency from appreciating against the reserve currency, the nonreserve central bank must buy foreign exchange (that is, reserve-currency-denominated deposits) in the foreign exchange market. This increases the nonreserve country's money stock and shifts its LM curve to the right. At the new equilibrium, both the reserve and nonreserve economies have higher levels of income and lower interest rates.

Policy makers in the reserve country clearly enjoy an advantage from their ability to conduct monetary policy under a fixed exchange rate regime. Put another way, the reserve country avoids responsibility for financing its own balance-of-payments surpluses or deficits; other countries must do so. Other countries will likely view the spillover effects of reserve-country policy as a mixed blessing. If reserve and nonreserve countries tend to experience similar economic situations (for example, simultaneous booms or recessions), then the across-border effects of reserve-country policy may cause no problem and may even be welcomed. However, if economic situations in the two countries differ, making expansionary policy appropriate for one and contractionary policy appropriate for the other, tensions are likely to rise as the nonreserve country inherits

---

21 Under Bretton Woods, exchange rates could fluctuate within bands of plus or minus 1 percent of the central rate.

22 The same logic applies to the case of triangular arbitrage in section 12.3.2.

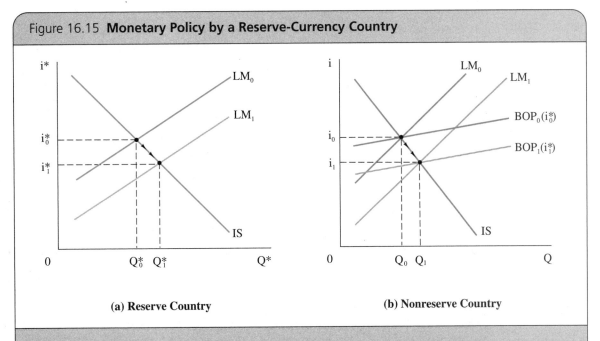

Figure 16.15 Monetary Policy by a Reserve-Currency Country

(a) Reserve Country

(b) Nonreserve Country

The reserve-currency country, in panel (a), doesn't face the usual balance-of-payments constraint on its monetary policy. Expansionary monetary policy by the reserve country shifts its LM curve to the right and lowers its interest rate. In the non-reserve country (panel (b)), the decline in the reserve-country interest rate shifts the BOP line down, because the fall in i^* lowers the expected return on deposits denominated in the reserve currency and makes portfolio owners content to hold nonreserve-currency deposits at a lower interest rate than before. At i_0, the nonreserve country has a balance-of-payments surplus. It intervenes by purchasing reserve-currency deposits in the foreign exchange market. The domestic money stock rises and shifts the LM curve to the right. Expansionary monetary policy by the reserve country expands not only its own money stock, but that of the nonreserve country as well.

the effects of the reserve country's policy. We'll see in Chapters Seventeen and Twenty that tensions such as these contributed to the demise of the Bretton Woods system of fixed exchange rates, as countries became unwilling to absorb the impact of U.S. inflationary policies during the late 1960s.

Germany

CASE ONE:
More on German Unification

The unification of the Federal Republic of Germany and the German Democratic Republic in 1990 occurred in the context of a fixed exchange rate regime among the (then 12) member countries of the European Community (EC), now the European Union. Within the group, the German Deutsche mark served as the unofficial reserve currency; and other member countries adjusted their policies to maintain the values of their currencies relative to the mark. This implied that Germany could conduct effective monetary policy while other member countries could not, as we saw in section 16.6.

This exchange rate regime played an important role in determining the economic effects of German unification on other EC members. In particular, the fixed-rate system caused Germany's unification-based economic boom to exert a contractionary effect on the country's European trading partners.

To keep our analysis simple, let's let Britain represent all non-German EC members. Figure 16.16 illustrates the pre-unification economic conditions in Germany and Britain, where all three markets in both countries are in equilibrium. Recall that the absence of a BOP^G curve reflects Germany's

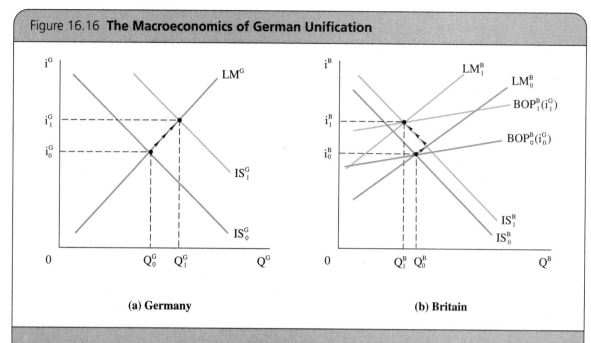

Figure 16.16 The Macroeconomics of German Unification

(a) Germany

(b) Britain

The accelerated expenditure and tight monetary policy that accompanied unification in Germany (panel (a)) exerted two influences on trading partners, represented here by Britain (panel (b)). First, increased demand for their exports shifted IS to the right and exerted an expansionary influence on trading-partner economies. Second, the increased German interest rate shifted trading partners' BOP lines upward. To keep their currencies from depreciating against the mark, trading partners had to intervene to supply marks, shifting their LM curves to the left and exerting a contractionary influence on the economy. The net effect on trading-partner economies—expansionary or contractionary—depends on the relative sizes of the two effects.

monetary independence as the reserve-currency country. The unification process caused German consumption, investment, and especially government expenditure to rise, so the IS^G curve shifted substantially to the right. German central bankers, fearful that too much expansion might cause inflation to rise, kept the money stock constant. Upward pressure on German interest rates shifted BOP^B up and caused a capital flow from Britain to Germany, resulting in a British balance-of-payments deficit and a German surplus. Increased German demand for imports also shifted the IS^B curve to the right.

To prevent the pound from depreciating against the mark, the Bank of England had to supply marks to the foreign exchange market. This shifted the LM^B curve to the left until it intersected the new BOP^B_1 and IS^B_1. Note that the *net* effect of German unification on Britain depends on the relative sizes of the shifts in IS^B and LM^B. The greater the increase in German demand for foreign goods and services, the bigger the rightward shift in Britain's IS curve and the more likely Germany's unification boom would be transmitted as a boom to Germany's European trading partners. The smaller the increase in German demand for foreign goods

and services, the smaller the shift in Britain's IS curve and the more likely Germany unification would push its partners into economic slumps through monetary contraction transmitted by the fixed exchange rate system.

How did the scenario actually play out? Following unification, Germany pursued tight monetary policy to avoid unification-induced inflation. As the German LM curve shifted to the left, European trading partners were forced to do likewise to maintain their exchange rates against the mark. *(Illustrate in a diagram similar to Figure 16.16.)* Germany entered a recession along with most of the other economies of Europe.

By late 1992, Germany's ability to force its partners to follow the Bundesbank's monetary policy threatened the whole process of monetary integration within the European Community. Participants in the foreign exchange market started to doubt the resolve of countries such as Britain and France to carry through with contractionary monetary policies when their economies were already in recession. Portfolio owners began to expect devaluations of the pound, franc, and other non-mark EU currencies. As e^e (defined as pounds or francs per DM) rose, the BOP lines of the nonreserve countries shifted further up—in September 1992, November 1992, and again in July 1993—requiring even more monetary contraction to maintain the exchange rate pegs against the mark. France continued to engage in large-scale intervention, buying francs to support the exchange rate. By the time the dust settled, the French franc was one of only a few EU currencies to survive with its pre-crisis exchange rate intact.

We'll see in Chapter Seventeen that Britain removed the pound from the EU's fixed exchange rate system in September 1992 and allowed the currency to float against the mark, permitting a more expansionary British monetary policy than would otherwise have been feasible. *(Illustrate in a diagram similar to Figure 16.16.)* The pound depreciated by more than 10 percent against the mark, but Britain began to move out of its recession, unlike France and Germany, whose unemployment rates continued to rise until 1995.

Thailand

CASE TWO:
Betting against the Baht

For 13 years, the Thai government pegged the country's currency, the baht, to an international currency basket composed of 80 percent U.S. dollars and the rest German marks and Japanese yen. After a decade of rapid economic growth of around 8 percent per year, the economy fell into a slump in 1997. Demand for electronics exports dropped. The appreciation of the dollar, which carried the baht with it, hurt other Thai export industries. *(Why?)* The banking system struggled under billions of dollars' worth of bad loans, many to the domestic real-estate sector, financial institutions, and inefficient manufacturers. The Stock Exchange of Thailand index had dropped 60 percent from its high in early 1996.

In the midst of these myriad economic problems, keeping the baht pegged required monetary contraction and higher interest rates. The Bank of Thailand repeatedly announced its plans to maintain the peg, but foreign exchange market participants started to wonder. *(Illustrate in an IS-LM-BOP diagram the combination of a slump in export demand and an expected currency devaluation. What would the central bank need to do to maintain the fixed exchange rate?)* The central bank held about $30 billion in foreign exchange reserves; but no one knew how much of that total the bank had already committed in the forward market to buy baht in 3, 6, 9, or 12 months. (Later, the answer would turn out to be more than $23 billion, although fulfilling the forward contracts would reduce reserves by much less than the full $23 billion.) A devaluation could devastate the country's already shaky banks and other firms that had borrowed heavily in dollars and lent in baht. Thai private firms owed over $67 billion in foreign debt, much of it with unhedged foreign exchange risk. On the other hand, the monetary restraint and high interest rates (initially around 13 percent) necessary to maintain the baht peg also took their toll. Interest rates continued to rise with expectations of an impending devaluation. The government imposed capital controls that prohibited foreigners from buying baht

except as required for trade transactions. *(Illustrate the effects in your IS-LM-BOP diagram.)* Capital outflows slowed, but so did capital inflows, since the controls prevented potential foreign investors from hedging their foreign exchange risk. More and more of the still-functioning Thai firms found themselves unable to get credit to cover their day-to-day operating needs.

The devaluation came on July 2, 1997. The government abandoned its peg and allowed the baht to float. It dropped over 16 percent against the dollar and 12 percent against the yen on the first day. Within a month, the Bank of Thailand and the Finance Ministry sought an IMF loan assistance package to finance the country's payments and replenish the Bank of Thailand's foreign exchange reserves. The IMF granted $4 billion in loans, contingent on the country meeting IMF-approved policy plans and economic targets. Additional assistance came from Japan, Australia, China, Hong Kong, Malaysia, Singapore, Indonesia, South Korea, the World Bank, the Asian Development Bank, and the Bank for International Settlements (the bank for central banks). As of August 1997, experts estimated that Thailand had spent over $32 billion in its failed effort to defend the baht's peg.

As we saw in Chapter Fifteen, economic crises with their roots in the banking sector tend to spread—and Thailand's certainly did. Soon Indonesia, South Korea, and Malaysia succumbed, as did Hong Kong, the Philippines, and even Japan and China—albeit to a lesser extent. In the year after the baht devaluation, Thai manufacturing production, private investment, and exports all fell between 10 and 20 percent, and imports by 40 percent. Analysts estimated that between 30 and 40 percent of all loans by Thai banks and finance companies were nonperforming. In January 1998, the government moved to explicitly guarantee all bank liabilities, including debts owed to foreigners. This amounted to a promise that the Thai government would, if necessary, use its foreign exchange reserves to service Thai banks' debts.

CASE THREE:
Pesos and Tequila

In 1987, after years of ineffective economic policies, failed efforts at reform, and a major external debt crisis, Mexico instituted a set of economic reforms that promised growth, stable prices, open trade, reduction of government's intrusive role in the economy, and a stable peso. Policy makers in other countries and participants in world markets viewed the reforms as evidence of Mexico's strong commitment to shift to a market-based economy as a means of supporting economic growth and development.

In 1994, events external and internal to Mexico interfered with the reforms. U.S. monetary policy shifted from expansionary to contractionary and pushed the U.S. interest rate sharply higher. Capital flows, which had rushed into Mexico in response to the country's reforms and growth prospects, slowed. Policy makers had to intervene to supply dollars from their foreign exchange reserves to keep the peso within its promised exchange-rate band against the dollar. *(Illustrate using an IS-LM-BOP diagram for Mexico.)* Internal political disturbances—including an uprising in Chiapas and the assassination of a leading presidential candidate—added to the political and economic uncertainty. Expectations of a pending devaluation mounted. *(Illustrate the impact of such expectations.)* By late December 1994, the Bank of Mexico's foreign exchange reserves had fallen by almost two-thirds from their March level. On December 22, after a December 20 devaluation failed to stabilize the currency, the new government abandoned its promise to peg the peso and allowed the currency to float. Market participants took the government's reneging on its peso commitment as a signal that the country's economic reforms and ability to make payments on its external debt were at risk. By the end of January, the peso had depreciated by more than 40 percent.

Adding to the pressure was the fact that the Mexican government had borrowed a large quantity of dollar-denominated short-term debt, called *tesobonos,* which were coming due.[23] The upcoming payments on the government's *tesobono* debt exceeded the country's foreign exchange reserves by several times. Lenders lost confidence in the country and its policies, leaving the government unable to borrow fresh funds to make its *tesobono* payments. Mexico received emergency loans and loan guarantees from several sources: $20 billion from the U.S. Treasury Exchange Stabilization Fund, $18 billion from the IMF, $10 billion from the Bank for International Settlements, and $1 billion from Canada.

Economists and policy makers have performed many "autopsies" on the Mexican crisis in hopes of understanding what went wrong and how it could have been avoided. Most analysts agree that several factors contributed to Mexico's rapid descent from promising emerging market to developing country on the verge of economic collapse. First, Mexico routinely sterilized its intervention in early 1994 in an attempt to prevent a contraction in the domestic economy prior to the upcoming presidential election. But, as we've seen, sterilized intervention can interfere with necessary macroeconomic adjustments, leading to a crisis. As foreign interest rates rose, especially in the United States, a decline in the Mexican money stock could have facilitated international adjustment; but sterilization foreclosed that adjustment. Second, Mexico by 1994 ran a current-account deficit of almost $30 billion because of the real peso appreciation caused by continuing inflation in excess of the nominal peso depreciation. The current-account deficit required financing by private capital inflows (that is, a capital-account surplus) or by intervention (that is, an official-settlements-balance surplus), which reduced the Bank of Mexico's reserves. At least part of the current-account deficit and associated international borrowing, no doubt, produced intertemporal gains from trade, but a portion went to consumption expenditure rather than investment. And the size of the deficit and the associated international borrowing rendered the Mexican economy vulnerable to a loss of confidence by international investors. The Chiapas rebellion and the political assassination contributed to just such a loss of confidence. Note, however, that Mexicans faced the same incentives as foreign investors to move funds out of the country in response to an expected devaluation.

Mexico and its foreign investors weren't the only ones affected by the peso experience. In what came to be known as the *tequila effect,* financial markets throughout Latin America, only recently recovered from their own 1980s debt crisis, became more volatile. Governments throughout the region, especially those of Argentina and Brazil, had to intervene to prevent their currencies from depreciating in foreign exchange markets, the result of market participants' expectations of devaluations similar to Mexico's.

---

23 The government had started issuing *tesobonos,* which promised repayment in dollars, to avoid paying the high interest rates lenders were demanding on *cetes* bonds denominated in pesos. In effect, *tesobonos* placed the foreign exchange risk on the Mexican government, while *cetes* placed it on the lenders.

The Mexican government made the Bank of Mexico, the central bank, formally independent in 1994 in an effort to reduce the political-business-cycle problem. The crisis-induced recession continued until mid-1996, when the Mexican economy began to grow. Once again able to borrow in international capital markets, Mexico in early 1997 paid off its 1995 emergency borrowing from the United States and the International Monetary Fund.

A weak banking system, the risk of political business cycles (especially overly expansionary monetary policy in pre-election periods), vulnerability to oil-price changes (especially since 35 percent of government revenues come from oil products), and the country's delicate political stability continue to constrain Mexico's economic performance. But, unlike 1994, the 2000 election passed without an economic crisis.

CASE FOUR:
The Two Faces of Capital Flows

In the wake of what have been dubbed the "first financial crises of the 21st century"—Mexico and Asia—a debate emerged about the appropriate role of and policy toward capital mobility, especially in developing economies. When most developing countries followed import-substitution policies during the 1950s and 1960s, they discouraged foreign direct investment, fearful that former colonial powers would simply buy up the economies to replace lost political control.[24] Private portfolio capital flows at the time were minimal because even industrial economies imposed capital controls and because many of the technologies and markets that exist today to facilitate such flows hadn't yet developed.

As import substitution failed and developing countries opened up to the world economy, they were encouraged to liberalize their capital markets. Figure 16.17 illustrates that countries did move toward more liberal policies toward capital-account transactions, although many restrictions remain in place.

Evidence indicates strongly that foreign direct investment plays complex and multifaceted roles in providing new technology, management skills, and other sources of enhanced productivity and growth to developing economies. Along with foreign direct investment, many developing economies allowed or encouraged private portfolio capital flows. Such flows allow savers around the world to seek the highest expected rates of return on their saving and permit investors with promising projects to borrow in international markets. Free flows of funds also permit markets to "judge" countries' policies by moving funds into countries with policies perceived as sound and out of countries whose economic policies seem problematic. Such capital movements can provide policy makers, especially those in developing economies, with early information about the perceived quality of their policy choices. Capital controls, in contrast, provide an opening for corruption, because policy makers can grant exemptions to

special interests. For all these reasons, economists generally encourage countries to eliminate controls on capital flows.

However, large-scale and sudden capital flows can contribute to financial crises. If market participants lose confidence in a country's prospects and suddenly withdraw funds, even a basically sound economy can find itself in trouble, just as a basically sound bank can be rendered illiquid by a run, as we learned in Chapter Fifteen. For economies with deep-rooted economic problems, sudden capital flows can turn painful episodes into genuine financial crises. When market participants in Mexico, Thailand, and Indonesia began to expect currency devaluations, they pulled funds from the countries and contributed to the deep economic crises that followed.

How does one weigh these two faces of capital mobility? Recently, some economists have suggested that *temporary* controls on *short-term* capital *inflows*, especially foreign borrowing by domestic banks, may have a role to play in developing economies that as yet lack well regulated, well supervised, and transparent financial systems. Permanent capital controls are judged unlikely to work, because the longer controls remain in place, the more adept market participants become at circumventing them. So long-term capital controls simply introduce distortions. Efforts to control capital outflows send a bad signal to potential foreign investors: You can put funds into the economy but you may not be able to get them out. Hardly a recipe for confidence! Any positive role for capital controls centers on short-term flows (pejoratively called *hot money*) because they're the ones more likely to contribute to crises. Long-term foreign direct investment, on the other hand, can't abandon a country quickly and brings needed technology and know-how.

Large-scale short-term capital inflows to banks can bring particular risks. Banks play such a vital role in a well-functioning economy that allowing them to engage in risky

---

24 Section 11.4 outlines the history of import-substitution policies and subsequent developments.

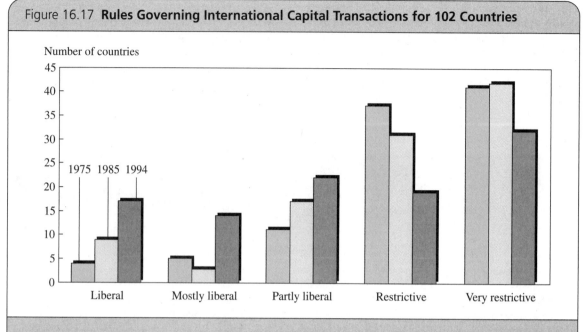

Figure 16.17 **Rules Governing International Capital Transactions for 102 Countries**

Note: *Liberal* means no restrictions; *mostly liberal* means a few restrictions by industry; *partly liberal* means many restrictions on the size and timing of transactions; *restrictive* means that domestic investment by foreigners or foreign investment by domestic residents requires official approval; *very restrictive* means that all cross-border transactions require official approval.

Source: World Bank, *World Development Report 1997* (Washington D.C.: The World Bank), p. 135.

behavior puts the entire macroeconomy in jeopardy. When banks overborrow and become unsound, governments tend to bail them out in an effort to insulate the rest of the economy from damage. But such bailouts, in turn, cause banks to be less than prudent in their choices, since they count on future bailouts.

Can a country really have too much capital flowing in? In a world of perfect information, such a thing couldn't happen. Market participants would know the true productivity of all potential assets and investment projects; no one would shift funds to a country that wouldn't invest them prudently and productively. In practice, especially in developing economies, information can be highly imperfect. Banks can be poorly supervised and regulated, allowed to borrow abroad and to lend to overly risky projects, counting on public bailouts if they get in trouble. A big capital inflow can quickly turn into a big capital outflow. However, it's important to recognize that evidence suggests that in financial crises—including those in Mexico and Asia—*domestic residents'* capital typically flees in advance of that of *foreign*

investors, presumably because locals are more attuned to early signs of trouble.

Capital-control proponents typically point to Chile as a success story. Chile required that a percentage of any non-equity capital entering the country be placed in a non-interest-paying deposit at the central bank for one year. This *encaje* policy acted as a tax on capital inflows, and the effective tax rate was higher the shorter the capital flow's time horizon. In addition, any foreign investment had to stay in the country for at least one year. Fans of the system claim it maintained overall capital inflows and shifted them from less-desirable short-term portfolio flows toward more-desirable long-term foreign direct investment. They also point to the fact that Chile suffered relatively little from the tequila effect after Mexico's 1994 devaluation. But capital-control opponents ask whether Chile's tequila immunity really came from its controls on capital inflows. Or did the immunity result from Chile's strong bank reform of 1986, which gave it one of the best-regulated banking systems in Latin America?[25] In any event, Chile surprised fans of its capital controls

25 The evidence for this view is that Chilean controls on capital inflows failed to prevent a major banking and currency crisis in the early 1980s, before the banking reform. At the time, Chile's banking system resembled that of many Asian countries during the 1990s—poor regulation, rampant real estate speculation, and questionable loans to bank insiders.

by eliminating the *encaje* in September 1998, after economic problems in Russia disturbed international financial markets. In 2000, Chile dropped the one-year-stay rule for direct investment, fearful that such requirements were pushing valuable foreign investment funds into other countries with more accommodating policies.

Part of the disagreement over capital controls stems from varying definitions of the term. Most economists agree that a sound banking system *requires* government supervision and prudential regulation of banks. For example, banks in the United States are restricted in their ownership of corporate stock, because the values of such stock are viewed as inappropriately volatile to form a major part of banks' asset portfolios. The prohibition extends to stock in foreign firms, so the rule is, in some sense, a capital control. But it is a very specific, narrowly defined control targeted at a very specific potential problem. Such prudential regulations are very different from, for example, the across-the-board currency and capital controls imposed by Malaysia after the height of that country's financial crisis. Malaysia abruptly outlawed trading of its ringgit abroad, restricted Malays' holdings of foreign currencies, and dictated that the proceeds of any foreigner's sales of any Malay asset or property had to remain in the country for a year unless the Bank of Negara (the central bank) granted an exemption.

An important risk posed by even temporary capital controls is that policy makers will view them as a substitute for needed policy changes. The most important lessons of recent financial crises are simple: (1) there's no substitute for sound, consistent macroeconomic policies or for prudent regulation of a transparent banking system, (2) a fixed exchange rate can't provide macroeconomic stability if policy makers pursue inconsistent policies, (3) protecting local banks from competition by foreign ones tends to generate a bloated, inefficient, and vulnerable banking sector, and (4) a lack of information (for example, markets not knowing in May 1997 that the Bank of Thailand had already committed many of its reserves to buy forward baht or how much short-term debt South Korea's private sector had accumulated) may postpone a crisis but not avoid one and is highly likely to make the eventual crisis more severe.

CASE FIVE:
Paying the Bills

Economists rarely have the opportunity to run laboratory experiments of the kind conducted by chemists or physicists. More often, we have to learn what we can from "experiments" that the world economy provides. The Mexican and Asian crises represent excellent recent examples. Economists and policy makers have scoured data about the two crises in search of insights. One question of particular interest is: What are the signs of an impending crisis? In other words, what variables might we monitor in order to spot potential trouble?

One answer seems to be the relationship between a country's short-term foreign borrowing and its international reserves. After all, short-term foreign borrowing represents debt that must be repaid soon (in a year or less) in foreign currency. If this debt exceeds available foreign exchange reserves, then the country is at least illiquid even if not insolvent. In early 1998, economists Steven Radelet and Jeffrey Sachs analyzed a sample of 22 developing countries and computed their short-term foreign debt to reserve ratios, which we report in Table 16.4. Radelet and Sachs found that in eight of the nine countries that had experienced a financial crisis, the ratio exceeded 0.8; the only exception was Malaysia.

With hindsight, another of their results proves even more revealing. Radelet and Sachs note that "This [0.8] value is exceeded by only three of the thirteen noncrisis economies: Russia, South Africa, and Zimbabwe. It is possible to have a high level of short-term debt without entering a crisis . . . but it does seem to indicate vulnerability" (p. 46). Shortly after this statement was written, all three countries *did* experience financial crises, with Russia's the most severe but Zimbabwe's still ongoing.

Table 16.4 Prelude to Crisis? Ratio of Short-Term Debt to Foreign Exchange Reserves

Country	Period	Short-Term Foreign Debt/ Foreign Exchange Reserves
Noncrisis:		
Brazil	1994–1997	0.71
Chile	1994–1997	0.50
Colombia	1994–1997	0.68
Hungary	1994–1997	0.40
India	1994–1997	0.36
Jordan	1994–1997	0.35
Peru	1994–1997	0.49
Poland	1994–1997	0.19
Russia	1994–1997	3.33
South Africa	1994–1997	3.17
Sri Lanka	1994–1997	0.24
Taiwan	1994–1997	0.22
Zimbabwe	1994–1997	1.40
Crisis:		
Argentina	1995	1.57
Indonesia	1997	1.70
Korea	1997	2.06
Malaysia	1997	0.61
Mexico	1995	5.28
Philippines	1997	0.85
Thailand	1997	1.45
Turkey	1994	2.06
Venezuela	1994	0.81

Source: Data from Steven Radelet and Jeffrey D. Sachs, "The East Asian Financial Crisis: Diagnosis, Remedies, Prospects," *Brookings Papers on Economic Activity* (1998), p. 47.

CASE SIX:
Pegged, but to What?

Choosing a fixed exchange rate isn't the end of policy makers' exchange-rate decisions. A fixed rate involves pegging the currency's value relative to the value of something else. This something else can be the currency of a major trading partner (such as Hong Kong's peg to the U.S. dollar), an accounting unit created by an international organization (such as Saudi Arabia's use of the International Monetary Fund's special drawing right, or SDR), or a "basket" containing several currencies (such as Thailand's pre-crisis peg to a basket containing 80 percent dollars and 20 percent yen and Deutsche marks).

The choice of "pegged to what" can be important because a pegged currency moves in lock step with its "anchor" against all other currencies. For example, when the U.S. dollar appreciated against most other currencies during the 1990s, it carried the Thai baht with it because of the heavy dollar weight (80 percent) in Thailand's currency-basket peg. The resulting real appreciation of the baht against nondollar currencies cut Thailand's ability to export at the same time demand for its electronics exports was falling for other reasons. To minimize this effect, many countries using a fixed exchange rate choose to peg either to the currency of the predominant trading partner or to a currency basket representative of the country's pattern of trade.

Sometimes countries change their peg anchor. Following years of triple- and quadruple-digit inflation, Argentina in 1991 introduced its Convertibility Plan, which pegged the peso to the U.S. dollar at a one-to-one exchange rate. The monetary authority pledged not to create more pesos than it could back with dollar reserves. This effectively took away the government's ability to conduct monetary policy, the inflationary consequences of which had wrecked the country's economy. After 1991, inflation fell dramatically, and the Convertibility Plan formed the bedrock of residents' confidence in the economy. But Argentina traded more with Europe than with the United States. So, when the dollar appreciated by about 30 percent against the new euro between 1999 and 2001, the dollar carried the peso with it. Argentina, already in recession, experienced a sharp real appreciation of the peso relative to both its neighbor currency, the Brazilian real, and the euro. As the country's economic situation grew worse, Argentina decided in 2001 that a peg against a currency basket containing half dollars and half euros would help. But changing from a dollar peg to a dollar-euro-basket peg at prevailing exchange rates would have amounted to a devaluation. Residents' confidence in

the Convertibility Plan would have been lost. And, because most public and private debt in Argentina was denominated in dollars, any devaluation would threaten the country's already shaky ability to pay its debts.

So Argentina passed a law that switched from the dollar peg to a dollar-euro-basket peg, but also delayed the switch for everyone but exporters and importers until the dollar-euro exchange rate reached $1/€1—in an effort to avoid charges of a clandestine devaluation. International investors worried that the de facto devaluation for international trade represented a step toward a general devaluation, and they responded to the move by selling peso-denominated assets. As expectations of either debt default or a devaluation rose, so did the interest rates the country had to pay to rollover its outstanding loans. Analysts agreed that getting Argentina's economy back on track would require politically difficult moves: getting government spending, especially that by provincial governments, under control; making labor markets more flexible; deregulating markets; and making the economy more hospitable to foreign investors. The economic situation shifted from bad to worse, and before the end of 2001, the government resigned amid a growing economic crisis.

Summary

With the price level and the exchange rate fixed, self-adjustment mechanisms exist for reaching external balance (balance-of-payments equilibrium) but not for attaining internal balance (full employment) in the short run. The effectiveness of short-run macroeconomic policy in achieving internal balance under fixed exchange rates depends on the degree of international capital mobility.

With completely immobile capital, neither fiscal nor monetary policy can bring the economy into internal balance. Only a change in the exchange rate can alter the income consistent with external balance to match that required for internal balance.

Increased capital mobility enhances fiscal policy's ability to alter income. Monetary policy remains ineffective even in the presence of capital mobility, and exchange rate policy retains its ability to affect income. Table 16.6 summarizes these results.

Looking Ahead

Capital mobility strongly influences the effectiveness of various tools of macroeconomic policy. Likewise, a change in the exchange rate regime alters the ability of fiscal and monetary policy to achieve simultaneous internal and external balance. Since policy makers can choose the type of exchange rate regime under which their

Table 16.6 **Short-Run Policy Effectiveness under Fixed Exchange Rates**

| Policy | Ability to Affect Income under a Fixed Exchange Rate | | |
	Immobile Capital	Imperfectly Mobile Capital	Perfectly Mobile Capital
Fiscal	0	Effective	Effective
Monetary	0	0	0
Exchange rate	Effective	Effective	Effective

currencies operate (in fact, individual countries can—and do—choose different systems), understanding the implications of the type of exchange rate regime for macroeconomic policy is particularly important. Chapter Seventeen explores the move to a more flexible exchange rate system made by the major industrial economies in the early 1970s and its implications for fiscal and monetary policy and for internal and external balance.

Key Terms

internal balance

external balance

targets

instruments

crowding out

sterilization policy

perfect capital mobility

risk premium

signal

reserve currency

Bretton Woods

Problems and Questions for Review

1. Consider an open market *sale* of 500 under a fixed exchange rate regime. Assume the money multiplier is 10 and the economy is at a general equilibrium before the policy.
   a. Explain carefully what action by the central bank would constitute such a policy.
   b. *Ignoring the foreign exchange market for a moment,* what would be the initial or direct effect of the open market sale on the domestic money stock (that is, by how much would M increase or decrease)? Explain.
   c. What would be the effect of such a policy on the domestic balance of payments? Why? Does your answer depend on the extent of capital mobility? Explain.
   d. To maintain the pegged exchange rate, what action would the central bank need to undertake, if any? What would be the effect on the domestic money stock (that is, by how much would this action increase or decrease M)?
   e. What is the total net effect of the open market operation on the domestic money stock (taking into account the effects in parts (b) and (d))?
   f. What are the implications of your answer to part (e) for discretionary or activist monetary policy under a fixed exchange rate?

2. Assume that the exchange rate is fixed and capital is perfectly mobile.
   a. *Scenario 1:* Country A's central bank devalues the domestic currency, the alpha (α); but the citizens of A do *not* expect the devaluation to be permanent. Illustrate the effect of the exchange rate policy on income and the interest rate.
   b. *Scenario 2:* Country A's central bank devalues the domestic currency, the alpha (α), by the same amount as in Scenario 1; but the citizens of A *do* expect the devaluation to be permanent. Illustrate the effect of the exchange rate policy on income and the interest rate.
   c. *Scenario 3:* Country A's central bank devalues the domestic currency, the alpha (α), by the same amount as in Scenario 1; but the citizens of A expect the devaluation to be permanent *and* it causes them to expect a further devaluation. Illustrate the effect of the exchange rate policy on income and the interest rate.
   d. Explain why you drew the graphs in parts (a), (b), and (c) as you did, and compare the policy effects in the three scenarios.

3. Comment on the following statement by the head of a central bank of a small country that has a fixed exchange rate and strict capital controls that prohibit capital inflows and outflows: "The reason for our capital controls is to prevent external events from affecting our domestic economy. For the same reason, we will not alter the pegged value of our currency by devaluing or revaluing, but rather we will rely on domestic monetary and fiscal policies to achieve our economic goals."

4. Hong Kong maintains a fixed exchange rate of its Hong Kong dollar against the U.S. dollar. During the Asian financial crisis, the currencies of most of Hong Kong's Asian trading partners depreciated sharply against the U.S. dollar. What would be the effect on Hong Kong? Why might this have caused market participants to expect a devaluation of the Hong Kong dollar? Why might Hong Kong policy makers have been eager to convince market participants that there would be no devaluation?

5. It is common for countries to complain about one another's interest rates. Assume that the domestic country operates under a fixed exchange rate regime, and capital is completely mobile. Illustrate and explain the effect on the domestic economy of a *decline* in the *foreign* interest rate (i*), beginning from a point of general equilibrium, using the IS-LM-BOP framework.

6. One effect of a one-time devaluation is to allow a central bank to replenish its foreign exchange reserves. Explain how this happens. Sometimes, a devaluation causes foreign exchange market participants to expect another devaluation in the future. When this happens, would you expect the initial devaluation to increase the central bank's reserves? Why, or why not?

7. Historically, it has been common for a country to pressure its trading partners to follow expansionary macroeconomic policies. Assume that the domestic country operates under a fixed exchange rate regime, and capital is completely mobile. Illustrate and explain the effect on the domestic economy of an *increase* in *foreign* income, beginning from a point of general equilibrium, using the IS-LM-BOP framework.

8. Explain the role of each of the following in Mexico's December 1994 currency crisis.
   a. The rise in the U.S. interest rate.
   b. Mexico's decision to sterilize its foreign exchange market intervention.
   c. Declining confidence by market participants in the credibility of the Mexican government's commitment not to devalue the peso.

References and Selected Readings

Baxter, M. "International Trade and Business Cycles." In *Handbook of International Economics,* Vol. 3, edited by G. M. Grossman and K. Rogoff, 1801–1864. Amsterdam: North-Holland, 1995.
Survey of research on the relationship between international trade activity and macroeconomic cycles; intermediate and advanced.

Bosworth, Barry P., and Susan M. Collins. "Capital Flows to Developing Economies: Implications for Saving and Investment." *Brookings Papers on Economic Activity* 1 (1999): 143–180.
How capital flows affect developing economies' domestic saving and investment.

Cooper, Richard N. "Should Capital Controls be Banished?" *Brookings Papers on Economic Activity* 1 (1999): 89–142.
A sympathetic view of capital controls to prevent or manage crises.

Cooper, Richard N., and Jane Sneddon Little. "U.S. Monetary Policy in an Integrating World: 1960 to 2000." In *The Evolution of Monetary Policy and the Federal Reserve System over the Past Thirty Years,* edited by R. W. Kopcke and L. E. Browne, 77–130. Boston: Federal Reserve Bank of Boston, 2000.
History of international influences on U.S. monetary policy.

Desai, Padma. "Why Did the Ruble Collapse in August 1998?" *American Economic Review Papers and Proceedings* 90 (May 2000): 48–52.
What caused the ruble crisis and what, if anything, might have prevented it?

Dominguez, Kathryn M., and Jeffrey A. Frankel. *Does Foreign Exchange Intervention Work?* Washington, D.C.: Institute for International Economics, 1993.
Study of the effect of sterilized intervention; intermediate.

Dornbusch, Rudiger, et al. "Currency Crises and Collapses." *Brookings Papers on Economic Activity* 2 (1995): 219–293.
Lessons from four currency crises; intermediate.

Dueker, Michael J., and Andreas M. Fischer. "The Mechanics of a Successful Exchange Rate Peg: Lessons for Emerging Markets." Federal Reserve Bank of St. Louis, *Review* (September/October 2001): 47–56.
Why did Austria's peg to the Deutsche mark work while Thailand's peg to the dollar failed?

Edwards, Sebastian. "How Effective Are Capital Controls?" *Journal of Economic Perspectives* 13 (Fall 1999): 65–84.
What capital flows can and cannot do to prevent or manage financial crises.

Eichengreen, Barry. *Globalizing Capital.* Princeton: Princeton University Press, 1996.
Readable account of the history of capital flows and macroeconomic policy.

Eichengreen, Barry, and Michael Mussa. "Capital Account Liberalization and the IMF." *Finance and Development* (December 1998): 16–19.
How to manage capital-account liberalization to obtain its benefits and control its risks.

Fleming, J. M. "Domestic Financial Policies under Fixed and Floating Exchange Rates." *IMF Staff Papers* 9 (November 1962): 369–380.
A classic paper on macroeconomic policy effectiveness in an open economy; for advanced students.

Garber, P., and L. Svensson. "The Operation and Collapse of Fixed Exchange Rate Regimes." In *Handbook of International Economics,* Vol. 3, edited by G. M. Grossman and K. Rogoff, 1865–1912. Amsterdam: North-Holland, 1995.
Survey of research on fixed-rate systems; intermediate and advanced.

Goldstein, Morris. *The Asian Financial Crisis.* Washington, D.C: Institute for International Economics, 1998.
Overview of the causes, cures, and implications; for all students.

Hume, David. "On the Balance of Trade." In *Essays, Moral, Political, and Literary,* Vol. 1. London: Longmans, Green, 1898 [1752].
The original statement of the automatic adjustment process under fixed exchange rates; for all students.

Isard, Peter. *Exchange Rate Economics.* Cambridge: Cambridge University Press, 1995.
Excellent survey of the literature on fixed exchange rates; for intermediate and advanced students.

Kaminsky, Graciela, and Sergio Schmukler. "Short- and Long-Run Integration: Do Capital Controls Matter?" *Brookings Trade Forum* (2000): 125–178.
Short- and long-run implications and effects of controls on capital flows.

Kharas, Homi, et al. "An Analysis of Russia's 1998 Meltdown: Fundamentals and Market Signals." *Brookings Papers on Economic Activity* (2001): 1–68.
Interaction of fixed exchange rate and fiscal policy in Russia's crisis.

Meade, James E. *The Balance of Payments.* London: Oxford University Press, 1951.
The definitive early work on the balance of payments; for advanced students.

Meltzer, Allan H. "U.S. Policy in the Bretton Woods Era." Federal Reserve Bank of St. Louis, *Review* 73 (May–June 1991): 53–83.
Excellent, readable survey of the functioning of the Bretton Woods system of pegged exchange rates.

Mundell, Robert A. "Capital Mobility and Stabilization Policy under Fixed and Flexible Exchange Rates." *Canadian Journal of Economics and Political Science* 29 (November 1963): 475–485.
The original presentation of capital mobility's impact on macroeconomic policy effectiveness in an open economy; for intermediate and advanced students.

Neely, Christopher J. "An Introduction to Capital Controls." Federal Reserve Bank of St. Louis, *Review* 81 (November/December 1999): 13–30.
What are capital controls, and what are their effects?

Obstfeld, Maurice. "International Currency Experience: New Lessons and Lessons Relearned." *Brookings Papers on Economic Activity* 1 (1995): 119–220.
Excellent survey of the current state of knowledge on exchange rates; intermediate.

Obstfeld, Maurice. "The Global Capital Market: Benefactor or Menace?" *Journal of Economic Perspectives* (Fall 1998): 9–30.
More on the two faces of capital flows.

Obstfeld, M., and K. Rogoff. "The Intertemporal Approach to the Current Account." In *Handbook of International Economics,* Vol. 3, edited by G. M. Grossman and K. Rogoff, 1731–1800. Amsterdam: North-Holland, 1995.
Survey of research on the current account from the perspective of intertemporal trade; intermediate and advanced.

Noland, Marcus, et al. *Global Economic Effects of the Asian Currency Devaluations.* Washington, D.C.: Institute for International Economics, 1998.
Estimates of the Asian crisis's effects on the rest of the world economy; intermediate.

Persson, T., and G. Tabellini. "Double-Edged Incentives: Institutions and Policy Coordination." In *Handbook of International Economics,* Vol. 3, edited by G. M. Grossman and K. Rogoff, 1973–2030. Amsterdam: North-Holland, 1995.
Survey of research on interactions between countries' macroeconomic policies; intermediate and advanced.

Schuknecht, Ludger. "A Trade Policy Perspective on Capital Controls." *Finance and Development* 36 (March 1999): 38–41.
Uses the basic trade model to illustrate the benefits of open international capital flows.

Summers, Lawrence H. "Distinguished Lecture on Economics in Government: Reflections on Managing Global Integration." *Journal of Economic Perspectives* 13 (Spring 1999): 3–18.
An overview of international financial integration by the former U.S. Treasury secretary, now president of Harvard University.

Tinbergen, Jan. *On the Theory of Economic Policy.* Amsterdam: North-Holland, 1952.
An early influential work on the theory of macroeconomic policy making in an open economy; for advanced students.

CHAPTER SEVENTEEN

Short-Run Macroeconomic Policy under Flexible Exchange Rates

17.1 Introduction

After World War II, the world economy operated under the **Bretton Woods system** of fixed, or pegged, exchange rates. The Bretton Woods agreement consisted of a commitment by each member country's central bank to intervene in foreign exchange markets to keep the value of its currency, in terms of U.S. dollars, within a certain range or band. If a currency's value threatened to rise above the upper limit of its band, the central bank would sell the currency for dollars in the foreign exchange market. If a currency's value sank to the lower limit of its band, the central bank would use dollars from its foreign exchange reserves to buy the excess supply of the domestic currency from the foreign exchange market. These intervention activities pegged each currency's value within its agreed-upon band relative to the U.S. dollar.[1]

By the late 1960s, the Bretton Woods system came under stress and threatened to disintegrate for two basic reasons. First, governments of the major industrial economies faced increasing domestic political pressure to pursue short-run macroeconomic policies that maintained full employment. As we saw in Chapter Sixteen, however, fixed exchange rates prevent countries other than the reserve-currency country from conducting independent monetary policies aimed at domestic goals such as full employment. Second, as we saw in section 16.6, the reserve country under a fixed exchange rate regime conducts monetary policy not only for itself, but for all the countries in the system. During the 1960s, the United States, the reserve-currency country under Bretton Woods, pursued increasingly expansionary monetary policies that generated inflation at home; and the rules of the Bretton Woods system transmitted that inflation to other countries.

By early 1973, after several years of gradual disintegration, the Bretton Woods system collapsed, and the major industrial countries allowed their currencies to float against the dollar.[2] The move to flexible exchange rates, viewed as unthinkable by most economists and policy makers only a decade before, occurred primarily as a response to the collapse of the former system and a lack of agreement on an alternative. The move was met with relief in some circles and dismay in others. Gradually the idea of a flexible exchange rate system gained support, though far from unanimous. Today, many countries, including the United States, Japan, Canada, and Mexico, operate under flexible exchange rate regimes (see Table 17.1). However, since the early 1970s, each disruption to the world macroeconomy has generated renewed skepticism regarding a flexible-rate regime, at

---

1 Chapter Twenty provides more detail on the mechanics of the Bretton Woods system.

2 In the post–Bretton Woods world, most central banks still intervene occasionally in foreign exchange markets. In other words, the current system is not a perfectly flexible one but a "managed" float (pejoratively called a "dirty" float). The extent of "management" or intervention varies over time and across countries. We'll examine the strengths and weaknesses of such a system later; for now, we focus on the effectiveness of macroeconomic policy under a perfectly flexible exchange rate regime.

Table 17.1 **IMF Members Maintaining Flexible Exchange Rates, March 31, 2000**

Exchange Rate Regime (Number of Countries)	
Independently floating[a] (49)	Afghanistan, Albania, Angola, Armenia, Australia, Brazil, Canada, Chile, Colombia, Democratic Republic of Congo, Eritrea, Gambia, Georgia, Ghana, Guinea, Guyana, Haiti, India, Indonesia, Japan, Kazakhstan, Korea, Liberia, Madagascar, Mauritius, Mexico, Moldova, Mongolia, Mozambique, New Zealand, Papua New Guinea, Peru, Philippines, Russian Federation, Rwanda, São Tomé & Principe, Sierra Leone, Somalia, South Africa, Sudan, Sweden, Switzerland, Tanzania, Thailand, Uganda, United Kingdom, United States, Yemen, Zambia

[a]The exchange rate is market determined, with any foreign exchange intervention aimed at moderating the rate of change and preventing undue fluctuations in the exchange rate, rather than at establishing a level for it.

Source: International Monetary Fund.

least among the world's major currencies, and a vocal constituency continues to support a return to some type of fixed exchange rate system. The arguments on both sides of this issue form the subject of Chapter Twenty. Before we can evaluate those arguments, though, we must understand how a flexible exchange rate system works and its implications for macroeconomic policy.

We'll continue to assume, as we did in Chapter Sixteen's analysis of fixed exchange rates, that policy makers' goal is to bring the economy into internal balance, and that domestic and foreign price levels are fixed.[3] With flexible exchange rates, the economy contains an automatic adjustment mechanism for effecting external balance.[4] The adjustment takes the form of currency appreciations that relieve balance-of-payments surpluses and depreciations that relieve BOP deficits. However, policy makers may not be content with this outcome. We've seen that changes in the nominal exchange rate with fixed price levels cause changes in the real exchange rate, or the relative price of domestic goods and services. This implies that different values of the nominal exchange rate carry different implications for the fortunes of various sectors of the economy—exporters, import-competing industries, consumers of imported goods, and users of imported inputs—as well as for the current-account balance. Therefore, the value of the exchange rate consistent with external balance or balance-of-payments equilibrium may prove unacceptable because of its distributional ramifications or its implications for the current account. In addition, the income at which the automatic adjustment mechanism produces external balance may prove unacceptable in terms of policy makers' internal-balance goal; for example, the unemployment rate may be unacceptably high. We'll begin our analysis of each policy at a point of external balance that reflects the outcome of the automatic adjustment mechanism. The question then becomes whether the policy under scrutiny can bring the economy into internal balance while allowing exchange rate changes to continue maintaining external balance. We'll also track the policies' implications for the current account.

A perfectly flexible exchange rate regime allows the supplies of and demands for different currencies to determine exchange rates. Central banks don't intervene in the foreign exchange market. The exchange rate moves to equate the quantity demanded and the quantity supplied for each currency; therefore, external balance is achieved through automatic adjustment in the form of exchange rate movements. The fact that achieving external balance with a flexible exchange rate doesn't require foreign exchange market intervention has important implications for macroeconomic policy.

Recall from Chapter Sixteen that under fixed exchange rates, a major determinant of the effectiveness of any macroeconomic policy is that policy's consequence for the balance of payments and, through intervention,

---

3 In Chapter Eighteen, we'll relax the fixed price level assumption. Price flexibility has two important implications. First, the economy will contain an automatic adjustment mechanism for reaching internal as well as external balance. Second, attempts to use macroeconomic policy to alter the economy's path may result in price level changes in addition to or instead of changes in real income or employment.

4 The economy also contains an automatic adjustment mechanism for reaching external balance under fixed exchange rates: changes in the money stock through foreign exchange market intervention.

for the domestic money stock. A flexible exchange rate breaks this link between a country's balance of payments and its money stock. By giving up the power to determine the exchange rate, the central bank gains the ability to affect the nominal money stock without causing offsetting changes through international reserves. Graphically, under a flexible exchange rate, the central bank's monetary policies, primarily open market operations, determine the position of the LM curve.[5] As long as the central bank doesn't purchase bonds from or sell bonds to the public, the money stock remains unchanged and the LM curve remains stationary.[6]

Exchange rate flexibility's role in breaking the link between the balance of payments and the domestic money stock was the primary argument used by early supporters of a move to flexible exchange rates. Proponents of flexible rates argued that freeing the domestic money stock from the constraint imposed by the balance of payments would allow policy makers to use monetary policy more effectively to pursue internal balance, or full employment.[7] We'll see in Chapter Twenty that, after the inflationary 1970s, opponents of flexible exchange rates reversed the argument and claimed that freeing monetary authorities to pursue internal balance permitted overly expansionary monetary policies that caused a dramatic increase in inflation rates.[8]

17.2 Macroeconomic Policy with Immobile Capital

Recall that with zero capital mobility, the balance of payments simply equals the current-account balance. For each value of the exchange rate, a unique income coincides with a zero current-account balance. Because the unique income that corresponds to external balance varies with the exchange rate, any policy capable of affecting the exchange rate has the potential to bring the economy into simultaneous internal and external balance by altering the income required for external balance to match that required for internal balance.

17.2.1 Fiscal Policy

In Figure 17.1, a rise in government purchases or a cut in taxes shifts the IS curve from IS^0 to IS^1 by raising total expenditure on domestically produced goods and services (see section 14.8 for a review). The initial effect raises income, because total expenditure has risen, and the interest rate. The rise in the interest rate is necessary to offset the effect of increased income on the demand for money, since the stock of money remains fixed at all points along LM^0 (see section 15.2.5). At the new, higher income, imports rise and the balance of payments shifts into deficit.[9] The exchange rate responds to the excess demand for foreign exchange by a domestic currency depreciation. The rise in the exchange rate lowers the relative price of domestic goods and services $(R \equiv P/eP^*)$ and, therefore, raises the current-account balance at each income. The current-account balance now equals zero at a higher income, so the BOP curve shifts to the right from BOP^0 to BOP^1. The same fall in the relative price of domestic goods and services shifts expenditure toward those goods and moves the IS curve still further to the right to IS^2. In other words, the depreciation shifts both the BOP and IS curves to the right until they intersect on the original LM curve.

At the new equilibrium, income, the interest rate, and the exchange rate are all higher. The rise in the interest rate that accompanies an expansionary fiscal policy prevents an even larger rise in income by crowding out a portion of private investment expenditure. In terms of Figure 17.1, crowding out causes income to rise to only Q^1_{EB} rather than to Q^2_{EB}.

---

5 Open market operations refer to central bank sales of government bonds to the public or purchases of government bonds from the public. Other tools of monetary policy include changes in the required reserve ratio, the percentage of their deposits that banks are required to hold in reserves, and changes in the discount rate, the interest rate that the central bank charges banks to borrow reserves.

6 For now, we ignore the possibility of changes in money demand other than those arising from changes in Q or i.

7 Note, however, that policy makers lose their ability to dictate the exchange rate. A fixed exchange rate regime allows control of the exchange rate but not the money stock. A flexible exchange rate allows control of the money stock but not the exchange rate.

8 These arguments will play prominent roles in Chapters Eighteen and Nineteen.

9 To work step by step through the policy's effects, we say that the balance of payments moves into deficit, which causes the currency to depreciate. In fact, the depreciation of the currency prevents the deficit from actually arising; such a deficit is called *incipient*. An incipient surplus would be a balance-of-payments surplus that would occur in the absence of a currency appreciation.

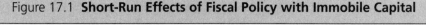

Figure 17.1 **Short-Run Effects of Fiscal Policy with Immobile Capital**

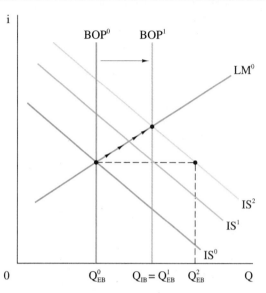

An expansionary fiscal policy shifts the IS curve from IS^0 to IS^1, raising income and the interest rate. The current-account balance moves into deficit, and the domestic currency depreciates. The depreciation raises the income consistent with external balance (shifting the BOP curve to the right) and lowers the relative price of domestic goods (shifting the IS curve from IS^1 to IS^2). At the new equilibrium, income, the interest rate, and the exchange rate are higher. The domestic crowding-out effect of the rise in the interest rate prevents income from rising to Q_{EB}^2.

Fiscal policy brings the external-balance requirement into harmony with that for internal balance *by generating a depreciation of the currency*.[10] However, governments often seem reluctant to permit their currencies to depreciate. This reluctance has at least two sources. First, a currency depreciation raises the price of imported goods to consumers and the cost of imported inputs to domestic firms. Both groups will lobby against policies that would cause a currency depreciation, although exporters and import-competing firms will lobby for them. Second, an increase in the exchange rate often is called a "weakness" of the currency and thus interpreted as a sign of weakness of the economy.[11] The combination of these two factors may cause governments to intervene in foreign exchange markets to prevent a currency depreciation even under a supposedly flexible-rate regime. Should this occur, the fiscal policy's expansionary effect disappears, and the appropriate analysis becomes that under a fixed exchange rate as discussed in section 16.3.1.

Note that the results in Figure 17.1 will be temporary if the increase in government purchases is a one-time policy. Sustaining the rise in income would require a permanently higher level of government spending, but analysis of the long-run effects of such a policy must await the introduction of price flexibility in the next chapter.

A second cautionary note in evaluating the effect of fiscal policy centers on the assumption of capital immobility. We'll see that fiscal policy's effectiveness under flexible exchange rates hinges on capital immobility. As capital becomes more internationally mobile, the prospects for fiscal policy restoring internal balance fade because such a policy tends to cause a currency appreciation rather than depreciation. As the world economy

---

10 Of course, internal balance doesn't happen automatically in response to *any* expansionary fiscal policy. The magnitude of the policy must be calibrated to the increase in income required to reach internal balance.

11 See section 14.4.1 for a discussion of the dangers of identifying a balance-of-payments surplus (deficit) or a currency appreciation (depreciation) with improvement (deterioration) of the economy.

becomes more integrated, capital tends to become more mobile. Efforts to achieve capital immobility often take the form of capital controls that are costly to administer, interfere with the efficient allocation of capital, lead to black markets and other means of circumvention, and tend to be ineffective at least in the long run.[12]

17.2.2 Monetary Policy

The major effect of a move to a flexible exchange rate is the elimination of foreign exchange market intervention and its effect on the domestic money stock. Once changes in the central bank's foreign exchange reserves are eliminated, the money stock changes only in response to open market operations:[13]

$$\Delta M = mm \cdot (\Delta GB + \Delta FXR) \qquad \textbf{[17.1]}$$

Thus, $\Delta FXR = 0$ implies that:

$$\Delta M = mm \cdot \Delta GB \qquad \textbf{[17.2]}$$

The requirement of external balance no longer constrains the size of the domestic money stock, although its size will affect the exchange rate. The central bank can choose any value for the money stock, but it must be willing to accept the implied exchange rate.[14]

The initial effect of a money stock expansion through an open market purchase is a drop in the domestic interest rate and a rise in income, as illustrated in Figure 17.2 by the shift from LM^0 to LM^1. The lower interest rate encourages private investment spending, which raises total expenditure and income. The change in the interest rate has no direct effect on the balance of payments, because capital is assumed to be completely unresponsive to changes in the international pattern of interest rates. The higher income leads to more imports and a current-account deficit, and the domestic currency depreciates. The depreciation shifts both the BOP and IS curves to the right, to BOP^1 and IS^1 *(Why?),* until they intersect on the new LM curve at a higher income.

In fact, monetary policy raises income precisely *because* it generates a currency depreciation that lowers the relative price of domestically produced goods and services. Again, depreciation may prove unpopular with consumers, who face higher prices for imported goods, and with producers who face higher prices for imported inputs. On the other hand, exporters and firms that sell import-competing products tend to view a currency depreciation favorably. Monetary policy therefore not only changes the level of income but also redistributes income among sectors of the domestic economy.

17.2.3 Summary of Policy Effects with Immobile Capital

With a flexible exchange rate and immobile capital, either fiscal or monetary policy can raise the economy's level of income or GDP in the short run. Both expansionary policies work through their ability to depreciate the domestic currency and shift expenditure toward domestically produced goods and services. Table 17.2 summarizes fiscal and monetary policies' effects on income, the exchange rate, and the current account. *(Compare Table 17.2 with Table 16.2, and make sure you can explain the reasons behind any differences.)*

---

12 See Chapter Sixteen, Case Four.

13 The central bank can also alter the money stock by using other policy tools, including changes in the discount rate and in the required reserve ratio. The introduction of these additional tools wouldn't alter the basic conclusion that the move to a flexible exchange rate breaks the link between the balance of payments and the money stock and places control over the nominal money stock in the central bank's hands.

14 Note that under a fixed exchange rate, the central bank could choose the level at which to peg the exchange rate but would have to accept the implied money stock.

Figure 17.2 **Short-Run Effects of Monetary Policy with Immobile Capital**

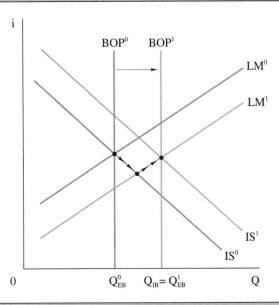

An increase in the money stock causes income to rise and interest rates to fall to equalize the quantity of money demanded with the new, higher stock. As income rises, the current account moves toward a deficit and the currency depreciates. The depreciation lowers the relative price of domestic goods, shifts spending toward domestic and away from foreign goods, and raises the income consistent with external balance.

Table 17.2 **Short-Run Policy Effects with Immobile Capital**

Policy	Effect on Equilibrium Q	Effect on Equilibrium Exchange Rate[a]	Effect on Equilibrium Current-Account Balance
Fiscal Policy:			
Increase in G	+	+	0[b]
Decrease in G	−	−	0[b]
Monetary Policy:			
Increase in M	+	+	0[b]
Decrease in M	−	−	0[b]

[a]A plus sign denotes a rise in e (domestic currency depreciation); a minus sign denotes a fall in e (domestic currency appreciation).
[b]With completely immobile capital, only a current-account balance of zero is consistent with balance-of-payments equilibrium.

17.3 **Macroeconomic Policy with Perfectly Mobile Capital**

The years since the move to more flexible exchange rates have also brought increased integration of world capital markets. The world's major trading economies now engage in extensive trade in stocks, bonds, and other financial assets as well as goods and services. These trends make the analysis of macroeconomic policies under flexible exchange rates and mobile capital particularly important. Of course, a number of smaller economies remain largely outside the growing world capital market and have tended to remain under some form of fixed exchange rate system (see Table 16.1).

17.3.1 **Fiscal Policy**

Highly mobile capital reduces fiscal policy's effectiveness under flexible exchange rates.[15] Recall that fiscal policy works to alter income with immobile capital because of the accompanying currency depreciation. With highly mobile capital, expansionary fiscal policy no longer causes a depreciation of the domestic currency but an appreciation. The appreciation causes a second form of the **crowding-out** phenomenon.[16] As the domestic currency appreciates (e falls), the relative price of domestic goods rises because $R \equiv P/eP^*$, and individuals shift their expenditures toward the now relatively cheaper foreign goods. This decline in private expenditure on domestic goods partially or totally offsets the increased government purchases, depending on whether asset holders perceive the fiscal policy as temporary or permanent.

Policy Expected to Be Temporary

In Figure 17.3, panel (a), expansionary fiscal policy initially raises spending on domestic goods and services and shifts the IS curve from IS^0 to IS^1. Income rises, and the interest rate must rise to keep the quantity demanded of money equal to the fixed money stock. As the domestic interest rate rises, capital flows into the economy and the balance of payments moves into surplus at point 2. The surplus causes the domestic currency to appreciate. If participants in the foreign exchange market perceive the increased government spending as temporary, they also will expect the accompanying currency appreciation to be temporary, leaving their expected future spot exchange rate, e^e, unaffected. The spot appreciation coupled with an unchanged expected future spot rate shifts the BOP line up to BOP^1. *(Explain why, using uncovered interest parity.)*[17]

The currency appreciation also shifts the IS curve leftward to IS^2 as the relative price of domestic goods and services rises. The temporary rise in government spending moves the economy to the intersection of IS^2, LM^0, and BOP^1 at point 3, with income and the interest rate higher than before the policy. The domestic currency has appreciated, and the current-account balance has shifted toward a deficit.

Panel (b) of Figure 17.3 allows us to view events in the foreign exchange market more explicitly. In the diagram, we denote the foreign currency simply as FX. We saw in panel (a) that the initial shift to the right in the IS curve due to increased government spending on domestic goods and services pushes up the domestic interest rate from i_0 to i_1. This raises the expected rate of return on domestic-currency-denominated deposits relative to that on foreign-currency ones. In the foreign exchange market in panel (b), the demand for foreign-currency deposits shifts to the left in response to the decline in their expected rate of return. At the original exchange rate of e_0, market participants now want to hold fewer foreign-currency deposits in their asset portfolios. Market participants' efforts to rid themselves of the extra foreign-currency deposits bids down the domestic price of foreign currency; that is, the domestic currency appreciates to e_1 at point 3.

Policy Expected to Be Permanent

If participants in the foreign exchange market expect the rise in government purchases to be permanent, they also will expect the accompanying appreciation of the domestic currency to persist, so e^e will fall along with e. In panel (a) of Figure 17.3, the currency appreciation no longer shifts the BOP curve because, as long as $e = e^e$, i_0 is consistent with foreign exchange market equilibrium for the given foreign interest rate. *(Show why, using the interest parity condition.)* With the BOP line unchanged at BOP^0, the balance-of-payments surplus at point 2 is larger than in the case of a temporary policy discussed earlier. The larger surplus requires a larger currency appreciation to restore balance-of-payments equilibrium on BOP^0. The larger appreciation shifts the IS curve further to the left, since the appreciation raises the relative price of domestic goods and shifts spending toward imports.

Equilibrium is restored when the IS and BOP curves again intersect on the LM curve, but this can't happen until income falls all the way back to its original level. As long as income remains above Q_{EB}^0, the demand for

---

15 Capital is highly mobile when small changes in international interest rate differentials generate large capital flows.

16 The first, or domestic, form of crowding out is the decline in private investment spending caused by a rise in government purchases.

17 Market participants expect the currency appreciation to be reversed; in other words, they expect a depreciation of the domestic currency. To compensate them for holding deposits denominated in the domestic currency during the expected depreciation, asset holders require a higher domestic interest rate (i_1 rather than i_0).

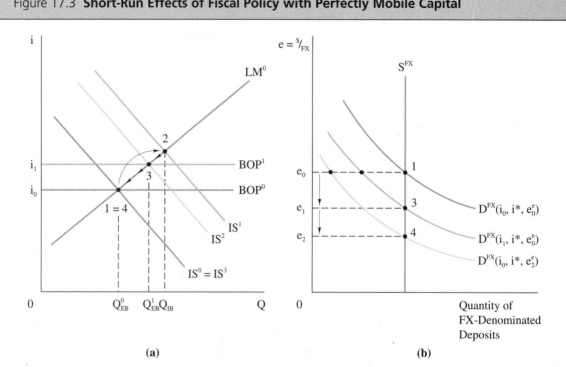

Figure 17.3 **Short-Run Effects of Fiscal Policy with Perfectly Mobile Capital**

In panel (a), the initial direct effect of an expansionary fiscal policy (illustrated by the movement of the IS curve from IS⁰ to IS¹) is to raise income and interest rates. The higher domestic interest rate (at point 2) generates a capital inflow and appreciation of the domestic currency. If the fiscal policy is perceived as temporary, the BOP line shifts to BOP¹. As the exchange rate falls, domestic goods and services become more expensive relative to foreign ones. Individuals respond to the change in relative prices by shifting expenditure to foreign goods. The fall in private expenditure shifts the IS curve back to IS², at point 3. If the policy is perceived as permanent, the appreciation doesn't shift the BOP line but shifts the IS curve all the way back to IS³, and equilibrium is restored at the original income level at point 4. Panel (b) traces the corresponding events in the foreign exchange market.

money exceeds the money stock at i_0; thus, the interest rate must be above i_0. Perfect capital mobility implies that capital will flow into the economy and cause the currency to appreciate as long as the interest rate remains above i_0. The IS curve continues to shift to the left until the appreciation stops. This can happen only when the interest rate has fallen back to i_0, restoring balance-of-payments equilibrium at point 4 in Figure 17.3, panel (a).

Panel (b) of Figure 17.3 focuses on adjustments in the foreign exchange market. When the expected future spot exchange rate drops below e_0^e, the demand for FX-denominated deposits shifts to the left as their expected rate of return falls. The result is a larger spot appreciation of the domestic currency than occurred in the case in which expansionary fiscal policy was expected to be temporary; e_2 denotes the new equilibrium exchange rate at point 4.

Expansionary fiscal policy that's expected to persist can't bring the economy into internal balance when capital is very responsive to interest rates because it generates a large appreciation of the domestic currency. The currency appreciation, acting through the current-account balance, crowds out enough private expenditure on domestic goods and services to offset the expansionary effect of the increased government spending. Although the expansionary fiscal policy leaves total income unchanged, it reallocates spending toward the public sector. It also reallocates income away from export-oriented and import-competing sectors of the economy and toward sectors insulated from the effects of foreign trade, such as construction and retailing. Just as depreciations prove unpopular with consumers and with firms that use imported inputs, currency appreciations are unwelcome in sectors of the economy tightly linked to international trade. For example, the appreciation of the dollar in the early 1980s proved unpopular with trade-oriented sectors of the U.S. economy and led to increased pressure for protectionism. What was the most commonly cited reason for that dramatic rise of the dollar during the early 1980s? The United States' expansionary fiscal policy, dramatically represented by the federal government's rapidly growing budget deficit.[18]

17.3.2 Monetary Policy

Although fiscal policy is largely or completely ineffective under a flexible exchange rate with mobile capital because of the resulting currency appreciation, monetary policy becomes effective in the same circumstances because it produces a currency depreciation. The depreciation lowers the relative price of domestic goods, which stimulates spending and income. Also unlike the fiscal-policy case, expectations that monetary policy changes are permanent rather than temporary enhance the policy's effectiveness.

Policy Expected to Be Temporary

An open market purchase of government bonds increases the money stock by an amount equal to the money multiplier times the magnitude of the purchase (from Equation 17.2) and shifts the LM curve in Figure 17.4, panel (a), from LM^0 to LM^1. As the money stock rises, income and the interest rate must adjust to keep the quantity demanded of money equal to the growing stock. Income rises, and the interest rate falls, both of which increase the quantity of money that individuals in the economy choose to hold at point 2. The fall in the interest rate causes capital to flow out of the country and moves the balance of payments toward a deficit. The deficit depreciates the domestic currency.[19]

If the expansionary monetary policy is expected to be temporary, the accompanying depreciation will be perceived as temporary as well, implying that e^e remains unchanged at e_0^e. The spot depreciation shifts the BOP line down to BOP^1. *(Why?)*[20] The depreciation also lowers the relative price of domestic goods and shifts the IS curve to the right (to IS^1) until it intersects the new BOP^1 curve on the new LM^1 curve at point 3. The expansionary monetary policy's overall effect is to raise income, depreciate the currency, and move the current-account balance toward a surplus.

Panel (b) of Figure 17.4 highlights adjustments in the foreign exchange market. Beginning from point 1, the increase in the money stock puts downward pressure on the domestic interest rate, originally at i_0. The decline in the interest rate to i_1 lowers the expected rate of return on domestic-currency-denominated deposits and, therefore, increases demand for foreign-currency ones. At the original exchange rate, e_0, market participants now want to hold more than the existing quantity of foreign-currency deposits. As portfolio owners try to accumulate such deposits, they bid up their price. In other words, the domestic currency depreciates from e_0 to e_1, the new exchange rate at which participants in the foreign exchange market willingly hold the existing stock of deposits in each currency. As the exchange rate rises, the expected future exchange rate doesn't change from e_0^e, because market participants perceive the current depreciation as temporary. The new equilibrium occurs at point 3.

Policy Expected to Be Permanent

If participants in the foreign exchange market expect the expansionary monetary policy to be permanent, they'll expect the currency depreciation to be permanent as well. The expected future exchange rate then rises with e. In this case, in panel (a), the depreciation does *not* shift the BOP curve, which remains at BOP^0. *(Why?)* The large balance-of-payments deficit at point 2 (larger than in the case of the temporary monetary policy) causes a larger currency depreciation, and shifts the IS curve further to the right to IS^2. At the new equilibrium

---

18 Case Four in this chapter investigates the relationship between the government budget deficit and the exchange rate.

19 Recall that the deficit is an incipient one. The actual deficit is prevented by the depreciation, but it is helpful in understanding the logic of the adjustment process.

20 This follows directly from uncovered interest parity. If the currency depreciates with no change in e^e, the currency is expected to appreciate. Because of the expected appreciation, portfolio owners are content to hold the existing quantity of domestic-currency deposits at a lower interest rate (i_1) than they would if the currency were not expected to appreciate (i_0).

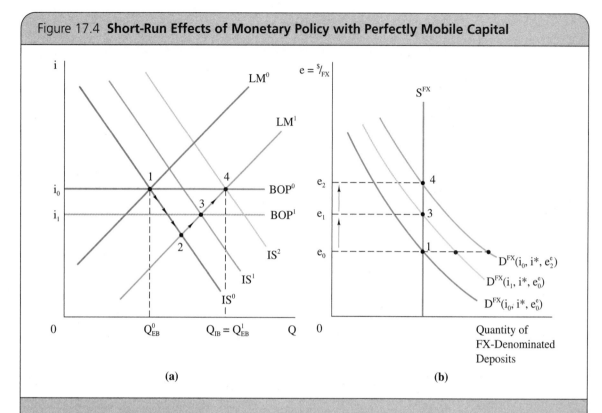

Figure 17.4 **Short-Run Effects of Monetary Policy with Perfectly Mobile Capital**

An open market purchase of government bonds by the central bank moves the LM curve from LM^0 to LM^1. Income rises and the interest rate falls to make individuals willing to hold the new, larger stock of money. Because capital flows are very sensitive to interest rate changes, the fall in the domestic interest rate causes a large capital outflow at point 2. The resulting balance-of-payments deficit causes the domestic currency to depreciate. As the exchange rate rises, domestic goods become less expensive compared to foreign ones and spending shifts in favor of domestic goods. The IS curve moves to the right. If the monetary policy is perceived as temporary, e^e doesn't change and the depreciation shifts the BOP line down to BOP^1; the new equilibrium is at point 3. If the policy is perceived as permanent, e^e rises along with e and the BOP line doesn't shift in response to the (now larger) depreciation, but the IS curve shifts further to IS^2, restoring equilibrium at point 4. Panel (b) illustrates the corresponding adjustment in the foreign exchange market.

at point 4 in panel (a), income is high enough to make individuals willing to hold the higher stock of money balances at the old interest rate. Only when this is true can the interest rate return to its original level at i_0, halting capital outflows and the currency depreciation.

In panel (b) of Figure 17.4, when the expected future exchange rate rises above e_0^e, the demand for foreign-currency-denominated deposits shifts to the right as their expected rate of return increases. *(Why?)* The result is a larger spot depreciation of the domestic currency than occurred in the case in which monetary policy was expected to be temporary; e_2 denotes the new equilibrium exchange rate at point 4.

Monetary policy—temporary or permanent—raises income because it causes the domestic currency to depreciate, and the depreciation again alters the distribution as well as the level of income. Export and import-competing sectors of the economy tend to gain relative to nontraded-goods sectors, consumers of imported goods, and firms that are heavy users of imported inputs. The current-account balance moves toward a surplus.

17.3.3 **Summary of Policy Effects with Perfectly Mobile Capital**

Table 17.3 summarizes fiscal and monetary policies' short-run effects on the macroeconomy. Perfectly mobile capital reduces fiscal policy's effectiveness under flexible exchange rates. With highly mobile capital, expansionary fiscal policy causes a currency appreciation, rather than a depreciation as in the zero capital mobility

Table 17.3 **Short-Run Policy Effects with Perfectly Mobile Capital**

Policy	Effect on Equilibrium Q	Effect on Equilibrium Exchange Rate[a]	Effect on Equilibrium Current-Account Balance
Fiscal Policy:			
Perceived as temporary			
Increase in G	+	−	−
Decrease in G	−	+	+
Perceived as permanent			
Increase in G	0[b]	−	−
Decrease in G	0[b]	+	+
Monetary Policy:			
Perceived as temporary			
Increase in M	+	+	+
Decrease in M	−	−	−
Perceived as permanent			
Increase in M	+	+	+
Decrease in M	−	−	−

[a]A plus sign denotes a rise in e or currency depreciation; a minus sign denotes a decline in e or currency appreciation.
[b]Completely crowded out through change in the real exchange rate.

case. The currency appreciation generates a second type of crowding out: As the domestic currency appreciates, the relative price of domestic goods rises, and expenditure shifts toward now-cheaper foreign goods. This expenditure shift away from domestic goods partially or totally offsets the increased government spending, depending on whether participants in the foreign exchange market perceive the fiscal policy as temporary or permanent. (*Compare Table 17.3 with Table 16.3.*)

Although fiscal policy generates partial or complete crowding out because of the accompanying appreciation, monetary policy becomes highly effective in the same circumstances because it produces a currency depreciation. The depreciation stimulates spending on domestic goods by lowering their relative price. Also unlike the fiscal-policy case, expectations that monetary policy changes are permanent rather than temporary enhance the policy's effectiveness because they generate a larger currency depreciation.

17.4 Macroeconomic Policy with Imperfectly Mobile Capital

Most countries operate under an intermediate degree of capital mobility represented by an upward-sloping BOP curve. If income rises, the current account moves into deficit, and a rise in the domestic interest rate is needed to bring about an offsetting capital inflow. The more sensitive capital flows are to the interest rate, the smaller the required rise in the interest rate and the flatter the BOP curve. As in Chapter Sixteen, we'll concentrate on the case in which capital is very sensitive to interest rates and the BOP curve thus is flatter than the LM curve. (*A good way to test your understanding of the following analyses: Construct analogous analyses for the low-mobility case in which the BOP curve is steeper than the LM curve.*)

17.4.1 Fiscal Policy

Fiscal policy may raise income with imperfectly mobile capital, but the expansionary effect is at least partially offset by an appreciating currency that induces a shift toward foreign goods and away from domestic ones. In Figure 17.5, the expansionary fiscal policy's initial effect is a shift of the IS curve from IS^0 to IS^1. Income rises

---

Figure 17.5 **Short-Run Effects of Fiscal Policy with Imperfectly Mobile Capital**

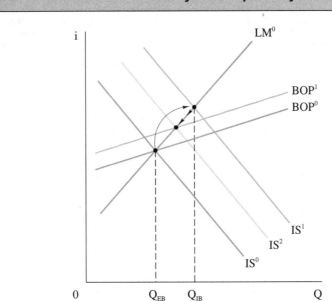

A rise in government purchases shifts the IS curve to the right and raises income and the interest rate. With high capital mobility, capital flows into the economy and the currency appreciates. As the exchange rate falls, the relative price of domestic goods rises. A shift in expenditure to now relatively cheaper foreign goods at least partially offsets the policy's initial expenditure-increasing effect by shifting IS back to the left. Perceptions that the policy is permanent rather than temporary make the policy less effective in raising income.

---

because of the increased spending on domestic output. The interest rate too must rise to keep the quantity demanded of money equal to the unchanged money stock. In response to the rise in the domestic interest rate, capital flows into the economy.

The balance of payments moves into surplus, and the currency appreciates. The BOP curve shifts to the left (BOP^0 to BOP^1) as a result of the appreciation. Because of the movement from domestic to foreign goods, at each interest rate balance-of-payments equilibrium requires a lower income. *(Why? For a review, see section 15.4.2.)* The IS curve also shifts to the left as individuals respond to the fall in e by switching spending from domestic to foreign goods. The new equilibrium occurs where the IS^2 and BOP^1 curves intersect on the LM curve.

The precise effects on income, the interest rate, and the exchange rate depend on whether the policy is perceived as temporary or permanent. If temporary, the leftward shift of the BOP line is relatively large because of the expected future depreciation, and the leftward shift of the IS curve is relatively small because of the relatively small BOP surplus; expansionary fiscal policy can then substantially raise income. However, if the policy is perceived as permanent, the leftward shift of the BOP line is small and that of the IS line is large *(Why?)*, leaving income little affected by the fiscal policy.

Regardless of whether the fiscal policy is perceived as temporary or permanent, income rises by less than it would were the policy not accompanied by a currency appreciation. The appreciation makes domestically produced goods more expensive relative to foreign ones, and the resulting shift away from spending on domestic goods at least partially offsets the expansionary effect of the fiscal policy. The more mobile capital, the larger the currency appreciation and the smaller the fiscal policy's impact on income. Likewise, the more permanent the policy is perceived as being, the larger the currency appreciation and the smaller the effect on income.

The crowding-out effect through the real exchange rate was the center of much attention in the United States during the early 1980s. Fiscal policy was expansionary, and the dollar appreciated dramatically against many trading partners' currencies. The dollar's appreciation, in turn, contributed to rising imports in indus-

Figure 17.6 **Short-Run Effects of Monetary Policy with Imperfectly Mobile Capital**

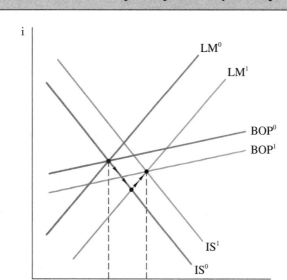

An increase in the money stock raises income and lowers the interest rate. A capital outflow depreciates the currency, lowering the relative price of domestic goods. Spending switches to domestic goods, and the IS curve shifts to the right. The depreciation of the currency makes monetary policy an effective instrument for reaching internal balance. Perceptions that the policy is permanent rather than temporary (resulting in a smaller shift in the BOP curve and a larger shift in the IS curve) make it more effective in raising income.

tries such as steel, automobiles, textiles, and footwear, and to reduced exports of agricultural products. The expansionary fiscal policy's net effect was to increase income, but the accompanying appreciation dampened the policy's impact on income and adversely affected trade-sensitive U.S. industries.

17.4.2 **Monetary Policy**

Capital mobility contributes to monetary policy's effectiveness in raising income under a flexible exchange rate regime. This follows from the fact that the currency depreciation that accompanies an expansionary monetary policy gives the economy an extra boost through its effect on domestic and foreign relative prices. The more mobile is capital, the larger the depreciation that follows a given monetary expansion and the greater the fall in the relative price of domestic goods. Similarly, the more permanent the expansionary monetary policy is perceived to be, the larger is the currency depreciation.

Figure 17.6 traces the effect of an expansionary monetary policy. The initial rightward shift of the LM curve from LM^0 to LM^1 lowers the domestic interest rate and creates a capital outflow. The outflow moves the balance of payments toward a deficit and generates a depreciation of the domestic currency. The depreciation shifts the BOP curve to the right to BOP^1. The more permanent the policy is perceived as being, the smaller will be the rightward shift in the BOP line and the larger will be the depreciation. *(Why? See footnote 20.)* As a result of the depreciation, the relative price of domestic goods falls and demand shifts toward domestic goods, moving the IS curve to the right to IS^1. Again, the more permanent the policy, the larger the deficit and the depreciation and the larger the shift in the IS curve. The new equilibrium occurs at the income at which the IS^1 and BOP^1 curves intersect on the LM^1 curve. Through the accompanying currency depreciation, the expansionary monetary policy favors export and import-competing sectors of the domestic economy.

17.5 The Policy Mix

The analysis in the preceding section suggests that fiscal and, to a greater extent, monetary policy can be used to pursue internal balance under a flexible exchange rate with imperfectly mobile capital. Which combination of the two available policies should policy makers use, or does it matter? The choice of fiscal and monetary **policy mix** does matter, because each combination results in a different domestic interest rate and exchange rate which, as we've noted all along, can dramatically affect distribution in different sectors of the domestic economy.

17.5.1 Examples of Policy Mixes

Figure 17.7 illustrates three policy mixes that policy makers could use to reach internal balance beginning from a point of external balance with unemployment, $Q_{EB} < Q_{IB}$. The economy begins at an identical point in each case. In panel (a), fiscal policy alone is used; panel (b) represents the use of monetary policy alone; and panel (c) illustrates the use of one of many possible combinations of fiscal and monetary policy. Each scenario is designed to achieve the same level of output: the one corresponding to internal balance, Q_{IB}. However, each policy mix has different implications for the allocation of expenditure between the private and public sectors, for the performance of various industries within the economy, and for the status of the current and capital accounts of the balance of payments.

In panel (a) of Figure 17.7, expansionary fiscal policy raises both income and the interest rate and appreciates the domestic currency. The rise in the interest rate reduces private spending in those sectors most sensitive to interest rates—consumer durables such as automobiles and appliances, firms' investment in new plants and equipment, and construction. The currency appreciation switches expenditure from domestically produced to foreign-produced goods by causing a change in relative prices. Export and import-competing industries suffer from this change in the expenditure pattern. Both effects of fiscal policy—crowding out by a rise in the interest rate and crowding out by currency appreciation—reduce private expenditure on domestic output, partially offsetting the policy's expansionary effect on income. The net effect is an increase in income, a rise in the share of spending accounted for by the public rather than the private sector, and a decline in both interest-sensitive and trade-oriented sectors of the economy.

Panel (b) of Figure 17.7 represents an expansionary monetary policy intended to have the same net effect on income as the fiscal policy illustrated in panel (a). The other effects of the two policies are quite different, however. The expansionary monetary policy lowers the domestic interest rate, and private investment expenditure rises. Interest-sensitive sectors, such as consumer durables and construction, may benefit. The domestic currency depreciates, and trade-oriented sectors may find their performances improved. Consumers with a taste for imported goods and firms that use imported inputs, on the other hand, will face higher prices as a result of the rise in the exchange rate.

The use of either expansionary fiscal policy or expansionary monetary policy obviously has important domestic implications. Each allows some groups to gain relative to others. One way to limit the extent of these distributional effects is to use a combination of both types of expansionary policy. A large number of such mixes exist that would move the economy to Q_{IB} in Figure 17.7.

Panel (c) illustrates a policy mix that leaves the exchange rate unchanged. The interest rate rises slightly, causing a small amount of crowding out of interest-sensitive industries. But teaming the expansionary fiscal policy with an expansionary monetary policy moderates the rise in the interest rate and reduces the magnitude of crowding out from the fiscal-policy-only case in panel (a). The accompanying monetary policy also keeps the currency from appreciating; this prevents a rise in the relative price of domestically produced goods. At the same time, the combination keeps the exchange rate from depreciating and prevents a rise in the domestic price of imported goods and inputs, as would happen if policy makers used monetary policy alone.

17.5.2 Responding to Disturbances

The policy mix with which policy makers choose to pursue internal balance depends on, among other things, the nature of the disturbance that pushed the economy below full employment.[21] Such disturbances fall into

---

21 Of course, the economy can experience expansionary disturbances that push income above the full-employment level. We concentrate on contractionary disturbances, which call for expansionary policy responses, because we've focused on the impact of expansionary policies.

Figure 17.7 **Use of Various Policy Mixes to Achieve Internal Balance**

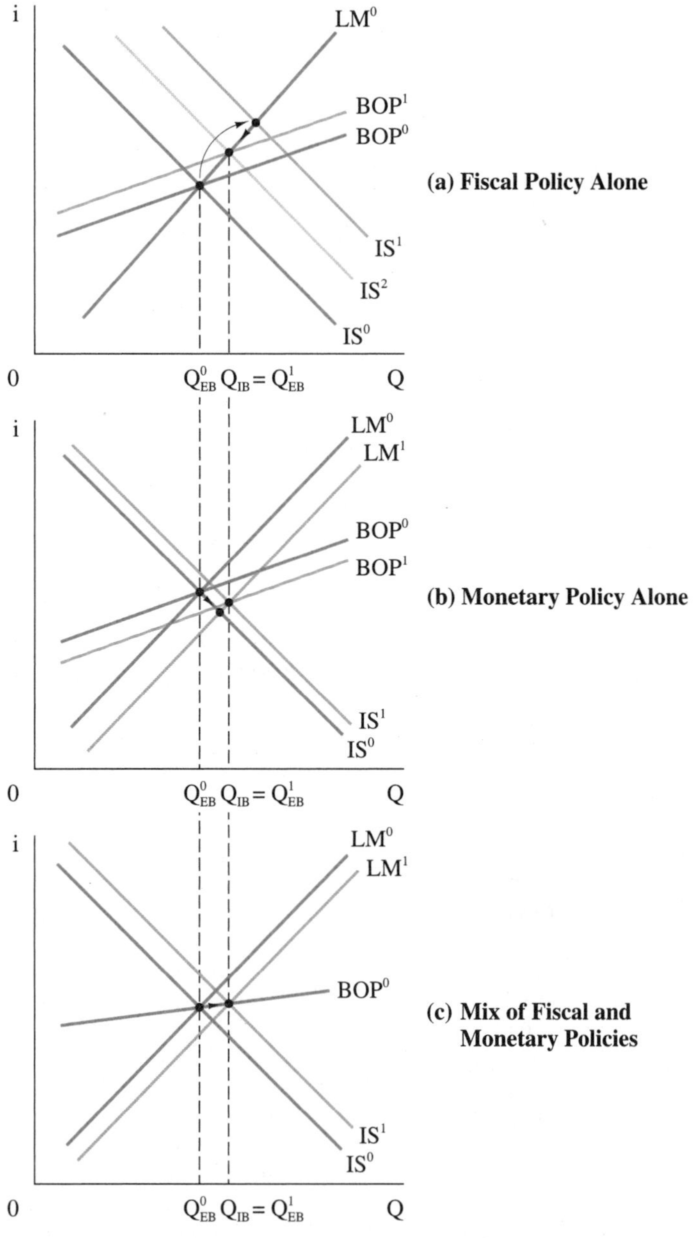

(a) Fiscal Policy Alone

(b) Monetary Policy Alone

(c) Mix of Fiscal and Monetary Policies

Policy makers can use many fiscal/monetary policy combinations to increase income to Q_{IB}. Each combination results in different values of the interest rate and the exchange rate. Expansionary fiscal policy alone (panel (a)) produces the highest interest rate, monetary policy alone the lowest (panel (b)), and a policy mix an intermediate value (panel (c)). Expansionary fiscal policy appreciates the domestic currency; monetary policy alone depreciates it; and the illustrated policy mix leaves the exchange rate unchanged.

Figure 17.8 **Policy Responses to a Spending Disturbance**

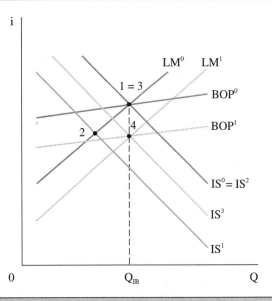

Policy makers can respond to a contractionary spending disturbance with an expansionary fiscal or monetary policy. A fiscal policy restores full employment at the original interest rate and exchange rate (point 3). A monetary policy restores full employment but magnifies the disturbance's effect on the interest rate and exchange rate (point 4).

two broad categories: shifts in tastes away from domestically produced goods and increases in the demand for real money balances.

Beginning from a position of internal balance (point 1 in Figure 17.8), suppose the economy experiences a shift in consumer tastes away from domestically produced goods and services. Potential causes of such a shift could include pessimism about the future leading to an overall reduction in consumption or investment spending or a shift in consumer preferences in favor of foreign goods and services.[22] We can represent such a spending disturbance by a shift to the left of the IS curve, from IS^0 to IS^1. Income falls below the level consistent with internal balance, and the domestic currency depreciates because of the decline in the domestic interest rate at point 2.

Policy makers might respond to the temporary shortfall in consumption or investment spending in one of two ways. An expansionary fiscal policy shifts IS back to the right to IS^2 and restores full employment at the same interest rate and exchange rate as before the disturbance (point 3). The alternative is an expansionary monetary policy. By shifting LM to the right to LM^1, such a policy puts further downward pressure on the interest rate and causes a further currency depreciation, which shifts the IS curve and BOP curve to the right, to IS^3 and BOP^1. Monetary policy restores full employment, but with a lower interest rate and a depreciated value of the domestic currency at point 4. As noted in section 17.5.1, the different values of the interest rate and the exchange rate implied by fiscal and monetary policies carry important implications for the performance of specific sectors of the economy, even though either can restore full employment.

A second type of contractionary economic disturbance consists of a rise in the demand for real money balances for a given value of income and the interest rate. Beginning from a point of full employment (point 1), such a shock shifts the LM curve to the left, as in Figure 17.9.[23] Again, output falls below the full-employment level. The disturbance raises the domestic interest rate and causes a currency appreciation (at point 2).

---

22 The exogenous spending disturbances under consideration here do *not* include changes in response to the domestic interest rate, domestic income, or the relative price of domestic goods and services, but rather shifts in spending for given levels of those variables.

23 Section 15.2.5 reviews why.

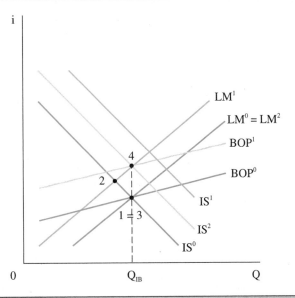

Figure 17.9 **Policy Responses to a Money-Demand Disturbance**

Possible policy responses to a contractionary monetary disturbance include expansionary fiscal or monetary policy. An expansionary fiscal policy restores full employment but exacerbates the rise in the interest rate and the currency appreciation (point 4). Monetary policy restores full employment at the pre-disturbance interest rate and exchange rate (point 3).

If policy makers respond with an expansionary monetary policy, LM shifts back to the right, restoring full employment at the original interest rate and exchange rate (point 3). If, instead, policy makers respond with expansionary fiscal policy, the IS curve shifts to the right to IS^1. This puts further upward pressure on the interest rate and causes further currency appreciation. As the domestic currency appreciates, the IS and BOP curves shift to the left to IS^2 and BOP^1. The economy returns to full employment at point 4, with a higher interest rate and a lower value of the exchange rate than prior to the disturbance to money demand.

17.5.3 **Constraints on the Policy Mix**

Several considerations not obvious in our analysis of Figures 17.8 and 17.9 considerably complicate policy makers' choice of policy mix. For example, we assumed that the level of output consistent with full employment is known, as is how the actual level of output compares with full employment (often called the *output gap*). However, as we saw in Chapter Sixteen, defining the full-employment level of output for an economy is a complex task, as is judging whether the current level of output is consistent with, above, or below full employment. Policy makers may disagree among themselves or with the public about the current state of the economy and, therefore, about the need for macroeconomic policies and the appropriate magnitudes of those policies.

We also assumed in our analysis that policy makers know the source of the disturbance to the economy, that is, whether the disturbance originates in the market for goods and services or in the money market. In fact, the nature of disturbances to the economy may be difficult to discern, particularly in the short run, during which policy makers must formulate their response. As Figures 17.8 and 17.9 make clear, responding to a spending disturbance with monetary policy or to a monetary disturbance with fiscal policy can exacerbate swings in the interest rate and the exchange rate and the accompanying distributional impacts on the economy.

Policy makers also must judge a disturbance's time horizon in order to make an appropriate policy response. If the decline in spending or increase in money demand is short-lived, then no response may be required, as the economy will return to full employment automatically as soon as the disturbance ends. If policy makers respond aggressively to a short-lived disturbance, they risk pushing output above the full-employment level and generating inflation. On the other hand, an overly passive response that relies too heavily on the temporary nature of the disturbance risks a prolonged period of unemployment. These timing decisions are complicated by the fact that macroeconomic policies typically affect the economy with lags.

Finally, policy makers may face political pressures that constrain their ability to use some macroeconomic policy tools. We've already mentioned one source of such pressure: the distributional implications of changes in interest rates and exchange rates. A second source of pressure comes from policy targets beyond internal and external balance. For example, the ability to use expansionary fiscal policy may be constrained by concerns over the implications of existing government budget deficits or debt. If a government accumulates a large debt during times of economic prosperity, it may find itself constrained against using fiscal policy to respond to a slump. Along similar lines, a government facing reelection may find it difficult to cut public spending—even if macroeconomic considerations point to the appropriateness of a contractionary fiscal-policy stance.

17.5.4 International Transmission and the Policy Mix

Domestic political considerations aren't the only constraints on macroeconomic policy makers. Different domestic macroeconomic policy mixes exert different effects on trading-partner economies, a phenomenon known as **transmission,** so the governments of those economies often attempt to influence the course of domestic macroeconomic policy.

With a high degree of capital mobility, if domestic policy makers respond to a contractionary disturbance with an expansionary fiscal policy, trading-partner economies typically experience an expansion as well. This happens because the fiscal policy appreciates the domestic currency or, equivalently, depreciates the foreign currency. The depreciation makes foreign-produced goods and services relatively cheaper, so expenditure on them rises. In contrast, if domestic policy makers respond to a contractionary disturbance with an expansionary monetary policy, trading partners are likely to feel the contraction. The domestic currency depreciates, or the foreign one appreciates. Foreign goods and services become more expensive relative to domestic ones, and consumers shift away from spending on foreign goods. Of course, how trading partners feel about these transmitted policy effects depends on the state of their economies. A country fighting inflation may welcome a contractionary effect initiated abroad, while a country suffering from excessive unemployment will resent the same effect.

17.6 Summary of Short-Run Policy Effectiveness under a Flexible Exchange Rate

The short-run effectiveness of fiscal and monetary policy in pursuing a goal of internal balance under a flexible exchange rate regime critically depends on the degree of capital mobility. As capital mobility rises, monetary policy becomes more effective than fiscal policy because of its different impact on the exchange rate. Policy-induced changes in the exchange rate are important because, with the assumption of fixed domestic and foreign price levels, they're reflected directly in changes in the real exchange rate or relative prices of domestic and foreign goods. In such circumstances, any policy that can alter the exchange rate can shift expenditure between domestic and foreign goods.

Table 17.4 summarizes the effects of fiscal and monetary policy under flexible exchange rates with differing degrees of capital mobility. Because of the importance of changes in the exchange rate that accompany each policy, the table reports those as well.

Japan

CASE ONE:
The Japan Slump

After years of envy-inspiring growth, the Japanese economy has struggled since the early 1990s. Growth has averaged only about 1 percent a year since 1992. Figure 17.10 traces the country's output gap, the percentage difference between actual real GDP and full-employment, or potential, real GDP since 1982. The positive output gap of 2.2 recorded

Table 17.4 Short-Run Policy Effectiveness under Flexible Exchange Rates

Policy	Ability to Affect Income under a Flexible Exchange Rate		
	Immobile Capital	Highly Mobile Capital	Perfectly Mobile Capital
Fiscal	Effective (currency depreciates)	Somewhat effective[a] (currency appreciates)	Ineffective[a] (currency appreciates)
Monetary	Effective (currency depreciates)	Effective[b] (currency depreciates)	Very effective[b] (currency depreciates)

[a]Less effective if perceived as permanent than if perceived as temporary.
[b]More effective if perceived as permanent than if perceived as temporary.

Figure 17.10 Japanese Output Gap, 1982–1999

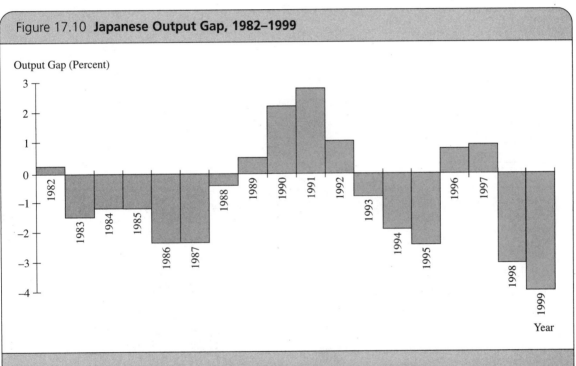

The output gap equals the percentage difference between actual real GDP and potential, or full-employment, real GDP. Positive gaps represent periods of economic boom; negative gaps represent economic slumps.

Source: Data from Organization for Economic Cooperation and Development.

for 1990, for example, means that actual output that year exceeded full-employment output by 2.2 percent, a situation that, had it persisted, we would expect to lead to inflation. The gap of −3.8 for 1999, on the other hand, indicates that real GDP fell short of its full-employment level by 3.8 percent, an indication of sluggish macroeconomic performance. Since 1982, Japan has experienced 11 years of negative output gaps and only 7 years of above-full-employment output.

Japanese property and stock markets declined precipitously during the 1990s, as illustrated in Figure 17.11. Figures 17.10 and 17.11 make clear that when the Asian financial crisis hit, in 1997, the Japanese economy was already weak.

Japanese policy makers repeatedly used expansionary fiscal policy in an attempt to get the economy moving. Nine separate fiscal-stimulus packages were enacted during the 1990s, as shown in Figure 17.12.

By the time of the Asian financial crisis, Japan hesitated to use further expansionary fiscal policy because of the heavy government debt already accumulated during 1992–1996. Much of that government spending had gone toward public

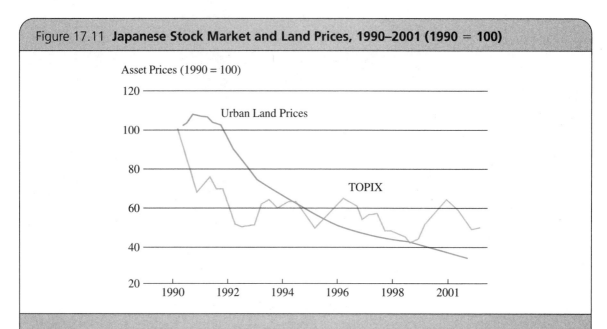

Figure 17.11 **Japanese Stock Market and Land Prices, 1990–2001 (1990 = 100)**

Asset Prices (1990 = 100)

Urban Land Prices

TOPIX

The Japanese TOPIX stock index and urban land prices fell dramatically during the 1990s.

Source: International Monetary Fund.

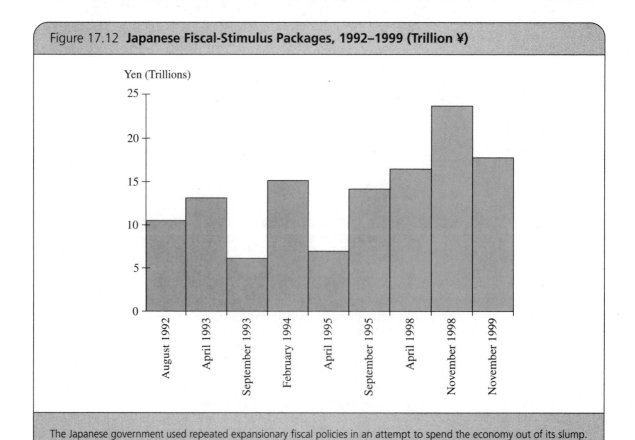

Figure 17.12 **Japanese Fiscal-Stimulus Packages, 1992–1999 (Trillion ¥)**

Yen (Trillions)

The Japanese government used repeated expansionary fiscal policies in an attempt to spend the economy out of its slump.

construction programs, notoriously expensive and inefficient in Japan. So while the number of yen spent on government purchases looked impressive, their actual macroeconomic impact was limited. By 1996, when policy makers sensed a small upturn in the economy, fiscal policy turned contractionary as the government tried to reduce its budget deficit by reducing public spending and instituting a tax increase. The quarter following the tax increase, GDP fell at a rate of 11 percent. Policy makers from other countries pressured Japan to postpone its government debt and budget concerns and use expansionary fiscal policy—in particular, permanent tax cuts—to stimulate the economy. *(If Japan suffered from a negative spending shock, why might fiscal rather than monetary policy be a recommended response?)*

Interest rates in Japan were at historic lows (around 0.5 percent) when the Asian crisis hit, but the rate of growth of the money stock was relatively low. Japanese banks held many bad loans, both domestically and in the rest of Asia, making them less-than-willing lenders, especially to small and medium-sized borrowers. Housing and business investment, two sectors through which expansionary monetary policy traditionally works, declined.

At first, trading partners (especially the United States, with its large trade deficit) criticized Japan's reliance on depreciating the yen and stimulating exports to the neglect of policies to stimulate the domestic components of demand (C and I). Also, while the yen depreciated against the dollar, the Japanese currency appreciated against the Asian-crisis countries, whose demand for Japanese exports fell. This made currency depreciation a less effective way of stimulating demand since over 40 percent of Japanese exports typically went to Asia. By early 1999, anxious for Japanese growth to accelerate and support recovery in the Asian-crisis countries, the United States switched gears and pushed

Japan toward expansionary monetary policy, despite that policy's likely effect of enlarging the politically sensitive U.S. trade deficit.

Regardless of the government's policies, Japanese consumers worried about their jobs and curtailed their expenditure. They saved rather than spent most of the temporary tax cuts provided by government fiscal policy makers.[24] Businesses found it harder to borrow as banks slowed their loans to comply with the higher bank-capital standards applied in 1998. Firm bankruptcies, failures of several big financial institutions, and corruption scandals, both public and private, further dampened confidence.

Overall, both fiscal and monetary policy were expansionary in Japan through the 1990s, but only erratically so. The nominal interest rate fell from over 8 percent in 1991 to near zero in 1999, but the money stock often grew only slowly. The government budget deficit, corrected for business-cycle effects, rose by about 6 percent of GDP over the same period, and the government's debt grew to about 130 percent of GDP (the highest among industrial economies).[25] Most economists, however, think that more fundamental structural reforms will be required before the Japanese economy really recovers. Those reforms include deregulating many industries, making the economy more open to new firms and new competitors, creating a more competitive and innovative banking and financial sector, reducing firms' reliance on banks as the main source of finance, and stopping the long-standing tendency for the government to insure special-interest groups against losses in return for the groups' political support. All these reforms would prove politically difficult even during a period of strong economic performance; accomplishing them during a long-running slump will challenge Japanese policy makers, their constituents, and their trading partners.

Japan

CASE TWO:
Policy Squeezes: To Do, or Not to Do?

Japan's situation in the 1990s provides excellent examples of several common dilemmas that confront policy makers. First, let's consider the country's fiscal policy; how expansionary should it be? Given the recessionary conditions prevailing during most of the decade, expansionary fiscal policy seemed appropriate from a short-run policy perspective. The United States, a major trading partner, encouraged Japan's

expansionary fiscal policy, in part because the resulting yen appreciation helped mitigate the growing U.S. trade deficit. But, of course, that same yen appreciation made the fiscal policy less expansionary for Japan. The main reason for Japanese policy makers' reluctance to continue such expansionary fiscal policy lies in the country's accumulating government debt. That debt quickly passed 100 percent of GDP

---

24 Both macroeconomic theory and experience in other countries indicate that temporary tax cuts tend to increase saving while permanent tax cuts tend to increase consumption expenditure.

25 International Monetary Fund, *World Economic Outlook May 2001*, p. 17.

and, while still modest by developing-country standards, eventually surpassed the debt of infamously profligate developed countries such as Italy. Policy makers feared, with some justification, that holders of Japanese assets would lose confidence in the country's ability to manage and repay its debt. Such a loss of confidence would push up interest rates and hurt already-shaky banks. Fiscal matters were further complicated by Japan's rapidly aging population, which implies an approaching responsibility, shared by firms and government, to pay millions of pensions. So fiscal policy makers were squeezed—between a short-run need for fiscal spending and longer-run pressures for fiscal consolidation.

Monetary policy makers didn't have life much easier. Again, the recessionary conditions suggested a need for expansionary monetary policy. But the United States was slower to support such a move because it risked a sharp yen depreciation and a bigger spurt in the already-large U.S. trade deficit. Japanese domestic politics also played a role. The central bank, the Bank of Japan, had won formal independence from the Ministry of Finance only in 1998 and was eager to demonstrate that independence. So pressure from politicians, including the Ministry of Finance, to follow expansionary monetary policy to alleviate the fiscal expansion's upward pressure on interest rates encountered resistance at the Bank of Japan. Monetary policy makers also worried that too much expansionary policy would let banks off the hook too easily after years of bad management and bad loans. Again, short-run policy considerations (getting out of the recession) conflicted with longer-term policy goals (get-

ting banks to reform in ways that would support a more efficient economy in the long run).

Other reforms and policy decisions involved similar dilemmas. Most analysts agreed that Japanese banks' large-scale ownership of stock in firms discouraged efficient channeling of saving to the most productive investment projects. The stock "cross-holdings" also presented risks for the banks' own balance sheets. So long-run considerations indicated that banks should sell (or "unwind") those assets. But with the stock market falling for much of the decade, large-scale sales by banks could simply exacerbate the short-run problem. Similarly, forcing banks to abide by international regulatory standards in their accounting and capital provisions seems essential if Japan's financial sector is to better support the country's economy. But forcing those standards on struggling banks with huge bad-loan problems risked forcing even more banks into bankruptcy, with the resulting loss of public confidence.

So what's the lesson from all these dilemmas (other than the fact that it isn't easy being an economic policy maker)? The importance of fixing structural weaknesses in the economy when times are good. Policy changes that have distributional consequences (for example, telling banks they're responsible for their own bad loans, or telling depositors that government will insure only part of their bank deposits) isn't ever easy. But politically difficult decisions need to be made when the economy is strong enough to absorb any bad side effects with minimal loss of confidence.

Great Britain

CASE THREE:
Floating the Pound, Part I

The policy dilemmas posed by fixed exchange rates and capital flows didn't arise first in the Mexican or Asian financial crises. Case One in Chapter Sixteen analyzed the effect of German unification on the country's European trading partners in the early 1990s. The combination of Germany's expansionary fiscal policies to finance unification and tight monetary policies to deter inflation kept the interest rate on Deutsche mark–denominated assets high and shifted trading partners' BOP curves upward. Fellow members of the European Union's Exchange Rate Mechanism of fixed exchange rates had to intervene to sell Deutsche marks from their foreign exchange reserves to prevent their currencies from depreciating against the mark. That intervention lowered trading partners' money stocks and placed contractionary

pressures on their economies, where unemployment already was high.

In September 1992, a period of increased uncertainty about the future of monetary integration in Europe, participants in the foreign exchange markets started to expect devaluations of several EU currencies, including the British pound. The expected devaluations implied that, to prevent actual devaluations, central banks would have to conduct even more intervention and monetary contraction. *(Why?)* But those policies posed political risks in countries such as Britain, already entering its third year of recession.

On September 16, 1992 (dubbed "Black Wednesday" by opponents of the move), rather than pursue further monetary contraction, the British government pulled the pound

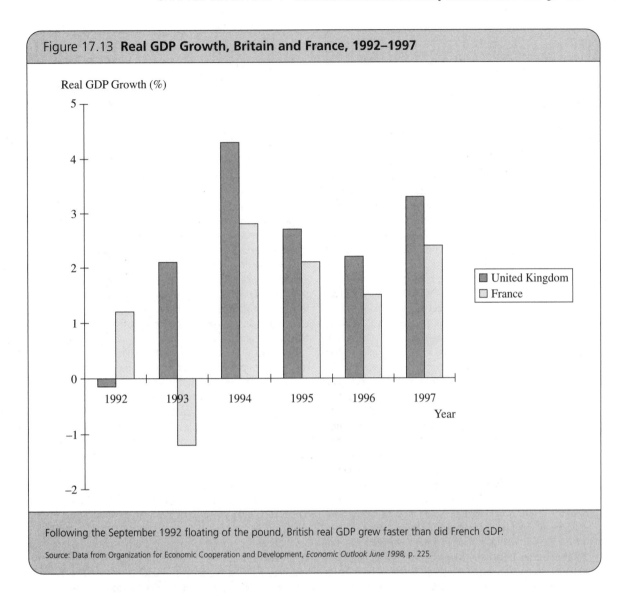

Figure 17.13 **Real GDP Growth, Britain and France, 1992–1997**

Following the September 1992 floating of the pound, British real GDP grew faster than did French GDP.

Source: Data from Organization for Economic Cooperation and Development, *Economic Outlook June 1998*, p. 225.

out of the fixed exchange rate system and allowed the pound to float against the Deutsche mark and other EU currencies. Britain's monetary policy became more expansionary, and interest rates on pound-denominated assets fell. The pound depreciated in foreign exchange markets from the fixed rate of DM2.85/£1 to a low of DM2.34/£1 in February 1993, lowering the relative prices of British goods and services; the country's current-account deficit shrank. By 1994, the British economy was growing faster than EU economies such as France that remained in the Exchange Rate Mechanism (see Figure 17.13).[26]

---

26 An obvious question is why more EU member countries didn't abandon their fixed exchange rates. There are at least two reasons. First, several economies had histories of excessively expansionary monetary policies, inflation, and currency devaluations. Those countries feared that escaping the discipline imposed by the Exchange Rate Mechanism would generate expectations of further currency depreciations. Second, countries that pulled out of the system ran the risk of having less voice in the process of European monetary integration.

CASE FOUR:
The Budget and the Dollar

During the early 1980s, when the dollar *appreciated* dramatically against the currencies of most U.S. trading partners, many commentators blamed the U.S. government budget deficit. Overly expansionary fiscal policy, they argued, placed upward pressure on U.S. interest rates, encouraged capital inflows, and caused the dollar to appreciate. *(Illustrate in the IS-LM-BOP framework.)* The period between 1985 and 1995 was one of substantial dollar *depreciation*. Yet commentators still blamed the U.S. government budget deficit! The result has been a lively debate about the likely impact on the dollar of a reduction in the budget deficit.

The link between a budget deficit and currency *appreciation* shows up clearly in the model developed in this chapter. Why, then, would anyone link the deficit to the dollar *depreciation* after 1985? There are three possibilities. First, prolonged, large, and growing budget deficits might cause market participants to anticipate more expansionary future monetary policies to mitigate the deficit's effect on the interest rate. If so, a future currency depreciation might be expected to follow from the monetary expansion. Those expectations could reduce the demand for domestic-currency-denominated deposits and cause the currency to depreciate. A second possibility also relies on expectations, but in a more general way. If a persistent budget deficit weakened overall confidence in the U.S. economy, it might reduce the demand for dollar-denominated deposits. However, note that the resulting depreciation would increase demand for U.S. goods and services and thereby tend to offset the lack of confidence in the economy's future performance. The third possibility involves a risk premium.[27] Recall that portfolio owners may demand a risk premium to hold assets denominated in a particular currency if such assets constitute a large portion of their portfolios, making the portfolios' value vulnerable to exchange rate changes. If the U.S.

government budget deficit, by requiring individuals to hold a large stock of dollar-denominated government bonds, generated a higher risk premium on dollar assets, then the U.S. BOP line would shift upward and the dollar would depreciate. As we noted in the earlier discussion of risk premiums, the empirical evidence on their importance is mixed.

So our basic model of an open macroeconomy suggests a currency appreciation would accompany budget deficits. But several expectations-based arguments may generate effects in the opposite direction. Figure 17.14 looks at the recent empirical evidence for the United States. Panel (a) reports the federal budget surplus (if positive) or deficit (if negative) as a percent of GDP. Panel (b) illustrates the real effective exchange rate, expressed as an index of the dollar price of foreign exchange.

The two dramatic trends of the 1980s in Figure 17.14 suggest a positive relationship between the size of the government budget deficit and the value of the dollar. During the early 1980s, the deficit grew dramatically and the dollar appreciated. During the late 1980s, the deficit shrank and the dollar depreciated. This supports the analysis based on the model presented in the chapter. However, the late 1990s appear to exhibit a different pattern. The deficit shrank (and, in fact, the government budget moved into surplus), and the dollar appreciated.

The large government budget deficits of the 1980s were a relatively new phenomenon for the United States, at least in peacetime. It's possible that had the deficit continued to grow, its impact on expectations could have become more significant. Similarly, it's too early to tell if the late-1990s disappearance of the budget deficit is (or is perceived by markets participants as) a permanent phenomenon or a temporary one generated by the extraordinary duration of the U.S. economic boom of the 1990s.

Summary

The switch from a fixed to a flexible exchange rate regime carries important implications for the effectiveness of various types of macroeconomic policy. Unlike a fixed exchange rate, a flexible rate allows the monetary authority to control the domestic nominal money stock through open market operations. Changes in the money stock, however, alter the exchange rate, and policy makers must tolerate these changes—with their distributional implications and their impact on the current-account balance—as a side effect of monetary policy. With high degrees of capital mobility, monetary policy becomes very effective in altering domestic income and

---

27 See section 16.4.2.

Figure 17.14 **The U.S. Government Budget and the Exchange Rate, 1973–2000**

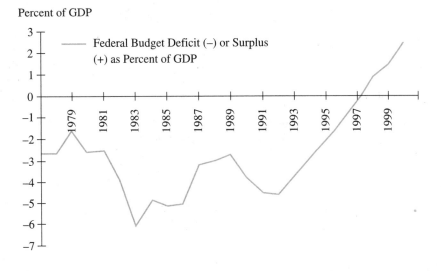

The basic open economy macroeconomic model predicts that a government budget deficit would be associated with a domestic currency appreciation and a budget surplus with a depreciation. Major trends during the 1973–2000 period in the United States conform to the expected pattern, but some years are exceptions.

Source: U.S. Department of the Treasury and Board of Governors of the Federal Reserve System.

fiscal policy loses its effectiveness. The choice of fiscal and monetary policy mix for pursuing internal balance affects the allocation of spending between the private and public sectors as well as the relative performances of various domestic industries and of trading partners' economies.

Looking Ahead

Throughout our discussion of macroeconomic policy in an open economy, we've assumed that the domestic and foreign price levels are fixed. This assumption implies that, despite the economy's automatic adjustment mechanisms for reaching external balance, no analogous mechanism ensures internal balance; that is, the market for goods and services may be in equilibrium at a level of income above or below the level consistent with full employment or internal balance. In Chapter Eighteen, we relax the fixed-price assumption and concentrate on long-run macroeconomic behavior, especially that of the exchange rate.

Key Terms

Bretton Woods system   **policy mix**
crowding out   **transmission**

Problems and Questions for Review

1. Countries A and B are trading partners. Both have a flexible exchange rate and highly but not perfectly mobile capital. Both want to pursue expansionary policies to raise the level of income.
   a. Country A pursues an expansionary fiscal policy and a tight monetary policy (that is, zero growth of the domestic money stock). Illustrate the effects of such a policy mix.
   b. Country B pursues a tight fiscal policy (that is, no change in government purchases or taxes) and an expansionary monetary policy. Illustrate the effects of such a policy mix.
   c. What would you expect to happen to the interest rate in country A relative to that in country B? What would happen to the exchange rate between country A's currency and country B's?
   d. What distributional effects would your results in part (c) have in the two economies?
   e. Use your answers to construct a brief argument in favor of international macroeconomic policy coordination (that is, for countries getting together to discuss and coordinate their macroeconomic policy actions).
2. A country hires you as its minister of macroeconomic policy. The country maintains strict capital controls that make any nonofficial capital inflows or outflows impossible. Up until now, the country has operated under a fixed exchange rate regime. The day you take office, exchange rate policy changes to a perfectly flexible exchange rate regime. Your first order of business is to give seminars for your subordinates, the assistant minister of fiscal policy and the assistant minister of monetary policy, to outline the implications of the change in exchange rate policy. Summarize the main points of your seminar presentations on the implications of the new policy, using the appropriate tools of analysis.
3. It is common for countries to complain about one another's interest rates. Assume that the domestic country operates under a flexible exchange rate regime, and capital is completely mobile. Illustrate and explain the effect on the domestic economy of a *decline* in the *foreign* interest rate (i^*), beginning from a point of general equilibrium, using the IS-LM-BOP framework. (Compare your answer with that of Question 5 in Chapter Sixteen.)
4. Historically, it has been common for a country to pressure its trading partners to follow expansionary macroeconomic policies. Assume that the domestic country operates under a flexible exchange rate regime and that capital is completely mobile. Illustrate and explain the effect on the domestic economy of an *increase* in *foreign* income, beginning from a point of general equilibrium, using the IS-LM-BOP framework. (Compare your answer with that of Question 7 in Chapter Sixteen.)
5. a. How does the expectation that the policy is temporary affect the efficacy of fiscal policy under a flexible exchange rate and perfect capital mobility? Explain.
   b. How does the expectation that the policy is temporary affect the efficacy of monetary policy under a flexible exchange rate and perfect capital mobility? Explain.

6. Question 5 distinguishes between the effects under a flexible exchange rate regime of macroeconomic policies perceived to be temporary and those perceived to be permanent. The analysis in Chapter Sixteen of macroeconomic policy under a fixed exchange rate regime made no such distinction. Explain why.

7. Suppose everyone expects a country's new government to follow much more expansionary monetary policy, although policy hasn't actually changed yet. How do you think these expectations would affect the country's exchange rate? Why?

8. Country A operates under a flexible exchange rate regime and is characterized by a high degree of capital mobility. The country is beginning to experience inflationary pressure, and policy makers decide that a contractionary macroeconomic policy is appropriate. They consider three policy packages, all of which would be designed to generate the same overall effect on income:

   Policy package 1: Contractionary fiscal policy combined with neutral monetary policy.
   Policy package 2: Contractionary monetary policy combined with neutral fiscal policy.
   Policy package 3: A combination of contractionary fiscal and contractionary monetary policy such that the exchange rate will remain the same.

   a. Suppose you own a residential construction firm. How might you rank your preferences for the three policy packages? Explain.
   b. Suppose you own a large soybean farm and typically export a large portion of your crop. How might you rank your preferences for the three policy packages? Explain.
   c. Suppose you own a small retail shop that sells handicrafts imported from developing countries. How might you rank your preferences for the three policy packages? Explain.

References and Selected Readings

Baxter, M. "International Trade and Business Cycles." In *Handbook of International Economics,* Vol. 3, edited by G. M. Grossman and K. Rogoff, 1801–1864. Amsterdam: North-Holland, 1995.
Survey of research on the relationship between international trade activity and macroeconomic cycles; intermediate and advanced.

Browne, L. E. "Does Japan Offer Any Lessons for the United States?" Federal Reserve Bank of Boston, *New England Economic Review* (2001), No. 3: 3–18.
Similarities and differences between Japan's economic downturns of the 1990s and the U.S. downturn of 2001.

Cooper, Richard N. "Is the U.S. Current Account Deficit Sustainable? Will It Be Sustained?" *Brookings Papers on Economic Activity* (2001): 217–226.
Emphasizes the role of capital flows into the United States as a source of the U.S. current-account deficit.

Cooper, Richard N., and Jane Sneddon Little. "U.S. Monetary Policy in an Integrating World: 1960 to 2000." In *The Evolution of Monetary Policy and the Federal Reserve System over the Past Thirty Years,* edited by R. W. Kopcke and L. E. Browne, 77–130. Boston: Federal Reserve Bank of Boston, 2000.
History of international influences on U.S. monetary policy.

Eichengreen, Barry. *Globalizing Capital.* Princeton: Princeton University Press, 1996.
Readable account of the history and implications of international capital flows.

Fleming, J. M. "Domestic Financial Policies under Fixed and Floating Exchange Rates." *IMF Staff Papers* 9 (November 1962): 369–380.
A classic paper on macroeconomic policy effectiveness in an open economy; for advanced students.

Frankel, J. A., and A. K. Rose. "Empirical Research on Nominal Exchange Rates." In *Handbook of International Economics,* Vol. 3, edited by G. M. Grossman and K. Rogoff, 1689–1730. Amsterdam: North-Holland, 1995.
Survey of research on the empirical behavior of exchange rates; intermediate and advanced.

Friedman, Milton. "The Case for Flexible Exchange Rates." In *Essays in Positive Economics,* 157–203. Chicago: University of Chicago Press, 1953.
One of the first serious calls for a change to flexible exchange rates; for all students.

Hetzel, Robert L. "Japanese Monetary Policy: A Quantity Theory Perspective." Federal Reserve Bank of Richmond, *Economic Quarterly* 85 (Winter 1999): 1–26.
Introduction to monetary policy's role in Japan's weak economic performance during the 1990s.

Hondroyiannis, George, et al. "Is the Japanese Economy in a Liquidity Trap?" *Economics Letters* 66 (2000): 17–23.
Argues that more rapid money growth would pull the Japanese economy out of its decade-long slump; advanced.

Krugman, Paul R. "It's Baaack: Japan's Slump and the Return of the Liquidity Trap." *Brookings Papers on Economic Activity* 2 (1998): 137–206.
Argues that Japan is experiencing a liquidity trap similar to that exhibited during the Great Depression.

Lincoln, Edward J. "Japan's Financial Problems." *Brookings Papers on Economic Activity* 2 (1998): 347–385.
The financial-sector basis of Japan's continuing macroeconomic malaise.

Mann, Catherine L. "Is the U.S. Current Account Deficit Sustainable?" *Finance and Development* 37 (March 2000): 42–45.
Are there reasons the U.S. current-account deficit must shrink?

McKinnon, Ronald I. "The International Dollar Standard and the Sustainability of the U.S. Current Account Deficit." *Brookings Papers on Economic Activity* (2001): 227–240.
Emphasizes the vehicle-currency role of the dollar as a source of sustainability for the U.S. current-account deficit.

Meltzer, Allan H. "U.S. Policy in the Bretton Woods Era." Federal Reserve Bank of St. Louis, *Review* (May–June 1991): 53–83.
Excellent survey of the Bretton Woods era; for all students.

Mühleisen, Martin, and Hamid Faruqee. "Japan: Population Aging and the Fiscal Challenge." *Finance and Development* 38 (March 2001): 10–13.
How can Japan reduce its fiscal deficit when it faces pension liabilities for an old and rapidly aging population?

Mundell, Robert A. "Capital Mobility and Stabilization Policy under Fixed and Flexible Exchange Rates." *Canadian Journal of Economics and Political Science* 29 (November 1963): 475–485.
The original presentation of capital mobility's impact on macroeconomic policy effectiveness in an open economy; for intermediate and advanced students.

Obstfeld, Maurice. "International Currency Experience: New Lessons and Lessons Relearned." *Brookings Papers on Economic Activity* 1 (1995): 119–220.
Excellent overview of lessons based on recent exchange rate experience.

Olivei, Giovanni P. "The Role of Saving and Investment in Balancing the Current Account: Some Empirical Evidence from the United States." Federal Reserve Bank of Boston, *New England Economic Review* (July/August 2000): 3–14.
The relationship among saving, investment, and the current-account deficit.

Persson, T., and G. Tabellini. "Double-Edged Incentives: Institutions and Policy Coordination." In *Handbook of International Economics,* Vol. 3, edited by G. M. Grossman and K. Rogoff, 1973–2030. Amsterdam: North-Holland, 1995.
Survey of interaction effects among countries' macroeconomic policies; intermediate and advanced.

CHAPTER EIGHTEEN

The Exchange Rate in Long-Run Equilibrium

18.1 Introduction

Thus far, in Chapters Fourteen through Seventeen, we've examined macroeconomic behavior in the short run, during which the price level remained fixed. Exchange rates sometimes move dramatically even in the very short run. For example, the Indonesian rupiah declined in value from Rp7,750/$1 to Rp10,550/$1 on January 8, 1998, in the midst of the Asian financial crisis. On August 26, 1998, the Russian ruble depreciated by more than 69 percent against the Deutsche mark, in response to Russia's default on its debt and more general doubts about Russian economic and political reform.

Longer-run trends in the world economy can be just as dramatic. In 1973, the dollar price of yen stood at $1/¥360; by early 1995, the price had risen to $1/¥80, a dollar depreciation of almost 80 percent. A reversal of trend brought the exchange rate to $1/¥147 on June 17, 1998, when the U.S. Federal Reserve intervened by buying $833 million worth of yen in an effort to slow the yen's depreciation. To understand such events, we must take into account the fact that in the long run prices *do* respond to macroeconomic policy, as well as to other events in the economy. This chapter and the next extend our model to incorporate those price-level changes. It's useful to proceed in two stages. In this chapter, we turn our attention to long-run equilibrium under a flexible exchange rate and explore the relationships we expect to observe among key macroeconomic variables *once the price level has adjusted completely to any change in the economy.* Chapter Nineteen focuses on the relationship between the short-run results and the long-run results, or on what happens in the economy *as the price level adjusts.*

In **long-run equilibrium,** the economy satisfies two related conditions. First, output reaches its full-employment level, determined by how much capital and labor the economy contains, as well as by the available technology and by how much individuals in the economy choose to work. Second, all prices in the economy, including the wage rate and the exchange rate, reach levels consistent with equilibrium in their respective markets. We call this a long-run *equilibrium,* because once the economy attains it, economic variables won't change until some new shock to the system disturbs them.

In this chapter, we examine how the exchange rate behaves in long-run equilibrium. This requires an understanding of the long-run relationships among the country's money stock, price level, and exchange rate.

18.2 Money in Long-Run Equilibrium

18.2.1 How Does Money Affect Real Output?

What effect does a one-time permanent change in the size of the money stock have on the economy's long-run equilibrium real output? The answer is none, and a simple thought experiment can help us see why. Suppose that, beginning from a position of long-run equilibrium, the U.S. government announced that, as of next January 1, the U.S. money stock would double. Each individual's bank balances would double, as would each worker's nominal wage rate, and the money price of every good and service.

Such a policy would have no effect on real output. No one would be any wealthier or poorer in *real* terms. And the *relative* prices of all goods in the economy would remain the same, because the relative price of two goods equals the ratio of the two goods' money prices, both of which would have doubled with the doubled money stock.[1] Output would remain at its full-employment level, determined by the economy's endowment of resources, its technology, and residents' tastes for income and leisure. Therefore, we can conclude that *a one-time permanent change in the money stock has no effect on the economy's long-run equilibrium real output.* This important result has a name: the **neutrality of money.**

18.2.2 **How Does Money Affect the Interest Rate?**

Just as a one-time change in the money stock leaves long-run output unaffected, such a change also has no effect on the long-run equilibrium interest rate. To understand why, recall that the equilibrium interest rate in the economy represents the rate of return a lender must receive to willingly lend funds to a borrower. A lender lends $1 today in return for a promised repayment of $1(1 + i) next year.

Suppose at the time the money supply doubled, the equilibrium interest rate in the economy equaled 5 percent, so that lending a dollar for one year brought a repayment of $1.05, or a rate of return of 5 percent. A bank willing to lend a firm $1 million to build a new factory (in return for $1,050,000) before the doubling of the money stock should still be willing to lend the firm $2 million for the same project after the doubling (in return for $2,100,000), because the bank's rate of return still would equal 5 percent. All borrowing and lending decisions in the economy should remain unchanged, so we can conclude that *a one-time permanent change in the size of the money stock doesn't alter the long-run equilibrium interest rate.*

18.2.3 **How Does Money Affect the Price Level?**

If one-time changes in the money stock don't change real output or the interest rate in long-run equilibrium, such changes in the money stock must cause proportional changes in the price level. For example, if the money stock doubles, the long-run equilibrium price level must double as well. We can see why by recalling from Chapter Fifteen the condition required for equilibrium in the money market.[2] The real money stock must equal the demand for real money balances, which depends positively on real income and negatively on the interest rate:

$$M/P = L(\overset{+}{Q}, \overset{-}{i})\qquad\qquad\text{[18.1]}$$

If, in long-run equilibrium, one-time permanent changes in the nominal money stock, M, don't alter either real income or the interest rate, Equation 18.1 implies that changes in M must generate proportional changes in P to maintain money-market equilibrium. In other words, if changes in the nominal money stock don't lead to changes in real money demand, then the price level must adjust to keep the *real* money stock (M/P) constant. So, *in long-run equilibrium, one-time changes in the money stock lead to proportional changes in the price level.* If the money stock doubles, for example, the price level doubles as well.

We can examine empirically the relationship between changes in countries' money stocks and changes in their respective price levels. Our theory implies that changes in the money stock should lead to proportional changes in the long-run price level. Actual data, of course, come from a world economy constantly bombarded by shocks of various kinds, not from one constantly in long-run equilibrium, so we shouldn't expect the predicted relationship to hold exactly. Nonetheless, countries with larger increases in their money stocks should experience larger increases in their price levels than countries whose money stocks exhibit smaller changes, especially if we focus on averages over a relatively long period to lessen the impact of short-run disturbances.

---

1 Section 12.2.1 covers the relationship between money prices and relative prices.

2 See section 15.2.4 for a review.

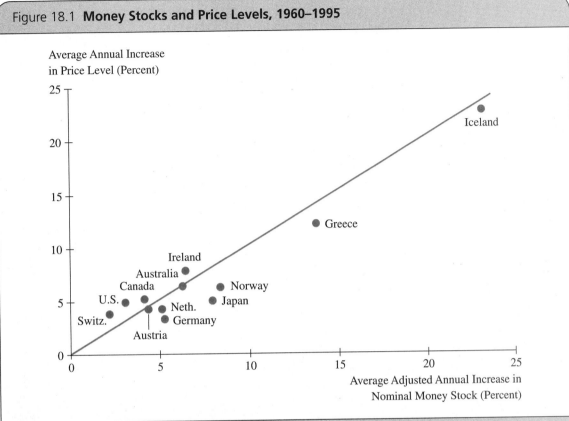

Figure 18.1 **Money Stocks and Price Levels, 1960–1995**

The horizontal axis measures the average annual percentage increase in each country's money stock, minus 3 percent to adjust for increases in full-employment real output. The vertical axis measures the average annual percentage increase in each country's price level (CPI). In the long run, countries with high rates of money growth experience higher rates of inflation than countries with lower rates of money growth.

Source: Data from Organization for Economic Cooperation and Development.

Figure 18.1 reports the average adjusted rates of money-stock growth (horizontal axis) and price-level growth (vertical axis) for a subset of industrial economies from 1960 through 1995.[3] If our predicted relationship held exactly, all points would fall along the upward-sloping 45-degree line in the figure. While few of the points actually lie on the 45-degree line, most are close to it, implying a close relationship between changes in countries' money stocks and price levels. Countries such as Iceland and Greece, with high rates of money growth, experienced higher rates of inflation than did countries such as Switzerland and the United States, whose money stocks grew at much slower rates.

We can use the graph of money-market equilibrium from Chapter Fifteen to summarize the long-run equilibrium relationship among M, P, Q, and i, as in Figure 18.2. Equilibrium requires that the real money stock (M/P) equal the public's demand for real money balances (L[Q, i]). If changes in M fail to move Q or i from their long-run equilibrium values of Q_0 and i_0, the money demand function remains stationary. To maintain equilibrium, the money-stock line must remain stationary as well, and this requires that the *real* money stock

---

3 To account for the fact that, over such a long period, the full-employment level of output grows, the money-stock growth rates have been reduced by 3 percent per year to cover real output growth.

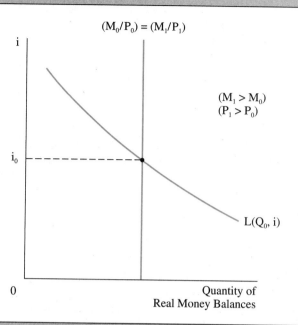

Figure 18.2 **Long-Run Equilibrium in the Money Market**

$$(M_0/P_0) = (M_1/P_1)$$

$(M_1 > M_0)$
$(P_1 > P_0)$

i_0

$L(Q_0, i)$

Quantity of
Real Money Balances

In long-run equilibrium, a change in the nominal money stock exerts no effect on real output or the interest rate. Money demand remains unchanged, and the price level must change proportionally with the nominal money stock to maintain equilibrium.

(M/P) not change. Therefore, the ratio of the new money stock and price level (M_1/P_1) must equal the ratio of the original money stock and price level (M_0/P_0). In other words, the nominal money stock and price level must change proportionally.

18.2.4 **How Does Money Affect the Exchange Rate?**

We've argued that in long-run equilibrium, all prices in the economy change proportionally with the money stock, while real output and the interest rate remain unchanged. The nominal exchange rate, e, is just the domestic-currency price of a unit of foreign currency. Therefore, under a flexible exchange rate regime, we would expect the exchange rate to move proportionally with any change in the money stock.[4]

Returning to our thought experiment in which the U.S. money stock doubled, we would expect the dollar price of a unit of each foreign currency to double, implying that each foreign good or service would cost twice as many dollars as before. Again, individuals would be no better and no worse off. They would own and earn twice as many dollars, but every item they bought—including imports—would also cost twice as many dollars.

Therefore, *in long-run equilibrium, increases in the money stock lead to proportional nominal depreciations of the domestic currency; and decreases in the money stock lead to proportional nominal appreciations.* Figure 18.3 depicts equilibrium in the foreign exchange market. Beginning from a long-run equilibrium at point I, a rise in the nominal money stock leaves the domestic and foreign interest rates unchanged at i_0 and i_0^*. But the expected future spot exchange rate rises proportionally with M, because market participants expect a proportional increase in all money prices, including the nominal exchange rate. The rise in e^e lowers the expected rate of

---

4 Under a fixed exchange rate, monetary policy fails to alter the nominal money stock, because the necessary foreign exchange market intervention offsets the policy's impact.

Figure 18.3 **Long-Run Equilibrium in the Foreign Exchange Market**

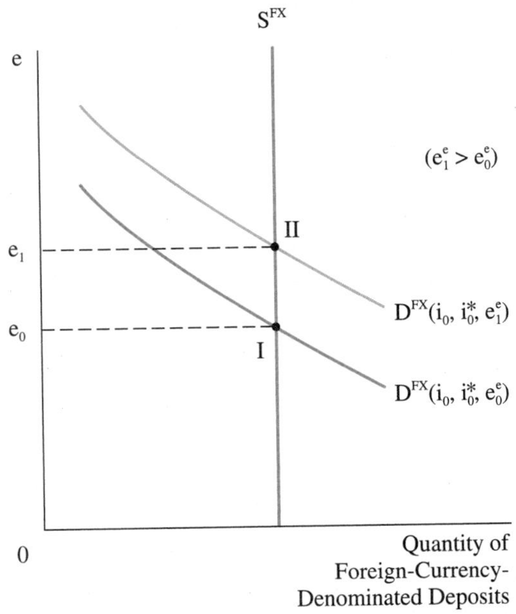

In long-run equilibrium, an increase in the nominal money stock doesn't change the interest rate. However, market participants anticipate proportional increases in all money prices, including the nominal exchange rate. The rise in e^e increases the demand for foreign-currency-denominated deposits and causes a proportional spot depreciation of the domestic currency.

return on deposits denominated in the domestic currency and shifts the demand for foreign-currency-denominated deposits to the right. This causes a spot depreciation of the domestic currency proportional to the original increase in the domestic money stock.

Note, however, that the *real* exchange rate, $R \equiv P/eP^*$, doesn't change. If a change in the money stock leads to proportional changes in both the domestic price level, P, and the nominal exchange rate, e, then the real exchange rate remains at its original value. This is simply another case of the long-run neutrality of money: one-time money stock changes don't change relative prices. After all, the real exchange rate represents the relative price of domestic goods and services compared with foreign ones. Just as a rise in the price level fails to change relative prices because all money prices change proportionally, a proportional rise in both the price level and the nominal exchange rate leaves the real exchange rate unaffected.

18.2.5 Summary: How Does Money Affect the Economy in Long-Run Equilibrium?

A one-time permanent change in the nominal money stock changes all money prices, including the nominal exchange rate, proportionally and leaves real output, the interest rate, relative prices, the real exchange rate, and the real money stock unchanged. Table 18.1 summarizes these results.

18.3 Purchasing Power Parity

We've seen that changes in countries' money stocks, in the long run, affect both price levels and nominal exchange rates. The interaction between these two relationships suggests a direct linkage between a country's price level and its nominal exchange rate. This linkage forms the basis for a view of long-run exchange rate

Table 18.1 **Summary of Money's Effects in Long-Run Equilibrium**

Variable	Effect of One-Time Permanent Increase in Nominal Money Stock	Effect of One-Time Permanent Decrease in Nominal Money Stock
Real output (Q)	0	0
Interest rate (i)	0	0
Price level (P)	$+^a$	$-^a$
Nominal exchange rate (e)[b]	$+^a$	$-^a$
Real exchange rate (R)	0	0
Real money stock (M/P)	0	0

[a]Proportional to change in nominal money stock.
[b]A plus sign denotes a rise in e, or domestic currency depreciation; a negative sign denotes a fall in e, or domestic currency appreciation.

behavior known as purchasing power parity (PPP), which focuses on exchange rates' role in defining the relative prices of domestic and foreign goods and services. The key building block for purchasing power parity is the law of one price.

18.3.1 The Law of One Price

The **law of one price** states that identical goods will sell for an equivalent price regardless of the currency in which the price is denominated. Arbitrage ensures that, with no transportation costs, barriers to trade, monopolies, or other restrictions, the law of one price will hold. Suppose, for example, that a stereo selling for £200 in London were priced at $500 in New York with the exchange rate equal to $2 per pound (e = $2/£1). This would violate the law of one price, because the pound price of the stereo would be £200 in London and £250 in New York *(Why?)* or, equivalently, the dollar price would be $400 in London and $500 in New York *(Why?)*. Arbitrageurs would find it profitable to buy stereos in London and sell them in New York; in fact, their profit would equal £50, or $100, per stereo. Arbitrage would raise the price of stereos in London by increasing demand there and lower the price of stereos in New York by increasing supply there.

Algebraically, we can represent this scenario as follows, letting P_S^{NY} and P_S^L denote the price of stereos in New York and London, respectively. Initially,

$$P_S^{NY} > e \cdot P_S^L,$$

or

$$\$500 > (\$2/£1) \cdot (£200) = \$400$$

Arbitrage causes P_S^{NY} to fall and P_S^L to rise until

$$P_S^{NY} = e \cdot P_S^L \qquad \qquad \textbf{[18.2]}$$

Equation 18.2 states the law of one price: The dollar price of a stereo must equal the dollar price of a pound multiplied by the pound price of the stereo. *(State the law of one price for stereos in terms of pounds.)*[5]

---

5 If e' denotes the pound price of a dollar, we can write the law of one price as $e' \cdot P_S^{NY} = P_S^L$. This is simply Equation 18.2 divided through by e because, by definition, e' = 1/e. In words, the pound price of a stereo must equal the pound price of a dollar times the dollar price of the stereo.

Complications such as transportation costs, tariffs, or nontariff barriers to trade can prevent the law of one price from holding. Nevertheless, the possibility of arbitrage links prices of homogeneous traded goods expressed in different currencies. Even when we include a consideration such as transportation costs, the prices in different currencies of a homogeneous good should differ by only a constant—equal to the amount of transportation cost involved in arbitrage. In other words, the prices still should move in tandem.

The degree to which the law of one price holds will differ depending on the characteristics of the good in question. Prices of identical, freely traded goods exhibit the tightest links. Equation 18.2 will hold more closely if both stereos are identical than if their brands, qualities, or technical characteristics differ. But empirical evidence indicates that, even for identical traded goods, surprisingly large deviations from the law of one price do occur.[6] For differentiated products (for example, three automobiles made by Chevrolet, Volkswagen, and Toyota), small differences among them can result in persistent price differences even with no transportation costs or trade barriers. We wouldn't expect the dollar price of a Chevrolet to be equivalent to the dollar price of a Volkswagen or a Toyota—because consumers don't perceive the automobiles as identical.

Trade barriers introduce artificial price differences across countries and can cause the law of one price not to hold. Japan, for example, maintains strict import quotas on rice to protect domestic rice farmers, who hold a special place in traditional Japanese culture and wield considerable political clout. Imported rice would be much cheaper for Japanese consumers than domestically produced rice. *(Write out the relationship among the dollar price of rice imported from the United States, the yen price of Japanese-grown rice, and the dollar price of yen.)* But import quotas effectively rule out the kind of arbitrage we used to argue for Equation 18.2 in the stereo example.

For nontraded items (that is, products not traded internationally) the law of one price may hold even more loosely. Many services are traded only infrequently because the buyer and seller must be in the same location; examples include health-care services, haircuts, and retailing. Even if the dollar price of a tonsillectomy exceeded the pound price of a tonsillectomy multiplied by the dollar price of a pound, few Americans needing a tonsillectomy would travel to London to get it. The inconvenience of some types of transactions limits the process of arbitrage in the case of these services. This implies that price differences among infrequently traded goods and services may persist; that is, we wouldn't expect the law of one price to hold for such items.

18.3.2 Going from the Law of One Price to PPP

Purchasing power parity (PPP) carries the law of one price one step further by applying the logic not to the price of a single good such as stereos, but to countries' overall price levels. The simplest version of purchasing power parity states that the price level in one country (such as the *United States*) equals the price level in a second (for example, *Britain*) multiplied by the exchange rate between the countries' currencies:

$$P^{US} = e \cdot P^B \qquad \textbf{[18.3]}$$

The U.S. price level measures the dollar price of a basket of goods and services, and the British price level measures the pound price of a basket of goods and services. Therefore, purchasing power parity holds when the two countries' price levels are equal once translated into a common currency using the exchange rate.

Equations 18.2 and 18.3 appear similar. Going from the law of one price to PPP represents only one small step for a typesetter, but requires a giant leap for economists. The apparently simple move from the law of one price's link between the prices of a good expressed in two currencies to purchasing power parity's link between two countries' price levels actually entails a number of important economic considerations. If the law of one price held perfectly for every good and service, and if the baskets of goods and services used to compute the two countries' price levels were identical, then purchasing power parity would follow. But we've argued that considerations such as transportation costs, product differentiation, and trade barriers render the law of one price ineffective for some goods and services. And the baskets of goods and services produced or consumed in various countries differ.

---

6 The most commonly cited sources of such deviations include imperfect competition and segmented markets. In particular, firms that face different amounts of competition in different submarkets may charge different prices in those markets if they can prevent resale from low-price to high-price markets.

Still, the forces of arbitrage that underlie the law of one price should keep price levels and exchange rates from deviating too far from the purchasing-power-parity relationship, at least in the long run. If goods and services in the United States become more expensive than those in Britain ($P^{US} > e \cdot P^B$), the demand for dollars and for U.S. goods and services should fall, while the demand for British goods and services should rise. This would lower P^{US} and raise both e and P^B, leading back toward purchasing power parity. Similarly, if goods and services in the United States become cheaper than those in Britain, market forces should place upward pressure on the U.S. price level and downward pressure on Britain's, as well as generating a dollar appreciation against the pound.

18.3.3 **Absolute and Relative PPP**

Economists call the version of purchasing power parity in Equation 18.3 **absolute purchasing power parity.** Absolute parity represents the strongest form, because it requires a strict relationship between the two countries' price levels to hold continually. In terms of the model of the macroeconomy we developed earlier, absolute purchasing power parity requires that the relative price of domestic and foreign goods or the real exchange rate ($R \equiv P/eP^*$) continually equal 1. Suppose R rose above 1. The dollar price of domestic (U.S.) goods would exceed the pound price of foreign (British) goods multiplied by the dollar price of pounds. Arbitrage would result in some combination of a fall in the dollar price of U.S. goods, a rise in the pound price of British goods, and a dollar depreciation. If the relative price of domestic and foreign goods fell below 1, the same types of adjustments would occur, but in the opposite direction. *(Why?)*

Under a weaker form of parity, **relative purchasing power parity,** the percentage change in the domestic country's price level equals the percentage change in the foreign country's *plus* the percentage change in the exchange rate between the two countries' currencies—or, letting "hats" over variables represent percentage rates of change in those variables:[7]

$$\hat{P} = \hat{e} + \hat{P}*$$

[18.4]

Equation 18.4 says that the rate of inflation in the domestic country (the percentage rate of change in its price level) equals the rate of its currency's depreciation against that of the foreign country plus the latter's inflation rate. Relative PPP may hold when absolute PPP fails. In particular, if the factors such as transportation costs and trade barriers that cause deviations from absolute PPP remain more or less constant across time, then the relative PPP relationship between inflation rates and changes in exchange rates will hold.

18.3.4 **How Can PPP Not Hold?**

We've already considered several factors that can cause purchasing power parity not to hold. The most obvious is the presence of transportation costs or trade barriers. These cause the law of one price—and therefore absolute purchasing power parity—not to hold, and they may do the same with relative PPP if transportation costs or trade barriers change over time.

Suppose two countries produced and consumed identical baskets of goods. We would then expect relative purchasing power parity to hold quite closely for them. But most countries produce and consume diverse combinations of goods, partly as a result of specialization according to comparative advantage and partly as a result of taste differences. Many items are nontraded; others are heterogeneous (such as Chevrolets, Volkswagens, and Toyotas). All these considerations imply that each country's price level, whether a production-based measure such as the GDP deflator or a consumption-based measure such as the consumer price index (CPI), measures the price of a unique combination of goods. The goods produced and consumed in the United States differ from those produced and consumed in Britain, which can cause either version of PPP to fail to hold. After all, the logic of PPP rests ultimately on the arbitrage that leads to the law of one price. But if each country's basket of goods and services is different, we shouldn't expect arbitrage to equalize the various baskets' prices.

---

7 For example, a P with a "hat" equals the percentage change in P, or $\hat{P} \equiv \Delta P/P$, where $\hat{P}$ denotes the inflation rate.

PPP is more likely to hold for traded goods or services than for nontraded ones, so the evidence in its favor tends to be stronger in tests that use wholesale rather than consumer prices. The wholesale (or producer) price index measures changes in the prices of goods bought by firms and includes mainly intermediate traded goods. The consumer price index, on the other hand, measures changes in the prices of items bought by typical consumers. This includes many services, such as housing and health care, for which the law of one price may be only a very weak long-term tendency.

Relative purchasing power parity links inflation rates among countries. The implied relationship between inflation rates assumes that *relative* prices of various goods *within* each country don't change. When relative prices within countries do change, purchasing power parity may not hold, because the baskets of goods that countries produce and consume contain differing amounts of the goods whose relative prices have changed. An increase in the relative price of rice, for example, would raise the price levels of many Asian economies relative to those of non-Asian economies, because rice constitutes the main staple of many Asian diets and is, therefore, weighted relatively heavily in the computation of those economies' price levels. Empirically, the PPP relationship holds more closely in periods of rapid inflation. This occurs because high inflation rates tend to overwhelm any changes in the pattern of relative prices that may occur simultaneously. During periods of little inflation, changes in relative prices may conceal any tendency toward PPP.

18.3.5 Does PPP Hold?

Evidence from many countries and time periods shows conclusively that the absolute form of purchasing power parity doesn't hold reliably. Nor does the law of one price hold for many goods, including some traded ones. The evidence provides somewhat more support for relative PPP. Generally it's true that when one country's rate of inflation exceeds another's, the first country's currency tends to depreciate against the second's. Of course, the precise relationship in Equation 18.4 doesn't always hold, but a trend toward relative purchasing power parity does hold, at least over the long run. For most country pairs, relative PPP held more closely prior to 1971, during the years of the Bretton Woods system of fixed exchange rates. Since 1973, and particularly since 1979, even relative PPP has failed to explain short- and medium-run movements in exchange rates and price levels. Short-run deviations from PPP often are large, volatile, and persistent. Deviations disappear at a rate of only about 15 percent per year, and their half-life runs about three to five years (that is, only half of a typical deviation will have disappeared three to five years after its appearance).

However, for the post-1973 flexible-exchange-rate period as a whole, relative purchasing power parity performs reasonably well in explaining the long-run behavior of industrialized countries' exchange rates against the dollar. Figure 18.4 demonstrates this relationship over the first quarter century after the breakdown of Bretton Woods, using changes in countries' consumer price indices to measure their rates of inflation relative to that of the United States. If relative purchasing power parity held perfectly, all points would lie on the upward-sloping 45-degree line, along which the currency's depreciation or appreciation relative to the dollar (measured along the vertical axis) equals the country's inflation rate relative to U.S. inflation (measured along the horizontal axis).

The countries below the 45-degree line in Figure 18.4—Japan, the United Kingdom, and Italy—experienced real currency appreciations relative to the dollar between 1973 and 1997. In the case of the United Kingdom, for example, the inflation rate exceeded the U.S. rate by 2.7 percent per year, but the pound depreciated against the dollar by only 1.7 percent a year. Therefore, the price of U.K. goods and services relative to U.S. ones rose by about 1 percent per year ($\hat{R} \equiv [\hat{P}^{UK} - \hat{P}^{US}] - (\hat{\pounds/\$}) = 2.7 - 1.7 = 1.0$). Real appreciations of a foreign currency always make the foreign country's goods and services more expensive relative to U.S. goods and services. Note that in the cases of the United Kingdom and Italy, the currencies *de*preciated in nominal terms but *appre*ciated in real terms; in other words, the nominal depreciation was smaller than the amount by which U.K. and Italian inflation exceeded that of the United States.

Countries above the 45-degree line in Figure 18.4 experienced real currency depreciations, as changes in their nominal exchange rates more than offset any excess of their inflation rates relative to that of the United States. Canada, for example, experienced inflation 0.3 percent above that in the United States, while the Canadian dollar depreciated by 1.3 percent against its U.S. counterpart. Therefore, the relative price of Canadian goods and services fell by approximately 1 percent ($\hat{R} \equiv [\hat{P}^C - \hat{P}^{US}] - (\hat{C\$/\$}) = 0.3 - [1.3] = -1.0$). Real depreciations of a foreign currency always make the foreign country's goods and services cheaper relative to U.S. goods and services. Germany experienced a nominal appreciation of its mark, but a real depreciation.

Figure 18.4 **Relative Purchasing Power Parity, 1973–1997 (Percent)**

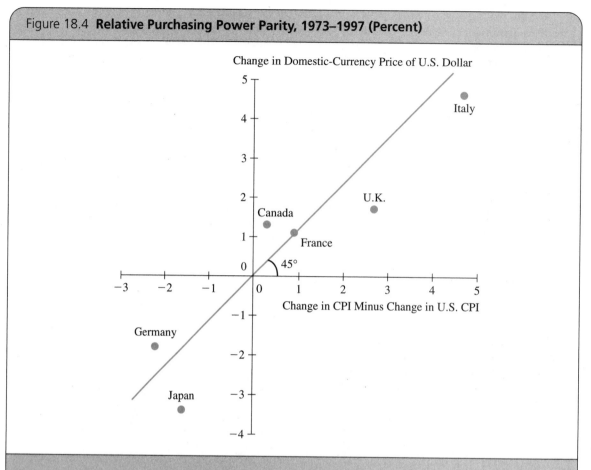

Relative purchasing power parity implies that the rate of change in the exchange rate between two countries' currencies equals the countries' inflation differential. The horizontal axis measures the percentage change in each country's price level minus the percentage change in the U.S. price level. The vertical axis measures the percentage change in the price of the dollar measured in each country's currency. If purchasing power parity held perfectly, all points would lie on the 45-degree line. Deviations from the 45-degree line represent real appreciations of the yen, pound, and lira, along with real depreciations of the mark and Canadian dollar.

Source: Data from *Economic Report of the President.*

Now that we've defined the basic concepts of purchasing power parity and examined them empirically, we add a few cautionary notes about what purchasing power parity does and doesn't imply, for the concept often is misinterpreted.

18.3.6 Cautionary Notes on PPP

Economist Gustav Cassel elaborated the concept of purchasing power parity following World War I. The gold standard of fixed exchange rates had broken down during the war, leaving economists and policy makers with the problem of how to choose new rates at which to peg postwar currencies. Cassel suggested using purchasing power parity as a guide in selecting the new rates. Purchasing power parity, according to Cassel, would capture the underlying equilibrium level of exchange rates, even if shocks temporarily drove rates away from their PPP levels.

Today, interpretation of purchasing power parity ranges from positive to normative.[8] Some economists perceive PPP as a positive statement of how the economy works. Others attach a more normative significance to PPP, arguing that it *should* hold and that, if it fails, policy makers should take actions to restore it. We've argued that the possibility of international arbitrage creates a linkage among various prices that drives them toward purchasing power parity, at least over the very long run. However, we have little reason to expect PPP to hold over the short or medium term, nor any justification for using PPP as a policy goal.

Arguments that a currency is under- or overvalued based on purchasing power parity rest on a misunderstanding of PPP. In fact, under a perfectly flexible exchange rate regime, the terms *undervalued* and *overvalued* carry little meaning, because supply and demand in foreign exchange markets determine exchange rates. A currency can be "wrongly" valued only if intervention by central banks holds the rate away from its equilibrium level. This does *not* imply that all individuals and firms in the economy will be happy with the exchange rate's value. We've repeatedly discovered that different exchange rate values benefit different groups within the economy. Export and import-competing industries benefit from currency depreciations, while consumers and non-traded-goods industries prefer currency appreciations, at least over the short run when changes in the nominal exchange rate imply changes in the relative prices of domestic and foreign goods.

A second caution deals with the cause-and-effect implications of PPP. Purchasing power parity can be interpreted as a theory of exchange rate behavior that attributes changes in the nominal exchange rate between two currencies to differences in the countries' inflation rates. We can make this view of PPP more explicit by rewriting Equation 18.4 with the exchange rate on the left-hand side and the inflation differential on the right-hand side:

$$\hat{e} = \hat{P} - \hat{P}*$$

[18.5]

This view of PPP treats inflation rates as exogenous and assumes that they determine changes in the exchange rate. For example, if the domestic inflation rate equals 10 percent per year and the foreign inflation rate 5 percent per year, Equation 18.5 predicts that the domestic currency will depreciate by 5 percent.

Alternatively, purchasing power parity sometimes is viewed as a theory of price-level determination. Given the foreign inflation rate and the rate of change in the exchange rate, we can solve the PPP expression for the domestic inflation rate ($\hat{P} = \hat{e} + \hat{P}*$). If the foreign inflation rate is 5 percent and the domestic currency is depreciating by 5 percent per year, the domestic inflation rate must equal 10 percent. *(Could you distinguish empirically between this case and the previous one, in which inflation rates determined the change in the exchange rate?)*

However, neither of these interpretations is really correct! Purchasing power parity does *not* imply that inflation rates determine exchange rates *or* vice versa. Domestic and foreign price levels and the exchange rate all are determined jointly and simultaneously within the macroeconomy. All three values result from the interrelationships among many variables. Neither the price level nor the nominal exchange rate is under policy makers' direct control, although their macroeconomic policy choices certainly affect both prices and exchange rates.

Another caution concerns "tests" of PPP frequently reported in the popular press. One of the most popular is the "hamburger standard" published each year since 1986 by *The Economist*. The *Economist* staff (1) collects the local-currency price of a Big Mac in several dozen of the more than 100 foreign countries in which McDonald's sells the burgers, (2) translates this price into dollars at the current exchange rate, and (3) reports that the foreign currency is overvalued (undervalued) against the dollar by the amount by which the dollar price of the foreign burger exceeds (falls short of) the dollar price of the U.S. burger. For example, in the December 2001 survey, the U.S. burger cost $2.59. A Big Mac in Britain cost £1.99, and the spot exchange rate was $1.45/£1. Converting the price of the British burger into dollars at that exchange rate yields a dollar price of $2.89, or about 12 percent higher than the dollar price of the U.S. burger. For the law of one price to hold would have required an exchange rate of $1.30/£1. So the market exchange rate made British goods about 12 percent more expensive than comparable U.S. goods, or the pound was "overvalued" by about 12 percent relative to the dollar.[9] At the other end of the spectrum, consider a Big Mac in South Africa. Converting the price of the South

---

8 The Isard book in the chapter references contains a useful discussion.

9 *The Economist*, December 22, 2001, p. 130.

African burger into dollars at the market rate yields a dollar price of $0.82, 68 percent lower than the dollar price of the U.S. burger. So the market exchange rate made South African goods about 68 percent cheaper than comparable U.S. goods, or the rand was "undervalued" by 68 percent.

Our discussion of the law of one price and purchasing power parity suggests at least two potential problems with the burger-based PPP test. First, the use of a single good, the Big Mac, means that the test can at best evaluate the law of one price, *not* purchasing power parity. Second, even as a test of the law of one price, the Big Mac represents a poor choice, because as a restaurant meal it isn't a traded good. The Big Mac market is difficult to arbitrage, although the availability of cheap restaurant meals might serve as a small inducement to tourism. Also, Big Macs differ around the world as a concession to local tastes. It may seem harsh to criticize the Big Mac survey, which was, after all, introduced as a lark (even though studies by economists have found that it predicts remarkably well). But many so-called tests of PPP use inappropriate goods. For example, another PPP test included a deluxe single hotel room, a hotel room-service American-style breakfast, the ubiquitous Big Mac, a one-mile taxi ride, a man's haircut, a drink of Johnnie Walker Black Label scotch on the rocks, a local phone call from a pay phone, and a first-run movie. *(Evaluate each good and service for inclusion in a test of PPP.)*[10]

We're now ready to combine our results on the long-run neutrality of money with those from purchasing power parity to develop a simple but very useful theory of long-run exchange rate behavior, known as the *monetary approach* because the model focuses exclusively on the role of monetary factors in explaining long-run movements in exchange rates.

18.4 The Monetary Approach to the Exchange Rate

18.4.1 History and Intuition behind the Monetary Approach

The **monetary approach to the exchange rate** assumes that the primary role of the exchange rate in the macroeconomy is to equate the quantities supplied and demanded of various monies or currencies.[11] Any event that alters either the quantity of money balances demanded or the money stock will alter the exchange rate according to the monetary approach.

The modern version of this view of the exchange rate dates from the 1970s and work by University of Chicago economists Robert Mundell, the late Harry Johnson, and Jacob Frenkel. Despite the monetary approach's relatively short modern history, its roots reach back to David Hume's 1752 elaboration of the specie-flow mechanism. Much of the monetary approach's renewed appeal rests on its simplicity. Unlike other models of exchange rate behavior, the monetary approach relies on the fundamental definition of an exchange rate as the relative price of two monies. Just as the supplies of and demands for, say, corn and wheat determine the relative price of those goods, so the supplies of and demands for dollars and yen determine their relative price. When the quantity demanded of a money exceeds the quantity supplied, its relative price rises—that is, the currency appreciates. When the quantity supplied exceeds the quantity demanded, the money's relative price falls, or the currency depreciates.

The monetary approach assumes that real output equals its full-employment level and that output and input prices adjust quickly to their long-run equilibrium levels. Therefore, we take the monetary approach as a long-run theory of exchange rate behavior, with little to say about short-run exchange rate fluctuations that occur before prices in the economy have time to adjust to shocks.

18.4.2 A Simple Monetary Model of the Exchange Rate

Equilibrium in the money market requires that the real money stock, defined as the nominal money stock divided by the price level, equal the quantity demanded of real money balances. The demand for real money

---

10 Additional information you might find useful: A large portion of the price of liquor in most countries consists of taxes; phone service typically is either government owned or a regulated private monopoly; and most countries subject movies to import restrictions.

11 The analogous theory under a fixed exchange rate regime is known as the *monetary approach to the balance of payments*.

balances depends positively on real income and negatively on the nominal interest rate. Equation 18.6 repeats the money-market equilibrium condition for the domestic country:

$$M/P = L(\overset{+}{Q}, \overset{-}{i})$$ [18.6]

Equation 18.7 presents the corresponding condition for the foreign country:

$$M^*/P^* = L^*(\overset{+}{Q}^*, \overset{-}{i}^*)$$ [18.7]

Because we're interested in the causes of *movements* in exchange rates rather than the particular *level* of the exchange rate, it's convenient to translate Equations 18.6 and 18.7 into relationships among the percentage rates of change of money stocks, price levels, and money demands. Letting "hats" continue to denote percentage rates of change:[12]

$$\hat{M} - \hat{P} = \hat{L} \text{ and } \hat{M}^* - \hat{P}^* = \hat{L}^*$$ [18.8]

Equation 18.8 says simply that the rate of growth of the real money stock (the left-hand side of each equation) must match that of the demand for real money balances (the right-hand side of each equation) for the country's money market to remain in equilibrium.

Subtracting the second expression in Equation 18.8 from the first and rearranging gives the fundamental relationship central to the monetary approach to the exchange rate:

$$\hat{P} - \hat{P}^* = (\hat{M} - \hat{M}^*) - (\hat{L} - \hat{L}^*)$$ [18.9]

The difference between two countries' inflation rates depends on the relative growth rates of their money stocks and money demands.

How can the monetary approach provide a theory of exchange rate behavior when the exchange rate doesn't even appear in Equation 18.9? The answer is that the monetary approach assumes that relative purchasing power parity holds. This implies that, in the long run, the inflation differential on the left-hand side of Equation 18.9 will equal the percentage rate of change in the exchange rate (from Equation 18.5), so that:

$$\hat{e} = (\hat{M} - \hat{M}^*) - (\hat{L} - \hat{L}^*) = (\hat{M} - \hat{L}) - (\hat{M}^* - \hat{L}^*)$$ [18.10]

This statement makes a simple but powerful prediction about the exchange rate: *The relative rates of growth of the supplies of and demands for different monies determine long-run movements in the exchange rate.* If the domestic money stock grows more rapidly than the foreign money stock and if money demands remain constant, the domestic currency will depreciate. If the stock of each money grows at the same rate as the demand for it, the exchange rate will remain stable. We can also use the simple monetary-approach expression for the exchange rate to highlight the inherent interdependence of exchange rate policies. Equation 18.10 makes clear that the exchange rate between two currencies depends on money supply and demand in *both* economies. Even a country with rapid money growth can experience an appreciation—if the other country's money stock grows even more rapidly.

---

12 The percentage rate of change of a ratio such as M/P equals the percentage rate of change of the numerator ($\hat{M}$) minus the percentage rate of change of the denominator ($\hat{P}$).

18.4.3 **What Does the Monetary Approach to the Exchange Rate Tell Us?**

As a theory of long-run exchange rate behavior, the monetary approach summarized in Equation 18.10 predicts the long-term effects of changes in domestic and foreign money stocks, real outputs, and interest rates on the exchange rate. Table 18.2 summarizes these results. *Other things being equal,* a one-time permanent rise in the domestic money stock causes a proportional increase in the domestic price level (from Equation 18.6) and, through PPP, a proportional depreciation of the domestic currency.[13] Similarly, a one-time permanent increase in the foreign money stock raises the foreign price level (from Equation 18.7) and appreciates the domestic currency proportionally in the long run.

The monetary approach in Equation 18.10 also predicts that economic events that raise the domestic demand for money ($L > 0$) will cause a domestic appreciation; examples include a rise in domestic income or a fall in the domestic interest rate. If domestic real output rises, for given levels of the nominal money stock and the interest rate, Equation 18.6 implies that the domestic price level must fall. According to purchasing power parity, a decline in the domestic price level causes the domestic currency to appreciate.

A rise in the domestic interest rate lowers the domestic demand for money according to Equation 18.6 and, for given values of M and Q, raises the domestic price level. Therefore, the domestic currency must depreciate to maintain purchasing power parity. Note that this seems to contradict the predictions of our short-run model from Chapters Fifteen through Seventeen, in which a rise in the domestic interest rate always caused a currency *appreciation*. Here, the monetary approach argues instead that a rise in the domestic interest rate should cause a domestic currency *depreciation*. Despite first appearances, the two predictions don't contradict one another; they simply rest on different assumptions about the relevant time horizon.

Table 18.2 **Implications of the Monetary Approach to the Exchange Rate**

Variable	Effect on the Exchange Rate[a]
Domestic Nominal Money Stock (M):	
Increase	+
Decrease	−
Foreign Nominal Money Stock (M*):	
Increase	−
Decrease	+
Domestic Money Demand (L):	
Domestic real output (Q)	
Increase	−
Decrease	+
Domestic interest rate (i)	
Increase	+
Decrease	−
Foreign Money Demand (L*):	
Foreign real output (Q*)	
Increase	+
Decrease	−
Foreign interest rate (i*)	
Increase	−
Decrease	+

[a]Plus signs denote increases in e or domestic currency depreciations. Minus signs denote decreases in e or domestic currency appreciations.

---

13 Recall from section 18.2 that a one-time change in M doesn't affect Q or i and, therefore, doesn't affect the demand for real money balances. For the money market to stay in equilibrium, P must rise to keep the real money stock constant.

The short-run model of earlier chapters assumes that the price level is fixed. This allows one-time changes in the money stock to alter the interest rate.[14] The monetary approach, with its long-run equilibrium focus, assumes that the price level adjusts to any monetary disturbance. As we saw in section 18.2.2, this implies that one-time changes in the money stock don't alter the interest rate. Therefore, when the monetary approach makes predictions about the impact of an interest rate change on the exchange rate, the cause of the change in the interest rate must be something *other than* a simple one-time increase in the money stock. If the interest rate changes for different reasons in the two models, we shouldn't be surprised that the interest rate's effect on the exchange rate also differs between the short-run model and the long-run monetary-approach model. To understand better the relationship between the two models' predictions, we must find the fundamental cause of interest rate changes in long-run equilibrium.

18.4.4 PPP and Long-Run Interest Parity with Inflation

If permanent one-time changes in the nominal money stock don't alter the interest rate in the long run, what kind of monetary disturbance would cause a change in the long-run equilibrium interest rate? The answer is a change in the *rate of growth* (as opposed to the *level*) of the money stock. Virtually all economies experience more or less continual growth in their money stocks. Actual monetary policy decisions typically concern the money stock's rate of growth, not one-time increases or decreases in its level. Table 18.3 reports recent percentage rates of growth of the money stocks for the major industrial economies. Notice that the growth rates exhibit substantial variation, both across years for a single country and across countries, and that growth rates are positive in most years for most countries.

When the money stock grows continually, prices in the economy must continually adjust. The result is **inflation,** which simply means a continuing rise in the price level. In long-run equilibrium, the money stock's growth rate doesn't affect real output, and the price level rises at the same rate as the money stock. We can incorporate the possibility of inflation into our theory of the long-run relationship among prices, interest rates, and the exchange rate simply by combining interest parity and purchasing power parity.

Recall that interest parity summarizes the relationship between interest rates and exchange rates required for portfolio owners to willingly hold the existing quantities of deposits in various currencies.[15] The interest parity relationship, written as

$$i - i^* = (e^e - e)/e = \hat{e}^e \qquad \qquad [18.11]$$

holds whenever the expected rates of return on deposits denominated in the domestic and foreign currencies are equal, so portfolio owners have no incentive to reallocate their portfolios between the two types of

Table 18.3 **Annual Growth of Nominal Money Stocks, 1990–1999 (Percent)**

Country	1990	1991	1992	1993	1994	1995	1996	1997	1998	1999
United States	5.0%	8.6%	11.7%	9.7%	0.1%	−0.9%	1.4%	3.5%	5.7%	10.4%
Japan	4.5	9.5	3.9	7.0	4.2	13.1	9.7	8.6	5.0	11.7
Euro area	21.2	2.3	5.2	5.3	4.2	37.0	10.6	11.8	10.0	10.6
United Kingdom	10.1	6.6	4.3	9.9	0.8	16.7	9.3	25.7	9.3	11.1
Canada	1.2	4.4	7.1	8.3	6.6	10.2	12.7	9.2	5.7	11.3

Source: Data from International Monetary Fund.

---

14 With P fixed, changes in M change the real money stock and, therefore, i.

15 Section 12.4 develops the theory of interest parity.

deposits.[16] This requires the interest differential (the left-hand side of Equation 18.11) to equal the expected rate of domestic currency depreciation (the right-hand side of Equation 18.11).

But, in the long run, what determines the expected rate of domestic currency depreciation? If relative PPP determines the behavior of the exchange rate in the long run, the *actual* rate of depreciation will equal the difference between the two countries' rates of inflation, as in Equation 18.5. And if individuals in the economy know that this is how the exchange rate behaves, they will *expect* the domestic currency to depreciate by whatever amount they *expect* domestic inflation to exceed foreign inflation. To summarize the argument algebraically, if relative purchasing power parity implies that

$$\hat{e} = (\hat{P} - \hat{P}*),$$

then market participants will form their expectations using the same relationship, so

$$\hat{e}^e = (\hat{P}^e - \hat{P}^{*e}). \qquad \textbf{[18.12]}$$

Combining Equations 18.11 and 18.12 tells us that in the long run, if relative purchasing power parity holds and market participants expect it to hold, the interest differential between deposits denominated in two currencies equals the expected inflation differential between the two countries:

$$i - i^* = (\hat{P}^e - \hat{P}^{*e}) \qquad \textbf{[18.13]}$$

This implies that *differences in countries' nominal interest rates, in long-run equilibrium, reflect differences in their expected inflation.* If the domestic country's expected inflation rate rises relative to the foreign country's, the interest rate on deposits denominated in the domestic currency must rise proportionally to maintain interest parity.[17] To understand why, we need to distinguish between two measures of an asset's rate of return.

Real and Nominal Rates of Return

The nominal interest rate, i, measures an asset's rate of return measured in units of the domestic currency. Suppose an individual purchases a $1,000 bond that promises to pay $1,100 in one year. The interest rate equals ($1,100 − $1,000)/$1,000 = 10%, because the individual earns 10 percent in dollars on the funds invested in the bond. This interest rate gives the **nominal rate of return** on the investment, or the rate of return measured in current dollars.

If the rate of inflation equals zero over the year the bond is held, the individual's purchasing power, or ability to purchase goods and services, also will increase by 10 percent. This increase in purchasing power represents the bond's **real rate of return,** or its return measured in real terms (that is, purchasing power over goods and services) rather than in dollars. Whenever the price level remains constant or the rate of inflation equals zero, the nominal and real rates of return on any asset are equal.

Suppose, instead, that the rate of inflation is 10 percent during the year of the investment. At the end of the year, $1,100 will buy the same quantity of goods and services that $1,000 would buy at the beginning. The investment still earns a nominal return (i) of 10 percent measured in dollars but now earns a real return (r) of 0 percent measured in purchasing power over goods and services; the difference just equals the rate of

---

16 The expected nominal rate of return on domestic-currency-denominated deposits equals the domestic interest rate. The expected nominal rate of return on foreign-currency-denominated deposits (expressed in terms of domestic currency) equals the foreign interest rate plus any expected rate of domestic currency depreciation. Equality between the two expected rates of return requires i = i* + ê^e, an expression equivalent to Equation 18.11.

17 The relationship between expected inflation and the interest rate is known as the *Fisher effect,* after Irving Fisher, an economist who did important work on interest rates and their role in the economy.

inflation ($\hat{P}$). Generally, the real return on any asset equals the nominal rate of return minus the rate of inflation, a relationship known as the **Fisher equation:**

$$r = i - \hat{P} \qquad \text{[18.14]}$$

Of course, an individual making an asset-portfolio decision can't know in advance what the actual inflation rate will be over the asset's life. Asset decisions must be made on *expected* real rates, or the difference between the observable nominal rate of return and the expected rate of inflation:

$$r^e = i - \hat{P}^e \qquad \text{[18.15]}$$

To keep the expected *real* rate of return on domestic-currency-denominated deposits constant, Equation 18.15 makes clear that the domestic nominal interest rate must rise by the amount of any expected inflation. This is exactly what Equation 18.13 predicts will happen in the long run. In long-run equilibrium, any inflation-induced interest rate increase doesn't make portfolio owners any better off or any worse off in real terms; it simply compensates them for inflation's expected erosion of the domestic currency's purchasing power.

Interest and Exchange Rates in the Monetary Approach

Now we can see more clearly the reasons for the monetary approach's surprising long-run prediction: An *increase* in the domestic nominal interest rate causes a domestic-currency *depreciation*. In the long run on which the monetary approach focuses, the nominal interest rate rises only in response to a rise in the money stock's rate of growth. Such a rise causes inflation, and market participants expect that inflation. They demand higher *nominal* rates of return in order to maintain a constant *real* rate of return as inflation erodes the domestic currency's purchasing power. We know that money growth leads to currency depreciations, so the monetary approach's link between increases in interest rates and currency depreciations makes perfect sense—once we understand that increases in the long-run equilibrium interest rate come only from inflation-inducing increases in the rate of money growth.

The monetary approach's link between inflation, the exchange rate, and the nominal interest rate suggests that, other things equal, high-inflation countries should have higher nominal interest rates than low-inflation countries and that a single country's nominal interest rate should vary positively with the country's rate of inflation. We can investigate these relationships empirically by illustrating recent interest rates and inflation for a sample of three industrialized economies, as in Figure 18.5. Within each economy, periods of higher inflation clearly are associated with higher nominal interest rates. Comparing across countries, the higher inflation rate in the United States than in Germany or Japan in most years translated into a higher nominal U.S. interest rate as well.

18.4.5 **What's Missing from the Monetary Approach?**

Purchasing power parity and the monetary approach to the exchange rate provide only one piece of a complete explanation of exchange rate behavior. We've seen that even relative purchasing power parity doesn't hold in the short run, making the monetary approach, which relies on purchasing power parity, an inappropriate model for predicting short-run behavior of the exchange rate or any other macroeconomic variable. The fixed-price model from Chapters Fourteen through Seventeen provides a better guide to the macroeconomy in the short run, and in Chapter Nineteen we'll turn our attention to the economy's adjustment from short-run to long-run results.

But even in long-run equilibrium, elements beyond PPP play an important role. Purchasing power parity explains how exchange rates respond to price level changes caused by changes in the money stock. Similarly, the monetary approach focuses exclusively on the long-run equilibrium effect of changes in the money stock or its rate of growth. When *nonmonetary* shocks hit the economy, the exchange rate may behave in ways not explained well by purchasing power parity and the monetary approach, even in long-run equilibrium. In other words, the *real* exchange rate may change.

Figure 18.5 **Inflation and Nominal Interest Rates**

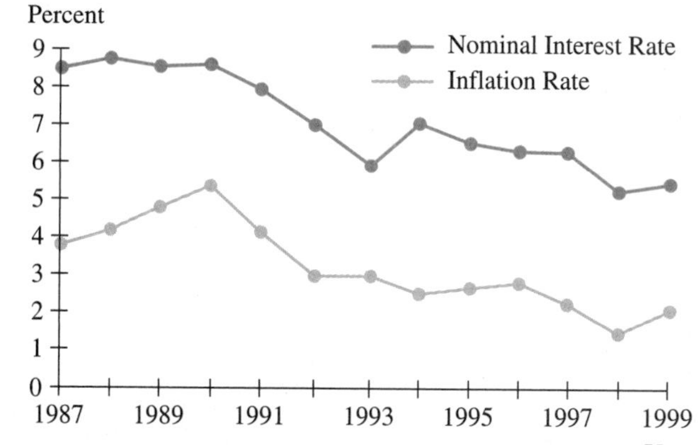

(a) United States

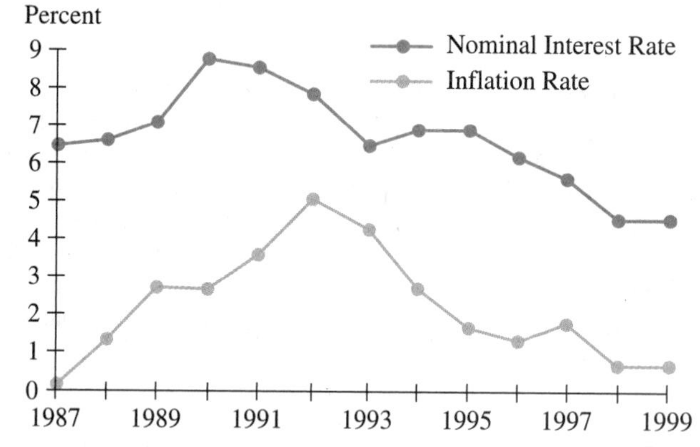

(b) Germany

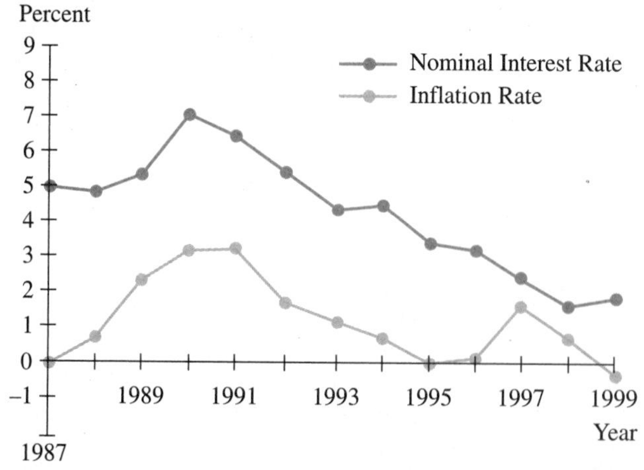

(c) Japan

To maintain assets' real rates of return, nominal interest rates must incorporate changes in the rate of inflation. Within each country, nominal interest rates rise and fall with inflation. Across countries, those with higher inflation exhibit higher nominal interest rates.

Source: Data from Organization for Economic Cooperation and Development.

18.5 The Real Exchange Rate

18.5.1 Changes in the Real Exchange Rate

The monetary approach to the exchange rate does a reasonably good job of explaining exchange rate movements in the long run when the disturbances to the economy come from the money market. However, to understand exchange rates better, we must be able to analyze disturbances that are nonmonetary in nature. Such shocks cause purchasing power parity not to hold. In other words, they cause changes in the *real* exchange rate. Recall that the real exchange rate or, equivalently, the relative price of domestic goods and services, equals the ratio of the domestic price level to the foreign price level expressed in terms of domestic currency:

$$R \equiv P/eP^* \qquad\qquad \textbf{[18.16]}$$

A decline in the real exchange rate constitutes a **real depreciation** of the domestic currency. When price levels are fixed, a nominal depreciation (a rise in e) leads directly to a real depreciation. We saw in earlier chapters that a real depreciation causes consumers to shift their spending from foreign to domestic goods. A rise in the real exchange rate represents a **real appreciation** of the domestic currency. A real appreciation can be caused by, among other things, a nominal appreciation (a decline in e) with price levels fixed. The major impact of a real appreciation is a shift of expenditure from domestic to foreign goods and services. But, as we've seen, price levels can't be assumed fixed in the long run.

Changes in the real exchange rate constitute deviations from purchasing power parity. If absolute purchasing power parity held continually in the long run (P = e · P* from Equation 18.3), the real exchange rate would always equal 1. Or, if relative purchasing power parity held continually ($\hat{P} = \hat{e} + \hat{P}^*$ from Equation 18.4), the real exchange rate would be a constant, because expressing the definition of the real exchange rate (from Equation 18.16) in rates of change shows that

$$\hat{R} = (\hat{P} - \hat{P}^*) - \hat{e}, \qquad\qquad \textbf{[18.17]}$$

so relative purchasing power parity implies that $\hat{R} = 0$. Or, we can rearrange Equation 18.17 to express changes in the nominal exchange rate in terms of two components as in Equation 18.18. The first component represents the inflation differential between the two countries—as predicted by purchasing power parity—and the second captures changes in the real exchange rate—deviations from purchasing power parity:

$$\hat{e} = (\hat{P} - \hat{P}^*) - \hat{R} \qquad\qquad \textbf{[18.18]}$$

Real exchange rates can change dramatically, and trends in real exchange rates can last for decades. The yen appreciation mentioned in the chapter opening, for example, has persisted since 1960 and has far exceeded the inflation differential between the United States and Japan during the same period; in other words, the yen has experienced a *real* appreciation against the dollar, with occasional interruptions, for decades. Such changes exert important influences on the international macroeconomy because they generate shifts in expenditure between domestic and foreign goods and services.

18.5.2 What Can Cause Changes in the Real Exchange Rate?

Unfortunately, economists don't yet understand as well as we would like all the causes of real exchange rate movements. Work to understand real exchange rates is in its relatively early stages in part because real exchange rates have exhibited much more volatility during the flexible-rate years since 1973 than they did during the fixed-rate years between World War II and the early 1970s. A full understanding of real exchange rates presents a formidable task because they involve the interaction of so many macroeconomic variables. However, we can gain substantial insight into several important causes of changes in real exchange rates by noting simply that the real exchange rate represents the relative price of domestic goods and services compared

Figure 18.6 Relative Output Demand Affects the Real Exchange Rate

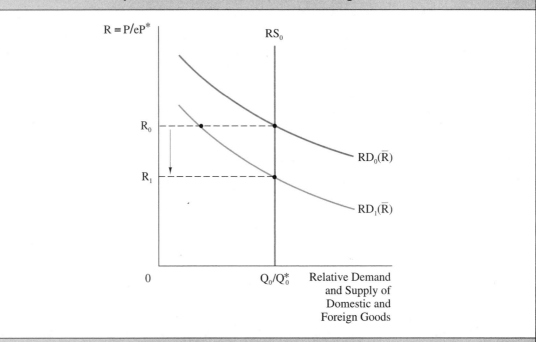

The real exchange rate ($R \equiv P/eP^*$) represents the relative price of domestic and foreign goods and services. When demand for foreign goods rises relative to demand for domestic goods, RD shifts to the left. At the old real exchange rate, R_0, there is excess supply of domestic goods and excess demand for foreign ones. The domestic currency depreciates in real terms to make domestic goods relatively cheaper, increase relative demand for domestic goods, and bring it back into equality with relative output supply at a real exchange rate of R_1.

with foreign goods and services. This focuses our attention on *output markets,* because the relative prices of domestic and foreign goods and services should be determined by the relative demands for and supplies of those goods and services.

Figure 18.6 illustrates how the relative demands for and supplies of domestic and foreign goods and services interact to determine the relative price of those goods and services, or the real exchange rate. We focus on the long run, so the supplies of both domestic and foreign output are at their full-employment levels, Q_0 and Q_0^*, respectively. This implies a vertical long-run *relative* supply curve, RS_0. Relative demands for domestic and foreign goods and services depend on their relative price. At high values of R, expenditures shift toward foreign goods and services, so the relative demand for domestic goods is low. At low values of R, expenditure shifts toward domestic goods and services, so the relative demand is high. Therefore, the *relative de*mand curve, RD_0, exhibits a negative slope in Figure 18.6. Just as in other product markets, the equilibrium price in Figure 18.6 is the one at which the relative supply of domestic goods equals the relative demand for them, or R_0.

Disturbances that shift either the relative supply curve or the relative demand curve lead to changes in the real exchange rate. Suppose consumers' tastes shift in favor of foreign goods and services. RD shifts to the left, from RD_0 to RD_1 in Figure 18.6. At the original real exchange rate, excess relative supply of domestic goods and services exists, or, equivalently, excess relative demand for foreign ones. This causes the relative price of domestic goods and services to fall to R_1. The foreign currency appreciates in real terms, and the domestic currency depreciates. This makes foreign goods and services relatively more expensive, shifts expenditure toward domestic ones, and reequates relative demands to the unchanged relative supplies of the two countries' outputs. *(Illustrate and explain why an increase in relative demand for domestic goods would lead to a domestic real appreciation.)*

Figure 18.7 **Relative Output Supply Affects the Real Exchange Rate**

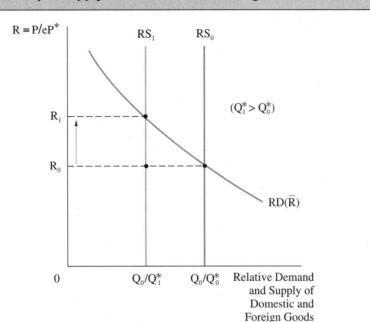

A rise in the long-run equilibrium level of foreign output (Q^*) relative to domestic output (Q) shifts RS to the left. At the original real exchange rate, R_0, there is excess demand for domestic goods and excess supply of foreign ones. The domestic currency appreciates to make domestic goods relatively more expensive, reduce relative demand for domestic goods, and bring it back into equality with relative output supply at a real exchange rate of R_1.

Changes in relative output supplies also influence the real exchange rate. Suppose the foreign economy enjoys an increase in its productivity due to a technological innovation. The long-run, or full-employment, level of foreign output rises relative to domestic output, shifting RS to the left to RS_1 in Figure 18.7. At the original real exchange rate, R_0, excess relative demand now exists for domestic goods. Their relative price rises to R_1. This constitutes a real domestic-currency appreciation, or a real foreign-currency depreciation. The change in the real exchange rate makes domestic goods relatively more expensive, shifts expenditure away from those goods, and reequates relative demands to the new lower relative supply of domestic goods. *(Illustrate that a rise in domestic relative supply leads to a domestic real depreciation and a foreign real appreciation.)*

18.6 **Long-Run Equilibrium Exchange Rates**

We've now seen through the monetary approach how *monetary* disturbances affect nominal exchange rates and through our theory of the real exchange rate how *nonmonetary* disturbances affect real exchange rates. We can combine these two insights to see how the long-run equilibrium exchange rate responds to various shocks to the economy; Table 18.4 summarizes these responses.

To examine the effect of a one-time change in the size of the domestic money stock, we need only the monetary approach to the exchange rate. Changes in the level of the money stock don't affect long-run equilibrium real output or the interest rate. Therefore, our money market equilibrium condition in Equation 18.6 implies that the price level moves in proportion to the change in the money stock. The domestic currency depreciates (appreciates) in nominal terms in proportion to the increase (decrease) in the domestic money stock. All *relative* prices in the economy, including the real exchange rate, remain unaffected.

Table 18.4 **Long-Run Equilibrium Nominal and Real Exchange Rates**				
Shock	Effect on $\hat{e}^a$	=	Effect on $(\hat{P} - \hat{P}*)$	−	Effect on $\hat{R}^b$
Relative Money Stock Levels (M/M*):[c]				
Increase	+		+		0
Decrease	−		−		0
Relative Money Growth Rates ($\hat{M}/\hat{M}*$):[c]				
Increase	+		+		0
Decrease	−		−		0
Relative Output Demands (RD):[d]				
Increase	−		0		+
Decrease	+		0		−
Relative Output Supplies (RS = Q/Q*):[d]				
Increase	?		−		−
Decrease	?		+		+

[a]A plus sign denotes a domestic nominal depreciation, and a minus sign a nominal appreciation.
[b]A plus sign denotes a domestic real appreciation, and a minus sign a real depreciation.
[c]Purchasing power parity holds.
[d]Purchasing power parity does not hold.

The monetary approach also suffices to understand the effect of a change in relative money growth rates. If the domestic money growth rate rises relative to foreign money growth, we saw in section 18.4.4 that the rate of domestic inflation rises proportionally. Purchasing power parity requires a proportional nominal domestic currency depreciation. Again, relative prices remain unchanged, including the real exchange rate.

A change in relative demand for domestic output (RD) doesn't change the long-run equilibrium price level, which is determined by the money market equilibrium condition in Equation 18.6.[18] However, section 18.5.2 implies that changes in relative output demands do alter the *real* exchange rate. In particular, a rise in relative demand for domestic output causes a domestic real appreciation, and a fall in relative demand causes a domestic real depreciation. But long-run price levels don't change, so nominal currency appreciations and depreciations are the mechanisms through which the real exchange rate changes occur.

Unlike changes in relative output demands, changes in relative output supplies (RS) do change the long-run equilibrium price level. Recall that the price level is determined by the money market equilibrium condition in Equation 18.6. If the relative supply of domestic output rises, the increase in full-employment Q increases the demand for domestic money. With a fixed nominal money stock, this requires a fall in the price level to maintain money market equilibrium. Through purchasing power parity, the fall in the domestic price level pushes the nominal exchange rate down (a nominal appreciation). But the change in relative output supplies also alters the equilibrium *real* exchange rate. The domestic currency depreciates in real terms. Therefore, the supply shock's effects through the money and output markets push the nominal exchange rate in opposite directions, and we can't be sure of the net effect.

18.7 More on Why Interest Rates Differ

At any time, the nominal interest rates paid on assets denominated in different currencies generally differ substantially. We encountered one reason why back in Chapter Twelve's introduction of the foreign exchange market: Interest parity suggests that interest-rate differences reflect market participants' expectations about future

---

18 Note that the Q term in Equation 18.6 isn't affected by a rise in demand for domestic output because, in long-run equilibrium, real output must be at its full-employment level, as determined by the supply side of the economy.

currency appreciations and depreciations. To hold assets denominated in currencies expected to appreciate, portfolio owners willingly accept lower nominal interest rates. For assets denominated in currencies expected to depreciate, portfolio owners demand higher nominal interest rates as compensation.

The monetary approach to the exchange rate in section 18.4 carried us one step further toward understanding international interest rate differences. Purchasing power parity implies that long-run equilibrium nominal exchange rate movements reflect differences in countries' rates of inflation. Hence, in long-run equilibrium, *expected* exchange rate movements should equal *expected* inflation differentials. This implies that long-run equilibrium differences in nominal interest rates equal differences in countries' expected inflation rates (see Equation 18.13).

We can take a further step by building in what we now know about changes in real exchange rates, or deviations from purchasing power parity. If, in long-run equilibrium, changes in the nominal exchange rate include both relative inflation rates (as in the monetary approach) *and* changes in the real exchange rate, then changes in the *expected* nominal exchange rate should include both *expected* relative inflation rates and changes in the *expected* real exchange rate:

$$\hat{e}^e = (\hat{P}^e - \hat{P}^{*e}) - \hat{R}^e \qquad\qquad [18.19]$$

Interest parity says that the interest differential equals the expected rate of change in the nominal exchange rate, or the left-hand side of Equation 18.19, so we can conclude that:

$$i - i^* = (\hat{P}^e - \hat{P}^{*e}) - \hat{R}^e \qquad\qquad [18.20]$$

Now we can see that international nominal interest-rate differences contain two components. The first reflects expected inflation differentials. The second reflects expected changes in the real exchange rate. Higher expected domestic inflation, lower expected foreign inflation, or an expected real domestic depreciation leads to a higher nominal interest rate differential.

We distinguished earlier between nominal interest rates, which measure an asset's rate of return in nominal or currency units, and real interest rates, which measure an asset's rate of return in real units of purchasing power. Equation 18.15, repeated here, indicated that the expected real interest rate equaled the nominal interest rate minus any expected inflation:

$$r^e = i - \hat{P}^e$$

We can combine the expressions for the domestic and foreign real interest rates to see what determines the difference between them:

$$r^e - r^{*e} = (i - i^*) - (\hat{P}^e - \hat{P}^{*e}) \qquad\qquad [18.21]$$

Simply plugging the expression for the nominal interest differential from Equation 18.20 into Equation 18.21 reveals that *international differences in expected real interest rates reflect expected real currency appreciations or depreciations:*

$$r^e - r^{*e} = (\hat{P}^e - \hat{P}^{*e}) - \hat{R}^e - (\hat{P}^e - \hat{P}^{*e}) = -\hat{R}^e \qquad\qquad [18.22]$$

Note that Equation 18.22 is simply a *real* form of interest parity. While *nominal* interest parity equates the *nominal* interest differential to the expected change in the *nominal* exchange rate, **real interest parity** equates the *real* interest differential to the expected change in the *real* exchange rate. This suggests that when all disturbances are monetary, implying that purchasing power parity is expected to hold (and, therefore, $\hat{R}^e = 0$), real expected interest rates should be equal across countries. But if nonmonetary shocks are expected to cause deviations from purchasing power parity, real interest rates can differ, *even in long-run equilibrium.*

CASE ONE:
Choose Your GNP

Economic policy makers—whether they work for a national government or for an international organization such as the World Bank or the International Monetary Fund—often need to compare countries' incomes or GNPs. For example, if policy makers determine that U.S. income has been growing faster than Japan's, they might base their policy choices on the likelihood that the U.S. bilateral current account would move toward a deficit and Japan's toward a surplus. Or, the World Bank staff, to allocate its development assistance, might want to know which countries suffer from the lowest per-capita incomes. Unfortunately, cross-country income comparisons are tricky. The main (but not the only) reason is that to compare, incomes must be stated in a common currency.

Each country calculates its income in its own domestic currency, so comparisons require a "translation" from one currency to another. If U.S. GDP in 1999 equaled $9,256,100,000,000 and Japan's equaled ¥495,375,000,000,000, which was bigger? The obvious path to an answer (and the most commonly taken one) is to multiply Japan's yen-denominated GDP by the 1999 exchange rate ($1/¥113.91) to get Japanese GDP denominated in dollars, which turns out to be $4,348,800,000,000, or about 47 percent of 1999 U.S. GDP.

Unfortunately, this estimation technique suffers a serious weakness: It is very sensitive to changes in the market exchange rate, which, as we've seen, can be very volatile in the short run. Consider January 8, 1998, in Indonesia. As we noted at the beginning of the chapter, the rupiah depreciated by about 36 percent against the dollar that day. But it makes little sense to conclude that Indonesian GDP fell by 36 percent relative to U.S. GDP in one day.

To get around this problem, policy makers and international organizations such as the World Bank increasingly perform their income comparisons by converting countries' incomes to dollars at purchasing-power-parity exchange rates rather than market ones. The result is a measure of income that provides a truer picture of countries' relative abilities to produce goods and services. Sometimes, the differences between the non-PPP and PPP measures, as reported in Table 18.5, are surprisingly large. This, after all, is just another way of saying that some short-run deviations from PPP are large. *(In the table, which income measure tends to be higher for very-low-income countries? For very-high-income countries?)*

Table 18.5 **Per-Capita GNP at Market and at PPP Exchange Rates, 2000 ($)**					
Country	Per-Capita GNP (at Market e)	Per-Capita GNP (at PPP)	Country	Per-Capita GNP (at Market e)	Per-Capita GNP (at PPP)
Albania	$ 870[a]	$ 3,550	Bolivia	$ 1,000	$ 2,380
Algeria	1,590	5,040	Botswana	3,300	7,190
Angola	240	1,230	Brazil	3,570	7,320
Argentina	7,440	12,090	Bulgaria	1,510	5,530
Armenia	520	2,570	Burkina Faso	230	1,020
Australia	20,530	25,370	Burundi	110	580
Austria	25,220	26,310	Cambodia	260	1,410
Azerbaijan	610	2,760	Cameroon	570	1,570
Bangladesh	380	1,650	Canada	21,050	27,330
Belarus	2,990	7,550	C. African Rep.	290	1,210
Belgium	24,630	27,500	Chad	200	860
Benin	380	970	Chile	4,600	9,110

(continued)

Table 18.5 (continued)

Country	Per-Capita GNP (at Market e)	Per-Capita GNP (at PPP)	Country	Per-Capita GNP (at Market e)	Per-Capita GNP (at PPP)
China	840	3,940	Moldova	400	2,240
Hong Kong	25,950	25,660	Mongolia	390	1,660
Colombia	2,080	5,890	Morocco	1,180	3,410
Congo, D. Rep.	100	682	Mozambique	210	820
Congo, Rep.	630	590	Namibia	2,050	6,440
Costa Rica	3,960	8,250	Nepal	220	1,360
Côte d'Ivoire	660	1,520	Netherlands	25,140	26,170
Croatia	4,510	7,780	New Zealand	13,080	18,780
Czech Rep.	4,920	13,610	Nicaragua	420	2,100
Denmark	32,020	27,120	Niger	180	760
Dominican Rep.	2,100	5,720	Nigeria	260	790
Ecuador	1,210	2,920	Norway	33,650	29,760
Egypt	1,490	3,690	Pakistan	470	1,960
El Salvador	1,990	4,390	Panama	3,260	5,700
Eritrea	170	950	P. New Guinea	760	2,280
Estonia	3,410	9,050	Paraguay	1,450	4,460
Ethiopia	100	660	Peru	2,100	4,720
Finland	24,900	24,610	Philippines	1,040	4,220
France	23,670	24,470	Poland	4,200	9,030
Georgia	590	2,470	Portugal	11,060	16,880
Germany	25,050	25,010	Romania	1,670	6,380
Ghana	350	1,940	Russia	1,660	8,030
Greece	11,960	16,940	Rwanda	230	930
Guatemala	1,690	3,770	Saudi Arabia	6,900	11,050
Guinea	450	1,930	Senegal	500	1,480
Haiti	510	1,500	Sierra Leone	130	460
Honduras	850	2,390	Singapore	24,740	24,970
Hungary	4,740	12,060	Slovak Rep.	3,700	11,000
India	460	2,390	Slovenia	10,070	17,390
Indonesia	570	2,840	South Africa	3,020	9,180
Iran	1,630	5,900	Spain	14,960	19,180
Ireland	22,960	25,470	Sri Lanka	870	3,470
Israel	16,310	19,320	Sweden	26,780	23,770
Italy	20,010	23,370	Switzerland	38,120	30,350
Jamaica	2,440	3,500	Syria	990	3,230
Japan	34,210	26,460	Tajikistan	170	1,060
Jordan	1,680	4,040	Tanzania	280	530
Kazakhstan	1,190	5,490	Thailand	2,010	6,330
Kenya	360	1,010	Togo	300	1,450
Korea, Rep.	8,910	17,340	Tunisia	2,090	6,090
Kyrgyz Rep.	270	2,590	Turkey	3,090	7,030
Lao PDR	290	1,530	Turkmenistan	840	4,040
Latvia	2,860	6,960	Uganda	310	1,230
Lebanon	3,750	4,530	Ukraine	700	3,710
Lesotho	540	2,490	United Kingdom	24,500	23,550
Lithuania	2,900	6,960	United States	34,260	34,260
Macedonia	1,710	4,960	Uruguay	6,090	8,880
Madagascar	260	830	Uzbekistan	610	2,380
Malawi	170	600	Venezuela	4,310	5,750
Malaysia	3,380	8,360	Vietnam	390	2,030
Mali	240	790	Yemen, Rep.	380	780
Mauritania	370	1,650	Zambia	300	750
Mexico	5,080	8,810	Zimbabwe	480	2,590

[a]1999.
Source: World Bank.

CASE TWO:
Purchasing Power Parity at Home?

Section 18.3 cited many possible reasons for the failure of purchasing power parity—trade barriers, nontraded goods, changes in relative prices, and differences in countries' production and consumption patterns among them. With so many possible causes of failure, it becomes difficult to sort out empirically which are genuinely important. A recent test took an unusual approach to testing purchasing power parity in order to circumvent this problem.[19]

The study tested whether purchasing power parity held among consumer price indices for Philadelphia, Chicago, New York, and Los Angeles. The four U.S. cities use the same currency, so exchange rate fluctuations could be ruled out as the explanation of any intercity deviations of prices. Along the same lines, macroeconomic policies could be assumed to exert similar influences on the four cities. And while consumption patterns differ somewhat regionally, the consumer-price-index data reflected the prices of similar consumption baskets.

The study found that purchasing power parity fails to hold in tests based on cities' overall consumer price indices.[20] However, when nontraded goods are excluded, purchasing power parity holds. These results indicate that the presence of nontraded goods, such as housing which contains a large real estate component, may explain much of the observed deviations from purchasing power parity. We can apply these insights in an international context. Suppose, for example, that each country's price level includes two components: One captures prices of *traded* goods and services (P_T) and one reflects prices of *nontraded* goods and services (P_{NT}):

$$P = (\alpha_T \cdot P_T) + (\alpha_{NT} \cdot P_{NT}) \text{ and}$$
$$P^* = (\alpha_T^* \cdot P_T^*) + (\alpha_{NT}^* \cdot P_{NT}^*), \quad \text{[18.23]}$$

where α_T and α_{NT} represent the weights of *traded* and *non-traded* goods in the domestic country's consumption basket, while α_T^* and α_{NT}^* denote the corresponding weights for the foreign country's consumption. If the law of one price holds for traded goods but not for nontraded ones, because arbitrage works for the former but not for the latter, then $P_T = e \cdot P_T^*$. This allows us to write the real exchange rate by plugging Equation 18.23 into the definition, $R \equiv P/eP^*$:

$$R = [(\alpha_T \cdot e \cdot P_T^*) + (\alpha_{NT} \cdot P_{NT})]/$$
$$[(\alpha_T^* \cdot e \cdot P_T^*) + (\alpha_{NT}^* \cdot e \cdot P_{NT}^*)] \quad \text{[18.24]}$$

Recall that absolute purchasing power parity holds if R equals 1, and relative purchasing power parity holds if R equals a constant. Equation 18.24 will equal 1 only if two conditions hold. First, the two countries' consumption weights for traded and nontraded goods must be equal ($\alpha_T = \alpha_T^*$ and $\alpha_{NT} = \alpha_{NT}^*$). Second, the prices of nontraded goods must be equal, or the law of one price must hold for those goods (that is, $P_{NT} = e \cdot P_{NT}^*$). Equation 18.24 will remain constant only if the two countries' weights remain constant relative to one another *and* if nontraded goods prices in the two countries remain constant relative to one another. The next case examines the importance of across-country changes in nontraded goods prices for purchasing power parity and real exchange rates.

CASE THREE:
Nontraded Goods and the Real Exchange Rate

For most countries, workers exhibit higher degrees of mobility between industries within the domestic economy than across international borders. This characteristic of world markets played an important role in our study of international trade theory in Chapters Two through Four. If workers are more mobile within than across countries, then similarly skilled workers in different sectors of the same economy will tend to earn similar wages, while even similarly skilled work-

---

19 Information for this case comes from the Tootell article in the chapter references.

20 The *Economist* Big Mac test reported in section 18.3.6 finds different burger prices in U.S. cities; the U.S. price used in the test is the average of the New York, Chicago, San Francisco, and Atlanta prices.

ers in different countries may earn very different wages (unless the countries follow free-trade policies).[21] In such a world, differences in countries' rates of productivity growth can cause changes in real exchange rates, or deviations from purchasing power parity. This link between differential productivity growth and the real exchange rate constitutes the **Balassa-Samuelson effect.**

Suppose the domestic country enjoys rapid productivity growth limited to its traded-goods sector. Wages will rise with productivity in that sector. And because workers are mobile between the domestic traded- and nontraded-goods sectors, wages will rise in the nontraded-goods sector as well, even though it hasn't shared in the productivity growth. The combination of rising wages and no productivity growth in the nontraded-goods sector leads to rising prices for nontraded goods (P_{NT}) relative to the prices of traded goods ($P_T = e \cdot P_T^*$) in the domestic economy. With no productivity growth in the foreign economy, the price of domestic nontraded goods rises relative to the price of foreign ones ($e \cdot P_{NT}^*$) as well. As Equation 18.24 indicates, such relative price changes cause purchasing power parity to fail in both its absolute and relative forms.

The Balassa-Samuelson effect often is cited as one possible explanation for the yen's dramatic real appreciation relative to the U.S. dollar over the last 30 years. Suppose that U.S. and Japanese nontraded-goods sectors enjoy productivity growth at about the same rate, but productivity growth in Japan's traded-goods sector (for example, autos) outpaces that in the U.S. traded-goods sector. Enhanced productivity in the traded-goods sector raises Japanese wages, and labor mobility within Japan transmits that wage increase to the nontraded-goods sector. The price of Japanese nontraded goods rises relative to the price of U.S. nontraded goods, and the yen appreciates in real terms against the dollar.

The patterns of traded-goods and nontraded-goods productivity and prices in the United States and Japan since

1960 suggest that the Balassa-Samuelson effect may explain much of the yen's real appreciation. Japanese productivity in tradable goods grew much more quickly than that of the United States, but not in nontradables. And the price of nontradables relative to tradables rose several times as fast in Japan as in the United States. From Equation 18.24, we can see that the predicted result is a real yen appreciation.

More generally, the Balassa-Samuelson story implies that rich countries' price levels should be higher than those of poor countries.[22] Again, the empirical evidence is broadly supportive. Figure 18.8 plots each country's per-capita GDP relative to that of the United States on the horizontal axis and each country's price level relative to that of the United States on the vertical axis. Across the entire sample, countries with high per-capita GDPs clearly tend to have higher price levels. However, in samples limited to just poor countries or just rich ones, income doesn't do as good a job at explaining the price-level variation within the group.

The Balassa-Samuelson effect also carries another potentially important implication: It may explain why nontraded goods tend to be much cheaper in relatively poor countries than in more affluent ones. If poor countries have lower labor productivity in traded goods than richer countries, but equal productivity in nontraded goods and services, then nontraded goods will be cheaper in poor countries. This follows because the low productivity in traded goods implies low wages in poor countries, and low wages imply low prices for nontraded goods. India may provide a classic example:

> A meal at a roadside diner costs the equivalent of about 35 U.S. cents, while lunch at a downtown Delhi cafeteria costs $1. A full-time housekeeper earns $25 a month; a private driver charges $80 a month. Monthly rent for a two-bedroom apartment in New Delhi is about $130.[23]

CASE FOUR:
Dry Cleaning in Tokyo and Mumbai

The Balassa-Samuelson theory indicates that services would be cheaper in relatively poor countries. Is this true? We can get a rough idea by investigating the relationship between

the prices of a basket of 19 services in 56 cities (compiled by Swiss financial-services firm UBS) and the per-capita GNPs in the corresponding countries. The services basket includes

---

21 Section 4.4 discusses the factor price equalization theorem.

22 This provides an explanation of why, in Table 18.5, GNP at market exchange rates tends to be lower (higher) than GNP at PPP exchange rates for low- (high-) income countries.

23 Miriam Jordan, "In India, Luxury Is within Reach of Many," *The Wall Street Journal,* October 17, 1995.

Figure 18.8 **Rich Countries' Price Levels Are Higher Than Those of Poor Countries**

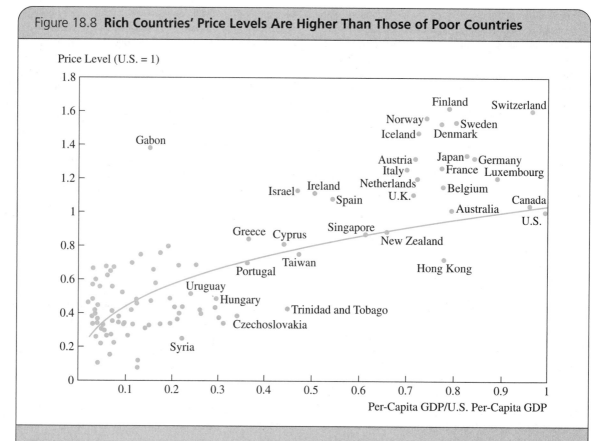

One implication of the Balassa-Samuelson theory is that countries' price levels should be positively related to their per-capita incomes. The evidence clearly supports this implication for the entire country sample, although the theory proves less successful in explaining variation either within rich countries as a group or within poor countries as a group.

Source: Kenneth Rogoff, "The Purchasing Power Parity Puzzle," *Journal of Economic Literature* (June 1996), p. 660.

items such as the cost of a house cleaner, a visit to the hairdresser, dry cleaning, monthly phone bills, a restaurant meal, a movie ticket, a daily newspaper, and a postage stamp. The price of the entire basket of 19 items varied from $110 in Mumbai to $520 in Tokyo. Figure 18.9 reveals that, on average, low-income countries do have cheaper services.

There are also outliers. At the time the data were gathered, services were cheaper in Vienna than one might have expected, given Austria's relatively high per-capita income. On the other hand, consumers in Buenos Aires and Caracas paid more for services than Argentina's or Venezuela's per-capita incomes would have led us to expect.

Summary

In long-run equilibrium, money has a neutral effect on the macroeconomy. In other words, changes in the money stock can affect nominal variables such as the price level and the nominal exchange rate, but not real variables such as real output, the real rate of interest, or the real exchange rate. The monetary approach to the exchange rate describes how the macroeconomy behaves in the long run when all shocks to the economy are monetary and purchasing power parity holds, at least in its relative form. When shocks can disturb the output market as well as the money market, even relative purchasing power parity can fail, resulting in long-run real currency appreciations and depreciations.

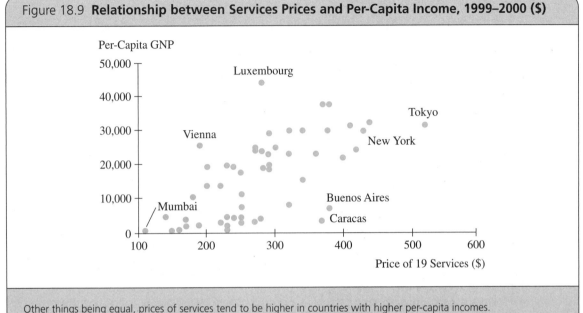

Figure 18.9 **Relationship between Services Prices and Per-Capita Income, 1999–2000 ($)**

Other things being equal, prices of services tend to be higher in countries with higher per-capita incomes.

Source: UBS, World Bank.

Looking Ahead

In Chapters Fourteen through Eighteen, we've examined how the macroeconomy behaves in the short run and in long-run equilibrium. In Chapter Nineteen, we focus on how the economy adjusts as it moves from its short-run response to its new long-run equilibrium. We'll see that economic policies may generate short-run effects that differ substantially from their long-run ones.

Key Terms

long-run equilibrium
neutrality of money
law of one price
purchasing power parity (PPP)
absolute purchasing power parity
relative purchasing power parity
monetary approach to the exchange rate
inflation

nominal rate of return
real rate of return
Fisher equation
real depreciation
real appreciation
real interest parity
Balassa-Samuelson effect

Problems and Questions for Review

1. Suppose an automobile air conditioner (an intermediate good or input into automobile production) sells for 6,000 pesos in Mexico, while an identical air conditioner sells for $500 in the United States. If the exchange rate between the peso and the dollar is 10 pesos per dollar, does the law of one price hold? Why or why not? If not, what adjustments would you expect in the peso price of air conditioners and in the dollar price of air conditioners? How would your answer differ if the item in question were the price of having a car washed rather than the price of an air conditioner? Why?

2. The following data are for 1983–1997.

Country	Percent Increase in Price Level (CPI)	Percent Change in Exchange Rate (e = $/FX)
United States	61%	—
United Kingdom	85%	–8%
Canada	56%	+18%
France	52%	–23%
Germany	37%	–32%
Italy	114%	+12%

   a. Generally, do the data seem to support purchasing power parity? Be sure to define purchasing power parity.
   b. Briefly outline three reasons why purchasing power parity might not hold between a particular pair of countries over a particular period.
3. Suppose the law of one price held for all goods and services. Would purchasing power parity necessarily hold? Why or why not?
4. For several decades in the United States, productivity grew more rapidly in traded-goods sectors such as manufacturing than in nontraded sectors such as services. Some analysts recently have argued that the "computer revolution" may finally be changing that trend, as automation raises productivity growth in many nontraded services.
   a. If increased productivity in the nontraded sector were *unique* to the United States, how would you expect it to affect the real exchange rate? Explain.
   b. Services (many of which are nontraded) typically comprise a larger share of economic activity in advanced industrial economies than in developing ones. If so, how might a *worldwide* rise in productivity in the service sector affect real exchange rates between advanced industrial economies and developing economies?
5. According to the monetary approach to the exchange rate, what would happen to the nominal exchange rate if:
   a. the domestic money stock grew at 10 percent, the foreign money stock grew at 10 percent, the demand for domestic money balances grew at 10 percent, and the demand for foreign money balances grew at 10 percent?
   b. the domestic money stock grew at 10 percent, the foreign money stock grew at 10 percent, the demand for domestic money balances grew at 5 percent, and the demand for foreign money balances grew at 5 percent?
   c. the domestic money stock grew at 5 percent, the foreign money stock grew at 10 percent, the demand for domestic money balances grew at 5 percent, and the demand for foreign money balances grew at 10 percent?
6. "If country A's nominal interest rate rises because everyone expects a higher real interest rate, A's currency will depreciate. If country A's nominal interest rate rises because everyone expects higher inflation, A's currency will depreciate." Do you agree or disagree? Why?
7. Suppose a developing country pegs its currency, the alpha (α), to the U.S. dollar at an exchange rate e = (α/$) that rises by a pre-announced amount each month. Such an arrangement is called a crawling peg. If the country's inflation rate exceeds that of the United States by more than the rate at which the α is devalued, what happens to the country's real exchange rate? What effect, if any, would you expect this to have on demand for the country's goods and services?
8. When policy makers in an economy with a history of high inflation rates attempt to change their macroeconomic policies to lower inflation, they often cite declining long-term nominal interest rates as evidence that the policy change is working. Explain. How might policy makers use changes in the exchange rate as an additional source of information about the success of their policy change? Explain.

References and Selected Readings

Coughlin, Cletus C., and Kees Koedijk. "What Do We Know about the Long-Run Real Exchange Rate?" Federal Reserve Bank of St. Louis, *Review* (January–February 1990): 35–48.
Theory and evidence on changes in the real exchange rate, or R, the relative price of domestic and foreign goods and services.

Engel, Charles. "Accounting for U.S. Real Exchange Rate Changes." *Journal of Political Economy* 107 (June 1999): 507–538.
Advanced model measuring the causes of changes in the real exchange rate.

Engel, Charles, and John H. Rogers. "How Wide Is the Border?" *American Economic Review* (December 1996): 1112–1125.
A study of PPP in U.S. and Canadian cities; for intermediate and advanced students.

Fieleke, Norman S. "The Soaring Trade in 'Nontradables.'" Federal Reserve Bank of Boston, *New England Economic Review* (November–December 1995): 25–36.
Excellent overview of the growing trade in services and other "nontradables"; for all students.

Frankel, J. A., and A. K. Rose. "Empirical Research on Nominal Exchange Rates." In *Handbook of International Economics,* Vol. 3, edited by G. M. Grossman and K. Rogoff, 1689–1730. Amsterdam: North-Holland, 1995.
Review of theory and evidence on exchange rate behavior; intermediate and advanced.

Frenkel, Jacob A., and Harry G. Johnson, eds. *The Economics of Exchange Rates.* Reading, Mass.: Addison-Wesley, 1978.
A classic collection on exchange rate theory's major developments during the 1970s, especially the monetary approach; for advanced students.

Frenkel, Jacob A., and Harry G. Johnson, eds. *The Monetary Approach to the Balance of Payments.* London: Allen and Unwin, 1976.
The classic collection on the monetary approach; for intermediate and advanced students.

Froot, K., and K. Rogoff. "Perspectives on PPP and Long-Run Real Exchange Rates." In *Handbook of International Economics,* Vol. 3, edited by G. M. Grossman and K. Rogoff, 1647–1688. Amsterdam: North-Holland, 1995.
Review of theory and evidence on long-run exchange rate behavior; intermediate and advanced.

Goldberg, Pinelopi Koujianou, and Michael M. Knetter. "Goods Prices and Exchange Rates: What Have We Learned?" *Journal of Economic Literature* (September 1997): 1243–1272.
Imperfect competition, market segmentation, and pricing to market; intermediate to advanced students.

Isard, Peter. *Exchange Rate Economics.* Cambridge: Cambridge University Press, 1995.
Survey of the state of knowledge about exchange rates; level of different sections of the book varies.

Johnson, Harry G. "The Monetary Approach to the Balance of Payments: A Nontechnical Guide." *Journal of International Economics* 7 (August 1977): 251–268.
An introduction to the monetary approach by one of its originators; for all students.

Lewis, K. "Puzzles in International Financial Markets." In *Handbook of International Economics,* Vol. 3, edited by G. M. Grossman and K. Rogoff, 1913–1972. Amsterdam: North-Holland, 1995.
Review of theory and evidence on exchange rate behavior and interest rates; intermediate and advanced.

Meltzer, Allan H. "Real Exchange Rates: Some Evidence from the Postwar Years." Federal Reserve Bank of St. Louis, *Review* (March–April 1993): 103–117.
Theoretical and empirical overview of real exchange rates; intermediate.

Obstfeld, Maurice. "International Currency Experience: New Lessons and Lessons Relearned." *Brookings Papers on Economic Activity* 1 (1995): 119–220.
Excellent survey of recent currency experience, including purchasing power parity. Intermediate.

Pakko, Michael, and Patricia S. Pollard. "For Here or to Go? PPP and the Big Mac." Federal Reserve Bank of St. Louis, *Review* (January–February 1996): 3–22.
Examination of The Economist's burger-based PPP test; for all students.

Rogoff, Kenneth. "The Purchasing Power Parity Puzzle." *Journal of Economic Literature* (June 1996): 647–668.
Excellent, accessible survey of what we know and what we don't about PPP.

Szapáry, György. "Transition Countries' Choice of Exchange Rate Regime in the Run-Up to EMU Membership." *Finance and Development* 38 (June 2001): 26–29.
Application of the Balassa-Samuelson effect to transition economies.

Taylor, Mark P. "The Economics of Exchange Rates." *Journal of Economic Literature* 33 (March 1993): 13–47.
Survey of recent literature on exchange rates; intermediate and advanced.

Tootell, Geoffrey M. B. "PPP within the United States." Federal Reserve Bank of Boston, *New England Economic Review* (July–August 1992): 15–24.
Tests find purchasing power parity fails to hold within the United States; for all students.

CHAPTER NINETEEN

Prices and Output in an Open Economy

19.1 Introduction

In Chapters Fourteen through Seventeen, we examined how fiscal, monetary, and exchange rate policies affect an open macroeconomy in the *short run*—that is, the time horizon over which the price level remains fixed. In Chapter Eighteen, we turned our attention to the *long run,* when output reaches and maintains its full-employment level and the price level adjusts fully to any shocks or policy changes in the economy. Now it's time to explore how the economy behaves *between* the short run and the long run. In other words, what happens *as the price level adjusts* to economic shocks and policy changes?

A quick examination of basic macroeconomic data for a sample of countries reveals that this medium-run period—in which both output and the price level adjust—appears to fit the situation in which most economies find themselves most of the time. This should come as no surprise. After all, economic shocks of all kinds constantly impinge on economies, and policy makers continually adjust their policy instruments. Long-run equilibrium, when all macroeconomic variables have reached states of rest, provides a useful conceptual benchmark, but it's unlikely to be observed often in the world economy, where new shocks and policy changes occur before the economy has adjusted fully to earlier events.

Countries rarely have a stable, unchanging price level. Typically, the price level rises in most years, but at variable and sometimes highly erratic rates. A sustained rise in the overall price level defines **inflation;** a sustained fall in the price level, rarely observed, represents **deflation.** Table 19.1 reports recent price-level behavior for a sample of countries. Note two patterns. First, inflation rates vary widely across countries. Second, inflation rates often change dramatically within a single country, even over a short period, confirming as we noted previously that economies constantly are adjusting to shocks and policy changes that influence their price levels.

Just as changes in countries' inflation rates differ, both across countries and across time, so do changes in their outputs. If an economy were perpetually in long-run equilibrium, of the type we examined in Chapter Eighteen, we would expect its real output to grow fairly smoothly over time, at a rate determined by growth in the country's resource endowment and improvements in its technology. Instead, we see output growth speeding up and slowing down as in Table 19.2, mirrored by changes in unemployment. This provides further evidence that we observe economies primarily in the process of adjusting to more-or-less constant economic shocks and policy changes.

To augment our model of the macroeconomy to incorporate price-level adjustment, we need to distinguish between the *supply,* or production, side of the economy and the *demand,* or expenditure, side, and then to combine the two. Our fixed-price model of Chapters Fourteen through Seventeen focused on the demand side alone; in fact, the IS, LM, and BOP curves that we used there together constitute the demand side of the economy. We assumed implicitly that firms willingly supplied at unchanged prices all the output demanded. If this condition were met, the quantity of output demanded, or what we've called *total expenditure on domestic goods*

Table 19.1 **Annual Change in Consumer Prices, 1991–2000 (Percent)**

Country	1991	1992	1993	1994	1995	1996	1997	1998	1999	2000
United States	4.2%	3.0%	3.0%	2.6%	2.8%	2.9%	2.3%	1.5%	2.2%	3.4%
Canada	5.6	1.5	1.8	0.2	1.9	1.6	1.6	1.0	1.7	2.7
Japan	3.3	1.7	1.2	0.7	−0.1	0.1	1.7	0.6	−0.3	−0.6
France	3.2	2.4	2.1	1.7	1.8	2.1	1.3	0.7	0.6	1.8
Germanyᵃ	3.5	5.1	4.5	2.7	1.7	1.2	1.5	0.6	0.7	2.1
Italy	6.3	5.3	4.6	4.1	5.2	4.0	1.9	2.0	1.7	2.6
United Kingdom	6.8	4.7	3.0	2.4	2.8	3.0	2.8	2.7	2.3	2.1
China	2.7	5.4	14.7	24.1	17.1	8.3	2.8	−0.8	−1.4	0.4
Thailand	5.7	4.1	3.4	5.1	5.8	5.9	5.6	8.1	0.3	1.5
India	13.0	9.8	6.4	10.2	10.2	9.0	7.2	13.2	4.7	4.0
Turkey	66.0	70.1	66.1	106.3	93.7	82.3	85.7	84.6	64.9	54.9
Mexico	22.7	15.5	9.8	7.0	35.0	34.4	20.6	15.9	16.6	9.5
Uganda	32.9	42.2	30.0	6.5	6.1	7.5	7.8	5.8	−0.2	6.3
Poland	70.3	43.0	35.3	32.2	27.9	19.9	14.9	11.8	7.3	10.1
Indonesia	9.4	7.5	9.7	8.5	9.4	7.9	6.2	58.0	20.7	3.8
Argentina	171.7	24.9	10.6	4.2	3.4	0.2	0.5	0.9	−1.2	−0.7
Peru	409.5	73.5	48.6	23.7	11.1	11.5	8.5	7.3	3.5	3.8
Brazil	414.8	991.4	1,927.4	2,075.8	66.0	15.8	6.9	3.2	4.9	7.0
D. R. of Congoᵇ	2,154.4	4,129.2	1,893.1	23,760.5	541.8	616.8	198.5	29.1	284.9	555.7

ᵃData for West Germany through 1991 and for unified Germany thereafter.
ᵇFormerly Zaire.

Source: International Monetary Fund, *World Economic Outlook*.

and services, would determine the level of output, as it did in Chapters Fourteen through Seventeen. However, once we introduce an independent supply side of the economy to represent firms' production decisions and workers' labor-supply decisions, things become more complex—and more realistic.

19.2 Apples versus GDP: Supply in Micro- and Macroeconomics

A microeconomic analogy with a market for a single good, such as apples, is useful here. For the price of apples to remain fixed and for demand alone to determine the equilibrium quantity of apples requires a horizontal supply curve for apples, as depicted in panel (a) of Figure 19.1. Changes in the demand for apples would then cause quantity to change in the same direction and leave price unchanged. But the horizontal supply curve in panel (a) of Figure 19.1 doesn't depict how microeconomic markets typically operate.

In microeconomics, changes in demand usually generate changes in *both* price and quantity. Figure 19.1 shows this in panel (b), where we draw the supply of apples as an upward-sloping line. The positive slope of the supply curve represents the role of price increases (that is, increases in the price of apples *relative* to the prices of other goods) in drawing resources into apple production and of price decreases in driving resources out of it. These resource movements in response to *demand*-induced price changes cause changes in the quantity *supplied* of apples. When the demand for apples rises, the relative price of apples rises and resources flow out of other endeavors (that is, production of goods whose prices have declined relative to the price of apples) and into apple growing. This resource movement allows the quantity of apples supplied to fluctuate in response to changes in consumers' demand for apples.

Table 19.2 **Annual Change in Real GDP, 1991–2000 (Percent)**

Country	1991	1992	1993	1994	1995	1996	1997	1998	1999	2000
United States	−0.9%	2.7%	2.7%	4.0%	2.7%	3.6%	4.4%	4.4%	4.2%	5.0%
Canada	−1.9	0.9	2.3	4.7	2.8	1.5	4.4	3.3	4.5	4.7
Japan	3.8	1.0	0.5	1.0	1.6	3.3	1.9	−1.1	0.8	1.7
France	0.8	1.2	−1.9	1.8	1.9	1.0	1.9	3.3	3.2	3.2
Germanyª	5.0	2.2	−1.1	2.3	1.7	0.8	1.4	2.1	1.6	3.0
Italy	1.1	0.6	−0.9	2.2	2.9	1.1	2.0	1.8	1.6	2.9
United Kingdom	−2.0	−0.5	2.3	4.4	2.8	2.6	3.5	2.6	2.3	3.0
China	9.2	14.2	13.5	12.6	10.5	9.6	8.8	7.8	7.1	8.0
Thailand	8.1	8.2	8.4	9.0	9.3	5.9	−1.4	−10.8	4.2	4.3
India	1.7	4.2	5.0	6.7	7.6	7.1	4.9	6.0	6.6	6.4
Turkey	0.8	5.0	7.7	−4.7	8.1	6.9	7.5	3.1	−4.7	7.2
Mexico	4.2	3.6	2.0	4.4	−6.2	5.2	6.8	4.9	3.8	6.9
Uganda	5.2	3.1	8.6	6.4	11.9	8.6	5.1	4.6	7.6	4.6
Poland	−7.0	2.6	4.3	5.2	6.8	6.0	6.8	4.8	4.1	4.1
Indonesia	8.9	7.2	7.3	7.5	8.2	8.0	4.5	−13.1	0.8	4.8
Argentina	10.5	10.3	6.3	5.8	−2.8	5.5	8.1	3.8	−3.4	−0.5
Peru	2.9	−1.8	6.4	13.1	7.3	2.5	6.8	−0.4	1.4	3.6
Brazil	1.0	−0.5	4.9	5.9	4.2	2.7	3.3	0.2	0.8	4.2
D. R. of Congoᵇ	−8.4	−10.5	−13.5	−3.9	0.7	0.9	−8.2	−3.5	−14.0	−4.9

ªData for West Germany through 1991 and for unified Germany thereafter.
ᵇFormerly Zaire.

Source: International Monetary Fund, *World Economic Outlook.*

Figure 19.1 **Price and Supply in the Apple Market**

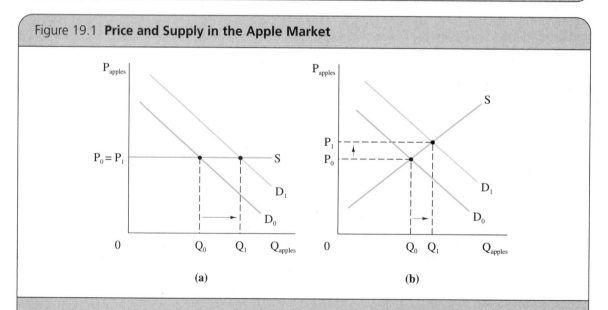

(a)   (b)

In panel (a), the supply curve for apples is perfectly horizontal. The price of apples is fixed, and demand determines quantity. In panel (b), the supply curve for apples is upward sloping, reflecting the movement of resources into and out of apple production in response to relative price changes.

Moving back to the macroeconomy, changes in the economy's overall output, or GDP, also require changes in the quantity of resources employed. Increased production requires more inputs. However, when we want to model changes in real GDP, or the economy's *total* output of goods and services, we can't explain increases and decreases in terms of resource movements among industries in response to relative price changes, as in the apple-market example. For the quantity of total output supplied to increase, resources previously unemployed must come into use or resources must be used more intensively (such as workers' overtime, running machines two shifts per day, or cultivating previously idle land). *If* a rise in the price level causes these types of adjustments, the economy's macroeconomic or aggregate supply curve (the relationship between the quantity of real output produced and the price level) will slope upward.

The relevant question then becomes: Will an increase in the price level cause resource utilization to rise? Economists' answer to this question has evolved with our understanding of the macroeconomy; in fact, the question represents one of the most fundamental and enduring issues of macroeconomics. A hundred years ago, most economists would have answered in the negative. Fifty years ago, most would have answered with a resounding yes. Today only a few would give such an unequivocal reply. Most would answer, "Yes, but not in the long run, and only if the economy hasn't experienced continual increases in its price level."

With this introduction to the problems at hand, let's proceed to translate our model of an open macroeconomy into a form more convenient for analyzing the economy's adjustment from short-run to long-run equilibrium. We must develop an aggregate demand curve and a more complete concept of an aggregate, or macroeconomic, supply curve. We can continue to use the microeconomic concepts of demand and supply as analogies, but we must also distinguish the features that make an *aggregate* demand or supply curve unique to macroeconomics.

19.3 Aggregate Demand under Fixed Exchange Rates

An economy's **aggregate demand curve** represents the relationship between the quantity demanded of domestic goods and services and the domestic price level. Note that this definition closely resembles that of a market demand curve for a single good in microeconomics. The differences in the case of the aggregate demand curve are that (1) the quantity examined represents the economy's total output of goods and services, or real GDP, rather than output of a single good or service, and (2) the relevant price represents the overall domestic price level, the GDP deflator, rather than the relative price of a single good. The form of the aggregate demand curve differs slightly depending on whether the economy operates under a fixed or flexible exchange rate regime, so we begin with the analysis under a fixed exchange rate.

19.3.1 The Slope of the Aggregate Demand Curve[1]

The aggregate demand curve slopes downward like a microeconomic demand curve, but for different reasons. Two reasons account for its negative slope. First, a rise in the domestic price level, P (with the foreign price level, P*, and the exchange rate, e, held constant), raises the price of domestic goods and services relative to that of foreign ones because $R \equiv P/eP^*$. Individuals respond by shifting expenditure from domestic to foreign goods; thus, the quantity demanded of domestic goods and services falls, resulting in a negative relationship between the domestic price level and the quantity demanded of domestic goods. *(To test your understanding, outline the effect of a fall in the price level on relative prices and on the quantity demanded of domestic goods.)*

The second reason for the aggregate demand curve's negative slope comes from the money market.[2] Recall that individuals demand real money balances to make transactions conveniently. The quantity demanded of real money balances (L) depends positively on real income (Q)—because the number and size of transactions depend positively on income—and negatively on the interest rate (i), which measures the opportunity cost of holding cash balances rather than interest-bearing bonds.

In equilibrium, the quantity of real money balances demanded by the public (L[Q, i]) must equal the stock of real money balances, which equals the nominal money stock (M) divided by the price level (P). Figure 19.2 illustrates such an equilibrium, along with the effects of a rise in the price level. Given a value for the nominal

---

1 The appendix to this chapter derives the aggregate demand curve from the IS-LM-BOP framework of Chapters Sixteen and Seventeen.

2 See section 15.2 to review the demand for money and the money stock.

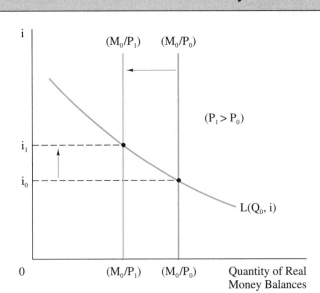

Figure 19.2 **Effect of a Rise in the Price Level in the Money Market**

A rise in the price level from P_0 to P_1 reduces the real money stock (M/P), assuming that the nominal money stock (M) is held constant. The equilibrium interest rate rises to reduce the quantity demanded of real money balances to equal the new, smaller stock.

money stock (M_0), a rise in the price level from P_0 to P_1 reduces the real money stock and shifts the money stock line to the left. At the original interest rate (i_0), the quantity demanded of money exceeds the new, smaller stock. Individuals try to sell bonds to raise their real money balances to the desired level. The price of bonds falls, which is reflected in a rise in the interest rate to i_1. At the new, higher interest rate, individuals are satisfied holding the new, smaller stock of real money balances.

The rise in the interest rate produced by adjustments in the money market discourages investment expenditure.[3] Total expenditure on domestic goods and services falls. This chain of events—from a rise in the price level to a decline in total expenditure—provides the second reason why the aggregate demand curve slopes downward. Again, a higher price level corresponds to a smaller quantity demanded of domestic goods and services. *(To test your understanding, go through the effects of a* fall *in the price level on the money market and total expenditure.)*

The effects of a change in the domestic price level on the relative price of domestic goods and on the real money stock both contribute to the negative relationship between the quantity demanded of domestic goods and services and the domestic price level represented by the downward-sloping aggregate demand curve in an open economy.[4] Besides the slope, we need to know what variables cause the entire aggregate demand curve to shift. Just as with a market demand curve in microeconomics, we draw an aggregate demand curve assuming that certain variables are held constant; when any of these variables changes, the entire demand curve shifts.

---

3 For a review, see the discussion of investment in section 14.5.3.

4 Note that the second effect, but not the first, exists in a closed economy; therefore, the aggregate demand curve in an open economy tends to be flatter than that in an otherwise comparable closed economy.

Figure 19.3 **Shifts in the Aggregate Demand Curve**

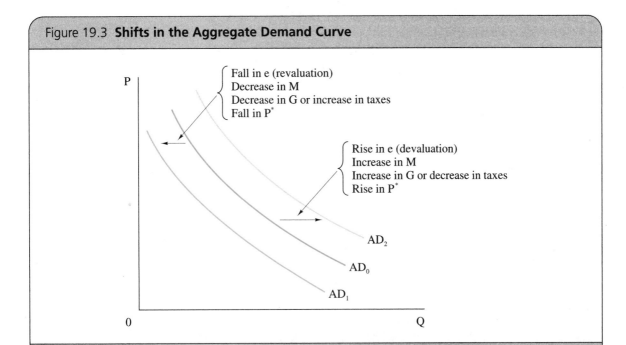

The demand for domestically produced goods and services is reduced at each domestic price level by a revaluation of the domestic currency, a decline in the domestic nominal money stock, a decrease in government purchases, a rise in taxes, or a fall in the foreign price level. The demand for domestically produced goods and services increases at each domestic price level due to a devaluation of the domestic currency, a rise in the domestic money stock, an increase in government purchases, a reduction in taxes, or a rise in the foreign price level. Changes in the domestic price level itself, other things equal, cause movements along a single aggregate demand curve rather than shifts in it.

19.3.2 Shifts in the Aggregate Demand Curve

For our purposes, the important variables fixed along a given aggregate demand curve include the nominal money stock, fiscal policy variables such as government purchases and taxes, the nominal exchange rate, and the foreign price level. A change in any one of these variables alters the demand for domestic goods *at each domestic price level* and, therefore, shifts the entire aggregate demand curve. Figure 19.3 summarizes the effects of changes in each variable on the aggregate demand curve.

Changes in the nominal money stock can arise through either open market operations or foreign exchange intervention in response to a balance-of-payments surplus or deficit (recall that we're examining aggregate demand under a *fixed* exchange rate regime). In either case, an increase in the nominal money stock raises the real money stock for a given price level. The interest rate must fall to make individuals willing to hold the new, larger stock of real money balances. The fall in the interest rate raises the investment component of expenditure on domestic goods and services, and the aggregate demand curve shifts to the right. A decrease in the nominal money stock shifts the aggregate demand curve to the left, for the same reason. Note that a change in the real money stock can cause *either* a movement along a single aggregate demand curve *or* a shift of the entire curve, depending on whether the change in (M/P) was caused by a change in the price level or in the nominal money stock.[5]

_____

5 This seemingly peculiar state of affairs arises because the price level is the variable plotted on the vertical axis in drawing an aggregate demand curve.

By raising total expenditure on domestic goods and services, expansionary fiscal policy increases demand for them at each price level and shifts the aggregate demand curve to the right. Expansionary fiscal policy can consist of either increased government purchases or tax cuts, which raise disposable income and increase consumption expenditure. Contractionary fiscal policy lowers demand and shifts the AD curve to the left.

A devaluation of the domestic currency (a rise in the nominal exchange rate, e) lowers the relative price of domestic goods ($R \equiv P/eP^*$) and increases demand for them at each level of domestic prices. The aggregate demand curve shifts to the right. A revaluation of the domestic currency has the opposite effect; it raises the relative price of domestic goods and shifts the aggregate demand curve to the left.

Changes in the foreign price level (P^*) also shift the aggregate demand curve because, for given values of the domestic price level and the nominal exchange rate, they alter the relative price of domestic goods. A rise in P^* switches expenditure toward domestic goods and shifts the aggregate demand curve to the right. A fall in the foreign price level switches spending toward now relatively cheaper foreign goods and shifts the domestic aggregate demand curve to the left. Note that changes in R can lead to either a movement along the AD curve (if R changes through P) or to a shift of the AD curve (if R changes through e or P^*).

19.3.3 Aggregate Demand Alone Can't Determine Output

The models of an open macroeconomy we considered in Chapters Fourteen through Seventeen constitute models of aggregate demand. They tell us, *given* the price level, the quantity of domestic goods and services demanded by individuals, firms, government agencies, and foreigners. However, goods and services don't appear magically; they must be produced by firms, using labor and capital inputs and the available technology. The economy's aggregate supply curves contain information about this production process.

19.4 Long-Run Aggregate Supply

Aggregate supply refers to the relationship between an economy's price level and the total quantity of goods and services produced. As in a microeconomic context, the theory of aggregate supply reflects the use of inputs and technology to produce output and the responses by firms and input suppliers to changes in prices.

The quantity of available resources and the existing technology constrain the total quantity of output an economy can produce. Changes in employment, the capital stock, natural resource inputs, or technology alter an economy's ability to produce goods and services. Macroeconomists typically assume that a country's capital stock, natural resource inputs, and technology are fixed over the time horizon under analysis. Over a long period, capital stocks grow or shrink, natural resources are discovered or exhausted, and new technologies permit the same resources to generate larger quantities of output.[6] These changes usually, but not always, occur gradually and largely outside macroeconomic policy makers' control, so macroeconomic analysis tends to focus on changes in the quantity of output produced holding constant the quantity of available resources and technology. Changes in output then must come from changes in employment or in the intensity with which firms use the given capital stock.

19.4.1 The Short, Medium, and Long Runs

When examining the supply or production side of the economy, we must distinguish among behavior in the short, medium, and long runs. Production inherently takes time, and firms can't adjust instantaneously to changes in their economic environment. For example, firms often hire workers at wage rates fixed contractually for a set period, such as a year or longer; and the cost of changing the wage rate within the contract period may be prohibitive. Firms also make contracts with raw-material suppliers, often well before actual input delivery. Toy makers must decide how many of the hottest toys to make for the Christmas season long before they can determine whether the toys' popularity will even last until Christmas. Auto makers must commit to produce a certain number and size of cars before knowing next year's gasoline prices. All these factors force firms to make hiring and production decisions based on less-than-perfect information and limit their ability to adjust quickly as new information becomes available.

---

6 See Chapter Ten for a discussion of the sources of economic growth.

The limited availability of information and firms' restricted ability to adjust speedily to new information create an important distinction between their medium- and long-run responses to changes in the price level. We define the **short run** as in Chapters Fourteen through Seventeen—the period during which the price level remains fixed in response to economic shocks or policy changes, so aggregate demand alone determines real output. The **medium run** is the period during which the price level begins to respond to shocks or policy changes, but individuals and firms may remain unaware of some price changes or may find it too costly because of contracts or other rigidities to adjust their behavior fully in response to those changes. The **long run,** on the other hand, denotes the time over which everyone in the economy knows the price level and has had time to adjust production decisions accordingly.

Economists can't attach concrete time periods, such as a month, six months, or a year, to the concepts of the short, medium, and long runs, because the time required to learn and adjust to price changes depends on the nature of the economy and on the past history of the price level. Generally, the more volatile prices have been in the past, the shorter will be the short and medium runs. When price movements have been very dramatic, individuals have an economic incentive to monitor and anticipate changes to avoid the large losses that drastic unexpected changes in the price level could impose. On the other hand, when prices have been stable histori-cally, individuals have less incentive to monitor prices closely and may be slow to perceive or react to changes when they do occur.

19.4.2 The Vertical Long-Run Aggregate Supply Curve

Because the theory of aggregate supply in the long run is somewhat simpler than that in the medium run, we begin with the long run. The **long-run aggregate supply curve** is a simple vertical line at the economy's full-employment output, implying that changes in the price level have no effect on the quantity of output supplied. Remember that along a *long-run aggregate supply* curve (LRAS in Figure 19.4), individuals and firms in the economy know about and have adjusted fully to any change in the price level.

The vertical long-run aggregate supply curve reflects the way individuals and firms make economic deci-sions. Firms decide how much to produce and workers how much labor to supply in response to relative prices.

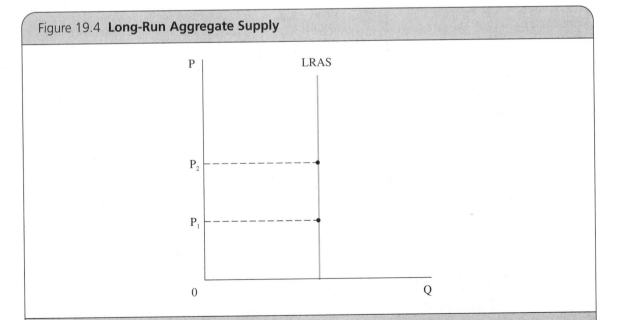

Figure 19.4 **Long-Run Aggregate Supply**

In the long run (when the price level is known and individuals and firms have time to adjust their decisions to any changes in it), the quantity of output supplied doesn't depend on the price level. The economy's quantity of resources and technol-ogy determine the horizontal placement of the LRAS curve.

If the price a firm receives for its product rises *relative to* the prices the firm must pay for its inputs, the firm increases production. But if the price a firm receives for its product rises while the prices of all the inputs it uses rise in the same proportion, the firm finds it not worthwhile to boost production. Similarly, if workers' wages rise *relative to* the prices of the goods workers buy, they will supply a larger quantity of labor to take advantage of the higher real wages. A similar wage increase wouldn't encourage additional work if the prices of all the goods workers purchase rose in the same proportion as wages, leaving real wages unchanged.

A change in the overall price level on the vertical axis of Figure 19.4 implies that *all* money prices in the economy (prices of all goods and services, nominal wages, and so on) change proportionally, leaving all relative prices unaffected. Real economic decisions (that is, how much to produce or how much labor to supply) depend on relative prices, so those decisions remain unaffected. Therefore, real output, on the horizontal axis in Figure 19.4, doesn't vary with the price level: *The long-run aggregate supply curve is vertical.*

Resource availability and technology determine the horizontal position of the long-run aggregate supply curve. As resource supplies increase over time or as technological progress allows given quantities of resources to produce larger quantities of output, the economy experiences economic growth and the LRAS curve shifts to the right. We noted earlier that this movement usually happens quite slowly and outside the direct control of macroeconomic policy makers, so we'll ignore the effects of growth by assuming a fixed position for the LRAS curve through most of our analysis.[7]

One final note about the LRAS curve is in order. The full-employment output corresponding to the position of the LRAS curve *doesn't* represent the maximum output the economy can produce. In fact, more output can be and often is produced for brief periods. But, given the pattern of relative prices in the economy, the equilibrium output in the long run (when all firms and workers have made their chosen adjustments to price changes) is given by the LRAS curve. This represents full-employment output, or the output firms can produce without resorting to overtime for workers, overtime for machines (which raises maintenance costs), and other short-term arrangements that put upward pressure on prices.[8]

Consider an economy operating at full employment. Could it produce a still higher output? Yes—for example, workers could work 45 hours per week rather than the 35 to 40 hours typical in modern industrial economies, and output clearly would rise. Societies settle for a smaller output in order to work fewer hours per week, because individuals value leisure as well as income. Given the wage rate, individuals choose how to allocate their time between work (to earn income) and leisure, a decision reflected in the position of the LRAS curve. *(What would happen to the long-run aggregate supply curve if everyone in the economy suddenly wanted to take more leisure and work less? If everyone suddenly wanted to take less leisure and work more?)* Similarly, firms could raise output by running machines for longer periods or using double shifts. When temporary considerations cause individuals to alter their decisions about how to divide time between work and leisure or firms to alter their decisions about how intensively to use their equipment, the economy temporarily moves off the LRAS curve.

19.5 Medium-Run Aggregate Supply

The **medium-run aggregate supply curve** captures the behavior of individuals and firms when lack of information about the price level, stickiness of some prices, or inability to adjust quickly to a change in the price level causes behavior to differ from what it would be with full information and instantaneous adjustment. Since macroeconomic policy decisions tend to center on medium-run considerations, understanding supply behavior in the medium run is critical.

19.5.1 The Slope of the Medium-Run Aggregate Supply Curve

The medium-run aggregate supply curve slopes upward, somewhat like the letter *J*. If the price level rises but individuals and firms don't fully perceive or adjust to that event, output increases. Of course, at some output the economy reaches an absolute resource constraint (for example, when all workers are working 100 hours

---

7 Section 19.10's analysis of supply shocks is an exception.

8 This long-run equilibrium level of real output often is called the *natural rate of output,* or *potential real output.*

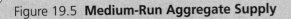

Figure 19.5 **Medium-Run Aggregate Supply**

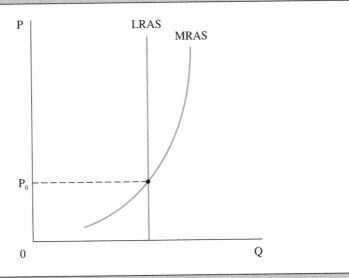

When individuals in the economy aren't fully aware of changes in the price level or able to adjust quickly to them (because of contractual rigidities, for example), a rise in the price level causes an increase in the quantity of output supplied. This is captured by the upward-sloping portion of the MRAS curve. At some point the economy reaches the constraint of resources and technology, causing the medium-run aggregate supply curve to become vertical.

per week and all machines are running 24 hours per day) that prohibits further production. At that point, the *medium-run aggregate supply* curve (MRAS in Figure 19.5) becomes vertical, since further price increases can't generate further production. However, the upward-sloping portion of the MRAS curve is of interest here; thus, we'll ignore the vertical section in the following discussion and figures.

Given the economic arguments for the vertical shape of the long-run aggregate supply curve, why would a rise in the price level ever cause output to increase? Economic theory and empirical evidence from many economies suggest several possible answers to this question. The key definitional differences between the medium-run and long-run supply curves are (1) the information available to individuals and firms within the economy and (2) their ability to adjust to that information; we'll focus on the roles these two factors play in explaining the positive medium-run relationship between the price level and quantity supplied.

Even if firms and workers always had complete information about events throughout the economy, contractual rigidities still would prevent instantaneous adjustment. Consider, for example, the case of an industry that sets its wages in nominal terms in year-long contracts. If the price level rises during the year, the price the firm can charge for its product rises, while the contractually fixed wage rate stays constant. The firm responds to the rise in the price of its output relative to the price of its labor input by producing more. Graphically, we illustrate this response by a movement up along the economy's medium-run supply curve. We'll see later that once the firm's wage contract expires and must be renegotiated, the nominal wage will tend to rise to compensate workers for the higher prices of the goods they buy. When this happens, the firm's relative price falls back to its original level, as does its output. This places the economy back on the long-run aggregate supply curve. Before we see more about this adjustment process, we turn to the role of limited information in causing workers' and firms' medium-run behavior to differ from their long-run behavior.

Firms base production decisions on information about the prices received for their products relative to the prices of their inputs. There are two major sources of information about these prices: government statistics and firms' own experience in selling their products and buying inputs. Each of these sources is subject to lags. Governments publish some price statistics monthly and others quarterly; all are subject to periodic revision that continues long after initial publication. Likewise, a firm's own experience can't provide full, up-to-date information on the state of prices throughout the economy. Suppose an automobile producer sees its sales rise, signaling an increase in demand. How should the producer interpret this information? There are two basic possibilities, and the appropriate (that is, profit-maximizing) response by the firm depends on which one occurs. If the increase in demand occurs *only* in the automobile industry or *only* for the output of that particular automobile producer, the price of the firm's output rises *relative to* those of other goods in the economy (including the firm's inputs) and the firm should increase output. The second possibility is that the increase in demand for the firm's output is part of a general increase in demand for *all* products (that is, in aggregate demand). In this case, the firm can charge a higher price for its product but also must pay proportionally higher prices for its inputs. The firm's *relative* price remains unchanged, and the profit-maximizing response keeps output at its original level.

In the medium run, the firm may be unable to tell which of these two possibilities has occurred. If firms mistakenly interpret a rise in the overall price level as a rise in the relative prices of their respective outputs and respond by raising output, the economy moves up along the medium-run aggregate supply curve. In other words, a rise in the price level, if misperceived by firms as an increase in their relative prices, causes output to increase. But eventually firms will discover their mistake—for example, when they go to buy additional inputs and find that input prices have risen by the same percentage as the prices of their products. When this happens, output falls back to its original level and the economy moves back onto the long-run aggregate supply curve. We'll examine this adjustment from the medium run to the long run by considering the causes of shifts in the medium-run aggregate supply curve.[9]

19.5.2 Shifts in the Medium-Run Aggregate Supply Curve

Each medium-run aggregate supply curve is drawn for given values of input prices and of firms' expectations about prices other than those of their own products. If the price level rises but contractual rigidities keep some input prices constant and firms don't immediately alter their expectations about other prices throughout the economy, firms will perceive the relative prices of their outputs as having risen and will increase output. This causes the economy to move up along a given MRAS curve.

Figure 19.6 depicts this situation, in which W denotes nominal *w*ages and P^e denotes firms' *e*xpectations about the price level. Beginning at point 1, the price level rises but input prices and firms' price expectations don't adjust immediately. Output rises, and the economy moves to point 2. Gradually, input prices adjust upward, firms detect the rise in all prices, the expected price level rises, and the economy moves to point 3, back on the long-run aggregate supply curve. (*What would happen to output in the medium run if the price level suddenly fell to $P_2 < P_0$? In the long run?*)

Of course, not every rise in the price level leaves input prices temporarily untouched or fools firms into thinking their relative prices have risen. If all input prices respond immediately and if firms immediately recognize a proportional rise in all prices, the economy moves directly from point 1 to point 3, leaving output completely unaffected by the rise in prices.

When the economy operates at a point to the right of the LRAS curve, two things happen. First, output is above the full-employment level, so wages and other input prices tend to rise, shifting the MRAS upward. Second, if the actual price level exceeds the expected price level ($P > P^e$), the expected price level will rise, again shifting the MRAS curve upward. When the economy operates at a point to the left of the LRAS curve, output is below the full-employment level and the expected price level may be higher than the actual price level ($P^e > P$). As input prices fall and information about the lower-than-expected price level spreads, the expected price level falls and the medium-run aggregate supply curve shifts downward.

19.6 Combining Aggregate Demand and Aggregate Supply

The simultaneous determination of output and the price level requires that we combine the aggregate demand curve with the aggregate supply curves, as in Figure 19.7. In the medium run, the economy can operate at any intersection of an aggregate demand curve and a medium-run aggregate supply curve. In the long run, there's the additional requirement that the aggregate demand and medium-run aggregate supply curves intersect at a

---

9 Several types of shifts in the medium-run aggregate supply curve can occur. We concentrate here on those caused by changes in input prices or perceptions of the price level. These shifts are vertical ones. Both the medium- and long-run supply curves may shift horizontally because of changes in the quantity of available resources or in technology, as we'll see in section 19.10.

Figure 19.6 **Vertical Shift in the Medium-Run Aggregate Supply Curve Due to a Rise in Input Prices or in the Expected Price Level**

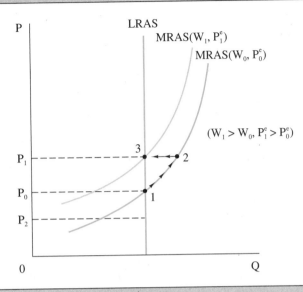

Each MRAS curve is drawn for given input prices (W) and expectations about the price level (P^e). A rise in input prices or in the expected price level shifts the MRAS curve upward.

Figure 19.7 **Medium-Run and Long-Run Equilibrium**

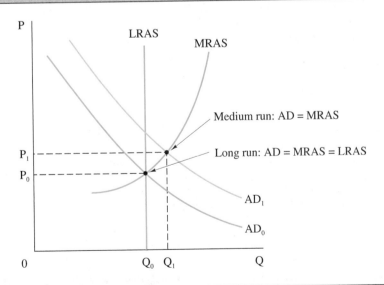

In the medium run, the economy must be at a point of intersection of an aggregate demand curve and a medium-run aggregate supply curve. In the long run, there is an additional requirement: The intersection of the aggregate demand and medium-run aggregate supply curves must occur on the long-run aggregate supply curve.

point *on* the long-run aggregate supply curve. This means that individuals and firms must know the price level and must have adjusted their pricing and output decisions accordingly.

   To analyze various policies' effects on output and prices, we must make an assumption about the degree of capital mobility for the country in question. Since the degree of capital mobility has increased in recent years, especially for the industrial economies, we choose the assumption of **perfectly mobile capital.** Recall that this means that portfolio owners, in deciding where to place their funds, consider only interest rates, exchange rates, and expected changes in exchange rates. Individuals have no inherent preferences for investments in one currency over those in another, and no government regulations restrict capital flows among countries. With perfectly mobile capital, the interest parity conditions discussed in Chapter Twelve determine the pattern of international interest rates.

19.7 Macroeconomic Policy under Fixed Exchange Rates

Once we relax the assumption of a fixed price level, the economy contains **automatic adjustment mechanisms** (that is, mechanisms that don't require an active response from policy makers) for reaching a long-run equilibrium in which (1) the quantity demanded of domestic goods equals the quantity supplied *at full employment* and (2) balance-of-payments equilibrium prevails. Changes in input prices and in the expected price level move the economy onto the long-run aggregate supply curve by shifting the medium-run supply curve until it intersects the aggregate demand curve at a point on the long-run supply curve. Changes in the money stock due to intervention in the foreign exchange market handle any imbalance in the country's international payments. A balance-of-payments surplus (deficit) causes a rise (fall) in the money stock that shifts the aggregate demand curve to the right (left) to restore balance-of-payments equilibrium. Therefore, the economy reaches long-run equilibrium only when these adjustment mechanisms have resolved problems of output, employment, and balance of payments.

   The primary shortcoming of the automatic adjustment mechanisms is their lack of speed. The price level, in particular, may adjust quite slowly, leaving the economy off the long-run supply curve for relatively long periods. Given this possibility, an obvious question arises as to whether macroeconomic policies can speed up the adjustment process. In Chapter Sixteen, we saw that, with a *fixed* price level, fiscal policy can affect domestic output with a fixed exchange rate and perfectly mobile capital. Monetary policy, on the other hand, proved completely incapable of affecting output. How does the introduction of price flexibility alter these results? The already pessimistic conclusion about monetary policy remains unchanged, but the previously optimistic view of fiscal policy becomes a bit more pessimistic. In the medium run, fiscal policy can alter income, but monetary policy can't. Neither policy can affect real output in the long run, although fiscal policy continues to affect the price level. Because price flexibility is important primarily in assessing a policy's medium- and long-run effectiveness, we focus on permanent changes in the level of government spending and the money stock.[10]

19.7.1 Fiscal Policy

We begin our initial analysis of fiscal policy from a point of long-run equilibrium (point 1 in Figure 19.8). In long-run equilibrium, the markets for goods and services, money, and foreign exchange are in equilibrium and everyone in the economy has adjusted fully to the actual price level (P_1).[11] A one-time permanent expansionary fiscal policy shifts the aggregate demand curve to the right from AD_1 to AD_2 (see section 19.3.2). The price level begins to rise. If some input prices don't adjust quickly, or if some individuals or firms mistake the rise in all prices for a rise in a specific relative price, the quantity of output supplied increases, as illustrated by point 2. However, the economy can't remain at point 2 in the long run for two reasons: (1) balance of payments disequilibrium, which implies additional movement of AD, and (2) lack of full adjustment to the new price level, which places the economy off the long-run aggregate supply curve.

   The balance of payments is in surplus at point 2, because the rise in income raises the demand for money with a fixed nominal money stock, implying a rise in the interest rate and a capital inflow. The resulting intervention increases the nominal money stock and shifts AD further to the right from AD_2 to AD_3. As individuals

---

10 Section 17.3 highlights the different effects of temporary and permanent fiscal and monetary policies when the exchange rate is flexible.

11 Recall that the AD curve incorporates the IS, LM, and BOP lines, as shown in more detail in the chapter appendix.

Figure 19.8 **Effect of Expansionary Fiscal Policy with Flexible Prices, Fixed Exchange Rates, and Perfectly Mobile Capital**

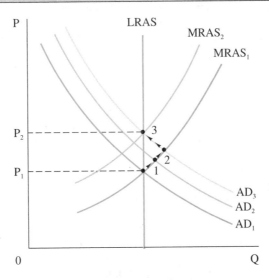

Beginning from a long-run equilibrium at point 1, an expansionary fiscal policy temporarily raises output. As firms and individuals adjust to the rise in the price level, the increase in output is offset, and the long-run effect is merely a rise in the price level.

and firms in the economy gradually come to realize that the price level has risen, and as input prices rise in response to output above the full-employment level, the MRAS curve shifts upward until long-run equilibrium is restored on the LRAS curve at point 3. *The net long-run effect of the expansionary fiscal policy is a rise in the price level with no effect on real output.*

If government purchases of goods and services increase while total output remains unchanged, some sectors of the economy must shrink. The growth of the public sector comes at the expense of other components of expenditure on goods and services. The rise in the domestic price level makes foreign goods more attractive by raising the real exchange rate ($R \equiv P/eP^*$), so export and import-competing industries in the domestic economy contract.[12]

Perhaps it isn't surprising to find that an expansionary fiscal policy that begins from a point of long-run equilibrium and attempts to expand output beyond full employment fails in the long run. In fact, it's unclear why policy makers would pursue expansionary policies when output already is at full employment and can be raised further only by generating a rise in the price level that firms and individuals in the economy misinterpret or respond to slowly.[13] A more appropriate test of fiscal policy's effectiveness might be its ability to bring the economy into long-run equilibrium from a point of less-than-full employment. In other words, if an exogenous disturbance pushed the economy below full employment, could fiscal policy help restore output to its long-run equilibrium in a timely fashion?

12 The capital inflow maintains balance-of-payments equilibrium in the face of a move toward a deficit in the current account. Note that the real appreciation under a fixed exchange rate comes through a rise in P, with the nominal exchange rate and foreign price level fixed. We'll see in section 19.9 that, under a flexible exchange rate, the real appreciation comes through a nominal currency appreciation with the domestic and foreign price levels fixed.

13 Political-business-cycle theory suggests that politicians, prior to elections, have an incentive to engage in overly expansionary policies to generate higher employment and output in the short run. The long-run effect is inflation, but only *after* the election.

Suppose policy makers executed an expansionary fiscal policy beginning at a point to the left of the LRAS curve to stimulate output. Could the policy then raise real output? The answer is yes, but the policy would still result in a rise in the price level. *(We leave the graphical demonstration to the reader.)* The domestic economy still experiences a real currency appreciation caused by the price-level increase, and the trade-oriented sectors still contract, but by less than the initial increase in government purchases.

However, this more optimistic result requires a proviso. With flexible prices, the economy contains a mechanism with which to move *automatically* to the LRAS curve without using expansionary policies. At any point to the left of the LRAS curve, output is below its full-employment level. Less-than-full employment puts downward pressure on input prices. And as a lower-than-expected actual price level (including input prices) becomes known, the expected price level falls and the medium-run supply curve shifts downward to restore a long-run equilibrium on the LRAS curve. Unfortunately, this process may unfold quite slowly, leaving output and employment at a low level for extended periods. This presents a possible role for fiscal policy in speeding up adjustment by shifting AD upward rather than waiting for MRAS to shift downward.

Figure 19.9 compares the two alternative paths to long-run equilibrium. Beginning at point 1, with low output and employment, automatic adjustment through a reduction in input prices and the expected price level would gradually shift the MRAS curve down, bringing the economy into long-run equilibrium at point 2a. If, instead, policy makers pursue expansionary fiscal policy in an effort to speed up the return of output to its long-run level, the aggregate demand curve would shift upward to AD_2 and the price level would rise to P_2 at point 2b. Both scenarios would end with the same level of real output, but the final price level would be higher under the expansionary fiscal policy (P_2) than under automatic adjustment (P_0).

The primary reason for using expansionary fiscal policy in such a situation is that empirical evidence suggests that sometimes the automatic adjustment mechanism may work slowly, leaving output and employment low for a long period. The fiscal-policy solution might be faster, at least ideally. However, as anyone who follows congressional debates on tax and spending policy knows, fiscal policy is hardly an instantaneous cure. In fact, many economists believe that by the time policy makers realize the need for an expansionary fiscal policy and implement it, the economy is likely to be well on the way to correcting itself through the admittedly slow process of price adjustment. If the expansionary policy arrives too late, the rightward shift of AD will push output above full employment and the price level will rise, as we saw in Figure 19.8.[14]

Automatic adjustment and expansionary fiscal policy lead the economy to the same level of real output in Figure 19.9, but the two alternatives imply different outcomes for other macroeconomic variables besides just the price level. Automatic adjustment lowers the price level to P_0, generates a real currency depreciation, improves the competitiveness of the country's export goods in world markets and its import-competing goods in domestic markets, and leads toward a surplus on the current account. Expansionary fiscal policy, on the other hand, raises the price level to P_2. The current account moves toward a deficit as the real currency appreciation makes domestic goods less competitive in world markets; public expenditure rises to offset the decline in net exports of goods and services. These effects imply that various interest groups within the economy are likely to disagree about the appropriate policy.

19.7.2 Monetary Policy

We learned in Chapter Seventeen that monetary policy can't affect income with a fixed price level, a fixed exchange rate, and perfectly mobile capital. This conclusion continues to hold when we introduce price flexibility. Recall that the economy's aggregate demand curve is drawn for a given value of the nominal money stock (see section 19.3.2). An open market purchase that attempts a one-time permanent expansion of the nominal money stock puts downward pressure on the interest rate and causes a capital outflow. The resulting balance-of-payments deficit requires foreign exchange market intervention by the central bank to supply foreign exchange. Foreign exchange reserves fall, and the money stock returns to its original level. Graphically, an open market purchase can shift the aggregate demand curve to the right (raising output and prices) only for the brief interval between the initial expansionary policy and the offsetting loss of foreign exchange reserves.

---

14 We ignore some economists' even more fundamental argument that fiscal policy cannot shift the AD curve. The simplest version of this view (known as *Ricardian equivalence*) is that increased government expenditures must imply eventual increased taxes to pay for them. When individuals in the economy realize that a rise in government spending means higher future taxes, they reduce consumption expenditures to save to cover their expected tax liability. The reduction in consumption expenditures offsets the rise in government purchases, leaving total expenditures and aggregate demand unchanged.

Figure 19.9 **Expansionary Fiscal Policy versus Automatic Adjustment**

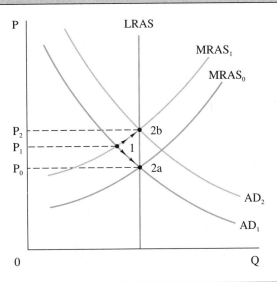

Beginning at point 1, expansionary fiscal policy brings the economy to a new long-run equilibrium at point 2b. Automatic adjustment leads to a long-run equilibrium at point 2a. In either case, the location of the long-run aggregate supply curve determines output. The equilibrium price level is higher in the case of expansionary fiscal policy (P_2) than in that of automatic adjustment (P_0).

Unlike the fiscal policy case, the pessimistic outlook for monetary policy with perfectly mobile capital doesn't depend on the output at which the policy experiment begins. Even if current output lies to the left of the LRAS curve, where the economy operates at less-than-full employment, the balance-of-payments constraint on the money stock still prevents monetary policy from affecting income. This does *not* mean, however, that the economy remains stuck at low levels of output and employment indefinitely.

Again, price flexibility eventually restores output to its long-run, full-employment level. Output remains below that level only as long as input prices fail to decline or the actual price level remains below the expected price level. As information about the price level spreads and input-price adjustments occur, the medium-run aggregate supply curve shifts downward to restore a long-run equilibrium. Therefore, as long as the price level is flexible, the **price adjustment mechanism** pushes output toward its long-run level, though not necessarily quickly. As for the balance of payments, the fixed exchange rate implies that the money stock adjusts—through changes in foreign exchange reserves—to equate the balance of payments.

19.7.3 **Exchange Rate Policy**

A third type of possible macroeconomic policy under a fixed exchange rate involves a permanent change in the exchange rate, such as a devaluation. Figure 19.10 illustrates the medium- and long-run effects of a devaluation.

The story begins at point 1 with the economy in long-run equilibrium. A devaluation shifts the aggregate demand curve to the right from AD_1 to AD_2.[15] At point 2, the rise in the price level from P_1 to P_2 has reduced the real money stock, placed upward pressure on interest rates, and generated a capital inflow. The combination of the capital inflow and the move toward a surplus on the current account due to the devaluation implies that the balance of payments exhibits a surplus at point 2. In the medium run, export and import-competing sectors gain from the decline in the relative price of domestically produced goods and services.

---

15 See section 19.3.2 for a review of the reasons why.

Figure 19.10 **Effect of a Devaluation with Flexible Prices, Fixed Exchange Rates, and Perfectly Mobile Capital**

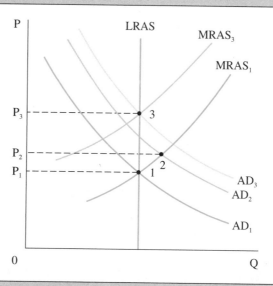

Beginning at point 1, a devaluation of the domestic currency lowers the relative price of domestic goods and services and switches expenditure toward them. The aggregate demand curve shifts to the right from AD_1 to AD_2. At point 2, the balance of payments is in surplus due to the devaluation. Intervention in the foreign exchange market increases the domestic money supply, and the aggregate demand curve shifts further to the right. The medium-run aggregate supply curve moves upward; long-run equilibrium is restored at point 3.

Under the fixed exchange rate regime, the central bank must intervene to buy foreign exchange, and the money stock rises with the accumulation of foreign exchange reserves. Aggregate demand shifts further to the right to AD_3. Output above full employment puts upward pressure on input prices, and the expected price level adjusts upward as information about rising prices spreads. These developments shift MRAS upward from $MRAS_1$ to $MRAS_3$. The new long-run equilibrium is at point 3. The domestic nominal money stock and the domestic price level have risen proportionally with the exchange rate. The real money stock remains unchanged (*Why?*), as do the relative price of domestic and foreign goods (*Why?*) and the interest rate (*Why?*). In the long run, distribution within the domestic economy as well as the overall level of output returns to its original configuration.[16]

What about the effects of a devaluation implemented when the economy's output has fallen below full employment? A devaluation can restore output to its full-employment level, but only by generating a rise in the price level. The devaluation shifts the AD curve to the right by lowering the relative price of domestic goods and services, or causing a short-run real devaluation, and shifting the current account toward a surplus. As the price level begins to rise, the real money stock falls, putting upward pressure on the domestic interest rate. Capital inflows add to the balance-of-payments surplus and require the central bank to intervene by buying foreign currency. The resulting increase in the domestic nominal money stock shifts the aggregate demand curve further to the right. The process ends when output is back at its full-employment level, on the long-run aggregate supply curve. The devaluation's long-run effects include restoring full employment, increasing the domestic

16 We'll see that devaluations and revaluations under a fixed exchange rate regime have identical effects, respectively, as increases and decreases in the nominal money stock under a flexible exchange rate regime (section 19.9). This shouldn't come as a surprise, because a fixed exchange rate requires policy makers to surrender their ability to control the nominal money stock in order to control the exchange rate, whereas a flexible rate requires that they surrender control over the exchange rate to gain control over the nominal money stock.

money stock, increasing the central bank's foreign exchange reserves, and a long-run real devaluation, because the price level rises less than proportionally with the initial nominal devaluation.

The economy's response to a currency devaluation depends in part on the economy's history. When past policy has been overly expansionary and currency devaluations have been common responses to balance-of-payments crises, then a devaluation may cause foreign exchange market participants to expect further devaluations and inflation. If so, the medium-run aggregate supply curve may shift up further and more quickly following a devaluation, as input suppliers and firms try to protect themselves from losses due to future price increases. Then the response to the devaluation will be a bigger price increase and less growth in real output. However, if a country has a history of stable prices and past devaluations have been rare events, a devaluation is likely to have less effect on price expectations, keeping the medium-run aggregate supply curve more stable. Such conditions lead to a longer-lasting effect on real output from a currency devaluation.

19.7.4 Summary of Long-Run Policy Effects under Fixed Exchange Rates

Table 19.3 summarizes the long-run effects of one-time permanent fiscal, monetary, and exchange rate policies under a fixed exchange rate with perfectly mobile capital. The table assumes that the policies pursued are expansionary ones; switch the signs of all nonzero entries in the table to evaluate the effects of the corresponding contractionary policies. Note that whether the policy is initiated from a point of full employment affects the long-run impact of fiscal and exchange rate policies. Monetary policies, in contrast, have no long-run impact on any economic variable reported in the table regardless of whether the economy is initially operating at full employment. This result reflects the fact that in the long run, policy makers can't alter the size of the domestic money stock under a fixed exchange rate regime from the size consistent with balance-of-payments equilibrium.

19.8 Aggregate Demand under Flexible Exchange Rates

Just as under a fixed exchange rate regime, the aggregate demand curve under a flexible-rate regime captures the negative relationship between the domestic price level and the quantity demanded of domestic goods and services.[17] Due to differences in how the economy adjusts to disturbances under the two types of regime, however, there are minor differences in the aggregate demand curve for each system, primarily in the variables held constant along a given aggregate demand curve. We continue to assume that capital is perfectly mobile among countries.

Table 19.3 **Long-Run Effects of Expansionary Policies under a Fixed Exchange Rate**

Policy	Effect on					
	Q	P	i	e	R	CAB
Fiscal:						
Initiated on LRAS	0	+	0	0	+	−
Initiated to left of LRAS	+	+	0	0	+	−
Monetary:						
Initiated on LRAS	0	0	0	0	0	0
Initiated to left of LRAS	0	0	0	0	0	0
Exchange Rate:						
Initiated on LRAS	0	+[a]	0	+	0	0
Initiated to left of LRAS	+	+	0	+	−	+

[a]Proportional to initial policy.

---

17 In both cases, the aggregate demand curve incorporates the requirements for equilibrium in the goods, money, and foreign exchange markets; that is, the aggregate demand curve is derived from the IS, LM, and BOP curves. The chapter appendix illustrates the derivation.

19.8.1 The Slope of the Aggregate Demand Curve

The aggregate demand curve under a flexible exchange rate slopes downward for the same reasons that the aggregate demand curve under a fixed exchange rate does. First, a rise in the price level raises the relative price of domestic goods and shifts expenditure toward foreign goods. Second, a rise in the domestic price level (given the nominal money stock) lowers the real money stock, raises the domestic interest rate, lowers investment, and causes capital inflows and a currency appreciation.[18] Both mechanisms cause a rise in the price level to correspond with a fall in the quantity demanded of domestic goods and services. The difference in the aggregate demand curve under a flexible exchange rate arises because any change in the price level may result in a change in the exchange rate.[19] Each aggregate demand curve is drawn taking these exchange rate changes into account; thus, the exchange rate isn't held constant along an aggregate demand curve, as was the case under a fixed exchange rate system, but adjusts to maintain balance-of-payments equilibrium.

19.8.2 Shifts in the Aggregate Demand Curve

Although a number of variables are held constant along each aggregate demand curve, we'll focus on the effects of changes in the nominal money stock due to monetary policy and of changes in expenditure due to fiscal policy.

A one-time permanent increase in the nominal money stock (holding the price level constant) raises the real money stock and lowers the interest rate. The fall in the interest rate causes a capital outflow, which depreciates the domestic currency and lowers the relative price of domestic goods. This implies a larger quantity demanded of domestic goods *at each price level* when the nominal money stock rises, represented graphically by a rightward shift in the aggregate demand curve. *(Go through the logic in the opposite direction, beginning with a fall in the nominal money stock, to see why the result would be a leftward shift in AD.)*

It's tempting to conclude that a one-time permanent rise in government purchases would shift the AD curve to the right in a manner similar to the effect of a rise in the money stock. However, this conclusion would be incorrect: Such changes in government purchases have *no* effect on aggregate demand under a flexible exchange rate and perfect capital mobility. When government purchases rise, any expansionary effect on income raises the quantity demanded of money. But the money stock remains fixed, so the interest rate must rise to make individuals content with the available stock of real balances. With perfectly mobile capital, the rise in the interest rate brings in capital flows that appreciate the domestic currency and raise the relative price of domestic goods. Net exports respond to the rise in relative prices by falling enough to offset the initial increase in government purchases. Total demand remains unchanged, but spending shifts from the trade-oriented sector (export and import-competing industries) to the public sector.

19.9 Macroeconomic Policies under Flexible Exchange Rates

19.9.1 Automatic Adjustment Mechanisms

With both a flexible price level and a flexible exchange rate, the economy contains automatic adjustment mechanisms for bringing it into equilibrium on the long-run supply curve with balanced payments. The price level adjusts to equate the quantity demanded of domestic goods and services with the quantity supplied at full employment, and the exchange rate adjusts to bring the balance of payments into equilibrium.

As in the case of fixed exchange rates, the automatic adjustment mechanisms may work slowly, especially the price adjustment mechanism. This can be particularly troublesome when shocks push the economy to the left of the long-run aggregate supply curve, to low output and employment levels. In such a situation, the question again arises whether an expansionary macroeconomic policy can speed up the economy's movement toward long-run equilibrium, minimizing the loss of output and the costs of unemployment.

---

18 Since we continue to operate under the assumption of perfectly mobile capital, changes in the interest rate are incipient just as under a fixed exchange rate.

19 For details, see section 19A.2 in the chapter appendix.

19.9.2 Macroeconomic Policy

Within the aggregate demand–aggregate supply framework, a policy clearly must shift the aggregate demand curve if that policy is to affect income.[20] Section 19.8.2 argued that monetary but not fiscal policy can shift the aggregate demand curve under a flexible exchange rate and perfectly mobile capital. In fact, this is just another way of saying that with a fixed price level, monetary policy can affect income but fiscal policy can't. Recall that when the price level is fixed, aggregate demand completely determines income; so any policy that can shift aggregate demand can affect income as long as the price level is fixed. A one-time permanent fiscal expansion fails because it generates a nominal and real appreciation of the domestic currency that fully offsets the policy's potential effect on output.[21]

Fiscal policy is ruled out by its inability to shift the aggregate demand curve, so we'll concentrate on the possibility of using monetary policy. Beginning from a point of long-run equilibrium, consider the impact of an open market purchase that raises the nominal money stock and shifts the AD curve to the right, as illustrated in Figure 19.11. The rise in aggregate demand pushes up the price level. In the medium run, contractual rigidities may prevent some prices (for example, nominal wages) from adjusting quickly, and firms or individuals may mistake the price increase for a change in relative prices. Output climbs along MRAS$_1$.

What causes the quantity demanded of domestic goods to rise to match the temporarily higher output? Domestic goods become temporarily cheaper relative to foreign goods even though the domestic price level has risen. This is caused by the depreciation of the domestic currency. The relative price of domestic goods is

Figure 19.11 Effect of Expansionary Monetary Policy with Flexible Prices, Flexible Exchange Rates, and Perfectly Mobile Capital

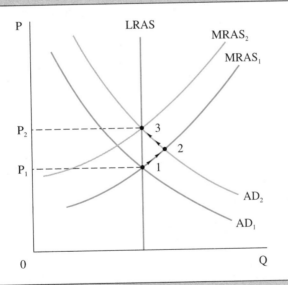

Beginning from a point of long-run equilibrium such as 1, expansionary monetary policy can raise output, but only temporarily. As individuals and firms recognize and adjust to the accompanying rise in the price level, output falls back to its original level. The policy's long-run effect consists solely of a proportional rise in the price level and a proportional depreciation of the domestic currency.

20 We ignore the possibility of "supply-side" policies that alter the position of the medium-run and/or long-run aggregate supply curve. Monetary and fiscal policy don't affect the supply curves directly, although they may shift the MRAS curve indirectly through their effects on the expected price level.

21 Note that under a fixed exchange rate, the real appreciation caused by a fiscal expansion works through a rise in P with no change in e. Under a flexible exchange rate, the real appreciation caused by a fiscal expansion works through a nominal appreciation with no change in P. See footnote 12.

defined as $R \equiv P/eP^*$, so a rise in e can more than offset a rise in P, lowering the relative price of domestic goods. We know from Chapter Eighteen (section 18.2) that in the long run, P and e must rise proportionally with M; in the short and medium runs, the price level lags behind, so the rise in e temporarily represents a real as well as a nominal depreciation.

The rise in output occurs either because of confusion over a change in the price level versus a change in the relative price that a firm receives for its output or because input prices fail to rise immediately. When firms and labor suppliers realize that the price level (including input prices) has risen and adjust their behavior accordingly, the medium-run supply curve shifts upward and output returns to its original level. As the price level rises to P_2, the relative price of domestic goods returns to its original level, with the total rise in P just matching the overall depreciation of the domestic currency and leaving R unchanged. The domestic interest rate also returns to its original level as the price level catches up with the increase in M. In the long run, the sole remaining effects of the expansionary monetary policy are a proportionally higher price level and a proportionally depreciated domestic currency. Note that these policy results match those of a currency devaluation under a fixed exchange rate.[22]

Exchange Rate Overshooting

The economy's adjustment to the new long-run equilibrium following an expansionary monetary policy reveals an interesting and important phenomenon known as exchange rate overshooting. **Overshooting** occurs when a variable responds to a disturbance more in the short or medium run than it does in the long run. Overshooting phenomena tend to occur whenever some variables adjust more quickly than others to a disturbance. Our model of the macroeconomy suggests that the exchange rate and interest rate adjust more quickly than do prices, which tend to be somewhat sluggish because of incomplete information and long-term contracts. In the case of a one-time permanent monetary expansion under a flexible exchange rate regime with perfectly mobile capital, the domestic currency depreciates sharply in the medium run and then undergoes a partially offsetting appreciation as the price level adjusts.

To understand exchange rate overshooting, we begin from the interest parity condition and trace the effect of the expansionary monetary policy on each of the relevant variables. Equation 19.1 repeats the uncovered interest parity condition from section 12.4:

$$i - i^* = (e^e - e)/e \qquad \text{[19.1]}$$

For simplicity, we assume that the story begins at a point where $e^e = e$ and, therefore, $i = i^*$. The foreign interest rate, i^*, remains constant throughout the whole process. The monetary policy is recognized as permanent, so the expected exchange rate, e^e, moves immediately to its new long-run level, which equals the value that the actual exchange rate will have at the new long-run equilibrium (point 3 in Figure 19.11). In the medium run following the monetary expansion, i falls because P rises by less than M, resulting in a rise in the real money stock. But if $i < i^*$ at point 2, it must be true that $e > e^e$ at point 2. *(Why?)* Since e^e equals the new long-run equilibrium value of e at point 3, it follows that e is higher at point 2 than at point 3. The monetary expansion generates a medium-run depreciation of the domestic currency that exceeds the long-run depreciation. In other words, the domestic currency *appreciates* in the adjustment from point 2 to point 3.

Why does overshooting depend on the slow adjustment of the price level? If the monetary expansion pushed the price level immediately to P_2, the real money supply wouldn't rise, even in the medium run. The domestic interest rate wouldn't fall below the foreign interest rate, and a period of expected appreciation ($e > e^e$) wouldn't be necessary to maintain interest parity.

Again the outlook for expansionary monetary policy beginning from a point of long-run equilibrium is pessimistic. However, a more important issue concerns its ability to move the economy to equilibrium from a point of low output and employment to the left of the long-run aggregate supply curve. Figure 19.12 demonstrates that expansionary monetary policy can move the economy into equilibrium, but only at the cost of a rise in the price level. At point 1, the economy suffers from low output and employment. An expansionary monetary policy shifts the AD curve to the right. The price level rises, and output returns to its long-run level at point 2a. The

---

22 See footnote 16.

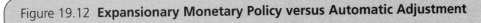

Figure 19.12 Expansionary Monetary Policy versus Automatic Adjustment

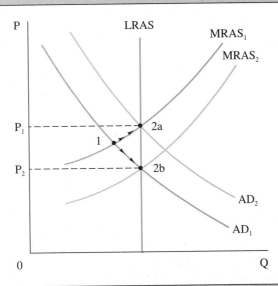

Beginning from point 1, expansionary monetary policy leads to a long-run equilibrium at point 2a with price level P_1. Automatic adjustment leads to a long-run equilibrium at 2b with price level P_2.

alternate course involves reliance on the economy's automatic adjustment mechanism. In that case, below-full-employment output at point 1 eventually causes input prices to fall and individuals in the economy to adjust downward their price-level expectations. The medium-run supply curve shifts downward, restoring output to its long-run level at point 2b—at a price level lower than that in the case of expansionary monetary policy.

19.9.3 Summary of Long-Run Policy Effects under Flexible Exchange Rates

Table 19.4 summarizes the long-run effects of one-time permanent expansionary fiscal and monetary policies under a flexible exchange rate, flexible prices, and perfectly mobile capital.[23] Fiscal policy exerts no long-run effects on output, the price level, or the interest rate. An expansionary fiscal policy generates a nominal and real appreciation of the domestic currency that shifts the current account toward a deficit and reduces other expenditure, in particular net exports, by the amount of the initial fiscal expansion.

Monetary policy, in contrast, can affect output, although only if instituted after some disturbance has pushed the economy away from long-run equilibrium. Otherwise, expansionary monetary policy leads only to a proportional increase in the price level and the nominal exchange rate, with no effect on output, the real exchange rate, or the current-account balance.

19.10 Supply Shocks

So far, we've considered how the macroeconomy responds to shifts in the aggregate *demand* curve, shifts that may reflect either exogenous shocks or policy makers' efforts to influence the economy. We've assumed that the long-run aggregate supply curve remains stable throughout the adjustment process and that the medium-run

---

23 For contractionary policies, simply switch the signs of all nonzero entries in the table.

Table 19.4	**Long-Run Effects of Expansionary Policies under a Flexible Exchange Rate**					
	Effect on					
Policy	Q	P	i	e	R	CAB
Fiscal:						
Initiated on LRAS	0	0	0	–	+	–
Initiated to left of LRAS	0	0	0	–	+	–
Monetary:						
Initiated on LRAS	0	+[a]	0	+[a]	0	0
Initiated to left of LRAS	+	+	0	+	+	+

[a]Proportional to initial policy.

aggregate supply curve shifts as input prices and price expectations adjust up or down in response to shifts in aggregate demand. Our discussion thus far has ignored the second major source of macroeconomic disturbances and the second major set of events to which policy makers must respond: **supply shocks.** Such shocks include any event that alters the economy's long-run equilibrium productive capacity.[24] Any newspaper suggests many possible examples, such as earthquakes, floods, and wars. The OPEC oil embargoes of the 1970s, which dramatically increased the real price of petroleum, provide the most famous case examined by macroeconomists. For now, we focus on the effects of a generic supply shock.

Point 1 in Figure 19.13 represents an economy in long-run equilibrium at the intersection of AD_0, $MRAS_0$, and $LRAS_0$. Output is at its full-employment level, Q_0; all prices have adjusted fully to long-run equilibrium in their respective markets, with an overall price level of P_1. Now suppose an adverse supply shock hits the economy and reduces its ability to produce goods and services. Both the medium-run and long-run supply curves shift to the left, although the relative magnitudes of the two shifts depends on the exact nature of the shock.

If policy makers don't respond right away to the decline in supply, the economy moves to point 2, at the intersection of the original aggregate demand curve and the new medium-run aggregate supply curve, $MRAS_1$. The price level rises sharply to P_2. The increase in price cuts the quantity demanded of domestic goods and services, along AD_0, to match the curtailed supply. This combination of rising prices and declining output often is called **stagflation,** a combination of stagnating real output and a rising price level or inflation.

What happens next depends on if and how policy makers respond. We can outline four basic possibilities, ranging from the most passive to the most active responses. First, macroeconomic policy makers can choose to do nothing to alter aggregate demand. From point 2, to the left of the new long-run aggregate supply curve, $LRAS_1$, input prices would fall in response to the less-than-full-employment level of output. The medium-run aggregate supply curve eventually would shift down with input prices, and a new long-run equilibrium would occur at point 3a. Output would be lower than prior to the supply shock, but this is inevitable; the price level (P_a) would be higher.

A more active response by policy makers would involve an expansionary policy to shift aggregate demand to the right to AD_1, rather than waiting for unemployment and falling input prices to shift the medium-run aggregate supply curve down. An expansionary policy would restore long-run equilibrium at point 3b. Again, real output is lower than before the shock; the price level rises to P_b, more than in the case where policy makers chose to avoid an expansionary policy.

Policy makers also might follow an even more aggressively expansionary policy in an attempt to restore real output to its preshock value. By shifting aggregate demand all the way up to AD_2, they could accomplish this goal at point 3c, but only temporarily. The new postshock, full-employment output is Q_1, not Q_0, so their

---

24 Temporary supply shocks that shift the medium-run supply curve to the left but leave the long-run supply curve unaffected also are possible. We restrict our attention to supply shocks that influence the economy's long-run ability to produce goods and services.

Figure 19.13 **An Adverse Supply Shock and Potential Policy Responses**

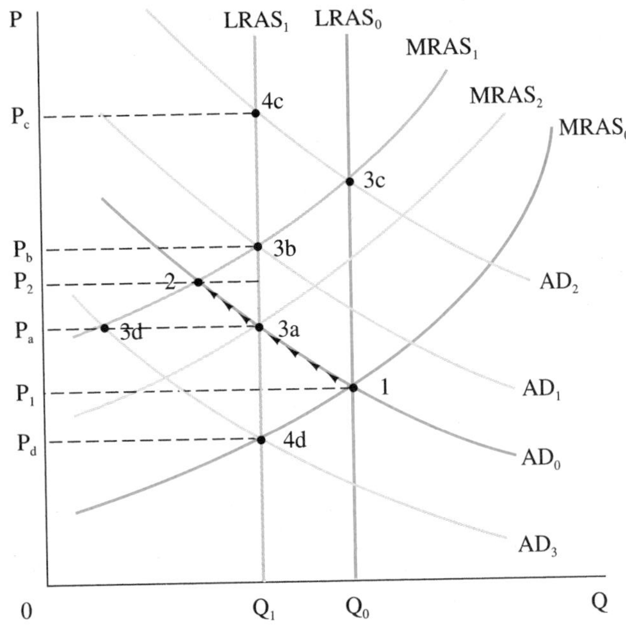

An adverse supply shock shifts the medium- and long-run aggregate supply curves to the left. Policy makers can choose from several policy options. First, they can leave AD unchanged at AD_0, so the new long-run equilibrium occurs at point 3a. Second, they can expand AD to AD_1 to speed the economy's return to full employment at point 3b, but such a policy raises prices. Third, policy makers can expand AD by more (to AD_2) and push output back to its preshock level, but only temporarily. The long-term cost of this aggressively expansionary policy is a much higher price level at point 4c. Finally, policy makers can contract AD to AD_3 and restore long-run equilibrium at point 4d. This keeps prices down but may require an extended period of exacerbated unemployment (at 3d). Regardless of policy makers' choice, the new long-run, full-employment output is at the lower Q_1.

attempts to keep output at Q_0 eventually push the price level up to P_c as the medium-run aggregate supply curve shifts up. Point 4c denotes the new long-run equilibrium under this scenario.

A final possibility involves policy makers pursuing policies designed to prevent the supply shock from generating a rise in the price level. For example, beginning from point 2, they could *cut* aggregate demand to AD_3. In the medium run, output would fall even further, to point 3d. Eventually, as input prices and price expectations adjusted, the MRAS curve would shift down and the economy would reach a new long-run equilibrium at point 4d, with prices at P_d, slightly below the preshock value.

The four policy paths just outlined suggest the menu of possibilities that policy makers faced in the aftermath of the OPEC oil embargoes of 1973–1974 and 1979–1980. The first shock, during which oil prices quadrupled, occurred shortly after the breakdown of the Bretton Woods system of pegged exchange rates. Many economists believe that exchange rate flexibility played an important role in facilitating adjustment to the shocks. Under a fixed-rate system, countries' abilities to choose among the various policy responses would have been constrained by the need to intervene in foreign exchange markets to prevent appreciations or depreciations of their currencies. Alternatively, a system of fixed exchange rates would have ruled out monetary policy as a tool for shifting aggregate demand in response to the supply shocks. But because exchange rates were flexible, most countries responded with monetary policies, although the degrees of expansion pursued by different countries varied substantially.

CASE ONE:
Unemployment—Structural and Cyclical

Economists distinguish at least two types of unemployment: structural and cyclical. Structural unemployment refers to individuals who lack jobs for long periods of time, despite looking for work, because of mismatches between their location or skills and the location or skill requirements of available job openings. This type of unemployment doesn't directly depend on the stage of the business cycle. A steel worker might be unemployed in Gary, Indiana, even during an economic boom when lots of job openings exist for computer programmers in Seattle. Cyclical unemployment, on the other hand, counts individuals who lack jobs because the economy

operates at less than its full-employment level of real output, or to the left of its long-run aggregate supply curve.

Actual unemployment rates vary significantly across countries; this variation reflects differences both in structural unemployment rates and in the timing of countries' economic booms and recessions. Figure 19.14 reports 1999 unemployment rates for 21 developed-country members of the Organization for Economic Cooperation and Development plus for the 11-member euro area.

The height of the bar for each country represents its structural unemployment rate. In terms of our aggregate demand–

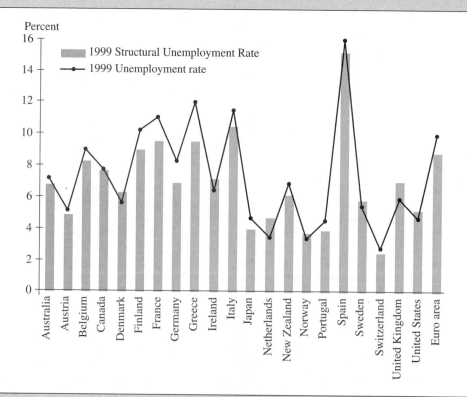

Figure 19.14 **Unemployment Rates' Structural and Cyclical Components, 1999 (Percent of Labor Force)**

Each country's actual unemployment rate (illustrated by the black dot) can be decomposed into a structural component (the shaded bar) and a cyclical component (the difference between the height of the bar and that of the line).

Source: Data from Organization for Economic Cooperation and Development.

aggregate supply model from the chapter, the structural unemployment rate is the one that corresponds to real output on the LRAS curve. The reported rates vary from less than 4 percent for Norway, Portugal, and Switzerland to over 10 percent for Italy and over 15 percent for Spain, with most countries falling in the 5–10 percent range. The black dots in Figure 19.14 report each country's actual unemployment rate, including both the structural and cyclical components. These rates vary from about 3 percent to over 10 percent, with most in the 5–10 percent range. Note that structural unemployment accounts for the vast majority of the total for every country. The cyclical component of unemployment rarely makes up more than 1.5 percent. Most countries in the figure exhibit positive cyclical unemployment; that is, they operated to the left of their respective LRASs in 1999. A few countries—Canada, Denmark, Ireland, the Netherlands, Norway, Sweden, the United Kingdom, and the United States—had negative cyclical unemployment, or actual unemployment less than

structural unemployment. These countries were in the midst of economic booms in 1999 and operated to the right of their LRASs.

Many western European economies have had high rates of structural unemployment for several decades; policy makers have started to focus on policies to bring those rates down. Such policies include job training, imposing job-search requirements for receipt of public-assistance and unemployment benefits, eliminating labor-market inflexibilities such as restrictions on firms' abilities to reassign workers or reduce their workforces, and shifting wage bargaining from the national to the local or firm level. During the 1990s, countries such as Ireland and the Netherlands succeeded in reducing their structural unemployment rates substantially, as mentioned in Table 19.5. Finland, Sweden, and several other European economies, on the other hand, continue to see their structural rates increase.

Table 19.5 **Structural Unemployment in the OECD, 1990–1999 (Percent of Labor Force)**

	1990	1999
Structural unemployment increased in the 1990s in:		
Finland	5.6%	9.0%
Germany	5.3	6.9
Greece	8.4	9.5
Italy	9.1	10.4
Japan	2.2	4.0
Sweden	3.8	5.8
Structural unemployment remained stable in the 1990s in:		
Australia	6.5%	6.8%
Austria	4.6	4.9
Belgium	8.4	8.2
Denmark	6.9	6.3
France	9.3	9.5
New Zealand	7.0	6.1
Norway	4.6	3.7
Portugal	4.8	3.9
Switzerland	3.0	2.4
United States	5.4	5.2
Structural unemployment decreased in the 1990s in:		
Canada	9.0%	7.7%
Ireland	14.1	7.1
Netherlands	7.5	4.7
Spain	17.4	15.1
United Kingdom	8.6	7.0

Source: Data from Organization for Economic Cooperation and Development.

CASE TWO:
Government Budgets—Structural and Cyclical

Unemployment isn't the only variable that economists divide into structural and cyclical components. The same division applies to government budgets. Suppose we look at a government's budget, T − G, where T denotes net taxes (or, tax revenues minus transfer payments) and G denotes government purchases of goods and services. The budget is in surplus if T − G is positive and in deficit if the difference is negative. Now suppose we look at the government budget for a mythical country that never conducts active fiscal policy by altering either T or G to affect output, unemployment, or prices. Even in the absence of such activist policy, the government budget still would vary over the business cycle. During a recession, tax revenue, which depends positively on income, would fall and transfer payments, especially unemployment benefits and public-assistance payments, would rise as more individuals found themselves out of work and in financial hardship. So, other things being equal, recessions tend to shift the government budget toward a deficit. This effect is often called an *automatic stabilizer* because it acts as an automatic expansionary fiscal policy to offset the recession. Booms, on the other hand, tend to produce more tax revenue as incomes rise and to reduce demands for unemployment and public-assistance benefits. So booms tend to move the government budget toward a surplus, which in turn exerts a needed contractionary effect on the booming economy to avoid inflation.

The government *structural budget* refers to what the deficit or surplus would be without these cyclical effects—in other words, what the budget would be given current fiscal policies if the economy were operating *on* its LRAS curve. The *cyclical* component of the budget measures the remainder, or the portion that results from the effects of the business cycle. When governments conduct active expansionary

or contractionary fiscal policy, they affect the structural budget. A shift of the structural budget toward surplus means a contractionary policy; and a shift toward deficit represents policy expansion.

Figure 19.15 traces Japanese fiscal policy through the 1990s. Panel (a) illustrates the structural and cyclical budgets as a percent of GDP. During 1990–1992, the structural budget was in surplus (T > G), and the cyclical component added to that surplus. In 1993, the structural budget shifted to a deficit (meaning that policy was deliberately expansionary) and the cyclical component also showed a deficit as the economy fell into a slump. As of the eve of the Asian financial crisis in 1996–1997, the structural budget continued to be in a deficit, but the cyclical component showed a tiny surplus. Once the financial crisis hit, deliberate fiscal expansion pushed the structural budget further into deficit, and the weakening economy caused a cyclical deficit as well.

Panel (b) translates this information into a commonly used measure of fiscal policy called *fiscal stance*. A government's fiscal stance is the *change* in its structural government budget expressed as a percent of GDP. When the structural budget moves toward a deficit, fiscal policy is expansionary; a move toward a structural surplus signals contractionary policy. Figure 19.15 reveals that Japanese fiscal policy was mildly expansionary until 1997, when it turned sharply contractionary as a result of a sizable tax increase. The Japanese economy already stood at the brink of recession, and the fiscal contraction pushed further in that direction. The Japanese government faced strong pressure from trading partners and international economic organizations to cut taxes and move its fiscal policy stance in the expansionary direction, which it did in 1998 and 1999.[25]

CASE THREE:
Greasing the World Economy

When policy makers or international organizations such as the International Monetary Fund or Organization for Economic Cooperation and Development (OECD) forecast the world economy's likely performance, oil prices always enter

the discussion. The OPEC oil embargo of 1973–1974 dramatically raised the real price of oil, and it also dramatically affected the way macroeconomists think about and model the world macroeconomy. In particular, the embargo's

---

25 Case One in Chapter Seventeen contains more about recent macroeconomic policy in Japan.

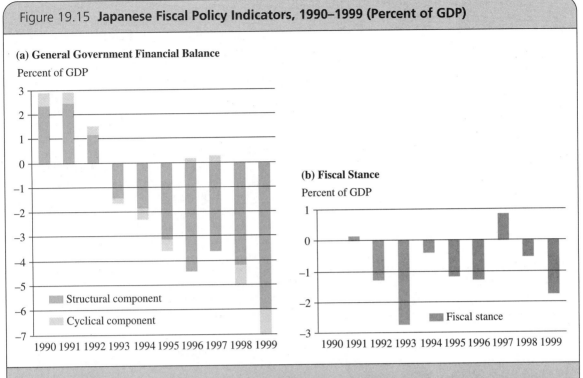

Figure 19.15 **Japanese Fiscal Policy Indicators, 1990–1999 (Percent of GDP)**

After several years of expansionary policy, Japan's fiscal policy stance turned contractionary in 1997 when the government increased taxes. The economy deteriorated, and the government resumed its expansionary fiscal policies.

Source: Data from Organization for Economic Cooperation and Development.

stagflationary impact on oil-importing economies brought the aggregate demand–aggregate supply model, which could explain such effects, to the forefront of analysis. Many things have changed since the 1970s. OPEC members now produce only about 40 percent of total oil supply, and the industrial countries depend far less on imported oil. But oil prices still play an important role in determining how the world macroeconomy functions.

During the late 1990s, oil prices once again displayed more than the usual amount of volatility. From around $25 per barrel in early 1997, the price sank to below $11 by early 1999; by 2000, the price had risen to $38.50. Both the decline and the rise that quickly followed reflected developments on both sides of the oil market. In early 1997 OPEC oil producers, operating in an environment of rapid economic growth and rising demand for oil, deliberately increased output. As more oil hit the market, the onset of the Asian financial crisis cut demand for oil. The combination of increased supply and decreased demand sent prices down sharply. By early 1999, oil-producing countries were suffering the economic effects of such low oil prices—including reduced rates of growth, rising current-account deficits, and growing government budget deficits. So both OPEC and several non-OPEC producers (Mexico, Norway, Oman, and Russia) agreed to cut production by a total of about 7 percent. Just as the supply cuts hit the market, the world economy, especially Asia, began to recover, and the combination of reduced supply and increased demand pushed prices to near $40 per barrel.

By early 2000, even oil exporters worried about the effect of the sharp price increases on the world economy, so OPEC agreed to increase production and informally to try to hold the price of oil in the $22–$28-per-barrel range. Several more agreements to increase production followed throughout 2000. However, with the exceptions of Saudi Arabia, Kuwait, the United Arab Emirates, Iran, and Mexico, producers already were pumping close to their short-run capacities. This made OPEC agreements to boost output difficult to reach, because members already producing at capacity had little to gain and much to lose by voting for an output increase.

How do oil-price changes such as those of 1998–2000 affect the world macroeconomy? They shift income between oil-producing and oil-importing countries. These shifts typically amount to less than 1 percent of GDP for most importing countries. The industrial economies, in particular, experience smaller effects from oil-price changes now than during the

1970s (when effects were 2–3 percent of GDP) because those economies have substantially reduced their dependence on imported oil. For example, members of the OECD now import about half the amount of oil per unit of output that they did in 1972. Another reason the shifts in income are relatively small is the fact that the oil-exporting countries typically spend about 75 percent of their increased oil revenues within three years, largely on imports from the industrial economies. Oil-importing developing countries, on the other hand, typically don't enjoy this offsetting benefit of higher oil prices because they don't export many goods to the oil exporters.

Oil prices also alter the costs of producing and transporting most goods. This is why macroeconomists represent an oil-price increase as a shift to the left of the MRAS curve. Other things equal, real output falls and the price level rises.[26] How big this effect is depends in large part on whether the initial price increase leads to higher wages or to a higher expected price level; either development increases the inflationary effect of the initial oil-price increase. Early analyses suggest that these secondary effects are likely to be smaller now than during earlier episodes of rising oil prices. Wage-indexation policies, in which wages automatically rise in response to any increase in the price level, have largely disappeared, at least in the industrial countries. Price-level expectations are less likely to rise now that citizens of most countries perceive that their policy makers have learned valuable lessons about the inflationary dangers of responding to supply shocks with overly expansionary monetary policies. So far, the increased oil prices of 1999–2000 have pushed up inflation rates in the industrial economies, but by modest amounts compared to experience during the 1970s.

Table 19.6 reports the OECD's estimates of the key macroeconomic effects of possible changes in the oil market. The OECD used its macroeconomic model, INTERLINK, to ask the question: If oil prices fell to $17.50 a barrel or rose to $38.50 a barrel, what would happen to real GDP and inflation rates in the major industrial economies? The answer: Lower oil prices do mean more output and lower inflation, while higher oil prices generate less output and higher inflation. But even the hypothesized large changes in oil prices suggested annual changes of no more than 0.5 percent for either output or inflation.

Table 19.6 OECD Oil Price Scenarios (Percent)

	Oil Price Falls to $17.50		Oil Price Rises to $38.50	
	2001	2002	2001	2002
Real GDP Level:				
United States	0.3%	0.3%	−0.3%	−0.2%
Japan	0.4	0.6	−0.4	−0.4
Euro area	0.4	0.4	−0.4	−0.2
OECD total	0.3	0.4	−0.3	−0.2
Consumer Price Inflation:				
United States	−0.5%	−0.3%	0.5%	0.2%
Japan	−0.5	−0.2	0.4	0.1
Euro area	−0.5	−0.4	0.5	0.2
OECD total	−0.5	−0.3	0.5	0.2

Source: Organization for Economic Cooperation and Development.

Summary

The introduction of price flexibility in this chapter has three major implications:

1. The economy now contains an automatic adjustment mechanism for bringing output to its long-run equilibrium level at full employment, unlike the situations of potentially chronic internal imbalance in Chapters Sixteen and Seventeen.

---

26 As we saw in section 19.10, whether these effects are temporary or permanent depends on the duration of the price increase and on how policy makers respond.

2. The remaining effective tools of macroeconomic policy (fiscal and exchange rate policy under fixed exchange rates, and monetary policy under flexible exchange rates) can permanently increase output *only* if the economy is operating temporarily to the left of the long-run aggregate supply curve and then *only* by raising the price level.
3. Expansionary macroeconomic policy, if pursued beginning from a point of long-run equilibrium, can permanently affect only the price level, not the level of real output or employment.

Table 19.7 summarizes the policy results derived in the chapter.

Looking Ahead

We've seen that macroeconomic policies' effectiveness depends critically on the exchange rate regime under which the economy operates. Recall from Chapters Sixteen and Seventeen that countries manage their exchange rates in a variety of ways, ranging from a fixed to a purely flexible exchange rate. Chapter Twenty traces recent macroeconomic history, considers the major arguments regarding the choice of exchange rate regime, and explores several possible arrangements other than a simple fixed or flexible rate.

Key Terms

inflation
deflation
aggregate demand curve
aggregate supply
short run
medium run
long run
long-run aggregate supply curve

medium-run aggregate supply curve
perfectly mobile capital
automatic adjustment mechanisms
price adjustment mechanism
overshooting
supply shocks
stagflation

Table 19.7 **Policy Effectiveness with Flexible Prices and Capital Mobility**

Policy	Fixed-Rate Regime	Flexible-Rate Regime
If instituted beginning at point of long-run equilibrium:		
Fiscal:		
Medium run	Effective[a]	Ineffective
Long run	Ineffective[a]	Ineffective
Monetary:		
Medium run	Ineffective	Effective[a]
Long run	Ineffective	Ineffective[a]
If instituted at point to left of long-run equilibrium:		
Fiscal:		
Medium run	Effective[a]	Ineffective
Long run	Effective[a]	Ineffective
Monetary:		
Medium run	Ineffective	Effective[a]
Long run	Ineffective	Effective[a]

[a]Results accompanied by changes in the price level.

Problems and Questions for Review

1. Use the aggregate demand–aggregate supply model to analyze the following policy dispute concerning an open economy with perfectly mobile capital and a fixed exchange rate. The economy currently operates at a long-run equilibrium, including the balance of payments.
    a. *Policy maker 1:* "We need to expand real output and lower the unemployment rate. If only we had a flexible exchange rate, we could undertake an expansionary monetary policy that would have the desired effect. But since our exchange rate is fixed, there's no way we can expand our money stock."
    b. *Policy maker 2:* "There are two things wrong with your argument. First, it *is* possible to increase our money stock even though our exchange rate is fixed; all we have to do is devalue our currency. Second, if we follow such a policy, the increase in real output and decrease in unemployment will be a medium-run effect only. In the long run, all it will accomplish is a rise in the price level."
2. This question asks you to examine the relationship between an economy's openness and the effects of fiscal policy.
    a. Country A is a closed economy. It engages in no transactions with other countries, so its current-account and capital-account balances always equal zero. Country A pursues an expansionary fiscal policy of cutting taxes and increasing government purchases. Illustrate and explain the effects of the policy on real output and on the price level in the medium run and in the long run. What is the effect on the interest rate? What are the long-run distributional effects of the policy?
    b. Country B is an open economy. It engages in trade in goods, services, and financial assets. It operates under a flexible exchange rate regime and has perfectly mobile capital. Country B pursues an expansionary fiscal policy of cutting taxes and increasing government purchases. Illustrate and explain the effects of the policy on real output and on the price level in the medium run and in the long run. What is the effect on the interest rate? What are the long-run distributional effects of the policy?
    c. Compare the effects of expansionary fiscal policies in countries A and B. (Assume that both countries follow identical, neutral monetary policies that can be ignored for purposes of this analysis.) As an economy becomes more open, how do the effects (especially the distributional effects) of fiscal policy change?
    d. In the early 1980s, the United States followed an expansionary fiscal policy of lower taxes and increased government purchases. Policy makers seemed surprised by two characteristics of the period, in comparison with earlier experience. First, the U.S. trade balance moved sharply into deficit. Second, private investment remained relatively high. Given your answers to parts (a), (b), and (c), can you explain the two observations? Should they have come as a surprise?

One of the major events in the international economic system was the unification of Germany and the accompanying macroeconomic adjustment. The next two questions ask you to analyze two aspects of that process.

3. One aspect of unification that had to be dealt with was the East German currency, the ostmark, which had been nonconvertible. Black market prices suggested that the market value of the ostmark relative to other currencies was about 10 percent of its official (East German) price or exchange rate. As a part of unification, (West) Germany decided to intervene in the foreign exchange market to buy up the ostmarks. But policy makers had to decide at what price to purchase the currency. Consider three possibilities: (i) Buy the ostmarks at the black market price of approximately DM0.08 per ostmark, (ii) buy the ostmarks at the official East German exchange rate of DM1.00 per ostmark, or (iii) buy the ostmarks at an intermediate value of, say, DM0.50 per ostmark.
    a. Write the expression for a country's money stock as a function of the assets held by the central bank.
    b. What would be the effects of the three cases of intervention listed above on the German money stock? (*Hint:* Remember that the foreign exchange reserve component of the monetary base is expressed in units of the *domestic* currency [the DM in the case of West Germany]. For example, if the U.S. Federal Reserve buys one pound sterling at an exchange rate of two dollars per pound, the foreign exchange reserve component of the U.S. monetary base rises by two dollars.)
    c. Assume that Germany decided to go with option (ii) and exchanged ostmarks for Deutsche marks at a one-for-one exchange rate. This might raise serious questions about inflation in historically inflation-conscious Germany. Illustrate and explain the logic behind this concern. Assume that unified Germany uses a flexible exchange rate and has perfectly mobile capital.

4. A second aspect of German unification concerned the supply or production side of the economy. East German factories were notoriously inefficient after years of central planning. Before unification, East German workers were paid in ostmarks. After unification, those same workers were to be paid in Deutsche marks. Again, a decision had to be made how to translate ostmark-denominated wages into DM-denominated wages. This question asks you to analyze the macroeconomic effects of a decision to translate wages on a one-for-one basis; in other words, a worker who previously made 100 ostmarks per week now would be paid 100 DM per week.
    a. Remember that the real value of DM is much higher than the real value of ostmarks; therefore, the one-for-one wage policy is equivalent to a large increase in real wages. Illustrate and explain the effects on real output and the price level of the change from ostmark wages to DM wages in the medium run. (*Hint:* How does a rise in real wages or other input prices affect the aggregate demand–aggregate supply model?)
    b. After unification, Germany had relatively high unemployment, particularly in the "new states" of former East Germany. Is this surprising, or not, given your analysis in part (a)? Can you think of a wage policy (that is, an alternative to the one-for-one translation of ostmark wages into Deutsche mark wages) that might have resulted in less unemployment? Explain.
    c. Given the one-for-one translation of wages, what adjustments would you expect to occur in the long run? Explain.

5. The countries of USia and Germania have flexible price levels, flexible exchange rates, and perfectly mobile capital.
    a. The USia economy currently operates to the left of its long-run aggregate supply curve. USia has a large government debt, so policy makers decide to pursue expansionary monetary policy rather than fiscal policy. Illustrate, showing the initial position, the effect of the policy, and the new long-run equilibrium. Explain.
    b. The Germania economy currently operates to the left of its long-run aggregate supply curve. Residents of Germania, for historical reasons, have an aversion to inflation. Germania has just undertaken political unification with a less-developed neighbor, and the unification involved substantial expansion of government purchases of goods and services. Because of the expansionary fiscal policy, Germania's policy makers decide to hold the money stock constant rather than pursue expansionary monetary policy. Illustrate, showing the initial position, the effect of the fiscal policy, and the new long-run equilibrium. Explain.
    c. Using your answers to parts (a) and (b), what would you expect to happen to the exchange rate between USia's currency (the dollie) and Germania's currency (the markie) in the medium run? What would you predict about the two countries' current and capital accounts? Explain.

6. Country A's government is running an actual budget surplus of $10 billion. The government's cyclical budget surplus is $20 billion. Is country A experiencing a boom, a recession, or a period in which the country operates on its long-run aggregate supply curve? How do you know? The president of country A claims that the government's fiscal policy stance is perfectly appropriate given the business-cycle situation. Do you agree, and why?

7. This question asks you to analyze the effects of a currency devaluation.
    a. Trustia is a country with perfectly mobile capital and a long history of price stability. The government pegs Trustia's currency to the currency of an important trading partner. Trustia's policy makers, especially its central bankers, always do exactly what they say they will do. Unfortunately, Trustia's economy has fallen into a recession. Policy makers decide that the appropriate response is a permanent, one-time devaluation of Trustia's currency, and they announce and enact such a policy. Illustrate and explain the devaluation's likely effects on Trustia's economy.
    b. Messia is another country with perfectly mobile capital but a long history of high inflation. The government pegs Messia's currency to the currency of an important trading partner. Messia's policy makers, especially its central bankers, rarely do what they say they will do, and the country has a long history of failed economic reforms. Unfortunately, Messia's economy has fallen into a recession. Policy makers postpone a devaluation as long as possible and deny publicly that they are even considering one. Finally, the central bank runs short of foreign exchange reserves and is forced to devalue. Illustrate and explain the likely effects of the devaluation on Messia's economy.
    c. Based on your answers to parts (a) and (b), is devaluation an effective policy tool for an economy operating under a fixed exchange rate and a high degree of capital mobility? Why or why not?

8. Mediate the following dispute between two macroeconomic policy makers. The economy they're discussing operates under a flexible exchange rate and has perfectly mobile capital.

   a. *Policy maker 1:* "To increase real output, we should use expansionary fiscal policy. After all, the primary problem with fiscal policy is crowding out. But because our country has perfectly mobile capital, expansionary fiscal policy can't push up the interest rate and discourage investment. Therefore, any increase in government purchases or any cut in taxes will go directly into increased real output."

   b. *Policy maker 2:* "You need to review the notes from your undergraduate macroeconomics course. Fiscal policy never works under a flexible exchange rate with perfectly mobile capital—an ideal combination to generate complete crowding out."

References and Selected Readings

Baxter, M. "International Trade and Business Cycles." In *Handbook of International Economics,* Vol. 3, edited by G. M. Grossman and K. Rogoff, 1801–1864. Amsterdam: North-Holland, 1995.
Survey of empirical evidence on the relationship between macroeconomic cycles and international trade, especially real business cycles; intermediate to advanced.

Blinder, Alan S. "What Central Bankers Could Learn from Academics—and Vice Versa." *Journal of Economic Perspectives* (Spring 1997): 3–19.
An academic and former central banker's discussion of the relationship between models of monetary policy and actual central-banking problems; for all students.

Browne, L. E. "Does Japan Offer Any Lessons for the United States?" Federal Reserve Bank of Boston, *New England Economic Review* (2001), No. 3: 3-18.
Similarities and differences between Japan's economic downturns of the 1990s and the U.S. downturn of 2001.

Cooper, Richard N., and Jane Sneddon Little. "U.S. Monetary Policy in an Integrating World: 1960 to 2000." In *The Evolution of Monetary Policy and the Federal Reserve System over the Past Thirty Years,* edited by R. W. Kopcke and L. E. Browne, 77–130. Boston: Federal Reserve Bank of Boston, 2000.
History of international influences on U.S. monetary policy.

Croce, Enzo, and Mohsin S. Khan. "Monetary Regimes and Inflation Targeting." *Finance and Development* 37 (September 2000): 48–51.
The interconnection between monetary policy tools and targets and inflation.

Frankel, J. A., and A. K. Rose. "Empirical Research on Nominal Exchange Rates." In *Handbook of International Economics,* Vol. 3, edited by G. M. Grossman and K. Rogoff, 1689–1730. Amsterdam: North-Holland, 1995.
Survey of empirical evidence on exchange rate behavior; intermediate to advanced.

Froot, K., and K. Rogoff. "Perspectives on PPP and Long-Run Real Exchange Rates." In *Handbook of International Economics,* Vol. 3, edited by G. M. Grossman and K. Rogoff, 1647–1688. Amsterdam: North-Holland, 1995.
Survey of the literature and empirical evidence on long-run exchange rate behavior; intermediate to advanced.

Fuhrer, Jeffrey C., and Scott Schuh. *Beyond Shocks: What Causes Business Cycles?* Boston: Federal Reserve Bank of Boston, 1998.
Collection of papers on causes of business cycles; most accessible to all students.

Garber, P., and L. Svensson. "The Operation and Collapse of Fixed Exchange Rate Regimes." In *Handbook of International Economics,* Vol. 3, edited by G. M. Grossman and K. Rogoff, 1865–1912. Amsterdam: North-Holland, 1995.
Survey of how fixed exchange rate regimes work—and fail; intermediate to advanced.

Isard, Peter. *Exchange Rate Economics.* Cambridge: Cambridge University Press, 1995.
Survey of the literature on exchange rates and the macroeconomy; intermediate.

Klitgaard, Thomas. "Exchange Rates and Profit Margins: The Case of Japanese Exporters." Federal Reserve Bank of New York, *Economic Policy Review* 5 (April 1999): 41–54.
How do exporting firms adjust their prices when exchange rates change?

Kouparitas, Michael A. "Are International Business Cycles Different under Fixed and Flexible Exchange Rate Regimes?" Federal Reserve Bank of Chicago, *Economic Perspectives* (First Quarter 1998): 46–64.
Finds that increased post–Bretton Woods correlation among G-7 real outputs is due to common shocks and common policy responses to them; intermediate.

Mishkin, Frederic S. "Inflation Targeting in Emerging-Market Countries." *American Economic Review Papers and Proceedings* 90 (May 2000): 105–109.
Is inflation-targeting a viable policy approach for emerging-market economies?

Mishkin, Frederic S., and Adam S. Posen. "Inflation Targeting: Lessons from Four Countries." Federal Reserve Bank of New York, *Economic Policy Review* (August 1997): 9–110.
An argument in favor of inflation targeting, based on the experiences of New Zealand, Canada, the United Kingdom, and Germany; for all students.

Obstfeld, Maurice. "International Currency Experience: New Lessons and Lessons Relearned." *Brookings Papers on Economic Activity* 1 (1995): 119–220.
Useful survey of recent theory and evidence on exchange rate behavior; intermediate.

Organization for Economic Cooperation and Development. *OECD Economic Outlook.* Paris: OECD, biannual.
Excellent source for recent macroeconomic events, data, and forecasts.

Persson, T., and G. Tabellini. "Double-Edged Incentives: Institutions and Policy Coordination." In *Handbook of International Economics,* Vol. 3, edited by G. M. Grossman and K. Rogoff, 1973–2030. Amsterdam: North-Holland, 1995.
Survey of strategic aspects of governments' macroeconomic policy choices; intermediate to advanced.

Sarno, Lucio, "Toward a New Paradigm in Open Economy Modeling: Where Do We Stand?" Federal Reserve Bank of St. Louis, *Review* 83 (May/June 2001): 21–36.
Survey of the newest theoretical models in open-economy macroeconomics; intermediate and advanced.

Symposium on "New Challenges for Monetary Policy." Federal Reserve Bank of Kansas City, 1999.
Domestic and international challenges facing monetary policy makers.

Tootell, Geoffrey M. B. "Globalization and U.S. Inflation." Federal Reserve Bank of Boston, *New England Economic Review* (July–August 1998): 21–34.
Argues against a big effect of foreign capacity on U.S. inflation; for all students.

CHAPTER NINETEEN APPENDIX

The Aggregate Demand Curve

In Chapter Nineteen, we used the aggregate demand curve to examine macroeconomic policies' effects on prices and output. This appendix demonstrates how to derive the aggregate demand curve from the IS-LM-BOP model of Chapters Sixteen and Seventeen. The aggregate demand curve differs slightly under fixed and flexible exchange rate regimes, so we'll consider the two cases separately, beginning with the aggregate demand curve under a fixed exchange rate.

19A.1 Derivation of the Aggregate Demand Curve under a Fixed Exchange Rate

As in Chapter Nineteen, we assume that capital is perfectly mobile among countries. This implies a horizontal BOP curve representing equilibrium in the balance of payments. At points above the BOP line, the balance of payments is in surplus; at points below it, the balance of payments is in deficit. With perfectly mobile capital, the economy will never actually be off its BOP line, but examining what would happen in such a case will help clarify the adjustment processes.

Panel (a) of Figure 19A.1 illustrates an initial equilibrium at the intersection of IS_0, LM_0, and BOP. The price level is P_0, and the equilibrium level of output is Q_0. Panel (b) represents that equilibrium price and output combination (P_0, Q_0) as a point on an aggregate demand curve.

Now suppose the price level rises from P_0 to P_1. The effects in the IS-LM-BOP diagram will include (1) a shift to the left of the IS curve because of the increase in the relative price of domestic goods and (2) a shift to the left of the LM curve due to the negative effect of the price rise on the real money stock. The more sensitive are the demands for imports and exports to changes in relative prices (that is, the higher are the price elasticities of the import and export demand curves), the larger will be the shift of the IS curve relative to that of the LM curve. IS_1 represents the low-elasticity case, in which the IS shift is relatively small. In this case, the new equilibrium occurs at the intersection of IS_1 and LM_1, implying a point corresponding to (P_1, Q_1) on the aggregate demand curve labeled *AD (fixed rate, low elasticity)* in panel (b). IS_2 represents the high-elasticity case, in which the IS shift is relatively large. In this case, the new equilibrium occurs at the intersection of IS_2 and LM_1, implying a point corresponding to (P_1, Q_2) on the aggregate demand curve labeled *AD (fixed rate, high elasticity)* in panel (b). As panel (b) demonstrates, the higher the elasticity values, the flatter the aggregate demand curve under a fixed exchange rate. *(To test your understanding, explain the points on the aggregate demand curve corresponding to a fall in the price level to $P_2 < P_0$.)*

Note that at points (P_1, Q_1) and (P_1, Q_2) on the two fixed-exchange-rate aggregate demand curves in panel (b) the balance of payments is *not* in equilibrium, but in surplus and deficit, respectively. *(Why?)* To restore balance-of-payments equilibrium given the fixed exchange rate, the central bank will have to intervene appropriately in each case. Intervention will alter the money stock and shift the aggregate demand curve.

19A.2 Derivation of the Aggregate Demand Curve under a Flexible Exchange Rate

The derivation of the aggregate demand curve from the IS-LM-BOP framework under a flexible exchange rate is quite similar to that under a fixed exchange rate. In fact, we can use Figure 19A.1 again. We continue to assume that capital is perfectly mobile inter-nationally. In panel (a), the initial equilibrium is at the intersection of IS_0, LM_0, and BOP; the price level is P_0 and the equilibrium output Q_0. This initial equilibrium is represented in panel (b) of Figure 19A.1 as a point on the *AD (flexible rate)* curve.

Figure 19A.1 Derivation of Aggregate Demand Curve from IS-LM-BOP with Perfectly Mobile Capital

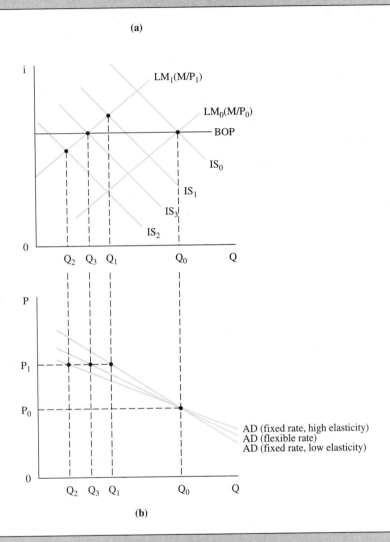

(a)

(b)

Real output and the price level are negatively related along an aggregate demand curve.

A rise in the price level to $P_1 > P_0$ shifts the IS curve to the left, because the relative price of domestic goods rises and consumers switch to imports. The LM curve also shifts to the left (to LM_1), because the rise in the price level reduces the real money stock. The new equilibrium output at price level P_1 is Q_3. This new equilibrium forms a second point on the flexible-rate aggregate demand curve in panel (b).

But how do we know exactly how much the IS curve shifts as a result of the rise in the price level? In particular, how can we be sure that IS_3 and LM_1 intersect *on* the BOP curve at output level Q_3? If the IS curve (such as IS_2) intersected LM_1 below the BOP line, the balance of payments would be in deficit. Under a flexible exchange rate regime, the domestic currency would depreciate and the relative price of

(continued)

domestic goods would fall. The change in relative prices would shift the IS curve to the right to IS_3. On the other hand, if the IS curve (such as IS_1) intersected LM_1 at a point above the BOP line, the balance of payments would be in surplus. With a flexible exchange rate, the domestic currency would appreciate and domestic goods would become more expensive relative to foreign goods. The IS curve would shift to the left to IS_3. This exchange rate adjustment in response to the balance of payments will ensure that the new IS curve intersects LM_1 on the BOP line at output level Q_3. *(As an exercise, explain the shifts in the IS and LM curves in response to a fall in the price level to $P_2 < P_0$.)*

Note that, unlike the fixed exchange rate case, the balance of payments is in equilibrium at each and every point on the flexible-rate aggregate demand curve. The slope of the flexible-rate curve falls between the slopes of the fixed-rate curves for the low- and high-elasticity cases.

CHAPTER TWENTY

International Monetary Regimes

20.1 Introduction

Chapters Twelve through Nineteen provided numerous examples of how the adjustment process and the effects of macroeconomic policy depend on the exchange rate regime. For the most part, we concentrated on differences between fixed and flexible exchange rate regimes and assumed that the regime was imposed exogenously. However, countries *choose* the systems to manage their currencies, and the choices countries make in this regard differ widely, as indicated in Table 20.1.

The goals of this chapter are to (1) examine the considerations that go into the choice of exchange rate regime, (2) outline some of the available alternatives other than pure fixed or flexible exchange rates, and (3) evaluate the strengths and weaknesses of alternate regimes as well as historical experience under each.

20.2 What Does a Monetary Regime Need to Do?

Any country that engages in international trade must make some provision for handling transactions that involve more than one currency. Countries use a variety of arrangements, ranging from barter or countertrade, which eliminates currencies altogether, to flexible exchange rates, which permit unrestricted exchange of one currency for another at market-determined exchange rates. That different countries choose different arrangements suggests that the decision involves trade-offs. We begin our study of alternative monetary regimes by examining some desirable goals that a hypothetical "ideal" regime would achieve.

An international monetary regime should promote efficient functioning of the world economy by *facilitating international trade and investment* according to the patterns of comparative advantage. The regime also should *support international borrowing and lending* that produce gains from intertemporal trade. Regimes that depend on trade restrictions or capital controls don't perform well in the long run. Such restrictions reduce the output of the world economy by encouraging inefficient production and by preventing resources and investment funds from flowing to their most productive uses. The ideal regime would allow trade and finance to proceed just as if the entire world used a single currency.

A successful international monetary regime should also *promote balance-of-payments adjustment* to prevent the disruptions and crises associated with large, chronic BOP imbalances. This means that the system needs to either contain automatic adjustment mechanisms for restoring BOP equilibrium or encourage policy makers to take steps to correct balance-of-payments problems promptly. A related requirement is that the system *provide countries with liquidity* sufficient to finance temporary BOP deficits. Under any arrangement other than a perfectly flexible exchange rate, some temporary imbalances are inevitable; adequate provisions for handling them play a vital role in avoiding and resolving crises.

Table 20.1 **Number of IMF Countries Using Various Exchange Rate Arrangements, 2000**	
Exchange Rate Arrangement	Number of Countries
Less-Flexible Regimes:	
Exchange arrangements with no separate legal tender	38
Currency board	8
Other conventional fixed peg (including de facto peg under managed floating)	45
Pegged exchange rates within horizontal bands	6
Crawling peg	5
Exchange rates within crawling bands	7
More-Flexible Regimes:	
Managed floating with no preannounced path for exchange rate	27
Independently floating	49
Total:	185

Source: International Monetary Fund.

Individuals and firms that engage in international trade and financial transactions face many types of uncertainty. An ideal international monetary regime would *avoid adding to this uncertainty,* which may discourage international transactions and cause countries to forgo gains from trade. Proponents of fixed exchange rates often present this criterion as an argument for using fixed rather than flexible exchange rates. As we'll see later in the chapter, however, fixed exchange rates don't necessarily involve less uncertainty than flexible ones.

We've learned that the choice of monetary regime interacts with the policy-making process to determine the effectiveness of various macroeconomic policies. The ideal monetary system would *enhance policy effectiveness* and provide policy makers with a number of policy instruments at least equal to the number of targets. The system would also *minimize the possibility of policy mistakes and cushion their negative impact.* It would encourage policy makers to take correct and timely policy actions and *shield the policy-making process from undue political pressure.*

The very definition of money demonstrates that confidence provides an essential ingredient in a successful monetary system. Money can function only as long as the public has confidence in the monetary unit and its acceptance as payment for goods and services. Expectations of disruptions in the world monetary system can themselves cause volatility, disorder, and poor economic performance, so the ideal monetary system would *generate confidence in its stability and continuity.*

Finally, any international monetary system involves costs to operate. The relevant costs include those of negotiating international agreements, maintaining international organizations such as the International Monetary Fund, and holding stocks of foreign exchange reserves, as well as the costs to individuals and firms of handling multiple currencies. Other things being equal, an international monetary system with *lower administrative and operating costs* is superior to one involving higher costs.

The list of attributes desirable for an international monetary regime is quite long. The following passage by Barry Eichengreen, a leading expert on international monetary history, summarizes the goals:

> The international monetary system is part of the institutional framework that binds national economies together. An ideally functioning system permits producers to specialize in goods in which the nation has a comparative advantage and savers to search beyond national borders for profitable investment opportunities. It does so by combining the virtues of stability and flexibility. Stability in the market for foreign exchange minimizes the volatility of import and export prices, permitting producers and consumers to exploit fully the advantages of international specialization. Flexibility in the operation of the international monetary system permits the divergent objectives of national economic authorities to be reconciled with one another.[1]

---

1 Barry Eichengreen, "Editor's Introduction," in *The Gold Standard in Theory and History,* edited by Barry Eichengreen (New York: Methuen, 1985), 1.

No system satisfies all these attributes perfectly; rather, the choice of international monetary system implies trade-offs among the various criteria. We now turn to an examination of the major monetary regimes and to the question of how each fares in terms of the preceding criteria. We begin with the gold standard.

20.3 The Gold Standard, 1880–1913: Panacea or Rose-Colored Glasses?

20.3.1 What Is a Gold Standard?

The use of precious metals, especially gold, as money dates back many centuries. Gold's characteristics make it well suited for this purpose; it's scarce, durable, transportable (at least in the quantities required for most economic transactions), easily measurable, and mintable into uniform coins.

The precise way gold functioned as money evolved as national governments assumed larger roles in the money-supply process. At first, unminted gold circulated in the form of dust or bullion. Market forces determined the relative price between gold and goods. For example, gold discoveries led to a fall in gold's relative price and a rise in the relative price of goods, as gold became more abundant relative to goods. Gradually, sovereigns began to mint gold into coins of a specified weight and to certify the coins' value. The value of these full-bodied coins equaled the value of their gold. Coining gold offered clear advantages, because it eliminated the need to weigh and measure at each transaction.

As economies grew and the number and size of economic transactions increased, the use of currency or paper money as a substitute for gold began to spread. Paper money was lighter and easier to transport, and each unit of it could represent a unit of gold actually held by the issuer of the currency. Currency was **convertible;** that is, holders of currency could convert it into gold on request, and vice versa. This type of **gold standard,** in which currency backed by gold circulated as the money stock, evolved independently in many countries. While the gold standard involved no explicit international agreement, the major trading economies—including Britain, Germany, the United States, and Japan—operated under a gold standard by around 1880, providing the basis for an international monetary regime that would last until World War I.

Simple rules governed the gold standard. First, each government defined the value of its currency in terms of gold; for example, the United States defined the dollar value of an ounce of gold as $20.67, and Britain defined the pound price of gold as £4.24 per ounce. The U.S. government committed itself to buy or sell gold at $20.67 per ounce, while the British government likewise stood ready to exchange pounds for gold, and vice versa, at £4.24 per ounce. Each government held gold reserves to back its commitment. Together, the two governments' commitments defined an implicit or **mint exchange rate** between dollars and pounds of ($20.67/oz.)/(£4.24/oz.), or about $4.87/£1.

Under a gold standard, the mint exchange rate fixes the market exchange rate between two currencies, not through direct intervention by the countries' monetary authorities, but by private arbitrage.[2] Suppose that the dollar price of pounds in the foreign exchange market rises above the mint exchange rate of $4.87/£1, say, to $5 per pound. Arbitrageurs then find it profitable to use dollars to buy gold in the United States at the official rate of $20.67 per ounce, ship it to Britain, sell it at the official rate of £4.24 per ounce, and exchange the pounds for (£4.24) · ($5.00/£1) = $21.20 in the foreign exchange market. The arbitrageurs earn a profit of $21.20 − $20.67 = $0.53 on each ounce of gold, ignoring transportation and other transaction costs. The arbitrage process raises the demand for dollars in the foreign exchange market and lowers the market exchange rate toward the mint rate of $4.87 per pound.

A fall in the dollar price of pounds to, say, $4.50 would cause arbitrageurs to ship gold from Britain to the United States at a profit of £0.35 per ounce. (*Why?*) Because of the transaction costs involved in shipping gold in response to deviations between the mint and market exchange rates, arbitrage can't keep the two rates identical at all times. However, it will keep the market rate within a band around the mint rate. The costs of gold shipments determine the width of the band, and the boundaries of the band are called *gold points.*

The combination of (1) government purchases and sales of gold to keep the price of each currency fixed in terms of gold and (2) private arbitrage to keep the market exchange rate approximately equal to the mint exchange rate ensures a fixed exchange rate between each pair of currencies under a gold standard. The viability

---

2 Recall that arbitrage is an effort to make a profit by taking advantage of price differentials that exist in two submarkets at a given time.

of the gold standard requires that each monetary authority issue no more currency than it can back with its stock of gold. If a central bank violates this rule, it faces the possibility of being unable to honor its promise to convert currency into gold on demand.

We can see how the gold standard disciplines monetary policy by considering a country that pursues an open market purchase to expand its money stock. Initially, the domestic real money stock rises and the interest rate falls. The decline in domestic relative to foreign interest rates makes foreign-currency-denominated assets more attractive. Asset owners sell the now unattractive domestic-currency-denominated assets to the central bank for gold, a transaction the central bank is obligated to fulfill under gold-standard rules. New owners of gold then sell it to foreign central banks in exchange for foreign currency that they use to purchase assets denominated in foreign currency—which pay higher interest rates. The net effect: The country that raised its money stock experiences a capital outflow, and other countries experience a matching capital inflow.

These capital flows reequilibrate the foreign exchange market. The money stock of the country that conducted the expansionary monetary policy shrinks back to its original size as the country loses gold reserves. Other countries experience money-stock growth as they accumulate gold reserves. Once interest parity reestablishes itself, capital flows cease. The total world money stock remains unchanged. Note two important results. First, both countries take part in the adjustment process. This makes adjustment under the gold standard *symmetrical,* as opposed to the *asymmetrical* adjustment under other fixed exchange rate systems, in which the reserve country controls its money stock and determines money growth for all members of the group.[3] Second, the rules of the gold standard link a country's money stock to its central bank's gold. This key characteristic of the gold standard—the tying of the money stock to the central bank's stock of gold—lies at the heart of arguments both in favor of and against use of a gold standard as an international monetary regime.

20.3.2 **How Is a Gold Standard Supposed to Work?**

The primary arguments in favor of a gold standard rest on the belief that such a system contributes to price stability (particularly to avoiding inflation) and contains an automatic adjustment mechanism for maintaining balance-of-payments equilibrium. The price-stability argument stems from a gold standard's limits on money-stock growth. At the worldwide level, the money stock can't grow faster than the total world stock of gold. At the national level, each country's money stock can't grow faster than that central bank's stock of gold, because gold must back all currency. The central bank can't create gold but must either buy existing gold from the public or promote mining to enlarge the available supply.[4] Insofar as this limit on money growth works, the gold standard imposes **price discipline** on central banks, both individually and collectively. This discipline keeps central banks from creating continual increases in the price level through excessively expansionary monetary policy.

The automatic adjustment mechanism for the balance of payments under a gold standard provides an example of David Hume's specie-flow mechanism, first discussed in Chapter Two. *Specie* is a term for money in the form of precious metals. In the **specie-flow mechanism,** international flows of gold (money) correct BOP disequilibria. Suppose, for example, that the United States has a balance-of-payments (or, more accurately, a current-account) deficit with Britain under a gold standard. The value of goods and services the United States imports from Britain exceeds that of U.S. exports to Britain. To cover the difference and settle its account, the United States must ship gold to Britain. This movement of gold reduces the U.S. money stock and increases Britain's. The fall in the U.S. money stock causes U.S. prices to fall, while the rise in the British money stock causes British prices to rise. The change in relative prices of American and British goods (or, equivalently, the real depreciation of the dollar) shifts demand away from British goods and toward American ones, correcting the original current-account imbalance. Under a gold standard, any such imbalance reduces the money stock of the deficit country and increases that of the surplus country. The resulting change in relative prices of the two countries' products, or the real exchange rate between their currencies, raises the deficit country's net exports and lowers those of the surplus country, moving the balance of payments toward equilibrium.

Hume presented his specie-flow mechanism in 1752 as a counter to mercantilist arguments for restricting trade. Recall from Chapter Two that the mercantilists saw trade policy primarily as a vehicle for the accumulation of specie, which they viewed as the source of wealth and power. The route to this accumulation involved restrictive trade policies designed to create BOP surpluses that would be settled in gold. Hume's logic, along with

---

3 See section 16.6 and Case One in Chapter Sixteen on reserve-currency countries.

4 The other way of increasing the domestic stock of gold, as we'll see, is to run a balance-of-payments surplus.

that of classical economists David Ricardo and Adam Smith, exposed the fallacies of the mercantilist view. The specie-flow mechanism contributed by demonstrating the inherently short-term nature of balance-of-payments surpluses. When a country succeeded in creating a surplus through mercantilist policies, it indeed experienced a gold inflow; but this swelled the money stock and raised prices, thereby encouraging imports, discouraging exports, and eliminating the surplus. On the basis of this automatic adjustment mechanism, Hume argued that mercantilist policies, *even if* they have been desirable, couldn't succeed in the long run.

The simple version of Hume's specie-flow mechanism emphasized price flexibility and focused on adjustment of the current-account balance rather than the overall balance of payments. However, we've seen that a similar adjustment mechanism works through the capital account. When the U.S. money stock falls and Britain's rises, U.S. interest rates rise relative to Britain's.[5] This causes the U.S. capital account to move toward a surplus and corrects the original deficit in the U.S. balance of payments. Thus, although Hume's treatment of the specie-flow mechanism analyzed the effect of price flexibility in promoting adjustment through the current account, the same basic idea can be applied to adjustment in the capital account.

In summary, a gold standard requires that individual governments peg their currencies' values in terms of gold, that arbitrageurs keep the market exchange rate approximately equal to the mint exchange rate, and that adequate gold stocks back countries' money stocks. The gold standard imposes a degree of price discipline on the central bank by limiting money growth to equality with gold-stock growth. It also contains an automatic adjustment mechanism in the form of Hume's specie-flow mechanism for solving balance-of-payments problems through symmetric changes in the relative sizes of countries' money stocks. As under any fixed exchange rate regime, the link between the balance of payments and the money stock plays an essential role in automatic adjustment. Given these proposed advantages of a gold standard, let's examine the historical evidence on operation of a gold-based international monetary regime.

20.3.3 How Did the Gold Standard Really Work?

A gold standard links the growth of the domestic money stock to that of the gold stock, so an accurate evaluation of its desirability depends on the pattern of growth in the gold stock, among other things. A smooth pattern of growth, which kept pace with full-employment output, would prevent shocks to the world economy. Consistently faster growth in gold than in output would put upward pressure on the price of goods relative to gold as countries accumulated gold reserves. Consistently slower growth in gold than in output would put downward pressure on the price of goods relative to gold and create a shortage of reserves for the growing economies. An erratic growth pattern in gold, on the other hand, could disrupt the world economy by generating business cycles.

Table 20.2 reports the growth rate of the U.S. monetary gold stock from 1880 to 1913, when the major economies operated under a gold standard. The annual rates of change ranged from a low of −7 percent to a high of 43 percent. Even if monetary authorities had closely followed the rule of creating no more money than they could back by gold, the rate of growth in the money stock would have been quite volatile.

But how closely did governments actually abide by the rules of the gold standard? Studies suggest that policy makers often disregarded the rules. If the growth of the gold stock proved insufficient to support the money growth that policy makers wanted, they could change the law to require less gold backing for each unit of currency issued or to exempt certain types of money creation (for example, bank deposits as opposed to currency) from gold backing. As under any fixed exchange rate regime, central banks could sterilize the effects of changes in the gold stock by engineering offsetting changes in domestic monetary policy.

In practice, the expediency of such policies limited the price discipline imposed by the gold standard, and the U.S. money stock grew erratically even by today's standards, as documented in Table 20.2. The table also reveals that changes in the gold stock explain most changes in the U.S. money stock during the gold-standard era. The years of the most rapid gold stock growth (1880–1881 and 1898–1899) correspond to those of fastest monetary growth. At the other extreme, during 1893 both the gold stock and the money stock suffered their biggest declines.

The gold standard in the United States doesn't appear to have promoted smooth, disciplined behavior of the money stock. However, the behavior of the money stock matters not in itself but for its implications for real

---

5 A rise in the money supply could cause expectations of inflation and a rise in the long-term nominal interest rate. However, short-term interest rates are of primary concern here; section 18.4.4 treats the relationship between inflation and long-term interest rates.

Table 20.2 **Annual Growth in the U.S. Monetary Gold Stock, 1880–1913 (Percent)**

Year	Annual Growth in U.S. Monetary Gold Stock	Annual Growth of U.S. M2	Year	Annual Growth in U.S. Monetary Gold Stock	Annual Growth of U.S. M2
1880	43%	22%	1897	13%	7%
1881	33	20	1898	23	13
1882	7	8	1899	18	16
1883	6	6	1900	7	8
1884	2	0	1901	10	13
1885	6	3	1902	5	9
1886	4	8	1903	7	6
1887	9	7	1904	6	6
1888	7	3	1905	2	11
1889	−2	6	1906	9	8
1890	0	9	1907	10	5
1891	−3	4	1908	10	−1
1892	−3	9	1909	1	11
1893	−7	−4	1910	1	5
1894	0	0	1911	6	6
1895	−5	4	1912	9	7
1896	0	−2	1913	3	4

Source: U.S. Department of Commerce, *Historical Statistics of the United States: Colonial Times to 1970.*

output and the price level. Recall the ultimate goal of an international monetary system: smooth functioning of the world economy as reflected in steady growth of real output and stable prices. Table 20.3 reveals that wide variations in both real output and the price level matched the instability in the money stock, as the model of Chapter Nineteen would lead us to expect.

Overall, the gold-standard era exhibited greater instability in terms of money growth, prices, and real output than some analysts admit. Apparently, rose-colored perceptions of the "good old days" filter some popular views of the gold standard. Efforts to smooth and limit money growth by tying the money stock to gold had limited success, for two basic reasons. First, the gold stock itself grew erratically due to new discoveries, new extraction technologies, and changing incentives for mining. Second, unless inclined to abide by the restrictions placed on money growth by the gold stock, central banks can circumvent the rules and eliminate much of the discipline credited to the gold standard. This second weakness of a gold standard seems likely to pose an even bigger problem for a gold standard today than during the early days of the twentieth century. A gold standard compels policy makers to focus on *external* balance, but throughout the postwar period, governments have accepted increasing responsibility for *internal*-balance targets, such as full employment. A government committed by law to the pursuit of full employment (as is, for example, the United States) seems unlikely to abide by the rules of a gold standard when those rules require behavior that may come at high short-run costs in terms of domestic economic targets.

20.4 The Interwar Years, 1919–1939: Search for an International Monetary System

World War I disrupted all aspects of the world economy, including the gold standard. Economic policy in the large trading economies focused on financing the war. Fiscal authorities borrowed to pay armies, buy arms, and later to finance reconstruction; monetary policy makers printed money to cover the fiscal expenditures.[6]

---

6 Other ways to finance government expenditures include raising taxes or borrowing from the public.

Table 20.3 **Annual Changes in U.S. Real GNP and Price Level under the Gold Standard, 1890–1913 (Percent)**

Year	Change in Real GNP (Q)	Change in GNP Deflator (P)	Year	Change in Real GNP (Q)	Change in GNP Deflator (P)
1890	7%	−2%	1902	1%	3%
1891	5	−1	1903	5	1
1892	10	−4	1904	−1	1
1893	−5	2	1905	7	2
1894	−3	−6	1906	12	2
1895	12	−1	1907	2	4
1896	−2	−3	1908	−8	−1
1897	9	0	1909	17	4
1898	2	3	1910	3	3
1899	9	4	1911	3	−1
1900	3	5	1912	6	4
1901	11	−1	1913	1	−1

Source: U.S. Department of Commerce, *Historical Statistics of the United States: Colonial Times to 1970.*

Except for the United States, countries abandoned their currencies' convertibility into gold, ushering in a period of flexible exchange rates. The dollar remained convertible into gold, but other governments stopped converting their currencies into either gold or dollars at fixed rates. Thus, the fixed mint exchange rates of the gold-standard era disappeared.

Few policy makers or economists viewed the flexible exchange rates as permanent, however. Discussion focused on when to reestablish the gold standard and how to choose the new rate at which to peg each currency to gold. The demands of financing the war and reconstruction had produced high rates of inflation in most economies (especially outside the United States), so most policy makers recognized a return to prewar rates as infeasible. The war had shaken confidence in the gold standard, and the relative strengths of the United States and Britain in the world economy had changed. A handful of countries reestablished a partial gold standard in 1925, but with unsustainable exchange rates. British war-generated inflation, combined with the British government's determination to return the pound to gold convertibility at its prewar rate, led to severe monetary contraction, a dramatic real appreciation of the pound, and a prolonged British recession. Germany—saddled with a devastated economy and war reparations that it attempted to pay by printing massive quantities of money—suffered a hyperinflation in which the price level rose by a factor of almost 500 *billion* between 1919 and 1925.

Beginning in 1931, the brief return to a gold standard collapsed in the midst of the Great Depression. One by one, countries again suspended their currencies' convertibility into gold. International monetary cooperation took a back seat to countries' self-interested attempts to regain control of their economies through competitive devaluations, tariffs, exchange and capital controls, and a variety of other desperate and often counterproductive policies.

Pervasive political and economic instability characterized the period between World War I and World War II. Table 20.4 summarizes the erratic macroeconomic performance. The lack of a smoothly functioning international monetary system was but one symptom of the overall problem. Neither the breakdown of the gold standard nor the spread of trade restrictions can shoulder blame for all the interwar economic problems, but narrowly nationalistic policies did little to alleviate them.

The interwar years left a historical record that still serves as a reminder of the world economy's interdependence and of the costs of beggar-thy-neighbor policies. Only after the Great Depression did macroeconomic stability and internal balance become central goals of government policy. One result of the interwar and Depression experiences was the major economies' determination to unite to build stable and open international trade and monetary systems following World War II.[7]

---

7 This determination was evidenced by the negotiations for a postwar international monetary system that began in 1941 and continued throughout the war.

Table 20.4 **Annual Changes in U.S. Real GNP and Price Level, 1919–1941 (Percent)**

Year	Change in Real GNP (Q)	Change in GNP Deflator (P)	Year	Change in Real GNP (Q)	Change in GNP Deflator (P)
1919	−4%	14%	1931	−8%	−9%
1920	−4	14	1932	−15	−10
1921	−9	−17	1933	−2	−2
1922	16	−8	1934	9	7
1923	12	2	1935	10	1
1924	0	0	1936	14	0
1925	8	1	1937	5	4
1926	6	−2	1938	−5	−1
1927	0	−2	1939	9	−2
1928	1	2	1940	9	−2
1929	7	0	1941	16	8
1930	−10	−3			

Source: U.S. Department of Commerce, *Historical Statistics of the United States: Colonial Times to 1970.*

20.5 Bretton Woods, 1945–1971: A Negotiated International Monetary System

In the 1940s, few scholars or policy makers viewed flexible exchange rates as a viable basis for an international monetary regime.. The Bretton Woods system established after World War II reinstated fixed exchange rates, but with three major changes from the prewar system:

1. The new regime represented a gold-exchange standard rather than a gold standard. This meant that a national currency—the U.S. dollar—played a central role along with gold.
2. The new system was an adjustable-peg exchange rate system rather than a fixed-rate system, because the Bretton Woods agreement contained provisions for altering exchange rates under certain, albeit vaguely specified, conditions.
3. The Bretton Woods system, unlike the gold standard, represented the outcome of international bargaining, even though the United States and Britain dominated the negotiations. Those negotiations created a major international organization, the International Monetary Fund (IMF), as a multilateral body to support the new agreement.

20.5.1 What Is a Gold-Exchange Standard?

The Bretton Woods system provides an example of a **gold-exchange, or gold-dollar, standard.** Nondollar currencies weren't convertible directly into gold, but they were convertible, at a pegged exchange rate, into dollars, which in turn were convertible into gold at $35 per ounce.[8] That the U.S. dollar served as the key currency in the Bretton Woods gold-exchange standard implied a distinction between the policy rules followed by the United States and those followed by other countries.[9] The **key, or reserve, currency** was convertible into gold. Maintaining this convertibility, initially at $35 per ounce, defined the primary U.S. responsibility under Bretton Woods. Fulfillment of this responsibility required the United States to (1) stand ready to buy or sell

---

8 At the war's end, most currencies weren't convertible. The Bretton Woods agreement urged member countries to establish convertibility, at least for current-account transactions, as soon as possible. Most major economies accomplished this move by the late 1950s or early 1960s. In Chapter Twenty-One, we'll look into the costs that nonconvertible currencies impose on economies.

9 Section 16.6 discusses the special status of reserve-currency countries.

gold in exchange for dollars at $35 per ounce at the request of other central banks and (2) create no more dollars subject to convertibility than the U.S. stock of gold could support. Other countries' central banks held responsibility for intervening in foreign exchange markets to buy and sell dollars, to keep the dollar values of their respective currencies at the agreed-upon pegged rates.

Notice the fundamental difference between a gold standard and a gold-exchange standard. Under a true gold standard, *each* currency is convertible into gold. Under a gold-exchange standard, *only* the reserve currency is convertible directly into gold. Other currencies, in turn, are convertible into the reserve currency at pegged exchange rates maintained through intervention by nonreserve-currency central banks.

20.5.2 How Was Bretton Woods Supposed to Work?

The gold standard had collapsed when policy makers no longer would subordinate their domestic, internal-balance goals to the gold standard's externally oriented rules. To fight unemployment during the Great Depression, governments resorted to abandoning their exchange-rate pegs, competitively devaluing, and imposing trade barriers. Negotiators at Bretton Woods, fresh from the interwar experience, recognized that any new international monetary system, if it was to succeed based on fixed exchange rates, would have to provide governments with some flexibility to address the domestic macroeconomic priorities for which electorates increasingly held governments responsible. The Bretton Woods agreement contained three important elements meant to incorporate this flexibility: an adjustable-peg exchange rate system, IMF lending facilities, and permission for countries to institute or continue to use exchange controls on some types of international transactions.

The Adjustable Peg

The designers of Bretton Woods recognized that the pegged exchange rates selected at the close of World War II would require periodic adjustment as countries' economic situations evolved. The major economies found themselves in widely divergent circumstances and pursuing diverse policies at the end of the war. Some economies were growing rapidly, while others struggled to reconstruct their basic productive capacities. For all these reasons, the negotiators at Bretton Woods recognized the need for periodic devaluations and revaluations to correct chronic balance-of-payments problems. Rather than permanently fixing exchange rates, the Bretton Woods agreement explicitly left open the possibility of occasional currency realignments and allowed countries to devalue or revalue their currencies under specified conditions with the consent of the rest of the group.[10] The framers of the agreement hoped that by providing a cooperative framework for these changes, through the IMF, policy makers could avoid future episodes of the destructive competitive devaluations that had occurred during the Great Depression. A system of fixed exchange rates that embodies rules for periodic adjustment of rates as economic conditions change is called an **adjustable-peg system.**

Bretton Woods' adjustable peg required a central bank to intervene to buy or sell foreign exchange whenever short-run disturbances caused a temporary disequilibrium at the pegged rate for that central bank's currency. If, however, economic circumstances changed permanently or dramatically such that the pegged rate clearly differed from long-run equilibrium, intervention to maintain the rate could be undesirable or even infeasible. In such cases of **fundamental disequilibrium,** policy makers could change the pegged exchange rate, under the guidance of the IMF, to a rate that corresponded more closely to equilibrium.

IMF Lending Facilities

A fixed exchange rate regime requires central banks to intervene in foreign exchange markets to maintain balance-of-payments equilibrium at the assigned exchange rates. This intervention alters the domestic money stock; in fact, we've seen that intervention's effect on the money stock represents the key step in the mechanism through which intervention restores balance-of-payments equilibrium.[11] However, these changes in the money stock may exacerbate problems of internal balance, particularly unemployment, and lead policy makers

---

10 Each exchange rate actually fluctuated in a band (of ±1 percent) around the pegged rate; minor exchange adjustments didn't require consent.

11 See section 15.7, especially Figure 15.19.

to circumvent the rules of the regime and cause crises. The Bretton Woods agreement recognized this possibility and incorporated provisions for lending reserves (either gold or foreign currencies) to governments that faced temporary balance-of-payments deficits but for which immediate monetary contraction presented unacceptable domestic economic consequences.

The International Monetary Fund consists of member countries that promise to abide by the organization's Articles of Agreement, which define the rules, privileges, and obligations of membership. Each country joins the IMF by contributing a sum called the *quota*, which consists of gold (25 percent) and the country's domestic currency (75 percent). The IMF, in turn, could lend these funds to countries that needed its assistance to meet their Bretton Woods obligations. Countries could use their quotas to buy specific currencies they needed for foreign exchange market intervention. This allowed countries to maintain their exchange rate pegs while postponing monetary adjustment.

A country's economic size determined the size of its IMF quota and, therefore, of its routine borrowing privilege. Voting within the IMF also was determined by the size of a country's quota. The IMF divided each country's borrowing privileges into several classes called **tranches. Conditionality** referred to the IMF's requirement that countries follow certain policy prescriptions as a condition for borrowing. When a country borrowed small sums from the fund, the borrowing came from the lower tranches subject to no conditionality requirements. As the country's borrowing rose into higher and higher tranches, which generally reflected increasingly serious and persistent economic problems, the number of conditions the IMF imposed increased. The most common conditions included adjusting the exchange rate to make it more consistent with balance-of-payments equilibrium, lowering deficit spending by the public sector, and lowering money growth rates. These conditionality prescriptions were designed to eliminate the balance-of-payments problems that required borrowing from the fund, while the IMF lending itself provided short-term relief to countries with high domestic unemployment and large balance-of-payments deficits.

Exchange and Capital Controls

At the end of World War II, most national currencies weren't convertible; that is, they couldn't be exchanged freely for other currencies. Nonconvertibility reduces the world economy's efficiency by making international trade more costly, because it limits the usefulness or the liquidity of foreign-currency-denominated export receipts. To encourage the reestablishment of international trade after the war, the Bretton Woods agreement urged member countries to restore currency convertibility quickly. However, the agreement limited the call for convertibility to current-account or international trade transactions and avoided requiring convertibility of capital-account or financial transactions.[12] The logic of the distinction was based on negotiators' perceptions that private capital flows, which could move quickly across national boundaries in response to expected changes in exchange rates, might add instability to the world economy. If policy makers constantly had to worry about foreign exchange market participants' perceptions of their economy and policy, this might further constrain their ability to manage the economy while maintaining fixed exchange rates.[13]

Currency nonconvertibility for capital-account transactions severely limited private capital flows in the years following the war. This implied that current-account deficits had to be financed in one of two ways: central banks' sales of foreign exchange, or official borrowing from other countries or the IMF.[14] At the same time, each government had to worry about keeping enough foreign exchange reserves to maintain the credibility of its exchange-rate commitments.

As currencies gradually became convertible for capital-account transactions, private capital flows increased. This development enhanced the opportunity for countries to reap gains from intertemporal trade. For some countries, private capital flows could offset current-account deficits or surpluses and reduce the need for foreign exchange intervention. For others, capital-account deficits or surpluses exacerbated their current-account counterpart and required large-scale intervention that generated huge swings in governments' foreign

---

12 Chapter Thirteen covers the distinction between current- and capital-account transactions.

13 Case Four in Chapter Sixteen provides more information about capital controls.

14 Recall from Chapter Thirteen that BOP = CAB + KAB = −OSB. If capital controls limit the private capital flow portion of KAB, then CAB < 0 requires either OSB > 0 or official (noncontrolled) capital inflows such that KAB > 0.

exchange reserves—and in domestic money stocks. Hints of an impending devaluation could cause immediate capital outflows and necessitate an actual devaluation, often one larger in magnitude than would have been required in the absence of the expectation-based capital outflow.[15]

20.5.3 How Did Bretton Woods Really Work?

Confidence in the international monetary system under Bretton Woods hinged on the credibility of two fundamental commitments: one tying countries' currencies to the dollar and the other tying the dollar to gold. Unfortunately, requirements for meeting the two commitments sometimes conflicted.

Immediately after World War II, reconstruction meant that the European and Japanese economies ran large current-account deficits. With private capital flows constrained by capital controls and currency nonconvertibility, those deficits required central banks to intervene on a large scale to maintain the countries' fixed exchange rates against the dollar. Such large-scale intervention was possible only if the central banks held sufficiently large stocks of foreign exchange reserves. This implied that the United States had to make available enough dollars to provide adequate world **liquidity** or reserves, because countries held the bulk of their reserves in U.S. dollars, the reserve currency.[16]

At the same time, continued confidence in the U.S. commitment to hold the price of gold at $35 per ounce required that the dollars in the hands of foreign central banks (and therefore subject to requests for conversion into gold) not exceed the value of the U.S. gold stock. The U.S. stock of gold reserves was large but finite. Figure 20.1 reports the U.S. gold stock during the Bretton Woods period, along with the dollar liabilities that the United States could have been asked to convert into gold. As the figure makes clear, dollar liabilities to foreign central banks surpassed the U.S. gold stock by the early 1960s. With dollars in the hands of foreign central banks exceeding the value of the stock of gold reserves (valued at $35 per ounce), the United States clearly could no longer convert all dollars into gold on request.[17]

An obvious conflict existed between the need to *create large stocks of dollars* to provide adequate liquidity for intervention and the need to *limit the creation of dollars* so as not to jeopardize confidence in their convertibility into gold. If the United States created a large quantity of dollars for use as reserves, confidence in its ability to honor its commitment to convert dollars into gold at $35 per ounce on foreign governments' request weakened. Thus, it isn't surprising that during much of the Bretton Woods era, failure to meet one or the other of these two goals was a source of concern. In fact, one can argue that the evolution and eventual demise of the Bretton Woods system resulted from the interplay of these two problems.

During the early postwar years, the first problem prevailed as other countries experienced large current-account deficits and a chronic "dollar shortage" as they sought dollars to supplement their gold reserves. The European economies maintained protectionist policies and controls on private capital flows in an effort to hold their balance-of-payments deficits at manageable levels.

In the mid-1960s, when the United States pursued more expansionary monetary policy and itself ran balance-of-payments deficits, the reserve-currency country obviously lost its ability to honor its commitment to convert dollars into gold.[18] The expansionary U.S. monetary policy meant that foreign central banks had to buy large quantities of dollars from the foreign exchange market to prevent their own currencies from appreciating against the dollar. For a while, foreign central banks willingly accumulated dollar reserves that, unlike gold, paid interest. As long as no one expected a dollar devaluation against gold, the United States, as the reserve-currency country, could continue to conduct expansionary monetary policy relatively unconstrained by its gold stock.[19]

---

15 See Cases One, Two, Three, and Five in Chapter Sixteen.

16 The remaining reserve stocks took the form of gold and a few other currencies, such as pounds.

17 As long as the Bretton Woods system enjoyed widespread confidence, the United States didn't have to redeem all dollars at the promised rate, but the belief that it *could* do so was crucial.

18 The classic explanation for U.S. expansionary macroeconomic policy during the mid-1960s goes as follows: The Johnson administration incurred mounting fiscal expenditures as it financed both its Great Society programs (including the War on Poverty) and its defense buildup to support the expanding Vietnam War. Economists publicly warned Johnson of the need to raise taxes to finance the expenditures. But the president, aware of the growing unpopularity of the Vietnam conflict, insisted on printing money rather than raising taxes. The result was a succession of large increases in aggregate demand and, eventually, inflation and currency devaluation.

19 Gold's constraint on money expansion eroded further in 1968 when institution of a two-tier gold market allowed private traders to buy and sell gold at a market-determined price not linked to the official $35 per ounce price at which central banks continued to trade.

Figure 20.1 **The U.S. Gold Stock and Dollars Eligible for Conversion into Gold during Bretton Woods (Gold Valued at the Official Rate)**

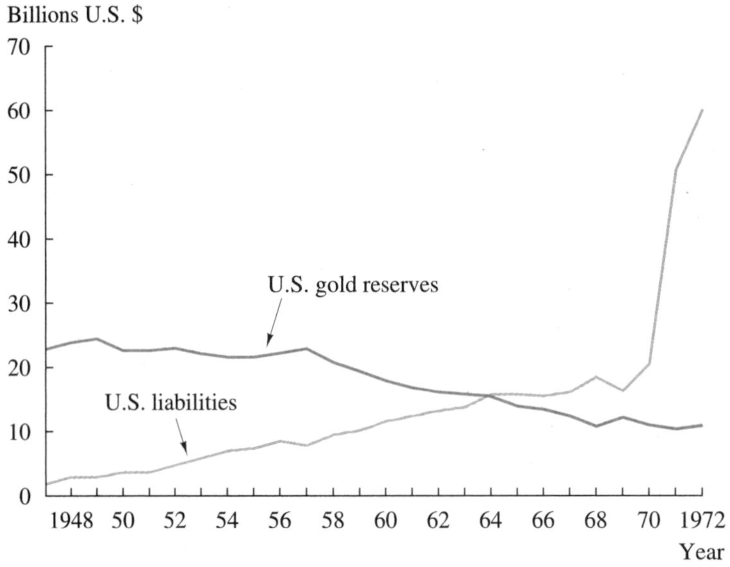

During the 1960s, the number of dollars eligible for conversion into gold grew to exceed the value of official U.S. gold reserves.

Sources: *Economic Report of the President;* International Monetary Fund, *International Financial Statistics.*

Intervention by foreign central banks swelled their money stocks and spread the inflationary effects of U.S. expansionary policy abroad.

Eventually, many foreign governments and market participants began to anticipate a devaluation of the dollar (that is, a rise in the dollar price of gold). Foreign policy makers grew increasingly unwilling to hold large stocks of dollars, because they no longer viewed the dollar as "good as gold." The chronic dollar shortage of the early postwar years had turned into a "dollar glut" by the mid-1960s. Some central banks, especially France's, hurried to exchange their dollars for gold before the expected devaluation, and pressures rose as the U.S. gold stock dwindled. Countries strongly opposed to inflation, particularly West Germany and Japan, ceased to support the Bretton Woods system, which had exported the inflationary effects of excessively expansionary U.S. policies (see Table 20.5).

Finally, in August 1971, the United States announced that it no longer would convert dollars to gold at the official $35 rate on foreign central banks' request. By the end of 1971, a makeshift arrangement—the Smithsonian Agreement—had replaced Bretton Woods, fixing the price of gold at $38 per ounce (later to become $42 per ounce) and pegging foreign currencies against the dollar at higher rates. The shift from Bretton Woods to Smithsonian amounted to a dollar devaluation imposed unilaterally by the United States against all other member currencies. The Smithsonian Agreement also differed from Bretton Woods in that the United States made no promise to convert dollars into gold at the new $38 rate; in other words, the new system represented a **dollar standard** rather than a gold-dollar standard. The Smithsonian Agreement couldn't reestablish the stability and confidence enjoyed under Bretton Woods. High rates of U.S. money growth continued, and foreign exchange market participants sold dollar-denominated assets in exchange for mark-denominated ones in anticipation of another dollar devaluation. By 1973, after several futile attempts to reestablish stable fixed exchange rates, the currencies of the major industrial economies floated against the dollar.

Table 20.5 **Inflation in the Major Industrial Economies, 1952–1973 (Percent Change in Consumer Prices)**

Year	U.S.	Canada	Japan	France	Germany	Italy	United Kingdom
1952	2%	2%	4%	12%	2%	4%	9%
1953	1	–1	7	–1	–2	2	3
1954	0	1	6	0	0	3	2
1955	0	0	–2	1	1	3	5
1956	1	1	0	2	3	3	5
1957	4	3	3	4	2	1	4
1958	3	2	0	15	2	3	3
1959	1	1	1	6	1	0	0
1960	2	1	4	4	1	2	1
1961	1	1	5	3	2	2	3
1962	1	1	7	5	3	5	4
1963	1	2	8	5	3	7	2
1964	1	2	4	3	2	6	3
1965	2	2	7	3	3	4	5
1966	3	4	5	3	4	2	4
1967	3	3	4	3	1	3	3
1968	4	4	5	5	2	1	5
1969	5	5	5	6	3	3	5
1970	6	3	8	5	4	5	6
1971	4	3	6	6	5	5	10
1972	3	5	5	6	6	6	7
1973	6	8	12	7	7	10	8

Source: *Economic Report of the President.*

The Bretton Woods system met with difficulties for three basic reasons. First, as we've seen, U.S. responsibilities under the system sometimes conflicted, so at least some of them weren't carried out. Second, central banks faced conflicts between their international responsibilities under the agreement and the macroeconomic policies acceptable to their domestic political constituencies. Finally, as capital mobility increased, perceived conflicts between a country's international and domestic economic obligations could quickly trigger a capital outflow and a balance-of-payments crisis whenever market participants began to expect a devaluation.

20.5.4 How Did the Macroeconomy Perform under Bretton Woods?

The Bretton Woods system clearly had imperfections: it implied potentially contradictory responsibilities for the United States and imposed the effects of U.S. policy on foreign economies. Although the underlying agreement allowed for exchange rate adjustments by design, actual devaluations or revaluations were rare, and chronic balance-of-payments deficits and surpluses were common. Despite these problems, however, the world economy performed respectably during the Bretton Woods years.

Table 20.6 summarizes the behavior of U.S. real output and prices during the Bretton Woods era. Output grew, if not smoothly, and the international system's increased openness led to rapid growth in world trade and investment. Inflation posed few problems during the early years once the immediate postwar adjustments passed, but it grew to be a bigger threat as U.S. expansionary policies produced growing balance-of-payments deficits and price increases.

Table 20.6 **Annual Changes in U.S. Real GNP and Price Level, 1946–1971 (Percent)**

Year	Change in Real GNP (Q)	Change in GNP Deflator (P)	Year	Change in Real GNP (Q)	Change in GNP Deflator (P)
1946	12%	12%	1959	6%	2%
1947	−1	12	1960	2	2
1948	4	7	1961	2	1
1949	0	−1	1962	7	1
1950	10	1	1963	4	1
1951	8	7	1964	5	1
1952	3	2	1965	6	2
1953	4	1	1966	7	3
1954	−1	1	1967	3	3
1955	8	1	1968	5	4
1956	2	3	1969	3	5
1957	1	4	1970	0	5
1958	−1	3	1971	3	5

Source: *Economic Report of the President.*

20.6 Post-Bretton Woods, 1973– : Another Search for an International Monetary System

The breakdown of the Bretton Woods system of pegged exchange rates led less to a regime based on exchange rate flexibility than to a world in which individual countries unilaterally choose their own exchange rate arrangements. This represented less of a break with the past than is commonly acknowledged. Historically, the exchange arrangement used by the dominant economies has been treated as characteristic of each period, as if the entire world economy operated under a unified exchange regime. In fact, this rarely has been the case. During the gold-standard era, many countries never tied their currencies to gold, and others entered and exited the system according to prevailing domestic political constraints on economic policies. Under Bretton Woods, the regime was subject to negotiation, but the United States and Britain dominated those negotiations. Many countries, including large ones such as France, never liked the system. Many currencies never became fully convertible into dollars—a requirement for a true gold-exchange standard. Government leaders postponed exchange rate adjustments until crises arose, actions that clearly violated the spirit, if not the letter, of the Bretton Woods agreement.

If economic history has taught any lessons, one is certainly that national governments are reluctant to relinquish sovereignty in any area, including international monetary relations and international trade policy. Nations jealously guard the prerogative to manage their respective currencies and never freely relinquish that prerogative to the dictates of an international monetary regime. Nor do countries easily relinquish power over other aspects of macroeconomic policy making.

Despite the problems inherent in characterizing a world monetary regime based on the policy choices of a handful of large countries, we examine today's system as a managed float, the arrangement in use by the major industrial economies. A **managed float** refers to a system in which the forces of supply and demand in foreign exchange markets determine basic trends in exchange rates but central banks intervene when they perceive markets as "disorderly" or dominated by short-term disturbances. Some opponents call this arrangement a **dirty float,** referring to the fact that central banks' intervention actions dirty, or interfere with, market forces. Nonetheless, the period since 1973 represents the longest in modern economic history during which the major currencies have been allowed to float.[20]

---

20 Garber and Svensson, p. 1866.

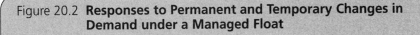

Figure 20.2 **Responses to Permanent and Temporary Changes in Demand under a Managed Float**

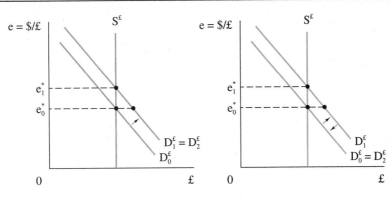

(a) Permanent Increase in Demand for Pounds

(b) Temporary Increase in Demand for Pounds

In panel (a), the demand for pounds increases permanently. The response under a managed float is to allow the exchange rate to move to a new equilibrium at e_1^*. In panel (b), the demand for pounds increases temporarily but then moves back down to its original level. Intervention would hold the exchange rate at its fundamental equilibrium level, e_0^*.

20.6.1 How Is a Managed Float Supposed to Work?

A managed float attempts, by combining market-determined exchange rates with some foreign exchange market intervention, to capture the more desirable aspects of both fixed and flexible exchange rates. The fundamental idea is to use intervention to avoid short-term exchange rate fluctuations that many believe contribute to uncertainty. At the same time, central banks avoid long-term intervention so that the supply of and demand for various currencies determine long-run movements in exchange rates, avoiding persistent fundamental misalignments.

Figure 20.2 illustrates the ideal working of a managed float. For simplicity, we maintain the simple two-country (Britain/United States) framework.[21] Each panel depicts the demand for pound-denominated deposits along with the supply of such deposits. Initially the demand for and supply of pounds are given by $D_0^£$ and $S^£$, respectively. With no central bank intervention, the exchange rate or dollar price of pounds equals e_0^*, at which the quantity demanded of pounds equals the quantity supplied. At that rate, portfolio owners willingly hold the existing stock of pound-denominated deposits in their asset portfolios.

In panel (a) of Figure 20.2, a permanent increase in the demand for pound-denominated assets disturbs the foreign exchange market. A number of events could cause such an increase—for example, an increase in the interest rate on pound assets. Once the demand for pounds shifts to $D_1^£$, the old exchange rate, e_0^*, no longer represents an equilibrium. At e_0^*, the quantity demanded of pounds exceeds the quantity supplied. Individuals want to hold more than the available quantity of pound-denominated assets. How should the central banks react? Policy makers face two options: (1) allow the exchange rate to float in response to the forces of supply and demand, moving to a higher dollar price of pounds at e_1^*, or (2) intervene by selling pound-denominated assets from foreign exchange reserves to hold the exchange rate at e_0^*.

Under a managed float, the appropriate response to a *permanent* increase in the demand for pounds is to allow the exchange rate to move to a new equilibrium at e_1^*. Using intervention in an attempt to hold the exchange rate at e_0^* would require a fall in the U.S. money stock relative to Britain's to eliminate the payments

---

21 Sections 12.5 through 12.7 develop the basic demand and supply model of the foreign exchange market and apply the model under fixed and flexible exchange rates.

imbalance. If the two countries are unwilling to allow balance-of-payments considerations to dictate their monetary policies, sterilization will result in a fundamental disequilibrium: a chronic U.S. balance-of-payments deficit and British surplus.[22] The managed float breaks the link between the countries' BOPs and money supplies by allowing movements in the exchange rate to act as the adjustment mechanism when demand or supply conditions in the foreign exchange market change permanently.

Panel (b) of Figure 20.2 represents the case of a *temporary* increase in the demand for pounds (that is, demand shifts upward from $D_0^£$ to $D_1^£$ and then back down). Under a floating exchange regime, the dollar price of pounds would move upward from e_0^* to e_1^* and then back to e_0^*. Many analysts view this type of short-term exchange rate volatility as one of the primary drawbacks to a flexible exchange rate system. It can cause uncertainty about the profitability of international trade and financial transactions, because the future value of the exchange rate partially determines that profitability. *(Why?)* Proponents of intervention argue that uncertainty about exchange rates discourages specialization and trade and thereby reduces the efficiency of the world economy. Under an ideal managed float, the appropriate response to the temporary disturbance would be temporary intervention to hold the exchange rate at its underlying equilibrium level, e_0^*. This would require a sale of pounds by central banks, but only for the brief period during which demand was at $D_1^£$. As soon as the disturbance ended, demand would return to $D_0^£ = D_2^£$ and intervention could cease.

A managed float aims to limit exchange rate uncertainty by using intervention in foreign exchange markets to smooth short-run fluctuations in exchange rates, thereby achieving one of the proclaimed virtues of a fixed exchange rate. At the same time, a managed float allows market forces to determine long-run exchange rates, breaking the link between the balance of payments and the money stock and preventing chronic payments disequilibria, thereby achieving two virtues of a flexible exchange rate.

20.6.2 What Are the Problems with a Managed Float?

The major criticism of managed floating exchange rates is practical rather than theoretical. Figure 20.2 makes clear the correct policy response to each disturbance in the foreign exchange market because the nature of the disturbance is obvious—we labeled each up front as permanent or temporary. With this knowledge, a regime with rules that require intervention in the case of temporary disturbances and no intervention in the case of permanent disturbances performs satisfactorily. But in practice, of course, disturbances to the world economy have no labels to reveal their precise nature and time horizon.

Figure 20.3 illustrates the problem. Movement along the horizontal axis represents the passage of time, while the vertical axis measures the exchange rate. The jagged line to the left of t_0 depicts the historical movement of the exchange rate until today (time t_0). Let's assume that the dollar suddenly begins to appreciate rapidly against the pound just before t_0. Policy makers must decide whether to intervene to stop, or at least dampen, the appreciation. Under a managed float, intervention should occur only if the appreciation represents a short-term "blip" and not a fundamental change in the equilibrium exchange rate between dollars and pounds. But without knowing the future (that is, the path of the exchange-rate line to the right of t_0), how can policy makers distinguish between the two?

If line I turns out to be the future path of the exchange rate, the dollar appreciation will have been temporary and intervention the correct policy under the rules of a managed float. On the other hand, if the future exchange rate ends up following line II, the appreciation will have signaled the beginning of a trend, or a permanent change in the equilibrium exchange rate between dollars and pounds, and the appropriate policy response will have been to allow the dollar to appreciate. In practice, central banks often intervene just enough to dampen or slow the exchange rate movement but not enough to stop it. Such policies are called **leaning against the wind.**

If central banks intervene often in foreign exchange markets, the heavily managed float will function much like an adjustable-peg exchange rate system. The primary advantage claimed for such active management of the exchange rate involves the greater reduction in exchange rate uncertainty than under a more flexible rate regime. For intervention to maintain the exchange rate successfully, monetary authorities must allow it to affect the money stock; that is, they must not sterilize.[23] If a currency depreciates in foreign exchange markets and the domestic central bank intervenes to stop the depreciation, the domestic money stock falls. This lowers

---

22 On the impact of sterilization, see sections 16.3.3 and 16.4.2.

23 On sterilization, see sections 16.3.3 and 16.4.2.

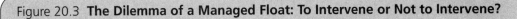

Figure 20.3 **The Dilemma of a Managed Float: To Intervene or Not to Intervene?**

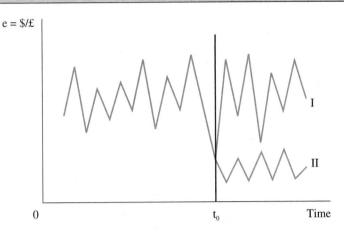

One interpretation of the "rules" of a managed float is to intervene in response to temporary disturbances in foreign exchange markets and to avoid intervention in response to permanent changes in the underlying equilibrium exchange rate. A practical difficulty arises because at the time of the disturbance (t_0), a policy decision must be made but policy makers cannot know the precise nature of the disturbance.

domestic prices, raises interest rates, and may lower output. These changes help eliminate the balance-of-payments deficit that caused the initial depreciation. If the monetary authority sterilizes by making open market purchases to offset the intervention's impact on the money stock, the sterilization blocks the adjustment mechanism and the balance-of-payments deficit becomes chronic.

A managed float doesn't change the basic rule that *correction of a payments imbalance requires a change in either the exchange rate or the money stock.* When central banks engage in sterilized intervention to attempt to circumvent this basic rule, crises develop. Any advantage that pegged exchange rates may have in reducing uncertainty quickly disappears if they are accompanied by balance-of-payments crises that come from interference with the economy's adjustment mechanisms. In other words, pegged exchange rates generate confidence and stability only if the chosen rates are sustainable, given policy makers' actions.

20.6.3 How Has the Macroeconomy Performed in the Post–Bretton Woods Years?

For several years following the collapse of Bretton Woods in 1971, most policy makers and many economists considered the managed float a temporary measure. Gradually, alternatives faded as the world economy endured serious shocks, especially the OPEC oil embargo and price increase in 1973–1974, which brought rising price levels along with rising unemployment rates to most oil-importing countries.[24] Judging a return to fixed exchange rates not viable in the face of such shocks, policy makers turned their attention to defining specific rules as to when intervention should and should not occur or how "managed" the float should be. Eventually these attempts also failed. The *de facto* system, under which the major currencies float subject to central banks' case-by-case intervention decisions, finally received official sanction in 1975 and in a 1976 revision of the IMF agreement.

The United States pursued expansionary policies in the mid-1970s in an effort to end its OPEC-induced economic slowdown. Other industrial countries, particularly West Germany and Japan, feared inflation more and waited several years before joining U.S. expansionary policies. The U.S. monetary expansion of the mid-1970s,

---

24 Section 19.10 examines supply shocks and policy responses to them under alternative exchange rate systems.

unaccompanied by expansions by trading partners, produced a substantial depreciation of the dollar against other currencies. Even intervention by the United States, West Germany, and Japan proved unable to stop the depreciation because of the continuing rapid U.S. money growth. In 1979, President Jimmy Carter appointed Paul Volcker, a respected financier with a strong anti-inflation reputation, chairman of the U.S. Federal Reserve Board. The appointment resulted in new Fed policies of lower monetary growth as well as renewed confidence in the dollar.

The effects of the slowdown in U.S. monetary growth hit the economy at about the same time as a second round of OPEC oil price increases in 1979–1980. Fearful of encouraging the inflation they had worked so hard to eliminate, U.S. policy makers didn't respond with expansionary monetary policies as they had after the 1973–1974 oil shock, and the economy underwent a severe recession that lasted through 1983. Money growth rates remained low, but fiscal policy grew more expansionary as tax rates fell and government spending rose during the Reagan administration. The dollar appreciated dramatically, which shifted demand away from U.S.-made goods and services toward foreign ones. *(Why?)* Gradually monetary policy loosened, but the dollar continued to appreciate into 1985, with virtually no intervention by the United States.

Although expansionary U.S. fiscal policies contributed to the recovery from the early 1980s recession, the resulting dollar appreciation also caused a significant redistribution of income. U.S. farmers found their overseas markets shrinking, while import-competing producers in U.S. industries such as automobiles, steel, and footwear endured increased competition from foreign rivals. Pressure mounted for protectionist policies, and Congress considered hundreds of bills ranging from import quotas for particular industries to across-the-board import tariffs.

In September 1985, the Reagan administration responded with the Plaza Accord. The Group of Five nations (known as G-5—the United States, Britain, Japan, Germany, and France) agreed to intervene in foreign exchange markets to bring about a depreciation of the dollar. The dollar actually had begun to depreciate in March, several months before the Plaza meeting; but in the months following the September accord, policy makers combined active intervention with public statements designed to "talk the dollar down" and with expansionary U.S. monetary policy, primarily cuts in the discount rate. The value of the dollar continued to decline against trading-partner currencies, most notably those of Germany and Japan. By November 1986 it had reached postwar lows against the yen.[25]

By 1987, attention had turned to slowing the dollar's decline. Based on the Louvre Accord of February 1987, the Group of Seven countries (G-7 consists of the G-5 plus Canada and Italy) engaged in coordinated foreign exchange market intervention through 1987 and 1988, attempting to hold the dollar's value within secret bands.[26]

The extent of intervention in foreign exchange markets has varied since 1988. The dollar has experienced periods of both appreciation and depreciation against the currencies of most major trading partners. As the models of Chapters Seventeen and Nineteen would lead us to expect, strong U.S. export performance accompanied the depreciations. During the recession of the early 1990s, exports proved one of the few sectors of the U.S. economy to grow strongly, although that growth slowed in 1992 as Germany and Japan entered recessions of their own and bought fewer U.S.-produced goods and services. Germany's expansionary fiscal policy (related to unification) and tight monetary policy caused both tensions between the United States and Germany and the near-breakdown in 1992–1993 of the European Union's efforts at monetary integration.[27]

By 1994, U.S. unemployment had fallen below many analysts' estimates of the full-employment level. Policy makers expressed concern about inflationary pressure, and the Federal Reserve tightened monetary policy. Most European economies experienced some recovery from their recessions, but European unemployment remained very high by U.S. standards. Large government budget deficits continued to constrain fiscal policy in both the United States and Europe.[28] Japan employed expansionary fiscal policy in an effort to emerge from its deepest slump since World War II, accumulating a rapidly rising level of government debt.

---

25 For a discussion of the differential depreciation of the dollar against various currencies, see section 12.8.

26 The G-7 countries never announced the band parameters, and financial market participants spent much time guessing about their values. Observing intervention activity by the central banks provided the major clues to the exchange rate values acceptable or unacceptable to the Group of Seven.

27 See Case Three in Chapter Fourteen, Case One in Chapter Sixteen, and Case Three in Chapter Seventeen, as well as section 20.8.

28 We'll see some of the reasons behind the constraints on European fiscal policy in section 20.8 on the European Monetary System.

Throughout most of the early 1990s, the dollar depreciated, especially against the Japanese yen and the German mark.[29] All three central banks intervened periodically to buy dollars. However, intervention occurred more rarely than during the Plaza-Louvre period of the late 1980s; macroeconomic policy in the major countries appeared less directed toward exchange rates, even when those rates exhibited dramatic movements. Table 20.7 reports the frequency and scale of U.S. foreign exchange market intervention in recent years.

During the late 1990s, attention centered on continuing macroeconomic problems in Asia, including both Japan's long slump and the severe financial crises facing South Korea, Indonesia, Malaysia, the Philippines, and Thailand, and on the European Union's plan to move to a single currency for most member countries (discussed in section 20.8). After several years of non-intervention, U.S. and Japanese central banks intervened in foreign exchange markets during the summer of 1998 in an effort to stop or at least slow the yen's depreciation against the dollar.

The conjunction of a booming U.S. economy and slumping Asian ones placed policy makers in a difficult position. Based on the U.S. economy alone, the Federal Reserve almost surely would have tightened its monetary policy to prevent inflation as the U.S. unemployment rate fell below most estimates of its full-employment level. But tighter U.S. monetary policy would have risked generating further capital outflows from Asia. By late 1998, as the Asian situation failed to improve and threatened to spread to emerging markets in other regions, speculation shifted to the possibility of looser U.S. monetary policy despite the historically low U.S. unemployment figures. European economies, many just starting to grow again after the early-1990s recession, hesitated to loosen their monetary reigns for fear of unsettling markets as the European Union entered the critical period leading up to the January 1, 1999, adoption of the common currency. Japan, as we saw in Case One in Chapter Seventeen, continued to pursue expansionary fiscal policy, but with little apparent effect. By the fall of 1998, Asia's lingering economic ills pushed central banks in other parts of the world to act. First the United States and then the countries of western Europe (singly at first and later as a group) undertook expansionary monetary policies in an effort to prevent the Asian recessions from spreading.

Table 20.7 **U.S. Intervention in Foreign Exchange Markets, 1989–2000**

Year	Total Intervention	Frequency (Days of Intervention)
1989	Sell $8.90 billion for DM; Sell $10.58 billion for ¥	97
1990	Sell $200 million for DM; Sell $2.18 billion for ¥	16
1991	Buy $1.34 billion with DM; Sell $520 million for DM; Sell $30 million for ¥	13
1992	Buy $1.27 billion with DM; Sell $250 million for ¥	8
1993	Buy $1.43 billion with ¥	5
1994	Buy $3.50 billion with DM; Buy $2.60 billion with ¥	5
1995	Buy $3.25 billion with DM; Buy $3.10 billion with ¥	8
1996		0
1997		0
1998	Sell $833 million for ¥	1
1999		0
2000	Sell $1.5 billion for €	1

Source: Federal Reserve Bank of New York.

---

29 Section 18.5 covers the long-run real depreciation of the dollar against the yen.

Even after the worst of the Asian crisis passed, the U.S. economy continued to grow faster than its counterparts in Japan or Europe. The dollar appreciated, especially against the new euro. Finally, on September 22, 2000, after the euro had dropped by more than 25 percent of its initial value against the dollar, world central banks (including both the European Central Bank and the U.S. Federal Reserve) intervened. Macro policy makers continued to be confronted with a fast-growing U.S. economy, slow growth in Europe, and stagnation in Japan. During 2000, a sudden slowdown in U.S. growth turned everyone's attention to that slowdown's effect on the rest of the world. Then on September 11, 2001, with many economies already on the brink of recession, analysts struggled to predict the economic implications of both terrorist attacks on New York and Washington and a long-term battle against terrorism around the world.

After experiencing several decades of sharp swings among the dollar, yen, and euro, policy makers and economists remain divided over the managed floating exchange rate system. On the one hand, many worry about exchange rate volatility, the resource-allocation effects of unpredictable changes in real exchange rates, and lack of effective policy coordination among the major players. On the other hand, most acknowledge both the difficulties of returning to a fixed-rate system in an environment of highly mobile capital and governments' reluctance to subordinate domestic economic interests to the requirements of external balance, as demanded by a fixed-rate regime.

In summary, the years since 1973 represent a period of widely varying degrees of management of exchange rates. Table 20.8 presents the yearly performance of U.S. real output and prices under the managed float.

Unfortunately, the history of international monetary regimes can't answer the fundamental question of which arrangement is best. The answer to that question depends in complex ways on an individual country's circumstances. We can't even rely on a comparison of past macroeconomic performance under the various systems, because each historical period brought unique challenges and shocks to the world economy. We can, however, determine the facets of the different systems that worked well and those that apparently contributed to instability or other problems. In the next two sections, we summarize and briefly evaluate the main arguments for using fixed versus flexible exchange rates as a basis for the international monetary system.

Table 20.8 Annual Changes in U.S. Real GDP and Price Level, 1973–2000 (Percent)

Year	Change in Real GNP (Q)	Change in GNP Deflator (P)	Year	Change in Real GNP (Q)	Change in GNP Deflator (P)
1973	5.8%	5.6%	1987	3.4	3.0
1974	−0.6	9.0	1988	4.2	3.4
1975	−0.4	9.3	1989	3.5	3.8
1976	5.6	5.7	1990	1.8	3.9
1977	4.6	6.4	1991	−0.5	3.6
1978	5.5	7.1	1992	3.0	2.4
1979	3.2	8.3	1993	2.7	2.4
1980	−0.2	9.2	1994	4.0	2.1
1981	2.5	9.3	1995	2.7	2.2
1982	−2.0	6.2	1996	3.6	1.9
1983	4.3	4.0	1997	4.4	1.9
1984	7.3	3.7	1998	4.3	1.2
1985	3.8	3.2	1999	4.1	1.4
1986	3.4	2.2	2000	4.1	2.3

Source: U.S. Department of Commerce (updates are available at www.stats.bls.gov).

20.7 The Fixed-versus-Flexible Debate

Since the collapse of Bretton Woods in 1971–1973, policy makers, economists, and myriad pundits have engaged in dialogue and debate over the history and future course of the international monetary system. Was Bretton Woods responsible for the economic growth and relative stability of the 1950s and 1960s? Or was it a flawed system that lasted as long as it did only because of the period's otherwise strong economic performance? Do flexible exchange rates doom the world economy to inflation and lack of policy coordination? Or does exchange rate flexibility free the world economy from the constraints and overemphasis on external balance imposed by a fixed-rate regime? Even well-informed analysts and scholars differ in their answers to these questions.

20.7.1 Pros and Cons of Fixed Exchange Rates

We came across two major arguments for fixed exchange rates earlier in the chapter. Proponents of fixed exchange rates believe that they impose price discipline by preventing central banks from engaging in excessively expansionary, and thus inflationary, monetary policies. Proponents also claim that fixed exchange rates reduce uncertainty about the future value of the exchange rate and thereby encourage international economic activity that enhances the world economy's efficiency.

Price Discipline

The price-discipline argument would be a solid one if a fixed exchange rate did indeed prevent inflationary monetary policies. Unfortunately, historical evidence suggests that central banks inclined to pursue overly expansionary policies tend to circumvent attempts at discipline. Under a fixed exchange rate, a country with a balance-of-payments deficit experiences a reduction in its money stock as the central bank intervenes to prevent a currency depreciation. Should the central bank be inclined to avoid this loss of control of the money stock (that is, the discipline of a fixed exchange rate), sterilization policies can offset the reduction in the money stock, resulting in a chronic deficit. In other words, a fixed exchange rate can impose price discipline only on central banks willing to submit to it. Also, a fixed exchange rate system based on a reserve currency, such as Bretton Woods, doesn't impose effective price discipline on the reserve-currency country, which conducts monetary policy for the entire system and exports any inflation it generates.[30]

Proponents of flexible rates counter the price-discipline argument by pointing out that voters can and do discipline governments that follow inflationary policies. Inflation did rise during the early years of the floating period; but voters have disciplined many governments for inflation, and governments have learned to control, at least to some extent, their inflationary tendencies. Since the switch to flexible exchange rates, voters in the United States, Japan, several countries of Western Europe, and many developing countries have voted governments out of power for the inflation generated by their policies. Overall, experience suggests that avoiding inflation requires vigilance and discipline on the part of both voters and policy makers; a stable exchange rate regime can help, but can't substitute for sheer willpower and determination in avoiding inflation.

Reduced Volatility and Uncertainty

Exchange rate volatility and uncertainty can cause two problems. First, they may discourage beneficial international economic activity, such as trade and foreign investment, by making the domestic-currency value of future receipts and payments less certain. Second, volatile exchange rates can cause costly movements of resources as hard-to-predict exchange rate changes alter relative prices and shift demand back and forth between domestic and foreign goods. We've seen that such shifts in demand alter the performance of trade- and nontrade-oriented sectors of the economy, and these resource reallocations can generate political pressure for protection and other beggar-thy-neighbor policies.

Empirical evidence suggests that real exchange rates have exhibited much more volatility since the shift to more flexible exchange rates. However, many analysts argue that exchange rate volatility actually exerts little negative effect on international trade and investment because of the availability of forward markets for

---

30 On reserve-currency countries, see section 16.6.

hedging.[31] Proponents of fixed exchange rates counter by pointing out that forward contracts involve costs and may not be available for many currencies or for long-term economic activities such as foreign direct investment—although innovative financial instruments to provide long-term hedges are evolving. Numerous empirical studies that attempt to quantify exchange-rate uncertainty's effect on international trade, investment, or economic growth provide mixed rather than definitive results. Most economists agree that increased exchange rate flexibility doesn't appear to have exerted a dramatic negative effect on the growth of international trade and investment.

Real Exchange Rate Adjustment

We've learned that changes in real exchange rates play a vital role in macroeconomic adjustment to the shocks that constantly impinge on economies. Under a fixed exchange rate regime, changes in real exchange rates ($R \equiv P/eP^*$) can occur in one of two ways: changes in countries' price levels or currency realignments. Proponents of fixed exchange rates claim that, by preventing unilateral devaluations and revaluations, a fixed-rate regime avoids the competitive devaluations that plagued the world economy during the Great Depression. Instead of such beggar-thy-neighbor policies, adjustment occurs when countries either allow their price levels to adjust or alter their pegged exchange rate in consultation with trading partners. Opponents of fixed rates point out that devaluations occurred too infrequently under Bretton Woods, resulting in chronic failure to adjust to shocks, and that price levels often adjust very slowly, leaving economies to endure extended periods of unemployment. They also note that Bretton Woods required countries to hand control of their money stocks over to the reserve-currency country—the United States.

Exchange Crises

Countries that operate under a fixed exchange rate regime can avoid crises only if central banks play by the rules and allow adjustments in the money stock to correct any balance-of-payments disequilibria. When a government intervenes, sterilizes, and refuses to adjust the exchange rate, pressures build and crises develop. Balance-of-payments crises hardly reduce uncertainty, and they discourage international trade and financial activities.[32] A fixed exchange rate regime builds confidence in the stability of exchange rates only when policy makers follow policies that facilitate adjustment. These policies include, first, not sterilizing the effects of the balance of payments on the money stock and, second, timely devaluations and revaluations when pegged exchange rates deviate too far from equilibrium. Both policies require a subordination of internal balance to external balance that may prove politically and economically painful in the short run. When market participants lose faith in a government's ability to withstand the domestic political pressures generated by this pain, a balance-of-payments crisis can develop as portfolio owners' willingness to hold the domestic currency drops because they expect an impending devaluation.[33]

Governments may attempt to avoid such crises by imposing capital controls that seek to limit the scale of payments imbalances, but controls can interfere with the economy's efficiency and tend to lose their effectiveness in the long run as individuals learn to circumvent them.[34] Sudden expectation-generated flows of short-term capital can clearly complicate policy makers' tasks. However, it's difficult to design controls that don't hamper desirable trade and investment activities. Often, governments attempt to limit capital *outflows* while allowing or even encouraging *inflows*. But, of course, asset owners hesitate to purchase assets in a country if they fear that the government will restrict their ability to sell those assets, so controls on capital outflows can also discourage inflows. Most economists agree that capital controls are no substitute either for appropriate exchange-rate adjustments, sound macroeconomic policies, or effective prudential regulation of banking and the financial sector.

---

31 Section 12.3.2 explains hedging. The Obstfeld paper in the Chapter Nineteen references reviews the evidence on real exchange rate volatility.

32 See sections 16.4.4 and 20.8, along with Case One in Chapter Sixteen and Case Three in Chapter Seventeen on recent crises within the Exchange Rate Mechanism of the European Monetary System.

33 See Cases One, Two, Three, and Five in Chapter Sixteen, and Case Three in Chapter Seventeen.

34 See Case Four in Chapter Sixteen.

20.7.2 Pros and Cons of Flexible Exchange Rates

Crisis Avoidance

The primary benefits claimed for flexible exchange rates are essentially the same as those for market-determined prices in any market: smooth, automatic, and continuous adjustment to equate quantity demanded with quantity supplied. Such adjustment under a flexible exchange rate has several advantages. It avoids large balance-of-payments deficits and surpluses, because the exchange rate moves in response to any tendency for either to develop. Needed adjustments in the real exchange rate can occur quickly through changes in the nominal exchange rate rather than slowly through changes in countries' price levels.[35] Flexible exchange rates also render many policy decisions unnecessary, thereby avoiding the potential for policy errors or delays. These characteristics, taken together, imply that floating rates may help avoid the crises that occur under fixed rates when expectations of an impending devaluation build.

The fact that flexible exchange rates respond to all disturbances in the foreign exchange market also is used as an argument *against* flexible rates—on the grounds that they produce unacceptable levels of volatility. Of course, this need not be true; exchange rates, like any other price, will be volatile only if the demand and supply conditions in the foreign exchange market are volatile. However, because expectations are so important in asset markets such as the foreign exchange market, the volatility of demand and supply conditions can be difficult to predict and to control.

Policy Independence and Symmetry

Flexible exchange rates allow each country to determine its monetary policy independently. Recall that a major problem during the late Bretton Woods years involved other countries' dissatisfaction with U.S. monetary policy, the inflationary effects of which were exported from the reserve-currency country through the rules of the adjustable-peg system. If one thinks, as some economists do, that policy makers will misuse their ability to control the money stock by creating excessive monetary growth and inflation, one could view the ability of flexible exchange rates to give policy makers such power as a *minus* rather than a *plus* for flexible rates. Flexible exchange rates do free up the money stock for use in pursuing domestic targets, but as we saw in Chapters Eighteen and Nineteen, once we introduce price flexibility, monetary policy can affect only the price level in the long run and not real output.

On the other hand, a floating rate does permit a country to determine its own inflation rate, rather than forcing the country to "import" the inflation rate chosen by the reserve-currency country. When domestic and foreign inflation rates differ, the exchange rate adjusts in the long run in accordance with purchasing power parity.[36] This allows countries to choose different rates of inflation, whereas a fixed exchange rate system such as Bretton Woods requires countries either to follow the same rate of inflation or to realign their currencies. Evidence since the early 1970s indicates that flexible exchange rates *have* allowed countries to choose more divergent money-growth and inflation rates.

Consistency with Capital Mobility

A country with a fixed exchange rate can avoid crises only as long as its policies convince foreign exchange market participants that no devaluation is forthcoming, because this confidence makes portfolio owners willing to hold assets denominated in the domestic currency. A loss of confidence in the future value of the domestic currency causes portfolio owners to sell assets denominated in that currency and requires the central bank to sell foreign exchange reserves to maintain the fixed exchange rate. If the crisis is large enough in magnitude, the central bank may run short of reserves or ability to borrow and may be forced to devalue, possibly leading to a further loss of confidence in the currency.

Economies become particularly sensitive to such crises when capital is highly mobile, because portfolio owners can move quickly and easily in and out of different currency holdings. Therefore, a common policy for governments seeking to avoid exchange crises under a fixed exchange rate involved controls on capital flows.[37]

---

35 On real exchange rate adjustment under fixed and flexible exchange rates, see sections 19.7 and 19.9.

36 See Chapter Eighteen, especially sections 18.3 and 18.4, on purchasing power parity.

37 See Chapter Sixteen, Case Four.

But we've seen that capital mobility serves an important economic function: It allows capital owners to move their resources to locations where those resources will be most productive. In other words, capital mobility allows countries to take advantage of the gains from intertemporal trade. Capital controls can interfere with this capital-allocation process and generate efficiency losses for the world economy. By eliminating the major source of crises—expected currency devaluations—flexible exchange rates can eliminate one of the most important reasons that governments institute capital controls.

Excessive Volatility and Real Exchange Rates

While a perfectly flexible exchange rate gives policy makers control over the money stock, it requires them to accept market-determined movements in the exchange rate. Many economists doubt policy makers' ability to do this because of the exchange rate's broad impact on the domestic economy. Evidence suggests that, in the short and medium runs, changes in the nominal exchange rate also affect the real exchange rate. This implies that movements in e lead to changing fortunes for the trade-sensitive sectors of the economy. Real appreciations, in particular, can cause dramatic increases in domestic political pressure for protectionism, as occurred in the United States in the early and mid-1980s. Domestic political pressures from trade-oriented sectors of the economy make policy makers sensitive to changes in the real exchange rate and may cause them to intervene in foreign exchange markets in an effort to maintain export competitiveness and domestic sectoral employment, even when the exchange rate is supposed to be flexible.

The empirically demonstrated link between changes in real and nominal exchange rates in the short and medium runs also limits a flexible exchange rate's ability to insulate an economy from foreign monetary disturbances. If changes in the foreign money stock, for example, lead to proportional changes in the foreign price level and in the exchange rate in the long run, then foreign monetary policy exerts no real influence on the domestic economy because it doesn't alter the real exchange rate. *(Why?)* But in the short run, empirical evidence suggests that changes in the nominal exchange rate do alter the real exchange rate, as the foreign price level adjusts slowly to the change in the money stock, reducing the claimed insulation properties of a floating exchange rate.

Since the early 1970s, exchange rates, both nominal and real, often have exhibited high short-term volatility, much of which economists can't explain based on existing models. Longer-run exchange rate movements, however, appear roughly consistent with relative purchasing power parity and with existing economic models' predictions concerning policy effects.

As the preceding discussion makes clear, there's no "ideal" international monetary system. Both fixed and flexible exchange rate regimes have their advantages, and it's not surprising that various countries use different arrangements. During periods of stability when countries pursue consistent policy paths, either system can work quite well. During periods of instability in the world economy, both systems encounter problems and each has strengths and weaknesses in the face of different types of shocks.

20.7.3 **Insulation from Economic Shocks**

Three major classes of shocks disturb economies and require responses from policy makers: demand shocks that originate in the money market, demand shocks that originate in spending patterns, and supply shocks. Fixed and flexible exchange rates provide an economy with differing degrees of insulation and ability to adapt to these various shocks. For an economy more prone to one type of shock than to others, these differences represent an important consideration in the country's choice of exchange rate regime.

Shocks to the Domestic Money Market

Fixed exchange rates tend to provide more insulation than flexible ones to economies subject to frequent shocks that originate in domestic money markets. Consider what happens when the domestic money stock falls (or, equivalently, domestic money demand rises). Under a fixed exchange rate, the balance of payments moves toward a surplus, and the central bank must intervene by buying foreign exchange to prevent an appreciation. The money stock rises and reestablishes equilibrium in the domestic money market. *(Analyze the effects using an aggregate demand–aggregate supply diagram.)* If, instead, the economy operated under a flexible exchange rate, the monetary shock would cause the domestic currency to appreciate, shift demand toward foreign and away from domestic goods, and require a fall in the domestic price level to bring the economy back to internal balance.[38] *(Analyze the effects using an aggregate demand–aggregate supply diagram.)* So, for economies prone to shocks to their domestic money market, fixed exchange rates can provide an advantage over flexible ones in the form of this insulating property.

Flexible exchange rates, however, provide insulation against foreign monetary disturbances, but only in the long run. In the short and medium runs, adjustment in the price level lags behind changes in money stocks, leading to changes in the real exchange rate that affect output in both the domestic and foreign economies.

Shocks to Spending on Domestic Goods and Services

Flexible exchange rates tend to provide more insulation to economies subject to frequent shocks that originate in output markets or spending patterns. Consider an economy that experiences a decline in demand for its exports. Under a fixed exchange rate, the decline in income reduces money demand, puts downward pressure on the interest rate, and causes a capital outflow. To keep the domestic currency from depreciating in response to the balance-of-payments deficit, the central bank must sell foreign exchange and reduce the domestic money stock. This accentuates the decline in aggregate demand and means that the price level must fall by more to restore full employment—a possibly slow and painful adjustment process. *(Analyze the effects using an aggregate demand–aggregate supply diagram.)* Under a flexible exchange rate, the balance-of-payments deficit depreciates the domestic currency rather than reduces the money stock. The depreciation shifts demand away from foreign goods toward domestic ones and mitigates the spending shock's negative impact on employment and output. A flexible exchange rate allows the economy to return to long-run equilibrium more quickly (because the exchange rate adjusts more quickly than the price level) and minimizes the shock's short-run recessionary impact. *(Analyze the effects using an aggregate demand–aggregate supply diagram.)* This implies that a flexible exchange rate regime can provide advantages to economies that face primarily spending shocks to their output markets.

Supply Shocks

As we saw in Chapter Nineteen, flexible exchange rates provide policy makers with more choices in their responses to supply shocks. When a country experiences a permanent negative supply shock, of the kind examined in section 19.10, no policy can restore output permanently to its pre-shock level. A permanent negative supply shock reduces the economy's ability to produce goods and services and shifts its long-run aggregate supply curve to the left. Different macroeconomic policies can, however, influence how long the economy takes to adjust to its new long-run equilibrium, the extent of unemployment and reduced output during the adjustment period, and the shock's eventual impact on the price level.

A fixed exchange rate constrains policy makers to pursue macroeconomic policies consistent with balance-of-payments equilibrium and rules out expansionary monetary policy as a temporary device to cushion a supply shock's impact on the economy. Many economists believe that, had the OPEC oil shock of 1973–1974 occurred while the major industrial economies still operated under the fixed exchange rates of Bretton Woods, the shock's short-term impact on unemployment could have been much more severe. The economies generally responded to the OPEC shock with expansionary monetary policy that, while it contributed to inflation, did mitigate the short- and medium-run rise in unemployment.[39] This experience, coming at a time when negotiations to replace the Bretton Woods system were underway, played a role in discouraging countries from committing themselves to another fixed exchange rate system. In general, flexible rates have helped economies adjust to supply shocks and other disturbances that require changes in real exchange rates, albeit sometimes at a cost in terms of higher inflation.

In sum, different exchange rate regimes carry different implications for economies' adjustments to various types of economic shocks. Fixed exchange rates may mitigate domestic monetary shocks but exacerbate spending shocks. Flexible exchange rates may mitigate spending shocks and foreign monetary shocks but exacerbate domestic monetary ones. Floating rates provide policy makers with more flexibility in responding to supply

---

38 Flexible exchange rates speed the responsiveness of the price level to changes in the domestic money stock, as currency depreciation raises import prices and causes workers to demand higher wages in compensation. Therefore, monetary policy influences real output and employment for shorter periods.

39 Such a policy corresponds to following path "b" rather than path "a" or "d" in Figure 19.13. Of course, flexible exchange rates also allow policy makers to choose the very inflationary path "c."

shocks, but also give policy makers the option of following overly expansionary policies in vain attempts to avoid the inevitable decline in output following a permanent negative supply shock. Overall, governments' willingness and ability to coordinate their macroeconomic policies appear to depend more on the state of their domestic economies than on the exchange rate regime.

20.8 Money in the European Union: From EMS To EMU

In 1991, members of the European Union set out to accomplish an unprecedented feat: to have most, if not all, of the sovereign nation-states that belong to the EU using a common currency (since named the *euro)* and operating under a common monetary policy run by a common central bank, the European Central Bank. To understand the pros, cons, and risks of such a historic project, we need to know a bit about recent European monetary history.

20.8.1 History, 1979–1999

The major Western European currencies, as well as the U.S. dollar, have operated under a managed float since the early 1970s, but the European arrangement has been somewhat more complicated. Since 1979, the currencies of most European Union members have been *fixed* relative to one another and have *floated* as a group against the dollar and other currencies, an arrangement called the **Exchange Rate Mechanism (ERM)** of the **European Monetary System (EMS).**[40] A weighted basket or composite of the EU currencies called the **European Currency Unit (ECU)** floated against non-EU currencies. Within the ERM, each central bank intervened in foreign exchange markets to keep the value of its currency fixed within a prescribed band against the ECU and, thereby, against other EU currencies.[41]

We know that attempts to maintain fixed but adjustable exchange rates among countries following divergent macroeconomic policies are fraught with difficulties, especially when capital is highly mobile, as is increasingly the case in Europe. When individual countries follow divergent policies, those policies create pressures for exchange rate realignments, because rates threaten to move outside their defined bands. Foreign exchange market participants begin to anticipate those realignments and start to buy currencies expected to face revaluation and to sell those subject to devaluation. Such speculative activity involves little risk because the official bands tell market participants which way the exchange rates must move; the process resembles buying or selling stock if you somehow knew the stock price could move only in one direction. Expectations become self-fulfilling prophecies as demand falls for already weak currencies and rises for already strong ones.

Given what we know about the difficulties of maintaining fixed exchange rates among economies that follow divergent economic policies and encounter diverse economic shocks, why did the European Union persist in its efforts, and how did the system survive? Proponents of European monetary integration hoped to accomplish several goals, some economic and some political. First, they hoped to improve European economic performance and make Europe more "competitive" with other industrial areas, especially the United States and Japan. For more than two decades, Europe had suffered much higher unemployment rates (an average of more than 10 percent), lower rates of job creation, and deteriorating technological leadership compared with its rivals.[42] Second, proponents hoped to present the United States with a more nearly equal macroeconomic counterpart in terms of economic size and voice in international negotiations. Third, within Europe, proponents believed that monetary integration would encourage intra-European trade and investment by lessening transaction costs associated with multiple currencies and exchange rate fluctuations. Fourth, proponents wanted to use the policy credibil-

---

40 All EU member countries joined the EMS; however, not all joined the ERM, which required intervening to enforce the fixed intra-EU exchange rates. For example, Britain avoided joining the ERM until 1990 and dropped out in 1992 (see Case Three in Chapter Seventeen and Case One at the end of this chapter).

41 Prior to 1993, the ERM bands allowed currencies to fluctuate up or down by 2.25 percent, or by 6 percent in some cases (Spain, Britain, Portugal, and Italy). After the European currency crises of 1993 (discussed later), the bands were widened to ±15 percent, and Italy and Britain left the ERM. Italy reentered the ERM in 1996, and Greece in 1998. Finland entered in 1996. Sweden did not participate in the ERM.

42 Case One in Chapter Nineteen reports on European unemployment.

ity of governments and other institutions with established policy making reputations (for example, Germany's Bundesbank) to help establish sound policies in countries that lack such credible institutions (for example, Italy and Greece).[43] Finally, supporters of European economic and political integration hoped that monetary integration would contribute to the momentum toward more unified policy making in Europe.

Given this ambitious agenda and the problems that face fixed exchange rate systems, how did the European Monetary System survive? During most of the post-1979 period, the pegged bilateral exchange rates within the EMS were adjustable and, in fact, periodically realigned, usually once or twice per year. The realignments involved revaluations of the Deutsche mark and the Dutch guilder, devaluations of the Italian lira and Greek drachma, and mixed changes in the other currencies. In addition, EU rules required that member countries with BOP surpluses lend to countries that encountered difficulties as a result of BOP deficits. Usually this involved Germany lending Deutsche marks to other central banks that, in turn, sold those marks in the foreign exchange market to support their respective currencies. Throughout much of the 1980s, many EU members maintained some degree of capital controls that limited the magnitude of BOP deficits and helped keep the required intervention and realignments manageable. But capital controls imposed costs on European economies by preventing capital from flowing to its most productive location. The European program to complete an open internal market by 1992 required elimination of capital controls and made currencies more vulnerable to crisis under the ERM adjustable-peg system. The increased capital mobility limited European governments' ability to realign their currencies without generating expectations-based crises. Beginning in 1987, facing the constraints of increasingly mobile capital, EU member countries began to place more emphasis on following convergent macroeconomic policies, thereby reducing pressure for exchange rate realignments; the periodic exchange-rate adjustments ceased. The period between 1987 and mid-1992 was one of relative quiet on the monetary front in Europe, but the quiet didn't last.

20.8.2 Maastricht, Monetary Unification, and Crisis

The EMS was part of a long history of attempts to integrate the Western European economies.[44] Like the policy coordination efforts of the G-7 or of the broader world economy, integration efforts within the EMS encountered resistance when they threatened national sovereignty over macroeconomic policy. However, in 1991 at the Dutch town of Maastricht, the EU governments outlined an ambitious plan for a three-stage process of **economic and monetary union (EMU)** that included "the irrevocable fixing of exchange rates leading to the introduction of a single currency" and the goal of "definition and conduct of a single monetary policy and exchange rate policy the primary objective of both of which shall be to maintain price stability."[45] Proponents of the Maastricht plan hoped to accomplish two goals: (1) by creating a common currency, minimize transaction costs and establish a stable exchange rate system not susceptible to crises generated by expected currency realignments, and (2) by creating a European system of central banks, give other EU countries a voice in monetary policy, dictated largely by Germany's Bundesbank under the pre-Maastricht EMS arrangements.[46]

The Maastricht plan turned out to be enormously controversial—in Europe and elsewhere. The timetable established at Maastricht required ratification by all (then) 12 member countries, a process temporarily waylaid by Denmark's *no* vote in the summer of 1992. The political and economic uncertainty generated by the lengthy process of ratification contributed to buildups of speculative pressure against some member currencies. EU members refused to discuss any possible currency realignments, fearful of contributing to the growing expectations that devaluations of the Italian lira, Spanish peseta, Portuguese escudo, and British pound were inevitable.[47]

43 On Germany's reserve- or key-currency role within the EMS, see section 16.6, along with Case Three in Chapter Fourteen and Case One in Chapter Sixteen.

44 For a discussion of integration in terms of international trade, see Chapter Nine.

45 Europe's Werner Report made a proposal similar in many respects to Maastricht back in 1971.

46 See section 16.6 and Case Three in Chapter Fourteen, Case One in Chapter Sixteen, Case Three in Chapter Seventeen, and Case One at the end of this chapter.

47 See section 16.4.4 on exchange rate expectations.

EU governments pressured German policy makers to expand the German money stock to lower German interest rates and ease the devaluation pressures on non-mark currencies. But German policy makers refused, not wanting to add monetary expansion to their dramatic fiscal expansion to cover the costs of unification.[48] This forced other EU members—some deep in recession—to continue to intervene to support their currencies against the Deutsche mark. In September 1992, rather than continue to intervene and contract their money stocks, Italy and Britain withdrew from the ERM and Spain devalued the peseta.[49] Denmark and Britain, in exchange for their ratification of Maastricht, won the right to "opt out" of its provisions for a common European currency.

A year of more-or-less constant crises followed. These crises forced several currency realignments, despite modest German monetary expansion. Ireland devalued its pound, and Spain and Portugal devalued their respective currencies several times. The EU reaffirmed each ERM member country's responsibility to intervene when its currency threatened to move outside its set trading band. Most European countries found themselves in recession and increasingly unwilling to constrain their monetary policies to maintain their exchange rates against the Deutsche mark. In August 1993, the exchange rate bands for ERM currencies were widened to ±15 percent except for the guilder-mark rate, making the system resemble more closely a managed floating exchange rate. By 1994, Europe showed signs of recovery from recession, and the exchange crises of 1992–1993 abated. The wide ±15 percent bands remained in place, but most currencies (with the exceptions of the pound and lira, which remained outside the ERM) returned to their earlier, narrower bands until March 1995, when the peseta and escudo were again devalued.

Historian Harold James, in his official IMF history, *International Monetary Cooperation since Bretton Woods*, summarized the basic dilemma confronting European efforts at monetary integration during the mid-1990s:

> [Intervention] could not be a substitute for policy adjustment. In this case, central bank intervention could not counter the perception that two fundamentally opposed political pressures were pulling the system apart. Germany, threatened by a large fiscal deficit as a consequence of the high costs of political unification, required monetary restraint. Tight money policies, however, elsewhere in Europe were blamed for the severity of the recession, and political pressure mounted for a relaxation. Germany's neighbors faced a dilemma: if they followed German monetary restraint, their recession would be intensified; if they failed to tighten, funds would flow out and lead to an exchange rate crisis.[50]

The early 1990s, especially the economic implications of Germany's unification, confronted the European Union with a dramatic economic shock originating in the system's reserve-currency country. That this shock seriously damaged the EU's fixed exchange rate system, just as U.S. policy during the late 1960s had seriously damaged Bretton Woods, shouldn't surprise us. In December 1995, members of the European Union reconfirmed their intention to proceed with monetary unification and announced a new post-crises timetable. They announced that the new European currency would be christened the **euro**.[51] As the countdown to the first key date began, attention focused on which countries would manage (or choose) to satisfy the economic criteria to participate.

Maastricht Convergence Indicators

Prior to participation in the planned common central bank, common monetary policy, and common currency, the Maastricht plan requires countries to conform to rules regarding exchange rate stability, inflation, interest rates, government budget deficits, and government debt. These rules are known as **convergence indicators,** because they measure whether the economies follow policies similar enough to make a common currency

---

48 For various perspectives, see Case Three in Chapter Fourteen, Case One in Chapter Sixteen, Case Three in Chapter Seventeen, and Case One at the end of this chapter.

49 See the cases cited in footnote 48.

50 Page 487.

51 Throughout years of discussion of a common currency, the unofficial name most often used was the *ecu* (note the similarity to the European Currency Unit, or ECU). When a last-minute decision resulted in *euro* instead, some commentators speculated that *ecu* had lost out because it sounded (especially to Germans) "too French."

viable. This raised a politically controversial issue: Should the subset of countries achieving policy convergence move ahead with plans for a common currency without the other EU members? The Maastricht plan's answer to this question was yes. All countries that satisfied the criteria were to embark on currency unification as of January 1, 1999; other EU members could join later as they met the convergence criteria.

The Maastricht treaty requires each EU member country to meet five economic convergence criteria before it can participate in monetary unification:

1. Currency must have remained within its ERM trading bands for at least two years with no realignment.
2. Inflation rate for the preceding year must have been no more than 1.5 percent above the average inflation rate of the three lowest-inflation EU members.
3. Long-term interest rate on government bonds during the preceding year must have been no more than 2 percent above the average interest rate of the three lowest-inflation EU members.
4. Budget deficit must not exceed 3 percent of the country's GDP.
5. Government debt must not exceed 60 percent of the country's GDP.

The number of EU members that satisfied the Maastricht convergence criteria fluctuated during the 1990s. Countries that failed did so primarily on the exchange-rate criterion (#1), a legacy of the exchange crises of 1992–1993, and on the government budget deficit (#4) and government debt criteria (#5), because of increased government spending and reduced tax revenues associated with the recession of the early 1990s. Most countries made substantial progress between 1993 and 1997 toward meeting the criteria, although in some cases the "progress" involved a bit of accounting smoke and mirrors. An EU conference in May 1998 determined, based on 1997 data, which countries could participate initially in the monetary union. Of the 15 EU members, Denmark, Sweden, and Britain opted out of participation in the common currency, at least temporarily. Of the remaining 12, only Greece was ruled to have made insufficient progress toward meeting the convergence criteria, in part because the drachma had only reentered the ERM in March 1998. The ruling admitting so many countries reflected a very flexible interpretation of the convergence criteria.

Throughout the early 1990s, most of the opposition to such a flexible interpretation came from Germany, which didn't want to tie itself to countries that lacked the policy discipline to meet the strict convergence criteria. Many German policy makers argued that Italy, in particular, shouldn't be admitted until it demonstrated further commitment to sustainable, sound, noninflationary macroeconomic policies. However, when the costs of unification and its early-1990s recession forced Germany itself to undertake some accounting wizardry to meet the criteria, German opposition to other countries' doing the same thing lost much of its force.

To get their government budget deficits below the 3 percent Maastricht limit, countries undertook a variety of one-time policies, implying that deficits were unlikely to stay below 3 percent in future years without further fiscal consolidation. Italy imposed a one-year "eurotax" to raise additional revenue. Spain froze public-sector wages to reduce its expenditure. France transferred the accumulated pension funds of state-owned France Telecom to the government account. Germany sold some of its government-owned oil reserves and raised its value-added tax.[52]

Some economists and policy makers agreed that a lenient interpretation of the convergence criteria was appropriate. They argued that any delay in monetary union because of EU members' failure to meet strict criteria would merely provide opportunity for yet another period of instability to disrupt the schedule. Proponents of leniency also argued that EU member countries would find it much easier to meet the criteria once monetary unification occurred and that a union excluding more countries would be hardly worth the trouble. Opponents of leniency argued that it threatened the monetary union because a single currency ultimately couldn't work among countries following divergent macroeconomic policies.

With the initial membership determined, attention turned to the mechanics of introducing the new currency and to the challenges of implementing a single monetary policy for countries in such different macroeconomic circumstances. Table 20.9 outlines the schedule for the key steps in the process.

As January 1, 1999, approached, the governments of many EU member countries had changed significantly from those that had negotiated the Maastricht agreement a decade earlier. Left-of-center parties controlled or shared power in 13 of 15 EU members, including 9 of the 11 initial euro participants. This political change,

---

52 The German government also proposed revaluing its gold stock from its historical price of $92 per ounce to the current market price of $344 per ounce to show additional government revenue. A storm of protest from both citizens and officials of the anti-inflation Bundesbank killed that proposal.

Table 20.9 **EU Monetary Unification Timetable**	
Date	Tasks
January 1, 1999	Set conversion rates of national currencies into euro European Central Bank conducts monetary and exchange rate policy National currencies still circulate as legal tender
January 1, 2002	Introduction of euro notes and coins
March 1, 2002	Euro becomes sole legal tender Withdrawal of national currency notes and coins

along with Europe's continued slow growth, raised questions about whether needed structural reforms and fiscal consolidation would move forward. Wim Duisenberg, the Dutch first president of the new European Central Bank, announced in the fall of 1998 that Europe didn't need expansionary monetary policies to offset the negative effect of the Asian crisis on European economies, despite the fact that the U.S. Federal Reserve had already responded with lower interest rates. With only weeks to go before the January deadline for introduction of the euro, interest rates in participating countries still differed. Then, on December 3, 1998, the 11 countries announced simultaneous interest rate cuts designed to bring rates in all 11 to 3 percent, an event many commentators proclaimed "the birth of the euro."

As of January 1, 1999, the European Central Bank conducted monetary policy for the euro area. The bank faced challenging tasks. The brand-new institution had no reputation or credibility on which to draw and lacked established procedures. As its key date approached, most member countries struggled with high rates of structural unemployment, as we saw in Case One in Chapter Nineteen. To make policy decisions even harder, some countries, especially Spain and Ireland, boomed, while others, including the all-important Germany and France, had just started to recover from recessions. A single monetary policy appropriate for all wasn't easy to find, but, as we'll see in section 20.8.3, this represents the most important ongoing problem for any attempt at monetary union.

As of 2001, policy makers in the European Central Bank faced a difficult policy-making environment. The euro had depreciated significantly since its introduction, especially against the U.S. dollar. "Euroland" economies were experiencing very different business-cycle conditions. Ireland, and to a lesser degree Spain and Portugal, boomed; their inflation rates exceeded the European Central Bank's 2 percent inflation target. Other countries, most notably Germany, lagged. Should the ECB slow money growth, as appropriate for Ireland, or speed it up to give the German economy a short-run lift? Higher oil prices combined with the ECB's inflation-target rule made the bank's position even less comfortable: Should it tighten monetary policy in response to rising inflation or to loosen monetary policy in response to slowing output? More-expansionary monetary policy would run the risk of further euro depreciation; policy makers worried that such depreciation might cause the public to lose confidence in the young currency, despite the short-run expansionary effects of a currency depreciation. On top of these problems, journalists and policy makers in other countries seemed to pounce on every statement ECB officials made, eager to point out inconsistencies.

Besides the obvious political or sovereignty-related arguments by politicians and policy makers against monetary union, there are economic arguments both in favor of and against such ventures. Those arguments attempt to shed light on the question, *"Who should use a common currency, or how large is the optimal currency area?"*

20.8.3 **Who Should Use a Common Currency?**

Two geographic regions that use a common currency encounter both advantages and disadvantages compared with use of two distinct currencies. As the common-currency area grows, the costs of a common currency tend to rise and the benefits to decline. The area that maximizes the benefits minus the costs of using a single currency is called an **optimal currency area.** Economist Robert Mundell developed the theory of optimal currency areas in the early 1960s, but the issue took on new urgency and interest with recent events in the European Union.[53]

---

53 The Tavlas articles in the chapter references contain detailed but accessible discussions of optimal currency areas.

The potential benefits of using a common currency include reduced exchange rate volatility, reduced transaction costs, and enhanced policy credibility. As we noted earlier, uncertainty about future changes in exchange rates may discourage international trade and financial activity. A common currency—the ultimate fixed exchange rate—eliminates this uncertainty and allows firms to specialize according to comparative advantage and to plan imports and exports without worrying about losses due to future exchange rate movements and without having to hedge in forward markets. *(What do you think would happen to trade between New York and California if the two states used different currencies?)* A common currency also allows individuals and firms to avoid the transaction costs of exchanging one currency for another when engaging in travel or cross-border transactions. During the early 1990s in the European Union, if you began with one currency and exchanged it step-by-step for each of the other EU currencies *without buying any goods or services,* the transaction cost of the currency exchanges alone reduced the original sum by approximately half. A single currency eliminates those costs.[54] The higher the share of intragroup trade and investment within a set of countries, the greater these benefits from a single currency.

A common currency also can provide an advantage to policy makers by allowing them to credibly commit to a future course for monetary policy. This argument proved particularly relevant for the European case. There, the German Bundesbank's strong anti-inflation reputation, if effectively transferred to a European Central Bank, might allow historically high-inflation countries such as Italy and Greece to commit themselves to non-inflationary policies. For this reason, much of the monetary-union debate in Europe centered on the proposed central bank's policy mandate; inflation-conscious citizens and policy makers wanted to ensure it would follow policies similar to those of the Bundesbank rather than the Banque d'Italia! The agreement establishing the European Central Bank requires it to follow an inflation target; the bank adjusts monetary policy to keep the average medium- to long-run inflation rate in member countries below 2 percent.

A common currency involves costs as well as benefits. Most important, countries lose the ability to pursue independent monetary policies. After all, a common currency represents the ultimate fixed exchange rate ($e \equiv 1$), and we know that a fixed exchange rate eliminates independent monetary policy as a macroeconomic policy instrument. A common currency also eliminates exchange devaluations or revaluations as a policy tool within the currency area. The entire region using a common currency binds itself to follow the same monetary policy.

Given the list of costs and benefits, how does a region determine whether a currency area would provide net benefits? The literature on optimal currency areas suggests that a region is likely to gain from a common currency if (1) a large share of members' trade occurs with other members, (2) the region is subject primarily to common shocks that affect the entire area similarly and not to shocks that affect its subregions differentially, (3) labor is mobile within the region, and (4) a tax-transfer system exists to transfer resources from subregions performing strongly to those performing poorly. We've already seen why criterion (1) matters: The higher the share of intragroup trade, the greater the transaction-cost saving of a single currency. Criteria (2) through (4) all relate to how likely countries are to need different monetary policies.

If different shocks buffet subregions, policy makers in those subregions may need to follow different monetary policies or to allow their exchange rate to move to offset the shocks' short-run effects. For example, suppose the German economy booms while Britain's languishes. Britain might follow an expansionary monetary policy relative to that of Germany, thereby depreciating (or devaluing) the pound and shifting demand toward British goods and services and away from German ones, at least in the short run. Such adjustment becomes impossible under a common currency.

When some subregions of a currency area grow quickly and others grow more slowly, movements of labor between subregions represent another possible adjustment mechanism. If cultural or institutional factors restrict such labor flows, then differential monetary policies and exchange rate realignment may be needed—ruling out a common currency. An alternative means of dealing with differential regional growth involves fiscal transfers from growing regions to stagnant ones. Suppose Florida booms while California suffers a recession. The U.S. federal tax and transfer system conducts an automatic transfer from Florida to California: Florida's tax payments rise with income, while California's fall; Florida's transfer-payment receipts (that is, unemployment benefits, welfare payments, and so forth) fall with rising income, and California's rise. These transfers partially offset the two states' differential economic performance and lessen the need for any exchange rate adjustment (impossible, of course, within the United States).

---

54 European banks' foreign-exchange trading revenues were predicted to drop by about 70 percent when the euro replaced national currencies.

How does the European Union measure up to these standards for an optimal currency area? Most empirical studies have compared Europe to the United States, which, after all, operates under a common currency. Members of the EU appear more subject to differential shocks than the regions of the United States. Labor is considerably less mobile between countries in Europe than between U.S. regions, perhaps because of greater language and cultural differences. In fact, labor is much less mobile even *within* countries in Europe than in the United States, but intra-European mobility does appear to be rising. Finally, the separate nation-states of the EU have no supranational tax and transfer system to reallocate resources across regions in response to differential shocks, although the EU does administer some development funds for less-developed or declining regions in the Union. All these findings have led many economists to question whether the EU really represents an optimal currency area, despite its relatively high level of intragroup trade. These questions take on even more significance as the EU extends its membership and announces plans to expand into Eastern Europe.[55] Euro optimists argue that once the euro transition process is completed, the economies will become more alike and their business cycles more synchronized. Pessimists point out that the countries may specialize more heavily as intercountry trade becomes easier, making the countries even more different and more prone to subregion-specific shocks.

In the end, two considerations will play central roles in the success or failure of the European monetary union. First, most economists agree that many EU members must undertake significant structural reforms to improve the flexibility of their labor markets and to reduce the sizes of their welfare policies if the European economies are ever to grow faster and to bring down their high rates of structural unemployment. These policy changes are always politically difficult, but timing is important. To be politically feasible, the reforms need to be enacted when the respective economies are performing relatively well. Second, the countries must prove willing to subordinate some of their national policy-making sovereignty to the union.

Great Britain

CASE ONE:
Floating the Pound, Part II

We learned in Case Three of Chapter Seventeen that Britain, faced with a choice of (1) reducing its money stock to maintain the pound's peg to the Deutsche mark or (2) dropping out of the EU's Exchange Rate Mechanism, chose in September 1992 to do the latter. Floating the pound permitted Britain to follow a more expansionary monetary policy in response to the country's recession. Britain's economy grew more rapidly over the next few years than did those of countries that chose to remain in the ERM and follow the tight monetary policies necessary to prevent devaluations of their currencies against the Deutsche mark.

Later Britain opted out, at least temporarily, of joining the European monetary union and adopting the euro. The decision wasn't without its costs, both political and economic. After the country's ERM withdrawal, Britain's voice within the European Union carried less weight in the informal negotiations that play a large role in determining the union's future course. The British government also faced the tricky domestic political problem of deciding if and when to rejoin. Economically, absence from the ERM put Britain on a distinct policy course from countries that remained commit-

ted to adopting the euro. At first, as we've seen, Britain's independent course allowed for faster growth. But, as usual, things were to change.

By late 1998, the British economy started to show some signs of weakness, especially in terms of employment in its export-oriented manufacturing industries. Table 20.10 reports EU countries' structural government budgets as a percent of their full-employment GDPs. Recall from Case Two in Chapter Nineteen that the *structural* budget refers to what the budget surplus (+) or deficit (−) would be, given policy makers' fiscal-policy stance, if the economy were operating a full employment, neither in a boom nor in a recession. In other words, the structural budget measures the effect of fiscal policy, taking out the effect of the business cycle on the budget. Countries that remained in the ERM had been forced to follow several years of tight fiscal policies in order to comply (or at least *try* to comply) with the Maastricht convergence criteria on government deficit and public debt. Britain, on the other hand, freed from the convergence criteria, faced less pressure to tighten its fiscal policy. The table reveals that Britain ran larger budget

---

Table 20.10 **Structural Government Budget Balances of EU Members, 1993–1997 (Percent of Full-Employment GDP)**

Country	1993	1994	1995	1996	1997
Germany	−2.8%	−1.6%	−2.6%	−4.0%	−2.6%
France	−3.9	−4.3	−3.8	−2.6	−1.8
Italy	−9.0	−8.8	−7.3	−5.8	−1.8
United Kingdom	**−6.1**	**−6.1**	**−5.2**	**−4.4**	**−1.9**
Austria	−3.4	−4.4	−4.7	−3.2	−1.8
Belgium	−5.4	−3.3	−2.5	−1.5	−0.8
Denmark	−0.7	−1.1	−1.0	−0.1	0.8
Finland	−1.6	−1.5	−2.2	−1.2	−0.8
Greece	−12.0	−8.3	−8.6	−6.2	−3.3
Ireland	0.3	0.7	−1.4	−0.7	−0.2
Netherlands	−2.5	−3.5	−3.4	−2.3	−1.5
Portugal	−6.3	−5.3	−4.8	−2.3	−1.8
Spain	−5.7	−5.1	−5.3	−3.1	−1.5
Sweden	−9.0	−8.4	−6.7	−2.9	0.1
Total of EU countries	−5.1	−4.9	−4.5	−3.4	−1.7

Source: Organization for Economic Cooperation and Development, *OECD Economic Outlook*, June 1998.

deficits than most EU members, except for Italy (long an EU laggard in terms of policy discipline), Greece (a recent EU entrant with little hope of approval for early euro participation), and Sweden (which didn't join the EU until 1995 and remained outside the ERM).

Expansionary fiscal policies tend to generate currency appreciations, so these fiscal differences caused the pound to appreciate against the ERM currencies.[56] The result: struggling British export industries. Most analysts predicted a current-account deficit for Britain in 1998, after a 1997 surplus. As the economy threatened to move into recession, the Bank of England undertook expansionary monetary policies during late 1998, following interest-rate cuts by the U.S. Federal Reserve and just before the coordinated interest-rate cuts by the 11 euro participants.

CASE TWO:
Do Floating Rates Really Float?

Member countries report to the International Monetary Fund what type of regime they use for their respective currencies (see, for example, Table 20.1 for recent data). Those reports indicate a dramatic shift from fixed to floating exchange rates since the early 1970s. Only 11 percent of countries pegged their rates in 1999, compared with 97 percent in 1970.

But do governments actually allow the forces of supply and demand to determine their exchange rates, or do they still control exchange rates while claiming to float? It's impossible to know for sure, since governments can use many policies to affect their exchange rates. Guillermo Calvo and Carmen Reinhart set out to try to find out.[57] They found that the exchange rates for supposedly floating currencies

---

56 Case Four in Chapter Seventeen investigates the relationship between fiscal policy and the exchange rate.

57 "Fear of Floating," National Bureau of Economic Research Working Paper W7993.

stay within 2.5 percent bands 80 percent of the time. And these countries' foreign exchange reserves varied by more than 2.5 percent in any given month 66 percent of the time. Both these observations suggest that many countries that claim to have floating exchange rates—including some developed industrial economies, but not including the United States, Germany, or Japan—in fact intervene extensively to limit their exchange rates' movements.

CASE THREE:
When Is a Central Bank Not a Central Bank?

We've implied thus far that all economies, at least market-oriented ones, have a central bank that both conducts open-market operations and intervenes in foreign exchange markets. In fact, some countries have a *currency board* instead of a central bank. A currency board intervenes in foreign exchange markets as needed to maintain its fixed exchange rate but doesn't conduct open-market operations. In other words, a currency board is a central bank that can't conduct expansionary monetary policies to cover the government's fiscal expenditures. A true currency board owns no domestic government bonds, so the board's foreign exchange reserves must back the entire domestic money stock.[58]

Whenever a balance-of-payments deficit arises, the currency board sells foreign exchange reserves and the domestic money stock falls. When the balance of payments moves into surplus, the currency board buys foreign exchange and the domestic money stock rises. In other words, operating under a currency-board system means allowing the balance of payments to determine changes in the money stock, with no opportunity to sterilize intervention's effects.[59] If the currency board "follows the rules," the system rules out overly expansionary (and thus inflationary) monetary policy. Many developing economies and economies in transition from central planning find this "policy commitment" element of a currency board advantageous, since their governments typically lack policy credibility. Countries with currency boards include Hong Kong, Estonia, Lithuania, Bosnia, Bulgaria, and (at least until late 2001) Argentina. All but Hong Kong introduced their boards during the 1990s, as part of economic reform programs.

Currency boards are somewhat controversial. Many economists recognize the system's potential benefits for historically inflation-prone economies trying to establish sounder macroeconomic policies. However, such a system limits policy makers' options for responding to shocks. When a financial crisis such as the one in Asia strikes, for example, a currency board, unlike a central bank, can't act as a lender of last resort to banks on the verge of failure. And the interest rate increases implied by a balance-of-payments deficit under a currency board can weaken poorly regulated or supervised banks.

Hong Kong has long experience with a currency board. Despite the former colony's historically strong banks and its large stock of foreign exchange reserves, the Hong Kong Monetary Authority's 1997 and 1998 defense of the HK$7.8 = US$1 peg (in effect since 1983) imposed substantial costs on the economy. As the currency board sold dollars to defend the peg, the domestic money stock fell and interest rates rose dramatically, with serious negative consequences for banks and the stock market. (*As of February 1998, Hong Kong interest rates were approximately 5 percent above comparable U.S. ones. What does this imply about market participants' exchange rate expectations?*)

In early 1998, in the midst of the Asian financial crisis, Indonesia proposed moving to a currency-board system after having been forced to abandon its traditional fixed exchange rate. Many economists, as well as the International Monetary Fund, were skeptical, not believing that Indonesia or its banks were in a position, either economically or politically, to accept the discipline such a board requires. Indonesia finally abandoned the plan.

---

58 Section 15.2.3 outlines how central-bank assets, usually government bonds *and* foreign exchange, form the basis for the country's money stock.

59 Some currency boards, including Hong Kong's, give it some characteristics of a central bank. This generated controversy in 1997 when many analysts claimed that the Hong Kong Monetary Authority's attempts to behave like a central bank rather than a currency board produced expectations of a devaluation of the Hong Kong dollar.

Ireland

CASE FOUR:
Standing Ireland in the Corner

Common-currency areas always face problems when some member economies boom while others languish. It didn't take long for this issue to confront the new European Central Bank. Just as countries prepared to adopt the euro, the Irish economy emerged from decades of doldrums. Growth in 2000 was predicted to reach 8 percent, following five years of growth over 5 percent per year. Unemployment fell, and living standards rose—but so did inflation. Housing prices and wages increased rapidly, and overall inflation reached 5 percent, more than three times the rates in France or Germany. With the introduction of the new currency, European interest rates fell and the euro depreciated, just the opposite of economists' prescriptions for a booming economy starting to experience rising inflation.

In late 2000, the Central Bank of Ireland, powerless as a euro member to affect monetary policy, called on the Irish government to restrain its fiscal policies of tax cuts and heavy government spending on infrastructure. Soon, the European Commission also expressed concern over Ireland's continued fiscal expansion in light of the country's rising inflation. This made Ireland the first EU member to be publicly and formally reprimanded for policies inconsistent with the common-currency project. Ireland refused to change its policies in response to the EU criticism; and the union lacks the power to compel such policy changes. Despite its controversial expansionary fiscal stance, Irish policy continued to satisfy the requirement of the EU's Growth and Stability Pact that government budget deficits must not exceed 3 percent of GDP except during exceptional circumstances such as deep recessions or natural disasters.

CASE FIVE:
Su Currency Es Mi Currency

In common-currency projects such as the European Union's euro, countries join to create a new currency. Sometimes, however, a country chooses to adopt as its domestic legal tender another country's existing currency. This general process is widely known as *dollarization,* although in principle the currency adopted need not be the U.S. dollar. Such practices aren't new; Panama has used the U.S. dollar since 1904. But interest in dollarization is rising. Ecuador adopted the U.S. dollar in 2000, after 116 years of the sucre as the national currency; El Salvador followed; and Argentina considered doing so as it confronted a 2000–2001 debt crisis under the currency board that had since 1991 tied the peso to the dollar at a 1:1 exchange rate.

Why might a country choose to abandon its national currency and adopt that of another country, thereby handing over its monetary policy to the other country's monetary authority? Typically because domestic policy makers have shown themselves—usually through long periods of high rates of inflation—to be unable to conduct monetary and exchange-rate policies consistent with stability and credibility. In such circumstances, "signing on" to another, more stable country's policies and institutions may help stabilize the domestic economy and rebuild confidence, but not without some costs.

Some analysts believe that dollarization promotes trade and financial integration, but the empirical evidence on this question appears mixed. If, by dollarization, a country can convince market participants that no possibility of a devaluation exists, then the country may enjoy lower interest rates as lenders no longer demand a premium to cover the fear of devaluation. For countries with high levels of debt, this possibility of lower borrowing costs serves as a powerful incentive for dollarization. But even dollarized economies can still face high interest rates to borrow if they follow unsustainable fiscal policies, because lenders must bear the risk of debt default even if not of devaluation.

Dollarization eliminates all possibility of a devaluation, even the small possibility preserved under a currency board. Escaping dollarization would require reintroducing a national currency; such an effort would likely encounter resistance and skepticism, especially during a crisis. Dollarization also eliminates the monetary authority's ability to act as a lender of last resort to banks during a banking crisis, because the domestic authorities can't create dollars. However, banking crises may be less likely to occur if dollarization increases public confidence in the banking system, and the government can still lend directly to banks in trouble.

Not all dollarization results from formal government policy decisions. In many economies, for example in Latin America, U.S. dollars handle many economic transactions, constitute large shares of bank reserves, and represent the currency of denomination for contracts such as wage agreements and borrowing and lending. With such informal dollarization already well advanced, formal dollarization provides both fewer benefits and fewer costs.

Policy makers in the country whose currency is being adopted by others aren't always enthusiastic about dollarization. After all, those policy makers' responsibility is to conduct policy appropriate for their own economy. But dollarizers experience those same policies, whether appropriate or not.

Summary

International trade and financial transactions require some means of exchanging one currency for another, known as an *international monetary regime*. The major types of regimes include fixed exchange rates (including Europe's common currency), flexible exchange rates, and managed floating. Each arrangement has benefits and costs, so the choice involves trade-offs depending on the individual country's economic situation.

The strengths claimed for fixed exchange rates include discipline against inflationary policies and reduction in exchange rate uncertainty. Flexible exchange rates, on the other hand, promote adjustment and eliminate the need for foreign exchange market intervention, thereby allowing each country to determine its own monetary policy independently.

Since 1973, the major currencies have operated under a managed float that attempts to capture the benefits of both fixed and flexible exchange rates. Ideally, a managed float would allow the forces of supply and demand to determine the long-run paths of exchange rates while using intervention to smooth out short-term fluctuations. In practice, the lack of information concerning the nature of disturbances when policy decisions must be made makes it difficult to choose the appropriate extent of intervention.

Looking Ahead

We've focused so far on developing general models that provide basic insights into macroeconomic policies, events, and performance for virtually any country. However, some countries face special challenges in designing and implementing sound macroeconomic policies. Two such groups are developing economies and countries in transition from central planning to more market-oriented economic systems. In Chapter Twenty-One, we turn our attention to the macroeconomic problems and prospects facing these countries.

Key Terms

convertible currency
gold standard
mint exchange rate
price discipline
specie-flow mechanism
gold-exchange (gold-dollar) standard
key (reserve) currency
adjustable-peg system
fundamental disequilibrium
tranches
conditionality

liquidity
dollar standard
managed (dirty) float
leaning-against-the-wind policies
Exchange Rate Mechanism (ERM)
European Monetary System (EMS)
European Currency Unit (ECU)
economic and monetary union (EMU)
euro
convergence indicators
optimal currency area

Problems and Questions for Review

1. Explain the determination and maintenance of the exchange rate between the German Deutsche mark and the French franc
   a. Under the gold standard.
   b. Under the Bretton Woods gold-dollar standard.
   c. Under the Exchange Rate Mechanism of the European Monetary System.
   d. Under the post-2002 EU common currency.

2. What considerations does the optimal currency area literature suggest that a group of countries should take into account in deciding whether to adopt a common currency? Explain.

3. Comment on the following statement: "A fixed exchange rate regime cannot work as long as policy makers place more importance on internal than on external balance."

4. What is the practical shortcoming of the following rule for policy makers under a managed floating exchange rate system: "Intervene in foreign exchange markets to offset the effects of temporary disturbances, and allow the exchange rate to change in response to permanent disturbances."

5. Some analysts argued that a common European currency could not work unless all members satisfied the Maastricht convergence indicators *prior* to joining. Others argued that EU member countries should adopt a common currency first and *then* satisfy the convergence indicators. What are some of the pros and cons of each argument?

6. When a central bank follows an inflation target rule, it loosens monetary policy if inflation falls below the target range and tightens monetary policy if inflation rises above the target range. Explain how such a policy response might exacerbate unemployment after a negative supply shock.

7. Some economies, especially those with histories of high inflation, operate under crawling-peg exchange rate regimes. Under a crawling peg, the domestic currency is devalued by a pre-announced amount on a regular schedule (for example, 1 percent per month). Suppose country A operates under such a regime.
   a. What relationship would you expect to hold between the domestic interest rate, i, and the interest rate of the foreign country, i*? Why?
   b. To keep the *real* exchange rate constant, what relationship would need to hold between P and P*?
   c. If the domestic inflation rate exceeded the foreign one by more than the crawling devaluation, what would happen to the real exchange rate? What would happen to the country's current-account balance? How might this contribute to the probability of a crisis?

8. One possible international monetary regime consists of a world central bank conducting monetary policy and issuing a single currency used throughout the world. What would be the advantages of such a system? The disadvantages?

References and Selected Readings

Antinolfi, Gaetano, and Todd Keister. "Dollarization as a Monetary Arrangement for Emerging Market Economies." Federal Reserve Bank of St. Louis, *Review* (November/December 2001): 29–40.
Accessible review article on the subject of Case Five.

Bayoumi, Tamim, et al. *Modern Perspectives on the Gold Standard.* Cambridge: Cambridge University Press, 1996.
Analyses of the pros and cons of a gold standard; intermediate.

Calvo, Guillermo A., and Carmen M. Reinhart. "Fixing for Your Life." *Brookings Trade Forum* (2000): 1–58.
Fixed exchange rates as a source of stability and credibility.

Chang, Roberto. "Policy Credibility and the Design of Central Banks." Federal Reserve Bank of Atlanta, *Review* (First Quarter 1998): 4–15.
Accessible overview of the theory and evidence on inflation and central-bank independence.

Chang, Roberto, and Andrés Velasco. "Exchange-Rate Policy for Developing Countries." *American Economic Review Papers and Proceedings* 90 (May 2000): 71–75.
Issues relevant to developing countries' choice of exchange-rate regime.

Chriszt, Michael. "Perspectives on a Potential North American Monetary Union." Federal Reserve Bank of Atlanta, *Economic Review* (Quarter Four 2000): 29–38.
What are the chances of an eventual North American monetary union similar to the one in Western Europe?

Cooper, Richard N., and Jane Sneddon Little. "U.S. Monetary Policy in an Integrating World: 1960 to 2000." In *The Evolution of Monetary Policy and the Federal Reserve System over the Past Thirty Years,* edited by R. W. Kopcke and L. E. Browne, 77–130. Boston: Federal Reserve Bank of Boston, 2000.
History of international influences on U.S. monetary policy.

Dueker, Michael J., and Andreas M. Fischer. "The Mechanics of a Successful Exchange Rate Peg: Lessons for Emerging Markets." Federal Reserve Bank of St. Louis, *Review* (September/October 2001): 47–56.
Why did Austria's peg to the Deutsche mark work while Thailand's peg to the dollar failed?

Eichengreen, Barry. *Globalizing Capital.* Princeton: Princeton University Press, 1996.
The history of capital flows in the world economy.

Enoch, Charles, and Anne-Marie Gulde. "Are Currency Boards a Cure for All Monetary Problems?" *Finance and Development* (December 1998): 40–43.
Introductory overview of what currency boards can and cannot accomplish.

Fischer, Stanley. "Exchange Rate Regimes: Is the Bipolar View Correct?" *Finance and Development* 38 (June 2001): 18–21.
Accessible overview of why softly pegged exchange rates—that is, those subject to devaluation or revaluation— may be disappearing.

Frankel, Jeffrey A., et al. "Verifiability and the Vanishing Intermediate Exchange Regime." *Brookings Trade Forum* (2000): 59–124.
Are regimes between a common currency and a float viable in a world of mobile capital?

Friedman, Milton. "The Case for Flexible Exchange Rates." In *Essays in Positive Economics.* Chicago: University of Chicago Press, 1953.
One of the first serious calls for a change to a flexible exchange rate regime; for all students.

Fuhrer, Jeffrey J. "Central Bank Independence and Inflation Targeting." Federal Reserve Bank of Boston, *New England Economic Review* (January–February 1997): 19–36.
A skeptical view of central-bank independence and inflation targeting; for all students.

Garber, P., and L. Svensson. "The Operation and Collapse of Fixed Exchange Rate Regimes." In *Handbook of International Economics,* Vol. 3, edited by G. M. Grossman and K. Rogoff, 1865–1912. Amsterdam: North-Holland, 1995.
Advanced survey of the theoretical and empirical literatures.

Gulde, Anne-Marie. "The Role of the Currency Board in Bulgaria's Stabilization." *Finance and Development* 36 (September 1999): 36–39.
An example of use of a currency board during transition.

Isard, Peter. *Exchange Rate Economics.* Cambridge: Cambridge University Press, 1995.
Intermediate- to advanced-level survey of the literature on exchange rate regimes.

James, Harold. *International Monetary Cooperation since Bretton Woods.* Oxford: Oxford University Press, 1996.
A comprehensive official history commissioned on the 50th anniversary of Bretton Woods.

Kopcke, Richard W. "Currency Boards: Once and Future Monetary Regimes?" Federal Reserve Bank of Boston, *New England Economic Review* (May/June 1999): 21–38.
What currency boards can and cannot do, and in what circumstances.

Krueger, Anne O. "Conflicting Demands on the International Monetary Fund." *American Economic Review Papers and Proceedings* 90 (May 2000): 38–42.
Introduction to the myriad pressures on the IMF in its assistance of developing economies.

LeBaron, Blake, and Rachel McCulloch. "Floating, Fixed, or Super-Fixed? Dollarization Joins the Menu of Exchange-Rate Options." *American Economic Review Papers and Proceedings* 90 (May 2000): 32–37.
Introduction to the pros and cons of dollarization.

Little, Jane Sneddon, and Giovanni P. Olivei. "Rethinking the International Monetary System: An Overview." Federal Reserve Bank of Boston, *New England Economic Review* (November/December 1999): 3–28.
An introduction to the challenges facing the international monetary system.

Little, Jane Sneddon, and Giovanni P. Olivei. "Why the Interest in Reforming the International Monetary System?" Federal Reserve Bank of Boston, *New England Economic Review* (September/October 1999): 53–84.
How recent challenges facing the international monetary system created a move toward reform.

Mundell, R. A. "A Reconsideration of the Twentieth Century." *American Economic Review* 90 (June 2000): 327–340.
A Nobel Prize winner's look back at the century's exchange rate regimes.

Obstfeld, Maurice, and Kenneth Rogoff. "The Mirage of Fixed Exchange Rates." *Journal of Economic Perspectives* 9 (1995): 73–96.
Argues that permanently fixed exchange rates have become infeasible for all but a few countries; accessible to all students.

Pakko, Michael R., and Howard J. Wall. "Reconsidering the Trade-Creating Effects of a Currency Union." Federal Reserve Bank of St. Louis, *Review* (September/October 2001): 37–46.
Cautions whether a common currency really increases countries' intra-group trade.

Pollard, Patricia S. "The Creation of the Euro and the Role of the Dollar in International Markets." Federal Reserve Bank of St. Louis, *Review* (September/October 2001): 17–36.
How will the euro affect international use of the dollar? For all students.

Quirk, Peter J. "Exchange Rate Regimes as Inflation Anchors." *Finance and Development* (March 1996): 42–45.
Argues that developing countries can be well served by flexible exchange rates; for all students.

Reinhart, Carmen M. "The Mirage of Floating Exchange Rates." *American Economic Review Papers and Proceedings* 90 (May 2000): 65–70.
Evidence that many countries that claim to allow their exchange rate to float do not.

Soltwedel, Rüdiger, et al. "European Labor Markets and EMU: Challenges Ahead." *Finance and Development* 37 (June 2000): 37–40.
How much of a barrier will Europe's labor immobility create for the monetary union?

Symposium on "Building an Infrastructure for Financial Stability." Federal Reserve Bank of Boston, 2000.
Infrastructure requirements for financial openness and stability.

Symposium on "Global Economic Integration: Opportunities and Challenges." Federal Reserve Bank of Kansas City, 2000.
Challenges of creating and managing an open international financial system.

Symposium on "Rethinking the International Monetary System." Federal Reserve Bank of Boston, 1999.
Thoughts on the international monetary system in the wake of the late-1990s financial crises.

Tavlas, George S. "On the Exchange Rate as a Nominal Anchor: The Rise and Fall of the Credibility Hypothesis." *The Economic Record* 76 (June 2000): 183–201.
Problems with use of a pegged exchange rate as a nominal anchor; intermediate.

Tavlas, George. "The 'New' Theory of Optimum Currency Areas." *The World Economy* (1993): 663–685.
Excellent, detailed survey of the current state of the literature on optimum currency areas; for all students.

Tavlas, George. "The Theory of Optimum Currency Areas Revisited." *Finance and Development* 30 (June 1993): 32–35.
Accessible overview of the renewed interest in optimal currency areas.

Velde, François R., and Marcelo Veracierto. "Dollarization in Argentina." Federal Reserve Bank of Chicago, *Economic Perspectives* (First Quarter 2000): 24–37.
The experience of an early unofficial adopter of the dollar, written prior to Argentina's latest crisis.

CHAPTER TWENTY-ONE

Macroeconomics of Development and Transition

21.1 Introduction

The models developed in Chapters Twelve through Twenty capture the fundamental knowledge that economists have acquired about how the international macroeconomy and monetary system work. Those models provide insight into macroeconomic events and policy options for *any* country, and we've used many diverse countries as examples and cases. However, we should remember that not all countries' macroeconomies are alike. The United States, Britain, Kazakhstan, Brazil, Singapore, India, and Ethiopia each face different macroeconomic challenges, policy options, and potentials. Important macroeconomic differences arise from countries' unique histories, economic and political systems, legal institutions, economic shocks, size, trading relationships, resource endowments, and many other factors.

Two groups of economies that exhibit distinctive macroeconomic characteristics and encounter special macroeconomic situations as a result are the developing economies and the countries in transition from central planning. Recall that in the *micro*economic portion of the book, we first developed economists' basic trade models in Chapters Two through Ten and then looked in Chapter Eleven at the unique trade-related issues and problems that face developing and transitional economies. Having now mastered the basic *macro*economic models, we're ready to take the analogous step and focus on the unique macroeconomic challenges that face developing and transitional economies.[1]

Macroeconomists have turned more attention to these countries over the past few years for several reasons. The internationalization of output and finance markets, represented by rapidly growing trade in goods, services, and financial assets, creates more numerous and more important linkages between developed and developing economies. These linkages sometimes grow largely unnoticed until a dramatic event—such as the OPEC oil shocks of the 1970s, the debt crisis of the 1980s, the Asian financial crisis of the late 1990s, or the Turkish and Argentinean crises of 2001—thrusts them onto newspapers' front pages. As developing economies grow and integrate themselves further into the world economy, macroeconomic interdependence becomes more pronounced. Events in Mexico following the December 1994 peso devaluation provide one example in which macroeconomic events in a single developing economy exerted dramatic influence on other countries, both developed and developing.[2] Events in Asia after the July 1997 devaluation of the Thai baht provide another.

---

1 Note that division of the problems facing developing and transitional economies into *micro*economic ones and *macro*economic ones is highly artificial, so we hope readers will read or review Chapter Eleven along with this chapter.

2 Case Three in Chapter Sixteen covers the Mexican crisis.

A second reason for macroeconomists' increased attention to development-related issues comes from the emergence of a large group of "new" developing countries in the wake of the political and economic revolutions that swept the Soviet bloc in 1989–1991. Those economies face the need not only to establish sound day-to-day macroeconomic policies, but also to design economic and political institutions that make such policies possible, sustainable, and credible.

We turn first to developing economies in general, and then to the newest group of developing economies—those making the transition toward market-oriented economic systems after decades of central planning.

21.2 Development and the Macroeconomy

Recall from Chapter Eleven the fundamental goal of economic development: an improvement in the well-being of a country's residents. Per-capita GDP is the most common, albeit imperfect, measure of development status. Based on 2000 per-capita income, the World Bank classifies countries with annual incomes below $9,266 as developing countries, which the bank further divides into middle-income ($756–$9,266) and low-income (<$756) countries.[3]

We also noted in Chapter Eleven that important differences exist *among* developing economies.[4] Most of sub-Saharan Africa, where economic development has progressed least, continues to exhibit very low per-capita incomes, and low or negative growth rates, along with high illiteracy and short life expectancy compared with other countries. In East Asia, many developing countries still have low per-capita incomes, but until the financial crisis of the late 1990s, growth rates had been very high, and life expectancy almost equals that in developed economies. A handful of developing countries, most notably in Latin America, have accumulated such large amounts of external debt that, even after substantial debt rescheduling and forgiveness by creditors, that fact continues to dominate their macroeconomies. The fragility of their macroeconomic reforms and prospects was further highlighted by their negative reactions to the volatility in world financial markets generated by the Asian crisis and by another round of crises in 2001 centered on Argentina. And, as we'll see later in the chapter, the formerly centrally planned economies of Eastern Europe and Central Asia enjoy high incomes relative to those in many developing economies, as well as relatively high life expectancy and literacy rates, but nevertheless experienced dramatically negative growth rates during the transitional 1990s.

21.2.1 Developing Countries' Pre-Reform Macroeconomic Characteristics

We must keep in mind the important differences among developing economies; still, we can highlight a set of macroeconomic characteristics historically shared by many of these countries prior to their recent reforms. Common characteristics include the following:

1. Pervasive government involvement in the economy, including widespread government ownership of infrastructure, industry, and land, as well as extensive control of day-to-day economic activity.
2. Poorly developed financial institutions.
3. Government finance through money creation rather than taxes or domestic borrowing.
4. Fixed exchange rates, accompanied by capital controls or direct government control of foreign exchange transactions.
5. Extensive foreign borrowing to cover current-account deficits.

Much of the reform undertaken by many developing countries during the 1980s and 1990s involved undoing or altering this web of characteristics, which most economists agree combined to hinder both macroeconomic performance and economic development. We can easily see, based on insights from the macroeconomic models developed in earlier chapters, how these five characteristics would interact to affect economic performance adversely.

---

3 Table 11.1 reports countries' per-capita incomes and other indicators of well-being.

4 Table 11.2 summarizes some of the relevant differences.

Government Ownership and Control

Government directly owned and controlled much of the productive capacity in many developing countries. This created a variety of microeconomic and macroeconomic problems.[5] Because government typically maintained its ownership and control through political power rather than by good economic performance that survived the test of the market, many state-owned enterprises exhibited low productivity, technological backwardness, and production patterns that ignored consumer preferences.

When government owned large sectors of the economy and engaged in detailed management of business enterprises, policy decisions often hinged more on politics than on economics. Plant managers, who realized that their fate depended more on political connections than on economic performance, had little incentive to enhance the productivity and efficiency of their plants. Wages often were set to reward the politically faithful with high-paying jobs, even if those wages outstripped labor productivity and resulted in uncompetitive products. As a result, many state-owned enterprises required constant government subsidies to keep them in operation. The inefficient enterprises also required protection from foreign competition, so economies with extensive government ownership and control often passed up substantial portions of the potential gains from international trade. After all, if state-owned domestic producers ignored consumer wants, consumers would try to import goods from abroad (or emigrate) to satisfy those wants. To maintain its control, the government had to stifle those attempts to circumvent its rules.

Poorly Developed Financial Markets and Institutions

In a context of such extensive government ownership and control, private capital markets could perform few of the functions they serve in industrial economies where government plays a more limited role. As a result, capital markets and financial services tended not to evolve in developing economies even when they weren't restricted legally. The absence of well-developed financial markets then provided a rationale for still *more* government involvement to allocate capital and make investment decisions—tasks performed largely by private capital markets in the major industrial economies. Developing-country governments' poor policy records, bad reputations, and lack of credibility made it difficult for them to borrow by selling long-term bonds. At the same time, widespread government ownership of industry precluded a stock market as a major means of raising private funds to finance investment. This left only bank loans as a source of domestic finance; since governments typically controlled the banking sector, government often determined which enterprises received financing and which didn't.[6] Government also used credit terms, such as the interest rate charged on loans, to subsidize favored activities and tax unfavored ones.

Money-Financed Fiscal Expenditures

Government's broad role in the typical pre-reform developing economy dictated high levels of fiscal expenditures. And, as in *all* economies, these expenditures had to be paid for. Developing countries often had poorly functioning tax systems for several reasons. Low incomes translated into a small tax base. Any high-income elites in the economy typically enjoyed a close political relationship to the government, thereby insulating themselves from pressures to pay taxes. And tax compliance and enforcement tended to be weak.[7] These characteristics combined to render tax finance of high levels of government expenditure infeasible.

An alternative means of finance was government borrowing from the domestic population. But, as we mentioned, governments with poor policy records and credibility problems found it difficult to borrow by selling long-term bonds to the domestic population. The basic reason was that governments could, after selling bonds, create excessive money growth and inflation, which would erode the real rate of return earned by those who bought the bonds. In fact, if the rate of inflation exceeded the nominal interest rate paid on the bonds, investors actually earned *negative* real rates of return—quite a deterrent to buying bonds.[8] This left just one source of

---

5 In addition to the problems discussed here, many economists think that a pervasive state role in the economy creates additional opportunities for corruption.

6 See section 15.3 on banking crises and their potential macroeconomic effects.

7 Poorly developed tax systems cause many developing countries to rely heavily on taxes on imports and exports. This imposes an additional cost on the economy by discouraging international trade and forcing the economy to forgo part of the potential gains from trade.

8 Recall the Fisher relationship from Chapter Eighteen. The nominal interest rate, i, can be divided into two components: the real interest rate, r, and the rate of inflation, $i = r + \hat{P}$.

domestic financing for government expenditure: money creation. In effect, the central bank printed money that the government then used to buy goods and services. This combination of expansionary fiscal policy and expansionary monetary policy, of course, produced inflation, along with a bigger "inflation tax," which further reduced governments' credibility and future ability to borrow.

To keep the required interest payments low on whatever borrowing the government undertook, policy makers had an incentive to keep interest rates artificially low. This discouraged domestic saving and encouraged capital flight, as domestic savers attempted to earn higher and more secure real rates of return by placing their funds in foreign assets.[9] Low interest rates combined with government control over bank lending allowed politically favored sectors to receive handsome subsidies in the form of cheap loans. But low interest rates also resulted in a shortage of capital to finance investment and more opportunity for the government to allocate the scarce capital on political criteria.

Government Control over Foreign Exchange

In an attempt to keep domestic funds in the domestic economy rather than allowing them to escape as capital flight, governments often used capital controls or foreign exchange controls. Regulations commonly required exporters who earned foreign currencies to sell them immediately to the government in exchange for domestic currency. More generally, exchange controls rendered the domestic currency nonconvertible for current-account or capital-account transactions or both. These policies gave governments even more control over the economy. By choosing to whom to allocate scarce foreign exchange and what exchange rate to charge for it, government could tax or subsidize each transaction. Controls also restricted the domestic population's opportunity to circumvent the government's inflation tax by using a foreign currency instead of the domestic one in everyday domestic transactions.[10] Despite governments' best efforts, black markets in foreign exchange usually developed and limited official attempts to control access to loans and foreign exchange.

External Debt

Finally, we come to the characteristic that put developing countries on newspaper front pages around the world during the 1980s: external debt. We've discussed the widely publicized debt problem of some developing countries at several points in the text. In Chapter Eleven, we analyzed external debt as one element of the general development problems facing developing countries and focused on the microeconomic aspects of their debt. *(We suggest a review of section 11.5.3.)* Here we note the relationship between the macroeconomic aspects of external debt and the other macroeconomic characteristics of developing countries.

Consider one of the fundamental macroeconomic relationships, the link between domestic investment, saving, the government budget, and the current-account balance. For every economy, by definition:[11]

$$I = S + (T - G) - CAB \qquad \textbf{[21.1]}$$

Equation 21.1 implies that a country can finance domestic investment (I) in three ways: through domestic private saving (S), through government saving in the form of a budget surplus ($T - G > 0$), or through a current-account deficit ($CAB < 0$) and the matching borrowing from abroad. We argued earlier that the typical pre-reform developing country exhibited a low rate of private saving, high government expenditure, and low tax revenues. Together, these characteristics limited the feasibility of the first two forms of finance.

Developing countries still could take advantage of domestic investment opportunities, but they had to run current-account deficits and borrow abroad to finance them. This is just the intertemporal-gains-from-trade argument again: If developing economies have good domestic investment opportunities but little current income with which to finance them, those countries can borrow from foreigners who have investment funds

---

9 A high rate of private saving is one of the important characteristics that distinguished the East Asian economies from most other developing countries.

10 This phenomenon is called *currency substitution* or, more specifically, informal *dollarization;* see Case Five in Chapter Twenty.

11 Section 14.7 develops this relationship.

available but few good domestic investment opportunities. Both parties can gain, but only so long as the borrowing finances investment projects that prove productive enough to generate an economic return sufficient to repay the loan.

Unfortunately, many developing economies in the 1970s borrowed to finance projects that failed this criterion.[12] The projects failed for several reasons. Many were chosen by governments on a political rather than economic basis. Some borrowed funds supported grossly inefficient state-owned enterprises; others paid for military buildups; still others went to unproductive "prestige projects" such as national airlines, steel mills, and new capital cities. Other projects failed because economic conditions changed between the time the projects were undertaken and the time repayment came due. The industrial-country recession of the early 1980s caused primary-product prices to plunge, real interest rates to soar, and the dollar to appreciate dramatically against most developing-country currencies. As a result, many borrowers suffered a decline in export earnings from which to make payments, a rise in interest payments, and a rise in the domestic-currency value of their outstanding foreign-currency-denominated loans. This unfortunate combination led many developing countries to the brink of default.

Only years of negotiations ended the crisis with no major defaults and minimal long-term damage to the international monetary system. However, as section 11.5.3 makes clear, the debt crisis left a painful legacy and continuing economic problems for many developing countries. It did, however, have some positive effects as well. The debt crisis reminded developed and developing countries once again of their interdependence. The crisis also forced many developing countries to undertake long-needed economic and political reforms.

21.2.2 Reform

In a contest to select the top three trends in the international macroeconomy over the past 20 years, policy reform in the developing countries would be a strong candidate for inclusion. One by one, following decades of dismal economic performance, many countries changed some or all of the five key pre-reform macroeconomic characteristics listed earlier.[13] The reforms differ from country to country in their timing and breadth, but the most common changes fall into two groups. **Stabilization reforms** refer to policy changes that aim to achieve macroeconomic *stability*. The most basic elements of this stage of reform include cutting excessive government spending and reducing excessive money growth. Together, these changes help stabilize the value of the domestic currency and reduce inflation. The other major component of reform, **structural reform,** or **structural adjustment,** refers to changes in the basic *structure* of the economy. The most important element involves reducing the extent of government involvement in the economy and increasing the role for markets. Structural reforms attempt to provide stronger incentives for productive economic activities, including production, saving, investment, and international trade based on comparative advantage. Note, however, that stabilization and structural reforms can't really be separated. After all, the primary forces that cause macroeconomic instability—excessive fiscal spending and money growth—follow directly from government ownership and control of the economy, and reducing government ownership and control requires structural reform.

Although the correspondence is rough and inexact, we can think of stabilization reform as improving control over the aggregate *demand* curve (especially, stopping continual large rightward shifts that lead to persistent high inflation) and structural reform as encouraging rightward shifts of the long-run aggregate *supply* curve, which represents the economy's basic productive capacity. Historically, many developing countries suffered a combination of (1) inefficient government management of the economy that mired supply far to the left of its potential position based on the countries' resources, and (2) excessively expansionary fiscal and monetary policies that continually shifted aggregate demand to the right and, given the economies' low productivities, generated persistent inflation and currency devaluations. Panel (a) of Figure 21.1 illustrates these effects. The fundamental policy reforms undertaken by many developing economies during the past 20 years attempt to undo this disastrous combination and move the economies to a situation more similar to that in panel (b) of Figure 21.1. The precise approach to reform and the relative emphasis on its many diverse aspects vary greatly from country to country; however, we can note some common themes.

---

12   Section 11.5.3 provides details.

13   In some cases, countries instituted reforms at least in part because of pressure from creditors and international organizations such as the International Monetary Fund.

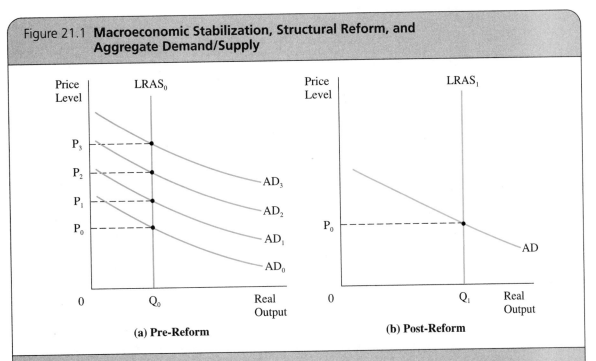

Figure 21.1 **Macroeconomic Stabilization, Structural Reform, and Aggregate Demand/Supply**

Panel (a) represents the typical macroeconomic situation in developing economies prior to reform. Overly expansionary fiscal and monetary policies shift aggregate demand (AD) continually to the right. Structural inefficiencies hold the long-run aggregate supply curve (LRAS) to the left of its potential position. This combination produces low levels of real output and rising prices. Reform shifts the situation to the one depicted in panel (b). Macroeconomic stabilization stops the continual rightward shift of AD, and structural reform allows LRAS to move to the right. This new policy combination produces higher real output and steady prices.

Privatization and Deregulation

The most basic structural reform involves reducing the role of government in the ownership and day-to-day control of the economy. Many state-owned enterprises have been privatized, sold to private investors. The goal is to confront the enterprises with a competitive economic environment, forcing them to become more productive, efficient, competitive, and responsive to consumer preferences. Managers and workers in this new environment face stronger incentives to improve production techniques, minimize costs, adopt new technologies, and otherwise improve the enterprises' economic performance.

   Privatization, as essential as it is to reform, can be a slow and difficult process. Emerging capital markets and investors find it hard to estimate reasonable prices for the enterprises up for sale, because their earlier performance under government ownership often provides a poor guide to their potential profitability. Foreign purchases of formerly state-owned enterprises can generate resentment of reform among the domestic population. Workers who held subsidized-wage jobs in the state-owned enterprises may oppose reforms that ultimately must limit wages to those justified by labor productivity. Some of the enterprises, established for political reasons, simply have no economic future and eventually must be closed or allowed to go bankrupt to avoid a continual drain on the government budget.

Financial Integration

Historically, many developing countries deliberately isolated themselves from world capital markets. Authorities prohibited or strictly regulated foreign investment in the domestic economy and tried to prevent any outflow of domestic funds. This isolation gave the domestic government a near monopoly over capital allocation. As a result, economically promising investment projects often went unfunded, while less promising ones received not only initial funding but an ongoing stream of government-financed subsidies.

Financial integration with world capital markets—the macroeconomic counterpart of trade liberalization—plays an important role in undoing this legacy by replacing government control of the capital-allocation process with more efficiently functioning markets.[14] These markets, by providing capital owners with vehicles to move their funds around the world, allow investors to compare investment projects across countries and to invest in the most economically promising projects. Governments lose their ability to channel funds into politically motivated "white-elephant" projects. Governments also acquire an external check on their macroeconomic policies. If a government strays too far from the reform path and begins to follow policies not conducive to strong economic performance, investors can shift their funds away from that economy, signaling to the government the riskiness of its path.[15]

The changes associated with financial market integration also encourage domestic saving and create domestic sources of funds to finance investment projects. Even given their low incomes, developing-country populations can generate impressive levels of saving—*if* convinced that government won't expropriate those savings, erode them through inflation, or force them into instruments that pay low or even negative real rates of return.

Like privatization, financial market integration can prove politically difficult. Enterprises favored under the government capital-allocation regime may attempt to block reform that would result in their evaluation on economic rather than political criteria. Opening the economy to foreign investment may generate resentment, particularly in economies with colonial histories. Powerful banking interests, accustomed to monopoly access to domestic depositors and borrowers, may generate political pressure to keep their protected position. And policy makers may not always appreciate the check on their policies provided by investors' ability to shift funds in response to policy changes.

Fiscal Consolidation and Tax Reform

Fundamental reforms of macroeconomic policy include reducing the level of government expenditure and shifting the finance of continuing expenditure away from money creation and toward taxes or government borrowing. The basic goal is reduction of the rate of growth in aggregate demand in order to reduce the exorbitant rates of inflation common in many pre-reform developing economies. Reducing government expenditure requires curtailing the role of government to include only those activities not well suited to markets, such as national defense, law enforcement, provision of a social-safety net, and some infrastructure projects. Government also must cut ongoing subsidies to enterprises that continue under state ownership.

To reduce inflation, post-reform government expenditures must be financed more through taxes and government borrowing and less through money creation. Other aspects of reform help accomplish this shift, at least in the long run. For example, as reform improves policy making and economic performance, the government's policy-making reputation may improve to the extent that the domestic population willingly purchases government bonds. Integration with world financial markets helps ensure that the rates of return on such bond offerings will be competitive with those available on foreign assets.

As with other aspects of reform, fiscal consolidation won't be universally popular. The country's elites may have adjusted to inflation and learned to circumvent government controls; so they may actually prefer continued inflation to either paying taxes to finance government expenditures or forgoing government services or subsidies. And, of course, enterprises that lose their government subsidies may oppose reform.

Currency Convertibility

A country can't enjoy the full gains from trade in goods and services or from intertemporal trade unless its currency is convertible. As long as government maintains control over foreign exchange and sets artificial exchange rates for those transactions, international activity can't be based on comparative advantage. Potential exporters, for example, have little incentive to produce for export if they know they must sell any foreign currency they earn to the government at artificially low prices. On the other hand, government-favored elites will import luxury consumption goods from abroad if provided with the requisite foreign exchange at reduced rates.

---

14 See Case Four in Chapter Sixteen.

15 Some analysts worry that capital markets may *overreact* to a government's policy missteps, such as Mexico's 1994 devaluation, thereby worsening macroeconomic performance.

Currency convertibility implies that the exchange rate, if fixed, can't be set too far from equilibrium in the foreign exchange market. Convertibility means that international traders and investors can demand that the central bank buy and sell foreign exchange at the pegged rate in amounts sufficient to cover the desired international trade and financial activities. If the pegged exchange rate strays too far from equilibrium, the excess demand or excess supply of foreign exchange will eventually exceed the central bank's ability to intervene and maintain the peg. If the central bank runs short of reserves, market participants may come to expect a devaluation and precipitate a currency crisis similar to Mexico's in December 1994, those within the European Monetary System in 1992 and 1993, those in East Asia in 1997, and those in Russia in 1998 and Brazil in 1999.

One way to avoid such crises is to operate under a flexible rather than a fixed exchange rate regime. Reforming developing countries often hesitate to make this move for two reasons. For very small developing economies, transactions in the domestic currency may be so infrequent and small that the foreign exchange market bears little resemblance to the active and competitive markets for dollars, yen, and euros. Forward and futures markets, in particular, may be thin or nonexistent, leaving individuals and firms with little opportunity to hedge foreign exchange risks under floating rates.

Perhaps more important, a fixed exchange rate, *if* crises can be avoided, can provide price discipline as part of the reform process by forcing the central bank to shrink the money stock when the balance of payments shifts to deficit (such policies are called using the exchange rate as a *nominal anchor*). However, we saw in Chapters Sixteen and Twenty that governments can circumvent such discipline if they're so inclined. Reforming governments may lean too heavily or too long on the exchange rate as the anchor of a disinflation program. If they refuse to devalue even when domestic inflation persistently outpaces foreign inflation, the result is a real currency appreciation (recall that the real exchange rate, or the relative price of domestic goods and services, equals $R \equiv P/eP^*$). This leads to declining exports, rising imports, and a growing current-account deficit that must be financed with either external borrowing or sales of foreign exchange reserves. *(Why?)* If foreign-exchange-market participants view this trend as unsustainable, as they did in Mexico and in Asia, a currency crisis erupts.

Another potential disadvantage of fixed exchange rates comes from interaction between the exchange rate regime and the production structure of the economy. For many developing economies, such as those in Africa, a mere handful of goods—often primary products—account for all export revenues. World demand for these primary products moves with business-cycle conditions in the major industrial countries, so a recession there can severely reduce demand for a developing country's two or three export products. We learned in section 20.7.3 that a fixed exchange rate can exacerbate the macroeconomic impact of negative shocks to export demand. This happens because the initial decline in demand pushes down the domestic interest rate and leads to a balance-of-payments deficit. To hold the pegged exchange rate, the central bank must place further contractionary pressure on the economy by intervening in the foreign exchange market and shrinking the money stock. Under a flexible exchange rate, on the other hand, the balance-of-payments deficit would cause the domestic currency to depreciate, lowering the relative price of domestic goods and services, and improving the competitiveness of the country's products on world markets. *(Illustrate these results in an aggregate demand–aggregate supply diagram.)*

Increased recognition of the limits on the discipline that fixed exchange rates can impose, of the crisis-generating potential of fixed rates with mobile capital, and of the interaction between fixed exchange rates and negative export-demand shocks has led growing numbers of developing economies to adopt more flexible exchange rate regimes as part of their reform packages.[16] Early empirical evidence from these economies suggests that a flexible exchange rate *can* work for developing countries—as long as they follow fiscal and monetary policies consistent with macroeconomic stability.

Investment Finance and Debt

The debt crisis of the 1980s reminded debtors and creditors alike of the fundamental rules for sound debt management: (1) to avoid insolvency crises, an investment project must produce a rate of return sufficient to cover loan payments; (2) to avoid illiquidity crises, loan maturity and project maturity must match so that returns from the project come in time to make loan payments; and (3) uncertainty regarding future economic events, both domestic and international, constrains the prudent amount of debt accumulation any country can undertake.[17]

---

16 However, recent evidence suggests that many governments who claim to allow their exchange rates to float in fact don't. See, for example, Case Two in Chapter Twenty.

17 Section 11.5.3 develops the economic logic underlying each rule.

Ideally, the aspects of reform already discussed can go a long way toward preventing a repeat of the debt crisis. With government playing more limited roles in the economy of most developing countries, future borrowed funds are less likely to be wasted on unproductive, politically motivated projects. Privatization facilitates the growth of stock markets and equity finance, in which the debtor's obligation to the creditor varies with economic outcomes.[18] This helps avoid the problem that arose in the 1980s when debtors—because their debt took the form of bank loans—owed fixed repayment schedules regardless of their investment projects' outcomes. Active capital markets help potential investors evaluate more accurately the return likely from various projects. Removal of capital controls and foreign exchange controls allows investors to express confidence or lack thereof in policy makers' decisions by "voting with their funds." Governments' improved reputations encourage domestic saving and make long-term government bonds a more feasible means of public finance. Early evidence indicates that the nature of developing-country borrowing has shifted away from the pre-reform pattern of predominantly bank loans to developing-country governments and toward debt and equity flows from private lenders to private borrowers. Still, the Asian financial crisis makes clear that accumulation of too much debt, regardless of the specific identities of the debtor and creditor, can plunge otherwise healthy economies into crisis.

21.2.3 Lingering Risks

Current concerns about developing countries' macroeconomies differ between two groups of economies: (1) those that cling to pre-reform characteristics and policy choices and remain relatively isolated from the world economy, and (2) those that are "emerging" or reforming and integrating themselves into the world economy.

Among the first group, countries still haven't embarked on meaningful stabilization and structural reform programs. As other developing countries do reform their macroeconomies, those that fail to do so run the risk of becoming even more isolated. International investors, faced with a choice between reforming and nonreforming countries as hosts for investment, are likely to choose those with the strongest reform programs. Empirical evidence already strongly supports these predictions.

The lowest-income countries, in particular, remain deeply indebted and largely isolated from participation in world markets. Many have lagged in instituting macroeconomic reforms, and several continue to suffer from wars, both civil and with neighbors. Foreign investors, with the exception of official lenders such as the World Bank, show little interest in investing in these economies.

The largest cluster of such countries lies in sub-Saharan Africa, where per-capita GNP *fell* by an average of 0.3 percent per year during 1965-1998. Inflation in the region averaged more than 17 percent in 2000. Government involvement in the economies remains high, and many continue to finance large-scale losses incurred by state-owned enterprises. Money growth rates are erratic, but averaged more than 18 percent per year in 2000; real interest rates often are negative as a result of high inflation along with government ceilings on nominal interest rates. The countries continue to run large current-account deficits (almost $7 billion in 2000), which implies that they continue to add to already large external debts. In 2000, after several programs of debt forgiveness by creditors, total external debt for sub-Saharan Africa equaled over 70 percent of its total GDP. Net foreign direct investment inflows to sub-Saharan Africa in 1999 totaled about $5.6 billion (less than 2 percent of GDP); most went to Ghana, South Africa, Uganda, and to the oil industries of Angola and Nigeria. Portfolio investment in the region rose to about $8 billion in 1997, but again, over half went to South Africa. Not all these problems result from poor macroeconomic policy. The countries suffered dramatic declines in prices for their highly concentrated primary-product exports during the industrial-country recession of the early 1990s and again in the late 1990s. But failure to undertake and maintain strong macroeconomic reforms exacerbated the negative shocks' impact on the economies.

For the "emerging" developing economies, the important policy challenges include building popular support to stay on the reform path even during economic downturns and periods of stressful volatility. Erratic approaches to reform fail to build credibility and impose larger cumulative costs on the economy than more-determined, steady approaches. The Mexican and Asian crises brought the financial sector to the forefront of

---

18 Section 11.5.3 treats the distinction between debt and equity finance and its role in the debt crisis.

debates over emerging markets' reform agendas. In many reforming developing countries, banks and other financial-sector institutions remain weak and vulnerable. They often lack effective, honest, transparent, and watchful government regulation. Even senior bank staff often lack experience in international markets, having become accustomed to a protected domestic market largely insulated from market forces. Banks and other firms may overborrow in international capital markets newly open to them, relying on implicit guarantees of government bailouts if they run into trouble. Weak corporate governance and accounting standards deter foreign investment and hinder fund flows even to firms with the best economic prospects.

Developing countries remain, as a group, heavily dependent on external sources of finance for investment. These capital inflows continue only as long as the recipient countries maintain macroeconomic stability and provide attractive real rates of return. Fortunately, the same policies conducive to establishing *foreign* investor confidence also promote *domestic* saving and discourage capital flight, so there is long-term potential for building domestic saving into a viable source of investment finance. In the meantime, the need to maintain foreign investor confidence constrains policy makers' options. This can help hold countries on the reform path, but it also can make economies prone to expectation-generated crises similar to those suffered by Mexico, the economies of East Asia, and Argentina.

21.3 Transition and the Macroeconomy

Prior to the revolutions of 1989–1991, most analysts considered the centrally planned economies of the Soviet bloc to be developed industrialized economies. In one sense, this analysis was correct, because we'll see that industrialization—in fact, *over*industrialization—was a key characteristic of many of these economies. Yet in other senses the analysis was wrong or misleading, due in part to the lack of reliable economic statistics. The revolutions raised the Iron Curtain to reveal economies with low levels of productivity; drastic shortages of consumer goods; outmoded technologies; severe environmental problems; and a dramatic lack of political, legal, and economic institutional infrastructure suited to a market economy. These characteristics gave the transitional economies much in common with developing ones, despite, in some cases, the presence of huge industrial plants, sophisticated military capabilities, and relatively high per-capita incomes and high literacy rates.

21.3.1 Centrally Planned Economies' Pre-Reform Macroeconomic Characteristics

Substantial differences exist *among* the transitional economies, and these differences carry important implications for the countries' prospects. For some, such as Poland and Hungary, the histories of central planning were relatively short, and central planning never fully enveloped their highly productive agricultural sectors. For others, such as most of the states of the former Soviet Union, the history of central planning was much longer, and that planning encompassed and often devastated agriculture.

A few countries, such as China, embarked on market-oriented economic reforms with no explicit political revolution. Another, the former East Germany, actually ceased to exist as an independent state in the reform process.[19] Still others, the 15 republics of the former Soviet Union, became new independent states.

For some countries, such as China, dramatic increases in international trade have been a hallmark and important engine of the reform process. For others, such as Bulgaria and some of the former Soviet republics, the events of 1989–1991 brought trade to a virtual halt—albeit temporary—as the Council for Mutual Economic Assistance dissolved.[20]

The transitional economies also differ substantially in the extent to which they have in place legal and institutional frameworks to support a market-based economy. Vital elements of these frameworks include many items taken for granted in the major industrial economies: laws to protect private property, laws to enforce contracts, accounting rules and standards, orderly bankruptcy procedures, and economic policy-making institutions such as central banks.

---

19 The article by the authors in the chapter references takes an economic approach to explaining the German choice to unify.

20 Section 11.6 examines trade-related aspects of transition, including the role of CMEA trade.

Despite the important differences among transitional economies, we can make substantial progress toward understanding the macroeconomics of the process by focusing on a few key characteristics of the "typical" pre-reform centrally planned economy. It will soon become obvious why we treat these economies in the same chapter as more traditional developing ones. Common macroeconomic features include the following:

1. Extensive government ownership of productive assets; government control over all aspects of economic activity, prices, and trade; and government resource allocation according to a central economic plan.
2. Overly industrialized economic structure, with underdeveloped financial and services sectors.
3. Government-set prices and investment-funding procedures that encourage capital- and military-goods production and discourage consumer-goods production.
4. Extensive money finance of government expenditure, especially subsidies to large state-owned enterprises.
5. Capital and exchange controls to maintain highly artificial fixed exchange rates.

Government Ownership and Control

Until the mid-1980s, more than 95 percent of production in the Soviet Union was in state hands.[21] This figure put the Soviet Union at the upper end of the spectrum of state ownership (Hungary, for example, represented the lower end of the spectrum), but the predominant economic role of the state defined centrally planned economies. Governments owned virtually all productive resources. Planners decided what would be produced, in what quantities, by which enterprises, using which inputs, on what schedule, to whom the output would be distributed, and at what prices.

Government planners allocated capital and other resources according to the economy's central plan. State-owned enterprises received government "credits" that they used to buy nonlabor inputs at state-determined prices. Different enterprises paid different prices for inputs, according to whether the government wanted to tax or subsidize the enterprise's activity. Enterprises that were "profitable" returned the profit to the government as tax revenue; enterprises that earned losses typically had their debt forgiven. The fact that losses didn't force enterprises into bankruptcy, because the government simply provided more loans and credits regardless of economic performance, meant firms faced a **soft budget constraint.** In other words, profitability wasn't a requisite for continued operation under such a system. Workers received government-set wages, often paid in cash, but the typical shortages of consumer goods implied that much of the cash went unspent. Officially recorded unemployment hovered close to zero—because planners assigned workers to jobs and prevented residential relocation or job changes.

The government's control also extended to international trade, handled through state trading companies rather than directly by individual enterprises. Comparative advantage, which rests on a comparison of relative prices across countries, can't determine trade patterns when prices are set bureaucratically without regard to market forces. Planners often attempted to keep the economy from relying on imports, especially from market-oriented economies, and state trading companies chose "surplus" goods to export in exchange for the necessary imports.[22]

Overindustrialization

Policy makers in some centrally planned economies used their power over prices and resource allocation to encourage production of capital and military goods and discourage production of consumer goods and services. Among other tools to accomplish this, governments provided the favored sectors with cheap energy, access to cheap foreign exchange for their imports, and heavy subsidies to cover wages and other costs. As a result, in the late 1980s, industry accounted for twice as large a share of output in the former Soviet Union as in the United States, while Soviet service-sector output fell short of a third of the U.S. figure. Among the major transitional economies, China appears to have recognized its overemphasis on industry relatively early; it shifted policy in 1978 to create marketlike incentives for agricultural production and build a better balanced productive structure.

---

21 David Lipton and Jeffrey D. Sachs, "Prospects for Russia's Economic Reforms," *Brookings Papers on Economic Activity* 2 (1992), p. 219.

22 In contrast to their disregard of comparative advantage, planners placed heavy emphasis on regional specialization and economies of scale. This produced a set of heavily dependent supplier-customer relationships that the events of 1989–1991 destroyed. This breakdown contributed to dramatic short-term declines in output and continues to constrain prospects for many transitional economies, particularly the former Soviet republics.

In addition to their heavy emphasis on industry, centrally planned economies typically exhibited a prevalence of very large-scale state-owned enterprises that held monopoly positions for their respective products.[23] The sheer size of the firms surpassed any possible economies of scale, and their protected monopoly status provided them little incentive to produce high-quality products or adopt new technologies.

Price Controls and Shortages

Government planners set prices administratively for both goods and resources, often ignoring supply and demand. The result, of course, was a situation of chronic shortages of goods that consumers and firms wanted and surpluses of goods that no one wanted. Shortages of consumer goods implied that citizens had to stand in line, often daily, to acquire basic goods. Workers hoarded their cash wages because of the lack of goods to purchase with them; these hoarded funds (called **monetary overhang**) gave the government a further incentive to levy an inflation tax that eroded the funds' purchasing power. Existence of a large monetary overhang also meant that lifting price controls would likely lead to a dramatic price increase because of the pent-up money balances.

Price controls resulted in shortages of productive inputs for which government planners had set prices too low. This led to production bottlenecks as downstream firms ran short of vital inputs. To avoid these bottlenecks that could cause firms to fall short of their government-assigned output targets, firms hoarded inputs and inventories and attempted to vertically integrate and be as self-sufficient as possible.

Money-Finance of Fiscal Expenditures

Unproductive state-owned enterprises relied on massive government subsidies to keep them in operation. These subsidies, along with other governmental functions, led to high rates of government expenditure. Tax systems often were poorly developed and overly reliant on the state-owned enterprises for revenues. Governments found it difficult to borrow because of their isolation from world capital markets, their poor credibility, and the domestic population's distrust of government promises to repay debts and avoid inflation that produces negative real rates of return. As a result, governments relied heavily on money finance of government expenditures. In essence, the central bank printed money to keep the state-owned enterprises in operation—an ideal recipe for inflation that price controls, in turn, attempted to suppress.

Capital and Exchange Controls

Government control over prices in centrally planned economies extended to the price of foreign exchange or the exchange rate. Currencies typically were nonconvertible, and governments maintained monopoly control over foreign exchange transactions. Because international trade was channeled through state-trading companies, the government controlled access to any foreign exchange acquired through exports. Planners then allocated the scarce foreign exchange by selling it at different prices to cover imports according to their different priorities under the central plan.

Currency nonconvertibility, along with price controls' distortion of comparative advantage, caused centrally planned economies to forgo most of the potential gains from trade. In particular, nonconvertibility imposed **bilateralism** on trade. Suppose Czechoslovakia exported tractors to the Soviet Union and received payments in rubles, the Soviet currency. The rubles couldn't be sold on the foreign exchange market for dollars, pounds, or any other foreign currency; so to use the rubles, Czechoslovakia had to import a good from a country willing to accept rubles as payment, that is, the Soviet Union. Therefore, each pair of countries ended up importing and exporting approximately equal values of goods from one another, a pattern that eliminated many opportunities for mutually beneficial trade.

Governments also restricted capital inflows and outflows, as well as use of foreign currencies, under central planning. The domestic population hoarded cash because government restrictions prohibited buying foreign assets and because domestic assets might be nonexistent or vulnerable to confiscation, inflation, or other risks. The government represented most enterprises' only potential source of investment funds. Many centrally planned economies reported high rates of investment, but the actual productivity of such investment often was

---

23 Chinese policy during the "Great Leap Forward" of the late 1950s and early 1960s represents a dramatic exception; the government mandated what amounted to backyard steel mills.

low. Government planners, with little knowledge of actual production processes in different sectors of the economy, often provided inappropriate resources and funded inappropriate investments. In the Soviet Union, in particular, newly available evidence suggests that the domestic population was asked to forgo consumption goods in order for the economy to invest in ways that ultimately failed to enhance productivity.

21.3.2 **Reform**

Transforming the centrally planned countries into functioning market-oriented economies represents a task of a magnitude unprecedented in modern economic history. One reason for this assessment is that so many types of reform—economic, political, social, legal, and institutional—are needed. A high degree of consensus exists on the basic outline of economic reform. Most lingering controversies concern issues of timing. For example, is it better to attempt dramatic and immediate reforms on all margins simultaneously (the so-called **big-bang approach,** often associated with Poland), or to reform more slowly and take the different elements of reform one-by-one (the **gradualism approach,** often associated with China)? One right answer probably doesn't exist; for example, big bangs may be required in cases of large-scale breakdown of political authority, as in the former Soviet Union, but not in cases of more subtle political transformation, as in China. In the following discussion, we mention several timing dilemmas that confront reformers. No historical counterpart exists of so many countries undertaking such a broad array of reforms, so economists' ability to answer important questions about the timing of reform is limited. All we can do is apply sound economic theory, watch as different countries take different approaches, and try to learn what works, what doesn't, and why.

Regardless of approach—big-bang or gradual—successful reforms must include both macroeconomic stabilization and structural reform. Stabilization seeks to halt excessive fiscal spending and money growth in order to prevent continual rightward shifts of the aggregate demand curve that generate chronic high inflation. Structural reform seeks to shift the long-run aggregate supply curve to the right in several ways. One is the elimination of gross productive inefficiencies and enhancement of market incentives; these move the economy onto its production possibilities frontier from the interior point associated with central planning. The second and third changes that can shift the supply curve involve improved knowledge and access to more productive technologies along with increased investment; these two processes should shift a country's production possibilities frontier outward.

Privatization

Privatization represents a central task of structural reform. Just as government ownership of productive assets defines central planning, private ownership defines a market-oriented or price-based economic system. Privatization means the sale of state-owned enterprises to private owners, who then run the enterprises on a market basis; that is, buying inputs and selling outputs at market-determined prices, deciding what and how much to produce, what production techniques to use, and so on. These changes play several key roles in reform. Together, they harden the soft budget constraint faced by firms; profitability becomes a requisite for continued operation. This contributes to macroeconomic stabilization because it eliminates enterprise losses as a continual drain on the government's budget and reduces the incentive to print money to cover those losses. Privatization can help absorb some of an economy's monetary overhang as individuals spend accumulated cash to buy shares in privatized enterprises, and the revenues raised through privatization also contribute (albeit on a one-time basis) to reduction of the government budget deficit. By giving investors a clear financial stake in the firm's future, privatization also enhances productivity incentives and avoids the tendency, prevalent in years just prior to reform, for workers to "decapitalize" firms by paying themselves exorbitant wages and counting on government subsidies to cover the shortfall.

Privatization has proven to be one of the more politically difficult and slow-moving reforms for most countries, especially in the large-enterprise sector. Some of the reasons are easy to see: Who should be eligible to buy the enterprises? Before other reforms, especially price liberalization, are in place, how can potential investors evaluate enterprises' potential values? What if the new owners are foreign? What if the new owners decide to cut employment? Despite these problems, countries have made progress. Estonia, Hungary, and the Czech and Slovak Republics have almost completed privatization programs. Others, such as Albania, have made substantial progress in privatizing small-scale enterprises but lag in dealing with large-scale ones, where

Figure 21.2 **Transitional Economies' Progress in Privatization, 2001**

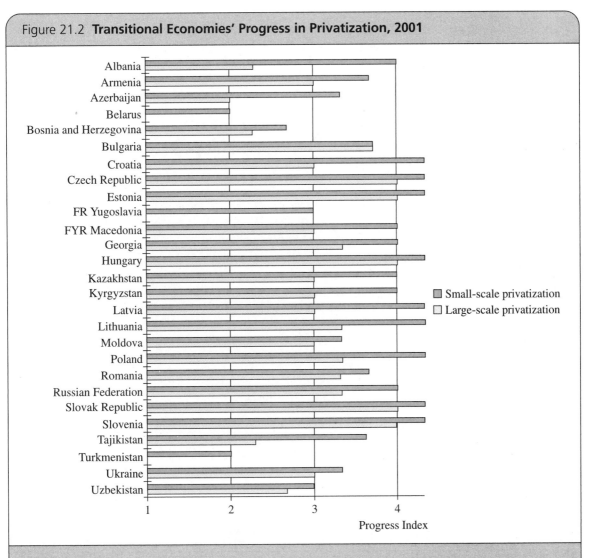

Note: For large-scale privatization: 1 = little private ownership; 2 = comprehensive scheme almost ready for implementation, some sales completed; 3 = more than 25 percent of large-scale enterprise assets in private hands or in the process of being privatized (with the process having reached a stage at which the state has effectively ceded its ownership rights), but possibly with major unresolved issues regarding corporate governance; 4 = more than 50 percent of state-owned enterprise and farm assets in private ownership and significant progress on corporate governance of these enterprises; 4+ = standards and performance typical of advanced industrial economies, more than 75 percent of enterprise assets in private ownership with effective corporate governance. For small-scale privatization: 1 = little progress; 2 = substantial share privatized; 3 = nearly comprehensive program implemented; 4 = complete privatization of small companies with tradable ownership rights; 4+ = standards and performance typical of advanced industrial economies, no state ownership of small enterprises, effective tradability of land.

Source: Data from European Bank for Reconstruction and Development, *Transition Report 2001.*

ownership and employment issues are more politically sensitive. Figure 21.2 documents countries' cumulative progress in privatization as of 2001, including the distinction between small- and large-scale enterprises. Note that no country has made more progress in the large-enterprise sector than in the small one. The European Bank for Reconstruction and Development, created to assist countries in their transition from centrally planned to market economic systems, ranks countries' progress on a four-point scale with pluses and minuses, much like grades in school.

In practice, privatization results have, in some cases, disappointed. First, before many of the positive effects of privatization could happen, some transitional economies (especially the former Soviet Union) experienced sudden drops in output as the government's coordination role in the economy—no matter how ineptly performed—disappeared with no short-term replacement. Basic input-supply relationships broke down, because enterprises had little experience interacting directly with one another without the state as an intermediary. Output declined by an average of about 20 percent before the reform process even began; in some cases, such as the Russian oil industry, the declines were even more dramatic. Even more important, privatization often failed to produce restructured, competitive firms with effective and honest corporate governance.

Governance and Restructuring

Central planning produces an economy in which the quantities supplied and quantities demanded for various goods and resources don't match. This is reflected in many ways, such as overindustrialization, queues for consumer goods, and the existence of large monetary overhangs. Sectoral restructuring occurs when market-determined prices begin to allocate resources so that the economy produces those goods that consumers and firms want.

Many large state-owned enterprises existed largely on government subsidies and produced poor-quality versions of goods no one wanted. These enterprises must be allowed to adapt or die as part of the reform process, because they represent a huge drain on the economy and a major barrier to stabilizing fiscal expenditures. In other words, the previously soft budget constraint facing state-owned enterprises must become a hard one—an essential step in both long-term macroeconomic stabilization and structural reform.

Many of the transitional economies suffer from poorly developed service and financial sectors, the mirror image of their overindustrialization. A shift toward markets means improvements in retailing and distribution, as well as creation of private financial and banking sectors to replace government control over financial activity in the economy. The new financial sectors often suffer from a lack of expertise, vulnerability to fraud, and lack of transparent accounting standards, regulation, and supervision.

A need for sectoral restructuring in *any* economy, centrally planned or otherwise, presents a difficult task. Workers in industries that must shrink have strong incentives to oppose reform, especially when they have been the long-time recipients of heavily subsidized high wages. Some workers may lack the skills to move to other employment in the growing private sector. The society must devise programs to alleviate the economic hardship imposed on such workers lest they block the necessary reforms and condemn the economy to continuing stagnation. Given this list of barriers to overcome, it isn't surprising that progress has been slow and erratic, as reported in Figure 21.3. However, as of 2001, all transitional economies except Belarus, Yugoslavia, and Turkmenistan had begun to address governance and restructuring.

The other major piece of restructuring involves designing policies to foster competitive markets and limit the scope for inefficient monopolies. This has proven one of the most difficult elements of transition for most economies. Because many state-owned enterprises were deliberately created as monopolies, privatization can leave those monopolies intact unless privatization is accompanied by effective antitrust policies. Figure 21.4 documents that this area is one in which many transitional economies have made little progress. Effective competition policy is complex and requires appropriate legal and economic institutions as well as a pool of expertise, all of which may be lacking in many transitional economies. And, of course, existing enterprises, privatized or not, have an incentive to lobby against policies that would promote entry by new rivals into their markets.

Price Liberalization

Privatization and sectoral restructuring can't occur without large doses of price liberalization. Private investors will be hesitant to purchase enterprises whose output prices are held down by government price controls, because such enterprises will earn losses rather than profits. And sectoral restructuring, or shifting resources toward the goods wanted by consumers and firms, requires that producers know what consumers and firms want. Prices convey this information by signaling how much buyers are willing to pay to obtain the good. From consumers' perspective, price liberalization is the means to eliminate shortages and queues.

All these salutary effects from price liberalization can't prevent controversy from surrounding this aspect of reform. After all, transition typically means that some workers lose their jobs in antiquated, unproductive

Figure 21.3 **Transitional Economies' Progress in Governance and Restructuring, 2001**

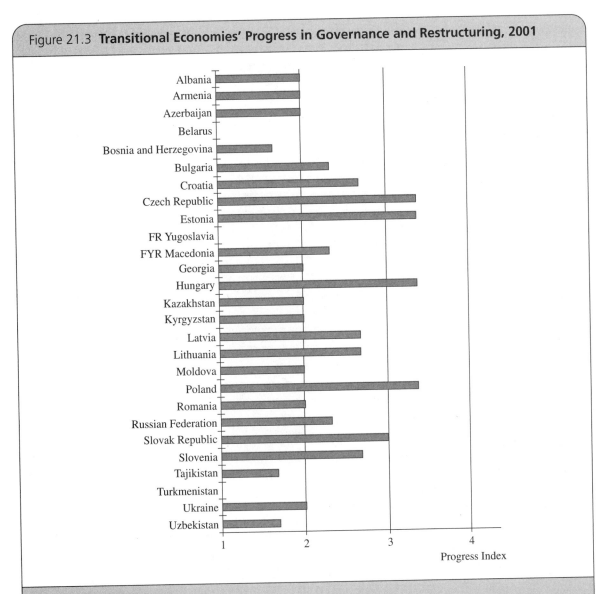

Note: 1 = soft budget constraints (lax credit and subsidy policies weakening financial discipline at the enterprise level), few other reforms to promote corporate governance; 2 = moderately tight credit and subsidy policy but weak enforcement of bankruptcy legislation and little action taken to strengthen competition and corporate governance; 3 = significant and sustained actions to harden budget constraints and to promote corporate governance effectively (for example, through privatization combined with tight credit and subsidy policies and/or enforcement of bankruptcy legislation); 4 = substantial improvement in corporate governance (for example, an account of an active corporate control market, significant new investment at the enterprise level); 4+ = standards and performance typical of advanced industrial economies, effective corporate control exercised through domestic financial institutions and markets, fostering market-driven restructuring.

Source: Data from European Bank for Reconstruction and Development, *Transition Report 2001.*

state-owned enterprises. For those who keep their jobs, the artificially high wages paid under central planning must give way to market-determined wages based on productivity if the products are to compete in world markets. In this context, a rise in consumer-goods prices due to price decontrol is bound to prove unpopular, even if it does fill previously empty store shelves with goods.

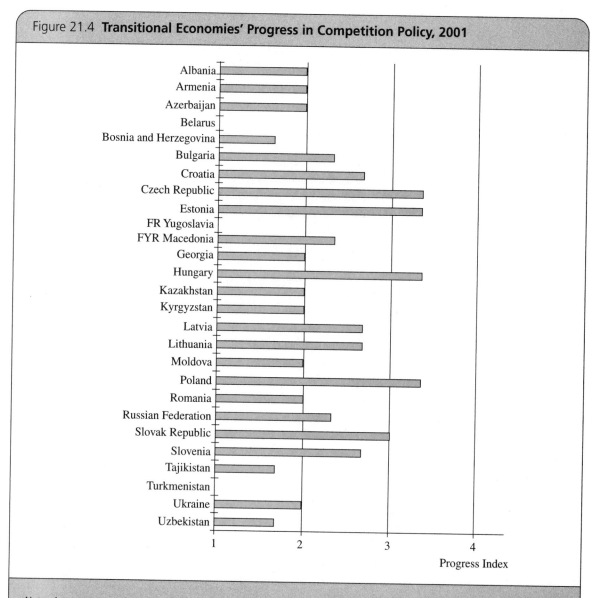

Figure 21.4 **Transitional Economies' Progress in Competition Policy, 2001**

Note: 1 = no competition legislation and institutions; 2 = competition policy legislation and institutions set up, some reduction of entry restrictions or enforcement action on dominant firms; 3 = some enforcement actions to reduce abuse of market power and to promote a competitive environment, including breakups of dominant conglomerates, substantial reduction of entry restrictions; 4 = significant enforcement actions to reduce abuse of market power and to promote a competitive environment; 4+ = standards and performance typical of advanced industrial economies, effective enforcement of competition policy, unrestricted entry to most markets.

Source: Data from European Bank for Reconstruction and Development, *Transition Report 2001.*

Note, however, that price decontrol leads to a one-time price increase, *not* to ongoing inflation. In the former Soviet Union, prices rose by between 350 and 400 percent on decontrol.[24] When—as in Russia—authorities decontrol prices *before* they establish macroeconomic stability and control inflation, they risk the populace mistakenly attributing the inflation to price decontrol. Such mistaken attribution can lead to a loss of popular

---

24 Stanley Fischer, "Stabilization and Economic Reform in Russia." *Brookings Papers on Economic Activity* 1 (1992), p. 78.

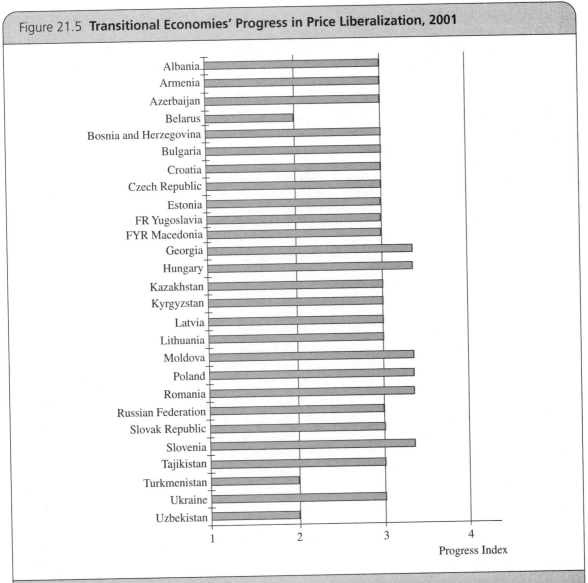

Figure 21.5 **Transitional Economies' Progress in Price Liberalization, 2001**

Note: 1 = most prices formally controlled by the government; 2 = price controls for several important product categories, state procurement at non-market prices remains substantial; 3 = substantial progress on price liberalization, state procurement at nonmarket prices largely phased out; 4 = comprehensive price liberalization, utility pricing that reflects economic costs; 4+ = standards and performance typical of advanced industrial economies, comprehensive price liberalization, efficiency-enhancing regulation of utility pricing.

Source: Data from European Bank for Reconstruction and Development, *Transition Report 2001*.

support for reform. Does this mean that price liberalization should always wait until *after* authorities can control inflation? Not necessarily. In Russia, policy makers feared that the growing shortages of consumer goods posed a greater threat to support for reform than did further inflation; the only way to fill store shelves was to liberalize prices.

By 2001, most transitional economies had liberalized most prices. Key exceptions include utilities prices and housing, which remain under government-administered prices even in the most advanced transitional economies, as reported in Figure 21.5. Laggards on this margin of reform include Belarus, Turkmenistan, and Uzbekistan.

Fiscal Consolidation

Extensive government control of the economy translates into extensive government expenditures. Macroeconomic stabilization, essential as a foundation for longer run structural reforms, requires that these expenditures be brought under control. There are two major parts of this task. The first is simply reduction in government expenditure, with much of the reduction coming from curtailed subsidies to unproductive state-owned enterprises. Military spending and unproductive investment expenditures are other candidates for cuts. The second part of fiscal consolidation involves shifting from money finance of expenditure to taxes and government borrowing. This requires both strengthening the tax system (often *ad hoc*, corrupt, and politicized under central planning) by making it simple, transparent, and enforceable, and improving the government's credibility to the point that it becomes able to issue bonds to finance its expenditure.

The whole process of fiscal consolidation involves not only changes in policy makers' day-to-day behavior but changes in the fundamental structure of policy-making institutions. Most notably, the money-supply process must be reoriented toward monetary control as a tool of macroeconomic policy rather than a passive accommodator of fiscal expenditure. This presented a particular challenge to the former Soviet republics, where runaway inflation during the early 1990s threatened to drive the economy back to barter; Russia continued well into the transition years to succumb periodically to the temptation to print money to cover wages at its unreformed state-owned enterprises and other fiscal expenditures.

Figure 21.6 illustrates 2000 government budget balances, as a percent of GDP, in the transitional economies. Positive numbers (there are only three: Azerbaijan, Macedonia, and Turkmenistan) reflect budget surpluses, and negative numbers reflect budget deficits.

Financial Integration

A system of central planning with its artificial prices requires isolation from world markets, where demand and supply determine prices. This holds true not only for goods markets, but for capital and foreign exchange markets as well. Uncontrolled contact with world markets makes the central plan's artificial prices unsustainable. Once reform begins, building contacts with world markets serves an important function by helping align prices to their market levels.

Removing capital controls means allowing domestic residents to invest abroad and allowing foreign investors to invest in the domestic economy. Under a market-oriented system, funds to finance investment flow toward projects that offer the most attractive mix of real rate of return and risk, regardless of location. If domestic residents distrust the government's promises, they can place their funds in foreign assets instead. Enterprises attract capital by promising to use it productively, not through their priority in the government's central plan.[25] The banking sector presents significant reform challenges. In the former Soviet Union, for example, the primary assets owned by banks consist of loans to unproductive state-owned industrial enterprises that eventually must go bankrupt. Yet many analysts believe the banks need to be saved in order to help in the privatization process.

Reform of banks and nonbank financial institutions has proceeded slowly (see Figure 21.7). Only Hungary had achieved a grade of 4 by 2001; Belarus, Yugoslavia, Tajikistan, and Turkmenistan had hardly begun reforms in this crucial sector. Many banks remain state-owned or subject to state interference. Most lack the expert staff, modern technology, and sophisticated accounting and information systems typical of financial institutions in industrial market economies. Regulation and supervision are lax; bankruptcy provisions to eliminate "zombie" banks don't exist or aren't enforced effectively.[26] Several transitional economies, including Russia, Albania, the Czech Republic, and Romania, have endured crises due to fraudulent financial institutions and pyramid schemes that cost many citizens their savings.

Reform also involves changing the system of state control over foreign-exchange allocation. The domestic currency must be made convertible, particularly for current-account transactions. This openness to international markets allows world market prices to bring artificial domestic prices into line. Governments can choose

---

25 Some estimates suggest that half to three-quarters of capital investment in Czechoslovakia, Hungary, and Poland under central planning was wasteful in the sense that it will be useless in a market economy. See Rudiger Dornbusch and Holger Wolf, "Economic Transition in Eastern Germany," *Brookings Papers on Economic Activity* 1 (1992), p. 252.

26 The term "zombie" has been suggested for banks that are dead by any market-oriented economic criteria but that nonetheless continue to operate because governments keep them alive for political reasons.

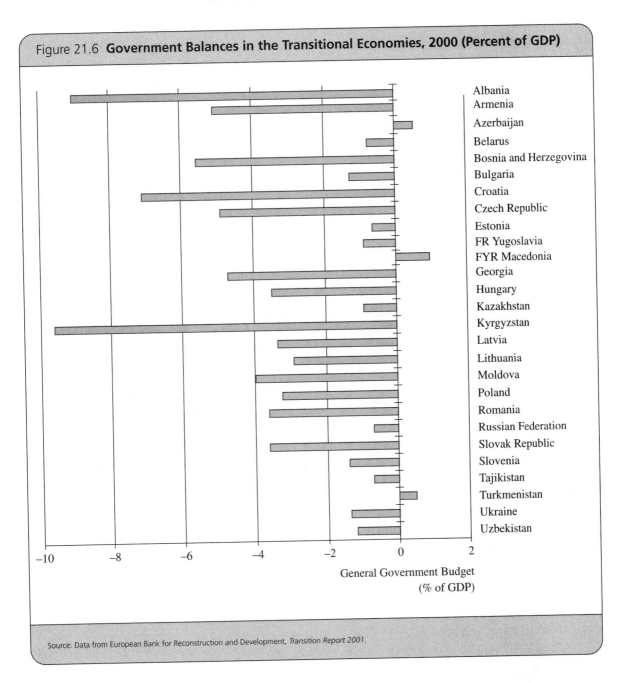

Figure 21.6 Government Balances in the Transitional Economies, 2000 (Percent of GDP)

General Government Budget
(% of GDP)

Source: Data from European Bank for Reconstruction and Development, *Transition Report 2001.*

between fixed and flexible exchange rate regimes, each of which carries advantages and disadvantages, just as is the case for developed and other developing economies. Transitional economies often select some type of pegged exchange rate regime in the hope that the exchange-rate anchor will provide credibility for the government's effort to reduce excessive growth of the money stock. If unaccompanied by fiscal consolidation and monetary restraint, however, a fixed exchange rate can lose credibility and become prone to balance-of-payments and currency crises. As long as high rates of inflation continue, failure to devalue the domestic currency sufficiently to offset the inflation differential results in real currency appreciation, rising imports, dwindling exports, and a growing current-account deficit to finance.

Figure 21.7 **Transitional Economies' Progress in Bank and Nonbank Financial Reform, 2001**

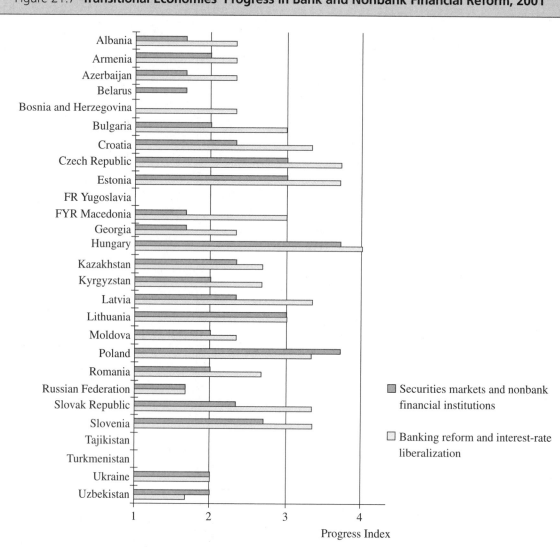

Note: For banking reform and interest-rate liberalization: 1 = little progress beyond establishment of a two-tier system; 2 = significant liberalization of interest rates and credit allocation, limited use of directed credit or interest-rate ceilings; 3 = substantial progress in establishment of bank solvency and of a framework for prudential supervision and regulation, full interest-rate liberalization with little preferential access to cheap financing, significant lending to private enterprises and significant presence of private banks; 4 = significant movement of banking laws and regulations toward BIS standards, well-functioning banking competition and effective prudential supervision, significant term lending to private enterprises, substantial financial deepening; 4+ = standards and performance norms of advanced industrial economies, full convergence of banking laws and regulations with BIS standards, provision of full set of competitive banking services.

For securities markets and nonbank financial institutions: 1 = little progress; 2 = formation of securities exchanges, marketmakers, and brokers, some trading in government paper and/or securities, rudimentary legal and regulatory framework for the issuance and trading of securities; 3 = substantial issuance of securities by private enterprises, establishment of independent share registries, secure clearance and settlement procedures, and some protection of minority shareholders, emergence of nonbank financial institutions (for example, investment funds, private insurance and pension funds, leasing companies) and associated regulatory framework; 4 = securities laws and regulations approaching IOSCO standards, substantial market liquidity and capitalization, well-functioning nonbank financial institutions and effective regulation; 4+ = standards and performance norms of advanced industrial economies, full convergence of securities laws and regulations with IOSCO standards, fully developed non-bank intermediation.

Source: Data from European Bank for Reconstruction and Development, *Transition Report 2001.*

Figure 21.8 **Transitional Economies' Progress in Trade and Foreign-Exchange Reform, 2001**

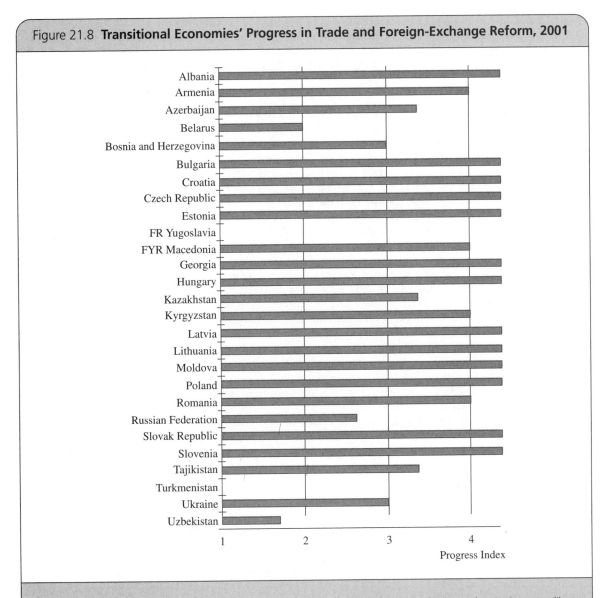

Note: 1 = widespread import and/or export controls or very limited legitimate access to foreign exchange; 2 = some liberalization of import and/or export controls, almost full current-account convertibility in principle but with a foreign exchange regime that is not fully transparent (possibly with multiple exchange rates); 3 = removal of almost all quantitative and administrative import and export restrictions, almost full current-account convertibility; 4 = removal of all quantitative and administrative import and export restrictions (apart from agriculture) and all significant export tariffs, insignificant direct involvement in exports and imports by ministries and state-owned trading companies, no major non-uniformity of customs duties for nonagricultural goods and services, full current-account convertibility; 4+ = standards and performance norms of advanced industrial economies, removal of most tariff barriers, WTO membership.

Source: Data from European Bank for Reconstruction and Development, *Transition Report 2001*.

Most transitional economies have made significant progress in reforming their foreign-exchange systems and in liberalizing international trade (see Figure 21.8). Some, such as Uzbekistan, however, have hardly started the needed changes. Others, after liberalizing trade, have encountered domestic political pressures for protection and reinstituted tariffs, quotas, and other trade restrictions. On the foreign-exchange front, crises have caused several countries, most notably Russia in late 1998, to abandon reforms at least temporarily and take large steps backward toward arrangements consonant with central planning rather than with a market-oriented economy.

21.3.3 Transition Prospects

Prospects for the transitional economies differ substantially depending on the degree of their economic problems, the wisdom and perseverance of their reforms, their political stability to endure the reform process, and their luck in avoiding adverse domestic and international shocks during the transition period. Each country faces unique advantages and disadvantages. Russia, for example, inherited a more complete set of economic institutions than did the other Soviet republics, but it also inherited the Soviet army payroll and the bulk of outstanding Soviet external debt, on which it defaulted in late 1998. Generally speaking, most countries' macroeconomic *stabilization* efforts have thus far been more sustained and successful than their *structural* reforms.

By 1992, Poland began to experience positive real GDP growth; other early reformers joined it during the next few years. This contrasted sharply with the experience of late or timid reformers. In Russia, legislative opposition to fiscal consolidation, along with rising military expenditures in 1994, damaged the earlier progress made toward macro stabilization, and the run-up to the June 1996 presidential election, along with massive corruption, stalled reform. Armed conflict complicated reform efforts in Armenia, Georgia, and the former Yugoslavia. As of 1995, reforms had barely begun in Azerbaijan, Belarus, Tajikistan, Turkmenistan, and Uzbekistan.

By 1995, small private capital flows into the transitional economies had begun, along with repatriation of flight capital. Both trends, however, applied primarily to those countries most advanced in the reform process—particularly the Czech Republic, the Slovak Republic, Hungary, and the Baltic states. And flows were modest compared with experts' earlier predictions. The same held true for foreign direct investment, which potentially can play a vital role in transition by transferring new technology, worker training, and managerial know-how. Opaque legal systems and uncertain governance structures appeared as responsible as macroeconomic instability for the dearth of investment inflows.

Table 21.1 reports the year in which each transitional economy first achieved positive real GDP growth. By 2000, all reported positive growth. As of 1999, only Poland, the Slovak Republic, and Slovenia had reached and surpassed their respective real GDPs from 1989. Continued success in the transition process depends on countries' abilities both to *maintain* the progress made in macroeconomic stabilization and to *move forward* on the difficult issues of structural reform.

Table 21.1 **Year of First Post-Transition Positive Real GDP Growth**

1992	1993	1994	1995	1996	1997	1998	1999	2000
Poland	Albania	Bulgaria	Georgia	Azerbaijan	Moldova	Turkmenistan		Ukraine
	Czech Rep.	Croatia	Estonia	Belarus	Russia			
	Romania	Hungary	Lithuania	Kazakhstan	Tajikistan			
	Slovenia	Latvia	Bosnia	Kyrgyzstan				
		Slovak Rep.		Uzbekistan				
		Armenia		Macedonia				
		Yugoslavia						

Source: Data from European Bank for Reconstruction and Development, *Transition Report Update,* April 2001.

CASE ONE:
The HIPC Initiative

During the developing-country debt crisis of the 1980s, large developing countries—Mexico, Argentina, Brazil, and Chile—took center stage as their debt threatened developed-country commercial banks. More recently, attention during the financial crises of the 1990s centered on the debt of (relatively) high-income developing economies—Korea, Thailand, Indonesia, and, again, Mexico and Brazil. However, the 41 countries classified by the International Monetary Fund and the World Bank as *Heavily Indebted Poor Countries* (HIPCs) include none of the countries mentioned. Instead, the list includes mostly small countries, many in Africa, for which the present value of debt averages at least 120 percent of GNP or 400 percent of annual export rev-

enues. Table 21.2 provides country-by-country debt information for the HIPCs.

The HIPCs' external debt totals about $200 billion. Approximately 600 million people live in these countries, and more than half live on less than one dollar per day. The countries' circumstances vary, but most suffer from low growth rates due to some combination of unstable macroeconomic policies, wars, civil unrest, weak governance, failure to undertake price liberalization and other economic reforms, and unfavorable movements in their terms of trade. And the sheer size of their debt places a drag on economic performance for several reasons. If the benefits of improved economic performance go to creditors rather than

Table 21.2 **Debt Indicators for HIPC Countries, 1998**

Country	Present Value of Debt as Percent of GNP	Total Debt Service as Percent of GNP	Total Debt Service as Percent of Exports	Country	Present Value of Debt as Percent of GNP	Total Debt Service as Percent of GNP	Total Debt Service as Percent of Exports
Africa:				Rwanda	34	1.0	16.9
Angola	280	33.0	34.4	São Tomé &			
Benin	46	2.7	10.6	Principe	n.a.	n.a.	n.a.
Burkina Faso	32	2.1	10.7	Senegal	58	6.9	23.2
Burundi	72	3.5	40.0	Sierra Leone	131	3.2	18.2
Cameroon	100	6.5	22.3	Somalia	n.a.	n.a.	n.a.
C. African R.	55	2.9	20.9	Sudan	172	0.7	9.8
Chad	38	2.1	10.6	Tanzania	70	3.0	20.8
Congo, D. R.	196	0.3	1.2	Togo	68	2.7	5.7
Congo	280	2.5	3.3	Uganda	35	2.4	23.6
Côte d'Ivoire	124	13.5	26.1	Zambia	175	6.4	17.7
Ethiopia	135	1.8	11.3	**Asia:**			
Ghana	54	7.7	28.4	Lao PDR	92	2.5	6.3
Guinea	72	4.6	19.5	Myanmar	n.a.	n.a.	n.a.
Guinea-Bissau	363	4.1	25.6	Vietnam	76	4.0	8.9
Kenya	45	4.8	18.8	**Middle East:**			
Liberia	n.a.	n.a.	n.a.	Yemen	79	3.2	4.2
Madagascar	89	3.4	14.7	**W. Hemisphere:**			
Malawi	77	4.7	14.7	Bolivia	59	5.6	30.2
Mali	82	3.1	12.6	Guyana	n.a.	n.a.	n.a.
Mauritania	150	11.6	27.7	Honduras	62	9.8	18.7
Mozambique	74	2.8	18.0	Nicaragua	295	14.1	25.5
Niger	55	3.1	18.4				

Source: World Bank.

the domestic economy, this can reduce the incentives for reform. High levels of debt can also discourage both domestic and foreign investment in the economy.

In 1996, the World Bank and International Monetary Fund responded with the Heavily Indebted Poor Country (HIPC) Initiative, which was enhanced and fine-tuned in 1999. The initiative has three main goals:

- Reduce the countries' debt to sustainable levels (that is, levels at which the countries could meet their future debt-service obligations without further debt relief or other outside assistance). The HIPC Initiative's debt-relief targets lower the net present value of debt to 150 percent of export earnings (because exports are how the countries earn foreign exchange to pay their foreign-currency-denominated debt) or 250 percent of government tax revenue (because the bulk of many countries' debt is owed by the public sector).
- Encourage anti-poverty programs, especially increased resources devoted to primary education and preventive health care, based on a Poverty Reduction Strategy Paper prepared by each country. The funds saved through debt relief are to be focused on poverty reduction and on the types of educational and health services that benefit primarily the poorest sector of the population.
- Encourage and reward successful macroeconomic and structural reforms that support growth and reduce the likelihood of future debt problems. Empirical evidence from earlier episodes of debt relief indicates that such reforms are necessary both for successful debt reduction and for growth.[27] Important reforms include macroeco-

nomic stabilization (for example, control of fiscal deficits), as well as structural reforms (for example, building institutions to facilitate the rule of law and systems of governance that credibly support individuals' saving and investment in the economy).

The first group of countries to qualify for HIPC debt relief included Bolivia, Burkina Faso, Côte d'Ivoire, Guyana, Mali, Mozambique, and Uganda; their debt-service relief totaled almost $7 billion (or $3.4 in net present value terms). Despite support and political pressure for debt relief by groups such as Jubilee 2000, evidence indicates that debt relief is no panacea. In fact, the HIPCs that received $33 billion in debt relief between 1987 and 1997 undertook net new borrowing of $41 billion during that same period.[28] William Easterly (2001, p. 136), author of many empirical studies of development and growth, summarizes:

> Our heart tells us to forgive debts to the poor. Alas, the head contradicts the heart. Debt forgiveness grants aid to those recipients that have best proven their ability to misuse that aid. Debt relief is futile for countries with unchanged government behavior. The same mismanagement of funds that caused the high debt will prevent the aid sent through debt relief from reaching the truly poor. A debt relief program could make sense if it meets two conditions: (1) it is granted where there has been a proven change from an irresponsible government to a government with good policies; (2) it is a once-for-all measure that will never be repeated.

CASE TWO:
Ownership Matters

Privatization involves the transfer of ownership of firms or other productive assets from the state to private investors. A comparison of Figures 21.2 and 21.3 reveals that transitional economies have made much more progress in privatization, even in the challenging large-scale sector, than in "governance and restructuring," which measures the extent to which firms operate in a competitive market-oriented environment, both internally and externally. How can a privatized firm lack restructuring and effective corporate governance?[29] Part of the answer lies in the various ways firms can be privatized.

Governments privatize enterprises in different ways for several reasons. In some cases, governments have been so eager to earn privatization revenues and to rid themselves of the budget drain of loss-making enterprises that they sold quickly to virtually anyone who made an offer. In other cases, workers and managers threatened to block privatization unless they maintained control over their enterprises, leading to sales to "insiders." Still another possibility is "mass privatization" in which governments issue vouchers to large groups of citizens, who can then use the vouchers to purchase stakes in various enterprises available for sale.

---

27 See the Easterly book in the chapter references.

28 Easterly (2001), p. 128.

29 For more information, see Chapter Three in the World Bank's *World Development Report 2002*.

Foreigners may or may not be allowed to participate in privatization. The main advantages of including foreigners are two. By enlarging the pool of potential buyers, governments may be able to obtain a better price. And foreign owners may bring expertise, management skills, and access to new technology and finance badly needed by formerly state-owned enterprises. On the other hand, selling formerly state-owned enterprises to foreigners can be politically controversial, especially among workers and managers who fear losing their jobs or their above-productivity wages. Even if excluded from initial privatizations, foreigners may be able to acquire firms later. In 1998, about 58 percent of all developing countries' privatization proceeds came from foreign investors.[30]

The privatization programs in the non-Baltic former Soviet republics including Russia (now members of the Commonwealth of Independent States), former Yugoslav republics, and Poland benefited primarily insiders, through insider-oriented voucher programs or management-employee buyouts. Generally, methods of privatization that place enterprises in insiders' hands, while sometimes necessary for political reasons, can leave lingering governance and restructuring problems, since they provide for no outside shareholders to judge managers' and workers' operating and financial performance. These problems are made worse if the privatization scheme makes no provision for outsiders to acquire the firm if they think they can improve its performance. Despite the problems of insider control, these programs represented substantial improvements over state ownership. And, given managers' and workers' effective pre-privatization control over the enterprises, some reformist governments faced little choice if privatization was to be politically feasible. These programs tended to treat all enterprises the same—whether commercially viable, potentially viable, or nonviable.

Eastern European and Baltic transitional economies faced less political pressure for insider-dominated privatization. Estonia and Hungary sold to outside owners. The Czech Republic, Latvia, and Lithuania provided vouchers to all citizens, with little or no preference to enterprise insiders. In both cases, the enterprises judged to be most commercially viable were singled out for sale to outsiders. Buyers of such enterprises often are called *strategic investors,* chosen for their ability to exert effective control over managers and to access finance for the firm.

One benefit of privatization is the revenue it generates for governments. The sums represent a combination of the *number* of enterprises privatized, the economic viability and therefore the *value* of those enterprises, and the *method* of privatization, which affects the prices the enterprises bring.

While privatization revenues certainly prove helpful to governments struggling with large budget deficits, it's important to keep in mind that they represent one-time inflows of funds. Such revenues, because of their one-time nature, can't be counted on as a source of funding for ongoing government expenditures.

Among the privatized assets are infrastructure facilities (such as power and telecommunications); manufacturing; oil, gas, and mining operations; and banking and other financial services. Figure 21.9 summarizes all countries' privatization revenues in 1990–1998 by sector. Countries engaging in recent privatizations include not just the Eastern European and Central Asian economies in transition from central planning, but Latin America and the Caribbean, plus East Asia. Figure 21.10 reports the various regions' privatization revenues for 1990–1998.

Countries in East Asia, especially Indonesia, Thailand, Malaysia, and South Korea, face renewed privatization tasks to undo nationalizations within the financial sector undertaken during the financial crisis of 1997–1998.

It's still early to draw firm conclusions about the success or failure of various approaches to privatization. However, some patterns have emerged. In the transitional economies outside the Commonwealth of Independent States (comprising the non-Baltic former Soviet republics), privatized firms have restructured more thoroughly and performed better than nonprivatized ones. This has not been the case in the Commonwealth of Independent States, where state subsidies and continuing softness of budget constraints have allowed even privatized firms to avoid restructuring, with negative consequences for their performance. Strategic foreign investors have produced the best performance results. And firms with relatively concentrated ownership have outperformed those with more dispersed ownership, especially in states where the legal framework for good corporate governance (such as protection of minority shareholders) is weak.

In the end, the same things matter for successful privatization that matter for strong economic performance more generally: open competition, hard budget constraints, open international trade, unrestricted entry for new firms, lack of corruption, transparent accounting and legal standards, and a healthy financial sector to provide investment funds based on sound economic criteria. It's a recipe for growth taken for granted in industrial market economies and, increasingly, in a subset of developing and transitional economies; but it's yet to spread to other areas of the world economy, where the recipe could do much to alleviate poverty.

---

30 World Bank, *Global Development Finance 2000*, p. 191.

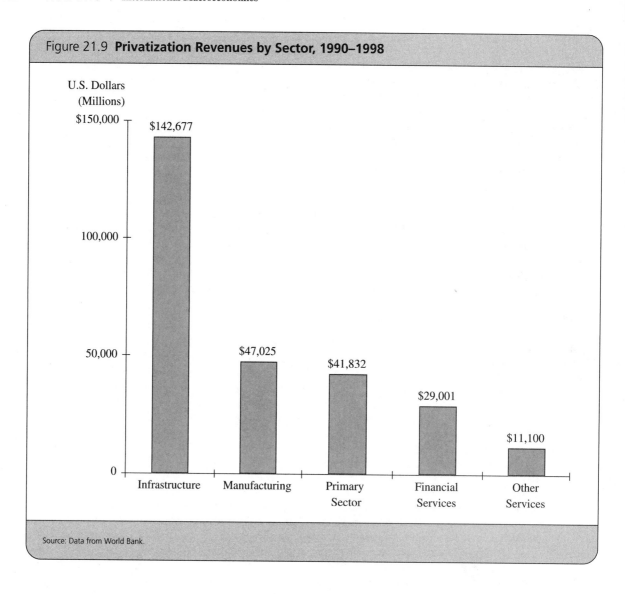

Figure 21.9 **Privatization Revenues by Sector, 1990–1998**

U.S. Dollars (Millions)

Source: Data from World Bank.

Summary

The developing and transitional economies share two major tasks in their pursuit of improved economic performance: macroeconomic stabilization and structural reform. Macroeconomic stabilization includes reformed fiscal and monetary policies that reduce the rate of inflation and stabilize the value of the domestic currency. Structural reform includes reduction of the government's role in the day-to-day management of the economy and development of the institutional infrastructure necessary for a market economy to function and grow. Most developing and centrally planned economies have embarked on these tasks. The timing and boldness of reforms differ significantly across countries; early evidence indicates that early, bold, and persistent reform contributes to improved economic performance. Most reforming economies have made greater progress toward macroeconomic stabilization than toward structural reform, and many continue to have weak and vulnerable financial sectors, leaving them vulnerable to crises.

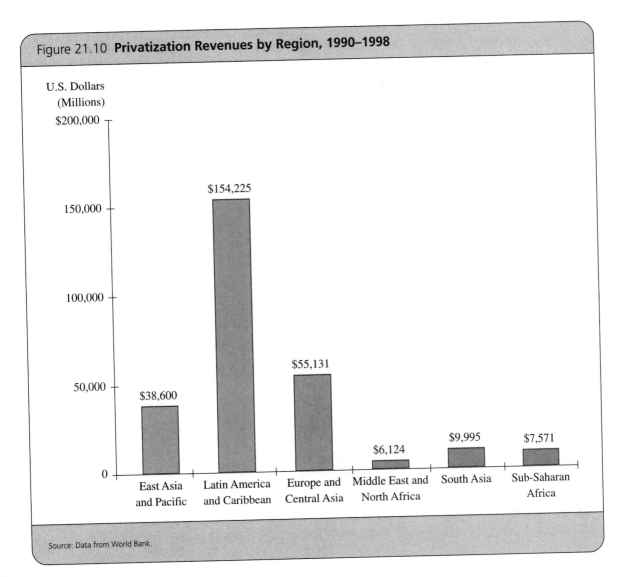

Figure 21.10 **Privatization Revenues by Region, 1990–1998**

Source: Data from World Bank.

Key Terms

stabilization reforms
structural reform (structural adjustment)
privatization
soft budget constraint

monetary overhang
bilateralism
big-bang approach
gradualism approach

Problems and Questions for Review

1. Describe several macroeconomic characteristics typical of pre-reform developing economies. Briefly explain each characteristic's likely effect on macroeconomic performance.
2. What are the two key types of economic reform for developing and centrally planned economies? Relate the two to the aggregate demand–aggregate supply model.

3. Describe how reform in developing economies alters the characteristics you listed in problem 1. How is each element of reform likely to affect a country's macroeconomic performance?

4. Describe several macroeconomic characteristics typical of pre-reform centrally planned economies. Briefly explain each characteristic's likely effect on macroeconomic performance.

5. Describe how reform in transitional economies alters the characteristics you listed in problem 4. How is each element of reform likely to affect a country's macroeconomic performance?

6. Explain why "hardening" enterprises' previously soft budget constraints plays an essential role in economic reform.

7. Consider the hypothetical transitional economy of Russokia, which lacks effective corporate governance laws. The government removes capital controls and privatizes many of the country's state-owned enterprises into the hands of political cronies. There's uncertainty about how long the current government will be in power. What would you expect to happen? If you're right, how would you expect events to affect political support for reform and the country's rate of economic growth?

8. In June 1998, the OECD's *Economic Outlook* (p. 151) reported about Bulgaria that "Since mid-1997, a currency board has pegged the lev to the DM. The restoration of confidence in the government and the currency has been reflected in a much higher domestic and international demand for lev-denominated assets. In this context, between 1 July 1997 and 1 February 1998, the foreign exchange assets of the currency board more than doubled to over DM4 billion and interest rates on government paper have actually fallen to levels close to those on German treasury bonds." Explain.

References and Selected Readings

Dornbusch, Rudiger, et al. "Currency Crises and Collapses." *Brookings Papers on Economic Activity* 2 (1995): 219–293.
Lessons from four currency crises; intermediate.

Easterly, William. *The Elusive Quest for Growth.* Cambridge, MA: MIT Press, 2001.
Readable account of recent development experience.

Edwards, Sebastian. *Crisis and Reform in Latin America.* New York: Oxford University Press for the World Bank, 1995.
Readable account of Latin American developments from 1982 through 1994.

European Bank for Reconstruction and Development. *Transition Report.* London: EBRD, annual.
Excellent annual survey of transitional economies and reform.

Goldstein, Morris. *The Asian Financial Crisis: Causes, Cures, and Systemic Implications.* Washington, D.C.: Institute for International Economics, 1998.
Accessible survey of the Asian crisis.

Harwood, Alison, et al., eds. *Financial Markets and Development.* Washington, D.C.: Brookings, 1999.
The role of well-functioning financial markets in facilitating development.

Heybey, Berta, and Peter Murrell. "The Relationship between Economic Growth and the Speed of Liberalization during Transition." *Journal of Policy Reform* 3 (1999): 121–138.
What economists do and don't know about the optimal speed of liberalization.

International Monetary Fund. *World Economic Outlook.* Washington, D.C.: International Monetary Fund, biannual.
Overview of current economic events and prospects relevant to the developing economies, with data.

Kharas, Homi, et al. "An Analysis of Russia's 1998 Meltdown: Fundamentals and Market Signals." *Brookings Papers on Economic Activity* (2001): 1–68.
Interaction of fixed exchange rate and fiscal policy in Russia's crisis.

Krueger, Anne O. "Whither the World Bank and the IMF?" *Journal of Economic Literature* (December 1998): 1983–2020.
The former Chief Economist of the World Bank, now at the IMF, addresses the current role for the two institutions.

Kutan, Ali M., and Josef C. Brada. "The Evolution of Monetary Policy in Transition Economies." *Federal Reserve Bank of St. Louis Review* 82 (March/April 2000): 31–40.
Overview of how the monetary policy-making process has changed during transition.

La Porta, Rafael, et al. "Government Ownership of Banks." *Journal of Finance* (February 2002): 265–301.
Finds government ownership of banks lowers productivity and growth.

Masson, Paul R., et al. "Can Inflation Targeting Be a Framework for Monetary Policy in Developing Countries?" *Finance and Development* (March 1998): 34–37.
Concludes developing countries lack the institutions to target inflation; for all students.

McKinnon, Ronald I., and Huw Pill. "Credible Economic Liberalizations and Overborrowing." *American Economic Review Papers and Proceedings* (May 1997): 189–193.
A useful model of overborrowing and crises; intermediate.

Nuti, Domenico Marco. "The Polish Zloty, 1990–1999: Success and Underperformance." *American Economic Review Papers and Proceedings* 90 (May 2000): 53–58.
The currency experience of one of the most successful transitional economies.

Obstfeld, Maurice. "The Global Capital Market: Benefactor or Menace?" *Journal of Economic Perspectives* 12 (Fall 1998): 9–30.
The benefits and risks to developing economies of capital liberalization.

Obstfeld, Maurice, and Kenneth Rogoff. "The Mirage of Fixed Exchange Rates." *Journal of Economic Perspectives* 9 (1995): 73–96.
Argues that permanently fixed exchange rates have become infeasible for all but a few countries; accessible to all students.

Rodrik, Dani. "Understanding Economic Policy Reform." *Journal of Economic Literature* (March 1996): 9–41.
The politics of economic reform.

Schneider, Friedrich, and Dominik H. Enste. "Shadow Economies: Size, Causes, and Consequences." *Journal of Economic Literature* 38 (March 2000): 77–114.
Intermediate/advanced discussion of underground economies.

Symposium on "Economies in Transition." *Finance and Development* 37 (September 2000): 2–47.
Recent macroeconomic developments in the transitional economies.

Symposium on "Latin America and the Caribbean: Reform and Recovery." *Finance and Development* 37 (March 2000): 7–41.
Recent macroeconomic events in the Western Hemisphere.

Symposium on "Transition: Achievements and Challenges." *Finance and Development* 36 (June 1999): 2–27.
Evaluation of the transition process after 10 years.

Williamson, John. *International Debt Re-Examined.* Washington, D.C.: Institute for International Economics, 1995.
A readable ex post examination of the 1980s developing-country debt crisis and responses by the debtors, international capital markets, creditors, developed economies, and international organizations.

Williamson, John, ed. *The Political Economy of Policy Reform.* Washington, D.C.: Institute for International Economics, 1994.
Collection of papers on the different experiences of various developing countries undergoing political and economic reform; for all students.

World Bank. *Bureaucrats in Business: The Economics and Politics of Government Ownership.* New York: Oxford University Press, 1995.
Detailed case studies of state-owned enterprises, privatization, and reform; for all students.

World Bank. *Global Development Finance.* Washington, D.C.: World Bank, annual.
Overview and data on capital flows to developing and transitional economies.

World Bank. *Global Economic Prospects and the Developing Countries.* Washington, D.C.: World Bank, annual.
Overview of current issues facing developing and transitional economies.

World Bank. *World Development Report.* Oxford: Oxford University Press, annual.
Devoted to examination of various aspects of development; accessible to all students. Also contains a large collection of data.

Yarbrough, Beth V., and Robert M. Yarbrough. "Unification and Secession: Group Size and 'Escape from Lock-In,'" *Kyklos* (1998): 171–195.
Simple model of German unification as a means of achieving reform in the former East Germany.

CREDITS

Table 2.4: Bart Van Ark and Dirk Pilat, "Productivity Levels in Germany, Japan, and the United States: Differences and Causes," *Brookings Papers on Economic Activity: Microeconomics* 2 (1993), p. 17. Reprinted by permission of The Brookings Institution.

Figure 3.11: World Bank, China: *Foreign Trade Reform* (Washington, D.C.: World Bank, 1994), p. 5.

Figure 4.8: Data from Cletus C. Coughlin and Patricia S. Pollard, "Comparing Manufacturing Export Growth across States: What Accounts for the Differences?" Federal Reserve Bank of St. Louis *Review* 83 (January/February 2001), p. 36.

Figure 5.9: World Bank, *Global Economic Prospects and the Developing Countries* (Washington, D.C.: World Bank, 1997) p. 98.

Figure 6.2: World Bank, *Global Economic Prospects and the Developing Countries* (Washington, D.C.: World Bank, 1997) p. 53.

Table 6.1: Data from Marcelo de Paiva Abreu, "Trade in Manufactures: The Outcome of the Uruguay Round and Developing Country Interests," in Will Martin and L. Alan Winters, eds., *The Uruguay Round and the Developing Countries* (Cambridge: World Bank, 1996), pp. 66, 75, 79.

Table 6.2: Data from Gary Clyde Hufbauer and Kimberly Ann Elliott, *Measuring the Costs of Protection in the United States* (Washington, D.C.: Institute for International Economics, 1994), p. 8.

Table 6.5: U.S. International Trade Commission, *The Year in Trade 1999* (Washington, D.C.: USITC, 2000), p. 59.

Table 7.1: Data from Gary Clyde Hufbauer and Kimberly Ann Elliott, *Measuring the Costs of Protection in the United States* (Washington, D.C.: Institute for International Economics, 1994), pp. 8–9.

Table 7.3: Data from U.S. Trade Representative, *2000 National Trade Estimate Report on Foreign Trade Barriers* (Washington, D.C., 2000). Available at www.ustr.gov.

Figure 7.7: World Trade Organization, *Annual Report 2001.*

Table 7.4: U.S. International Trade Commission, *The Year in Trade 2001.*

Table 8.6: Table from Richard Beason and David E. Weinstein, "Growth, Economies of Scale, and Targeting in Japan (1955–1990)", *The Review of Economics and Statistics,* 78:2 (May, 1996), pp. 286–295. Copyright © 1996 by the President and Fellows of Harvard College and the Massachusetts Institute of Technology. Reprinted by permission of MIT Press Journals.

Figure 9.8: *China Statistical Yearbook 2000.*

Table 9.3: Data from John E. Cremeans, ed., *Handbook of North American Industry: NAFTA and the Economies of Its Member Nations* (Lanham, MD: Bernan Press, 1998), p. 30.

Table 10.9: Data from Chrys Dougherty and Dale W. Jorgenson, "International Comparisons of the Source of Economic Growth," *American Economic Review Papers and Proceedings* (May 1996), p. 26. Reprinted by permission of the American Economic Association.

Figure 10.10: Data from United Nations, *World Investment Report 2000.*

Table 10.10: Data from Financial Action Task Force Report. Updates available at the OECD Web site at http://www.oecd.org/faft/contactfaft_en.htm. Reprinted by permission of Organization for Economic Development.

Table 10.11: Data from Multilateral Investment Fund, Inter-American Development Bank.

Figure 10.15: From "Global Capital Flows" by Martin Feldstein in *The Economist,* June 24, 1995, p. 73. Copyright © 1995 The Economist Newspaper Ltd. All rights reserved. Reprinted with permission. Further reproduction prohibited. www.economist.com.

Table 11.1: Data from World Bank, *World Development Report 2001/02.*

Table 11.2: World Bank, *World Development Indicators 2000 and World Development Report 2001/02.*

Table 11.3: Data from World Bank, *Global Development Finance 2000.*

Table 11.4: Central Intelligence Agency, *World Factbook 2001.*

Table 11.6: Data from World Bank, *Global Development Finance 2000.*

Table 11.7: Data from World Bank, *World Development Indicators 2000.*

Table 11.9: Data from European Bank for Reconstruction and Development, *Transition Report 2001.*

Table 11.11: Data from European Bank for Reconstruction and Development, *Transition Report 2001.*

Figure 12.1: "Currency Trading" from *The Wall Street Journal,* December 14, 2001. Copyright © 2001 Dow Jones & Co., Inc. Reprinted by permission of Dow Jones & Co., Inc. via Copyright Clearance Center.

Figure 12.2: "World Value of the Dollar" from *The Wall Street Journal,* December 14, 2001. Copyright © 2001 Dow Jones & Co., Inc. Reprinted by permission of Dow Jones & Co., Inc. via Copyright Clearance Center.

Figure 12.3: "Key Currency Cross Rates" from *The Wall Street Journal,* December 14, 2001. Copyright © 2001 Dow Jones & Co., Inc. Reprinted by permission of Dow Jones & Co., Inc. via Copyright Clearance Center.

Figure 12.4: "Futures Prices" from *The Wall Street Journal,* December 14, 2001. Copyright © 2001 Dow Jones & Co., Inc. Reprinted by permission of Dow Jones & Co., Inc. via Copyright Clearance Center.

Figure 12.11: "Futures Options Prices" from *The Wall Street Journal,* December 14, 2001. Copyright © 2001 Dow Jones & Co., Inc. Reprinted by permission of Dow Jones & Co., Inc. via Copyright Clearance Center.

Table 12.2: Data from Board of Governors of the Federal Reserve System (updates are available at www.federalreserve.gov).

Table 12.3: Bank for International Settlements.

Table 13.1: Data from World Bank, *World Development Indicators.*

Table 13.3: Data from World Bank, *World Development Indicators.*

Table 13.4: U.S. Department of Commerce (updates are available at the department's Web site, www.bea.doc.gov).

Table 13.5: U.S. Department of Commerce (updates are available at the department's Web site, www.bea.doc.gov).

Table 13.7: U.S. Department of Commerce (updates are available at the department's Web site, www.bea.doc.gov).

Table 13.9: U.S. Department of Commerce (updates are available at the department's Web site, www.bea.doc.gov).

Table 13.11: U.S. Department of Commerce (updates are available at the department's Web site, www.bea.doc.gov).

Table 14.1: U.S. Department of Commerce (updates are available at the department's Web site, www.doc.gov).

Table 14.2: U.S. Department of Commerce (updates are available at the department's Web site, www.doc.gov).

Figure 14.11: U.S. Department of Commerce (updates are available at the department's Web site, www.doc.gov).

Figure 14.12: Data from U.S. Census Bureau and International Monetary Fund.

Table 15.1: Data from Board of Governors of the Federal Reserve System (updates are available at www.federalreserve.gov).

Figure 15.7: Data from Morris Goldstein, *The Asian Financial Crisis: Causes, Cures, and Systemic Implications* (Washington, D.C.: Institute for International Economics, 1998), p. 8.

Figure 15.8: Data from Morris Goldstein, *The Asian Financial Crisis: Causes, Cures, and Systemic Implications* (Washington, D.C.: Institute for International Economics, 1998), p. 3.

Table 15.8: Data from Morris Goldstein, *The Asian Financial Crisis: Causes, Cures, and Systemic Implications* (Washington, D.C.: Institute for International Economics, 1998), p. 48.

Figure 15.9: Data from Transparency International (updates are available at www.transparency.org).

Figure 15.10: Data from Morris Goldstein, *The Asian Financial Crisis: Causes, Cures, and Systemic Implications* (Washington, D.C.: Institute for International Economics, 1998), p. 2.

Figure 15.22: International Monetary Fund, *International Financial Statistics Yearbook 2000.* Reprinted by permission of International Monetary Fund.

Table 16.1: International Monetary Fund. Reprinted by permission of International Monetary Fund.

Table 16.4: Data from Steven Radelet and Jeffrey D. Sachs, "The East Asian Financial Crisis: Diagnosis, Remedies, Prospects," *Brookings Papers on Economic Activity* (1998), p. 47. Reprinted by permission of The Brookings Institution.

Figure 16.17: World Bank, *World Development Report 1997* (Washington D.C.: The World Bank), p. 135.

Table 17.1: International Monetary Fund. Reprinted by permission of International Monetary Fund.

Figure 17.10: Data from Organization for Economic Cooperation and Development. Reprinted by permission of OECD.

Figure 17.11: International Monetary Fund. Reprinted by permission of International Monetary Fund.

Figure 17.13: Adapted from Organization for Economic Cooperation and Development, *Economic Outlook* June 1998, p. 225. Copyright © 1998 OECD. Reprinted by permission of OECD.

Figure 17.14: U.S. Department of the Treasury and Board of Governors of the Federal Reserve System.

Figure 18.5: Data from Organization for Economic Cooperation and Development. Reprinted by permission of OCED.

Figure 18.8: Kenneth Rogoff, "The Purchasing Power Parity Puzzle," *Journal of Economic Literature* (June 1996), p. 660. Reprinted by permission of American Economic Association.

Figure 18.9: UBS, World Bank.

Table 19.1: International Monetary Fund, *World Economic Outlook.* Reprinted by permission of International Monetary Fund.

Table 19.2: International Monetary Fund, *World Economic Outlook.* Reprinted by permission of International Monetary Fund.

Figure 19.14: Data from Organization for Economic Cooperation and Development. Reprinted by permission of OECD.

Figure 19.15: Data from Organization for Economic Cooperation and Development. Reprinted by permission of OECD.

Table 19.5: Data from Organization for Economic Cooperation and Development. Reprinted by permission of OECD.

Table 19.6: Data from Organization for Economic Cooperation and Development. Reprinted by permission of OECD.

Table 20.1: International Monetary Fund. Reprinted by permission of International Monetary Fund.

Table 20.7: Federal Reserve Bank of New York.

Table 20.8: U.S. Department of Commerce (updates are available at www.stats.bls.gov).

Table 20.10: Adapted from Organization for Economic Cooperation and Development, *OECD Economic Outlook,* June 1998. Copyright © 1998 OECD. Reprinted by permission of OECD.

Figure 21.2: Data from European Bank for Reconstruction and Development, *Transition Report 2001.*

Figure 21.3: Data from European Bank for Reconstruction and Development, *Transition Report 2001.*

Figure 21.4: Data from European Bank for Reconstruction and Development, *Transition Report 2001.*

Figure 21.5: Data from European Bank for Reconstruction and Development, *Transition Report 2001.*

Figure 21.6: Data from European Bank for Reconstruction and Development, *Transition Report 2001.*

Figure 21.7: Data from European Bank for Reconstruction and Development, *Transition Report 2001.*

Figure 21.8: Data from European Bank for Reconstruction and Development, *Transition Report 2001.*

Table 21.1: Data from European Bank for Reconstruction and Development, *Transition Report 2001.*

Table 21.2: World Bank.

Figure 21.9: Data from World Bank.

Figure 21.10: Data from World Bank.

AUTHOR INDEX

COUNTRY OR ECONOMY INDEX

SUBJECT INDEX